BUSINESS LAW
PRINCIPLES AND CASES

by

HAROLD F. LUSK, S.J.D.
Professor of Business Law
Indiana University

THIRD EDITION

1949

RICHARD D. IRWIN, INC.
CHICAGO

THIRD EDITION
First printing, June 1946
Second printing, October 1946
Third printing, December 1946
Fourth printing, May 1947
Fifth printing, November 1947
Sixth printing, September 1948
Seventh Printing, May 1949
Eighth Printing, December 1949

PRINTED IN THE UNITED STATES OF AMERICA

PREFACE

THE same plan of presenting the materials has been followed in this revision as was used in the earlier editions. However, in this revision the text materials have been expanded; and, in many instances, related matters have been discussed under one heading, whereas in the previous editions they were discussed under several separate headings. The cases selected are outstanding recent decisions, with a few exceptions, in which early leading cases have been used. The cases are carefully edited with the aim of eliminating confusing technical discussion which is not material in developing the point in issue. Each case is prefaced by a statement of (1) the party or parties plaintiff and the party or parties defendant in the trial court; (2) for whom judgment was rendered in the trial court; (3) who appealed; and (4) the disposition of the case by the court of appeal.

The subject of crimes and torts has been expanded and discussed in a separate chapter. The order of the treatment of the subject matter of contracts has been revised, especially the chapters on third parties, performance, discharge, and remedies. The part on property has been completely re-written and now includes the materials formerly treated in the part on security transactions. The part on sales has been revised, and new material on the liability of the seller for negligence in inspecting goods sold, etc., has been added. The parts on negotiable instruments and corporations have been re-written and new material has been added. Chapters on bankruptcy and Labor relations have been added.

Although the passage of time and social upheavals bring about little change in the basic legal principles of a legal system, they do present new problems to be solved. The cases selected illustrate new problems with which the courts have had to deal during the past decade. This gives the student an opportunity to study the recent developments in the field of business law and also gives him a logical explanation of some of the recent changes which have taken place in the field.

The writer is indebted to the teachers of business law who have contributed many valuable suggestions for the improvement of this work. Most of these debts must remain unacknowledged. However, the obligation to Professor Harvey H. Guice of Southern Methodist University, Mr. Erwin E. Schowengerdt of St. Louis University, and Professor W. J. Eiteman of Duke University for their detailed criticism of the earlier edition, and to Professor Guice and Mr. Schowengerdt for the reading of the manuscript of this edition is such that it deserves special mention. Without the faithful assistance of Mrs. Vivian Crum, who prepared the manuscript, it would have been impossible to have completed this revision at this time.

Harold F. Lusk

Bloomington, Indiana
April 1946

TABLE OF CONTENTS

PART I

INTRODUCTION

PART II

CONTRACTS

PART III

PROPERTY

PART IV

SALES

PART V

NEGOTIABLE INSTRUMENTS

PART VI

AGENCY

PART VII

PARTNERSHIPS

PART VIII

CORPORATIONS

PART IX

MISCELLANEOUS

APPENDICES

GLOSSARY

INDEX

INDEX OF CASES

I

J

K

L

M

Mc

N

O

P

R

PART I

INTRODUCTION

CHAPTER I

NATURE AND SOURCE OF LAW

Nature of Law

The word law has many meanings, as will be disclosed by the definitions of the word in any unabridged dictionary, yet it always suggests a rule which is followed with consistency. If we use the term as it is used in the field of science, it denotes absolute consistency in action; but, if we use the term as it is used by the courts when referring to the "law of the land," it denotes a rule of conduct which should be followed consistently by the members of society, but the idea of absolute certainty of action is lacking.

In this discussion we shall use the word law in referring to that body of rules, customs, and usages which have been adopted and built up by a society, and to which the individuals of society are required to conform so that society can continue to exist as an organized unit. The "laws" in the aggregate are the result of a long period of social development. A society of men cannot exist without some rules or standards of conduct to which all of the members of society conform to a high degree. If we analyze our society, we shall find that even the most lawless individual in society conforms to the "laws" of that society in all but a few respects. This conformance is necessary to the continued existence of both the individual and the society. If one were driving an automobile in New York City on Fifth Avenue near Forty-second Street during the rush hour, the failure to comply with the traffic laws would in all probabilities result in serious injury to the one violating the law and also to other members of society using the street at that time. Some inconvenience to all concerned would be almost certain.

The nature of our law is such that the members of society comply with the majority of the requirements of the law unconsciously. The laws are in one sense a part of each member of society. They have been developed by that society over a long period of time, and each member of the society is trained from his earliest childhood to conform to the laws of the society into which he is born.

This does not mean that all members of the society comply with all of the laws of that society unconsciously. A society is constantly confronted with new social problems arising from changing conditions, and it adopts new rules of law as an aid in solving such problems. Also, within a society special rules of law will be adopted which can apply only to a limited number of the members of that society. Laws controlling various phases of the transaction of business are examples of such laws. Laws which fall into this category are, for the most part, consciously complied with by the members of society who are affected thereby. Some members of society may refuse to comply with some of the rules of law adopted by that society, but the number of members refusing to live up to the laws are relatively few and no single member of society will violate any appreciable number of its laws.

Origin of the Law

No known society, no matter how primitive, exists which does not have established laws. Law is one of the foundation stones of any society; consequently, if one is to account for the origin of law, he must at the same time account for the origin of society. The beginning of society is so remote that we cannot have any accurate history of its origin. Like the origin of language, its beginning is shrouded in antiquity. From the history of ancient peoples we can draw a few conclusions which will aid in describing the legal institutions of the earliest times, even though history does not account for their presence.

In most, but not all, legal systems of an early date, there is no clean-cut distinction between law and religion. We find that the basic laws of the society are of divine origin. The stories of the origin of these rules vary with the different societies or civilizations. In some the king, who also acts as judge, has some mysterious power of communication with the divine, and, through the medium of the king, the divine reveals his will. The story of the Mosaic law is illustrative of the conception of the divine origin of law. Moses went up on the mount and received from God the tablets of stone with the Ten Commandments written on them. These Ten Commandments were accepted as the foundation of the Hebrew law. We no longer accept the theory of divine guidance in law, yet there is a very close relationship between our laws and our religious beliefs. In the Christian countries the Ten Commandments are, for the most part, accepted and enforced as basic law.

Although we cannot trace law to its origin, we can trace it far enough to be convinced that it is an essential element in the development of any social order, and we are justified in concluding that its origin is synonymous with the origin of society.

Common Law

Before the Norman Conquest the right of litigants in England were determined by tribunals which relied on the elders or leaders of the community and on the decisions directed by God and revealed through the results of ordeals carried out under the auspices of a church official, usually the priest. No body of written law, stating the basic principles which should be followed in deciding controversies, was adopted. The customs of the community, as handed down from one generation to another, were of outstanding importance and in most instances determined the rights of the parties or dictated the formal procedure which would be followed in the trial of the controversy. After the Norman Conquest no abrupt change was made in the administration or in the basic laws of England. The Normans did establish a strong, centralized government and introduced the feudal system of land tenure which gave a unity to England such as had not existed since the time of the Roman occupation. At an early date the King's Court was established, primarily, to hear and determine the rights of the crown. By easy stages the jurisdiction of the King's Court was expanded until it accepted jurisdiction of controversies between citizens of the realm.

The King's Court was established in London; Westminster Hall was considered the seat of justice for the entire realm. At first all litigants came to Westminster Hall, but, as the country developed and the number of cases increased, the judges, who were by that time trained in the law, began to go on circuit, i.e., to hold court in the various towns, holding for a term in one town and then moving to another town. By gradual expansion and development a centralized court system (Westminster Hall continued to be the center of legal activity) was developed with courts of original jurisdiction and courts of appeal basically like the present court system. This stage of development was reached by about 1300 A.D.

The King's Courts professed to find and enforce as law the customs and usages of the people as they had existed from times immemorial. However, the customs and usages of the people were not uniform throughout England, but this did not seriously trouble the common law judges and lawyers. At an early date the judges and lawyers referred to earlier decisions of the courts as proof of the established law. By this time a centralized court system was well established; consequently, the law, as found and applied by the courts, became uniform.

In deciding a case the courts, especially the courts of appeal, considered that they were confronted with a double duty—the deciding of the controversy and the stating of the principle of law on which they based their decision. The statements of principles of law contained in the courts' decisions were treated as binding on the courts in subsequent cases in which the same problem was presented and were treated as the foundation on which analogies could be built in the deciding of similar cases. As a result of this practice, a vast body of law, treating of almost all conceivable types of situations, was built up, and it is customarily referred to as the common law.

Doctrine of Stare Decisis

The doctrine of *stare decisis* is the keystone of the common law. Its acceptance has made possible that nice balance between the desire for certainty in the law and the demand for justice in the individual case. As mentioned above, at an early date the courts began to refer to earlier cases and follow the decision when applicable. The practice of following earlier decisions is known as the doctrine of *stare decisis.* It might appear that under such a system there would be no opportunity for progress; however, the courts do not blindly follow an earlier case without giving consideration to the principles of law involved. In deciding a case the courts will refer to the prior cases which have presented a similar problem, analyze the facts in the decided cases, compare them with the facts of the case under consideration, and then by analogy arrive at a decision of the case under consideration. As society develops, the setting of a case changes; consequently, the courts are never confronted with two cases exactly alike in every respect. If the social development is of importance, this change in the fact situation may prompt the courts to distinguish the case from the earlier cases and adopt an altered principle for the decision of future cases. In some instances the courts may refute an earlier decision and definitely overrule it, but not unless the court is convinced that the earlier decision is erroneous.

Equity

Under the common law the remedies available to litigants were limited. Three general remedies were developed: (1) money damages, (2) recovery of possession of personal property, and (3) recovery of possession of real estate. These remedies have been applied in widely varying situations and have proved adequate in many types of disputes; yet, as society developed, they proved inadequate in many instances.

At the time of the reign of the Norman kings in England, the king was supreme and had the right to grant relief to his subjects whenever he desired. The king exercised this prerogative to relieve from the injustice of a situation over which the common law courts would not accept jurisdiction because under their organization there was no available remedy. The practice of appealing to the king to settle disputes, when the remedy at law was inadequate, grew with the development of the country until the number of cases brought before the king became burdensome.

The king then delegated the power to hear and determine such cases to the chancellor, who at that time was a high churchman usually learned in both Canon law and Roman law. With the development of the country, the number of cases brought before the chancellor increased to such an extent that the chancellor organized this part of his work and adopted a systematic scheme of disposing of these cases. After a period of time, a separate court was organized to handle this type of litigations. At a later period lawyers were trained to practice in the courts of chancery, and finally chancellors were appointed from this group. The procedure in the courts of chancery, or equity courts as they are now called, became stabilized and almost as rigid as the procedure in the courts of law. Also, the doctrine of *stare decisis* was adopted by the courts of chancery; however, the courts always heard and determined the rights of the parties in any case irrespective of how new or novel the case might be if the remedy at law was inadequate.

The courts of chancery (now generally called equity courts in the United States) developed certain remedies which have a wide and constant use, e.g., injunctions, specific performance, foreclosure of mortgages, accountings, receivership, bills to quiet title to real estate, and divorces, but the court is not limited in the remedy which it may grant. If, in the exercise of his discretionary powers, the judge deems the usual remedies inadequate to a just settlement of a case under consideration, he has the power to grant any remedy which is desirable.

Law Merchant

From an early period in England there existed a body of substantive law outside the jurisdiction of the common law and equity courts which was called the law merchant. The common law courts, and to a lesser extent the equity courts, treated of the feudal rights of the people and were ignorant of the practices of the trader. Traders were treated as a separate class. Trade was carried on at fairs and was international in character. Foreign traders were not trusted and often were treated harshly and unjustly. To protect themselves against the lawlessness and piracy of the times, traders organized guilds. These guilds were organized to facilitate trade, and the membership was made up of all merchants trading in the market town, whether domestic or foreign. They often sought and obtained the aid of the rulers to protect their business.

Certain towns were designated as fair towns, and the merchants of the fair established a court of their own, presided over by a master who heard and decided merchants' disputes. The law administered by these merchants' courts was a private, international law of commerce. It was drawn from the early Maritime law, the Canon law, and the Roman law. On the continent codes of commercial law had been adopted which were based on the customs of merchants, and, the mercantile trade of the time being international in character, it was only natural that some of the laws of the continent were recognized and enforced by the merchants' courts.

Another feature of the administration of the law merchant was its lack of procedural formality and the speed with which matters presented to the court were decided. Merchants were traveling men, and long delays in the deciding of disputes would be intolerable. It has been said that the sun never set on an undecided case. There were no formal pleadings, no records or writs. The disputing parties presented their dispute to the master of the fair who decided the case immediately. In some cases a jury of merchants heard the case, and the defeated party might appeal the case. These appeals were usually taken to the equity court. The law merchant in its operations was more like equity than like the common law.

As trade developed, the merchants' courts broke down and the common law courts began to hear and determine merchants' causes. At first the cases were handled in a cumbersome and inefficient manner. The parties would plead that they were merchants, and then at the trial of the case, the parties would give in evidence the mercantile law controlling their rights as the usage of merchants. The judges were not familiar nor in sympathy with the law merchant, and the results were not always all that could be desired. However, over a period of time, the law merchant was gradually accepted by the common law courts as a part of the common law of England.

Our insurance law, negotiable instruments law, partnership law, and law of sales originated in the merchants' courts, and was incorporated into the common law system between 1600 and 1800.

Statute Law

Statute law is law enacted by a body having legislative power. In England, Parliament has this power; in the United States, Congress and the various state legislatures have this power. A limited power to legislate is also granted to lesser political subdivisions, especially to incorporated cities. Statute law is frequently termed "written law" in contrast with the common law which is frequently termed the "unwritten law." This distinction is based on the fact that statutory enactments are formally drawn statements of law, while the common law is not formally stated but is found in the pronouncements of the courts in the decided cases.

Parliament, Congress, and state legislatures perform a dual function: they enact laws and perform purely administrative functions. The majority of the acts passed at a session of Congress or of any state legislature will be administrative in their nature, such as the acts making appropriations for the fiscal period. The acts which are not merely administrative in their scope may enact existing rules or principles which have been established by the common law, may add to or subtract from existing common law rules or principles, or may establish new rules or principles of law.

During the existence of the United States as a nation, our law has been developed both by court decisions and legislative enactments. The courts have recognized the rights of the legislatures and have refrained from making material changes in the law. Their contribution has been in the nature of a step-by-step development. They have reasoned by analogy from one case to the next, leaving the more far-reaching changes in the law to the legislatures. Yet, in interpreting statutes, the courts have tended to limit the scope of the statutes both by giving them a strict construction and by holding them strictly within the confines of the constitution. Statutes have, for the most part, set up the framework for our social development, and the courts have completed the structure through court decisions.

City Ordinances

We recognize the state as the sovereign unit in our governmental system, and the state legislature as the law-making body of that unit. The state legislatures have permitted the organization of smaller units and have given these smaller units certain legislative powers. From the standpoint of their law-making power, the city—the municipal corporation—is the most important. Each city has the right to enact laws—ordinances—for the regulation of its internal affairs. These ordinances must not exceed in their scope the delegated powers of the city. Usually such ordinances regulate such matters as traffic, zoning, licensing of certain types of businesses, etc. These ordinances have the same force as laws passed by the legislature so long as they are within the scope of the power delegated to the city, do not violate or conflict with existing state statutes, and do not infringe on the constitutional rights of the people.

Constitutions

When the original thirteen colonies gained their freedom from the mother country, they considered themselves as thirteen separate independent countries. Yet they had fought as a unit and there existed a strong tie between them. At first the colonies expressed an intention to remain independent but to form some sort of league, so they first adopted the "Articles of Confederation," but it was apparent that this arrangement would not meet their needs. Each of the colonies wished to retain its independence, yet all felt that the ties of tradition and the war had made them essentially one. The outcome was the formation of a central government based upon the Constitution. This recognized the people as the fundamental source of power. The people granted to the central government certain powers, carefully reserving to the states all powers except those granted to the central government. The Constitution of the United States, which took effect March 4, 1789, together with the amendments since adopted, is a statement of the powers of the federal government.

In the early days of the new country the question arose as to who should interpret and construe the Constitution. Some contended that Congress had the power to determine whether or not its legislation was within the powers granted by the Constitution; others, that it was the duty of the Supreme Court. The final outcome was in favor of the Supreme Court. It is now well settled that the United States Supreme Court is the final judge of the constitutionality of a statute. This applies to state as well as federal statutes. The states do not have a right to exercise those powers granted to the federal government if the federal government has acted.

The various states have drafted and adopted constitutions, which are not essential to the existence of the state governments but are instruments by which the states organize their own governments. Usually they limit the power of the state legislatures so that any act passed must be consistent with the state constitutions. Both the state constitutions and state legislation must be consistent with the federal Constitution.

Function of the Law

The function of the law is to provide principles, standards, and rules by which society may develop to the highest levels of civilization. Law provides orderliness in our social scheme. The people in society experience many conflicting desires. In a primitive society the conflict would be decided by physical combat; in a less primitive society some rule or some quasi-religious test might be applied to determine the rights of the parties. In some countries in the Middle Ages, many disputes were referred to arbitrators. In the more complex societies the legal system provides the machinery for determining the rights of parties when their interests conflict. To serve effectively the legal system must provide a nice balance whereby each individual obtains fair and just treatment. What is fair and just treatment will be determined in accordance with the established mores of the times.

In our society two concepts of the function of law appear to be competing for supremacy in the beliefs of the public. One, and the older, is that the laws should provide the greatest degree of freedom of action for the individual which is consistent with like freedom on the part of all other members of society. The other concept is that the function of the law is to provide the greatest good to the largest number of the members of society.

QUESTIONS AND PROBLEMS

1. What is the function of law in our society?
2. Why do the majority of people comply with the laws?
3. Does a person's willingness to pay the penalty justify his breaking the law? Give four reasons for your answer.
4. Are all the people affected by all of the laws?
5. Give some examples of instances in which a person may not be affected by a particular law.
6. What is the origin of our law?
7. Are all customs law? Give some examples of customs which are not law.
8. Give some examples of customs which have become law.
9. Are all of our laws in accord with existing customs?
10. What is the common law?
11. What is the doctrine of stare decisis?
12. Can a rule of law established by a decision of the United States Supreme Court be reversed by a later decision of the same court?
13. What is the basis of the jurisdiction of a court of equity?
14. In the following instances would suit be brought in equity or in law? (1) Suit for damages for breach of contract. (2) Suit for a divorce. (3) Suit to foreclose a mortgage. (4) Suit to recover the possession of an automobile.
15. What was the Law Merchant?
16. What is the nature of statute law?
17. What is the scope of city ordnances?
18. What is the function of the Constitution of the United States? The constitution of a state?

CHAPTER II

CRIMES AND TORTS

Nature of a Crime

In any human society there exists some concept of crime. Many studies have been made of the causes of crime, and these studies have answered many of the questions relative to the existence of crime in society, but as yet we have no complete answer to the fundamental "why" of crime. The term "crime" is used with many and varied meanings. It may be used to designate antisocial action or it may be given a more restricted meaning as, for example, that action which is punishable by organized society. This latter meaning substantially coincides with the definition of the term as used in law. A crime has been defined as "A wrong which the government notices as injurious to the public, and punishes in what is called a criminal proceeding in its own name." [1]

The central idea in all concepts of crime is action by the individual which is injurious to the society of which he is a member. This concept raises the question of how shall we determine what action is injurious to society. This question is answered for the most part by social development. Any organized society in its development embraces a vast number of beliefs, traditions, and customs which are accepted as indispensable to the welfare of that society. Institutions are built up which are considered as the very foundation of the society, and it is only natural that any act on the part of a member of that society which violates an accepted belief, tradition, or custom or which tends to weaken an existing institution is detrimental to the welfare of that society and therefore antisocial. However, in our modern society all antisocial action would not be classed, under the legal definition of crime, as criminal. One of the problems confronting modern society is where to draw the dividing line between antisocial action, which will be punished by society as crime, and antisocial action, which will be condemned by society by some means at its disposal other than the machinery of our law-enforcing agencies.

[1] Bouvier's *Dictionary*, 3d Revised Ed. (Rawles), Vol. 1, p. 729.

Nature of Criminal Law

The first task of the criminal law, which is to develop a body of laws which adequately defines those acts that are injurious to society, is complex, and, even if it were possible to perform this task to perfection, the problems of criminal law would not be completely solved. In addition to defining the act which is to be deemed criminal, the criminal law must prescribe the punishment to be inflicted on those committing a crime.

This concept of criminal law is much narrower than the concept held by people generally. It confines its scope to the definition and classification of crimes generally. In defining the crime the definition must state (1) the criminal act, (2) whether or not criminal intent is an essential element of the crime, (3) who has capacity to commit the crime, and (4) who shall be exempt.

Classification of Crimes

In the United States crimes are generally classified as treason, felonies, and misdemeanors. Treason is defined in the federal Constitution as follows, "Treason against the United States shall consist only in levying war against them, or in adhering to their enemies, giving them aid and comfort" (Art. 3, § 3, cl. 1). A felony is a serious crime. In its earliest use it was a crime punishable by death, but today the term usually signifies a crime punishable by imprisonment in a state prison. The definitions of felony speak in terms of punishment not in terms of acts; consequently, an act which might be a felony under the statutes of one state might not be a felony under the statute of a neighboring state. The meaning of the word has become indefinite and uncertain. Statutory definitions of the word "felony" are to be found in most states; however, there is no uniformity in the definitions. Lesser crimes are misdemeanors. As a general rule, all indictable offenses less than a felony are misdemeanors.

The Criminal Act and Criminal Intent

At common law every crime consisted of two elements—the criminal act and criminal intent. An act may be criminal in nature, yet, if the person performing the act does not entertain a criminal intent at the time he acts, he will not be guilty of crime, and conversely, if a person thinks evil but does not act, he will not be guilty of crime. If Archer while hunting with Burch accidentally shoots and kills him, Archer is not criminally liable, but if Archer intentionally shoots and kills Burch, he is criminally liable. Many attempts have been made to define criminal intent, none of which is completely successful. The idea is synonymous to "knowingly," "willfully," or "maliciously" doing the criminal act. It includes the doing of the act with knowledge of the results which will follow and a desire to accomplish that result. The reason infants of tender years and insane persons cannot be guilty of a crime which includes criminal intent is because they do not have the mental capacity to entertain a criminal intent. Some statutory crimes do not require criminal intent. The statutes are so framed that anyone performing the criminal act is criminally liable.

Nature of a Tort

A tort involves the invasion of the rights of a fellow-member of society. As stated above a crime is a violation of one's duty to society, and, if one commits a crime, society imposes a penalty. The relation in criminal law is between the individual and society and the action is brought by society. A criminal case is usually titled *State* v. *the name of the accused*. A tort is the violation of one's general duty to another individual which results in an injury. The recovery permitted is in the nature of reimbursement for injury suffered, and the action is brought by the party suffering the injury. Intent is not an essential element of a tort. The same act may be both a tort and a crime. Archer attacks Burch with the intent of killing him, but does not accomplish his purpose; however, he does injure Burch seriously. Archer is guilty of the crime of assault and battery with intent to commit murder and in an action by the state will be convicted and punished for the crime. Archer has also invaded Burch's individual rights, causing Burch injury. Burch may, if he elects to do so, sue Archer and recover for the injuries suffered. If Burch sues Archer, the case will be titled *Burch* v. *Archer*.

A tort differs from a contract in that tort liability is not voluntarily assumed by the individual but is imposed on him by general law, while a contractual obligation is voluntarily assumed. The lines of distinction between tort liability and contract liability are not clearly drawn, and in many situations the injured party may be permitted to bring suit either in tort or in contract. Archer stores goods in Burch's warehouse and, as the result of Burch's negligence, the goods are damaged. Burch has breached his contract and is liable to Archer for the resulting damage. He has also committed a tort in that, as a result of his negligence, Archer's property has been damaged. Archer may elect to base his suit against Burch on the breach of the contract or on the tort. He cannot bring two suits.

Elements of a Tort

Not all acts which result in an injury to another are tortious. Certain risks are incident to life and each individual must bear the burden of the normal risks of living. If a person, either as the result of an intentional invasion of the rights of another or through his negligent conduct or because he has created an extra-hazardous condition, injures another, he is guilty of tortious conduct and will be liable in tort for the injuries resulting from his conduct. Tortious conduct without injury does not give rise to tort liability. If one drives an automobile on a city street in a most reckless manner but no injury results, he is not liable in tort. If an injured person consented to the conduct which caused the injury, no tort liability arises. If a football player is injured during the normal course of a football game, he does not have a cause of action against his opponent.

If one indulges in extra-hazardous conduct which results in injury to another, he will be liable for the resulting injury. If Archer is making an excavation on a city lot and uses dynamite to blast out some stone and in the process damages Burch's house which is on an adjoining lot, Archer will be liable for the damage even though he has used every known precaution to prevent injury.

Classes of Torts

Torts may be classified according to the nature of the right invaded. One has a right to safety of person, and an invasion of this right may give rise to a right to tort damages. Torts against the person are classified as assault, battery, and false imprisonment. An assault is to put a person in apprehension of injury. It is purely emotional. If Archer points a gun at Burch under circumstances which justify Burch in believing that Archer will shoot him, Archer is guilty of an assault. There can be no assault resulting from negligent conduct. A battery involves an offensive touching of the body, usually intentional, which causes injury. False imprisonment is the confining of another for an appreciable time within limits fixed by the one causing the confinement.

One also has the right to safety of property, and an invasion of property rights may give rise to a right to tort damages. Torts arising from invasion of property rights are trespass to goods, conversion, and trespass to land. Trespass to goods is the taking possession of goods unlawfully or the damaging of another's goods. Intent is an element of trespass to goods. Conversion is the wrongful disposition of goods, the possession of which has been obtained lawfully. Trespass to land is the interference with one's right to possess, use, and control land. One's interest in commercial transactions are also protected. The tort of deceit is the obtaining of an unfair advantage through misrepresentation of material facts. The courts have also recognized and protected contractual relations and have granted a remedy for the interference with contractual rights.

One has a right to a good reputation, and an invasion of this right may give rise to tort damages. If one gives publication to harmful falsehoods concerning another, he has committed a tort. If the publication is spoken, the tort is slander; if written, it is libel.

Negligence

If one is guilty of negligent conduct which causes injury to a person or property of another, the injured party may recover damages for the injury. If two parties are guilty of negligent conduct and, as a result of their combined negligence, one or both are injured, neither is entitled to recover damages from the other. Also one's negligence must be the direct cause of the injury. In determining whether or not one has been negligent, the courts apply the "reasonably prudent man" test. Has the person exercised that degree of care which would be exercised by a reasonably prudent man under the same or like circumstances? If one has fulfilled this requirement, he is not negligent and will not be liable; but, if he has not fulfilled this requirement, he is guilty of negligence. The majority of tort cases grow out of injuries resulting from negligent conduct.

Torts and tort liability will be discussed in connection with specific situations in subsequent chapters.

Workmen's Compensation Laws

At common law an employer was not responsible to an employee for injuries suffered in the course of the employment unless the injury was the direct result of some negligence on the part of the employer. The employee assumed all the normal risks of the employment. If the injury was the result of the negligence of a fellow-employee, the employer was not liable unless it could be shown that the employer knew, at the time the fellow-employee was hired, that the latter was irresponsible and generally negligent. Under modern factory conditions the common law remedy proved entirely inadequate in employee injury cases. The employee, who was least able to bear the risks of injury incident to factory employment, had to bear the major portion of such risks. To correct this situation Workmen's Compensation Acts were passed by the states and also by the federal government.

Although these acts vary widely in detail, they follow the same basic principles. The employer is made responsible for the injuries to his employees suffered during the course of the employment; however, the amount to which the injured employee is entitled is stated in the act. For example, if an employee while operating a band saw should cut off his thumb, he would receive as compensation a stated percentage of his average wage for a stated period of time. Generally the costs of hospital and medical care will also be paid by the employer. The employer must either deposit cash or securities with a state officer or carry insurance in an approved insurance company and thereby assure the employee that compensation to which he is entitled under the act will be paid. Under the Workmen's Compensation Acts the injured employee, with very few exceptions, will receive medical care and a predetermined amount of compensation; the employer's liability is stabilized and he can insure the risk. The ultimate result is that the hazards incident to production are passed on to the consumer and not borne by either the employer or employee.

QUESTIONS AND PROBLEMS

1. What is the nature of a crime?
2. What is the function of our criminal law?
3. What is a misdemeanor? Give some examples of misdemeanors.
4. What is a felony? Give some examples of felonies.
5. At common law, what were the two essential elements of a crime?
6. Under present-day criminal law, may a person be guilty of a crime if he does not entertain a criminal intent at the time he does the criminal act?
7. What is the nature of a tort?
8. May the same act be both a tort and a crime?
9. Give some examples of acts which would be torts but not crimes.
10. In tort law, what is the standard test of negligence?
11. Why were the Workmen's Compensation Laws passed? How do they function?

CHAPTER III

COURTS AND COURT PROCEDURE

Federal Courts

In the United States we have a dual system of courts—the state system and the federal system. In some matters, the federal court has exclusive jurisdiction, while in other matters the state court has exclusive jurisdiction. In many matters the state and federal courts have concurrent jurisdiction, that is, the case may be tried in either the federal or the state courts.

A federal system is provided for by Article III, Section I, of the Constitution: "The judicial power of the United States shall be vested in one Supreme Court, and such inferior courts as the Congress may from time to time ordain and establish." The Supreme Court exists by virtue of an express constitutional provision, but Congress has the power to establish and also to abolish inferior courts. Both powers have been exercised. At present, through the action of Congress, we have district courts and circuit courts of appeals.

The federal courts have jurisdiction of all crimes and offenses, under the authority of the United States, and of admiralty causes, seizures, and prizes; internal revenue, customs, and tonnage laws; patent, copyright, and trade-mark suits; suits by the United States against national banks and suits arising in the course of the winding up of the affairs of a national banking association; suits in bankruptcy; suits arising under any law regulating interstate commerce, and in the enforcement of orders of the Interstate Commerce Commission. The federal courts also have jurisdiction of civil actions, at common law and equity, where the matter in controversy exceeds, exclusive of interest and costs, the sum or value of $3,000, and (1) arises under the Constitution or laws of the United States, or treaties made, or which shall be made, under their authority; or (2) is between citizens of different states; or (3) is between citizens of a state and foreign states, citizens, or subjects.

Under the federal system the District Court is the court of original jurisdiction. With the exception of a very small class of cases involving questions reserved to the Supreme Court, all cases must be brought in the District Court. It is here that suits are started, and it is here that issues of fact are determined. Each state constitutes at least one judicial district. The more populous states may be divided into two or more districts. Pennsylvania is divided into three and New York into four. Each court has from one to three judges, depending on the amount of business coming before the court. These courts have criminal, civil, and equity jurisdiction and are empowered to hear certain cases against the United States if the sum involved is not over $10,000.

The Bankruptcy Court and the Master in Chancery are attached to, and are a part of, the District Court. Cases in bankruptcy after adjudication are referred to the Bankruptcy Court for the purpose of having the estate administered. They are then returned to the District Court where the hearing on the petition for discharge is heard. The Referee in Bankruptcy has judicial powers, but his acts are reviewable by the District Judge. The District Judge may refer matters arising in equity cases to the Master in Chancery for hearing. The Master in Chancery reports his findings back to the District Judge. The District Judge is relieved of much detail in receivership cases and similar cases by referring certain matters, such as hearings on claims, to the Master in Chancery.

After a case has been tried and determined by the District Court, either party has the right to appeal to the Circuit Court of Appeals. There are a few matters which may be taken direct from the District Court to the Supreme Court, but in the majority of cases appeals from the district courts must be to the circuit courts of appeals. The Circuit Court of Appeals does not have original jurisdiction in any cases. The United States is divided into ten circuits, a circuit court of appeals being located in each circuit. Each court consists of three judges, and the district judges are competent to sit as judges in their respective circuits.

Appeals may be taken from the circuit courts of appeals to the Supreme Court, but such appeals, as a general rule, are a matter of privilege and not a matter of right. The litigant wishing to take such an appeal must petition the Supreme Court for permission to appeal. The circuit court of appeals may certify a question to the Supreme Court for decision. In such instances the Supreme Court may answer the question or may call for and hear the entire case. The Supreme Court also has the right to require the circuit court of appeals, and also the highest court of a state, to transmit the records of the case to it for decision where the validity of a treaty or statute of the United States, or the validity of a state statute is attacked on the grounds that it is repugnant to the Constitution, treaties, or laws of the United States or where either party to a controversy sets up that his federal constitutional rights have been violated. Where the highest state court has held invalid a treaty or statute of the United States or where a statute has been attacked on the grounds that it is repugnant to the Constitution or laws of the United States and has been held valid, an appeal may be taken to the Supreme Court by its permission. The Supreme Court has original jurisdiction in cases affecting ambassadors, public ministers, and consuls of foreign countries, and in cases where a state is a party.

The Court of Claims, etc.

A Court of Claims was established to adjudicate claims against the government of the United States. Formerly such claims were handled by Congress and paid by direct appropriation. The court is composed of five judges and has jurisdiction throughout the United States.

The Contract Settlement Act of 1944 conferred on the Court of Claims jurisdiction over controversies arising out of the settlement of contracts under the provisions of the act.

In addition to our federal court system, we have a number of boards and commissions having quasi judicial powers. These are in no sense a part of the judicial system, but they do have a right to hear and determine certain controversies. In all cases their decisions are reviewable by a regular court.

The Interstate Commerce Commission, the Board of Tax Appeals, the Federal Reserve Board, the Federal Trade Commission, National Labor Relations Board, and Securities Exchange Commission are examples of such boards and commissions. The various states have also established boards and commissions having similar powers.

State Courts

In each of the states the court system is like the federal system in that there are inferior courts and courts of appeals. The justice's court, presided over by a justice of the peace and having a limited jurisdiction as to amount, territory, and subject matter, is at the base of the state system. These courts, as a general rule, are established and their jurisdiction defined by statute, so although the part they play in the court systems of the various states is similar, they differ widely as to the details of their jurisdictions and methods of procedure.

Usually the justice of the peace need not be learned in the law, is elected by popular vote, has jurisdiction over petty criminal matters, can hold preliminary hearings in graver offenses and commit the accused, and in civil matters can hear controversies arising out of contract where the amount involved does not exceed a set limit (this limit varies from $50 to $1,000). In some states the justice has jurisdiction over tort cases where the damages claimed do not exceed a set amount. His territorial jurisdiction seldom exceeds the county and more often is confined to the township, city, or ward. He has no equity jurisdiction and cannot determine questions of title to land. No formal pleadings are required, and no record of testimony or proceedings is kept. A record of judgments rendered, executions, garnishments, etc., issued, and payments made into court is kept. An appeal may be taken from the justice court to the circuit court where the case is tried *de novo*. (This means the whole case is tried over again.)

The local courts of original jurisdiction, or trial courts, handle the great majority of the cases disposed of by the courts of the country. They are known as circuit, superior, district, common pleas, or county courts. They are courts of record; that is, a complete record is kept of all proceedings. They have general jurisdiction over criminal, civil, equity, and probate matters and are not limited in amount. Their territorial jurisdiction is limited in some types of cases to the county and in other types to the state. Through special legislative acts in some cases all territorial limitations have been removed.

In cities and other populous sections the duties of the judges may be specialized, and separate courts are established to handle particular types of cases, as criminal courts, civil courts, equity courts, probate courts, and juvenile courts; or a court may be given jurisdiction over any combination, as civil and equity cases or probate and juvenile. Also, where the amount of business warrants it, special courts with more limited jurisdiction, either as to territory or as to subject matter, are established to relieve the regularly established courts. These courts have concurrent jurisdiction with the regularly established courts, subject to some limitations, and appeals are allowed from these special courts to the higher courts of appeals on the same grounds and under the same rules governing the regular courts. As a general rule the power to establish inferior courts is vested in the legislative body. Hence courts have been established to meet particular needs, with the result that a great variety of special courts having jurisdiction fitting the needs of a community have been established. Traffic courts, police courts, and petty claims courts are examples of courts created to take care of special needs arising in cities.

Three systems of higher courts of appeals have been adopted by the various states. In some states there is only one court having general appellate jurisdiction. All appeals are taken from the court of original jurisdiction to the court of appeals, usually called the Supreme Court, and its decision is final unless the questions to be decided are such that the case may be carried to the United States Supreme Court. Other states have two courts having appellate jurisdiction. Under some state systems one of the courts of appeals, usually called the appellate court, is a court of intermediate jurisdiction; that is, appeals from the courts of original jurisdiction are taken to the appellate court, and after the matter has been passed on by this court an appeal may be taken to the higher court of appeals, usually called the supreme court. The federal system follows this plan. In other states having two courts of appellate jurisdiction, each court is a court of final appeal but is given jurisdiction over certain classes of appealed cases. Even though both courts have final jurisdiction, one court is considered inferior to the other. The one considered as the inferior is given jurisdiction over cases of lesser importance, and its decisions are often subject to review by the superior court. Excepting the few questions which may be appealed to the United States Supreme Court, the decision of the highest state court of appeals is final.

The function of a court of appeals is to review the work of the trial court in order to determine whether or not a material error has been made by the trial court during the course of the trial. The court of appeals reviews the record of the case, reads the briefs, and hears the arguments of the attorneys for the parties to the suit and decides the issues raised on the appeal. If no material error has been committed, the judgment of the trial court will be affirmed. If material error has been committed, the court of appeals may grant a judgment for the appellant thus disposing of the case, or it may set aside the judgment of the lower court and send the case back for retrial, i.e., the case is reversed and remanded or, as stated by some courts, reversed and new trial ordered. In some instances the judgment of the lower court may be affirmed in part and reversed in part. If the case is an equity case, the court of appeals may modify the decree of the trial court, may set it aside and order a new trial, or it may affirm it.

Procedure

The procedure followed in starting suit and trying a case varies in each jurisdiction; however, a general pattern is followed throughout the United States. The party plaintiff, usually through an attorney, starts suit by filing a declaration, which in final form will state the plaintiff's claims, including the remedy asked. In equity the term complaint or petition is generally used. The clerk will then issue a summons which will be addressed to the defendant and will notify him that suit has been entered against him by the plaintiff. The summons will also state the nature of the suit and the time within which the defendant must enter his appearance in the case if he wishes to defend. The summons is usually served on the defendant by the sheriff or a deputy. Service by mail or service by publication are provided for by statute in some types of cases. After being served, if the party defendant has a defense, he must enter his appearance—this is usually done through an attorney—and file an answer to the declaration. The declaration and answer will state the issues in the case.

When the pleadings are complete and the issue thereby determined, the case is ready for trial and will be set for trial. The parties, if the case is a law case, may have a jury trial or they may waive a jury. A jury is not used in the trial of equity cases. If the case is a jury case, the first step will be to select the jury. After the jury is selected and sworn in, generally the attorneys will make a statement to the jury in which each attorney outlines the claims which his client makes in regard to the controversy. Next the plaintiff's witnesses will be sworn, examined, and cross-examined. When all the plaintiff's evidence has been presented, the plaintiff's attorney will so indicate, and the defendant's witnesses will be sworn, examined, and cross-examined. When all of the evidence has been presented, the attorneys sum up the case and make their arguments before the jury. The judge then instructs, or as it is usually termed, charges the jury. The judge, in charging the jury, as a general rule, must not comment upon the weight of the evidence or the credibility of the witnesses but must confine himself to expounding the rules of law which the jury should apply in reaching the verdict.

When the jury has brought in its verdict, the court will enter a judgment based on the verdict. During the course of the trial certain motions may be made which will be ruled upon by the court.

If the defeated party thinks that an error has been committed during the course of the trial, he may wish to appeal the case.

QUESTIONS AND PROBLEMS

1. Why do we have a dual court system?
2. (*a*) If Archer, who is a resident of Chicago, enters into a contract with Burch, who is a resident of New York, and Burch breaches the contract, causing Archer to suffer damages in the amount of $2,000, in what court would Archer start suit against Burch? (*b*) Would it make any difference if the damages suffered were $5,000?
3. Is a case which has been appealed from a trial court retried in the appellate court?
4. What is the function of the Court of Claims?
5. What is a court of original jurisdiction?

6. What is a special court? How is it created?
7. Archer sues Burch on an account which Burch has paid in full. What should Burch do?
8. What is the purpose of serving a summons on the party defendant?
9. If Archer and Burch are partners and the partnership is dissolved and Archer sues Burch for an accounting, will Burch be entitled to a jury trial if he demands one?
10. What is the nature of the judge's charge to the jury?

PART II

CONTRACTS

CHAPTER IV

INTRODUCTION

Nature of a Contract

In theory, a contractual obligation or duty is voluntarily assumed by the parties to a contract. The courts have often said that they will not make a contract for the parties; that the duty of the court is to interpret and enforce the contract of the parties, not to make the contract. A contract has its origin in agreement, but all agreements are not contracts. A contract has been defined as follows: "A contract is a promise or a set of promises for the breach of which the law gives a remedy, or the performance of which the law in some way recognizes as a duty."[1] If your friend invites you to his home for dinner and you accept the invitation, you have entered into an agreement, but such an agreement is not a contract. If you do not go to your friend's home for dinner, you have failed to fulfill your part of the agreement, but you have not rendered yourself legally liable to your friend, and he cannot recover a judgment if he should bring suit. In accepting the invitation you assumed a social duty, but you did not assume a legal duty.

If you make an appointment with a business acquaintance for the purpose of discussing a contemplated business transaction, you have entered into an agreement, and if you fail to keep the appointment, you have failed to fulfill your part of the agreement. Your business acquaintance may have been injured in that he might have used to advantage the time set aside for you. However, if he should bring suit, he could not recover a judgment. In making the appointment you did not assume a legal duty. The failure to keep a business appointment is a breach of business ethics, but it is not a breach of a legal duty.

If you make an appointment with your dentist for the purpose of having dental work performed and your dentist sets aside one hour of his time for you and you fail to keep the appointment, can the dentist recover a judgment if he brings suit? The answer in this case is uncertain. If the dentist has so arranged his day's work that he can-

[1] *Restatement of the Law of Contracts,* sec. 1, p. 1.

not use this time profitably, he should be allowed to recover. When you make the appointment with the dentist you are in effect agreeing to hire him for one hour. A dentist sells services primarily. His time is his stock-in-trade. The custom of dentists in the community would be of outstanding importance in deciding a case of this type.

If you enter into an agreement to work for Smith for six months at an agreed wage, and after entering into the agreement you refuse to work, Smith can bring a suit and recover a judgment. Such an agreement creates a legal obligation on the part of both parties to the agreement.

The Essentials of a Contract

The fundamental objective of the law of contracts is to enforce those agreements which organized society deems of importance from the standpoint of the general welfare of society, and to leave the fulfillment of other agreements to the wish of the individual. To accomplish this objective, standards have been developed by which we may determine which agreements will create legal obligations. To have such an agreement, we must have an offer made by one party and communicated to a second party who accepts the offer—the legal elements of an agreement. The agreement must be supported by consideration.[2] The parties to the agreement must have capacity to contract, and the objective of the agreement must not be violative of the general interests of society.

The elements of a binding contract may be stated as a mutual agreement between parties having capacity to contract, which is supported by a sufficient consideration and the objective of which is legal.

Classification of Contracts

For the purpose of convenience of reference, contracts have been divided into various classes, depending on their form or other characteristics which they may have. These classes are not all-inclusive or all-exclusive. The same contract may fall into two or more of the classes. We may have an informal, bilateral, voidable contract. Contracts are classified as formal and informal. Informal contracts are also called simple contracts. Formal contracts are further classified as contracts under seal, recognizances, and negotiable instruments. A formal contract derives its validity from its form alone. A contract under seal must be in writing, sealed by the promisor, and delivered. It derives its validity from the formality of sealing the instrument and the delivery of the instrument. "A recognizance is an acknowledgment in

[2] Some exceptions will be taken up under "Consideration," chap. VII.

court by the recognizor that he is bound to make a certain payment unless a specific condition is performed."[3] It derives its validity from the circumstances and formality surrounding the making of the promise. Negotiable instruments, although they do not derive their validity from their form alone, are often classified as formal contracts because their form does give them special characteristics. All contracts other than those mentioned are classified as informal or simple contracts. State statutes require certain contracts to be in writing before the courts will enforce them. Such contracts are not formal contracts. They must have all the characteristics of other contracts and in addition must be in writing, so they do not derive their validity from their form even though their enforceability depends on their form.

Contracts are also classified as unilateral and bilateral. "A unilateral contract is one in which no promisor receives a promise as consideration for his promise. A bilateral contract is one in which there are mutual promises between two parties to the contract, each party being both a promisor and a promisee."[4] A reward contract is an example of a unilateral contract. The promisor offers the reward. His offer is accepted by the doing of the act required in the offer. The party accepting makes no promise; instead of promising, he acts in fulfillment of the requirements of the offer. The ordinary business contract is commonly a bilateral contract. Archer agrees, for a price, to sell and deliver goods to Burch, and Burch agrees to pay the agreed price and accept the goods. Archer is promisor in that he agrees to deliver the goods to Burch. Burch is promisee in that he is recipient of the promise. Burch is promisor in that he agrees to pay the agreed price, and Archer is promisee in that he is recipient of the promise. The parties to a bilateral contract exchange promises, while in a unilateral contract we have the exchange of a promise for an act.

Contracts may also be classified as unenforceable, voidable, and void. An unenforceable contract is one which cannot be enforced by court action, although it creates, in an indirect way, a duty of performance. If one deals with the United States government, he cannot sue the United States unless it consents, and even then he could not levy an execution. Such a transaction is classed as a contract, although it is not enforceable without the consent of one of the parties. Agreements required by statute to be in writing to be enforceable may create a moral obligation, which under some circumstances is enforced in a court of equity and which may create collateral rights even though not enforceable in a law court. Such

[3] American Law Institute, *Restatement of the Law of Contracts,* sec. 9.
[4] *Ibid.,* sec. 12.

agreements are unenforceable contracts. If one of the parties has the right at his election not to perform, the contract is a voidable contract. Infants, as a shield against others taking advantage of their immature judgment, are given the right to avoid their contract; also, one whose consent has been obtained by fraudulent representations is given the right to elect not to be bound. However, if the infant, after coming of age, wishes, he may elect to perform, and the other party will be bound. The defrauded party may think the deal is a good one and elect to be bound and hold the other party to his promises. A void contract is one that is a nullity; it has no legal effect. If the agreement is of no legal effect, it is inaccurate to call it a contract. The term is used usually to designate contractual transactions in which, owing to the lack of some essential element or to the effect of a statute, none of the parties to the transaction is bound.

A contract becomes executed when all the parties to the contract have fulfilled all their legal obligations created by the contract. Until all such legal obligations have been fulfilled, the contract is executory. If one of the parties has partially fulfilled his obligations under the contract, the contract is often referred to as a partially executed contract. The contract might be executed as to one of the parties to the contract and executory as to the other party.

Express and Implied Contracts

It is not necessary in entering into a contract that the parties express the terms of their agreement either in written or spoken language. They may by their acts indicate their intention to be bound to a contractual obligation. If the parties state their agreement in spoken or written language, the agreement is termed an express contract. If the terms of the contract are not stated by the parties and yet it is clear from their acts that they intended to contract, a contract implied in fact will have been entered into. There is no fundamental difference between an express contract and a contract implied in fact. In the express contract the terms and conditions are expressed by the parties, while in the contract implied in fact some or all of the terms and conditions are implied from the conduct of the parties.

Archer calls Burch, with whom Archer is not acquainted, and tells him he is in desperate need of help to get his hay in. Burch helps Archer for two days. At no time is anything said about paying Burch. Burch can recover the reasonable value of his services. A promise to pay will be inferred from the conduct of the parties. If Burch were a neighbor and the men had helped each other gratuitously in similar situations in the past, no promise to pay would be implied.

Quasi Contracts

Certain legal duties which are contractual in their nature but which are not based on the consent of the parties are enforced by the courts in contract actions. These contracts are often called contracts implied in law but are more properly called quasi contracts. Sometimes they are referred to as constructive contracts. In such cases the intentions of the parties are entirely disregarded. In quasi contracts the duty of the parties arises not from the consent of the parties but from justice and equity. The duty is generally based on unjust enrichment. One of the parties has been unjustly enriched to the detriment of the other party, and in justice and equity he should pay for the benefits which he has received.

Archer enters into an oral contract whereby he agrees to work for Burch for two years. Archer works for Burch for two months and Burch discharges him without cause. If Archer sues Burch for breach of contract, Burch can plead the statute of frauds as a complete defense to the contract. The contract is unenforceable. Archer can sue Burch in quasi contract and recover for the benefits conferred on Burch as a result of the two months' services.

The cases which come under the heading of quasi contracts are of infinite variety, and it is impossible to list the situations that may arise which will justify a recovery in quasi contract. In any situation in which a party is justified in believing that a binding contract exists and performs under such belief, thereby benefiting the other party, he can recover, for the benefits conferred, in a suit in quasi contract. One who has been injured by the tortious acts of another can, in most states, elect to sue for the injuries sustained in quasi contract.

Conkling's Estate et al. v. Champlin et al.
193 Okl. 79, 141 P. (2d) 569 (1943)

This was an action on a claim filed by H. H. Champlin as claimant in the estate of Nettie Conkling, deceased. The claim was opposed by Allen H. Blackledge and Ethel B. Dennis. The claim was allowed and Blackledge and Dennis appealed. Affirmed.

Mrs. Nettie Conkling was old and blind and had been a widow for 25 years. She had ceased to earn a living as a house mother of a fraternity at Oklahoma University. On account of family friendship and in the belief that Mrs. Conkling was destitute Mr. Champlin paid Mrs. Conkling \$100 a month for a period of three years immediately preceding her death. Mrs. Conkling was guilty of no fraud or misrepresentation. It is doubtful if she was mentally capable of comprehending fully her financial situation. After her death it was found that Mrs. Conkling was not destitute but that she had a farm in Kansas near a gas field and that she had $3,634.74 in the bank. It is admitted that Champlin did not expect to be reimbursed at the time he advanced the money to Mrs. Conkling, yet there is no clear indication that he was making a gift. Champlin filed a claim in Mrs. Conkling's estate for the money advanced contending that the estate was unjustly enriched by his advances and that he should be repaid.

Riley, J. It is contended that under the facts stated no contract between H. H. Champlin and decedent arose either by implication of law or fact. We consider the former. It is a constructive or quasi contract which in fact is a mere fiction, but imposed by law to afford a remedy in cases where a duty devolves upon a party as a matter of law and irrespective of intention.

This court is committed to the doctrine that: "A 'quasi' or constructive contract is an implication of law. An 'implied' contract is an implication of fact. In the former the contract is a mere fiction, imposed in order to adapt the case to a given remedy. In the latter, the contract is a fact legitimately inferred. In one, the intention is disregarded; in the other, it is ascertained and enforced. In one, the duty defines the contract; in the other, the contract defines the duty."

The relations are remedial in assumpsit and hence contracts arising from facts and circumstances independent of agreements or presumed intention; whereas in express and implied contracts the intention of the parties is the essence of the transaction. The duty is not infrequently founded on the doctrine of unjust enrichment.

The basis of recovery allowable is under the doctrine of unjust enrichment. As stated in *Restitution* (chap. 2, § 9, p. 36, American Law Institute):

"Where innocent misrepresentation or non-disclosure is the sole ground for restitution, restitution is granted only if the misrepresentation or non-disclosure was material.

"Where mutual mistake is the sole ground for restitution, restitution is granted only if the mistake was basic."

Moreover, as stated in section 26, *idem:*

"A person is entitled to restitution from another to whom gratuitously and induced thereto by a mistake a fact he has given money if the mistake was caused by fraud or material misrepresentation, or . . . as to some other basic fact. . . . .

"A person who has transferred money to another without intention to make a gift thereof may be entitled to restitution although at the time of transfer he manifested that the money was transferred as a gift."

The reason underlying the latter rule is that such a transaction involved no manifestation of intention to make an agreement based upon consideration. Therefore, the payee has neither given nor promised anything in return. Consequently, mere manifestation of intention to make a gift is not controlling, as intention would be in the case of agreements based upon consideration, but the payer is entitled to restitution if, in finality, it appears that payments were not intended to be gifts.

QUESTIONS AND PROBLEMS

1. Define a contract.
2. How does a contract differ from an agreement?
3. What are the essential elements of an enforceable contract?
4. Are all contracts in writing formal contracts?
5. Are oral contracts enforceable?
6. What is an informal or simple contract?
7. In what respect does a bilateral contract differ from a unilateral contract?
8. What is the difference between a void contract and an unenforceable contract?
9. What is the difference between a valid and a voidable contract?
10. What is an implied contract?
11. Are all express contracts also contracts in writing?
12. What is the nature of a quasi contract?
13. What is the basis for recovery in a suit in quasi contract?
14. When is a contract executed?

CHAPTER V

THE AGREEMENT

The Offer

Since an agreement is the basis of all contracts, it follows of necessity that one of the parties must make a proposition and the other party must accept that proposition, or, as stated in a note in the *Restatement of the Law of Contracts*, page 30, "An offer looks to the future. It is an expression by the offeror of his agreement that something over which he at least assumes to have control shall be done or happen or shall not be done or happen if the conditions stated in the offer are complied with." From this statement we see that an offer is composed of two essential parts: (1) a statement of what the offeror is willing to do, and (2) a statement of what is demanded of the offeree in return. Although some special instances might not come within this formula, substantially all offers for business contracts will be of this type.

We have said that the offer is "a statement"; this is not literally true. An offer may be made by an act, by spoken words, by written words, or by any combination of these. All that is necessary is that the one making the offer convey, by some means, to the offeree his proposition. If one goes into a store, picks up an article, shows it to the storekeeper, and walks out with the article without speaking, he has offered to purchase the article and pay to the storekeeper its value. The storekeeper, by permitting him to take the article, has accepted his offer.

The parties have come to an understanding or, as the early English judges expressed the situation, there was "a meeting of the minds" of the parties. Although we no longer require a "meeting of the minds," we do require that the parties must enter into an agreement with the intent to contract, thus making "intent" an essential of a binding contract. The only way a court can determine the presence of contractual intent is by an objective test; consequently, the courts have set up the "reasonable man" standard as a test for determining the presence or absence of contractual intent in those cases where its existence has been questioned. The circumstances surrounding the parties, their acts, their words, and any other facts which may aid the court are offered in evidence, and from this reconstruction of the entire happening the court decides whether under the circumstances a reasonable man would be justified in concluding that the parties intended to contract. Under this standard the parties will not be permitted to state what they "intended," i.e., what their mental reaction was—that is not material.

If Burch claims that Archer made him an offer and Archer claims that he did not intend to make an offer, Archer's stated intent would be immaterial; also what Burch thought would be equally immaterial. The court would determine whether or not, considering all the circumstances, Burch, acting as a reasonable person, was justified in thinking that Archer intended to make him an offer. Problems of intent are difficult to solve in that the vagaries of human transactions do not permit the adoption of any "rule of thumb" by which such problems can be satisfactorily solved.

The parties must make the terms of their agreement reasonably clear, else the court will be unable to enforce the agreement as a contract. It is impossible for a court of law to determine and enforce an unexpressed intent. If in negotiating an agreement the parties have used such vague expressions that, by the aid of surrounding circumstances and by the use of the "reasonable man" rule, the intentions of the parties cannot be determined with a reasonable degree of certainty, the court will hold that no contract came into existence because of "uncertainty of terms." The judges frequently make the statement that if the parties have not made a contract the court will not make one for them.

In the business world, however, certain practices have become common and the courts, in determining the intentions of the parties, assume that, when the common practices are followed, the parties intend the ordinary implications drawn from these practices. For example:

One wishing to enter into a contract with another person will not want to make an offer but will want to induce the other party to make the offer. To accomplish this, he will extend an invitation to negotiate. If Archer owns a house which he wishes to sell, he may approach Burch and say, "I should like to sell my house to you. How much will you offer me for it?" Archer has not made an offer. If Archer says, "I should like to sell my house. I think I should get $5,000 for it," he has not made an offer. The courts have recognized that in the transaction of business, it is often to the advantage of the parties to dicker. The seller will make statements as to what he thinks he should receive, and the buyer will make statements as to what he thinks the value of the property is, neither one making a definite proposition until one or the other feels certain that he has ascertained the best price he can get; then he will make a definite offer. Such dickering is generally termed preliminary negotiations and is not an offer. It is often difficult to determine whether the language used is an offer or not. In determining whether we have an offer or merely an invitation to negotiate, we must give due consideration to the surrounding circumstances, remembering to weigh them in the light of business practices and determine from these the intention of the parties. Some general rules have been established which aid the courts in distinguishing between offers and negotiations.

However, the courts have not and probably could not establish one all-inclusive general rule by which they could definitely determine whether or not any given expression is an offer or an invitation to negotiate. Each case must be analyzed, and from its facts the court must answer the question, what did the parties intend? It is true that the courts have given special weight to certain circumstances. In the case of advertisements of goods for sale, published either in newspapers and periodicals or by circulars sent out by mail or distributed by private agencies, the courts generally have held that these are not offers which become contracts as soon as anyone to whose notice the advertisement has come notifies the advertiser that he will take a certain quantity at the price. Such advertisements are intended as and are generally understood to be invitations to negotiate. However, an offer may be made by advertisement. If one clearly signifies by the wording of the advertisement his intention to make an offer, a contract will result from its acceptance.

The advertising of rewards for the return of lost property or capture of criminals are common examples of offers made through advertising. However, the advertising for bids on construction work is generally considered as inviting those interested to make an offer. Unless the advertisement for bids expressly states that the job will be let to the lowest bidder without reservation, the job need not be let to the lowest bidder. The bidder is the offeror, and no contract results until the bid is accepted. Substantially the same applies to sales by auction. Unless, in the terms governing the auction, language clearly expressing an intention to sell without reservation to the highest bidder is used, the bidder will be the offeror and the seller will be free to accept or reject bids as he may choose. No contract comes into existence when the highest bidder makes his bid. The contract is completed when the auctioneer strikes the goods off to the bidder, thus accepting the bid for the seller.

Some practices are of such long standing and of such universal use that the meaning attached is definite and inflexible. However, in all instances, the principal objective of the court is to determine the intention of the parties, and if surrounding circumstances indicate that the parties did not attach the ordinarily accepted meaning to the practice but did attach another reasonable meaning to it, the court will accept the meaning attached to the practice by the parties. In case of doubt it is assumed that the parties attached the ordinary meaning to a practice.

Higgins v. Lessig
49 Ill. App. 459 (1893)

This was an action by Lessig (plaintiff and appellee) against Higgins (defendant and appellant) to recover a reward. Judgment for Lessig in the trial court and Higgins appealed. Judgment of the trial court was reversed and a new trial ordered.

Higgins owned a set of double harness, worth perhaps $15, which was taken from his premises. The next morning while in his blacksmith shop he told the men who were in the shop at the time about the theft of the harness and said, "I will give $100 to any man who will find out who the thief is, and I will give a lawyer $100 for prosecuting him," using rough language and epithets concerning the thief. There was evidence of substantial repetitions of the statement, together with the assertion that he would not have a second-class lawyer, either, and that he would not hire a cheap lawyer, but a good lawyer.

The harness had been taken by a man called Red John Smith who had been adjudged insane. A Mrs. Philips told the plaintiff that she had seen Smith walking by with the harness on his back on Sunday morning which was the time when the harness was taken. During the day a boy found a part of the harness in Lessig's berry patch and Higgins and Lessig went to the berry patch and brought that part of the harness into Lessig's blacksmith shop. At the time Higgins gave the boy a quarter of a dollar and said that he would give him a dollar if he found the rest of the harness. Plaintiff watched Smith that night and saw him hiding the collars. The next day he waited for the return of defendant from Galesburg and told him that Red John Smith had the harness. A search warrant was procured and the remainder of the harness was found.

Cartwright, J. We do not think that the language used was such as, under the circumstances, would show an intention to contract to pay a reward, and think plaintiff had no right to regard it as such. Defendant had previously offered a very liberal reward for the return of the old harness and the conviction of the thief. On this occasion he paid the boy only a trifling sum, and offered only $1 for finding the rest of the property. His further language was in the nature of an explosion of wrath against some supposed thief who had stolen the harness, and was coupled with boasting and bluster about the prosecution of the thief. It was indicative of a state of excitement so out of proportion to the supposed cause of it, that it should be regarded rather as the extravagant exclamation of an excited man than as manifesting an intention to contract.

Davis v. Davis
119 Conn. 194, 175 Atl. 574 (1934)

This was an action by Robert Francis Davis (plaintiff) against Ann Smaley Davis (defendant) to annul a marriage. The lower court dismissed the case and plaintiff appealed. The case was remanded with direction to enter judgment for plaintiff.

The plaintiff and the defendant went on an automobile ride with several young people. It was a joyous occasion and to add to the excitement the defendant dared the plaintiff to marry her. The plaintiff accepted the dare, a license for the marriage was procured in New York state, and the ceremony was at once performed by a justice of the peace there. Neither party intended at the time to enter into the marriage status. They returned to their respective homes after the ceremony and have never cohabited. The claim of the plaintiff is that the parties never were in fact married despite the ceremony which was performed, because of the lack of real consent on the part of either to enter into that relationship.

Maltbie, C. J. "Marriage is that ceremony or process by which the relationship of husband and wife is constituted. The consent of the parties is everywhere deemed an essential condition to the forming of this relation. To this extent, it is a contract. But, when the relation is constituted, then all its incidents, as well as the rights and duties of the parties resulting from the relation, are absolutely fixed by law. Hence, after a marriage is entered into, the relation becomes a status, and is no longer one resting merely on contract."

It is an accepted principle that, where two parties go through the form of entering into a contract, both understanding that there is no intent thereby to incur legal obligations, no contract is in fact created. In a case very similar to the one before us, Chancellor Zabriskie applied this principle to the marriage contract in the following language: "Mere words without any intention corresponding to them, will not make a marriage or any other civil contract. But the words are the evidence of such intention, and if once exchanged, it must be clearly shown that both parties intended and understood that they were not to have effect. In this case the evidence is clear that no marriage was intended by either party; that it was a mere jest got up in the exuberance of spirits to amuse the company and themselves. If this is so, there was no marriage." It has been said that, where, after such a marriage, cohabitation has followed, "the interests of society become involved, and in many cases prevent the courts from interfering, except in extreme cases." We do not, however, in this case need to consider the extent to which that view is sound, for in this instance the parties separated after the ceremony and never have cohabited.

We find no decision of the New York courts declaring its common law as applied to such a situation as we are considering. Cases like this are naturally rare, because not often will people even young in years so trifle with such a vital relationship as that of marriage. But so fundamental is the principle that there can be no marriage without the consent of the parties, and so accepted is the rule that, though parties go through the form of a contract, if both understand that neither intends to assume a contractual obligation, no real contract is created, that we deem it a part of the general common law that in such a situation as this no marriage ever came into existence. In the absence of some contrary decision of the New York courts, we assume that this is as true in that state as we hold it to be in ours. Upon the facts found by the trial court, the purported marriage between the parties to this action was void under the law of New York, and the court should have decreed it to be void.

Corthell v. Summit Thread Co.
132 Me. 94, 167 Atl. 79, 92 A. L. R. 1391 (1933)

This was an action by Robert N. Corthell (plaintiff) against Summit Thread Company (defendant) to recover damages for breach of a written contract. The trial court reported the case to the Supreme Court for decision. Judgment for plaintiff.

Corthell was employed by the Summit Thread Co. as a salesman. Corthell had patented two bobbins and the company had taken a thirty days' option on the patents. On March 23, 1926, Corthell and the Summit Thread Co. entered into a written contract covering his services as salesman, pay for patent rights, and an agreement for the right to future patents and further provided as follows:

"Furthermore, in consideration of the increased salary to Corthell for five years and the payment of $3,500 to Corthell for the three patents, R. N. Corthell agrees that he will turn over to the Summit Thread Company all future inventions for developments, in which case, reasonable recognition will be made to him by the Summit Thread Company, the basis and amount of recognition to rest entirely with the Summit Thread Company at all times.

"All of the above is to be interpreted in good faith on the basis of what is reasonable and intended and not technically."

Sturgis, J. Corthell turned several patents over to the company during the term of the contract. The plaintiff has never received any compensation for these inventions.

No contention is made that the term "reasonable recognition," as used in the contract under consideration, means other than reasonable compensation or payment for such inventions as the plaintiff turned over.

There is no more settled rule of law applicable to actions based on contracts than that an agreement, in order to be binding, must be sufficiently definite to enable the court to determine its exact meaning and fix exactly the legal liability of the parties. Indefiniteness may relate to the time of performance, the price to be paid, work to be done, property to be transferred, or other miscellaneous stipulations of the agreement. If the contract makes no statement as to the price to be paid, the law invokes the standard of reasonableness, and the fair value of the services or property is recoverable. If the terms of the agreement are uncertain as to price, but exclude the supposition that a reasonable price was intended, no contract can arise. And a reservation to either party of an unlimited right to determine the nature and extent of his performance renders his obligation too indefinite for legal enforcement, making it, as it is termed, merely illusory.

In the instant case, the contract of the parties indicates that they both promised with "contractual intent," the one intending to pay and the other to accept a fair price for the inventions turned over. "Reasonable recognition" seems to have meant what was fair and just between the parties, that is, reasonable compensation.

Patrick v. Kleine
215 N.Y.S. 305 (1926)

This was an action by George J. Patrick (plaintiff) against Antoinette F. Kleine (defendant) asking specific performance of a contract. Judgment for defendant.

Hagarty, J. The contract, if any there be, is to be found in the letters and a telegram that passed between the parties. The defendant denies that a contract was made.

On December 15, 1925, the plaintiff wrote defendant, concerning a lot owned by her: "If you have not sold, I, of course, am the logical purchaser, as it is worth more to me than anybody else. . . . . I hope I shall have the pleasure of hearing from you shortly."

On the 16th day of December, defendant acknowledged plaintiff's letter, and wrote: "If you should be interested in this (my lot) would be glad to hear from you. Size of lot 20 x 100, price $1,000.00 (one thousand dollars)."

Two days later plaintiff telegraphed defendant: "Will accept your proposition of one thousand dollars for lot thirty-five in block seventy-nine aught six and will get contract and check to you within a day or so."

The next day, the following letter was written the defendant by the plaintiff: "Inclosed you will find contracts in the usual form and also my check for $100 as an evidence of good faith, and will you please sign and return one copy to me, so that the title company can institute search?"

On the 23rd day of December the defendant returned the contract and check, and advised plaintiff that the lot had been sold.

The sole question for determination is whether defendant's letter of December 16th is an offer to sell to the plaintiff or an invitation to negotiate. The property is sufficiently described and the price fixed, but the statement that "if you should be interested in this would be glad to hear from you" is indicative of mental reservations, such, for instance, as that she would not agree to sell until she knew the purposes for which the property was to be used. The letter was not an unqualified offer to sell, which became a contract upon acceptance.

While informal communications may constitute a contract, even though they contemplate the execution of a formal agreement, plaintiff's telegram and his letter of December 19th indicate that, in plaintiff's mind, the negotiations did not constitute a contract, or contain the terms of an agreement with the defendant.

Fairmount Glass Works v. Grunden-Martin Woodenware Co.
106 Ky. 659, 51 S.W. 196 (1899)

This was an action by Grunden-Martin Woodenware Company (plaintiff and appellee) against the Fairmount Glass Works (defendant and appellant) to recover damages for breach of contract. Judgment for plaintiff and defendant appeals. Judgment affirmed.

Hobson, J. On April 20, 1895, appellee wrote appellant the following letter:

"St. Louis, Mo., April 20, 1895. Gentlemen: Please advise us the lowest price you can make us on our order for ten carloads of Mason green jars, complete, with caps, packed one dozen in a case, either delivered here, or f. o. b. cars your place, as you prefer. State terms and cash discount. Very truly, Grunden-Martin W. W. Co."

To this letter appellant answered as follows:

"Fairmount, Ind., April 23, 1895. Grunden-Martin Wooden Ware Co., St. Louis, Mo. Gentlemen: Replying to your favor of April 20, we quote you Mason fruit jars, complete, in one-dozen boxes, delivered in East St. Louis, Ill.: Pints \$4.50, quarts \$5.00, half gallons \$6.50, per gross, for immediate acceptance, and shipment not later than May 15, 1895; sixty days' acceptance, or 2 off, cash in ten days. Yours truly, Fairmount Glass Works."

For reply thereto, appellee sent the following telegram on April 24, 1895:

"Fairmount Glass Works, Fairmount, Ind.: Your letter twenty-third received. Enter order ten car loads as per your quotation. Specifications mailed. Grunden-Martin W. W. Co."

In response to this telegram, appellant sent the following:

"Fairmount, Ind., April 24, 1895. Grunden-Martin W. W. Co., St. Louis, Mo.: Impossible to book your order. Output all sold. See letter. Fairmount Glass Works."

Appellee insists that, by its telegram sent in answer to the letter of April 23, the contract was closed for the purchase of 10 carloads of Mason fruit jars. Appellant insists that the contract was not closed by this telegram, and that it had the right to decline to fill the order at the time it sent its telegram of April 24. This is the chief question in the case.

We are referred to a number of authorities holding that a quotation of prices is not an offer to sell, in the sense that a completed contract will arise out of the giving of an order for merchandise in accordance with the proposed terms. There are a number of cases holding that the transaction is not completed until the order so made is accepted. But each case must turn largely upon the language there used. In this case we think there was more than a quotation of prices, although appellant's letter uses the word "quote" in stating the prices given. The true meaning of the correspondence must be determined by reading it as a whole. Appellee's letter of April 20, which began the transaction, did not ask for a quotation of prices. It reads: "Please advise us the lowest price you can make us on our order for ten car loads of Mason green jars. . . . . State terms and cash discount." From this appellant could not fail to understand that appellee wanted to know at what price it would sell it ten car loads of these jars; so when, in answer, it wrote: "We quote you Mason fruit jars . . . . pints $4.50, quarts $5.00, half gallons $6.50 per gross, for immediate acceptance; . . . . 2 off, cash in ten days," it must be deemed as intending to give appellee the information it had asked for. We can hardly understand what was meant by the words "for immediate acceptance," unless the latter was intended as a proposition to sell at these prices if accepted immediately. In construing every contract, the aim of the court is to arrive at the intention of the parties. In none of the cases to which we have been referred on behalf of appellant was there on the face of the correspondence any such expression of intention to make an offer to sell on the terms indicated. In *Fitzhugh* v. *Jones*, 6 Munf. 83, the use of the expression that the buyer should reply as soon as possible, in case he was disposed to accede to the terms offered, was held sufficient to show that there was a definite proposition, which was closed by the buyer's acceptance. The expression in appellant's letter, "for immediate acceptance," taken in connection with appellee's letter, in effect, at what price it would sell it the goods, is, it seems to us, much stronger evidence of a present offer, which, when accepted immediately, closed the contract. Appellee's letter was plainly an inquiry for the price and terms on which appellant would sell it the goods, and appellant's answer to it was not a quotation of prices, but a definite offer to sell on the terms indicated, and could not be withdrawn after the terms had been accepted.

Moulton v. Kershaw and another
59 Wis. 316, 18 N.W. 172 (1884)

This was an action by J. H. Moulton (plaintiff and respondent) against C. J. Kershaw and another (defendants and appellants) to recover damages for breach of contract. Decision on the pleading in favor of J. H. Moulton. Kershaw and another appealed. Decision reversed and cause was remanded to the trial court for retrial.

Taylor, J. The complaint of the respondent alleges that the appellants were dealers in salt in the city of Milwaukee, including salt of the Michigan Salt Association; that the respondent was a dealer in salt in the city of La Crosse, and accustomed to buy salt in large quantities, which fact was known to the appellants; that on the nineteenth day of September, 1882, the appellants, at Milwaukee, wrote and posted to the respondent at La Crosse a letter of which the following is a copy:

"Milwaukee, September 19, 1882.

"J. H. Moulton, Esq., La Crosse, Wis.—Dear Sir: In consequence of a rupture in the salt trade, we are authorized to offer Michigan fine salt, in full car-load lots of 80 to 95 bbls., delivered at your city, at 85¢ per bbl., to be shipped per C. & N. W. R. R. Co. only. At this price it is a bargain, as the price in general remains unchanged. Shall be pleased to receive your order.

"Yours truly, C. J. Kershaw & Son."

Moulton sent the following telegram to Kershaw in reply:

"La Crosse, September 20, 1882.

"To C. J. Kershaw & Son, Milwaukee, Wis.: Your letter of yesterday received and noted. You may ship me two thousand (2,000) barrels Michigan fine salt, as offered in your letter. Answer.

"J. H. Moulton."

The only question presented is whether the appellants' letter, and the telegram sent by the respondent in reply thereto, constitute a contract for the sale of 2,000 barrels of Michigan fine salt by the appellants to the respondent at the price named in such letter. We are very clear that no contract was perfected by the order telegraphed by the respondent in answer to appellants' letter.

We hold that the letter of the appellants in this case was not an offer. If the letter had said to the respondent we will sell you all the Michigan fine salt you will order, at the price and on the terms named, then it is undoubtedly the law that the appellants would have been bound to deliver any reasonable amount that the respondent might have ordered, possibly any amount, or make good their default in damages.

We place our opinion upon the language of the letter of the appellants, and hold that it cannot be fairly construed into an offer to sell to the respondent any quantity of salt he might order, nor any reasonable amount he might see fit to order. The language is not such as a business man would use in making an offer to sell to an individual a definite amount of property. The word "sell" is not used. They say, "we are authorized to offer Michigan fine salt," etc., and volunteer an opinion that at the terms stated it is a bargain. They do not say, we offer to sell to you. They use general language proper to be addressed generally to those who were interested in the salt trade. It is clearly in the nature of an advertisement or business circular, to attract the attention of those interested in that business to the fact that good bargains in salt could be had by applying to them, and not as an offer by which they were to be bound, if accepted, for any amount the persons to whom it was addressed might see fit to order. We think the complaint fails to show any contract between the parties.

Lovett v. Frederick Loeser & Co., Inc.
207 N.Y.S. 753 (1924)

This was an action by Charles H. Lovett (plaintiff) against Frederick Loeser & Co. (defendant) to recover damages for breach of contract. Defendant made a motion to dismiss the case on the ground that the facts stated in the pleadings were not sufficient to constitute a cause of action. The motion was granted.

Spiegelberg, J. The complaint alleges in substance that the defendant conducts a department store; that on September 19, 1924, it inserted an advertisement in one of the newspapers published in the city of New York to the effect that it would sell and deliver and install for any one who would purchase and pay for the same, certain "well-known standard makes of radio receivers at 25 per cent. to 50 per cent. reduction" from the advertised list prices thereof; that among the standard radio receiving sets thus advertised were those made by the makers of the "Radiola, Crosley, De Forest, Malone-Lemmon, Neutrodyne, Colon B. Kennedy, and Sleeper Monotrol" radio receiving sets. The complaint then sets forth in great detail that, among the De Forest radio receiving sets, there were types known as the "D-12 reflex radiophone receiving sets"; that on September 20, 1924, the plaintiff offered to buy two of said sets upon the terms and conditions named in the defendant's advertisement, but that the defendant repudiated its offer to sell; that thereupon on September 22, 1924, the plaintiff unconditionally accepted the defendant's said offer to sell to the plaintiff the two De Forest D-12 reflex radiophone receiving sets and tendered his certified check for the amount of the list price of said sets, less 25 per cent.

The complaint demands judgment for the damages suffered by the plaintiff by reason of the alleged breach of the defendant's contract to sell said sets.

The plaintiff's theory is that the offer of the defendant contained in the advertisement ripened into a contract by his acceptance thereof. Although the plaintiff in his complaint specifically and in great minuteness alleges that a contract of sale was made between the parties, his right must be determined by the contents of the advertisement itself.

I am of opinion that the plaintiff sets forth no cause of action. The defendant's advertisement is nothing but an invitation to enter into negotiations, and is not an offer which may be turned into a contract by a person who signifies his intention to purchase some of the articles mentioned in the advertisement. In *Georgian Company* v. *Bloom*, 27 Ga. App. 468, 108 S.E. 813, the court says: "A general advertisement in a newspaper for the sale of an indefinite quantity of goods is a mere invitation to enter into a bargain, rather than an offer."

"Frequently negotiations for a contract are begun between parties by general expressions of willingness to enter into a bargain upon stated terms and yet the natural construction of the words and conduct of the parties is rather that they are inviting offers, or suggesting the terms of a possible future bargain than making positive offers. Especially is this likely to be true where the words in question are in the form of an advertisement. Thus, if goods are advertised for sale at a certain price, it is not an offer, and no contract is formed by the statement of an intending purchaser that he will take a specified quantity of the goods at that price. The construction is rather favored that such an advertisement is a mere invitation to enter into a bargain rather than an offer." 1 Williston, Cont. 32, 33.

As stated by Professor Williston (supra, at page 35), a positive offer may be made even by an advertisement or general notice, and the only general test is the inquiry whether the facts show that some performance was promised in positive terms in return for something requested. But that is not the situation here. This is the ordinary case of an advertisement which extends an invitation to all persons that the advertiser is ready to receive offers for the goods upon the terms stated.

The Acceptance

Since in making an offer the offeror states what he is willing to do, it would seem that all that would be necessary for an acceptance would be compliance with the demands made in the offer. However, this is not all that is required. The courts require that the offeree, in complying with the demands, must do so with the intent of entering into a contractual obligation. For example, if Archer posts an offer to pay a reward to the person who finds and returns to him his lost watch and Burch, a friend of Archer's, finds the watch, recognizes it as Archer's watch, and returns it to him without any knowledge of the offer of the reward, Burch cannot recover the reward offered. Burch did not return the watch with the intent of accepting Archer's offer.

In offers of rewards for the apprehension of criminals some courts have held that the offer of a reward is in the nature of an offer of a bounty and not in the nature of an offer to contract. These courts allow a recovery if the requested act is performed, and knowledge of the offer of a reward is immaterial. A few courts have refused to apply the intent test in all reward cases, holding that if the person offering the reward received the benefits he desired, public policy would demand that he pay the promised reward.

The question of intent is important in those situations in which the offeree replies to the offeror's offer but his reply is not a definite statement that the offeree accepts the offer. The problems involved in these situations are of the same nature as those involved in determining whether or not one intends to make an offer. Archer advertises for bids on a construction job. Burch submits a bid. Archer telegraphs Burch, "You are low bidder. Come on the morning train." Is this an acceptance of Burch's bid? Does the language used clearly express an intent to accept Burch's offer? In situations of this type the courts have generally held that such language does not express an intent to accept the offer. Unless the offeree by his acts, his language, or by his acts and language clearly expresses an intention to accept an offer, the courts hold that no contract results.

What is necessary to accept an offer? The general rule is that, if the offeree wishes to accept an offer, he must comply strictly with the conditions stated in the offer. It is the offeror who is making the offer and he is free to dictate the terms of the offer. He is privileged to include any terms or conditions he wishes in the offer irrespective of how unreasonable they may be. The offeree is under no obligation to give any attention to the offer, and, if he thinks the conditions in the offer are unreasonable, he is free to ignore the offer. However, if he wishes to accept the offer, he must comply with all the material conditions in the offer.

If the offer is for a unilateral contract, in order to accept, the offeree must perform the act requested as requested. If the offer is for a bilateral contract, in order to accept, the offeree must make the promise requested as requested. The offeror may make the time, the place, the manner of performing the act or of communicating the promise conditions in his offer; if he does, in order to accept, the offeree must comply with all of these conditions. If the offeree does not comply with all the conditions of the offer, no contract will result.

In the negotiation of bilateral contracts frequently certain conditions in the offer are not expressly stated, but are included either by usage of trade or operation of law. Archer writes Burch, "I will sell you 100 cans of lard at 13¢ per lb." Burch replies, "I accept your offer." In the offer the quantity is stated in units of "cans," the price is stated in units of "pounds." By usage of trade a can of lard weighs 50 pounds; consequently, the court will find that the parties intended—understood—that each can of lard would weigh 50 pounds. Also, Archer does not state in his offer that he will transfer good title to the lard to Burch; yet, by operation of law, whenever one offers to sell and no statement is made as to title, it is implied that the seller has good title and will pass good title to the buyer.

Where the parties contemplate reducing their agreement to a

formal written contract, whether a binding contract results before the formal draft is signed depends entirely on the intentions of the parties. If they consider the writing as merely a memorandum of the agreement for the purpose of having a written record, the contract comes into existence as soon as the parties have come to a final agreement; but if the parties consider the written document when put into final form and signed as the contract, and do not intend to be bound until such formal writing is signed by them, then they will not be bound until the written instrument is signed. The intentions of the parties will be determined from all the circumstances surrounding the transaction together with their declarations.

If the agreement is reduced to writing and signed by one of the parties and sent to the other party for his signature and he does not sign, but both parties start to perform the contract, such acts will amount to an acceptance even though the instrument is not signed by both parties. Actual performance is conclusive evidence of an intention to be bound without signing.

As a general rule silence on the part of the offeree will not amount to an acceptance. This rule is based on the well-established legal principle that one cannot impose a contractual obligation on another without the consent, either expressed or implied, of that person. The application of this legal principle prevents an offeror from so wording his offer that the offeree must act or be bound by a contract. For example, if the offeror states in his offer, "If I do not hear from you I shall consider my offer as accepted," and the offeree makes no reply, no contract will result unless previous dealings of other circumstances impose on the offeree a duty to reply.

Owing to a prior agreement, a course of dealing, a usage of trade, or other circumstances, an offeree may be in such a position that he will owe a duty to the offeror to reply. If this is true the offeree's silence will amount to an acceptance and a contract will result. Also, if benefits are conferred on the offeree under circumstances where it is clear that the benefits are not intended as a gift and the offeree accepts the benefits, he will be bound to pay at least the reasonable value of the benefits conferred. For example, if one continues to accept a newspaper or magazine after his subscription expires, he will be liable for the subscription price.

Smith v. Vernon County
188 Mo. 501, 87 S.W. 949 (1905)

This was an action by Ed Smith (plaintiff) against Vernon County (defendant) to recover a reward. Judgment for plaintiff and defendant appealed. Judgment reversed.

One Paxton was murdered and the county offered a reward for the apprehension and conviction of the murderer. Smith apprehended and took the murderer into custody, and the murderer was later convicted. The county refused to pay the reward and Smith brought suit. On the trial no proof was offered that Smith knew of the reward at the time he took the murderer into custody, and from the circumstances it is most probable that he did not know of the reward.

Lamm, J. The cases are in hopeless conflict on this question.

On the one side is a line holding to the theory that knowledge of the offer of a reward is not necessary. The reasoning of this line of cases is felicitously expressed in *Auditor* v. *Ballard*, 72 Ky. 572, thus: "But it is said that the appellee is not entitled to the reward because he did not know, at the time he arrested the fugitive and delivered him to the jailor, that one had been offered, and therefore the services could not have been performed in consideration of the reward. If the offer was made in good faith, why should the state inquire whether appellee knew that it had been made? Would the benefit to the state be diminished by a discovery of the fact that the appellee, instead of acting from mercenary motives, had been actuated solely by a desire to prevent the escape of a fugitive and to bring a felon to trial? And is it not well that all may know that whoever in the community has it in his power to prevent the final escape of a fugitive from justice, and does prevent it, not only performs a virtuous service, but will entitle himself to such reward as may be offered therefor?"

On the one side is a line holding to the theory that knowledge of the offer and a resulting reliance upon it in performing services are essential elements in the recovery of a reward. This line of cases is based on the theory, everywhere recognized, that an offer of a reward is the same as any other contractual offer, and must be known and accepted by being acted upon. If the promise of a reward is to be brought, as seems sensible, within the classification of a contract, it is impossible to see how any other conclusion can be logically arrived at; for in every contract there must be an *aggregatio mentium*, and how can a meeting of the minds exist without the acceptance of an offer, express or implied, or arising, at least, from some fiction of law? That the absence of knowledge of the offer and the absence of performance of services on the faith of the offer, are barriers to recovery is reasoned out on principle by a philosophical writer, Dr. Wharton, and other authors, and is the doctrine of many courts of last resort, and is within the rationale of other cases, where the point was not directly involved.

Scott v. People's Monthly Co.
209 Iowa, 503, 228 N.W. 263, 67 A.L.R. 413 (1929)

This was an action by Scott (plaintiff) against People's Popular Monthly Co. (defendant) to recover $1,000 offered by defendant as first prize in a "Word-building Contest." Judgment for defendant and plaintiff appealed. Judgment affirmed.

The plaintiff submitted a list of words in a "Word-building Contest." It was her claim that she was entitled to the first prize ($1,000) for submitting to the defendant the "largest correct list of words." The plaintiff admitted that she was familiar with the rules of the contest and also admitted that 2,481 of the 4,137 words submitted by her were incorrect, that 122 words were duplications, and that there were words in her list which did not appear in their vocabulary places. The rules expressly set out the words which were permissible and also required the list to be "in alphabetical order and numbered consecutively."

Wagner, J. Appellant's action is founded upon contract. Did the action of the appellant, in submitting her list, containing a vast volume of words known by her to be incorrect under the rules, amount to an acceptance of appellee's offer? Was it substantial performance under and in accordance with the rules? In 23 R.C.L. 1115, it is aptly stated:

"A binding and enforceable contract to pay a reward rests on one side on a valid offer, and on the other side on an acceptance of such offer, *including its terms and conditions,* by a performance of the services requested in the offer. . . . . The matter rests exclusively in the domain of contract, involving an offer and its acceptance. One desiring to offer a reward may fix *his own terms and conditions.* If they are satisfactory, they must, like other propositions, be accepted as made. If unsatisfactory, no one need accept them." [The italics are ours.]

It was appellee who made the offer and fixed the rules. To constitute an acceptance by the appellant, it was necessary for her to substantially comply with the terms and conditions fixed in appellee's offer. Unless she did so, then there was no meeting of the minds, and no contract. Intentional violation of the rules, the terms of the offer, is not substantial performance. Other contestants, who substantially complied with the rules, should not lose to one who intentionally and deliberately violated them. Appellant was under no obligation to send appellee a list of words. She could do so or not, at her own election, but, to be entitled to a prize, it was incumbent upon her to substantially comply with the terms and conditions of appellee's offer. She could not, by making her list, make a rule to suit herself.

Servicised Premoulded Products, Inc. v. American Insulation Co. 104 Pa. Super. Ct. 469, 159 Atl. 228 (1932)

This was an action by Servicised Premoulded Products, Incorporated (plaintiff and appellee) against the American Insulation Company (defendant and appellant) to recover an amount due for goods sold. Defendant set up breach of contract to sell goods as a counterclaim. The issue on the trial was the existence of the alleged contract. Judgment for plaintiff and defendant appealed. Judgment affirmed.

This suit was brought to recover for merchandise sold and delivered to defendant on September 13, 1930. Defendant does not dispute this claim, but claims that plaintiff contracted to sell and deliver to him fifteen car loads of expansion joints and that they now refuse to deliver the expansion joints to his injury in excess of the amount of the plaintiff's claim.

On October 10, 1930, defendant gave the plaintiff's agent an order for fifteen car loads of expansion joints at a specified price. The defendant was to mail delivery dates to plaintiff. On October 11, defendant mailed plaintiff a schedule of shipping dates and on receipt of this schedule plaintiff wrote, "I have your letter under date of October 11th. I suggest that these cars go forward, one car this month, one car in November, four cars in December, four in January and four in February. We wish to thank you very much for your business."

These shipping dates differed materially from the shipping dates stated in defendant's letter. November 11, 1930, defendant received from plaintiff a letter of the same date informing it of "a change in the schedule of discounts," and "in view of this notice, we, of course, are obliged to withdraw any and all offers made prior to November 7th."

Gawthorp, J. Appellant contends that upon the facts above recited there was a binding contract between the parties. The learned judge of the court below decided otherwise, and we agree with him. The original order of October 10, 1930, discloses that it fails to cover all the details of the order, to wit, the dates of delivery. But even if it were to be conceded for present purposes that this incomplete order, if accepted, could form the basis of a binding contract, the fact is that appellant on October 14, 1930, before receiving any acknowledgment or acceptance whatsoever, submitted to appellee definite information as to its requirements on that subject, specifying the dates of delivery, and said "I trust the above is satisfactory to you and if it is we will send our orders for delivery as noted above." When appellee's president wrote the letter of October 14, acknowledging appellant's letter of October 11 and thanking the latter for the business, he suggested a shipping schedule considerably different from that proposed by appellee in its letter of October 14. In view of the facts that appellant made its order conditioned upon the observance of certain shipping directions to be furnished by it, and appellee made a counter-proposal as to those dates without making any formal acceptance of the order, it would seem that both parties regarded the dates of shipments as a vital matter. Inspection of the counter-claim discloses that appellant's view was that the shipping dates were not a negligible factor in the transaction, as there were great variations of prices from month to month. It is very clear that there was no meeting of the minds of the parties on the subject of shipping dates, and hence no contract. We adopt the reasoning and language of the court below that "in using the phraseology, 'if it is (i. e., shipment schedule satisfactory), we will send our orders, etc.,' defendant certainly reserved the right to reject shipments made at other intervals." We are of one mind that appellee's letter of October 14 was at most a polite reply to appellant's letter of October 11, with a counter-proposal, and not an unconditional acceptance of appellant's original order. It follows that no contract arose either by an acceptance of the original order or from the order and the correspondence which followed. A contract must arise from the acceptance of the last-stated terms, and the acceptance must be identical, in order to bring the minds of the parties together. "If an act is requested that very act and no other must be given . . . . and if any provision is added to which the offerer did not assent, the consequence is not merely that the provision is not binding and that no contract is formed; but that the offer is rejected." 1 Williston on Contracts, p. 73.

Curtis Land and Loan Co. v. Interior Land Co.
137 Wis. 341, 118 N.W. 853 (1908)

This was an action by the Curtis Land and Loan Company (plaintiff) against the Interior Land Company (defendant) to recover a certain tract of land. Judgment for plaintiff and defendant appealed. Judgment affirmed.

After some preliminary negotiations defendant offered to sell to plaintiff "S.W. S.W. 6-35-8" for $6.00 per acre. The offer was silent as to the acreage in the description, the county and state in which the described property was located, where the deed would be delivered, and delinquent taxes. On December 17th, plaintiff, replying to this letter, wrote as follows: "Your favor of the 12th inst. received. We will take your SW SW 6-35-8 Lincoln county, Wisconsin, for your cash price of $6.00 per acre. Your records probably show the acreage which is 22. 13 acres. If it is just as satisfactory to you, will you please send your deed to National Bank of Merrill for collection. Kindly have it made out to Curtis Land & Loan Co., a Wisconsin corporation. We note that this description was sold in 1903 and 1904 to F. J. Smith for delinquent taxes. Please take care of these taxes." On December 19th the defendant acknowledged receipt of this letter as follows: "Your letter of the 17th at hand and noted. Will say that our records do not show that this is a fractional forty, and we would have to investigate this further but we could sell it to you as we understand that this is a full forty. With reference to this description being sold for taxes to F. J. Smith, or in the name of F. J. Smith, are tax certificates we had him buy in for us. We will look this matter up promptly and let you know just as soon as we can have it looked up. We do not anticipate selling this forty for less than $240.00, which was the rate of $6.00 per acre for the full forty. We will investigate and let you hear from us promptly." The remaining portion of the correspondence consisted largely of claims made by the plaintiff that the foregoing letters constituted a complete contract, and of denials of such claims on the part of the defendant.

Barnes, J. The cases cited hold that such letters must contain all the elements necessary to constitute an unambiguous contract, and that there must be contained therein a definite offer to sell on the part of the owner of the land and an unqualified acceptance of such offer on the part of the purchaser. The vendee in his letter of acceptance may not attach any condition to such acceptance, even to the extent of undertaking to dictate the place where payment shall be made. If his attempted acceptance is coupled with any condition that varies or adds to the offer to sell, it is not an acceptance, but is in reality a counter proposition. Where the letter of acceptance contains a mere suggestion or request that payment be made at a particular place, but such request is not a condition attached to the acceptance, it does not amount to an attempt to vary the terms of the offer to sell, and will not defeat an action for specific performance.

The letter of defendant written December 12, 1906, was ambiguous as to the parcel of land which was the subject thereof, although both parties undoubtedly understood it to refer to the southwest quarter of the southwest quarter of section 6, township 35 north, of range 8 east, in Lincoln county. The ambiguity consisted in the correspondence up to this point not showing the state in which the land was located, or whether the township was north or south or the range east or west. Plaintiff's letter of acceptance referred to the land as being located in Lincoln county, Wis., and with this addition to the description referred to in the former correspondence there was no ambiguity about it whatever. This was the letter that resulted in the final consummation of the agreement. In addition to accepting defendant's offer, it cleared up something that the parties had in mind by making it a part of the writings. The defendant made no protest against the declaration that the land was located in Lincoln county, and does not now make any claim that both parties did not perfectly comprehend and understand that they were dealing with land correctly described in the letter last referred to. The addition of the words "Lincoln county, Wisconsin," to the description in plaintiff's letter of acceptance, attached no condition to the offer to sell, but elucidated something that was perfectly apparent to the contracting parties, and clarified the situation by obviating the objection that the writings were not sufficiently definite as to description. Plaintiff's letter of acceptance also contained the following statement: "We note that this description was sold in 1903 and 1904 to F. J. Smith for delinquent taxes. Please take care of these taxes." This letter makes it clear that the plaintiff expected the defendant to take care of the outstanding tax certificates mentioned in the letter. If this portion of the letter contained any requirement that was not comprehended in the defendant's offer to sell, then it may well be asseverated that plaintiff did not make an unqualified acceptance, but a conditional one, and that therefore no contract was made. If the legal effect of defendant's offer to sell the land at a stated price was that it should furnish a marketable title free and clear of outstanding liens and encumbrances, then the paragraph quoted added nothing to the defendant's proposition to sell, and did not constitute a counter proposition. The defendant's offer to sell is silent as to the nature of its title and as to the character of the conveyance which it purposed giving. But the law seems to be well settled that an agreement in general terms to convey real estate, without specifying the nature of the title held by the vendor, or the kind of a deed which is to be given, calls for a conveyance of the entire interest in the land sold by a good and sufficient deed. In other words, an agreement to sell at a sound price, without reservation or exception, implies that a marketable title free of incumbrances will be passed to the vendee upon compliance with his obligations. On an agreement by the vendor of lands to execute a good and sufficient conveyance, the purchaser may demand a clear title, as well as that it be assured him by proper covenants. The decisions outside of this court are generally to the effect that an agreement to convey, in the absence of any reservation or exception therein, requires the vendor to convey a marketable title free of incumbrances. The tax certificates referred to in the plaintiff's letter of December 17th were outstanding liens against the land. The statement in plaintiff's letter, "If it is just as satisfactory to you, will you please send your deed to National Bank of Merrill for collection," was a mere suggestion or request, and not an attempt to impose a condition upon the defendant not in consonance with its offer. It is apparent that there was no intention on the part of the plaintiff to make its acceptance conditional upon the deed being sent to Merrill for collection.

Clark et al. v. Fiedler
44 Cal. App. (2d) 838, 113 P. (2d) 275 (1941)

This was an action brought by Thomas Clark and others (plaintiffs and appellants) against Marty Fiedler (defendant and respondent) for damages for breach of contract. Judgment for defendant and plaintiffs appealed. The judgment was reversed and the case sent back to the trial court for a new trial.

Plaintiffs operated a public soft baseball park in Santa Monica. About June 1 the defendant proposed that the plaintiffs purchase an interest in two similar parks which the defendant was operating in Los Angeles. The parties negotiated for the purchase of a 50 per cent interest in defendant's parks. They sold their park and took over the operation of the defendant's parks. On June 28 it was agreed that the parties would meet on June 30 and sign a written agreement and that plaintiffs would make a payment of $6,000, which was the agreed initial payment to be made on the purchase price of the 50 per cent interest in defendant's parks. On the agreed date defendant did not arrive at the agreed place to sign the contract, and on July 1 the plaintiffs learned that the defendant had given an option on the 50 per cent interest to others. Defendant claimed that no binding contract was entered into and that he was not to be bound until the written contract was signed by him.

White, J. We are therefore called upon to determine whether the finding "that by reason of the failure of the parties to reduce their agreement to writing in order to make the same binding, no damage has been suffered by the plaintiffs" is supported by the evidence. We have no hesitancy in saying that the proof is overwhelming and without any creditable contradiction that respondent accepted the written contract on the night of June 30 and agreed to meet on July 1 for the purpose of signing the same and to receive the initial payment thereunder. Having thus assented to the terms and conditions of such contract, respondent is bound by them, and the court should have so found under the evidence herein. The testimony clearly shows that respondent at no time expressed an intention not to be bound until the writing was executed, but his every act and declaration was to the contrary. After all, the formal written contract is not the agreement of the parties, but only evidence of that agreement. In all the cases cited by respondent it appears from the facts thereof that the parties therein understood that their agreement was not to become binding upon any of them until evidenced by the written form; and under those circumstances, of course, their understanding does not become a binding agreement until it is reduced to writing and signed by the parties to it. However, where, as in the instant case, the contract is of such a nature that the law does not require it to be in writing, and it is conceded that a contract of partnership may be oral, and where the terms of the contract are definitely agreed upon and complete, then the fact that contemporaneously with the making of their full and complete oral agreement, they decide to evidence the same by a written instrument, the force and effect of the oral agreement is not thereby impaired or interfered with. We believe this rule to be sound and that it should be so held in the present case.

In *Pratt* v. *Hudson River Railroad Co.*, 21 N.Y. 305,308, it was said: "A contract to make and execute a certain written agreement, the terms of which are . . . . mutually understood, is, in all respects, as valid and obligatory, where no statutory objection interposes, as the written contract itself would be, if executed. If, therefore, it should appear . . . . that the minds of the parties had met; that a proposition for a contract had been made by one party and accepted by the other; that the terms of this contract, were, in all respects, definitely understood and agreed upon, and that a part of the mutual understanding, was, that a written contract, embodying those terms, should be drawn and executed by the respective parties, this is an obligatory contract, which neither party is at liberty to refuse to perform. . . . ."

When, as here, the evidence indisputably shows that all the terms and conditions of the understanding between the parties were definitely agreed upon and the written memorial thereof itself accepted, though not signed, the parties are bound.

Bowley v. Fuller
121 Me. 22, 115 Atl. 466, 24 A.L.R. 964 (1921)

This was an action by Raymond T. Bowley (plaintiff) against John Fuller (defendant) to recover for the storage of hay. Judgment for plaintiff and defendant appealed. Judgment reversed.

The defendant had been a tenant on a farm and had stored a

quantity of hay in the barn. The plaintiff leased the farm and took possession October 28, 1919, four days after the defendant moved. The hay was left in the barn because the defendant had given the plaintiff an option to purchase the hay at a certain price, and the option was continued for two months. The plaintiff did not see fit to purchase, however, leaving the defendant still the owner of the hay which remained in the barn until April 26, 1920.

On March 11, 1920, the plaintiff notified the defendant by letter that if he did not remove the hay by March 15, he would charge the defendant $1.00 per day for the storage after that date. To this the defendant made no reply and he took no steps to remove the hay. On March 30, 1920, the plaintiff again wrote the defendant that if he did not remove the hay before April 1, 1920, the rate of storage would be increased to $2.00 per day after that date. The defendant made no answer and did not remove the hay until April 26, 1920.

The plaintiff claims that he is entitled to the reasonable value of the storage from October 28, 1919, to March 15, 1920; that he is entitled to $1.00 per day storage from March 15, 1920, to April 1, 1920, and $2.00 per day storage from April 1, 1920, until the hay was removed April 26, 1920.

Cornish, C. J. The plaintiff's contention is that, while the price of storage prior to March 15, 1920, should be fixed by the jury at a reasonable rate under an implied contract, defendant's silence gave assent to the plaintiff's proposed increase to $1.00 and again to $2.00 per day, and that the defendant was bound thereby as under a perfected express contract.

The defendant answers that no express contract at any figure was made, because there was no acceptance on his part, and that the most that the plaintiff can recover is a reasonable compensation under an implied contract during the entire period for which he was liable.

In our opinion it cannot be said as a matter of law that an express contract was completed. Plaintiff's letters constituted nothing more than an offer communicated to the defendant. In order to perfect the contract and bind the defendant there must have been an acceptance by him. But he neither accepted nor rejected the offer. He did nothing which could be construed into an acceptance. He simply remained silent. He was under no obligation to speak or to act, and under those circumstances silence and inaction cannot be converted into acceptance.

The amount of storage to be paid rested entirely in contract. When the letters were written there was a subsisting implied contract which obligated the defendant to pay a reasonable sum. There was no existing obligation on the defendant to pay the increased demand, and it could not be inferred as a matter of law from merely allowing the hay to remain in the barn because the continuing liability for rent could be referred to that subsisting contract, and in the absence of any new contract, would be referred to it. A mere failure to reject cannot be converted into an acceptance unless the offeree has agreed in advance that such silence should be so construed or there was some legal duty resting upon him to that effect. There was no such preliminary agreement here and no such duty. Even if the plaintiff had attempted in his offer to make silence on defendant's part a constructive acceptance, the law would not permit it. The governing principles are summarized as follows:

"Acceptance of an offer may often be inferred from silence as when goods sent to another without request are used or dealt with as his own. Silence alone does not give consent, even by estoppel, for there must not only be the right but the duty to speak before the failure so to do can estop a person from afterward setting up the truth. It is otherwise of course if the relation of the parties, their previous dealings or other circumstances are such as to impose a duty to speak. An offer made to another either orally or in writing cannot be turned into an agreement because the person to whom it is made or sent makes no reply, even though the offer states that silence will be taken as consent for the offeror cannot prescribe conditions of rejection so as to turn silence on the part of the offeree into acceptance." 13 C. J. p. 276, § 74.

Of course, the conduct of the offeree may be of such a character that although he remains silent his acts import acceptance or assent and therefore in the eye of the law may be regarded as such. In this class of cases the question of acceptance inferable from conduct would be one of fact for the jury.

Communication of Offer

The mere intent to make an offer is not sufficient to bring an offer into existence; nor is the writing of an offer addressed to a named offeree sufficient to satisfy the legal requirements of a valid offer. In addition to intent and formulation of the offer, it must be communicated to the offeree. The term "communication of the offer" means more than that the offeree has learned of the offer. To have an offer communicated, the offeree must learn of the offer as a result of an act of the offeror which was intended to result in the offeree's learning of the offer. If the offeror relates the offer to a third person, stating that he intends to make such an offer to a named offeree, and the third person, without authority, conveys the information to the offeree, the offer has not been communicated, and the attempted acceptance by the proposed offeree would create no legal obligations.

The posting of a notice, the printing of terms on a baggage check or on a railroad ticket, or the inclosing of terms in a bill for moneys due from customers will not bind the party unless the terms are called to his attention. The mere posting of a notice or the mere printing of terms on a baggage check, etc., is not a communication of the notice or terms to the other party. Under some circumstances a person may be under a duty to read the notice or the terms on the check or ticket. If he is under such duty, his failure to read the notice or terms will not relieve him from legal liability, but if he is under no duty to read the notice or terms and such notice or terms are not brought to his attention and he does not read them, he will not be legally bound by them In such instances the notice or terms have not been legally com municated to the party.

Mayor, etc., of Jersey City v. Town of Harrison et al.
72 N.J. L. 185, 62 Atl. 765 (1905)

This was an action by the Mayor and Aldermen of Jersey City (plaintiff) against the Town of Harrison (defendant) to enforce a contract. Judgment for defendants and plaintiff appealed. The judgment was affirmed.

A resolution of the town council of Harrison directed the president and clerk to execute a contract with Jersey City for a supply of water on certain terms. It was adopted by a unanimous vote of the members of the town council of Harrison. But there was no proof in court to show that the town council directed that the resolution should be transmitted to Jersey City, or gave any one authority to present the resolution to Jersey City for its action thereon. Jersey City, learning of the resolution, secured a copy and drew up a contract in accordance with the provisions of the resolution and tendered it to the president and clerk for execution. At a later date the council of Harrison repealed the resolution and the town of Harrison refused to allow Jersey City to supply them water in accordance with the terms of the first resolution. Jersey City sued, claiming that the passing of the resolution was an offer and that the tendering of the contract drawn in accordance with the resolution was an acceptance and therefore a binding contract resulted. Harrison claimed no offer was communicated to Jersey City.

Magie, Ch. A proposition for a contract, to be competent to be accepted, must be communicated to the party with whom the contract is proposed. It will not be sufficient that the latter acquire knowledge of it, unless the knowledge is acquired with the express or implied intention of the proposing party. An owner of land contemplating a sale thereof, might direct his stenographer or other agent to draft a contract for sale to a particular person on specified terms. If the owner has not communicated the proposed contract to that person, the latter having acquired knowledge thereof, could not by acceptance bring the owner into a contractual relation of sale. The owner might leave his uncommunicated draft in his agent's hands without liability, and retract his agency and abandon his plan at any time. Until communicated there is no efficacious proposal which could be accepted. In like manner, the resolution never having been communicated to Jersey City by any out of the town of Harrison, did not constitute a proposal, and could not be raised to a binding contract by any acceptance.

Green's Executors v. Smith
146 Va. 442, 131 S.E. 846, 44 A.L.R. 1175 (1926)

This was an action by Howard A. Smith (plaintiff) against the estate of Mrs. A. D. Green, deceased (defendant) to recover an amount claimed payable under the terms of a contract. Judgment for plaintiff and defendant appealed. The judgment was reversed and judgment entered for defendant.

Mrs. Green stored her electric automobile in Smith's garage in the early part of 1918. At the time the car was left at the garage there was no written contract signed by the parties but Smith advised Mrs. Green of the terms and regulations then in effect at his garage for the regular monthly storage of automobiles. Smith, in addition to other specified services, contracted to deliver the car to the owner's residence and take it back to the garage once each day when requested by the owner with the further understanding that Smith should not be responsible for any damages to the car while in the hands of his employees during such movements.

In January, 1920, Smith had printed what he called a "folder" which bore on the title page this inscription:

"Service Rates of the Richmond Electric Garage
"Howard M. Smith, Proprietor,
"2035 W. Broad Street, Richmond, Va.
"Effective on and after January 1, 1920."

The center, or inside pages, of the folder contained a schedule of charges for divers specified services performed by the garage and other printed matter, including the following:

"Note: The owner agrees to accept our employees as his or her agent and to absolve this garage from any liability whatsoever arising while his or her car is in the hands of said employee at the request of and as agent of the owner. . . ."

The back of the folder contained only a schedule of rates and terms relating to work and services in connection with automobile batteries.

The folder was mailed to all the patrons of the garage, including Mrs. Green, with the bills sent out in the early part of January, which action was repeated the following month; and copies were also placed by the employees of the garage, on several occasions, in defendant's car as well as all other cars kept at the garage on regular storage. It also appears that the above-mentioned folder was the only document of the kind that plaintiff ever had printed and sent out to his customers.

On October 1, 1920, Mr. Moore was injured by one of the garage employees while taking Mrs. Green's car from her residence to the garage to be stored for the night. Moore sued Smith and obtained a judgment for $2,500 and costs. Smith sued Mrs. Green to recover the amount paid to Moore on his judgment together with $300 in attorney's fees which Smith incurred in defense of the suit. Mrs. Green contends that she never read the folder and never accepted the terms printed in the folder.

Chinn, J. It is elementary that mutuality of assent—the meeting of the minds of the parties—is an essential element of all contracts, and, in order that this mutuality may exist, it is necessary that there be a proposal or offer on the part of one party and an acceptance on the part of the other. Both the offer and acceptance may be by word, act or conduct which evince the intention of the parties to contract, and that their minds have met may be shown by direct evidence of an actual agreement, or by indirect evidence of facts from which an agreement may be implied. It is manifest, however, that before one can be held to have accepted the offer of another, whether such offer is made by word or act, there must have been some form of communication of the offer; otherwise there could be no assent and, in consequence, no contract. In the instant case the plaintiff relies upon the "note" printed in the folder as constituting the terms of the proposed contract; on the fact that said folder was mailed to Mrs. Green on several occasions with her monthly bills and placed in her car, as a communication of said terms; and on her conduct in continuing to keep her car in his garage as an implied acceptance of the terms specified in said note. The question, therefore, of whether Mrs. Green agreed to, and is bound by, the terms of the "note" in the main depends upon whether the means employed by the plaintiff to communicate such terms were sufficient, under the circumstances, to constitute her act in the premises an implied acceptance of the said terms. The rule as to when the delivery of a paper containing the terms of a proposed contract amounts to an acceptance is thus stated in 13 Corpus Juris, at page 277: "A contract may be formed by accepting a paper containing terms. If an offer is made by delivering to another a paper containing the terms of a proposed contract and the paper is accepted, the acceptor is bound by its terms; and this is true whether he reads the paper or not. When an offer contains various terms, some of which do not appear on the face of the offer, the question whether the acceptor is bound by the terms depends on the circumstances. He is not bound as a rule by any terms which *are not communicated* to him. But he is bound by all the legal terms which are communicated. This question arises when a person accepts a railroad or steamboat ticket, bill of lading, warehouse receipt, or other document containing conditions. He is bound by all the conditions whether he reads them or not, *if he knows that the document contains conditions.* But *he is not bound by conditions of which he is ignorant, even though the ticket or document contains writing, unless he knows that the writing contains terms, by reason of previous dealings, or by reason of the form, size, or character of the document.*"

There was nothing on the face of the folder, nor in its form or character, to indicate that it contained the terms of the contract which plaintiff has attempted to establish in this case, or any other contract imposing obligations of such a nature upon the defendant. The paper only purported to contain a schedule of rates for services at plaintiff's garage, and defendant had no reason, on account of her previous dealings with the plaintiff or otherwise, to know that plaintiff proposed, by mailing the folder to her along with his monthly bill, and placing a copy of it in her car, to commit her to a new contract of such unusual terms.

Communication of Acceptance

The question of communication of an acceptance raises many problems. If the offer is an offer for a unilateral contract, the performance of the required act is an acceptance. This rule is adhered to by the courts, but if, in the normal course of events, knowledge that the requested act has been performed will not come to the notice of the offeror, the general rule is that the offeree must notify the offeror that he has performed the requested act, and failure to give such notice within a reasonable time after the performance of the act will relieve the offeror from contractual liability.

If the offer is for a bilateral contract, in order to accept, the offeree must communicate his intention to make the requested promise to the offeror. If the parties are dealing face to face, the acceptance is communicated as soon as the words are spoken. Apparently the same view is taken when the contract is negotiated over the telephone. If the negotiations are carried on by mail, telegraph, or other method of communication, two questions arise: (1) What agency of communication must the offeree use in accepting the offer? (2) When does the acceptance become effective? Both of these questions may become immaterial if the offeror makes the use of a designated method of communication a condition of his offer, and if he also states as a condition of his offer the time the acceptance will become effective. Archer writes Burch making Burch an offer and then states, "acceptance of this offer must be by telegraph and your telegraphic acceptance must be delivered to me not later than noon Tuesday next." If Burch wishes to accept the offer, he will have to send his acceptance by telegraph, and the telegram of acceptance will not be effective until it reaches Archer and then only if it reaches Archer by noon "Tuesday next."

In normal business transactions it is not customary for the offeror to state either the method of communication to be used or the time the acceptance will become effective. To fill in this gap and thus lend certainty to an uncertain situation, the courts have adopted rules to aid in answering these two questions when the offer is silent on these two points. The courts are universal in holding that if the offer does not designate a means of transmitting the acceptance, the offeree is authorized to use the same means of transmitting the acceptance as the offeror used in transmitting the offer, and if so transmitted, the acceptance is operative and completes the contract as soon as it is put out of the offeree's possession, without regard to whether or not it ever reaches the offeror.

If an offer is sent by mail and the acceptance is sent by telegraph, when is the contract completed? The courts are not in complete accord on this question. The Iowa court held (quoting from the syllabus): "An acceptance by telegram of an offer by mail, which does not specify any mode of acceptance, does not complete the contract until the telegram is delivered to the sendee." The Federal Circuit Court of Appeals accepted this view in *Dickey* v. *Hurd*, 33 F. (2d) 415. But in *Weld* v. *Victory Mfg. Co.*, 205 Fed. 770, Connor, D. J., held: "The letter of defendant to plaintiff of September 7, 1911, was a 'firm offer . . . . subject to withdrawal before execution.' When the plaintiffs on September 20th filed with the Telegraph Company at 10:15 A.M. the telegram accepting the offer, the contract was complete. There was a proposal on the one part, and an acceptance on the other. The withdrawal of the offer or proposal was not completed by filing with the Telegraph Company the message at 9:55 A.M.—it was only effectual for that purpose when received by the plaintiff at 10:40 A.M. The contract is complete 'when the answer containing the acceptance of a distinct proposition is dispatched by mail or other usual mode of communication . . . . and before any intimation is received that the offer is withdrawn. Putting a letter in the mail containing the acceptance, and thus placing it beyond the control of the party, is valid as a constructive notice of acceptance.' "

From the cases it is clear that the majority of courts hold that, if the offeror does not expressly designate the agency of communication to be used in accepting the offer, a contract is completed when the acceptance is received, provided the offer has not terminated before receipt of the acceptance, irrespective of the mode used to communicate the acceptance. If the offeror has expressly or impliedly authorized the use of the means of communication used by the offeree, the contract is complete when the acceptance is dispatched. The question of what conduct on the part of the offeror will be construed as authorizing the use of a particular mode of communication is not settled except in those cases in which the offeror expressly states the mode of communication to be used, and in those cases in which the offeree uses the same means of communication as that used by the offeror.

Ross v. Leberman
298 Pa. 574, 148 Atl. 858 (1930)

This was an action by Edward Ross (plaintiff) against Maurice A. Leberman, individually and as executor of the estate of Sidney A. Leberman, deceased (defendant). Judgment for plaintiff and defendant appealed. Judgment reversed and new trial ordered.

The Lebermans owed Ross $36,512.50, less some agreed reductions for insurance and other expenses, which they refused to pay claiming that Ross owed them an amount in excess of this sum. Ross sued and the Lebermans set up their claim as a set-off. On the trial the only matter in dispute was the validity of the Lebermans' claim against Ross. Ross, Maurice Leberman, Sidney Leberman, and another owned all the stock of Edgar & Co., a corporation. The corporation was in financial difficulties and Ross promised to pay one-third of any sum advanced by the Lebermans to keep the corporation going. The fourth party was financially unable to contribute. Between 1923 and 1926 the Lebermans advanced $105,769.33 to Edgar & Co. No notice was given Ross at the time the sums were advanced, nor was notice given at any time. Ross contended that the failure to give notice within a reasonable time discharged him from all liability for the sums advanced.

Sadler, J. The argument is made that the contract set up was unilateral in nature, and therefore without effect, unless a notice of acceptance was given, which fact is not averred, but the act agreed upon as a condition of liability was performed without revocation. "It is often said that notice of acceptance is necessary for the completion of a contract, but it is not true and never has been true, as a general proposition, that, where an offeror requests an act in return for his promise, and the act is performed, notice to the offeror of the performance is necessary to create a contract." Williston on Contracts, 117.

The general rule applicable has been thus stated: "In reference to the sufficiency of an acceptance there is a distinction between an offer to make a contract executory on both sides and an offer or promise for an act. In the latter case the only acceptance of the offer that is necessary is the performance of the act. In other words, the promise becomes binding when the act is performed." 6 R.C.L. 607.

The opinion of the court in this case shows that summary judgment was entered, not because of lack of notice of acceptance of the offer, before revocation, but for failure to inform Ross when the actual expenditures were made, which it held was required if the counterclaim was to be sustained.

"Notice in such a case, however, is not a necessary element in the creation of the contract. If this were true, the offeror might revoke his offer after performance of the act requested, but prior to notification. Such a result would be unjust, and is required neither by the necessities of the case nor the authorities. The contract is complete on the performance of the act but is subject to a condition subsequent that if notice of the performance of the act is not given within a reasonable time by the promisee, the promisor is freed from obligation."

An attempt has been made to formulate a rule by the American Law Institute in section 56, when it states: "But if the offeror has no adequate means of ascertaining with reasonable promptness and certainty that the act or forbearance has been given, and the offeree should know this, the contract is discharged unless, within a reasonable time after performance of the act or forbearance, the offeree exercises reasonable diligence to notify the offeror thereof." But, as there said by the authors: "It is only in the exceptional case where the offeror has no convenient means of ascertaining whether the requested act has been done that notice is requisite. Even then, it is not the notice which creates the contract, but lack of the notice which ends the duty."

Ross had agreed that advances should be made to Edgar & Co., in the success of whose business he was interested, and stipulated that the balance owing him should be used by the Lebermans, provided they furnished twice the sum which he agreed to pay. This they did, without receiving notice of revocation of their authority to so act.

Spratt v. Paramount Pictures, Inc.
35 N.Y.S. (2d) 815 (1942)

This was an action by John M. Spratt (plaintiff) against Paramount Pictures, Inc. (defendant) to compel defendant to issue to plaintiff shares of defendant's common stock. Judgment for defendant.

Bevenga, J. The plaintiff brought this action to compel defendant to issue to plaintiff ninety shares of its common stock, to which plaintiff claims he is entitled by reason of the privilege of conversion granted to holders of defendant's preferred stock under the terms of defendant's certificate of incorporation.

The certificate of incorporation provides that, in the case of shares called for redemption, the preferred stock shall be convertible "only up to and including the day which shall be two weeks prior to the redemption," and that before the holder of such preferred stock shall be entitled to convert the same into common stock, "he shall surrender the certificate or certificates for the stock to be converted to the corporation at the office of any transfer agent for the common stock." Concededly, plaintiff's stock was called for redemption. The redemption date was February 3, 1942. The last day, therefore, on which the preferred stock was convertible was January 20, 1942. The question presented is whether the mailing by plaintiff of his certificate for shares of preferred stock on January 20, 1942, at York, S.C., so that it was not received at the office of the transfer agent in New York until January 22, 1942, is sufficient compliance with the provisions of the certificate of incorporation.

Plainly, the certificate of incorporation not only fixes the time within which the privilege of conversion must be done, but also prescribes the manner in which it must be exercised. The preferred stock is convertible "only up to and including January 20, 1942, by surrendering the certificates of stocks to be converted to the corporation." In other words, the certificate of incorporation calls not only for the acceptance of the offer within the time fixed, but the surrender of the certificate within that time. Compliance with both of these conditions is a prerequisite to the plaintiff's right to convert his preferred stock into common stock. Since the plaintiff failed to comply with these conditions, he has waived or lost that right.

It is true, as plaintiff argues, that an offer is deemed to be accepted as soon as a letter of acceptance, duly addressed and stamped, is deposited in a post office or letter box. But this rule applies only in cases where the offer is transmitted by mail. The theory is that the offeror, by using the mail as his agent to transmit the offer, has given the offeree implied authority to use the same agency to receive the reply. The rule does not apply where the offer prescribes the time, place, mode of acceptance, or other matters which the offeror may insert in and make a part of the offer. In such a case, "the acceptance, to conclude the agreement, must, in every respect, meet and correspond with the offer, neither falling short of or going beyond the terms proposed, but exactly meeting them at all points and closing with them just as they stand."

It follows, therefore, that where, as here, the offer specifies the time, place, and mode of acceptance, an acceptance after that time, or at any other place, or in any other manner, is wholly nugatory and ineffectual as an acceptance.

Trevor v. Wood
36 N.Y. 307 (1867)

This was an action brought by John B. Trevor, Jr., and James B. Colgate (plaintiffs and appellants) against John Wood, George W. Wood, and James Cullen (defendants and respondents) to recover damages for breach of a contract. Judgment for defendants and plaintiffs appealed. Judgment reversed.

The appellants are dealers in bullion in New York, and the respondents are dealers in bullion in New Orleans. In 1859 they agreed to deal with each other in the purchase and sale of dollars, and they also agreed that all communications between them in reference to such transactions should be by telegraph.

On the 30th of January, 1860, the appellants telegraphed from New York to the respondents at New Orleans, asking at what price they would sell one hundred thousand Mexican dollars. On the 31st of the same month, the respondents answered that they would deliver fifty thousand at seven and one-quarter; and on the same day the appellants telegraphed from New York to the defendants at New Orleans as follows:

"To John Wood & Co. —Your offer fifty thousand Mexicans at seven and one-quarter accepted; send more if you can.

TREVOR & COLGATE."

On the next day (1st February, 1860), the appellants again telegraphed to the respondents as follows:

"To John Wood & Co. —Accepted by telegraph yesterday, your offer for fifty thousand Mexicans; send as many more, same price. Reply.

TREVOR & COLGATE."

This telegram, as well as that of the 31st of January, from the appellants did not reach the respondents until 10 A.M. on the 4th of February, 1860, in consequence of some derangement in a part of the line used by the appellants. This fact was not known to the appellants until the 4th of February, when the telegraph company reported the line down. On the 3rd of February the respondents telegraphed to the appellants as follows: "No answer to our dispatch—dollars are sold"; and on the same day they wrote by mail to the same effect. The appellants received this dispatch on the same day, and answered it on the same day as follows: "To John Wood & Co.—Your offer was accepted on receipt"; and again the next day: "The dollars must come, or we will hold you responsible. Reply. TREVOR & COLGATE." And again on the 4th of February insisting on the dollars being sent "by this or next steamer," and saying "don't fail to send the dollars at any price."

On the same 4th of February the respondents telegraphed to appellants, "No dollars to be had. We may ship by steamer twelfth, as you propose, if we have them." No dollars were sent, and this action was brought to recover damages for an alleged breach of contract in not delivering them.

Scrugham, J. Mr. Justice Marcy in delivering the leading opinion in *Mactier* v. *Frith*, says: "What shall constitute an acceptance will depend in a great measure upon circumstances. The mere determination of the mind unacted on can never be an acceptance. Where the offer is by letter the usual mode of acceptance is by the sending of a letter announcing a consent to accept; where it is made by a messenger a determination to accept returned through him or sent by another would seem to be all the law requires if the contract may be consummated without writing. There are other modes which are equally conclusive upon the parties; keeping silent under certain circumstances is an assent to a proposition; anything that shall amount to a manifestation of a formed determination to accept, communicated or put in the proper way to be communicated to the party making the offer, would doubtless complete the contract."

It was agreed between these parties that their business should be transacted through the medium of the telegraph. The object of this agreement was to substitute the telegraph for other methods of communication, and to give to their transactions by it the same force and validity they would derive if they had been performed through other agencies. In accordance with this agreement the offer was made by telegraph to appellants in New York, and the acceptance addressed to the respondents in New Orleans, and immediately dispatched from

New York by order of the appellants. It cannot, therefore, be said that the appellants did not put their acceptance in a proper way to be communicated to the respondents, for they adopted the method of communication which had been used in the transaction by the respondents, and which had been selected by prior agreement between them as that by means of which their business should be transacted.

Under these circumstances the sending of the dispatch must be regarded as an acceptance of the respondents' offer and thereupon the contract became complete.

Termination of Offer

In an early English case (*Cook* v. *Oxley*, 3 Term Rep. 653) the court held that, if the offer was not accepted at the time it was made, it could not be accepted at a later time unless it was again repeated by the offeror. Had this rule been adhered to it is difficult to conceive how business could be successfully conducted under modern conditions. The rule was soon changed and now when an offer is made it remains open for acceptance until it is terminated.

This change in the rule has resulted in the development of several rules relative to the termination of offers. When the offeror states in his offer that the offer must be accepted within a designated time, the offeree does not have the privilege of accepting after the expiration of the designated time. After the stated time has elapsed it is impossible for the offeree to comply with all the terms of the original offer. If the offeror communicates his intentions to be bound by the delayed acceptance, a contract results. It would be more correct to consider the delayed acceptance as an offer and the communication of intention to be bound as the acceptance. Often in limiting the time for acceptance the offeror will use such expressions as "by return mail," "for immediate acceptance," "prompt wire acceptance." "By return mail" does not of necessity require the acceptance to go out by the next mail, especially in large cities where mails are leaving hourly, but it does require an answer the same day the offer is received unless received at too late an hour to answer that day, and in that event the acceptance must be dispatched on the opening for business the succeeding day. "Immediate acceptance" and "prompt wire acceptance" give the offeree a shorter time than "by return mail." The time would depend to some extent on the nature of the transaction; in any event, a few hours at the longest would be the limit of time allowed in which to accept.

If no time for acceptance is stated in the offer, the offer must be accepted within a reasonable time. This is a rule of law adopted by the courts and is very flexible. The time may vary from a few seconds to several days. The length of time which is reasonable must depend on the circumstances of the case. Each case will have to be decided as a separate proposition, and general rules will be of little help. However, there are certain things that are of particular importance in determining the length of time which is reasonable, e.g., the nature of the transaction and the state of the market. If the proposed contract is of a nature that does not require haste, a much longer time will be allowed than if the proposed contract involves property having a rapidly fluctuating market price. Also, if the proposed contract is for the sale of property and at the time the proposal is made the market is stable, a longer time will be allowed for acceptance than if the market is fluctuating.

If the offeror makes an offer, he has a right to withdraw it at any time before it has been accepted, with the exception of offers under seal in those states which recognize the efficacy of the seal, and offers containing a promise to hold the offer open for a stated time in which the promise is supported by consideration. This rule recognizes the right of the offeror to change his mind, but it requires him to inform the offeree that he has changed his mind. The fact that one has made an offer and agreed not to withdraw it, or has agreed to keep it open for a stated time does not prevent him from withdrawing the offer unless the promise not to revoke it is under seal or supported by consideration.

An offer to the general public is made by making a general announcement of the offer. This announcement may be made through the newspapers, magazines, posters, handbills, radio, or by any other means suitable to the purpose of the offeror. If the offeror, after having made the offer, wishes to withdraw it, he must announce his withdrawal in substantially the same manner which he used in announcing the offer. He must give the withdrawal the same publicity which he gave his offer. The fact that one read or heard the offer but did not read or hear of the withdrawal is of no moment. If the same publicity has been given to the revocation as was given to the offer, the offer is revoked as to the entire public, and an attempt to accept after the publication of the withdrawal is ineffective.

The general rule, that an offer may be revoked at any time before acceptance, applies to some types of offers for unilateral contracts, but there is some question whether the courts will apply the rule in all cases. If an offer for a reward is made and the offeror revokes the offer before the reward is claimed, the revocation will be effective. If the act requested is of such a nature that an appreciable period of time is required for its performance, should the offeror be permitted to revoke the offer an instant before the act is performed and the offer accepted? If the nature of the act is such that the offeror receives benefits from the performance, a recovery for the benefits conferred would be allowed in a suit in quasi contract. If the act is such that, although the performance is detrimental to the offeree, it is not beneficial to the offeror, no recovery can be had in quasi contract. Justice would dictate in such a case that the offer should be held to be irrevocable until the offeree, having started performance, would have a reasonable time to complete the performance. Cases involving the revocation of an offer for a unilateral contract are not very common. Business contracts are generally bilateral and the courts will, if the facts permit, hold that the contract is bilateral.

The general rule, that an offeror may withdraw his offer at any time before it has been accepted, does not serve to answer the two important questions: "When is the offer accepted?" and "When is an offer withdrawn?" If the parties are dealing face to face, the one who speaks first has the law with him; but when the parties are using some of the agencies of communication to carry on their negotiations, the questions are not answered so easily. The courts have adopted the general rule, that when the mails or other agencies of communication are used to negotiate a contract, the acceptance becomes effective as soon as it has been delivered to an authorized agency of communication. The general rule is that a revocation does not become effective until it is delivered to the offeree. Under this rule, if the offeree cannot be reached, some hardship may result, but the courts have the power to deal with exceptional cases so that no great injustice will result. The rule is to some extent arbitrary but is supported by business convenience.

When the offeree notifies the offeror that he does not wish to accept his offer, the offer is terminated. When the offeree has refused the offer, certainly the offeror should be free to seek a contract elsewhere. If the offeree makes a counter-offer or conditional acceptance, the original offer is terminated. If the offeree makes a counter-offer or conditional acceptance, he thereby indicates an intention not to accept the offeror's offer, thus terminating the offer, and at the same time the offeree makes the offeror an offer, thereby reversing the relationship of the parties. In some instances an offeree will unintentionally terminate an offer in an effort to obtain better terms. If the offer has been terminated by a counter-offer, rejection, or conditional acceptance, it cannot be revived by any act of the offeree.

There are some situations over which the parties have no control which will terminate an offer. It is a well-established rule that the death or insanity of either party will terminate the offer. This rule was developed in the English courts at the time that a "meeting of the minds" of the parties was the test of the existence of a contract. After death one has no mind and, at that time, the courts held that an insane person had no mind; consequently, if one of the parties died or became insane, it was impossible to have the essential "meeting of minds." In the case of death, the courts have held that the notice of the death is not necessary to terminate the offer. This rule is not in full accord with the general rules governing the termination of offers and sometimes results in injustice, but it is so well established that it will no doubt require legislative action to change it. There are a few cases in agency holding notice of death necessary. Where, without the knowledge or fault of either party, the subject matter of the proposed contract is destroyed, the offer is considered as terminated.

Archer, who lives in the city, offers to sell Burch a stack of hay which is on his farm. Without the knowledge or fault of either party the stack of hay is destroyed by fire before Burch accepts the offer. The courts will hold that when the stack of hay burned the offer was terminated.

Also, if, after the offer is made, legislation is passed or regulations adopted which would render the performance of the proposed contract illegal, the offer is terminated.

On December 1, 1941, Archer offered to sell Burch four new automobile tires and agreed to hold the offer open until March 1, 1942. When, as the result of the war, restrictions were put on the sale of automobile tires which made the performance of the proposed contract illegal, the offer was terminated.

Herndon v. Armstrong et al.
148 Or. 602, 38 P. (2d) 44 (1934)

This was an action by R. L. Herndon (plaintiff) against Evelyn G. Ramsay and Stanley Armstrong and wife (defendants) for the specific performance of a contract to sell land. Judgment for plaintiff and defendants Armstrong and wife appealed. Judgment affirmed.

Mrs. Ramsay leased a dwelling and ten acres of land to Armstrong. The lease gave Armstrong an option to purchase the property. By its terms the option expired January 15, 1934. Armstrong was negotiating for a loan from Federal Land Bank, but the loan was not granted until January 23, 1934. On January 22, 1934, Mrs. Ramsey contracted to sell the property to Herndon. Armstrong claims he exercised his option on January 23, 1934, and filed a cross-complaint to recover the property.

Bean, J. Options to purchase real estate are merely offers to sell property, and until acceptance and their conditions unconditionally performed, they confer no title to the realty. To develop an offer into a contract requires its acceptance in precise terms. An option to purchase real estate does not pass to the optionee any interest in the land, but a contract of sale does transfer to the vendee an interest in the land, and therefore a person appearing in the character of an optionee possesses nothing except the right to buy, and he has no interest in the land unless by his acceptance of the option he transfers the option into a contract of sale and changes his character from that of optionee to that of vendee. When an offer is made for the time limited in the offer itself, no acceptance afterwards will make it binding. An offer which in its own terms limits the time of acceptance is withdrawn or terminates by the expiration of the time.

Ward v. Board of Education of Harrison Tp. Rural School Dist.
36 Ohio App. 557, 173 N.E. 634 (1930)

This was an action by Ina A. Ward (plaintiff) against Board of Education of Harrison Township Rural School District (defendant) for wages claimed to be due under a contract of employment. Judgment for defendant and plaintiff appealed. Judgment affirmed.

Miss Ward was employed by the defendant to teach school for the 1928-29 school year. June 15, 1929, the clerk of the defendant board mailed a renewal contract for plaintiff to sign which she received June 18. This contract was retained by the plaintiff and not returned to the board until July 5, and in the meantime the board, at a meeting on July 2, employed another person in the place of the plaintiff to teach the school for which the plaintiff had been employed during the 1928-29 school year. The plaintiff knew at the time she returned her contract that the board had taken such action and that another teacher had been employed in her place.

Middleton, P. J. As long as the contract remained in her hands, or under her control, there was no acceptance on her part and the most that she may claim under such facts is that the time within which and during which she held the contract was a reasonable time, and that she acted with due diligence in signing and returning the contract to the board. It is a primary rule that a party contracting by mail, as she did, when no time limit is made for the acceptance of the contract, shall have a reasonable time, acting therein with due diligence, within which to accept. In *New* v. *Germania Fire Ins. Co.*, 171 Ind. 33, 85 N.E. 703, 706, 131 Am. St. 245, 250, this rule is well stated as follows: "It is true that where an offer is made by mail . . . . in the absence of notice of revocation . . . . that the writer continues willing to contract down to the time that the other party may, with due diligence, accept the proposition."

This rule does not permit the accepting party to sign a contract at his pleasure. It does not give him the unqualified right to hold the contract, as the plaintiff did in this case, for seventeen days; nor does it allow him undue delay to determine whether another contract in contemplation might be more advantageous to him if it could be obtained. The evidence in this case may have moved the trial court to find that the delay of the plaintiff was due to her pending application before another board for another school. The evidence at least tends strongly to show that she did not return her contract until the other outstanding application was denied.

In a note to *Maclay* v. *Harvey*, 32 Am. Rep. at page 51, the rule is thus stated: "If any undue delay or failure of delivery of the letter of acceptance is caused by the fault of the accepting party, there is no contract."

Manifestly the question of whether or not the plaintiff had acted with due diligence was a question for the jury, as was also the question whether the board, meeting again on July 2, and then having no return from the contract offered to the plaintiff, was justified in employing another in her place. If, as we have observed, the trial court reached the conclusion that the plaintiff did not act with due diligence, and that under the admitted circumstances of the case the board was not at fault, we regard the evidence as sufficient to support such finding and determination of the rights of the parties.

Durham Life Ins. Co. v. Moize et al.
175 N.C. 344, 95 S.E. 552 (1918)

This was an action by Durham Life Ins. Co. (plaintiff) against Moize and others (defendants) for breach of contract to sell stock. Judgment for defendants and plaintiff appealed. Judgment affirmed.

The defendants offered the plaintiff 90 shares of its capital stock at $125 per share. Plaintiff corporation immediately issued a call for a meeting of its board of directors to consider the offer. The day before the board meeting the defendants gave notice of the withdrawal of the offer. Plaintiff board decided to accept the offer and gave notice of their acceptance. Defendants refused to sell and deliver the stock. Plaintiff claimed it had a reasonable time in which to accept or reject the offer.

Brown, J. It is well settled that no contract is complete without the assent of both parties, and an offer to sell imposes no obligation until it is accepted according to its terms. The undisputed evidence shows that defendants' offer to sell was withdrawn before acceptance. Therefore no contract was entered into between the parties.

The offer to sell was without consideration, was an option merely, and could be withdrawn at any time before acceptance.

Sunburst Oil and Gas Co. v. Neville et al.
79 Mont. 550, 257 Pac. 1016 (1927)

This was an action by the Sunburst Oil and Gas Co. (plaintiff) against Neville and others (defendants) to force the delivery of a written contract. Judgment for plaintiff and defendant appealed. Judgment reversed and case remanded.

Neville et al. signed a written contract whereby the rights of the Sunburst Oil and Gas Co. and Neville et al. were adjusted. It was agreed, and there was a provision in the contract to that effect, that Sunburst Oil and Gas Co. was to have ten days from October 5 in which to accept the terms of the written contract. On October 9 Neville et al. withdrew their offer, and on October 11 Sunburst Oil and Gas Co. attempted to accept. Sunburst Oil and Gas Co. contend that they had until October 15 in which to accept the offer and that they accepted before that time.

Callaway, Ch. But it is earnestly argued that the defendants made the plaintiff an offer. An offer is a promise; it is a statement made by the offeror of what he will give in return for some promise or act of the offeree (1 Williston on Contracts, Sec. 25). The offer must be communicated to the offeree. Before it will become a binding promise the offer must be accepted. There must be mutual consent to create the contract. In order to form a contract there must be an offer by one party and an acceptance of it by the other. Unless there be consideration for the offer, until the moment of acceptance it may be revoked and a subsequent acceptance will be inoperative (Clark on Contracts, Sec. 23; 13 C. J. 293).

"So long as the offer has been neither accepted nor rejected, the negotiation remains open, and imposes no obligation upon either party; or one may decline to accept, or the other withdraw his offer; and either rejection or withdrawal leaves the matter as if no offer had ever been made" (*Minneapolis, etc. Ry.* v. *Columbus Rolling Mills*, 119 U.S. 149). . . . .

An offer may be revoked at any time before its acceptance is communicated to the offeror. Since an offer, unaccepted, creates no rights and is not binding on the party making it, it follows that it may be revoked at any time before acceptance. An order, for instance, given to the agent of the party for whom it is made, who has no authority to accept it, is a mere proposal and revocable at any time before its principal accepts it (Clark on Contracts, p. 47).

That the offer was not accepted is clear. But it is argued that the defendants did not have the right to revoke it when they did; it is said that if plaintiff's position that it had ten days in which to signify its acceptance is untenable, nevertheless it had a reasonable time in which to do so. Neither position may be maintained. An offer, unless for consideration, may be revoked by the offeror at any time prior to the creation of a contract by acceptance, even though a definite time in which acceptance may be made is named in the offer.

Petterson v. Pattberg
248 N.Y. 86, 161 N.E. 428 (1928)

This was an action by Jennie Petterson, as executrix (plaintiff) against George Pattberg (defendant) for damages for breach of contract. Judgment for plaintiff and defendant appealed. Judgment reversed.

Pattberg held a mortgage on property owned by Petterson. Pattberg offered to allow a discount if the mortgage was paid before due.

He wrote Petterson, "I will allow you $780 providing said mortgage is paid on or before May 31, 1924." The latter part of May Petterson went to Pattberg's house prepared to pay off the mortgage. When he knocked on the door, Pattberg demanded the name of his caller and Petterson replied, "It is Petterson; I have come to pay off the mortgage." Pattberg answered that he had sold the mortgage. Petterson contends that Pattberg's offer was accepted before notice of withdrawal was received.

Kellogg, J. In this instance Petterson, standing at the door of the defendant's house, stated to the defendant that he had come to pay off the mortgage. Before a tender of the necessary moneys had been made, the defendant informed Petterson that he had sold the mortgage. That was a definite notice to Petterson that the defendant could not perform his offered promise, and that a tender to the defendant, who was no longer the creditor, would be ineffective to satisfy the debt. "An offer to sell property may be withdrawn before acceptance without any formal notice to the person to whom the offer is made. It is sufficient if that person has actual knowledge that the person who made the offer has done some act inconsistent with the continuance of the offer, such as selling the property to a third person." Thus it clearly appears that the defendant's offer was withdrawn before its acceptance had been tendered. It is unnecessary to determine, therefore, what the legal situation might have been had tender been made before withdrawal. It is the individual view of the writer that the same result would follow. This would be so, for the act requested to be performed was the completed act of payment, a thing incapable of performance, unless assented to by the person to be paid. Williston on Contracts, § 60b. Clearly an offering party has the right to name the precise act performance of which would convert his offer into a binding promise. Whatever the act may be until it is performed, the offer must be revocable. However, the supposed case is not before us for decision. We think that in this particular instance the offer of the defendant was withdrawn before it became a binding promise, and therefore that no contract was ever made for the breach of which the plaintiff may claim damages.

Judge Lehman wrote a dissenting opinion in which he contended that Petterson's act should be held to be an acceptance.

I recognize that in this case only an offer of payment, and not a formal tender of payment, was made before the defendant withdrew his offer to accept payment. Even the plaintiff's part in the act of payment was then not technically complete. Even so, under a fair construction of the words of the letter, I think the plaintiff had done the act which the defendant requested as consideration for his promise. The plaintiff offered to pay, with present intention and ability to make that payment. A formal tender is seldom made in business transactions, except to lay the foundation for subsequent assertion in a court of justice of rights which spring from refusal of the tender. If the defendant acted in good faith in making his offer to accept payment, he could not well have intended to draw a distinction in the act requested of the plaintiff in return, between an offer which, unless refused, would ripen into completed payment, and a formal tender. Certainly the defendant could not have expected or intended that the plaintiff would make a formal tender of payment without first stating that he had come to make payment. We should not read into the language of the defendant's offer a meaning which would prevent enforcement of the defendant's promise after it had been accepted by the plaintiff in the very way which the defendant must have intended it should be accepted, if he acted in good faith.

Geary v. Great Atlantic & Pacific Tea Co.
366 Ill. 625, 10 N.E. (2d) 350 (1937)

This was an action by Jean S. Geary, assignee of Foreman Trust and Savings Bank, receiver (plaintiff) against Great Atlantic and Pacific Tea Co. (defendant). Judgment for plaintiff in the trial court and defendant appealed to Appellate Court which reversed the judgment of the trial court; plaintiff appealed to the Supreme Court where the judgment of the Appellate court was reversed and the judgment of the trial court was affirmed.

February 25, 1931, defendant held a lease on the premises at 3309 W. Madison Street. The lease was about to expire and the defendant wrote the Foreman Bank who was in charge of the leasing of the premises, as receiver of the owner, offering to lease the premises for the ensuing year.

On March 7 at 10:30 A.M. Foreman Bank mailed a letter accepting the defendant's offer. On the same day at 1:30 P.M. defendant mailed a letter revoking this offer.

Stone, J. It is stipulated that appellee did not, when it mailed this letter, know of the mailing of the executed leases by the receiver, and that the receiver, when mailing them to appellee, had no notice of an intention on the latter's part to withdraw its offer to lease.

The rule of law, accepted by counsel on both sides of this lawsuit, is that a contract is ordinarily effected by offer and acceptance, and that when an offer is made by letter and the offeree posts his acceptance, the contract is complete, notwithstanding a revocation or withdrawal of the offer is mailed before the letter of acceptance is received. This is the generally accepted rule. *Wagner* v. *McClay*, 306 Ill. 560, 138 N.E. 164. In the last-cited case the rule is also announced that a withdrawal of an offer is not effectual until communicated, and an acceptance prior to a communicated withdrawal completes the contract, and so, where an offer is accepted by posting a letter of acceptance before notice of the withdrawal of the offer is received, the contract is completed.

Minneapolis & St. Louis Railway v. Columbus Rolling Mill
119 U.S. 149, 30 L. Ed. 376 (1886)

This was an action by Minneapolis and St. Louis Railway (plaintiff) against Columbus Rolling Mill (defendant) to recover damages for breach of contract. Judgment for defendant and plaintiff appealed. Judgment affirmed.

The plaintiff alleged that on December 19, 1879, the parties made a contract by which the plaintiff agreed to buy of the defendant, and the defendant sold to the plaintiff, two thousand tons of iron rails of the weight of fifty pounds per yard, at the price of fifty-four dollars per ton gross, to be delivered free on board cars at the defendant's rolling mill in the month of March, 1880, and to be paid for by the plaintiff in cash when so delivered. The answer denied the making of the contract. It was admitted at the trial that the following letters and telegrams were sent at their dates, and were received in due course, by the parties, through their agents:

December 5, 1879. Letter from plaintiff to defendant: "Please quote me prices for 500 to 3000 tons 50 lb. steel rails, and for 2000 to 5000 tons 50 lb. iron rails, March 1880 delivery."

December 8, 1879. Letter from defendant to plaintiff: "Your favor of the 5th inst. at hand. We do not make steel rails. For iron rails, we will sell 2000 to 5000 tons of 50 lb. rails for fifty-four ($54.00) dollars per gross ton for spot cash, F.O.B. cars at our mill, March delivery, ... If our offer is accepted, shall expect to be notified of same prior to Dec. 20th, 1879."

December 16, 1879. Telegram from plaintiff to defendant: "Please enter our order for twelve hundred tons rails, March delivery, as per your favor of the eighth. Please reply."

December 16, 1879. Letter from plaintiff to defendant: "Yours of the 8th came duly to hand. I telegraphed you to-day to enter our order for twelve hundred (1200) tons 50 lb. iron rails for next March delivery, at fifty-four dollars ($54.00) F.O.B. cars at your mill. Please send contract. Also please send me templet of your 50 lb. rail. Do you make splices? If so, give me prices for splices for this lot of iron."

December 18, 1879. Telegram from defendant to plaintiff, received same day: "We cannot book your order at present at that price."

December 19, 1879. Telegram from plaintiff to defendant: "Please enter an order for two thousand tons rails, as per your letter of the sixth. Please forward written contract. Reply." (The word "sixth" was admitted to be a mistake for "eighth.")

December 22, 1879. Telegram from plaintiff to defendant: "Did you enter my order for two thousand tons rails, as per my telegram of December nineteenth? Answer."

After repeated similar inquiries by the plaintiff, the defendant, on January 19, 1880, denied the existence of any contract between the parties.

Mr. Justice Gray. The rules of law which govern this case are well settled. As no contract is complete without the mutual assent of the parties, an offer to sell imposes no obligation until it is accepted according to its terms. So long as the offer has been neither accepted nor rejected, the negotiation remains open, and imposes no obligation upon either party; the one may decline to accept, or the other may withdraw his offer; and either rejection or withdrawal leaves the matter as if no offer had ever been made. A proposal to accept, or an acceptance, upon terms varying from those offered, is a rejection of the offer, and puts an end to the negotiation, unless the party who made the original offer renews it, or assents to the modification suggested. The other party, having once rejected the offer, cannot afterwards revive it by tendering an acceptance of it. If the offer does not limit the time for its acceptance, it must be accepted within a reasonable time. If it does, it may, at any time within the limit and so long as it remains open, be accepted or rejected by the party to whom, or be withdrawn by the party by whom, it was made.

The defendant, by the letter of December 8, offered to sell to the plaintiff two thousand to five thousand tons of iron rails on certain terms specified, and added that if the offer was accepted the defendant would expect to be notified prior to December 20. This offer, while it remained open, without having been rejected by the plaintiff or revoked by the defendant, would authorize the plaintiff to take at his election any number of tons not less than two thousand nor more than five thousand, on the terms specified. The offer, while unrevoked, might be accepted or rejected by the plaintiff at any time before December 20. Instead of accepting the offer made, the plaintiff, on December 16, by telegram and letter, referring to the defendant's letter of December 8, directed the defendant to enter an order for twelve hundred tons on the same terms. The mention, in both telegram and letter, of the date and the terms of the defendant's original offer, shows that the plaintiff's order was not an independent proposal, but an answer to the defendant's offer, a qualified acceptance of that offer, varying the number of tons, and therefore in law a rejection of the offer. On December 18, the defendant by telegram declined to fulfill the plaintiff's order. The negotiation between the parties was thus closed, and the plaintiff could not afterwards fall back on the defendant's original offer. The plaintiff's attempt to do so, by the telegram of December 19, was therefore ineffectual and created no rights against the defendant.

Home Gas Co. of Cushing v. Magnolia Petroleum Co.
143 Okl. 112, 287 Pac. 1033 (1930)

This was an action by the Magnolia Petroleum Company (plaintiff) against Home Gas Co. of Cushing (defendant) for money due under a contract. Judgment for plaintiff and defendant appealed. Judgment affirmed.

Plaintiff and defendant had oil and gas leases on adjoining property. Defendant had drilled a test well on its leasehold which served as a test well for the holdings of both plaintiff and defendant. The well was a "dry hole," and plaintiff paid defendant $2,000 to help defray the expense of drilling the well. Plaintiff proposed that it would drill a second well which would also serve as a test well for the holdings of both parties. In the preliminary negotiations defendant's representative stated that defendant would make the same payment and under the same terms as the payment made toward the first test well. Later defendant's president wrote a letter offering to pay $2,000 of the expense of a test well if it were a "dry hole" and concluded his letter, "and to be drilled to second break in the lime at an approximate depth of 3,700 feet."

Plaintiff replied accepting the offer but adding to his letter of acceptance the following statement: "I have looked up the letter we wrote you and find that we gave you $2,000 for a 3,500 foot hole. I feel sure that you will want to change your letter to this depth." Defendant did not answer. Plaintiff drilled a test well to a depth of 3,970 feet and it was a "dry hole."

Reid, C. The defendant claims there was no contract of any kind by which it was bound to pay the $2,000 for the reason that the reply of plaintiff on May 24 was not an unconditional acceptance of the offer made by defendant's letter of May 22.

In the case of *Foster* v. *West Publishing Co.*, 77 Okl. 114, 186 P. 1083, this court stated the rule applicable to this case in the syllabus as follows: "If an offer is accepted as made, the acceptance is not conditional, and does not vary from the offer because of a suggestion that the terms are unfair, or the expression of a hope, or suggestion, that the offerer will modify the terms."

The opinion in the foregoing case reviews the decision of this and other courts and text-writers on the question; all to the effect, as applied to the particular facts of this case, that the acceptance does not become conditional simply by the fact that the acceptor suggests, in his reply, that the offeror will modify his offer in a certain particular, upon reflection.

The Massachusetts case of *Nelson* v. *Hamlin*, 258 Mass. 331, 155 N.E. 18, 21, is peculiarly in point. In that case the plaintiff sued defendant for breach of contract of employment claimed to have been made by letter, and recovered. The court in the opinion said:

"The finding that the letters of April 19 and April 21, 1920, constituted a valid contract in writing was warranted. The acceptance was in accordance with the terms of the offer. The statement in the plaintiff's letter, 'it being understood that you wish me to stay in my present position with the Phillips Company pending the working out of your present dealings or until conditions make it necessary to place me elsewhere,' does not render the acceptance qualified or conditional. By the use of the words, 'you wish,' the judge could have found that the plaintiff did not intend them to be a condition of the acceptance and the defendant did not so construe them.

" 'Frequently an offeree, while making a positive acceptance of the offer, adds as a request or suggestion that some addition or modification be made. So long as it is clear that the meaning of the acceptance is positively and unequivocally to accept the offer whether such request is granted or not, a contract is formed.' "

Plaintiff's letter of May 24, 1922, must be regarded as an acceptance of defendant's offer. It sought to impose no new condition, but simply expressed the belief that defendant would change its condition to a well of lesser depth when its attention was called to their previous contract under which defendant had drilled the well under similar circumstances.

Achenbach et al. v. Kurtz et al.
306 Pa. 384, 159 Atl. 718 (1932)

This was an action by Jacob D. Achenbach and another, administrators of the estate of Samuel Achenbach, deceased (plaintiffs) against F. Kurtz and another (defendants) for breach of a contract to purchase bonds. Judgment for defendants and plaintiffs appealed. Judgment affirmed.

Samuel Achenbach in his lifetime purchased six $500 bonds from defendants. Four days later defendants offered to repurchase the bonds on the following terms: "Referring to the six $500 bonds . . . . which you purchased April 17, will say that if at the end of one year you so desire, we will buy back these bonds for $2,850, the amount you paid for same. Should you, however, keep the above-mentioned bonds two years we agree to give you the sum of three thousand dollars for same and should you keep them until we call for same in four or five years, we will pay $50 bonus for each $1,000 bond." Achenbach died July, 1930, six years subsequent to his purchase, having the bonds still in his possession. Upon refusal of Kurtz Brothers to repurchase the obligations, his administrators sold them at public sale, and their claim is for the difference between the selling price and the amount at which they allege Kurtz Brothers were obligated to repurchase by the terms of their letter above quoted.

Per Curiam. The court below states in its opinion that plaintiffs admitted at argument their inability to show that Samuel Achenbach had at any time moved to accept the offer of Kurtz Brothers; under this situation the learned trial judge properly held that, "If Samuel Achenbach in his lifetime showed no desire to accept defendants' proposal to purchase his bonds, his administrators cannot now come along and make a demand for him and thus endeavor to create a contract uncompleted by the deceased while living." "The death of either party before acceptance is communicated, causes an offer to lapse. An acceptance communicated to the representatives of the offeror cannot bind them, nor can the representatives of a deceased offeree accept the offer on behalf of his estate." Inasmuch as acceptance is an indispensable part of a contract and no valid acceptance of the contract here alleged appears, the court below properly entered judgment for defendants.

QUESTIONS AND PROBLEMS

1. What are the essential elements of a valid offer?
2. Archer while playing cards with Burch, Drew, and Fox said: "I would willingly give $500 if my son Jim could be relieved from the draft." Later Burch succeeded in obtaining a deferment for Archer's son, Jim. The deferment was obtained legally. Archer refused to pay Burch $500. Burch sued Archer to recover the $500. Can Burch recover a judgment?

3. The Oil Co. entered into an agreement with Marble whereby it agreed to give Marble the exclusive agency for its refined oils within a stated territory, and Marble agreed to sell the Oil Co.'s refined oils exclusively. The price was stated to be "such reasonable terms as to enable Marble to compete with other parties selling refined oil in the territory." The Oil Co. sold to other dealers in the territory and Marble sued the Oil Co. for damages. Did a binding contract exist?
4. If the Oil Co. had agreed to sell refined oil to Marble at ¼ cents per gallon less than the price quoted on the New York market, would it make any difference in your decision?
5. Sellers offered to sell land to Warren for $4,000. Warren replied, "I would not pay more than $3,500 for your land." Sellers replied, "I accept your offer to pay $3,500 for my land." Did a contract result?
6. Knight wrote Cooley, "Do you own lot 469? What is your price on it?" Cooley answered, "Yes. The lot is so incumbered that it would be difficult to transfer a good title at once. Price, $1,700." Is Cooley's letter an offer?
7. Archer offers to sell his auto to Burch for $300. Burch replies, "I will pay you $300 for your auto if you will have the motor overhauled." Does a contract result?
8. United Oil Co. wrote Miles, "You are hereby authorized to sell the United Oil Co.'s oil leases in Kentucky comprising leases on 1,280 acres for $1,500,000 net to us." Miles found a customer who was willing to purchase the leases for $1,680,000 and negotiated a sale to him. United Oil Co. refused to transfer the leases. Miles sued United Oil Co. to recover $180,000 damages. Did a contract result when Miles found a purchaser for the leases?
9. Morrison wrote Parks: "I have about 80,000 feet of oak left yet, for which I will take $16 per M. delivered on cars at Bridgewater 'log run.' I will take $8 per M. for the mill culls I have at Bridgewater, cut and delivered." Parks answered: "We will take your 4/4 oak at $16, mill culls out, delivered on cars at Bridgewater. We will handle all your mill culls but not at the price you are asking. We are buying from A. L. & Co. at $4.50 on board the cars. We would be glad to handle yours at this price." Did a contract result?
10. Bills offered to trade Harris 80 acres of land and pay $5,000 in cash for 100 shares of the capital stock of the Farmer's Bank. Harris replied, "I have decided to accept your offer of $5,000 and 80 acres free from encumbrances." Bills refused to pay the $5,000 and convey the 80 acres, claiming that Harris's reply was not an unconditional acceptance because he stipulated that the land must be free from encumbrances. Is Bills' contention correct?
11. Cole operated a wholesale house. A traveling salesman representing Cole called on Holloway regularly. The salesman solicited from Holloway an order for meal to be delivered 60 days later. The written order signed by Holloway stated that it would not be binding on Cole until accepted by the home office. In the past Holloway had signed similar orders but had never been given notice of the acceptance of the order; however, the goods ordered were shipped. Cole did not give Holloway notice that the order for meal was accepted nor did he give notice of rejection. The meal was not delivered, and when Holloway inquired about the delivery of the meal, Cole refused to deliver claiming that the order had never been accepted. Is Holloway entitled to delivery of the meal?
12. Archer offers to sell his horse to Burch for $200. Shortly thereafter Burch told Clark about the offer. Clark wrote Archer, "I accept your offer to sell your horse for $200." Does a contract result?
13. Archer wrote Burch offering to sell Burch his farm for $5,000 stating the offer must be accepted in ten days. On the tenth day Burch telegraphed an acceptance which was delayed and was not delivered to Archer until the twelfth day. Did a contract result?
14. Beach offered to contribute $2,000 to a church building fund on condition that

the church would first raise $8,000. Before the church had raised $8,000 Beach was declared insane. After the church had raised $8,000 it demanded the payment of the $2,000, but Beach's conservator refused to pay. The church brought suit. Can the church recover a judgment?

15. If the church had raised $8,000 and had notified Beach before he became insane that $8,000 had been raised, could the church recover judgment in a suit against Beach's conservator?
16. Harvey wrote Maclay offering her a position and stating, "You will confer a favor by giving your answer by return mail." Maclay received the letter on March 21 and on March 25 mailed an acceptance. Was a contract consummated between the parties?
17. If in the foregoing case Harvey had stated no time for the acceptance of his offer, would a contract have been consummated between the parties?
18. The bank signed the following: "Please send to our address for 5 years 'The Merchant's Bank Directory' for which we agree to pay the sum of $200.00 per year on receipt of the first copy following date of contract, and annually thereafter."

    The bank accepted and paid for the directory for two years and then wrote the publisher, "We now desire to inform you that we wish to cancel our request for the directory, as we find that this service is of no use to us whatever." The publisher of the directory tendered the directory to the bank for the balance of the five-year period. The bank refused to accept and pay for the directory. Is the bank liable for refusing to accept and pay for the directory for the balance of the five-year period?
19. After some preliminary negotiations, Hamlin wrote Nelson, "I hereby offer you the sum of twelve thousand dollars per year for two years." Nelson replied, "I hereby accept your offer to employ me for a period of two years at a salary of twelve thousand dollars per year . . . . it being understood that you wish me to stay in my present position . . . . until conditions make it necessary to place me elsewhere." Nelson started to work for Hamlin, but the plant in which Nelson was working was shut down, and Hamlin did not give Nelson employment in any of his other plants. Nelson sued to recover damages for breach of contract, and Hamlin claimed that Nelson's acceptance was conditioned and no contract resulted. Is this claim correct?

CHAPTER VI

REALITY OF CONSENT

Nature of Defenses

If we accept the theory that a contractual obligation is an obligation voluntarily assumed by the party to be bound, it would logically follow that, if one has not voluntarily assumed the obligation, he could not be held for failure to perform. This is substantially the view of the courts in those cases in which one of the parties has been induced to enter into a contract by misrepresentation, fraud, or duress. If the party has been induced to consent through misrepresentation, fraud, or duress, his consent is not his own free act, and he has not voluntarily assumed the obligation of the contract.

A misrepresentation is an innocent misstatement of a material fact which is relied on and which induces the party to whom it is made to enter into the contractual relationship, while fraud is either an intentional misstatement or a misstatement made with reckless disregard of the truth which is relied on and which induces the party to whom it is made to enter into the contractual relationship. Duress is the forcing of a person to consent through active or threatened violence or injury. In all of these situations one of the parties has been led to give his consent to the agreement because he has been either misled or coerced, and from one viewpoint we do not have actual consent. If there is no consent, no contract will come into existence. There will be no acceptance, which is one of the essentials of a binding contract. Instead of treating such agreements as a nullity, the courts have treated them as voidable contracts. The party whose consent has been obtained through misrepresentation, fraud, or duress has the right to elect whether or not he will perform the contract. If he elects to avoid the contract, it then becomes of no force or effect. If he elects not to perform the contract, the other party to the contract is relieved of his duties. If he elects to perform after full knowledge, the contract becomes a valid enforceable contract.

In the event the parties have entered into a contract upon the assumption that certain material conditions exist, but they are mistaken in their assumption without fault on the part of either party, courts will grant relief from the burdens of the contract. No set rule has been developed. Each case will be tried as a separate problem and the nature of the mistake, the relation of the parties, the effect on the rights of intervening third parties, and all other facts and circumstances are taken into consideration in determining whether or not relief will be granted. In some instances courts of law have held that a mutual mistake of fact may prevent the parties from coming to an agreement and have held that no contract results.

Misrepresentation

The misrepresentation of a material fact which is relied on and induces a party to enter into a contract is grounds for the rescission of the contract. Knowledge of the falsity of a statement is not essential, and the mode by which the misrepresentation is made is not material. If one of the parties to the contract by his words or acts causes the other party to believe that certain material conditions exist when they do not exist, and the party enters into the contract in reliance on the existence of the conditions as represented, the courts will find that there existed a misrepresentation and will grant the relief of rescission of the contract. The misrepresentations must be of material facts. Sales talk, opinions, expressions of what one expects in the future, etc., are not representations of fact.

Archer wishes to insure his building against fire with the Burch Insurance Co. In the application for the insurance the following question is asked: "Of what construction are the adjoining buildings?" Archer answers this question, "Steel frame—brick veneer." The adjoining buildings are of wood frame construction with brick veneer fronts, but Archer honestly believes that the adjoining buildings are of steel frame and brick veneer. The Burch Insurance Co. issues a policy relying on Archer's statements. The Burch Insurance Co. could rescind the policy because of Archer's misrepresentations.

In many states, statutes have been enacted which provide that an error made in answering questions in an application for insurance are not actionable unless intent to defraud or bad faith can be shown.

Traut v. Pacific Mutual Life Insurance Co.
321 Ill. App. 374, 53 N. E. (2d) 262 (1944)

This was an action by Eugene F. Traut (plaintiff) against Pacific Mutual Life Insurance Co. (defendant) on certain accident and health policies. Defendant filed a counterclaim in equity to rescind and cancel the policy. Judgment for defendant and plaintiff appealed. Judgment affirmed.

The plaintiff had taken out non-cancelable accident and health insurance policies with the defendant. The plaintiff was totally disabled from practicing his profession, and the defendant refused to pay the benefits provided for in the policies of insurance. Plaintiff sued and defendant filed a counterclaim in equity to rescind and cancel the policies upon the ground that the plaintiff made certain misrepresentations in his application for the policies. On the trial of the case the evidence proved that certain questions in the application in regard to plaintiff's health, both past and present, were not answered correctly and that the matters involved were material to the risks assumed by the defendant. There was no proof that the plaintiff knew that his answers were false.

Burke, J. The brief asserts that in an equitable proceeding to cancel a contract of insurance it is not necessary to prove that the material misrepresentation was made in bad faith or with an intent to deceive, and that all defendants were obliged to prove by a preponderance of the evidence was that plaintiff made certain misrepresentations which were in fact false and material to the risk or the hazard assumed by the defendants. We are of the opinion that this contention is sustained by the authorities. In *Western & Southern Life Ins. Co. v. Tomasun*, 358 Ill. 496, at page 502, 193 N. E. 451 at page 453, the court said: "In an equitable action for the cancellation of an insurance policy upon the ground that misrepresentations had been made as to facts material to the risk, it is not essential that the applicant should have willfully made such misrepresentations knowing them to be false. They will avoid the policy if they are, in fact, false and material to the risk even though made through mistake or in good faith."

Fraud

Honesty and good faith are necessary elements in business dealings, and the courts will not sanction dishonesty and deceit. No precise definition of fraud can be given. If the courts attempted to definitely define the scope of fraudulent conduct, someone would be ingenious enough to perpetrate frauds which would not come within the scope of the definition. The courts recognize certain elements which are essential to an actionable fraud: (1) There must be a misrepresentation of a material fact, (2) the misrepresentation must be knowingly made or made with reckless disregard of the truth, (3) it must be made with intent to deceive and for the purpose of inducing the other party to act upon it, (4) the other must in fact act in reliance upon it, and (5) must thereby suffer an injury.

Just how the misrepresentation is made is immaterial; the result is the important thing. It may be accomplished by direct statements, by concealments, by half-truths, with the aid of others, or by some other means. The misrepresentation must be of a material fact. This requirement eliminates from consideration sales talk, puffing, and statements of opinion unless a false opinion is given as a means of accomplishing the fraud. The statement must be of an existing fact. Archer wishes to sell Burch stock in Ye Wilde Catte Oil Co. and says, "When we are operating to full capacity this stock will pay a 20 per cent dividend." Such a statement is not a statement of fact. At most it is a statement of opinion as to what will happen in the future. If Archer says, "The company has made a net profit of not less than $100,000 each year for the past ten years," he has made a statement of fact, and if it is not true it is a misrepresentation. What facts are material depends on the circumstances. The test generally applied is whether or not the fact induced the party to enter into the contract. It need not be the sole inducement, but, if the party would not have entered into the contract had he known the truth about the misrepresented fact, the fact is a material fact. The elements of knowledge and intent of the party making the misrepresentation are intangible elements and must be established by proof of the surrounding circumstances. One is held to know those things which one with his skill and training in his position and with his opportunities to observe would under normal conditions learn. Intent as in other situations is based on all the facts and circumstances. One is held to have intended the natural results of his acts.

One must show that he entered into the contract in reliance on the misrepresentations before he can claim fraud as a defense. If one has at hand the means of determining the truth of statements made, he must avail himself of them. One cannot prove unwarranted gullibility as a substitute for reliance. The courts demand that a person exercise some caution, that he use his powers of observance, and that he not rely entirely on what the other party tells him. Archer, a used-car dealer, is showing Burch a used car and tells Burch that the car is in good repair. The windshield is broken out of the car, a defect which anyone looking at the car would notice. Burch purchases the car and later brings an action against Archer based on fraud, setting up that Archer represented that the car was in good repair when in fact the windshield was broken out. Burch could not recover because the broken windshield was an apparent defect and would not be included in Archer's statement that the car was free from defects.

If a party has been induced to enter into a contract by fraud, he has an election of remedies. He can rescind the contract, return what he has received, and recover what he gave, or he can retain what he has received and recover for any damage he has suffered as a result of the fraud. If he elects the latter remedy, it is necessary that he show injury or damage. If he elects to rescind the contract, it is not necessary that he show that he has been damaged. However, a court of equity might refuse relief if no injury had been suffered.

Horner v. Wagy
173 Or. 441, 146 P. (2d) 92 (1944)

This was an action by Clarence D. Horner (plaintiff) against Marie H. Wagy (defendant). Judgment for plaintiff and defendant appealed. Judgment reversed and remanded.

Defendant sold plaintiff a laundry and dry cleaning business for $17,000. The plaintiff claims that the defendant made certain fraudulent representations in regard to the income from the business and other matters which were relied upon by him to his damage of $11,200.

Lusk, J. We think that the evidence that the defendant told the plaintiff that the business had earned during the preceding year $450 to $600 a week, together with the proof of the actual earnings, made a jury question. It was a material misrepresentation of positive fact, and, if it was made by the defendant for the purpose of inducing the plaintiff to purchase the property and was knowingly or recklessly false, and if the plaintiff relied upon it and was misled to his injury, a verdict in his favor was warranted.

As stated, the plaintiff swore that the record of weekly earnings shown to him covered only a part of the month of July and a part of August. While he admitted that nothing was done by the defendant to prevent him from examining all the books, still, in view of this testimony, it was a question for the jury whether the plaintiff exercised reasonable prudence for his own protection in the circumstances, and that question was properly submitted to the jury in the court's instructions.

The contention that the plaintiff is, as a matter of law, precluded from asserting that he relied on the representation because he could have learned the truth by an examination of the defendant's books does not accord with the law as announced in the decisions of this court. The cases cited by the defendant have to do with representations as to the value or condition of land or personal property, where the person claiming to have been defrauded has made an investigation and the subject of the representations is "open, patent, and visible." The doctrine of these cases is not controlling where the representation relates to something intangible, such as the earnings of a business.

Different considerations, however, apply to the representations respecting the profits of the business.

Mere expressions of opinion, it is well settled, are not actionable. It is not always easy, however, to determine whether a representation is to be taken as an opinion or as a statement of positive fact. Generally, statements by the vendor commendatory of the thing which he is trying to sell, such as that it is a good investment, or a money maker, or that it is of great value, or statements or representations as to the future profits of a business, are held to be merely expressions of opinion upon which the vendee has no right to rely; although representations couched in similar language, may, according to the circumstances, be deemed misrepresentations of fact. Thus, in *Patterson* v. *Western Loan & Building Co.*, 155 Or. 140, 144, 62 P. 2d 946, it was held that a false statement that stock, to be issued by an insolvent corporation, would be a good investment, made to a person ignorant of the fact who believed it to be true and acted upon it to his detriment, was not a mere expression of opinion but a fraudulent misrepresentation of an existing fact or condition of things.

The rule is said to be that "in order to amount to fraud a representation as to value must be coupled with some untrue or misleading statement of fact used to reinforce the opinion, and not only so, but, further, that the person alleged to have been defrauded must have been thereby induced to forego further inquiry as to the worth of what he would acquire." "An expression of opinion," it is said, "may be so blended with statements of fact as to become itself a statement of fact."

The facts of the instant case are, perhaps, unique, for the plaintiff is forced to take the position that the defendant made a statement of positive fact concerning a matter of which she professed to be ignorant. If she did not know what the net profits were she could have only an opinion as to whether the business was very profitable or sufficiently so to enable the plaintiff to make the payments required by the proposed contract, and, since she told the plaintiff that she did not know, it must have been apparent to him that she was expressing only an opinion or a prediction. The parties were dealing at arm's length. There was no relationship of trust or confidence. He was an intelligent man with twenty-one years' experience in the very kind of business they were discussing, and he had spent the better part of six days in investigating the subject matter of their negotiations.

The defendant's statement that she did not know what the net profits were, and could not tell because the books were in the hands of her attorney, so far from inducing the plaintiff to forego further inquiry, should have put him on his guard. In the circumstances, it stamps the accompanying representations concerning the net profits of the business as nothing but her opinion, known to him to be such, upon which he was not entitled to rely, and therefore not actionable.

Berry et ux. v. Stevens

168 Okl. 124, 31 P. (2d) 950 (1934)

This was an action by David Berry and wife (plaintiffs) against A. J. Stevens (defendant). Judgment for defendant and plaintiffs appealed. Judgment reversed and remanded.

Berry and wife owned a two-fifths' interest in 160 acres of land located in Caddo County, Oklahoma. They had lived in Caddo County most of their lives and knew the defendant A. J. Stevens, a real estate dealer, intimately. In 1927 Berry and wife moved to Craig County which was about 270 miles from Caddo County. In October, 1929, Stevens wrote Berry asking him if he wished to sell his interest in the 160 acres. Berry wrote that he would sell and stated a price of $2,500. Berry knew that the land was in oil territory. Some wells had been drilled in a shallow oil sand and had been pumped for several years but the production was light. Berry also knew that a new oil-bearing stratum had been discovered at something over 3,200 feet but the wells were not heavy producers. On October 30 or 31, 1929, a new well was brought in which produced 1,000 barrels a day. The Berrys knew nothing about this well. October 31, 1929, Stevens communicated with Berry by telephone and Stevens and Roberts, who was Steven's son-in-law, called on Berry November 1, 1929. Stevens introduced Roberts to Berry as a man interested in buying land in Craig County. Stevens talked to the Berrys about their land; the oil prospects were discussed but Stevens said nothing about the 1,000 barrel well which had just been brought in. As a result of the conversation Berry agreed to sell his interest in the 160 acres for $2,200. It was not until Stevens brought the deed to be signed that Berry knew that Stevens was purchasing an interest in the land. The deed named Stevens, Pruett, and Wamsley as grantees. Berry learned of the 1,000 barrel oil well two or three days after the execution of the deed and immediately brought this suit to have the deed rescinded and canceled because of fraud.

Per Curiam. The defendants, in their brief, stoutly contend that Stevens made no false representations to Berry, and that he was guilty of no act of fraud or deceit.

" 'Confidential relation' exists between parties to a transaction, wherein one of the parties is in duty bound to act with the utmost good faith for the benefit of the other party, and includes legal and all other relationships where confidence is rightfully reposed.

"In determining the existence of fraud, any evidence, direct or circumstantial, which is competent by other rules of law, and has a tendency to prove or disprove such issue, is admissible. The whole transaction involving the alleged fraud may be given in evidence.

"The gist of a fraudulent 'misrepresentation' is the producing of a false impression upon the mind of the other party, and, if this result is actually accomplished, the means of accomplishing it are immaterial. . . . .

"When fraud is alleged great latitude of proof is allowed, and every fact or circumstance from which a legal inference of fraud may be drawn is admissible. . . . .

"Fraud may be committed by suppression of truth as well as by the suggestion of falsehood . . . ."

In this case, the most potent contention made by the plaintiffs is that Stevens, while giving plaintiffs information as to the oil field in the vicinity of the lands involved in the action, gave them only such information as they already had, at least in part, but that he did not disclose to them the existence of the large well that had come in from the new and deeper sand just a day or two prior to the purchase of their lands, and, on this point, the record discloses that Stevens testified as follows:

"Q. Do you recall, in that conversation, that anything was said about the Magnolia well? A. No sir, the Magnolia activities were never mentioned."

Although a party may keep absolute silence and violate no rule of law or equity, yet, if he volunteers to speak and to convey information which may influence the conduct of the other party he is bound to discover the whole truth. A partial statement, then, becomes a fraudulent concealment, and even amounts to a false and fraudulent misrepresentation.

Though one may be under no duty to speak, if he undertakes to do so, he must tell the truth and not suppress facts within his knowledge or materially qualify those stated.

Fraudulent representations may consist of half-truths calculated to deceive, and a representation literally true is actionable, if used to create an impression substantially false.

A duty to speak may arise from partial disclosure, the speaker being under a duty to say nothing or to tell the whole truth. One conveying a false impression by the disclosure of some facts and the concealment of others is guilty of fraud, even though his statement is true as far as it goes, since such concealment is in effect a false representation that what is disclosed is the whole truth.

Welsh v. Kelly-Springfield Tire Co.
213 Ind. 188, 12 N.E. (2d) 254 (1938)

This was an action by Kelly-Springfield Tire Co. (plaintiff) against Robert J. Welsh (defendant). Judgment for plaintiff and defendant appealed. Judgment affirmed.

Defendant was engaged in the retail business selling casings, tires, tubes, and automobile accessories. In 1931 he entered into a written contract with plaintiff whereby defendant agreed to purchase all his requirements of casings, tires, tubes, and other automobile accessories from plaintiff. The contract was a "continuous credit" agreement whereby plaintiff was to extend to defendant credit in the sum of $1,500. The provisions required the defendant on the termination of the contract to pay the plaintiff in full in cash or in returned merchandise. In subsequent years similar contracts were entered into but some changes in the terms of the contracts were made from time to time. On January 2, 1934, a new written contract was signed by defendant which contained a "continuous credit" provision for $2,000. It provided that on the termination of the contract all sums owing the plaintiff would be paid immediately in cash. The clause regarding the returns of merchandise was not included in the 1934 contract. The contract was terminated and defendant tendered merchandise in payment of sums due. The plaintiff refused to accept the merchandise and on defendant's refusal to pay in cash brought suit. Defendant contended that he was induced to sign the contract by fraudulent representations.

Roll, J. The rule which we consider as controlling in this case is aptly stated by Pomeroy, Eq. Jurisp., 2d Ed., § 892, as follows:

"As a generalization from the authorities, the various conditions of fact and circumstance with respect to the question how far a party is justified in relying upon the representation made to him may be reduced to the four following cases, in the first three of which the party is not, while in the fourth he is, justified in relying upon the statements which are offered as inducements for him to enter upon certain conduct: (1) When, before entering into the contract or other transaction, he actually resorts to the proper means of ascertaining the truth and verifying the statement. (2) When, having the opportunity to make such examination, he is charged with the knowledge which he necessarily would have obtained if he had prosecuted it with diligence. (3) When the representation is concerning generalities equally within the knowledge or the means of acquiring knowledge possessed by both parties. (4) But when the representation is concerning facts of which the party making it has, or is supposed to have, knowledge, and the other party has no such advantage, and the circumstances are not those described in the first or second case, then it will be presumed that he relied upon the statement; he is justified in doing so."

In *American Insurance Company* v. *McWhorter*, 1881, 78 Ind. 136, the court quotes with approval from *Seeright* v. *Fletcher*, 6 Blackf. 380, as follows:

"It does not appear that the defendant was deceived by the representations made to him, or if he was, it is manifest that it was the consequence of his own folly. If the defendant were an illiterate man, and the bond had been misread to him, he not being able to detect the imposition, the case would have been different. But it appears that he signed the bond without reading it himself, or hearing it read, and with all the means of knowing the truth in his power, reposed a blind confidence in representations not calculated to deceive a man of ordinary prudence and circumspection. In such a case the law affords no relief."

In *Ray* v. *Baker et al.*, 1905, 165 Ind. 74, 74 N.E. 619, we have a different statement of fact. In this case the execution of the note was secured by fraud. Baker was very illiterate, unable to speak or write the English language, unacquainted with the transactions of business matters, and was wholly ignorant of the meaning of legal terms and proceedings, while, on the other hand, Junkens (who secured the execution of the note) was one who had had much experience in business, and was a man of pronounced business ability, and had transacted much business with Baker. The facts showed that Baker was justified, under all the circumstances, in placing confidence in Junkens. In other words, there existed a confidential relationship which distinguishes it from the present case. Here there was no contention that any relationship of trust or confidence existed between the parties. It appears that appellant was a business man of experience. No showing is attempted to be made that any trick or artifice was practiced to prevent appellant from reading the contract for himself. He had the contract in his possession and the fact that he did not read it and discover its contents for himself was clearly the result of his own carelessness and blind folly. Under such circumstances, he cannot obtain relief from the hands of the court. We think the law on this point is so well settled that further citations are not necessary.

Duress

Contractual obligations are created by the voluntary agreement of the parties. If the agreement is not entered into voluntarily, no contractual obligation comes into being. Duress is the coercion of one to do an act because of fear created by the other party to the agreement. A person is presumed to possess some courage; consequently, to establish the defense of duress one must not only show that threats were made but must show that they were sufficient to and did overcome the free exercise of his will.

The early courts confined duress to the threat of imprisonment, loss of life, or of severe personal violence coupled with the power to put the threat into immediate execution. The modern view has enlarged the scope of duress until it now includes substantially all cases where one has been deprived of freedom of will through fear of the results of his failure to act as required by the party guilty of the duress.

Winget v. Rockwood et al.
69 F. (2d) 326 (1934)

This was an action by Nell F. Winget (plaintiff) against C. J. Rockwood, receiver of W. B. Foshay Co., and others (defendants). Judgment for defendants and plaintiff appealed. Judgment reversed and remanded.

Plaintiff and her husband owned the Winget Company which manufactured wearing apparel. In 1922 Winget Company was in need of funds for expansion and entered into a contract with E. C. Warner Co., which was owned by E. C. Warner, whereby Warner Co. was to assist Winget Co. by guaranteeing its promissory notes not in excess of $50,000. Warner Co. was to be paid $5,000 a year for their services. The true situation was that Warner Co. merely loaned money to Winget Co. and the annual payment of $5,000 was usurious interest on the loan. The contract was entered into for the purpose of concealing the payment of the usurious interest. Warner Co. loaned Winget Co. $90,000 and without prior notice demanded payment of the entire sum. Winget Co. could not make immediate payment and Warner Co. threatened suit. At this point W. B. Foshay Co. offered to act as the fiscal agent for Winget Co. and sell its Gold Notes up to $90,000. Winget Co. contracted with Foshay to market the notes and was to pay Foshay 10 per cent for his services. After entering into the contract Foshay refused to market the notes unless plaintiff transferred to him 1,250 shares of stock in the Winget Co. which would give Foshay control of the Winget Co. Foshay told plaintiff that if she did not comply with his request he would not sell the notes, and the creditors and Warner would start suit and the Winget Co. would be "sunk." The entire deal was a conspiracy between Foshay and Warner to obtain control of the Winget Co. Plaintiff transferred the stock to Foshay who transferred one-half of the stock to Warner but the stock was not transferred on the books of the corporation. When Foshay was petitioned into receivership he had 625 shares of Winget Co. stock. This suit was brought claiming the stock on the ground that Foshay obtained it by duress.

Gardner, C. J. Under the ancient common-law rule, legal duress existed only where there was such a threat of danger as was deemed sufficient to deprive a "constant and courageous" man of his free will. Under this doctrine the resisting power which every person was bound to exercise for his own protection was measured not by the standard of the individual affected, but by the standard of a man of courage. This rule was later modified to the extent that the standard was changed from that of a "constant and courageous" man to that of a "person of ordinary firmness"; but in these modern and less heroic days, the standard of resistance by which to test the alleged wrongful acts of duress and coercion has been further modified and softened. The trend of modern authority is to the effect that a contract obtained by so oppressing a person by threats as to deprive him of the free exercise of his will may be voided on the ground of duress. What constitutes duress is a matter of law, but whether duress exists in a particular transaction is usually a matter of fact. There is no legal standard of resistance with which the victim must comply at the peril of being remediless for a wrong done, and no general rule as to the sufficiency of facts to produce duress. The question in each case is whether the person so acted upon, by threats of the person claiming the benefit of the contract, was bereft of the quality of mind essential to the making of a contract, and whether the contract was thereby obtained. In other words, duress is not to be tested by the character of the threats, but rather by the effect produced thereby on the mind of the victim. The means used, the age, sex, state of health, and mental characteristics of the victim are all evidentiary, but the ultimate fact in issue is whether such person was bereft of the free exercise of his will power.

In the instant case it is alleged, and we must accept the allegation as true, that the defendants Warner and Foshay, and their companies, conspired to create a condition of financial jeopardy. Loans were freely extended to the Winget Company, and its officers were encouraged to embark upon plans of expansion, and then, without warning, these large loans were called and immediate payment demanded. Under these circumstances, the conspirator Foshay entered upon the scene. Plaintiff and her company were not financial wizards. They had had no training or experience in grappling with or solving such financial problems or situations as confronted them. In this predicament they employed Foshay as a captain of finance, and after he had executed for his company a contract under which his company undertook the sale of the Winget Company's notes, he then began a process of intimidation and threats of financial calamity and disaster, and as a climax extracted from plaintiff this written contract through which she turned over to him as his property 1,250 shares of the stock of the Winget Company, of the value of $135 per share, in consideration for which he agreed that he would have his company fulfill its contract.

The contract was so unfair and unconscionable as to shock the conscience of a court of equity. It gave Foshay and his company over $177,000 in money and property for the service of selling $90,000 worth of notes. Plaintiff says this contract was extracted from her through duress, coercion, threats, intimidation, and undue influence. The test, as we have observed, is what was the condition of her mind as the result of the threats, coercion, intimidation, and undue influence.

Mistake

Owing to the varied shades of meaning and the great variety of situations arising together with the diversity of the court decisions, it is difficult, if not impossible, to state an all-inclusive or all-exclusive rule as to the effect a mistake will have on a contract relationship. The mere fact that the results growing out of the relationship are other than either or both of the parties anticipated clearly has no effect on the contractual liabilities assumed.

In deciding cases involving questions of mistake, in both law and equity, the courts have shown a tendency to give great weight to the fact situation in each individual case. Although some general rules have been formulated and some attempt has been made to classify the cases, it is apparent that the justice of the individual case has played as important, if not a more important, rôle in the deciding of the case than formal rules. Clearly, the courts will not grant relief merely on the ground that one or both of the parties deem the contract a bad deal or, in other words, made a mistake when they entered into the agreement, nor is the court very apt to grant relief when the mistake is due to the negligence of the party. One asking relief on the basis of mistake ordinarily must have strong equities in his favor or he will not be entitled to relief.

Mutual mistake of material fact is ground for granting relief both in law and in equity. To come within this rule both of the parties must have contracted in the mistaken belief that certain material facts existed. The mistake must be as to existing or past facts. A court might grant relief if the mistake was as to future happenings, but, as a general rule, it is presumed that the contracting parties assume the risks of future events.

Archer agrees to sell his horse to Burch and Burch agrees to buy the horse and pay Archer $300 for it. At the time the contract is entered into the horse is dead. When the contract was entered into both Archer and Burch believed that the horse was alive. The contract will not be enforced. A mistake as to the quality of the goods sold is not, as a general rule, grounds for granting relief. In the foregoing example if, at the time the contract was entered into, both Archer and Burch believed that the horse would develop into a first-class race horse but it did not, the mistake would not be grounds for granting relief. In any situation one of the parties may assume the risks of the existence of certain facts and take the risk of their nonexistence. If one of the parties assumes such risk, no relief will be granted in the event the facts do not exist.

If the mistake is unilateral, that is, only one of the parties is contracting under the mistaken belief that certain facts exist which do not exist, as a general rule, no relief will be granted. This rule is subject to many exceptions. If one party knows that the other party is mistaken in his belief that certain facts exist and enters into the contract for the purpose of taking advantage of the situation, the courts will grant relief. The courts will also grant relief where hardship amounting to injustice would result if relief were denied.

Courts of equity will grant relief in those cases in which a mistake has been made in drafting a written contract, deed, or other document. Archer bargains to sell to Burch a vacant lot which adjoins Archer's home. The vacant lot is "Lot 3 block 1"; Archer's house is on "Lot 2 block 1." In drawing the contract the stenographer strikes the wrong key and the contract reads "Lot 2 block 1." Neither Archer nor Burch notices this error when they read and sign the contract. A court of equity will reform the contract. Usually no relief will be granted if one of the parties is mistaken as to the meaning of language used in a contract; however, if the language is ambiguous, or both parties are mistaken as to the meaning and it does not express the intentions of the parties, no contract is formed.

Mistake as to one's legal rights under a contract is generally accepted as not sufficient justification for granting relief. If the mistake of law is coupled with mistake of fact, relief may be granted. Some courts have attempted to distinguish between mistake of law—error of judgment as to legal rights—and ignorance of law—lack of knowledge of the existence of the law. Such a distinction is difficult to apply and has no secure foundation because one's error in judgment as to his legal rights usually is the result of some degree of ignorance of the law.

Steinmeyer et al. v. Schroeppel
226 Ill. 9, 80 N. E. 564, 10 L.R.A. (N.S.) 114 (1907)

This was an action by Henry Steinmeyer and another (plaintiffs) against John Schroeppel (defendant) which was consolidated with an action by Schroeppel (plaintiff) against Steinmeyer and another (defendants). The trial court granted a decree canceling a contract between the parties, and Steinmeyer and another appealed to the Appellate Court where the decree was reversed and an appeal was taken to the Supreme Court. The decree of the Appellate Court was affirmed.

Mr. Justice Cartwright delivered the opinion of the court:

Appellants are in the lumber business at Collinsville, Illinois, and appellee is a building contractor at the same place. On June 10, 1905, appellee was about to erect a building for himself, and left at the office of appellants an itemized list of lumber, containing thirty-four items, on which he desired them to give him a price. Appellants' book-keeper set down upon that list, opposite each item, the selling price, but did not add up the column. If correctly added the column would have footed up $1867. One of the appellants made the addition and by mistake made the total $1446. The book-keeper copied the list on one of appellants' bill-heads without the prices opposite the different items, and wrote at the bottom, "Above for $1446," and delivered the paper to appellee the same evening. Appellee received bids for the lumber from two other firms, which were in the neighborhood of $1890. On June 16 appellee called at the office of appellants and accepted their offer. He did not bring the paper with him, but the book-keeper made another copy and at the bottom of it wrote the same memorandum, "Above for $1446." One of the appellants signed it. The same evening one of the appellants, looking over the bill, found that he had not added the amounts correctly, and the next morning one of them notified appellee by telephone of the mistake and refused to furnish the lumber for less than $1867. Appellants also sent appellee a notice that they had found an error of $421, and the estimate should read $1867 instead of $1446. Appellants did not furnish the lumber, and appellee purchased it at the next lowest bid from another firm and sued appellants for the difference between what he paid for the lumber and what they had agreed to furnish it for. The circuit court entered a decree canceling the contract.

The jurisdiction of equity to grant the remedy of cancellation because of a mistake of fact by one party to a contract is well recognized. Mutual consent is requisite to the creation of a contract, and if there is a mistake of fact by one of the parties going to the essence of the contract, no agreement is, in fact, made. If there is apparently a valid contract in writing, but by reason of a mistake of fact by one of the parties, not due to his negligence, the contract is different with respect to the subject matter or terms from what was intended, equity will give to such party a remedy by cancellation where the parties can be placed *in statu quo*. The ground for relief is, that by reason of the mistake there was no mutual assent to the terms of the contract. The fact concerning which the mistake was made must be material to the transaction and affect its substance, and the mistake must not result from want of the care and diligence exercised by persons of reasonable prudence under the same circumstances. In this case the mistake was in the addition of the figures set down by the book-keeper. The price of each item was written correctly, but appellants claimed that one item of about $400 was placed somewhat to the right, and in adding the column the 4 was counted in the ten-column instead of the hundred-column. If that was done it does not account for the difference of $421. But if it did, it would only show a want of ordinary care and attention. If the figures were not exactly in line, the fact could hardly escape notice by a competent business man giving reasonable attention to what he was doing. There was no evidence tending to prove any special circumstances excusing the blunder.

The case of *Board of School Comrs.* v. *Bender*, 72 N.E. Rep. 154, relied on by appellants, differs from this in various respects, one of which is that Bender was excusable for the mistake. His complaint alleged that he was misinformed by the architect that his bid must be in at or before four o'clock, when, in fact, he was allowed until eight o'clock; that in ignorance of the fact and for want of time he was hurried in submitting his bid and had no opportunity for verification of his estimate, and that under those circumstances he turned two leaves of his estimate book by mistake and omitted an estimate on a large part of the work. The case involved the question whether the bidder had forfeited a sum deposited as a guaranty that he would enter into a contract, and when notified that his bid was accepted, having discovered his mistake, he informed the architect and immediately gave notice that he would not enter into the contract. By the terms of the bid it was intended that if the bid was accepted a contract would be made, but the bid was not the contract contemplated by the parties and the bidder never did enter into the contract. The court concluded that the minds of the parties never, in fact, met, because the bidder fell into the error without his fault.

In the case of *Harron* v. *Foley*, 62 Wis. 584, there was no agreement, for the reason that the minds of the parties never met. The plaintiff claimed to have purchased of the defendant some cattle for $161.50, but the defendant intended to state the price at $261.50. When the defendant was informed that the plaintiff understood the price to be $161.50 he refused to deliver the cattle and tendered back

$20 received on the purchase price. No agreement was, in fact, made, since the statement of the price by the seller was clearly a mistake.

A mistake which will justify relief in equity must affect the substance of the contract, and not a mere incident or the inducement for entering into it. The mistake of the appellants did not relate to the subject matter of the contract, its location, identity or amount, and there was neither belief in the existence of a fact which did not exist or ignorance of any fact material to the contract which did exist. The contract was exactly what each party understood it to be and it expressed what was intended by each. If it can be set aside on account of the error in adding up the amounts representing the selling price, it could be set aside for a mistake in computing the percentage of profits which appellants intended to make, or on account of a mistake in the cost of the lumber to them, or any other miscalculation on their part. If equity would relieve on account of such a mistake there would be no stability in contracts, and we think the Appellate Court was right in concluding that the mistake was not of such character as to entitle appellants to the relief prayed.

Nilsson v. Krueger et al.
—S. D.—, 9 N. W. (2d) 783 (1943)

This was an action by Loyal T. Nilsson (plaintiff) against Harry J. Krueger and others (defendants). Judgment for defendants and plaintiff appealed. Judgment affirmed.

Plaintiff was employed by the defendants who operated a fruit and vegetable market. While lifting a sack of potatoes plaintiff strained his back. He was examined by a physician and was paid compensation in accordance with the provisions of the Workmen's Compensation Law. He went to the Mayo Clinic where his injury was diagnosed and he was treated. The doctors who treated plaintiff told plaintiff and defendants that they thought that eventually plaintiff's disability would clear up; that he could return to work, but that he should take it easy and not do any heavy lifting but gradually work into it. In reliance on this statement of plaintiff's condition plaintiff and defendants made a lump sum settlement of $490 and plaintiff signed "in final settlement and satisfaction of all claims for compensation." After plaintiff returned to work his back pained him and his condition did not clear up. It is now apparent that he has suffered a permanent partial disability. Plaintiff asked the court to set the release aside because of mistake of a material fact.

Roberts, P. J. A release is a contract and as such is subject to rescission for the same reason as other contracts, including mistake of fact. This is in accordance with the elementary rule that no contract results where the parties labored under such a mistake of fact that their minds never met. "Mistake of fact is a mistake not caused by the neglect of a legal duty on the part of the person making the mistake and consisting in: (1) an unconscious ignorance or forgetfulness of a fact, past or present, material to the contract; or (2) belief in the present existence of a thing material to the contract which does not exist, or in the past existence of such a thing which has not existed." The fact concerning which the mistake was made must be material to the transaction and must not result from the want of such care and diligence as would be exercised by a person of reasonable prudence under the same circumstances and must relate either to a present or past fact. The annotations appearing in 48 A.L.R. 1462 and 117 A.L.R. 1022 state the following conclusions with respect to the avoidance of releases of claims for personal injuries on the ground of mistake: "It has often been said that the law favors compromise. But . . . . this rule has not been permitted to defeat substantial justice, where a release of a claim for personal injuries is executed under mutual mistake of fact. . . . . The rule is well settled, according to the great weight of authority, that a general release of a claim for personal injuries may, under proper circumstances, be avoided on the ground of mutual mistake as to the nature or seriousness of the injury."

Plaintiff concedes that the mistake must be as to a past or present fact and not a mere prophecy as to a future condition to entitle plaintiff to prevail, but cites and relies upon the cases of *Granger* v. *Chicago, M. & St. P. R. Co.*, 194 Wis. 51, 215 N.W. 576 and *Atchison, Topeka & Santa Fe R. Co.* v. *Peterson*, 34 Ariz. 292, 271 P. 406, and other authorities, in support of the contention that a statement made by a physician as to the condition of a releasor and his prospects of recovery is an expression as to an existing fact and not a mere opinion as to a future event. Plaintiff contends that the facts as disclosed by the record show that he was advised by Dr. Woltman that his injury was of a temporary nature and that eventually his disability would disappear and requested an additional finding to this effect. We need not enter into a consideration of decisions construing statements made by physicians with respect to whether they constitute expressions as to a present, existing fact or are mere prophecies as to a future condition. The alleged mistake of fact is premised upon the representations of Dr. Woltman as we have stated concerning plaintiff's injury and his ability to resume work. We have only plaintiff's testimony with respect to such statements. He testified:

"Q. You had a conversation with Dr. Woltman about a surgical operation, what did he tell you? A. Well, he told me that eventually the thing would clear up he figured, but in case it didn't (he would) have to make an exploratory operation and what the outcome of that would be they didn't know, it would be a serious operation, but what the outcome was he couldn't state."

The requested finding that the physician represented that the injury was of a temporary nature and that eventually plaintiff would fully recover could not be sustained. The testimony of plaintiff considered as a whole is open only to the conclusion that there was an element of doubt and uncertainty and that he should at least have suspected that there might be a development from his injury that was not then apparent. The effect of the injury was problematical and it cannot be said that plaintiff acted under a mistake of fact.

QUESTIONS AND PROBLEMS

1. Archer was negotiating the sale of a house to Burch. In describing the house Archer told Burch that the house was painted gray. The house was painted white. Burch purchased the house relying on Archer's representations. Burch brings suit to have the transaction set aside on the ground that Archer misrepresented the house in that he said it was painted gray when it was painted white. Should the transaction be set aside?
2. Hundley was induced to buy the capital stock of the Rivermont Corp. on the fraudulent representation that a certain syndicate had purchased a large block of the stock. Later, Wilson who had sold the stock to Hundley told Hundley that he had misrepresented the syndicate deal; that the syndicate had taken an option on the stock but had not purchased it. Wilson offered to repurchase Hundley's stock but Hundley refused to sell stating that he was fully satisfied with the deal. At a later date, the Rivermont Corp. suffered financial reverses and Hundley tendered the stock to Wilson and demanded the purchase price. Hundley based his claim on the fraudulent representations made at the time he purchased the stock. What are Hundley's rights?
3. Foster installed a heating plant for Dwire. The plant did not operate satisfactorily and Dwire refused to pay the balance due on the contract—$2,068.78. Foster told Dwire that if he (Dwire) would pay the balance due, he (Foster) would remedy all the deficiencies in the heating system. Dwire paid Foster the balance of $2,068.78, but Foster did not fulfil his agreement. Dwire sued Foster in an action of tort for damages for deceit. Should Dwire recover a tort judgment?
4. International Harvester Co. sued Anna Voboril on her promissory notes which were given by her to pay the debts of her husband. Anna Voboril was uneducated, a foreigner, and knew nothing about court procedure. The representative of the company told her that if she did not give the notes, they would put her husband in jail and keep him there. When sued on the notes, Anna Voboril set up duress as a defense. Should a judgment be granted?
5. Would it have made a difference in Problem 4 if Anna Voboril had been a native American, well-educated, and familiar with court procedure?
6. The Southern Railway Co. had some rail which it wanted to sell. The rail was pointed out to a representative of the Locomotive Co. and the Locomotive Co. offered $12.50 per ton for the rail. This offer was accepted by the Southern Railway Co. When the rail was loaded, Southern Railway Co. discovered that about one-half of it was "relay rail." The Southern Railway Co. thought at the time it accepted the Locomotive Co.'s offer that all the rail was "scrap rail." "Relay rail" was worth about twice as much as "scrap rail." Southern Railway Co. refused to deliver the rail and when sued set up mistake as a defense. Is the defense good in this case?
7. Wells agreed to sell and Talbott agreed to buy one hundred tons of "Indiana Egg" coal, to be delivered during January and February, 1946. There were two grades of such coal commonly sold. One was screened twice and was used for domestic purposes; the other was screened once and was used as steam coal. Wells had in mind the coal screened once and Talbott had in mind the coal that was doubly screened. Did a binding contract result?

CHAPTER VII

CONSIDERATION

Nature of Consideration

Social experience has demonstrated the fact that it is undesirable to attempt to enforce all agreements through court action. The element of a legally binding contract which serves to distinguish a legally enforceable agreement from a legally unenforceable agreement is consideration. We do not have one clear-cut theory of consideration which is applicable to all situations. At one time in the development of our law the only agreements which were enforced by court action were sealed written agreements. The seal was at that time a wax wafer bearing a distinguishing mark. The formality of the sealing was the thing that gave the agreement legal standing. Today, the efficacy of the seal is recognized in only a few states. Several states have adopted statutes which declare, in effect, that there shall be no distinction made between sealed and unsealed contracts. Other states have adopted statutes which declare that the seal shall be prima facie evidence of consideration—i.e., that the party plaintiff will not have to prove the existence of consideration, but if consideration is not present the party defendant is free to set up lack or failure of consideration as a defense. The form of the seal is no longer important. The word "seal" or the letters "L. S." ("locus sigilli" meaning place of the seal) following the signature is sufficient.

In the majority of cases the idea of exchange is the basis of consideration. This theory of consideration is called the bargain theory. The idea is that one party bargains for and receives something in exchange for his promise. Archer offers to sell his horse to Burch for $300. In this case Archer is promising to transfer his ownership of the horse to Burch in exchange for Burch's promise to pay in return $300. Archer offers a reward of $20 to the person who finds and returns to him his lost watch. Archer is promising to pay $20 in exchange for the return of his lost watch. In both of these cases consideration is present. Archer promises to give Burch $50 on his twenty-first birthday as a birthday present. There is no consideration in this case. Archer has bargained for and received nothing in exchange for his promise.

It is not necessary that the party or parties to the agreement receive personally the consideration bargained for. Archer goes to Burch and orders an orchid sent to Clark and promises to pay Burch $10. The sending of the orchid to Clark is the thing bargained for and given in exchange for Archer's promise to pay Burch $10.

The injurious reliance theory—or promissory estoppel theory—is illustrated by the charitable subscription contract. Archer promises to contribute $5,000 to the trustees of Burch College to be used to build an auditorium. In reliance on this promise the trustees of Burch College contract for the building of an auditorium. Archer's promise to contribute the $5,000 will be enforced by the courts. Consideration is found in the fact that the trustees of Burch College, in reliance on Archer's promise, assumed a legal obligation—the contract for the building of an auditorium—which they would not have assumed otherwise.

A third theory of consideration generally recognized by the courts is the moral consideration theory. The scope of this theory is uncertain. However, it is generally applied in those cases in which a legal obligation is discharged by operation of law, and thereafter a new promise is made to perform the discharged obligation. Archer owes Burch $500. Archer is adjudged bankrupt and the obligation to pay the $500 is discharged in bankruptcy. Thereafter Archer promises to pay Burch the $500. The courts will enforce the new promise. The reasoning which is commonly followed is that, although the obligation to pay is discharged, the debt is not paid, and the debtor is morally obligated to pay the debt. This moral obligation to pay is sufficient consideration to support the new promise made after the legal obligation is discharged by operation of law.

Another theory sometimes followed is that the discharge in bankruptcy does not relieve the debtor of his duty to pay the debt but is a bar to an action to enforce the obligation, and that the promise to pay is a waiver of his right to set up his discharge in bankruptcy as a bar to the suit.

The Trustees of Amherst Academy v. Jonathan Cowles
23 Mass. 427, 17 Am. Dec. 387 (1828)

This was an action brought by the trustees of Amherst Academy (plaintiffs) against Jonathan Cowles (defendant) to recover the amount of his subscription to a charitable fund. Judgment for plaintiff and defendant appealed. Judgment affirmed.

Jonathan Cowles subscribed one hundred dollars to the charitable fund established at Amherst "for the classical education of indigent pious young men." Cowles refused to pay the amount of his subscription and when sued set up lack of consideration as a defense.

Parker, C. J. The law undoubtedly allows men, who have inconsiderately undertaken to bind themselves in contracts for which they have received no equivalent, to avoid such engagements by showing that they received nothing for them, or that the party with whom such contract was made would lose nothing by the non-performance of it. And this rule of law is frequently taken advantage of by those, who, without any pretense of mistake or inconsideration, have made their written promises. All that the court can do to discourage such dishonorable conduct is to require strict and unquestionable evidence that the case comes within the rule, the burden of proof, where a consideration is expressly admitted, being altogether on the defendant.

Was there a consideration for this note when it was given? In one sense there was not; that is, the promisor had received nothing at the time from the payees which was of any pecuniary value. But it is quite sufficient to create a consideration, that the other party, the payee, should have assumed an obligation in consequence of receiving the note, which he was compellable either at law or equity to perform, unless the promisor should be able to show when sued that the payee had refused, or was unable, or had unreasonably neglected to perform the engagement on his part; in which cases a defence might be raised on the ground of a failure of the consideration.

On the contrary, in all the cases cited except the first, it is decided expressly, that promises of this nature, if inefficient at first for want of a payee, or because at the time there was no actual consideration, but one in contemplation only, it is a legal basis for a subsequent promise, and that the execution of or beginning to execute the trust for which the fund is raised forms a sufficient consideration for such subsequent promise.

We have then in the present case a subscription to a charitable fund made after the incorporation of the body who were its trustees, and more than a year after that a promissory note, made for value received, payable to the same party, referring expressly to the subscription and the purposes of it as the consideration of the note. And we find that those purposes are in process of execution, the funds being needed for and applied to the faithful execution of the trust. We cannot doubt that the note is valid, and that the defence is maintainable neither in law nor in conscience.

Edwards v. Nelson
51 Mich. 121, 16 N.W. 261 (1883)

This was an action brought by Edwards, Townsend & Co. (plaintiff) against Nelson Braasted & Co. (defendants) to recover the amount due on a promissory note. Judgment for plaintiff and defendants appealed. Judgment affirmed.

The defendants owed plaintiff $412.40 which was discharged by a composition in bankruptcy. A 50% dividend was paid to creditors out of the bankruptcy court. Later defendants gave the plaintiff their promissory note in payment of the portion of the debt which was not paid by the dividend paid by the bankruptcy court. When the note fell due defendants refused to pay and when sued set up lack of consideration as a defense.

Sherwood, J. The bankrupt law, it is true, suspends the right of action on the balance of a debt partially paid under its discharge of the debtor, but the indebtedness remains the same after as before the discharge, and the moral obligation to pay still continues, and requires payment to be made by the debtor whenever he is of sufficient ability to do so. We know of no law which prevents a man from voluntarily paying his honest debts, or securing the payment thereof, if he desires, although the right of creditors to enforce payment may by the law be suspended; and this moral obligation to pay has always been held a good consideration to support a written contract for payment in a case like the present.

Legal Detriment as Consideration

In our discussion of the bargain theory of consideration we made the statement that consideration was something bargained for and given in exchange for a promise. What is that "something"? In business contracts it is usually property having an economic value, but the "something" in consideration need not be property. The surrendering of some legal right or privilege, or the doing of an act which one is not legally bound to do is sufficient. The surrendering of a legal right or privilege or the assuming of some burden one is not legally bound to assume is generally termed "legal detriment." Consequently, a simple and reasonably accurate test of the presence of consideration is "detriment to the promisee suffered or given in exchange for a promise." This test will prove adequate in most cases but not in all.

In the application of this test to a given situation, there are two important limitations which should not be overlooked: (1) the act must be one which the promisee is not legally bound to perform, and (2) it must be performed in exchange for the promise.

One has not suffered a detriment if he does only those things which he is already legally bound to do. This is the general rule followed by the majority of the courts, but the courts are not in accord in their holdings. The cases in which the performance of an act which one is already legally bound to perform is set up as consideration may be divided into three groups: (1) the doing of an act which one is already under a duty to the public to perform; (2) the performance of an act which one has already bound himself by contract to perform;

(3) the performance of an act which one has already bound himself by contract to perform, but the performance of which, owing to unforeseen factors, is more burdensome than either of the contracting parties contemplated at the time the contract was entered into.

In those cases falling under group 1, the courts have consistently held that the performance of the act which one is already legally bound to perform is not consideration. This position is supported by both logic and public policy. If one does only that which he is duty bound to do, he has given nothing in exchange as consideration for the benefits he receives. If we permitted one owing a duty to the public to contract for additional compensation if he performed that duty, we would be recognizing and sanctioning the bribing of public officials.

The element of public policy is not as apparent in group 2. These transactions are between individuals, and the public in general is not directly involved. However, if we should recognize the performance of an act which one is already bound by contract to perform as consideration to support a new promise, we would encourage fraudulent practices in that if one party to the contract was in a position where he would suffer serious injury if performance was not completed, the other party could force the payment of additional compensation by refusing to complete performance. The majority of the courts has held that the performance of an act which one is already bound by contract to perform is not consideration.

If the parties to the contract assume that certain conditions exist, but, on performance, unforseen and unforseeable difficulties are encountered and, as a result, additional compensation is promised for the performance of the promised act, the courts, as a general rule, will enforce such a promise. These cases are treated as exceptions to the general rule. The decisions can be supported on the basis of fair dealing.

The courts have consistently held that a promise to discharge a liquidated debt on payment of part of the debt at the place where the debt is payable and at or after the time when the debt is due, is not enforceable because of lack of consideration. This rule is the result of following to its logical conclusion the rule that the performance of an act which one is already bound to perform is not sufficient consideration to support a promise. The courts have expressed dissatisfaction with the rule on the ground that it is contrary to general business practices, yet the rule is so firmly established that the courts hesitate to overrule it. Although the courts adhere to the rule, they have narrowed its application to those cases in which the debt is liquidated; i. e., the amount of the debt is a sum certain which has not been disputed by either of the parties; it must be due or past due, and the part payment must be made at the place where the debt is payable. If the debtor does anything he is not bound to do or gives anything he is not bound to give, such as making payment in goods instead of money, the courts will hold that a consideration has been given and the promise to discharge the balance is enforceable. This rule also applies to promises to extend the time of payment of the debt.

In some cases the courts have sustained such agreements on the ground that there is an executed gift of the balance by the creditor to the debtor. If the creditor intends to make a gift of the balance and does execute the gift of the balance, he cannot repudiate the gift and recover the balance. In the majority of cases there is no evidence of an intent to make a gift of the balance, and the acts necessary to the execution of such a gift are not performed.

If the debt is unliquidated—i. e., the parties are not in agreement as to the amount of the debt or one party denies the existence of the debt—a promise to pay an agreed sum will be enforced. In this situation, the party making the payment is not doing something which he is already bound to do. He may have been legally bound to pay some amount, but he was not necessarily legally bound to pay the sum agreed upon in the settlement. Each party has the right to have the amount of the unliquidated claim determined by the court. The surrender of this right is sufficient consideration to support the promises to pay and accept the agreed amount in settlement of the claim.

Forbearance or the promise to forbear to prosecute a claim on which one has a right to sue is a sufficient consideration to support a contract. Forbearance or the promise to forbear to prosecute a groundless claim on which suit is threatened for the purpose of harassing the other party is not a sufficient consideration. Just where to draw the line between these two extremes is difficult to say. The courts are not in accord. The early English courts held that if one could not prosecute his claim to a successful conclusion, he gave up nothing by not bringing suit, and a promise to forbear or forbearance would not be sufficient consideration, but this rule has been relaxed because one could not tell the outcome of a close case without actually trying the case, thus making the practical application of the rule unsatisfactory. Some courts have favored the rule that if the party threatening suit thinks, in good faith, that he has a valid claim, his promise to forbear or forbearance is a sufficient consideration. The rule more widely adopted is that if the party has reasonable ground to believe that he has a valid claim, or in other words if the claim is reasonably doubtful, a promise to forbear or forbearance is a sufficient consideration. The general rule is based on the ground that one has a legal right to resort to the courts to have his claims adjudicated, and if he foregoes this right, he has suffered a legal detriment. One's right to sue is limited to actions on valid claims. If one maliciously sues, he renders himself liable for damages in a tort action, and a promise to forbear or forbearance on such a suit is never a sufficient consideration. However, one may sue on a cause in which no one but himself has any faith, and if the suit is brought in good faith and without malice, he will not render himself liable in a tort action. The better view is that a promise to forbear or forbearance to prosecute such a cause will not be a sufficient consideration.

The compromise of disputed claims is in effect a mutual agreement to forbear suit; hence, compromise agreements are supported by consideration and are enforceable. In the compromise of a disputed claim, each party gives up his right to have the court decide the controversy. As the basis of a compromise, one must have an honest dispute. If one has two claims, one admitted and the other disputed, it has been held that the payment of the admitted claim is no consideration for the promise to discharge the disputed claim.

If a debtor enters into an agreement with two or more of his creditors whereby he agrees to pay each creditor a stated percentage of his claims and the creditors each agree to accept the amount in full satisfaction of his claim, the courts will enforce the agreement, and no creditor can recover the balance of his claim. Such agreements are known as composition agreements. Under the terms of the composition agreement the debtor has discharged his debt by the payment of a lesser sum at or after the due date. Some courts find consideration in the mutual promises of the creditors to accept the agreed percentage of their claims as payment in full. Other courts hold that the composition agreement is an exception to the general rule, basing their decisions on sound business practice.

Talbott v. Stemmons' Executor
89 Ky. 222 (1888)

This was an action by Albert R. Talbott (plaintiff) against the executor of Sallie D. Stemmons, deceased (defendant). Judgment for defendant and plaintiff appealed. Judgment overruled and case remanded to lower court.

The plaintiff and his step-grandmother entered into the following agreement: "I do promise and bind myself to give my grandson, Albert R. Talbott, five hundred dollars at my death if he will never take another chew of tobacco or smoke another cigar during my life from this date up to my death . . . ."

The grandmother died and the grandson brought an action against her estate to recover the five hundred dollars. The grandson had fulfilled his part of the agreement.

Pryor, J. There is nothing in such an agreement inconsistent with public policy, or any act required to be done by the plaintiff in violation of law, but, on the contrary, the step-grandmother was desirous of inducing the grandson to abstain from a habit, the indulgence of which, she believed, created an useless expense, and would likely, if persisted in, be attended with pernicious results. An agreement or promise to reform her grandson in this particular was not repugnant to law or good morals, nor was the use of what the latter deemed a luxury or enjoyment a violation of either, and so there was nothing in the law preventing the parties from making a valid contract in reference to the subject-matter.

In the classification of contracts by the elementary writers, it is said: "An agreement by the one party to give, in consideration of something to be done or forborne by the other party, or the agreement by one to do or forbear in consideration of something to be given by the other, are such contracts, when not in violation of law, as will be held valid." Whether the act of forbearance or the act done by the party claiming the money was or was not of benefit to him is a question that does not arise in the case. If he has complied with his contract, although its performance may have proved otherwise beneficial, the performance on his part was a sufficient consideration for the promise to pay.

The right to enjoy the use of tobacco was a right that belonged to the plaintiff and not forbidden by law. The abandonment of its use may have saved him money or contributed to his health; nevertheless the surrender of that right caused the promise, and having the right to contract with reference to the subject-matter, the abandonment of the use was a sufficient consideration to uphold the promise.

Mr. Parsons, in his work on Contracts, says: "The subject-matter of every contract is something which is to be done or which is to be omitted," and where the consideration is valuable, need not be adequate. If, therefore, one parts with that he has a right to use and enjoy, the question of injury or benefit to the party seeking a recovery, by reason of a full performance on his part, will not be inquired into, because if he had the legal right to use that which he has ceased to use by reason of the promise, the law attaches a pecuniary value to it.

White v. Bluett

2 C. L. R. 301, 23 L. J. Ex. 36 (1853)

This was an action brought by White, executor of the estate of John Bluett, deceased (plaintiff) against William Bluett (defendant) to recover on a promissory note. Judgment for plaintiff.

The defendant complained to his father that he had not treated him as well as the other children. After the lapse of some time and considerable complaining on the part of the defendant, the father agreed to discharge a note of the defendant which he held if the defendant would cease to complain. After the father's death the executor sued on the note and the defendant set up the father's agreement to discharge the note as a defense. The executor claimed the agreement was not supported by consideration and was not enforceable.

Pollock, C. B. By the argument a principle is pressed to an absurdity, as a bubble is blown until it bursts. Looking at the words merely, there is some foundation for the argument, and, following the words only, the conclusion may be arrived at. It is said, the son had a right to an equal distribution of his father's property, and did complain to his father because he had not an equal share, and said to him, I will cease to complain if you will not sue upon this note. Whereupon the father said, if you will promise me not to complain I will give up the note. A man might complain that another person used the public highway more than he ought to do, and that other might say, do not complain, and I will give you five pounds. It is ridiculous to suppose that such promises could be binding. . . . . In reality, there was no consideration whatever. The son had no right to complain, for the father might make what distribution of his property he liked; and the son's abstaining from doing what he had no right to do can be no consideration.

Mason v. Manning
150 Ky. 805, 150 S.W. 1020 (1912)

This was an action by J. L. Manning (plaintiff) against Robert Mason, Jr. (defendant). Judgment for plaintiff and defendant appealed. Judgment reversed and remanded for further proceedings.

On a Friday afternoon in June, 1909, Hiram Mason was shot from his horse and killed as he was passing from Greasy creek across Pine Mountain to his home on Big Clear creek in Bell county, Ky. On the following Saturday he was buried in the family burying ground near his home. At the burial, appellant, Robert Mason, Jr., announced publicly that he would give $200 for the arrest and conviction of the party who killed his brother, Hiram. J. L. Manning was present at the burial, and heard the announcement. After the burial Manning went to the house of Robert Mason, Sr., father of Hiram Mason, who lived a short distance from the graveyard, and inquired of the old man what they proposed to do. At the same time he stated that he did not think $200 was enough, and wanted $350 to work up the case and capture and convict the guilty party. The old gentleman referred him to his sons with a statement that whatever they did would be all right with him. Manning then started out to find appellant, and overtook him and others on the county road. Manning made about the same inquiry of appellant, wherupon appellant stated that he did not know what Franklin Mason or the other boys would do, but that he would pay Manning $200 to work up the case, and secure the arrest and conviction of the guilty party. Manning worked on the case and discovered evidence which justified the arrest of Alex Webb.

At the trial of Webb, Manning was present, and testified and gave the prosecution all the information that he had.

Webb was convicted. On cross-examination it developed that Manning was a deputy sheriff of Bell county when Hiram Mason was killed, and when Webb was arrested and convicted. Manning claims that, in addition to his work as deputy sheriff, he sometimes did private detective work when called upon.

Manning brought this action against Robert Mason, Jr., and Robert Mason, Sr., to secure the reward of $200.

Clay, C. The question presented is: "Is an agreement to pay the deputy sheriff of a county where a felony is committed a reward for investigating the crime, arresting the offender and securing his conviction, enforceable?" From an early day it has been established and continues to be the rule that an agreement to pay money to a sheriff or other public officer for doing what he ought to do is void and against public policy. Accordingly, a public officer, such as a sheriff, constable, or policeman, is not entitled to a reward offered for the arrest or conviction of a criminal where the service performed is within the scope or line of the duties of such office. Such promises are void, not only because of want of consideration, but because they are contrary to public policy. The above rule was first announced by this court in *Marking* v. *Needy*, 8 Bush, 22, and has been uniformly adhered to. The reason underlying the rule is that, were it otherwise, law officers whose official duty it is to make arrests might be induced to delay making them until rewards should be offered and consequently criminals might escape arrest or punishment.

Leggett et al. v. Vinson
155 Miss. 411, 124 So. 472 (1929)

This was an action by M. M. Vinson (plaintiff) against Dr. T. Ford Leggett (defendant). Judgment for plaintiff and defendant appealed. Reversed and judgment entered for defendant.

Vinson entered into a contract with Dr. Leggett whereby he agreed to build a house for Dr. Leggett according to certain plans and specifications for the sum of $3,950. When the house was partly completed, Vinson went to Dr. Leggett and told him "that the job could not be carried through under the written contract." Dr. Leggett answered, "Go ahead and complete the job as we started and I will pay you time and pay the bills." On completion of the house Vinson submitted the bills and his time and the total exceeded the contract amount ($3,950) by $2,200.89. Dr. Leggett paid Vinson $3,950 but refused to pay the additional $2,200.89.

Cook, J. While there is some authority to the contrary, notably from the courts of Massachusetts, Indiana, and Illinois, the great weight of authority seems to establish as the general rule that the proposition that a promise to do that which a party is already legally bound to do is not a sufficient consideration to support a promise by the other party to the contract to give the former an additional compensation or benefit, and such a promise cannot be legally enforced although the other party has completed his contract in reliance upon it; and with this general rule, prior decisions of this court are in accord.

The Supreme Court of Minnesota, in the case of *King* v. *Duluth, M. & N. Ry. Co.*, 61 Minn. 482, 63 N.W. 1105, 1106, held that: "Where the refusal to perform and the promise to pay extra compensation for performance of the contract are one transaction, and there are no exceptional circumstances making it equitable that an increased compensation should be demanded and paid, no amount of astute reasoning can change the plain fact that the party who refuses to perform, and thereby coerces a promise from the other party to the contract to pay him an increased compensation for doing that which he is legally bound to do, takes an unjustifiable advantage of the necessities of the other party. To hold, under such circumstances, that the party making the promise for extra compensation is presumed to have voluntarily elected to relinquish and abandon all of his rights under the original contract, and to substitute therefor the new or modified agreement, is to wholly disregard the natural inference to be drawn from the transaction, and invite parties to repudiate their contract obligations whenever they can gain thereby. . . . . Surely it would be a travesty on justice to hold that the party so making the promise for extra pay was estopped from asserting that the promise was without consideration. A party cannot lay the foundation of an estoppel by his own wrong. If it be conceded that by the new promise the party obtains that which he could not compel, viz., a specific performance of the contract by the other party, still the fact remains that the one party has obtained thereby only that which he was legally entitled to receive, and the other party has done only that which he was legally bound to do. How, then, can it be said that the legal rights or obligations of the party are changed by the new promise? . . . . Where the promise to the one is simply a repetition of a subsisting legal promise there can be no consideration for the promise of the other party, and there is no warrant for inferring that the parties have voluntarily rescinded or modified their contract. . . . . And the promise cannot be legally enforced, although the other party has completed his contract in reliance upon it."

This principle is announced in 1 Williston on Contracts, § 130, in the following language: "Where A and B have entered into a bilateral agreement, it not infrequently happens that one of the parties, becoming dissatisfied with the contract, refuses to perform or to continue performance unless a larger compensation than that provided in the original agreement is promised him. Especially common is the situation where a builder or contractor undertakes work in return for a promised price and afterwards finding the contract unprofitable, refuses to fulfill his agreement but is induced to fulfill it by the promise of added compensation. On principle the second agreement is invalid for the performance by the recalcitrant contractor is no legal detriment to him whether actually given or promised, since, at the time the second agreement was entered into, he was already bound to do the work; nor is the performance under the second agreement a legal benefit to the promisor since he was already entitled to have the work done. In such situations and others identical in principle, the great weight of authority supports this conclusion."

Some of the cases supporting the general rule, as herein approved, recognize as an exception to this rule cases where a party refused to complete his contract on account of exceptional circumstances or unforeseen difficulties and burdens which would justify such party in rescinding the contract; but it will be unnecessary for us to here consider any question of exceptions, if any, to the general rule, for the reason that there is in the record now before us no evidence of any exceptional circumstances or unforeseen and substantial difficulties that would justify the appellee in rescinding the contract. Mere inadequacy of the contract price which is the result of an error of judgment on the part of the contractor is insufficient, and nothing more is made to appear in this record.

It is undoubtedly true that the parties to a contract may modify it, or waive their right under it, and ingraft new terms upon it, and in such case the promise of one party will be sufficient consideration for the promise of the other. But where the promise of one is merely a repetition of a subsisting legal promise, and the duties, obligations, and burdens imposed upon such party by the contract are in no way varied, altered, or changed, there is no consideration for the promise of the other. Such is the case made by the appellee's proof, and therefore the alleged promise of appellant was without consideration.

Michael v. Holland

111 Ind. App. 34, 40 N.E. (2d) 362 (1941)

This was an action by Joseph L. Michael (plaintiff) against Albert Holland (defendant). Judgment for defendant and plaintiff appealed. Judgment reversed and new trial ordered.

Holland became indebted to Michael in the sum of $450. Holland operated a restaurant and Michael was engaged in selling groceries for J. P. Michael Co., a wholesale grocery company. Holland purchased foodstuffs from J. P. Michael Co. After the debt was due, Holland went to Michael to pay the debt and at that time Michael said $150 was all he wanted. Holland offered to pay the full amount but Michael said that Holland had purchased considerable merchandise from J. P. Michael Co. and that Michael wished to show his appreciation for such orders. No payments were made on the account of such debt except the $150 and no demand was made by Michael for the balance until about four years after the payment of the $150 when this suit was brought to recover the $300 balance. Holland claimed that Michael had made him a gift of the balance of the debt; also that the payment made discharged the debt.

Bedwell, P. J. In this case the subject of the claimed gift had no corporeal existence. It was a pure chose in action without palpable form, and there was no document, symbol, or token that was evidence of title to it. As far as the evidence indicates there was not even a book account kept by appellant evidencing the indebtedness of appellee. While there is authority to the effect that where there is no written evidence of a debt, since no delivery can be made, there can be no gift, the great weight of authority in other jurisdictions, and we think the better rule, is that a gift of a simple debt without palpable form by the creditor to the debtor cannot be made effective without the execution and delivery of some instrument or the performance of some act or acts placing the debt beyond the legal control of the creditor.

It is well established that the payment of a smaller sum than is due on a liquidated claim, with no other element of accord in the transaction, is not satisfaction of the debt even though accepted as such at the time.

Union Central Life Insurance Co. v. Weber et al.
285 Ill. App. 568, 2 N.E. (2d) 746 (1936)

This was an action by Union Central Life Insurance Company (plaintiff) against Charles A. Weber and others (defendants) to foreclose a mortgage. From a decree granting plaintiff partial relief the plaintiff appealed. Decree affirmed.

Weber was in financial difficulties and could not pay his creditors in full. He proposed as a settlement that he would obtain a loan of $15,000 from the Federal Land Bank if his creditors would accept this sum on a pro rata basis in full discharge of their claims. Weber owed plaintiff $9,804.37. The plaintiff together with Weber's other creditors agreed to accept the $15,000 to be distributed on a pro rata basis in full settlement of their claims. Under this agreement plaintiff's claim was reduced to $8,250. Plaintiff now repudiates the agreement and brings suit to recover $9,804.37 and to foreclose the mortgage given to secure this sum.

Wolfe, J. We think that the evidence clearly shows that there was an agreement among all the creditors of the defendants to scale down their indebtedness and accept a smaller sum in full satisfaction of their claims, and that the same were dependent upon the defendants' procuring a federal loan for $15,000. Since the earliest cases, courts have recognized the rule that the payment of a smaller sum in satisfaction of a larger sum is not full discharge of the debtor, but there is a well-known exception to this rule, which is, that it does not apply in bona fide cases of compromise and settlement. In the case of the *National Time Recorder Company* v. *Feypel*, 93 Ill. App. 170, the court, in discussing what is a good consideration for a compromise of an indebtedness, have this to say: "We understand the rule to be that where several creditors join in an agreement of this kind with their common debtor, and in so doing give up their present rights for the general advantage, no other consideration need be shown—the consideration to each creditor being the undertaking by the others—and all are bound, unless it can be shown that the debtor has refused to fulfill his part of the agreement.

It is our conclusion that the agreement of the various creditors of the defendants that they would scale down and compromise their indebtedness was a valid consideration for the various agreements and cannot be avoided on the ground of lack of consideration.

Intention

It is well settled that an act, in order to be consideration, must be performed at the request of the promisor and in exchange for his promise. In determining whether an act has been performed at the request of the promisor and *in exchange for* the promise, the intent of the parties will be controlling.

Archer says to Burch, "I understand you want an old print of Brooklyn Bridge. I have several and if you will come to my apartment I will give you one." Burch goes to Archer's apartment for one of the prints and Archer refuses to give him one. If Burch sued Archer on his promise to give Burch one of the prints, Burch could not recover unless he could prove that both Archer and Burch intended the trip to Archer's apartment as consideration for the promise to give Burch a print. A promise to make a gift on a condition is not an enforceable agreement for lack of consideration. As in other cases, the intent of the parties is gathered from all the facts and circumstances surrounding the transaction.

Another problem which is closely related to that of intent in consideration is that of adequacy of consideration. It is well established that the courts will not inquire into the adequacy of the consideration. If the parties have entered into a contract intending a slight detriment as consideration to support a burdensome promise, the courts have taken the stand that the parties to the contract are the judges of the adequacy of the consideration and not the court. Closely associated with the question of the adequacy of the consideration are the question of intention and the question of fraud. If the consideration is entirely inadequate, it is at least evidence that it was not intended as consideration, and if the intent is lacking, the courts will hold that there is no consideration. In other cases where a burdensome promise is supported by an insignificant consideration, it may be evidence of fraud. If fraud is present, it may be set up as a defense to a suit on the contract.

Another closely associated question arises in regard to agreements reciting a nominal consideration such as "one dollar" or "six cents," etc. If the parties pay the recited consideration intending it as consideration, the courts will hold the agreement to be an enforceable contract, but if the recitation of consideration is for the purpose of formally complying with the requirement of consideration, the better view is that the agreement is unenforceable because of lack of consideration. In an early United States Supreme Court case,[1] Judge Story stated that the recitation of consideration, even though the recited consideration was not paid, was sufficient in that it gave rise to an obligation to pay which would be a sufficient consideration to make the agreement enforceable.

There is one exception to the rule that the courts will not inquire into the adequacy of the consideration and that is in an agreement to exchange a larger sum of money or fungible goods for a smaller sum of money or fungible goods at the same time and place. Such an agreement is equivalent to a promise to make a gift of the difference. Archer promises to deliver Burch 1,000 bushels of number one red wheat at Burch's mill on Tuesday next, and Burch promises to pay Archer 100 bushels of number one red wheat at the same time and place. This agreement would not be enforceable because of inadequacy of consideration.

Fire Insurance Association v. Wickham
141 U.S. 564, 12 S. Ct. Rep. 84 (1891)

This was an action brought by John W. Wickham (plaintiff) against Fire Insurance Association (defendant). Judgment for plaintiff and defendant appealed. Judgment affirmed.

Wickham owned the vessel, St. Paul, which navigated on the Great Lakes. The vessel was insured in the Fire Insurance Association. A fire broke out in the hold of the vessel and to save her and her cargo she was skuttled and sunk and the fire extinguished in this way. Later the vessel was raised and brought to Detroit. While unloading, another fire broke out and the vessel was again sunk and later raised and repaired. A statement of the fire loss was submitted to the insurance company which was approved, but this statement did not include the cost of raising the vessel, which cost was admitted to be covered by the policies. The insurance company paid the amount of the fire loss five days after the statement was submitted which was fifty-five days before it was due. Wickham signed a receipt which was broad enough in its terms to cover both the loss by fire and the cost of raising the vessel. The insurance company refused to pay the cost of raising the vessel claiming the payment of the fire loss

---

[1] *Lawrence* v. *McCalmot,* 2 Howard 426, 452, 11 L. Ed. 326.

fifty-five days before due was consideration to support an agreement to discharge them from their liability for the cost of raising the vessel.

Mr. Justice Brown. But assuming that the receipts upon their face show a complete settlement of the entire claim for one-half the total amount, what was the consideration for the release of the other half? The only one that is put forward for that purpose is that payment was made five days after proofs of loss were furnished, or fifty-five days before anything was actually due by the terms of the policy. That prepayment of part of a claim may be a good consideration for the release of the residue is not disputed; but it is subject to the qualification that nothing can be treated as a consideration that is not intended as such by the parties. Thus in *Philpot* v. *Gruninger*, 14 Wall. 570, 577, it is stated that "nothing is consideration that is not regarded as such by both parties." To constitute a valid agreement there must be a meeting of minds upon every feature and element of such agreement, of which the consideration is one. The mere presence of some incident to a contract which might under certain circumstances be upheld as a consideration for a promise does not necessarily make it the consideration for the promise in that contract. To give it that effect it must have been offered by one party and accepted by the other as one element of the contracts. In *Kilpatrick* v. *Muirhead*, 16 Penn. St. 117, 126, it was said that "consideration, like every other part of a contract, must be the result of agreement. The parties must understand and be influenced to the particular action by something of value or convenience and inconvenience recognized by all of them as the moving cause. That which is a mere fortuitous result flowing accidentally from an arrangement, but in no degree prompting the actors to it, is not to be esteemed a legal consideration." Now evidence of what took place at the meeting, if admissible for no other purpose, was competent as bearing upon the question whether the prepayment was mentioned or treated as an inducement or consideration for the release of the residue of the claim.

Rust v. Fitzhugh
132 Wis. 549, 112 N.W. 508 (1907)

This was an action by Dora Rust, executrix of the estate of W. A. Rust (plaintiff) against Daniel Fitzhugh (defendant). Judgment for the plaintiff and defendant appealed. Judgment affirmed.

Rust and Fitzhugh had engaged in a series of joint ventures involving the purchase and resale of lands. One of these transactions involved the purchase of 8,080 acres of land for $10,000. This land was held for resale in smaller tracts. Rust and Fitzhugh entered into a written agreement by the terms of which Fitzhugh agreed as follows: "Now, in consideration of one dollar to me in hand paid, receipt whereof is hereby confessed and acknowledged, I hereby agree to account for and pay over to W. A. Rust, his heirs and assigns, the one-fourth (1/4) of the net proceeds derived from the sale of said lands above referred to." At the time this suit was brought the lands referred to had been resold and one-fourth of the net proceeds amounted to $11,206.09. Fitzhugh refused to pay this sum to Rust's estate, contending that the contract was void for lack of consideration.

Marshall, J. It is contended that the contract is void for want of a sufficient consideration. Generally speaking, a valuable consideration however small is sufficient to support any contract; that inadequacy of consideration alone is not a fatal defect. That rule is recognized in *Wood* v. *Boynton,* in these words: "In the absence of fraud or warranty, the value of the property sold, as compared with the price paid, is no ground for a rescission of a sale."

Where the consideration to support a contract is so small as under all the circumstances to show fraud the agreement is void, but the defect consists in the element of fraud, not at all in the insignificance of the consideration.

There was no element of fraud established in this case or found. The parties seem to have contracted understandingly; no undue advantage being taken of one by the other. The evidence shows that they were business associates and had been for many years, and that they had been accustomed to have important dealings with each other of a character explainable only upon the theory that each deemed himself thoroughly competent to protect his own interest, and that he did so to his satisfaction at the time of each transaction.

A so-called exception, upon which counsel for appellant rely, that a trifling consideration, as one cent or one dollar, will not support a promise to pay a considerable sum of money, the agreement not being characterized by any uncertainty as to time or amount, is really not an exception at all since under circumstances fraud of some sort is presumed. The rule is thus recognized in Langdell's *Summary of the Law of Contracts, 55*: "Though the smallest consideration will in most cases support the largest promise, this is only because the law shuts its eyes to the inequality between them; and hence any inequality to which the law cannot shut its eyes is fatal to the validity of the promise. . . . ." But this reasoning is obviously inapplicable to a case in which "the value both of the consideration and the promise is conclusively fixed by law; and a promise to pay money in consideration of a payment of money is such a case, provided the elements of time and uncertainty be wholly excluded." That does not apply to the case in hand. The sum of money that might in the end come out of the speculation was, when the contract was made, involved in much uncertainty. The time when there would be profits for division was involved in like uncertainty. It was liable to take many years, as proved to be the case, to work the matter out. While large profits may have seemed probable, it could not have been regarded but that the result might be otherwise, especially in case of the value of the services required to market the land and collect the proceeds being charged up to the deal. There were many possible circumstances liable to materially affect the final result, making the same very profitable to the parties concerned or not so. It was not impossible that the value of the land might go down instead of up, or be largely absorbed by high taxes or other matters. The rule on this branch of the case is that, in the absence of satisfactory proof of fraud the smallness of the consideration to support a contract, so long as it is large enough to be measurable, is immaterial, except in case of a contract to pay a sum of money. Applying that to the facts the contract in question is valid.

Hogan et al. v. Richardson et ux.
166 Ark. 381, 266 S.W. 299 (1924)

This was an action by Charles Richardson and wife (plaintiffs) against C. B. Hogan and another (defendants). Decree for plaintiffs and defendants appealed. Decree affirmed.

Charles Richardson and Harriet Richardson, his wife, brought this suit in equity against C. B. Hogan and W. H. Strong to cancel a written option contract executed by the plaintiffs to the defendants on the ground that they had withdrawn their offer before it was accepted by the defendants. The defendants admitted that the instrument which is the basis of this suit was in law an option to purchase the oil, gas, and other minerals therein described at the price of $6,000; but aver that the contract is a valid and binding one, because it is based on a valid consideration; and asked for a specific performance of the same.

The instrument upon which the suit is based reads in part as follows:

"That said party of the first part, for and in consideration of one ($1) dollar, and other good and valuable consideration given by party of the second part, hereby agrees to sell and deliver by warranty deed an undivided one-half (½) interest in and to all the oil, gas and other minerals in, under and upon the following described lands.

"(Signed) Chas. Richardson
her
"Harriet X Richardson
mark

"Witness as to signature: J. Morgan Russell."

The evidence shows that the option was worth $3,000.

Hart, J. The consideration recited in the option contract was one dollar, and the defendants did not complete the contract by the payment of the $6,000 recited in it before the plaintiffs withdrew their offer. There is some conflict in the authorities as to whether or not there must be a valuable consideration for the option to render it more than an offer revocable before acceptance; but this court has recognized the rule to be that a recited consideration of one dollar is merely nominal, and that the offer may be revoked at any time before it is accepted. In the earlier case of *Greenfield* v. *Carlton*, 30 Ark. 548, the court recognized that in a complaint to enforce the specific performance of a contract for the sale of land, among other things, it was necessary to allege the execution of a binding agreement for a sufficient consideration.

The distinction between an option for the sale of land for a nominal consideration and one for a valuable consideration is that the former is merely an offer to sell and may be withdrawn at any time before acceptance upon notice to the vendee; but in the latter, where a valuable consideration is paid for the option, it cannot be withdrawn by the vendee before the expiration of the time specified in the option.

The contract in the case at bar was a mere option given by Charles Richardson and wife to C. B. Hogan and W. H. Strong to purchase an undivided one-half interest in all of the oil, gas, and other minerals in 240 acres of land, and there was no consideration to support the contract until Hogan and Strong should accept the offer of Richardson, unless one dollar should be considered a valuable one. It would be, therefore, in the power of Richardson to withdraw his offer before it was accepted if the consideration was nominal, and he in effect did withdraw it by bringing the present suit.

It is insisted by counsel for appellant, however, that the sum of one dollar named in the option contract is a valuable, or at least an adequate, consideration. The authorities on this point are in direct conflict, and we do not deem it necessary to cite or review them in this opinion. We consider that the better reasoning and the right of the matter is that one dollar is not an adequate consideration for such an option. It is merely a nominal consideration and should be disregarded by a court of equity. It cannot be said that the consideration for the option extends to and includes the purchase price named therein. The persons to whom the option was given were not to take possession of the property, nor were they to make any improvements thereon. The sole consideration for the option was the sum of one dollar.

In Bilateral Contracts

The consideration in a bilateral contract is the mutual promises of the parties to the contract. Not all promises will be sufficient consideration to support a bilateral contract. Since the performance of an act which one is already legally bound to perform is not consideration, obviously the promise to perform an act which one is already legally bound to perform will not be consideration. If the act or forbearance promised will not be sufficient consideration for a unilateral contract, the promise will not be sufficient consideration for bilateral contract. The rule is stated in the *Restatement of the Law of Contracts* as follows: "A promise is insufficient consideration if the promisor knows or has reason to know at the time of making the promise that it can be performed by some act or forbearance which would be insufficient consideration for a unilateral contract." [1]

[1] Sec. 78, p. 87.

To have a binding bilateral contract both parties to the contract must make binding promises. It is frequently stated by the courts and writers that if one party is not bound, neither party is bound, or, stated in other words, a contract that lacks mutuality is unenforceable. In business transactions it sometimes happens that although from a cursory reading of the agreement it appears that each party has made a binding promise, close analysis reveals that one of the parties has actually made no binding promise or that the effect of what appears to be a promise is counteracted by some other provision, so that the party is not actually bound to do anything. An example of the latter is a contract in which one of the parties to an agreement is given the power to cancel the contract at will.

Archer and Burch enter into an agreement by the terms of which Archer agrees to purchase a refrigerator of a designated size and model from Burch and makes a $50 down payment. The contract contains the following provision: "Burch hereby reserves the right to cancel this agreement at any time before delivery of said refrigerator by notifying Archer and returning the down payment made herewith." The agreement will not be a binding contract until the delivery and acceptance of the refrigerator. If Burch is not bound Archer will not be bound. Archer and Burch enter into an agreement by the terms of which Burch agrees to sell and deliver to Archer at Archer's residence all the Number 3 fuel oil Archer wishes to order during the winter of 1945-46. No binding contract will result because Archer has not promised to purchase oil. If the agreement was: Burch agrees to sell and deliver to Archer at Archer's residence all the Number 3 fuel oil Archer will need to heat his residence during the winter of 1945-46, and Archer agrees to purchase all the fuel oil he needs to heat his residence during said period, a binding contract will result. Although the quantity is not stated definitely, Archer has promised to buy fuel oil from Burch and impliedly contracted to buy from no one else in exchange for Burch's promise to sell to Archer.

International Shoe Co. v. Herndon
135 S. C. 138, 133 S. E. 202 (1926)

This was an action by International Shoe Company (plaintiff) against C. H. Herndon (defendant) to recover the purchase price of goods sold and delivered. Defendant set up the breach of an exclusive sale agreement as a counterclaim. Motion to dismiss counterclaim denied and plaintiff appealed. Reversed and remanded.

International Shoe Company sued Herndon upon an account for goods sold and delivered, amounting to $467.59. Herndon admitted the sale but set up a counterclaim as follows: That in March, 1915, he bought a bill of shoes from the plaintiff, in consideration of which the plaintiff "entered into a parol agreement with the defendant, C. H. Herndon, trading as Herndon Clothing Store, wherein it contracted and agreed that the defendant should have the exclusive sale of plantiff's shoes at Walterboro, and should be the only person, firm, or corporation to handle said line of shoes at said place, said parol agreement further providing that the defendant should have the exclusive agency as long as he would handle said shoes and as long as he wished to handle same"; that acting upon said agreement the defendant bought bills of goods from the plaintiff from year to year, up to June, 1923, and paid for them, aggregating more than $15,000, and expended in advertising the plaintiff's shoes not less than $1,500; that in May, 1923, the plaintiff violated said agreement by selling its shoes to two or more merchants in Walterboro, all to his damage in loss of profits and injury to his reputation as a merchant, in the sum of $2,500.

Cothran, J. The contract set up in the counterclaim is not declared upon as a unilateral contract, but as a bilateral one—a contract by which the defendant agreed to buy a certain bill of goods, and in consideration thereof the plaintiff agreed to give him the exclusive sale of the shoes at Walterboro, S.C.

It is very true that mutuality of obligation is not an essential element in unilateral contracts, such as option contracts, contracts evidenced by a subscription paper, contract of offers of rewards or a guaranty, or in many other instances readily put in ordinary business affairs. The non-requirement of mutuality in such contracts, however, does not dispense with the necessity of a valuable consideration. But in bilateral contracts, where the consideration is sought to be sustained upon mutual promises, the contract consists of the several engagements of the parties; the engagement of one being the consideration for the engagement of the other, and the combined engagements constituting the contract. In order to accomplish this result, it is manifest that the promise or engagement of one of the parties, which is sought to be held as the consideration for the promise or engagement of the other, must be an absolute engagement of such party; for if it is not, the contract is lacking in mutuality, notwithstanding the absolute character of the engagement of the other party.

The rule is thus stated in Elliott on Contracts, Vol. 1, § 231;

"A promise may constitute the consideration for another promise. But a promise is not a good consideration for a promise unless there is absolutely mutuality of the engagement, so that each party has the right to hold the other to a positive agreement. In case the promise of one of the parties impose no legal duty upon the party making it, such promise furnishes no consideration for a promise."

Thus, in the case at bar, the defendant seeks to hold the plaintiff to the alleged contract of March, 1915, by which he engaged to buy a bill of shoes from the plaintiff, and the plaintiff engaged to give him the exclusive sale of its shoes at Walterboro. There is no question as to the absolute character of the defendant's engagement; but if the plaintiff's engagement was not an absolute enforceable one, it is clear that the contract, which must consist of an absolute enforceable engagement on each side, is lacking in mutuality and therefore wanting in consideration. So the question of the validity of the alleged contract is to be resolved by the further question of the validity of the plaintiff's alleged engagement to give to the defendant the exclusive sale of its shoes.

It will be observed that this alleged engagement is not only indefinite as to time, quantity, price and terms, but it is accompanied by no corresponding engagement on the part of the defendant; he binds himself to nothing; he could, under it, order one or a thousand pairs of shoes, or none at all; at a price unknown, not agreed upon, and upon indefinite terms.

Under such circumstances, it cannot be considered as partaking of any of the elements of an absolute, binding, enforceable engagement, such as will constitute the consideration for the defendant's engagement, the essential element of a valid contract.

In *American Co.* v. *Kirk,* 68 F. 791, 15 C.C.A. 540, quoting syllabus, it is held:

"A contract to sell and deliver 10,000 barrels of oil, at a stipulated price, in such quantities per week as the buyer may desire, to be paid for as delivered, but which contains no agreement on the part of the buyer to purchase and receive any particular quantity of oil, is not binding, for want of mutuality."

In *Calvary Baptist Church* v. *Dart*, 68 S.C. 221, 47 S.E. 66, it was held that a contract to purchase property at foreclosure sale and resell to the original owner at the same price with only seven per cent interest was lacking in mutuality, upon the ground, it is assumed, that there was no reciprocal obligation on the part of the owner to repurchase.

We think therefore that the alleged contract, for the breach of which the defendant asks damages, was lacking in consideration and mutuality.

The court is not unmindful of the principle that where the contract has been fully executed, the party who has received the benefit of such performance will not be heard to urge the lack of mutuality of obligation on the part of the party performing in the contract as originally appearing. 13 C.J. 334. But this is not such a case; the defendant is not seeking recovery for any act of performance upon his part; but for profits which he would have made under a contract which must be held to have been lacking in consideration and mutuality.

American Agricultural Chemical Co. v. Kennedy & Crawford
103 Va. 171, 48 S. E. 868 (1904)

This was an action brought by American Agricultural Chemical Company (plaintiff) against Kennedy & Crawford (defendants). Judgment for defendants and plaintiff appealed. Judgment affirmed.

The American Agricultural Chemical Company and Kennedy & Crawford entered into a written agreement by the terms of which the American Agricultural Chemical Company agreed to manufacture and deliver to Kennedy & Crawford 200 bags of fertilizer at stipulated prices. The contract set out in detail the price, quantity, time and place of delivery, and credit terms and concluded as follows: "We [The American Agricultural Chemical Company] reserve the right to cancel this contract at any time we deem proper, but in the event of such cancelation the provisions of this contract shall govern the closing of all business begun thereunder."

The American Agricultural Chemical Company manufactured the fertilizer, packed it in bags, marked it for Kennedy & Crawford, and tendered delivery to them, but they repudiated the contract and refused to accept and pay for the fertilizer. This suit is brought to recover damages for breach of the contract.

Buchanan, J. The general rule of law is—and this seems to be conceded by the plaintiff company—that, where the consideration for the promise of one party is the promise of the other party, there must be absolute mutuality of engagement, so that each party has the right to hold the other to a positive agreement. Both parties must be bound, or neither is bound. The plaintiff insists that the averments of its declaration take this case out of the general rule, upon the ground that, while the contract sued on may have lacked mutuality of obligation in its inception, yet that the plaintiff had performed and executed the contract on its part by manufacturing the fertilizer, putting it in sacks, and tendering it to the defendants, and that such performance cured any lack of mutuality in the contract in its inception, and rendered it absolutely binding. Although the contract did not bind the plaintiff to furnish the fertilizer which the defendants agreed to purchase, yet, if the defendants had actually received it, they would have been bound to pay for it; and this would be so even if the agreement in question had never been entered into. But the defendants did not receive it. The offer of the plaintiff to deliver the fertilizer which it had never bound itself to sell could not make the defendants liable in damages for refusing to receive what they, in legal contemplation, had never agreed to purchase. The defendants never having had the right to compel the plaintiff to deliver the fertilizer, the plaintiff could not by its own act make it the duty of the defendants to receive it, nor impose any liability upon them.

The promise of the defendants to purchase from the plaintiff was not a continuing offer, which, when accepted, was mutually binding upon both parties, as was the case in most of the decisions cited and relied on by the plaintiff. In those cases, while one party was not bound when the proposition of the other was made, he afterward, before the proposition was withdrawn, either did, or bound himself to do, the thing which was the condition of the other's promise.

In a contract of sale the proposed buyer says, "I will give so much for these goods," and he may withdraw his offer before it is accepted, and, if his withdrawal reaches the seller before the seller has accepted, the obligation of the buyer is extinguished; but if not withdrawn it remains a continuing offer for a reasonable time, and, if accepted within this time, both parties are bound, as by a promise for a promise. There is entire mutuality of obligation. The buyer may tender the price and demand the goods, and the seller may tender the goods and demand the price.

In this case the plaintiff made a proposition to sell, which the defendants accepted, but the plaintiff's offer left it optional with it whether or not it would sell. It did not bind itself to sell. The defendants made no continuing offer to purchase. Their engagement was to purchase upon the terms and conditions stated in the plaintiff's proposition to sell. As that proposition did not bind the plaintiff to sell, there was no consideration for the defendant's promise to purchase, and, as we have seen, neither party was bound at that time. The plaintiff after that time never did any act or made any promise which bound it to complete the contract. There never was a time when the defendants had the right to tender the price and demand the fertilizer. In the absence of such obligation on the part of the plaintiff, and of such right on the part of the defendants, there never was a binding engagement between the parties which a court of law would enforce.

Past Consideration

The rule is generally expressed as follows: Past consideration will not support a present contract. The use of the term "past consideration" is confusing because it is used in the popular sense and not in the strict legal sense. The meaning of the rule may be clarified by the use of illustrations. (1) If Archer gives Burch an automobile as a present and later Archer meets with reverses and Burch promises Archer that he will pay him $1,000, the value of the automobile, Burch's promise is unenforceable. At the time Archer gave the automobile to Burch there was no legal obligation on the part of Burch to make any return to Archer. Burch might be under a social obligation to make some return, but the courts do not enforce social obligations of this nature. Consequently, Burch's promise to pay Archer $1,000 is in legal effect a promise to make a gift, is not supported by consideration, and is not enforceable. Archer's past gift will not support Burch's present promise. (2) If Burch calls Archer, a carpenter, and says, "Come over and fix my roof. It leaks," and Archer does fix the roof and at a later date Burch promises to pay Archer $25 for fixing the roof, Burch will be bound by his promise. In this case, owing to the circumstances, a promise to pay is implied at the time the act of repairing the roof is performed. Burch is under a legally binding obligation to pay Archer for his services, and if he does not pay, Archer can recover a judgment against Burch for the reasonable value of his services. It is an unliquidated debt. Burch's promise to pay $25 is reducing to a certainty an uncertain but existing obligation. If the relationship between Archer and Burch is such that the presumption would be that Archer's services were rendered as a gratuity, for example, if Archer were Burch's son and had in the past kept his father's (Burch's) house in repair without charge, then Burch's subsequent promise to pay would not be enforceable.

Brown v. Addington
114 Ind. App. 404, 52 N.E. 2d 640 (1944)

This was an action by Francis W. Brown, administrator of the estate of William E. Brown, deceased (plaintiff), against Claude L. Addington (defendant). Judgment for defendant and plaintiff appealed. Judgment affirmed.

Addington, a nephew of William E. Brown, became homeless when eight years old. Although under no legal obligation to do so, Brown took Addington into his own home where during the next six years he was fed, clothed, educated in the public schools, and otherwise cared for by Brown. In 1929, Brown had reached an advanced age and at Brown's suggestion the following agreement was drawn:

"July 20, 1929

"I, Claude L. Addington, remembering and appreciating the many favors and acts of kindness, rendered to me, during the years that have passed, by my beloved uncle William E. Brown, and desiring to express my gratitude to him in something more than empty words, hereby promise and pledge that I will pay to my said uncle William E. Brown, the sum of One Hundred Dollars ($100.00) during each year that the said William E. Brown shall live. Payment to be made on or about the first day of January of each said year, beginning with the year 1930.

"(Signed) Claude L. Addington."

Addington paid nothing during Brown's lifetime. The administrator of Brown's estate now sues to recover the amount due under the agreement. Addington sets up that the agreement is not supported by consideration.

Crumpacker, C. J. If a person has been benefited in the past by some act or forbearance for which he incurred no legal liability and "afterward, whether from good feeling or interested motives, he makes a promise to the person by whose act or forbearance he has benefited, and that promise is made on no other consideration than the past benefit, it is gratuitous and cannot be enforced; it is based on motive and not on consideration." 17 C.J.S., Contracts, p. 470, § 116, and cases cited. Although natural love and affection is sufficient consideration for an executed contract, it is generally held insufficient to support an executory promise. Indiana is in line with this general rule and the courts of this state have held frequently that such promises are mere gratuitous engagements to give and not gifts inter vivos or causa mortis.

By the great weight of authority a past consideration, if it imposed no legal obligation at the time it was furnished, will support no promise whatever. A past consideration is insufficient, even though of benefit to the promisor, where the services rendered or things of value furnished were intended and expected to be gratuitous.

Friedman v. Suttle
10 Ariz. 57, 85 Pac. 726 (1906)

This was an action by F. C. Friedman (plaintiff) against H. A. Suttle (defendant). From a judgment in favor of defendant plaintiff appealed. Judgment reversed and new trial ordered.

Campbell, J. There is testimony in the record tending to prove the following facts: The business of the defendant was that of a mine promoter and owner. The plaintiff at different times had been in the employment of the defendant "looking up" and "writing up" mining properties for him. Some time prior to the transaction involved in this action plaintiff had been engaged in traveling about the country surrounding Prescott, seeing different mining properties and writing descriptions of them for newspapers. Defendant instructed him to look for good prospects for him, telling him that he would examine any property that plaintiff would bring to his notice and if satisfactory, purchase it. He brought the property known as "Three Black Buttes" to the notice of the defendant, showed him written reports concerning it and samples of ore from it and told him the name of the owner and its location. He advised him that the purchase price was $36,000 and that he desired a commission of $4,000 for his services. Defendant manifested an interest in the property and told plaintiff that he would at once investigate it and if satisfactory would purchase it and pay plaintiff the $4,000 commission. All of the information was given before the promise of the defendant was made. At defendant's request plaintiff communicated with another person whom defendant desired to examine the property, giving him its location and the name of the owner. Defendant subsequently purchased the property. Conceding that the promise made by defendant was wholly in consideration of the information previously given him by plaintiff and did not contemplate other or further services from the plaintiff, does the case fall within the rule contended for by the appellee? (That said testimony fails to show any consideration for the alleged contract, promise or agreement, but shows that alleged contract is attempted to be based upon past consideration, to wit: Services or information rendered or given by plaintiff as a volunteer.) He had previously requested plaintiff to furnish information as to such promising prospects as he should discover. In laying the information before defendant plaintiff was not acting entirely as a volunteer. We think it fairly may be said that plaintiff furnished this information to defendant at his request and that the request is such a one that, if complied with, the law would imply a promise to pay, especially if the information given is accepted and acted upon. The rule is that an executed consideration given upon such a request will sustain a promise founded upon it.

QUESTIONS AND PROBLEMS

1. What is the nature of consideration?
2. Hamer's uncle promised to pay Hamer $5,000 if he would refrain from drinking liquor, using tobacco, swearing, and playing cards for money until he should become twenty-one years of age. Hamer did refrain, but his uncle refused to pay the $5,000. Can Hamer recover a judgment against his uncle?
3. Hewitt purchased a farm from the Loan Co., paying $6,000 down and signing a contract whereby Hewitt agreed to pay the unpaid balance ($1,900) at the rate of $300 per year. The contract further provided that if Hewitt defaulted in his annual payments, he would surrender possession of the farm and all payments made would be forfeited as rent.

   Hewitt paid only one yearly payment, and when he was two years in default, the Loan Co. declared the contract forfeited and demanded possession of the property. Hewitt complained to the Loan Co. stating that it was unfair to forfeit the contract when he (Hewitt) had made such a substantial down payment. The Loan Co. finally promised Hewitt that if he would vacate the premises on or before September 10, 1939, the Loan Co. would pay Hewitt $400. Hewitt vacated the place before September 10, 1939, and the Loan Co. refused to pay Hewitt the $400. Hewitt sued to recover a judgment for the $400. Should a judgment be granted?
4. Green purchased a cold-storage plant from S. W. Co. The purchase price was to be paid in installments. The plant was guaranteed for six months. After the expiration of the guaranty, Green had trouble with the plant in that it did not operate satisfactorily. S. W. Co. promised Green that, if he would pay the remainder of the unpaid installments in advance, the S. W. Co. would make the plant work perfectly. Green paid the unpaid installments in advance, but S. W. Co. did not make the plant work perfectly. Green sued and S. W. Co. set up as a defense lack of consideration, claiming that the payment of the debt was not consideration to support a contract. Is the S. W. Co.'s contention correct?
5. Archer had a set of false teeth made by Dr. Burch. Dr. Burch sent Archer a bill for $500 which Archer considered exorbitant. Archer sent Dr. Burch a check for $250 on which he wrote, "Payment in full for set of teeth and all dental work to date." Dr. Burch cashed the check and immediately sued Archer for the remaining $250. Can Dr. Burch recover a judgment?
6. Would your answer be the same in Problem 5 if Archer had agreed to pay Dr. Burch $500 for the set of false teeth, and the teeth were satisfactory in all respects, and the check was sent after payment was due?
7. Archer entered into a contract with his creditors whereby he conveyed to a creditors' committee all of his property, both personal and real, except his home, and his creditors agreed to accept the property in full payment of their claims against Archer. When the property was liquidated and the proceeds distributed, each creditor received 32 per cent of his claim. About three months thereafter, Archer promised Burch that he would pay Burch $285.76, the unpaid balance of Burch's claim. Burch had accepted the 32 per cent paid by the creditors' committee. Archer did not pay and Burch sued. Can Burch recover a judgment?
8. Fred Smith, Alfred Smith, and Cora Smith conveyed all their interest in their deceased mother's estate to their father. In consideration of the conveyance and

$1 paid by each of the children, the father contracted to convey before his death or to will the property to the children in equal shares. The father remarried and did not convey or will the property to the children. On suit the father's second wife claimed the contract was void because of inadequacy of consideration. Is her contention correct?

9. Archer entered into a written agreement whereby he agreed that, if Burch would solicit and sell ice in the city of Carson, Archer would manufacture and sell to Burch at $1.50 per ton all the ice Burch would require to fill his order during the year 1945-46, and that Archer would not sell ice to any other dealer in Carson. Archer furnished Burch ice for a period, but later during the year 1945-46 he refused to do so. Burch sued. Is Burch entitled to a judgment?

10. Allen and Bryson were engaged in the practice of law. They were in the habit of assisting each other as a matter of mutual accommodation. Allen had worked with Bryson on a case in the customary manner. After the case was closed, Bryson promised to pay Allen one-half of the fee. Bryson did not pay and Allen sued. Is Allen entitled to a judgment?

CHAPTER VIII

PARTIES

Parties to a Contract

To have a binding contract there must be two contracting parties—a promisor and a promisee. There is no legal limit on the number of persons who may be parties to a contract; however, there is a practical limit. The parties must be so indicated that they can be identified. A person may be acting in a special capacity, such as the trustee of a trust fund or the administrator of an estate. The courts have held that under such circumstances one cannot enter into a contract in his special capacity with himself in his individual capacity. Archer is administrator of Burch's estate. Archer owes Burch's estate $100 and draws a promissory note in which Archer as maker promises to pay "Archer, administrator of the estate of Burch, deceased" the sum of $100. The instrument in this form would not be considered a valid contract for lack of proper parties.

The law presumes that everyone has capacity to contract. Archer enters into an agreement with Burch which is supported by consideration and Burch has breached the agreement. If Archer sues Burch, Archer will not have to allege and prove that he (Archer) has capacity to contract nor will Archer have to allege and prove that Burch has capacity to contract. Unless the question of the capacity of the parties is raised by proper pleadings, the courts presume that all parties have the capacity to contract.

Certain classes of persons do not have full capacity to contract, the most important of which are: (1) infants; (2) married women; (3) insane persons; (4) drunken persons; (5) aliens; (6) corporations.

Infants' Contracts

At an early date the courts recognized the desirability of protecting the estates of persons who were too young and inexperienced to adequately protect their own interests. Two problems were presented: (1) how old must a person be before he has the ability to protect his own interests and (2) by what means can the desired protection be accomplished. The courts realized that age alone did not determine one's ability to compete in the business world, yet the desire for some definite means of determining who were infants resulted in the adoption of an age test. At common law both men and women attained this majority at the age of twenty-one years. A majority of the courts hold that one is twenty-one years of age at the beginning of the day before his twenty-first birthday. It is a well-established rule that the law does not recognize parts of days. Reasoning from this rule the courts arrived at the rule that the infant attains his majority the day before his twenty-first birthday. The reasoning followed is not very satisfactory but the rule is well established and is followed by the majority of the courts. The rule has been changed by statute in at least one state so that the infant becomes of age at the beginning of his twenty-first birthday. The age of infancy is fixed by statute in the United States. Most of the states have followed the common law and fixed the period of infancy as twenty-one years. Most states make no distinction between men and women. A few states have fixed the period of infancy at eighteen years, a few provide that if a man marries before he is twenty-one the incapacity of infancy will be removed, and a few states make a distinction between men and women. The statutes relative to the age at which one may marry without the consent of his parents should not be confused with the statutes fixing the period of infancy—age at which one may contract.

The infancy statutes apply to the parties' capacity to contract and in no way affect his capacity to own property. They do affect his capacity to sell property he owns and his capacity to purchase property, but an infant of tender years may become the owner of property by way of gift or inheritance. To protect the infant's estate the court granted the infant the privilege of disaffirming his contracts.

The statement is frequently made that an infant does not have capacity to contract. If one takes this statement literally, it is incorrect. An infant can enter into contracts, and his contracts are enforceable; however, the infant may disaffirm his contracts at his election. If an infant enters into an agreement with an adult whereby the infant makes promises, and the adult makes promises in exchange for the promises of the infant, the infant's promises are consideration and an enforceable contract results. The adult cannot, by any act on his part, escape his obligation to perform; but the infant is given the right to elect not to perform his obligations, or, in other words, the infant has the right to disaffirm the contract. The contract is an enforceable, subsisting contract, binding on both parties until the infant exercises his right to disaffirm it, and if the infant does not exercise his right of disaffirmance, the result of the agreement is the same as though two parties having full capacity to contract had entered into the agreement. The infant's contract would be classed as a voidable contract, not a void contract.

If the disaffirmed contract is wholly executory, the disaffirmance cancels all the legal obligations brought into existence by the contract. If the infant has received consideration, on disaffirmance of the contract he will be required to return any of the consideration or the benefits from such consideration which he still has in his possession at the time he disaffirms the contract. However, his right to disaffirm his contract, as a general rule, does not depend on his ability to return the consideration which he has received.

Archer, an infant, purchases an automobile from Burch, an adult. Archer pays nothing at the time the automobile is delivered to him but promises to pay the agreed purchase price in thirty days. Archer uses the automobile and at the expiration of the thirty days does not pay Burch. Burch brings suit and Archer gives notice that he disaffirms the contract. Archer has the right to disaffirm the contract. However, some courts will require him either to return the automobile to Burch or to pay Burch the reasonable value of the automobile, not to exceed the contract price. If Archer has wrecked the automobile during the time he has had it in his possession, he will be permitted to return the wreck and be relieved from all obligation to pay. (A few courts require the infant to pay for any benefits which he has received as a result of the use of the automobile.) If Archer has traded the automobile or sold it, he can disaffirm the contract; however, on disaffirming the contract, some courts will require him to pay Burch an amount equivalent to the value he received for the automobile or the purchase price, whichever is the smaller.

If Archer paid part or all of the purchase price to Burch at the time of the delivery of the automobile, Archer could disaffirm the contract, return the automobile and in the majority of states he could recover the entire amount paid irrespective of the condition of the automobile when returned.

As a general rule, if an infant disaffirms his contract, he can recover what he has parted with even though it has been transferred to an innocent third-party purchaser. This rule does not apply to goods sold by an infant in those states which have adopted the Uniform Sales Act.

The infant does not have to wait until he attains his majority to disaffirm his contracts. He may disaffirm at any time before he attains majority or within a reasonable time after he attains his majority. How long he will have, after he attains his majority, to disaffirm will depend on the circumstances of the case.

Sales of real estate are not controlled by this general rule. The infant cannot disaffirm the sale of real estate until he attains his majority. However, in some jurisdictions he may recover possession of the property while an infant; in other jurisdictions the courts will require the adult to account to the infant for the use of the property during the term of infancy.

In some cases the courts have resorted to equitable principles to solve the problems of infants' contracts. In these cases the courts take into consideration all the facts and circumstances and grant such relief as they deem fitting. Such a procedure gives more flexibility to the law and permits the protection of the infant's estate without imposing undue hardship on the adult.

McGuckian v. Carpenter
43 R.I. 94, 110 Atl. 402 (1920)

This was an action by Hugh McGuckian (plaintiff) against Arthur H. Carpenter (defendant) in which Arthur H. Carpenter also brought action as plaintiff against Hugh McGuckian as defendant. Judgment for Carpenter in both cases and McGuckian appealed. Judgments affirmed.

McGuckian sold a horse, harness, and wagon to Carpenter, a minor, 18 years of age, married, and with one child. Carpenter had no use for the outfit except driving for pleasure. Carpenter disposed of the harness and wagon, and the horse became so emaciated and disabled, either by disease or neglect, that by order of the agents of the Society for Prevention of Cruelty to Animals it was shot. Consequently, none of the property was returned to McGuckian. McGuckian sued for the unpaid balance of the purchase price. Carpenter disaffirmed the contract and sued for the amount paid to McGuckian.

Sweetland, C. J. In the suit against McGuckian to recover the cash paid on the purchase price the defendant takes the position that, as Carpenter has not returned the property, he ought not to be permitted to disaffirm the sale and obtain a return of the money paid. . . . He (McGuckian) also excepted to that portion of the charge of said justice in which he instructed the jury "that, if Carpenter had disposed of the chattels which came to him or if they were not in his possession or control, it would not be necessary for him to restore them to McGuckian before he could maintain the action." In support of these exceptions before us counsel for McGuckian has called to our attention the opinions of courts in some jurisdictions that in all cases an infant, on his avoidance of an executed contract, must return the property or consideration received before he can maintain his action for the money or property which he gave in the transaction, and, if he has disposed of the money or goods or has so misused them that he cannot restore them, then he cannot be permitted to disaffirm his contract. These cases are based on the consideration that minors should not be permitted to use the shield of infancy as a cover for dishonesty and the doing of injury to others dealing with them in good faith. . . . . We are of the opinion that, when an executed contract is not one for his necessaries, an infant should be permitted to disaffirm it and recover the consideration moving from him, and should be required on his part to return the consideration that remains in his hands; but, if he has dissipated the consideration or lost it, or for any reason is unable to restore it to the other party, he none the less should be permitted to disaffirm the contract and recover back the consideration moving from him. The law gives to a minor the right to disaffirm his contracts on the ground of the disability of infancy. This has been provided as a protection to him from the consequences of his own improvidence and folly. It is the same lack of foresight that in most instances leads to his dissipation of the proceeds of his voidable contracts. To say that he shall not have the protection by disaffirmance with which the policy of the law seeks to guard him, unless he has had sufficient prudence to retain the consideration of the contract he wishes to avoid, would in many instances deprive him, because of his indiscretion, of the very defense which the law intended that he should have against the results of his indiscretion.

A determination made in accordance with either view as to an infant's right to disaffirmance, when he is unable to return the consideration of the contract, will in many cases result in considerable hardship to one party or the other. Not infrequently, even in cases where the infant still has the consideration and returns it to the other party to the contract, such other party is far from being placed in status quo. It has been said that the right of an infant to avoid his contract is absolute and paramount to all equities.

The view which we have taken appears to us to have the support of the weight of authority. In the early case of *Bartlett* v. *Cowles*, 15 Gray (Mass.) 445, the court appears to have taken the contrary view and to have held that an infant might avoid his contract only by restoring the consideration. In the later case of *Bartlett* v. *Drake*, 100 Mass. 174, 97 Am. Dec. 92, 1 Am. Rep. 101, the doctrine of *Bartlett* v. *Cowles*, supra, was expressly repudiated, and in *Chandler* v. *Simmons*, 97 Mass. 508, 93 Am. Dec. 117, it was held that an infant's deed may be avoided "without the previous return, or offer to return, the consideration paid therefor." The rule in *Chandler* v. *Simmons* has been followed in the later Massachusetts cases.

Egnaczyk v. Rowland
267 N.Y.S. 14 (1933)

This was an action by Thomas Egnaczyk (plaintiff) against William Rowland (defendant) to recover the possession of an automobile. Judgment for plaintiff and defendant appealed. Judgment reversed.

Egnaczyk, a minor, owned an automobile. He took it to Rowland, a garageman, and requested him to make certain repairs on it. Rowland repaired the car. The bill for the repairs was $69.34. Egnaczyk refused to pay the bill, but demanded possession of the car. Rowland claimed the right to hold the car under the lien law. Egnaczyk replevined the car claiming that, having rescinded his contract for repairs, he was entitled to the possession of the car.

Hazard, J. We have thus the question presented as to whether a minor can take his automobile to a garage and order repairs thereon, and, when they are completed, refuse to pay therefor and demand that his repaired car be turned over to him. It seems that the court below has decided that he can do just that. That decision rather definitely and emphatically shocks one's sense of justice and fairness and decency. If it is upheld, it would lead to some curious results, as apparently the repairs might go to any extent, even including an entirely new motor, for instance, as the amount of the repair bill would have no bearing upon the question involved.

Of course it is fundamental that, aside from necessaries, an infant may rescind his contract. . . . .

Generally, and I think almost universally, the rule above mentioned, that an infant may rescind his contract, is subject to the provision that he must surrender any benefits which he had received under the contract which he seeks to disaffirm. The principle was quoted from Kent's Commentaries by Judge Haight in *Rice* v. *Butler*, 160 N.Y. 578, on page 582, 55 N. E. 275, 276, 47 L. R. A. 303, 73 Am. St. Rep. 703, succinctly as follows: "The privilege of infancy is to be used as a shield and not a sword. He cannot have the benefit of the contract on one side without returning the equivalent on the other."

In that case plaintiff had purchased a bicycle upon contract and made some payments thereon and then returned the bicycle to the vendor and demanded repayment of the amount she had paid upon the contract. It was proven upon the trial that the deterioration and the use of the wheel while the plaintiff had it in her possession was equal to the value of the amount she had paid on the contract; and it was held by the Court of Appeals that plaintiff could not recover. . . . .

Keeping in mind Kent's illustration about the sword and the shield, and applying it to this case, it is very clear that the court below has permitted the infant plaintiff here to use his infancy as a sword and not restricted it to use as a shield. In other words, he seems to have approved of the plaintiff perpetrating what seems like a bald swindle by permitting him to deliberately order certain repairs to his car and then deliberately refuse to pay for them. There is nothing defensive about such a situation as that; on the contrary it is decidedly aggressive. I think the justice's decision was not right.

Myers v. Hurley Motor Co. Inc.
273 U.S. 18, 47 S. Ct. 227, 50 A.L.R. 1181 (1927)

This was an action by Clarence H. Myers (plaintiff) against Hurley Motor Co. (defendant). Judgment for defendant and plaintiff appealed. Affirmed in part and reversed in part.

Clarence H. Myers purchased a Hudson automobile from Hurley Motor Co. on April 28, 1923. Myers was an infant 20 years old at this time but he represented that he was 24 years of age. Myers paid $250 at the time he purchased the automobile; the unpaid balance was secured by a conditional sales contract. Myers subsequently made payments on the contract to the amount of $156.12. Myers defaulted in his payments and Hurley Motor Co. repossessed the automobile. Myers attained the age of 21 years on October 21, 1923, and on the first day of November following disaffirmed his contract and demanded the return of $406.12, the amount paid on the contract. Hurley Motor Co. refused to refund any part of the money paid and when sued set up as a counterclaim $525.96, the cost of placing the Hudson automobile in as good condition as it was when sold to Myers. The trial court allowed Hurley Motor Co.'s counterclaim in full.

Mr. Justice Sutherland. "The misrepresentation by plaintiff of his age, supported by evidence that he had the appearance of a man of 24, at the time the contract was made, and depreciation in the value of the Hudson car from hard and abusive usage, are not denied by plaintiff, and may be accepted for the purpose of this case as conceded facts. Neither does it appear that any deception or misrepresentations were made by the defendant in order to induce the making of the contract, nor that the contract was in any respect an unfair one. Plaintiff rests his case entirely upon his absolute right, on becoming of age, to disaffirm his contract, and recover the amount which he had paid thereon, regardless of any damage the defendant may have sustained, either from his misrepresentation as to his correct age, or from his abusive use of the Hudson car which resulted in the depreciation above set forth."

Here the action brought by the quondam infant is one for money had and received—the payments under the disaffirmed contract having been either in money or in property converted into money before the disaffirmance. Such an action, though brought at law, is in its nature a substitute for a suit in equity; and it is to be determined by the application of equitable principles. In other words, the rights of the parties are to be determined as they would be upon a bill in equity. The defendant may rely upon any defense which shows that the plaintiff in equity and good conscience is not entitled to recover in whole or in part.

It has been held that, where an infant, after coming of age, seeks the aid of a court of equity to avoid a contract, under which he has received property, and restore to him the possession of obligations with which he has parted, he will be required, wholly irrespective of his own good faith in the transaction, to do equity, which may extend to compelling him to make full satisfaction for the deterioration of the property due to his use or abuse of it.

How far the equitable maxim, that he who seeks equity must do equity, applies generally in suits brought for relief because of infancy, we need not inquire. The maxim applies, at least, where there has been, as there was here, actual fraud on the part of the infant. When an infant of mature appearance, by false and fraudulent representations as to his age, has induced another person to sell and deliver property to him, it is against natural justice to permit the infant to recover money paid for the property without first compelling him to account for the injury which his deceit has inflicted upon the other person.

Our conclusion that the affirmative defense is available in this action does not rest upon the doctrine of estoppel, though the result may be the same. It recognizes the plaintiff's right to repudiate his promise and sue for the return of his payments, and his immunity from a plea of estoppel in so doing. Its effect is not to enforce the disaffirmed contract directly or indirectly, but to allow him to invoke the aid of the court to enforce an equitable remedy arising from the disaffirmance only upon condition that, "seeking equity, he must do equity." And the application of the maxim is not precluded because defendant's claim might not be enforceable in any other manner.

Hurley Motor Co., Inc., may set off the amount paid for the repair of the damaged car.

Ratification

Although, as a general rule, an infant may disaffirm his contract during infancy, he cannot ratify his contract until he attains his majority. The reason for this rule is rather obvious. If, owing to disability, the original act is voidable, he should not be allowed to do an act while still under the disability which will amount to a removal of the disability. His ratification, on reaching majority, may be either expressed or implied. If, on reaching his majority, the infant wishes to abide by the terms of the contract and expressly declares his intention to do so, he will be bound and cannot at a later day avoid the contract. He may by his acts as clearly indicate his intention to be bound. All that the law requires is a clear indication of intention to be bound. Retaining property an unreasonable length of time after attaining majority, accepting benefits under the contract after attaining majority, or recognizing the existence of the contract and continuing to perform are acts usually declared as amounting to ratification. In real estate transactions the courts have held that failure to avoid the sale within a year amounted to a ratification, while in another case it has been held that failure to avoid the sale for five years was not a ratification. Inaction for a period less than the running of the statute of limitations, standing alone, has been declared not to amount to a ratification; however, this cannot be accepted as an established rule. Inaction for an unreasonable time, all conditions and circumstances considered, is usually held to amount to a ratification of the contract.

In some states the requirements for a valid ratification of an infant's contract are set out by statute. For example, see Sec. 3358 of Revised Statutes of Missouri, 1939.

Fletcher v. A. W. Koch Co.
Ct. of Civ. App., Texas, 189 S.W. 501 (1916)

This was an action by B. J. Fletcher (plaintiff) against A. W. Koch Co. (defendant). Judgment for defendant and plaintiff appealed. Reversed and remanded for a new trial.

Fletcher, while an infant, purchased on land contract an unimproved city lot. The contract required a down payment of $12.50 and the payment of $12.50 each month until a total of $300 was paid. Fletcher also gave two promissory notes for $220 each, one payable three years from date and the other four years from date. The vendor was to pay the next year's taxes. Fletcher paid the stipulated monthly payments before he attained his majority. About two months after he attained his majority he wrote defendants, "on the purchase contract on lot 13 of block 17 of Highland Place addition it appears that I am to pay state and county taxes on the lot hereafter. Please let me know promptly the amount of the state and county taxes due on this lot for the year 1914, and also advise me whether I shall remit to you or to the county tax collector." Vendors replied stating they had paid the taxes and to remit to them, but Fletcher never remitted. Shortly after the first of the notes fell due Fletcher disaffirmed the contract and brought this action to recover the money paid to the defendant. This was 8 months after he attained his majority. Defendants contended that his letter amounted to a ratification, and that he waited an unreasonable length of time before disaffirming.

Key, C. J. That a contract made by a minor, except for necessaries is not binding upon him unless made so by such conduct as will create an estoppel, or by a ratification after the disability of minority had ceased to exist is a proposition of law too well established to require citation of authorities. It is true that such contracts are not absolutely void and they may be ratified by the minor after his minority ceases. It is also true that some authorities seem to teach the doctrine that the minor's failure to disaffirm or repudiate the contract within a reasonable time after reaching his majority will render the same binding upon him. Other authorities hold that the doctrine referred to should be limited to executed contracts and that it has no application to those where the contract is executory such as the one involved in this case.

The trial court seems to have regarded the letter written by the plaintiff to the defendant, 2½ months after he reached his majority, as an express ratification of the contract. In fact ratification may be shown without proving an express promise to fulfill the obligations of the contract. If the minor, after reaching the age of majority, and with full knowledge that the contract is not binding upon him, declares to the other party that he adopts it, or intends to abide by it, such conduct on his part would constitute a ratification without a specific promise to perform the several obligations of the contract. In other words, as applied to this class of contracts, ratification means that the late minor, knowing that the contract is not binding upon him on account of his minority at the time he made it, determines in his own mind to waive that defect and adopt the contract, and signifies such intention by such spoken or written words or other conduct as will render such intention manifest. He may do or say things that are consistent with such intention, and therefore, by implication, such conduct may tend to prove the existence of an intention to ratify. But unless such acts or words make it clearly and distinctly appear that such intention to ratify existed, they do not constitute sufficient proof of ratification.

Few, if any, law-writers have ever ranked higher than Mr. Parsons, and he states the rule upon the subject of confirmation of contracts made by infants in the following language:

"As the liability of an infant is defeated by law for his protection, therefore, when he is of full age he may ratify and confirm a contract entered into by him during infancy, and this by parol; but for this ratification a mere acknowledgment that the debt existed, or that the contract was made, is not enough. It need not be a precise and formal promise, but it must be a direct and express confirmation, and substantially—though it need not be in form—a promise to pay the debt or fulfill the contract. It must be made with the deliberate purpose of assuming a liability from which he knows he is discharged by law, and under no compulsion, and to the party himself or his agent." 1 Parsons on Contracts, 270.

Contracts for Necessaries

The statement is generally made that an infant is liable on his contracts for necessaries. Although a few courts have so held, a majority of courts have adopted the principle that an infant is liable for the reasonable value of necessaries furnished him. This theory places the infant's liability on a quasi contractual basis rather than on a strict contractual basis.

If the infant's parents or guardian furnishes him with necessaries, the infant will not be held liable for articles furnished to him which might be classed as necessaries but with which the infant is already supplied.

There is no set rule by which one can determine with exactness whether or not an article will be classed as a necessary. As a general rule, to be a necessary it must be personal to the infant and the infant must be in need of the article. The infant's station in life will be taken in consideration in determining whether an article is a necessary; however, if the article is not personal to the infant, it will not be classed as a necessary, no matter how wealthy the infant may be.

Food, clothing, lodging, medical care, an elemental or vocational education, and the tools of a trade are generally recognized as necessaries. The amount which an infant might be bound to pay for these items will depend on his station in life. If he is already adequately supplied with these items, he will not be bound.

As to food, clothing, and lodging, there can be no question as to the infant's liability if the infant is not already supplied and the quality and quantity is reasonable.

The courts have held that an elemental education or vocational training comes within the class of necessaries but have refused to hold a college education to be a necessary; however, one judge expressed the opinion that it might be held to be a necessary for some infants, depending on their station in life.

Medical and dental care are generally recognized as necessaries, providing the services are reasonably required by the infant. The services of an attorney present a more controversial question. In some instances contracts for the services of an attorney have been held to be voidable at the election of the infant. If the attorney's services are for the protection of the infant—i.e., as attorney in a criminal prosecution—the courts have held that the infant will be liable for a reasonable fee. Also, in cases in which property or a judgment was recovered which benefited the infant, the attorney has been allowed to recover a reasonable fee.

As a general rule, an infant is not liable on his business contracts even though he may be dependent on the income from a business for his living. Archer, an infant, may contract with Burch, an adult, for a course in Burch's barber college. Archer will be liable for the reasonable charge for such training. If Archer purchases the tools of a journeyman barber from Burch upon completion of his course, he will be held liable for the reasonable value of such tools; but if Archer contracts to purchase a barber shop from Burch, such a contract will be voidable. It is a business contract and voidable at the election of the infant.

Some states have passed statutes making infants engaged in business liable on their contracts unless the person dealing with them knows they are infants. Iowa has passed such a statute, Code of Iowa, 1931, Section 10495, *Misrepresentations in engaging in business.* No contract can be thus disaffirmed in cases where, on account of the minor's own misrepresentations as to his majority or on account of his having engaged in business as an adult, the other party had good reason to believe him capable of contracting.

In the event an infant engages in business as a member of a partnership, he cannot be held individually liable for the partnership debts nor can he be held to the partnership agreement, but on withdrawal from the partnership or on a dissolution of the partnership, he is not entitled to the return of money invested until partnership creditors have been paid, and then he is not entitled to the return of capital invested unless there are sufficient assets to repay the total capital investment of the partners. After partnership creditors are paid, he is entitled along with the other partners to a pro rata distribution of the assets.

Barger v. M. & J. Finance Corporation, Inc., et al.
221 N.C. 64, 18 S.E. (2d) 826 (1942)

This was an action by Roy J. Barger (plaintiff) against M. & J. Finance Corporation, Incorporated, and the Ashville Nash Company (defendants). Judgment for plaintiff and defendants appealed. Judgment affirmed.

In the fall of 1939 Barger, who was an infant, purchased a Graham-Paige automobile from the Ashville Nash Company for the sum of $275, making a down payment of $38.45. On December 29, 1939, Barger traded the Graham-Paige to the Ashville Nash Company for a Nash automobile. Barger entered into a new contract and agreed to pay a difference of $257 for the Nash automobile. This contract was purchased from the Ashville Nash Company by the M. & J. Finance Corporation, Inc., and Barger paid to that concern $116.50. Barger defaulted and the automobile was repossessed on October 14, 1940. Barger attained the age of 21 on October 21, 1940, and immediately thereafter sued the Ashville Nash Company and the M. & J. Finance Corporation, Inc., to recover the $38.45 down payment and the $116.50 of monthly payments. The defense that the automobile was used by Barger in his work and was a necessary was set up.

Denny, J. The general rule, and one consistently followed by this court, is that a minor may elect to disaffirm a contract, relative to the sale or purchase of personal property, other than one authorized by statute or for necessaries.

In the case of *Chandler* v. *Jones*, the court said, at page 572 of 172 N.C., at page 581 of 90 S.E.: "The contract of an infant is voidable and not void, and it may be either ratified or disaffirmed upon attaining majority at the election of the infant. If the money is paid to an infant upon a contract and it is consumed or wasted, the infant may recover the full amount due under the contract, but if the money is used for his benefit and he has in hand property in which it has been invested, he cannot retain the property without allowing a just credit for the money paid to him, and if after becoming of age he continues to hold the property and uses it or disposes of it, this is evidence of a ratification."

The question as to what are necessaries often arises. In *Freeman* v. *Bridger*, 49 N.C. 1, 67 Am. Dec. 258, Pearson, J., speaking to the subject: "Lord Cole says, Co. Lit., 172, a, 'It is agreed by all the books, that an infant may bind himself to pay for his necessary meat, drink, apparel, physic and such other necessaries.' These last words embrace boarding; for shelter is as necessary as food and clothing. They have also been extended so as to embrace schooling, and nursing (as well as physic) while sick. In regard to the quality of the clothes and the kind of food, etc., a restriction is added, that it must appear that the articles were suitable to the infant's degree and estate."

The evidence in the instant case tends to show that the ownership of an automobile was advantageous to the plaintiff and that he would not have been promoted without an automobile available for his use. Nevertheless it does not appear that an automobile was necessary for him to earn a livelihood. Hence we are of opinion and hold that an automobile is not among those necessaries for which a minor may be held liable.

Leonard v. Alexander et al.
50 Cal. App. (2d) 385, 122 P. (2d) 984 (1942)

This was an action brought by Jack P. Leonard (plaintiff) against Adin Alexander, Jr., and another (defendants). Judgment for defendants and plaintiff appealed. Judgment affirmed in part and reversed in part.

Adin Alexander, Jr., an infant, brought an action to recover damages in a malpractice action. Jack P. Leonard, an attorney-at-law, rendered legal services in connection with the suit. After Alexander attained his majority he settled the case out of court, receiving $8,000 damages. Alexander refused to pay Leonard his attorney fee and Leonard sued. Alexander disaffirmed the contract and set up infancy as a defense.

Marks, J. The general rule concerning the fees of attorneys for services rendered a person under disability to contract is thus stated in 6 Corpus Juris, p. 748, section 330, as follows:

"The services of an attorney are usually considered as necessaries, and a promise to pay for them is implied when they are rendered in a proceeding personal to an infant, or to any other person incapable of entering into a contract, such as a habitual drunkard or an insane man."

Under these authorities we have reached the conclusion that the services rendered by plaintiff were for necessaries of life of the minor and that their reasonable value is recoverable from him.

Sanger et al. v. Hibbard et al.
104 Fed. 455 (1900)

This was an action by Hibbard Bros. and another (plaintiffs) against S. S. Sanger, Jr. (defendant). Judgment for plaintiff and defendant appealed. Judgment reversed.

Sanger while a minor purchased a stock of goods and conducted a retail store. Several of his merchandise creditors levied attachments on the stock. The stock was sold under court order and Sanger gave bond to dissolve the attachments. On the trial Sanger set up infancy as a defense.

Caldwell, C. J. . . . . Was it error to render judgment in action at law against him for the goods purchased while a minor? This question must be answered in the affirmative. The rule is well settled that an infant has an absolute right to disaffirm and avoid his contract for the purchase of property with which to enter into trade. He can repudiate his contract to pay for the property purchased for such a purpose, and the seller has no redress, unless the property purchased remains in the possession and control of the infant. In such case the infant's repudiation of his contract revests the title to the property sold in the vendor, who may recover it in a proper action for that purpose. But this suit is upon the contract for the purchase of the goods, and there is no claim that the property, or any part of it, or the proceeds thereof, are in the possession or control of the defendant.

Married Women's Contracts

At common law a married woman could not contract. When a woman married, her legal existence ceased, the husband being the sole representative of the family. It is often said that under the common law the husband and wife are one and the husband is that one. The wife had no standing in court, except in suits for dissolution of the marital relation; her personal property became the property of the husband, and the husband had the right to use her real estate during the duration of the marital relationship. At an early date the courts of equity recognized the right of the wife to a separate estate, and through equitable proceedings a separate estate could be created for the wife. The wife, having no separate existence in the eyes of the law, had no power to create a legal relationship; therefore any attempt on her part to create a contract relationship was futile. Her contracts were void. Her acts were not recognized by the law, so the result of an attempt to contract was as though nothing at all had been done.

This disability has been partially or totally removed by statutes adopted by the various states. Some statutes give married women full power to contract, while others are so drafted that she cannot enter into contracts of suretyship or contract with her husband. In interpreting these statutes one should keep in mind the common law rule, that a married woman has no power to contract, because her power to contract is limited to the power granted in the statute. If the statute does not give her power to enter into a particular type of contract, she will continue to be under the old common law disability. To determine the limits of married women's power to contract, one has to consult the statutes of the various states.

Insane and Drunken Persons' Contracts

In some early cases the courts announced the doctrine that an insane person's contracts were void. They based their conclusion on the grounds that to have a contract there must be a meeting of the minds of the contracting parties, that an insane person had no mind, being *non compos mentis;* therefore there could be no meeting of the minds and consequently no contract came into existence. Although the modern courts frequently state that an insane person's contract is void, the term is so used that it is apparent they mean voidable. In most respects an insane person's contract is treated the same as an infant's contract. The insane person is under a disability. He does not have the mental capacity to deal with others on an equal plane, so he is afforded protection. In some jurisdictions the courts distinguish between instances where the other party knew or should have discovered the insanity and those where the other party dealt in good faith and in ignorance of the existing insanity, holding as valid the contracts in the latter situation. In recent cases the courts have recognized the existence of different degrees of insanity and have recognized the fact that a person may be insane in respect to certain things while sane in respect to others. As a general rule, the insane person, on regaining his reason, may avoid his contract, but the majority of courts make his avoidance and recovery of the consideration parted with contingent on his ability to return the consideration received. As in infants' contracts, the courts all attempt to give the insane person protection, but with the least possible injury to the other party. There is no little diversity of opinion as to how this result can be best accomplished.

As a general rule, the contracts of an insane person under the guardianship of a legally appointed guardian are void. The finding of insanity and the appointment of the guardian are matters of public record and notice to everyone. The guardian is the one duty bound to transact all business for the estate of the insane person.

Intoxicated persons are treated the same as insane persons—their contracts are voidable. Before intoxication can be interposed as the ground for avoiding a contract, the intoxicated person must show that the degree of intoxication was great enough to rob him of his mental faculties. Unless at the time of entering into the contract the person was so intoxicated that he could not understand the business he was transacting, the contract will be held to be valid. In some states, intoxication is not accepted as ground for setting aside a contract. They hold that it is a voluntary state and the person should suffer the consequences. However, if one has been taken advantage of while intoxicated, he may avoid the contract on the ground of fraud, showing that his condition was such that he was susceptible to fraudulent misrepresentations.

Lynder v. Schulkin et al.
305 Mich. 451, 9 N.W. (2d) 672 (1943)

This was an action by Max J. Lynder (plaintiff) against Abraham Schulkin and Ida Schulkin (defendants). Judgment for defendants and plaintiff appealed. Judgment affirmed.

On October 30, 1940, Abraham and Ida Schulkin contracted to sell Lynder certain parcels of real estate for $4,400. Lynder paid $100 at the time the contract was signed and was to pay the balance within five days after the abstract had been delivered and approved. Ida Schulkin refused to carry out the terms of the agreement, and Lynder brought this action asking for specific performance of the contract.

Ida Schulkin, by her guardian, set up insanity as a defense. After the contract was signed but before this action was brought, Ida Schulkin was declared insane and Abraham Schulkin was appointed her guardian. On the trial of the case it was established that Ida Schulkin was insane at the time she signed the contract and did not understand the significance of the contract. The lower court refused specific performance and ordered that Schulkin return to Lynder the $100 down payment and also reimburse him for the costs of having the abstract brought down to date.

Sharpe, J. The general rule is that contracts or conveyances of mentally incompetent persons made prior to an adjudication of mental incompetency are voidable. Such contracts may be enforced or repudiated in a court of equity upon equitable grounds. Where a grantor is incompetent to make a contract and has suffered financially in consequence, courts will set the transaction aside.

In the case at bar the burden of proof is upon defendants to show that Ida Schulkin was an incompetent person at the time she entered into the contract and having made such a showing it then becomes the duty of the plaintiff to satisfy the trial court that he (plaintiff) is entitled to equitable relief. It is apparent that the trial court concluded that plaintiff was not entitled to specific performance of the land contract. The record satisfies us that plaintiff failed to make such a showing as would entitle him to relief other than that which was granted.

Aliens, Corporations, etc.

As a general rule, there are no restrictions on an alien's power to contract. During a war, under "trading with the enemy" legislation, one is not permitted to enter into contracts with alien enemies, yet these statutes do not prohibit all contracts with aliens of an enemy country who may be in the United States. Ownership of land and some other rights of certain aliens are controlled either by treaty or state laws. Contracts in violation of such treaties or statutes are void.

In theory a corporation has capacity to enter into only such contracts as its charter permits. The capacity of a corporation to contract will be studied under the title of "Corporations."

Trustees of trust funds, trustees in bankruptcy, administrators or executors of the estates of deceased persons, guardians of infants and insane persons, receivers, etc., may enter into contracts in their official capacity. As a general rule, the contracts of the trustee of a trust fund bind the trustee personally. If the contract is permitted under the terms of the trust agreement, the trustee may charge it against the trust on his accounting. The extent to which a trustee in bankruptcy, the administrator or executor of the estate of a deceased person, the guardian of an infant or insane person, or a receiver may enter into contracts is set out in the statutes of the various states.

QUESTIONS AND PROBLEMS

1. Archer, an adult, sold Burch, an infant, a horse for $150. Shortly thereafter Archer tendered Burch $150 and demanded the return of the horse. Burch refused to return the horse and Archer replevied the horse. Is Archer entitled to the horse?
2. McFerren, when twenty and one-half years old, leased a business building from Carter. McFerren paid six months' rent in advance at the time of signing the lease. Three weeks after McFerren became of age he gave Carter notice that he disaffirmed the lease and demanded the return of the money paid at the time of the signing of the lease. McFerren never occupied the building. Is McFerren entitled to the return of the rent money paid?
3. Inman, a minor and a freshman at college, was adequately supplied with clothing by his father. Nash, a tailor, sent a salesman to the college to solicit orders who, hearing that Inman was spending money freely, called upon him and between October and June sold him clothing in the amount of $1,451. Inman did not pay and Nash sued. Inman set up his infancy as a defense. Can Nash recover a judgment?
4. Ryan, an infant, eighteen years of age and a graduate of a barber's school, contracted to purchase a barber shop consisting of a barber's chair, tools, mirrors, furnishings, and other articles used in the operation of a barber shop. Ryan was an orphan and not under guardianship and had no means of support except what he earned. Ryan defaulted in his payments on the barber shop and Smith, who sold the shop to Ryan, brought suit. Ryan set up infancy as a defense. Is the defense good?
5. If Ryan had purchased from Smith the barber tools of a journeyman barber, could Smith recover a judgment for the purchase price of the barber tools?
6. How would you determine a married woman's capacity to contract?
7. (*a*) What is the status of the contracts of an insane person? (*b*) Is an insane person liable for necessaries furnished? (*c*) If a person has been adjudged insane by a court having jurisdiction of his case and a guardian has been appointed, what is his capacity to contract?
8. After having two or three drinks of liquor, Burch contracted with Archer to sell a horse to Archer for $150. The price was the reasonable value of the horse. The next day Burch refused to perform the contract and, when sued, set up drunkenness as a defense. Is the defense good?

CHAPTER IX

ILLEGALITY

Nature of Illegality

Freedom to act as one wishes is one of the fundamental concepts of our law, yet we always add to this statement the limiting clause, "as long as one's acts do not interfere with like rights of others." This idea applies with particular force to contracts. We have always recognized and protected the right to contract; however, we do limit one's right to contract. If the performance of a contract will necessarily result in an injury to another person or if its performance is contrary to the best interests of society, the contract will be declared illegal and will not be enforced by the courts. The dividing line between a legal contract and an illegal contract is not clean cut. A contract which might be declared legal in one state might be declared illegal in another state. There are general principles, however, which are universally applied. If the parties enter into a contract, both parties intending thereby to bring about an illegal result, the contract will be declared illegal. If Archer and Burch enter into a series of contracts with Clark intending to defraud Clark, the contracts will be held to be illegal even though standing alone each contract would appear to be legal. If the objective of the contract is clearly illegal, the contract will be illegal even though the parties did not know of its illegality. Archer contracts to sell Burch a quantity of tobacco. A statute makes the purchase and sale of tobacco on which certain taxes have not been paid a crime. The tax has not been paid on the tobacco contracted for. Both Archer and Burch are ignorant of the existence of the law. The contract is illegal. If an agreement is capable of being performed either in a legal or an illegal manner and one of the parties intends to perform illegally but the other party is ignorant of this intent, the contract is legal.

If one party has knowledge of the other party's intent to use the subject matter contracted for to accomplish an unlawful act, as a general rule, the contract will not be held to be illegal. Archer sells Burch a quantity of malt. The sale of malt is legal and even though Archer knows that Burch will use the malt in the illegal manufacture of intoxicating beverages, the majority of the courts will hold that the contract is legal. However, if Archer participates in any way in the illegal act—for example, if he is to receive a part of the beverage illegally manufactured in payment for the malt—the contract will be held to be illegal.

The fact that an injurious act may result from the performance of the contract does not render it illegal. However, if the performance of the contract requires the performance of an injurious or illegal act, the contract will be illegal. Archer hires Burch to drive his truck from New York to Chicago. On the trip Burch may operate the truck negligently and injure someone. The fact that someone may be injured in the performance of the contract does not make it illegal. Archer hires Burch to go on Clark's land and without Clark's knowledge or consent cut tie timber. The contract is illegal because to perform the contract Burch must injure Clark, i.e., must trespass on Clark's property.

People v. Brophy
49 Cal. App. (2d) 15, 120 P. (2d) 946 (1942)

This was a criminal action brought by the State of California (plaintiff) against Russell L. Brophy (defendant). Brophy was convicted of perjury and appealed. Judgment reversed.

Russell L. Brophy and Leonard J. Nevans contracted with the Southern California Telephone Company for a telephone connection and service consisting of ten No. 51 order tables, one hundred trunk lines and four business trunk lines. Brophy and Nevans were engaged in furnishing information to "bookmakers" which was against the laws of California. At the request of the attorney general the telephone company threatened to cancel the contract and discontinue their services to Brophy and Nevans. Brophy and Nevans brought an injunction to prevent the telephone company from discontinuing the service. The criminal action (indictment for perjury) grew out of the suit for the injunction. In the course of the trial it was necessary to determine the legality of the service contract between Brophy and Nevans and the telephone company.

White, J. The law is clear and decisive on the question of the enforceability of a contract even though one of the parties thereto has knowledge of an intended purpose of the other party, by means of the contract, or the performance thereof, to violate some law or public policy of the state. The rule in that regard is thus stated in 53 A.L.R. 1364 at page 1366:

"The rule, according to the great weight of authority, is to the effect that a contract legal in itself is not rendered unenforceable by the mere fact that one of the parties thereto has knowledge of an intended purpose of the other party thereto, by means of the contract or subject-matter thereof, to violate some law or public policy of some state; or, as is stated in 6 R.C.L., p. 696, 'where there is no moral turpitude in the making or in the performing of the contract, the mere fact that an agreement the consideration and performance of which are lawful incidentally assists one in evading a law or public policy, is no bar to its enforcement, and that, if the contract has been performed by the promisee, it is no defense that the promisor knew that the agreement or its performance might aid the promisee to violate the law or to defy the public policy of the state, when the promisor neither combined nor conspired with the promisee to accomplish that result, nor shared in the benefits of such a violation.' "

In the case of *Gallick* v. *Castiglione*, 2 Cal. App. 2d 716, 38 P. 2d 858, it was held that knowledge on the part of the seller of sugar that the purpose of the purchaser thereof was to illegally manufacture whiskey was no defense to an action for the purchase price where the illegal purpose was not a part of the contract. Without doubt, therefore, the telephone company in the injunction case could have enforced its contract against appellant notwithstanding the letter written by the attorney general, because no claimed illegal purpose was part of the contract itself.

Contracts To Commit a Crime, Tort, etc.

It is axiomatic that a contract to commit a common law crime is illegal. A contract which does not require the commission of a crime but which induces the commission of a crime is, as a general rule, held to be illegal. The fact that one of the parties might benefit from the commission of a crime does not make the contract illegal. The inducement to commit a crime must be strong enough to be injurious to the general public welfare. Archer, an elderly person, agrees to leave his property to Burch, a nephew, who in payment agrees to support and care for Archer for the rest of Archer's life. The courts will usually enforce such contracts, even though Burch would profit by the early death of Archer. In some states life insurance contracts are not enforceable by the beneficiary unless the beneficiary has an insurable interest in the insured's life—i.e., one who is a close relative or one who would suffer a material loss through the death of the insured.

Contracts to commit a tort are also illegal and unenforceable. In many instances it is difficult to distinguish between a contract to commit a tort and a contract to commit a crime, because the same act may be both a tort and a crime. Contracts to bribe a public officer or an employee or to withhold evidence either in a criminal or civil case are illegal.

A contract to defraud a third person is illegal. Contracts which require fraudulent or deceitful conduct are also illegal. Contracts entered into by a trustee, the director of a corporation, an agent, a guardian, or other fiduciaries whereby their personal interests will be served by the violation of their fiduciary duties are examples of this type of illegal contract. The fact that the fiduciary does not actually benefit by the contract does not purge the contract of its illegality. The fact that the contract places the fiduciary in a position in which his personal interests conflict with his official duties is sufficient grounds for refusing to enforce the contract.

Under some circumstances a contract to breach an existing contract is illegal. The law on this point is not well settled. If the breach of the contract is an incident of the contract which induces the breach, the contract will be enforced.

Many statutes have been passed which declare certain acts to be crimes or torts or which expressly declare certain contracts to be illegal. There are other statutes which are regulatory. Contracts in violation of the former are clearly illegal and unenforceable. However, whether or not a contract which contravenes the latter is illegal and unenforceable will depend on the intent of the legislature which passed the statute. A common type of regulatory statute is one which requires those engaging in certain professions or business to obtain a license and which imposes a penalty on those who engage in the profession or business without having obtained the required license. As a general rule, any contract entered into by one who is not licensed is illegal. One who engages in the practice of medicine without first obtaining a license cannot collect fees for his services. Contracts for fees will be unenforceable. Some licensing statutes are passed for the purpose of raising revenue. A contract entered into by one who is not licensed under such a statute is, as a general rule, enforceable. If the licensing is adopted as a means of protecting the public against unskillful service or fraudulent dealing, a contract in violation of the statute will be unenforceable.

Most states have adopted usury laws which regulate the rate of interest which may be charged for the use of money. The usury laws of some states expressly declare that a contract which provides for a usurious rate of interest is void; others provide for the forfeiture of all or a part of the interest. In most states the usury laws do not apply to loans made to corporations.

K. & S. Sales Co. v. Lee
164 Ark. 449, 261 S.W. 903 (1924)

This was an action by Frank A. Lee (plaintiff) against K. & S. Sales Co. (defendant) to vacate a judgment which had been entered because plaintiff did not appear and defend the original case. Judgment for plaintiff and defendant appealed. Judgment affirmed.

K. & S. Sales Co. sued to recover the agreed price of a "punch-board." Judgment was taken against Lee by default and Lee brought this action to have the judgment set aside, setting up as his defense that the "punch-board" was a gambling device and its use was a violation of the statute prohibiting gambling and that he had been notified by the district attorney that it was a violation of the law to use or operate the same.

Wood, J. Any act which is forbidden either by the common or the statutory law, whether it is *malum in se* or merely *malum prohibitum*, indictable or only subject to a penalty or forfeiture, or however otherwise prohibited by a statute or the common law, cannot be the foundation of a valid contract; nor can anything auxiliary to or promotive of such act.

Reiner v. North American Newspaper Alliance
259 N.Y. 250, 181 N.E. 561 (1930)

This was an action by Robert Reiner (plaintiff) against North American Newspaper Alliance (defendant). During the course of the trial of this case a special question was certified to the court of appeals.

Reiner contracted with the North American Newspaper Alliance to engage passage on the Graf Zeppelin on its flight from Germany to New York. Arrangements were made with certain of Reiner's friends to send radio messages to him while he was on the Graf Zeppelin and Reiner was to answer these messages. A code had been worked out so that when decoded Reiner's messages would be a report on the progress of the flight. The messages were to be turned over to the North American Newspaper Alliance. In this way it could get a report on the progress of the flight. Both Reiner and the North American Newspaper Alliance knew at the time this agreement was entered into that the exclusive news rights on the flight had been sold to third parties. They also knew that to obtain passage Reiner would have to sign an agreement that he would send no reports of the passage while en route and would give no interviews for eight days after completion of the flight. North American Newspaper Alliance agreed to pay Reiner $5,000 for the reports. Reiner sent the reports as agreed but the North American Newspaper Alliance refused to pay and when sued set up illegality as a defense. The adequacy of this defense was certified to the court of appeals.

Hubbs, J. Assuming, as we must, the truth of the allegations contained in the answer, it appears that the conduct of the plaintiff was unconscionable, in violation of his contract of passage, and in violation of the exclusive privilege which, to his knowledge, had been granted to a third party.

Plaintiff, when he entered into the agreement with the defendant, was seeking to obtain for himself the promised advantage which had been contracted to another. That his conduct was vicious and has an evil tendency cannot be questioned. Did it have the effect of rendering his contract with the defendant unenforceable?

It has become the settled law of this State that an action will lie for intentionally and knowingly, and without reasonable justification or excuse, inducing a breach of contract.

The law endeavors to protect the interest of parties in existing contractual relations from intentional and wrongful interference by strangers. The principle constitutes a limitation upon the doctrine of freedom of contract, which courts have imposed in an attempt to promote justice and fair dealing and to prevent wrongs.

The plaintiff is undoubtedly liable to the parties in the exclusive rights contract for all damages caused by his wrongful conduct. Such an action would sound in tort. The gravamen of the action would be plaintiff's wrongful conduct in making it impossible for the third party to reap the full benefits of the contract with the owners of the *Graf Zeppelin.*

We do not mean to say that in all cases one who knowingly causes a breach of contract between others is liable for the damage caused by such breach. Whether liability will attach for causing such a breach of contract depends upon whether there exists sufficient justification. For a detailed discussion of that question see 36 *Harvard Law Review*, 663. It is sufficient for the decision of this case that no such justification exists.

The exclusive privilege contract with a third party vested in the parties thereto rights which the law protects, contract rights. It would be strange indeed if the law should protect such contract from wrongful interference by a stranger, but after such interference assist the stranger in reaping the fruits of his unjust and illegal act.

The wrongful acts of the plaintiff constituted a tort. The contract between plaintiff and defendant was a part of the scheme which resulted in the breach of the contract of passage entered into by plaintiff and interfered with the contract between the owner of the *Graf Zeppelin* and the third party. It was in effect a contract to commit a tort.

The plaintiff's act in entering into the contract cannot be said to have been negligent, incidental, or foreign to the purpose of the contract with the third party. It was made with full knowledge of the third party contract. Not only did plaintiff have knowledge of that contract, but in his contract of passage he had expressly agreed not to do anything to prevent the carrying out of that contract. In utter disregard of both contracts, he entered into the agreement with defendant, knowing that the effect of the contract would be to nullify the third party contract and make its fulfillment impossible and at the same time breach his contract of passage. By his contract with the defendant, the plaintiff robbed the third party of the exclusive right to the news rights of the voyage and attempted to take for himself the advantage which had been contracted to the third party.

A court will not lend aid to a party who has committed a tort to enable him to recover from another the price agreed to be paid for his wrongful act. The defense is allowed not as a protection to a defendant, but as a disability to the plaintiff.

Mees v. Grewer
63 N.D. 74, 245 N. W. 813 (1932)

This was an action by Fred Mees (plaintiff) against Matt Grewer (defendant). Judgment for the plaintiff and defendant appealed. Judgment reversed and action dismissed.

Mees was employed by the Minneapolis Threshing Machine Company as block salesman. He was employed to devote his entire time, talents, and energy to the services of said company; to make sales, write contracts, help local dealers, make collections for said company, and to represent it in his territory. He was paid a monthly salary for his services. Grewer was a dealer in Mees's territory. Grewer's territory was much smaller than that of Mees's. Grewer's contract provided that he was to receive a 25 per cent commission on all machines sold and if sold for cash he was to receive an additional 10 per cent commission on the amount remaining after the deduction of the 25 per cent commission.

Grewer proposed to Mees that, if Mees would help him establish subdealers and help the subdealers work their territory, he (Grewer) would split the commission he received from subdealers' sales with Mees. Under Grewer's contract subdealers were to receive 50 per cent of the total commissions and Grewer received 50 per cent. During the years 1923 and 1924 Mees aided Grewer according to their agreement, but Grewer refused to pay the commissions to Mees. When sued Grewer set up illegality as a defense.

Englert, D. J. The relation of an agent to his principal is ordinarily that of a fiduciary. The courts hold those acting in such fiduciary capacity to the strictest fairness and integrity.

In *Stephens* v. *Gall* (D.C.) 179 F. 938, the court held that all acts of an agent which tend to violate his fiduciary duty are regarded as frauds upon the confidence bestowed, and are not only invalid as to the principal, but are also against public policy.

But the plaintiff contends that the contract in question does not contravene any principle of good morals. We cannot agree with this contention. As said in *Ferguson* v. *Gooch,* 94 Va. 1, 26 S.E. 397, 40 L.R.A. 234: "To be secretly in the service of one party, while ostensibly acting solely for the opposite party is a fraud upon the latter, and a breach of public morals which the law will not permit."

It is a well-established rule that one acting in a fiduciary capacity is required to exercise perfect fidelity to his trust, and the law, to prevent the abuse of such fidelity, and to guard against any temptation to serve his own interest, to the prejudice of his principal's, will not lend itself to enforce any agreement in violation thereof. That the plaintiff by this agreement intended to obtain some advantage to himself cannot be seriously questioned. But such agreements, to be contrary to good morals, and against public policy, do not necessarily depend upon whether the fiduciary intended to gain an advantage to himself. If it affords the agent an opportunity, and subjects him to the temptation, to obtain such advantage, it offends against good morals. It is no answer against a wrong to say that the principal did not suffer as a result of the agreement. He may even have profited thereby. The test is the evil tendency of the contract, not its actual result. If the transaction is inconsistent with fair and honorable dealing, and contrary to sound policy, it contravenes good morals.

In *Atlee* v. *Fink*, 75 Mo. 100, 42 Am. Rep. 385, the court said: "One employed by another to transact business for him, has no right to enter into a contract with a third person, which would place it in his power to wrong his principal in the transaction of the business of the latter, and which would tempt a bad man to act in bad faith toward his employer." The court further said: "His compensation could be increased by such conduct, and it is no answer that nothing of the kind occurred."

That is exactly the situation here. The plaintiff, by the agreement on which he claims to recover here, increased his compensation to a very considerable extent.

Firpo v. Murphy et al.
72 Cal. App. 249, 236 Pac. 968 (1925)

This was an action brought by E. Firpo, assignee (plaintiff) against Leland S. Murphy (defendant). Judgment for plaintiff and defendant appealed. Judgment reversed.

This was an action to recover a broker's commission in the sum of $770 for securing a lease. The defense was that the salesman who negotiated the lease was not duly licensed under and pursuant to the provisions of the act of the legislature regulating such brokers and salesmen, that plaintiff therefore could not recover, because the contract for a commission was unlawful and contrary to express law. The statute in question required that real estate salesmen be licensed. If a salesman changed employers he had to surrender his license under his old employer and obtain a new license under his new employer. Also, all salesmen's licenses terminated December 31 of each year and had to be renewed each year.

Thomas L. Ricks, the salesman who negotiated the lease, was employed by another broker in 1922, but when he entered the employ of Ricker &Tharp (plaintiff's assignors) his license was not surrendered and he did not obtain a new license. The negotiations for the lease were begun in December, 1922, and were completed and the lease executed on January 22, 1923. At no time during this period did Ricks hold a license in accordance with the terms of the statute. Section 17 of the statute made it a criminal offense to act as a real estate salesman without a license.

Section 20 denies to any person, copartnership, or corporation engaged in the business or acting in the capacity of a real estate broker or a real estate salesman the right to maintain any action in the courts of this state for the collection of compensation for the performance of any of the acts mentioned in section 2 without alleging and proving that such person, copartnership, or corporation was a duly licensed real estate broker or real estate salesman at the time the alleged cause of action arose.

Tyler, P. J. Whenever a statute is made for the protection of the public, a contract in violation of its provisions is void. The pawnbroker's act provides that it is a misdemeanor to carry on the business of pawnbroker without a license.

While there is no express declaration in these sections that the transactions condemned are unlawful, or that no recovery shall be had thereon in the event that the provisions are violated, still it has been held that they, being designed for the protection of the public, and a penalty prescribed for a violation thereof, that such penalty is the equivalent of an express prohibition, and that a contract made contrary to the terms thereof is void, and further that whenever the illegality appears, whether the evidence comes from one side or the other, the disclosure is fatal to the case.

So, also, it has been held that a physician or surgeon, who is employed before he has procured the certificate required by the laws of this state regulating the practice of medicine, cannot recover any compensation for the services rendered before the procuring of the certificate upon any contract, express or implied, the contract being illegal and against public policy.

The principle is in accord with the positive provisions of our Civil Code, which makes that unlawful which is either contrary to the express provisions of law or contrary to the policy of express law, though not in terms prohibited.

The rule is universally established that, where a broker fails to procure the license required by law to carry on his business, he cannot recover commissions for acts as such.

In some of the states courts have allowed the recovery of a commission by a non-licensed broker where the license laws are enacted solely as revenue measures, in which case it has been held that such laws have no effect on the rights of the parties inter se.

That situation is not here presented. The cause of action here relied upon is founded on the violation of a state law. Plaintiff's assignor, having carried on its business in violation of law, any rights arising out of such unlawful transaction can form no proper cause of action.

Matlack Properties, Inc. v. Citizen & Southern National Bank
120 Fla. 77, 162 So. 148 (1935)

This was an action by Citizens & Southern National Bank, as administrator of the estate of John L. Slater, deceased (plaintiff) against Matlack Properties, Incorporated (defendant). Judgment for plaintiff and defendant appealed. Judgment affirmed.

Slater loaned money to Matlack Properties, Incorporated, a Florida corporation, at a rate of interest in excess of the ordinarily allowed contract interest rate of 10 per cent fixed by the Florida usury law. When suit was brought the defendant set up usury as a defense.

Davis, J. The common law of England, as adopted and approved in the United States, has never forbidden the exaction of usury on loans of money as a matter of general law irrespective of statute. So the subject is one entirely of statutory regulation and prohibition, despite the observation found in the Scriptures (15th Psalm, verses 1 and 6) that only those shall abide in the Lord's tabernacle "that putteth not out his money to usury, nor taketh reward against the innocent."

The court below held, and we approve its holding, that a Florida corporation is authorized to enter into a valid contract to borrow money at such rates of interest, and upon such terms, as the company or its board of directors shall authorize or agree upon, irrespective of the limitations on interest rates and devices for excessive interest exactions set forth in the general usury laws of Florida hereinbefore cited.

Wagering Contracts

At common law wagering contracts were enforceable, but in the United States certain types of wagering contracts are, by statutory enactment, illegal. These statutes vary in their scope, but their aim generally is to prevent "gaming" or "betting" and do not prevent "risk-bearing" business contracts. The element of a wager is that one party is to win and the other to lose something of value upon a future event which, at the time of the contract, is of an uncertain nature or upon something in existence which is uncertain in the minds of the parties. This statement is broad enough to include all types of insurance agreements and hedging contracts as well as many other contracts where the course of future events will determine the rights of the parties under the contract. Whether the contract is legal or not depends on the purpose or object of the contract. If it is a contract based on a legitimate business transaction and serves to facilitate the carrying on of trade, it will be a legal contract, but if its purpose or objective is to gamble on an uncertainty, it will fall within the prohibited class and be unenforceable. It is often difficult to determine from the facts and circumstances in just which class a certain transaction should fall. In stock and grain trading if the parties intend delivery, although at some future date, and the agreement is so drawn that one is bound to deliver and the other to accept delivery, the contract is valid even though at the time for performance delivery is waived and settlement made by paying the difference. However, if at the time the contract was entered into, neither party intended delivery to be demanded or made, but both intended merely a payment of differences at the named future date, the contract will fall within the prohibited class and be illegal and unenforceable.

If a risk is created for the purpose of assuming it, the contract will be a wagering contract. Archer and Burch are playing cards. Archer says to Burch, "I will pay you $10 if the next card I turn is above the seven if you will pay me $10 if it is below the eight." The contract is illegal because no risk existed, but the risk was created for the purpose of assuming it. The same rule has been applied to property insurance contracts. If the insurer has no interest in the property insured, he is, by insuring the property, creating a risk for himself which did not exist. Such contracts of insurance are illegal for two reasons. They are wagering contracts and they tend to induce the crime of arson or malicious destruction of property. If one has a property interest in the property, there is an existing risk that the property will be destroyed. If one insures against such risk, the insurance contract will be enforceable. It is not a wagering contract but a risk-shifting contract. To pool the risks of ownership through insurance contracts contributes to the welfare of society.

Becher-Barrett-Lockerby Co. v. Hilbert et al.
197 Minn. 541, 267 N.W. 727 (1936)

This was an action by Becher-Barrett-Lockerby Co. (plaintiff) against Joe Hilbert and Munster Equity Elevator Co. (defendants). Judgment for plaintiff and the Munster Equity Elevator Co. appealed. Judgment reversed and remanded with directions.

The plaintiff was a broker dealing in grain on the Chamber of Commerce in Minneapolis and on the Duluth Board of Trade. Joe Hilbert was a substantial grain farmer. Hilbert was dealing in grain futures through the local manager of Munster Equity Elevator Co. The purchases were made through plaintiff as broker. The elevator company guaranteed Hilbert's account with plaintiff. In 1928 Hilbert, through the elevator company, purchased through plaintiff 10,000 bushels of durum wheat for December delivery at 99 cents a bushel. Hilbert, through the elevator company, advanced $1,000 for margin. The parties signed the standard form contract used in such transactions which provided that the wheat would be delivered and paid for in December. From time to time the delivery of the wheat was postponed until July, 1930, when the transaction was closed out with a loss of $1,637.76. During the course of the transaction Hilbert had advanced a total of $5,000 as margins. Plaintiff sued to recover $1,637.76, the loss suffered on the transaction. The defense was that the transaction was a wager on wheat futures. The correspondence between the parties showed that none of the parties intended delivery of the wheat.

Loring, J. It is conceded by the plaintiff that a contract for the future delivery of a commodity is invalid when the parties to the contract do not intend the delivery of the subject-matter but a settlement based on the differences between the contract and the market price. Tested by this rule, we conclude that as a matter of law the record compels a finding that Hilbert and the plaintiff were engaged in a gambling transaction, and that there was no intent on the part of either that the actual grain contracted for should be delivered. Such had been the character of the transactions previously handled by the plaintiff. Such was also the character of the transaction here under scrutiny. The testimony of Hilbert shows clearly that he so regarded it, and the correspondence with McKay clearly indicates that defendant so regarded it. No amount of subsequent oral testimony denying such intent would be considered by reasonable men as changing the conclusion to be drawn from the evidence.

Such being the evidence, reasonable minds could arrive at no other conclusion than that this transaction was a wager by Hilbert upon the future price of durum without intent to take delivery of the actual grain and this with full knowledge by plaintiff of the nature of the transaction. To hold otherwise would be to ignore actualities.

The trial court was evidently led astray by some of the evidence in regard to what constituted a hedge. In the nature of things this transaction by Hilbert was not and could not be a hedge. We are therefore constrained to reverse the order of the trial court and remand the case with directions to enter judgment for the defendant.

Crossman v. American Insurance Company of Newark, New Jersey
198 Mich. 304, 164 N.W. 428, L.R.A. 1918 A. 390 (1917)

This was an action by John Crossman (plaintiff) against American Insurance Company of Newark, New Jersey (defendant). Judgment for plaintiff and defendant appealed. Judgment affirmed.

Donaldson Craig held an option to purchase certain property. On learning that the property was not fully covered by insurance, Craig insured it against fire. After the policy was issued, a fire loss was suffered. Craig assigned his interests under the policy to Crossman who was title owner of the property. The insurance company refused to pay the loss and Crossman sued. The insurance company set up as a defense that the policy was void because Craig did not have an insurable interest in the property.

Fellows, J. It was pressed upon the court at the argument with vigor that Craig did not have an insurable interest in the property, and for this reason plaintiff must fail in his right of recovery. This presents the meritorious question in the case. Policies of insurance founded upon mere hope and expectation and without some interest in the property, or the life insured, are objectionable as a species of gambling, and so have been called wagering policies. All species of gambling policies were expressly prohibited in England by St. 19

Geo. II, c. 37, and have been treated as illegal in this country upon the principles of that statute, without acknowledging it as authority. Here, such contracts of insurance are treated as contravening public policy, and are therefore void. If this policy falls within this class, it is void, and prevents plaintiff's recovery. If it does not, this judgment must be affirmed.

The unrippled current of authority is to the effect that title to, or lien upon, property is not essential to an insurable interest. Measured by the standard fixed in the cases quoted from, and cited, did Craig have an insurable interest in this property? He had an option upon this property, a right to buy it, an enforceable right, for which he paid over $2,500. Was that right of more value with the building standing than with the building destroyed? Would he suffer direct pecuniary loss in the value of his right by its destruction? Would he be damaged pecuniarily by the loss of the building? To ask these questions is to answer them. Obviously this contract of insurance was not a wagering, gambling contract prohibited by public policy, but was valid and enforceable.

Contracts against Public Policy

A contract to commit a crime or tort, or one which is in violation of the provisions of a statute, is against public policy and unenforceable; but it does not follow that, if the contract does not require the commission of a crime or tort and is not in violation of a statute, it is not an illegal contract. Many acts which are not crimes or torts and which are not expressly prohibited by statute are, nevertheless, injurious to society. A contract to perform such an act is said to be against public policy. Whether or not a certain contract is illegal because it is against public policy will depend on our conception of public policy. Public policy changes with both time and place. It is of such a nature that it cannot be made stable and certain.

Basically, a contract to perform any act which is injurious to the interests of the public is unenforceable on the grounds that it is against public policy.

From an early date courts have held that contracts in unreasonable restraint of trade are against public policy and unenforceable. A large variety of transactions is included in the term, contracts in restraint of trade, but all contracts, the performance of which results in some curtailment or restraint of trade, are not necessarily unenforceable. If the restraint is for the purpose of protecting the interests of the party in favor of whom it is given and the restraint is no greater than is necessary to protect his interests, the agreement will be enforced. However, the interests of the public are paramount, and if the restraint is actually injurious to the public, the agreement will be void.

The courts recognize good will as an element of value and recognize that an agreement on the part of the seller not to compete with the buyer is, in many instances, the only feasible method of assuring to the buyer the full value of the good will he has purchased with the business. Such contracts are enforced if the restraint is reasonable. If the restraint placed on the seller is greater than is reasonably necessary to protect the buyer of the business, the contract will be declared illegal.

No attempt has been made to enumerate the acts which are against public policy and those which are not against public policy; however, the decided cases are uniform in holding certain types of contracts to be against public policy. Contracts or clauses in contracts which relieve one of the contracting parties from liability for his own frauds or negligence are against public policy and illegal if a public interest is involved. Contracts to stifle bidding at public sales, contracts which promote immorality, contracts to hinder, delay, or defraud creditors in the collection of their claims, contracts to interfere with legislative action, contracts to influence public officials in the performance of their official duties, contracts which tend to obstruct the course of justice, and in many situations contracts to split fees are against public policy. The final test in all cases is the effect of performance of the proposed contract on the public. If its performance will be injurious to the public, the contract is against public policy and unenforceable.

Zeigler v. Illinois Trust & Savings Bank
245 Ill. 180, 91 N.E. 1041 (1910)

This was an action by Lord Clarence H. E. Zeigler (plaintiff) against Illinois Trust and Savings Bank, executor of the estate of Harriet G. McVicker, deceased (defendant). Judgment for plaintiff in circuit court and defendant appealed. The judgment was reversed in the appellate court and plaintiff appealed to the Supreme Court. Judgment of trial court affirmed.

Mrs. McVicker, a widow about 78 years of age, was in poor health and went to Dr. Zeigler, a licensed physician, for treatment in October, 1899. Shortly thereafter Mrs. McVicker had a written contract drawn which provided that Dr. Zeigler would give her such medical attention as she should require during her lifetime, and at her death he should be paid $100,000. After some changes in the wording of the contract it was executed by both parties. Dr. Zeigler performed all his duties under the contract. Mrs. McVicker died in 1904, and the Illinois Trust & Savings Bank, executor of her estate, refused to pay Dr. Zeigler the $100,000.

Cooke, J. The position of appellee is that the original and confirmatory contracts entered into between Mrs. McVicker and Dr. Zeigler are void, as against public policy, for the reasons, first, that they furnish an incentive to the commission of a crime; and, second, that they substantially form a wager on the length and continuance of the life of Mrs. McVicker. There is no precise definition of public policy, and consequently no absolute rule by which a contract can be measured or tested to determine whether or not it is contrary to public policy. Each case, as it arises, must be judged and determined according to its own peculiar circumstances. The public policy of the state or of the nation is to be found in its Constitution and its statutes, and, when cases arise concerning matters upon which they are silent, then in its judicial decisions and the constant practice of the government officials.

United States v. Addyston Pipe & Steel Co. et al.
85 Fed. 271 (1898)

This was an action by the United States (plaintiff) against Addyston Pipe & Steel Co. and five other corporations (defendants) charging them with unlawful restraint of interstate commerce. Judgment for defendants and plaintiff appealed. Judgment reversed.

The six corporations against which this action was brought were engaged in the manufacture of cast-iron pipe. They had entered into a series of contracts in which they agreed to divide the United States into districts in which they defined the rights of each to trade in that district and in which they agreed in general as to what course each would follow in the marketing of its products.

The question of the validity of these contracts was one of the questions before the court.

Taft, C. J. Contracts that were in unreasonable restraint of trade at common law were not unlawful in the sense of being criminal, or giving rise to a civil action for damages in favor of one prejudicially affected thereby, but were simply void, and were not enforced by the courts. . . . .

From early times it was the policy of Englishmen to encourage trade in England, and to discourage those voluntary restraints which tradesmen were often induced to impose on themselves by contract. Courts recognized this public policy by refusing to enforce stipulations of this character. The objections to such restraints were mainly two. One was that by such contracts a man disabled himself from earning a livelihood with the risk of becoming a public charge, and deprived the community of the benefit of his labor. The other was that such restraints tended to give to the covenantee, the beneficiary of such restraints, a monopoly of the trade, from which he had thus excluded one competitor, and by the same means might exclude others.

The inhibition against restraints of trade at common law seems at first to have had no exception. After a time it became apparent to the people and the courts that it was in the interest of trade that certain covenants in restraint of trade should be enforced. It was of importance, as an incentive to industry and honest dealing in trade, that, after a man had built up a business with an extensive good will, he should be able to sell his business and good will to the best advantage, and he could not do so unless he could bind himself by an enforceable contract not to engage in the same business in such a way as to prevent injury to that which he was about to sell. It was equally for the good of the public and trade, when partners dissolved, and one took the business, or they divided the business, that each partner might bind himself not to do anything in trade thereafter which would derogate from his grant of the interest conveyed to his former partner. Again, when two men became partners in a business, although their union might reduce competition, this effect was only an incident to the main purpose of a union of their capital, enterprise, and energy to carry on a successful business, and one useful to the community. Restrictions in the articles of partnership upon the business activity of the members, and with a view of securing their entire effort in the common enterprise, were, of course, only ancillary to the main end of the union, and were to be encouraged. Again, when one in business sold property with which the buyer might set up a rival business, it was certainly reasonable that the seller should be able to restrain the buyer from doing him an injury which, but for the sale, the buyer would be unable to inflict. This was not reducing competition, but was only securing the seller against an increase of competition of his own creating. Such an exception was necessary to promote the free purchase and sale of property. Again, it was of importance that business men and professional men should have every motive to employ the ablest assistants, and to instruct them thoroughly; but they would naturally be reluctant to do so unless such assistants were able to bind themselves not to set up a rival business in the vicinity after learning the details and secrets of the business of their employers.

In a case of this last kind, *Mallan* v. *May*, 11 Mees. & W. 652, Baron Parke said:

"Contracts for the partial restraint of trade are upheld, not because they are advantageous to the individual with whom the contract is made, and a sacrifice protanto of the rights of the community, but because it is for the benefit of the public at large that they should be enforced. Many of these partial restraints on trade are perfectly consistent with public convenience and the general interest, and have been supported. Such is the case of the disposing of a shop in a particular place, with a contract on the part of the vendor not to carry on a trade in the same place. It is, in effect, the sale of a good will, and offers an encouragement to trade by allowing a party to dispose of all the fruits of his industry. . . . . And such is the class of cases of much more frequent occurrence, and to which this present case belongs, of a tradesman, manufacturer, or professional man taking a servant or clerk into his service, with a contract that he will not carry on the same trade or profession within certain limits. . . . . In such a case the public derives an advantage in the unrestrained choice which such a stipulation gives to the employer of able assistants, and the security it affords that the master will not withhold from the servant instruction in the secrets of his trade, and the communication of his own skill and experience, from the fear of his afterwards having a rival in the same business."

For the reasons given, then, covenants in partial restraint of trade are generally upheld as valid when they are agreements (1) by the seller of property or business not to compete with the buyer in such a way as to derogate from the value of the property or business sold; (2) by a retiring partner not to compete with the firm; (3) by a partner pending the partnership not to do anything to interfere, by competition or otherwise, with the business of the firm; (4) by the buyer of property not to use the same in competition with the business retained by the seller; and (5) by an assistant, servant, or agent not to compete with his master or employer after the expiration of his time of service. Before such agreements are upheld, however, the court must find that the restraints attempted thereby are reasonably necessary (1, 2, and 3) to the enjoyment by the buyer of the property, good will, or interest in the partnership bought; or (4) to the legitimate ends of the existing partnership; or (5) to the prevention of possible injury to the business of the seller from use by the buyer of the thing sold; or (6) to protection from the danger of loss to the employer's business caused by the unjust use on the part of the employé of the confidential knowledge acquired in such business.

It would be stating it too strongly to say that these five classes of covenants in restraint of trade include all of those upheld as valid at the common law; but it would certainly seem to follow from the tests laid down for determining the validity of such an agreement that no conventional restraint of trade can be enforced unless the covenant embodying it is merely ancillary to the main purpose of a lawful contract, and necessary to protect the covenantee in the enjoyment of the legitimate fruits of the contract, or to protect him from the dangers of an unjust use of those fruits by the other party.

Mahoney v. Lincoln Brick Co.
304 Mich. 694, 8 N.W. (2d) 883 (1943)

This was an action by Edward J. Mahoney (plaintiff) against Lincoln Brick Co. (defendant). Judgment for defendant and plaintiff appealed. Judgment affirmed.

Mahoney, who inferred that he had political influence with the governor and "a number of the boys that did things in Lansing," entered into a contract with defendant to act as its selling agent, selling to the contractors who had state contracts to construct buildings for the state institutions. Plaintiff was to contact the architects on the jobs who were state employees and who, as a part of their duties, passed on contracts for materials. The trial court found that plaintiff was to use his political influence to coerce the state architects to favor defendant in awarding contracts for brick and tile. Plaintiff claims he was to get $2.00 per thousand commission on brick sold and 6 per cent on tile. Plaintiff sued to recover commissions which he claimed were due. Defendant set up illegality as a defense.

Boyles, C. J. Plaintiff admits that he was to receive commissions only on brick and tile sold to contractors for use in the construction of state buildings, but contends that, because the oral contract in question provided for the sale of brick and tile to contractors and not to the state, the question of political influence and public policy was not involved. Plaintiff testified that he was "to contact the architects on all these state jobs." The architects employed by the state to supervise the construction work were state employees and had some control over the selection of materials by the contractors. Plaintiff testified, "Of course the architect is the big influence in any construction job. . . . . I would say after the final recourse the architect would overrule the contractor." Any contract under which the parties proposed and intended by political influence or coercion to affect the judgment and decision of such architects in the selection of materials would be contra bonos mores and void. The testimony is convincing that the parties intended that plaintiff would use or attempt to use such political influence, pressure, and means as he could to induce the purchase of defendant's brick and tile. This was clearly an attempt to exercise improper influence on state-employed architects in respect to public business entrusted to them. The record is barren of any proof that plaintiff had the influence he claimed for himself, except by inference. However, such type of contract is against the public good and is void.

The rule directly applicable to the contract in the present case is stated in 46 A.L.R. p. 198, as follows: "However, beyond question, any agreement entered into because of the actual or supposed influence which the employee has, engaging him to influence administrative or executive officers in the discharge of their duties, which contemplates the use of personal influence and personal solicitation rather than any appeal to the judgment of the officer on the merits of the object sought, is contrary to public policy and void."

In 17 C.J.S., Contracts, § 211, pp. 563-565, it is stated:

"Contracts contrary to public policy, that is, those which tend to be injurious to the public or against the public good, are illegal and void, even though actual injury does not result therefrom. This rule is applied in both state and federal courts, in cases arising in law and in equity, to contracts involving numerous and steadily increasing types of subject matter, regardless of the character of the contracting parties. . . . .

"The test to be applied is not what is actually done, but that which may or might be done under the terms of the contract; it is the evil tendency of the contract and not its actual injury to the public in a particular instance. The law looks to the general tendency of such agreements, and it closes the door to temptation by refusing them recognition in any of its courts."

Otis Elevator Co. v. Maryland Casualty Co.
95 Colo. 99, 33 P. (2d) 974 (1934)

This was an action by the Maryland Casualty Company (plaintiff) against Otis Elevator Company (defendant). Judgment for plaintiff and defendant appealed. Judgment modified and affirmed.

The Otis Elevator Company installed a passenger elevator in the Oil Exchange Building, a five-story building, and contracted to "repair, inspect, examine, clean, and lubricate the elevator twice each month and to keep it in a safe condition as a passenger elevator." The contract contained a provision relieving the Otis Elevator Company from all liability for injury resulting from defects in the elevator. As a result of the failure of the Otis Elevator Company to use due care in keeping the elevator in working order, the elevator fell from the third floor to the basement injuring the passengers on the elevator at the time. Oil Exchange Building, Inc., owner of the building, was insured with the Maryland Casualty Company which has paid the damages resulting from the accident and now sues the Otis Elevator Company to recoup the loss. Otis Elevator Company sets up the clause in the contract relieving it from liability as a defense and the Maryland Casualty Company claims that the clause is illegal.

Holland, J. The trial court held that the terms of these contracts did not constitute a defense for Otis Company, for the reason that the terms thereof exonerating Otis Company from liability were void as against public policy. Counsel for Otis Company contend that a carrier may exempt itself from liability by contract for negligently performing a service which it is not compelled by law to perform, but not a service which it has a legal duty to perform, and places first reliance in the case of *Denver & Rio Grande R. Co.* v. *Whan,* 39 Colo. 230, 89 P. 39, 11 L.R.A. (N.S.) 432, 12 Ann. Cas. 732, for support of their contention. We do not believe this case and others cited to be in point, for there an employee of the carrier, as a consideration for his employment, contracted to assume the risks attendant thereon. The contract was held to exempt the carrier as to liability to the employee, but its liability to the public, whose interest was involved, still remained. In the case at bar, the public was concerned with the security of such of its citizens as would use the elevator maintained for such use. The public had the right to expect and demand that the elevator as a carrier of the public would be kept safe for its use. It was the business of Otis Company—contracted for consideration—to inspect and repair said elevator, with that safety for the public in view, and the law will not permit it to escape liability for its negligence therein by a contract which is against public policy such as is the one relied on here. Such contracts do not change the law of public liability. No such opportunities are extended, neither can they be made a privilege by contract.

Effect of Illegality

If a contract is illegal, as a general rule, the courts will not grant relief to either party but will leave the parties where it finds them.

The courts do not follow this rule as a means of punishing one of the parties, but because the results obtained thereby best serve the interests of the public. If the interests of the public can be best served by granting relief, the courts will grant such relief as the facts of the case warrant. It is immaterial whether the illegal act is the direct objective of the contract or whether the illegal objective is to be accomplished indirectly. If the contract is based on an illegal consideration, it will be treated as an illegal contract. One cannot ratify an illegal contract and purge it of the illegality. One exception to this rule is recognized by most courts. If a contract is declared illegal by statute because it is entered into on Sunday, the parties may avoid the illegality by affirmance of the contract on a subsequent week day. The reason for this rule is that such contracts are not tainted with any general illegality; they are illegal only as to the time in which they are entered into.

A contract which is collateral to but not a part of an illegal contract is enforceable if the collateral contract can be enforced without requiring the performance of the illegal act. Also, if one is not a party to the illegal agreement but the contract with him grows out of an illegal agreement, the agreement with the third party will be enforced. Archer bets Burch $100 that State will win the State-University football game. Clark acts as stakeholder. Burch wins the bet but Clark refuses to pay Burch the $200 which he has as stakeholder. Burch can recover in a suit against Clark.

If the parties are equally guilty in an illegal transaction, the courts usually follow the general rule. However, in some situations the public interest may be best served by allowing one of the parties to recover. Following this theory some states have passed statutes which allow one who has lost money while gambling to recover his losses. Frequently, confidence men induce their victim to participate in a scheme to defraud a third person or to enter into some other illegal deal as a means of defrauding him. The courts allow the victim of such schemes to recover his losses.

If one of the parties to an executory illegal agreement withdraws before the performance of the illegal act, the courts will allow him to recover any consideration he has parted with. One may recover money bet if he withdraws from the wager before the happening of the event.

If parts of a contract are illegal and parts legal, the courts will enforce the legal parts of the contract if they can be enforced without also enforcing the illegal parts. Archer sells his store to Burch and inserts a clause in the sales contract whereby he agrees not to operate a store anywhere in the world for a period of twenty-five years. The court will refuse to enforce the restraint clause because it is illegal, but they will enforce the legal provisions of the contract.

Tucker v. Binenstock
310 Pa. 254, 165 Atl. 247 (1933)

This was a bill for an accounting brought by Thomas A. Tucker (plaintiff) against Joseph Binenstock (defendant). Decree for plaintiff and defendant appealed. Decree reversed and bill dismissed.

Tucker and Binenstock together with four others organized in 1923 the New Century Realty Co., allegedly to carry on a real estate business, but actually to purchase a brewery. Later, under the name of others, they organized the Atlantic Brewing Co. to operate a brewery, manufacturing near beer. Actually, they manufactured and sold 4 per cent beer. The brewery was padlocked by the federal agents, but the seals were broken and all beer on hand taken away. This is a suit for an accounting of the profits of the business.

Kephart, J. There is no principle more clearly established than that the law will not enforce an illegal transaction, nor will it be an instrument for distribution of moneys illegally gained. It simply leaves the wrongdoers where it finds them. The rule is not designed for the protection of the more dishonest of the partners, although the latter may benefit from its application, but rests upon a broad principle of public policy; the government seeks to punish transgressions of the law, not to reward or aid them by countenancing any phase of the illegality. Therefore, in litigation where the government is not a party, where transactions are tainted with wrongdoing, as violations of statutes intended for the upbuilding of the moral structure of the body politic, no court will lend its aid where the cause of action is grounded on such immoral or illegal acts. . . . .

Appellee hopes to escape the consequences of these acts and of the rules set forth in the above cases, because the court did not find as a fact that the business was illegal, nor was it requested to so find, and the answer of appellant did not raise any such issue. The court below, in substance, found the fact of illegality; but, if the court below had not so found, that would not prevent this court from appraising the evidence of its true value. . . . . It is not necessary that the defense of illegality appear in the pleadings or record. . . . .

We find that the business as conducted by these partners was illegal, and the profits received therefrom were moneys received from illegal transactions.

Thomas v. Little et al.
209 Ala. 590, 96 So. 896 (1923)

This was an action by J. A. Thomas (plaintiff) against E. H. Little and Mary K. Little (defendants). Judgment for defendants and plaintiff appeals. Judgment reversed and remanded for new trial.

Little at the request of his uncle came to Alabama City and aided his uncle in purchasing a poolroom. Little was to operate the poolroom and sell liquor, in violation of the prohibition laws, which was to be furnished by the uncle. After the poolroom had been obtained and operated for a short time, the uncle purchased a lot, built a house on it, and sold it to Little to be used as a home for Little and his wife. Notes secured by a mortgage were given in payment, it being understood that payment was to be made out of the profits derived from the illegal sale of liquor. However, no such provision was included in either the notes or the mortgage. Little defaulted and the mortgage was foreclosed. Thomas acquired the property on the foreclosure sale. Little refused to surrender possession of the property and when Thomas sued, in ejectment, Little set up illegality as a defense.

Gardner, J. The defendants rely upon the principle, as sustained by the authorities, that where the consideration is illegal, or is a part of a transaction prohibited by law, the contract is void and unenforceable.

It is to be noted, however, that the purchase and sale of this house and lot, to be used by Little and wife as a home, took place some time subsequent to any unlawful arrangement concerning the traffic in prohibited liquors. Upon the question here presented, much may be written and many authorities cited, but we are persuaded that the facts in the instant case come within the rule noted in 3 Williston on Contracts, § 1752, as follows:

"Where the contract is merely collaterally connected with an unlawful purpose or act, the rule generally adopted is that where the contract is only remotely connected with an unlawful transaction and rests upon an independent and legal consideration, and the plaintiff can establish his case without relying upon the unlawful transaction, the contract is valid."

The transaction of purchase and sale of the house and lot here in question was based upon a legal consideration. It was not immediately connected with any illegal sale of liquor, but was only collateral and incidental thereto.

We are persuaded upon the undisputed facts in regard to the purchase and sale of the house and lot here in question, the principle invoked by the defendants in this cause was without application, and that the case comes within the influence of those decisions construing the contract as merely collaterally connected with an unlawful purpose.

Wassermann v. Sloss

117 Cal. 425, 49 Pac. 566, 38 L.R.A. 176, 59 Am. St. Rep. 209 (1897)

This was an action by Max Wassermann (plaintiff) against Louis Sloss (defendant). Judgment for defendant and plaintiff appealed. Judgment reversed.

Wassermann was a stockholder in the Alaska Commercial Company and Sloss was president of the company. Certain leases held by the company from the government of the United States and also that of Russia were about to expire. Sloss represented to Wassermann that to obtain renewal of the leases it would be necessary to transfer, as a gratuity, stock in the Alaska Commercial Company to high officials of both governments. Wassermann transferred 400 shares of the stock to Sloss to be used for this purpose. Sloss did not use the stock as contemplated but refused to return it to Wassermann. Suit was brought to recover the stock and Sloss set up illegality as a defense.

Garoutte, J. As we view this whole question, the good or bad morals of this undertaking are immaterial, for the reason that the venture was in no sense executed, and until executed both parties are given an opportunity for repentance and rescission. Seeing the error of his ways, the law says a party may withdraw from the transaction; and it extends to him a helping hand by offering the inducement of giving back to him anything of value with which he has parted. Putting this case against plaintiff as bad as may be imagined, he transferred his stock to defendant to be used by defendant in corrupting servants of the respective governments. The transaction progressed no further. The stock was not so used. The precipice which would have been death to plaintiff's cause of action was never reached. No one was corrupted, and the stock was not stained. The parties' intentions as to the use to which this stock was to be put are not the controlling factor. It is not what was intended to be done with the stock that christens the transaction, but rather what was actually done. If defendant had disposed of the stock as contemplated, plaintiff would have had no remedy, for the evil would have been accomplished, the harm would have been done, and of necessity his plea for relief would not have been heard. In this case plaintiff gave certain stock to defendant to be used for a certain purpose. He was plaintiff's bailee of the stock. The bailee did not use it for the purpose agreed upon, but took it to his own use. There is no principle of law to justify such a transaction. If plaintiff, upon the second day subsequent to the transaction, had changed his mind, and notified defendant of such change, and demanded a return of his stock, upon principle and authority he would have been entitled to such return. The authorities all hold that, if he had done this any day prior to the time when the agreement was fully executed, he would be entitled to a return of his stock. That this agreement was purely executory cannot be questioned.

QUESTIONS AND PROBLEMS

1. What is the basis for determining "public policy"?
2. Were Sunday contracts illegal at common law?
3. Archer makes an application to the Fire Insurance Co. for insurance on his farm buildings. Burch, the inspector for the Fire Insurance Co., inspects Archer's buildings and writes up his report on Sunday. The report is dated Monday, and on Monday the report is received by the Fire Insurance Co. and the policy of insurance is executed on Monday. Is the contract of insurance valid?
4. If Smart, who is not licensed to practice law, drafts a will for Jones and gives Jones advice as to his legal rights in connection with the disposal of his estate, can Smart recover a judgment against Jones for the amount of the fee which Jones promised to pay Smart for his services?

5. Levison is conducting the business of a pawnbroker but has not obtained a license as required by the state statutes. Levison loans Boas $100, and Boas pledges his diamond ring to Levison as security for the loan. Does Levison have a valid lien on the ring?
6. What is the difference between a wagering contract and a risk-bearing contract?
7. To stimulate trade Archer puts a jar of beans in his window and puts a sign on it to the effect that he will give $5 to the customer who guesses the number of beans in the jar. The statutes of the state prohibit lotteries. Is Archer's scheme a violation of the lottery laws?
8. Would Archer be violating the lottery laws if he charged 50 cents for the right to participate in the guessing contest?
9. (*a*) Tony who operates a boot-black parlor at the corner of Lexington and 23d St. sells his parlor to Pete and agrees not to operate a boot-black parlor in the New York City metropolitan area for a period of five years. Is the clause enforceable? (*b*) Wanamaker sells his New York City department store to Macy and agrees not to operate a department store in the New York City metropolitan area for a period of five years. Is the clause enforceable?
10. The president of the Island Club requested Halcomb to find a competent builder who would erect a building for the club for less money than the bids made by New York contractors. The president told Halcomb, "We only want parties that you can indorse in every way and who are responsible and reliable." Halcomb recommended Weaver to the club and, relying on Halcomb's recommendation, the club engaged Weaver to erect the building. Weaver, without the knowledge or consent of the club, promised to pay Halcomb a $250 commission. Weaver refused to pay and Halcomb sued. Can Halcomb recover a judgment?
11. Archer kept a billiard parlor and soft drink bar. The sale of intoxicating liquor was illegal. Archer employed Burch to work generally. He not only attended the billiard tables and sold soft drinks, but also served customers with intoxicating liquors. In Archer's absence Burch had entire charge of the business. Archer did not pay Burch for his services and Burch sued. Is Burch entitled to a judgment?
12. Burch was playing at cards and had lost all of his money. Burch asked Archer, who was watching the game, to loan him $100 so that he could recover his losses. Archer loaned Burch $100 which Burch lost. Burch refused to repay Archer and Archer sued. Is Archer entitled to a judgment?

CHAPTER X

STATUTE OF FRAUDS

Provisions of the Statute

The original English Statute of Frauds was passed in 1677—29 Car. II, Cap. 3 (1677). The purpose of the statute was to prevent certain fraudulent practices prevalent at the time, especially the practice of using perjured evidence to establish a cause of action. As a means of accomplishing this end, certain classes of contracts were required to be in writing before the courts would enforce them. Contracts falling within the provisions of the statute in order to be enforceable must comply with all the requirements of an enforceable contract—offer, acceptance, consideration, parties having legal capacity to contract, a legal objective—and in addition to these requirements there must be some note or memorandum in writing signed by the party to be bound. The statute does not require a formally drawn, written instrument, but it does require a writing sufficient to establish the material provisions of the contract.

The original English statute was extensive in its scope and included many provisions in addition to those requiring writings. There are eight sections requiring writings, but we are primarily interested in only two of these, sections 4 and 17. These sections of the original English statute read as follows:

"Section 4. No action shall be brought (1) to charge any executor or administrator on any special promise to answer damages out of his own estate; (2) or to charge the defendant upon any special promise to answer for the debt, default, or miscarriage of another person; (3) or to charge any person upon any agreement made upon consideration of marriage; (4) or upon any contract or sale of lands, tenements, or hereditaments, or any interest in them; (5) or upon any agreement that is not to be performed within one year of the making thereof; (6) unless the agreement or some memorandum or note thereof shall be in writing and signed by the party to be charged, or by some person thereunto by him lawfully authorized.

"Section 17. No contract for the sale of any goods, wares, and merchandises for the price of £10 sterling, or upwards, shall be allowed to be good, except the buyer shall accept part of the goods so sold, and actually receive the same, or give something in earnest to bind the bargain, or in part payment, or that some note or memorandum in writing of the said bargain be made and signed by the parties to be charged by such contract, or their agents thereunto lawfully authorized."

In the United States, the various states have re-enacted, with slight change in wording, sections 4 and 17 of the original English Statute of Frauds. Section 17 has been omitted by some states. In addition to the contracts required to be in writing under sections 4 and 17, some states require a promise to pay a debt, barred by the running of the statute of limitations, or a debt discharged in bankruptcy, to be in writing. Also, an increasing number of states require an agreement for the commissions of a real estate broker to be in writing. The statutes adopted by the various states are not uniform in their wording and scope, and in interpreting the various statutes the courts have approached the problem from many angles so the court decisions are frequently conflicting, especially on certain controversial points.

Secondary Promises

Under existing probate procedure if an administrator or executor promises to pay the debts of the estate which he is administering out of his own property, he is promising to answer for the debt of another person, and the contract will come within the provisions of subsection 2 of the statute.

The requirement that any promise to answer for the debt, default, or miscarriage of another person must be evidenced by some note or memorandum in writing to be enforceable covers all guaranty and surety contracts. Such a contract is composed of two parts, (1) the primary promise and (2) the secondary promise which must be noted in writing. Debtor promises to pay creditor $100. This is the primary promise and is not required to be in writing. Surety promises to pay creditor if debtor does not. This is the secondary promise and must be in writing to be enforceable.

If Archer should say to Burch, "You let Clark have a suit of clothes when he comes in this afternoon and I will pay you for it," Archer's promise to Burch would be a primary promise and need not be in writing to be enforceable.

The promise to pay the debt of another must be a promise which will charge the estate of the promisor; otherwise it need not be in writing. Archer has property in his possession which belongs to Burch.

Burch is negotiating a contract with Clark. Archer promises Clark that, if Clark gives credit to Burch and Burch does not pay, Archer will pay out of Burch's property which he has in his hands. Archer's promise to Clark is a primary promise and need not be in writing.

An indemnity contract need not be in writing. Frequently indemnity contracts are confused with surety or guaranty contracts because no liability arises on the indemnity contract until the person indemnified becomes obligated to a third person. An automobile property damage and public liability contract is usually an indemnity contract. Burch owns an automobile. Archer, for a premium, contracts that if as the result of the operation of the automobile Burch becomes liable for the injury of some person he will pay the damage and relieve Burch from liability. Burch injures Clark. Archer under the indemnity contract owes a duty to Burch to pay Clark, but Archer is under no obligation to Clark. Archer's promise to Burch is a primary promise and need not be in writing to be enforced.

If one promises to pay the debt of a third person, as part of the purchase price of property which has been pledged as security for the indebtedness, the promise need not be in writing. It is considered as an original undertaking. This is also true in a situation where Archer owes Burch and Burch owes Clark, and the parties agree among themselves, each consenting to the arrangement, that Archer will pay Clark the debt Burch owes Clark, thus discharging Burch's obligation, and in turn Burch discharges Archer of his obligation to Burch, leaving as a result Archer owing Clark, Burch being completely discharged of all obligation. Such an agreement is called a novation and need not be in writing to be enforceable. Archer's obligation to Clark is primary. Another situation similar in some respects is where Archer promises Clark that he will perform Burch's obligation to Clark in consideration of Clark's immediately discharging Burch from the obligation. In this case Archer's promise is primary, and Burch's obligation being discharged, it leaves only one obligation, that of Archer to Clark. Although the result of Archer's action is the discharge of Burch's obligation, Archer's promise to Clark is primary. It is not an agreement to pay if Burch does not, but an agreement to pay in consideration of Clark's discharging Burch. Burch's obligation being discharged leaves but two parties to the contract, Archer and Clark. Obviously a contract to purchase a debt from the creditor is not required to be in writing by the Statute of Frauds. Where the result of the contract is the discharge of the third person's obligation to the creditor and the substitution therefor of the promisor's obligation, the promise is primary and need not be in writing to be enforceable.

Another type of transaction not required to be in writing by the Statute of Frauds but frequently confused with agreements which are required to be in writing is an agreement, on the sale of stock in a corporation, to guarantee the payment of a stated dividend or an agreement to repurchase if the market value of the stock declines below a stated price within the time set. Contracts of this type are between the seller and the purchaser of the stock and are not collateral agreements guaranteeing the obligations of the corporation. Even though the result of such an agreement may be the discharge of a corporate obligation, it would not necessarily have to be in writing. However, if the promise was secondary in nature and the guaranteeing of the corporate obligation was the controlling incentive for the promise, it would have to be in writing.

The courts have held, perhaps unwisely, that if one promises to pay the debt of a third person primarily to gain some advantage accruing to himself, the promise is an original promise and enforceable although not in writing. Usually, although not necessarily, in such cases the consideration for the promise is forbearance to sue on a debt. In these cases the debtor continues to be primarily liable and the promisor's obligation is secondary or collateral. These are distinguished from other cases solely on the ground that the promisor is prompted to make the promise to gain some advantage accruing to himself.

Archer loans money to Burch and as security Burch gives Archer a mortgage on his (Burch's) farm. Later Clark loans money to Burch, and as security Burch gives Clark a second mortgage on the same farm. Burch defaults and Archer starts foreclosure proceedings. The farm has depreciated in value and the proceeds from a foreclosure sale will not be sufficient to pay both Archer and Clark. Clark orally promises Archer that if Archer will dismiss his foreclosure suit he (Clark) will pay Burch's debt if Burch does not. Clark's promise need not be in writing.

Sanders v. Hodges et al.
109 Fla. 391, 147 So. 571 (1933)

This was an action by J. D. Sanders (plaintiff) against G. L. Hodges and G. B. Stallings (defendant). Judgment for defendant and plaintiff appealed. Judgment reversed.

The suit was brought against Hodges and Stallings but on plaintiff's motion the suit was dismissed as to Hodges.

Sanders claimed that Stallings requested Sanders to extend to him (Stallings) credit for goods to be delivered to Hodges. Stallings' request was oral. The trial court ruled out all evidence offered for the purpose of proving that the credit was extended to Stallings and ruled that the promise to be enforceable must be in writing.

Terrell, J. We are first confronted with the question of whether credit was extended by Sanders direct to Stallings or to Hodges on Stallings' guaranty, but in either event was the agreement to extend it within the statute of frauds?

The declaration sounds against Stallings for goods, wares, and merchandise delivered to Hodges at Stallings' request and promise to pay for them. The cause of action in other words rests on Stallings' promise to pay rather than on his promise to pay if Hodges did not. The statute of frauds, section 3872, Rev. Gen. St. of 1920, section 5779, Comp. Gen. Laws of 1927, in effect provides that no action shall be brought to charge the defendant on a "special promise to answer for the debt, default or miscarriage of another person," unless the agreement or promise or some memorandum of it be in writing signed by the party to be charged.

There is a marked distinction between an original or direct promise on the part of a third person to pay for goods sold and delivered to another solely on the credit of the third person and a collateral promise on the part of such third person to pay for goods sold and delivered to another in the event the one to whom sold fails or refuses to pay for them. The latter or collateral promise is within the statute of frauds, while the former or direct promise is not considered to be.

The pith of the holding in these cases is that, if a third person makes a direct unconditional promise or agreement to pay for goods delivered or to be delivered to another, the delivery being contemporaneous with or flowing from the agreement, and it being intended by the parties that the third person is liable in the first instance for the payment of the goods, the promise or agreement will be treated as an original one, and not within the statute of frauds.

The agreement or promise or some memorandum of which the statute of frauds requires to be in writing does not have reference to the promisor's own debt, but refers to the debt of another which he agrees to protect. The question of whether the promise was direct or collateral, that is to say, to whom credit was extended, is one of fact to be determined by the jury from the evidence adduced.

Collins et al. v. Herwick
109 Pa. Supr. Ct. 413, 167 Atl. 474 (1933)

This was an action by F. C. Collins and another, partners (plaintiffs) against A. C. Herwick (defendant). Judgment for plaintiffs and defendant appealed. Judgment affirmed.

Mabel Utts owned a house to which she wished to make certain additions, changes, and repairs. She entered into a contract with Herwick whereby Herwick was to loan Mrs. Utts $6,500 secured by a mortgage on the house. Herwick was to retain the money and out of it was to discharge certain liens against the house, was to do the carpenter work and pay himself, and was to pay for certain plumbing. The amount paid to said plumbing contractor was not to exceed the amount remaining in Herwick's hands after the payment of the items mentioned. Mrs. Utts was to select the plumber and make the contract with him. Plaintiffs took the plumbing contract, but before entering into the contract they went to Herwick and Herwick told them that he had the money to pay them and would pay them out of the moneys in his hands when they completed their contract. Plaintiffs completed their contract and demanded payment from Herwick. Herwick refused to pay, stating that he had already exhausted the funds. When sued he set up as a defense that the promise was a promise to pay the debt of another, was not in writing, and, therefore, it was unenforceable.

Stadtfeld, J. The contract sued upon is the oral promise to pay the debt of another in consideration of property or funds received or to be received of the debtor for that purpose. Such a promise is not within the statute of frauds.

The verdict establishes the facts (1) that on or about October 8, 1927, appellant orally promised to pay to appellees the sum of $698 upon completion of their plumbing contract with the owner, out of the funds to be received by appellant from owner for that purpose, and (2) in January, 1928, appellant orally promised to pay to appellees said sum upon completion of their plumbing contract with the owner out of the funds received on or about December 5, 1927, by appellant from the owner for that purpose.

It is not material under these circumstances whether appellant retained the moneys paid to him for the appellees. If he saw fit to disburse the amount for other purposes, in disregard of his promise to appellees, that was his own affair.

Appellant cites the case of *Shannon* v. *American Iron & Steel Mfg. Co.*, 66 Pa. Super. Ct. 211, 214, in support of the proposition that "where one undertakes to enforce a verbal promise to answer for the debt or default of another if the original debt remains, it is necessary to show that his case is of a character that is recognized as exceptional." Quoting from the same case, page 215, the court says: "It is a recognized principle that a promise to pay the debt of another in consideration of property received or to be received of the debtor for that purpose is not within the statute. The promisor thereby makes the debt his own and incurs a primary liability."

The principle governing this case is well stated in Browne on the Statute of Frauds, cited with approval in *Stoudt* v. *Hine*, 45 Pa. 30, 31: "It is obvious . . . . that an engagement in terms to apply the debtor's own funds received, or to be received by the defendant to the payment of the demand against him, creates a duty as agent rather than as surety; the defendant's promise is not to pay the debt, but merely to deliver certain property to the nominee of the original debtor, and the right of action of such nominee against the defendant for a breach of his promise is not at all affected by the Statute of Frauds."

And this is true even if the liability of the original debtor continues. A promise to pay the debt of another is not within the statute of frauds, even though liability of the original debtor continues, if the promisor has received a fund pledged, set apart or held for the payment of the debt."

Gilinsky v. Klionsky
251 N.Y.S. 570, (1931)

This was an action by Nathan Gilinsky (plaintiff) against Bernet Klionsky (defendant). A motion was made to dismiss the suit. Motion was denied and defendant appealed. Judgment affirmed.

Israel Klionsky wished to borrow money from the Morris Plan Bank. Defendant, Israel Klionsky's brother, asked plaintiff to sign Israel's note as surety and orally promised that, if plaintiff signed Israel's note as surety, defendant would make good any loss plaintiff might suffer. Plaintiff (Gilinsky) signed as surety and as a result was required to pay to the bank a substantial balance on the note. This suit was brought to recover the balance paid from defendant, and defendant set up the Statute of Frauds as a defense.

Personius, J. Succinctly the question is whether a promise, by one not a party to a note, to one who becomes a surety thereon, to save the latter harmless, is within the Statute of Frauds. We hold that it is not.

There is much diversity of opinion in the several states. It appears that the English decisions were conflicting, accounting to a large extent for the divergent views in the United States. Ultimately the doctrine prevailed in England and a majority of the states, including New York, that such a promise was not within the Statute of Frauds. The contrary is still held in a few of our states, for instance, *Posten v. Clem*, 201 Ala. 529, 78 So. 883, 1 A.L.R. 381, where it is frankly admitted that the Alabama decisions must be classed with the minority line.

The defendant's promise was not to pay the indebtedness of his brother Israel to the banks; his promise was to pay an indebtedness not then in existence, but which would come into existence if and when these plaintiffs as guarantors of the banks' indebtedness were required to pay and did pay that indebtedness. Such a promise is not within the Statute of Frauds. To quote from 25 R.C.L. 525: "The better view, however, seems to be that a promise to indemnify a person against liabilities he may incur by reason of some act he may do or perform for a third person, though such third person may also by reason of such act be liable to reimburse the person to whom the promise is made, is not within the statute."

Kilbride v. Moss et al.
113 Cal. 432, 45 Pac. 812 (1896)

This was an action by J. J. Kilbride (plaintiff) against George D. Moss (defendant). Judgment for plaintiff and defendant appealed. Judgment affirmed.

The California Lustral Company, a corporation, was in need of money. Moss, a large stockholder, director and vice-president of the corporation, asked plaintiff to loan the corporation $1,500 which the plaintiff refused to do. Thereupon it was verbally agreed between plaintiff and defendant (Moss) that plaintiff should purchase 6,000 shares of stock in the corporation, pay $1,500 therefor to the corporation, and in the event the stock became worthless or of no value he, the defendant, would purchase the stock and pay plaintiff $1,500 therefor. The stock became of no value and plaintiff tendered the stock to defendant and demanded the defendant pay $1,500 therefor. Defendant refused and when sued set up the statute of frauds as a defense.

Searls, C. Appellant contends that defendant was a guarantor, and that the action is brought against him as such. If these facts constitute him a guarantor, the contention of appellant is sound, but, if the converse of the proposition is maintained, defendant is neither a guarantor nor surety. Much learning has been exhibited, many fine distinctions drawn, and, we may add, a good deal of discrepancy is to be found upon some of the many branches of the law relating to guaranty. The present case, however, seems to us to involve but a single, plain, fundamental principle, not calling for extended discussion. It is this: The contract of guaranty is a collateral undertaking. It cannot exist without the presence of a main or substantive liability to which it is collateral. If there is no such substantive liability on the part of a third person, either express or implied—that is to say, if there is no debt, default, or miscarriage, present or prospective—there is nothing to guaranty, and hence can be no contract of guaranty. If there is no primary liability of a third person to the promisee which continues after the promise is made, it is an original promise, and need not be in writing. Applying this doctrine to the case at bar, and we fail to discern any primary liability on the part of any one to the plaintiff upon which to base a guaranty. The corporation from which he purchased the shares of capital stock owed him no duty in the premises after such purchase was consummated, except the general obligation to him, in common with all other shareholders, to fairly and impartially conduct the business of the company in such manner as would best promote the interests of all concerned. The corporation simply sold him 6,000 shares of its stock, and received payment therefor. This closed the incident so far as the company was concerned. It was the defendant who entered into contract with him, whereby, as an inducement for plaintiff to purchase, he promised to refund his money should the stock become worthless. This was an original contract. *Moorehouse* v. *Crangle*, 36 Ohio St. 130, is in point. There C., who was a large stockholder of a business corporation, and president thereof, verbally promised M. that, if he would subscribe and pay $500 to the capital stock of the company, he should, within one year, receive 15 per cent on the amount invested. M., in consideration of this promise, subscribed and paid for the stock. No dividends were made or earned within the year. Held that this was not a contract to answer for the debt, default, nor miscarriage of another, but an original contract, upon the proof of which plaintiff was entitled to recover. Johnson, J., in discussing the case, said: "The terms of the statute make it clear that a collateral promise, or one to answer for the liability of another, is one where there is a debt or obligation of another than the promisor for whose default he undertakes to be liable. An original liability of another is the foundation of the collateral liability of the promisor. . . . . If this contract is not within the statute of frauds, the plaintiff is entitled to recover, as it is not doubted but that the consideration stated is sufficient. Was there any debt, obligation, or legal duty, express or implied, owing by the corporation to the plaintiff as a stockholder, for which the defendant undertook to answer upon default of the corporation?" The learned judge, after defining the duties of the corporation to its stockholders, adds: "The defendant did not undertake to answer for any debt, default, or miscarriage by the corporation growing out of a failure to perform any of these duties. . . . . Defendant's contract was, in legal effect, essentially different from the obligations of the corporation in favor of plaintiff as a stockholder, and the liability created was wholly independent of any default by the corporation. It was not an undertaking to answer for the default of the corporation."

Upon Consideration of Marriage

Subsection 3 of section 4 requires that an agreement made upon consideration of marriage must be in writing to be enforceable. The courts have uniformly held that mutual promises to marry need not be in writing to be enforceable. Many states have, by express provision, excluded mutual promises to marry from the operation of the statute. This provision applies more particularly to marriage settlement agreements where the consideration supporting the agreement is the marriage. The European practice of dowry agreements has never been followed extensively in the United States; consequently this subsection of the statute is of little importance in the United States.

An Interest in Land

Land and land ownership was of outstanding importance in England. From an early date the desirability of having a written record of transactions involving real estate was recognized. Several of the sections of the English Statute of Frauds deal with the transfer of interests in real estate. Subsection 4 of section 4 is the only clause which affects contracts. Actual conveyances of real estate—deeds, mortgages, etc.—are covered by special statutes. It is generally held that the earth's surface and everything firmly attached thereto is real estate. This simple rule does not serve to solve all the problems arising and in some instances is not followed.

The courts have generally enforced oral contracts to sell growing trees, crops, fruit on the trees, grass on a meadow, etc., if it is the intent of the parties that the title is to pass after severance from the land.

Archer owns an orchard. In the early summer Burch orally contracts for all the crop of fruit to be picked as the fruit matures, making a down payment on the purchase. The contract is not required to be in writing by the Statute of Frauds.

Purner v. Piercy
40 Md. 212 (1874)

This was an action by Piercy (plaintiff) against Purner (defendant). Judgment for plaintiff and defendant appealed. Judgment affirmed.

By parol contract the plaintiff agreed to sell the defendant a crop of peaches then on the trees. Some of the fruit was ripe at the time. The defendant was to gather and remove the peaches as they matured. Part of the purchase price was paid at the time the contract was entered into; another payment was made while defendant was gathering the peaches. This suit was to recover the balance of the purchase price. The defendant contended that the peaches on the trees were real estate, that a contract for their sale was a contract for the sale of an interest in real estate, that the contract was not in writing and therefore not enforceable.

Stewart, J. There is certainly some conflict in the adjudged cases in regard to the interpretation of contracts for the sale of crops and the natural products growing upon the land; and it is difficult to deduce therefrom any clearly defined rule upon the subject.

Mr. Alexander . . . . has carefully referred to numerous cases, both English and American, and deduced therefrom the distinctions which seemed to have prevailed in regard to the operation of the Statute in relation to growing crops and other produce of land. At page 532, et seq., contracts, as to the natural product of the land, are distinguished from such as relate to crops raised by the industry of man, and yielding an annual profit. A distinction is also noted between the natural produce when severed by the seller or by the buyer. He refers to the recent work of Benjamin on Sales, 84 et seq., for a fuller discussion. Mr. Benjamin, at p. 99, remarks, from all that precedes, the law on the subject of the sale of growing crops, may be summed up in the following proposition, viz.: growing crops, if *fructus industriales,* are chattels, and an agreement for the sale of them, whether mature or immature, whether the property in them is transferred before or after severance, is not an agreement for the sale of any interest in land, and is not governed by the 4th section of the Statute of Frauds. Growing crops, if *fructus naturales,* are part of the soil, before severance, and an agreement therefor vesting an interest in them in the purchaser before severance, is governed by the 4th section; but if the interest is not to be vested till they are converted into chattels by severance, then the agreement is an executory agreement for the sale of goods, wares and merchandise, governed by the 17th, and not by the 4th section of the Statute.

Not To Be Performed within One Year

Contracts, not to be performed within one year from the making thereof, must be in writing to be enforceable. In determining whether or not the contract is to be performed within a year of the date of the making of the contract, the date when both parties have assented, and not the date when performance is to begin, is the date from which time is computed.

If the contract expressly states the time within which it is to be performed, the question of whether or not it is within the statute is easily answered. If the time, counting from the date on which the parties made the contract to the stated date of the completion of performance, is one year or less, the contract need not be in writing, but if such period exceeds one year, it must be in writing. In computing the time, some courts hold that the day on which the contract is made is not counted, on the theory that parts of days are not recognized in computing time, while other courts hold that the day on which the contract is made should be counted. As a result, there is a conflict as to whether a contract to work for one year made today, work to begin tomorrow, must be in writing.

If by the terms of the contract it is to be performed within a year, and later, by agreement of the parties, the time is extended so that the contract will not be performed within a year from the time it was originally entered into, it need not be in writing, nor does the agreement to extend the time of performance have to be in writing if the extension is for less than a year from the time of the agreement, but if the extension is for more than one year, it must be in writing. In determining whether the contract is not to be performed within a year from the making thereof, the courts look to the terms of the agreement at the time it was entered into, and if from the terms of the agreement the time of performance will not, of necessity, be more than one year, the contract need not be in writing. The fact that the contract was not actually performed within one year does not bring the contract within the statute.

When the time stated in the contract is indefinite as "for life," "until I move from my present residence," "as long as needed," etc., if, under the conditions existing at the time the contract is entered into, it is possible to perform the contract within a year, it need not be in writing to be enforceable, even though the actual time of performance is more than one year.

The following are typical examples of problems arising under this section of the Statute of Frauds.

1. Archer agrees to support Burch for life.
2. Archer agrees to work for Burch for life.
3. Archer agrees to work for Burch for five years.
4. Archer agrees to support Burch for five years.
5. Archer agrees not to compete with Burch for five years.

Examples 1 and 2 are uniformly held not to be within this provision of the statute. The provision is framed in the negative "not to be performed within the space of one year." Applying the interpretation of the courts that if the agreement is capable of performance within the space of one year it does not come within the provisions of the statute, a contract to continue for the life of a person is capable of performance within the space of a year because the person may die within that time. Although examples 3, 4, and 5 are worded alike, that is, the duration of the contract is expressly stated to be five years, the courts have not treated them as alike. The courts are in accord in holding that example 3 must be in writing. Even though the death of Archer may render performance impossible, a contract to work for five years cannot be performed within the space of one year. This same reasoning could logically be applied to both examples 4 and 5, but all the courts have not followed it. In example 4, the majority of the courts have held that the statute does not apply on the grounds that on Burch's death the contract will be fully performed and Burch may die within one year. In other words, the courts have interpreted the agreement as though it were to support Burch for life not to exceed five years. There is considerable diversity in the holdings on example 5. Some courts class this type of agreement with 1 and 2, while others class it with 3.

An oral unilateral contract is not required to be in writing by this section of the statute. Archer loans Burch $100. Burch orally promises to repay Archer two years from date. Burch's promise need not be in writing to be enforceable.

Deucht v. Storper
44 N.Y.S. (2d) 350 (1943)

This was an action by Herta Deucht (plaintiff) against Dunziu Storper (defendant). A motion was made to dismiss the suit. Motion was denied and defendant appealed. Judgment affirmed.

Plaintiff had trained a group of skilled workers for the defendant. The defendant orally contracted to employ the plaintiff as a manager in his plant for so long a time as the defendant "continued to employ workers, trained, developed and gathered by plaintiff." The "skilled workers" were not under contract and could quit or be discharged at any time. Defendant discharged plaintiff while a number of such workers were still employed by defendant. When sued defendant set up as a defense that the contract could not be performed within one year from the making thereof, was not in writing, and was therefore unenforceable.

Coleman, J. Since the employment was to continue so long as the trained workers were retained and since their employment was at will, the contract with the plaintiff could be performed within a year and need not be in writing. For reading the words of the statute dryly as we should, we cannot say that the contract "by its terms is not to be (i.e. cannot be) performed within one year from the making." That is the test, even though the agreement, by the very fact that no calendar date for termination has been fixed, conceivably may extend beyond the year. By that test, as the defendant was free to discharge the group of other workers at any time, there is, therefore, nothing in the terms of the agreement that is "inconsistent with complete performance within a year."

Bashein et al. v. 2682 Broadway, Inc.
39 N.Y.S. (2d) 137 (1942)

This was an action by Bashein and Levy (plaintiffs) against 2682 Broadway, Inc. (defendant). Judgment for plaintiff.

Plaintiffs negotiated a lease for defendant. The lease was for seven years and contained a clause giving the lessee the option to renew the lease for seven years. The clause provided that the option to renew "must be exercised by the giving of written notice to the landlord not later than February 1, 1941." The lease was negotiated on September 15, 1934, and at the time the lease was negotiated it was orally agreed that, in the event the lessee exercised the option, plaintiff was to be paid a commission in the sum of $1,417.50. The lessee exercised the option September 30, 1940. Defendant refused to pay the agreed commission and when sued set up the Statute of Frauds as a defense.

Carlin, J. Upon the exercise of the option by the tenant a new tenancy was not created to begin at the end of the original term; it is deemed to have effected the continuance of the first seven years for seven years more, thus constituting a lease for fourteen years in legal contemplation.

The defendant contends that because the plaintiffs' claim to commissions is not evidenced by a writing that any agreement by the defendant to pay them in addition to the commission paid for the original term is void under the Statute of Frauds as the option provided for in paragraph 25 of the lease could not be performed within one year from the execution of the lease; with this contention the court is not in accord as the provision for the exercise of the option placed a limit beyond which the tenant would lose its right so to act; the limit therefor was "not later than February 1, 1941"; it, therefore, could be exercised any time intervening the date of execution of the lease and the date beyond which the right would cease and as a consequence is not within the Statute of Frauds as it could be performed within one year.

Sale of Goods

The Uniform Sales Act which has been adopted by a majority of the states has a statute of frauds section which is patterned after the English act, but does not follow its language strictly. The Uniform Sales Act, as originally drafted, applies to a "contract to sell or a sale of any goods or choses in action of the value of $500 or upwards." Some states require all such agreements to be in writing, irrespective of the amount involved, while Ohio places the amount at $2,500, it being the highest.

This section of the statute differs from section 4 in that certain acts other than a written memorandum will satisfy the statute. If the buyer accepts part of the goods, the statute is satisfied, or if something in earnest is paid or if a part payment is made, the statute is complied with. If none of these things is done, then the agreement or some note or memorandum thereof must be in writing and signed by the party to be charged.

There is a conflict and no little controversy as to what should be termed a contract for work and labor as distinguished from a sale or contract to sell goods. There are three rules recognized and known as the English, the New York, and the Massachusetts rules. The English rule is that if, as a result of the contract, property in a chattel is to pass, it is a sale of goods and within the statute, even though the chattel had no existence at the time of the making of the contract and although the principal value of the chattel, when created, will be the work and labor expended in its creation. The New York rule takes the opposite view and holds that, if the goods are not in existence when the contract is entered into but are to be made afterwards, the contract is for work and labor. The Massachusetts rule holds that, if the goods are not in existence and are not goods ordinarily manufactured or produced by the seller for sale on an established market, the contract is for work and labor. This is the rule adopted by the Uniform Sales Act.

Henry J. Handelsman, Jr., Inc. v. S. E. Schulman Co. et al.
319 Ill. App. 479, 48 N.E. (2d) 416 (1943)

This was an action by Henry J. Handelsman, Jr., Inc. (plaintiff) against S. E. Schulman Company and Philip Lome (defendants). Judgment for defendants and plaintiff appealed. Judgment reversed and remanded.

Plaintiff brought suit against defendants for specific performance of a contract to manufacture and deliver 100,000 cameras. Plaintiff and defendant Lome entered into an oral agreement whereby Lome agreed to have manufactured exclusively for plaintiff 100,000 cameras and cases of a specified size and design and marked "Photo Master Camera and Case." Afterward Schulman Company became a party to the agreement. The cameras and cases were not delivered according to the contract and plaintiff brought this suit. Defendants set up that the agreement was not in writing, and that the amount involved exceeded $500; therefore the agreement was unenforceable.

O'Connor, J. One of the contentions made by defendants was that the oral contract for the purchase of the cameras and cases, for which the price to be paid was over $500, was void under section 4 of the Uniform Sales Act. That section provides: "(1) A contract to sell or a sale of any goods . . . . of the value of five hundred dollars . . . . shall not be enforceable by action unless the buyer shall accept part of the goods . . . . or give something in earnest to bind the contract, or in part payment, or unless some note or memorandum in writing of the contract or sale be signed by the party to be charged or his agent in that behalf.

"(2) The provisions of this section apply to every such contract or sale, notwithstanding that the goods may be intended to be delivered at some future time or may not at the time of such contract or sale be actually made . . . .; but if the goods are to be manufactured by the seller especially for the buyer and are not suitable for sale to others in the ordinary course of the seller's business, the provisions of this section shall not apply." This section is referred to in the record and briefs as the "Statute of Frauds." We think the oral contract was enforceable and that no note or memorandum need have been signed to make it binding for the reason that the cameras and cases were to be "manufactured by the seller especially for the buyer" and were not suitable for sale to others in the ordinary course of the seller's business because they were to be marked "Photo Master Camera and Case" and from the allegations this designation indicated that they were being sold by plaintiff. Such a contract as the one involved may be enforced by either party.

Buchanan et al. v. Remington Rand, Inc.
130 N.J. L. 10, 30 A. (2d) 832 (1943)

This was an action by Joseph Buchanan and another (plaintiffs) against Remington Rand, Inc. (defendant). Judgment for plaintiff and defendant appealed. Judgment reversed.

Plaintiffs contracted to buy from the defendant 100 Remington Rand No. 1 portable typewriters at a cost in excess of $3,000. The contract was not in writing. There were no typewriters delivered, nor was there any note or memorandum signed by the defendant. The defendant did deliver to the plaintiffs a cut of the typewriter to be used for advertising purposes. The defendant set up the Statute of Frauds as a defense.

Bodine, J. Our statute (sec. 4 of the Uniform Sales Act) provides as follows: "(1) A contract to sell or a sale of any goods or choses in action of the value of five hundred dollars or upwards shall not be enforceable by action unless the buyer shall accept part of the goods or choses in action so contracted to be sold or sold, and actually receive the same, or give something in earnest to bind the contract, or in part payment, or unless some note or memorandum in writing of the contract or sale be signed by the party to be charged or his agent in that behalf."

The contention of the defendant was that the contract was for the sale of six typewriters and that when it delivered those typewriters, or attempted to, the plaintiffs refused to accept them. Since the statute was not complied with there was no cause of action. The respondents concede this point to be well taken, but seek to take the case out of the bar of the statute by showing that the defendant gave them a cut of the typewriters to be sold, which they used in inserting an advertisement in a newspaper. Obviously, this gift was no part of the goods to be sold—which were typewriters. Since there was no written note or memorandum and no acceptance and receipt of part of the goods sold, and since the cut was not part of the goods and since there was no giving by the alleged buyer of an earnest or part payment, we fail to see where there was any question for the jury.

In the case of *Garfield* v. *Paris*, 96 U.S. 557, 24 L. Ed. 821, involving the sale of whiskey and labels, a set of labels were given by the seller to the buyer. The question of whether the labels were part of the goods sold was submitted to the jury and they so found. There was no such finding in this case, nor was such issue submitted to the jury, nor were there proofs that the newspaper cut was other than a gift.

Sufficiency of Memoranda

What writing is required to satisfy the Statute of Frauds? Clearly, the statute does not require a formally drafted contract signed by both parties. The usual wording of the statute is "unless the agreement upon which such action shall be brought or some memorandum or note thereof, shall be in writing, and signed by the party to be charged therewith, etc." From the wording of the statute it is clear that some writing less than the entire agreement will satisfy the statute. As a general rule, the courts have required the memorandum or note to contain the material provisions of the agreement, the names of the parties, identity of subject matter, etc. Some courts require a statement of the consideration, but in some states this requirement is expressly dispensed with by statute. The memorandum need not be all on one paper, but if more than one paper is relied on, their connection must be established from the papers themselves. No particular form or language need be used. All that the courts require is a writing sufficient to establish the basic agreement between the parties.

The writing does not have to be signed by all the parties to the agreement. The words of the statute are in the singular—"party to be charged therewith." If the party defendant has signed the writing, that is sufficient. This brings about an inequitable result. Where one party signs the writing and the other party does not, the contract can be enforced against the one signing, but the defense of the Statute of Frauds would render the agreement unenforceable against the party not signing. The fact that one of the parties may be bound and the other may not be bound does not render the contract void on the grounds of lack of consideration.

The memorandum need not be drawn and signed at the time the agreement is entered into. It is immaterial when the memorandum is drawn and signed. If the party plaintiff has a note or memorandum of the agreement signed by the defendant at the time the suit is filed, the requirements of the statute are fulfilled.

Simmons v. Birge Company, Inc.
52 F. Supp. 629 (1943)

This was an action by John B. Simmons (plaintiff) against the Birge Company, Inc. (defendant). Judgment for defendant.

This was an action to recover damages for breach of contract. C. S. Smith Co., Inc., a corporation, had been in the wholesale wallpaper business on the west coast for ten years. It had the agency for a line of wallpaper manufactured by Birge Co., Inc. One line of wallpaper manufactured by Birge Co., Inc., and sold by Smith Company was known as the Blue Book line. Simmons was negotiating with Smith Company for the wallpaper division of the Smith Company. Simmons planned to organize a corporation, John B. Simmons, Inc., which was to purchase the wallpaper division of the Smith Company, providing arrangements could be made with the wallpaper manufacturer for the agency for their line of wallpaper. Negotiations were carried on between Simmons and Birge Company which Simmons contends resulted in a contract for the agency for the Blue Book line of the Birge Company for the year 1940. It was admitted that the contract could not be performed within one year from the making thereof. Simmons offered a series of letters and telegrams as the written note or memorandum required by the Statute of Frauds. The question presented to the court was whether the letters and telegrams which passed between the parties were a sufficient compliance with the Statute of Frauds.

J. F. T. O'Connor, D. J. "It is settled law . . . . that a correspondence through letters or telegrams, or both, if they show clearly what the contract was, is sufficient under the Statute of Frauds. . . . . In *Ryan* v. *United States*, 136 U.S. 68, 10 S. Ct. 913 (34 L. Ed. 447), the court held that 'a complete contract, binding under the Statute of Frauds, may be gathered from letters, writings, and telegrams between the parties relating to its subject matter, and so connected with each other that they may fairly be said to constitute one paper relating to the contract.' " It is not necessary that there be a formal contract, drawn up with technical exactness. Restatement of the Law of Contracts, sec. 207, which is in accord with the laws of California, declares: "A memorandum, in order to make enforceable contract within the Statute, may be any document or writing, formal or informal, signed by the party to be charged or by his agent actually or apparently authorized thereunto, which states with reasonable certainty (*a*) each party to the contract . . . . as will serve to identify him; . . . . and (*b*) the . . . . subject matter to which the contract relates, and (*c*) the terms and conditions of all the promises constituting the contract and by whom and to whom the promises are made." The letters alleged to contain the contract between the parties are signed by the party charged, viz.: Birge Co., Inc. The parties to the agreement are identified with reasonable certainty. In its letter of June 14, 1939, addressed to C. S. Smith Co., Inc., Birge Co. states: "We are given to understand that Mr. John B. Simmons of Los Angeles, California, proposes to organize a new corporation to take over your wallpaper division; . . . . we are willing to accept the new corporation as our debtor, releasing you from liability. . . . ."

Letters to a third person are sufficient to constitute a memorandum. While the John B. Simmons Company was not organized at the time this letter was written, Birge's letter of June 15, 1939, addressed to Mr. Simmons, stated: "We are willing to allow you to handle our Blue Book next season on the same basis as applied this year, provided your deal is fully consummated. . . . ."

In this letter and the letter of June 24, 1939, directed by Birge to Simmons, the subject matter with reference to which the parties intended to contract, viz., the Blue Book, is sufficiently identified.

Ascertaining the terms and conditions of all of the promises constituting the contract is the final determining factor in considering the applicability of the Statute of Frauds.

"To satisfy the Statute of Frauds a memorandum 'must contain the essential terms of the contract expressed with such a degree of certainty that it may be understood without recourse to parol evidence to show the intentions of the parties.' "

The door must not be opened to possible fraud, perjury, or to honest but mistaken recollection of memory. That which makes for certainty in business transactions is to be encouraged to prevent injustice by loss of property rights. Without elaborating upon the contents of the letters relied upon by the plaintiff, this court has been unable to discover any specification of the terms and conditions of the purported contract wherein the amount to be paid is ascertainable, and the geographical limits, in which the plaintiff is to exercise the exclusive agency of the Blue Book.

Failure To Comply

The Statute of Frauds expressly provides that "no action shall be brought, etc." The effect of this provision is to deny the parties the right to have an oral contract, required by the Statute of Frauds to be in writing, enforced by the courts. The contract is not void or voidable but it is unenforceable. It is not illegal and will be recognized for some purposes. If one of the parties, in reliance on an oral contract, performs his promises and thereby enriches the other party to the agreement, he will be permitted to recover for the benefits conferred in an action in quasi-contract. The courts of equity recognize and enforce the Statute of Frauds, yet the courts will refuse to permit the defense of the Statute of Frauds if permitting the defense will bring about an inequitable result. This rule is frequently applied in cases in which one party, in reliance on an oral agreement to sell real estate, has taken possession of real estate and made substantial improvements thereon. Archer agrees to sell Burch 80 acres of unimproved land for $1,000, and agrees to give him a deed to the land when the $1,000 is paid. There is no written note or memorandum of the agreement. Burch takes possession of the land, clears it, builds a house, barn, and other farm buildings, fences and improves it until it is a productive farm. Burch pays Archer the agreed $1,000, but Archer refuses to give Burch a deed to the farm. When sued in equity for specific performance Archer sets up the Statute of Frauds as a defense. The court of equity will grant specific performance.

If the parties have fully performed the contract, the courts will not disturb them. Also, if one is sued on an oral contract which is required by the Statute of Frauds to be in writing and the party defendant does not set up the failure to comply with the Statute of Frauds as a defense, the court will enforce the oral agreement. The parties have the right to waive the defense.

As a matter of good business practice all important contracts should be in writing whether coming within the provisions of the Statute of Frauds or not. To recover on a contract one must prove the existence of the contract and its terms. If one has a written contract, its existence and terms are easily established. Even though one does not wish to bring suit on a contract it is best to have it in writing.

QUESTIONS AND PROBLEMS

1. Does the Statute of Frauds provide that all contracts are unenforceable unless in writing?
2. What is a primary promise? What is a secondary promise?
3. Marr entered into an oral contract with the Railway Co. by the terms of which Marr agreed to board at least sixty of the Railway Co.'s employees at an agreed price for each employee. The Railway Co. agreed to furnish Marr at least sixty boarders and pay the stipulated price for each boarder. The contract was to run for six months. The Railway Co. furnished only twenty boarders and when sued set up the Statute of Frauds as a defense. Is the defense good?
4. Archer purchased an automobile from Burch, paying $100 down and promising to pay the $900 balance in nine equal installments. After paying two installments, Archer sold the automobile to Clark who paid Archer $150 and agreed to pay Burch $700, the unpaid balance of the purchase price. Archer and Clark called on Burch and informed him of the deal, and Clark orally promised to pay Burch the $700 balance. Burch agreed. Clark did not pay and Burch sued Clark. Clark set up the Statute of Frauds as a defense. Is the defense good?
5. Sams sold Austin one hundred shares of the capital stock of the Chix Corporation. At the time of the sale, Sams orally promised that if the Chix Corporation paid less than a 10 per cent dividend during the next five years, Sams would make up the deficiency. The corporation failed to pay a dividend within the five-year period and Sams refused to make up the deficiency. Austin sued and Sams set up the Statute of Frauds as a defense. Is the defense good?
6. In Problem 5 if the sale had been a sale of corporate bonds, and the oral promise had been to pay the interest on the bonds if the corporation defaulted, would the promise be enforceable?
7. On Friday, Chase orally agreed to work for Hinkley for one year beginning the following Monday. Chase worked for only a short time and quit. Hinkley sued Chase for damages for breach of the contract and Chase set up the Statute of Frauds as a defense. Is the defense good?
8. Paul Kent agreed orally to work his father's farm and to accept what his services were worth, payable at the death of his father. When the father died, Paul Kent filed a claim for his services and the executor refused to pay the claim. When sued the executor set up the Statute of Frauds as a defense. Is the defense good?
9. Goddard, a carriage maker, orally contracted to make a buggy for Binney. Binney gave directions as to how the buggy was to be painted, and also directed that the lining should be drab and the outside seat should be of cane. He also ordered his monogram and initials on it. The sum of $675 was agreed as the price. When the buggy was completed, Binney refused to accept and pay for it. Goddard sued and Binney set up the Statute of Frauds as a defense. Is the defense good?
10. On March 2, Bird and Munroe entered into an oral contract which could not be performed within one year from the making thereof. The contract was breached by Bird on March 10. On March 24, Bird wrote Munroe a letter in which he gave the terms of the contract and stated that he was unable to carry the contract out. He signed the letter. Munroe sued Bird and Bird set up the Statute of Frauds as a defense. Was the letter a sufficient memorandum to satisfy the Statute of Frauds?

CHAPTER XI

RIGHTS OF THIRD PERSONS

Introduction

Ordinarily, the only persons who have any interest in a contract are the parties to the contract. The contract is of their creation; they determine the nature of the rights and duties under the contract and do not have the right, by their agreement, to affect the legal status of third parties. This conception was carried to its logical conclusion by the early courts.

Two questions relative to third parties arose at an early date. (1) If, for a consideration, Archer promised Burch to perform a service for Clark, who was not a party to the agreement, did Clark have the right to sue Archer if he did not render the promised service? (2) If Archer and Burch had entered into a contract, could either Archer or Burch transfer his interest in the contract to Clark? Both of these questions were answered in the negative by the early courts. A contract was an agreement between the two parties to the agreement, and strangers to the agreement could obtain no right in it.

However, very early, exceptions to the second rule were recognized. Under the Law Merchant, bills of exchange and later promissory notes, if properly drawn, were negotiable before maturity and were readily assignable after maturity. Under special circumstances, contracts were assignable by operation of law; for example, all the contract rights of a bankrupt became the property of the trustee in bankruptcy.

Later, the desirability of permitting the assignment of certain classes of rights was recognized. The right to assign duties has never been recognized, but under some circumstances a party may assign his rights and delegate his duties to a third party, thus approximating a complete assignment of the contract.

The courts have also recognized the desirability of permitting the third party beneficiary under certain types of contract to bring an action to enforce the promises given, but this privilege is confined within narrow limits.

Assignment of Contracts

The courts now generally hold that one can assign rights under a contract unless the rights assigned are to the personal services of the other contracting party. This limitation on one's right to assign is based on the early conceived idea that one should not be forced into a personal relationship against his wishes. Suppose that Archer has contracted with Burch for Burch's services as personal secretary. If Archer were permitted to assign his right to Burch's services to Clark, Burch would be placed in a position where he would either have to render a personal service to Clark or breach the contract. This the court will not permit. If the right is not personal in its nature, it can be assigned unless the parties to the contract have expressly agreed that such right shall not be assigned.

Strictly speaking, one cannot assign his duties under a contract, but he may delegate those duties if they are not personal in their nature. By delegating the duties he does not relieve himself from all liability under the contract. If the person to whom the duties have been delegated does not perform the duties in full compliance with the terms of the contract, the assignor will be liable to the promisee for breach of contract. If the promisee agrees to accept the performance of the assignee in the place of that of the assignor, we have a novation and the assignor is relieved from all liability.

The courts have, as a general rule, held that the liability of the assignor is similar to that of a guarantor or surety. If the promisee deals with the assignee directly, especially if the promisee and assignee enter into any agreement which alters the terms of the contract without the knowledge or consent of the assignor, the courts will hold that the assignor is discharged.

The courts generally recognize assignments of contracts where the right assigned is the right to receive money and also generally recognize that the assignor has the right to delegate the duty to pay money. If the duty delegated is something other than the payment of money, the courts will not recognize the validity of the delegation of the duties unless they are impersonal in nature.

Archer has leased a building to Burch. Burch assigns the lease to Clark. If Clark does not pay the rent when due, Archer can recover from Burch. If Archer recognizes Clark as his tenant by dealing with him directly, and especially if, by subsequent agreement between Archer and Clark, some change is made in the lease without Burch's consent, Burch will be released from liability on the lease.

Archer lets his farm to Burch on a crop-sharing lease. Burch assigns the contract to Clark. The courts will not recognize the validity of the assignment, since on a crop-sharing lease the ability of the tenant is material.

Gargiulo v. California Wineries & Distilleries
171 N. Y. S. 855 (1918)

This was an action by Pasquale Gargiulo (plaintiff) against California Wineries and Distilleries (defendant). Judgment for plaintiff. Defendant made a motion to set the judgment aside and for a new trial. Motion denied.

Gargiulo entered into a contract with defendant for 750 barrels of wine to be delivered by monthly deliveries. The wine was to be paid for 30 days after each shipment. Gargiulo incorporated his business and assigned the contract to the corporation. Defendant refused to make deliveries.

Ford, J. Defendant's defense is that by the assignment or attempted assignment of the contract to the corporation it was relieved of its obligations to the plaintiff, because, as it contends, the contract was not assignable without its consent. Upon this question *Devlin* v. *City of New York*, 63 N.Y. 8, is the leading New York case. It involves the assignability of a street-cleaning contract which contained no provision relating to its assignability as the appeal book discloses. In that case the Court of Appeals laid down these general principles:

"The assignability of a contract must depend upon the nature of the contract and the character of the obligations assumed, rather than the supposed intent of the parties, except as that intent is expressed in the agreement. Parties may, in terms, prohibit the assignment of any contract, and declare that neither personal representatives nor assignees shall succeed to any rights in virtue of it, or be bound by its obligations. But when this has not been declared, expressly or by implication, contracts other than such as are personal in their character, as promises to marry, or engagements for personal services requiring skill, science, or peculiar qualifications, may be assigned, and by them the personal representatives will be bound.

In brief, public policy favors the assignability of contracts as facilitating commerce and its complex transactions, unless forbidden by the contract itself or by the other consideration mentioned. There are dicta to be found in some New York cases which indicate that an extension of credit, as in a contract of sale, for example, would destroy its assignability, unless the other party assented to the assignment. But in no case called to our attention in the voluminous brief submitted by defendant's counsel is this question squarely passed upon.

But upon the bare question of the assignability of the contract I am of the opinion that it could be assigned without the defendant's consent notwithstanding the extension of credit to the plaintiff. In the Rochester Lantern Co. case the court said: "The contract was not purely personal, in the sense that Kelly was bound to perform in person, as his only obligation was to pay for the dies when delivered, and that obligation could be discharged by any one. He could not, however, by the assignment, absolve himself from all obligations under the contract. The obligations of the contract still rested upon him, and resort could still be made to him for the payment of the dies, in case the assignee did not pay for them when tendered to it. After the assignment of the contract to the plaintiff, the defendant's obligation to perform still remained, and that obligation was due to the plaintiff, and for a breach of the obligation it became entitled to some damages."

Corvallis & A. R. R. Co. v. Portland, E. & E. Ry. Co.
84 Or. 524, 163 Pac. 1173 (1917)

This was an action by Corvallis & Alsea River Railroad Company (plaintiff) against Portland, Eugene & Eastern Railway Company (defendant). Judgment for plaintiff and defendant appealed. Judgment affirmed.

The Corvallis & A. R. R. Co. owned and operated a railroad line from Corvallis to Monroe. It entered into a contract with the Corvallis Lumber Manufacturing Co. whereby it agreed to build and operate a spur track to property of the Lumber Company. Corvallis & A. R. R. Co. sold its line, rolling stock, equipment, etc., together with its franchises, contracts, and other holdings, to Portland E. & E. Ry. Co. At the time of this sale the spur track had not been completed. The Corvallis & A. R. R. Co. assigned the contract for the building of the spur track to Portland E. & E. Ry. Co. at the time of the sale, and the Portland E. & E. Ry. Co. agreed to perform all the obligations of the contract. Portland E. & E. Ry. Co. did not complete the spur track and the Lumber Company sued Corvallis & A. R. R. Co. and recovered a judgment for damages. Corvallis & A. R. R. Co. brought this suit against Portland E. & E. Ry. Co. to recover the amount paid out on the judgment.

Bean, J. Defendant contends that the contract to build the extension was not assignable so as to obligate it to construct the same.

In the present case the contract involves no peculiar or special skill or personal element so far as the Lumber Company is concerned. A temporary road sufficient to transport the timber would fulfill the requirements of the contract. It appears that the Lumber Company assented to the agreement. We think the contract between the plaintiff and the Lumber Company was assignable.

The general rule is that an executory contract which is not necessarily personal in its character and which can consistently with the rights and interests of the adverse party be sufficiently executed by the assignee is assignable, where there is an absence of an agreement in the contract in regard to the assignability. In its very nature the contract in question was one which would have to be performed by many men. It is for that reason assignable.

In the case at bar the original contract was made between two different corporations. It necessarily follows that the work was to be done through agents and servants, and there could be no personal element involved. The Lumber Company was perfectly willing that the branch line of railroad should be constructed by plaintiff or any contractor or assignee with whom plaintiff might deal to that end. In 2 R. C. L. p. 601, 602, it is stated:

"As a general rule it may be stated that building and construction contracts, which of necessity usually require the labor and attention of a number of men, are assignable, unless it appears that the contract was made because of the knowledge, experience, or pecuniary ability of the contractor, or that for some reason he was especially fitted to carry it out, or that it involved some feature of a personal nature."

The usual test laid down in the cases is that a contract is generally assignable unless forbidden by public policy, or by the contract itself, or when its provisions are such as to show that one of the parties reposed a personal confidence in the other which he would not have been willing to repose in any other person. It is not pleaded in the present case that the Lumber Company would not have confided to any other company the duty of building the branch line. The work to be done by both parties was common ordinary work necessarily to be performed by many men.

In *Cutting Packing Co.* v. *Packers' Exchange*, the plaintiff made a contract to purchase and one Blackwood to sell crops of apricots for certains years, stating the minimum and maximum amounts. The agreement was assigned by plaintiff to defendant, but Blackwood refused to accept the defendant in place of the plaintiff. It was performed for two years. During the third year the defendant refused to accept the apricots, and the plaintiff received them, sold them upon the market for a less price than that stipulated by the contract, and thereupon brought action against the defendant for the deficiency by reason of the breach of the agreement. Mr. Justice Works, speaking for the court, said:

"The obligation thus assumed was apparent on the face of the contract. We therefore think it plain that, as the plaintiff, as assignor, was still bound to Blackwood to pay the price stipulated in the contract, notwithstanding the assignment, and as the defendant, as assignee, assumed such obligation, the plaintiff, as between it and the defendant, stood in the nature of a surety for the latter for the performance of the obligation. If this be correct, it then follows that from the assignment an implied contract arose between the plaintiff and defendant whereby the latter became bound to the former to receive and pay for the apricots according to the terms of the original contract."

The assignment of a contract does not discharge the assignor from his original undertaking.

Rights Acquired by Assignee

One who buys property, as a general rule, acquires no greater interest in the property than the seller of the property has. This rule of property law applies to the assignment of contracts. The assignee of a contract acquires no greater rights than the assignor has. Burch contracts to build a house for Archer for $5,000. Burch assigns the right to receive the $5,000 to Clark. Burch does not perform the contract according to its terms, and Burch's breach damages Archer in the amount of $1,000. Clark demands that Archer pay him (Clark) $5,000. Clark is entitled to $4,000. If Burch had sued on the contract, Burch could have recovered only $4,000 because of his breach of the contract. Clark acquired no greater rights than Burch had.

Archer borrows $1,000 from Burch. Archer sells Burch on credit $500 worth of materials. Later, Burch assigns his $1,000 claim against Archer to Clark. Clark can recover $500 from Archer. Had Burch sued Archer to recover the $1,000, Archer could have claimed credit for the $500 Burch owed Archer and the court would have allowed a judgment for the balance. Clark can acquire no greater rights than Burch had.

Notice plays an important part in the assignment of contracts. To protect the interests acquired in the contract, the assignee must give the obligor notice of the assignment. If the assignee or some person acting in his behalf does not give the obligor notice of the assignment of the contract and the obligor renders performance to the original obligee, the obligor has discharged his duties under the contract and the assignee cannot hold the obligor under the contract. The assignee will have a right of action against the assignor for the benefits the latter has wrongfully received. Archer borrows $1,000 from Burch. Burch assigns his rights to Clark. Clark does not give Archer notice of the assignment and when the debt falls due Archer pays Burch. The debt is discharged. If Clark had notified Archer of the assignment, payment to Burch would not have discharged the debt.

If a creditor assigns an account receivable and the debtor is not notified and at a later date the creditor assigns the same account to another assignee who does give notice to the debtor and the debtor pays the second assignee, the debtor is protected. The courts are not in accord as to the rights of the two assignees. Some hold that the assignee who first gives notice of the assignment has prior rights, while others hold that after a contract has once been assigned, the assignor has no further interest in it and cannot transfer any interest by an assignment, even though the assignee takes in good faith for value and without notice. Each view may be supported by logical arguments.

Archer borrows $1,000 from Burch. Burch assigns his rights to Clark who does not give notice. Thereafter Burch assigns the same right to Drew who gives Archer notice of the assignment. Archer pays Drew when the debt matures. The debt is discharged. If Drew gives notice of the assignment first and later Clark gives notice of the assignment, whom should Archer pay? The courts are not in accord in their answer to this question.

The right to assign future wages, the effect of such an assignment, and the formalities necessary to a valid assignment of future wages are matters which are for the most part controlled by state statutes. The statutes vary greatly in their nature and scope. At common law, an assignment of future wages was void unless the assignor had a contract of employment. The courts held that if one did not have a contract of employment, he had no present interest in future wages in that the employment might be terminated at any time by either party and, having no present interest in future wages, the employee had nothing which could be transferred. Later the courts held that if one was regularly employed, an assignment of future wages would be enforced, but the assignment would not apply if he quit the employment in which he was engaged at the time the assignment was made and obtained other employment. A few courts have held assignments of future wages enforceable even though the assignor had no employment at the time the assignment was made. Substantially all of the states have some statutes regulating the assignment of future wages which would alter or qualify the aforementioned rules. The statutes range from those making all assignments of future wages void to rather elaborate statutes regulating their assignment.

Sinclair Refining Co. v. Rosier
104 Kan. 719, 180 Pac. 807 (1919)

This was an action by Sinclair Refining Co. (plaintiff) against W. Lacy Rosier, doing business as the Hutchinson Oil Company (defendant). Judgment for defendant and plaintiff appealed. Judgment affirmed.

Defendant purchased a car of oil and a car of gasoline from the Chanute Refining Company on open account. The unpaid balance of the purchase price, $1,516.58, was assigned by the Chanute Refining Company to Sinclair Refining Company. Defendant refused to pay Sinclair Refining Company claiming that $289.70 had been paid on account and setting up a cross-demand for $1,477.30. The cross-demand arose from prior dealings between defendant and Chanute Refining Company. The state had an inspection law which was declared invalid. Defendant had paid inspection fees in the amount of $1,477.30 which were held by Chanute Refining Company and which, when the inspection law was declared invalid, should have been returned to the defendant.

Johnston, C. J. Plaintiff's objection to the rulings raises the question whether the defendant is entitled to set off his claim against the assigned account on which the action was brought. It was money had and received by plaintiff's assignor, to which the defendant was entitled, and it certainly constituted an actionable demand as against the Chanute Refining Company. We have the question, then, whether the assignment of the account to plaintiff cut off defenses which the defendant might have used against plaintiff's assignor. The thing assigned was an open account, which lacks the qualities of negotiable paper, and the plaintiff took it subject to any set-off or demand which the defendant held against the assignor at the time of the transfer.

It has been determined that, when demands exist between parties, one of them cannot defeat the demands of the other by an assignment, but that the assignee takes the assigned claim subject to any defense or demand that the other party holds against the assignor prior to the assignment. The larger demand is deemed to be satisfied up to the amount of the smaller demand.

The claim of defendant, based as it is on the fees charged against and paid by the defendant, and which were collected by plaintiff's assignor for the use of benefit of the defendant, amounted to a cross-demand, and from the time they were collected by the assignor cross-demands existed between the original parties, and for his demand the defendant had a right of action against the plaintiff's assignor.

It is alleged that the money had been collected by the assignor for the benefit of the defendant, and the demand had ripened into a right of action in his favor prior to the assignment of the account to the plaintiff. It being a subsisting claim, upon which he could maintain an action at the time the plaintiff's cause of action was in existence under the statute, the demand of either party is available in an action brought against the other, and the two demands must be deemed compensated so far as they equal each other.

Although it may not be important, it is alleged that the assigned account was received by plaintiff with full knowledge of the existence of the defendant's demand. The answer of the defendant was sufficiently definite, and it set forth a good ground of defense upon the cross-demand of the defendant.

Nanny v. H. E. Pogue Distillery Co. et al.
56 Cal. App. (2d) 817, 133 P. (2d) 686 (1943)

This was an action by J. V. Nanny (plaintiff) against H. E. Pogue Distillery Company (defendant) and City National Bank & Trust Company of Chicago as third party claimant. From a judgment for City National Bank & Trust Company of Chicago plaintiff appealed. Judgment affirmed.

On October 27, 1941, Pogue Distillery Company of Marysville, Kentucky, sold Sawelson Wholesale Company of Los Angeles, California, a car load of whiskey on open account. The whiskey was invoiced at $13,785.25 payable in thirty days and was shipped f.o.b. Marysville on November 21, 1941. On November 21, 1941, this account receivable was assigned by Pogue Distillery Company to City National Bank and Trust Company of Chicago. On November 22, 1941, City National Bank & Trust Company gave Sawelson Wholesale Company notice of the assignment. On December 2, 1942, Nanny, who had a claim against Pogue Distillery Company, garnisheed Sawelson Wholesale Company. The question raised on this suit was whether Sawelson Wholesale Company at the time the garnishment was served owed Pogue Distillery Company or City National Bank & Trust Company. If the assignment transferred the account to City National Bank & Trust Company, Nanny would get nothing through his garnishment.

York, P. J. "A mutual, open and current account, like an ordinary account, is property consisting of a chose in action, which is the subject of transfer, sale or assignment. . . . . And where an instrument was clearly intended as an assignment of the accounts, bills, and debts mentioned—whether absolutely or as security is immaterial—as between the parties, it was held to operate so as to transfer them to the assignee and *give him a right to have the moneys when collected applied to the payment of his debt. Kirk* v. *Roberts,* 3 Cal. Unrep. 671, 31 P. 620. To complete the assignment of an account as against the debtor, it is universally conceded that the debtor must have notice, or otherwise his debt will be discharged by payment to the assignor." 1 Cal. Jur. 150, 151. (Emphasis added.)

State ex rel. Crane Co. of Minnesota v. Stokke et al.
(Cochran Sargent Co. et al., Interveners)
65 S.D. 207, 272 N.W. 811 (1937)

This was an action by the state of South Dakota on the relation of the Crane Company of Minnesota (plaintiff) against Iver Stokke and the Aetna Casualty & Surety Company (defendants). Cochran Sargent Company, William D. Evans, and Fred J. Huhn intervened. From a portion of the judgment in favor of William D. Evans, both the Aetna Casualty Company and Cochran Sargent Company appealed. Judgment reversed and remanded with directions.

Iver Stokke entered into a series of contracts with the state of South Dakota whereby he contracted to install heating and plumbing in the School for the Deaf. Aetna Casualty Company signed bonds for Stokke guaranteeing performance of the contracts. The applications for the bonds contained an assignment clause which became effective as of August 10, 1929, and operated as an assignment of all sums due to Stokke from the state. No notice of this assignment was given to the state. Stokke was indebted to Cochran Sargent Company and on April 14, 1930, assigned to it an amount due and owing to him in the sum of $1,560. Cochran Sargent Company immediately gave written notice of the assignment to the proper state official. Stokke has been adjudged bankrupt.

Per Curiam. There is no question but that Stokke made an assignment to The Aetna and likewise to Cochran Sargent Company. What Stokke had to assign and did assign was a contract right to receive money—a chose in action.

The Aetna and Cochran Sargent Company occupy the position of successive assignees of a chose in action. Cochran Sargent Company admits that the assignment to The Aetna was prior in point of time. The record also shows that when Cochran Sargent Company took its assignment it had no notice of the prior assignment, and the record further shows that Cochran Sargent Company, although the subsequent assignee, was the first to give notice to the debtor.

The Aetna maintains that the first assignee should prevail; Cochran Sargent Company maintains that the assignee who first gave notice to the debtor should prevail. These contentions present squarely a most interesting and much contraverted question. The Aetna contends for what is frequently known as the American rule, which has been the law in a numerical minority of our state jurisdictions and which became the law of the federal courts by the decision in the leading case of *Salem Trust Co.* v. *Manufacturers' Finance Co.* (1924) 264 U.S. 182, 44 S. Ct. 266, 68 L. Ed. 628, 31 A. L. R. 867. Cochran Sargent Company advocates what is generally denominated the English rule arising out of the case of *Dearle* v. *Hall* (1828) 3 Russ. 1, 38 Eng. Rep., Full Reprint, 475. The situation is well stated by a commentator in 33 *Yale Law Journal*, 767, as follows:

"In the leading case of *Dearle* v. *Hall* the English courts early established the rule later broadened to cover all assignments of choses in action that a subsequent assignee of a cestui's interest who inquired of the trustee and gave him notice of his assignment was entitled to priority over a former assignee who failed to give such notice. This doctrine was based on the analogy to the sale of chattels to a later vendee by a vendor who has been allowed to remain in possession, and also on the theory that it was the only way to protect against the fraud of the assignor. A few years later the requirement of inquiry was eliminated, and prior notice to the debtor alone was held sufficient. This is the present so-called English doctrine. The rule does not apply to assignments of equitable interests in land, or to cases where recordation of assignments is provided for. Nor can the second assignee recover unless he is a purchaser for value and without notice of the prior assignment. Other courts, however, refused to adopt this doctrine, and applied the general rule that between equal equities, the one prior in time prevails regardless of notice. The basis of this latter rule is often said to be that the assignor has conveyed all his 'title' to the first assignee and has nothing left to convey to the second, and that notice is not necessary to consummate the right of the first assignee. Even under this theory if the second assignee obtains payment from the debtor, or effects a novation with the debtor, or reduces his claim to a judgment, he prevails over the first assignee. And the first assignee may by his conduct be estopped from claiming priority. In the United States the authorities are almost evenly divided between the two views. The United States Supreme Court has recently in the case of *Salem Trust Co.* v. *Manufacturers' Finance Co.* definitely adopted the rule preferring the first assignee."

Even the courts adhering to the American view of protecting the first assignee require him to yield to a subsequent assignee first giving notice in some instances and under some circumstances.

As stated by the United States Supreme Court in the Salem Trust Co. Case, supra: "If equities are equal, the first in time is best in right. Otherwise the stronger equity will prevail."

We think therefore that because of the stronger equity of the Cochran Sargent Company, so far as concerns the sum of $1,281.54 for which they might have enforced a claim against The Aetna, that under either view Cochran Sargent Company must prevail over The Aetna to this extent. In this case we are dealing with a surety.

So in this case we believe that Cochran Sargent has a stronger equity than The Aetna to the extent of $1,281.54. Cochran Sargent took its assignment to protect the surety as much as itself, and now the surety is claiming an assignment of the same fund at the expense of the creditor whose claim it has undertaken to secure. Clearly, it seems to us, equities are not equal in this case. As between the two, Cochran Sargent Company has a stronger equity than the Aetna in the $1,281.54 and to that extent must prevail. As to the balance of the fund we believe the Aetna should prevail. We are convinced that the American doctrine has the support of the better reason and we are content to adopt it as the law of this state, and give it application whenever the equities are equal.

Third Party Beneficiaries

As a general rule, a person not a party to a contract cannot bring suit on the contract. However, certain third party beneficiaries under a contract, although they are not parties to the contract, may bring a suit on it. Third party beneficiaries have been divided into three classes: (1) donee beneficiaries, (2) creditor beneficiaries, and (3) incidental beneficiaries. Ordinarily, a donee beneficiary or a creditor beneficiary can bring an action against the promisor, but an incidental beneficiary has no right of action against the promisor or the promisee.

Life insurance contracts payable to a named beneficiary are treated as a separate class of contracts. The relation of the parties to the contract depends upon the nature of the policy of insurance. All the courts permit the beneficiary under a life insurance policy to enforce the policy by a direct action. It is true that in some states persons not having an "insurable interest" in the insured's life may not be named beneficiary; and if they are named, they cannot take under the policy.

Archer agrees to paint a picture for Burch if Burch will pay Clark $100 within 30 days after the picture is completed and delivered to Burch. If Burch does not pay Clark, Clark can sue Burch and recover.

Clark is a donee beneficiary in that he is the recipient of the benefits of Burch's promise but has not furnished the consideration. Archer purchases an automobile from Clark on open account. Archer sells the automobile to Burch and Burch pays Archer $100 in cash and agrees to pay Clark the unpaid balance of the purchase price which Archer owes to Clark. Burch does not pay this balance. Clark can sue Burch and recover. Clark is a creditor beneficiary. Burch's promise to pay Clark the debt which Archer owes Clark on the purchase price of the article sold is part of the purchase price which Burch has paid for the article, and the courts will permit Clark to recover in a suit against Burch.

Burch contracts to dig a ditch which will drain a low place on Archer's farm. The draining of this low place on Archer's farm will improve Clark's farm which adjoins Archer's farm. Burch does not perform the contract. Clark will not be allowed to recover in a suit against Burch for damages for breach of the contract. Clark is an incidental beneficiary, and although he would benefit from the performance of the contract, the contract was not entered into for the purpose of benefiting Clark; therefore, Clark has no legal interest in its performance.

Another type of contract on which a third party may bring an action is one made for the benefit of the community. Not all contracts made by a municipality or any other governmental division may be sued on by an inhabitant, but if the contract provides for the performance of a duty owed to the public or is intended for the benefit of the individual inhabitants, an inhabitant may sue in his own right on the contract if he has been injured by a breach of the contract.

Le Ballister v. Redwood Theatres, Inc., et al.
— Cal. App. —, 36 P. (2d) 827 (1934)

This was an action by Homer L. Le Ballister (plaintiff) against Redwood Theatres, Inc., and another (defendants). Judgment for defendants and plaintiff appealed. Judgment reversed.

Defendants purchased from the National Theatres Syndicate certain stock for the sum of $43,937.50. The agreement of purchase and sale contained the following provision: "It is further understood and agreed that . . . we will retain your Mr. Homer Le Ballister, now employed by you as manager, in some suitable position for a period of one year at a salary of not less than eighty-five dollars per week." Defendants discharged plaintiff before the expiration of the one-year period. Plaintiff sues to recover damages for breach of the contract. Defendants contend that plaintiff was not a party to the contract and has no right to bring suit on the contract.

Spence, J. Appellant contends that said contract was one made expressly for his benefit and that the trial court erred in denying the recovery upon the ground stated. In our opinion this contention must be sustained. While the contract was not made solely and exclusively for appellant's benefit, it was not necessary that it should have been so made in order to entitle him to recover. The word "expressly" means "in an express manner; in direct or unmistakable terms; explicitly; definitely; directly." Here the respondent corporation agreed in direct and unmistakable terms to employ appellant for a definite period at a salary of not less than $85 per week. It could have done nothing more than it did do to make this provision one "expressly" for appellant's benefit.

Respondent cites certain authorities from this jurisdiction, but we find none of them in point. In the California Annotations of the Restatement of the Law of Contracts, the author deals with this subject under section 133 as follows: "The present rule is codified in Cal. Civ. Code Sec. 1559: 'A contract, made expressly for the benefit of a third person, may be enforced by him at any time before the parties thereto rescind.' It is evident, therefore, that the only statutory requirement is that the beneficiary be express. Whether or not a contract is one for the express benefit of a third person is a fact sometimes difficult to determine. The test appears to be whether an intent so to benefit the third party appears from the terms of the contract." From a reading of the agreement before us, we believe that the intent to benefit appellant clearly appears from its terms.

QUESTIONS AND PROBLEMS

1. Floyd entered into a contract with the Woodburn Public Schools whereby he agreed to convey to school the children living in a designated district. The contract was for a five-year period. When the contract had three years to run, Floyd assigned the contract to Wells. Woodburn Public Schools refused to permit Wells to convey the children. Is the contract assignable?
2. Dix entered into a contract of employment with Armour & Co. The contract provided that Dix would not assign wages due under the contract, and that any such assignment would be void unless Armour & Co. consented to the assignment in writing. Dix assigned all of his wages due under the contract to Furniture Co. Armour & Co. refused to recognize the validity of the assignment. Is the assignment valid?
3. Archer was negotiating with Burch for employment. Archer executed an assignment purporting to assign to Clark all moneys to become due to Archer under the contract when executed. Thereafter Archer and Burch entered into the contemplated contract. Is the assignment valid?
4. Bell had a contract with the City of New York whereby he was to do all the printing for the city and was to furnish the city with paper and stationery for one year. Bell assigned to Field all the bills which might become due under the contract to the amount of $1,500. Field gave the City of New York notice of the assignment. After notice of the assignment the City of New York paid Bell sums in excess of $1,500 for work done and materials furnished under the contract. Bell was nsolvent. Field sued the City of New York to re over $1,500. Is Field entitled t a judgment?

5. In Problem 4 would the City of New York be liable to Field if he had failed to give the City notice of the assignment?
6. Archer owes Burch $100. Burch assigns the claim to Clark. Thereafter Burch buys goods of the value of $75 from Archer on credit. After this transaction, Clark gives Archer notice of the assignment. How much does Archer owe Clark?
7. In Problem 6 if Archer had extended credit to Burch after Clark had given Archer notice of the assignment, how much could Clark recover from Archer?
8. Biggs sold a horse to Sims for $200, which sum Sims agreed to pay to Wade in thirty days. Sims did not pay and Wade sued Sims. Could Wade recover a judgment?
9. Magnier and several other hatters in the city of New Orleans entered into a contract to close their respective stores on Sunday. The contract provided that, in the event one of the contracting parties opened his store on Sunday, the violator of the obligation would pay $100 for the benefit of the asylum of St. Joseph's Orphans. Magnier violated the contract and St. Joseph's Orphans Association sued to recover the $100 penalty. Can the St. Joseph's Orphans Association recover a judgment?

CHAPTER XII

DISCHARGE

Interpretation

In the ordinary course of business, agreements entered into by business men are performed by both parties to the agreement without misunderstanding or controversy. In the exceptional case, the agreement is not fulfilled and one of the parties resorts to the court for aid. The court has at least two duties to perform: it must determine whether the agreement into which the parties have entered is a binding contract; and if a binding contract does exist, the court must determine what rights are awarded and what duties are imposed by the contract. This latter process is generally termed interpretation.

The statement is frequently made that in interpreting a contract the court endeavors to carry out the intentions of the parties; however, to determine the actual intention of each party to a contract approaches the impossible. The court determines the intention of the parties by applying an objective test to the words and other manifestations of intention of the parties and then declares this result to be the intention of the parties. This system is not perfect but has met with a reasonable degree of success from a practical standpoint.

To lend certainty to the interpretation of contracts, the courts have adopted certain standards which they follow. The contract is read as a whole, and taking the circumstances surrounding the transaction into consideration, the court determines the principal objective of the parties. In reading the contract the courts give words their usual meaning unless, from the entire writing and the surrounding circumstances, it appears that a different meaning was intended. Technical words are given their technical meaning unless a different intention appears. In cases of doubt an interpretation which gives a reasonable and lawful result is favored. If the parties have used general terms followed by special terms, the court will assume that the special terms qualify the general terms. If the parties use a form contract or a contract which is partly printed and partly in writing and there is a conflict between the printed terms and the written terms, the written terms will control. If there is an ambiguity in a contract and one of the parties has drawn the contract, the contract will be construed more strongly against the party who drew it.

Archer sells an automobile to Burch on a conditional sales contract. Archer has a printed contract which he has had drawn for his use in such transactions. Burch signs Archer's standard form contract. In case of dispute if a provision of the contract is ambiguous, the interpretation which favors Burch will be given to it.

If an individual, not legally trained, wishes to draw a contract, he should express his intentions in simple, well-selected words, avoiding technical terms and verbosity. Such a contract will stand the test in court. If the proposed contract deals with a complicated technical transaction where nicety of expression is essential, the parties should have a well-trained, experienced attorney draft the contract.

In business transactions the courts, in interpreting the agreement of the parties, take into consideration usage or custom. In some markets a gesture may be sufficient expression of intention to bring into existence a binding contract involving a substantial sum and entailing many detailed duties. Usage in the market supplies all the unexpressed terms of the agreement. Usage is habitual or customary practice. A particular usage may be followed by a large number of persons in a large area or by a few persons in a small area; it may be followed by a geographic area or a city, county, state or section of the country, or it may be followed by a special group of persons, as those employed in a certain trade or members of an association.

Usage may give to certain words a meaning differing from the general meaning of the words. It may add to a written contract provisions not actually written into the writing. This practice is not a violation of the parol evidence rule. The courts have held that there is a presumption that the parties did not intend to reduce the entire agreement to writing but intended to contract with reference to those known usages. If both contracting parties live in the same community or are members of the same trade or association, the presumption is that they contract with reference to the usages of the community or trade and that they are both familiar with such usages. If the parties do not wish so to contract, they should express an intention not to be bound by such usages. Where the parties are not residents of the same community or trade group, the presumption is that they contract in regard to general usages and not in respect to local or special usages. It may be shown, however, that the local or special usages were known to both parties and that they contracted in reference to them. Where different usages prevail in different sections, the presumption is that the parties contracted in reference to the usage prevailing at the place where the contract was made and is to be performed.

Jacobs et al. v. Danciger et al.
328 Mo. 458, 41 S. W. (2d) 389 (1931)

This was an action by Floyd E. Jacobs (plaintiff) against Abe Danciger and others (defendants). Judgment for plaintiff and defendants appealed. Judgment reversed and remanded. [NOTE: the reversal was based on points of law not included in this abstract.]

A contract for sale of 150 bales of hops at 85 cents per pound, to be delivered, 50 bales in October, 50 bales in November, and 50 bales in December, 1920, was entered into. The market price of hops dropped to 47 cents per pound and defendants notified plaintiff that they would not accept delivery of the hops. Plaintiff brought suit to recover damages for failure to accept and pay for hops. Defendants claimed the contract was void because the quantity of hops contracted for was indefinite (150 bales at 85 cents per pound). The plaintiff offered evidence to show that by custom and usage a "bale" of hops weighs 200 pounds, and defendants objected to its admission.

Gantt, P. J. Defendants contend the quantity of hops is not fixed by the contract, and for that reason the contract is void under the Statute of Frauds. The quantity is fixed at 150 bales at 85 cents per pound. There was evidence tending to show, and the jury found, that by trade usage a bale of hops weighed 200 pounds. The evidence was admissible under the well-settled rule, which follows: "Valid usages concerning the subject matter of a contract of which the parties are chargeable with knowledge, are by implication incorporated therein, unless expressly or impliedly concluded by its terms and are admissible to aid in its interpretation, not as tending in any respect or manner to contradict, add to, take from or vary the contract, but upon the theory that the usage forms a part of the contract."

This trade meaning of the word "bale" became a part of the contract and fixed the quantity purchased at 30,000 pounds.

Parol Evidence Rule

When one signs a written contract it is of outstanding importance that the writing covers the entire agreement and that it expresses the intentions of the parties in language that is clear and free from ambiguities. If suit is brought on the written contract, the writing is accepted in court as the final expression of the parties and parol (oral) evidence is not admissible for the purpose of adding to, varying, or contradicting the terms of the writing. The rule of law is based on the presumption that the parties have given careful consideration to the writing and have embodied in it the final expression of their intentions. Archer and Burch are negotiating a lease and during the preliminary negotiations certain alterations to the building are discussed, and

Archer declares his intention to make the alterations. A written lease is drawn and signed by the parties. The lease makes no provisions for alterations. Archer refuses to make alterations and Burch brings suit. Burch offers oral evidence to prove that alterations were to be made. The oral evidence will not be admitted. Such evidence would add to or alter the written lease.

Oral evidence is admissible for the purpose of attacking the validity of the contract or for the purpose of attacking the existence of a contract. In the hypothetical case stated above, oral evidence, which might be offered to prove that Burch was induced to sign the lease by fraudulent representations, would be admissible. Also, evidence to prove that the lease was illegal because the building was to be used for an illegal purpose in which Archer (the lessor) was a participant would be admissible. Burch could also bring an action in equity to have an alteration provision added to the lease on the ground that its omission was a mistake. Before a court of equity will reform a writing on the ground of mistake, the party bringing the action must convince the court beyond a reasonable doubt that the omission of the provision was a mutual mistake of the parties. Parol evidence is admissible to establish the existence of an agreement that the writing was not to become binding until a future day or on the happening of some future event. In short, parol evidence is not admissible to show that the parties intended something different than their writing imparts, but it is admissible to show that the writing is not an enforceable contract.

Union Fur Shop v. Max Melzer, Inc.
133 N.J. Eq. 416, 29 A. (2d) 873 (1943)

This was an action by the Union Fur Shop, Inc. (plaintiff) against Max Melzer, Inc. (defendant). From a decree for defendant, plaintiff appealed. Decree affirmed.

Plaintiff was the owner of a retail fur business in Union City, New Jersey, and in 1936 sold the business to the defendant. The bill of sale contained the following clause: "6. The Party of the first part hereby grants to the parties of the second part, the right to use the trade name such as the Union Fur Shop, or any name similar thereto, in the conduct of its business on the premises herein mentioned. . . . ." The premises mentioned were 4539 Bergenline Avenue. The building was owned by plaintiff who owned the controlling interest in the business sold. On the expiration of the lease the plaintiff refused to renew the lease and the defendant moved about five doors up the street. The plaintiff immediately started a new business in the vacated building under the name of the Union Fur Shop and brought this action to prevent the defendant from continuing to use the name on the ground that under the terms of the bill of sale the defendant had the right to use the name only in the conduct of its business at the premises herein mentioned. Oral evidence was offered to show that the parties intended to convey to defendant the ownership of the trade name Union Fur Shop.

Heher, J. A deed of conveyance absolute on its face may in equity be shown to be a mere security and treated as such. And parol evidence is admissible to prove that the writing has not become effective as a contract, or that the assent has been induced by fraud, mistake, or duress. It is the general rule that a parol condition deferring the effect of a sealed instrument is inadmissible, but that lack of the intent essential to delivery may be shown. There is a substantial difference in this regard between parol evidence elicited to demonstrate that the instrument does not express the true intention of the parties and that educed to reveal circumstances making it unconscionable and inequitable to effectuate the common intention. In the latter event, the language is not thereby varied by parol. "Oral evidence is admissible to reform a written instrument, or to subvert or overthrow it entirely, but not to vary or alter it."

Here, by appropriate averments and prayers in the answer and the counterclaim, respondent sought a reformation of the bill of sale to express the intention of the parties as found by the vice chancellor; and so it may have relief in that form. The proof of mistake in the expression of the common intention is of the requisite quality. It meets the standard of conviction which moves the conscience of the Chancellor to a decree of reformation.

Parol evidence was admissible to establish and rectify a mistake of this character, and thus to subserve the plainest requirements of justice. The writing may be reformed to accord with the contract that was in fact made but erroneously expressed.

Conditions

The parties, by the terms of their agreement, may make the duty of performance dependent on the happening of some event. Such a provision in a contract is known as a condition precedent, i.e., the duty of performance does not arise until the fulfillment of the condition. Such clauses are usually introduced by such terms as "if," "as soon as," "when," etc. Archer agrees to build a fish pond for Burch and Burch agrees to pay Archer $1,000 for the job, the work to be done during the summer of 1946-47, if Burch can obtain a permit from the state. The performance of the contract is conditioned on the obtaining of the permit, and if the permit is not obtained, the parties will be discharged from their obligations on the contract.

In some contracts, by the terms of the contract, the parties assume legal liabilities at the time the contract is entered into, but the agreement contains a clause which provides that on the happening of a stated event one of the parties will be discharged from his obligation.

Such a provision is known as a condition subsequent. Archer insures his house against fire with the Burch Insurance Company. The policy contains a clause that in the event gasoline in excess of thirty gallons is stored on the premises the insurance policy shall become null and void and of no effect. If Archer stores gasoline on the premises in excess of thirty gallons, Burch Insurance Company will be discharged from their liability on the fire insurance policy.

In many situations the courts will interpret the provisions of a contract as dependent, i.e., neither party is required to perform unless the other party tenders performance and if neither party takes the initiative and tenders performance both parties will be discharged from their legal obligations. Archer agrees to sell Burch his white-face horse for cash, and Burch agrees to buy and pay Archer $500 cash for his white-face horse. If neither party makes a tender within a reasonable time, both will be discharged from legal liability. If either of the parties wishes to enforce the contract, he must first make a tender. To make a tender, Archer will have to take the horse to Burch and offer the horse to Burch on payment of the $500. If Burch wishes to make a tender, he will have to take $500 in money to Archer and demand the horse. Neither party will have the right to recover in a suit for breach of the contract until he has made a tender of performance and the other party has refused to perform.

In many contracts the promises are independent, i.e., the duty of one of the parties to perform is not conditioned on the happening of any event nor on the other party's tender of performance. In all contract situations if one of the parties is guilty of a material breach of the contract, the injured party will be discharged from his duty to perform. The effect of a breach of contract will be discussed under "Performance."

All conditions in contracts need not be expressly written into the contract. The circumstances of the case may be such that the courts will be justified in finding that the duty of one of the parties to perform is conditioned on the happening of some event.

Mascioni et al. v. I. B. Miller, Inc.
261 N.Y. 1, 184 N.E. 473 (1933)

This was an action by John Mascioni and another (plaintiffs) against I. B. Miller, Inc. (defendant). From a judgment of the Appellate Division, reversing a judgment of the trial court for the defendant, the defendant appealed. Judgment of the trial court affirmed.

The defendant as general contractor contracted to construct an apartment building for Village Apartments, Inc., described in the contract as "Owner." Defendant subcontracted the cement work to plaintiffs. The subcontract contained the following clause in regard to payments: "Payments to be made as received from the Owner." Defendant has received no payments from the owner.

The problem presented on this appeal is whether the defendant assumed an absolute obligation to pay, though for convenience payment might be postponed till moneys were received from the owner, or whether the defendant's obligation to pay arose only if and when the owner made payment to the defendant.

Lehman, J. A provision for the payment of an obligation upon the happening of an event does not become absolute until the happening of the event. Whether the defendant's express promise to pay is construed as a promise to pay "if" payment is made by the owner or "when" such payment is made, "the result must be the same; since, if the event does not befall, or a time coincident with the happening of the event does not arrive, in neither case may performance be exacted."

True, a debt with consequent obligation to pay may exist aside from any express promise to pay. Then a condition annexed to an express promise to pay the debt may render the promise to pay conditional without making the debt subject to the same condition. "It must be admitted, however, that a condition annexed to a promise to pay a debt will commonly, upon the true construction of the instrument in which it is contained, extend to the debt itself. There is a difference also between a promise to pay a debt on a certain condition, and a proviso that the debt shall be payable only upon a certain condition; for the latter necessarily renders the debt itself conditional." Langdell, *Summary of the Law of Contracts*, Sec. 36. In this case, if there were no express promise to pay a stipulated price for stipulated work, such a promise would be implied. There is, however, an express promise to pay moneys "as received from the Owner," and the event upon which that promise would ripen into an absolute, immediate obligation has not occurred. From the express promise to pay upon the happening of an event, an inference may be drawn that the parties did not intend or impliedly agree that payment should be made even if the event does not occur.

Here on its face the contract provides for a promise to perform in exchange for a promise to pay as payments are "received from the Owner." Performance by the plaintiff would inure directly to the benefit of the owner and indirectly to the benefit of the defendant, because the defendant had a contract with the owner to perform the work for a stipulated price. The defendant would not profit by the plaintiffs' performance unless the owner paid the stipulated price. That was the defendant's risk, but the defendant's promise to pay the plaintiffs for stipulated work on condition that payment was received by the defendant shifted that risk to the plaintiffs, if the condition was a material part of the exchange of plaintiffs' promise to perform for defendant's promise to pay.

NOTE.—In the second paragraph of Judge Lehman's opinion he states, "True, a debt with consequent obligations to pay may exist aside from any express promise to pay." In this statement the judge refers to the following type of situation: Archer purchases a suit of clothes from Burch. He explains that he is doing some special work for Clark for which he expects to receive payments every two weeks, and promises to pay Burch as "this money comes in." If Archer does not receive payment from Clark, he (Archer) will not be discharged from his obligation to Burch, but will be obligated to pay after the lapse of a reasonable time. The circumstances are such that it is clear that in extending credit to Archer, Burch was not assuming the risk of Archer receiving the expected payments from Clark. Here a condition annexed to an express promise to pay the debt has rendered the promise to pay conditional without making the debt subject to the same conditions.

First National Bank of Salem v. Morgan et al.
132 Or. 515, 286 Pac. 558 (1930)

This was an action by First National Bank of Salem (plaintiff) against Hector Morgan and another (defendants). Judgment for plaintiff and defendants appealed. Judgment reversed and remanded with directions to enter judgment for defendants.

Plaintiff brought suit on a promissory note given in payment for certain corporate stock. The note contained the following provision: "Said units of stock are not to be issued or delivered until this note is paid in full and then the said unit shares of stock are to be issued and delivered." The note was not paid when due. The bank brought suit on the note, but it did not tender the unit shares of stock before bringing suit and has never tendered said stock. The defendants contended that the promises were dependent and the bank not having tendered the stock had no right to recover on the note.

Rand, J. Whether covenants are dependent or independent is a question of the intention of the parties as deduced from the terms of the contract. If the parties intend that performance by each of them is in no way conditioned upon performance by the other, the covenants are independent, but if they intend performance by one to be conditioned upon performance by the other, the covenants are mutually dependent.

In determining whether the parties in the instant case intended that payment of the entire amount due upon the note was to be conditional upon the delivery of the stock at the time the note was paid, we must consider not only the words of the particular clause quoted above but also the language of the whole contract as well as the nature of the act required and the subject-matter to which it relates. When so considered, it will be seen that the mutual covenants go to the whole consideration on both sides—the payment of a certain definite sum of money by one side and the issuance and delivery of a specified number of shares of stock by the other. While there is no fixed definite rule of law by which the intention in all cases can be determined, yet we must remember, as stated by Professor Williston, that, since concurrent conditions protect both parties, courts endeavor so far as is not inconsistent with the expressed intention to construe performances as concurrent conditions. The necessity of construing these covenants as concurrent in order to avoid gross injustice in the instant case is apparent, for without a delivery of the stock the whole consideration for which the note was given must of necessity fail. While it is true that it is the intention which the parties had at the time the contract was entered into, and not an intention which later arose because of subsequent events, yet it is very apparent that the intention, as expressed in the contract, was that upon payment of the note the stock was to be delivered at and when the note was paid. In this action the bank is seeking to enforce payment of the note without delivering or offering to deliver the stock. If successful in the action, the bank will recover the entire consideration without defendants receiving anything in exchange therefor.

Zambetti v. Commodores Land Co.
102 Fla. 586, 136 So. 644 (1931)

This was an action by Victor Zambetti (plaintiff) against the Commodores Land Company (defendant). Judgment for defendant and plaintiff appealed. Judgment affirmed.

Zambetti purchased a lot on a contract for a consideration of $8,500 payable as follows: $1,500 cash on execution and delivery of contract, and the balance in three equal installments, payable one, two, and three years from date. The contract was dated March 1, 1927, and bound the vendor to perform the following covenants:

"(a) Within sixty days after the date of this contract to let a contract for, or itself commence, the construction of and thereafter within a reasonable time cause to be completed or to complete the paving at its own expense with some appropriate material to a width of twenty-four (24) feet of the street, if any, shown upon said plat in front of said lot, if such street has not been then already paved.

"(b) Within said sixty days after the date of this contract, to let a contract for, or itself begin, the construction at its own expense of a water main under the street, if any, shown upon said plat in front of said lot, according to the requirements of the public officials of the City of Jacksonville in charge of the water works department of said city, and thereafter to prosecute such work to completion and cause said water main to be connected with the public water system of the City of Jacksonville, if such water main has not been already so constructed and connected."

The Land Co. did not perform and Zambetti brought this action to rescind the contract and recover the cash payment made.

Terrell, J. The case turns on the question of whether the covenants, (a) and (b), as here quoted, are dependent or independent. The appellant contends that they are dependent to be performed concurrently with the covenant to pay the purchase price. Not having been performed nor contract let for their performance as per nomination in the main contract, appellant, as complainant below, brought this suit to rescind.

Generally, covenants to an agreement are said to be dependent when made by two parties to a deed or contract and are such that the thing covenanted to be done on the part of each enters into the whole consideration for the covenant on the other part, or where the acts or covenants of the parties are concurrent, and are to be done or performed at the same time, and neither party can maintain an action against the other without averring and proving performance on his part. Covenants for conveyance and payment of the consideration for land as do covenants by a lessee to pay rent and by a lessor to make essential improvements or repairs without which the premises would be useless are typical examples of dependent covenants. Covenants are construed to be dependent or independent according to the intention and meaning of the parties as gleaned from all the circumstances of the case and any technical application of words should give way to such an intention.

In the case at bar, the covenants on the part of vendor to pave and extend the water main and the vendee to pay the purchase price did not run concurrently. The covenant to pay the purchase price ran over a period of three years, while the covenant to pave the street in front of and extend the water main to the lot involved in this litigation was to be contracted to be done within sixty days. The unpaved portion of the street in front of lot 4 was between three and four hundred feet long, and whether this portion was to be paved in full or only in front of lot 4 (which we do not here decide) is immaterial to the disposition of this cause, as from the showing in the record the cost of the paving in either event will be but a small part of the cost of the lot. The cost of executing the covenant to pave and extend the water main can be easily ascertained, and while the execution of this covenant will add to the accessibility and desirability of lot 4, it will not add materially to its intrinsic value, nor will it affect a particle the value, accessibility, or desirability of the lots or community generally in the vicinity of lot 4.

The record discloses that lot 4 was purchased to build a warehouse upon, that there were other warehouses in the same vicinity, and that it was in all respects suitable for that purpose. The covenants provoking this litigation were to be performed at different times and there is no indication whatever in the contract that the parties considered them as dependent. By the very terms of the contract the complainant could have prosecuted an action for damages against defendant for its failure to comply with the contract and could have reduced the same to judgment long prior to the due date of his final payment. Where this can be done and his damages can be readily ascertained, his remedy at law is adequate and he cannot seek the aid of a court of equity to rescind.

The rule seems to be well settled that when covenants on the part of different parties to a contract are to be performed at different times or when covenants to make improvements are independent of covenants to purchase, or when a covenant goes only to part of the consideration on both sides and a breach of such covenant may be compensated in damages and will not defeat the purpose of the contract, the covenant is independent and an action at law may be maintained for its breach by the party or parties interested.

Architects' and Engineers' Certificates

The building or construction contracts in common use usually contain a clause making the payments provided for in the contract conditional on the production of the certificate of a named architect or engineer. The courts enforce such a provision and will deny the contractor the right to recover in a suit on the contract unless he produces the certificate or can excuse his failure to produce it. The production of the certificate is excused by showing that the named architect or engineer is dead, insane, or otherwise incapacitated and cannot issue the certificate; that the certificate is fraudulently, collusively, or arbitrarily withheld; and in some instances the courts have excused the production of the certificate if it can be shown that the withholding is unreasonable. As a general rule if the architect or engineer is acting honestly and has some reason for withholding the certificate, the courts will not allow a recovery unless it is produced. The parties have contracted for the expert judgment of the named architect or engineer and if he has exercised that judgment honestly the courts will not substitute their judgment for that of the architect or engineer and hold that the architect or engineer is mistaken or his decision is incorrect. If a mistake has been made in computation, the courts will correct it.

City of San Antonio et al. v. McKenzie Construction Co.
S. Ct. of Texas, 150 S.W. (2d) 989 (1941)

This was an action by the McKenzie Construction Company (plaintiff) against City of San Antonio (defendant). A judgment for plaintiff was reversed by the Court of Civil Appeals and both plaintiff and defendant joined in this appeal. Judgment of the Court of Civil Appeals affirmed.

McKenzie Construction Company brought suit to recover a judgment for $104,639.48, alleged to be due it by the City of San Antonio under an express written contract for the construction of a dam. During the trial of the case the plaintiff claimed that certain unauthorized charges were made by the city and its engineer. By the terms of the contract certain decisions were to be made by the engineer during the performance of the work.

Critz, J. When parties to a building contract agree to submit questions which may arise thereunder to the decision of the engineer, his decision is final and conclusive, unless in making it he is guilty of fraud, misconduct, or such gross mistake as would imply bad faith or failure to exercise an honest judgment. Under this rule it would be hard to define the exact character or quantum of proof required to show that an umpire or arbitrator has been guilty of fraud, misconduct, or gross mistake. However, it certainly can be said that when an engineer is called on to make a decision under a construction contract such as this his decision cannot be set aside for fraud, misconduct, or gross mistake, simply by proving that some other engineer would have acted differently or given a different decision. Also, we think an engineer's decision under a contract like this cannot be impeached simply on a conflict of evidence as to what he ought to have decided. This must be true, because any other rule would simply leave the matter open for a court or jury to substitute its judgment and discretion for the judgment and discretion of the engineer; and such a procedure or rule would practically nullify the arbitration or umpire agreement. The decision of an engineer or architect under a contract like this is presumed to be correct, and to have been given while acting within the scope of his authority.

Performance

The majority of contracts are discharged by performance. In some types of transactions absolute performance is expected, while in other types of transactions absolute performance is not required. If Archer owes Burch $10, Archer will not be discharged by performance of the obligation unless he pays Burch $10. If Archer contracts to build a cement driveway for Burch, the cement to be four inches in thickness, Archer will be discharged even though the cement is not uniformly four inches thick on the entire driveway. In a contract of this nature, perfection of performance is not possible. If the thickness of the cement does not vary more than is customary in work of this type, Archer will have performed his obligations under the contract and will be discharged.

If one of the parties does not perform the contract in accordance with its terms but he does make an honest effort to perform and his performance approaches that required under the circumstances, the courts will allow a recovery of the contract price less the damages resulting from the failure to completely perform. This is known as substantial performance.

If one of the parties performs the contract in part and then wilfully abandons the contract and refuses to complete performance, he will not be permitted to recover any part of the contract price. If the other party to the contract voluntarily accepts the part performance and is benefited by it, the courts will allow a recovery of the value of the benefits conferred. The recovery is based on quasi contract and not on the contract.

When one of the parties to a contract is guilty of a material breach of the contract, the other party is discharged from his obligations under the contract. The breach may be either a failure to perform on time or a failure to do those acts required by the contract.

Whether or not failure to perform on time will be a material breach of the contract and discharge the other party from his obligations depends on the facts and circumstances of the case and on the intentions of the parties. If performance must be completed within a stated time, "time is of the essence of the contract." It has been stated that in contracts of merchants time is of the essence, but this is too broad a statement to be accepted as a rule of law. Archer purchases 1,000 bushels of wheat from Burch, and Burch agrees to deliver the wheat at Archer's mill on Tuesday next before noon. If Burch tenders the wheat at any time after noon on Tuesday next, Archer will be within his legal rights in refusing to accept the wheat. In a transaction of this nature time is generally considered as of the essence of the contract. Burch contracts to build a warehouse for Archer and agrees to have it completed by July 1. Burch does not have the warehouse completed by July 1. Archer cannot refuse to accept the warehouse. Archer can recover damages from Burch for breach of the contract in not completing the warehouse on time. If no time of performance is stated in the contract, the courts imply that the contract must be performed within a reasonable time.

One of the parties to the contract may stipulate that performance must be to his satisfaction. The courts have tended to distinguish between situations where personal taste and comfort are involved and those where fitness for a particular purpose is involved. In the former, failure to perform as agreed will bar a recovery on the contract. The courts require that the dissatisfaction must be real and not feigned. Whether or not one is satisfied is a question for the jury. However, the question is not whether one should be satisfied but whether one is actually satisfied. If the agreement provides that recovery will depend on the expressing of satisfaction, it is doubtful whether it would be a binding contract. It might well be held unenforceable because the promise of one of the parties was illusory. Where the determination of satisfaction depends merely upon the market value or mechanical fitness and utility of the subject matter of the contract, the courts have applied the "reasonable man" test. In interpreting such contracts, as in all contracts, the intentions of the parties are of primary importance. In contracts where personal taste is involved, the courts have found, as a general rule, that the parties intended personal satisfaction to be the test, while in cases where market value or mechanical fitness and utility were involved, the parties intended the rule of reason to apply. "A promise in turn conditional on the promisor's satisfaction with an agreed exchange, gives rise to no duty of immediate performance until such satisfaction; but where it is doubtful whether words mean that a promise is conditional on the promisor's personal satisfaction with an agreed exchange, or on the sufficiency of that exchange to satisfy a reasonable man in the promisor's position, the latter interpretation is adopted." [1]

Drew et al. v. Goodhue
74 Vt. 436, 52 Atl. 971 (1902)

This was an action by W. E. and J. W. Drew (plaintiffs) against E. G. Goodhue (defendant). Judgment for plaintiffs and defendant appealed. Judgment affirmed.

Plaintiffs contracted to haul for the defendant all the pulp wood that should be cut upon a certain tract, and were to be paid therefor 85 cents per cord, of which 25 cents per cord was to be held back until completion of the contract.

The whole number of cords cut was 8,345. Defendant refused to pay plaintiffs the 25 cents per cord withheld, claiming that they had not completed the contract, and plaintiffs brought this suit to recover the sum withheld. After the suit was brought plaintiffs went over the tract and found 7½ cords which had been concealed by snow and overlooked. This amounted to about one stick in eleven hundred which had been overlooked.

Stafford, J. In New York, and perhaps in many of the states, one who has in good faith performed his contract substantially, although he has not done all he should have done within its fair intent and meaning, may recover, not upon a quantum meruit, as it is said, but upon the contract itself, the contract price, suffering a deduction of such damages as his failure has occasioned. To be a substantial performance under those cases, it is only necessary that the defects should not run through the whole, nor be so essential as to defeat the object of the parties to have a specified amount of work done in a particular way.

We do not treat the present as a case of substantial performance in this sense merely, but hold that the contract, in view of the subject-

[1] *Restatement of the Law of Contracts*, Sec. 265.

matter to which it was to be applied, had been performed, within its fair intent and meaning before action was brought. The parties could not have expected nor intended that every single stick should be delivered; and we think the quantity undelivered, for the reason and in the circumstances stated, was no greater than they would naturally have expected to be overlooked or dropped and left ungathered. It is much as though a farmer, who had engaged to harvest all the hay upon a large farm, should be met with the claim that he could not recover the stipulated price because, by raking all the fields over again, at an enormously disproportionate expense, a few forkfuls, or even a small load, might be obtained. It is not that the law does not concern itself with trifles, for in the case supposed and in the case at bar the quantity is not in itself trifling; but that the contract has been fully performed, judged by any fair and sensible construction. When the contract is to do a large piece of work, like the one in question, in the doing of which by the common and ordinary process some residuum or fragments would naturally be neglected or overlooked, of slight consequence in themselves and for the securing of which great and disproportionate expense would be required, we think it becomes a question of fact, within reasonable legal limits, whether the contract has been performed to its fair meaning and intent, notwithstanding it has not been fulfilled to the letter. So far as it was a question of fact, we understand and treat the report as finding that this contract had been performed in the sense we have indicated, and we discover no legal obstacle to the finding.

Boljen v. Ellegaard
43 N.Y.S. (2d) 527 (1943)

This was an action by Otto Boljen (plaintiff) against George R. Ellegaard and another (defendants) wherein defendants filed a counter-claim. Judgment was in accordance with the opinion.

Plaintiff contracted to erect "new buildings as per plans and specifications, same to be made by Louis Danancher, registered Architect."

Cuff, J. Two important questions are presented, (1) . . . . , and (2) was there substantial performance of the contract by the plaintiff?

A glaring error was made by plaintiff in the construction of the staircase. The head room was only 5′7″ instead of 6′3″ as specified. The building is comparatively small. That stairway is in the center on the main floor. It is the only stairway. It is an outstanding feature of the interior of the building. The head room provided is woefully insufficient. The defendants are not obliged to accept the numerous makeshifts proposed to cure the defect. While substantial performance of a building contract by a contractor in constructing a building is all that the law requires, the phrase "substantial performance" is relative. What would be substantial performance in the construction of cellar stairs would not be accepted as such for the main stairway of the premises. The staircase in question was intended to be put to constant use. It was also designed to add beauty to the house. The defendants are entitled to a stairway which accomplishes the ends of usefulness and decoration which they had in mind.

If the doctrine of substantial performance is to be applied, there should be deducted from the unpaid balance due on the contract sufficient to allow for the reconstruction of that stairway in accordance with the plans and specifications, eliminating any appearance of patch work.

Defendants contend that deviation from the contract has been so radical that substantial performance is not applicable. (The Greater New York Savings Bank had contracted to loan the defendants the money to make the required payments on the building, the money to be paid on the production of a "certificate of completion." Because of the errors the "certificate of completion" has been withheld.)

The bank has declined to advance the money until the "certificate of completion" of the house is issued by the Federal Housing Administration. These happenings cannot be charged to defendants. They are attributable to plaintiff. No obligation may be placed upon them to make another and different loan in order to finance the alterations on the house which may be found necessary.

To dismiss this complaint the court considers drastic judicial action, indeed. Yet there is no alternative.

The fact remains when this complaint is dismissed that defendants find themselves in possession of a building for which they paid $3,060 which is worth considerably more, solely by reason of an honest mistake by plaintiff, which could have been and still can be correctable. This court may not subscribe to such a result. It will be held therefore that this proceeding has been prematurely brought; that judgment dismissing the complaint, with costs, will be entered without prejudice, however, to plaintiff instituting a new proceeding when and if he is able to obtain a proper certificate of completion of his contract from the Federal Housing Administration and the completion of the mortgage loan by the Greater New York Savings Bank and upon condition that he pays $200 terms to partially cover the expenses to which defendants have been subjected in defending this action.

Kelley v. Hance
108 Conn. 186, 142 Atl. 683 (1928)

This was an action by H. E. Kelley (plaintiff) against I. I. Hance (defendant). Judgment for plaintiff and defendant appealed. Judgment reversed.

In September plaintiff contracted to excavate to the proper level and construct a cement sidewalk and curb in front of defendant's property for the agreed price of $420. The plaintiff agreed to start the work within a week and complete it before cold weather set in. Plaintiff did nothing until December when he excavated a strip 12 feet wide and 8 feet deep along the front of the premises. Nothing further was done by plaintiff, and the following March 2 defendant notified plaintiff that he cancelled the contract. Plaintiff sued defendant to recover $158.60, the reasonable value of the excavating. Defendant set up a counter-claim for the value of the dirt removed. The lower court gave judgment to the plaintiff for $133.60, allowing $25.00 for the dirt.

Banks, J. The trial court reached the conclusion that the defendant was justified in cancelling the contract because of the failure of the plaintiff to perform, but that the latter was entitled to recover the reasonable value of the benefits accruing to the defendant from the work done by the plaintiff.

While the plaintiff's contract was for the construction of a sidewalk and curb at a unit price per running foot, no section of the walk and curb was completed, and it is not claimed that plaintiff could recover upon the theory of a performance of a divisible portion of the contract; nor was he entitled to recover upon the theory of a substantial performance. This was in the nature of a construction contract as to which class of contracts the rule is liberally applied permitting a recovery where a contractor has deviated slightly from the terms of the contract, not willfully, but in good faith, and there has been a substantial performance of the contract of which the other party has received the benefit. Here, however, not only is there no finding of substantial performance, but it appears from the finding that no portion of the sidewalk and curb was actually constructed by the plaintiff, who, after making an excavation along the front of defendant's premises, left the work and has not done anything since toward its completion. The court has found that the reasonable worth of the work done by the plaintiff was $158.60, slightly more than a third of the contract price, and that the defendant has benefited to that extent from the plaintiff's work. The case, therefore, is one where a contractor has without justification abandoned his contract before completion, but seeks to recover from the defendant the reasonable worth to the latter of the work done prior to the abandonment.

Though a contractor has failed of performance for reasons which would not excuse a breach, and where there has not been even substantial performance, the breach being merely negligent, many of the more recent decisions have held that he could recover the value of his work, less the damages caused by his default. Such recovery is allowed, not upon the original contract, for that has been breached, but in quasi contract upon the theory that, if such recovery were not allowed, the other party would be unjustly enriched at the expense of the contractor. Some cases have gone so far as to allow an employee who has performed part of his employment to recover reasonable compensation, though his failure to render further performance was due to his willful abandonment of his contract. By the weight of authority, however, there can ordinarily be no recovery where the contractor has willfully abandoned his contract without justification.

While the mere fact that part performance has been beneficial to the defendant will not entitle the plaintiff to recover where he has abandoned performance without justification, the defendant may nevertheless make himself liable by his voluntary acceptance of the benefits under circumstances sufficient to raise an implied promise to pay for them notwithstanding the nonperformance of the contract. Where one retains goods received in part performance of a contract, a promise to pay for them is ordinarily implied since he has the option either to pay for or return them. Where, however, work has been done upon one's land, the benefit cannot well be returned and an acceptance of the benefit cannot be implied from the mere retention of possession of the land. In such cases, therefore, the better rule would seem to be that, except where there has been an actual acceptance of the work prior to its abandonment by the plaintiff, mere inaction on the part of the defendant will not be treated as an acceptance of the work from which a promise to pay for it may be implied.

We have held that recovery can be had for partial performance which has been beneficial only when the benefit has been appropriated by the defendant under circumstances sufficient to raise an implied promise to pay for the reasonable value of what has been received.

The finding discloses an abandonment of his contract by the plaintiff after the excavation was made, but before any portion of the sidewalk and curb had been constructed. No justification for this abandonment appears and the plaintiff cannot therefore recover the reasonable value of the work done, unless there has been such an acceptance of it by the defendant as to raise an implied promise on his part to pay for it. No acceptance of the work by the defendant prior to the breach is found and no promise to pay for the benefit received can be implied from the mere fact that he has received a benefit which from the nature of the case he could not avoid receiving and was powerless to return.

Neumann et al. v. Gorak et al.
243 Wis. 503, 11 N.W. (2d) 155 (1943)

This was an action by Herman E. Neumann and others (plaintiffs) against Thomas Gorak, Jr., and others (defendants). Judgment for defendants and plaintiffs appealed. Judgment affirmed.

Plaintiffs and defendants entered into a contract for the purchase and sale of certain real property. The contract provided that payment should be made and the property conveyed "on or before November 1, 1941." Plaintiffs delayed in arranging for the money necessary to make payment until October 30, 1941, and were not able to obtain the money until November 5, 1941. Defendants, between the time the contract was signed, October 11, 1941, and the time for performance, had urged plaintiffs to close the deal. Plaintiffs requested an extension of time which was refused by the defendants. On November 2, 1941, defendants wrote plaintiffs that because of the plaintiffs' failure to consummate the purchase they declared plaintiffs' rights forfeited. Plaintiffs brought this action for specific performance of the contract.

Martin, J. Plaintiffs' principal contention is that time was not of the essence of the contract. Quoting from *Hermanson* v. *Slatter*, the court said, "It is the modern tendency, especially in equity, not to treat time as of the essence unless there is some express term in the contract so providing."

Further, the court said: "It is also held that, while the contract may contain no express language making time of the essence, a consideration of all the facts and circumstances of a particular case may lead to the conclusion that the parties did intend to make time of the essence."

In *Miswald-Wilde Co.* v. *Armory Realty Co.*, 210 Wis. 53, 55, 243 N.W. 492, 494, which involved installment payments on land contracts, the court said: "There were no express provisions and no facts or circumstances, because of which the times of the payments of the specified installments are to be considered of the essence of the contract. The fact that the contracts set dates for such payments did not of itself make time of the essence of the contracts."

If time was of the essence of the contract the judgment must be affirmed. The trial court's decision and findings are grounded on the theory that time was of the essence of the contract. We have in the instant case the additional fact that at no time within the contract period were defendants advised that plaintiffs would or could make the necessary financial arrangements to complete the transaction. It is clear that the real estate broker and plaintiffs' counsel considered time as of the essence of the contract. Counsel endeavored to get an extension of the time within which to close the transaction. In *James* v. *Knox,* 155 Wis. page 121, 143 N.W. page 1072, the court, speaking of the provision in a contract fixing the date for closing the transaction, said: "These are plain words, and clearly indicate an intention by both parties that the deal should be fully closed on or before the date specified. That both parties so understood it is also clearly manifest from the evidence of plaintiff Euclid W. James, that on or about March 1st the defendant sought to have him sign a paper extending the time of performance of the agreement to March 11, 1912 (the date set in the contract was March 1st), which he refused to do. He further testified that on March 1st he notified Rohr, who held the deed in escrow, that, if defendant wanted to close the deal, he could come to his home at any time until midnight, and he would be there to close the transaction. In view of the provisions of the agreement, and the evidence, the trial court properly held that time was of the essence of the contract. Cases holding that a failure to pay a given sum of money upon a date designated, or that a failure to perform some other act within a specified time, does not avoid the contract in the absence of any language therein, or evidence showing that the time for such performance has been made material by agreement of the parties, rest upon a different basis."

In *Green* v. *Kaempf*, 192 Wis. 635, at page 641, 212 N.W. 405, at page 407, which involved a contract for the exchange of real property, the court said: "They cannot be excused upon the ground that they were unable to perform the contract which they entered into. Whether they were unable or unwilling is immaterial so far as the rights of the defendant Kaempf are concerned. It would constitute an innovation in the law to hold that mere inability to perform excuses performance."

Wolff v. Smith
303 Ill. App. 413, 25 N.E. (2d) 399 (1940)

This was an action by Henry L. Wolff (plaintiff) against Carl A. Smith (defendant). From a judgment for plaintiff defendant appealed. Judgment reversed, and case remanded.

Plaintiff contracted to paint a portrait of defendant's father. The following is a provision of the contract entered into: "The price will be $500.00 for the canvas if my work is found to be to the entire satisfaction of all concerned." The defendant refused to accept the portrait when completed because it was not satisfactory. Plaintiff brought suit to recover the contract price of the painting.

Dove, J. In 13 C. J. page 675, it is said: "Contracts in which one party agrees to perform to the satisfaction of the other are ordinarily divided into two classes: (1) where fancy, taste, sensibility or judgment are involved: and (2) where the question is merely one of operative fitness or mechanical utility. In contracts involving matters of fancy, taste, or judgment, when one party agrees to perform to the satisfaction of the other, he renders the other party the sole judge of his satisfaction without regard to the justice or reasonableness of his decision, and a court or jury cannot say that such party should have been satisfied where he asserts that he is not." In a note, cases illustrating and supporting the text are cited and the statement is made that contracts have been held to fall within the first class and support the rule stated in the text where they have related to portraits, a portrait bust, a legal, literary or scientific article for an encyclopedia, a play to be written by an author for an actor, a set of artificial teeth, a suit of clothes, a fur coat, a carriage, a cabinet organ, support of a parent, and others.

In *Erikson* v. *Ward*, 266 Ill. 259, 107 N.E. 593, 595, Ann. Cas. 1916B, 497, cited and relied upon by both parties, a contract which provided that a building was to be constructed according to an architect's plans and specifications, in a good, workmanlike, and substantial manner, to the satisfaction of the defendant, was construed to mean a reasonable satisfaction not arbitrarily exercised. After so holding the court said: "It has been held that, where one contracts to furnish another personal property, personal services or works of art that will give satisfaction, if the property or the services furnished are not satisfactory there can be no recovery. The same strictness has not usually been applied to contracts for the construction of buildings."

Impossibility of Performance

Impossibility of performance should be distinguished from inability to perform. Impossibility of performance arises in three classes of situations: (1) when the performance of the contract has been declared illegal by a statute or governmental regulation enacted or issued after the contract was entered into, (2) when the subject matter essential to the performance of the contract has been destroyed, and (3) when a person who has contracted to perform personal services dies or is incapacitated by illness. Some courts have also held that where conditions essential to performance of the contract do not exist the contract is discharged.

When one enters into a contract, risks are involved. These risks are placed on one or the other of the contracting parties. However, if the parties wish to shift the risks, they may do so by an agreement to that effect. The only limitation is that a contract which relieves the party from his own fraudulent act is illegal because it is against public policy. If a party contracts to produce a stated result, he thereby assumes all the risks incident to the production of that result except in those cases in which his failure is the result of impossibility.

Archer enters into a binding contract to sell and deliver to Burch 100,000 automobile tires to be delivered 10,000 per month beginning in January, 1942. The war and the resulting restrictions on the sale of automobile tires will make the performance of the contract illegal. The contract is discharged because of impossibility of performance.

Archer enters into a binding contract to sell and deliver to Burch 100 suits of clothes. Archer's factory burns and he does not deliver the suits. Burch can hold Archer liable for breach of the contract. If Archer had contracted "to make in his factory at X" and to sell and deliver to Burch 100 suits of clothes and Archer's factory had burned, Archer would be discharged because of impossibility of performance. The continued existence of the factory would be essential to the performance of the contract. In the first case Archer's promise was to deliver 100 suits without reservation, while in the second case Archer's promise was "to make in his factory at X" 100 suits. If the factory is destroyed, the subject matter essential to the performance of the contract has ceased to exist. Fire, strike, and flood clauses are common in sale contracts of manufacturers. These clauses relieve the manufacturer from his duty to deliver the goods in the event he is prevented because of fire, strike, flood, or other causes beyond his control.

Archer contracts to work for Burch as his secretary for one year. Archer dies or is incapacitated by illness. The contract is discharged.

Archer agrees to build a rocket plane and fly Burch to Mars on a scientific expedition. Some courts will hold that the contract will be discharged by impossibility because conditions essential to the performance of the contract do not exist.

Deibler et al. v. Bernard Bros., Inc.
385 Ill. 610, 53 N.E. (2d) 450 (1944)

This was an action by May H. Deibler and another (plaintiffs) against Bernard Brothers, Inc. (defendants). Judgment for defendants and plaintiffs appealed to appellate court. Judgment reversed by appellate court and defendants appealed to the supreme court. Judgment of appellate court affirmed.

On June 18, 1940, plaintiffs leased certain premises to the defendants for a term of five years. The premises were used by the defendants as a show room and sales room for new automobiles. There were no provisions in the lease restricting the use of the building. As the result of certain orders of the Federal Director of Priorities, the defendants were unable to carry on their business of selling new automobiles. The defendants contend that as a result of these orders their business was destroyed and that the continuance of their business was essential to the performance of the lease contract.

Smith, C. J. The record furnishes a conclusive answer to this contention. It is predicated on the false premise that the property was leased for the sole purpose of conducting therein the business of the sale of new automobiles and could not be used for any other purpose without violating the lease. From this erroneous assumption the well-known rule is relied on that when the continued existence of a particular person or thing is necessary to the performance of a contract, the death of the person or the destruction of the thing will terminate the contract.

This reference to the lease shows conclusively that the continued existence of any particular thing or business was not within the contemplation of the parties or inherently necessary to the full performance of the contract. It is not claimed that the performance of the contract has been prohibited by law or that such performance is inherently impossible. The only claim is that by reason of certain restrictions, relating to the manufacture and sale of new automobiles, imposed by federal authority, it has become more difficult for the lessee to carry on the particular business for which the leased premises were used by it prior to the imposition of such restrictions. The fact that the inability of appellant to obtain its usual and normal former supply of new cars for sale, or its inability to obtain any such cars, has rendered its business less profitable and its ability to pay the rentals more burdensome, does not relieve it from the obligations of the lease.

It is elementary law that, when the contract is to do a thing which is possible in itself, the promisor will be held liable for a breach thereof, notwithstanding it was beyond his power to perform it, for it was his own fault to run the risk of undertaking to perform any impossibility, when he might have provided against it by his contract. The general doctrine is that where parties, by their own contract and positive undertaking, create a duty or charge upon themselves, they must abide by the contract and make the promise good. Inevitable contingencies afford them no relief, for they are regarded as insurers to the extent of making good the loss. It is a principle of the law that, in contracts in which the performance depends on the continued existence of a given or specified person or animal or thing, a condition is implied that the impossibility of performance, arising from the perishing of the person, animal, or thing, shall excuse the performance. But there is no place for the application of that rule to a contract not dependent upon the continued existence of some particular person, animal, or thing.

It would certainly be an innovation to establish a rule that all lessees, affected in the same way, were relieved from the obligations of their leases. It would be most difficult to suggest a business which has not been affected in some way by the prevailing conditions. It would not be an exaggeration to assert that the business of every retail dealer and merchant in the land has been reduced because of his inability to obtain an adequate supply of goods to meet the necessities of his former customers.

Lloyd et al. v. Murphy
— Cal. App. —, 142 P. (2d) 939 (1943)

This was an action by Caroline A. Lloyd and others (plaintiffs) against William J. Murphy (defendant). Judgment for plaintiffs and defendant appealed. Judgment reversed and remanded with directions.

Plaintiffs brought this action for a declaration of rights under a lease. The lease provided as follows:

"Use of Premises

"The demised premises shall be used by lessee for the sole purpose of conducting thereon the business of displaying and selling new automobiles (including the servicing and repairing thereof and of selling the petroleum products of a major oil company) and for no other purpose whatsoever without the written consent of lessor, provided, however, that lessee shall be privileged to make an occasional sale of a used automobile from said premises."

On January 1, 1942, the United States government issued its mandate prohibiting the sale of new automobiles. Defendant contends that because the lease restricted the use of the premises to the sale of unused automobiles, and such use was rendered illegal by wartime governmental regulations, he was thereby relieved from performance of the obligations of the lease.

White, J. While not new, the doctrine of commercial frustration came into greater prominence, its scope was widened, and its application was increased following the World War of 1914, when the impossibility of performance of contracts for the sale of certain materials or for the shipment on specified vessels to specified ports was affected by restrictions, occasioned by the war, declaring embargoes upon and seizure of vessels named in particular contracts. The doctrine of frustration was thus stated in *Straus* v. *Kazemekas*, 100 Conn. 581, 124 A. 234, 238: "Where from the nature of the contract and the surrounding circumstances the parties from the beginning must have known that it could not be fulfilled unless when the time for fulfillment arrived, some particular thing or condition of things continued to exist so that they must be deemed, when entering into the contract, to have contemplated such continuing existence as the foundation of what was to be done; in the absence of any express or implied warranty that such thing or condition of things shall exist the contract is to be construed as subject to an implied condition that the parties shall be excused in case, before breach, performance becomes impossible or the purpose of the contract frustrated from such thing or condition ceasing to exist without default of either of the parties."

We are not unmindful of the cases cited by respondent wherein it is held that a change in the law during the term of a lease, which merely restricts but does not wholly prohibit the conduct of the business carried on, does not relieve the tenant from his obligation to pay rent, but in all of such cases the leases did not, as does the one with which we are here concerned, contain a provision similar to the one herein which provides that the demised premises "shall be used by lessee for the sole purpose of conducting thereon the business of displaying and selling new automobiles." Under the circumstances here present, we are persuaded that it is firmly established in the law that the use of the premises being restricted to a particular and specified purpose, which main and principal purpose is frustrated by governmental decrees or regulations, the subject matter of the contract is destroyed and the covenants of such lease will not be enforced against either party thereto.

Matthews Construction Company v. Brady
104 N.J. L. 438, 140 Atl. 433 (1928)

This was an action by Matthews Construction Company (plaintiff) against James C. Brady (defendant). Judgment for defendant and plaintiff appealed. Judgment affirmed.

The plaintiff contracted to provide the materials and perform the work necessary for certain alterations and additions to the defendant's residence. The alterations and additions provided for included the rebuilding of a private chapel especially around the altar, which required a large amount of specially designed mill work. Plaintiff ordered these materials from the Butler-Howell Company. On March 15, 1923, the residence building was destroyed by fire without the fault of either party. The special millwork had been completed by Butler-Howell Company before the destruction of the residence by fire but had not been delivered or accepted and approved by the architect. Defendants paid plaintiff $10,522.08 for work done and materials installed in the residence before the fire, but refused to pay the sum of $4,407.84 claimed by plaintiff for the mill and cabinet work and labor performed by the Butler-Howell Company, which remained in the latter's mill undelivered at the time of the fire.

Per Curiam. The opinion of Judge Lawrence filed in the circuit court is adopted by this court.

"Plaintiff is not entitled to recover of defendant the sum in question. The materials had not been delivered and accepted by defendant or incorporated in the alterations and additions to his residence. The continued existence of the building to which the alterations and additions were to be made under the general contract was an implied condition of its performance, and its destruction without fault of either party before completion of the contract released both from further liability, excepting that defendant was obliged to pay plaintiff for the work done and materials provided and delivered and accepted to the date of the fire. This he did. Considering the circumstances here presented, it is of no consequence that the materials in question were in part peculiar in design and of special character to adapt them to the building operation contemplated by the general contract.

"Rulings.

"(a) When a builder is to furnish the materials and labor for the performance of a contract requiring the erection of structures on the land of the owner, the materials generally remain the property of the former until they are affixed to the land, or are delivered and accepted by the latter, and this rule is not altered by the fact that the materials are purchased by the builder with the intention of working them into such structures, and that preliminary work has been done on them so as to fit them for annexation.

"(b) Where, under a contract for alterations and additions to an existing building, performance depends on the continued existence of the structure, a condition is implied that impossibility of complete performance arising from its destruction without fault of the parties will absolve them from further liability, with the exception that the owner remains liable, and the builder may recover for the value of the work done and materials delivered and accepted prior to such destruction.

"(c) There is a distinction as to continuing liability under a building contract involving the erection of a new structure on land of the owner and that which relates to the making of additions and alterations to an existing building (the continuance of which is necessary to complete the contract) in the event of destruction without fault before completion. In the former case the builder remains liable for failure to complete, while in the latter both parties are relieved, and the contract is at an end in that respect.

Discharge by Agreement

A contract is the result of agreement between the parties. The contract having been created by agreement, it can be discharged by agreement. If the parties to the contract agree that the contract shall no longer bind them, the contract is discharged. The duty to perform may also be discharged by entering into a new contract covering the same subject matter, the terms of which are inconsistent with the old contract. When the parties have entered into a new contract inconsistent with the old contract, they have, in fact if not in words, indicated their intention not to fulfill the terms of the old contract. They have discharged the old contract by agreement.

A party to the contract may voluntarily relinquish a right which he has under the contract. Such a relinquishment is known as a waiver. If one party tenders an incomplete performance, and the other party accepts such defective performance without objection, knowing that the defects will not be remedied, he will have waived his right to strict performance. If he wishes to insist on strict performance, he should have objected to the incomplete or defective performance. In any instance in which performance is defective, notice should be given within a reasonable time that the defects must be remedied or that damages will be claimed. If failure to give notice would justify a belief that strict performance will not be claimed, failure to give notice will amount to a waiver. Archer sells goods to Burch and agrees to deliver them to Burch on June 15. Archer delivers the goods to Burch on June 17, and Burch accepts the goods without objection. Burch will have waived his right to have the goods delivered on time. Archer delivers goods which are not in compliance with the contract and Burch accepts, inspects the goods, and knows of the defects in the goods but makes no objection. Burch will have waived any rights he might have claimed as a result of the defects in the goods. If Burch wishes to protect his rights, he must give notice to Archer. Whether or not one's conduct results in a waiver of rights depends on the circumstances.

A party to a contract may be discharged by a novation. A novation is a three-party agreement whereby there is a substitution of obligations, resulting in the complete discharge of one of the parties. For example, Archer owes Burch $100, and Burch owes Clark $100. Archer, Burch, and Clark agree that Archer will pay Clark $100 and that Burch will be discharged from all liability. Such an agreement is supported by consideration. The consideration to support Archer's promise to pay Clark is Clark's discharge of Burch, and the consideration to support Burch's promise to discharge Archer is the extinguishment of Burch's debt to Clark.

Riverside Coal Company v. American Coal Company
107 Conn. 40, 139 Atl. 276 (1927)

This was an action by the Riverside Coal Company (plaintiff) against American Coal Company (defendant). Judgment for plaintiff for part of their claims and plaintiff appealed. Judgment affirmed.

About February 1, 1926, defendant agreed to purchase 1,500 net tons of Scotch coke to be imported by the plaintiff at a price of $12.00 per ton unloaded at New Haven and shipped by rail to Hartford. The coke was to be delivered in February. The coke did not arrive in New Haven until March 8, and defendant refused to accept delivery. After some negotiations the defendant agreed to accept the coke at New Haven and pay $6.50 per ton for it. Plaintiff now sues for the original contract price of the coke, $17,996.40 less a $2,000 down payment. The court gave a judgment for plaintiff for $7,441.05.

Hinman, J. The court refers to the transaction as a "novation," which term is usually used with reference to instances in which a new party is introduced into the new contract, while "substitute contract" is the designation commonly employed to cover agreements between the same parties which supersede and discharge prior contract obligations. There is, however, no distinction so far as concerns the legal effect.

We think that the language of the second contract is, of itself, clearly sufficient to place it in the category of substitute contracts. Its plain intent and effect is that instead of the February arrangement, therein described, by which the plaintiff agreed to sell and the defendant agreed to buy the specified quantity of coke at $12 per ton, delivered at Hartford, the same parties agreed to sell and to buy, respectively, a like quantity, but at a price of $6.50 per ton (instead of the $12 called for by the first agreement), delivery to be at New Haven (instead of at Hartford), and making provisions concerning payment of freight, division of demurrage, and other incidents of the transaction not present in the first agreement. Being thus "made by the same parties, but containing terms inconsistent with the former contract so that the two cannot stand together," it exhibits the characteristics and responds to recognized tests indicating a substitute contract. Furthermore, we think that an intent that the agreement to so sell and buy, on the substituted terms, shall discharge the prior contract and all claims and demands growing out of it is unmistakably expressed by the language used.

As a general rule, when the new contract is in regard to the same matter and has the same scope as the earlier contract and the terms of the two are inconsistent either in whole or in a substantial part, so that they cannot subsist together, the new contract abrogates the earlier one in toto and takes its place, even though there is no express agreement that the new contract shall have that effect.

Pabst Brewing Co. v. City of Milwaukee
126 Wis. 110, 105 N.W. 563 (1903)

This was an action by Pabst Brewing Co. (plaintiff) against the City of Milwaukee (defendant). Judgment for defendant and plaintiff appealed. Judgment affirmed.

The City of Milwaukee graded and paved the street in front of plaintiff's property and assessed the benefits accruing against plaintiff. Plaintiff paid the assessment without protest and sued the city in this action to recover part or all of the assessment claiming that the assessment was illegally or improperly made. The city contended that by paying the assessment without protest the plaintiff waived any and all objections to the legality or propriety of the assessment.

Marshall, J. It would seem that the more satisfactory ground to support the doctrine of waiver on is that it is a rule of judicial policy—the legal outgrowth of judicial abhorrence, so to speak, of a person's taking inconsistent positions and gaining advantages thereby through the aid of courts. A rule by which regardless of any element of estoppel or consideration, as those terms are popularly understood, the saying that one should not be permitted to blow hot and with advantage to himself turn and blow cold, within limits sanctioned by long experience as required for the due administration of justice, has been prohibitively applied. It is applied where one with knowledge of the facts voluntarily pays a demand upon him. It is applied when one with knowledge, or reasonable means of knowledge, of the facts having two inconsistent remedies chooses one of them. It is applied where one without objection and with such knowledge, or means of knowledge, receives property in consummation of an executory contract. The tendency of courts is to consider as within one of the exceptional classes any situation which is within the principle of it, both as regards the mere fact of waiver and the importance in the administration of justice of holding the waivee to the position he voluntarily and with knowledge of the facts has elected to take.

It is suggested that there can be no waiver without intent to waive based on knowledge of the facts. True, but one is presumed to know that which in contemplation of law he ought to know, and one is presumed to waive that which is necessarily implied from his conduct. Constructive as well as actual knowledge of the facts, and implied as well as express intent, satisfies the prime essential of a conclusive waiver. A standard reference work puts the matter thus:

"The intent to waive may appear as a legal result of conduct. The actuating motive, or the intention to abandon a right, is generally a matter of inference to be deduced with more or less certainty from the external and visible acts of the party, and all the accompanying circumstances of the transaction, regardless of whether there was an actual or expressed intent to waive, or even if there was an actual but undisclosed intention to the contrary."

Buerger Bros. Supply Co. v. El Rey Furniture Co.
43 Ariz. 472, 32 P. (2d) 1029 (1934)

This was an action by El Rey Furniture Co. (plaintiff) against Buerger Bros. Supply Company (defendant). Judgment for plaintiff and defendant appealed. Judgment affirmed.

Frank J. Kuckem was engaged in the barber shop and beauty parlor business in Tucson. Kuckem bought supplies from defendant and was indebted to it for both supplies and moneys advanced. Kuckem had purchased about $700 worth of furniture from El Rey Furniture Co. on credit. Kuckem's creditors, including El Rey Furniture Co., were pressing him for payment. Buerger Bros. Supply Co. requested Kuckem to make a list of all his creditors and the amount due each. Kuckem owed $2,645. Buerger Bros. Supply Co. agreed to pay all of Kuckem's creditors and took a mortgage on all of his shop equipment as security. Buerger Bros. Supply Co. gave a letter to Kuckem in which this agreement to pay Kuckem's creditors was set out, and Kuckem showed this letter to the El Rey Furniture Co. and also delivered to it a check drawn by Buerger Bros. Supply Co. in part payment. El Rey Furniture Co. agreed to the arrangement. Kuckem defaulted on his agreed payments to the Buerger Bros. Supply Co. and it refused to make further payments to Kuckem's creditors. El Rey Furniture Co. sued claiming a novation.

Lockwood, J. We consider then whether the letters, together with the acts of the parties, as shown by the testimony, constitute a novation. In the case of *Dunbar* v. *Steiert*, 31 Ariz. 403, 253 P. 1113, we have set forth the requisites of a novation as follows: ". . . . In every novation there are four essential requisites. A previous valid obligation; the agreement of all the parties to the new contract; the extinguishment of the old contract; and the validity of the new one. . . . ." There is no doubt that there was a valid obligation existing between plaintiff and Kuckem on the conditional sales contract.

The next question is whether the three parties agreed to a new contract, substituting defendant as debtor in the place of Kuckem. This involves a consideration of the letters referred to. Under date of January 5th, defendant wrote to Kuckem,

"We therefore feel when you approach these various creditors with these substantial amounts at this time and with the assurance that they will receive the balance in a more assured way now than previously, that they should be satisfied, in fact, such is to be expected of them, each and every one, before presenting any one of them with their check and which you should ascertain."

We think the statement just quoted could only be reasonably construed by a creditor seeing them as a promise on the part of the defendant to pay the bill in question; that this was the idea of defendant is confirmed by the following extract from a letter of January 28th:

"We also wish to acknowledge receipts from five respective creditors as paid by you to them with our checks amounting to $603.00 and we are more than pleased to note that these various creditors are taking a more pleasant attitude towards you and are now assured of matters being properly taken care of with your cooperation as well as that of ours.

"We take it for granted inasmuch that these various creditors will not be pressing you directly for payments but will rather be receiving similar payments from us again in the near future, that it is your intention to favor us direct with a payment of at least $100.00 per month for the time being to apply on your principal account in addition to the interest payment which you are to make. We shall be pleased to hear from you further regarding this."

The writing of these letters by defendant and receipt by Kuckem and the presentation of them by Kuckem to plaintiff, and the acceptance by plaintiff of the $100 check of defendant inclosed in the letter of January 20th, certainly justified the trial court in concluding there was an agreement of all the parties that defendant should assume the obligation of paying the balance due under the conditional sales contract, the consideration therefor being the forbearance on the part of the plaintiff to sue Kuckem. Such an agreement would of course be a legal one. The only remaining requisite of a novation was the extinguishment of the old contract, and this is established by the uncontradicted testimony of plaintiff's manager that it did not thereafter expect Kuckem to pay anything, but from that time looked to defendant for payment. Such being the case, we think the evidence sufficiently establishes a novation substituting defendant for Kuckem, as debtor under a new contract.

Discharge by Operation of Law

From the earliest times it has been held that if a party to a written instrument intentionally alters it in any material respect, the other party to the instrument is discharged from all his duties. If the instrument is altered by one not a party to it and without the knowledge and consent of one of the contracting parties, the alteration does not affect the rights of the parties. If an alteration is made with the consent of the other contracting parties or the other contracting parties consent to the alteration after they learn of it, they are not discharged.

From the earliest times the courts have refused to grant a remedy to one who has delayed an unreasonable time in bringing suit. In modern times the various states have by statute declared that an action must be brought within a stated time after the action accrues. Such statutes are known as Statutes of Limitation.

The time limit for bringing suit for breach of contracts differs in the various states and in many states the statutes distinguish between oral contracts and written contracts; for example, in Indiana, the time limit for bringing suit on an oral contract is six years and on a contract in writing it is ten years. In Illinois the time limit is five years on oral contracts and ten on written contracts. The time is computed from the time the cause of action accrues. If Archer enters into a contract with Burch on January 1, 1946, whereby he agrees to deliver goods to Burch on July 1, 1946, and then does not deliver the goods on July 1, 1946, he will have breached his contract and at that time the cause of action accrues. The time for bringing an action would start to run on July 2, 1946. On open accounts, promissory notes, and other contracts of this general type the time is computed from the time the last payment is made or the last charge is made. Archer owes Burch $100 which is due July 1, 1945. On July 1, 1945, Archer pays Burch $5.00 on account. The time of the running of the statute will be computed from July 1, 1945. Each payment will be considered as a renewal of the promise to pay and will start the running of the statute anew. If one is incapacitated or beyond the jurisdiction of the court, the time during which the incapacity continues or the time during which one is beyond the jurisdiction of the court is not, by the terms of many statutes, counted in computing the statutory time for bringing suit.

A contractual obligation may be discharged by a discharge in bankruptcy. The Bankruptcy Act is a federal statute and is substantially uniform in its operation throughout the United States. When one has been adjudged bankrupt and has complied with all the requirements of the act, he is entitled to a discharge which operates to bar any action on provable claims which have been properly scheduled. Contract claims are, as a general rule, provable claims and, if properly scheduled, will be discharged.

Griffin Grocery Co. v. Carson Grocery Co.
174 Okla. 96, 50 P. (2d) 368 (1935)

This was an action by the Griffin Grocery Co. (plaintiff) against Carson Grocery Co. (defendant). Judgment for defendant and plaintiff appealed. Judgment affirmed.

Plaintiffs brought suit to recover damages for breach of a contract to purchase 500 barrels of flour. An agent of plaintiff solicited the order and the defendant gave the plaintiff's agent a written order for 500 barrels of flour to be shipped on open account. After the order was received the plaintiff changed the credit terms from shipment on open account to payment on delivery by the railway company. Defendant refused to accept and pay for flour shipped on these terms.

Per Curiam. In the brief, the plaintiff urges three propositions: First, that any notation made by the salesman on the copy of the contract left with the defendant is immaterial, especially in view of the undisputed fact that he had no authority to fix terms of payment, citing the first syllabus in *Orr* v. *Murray*, 95 Okl. 206, 219 P. 333, to the effect that an alteration of a written contract by an agent of one of the parties does not avoid the contract unless the agent had express or implied authority to make the alteration. The terms of payment written by the salesman into the blank space provided for that purpose was not a mere notation for the word "open" represented a material part of the contract, which word remained unchanged in the carbon copy left with the defendant. As to the authority of the salesman to fix terms of payment, the salesman was the agent of the plaintiff and the terms of payment in the printed contract prepared by plaintiff were in blank; and, therefore, under the rules of law applicable thereto, the salesman had implied authority from his principal to fill in the blank space in conformity to the contract made with the defendant. The law applicable hereto is fully stated in 2 C. J. §§ 119 to 144, in the article, "Alteration of Instruments." The assertion on the part of the plaintiff that its salesman had no authority to fix terms of payment was a fraud on the defendant partners who appear to be entirely ignorant of any such limitation on the authority of the salesman. 2 C. J. § 121, p. 1244. There was no alteration in filling the blank showing the terms of payment as per agreement, but the alteration consisted in the salesman altering the agreement without consent of the defendant partners. At the time of the alteration, the original and one carbon copy of the contract had not been submitted to the plaintiff for its confirmation. Plaintiff's salesman had no express or implied authority from the defendant partners to make the alteration. The contract confirmed by the plaintiff was not the contract which had been executed by the defendant. We are not concerned here with the authority of plaintiff to its salesman to make the alteration. We are concerned with the lack of authority from defendant to plaintiff's salesman to make the alteration.

As a second proposition, the plaintiff contends the purchase contract contained no material alterations, citing the first syllabus in *Bailey* v. *Evans*, 100 Okl. 278, 229 P. 221, to the effect it was the duty of the defendant, on the receipt of the altered carbon copy of the contract, to make an investigation as the circumstances would suggest, etc. The record shows the defendant partners did make an investigation and the jury evidently concluded, and we think rightfully, that the investigation made by the defendant partners complied with the law announced in the foregoing decision of this court. But, in support of the proposition urged, the plaintiff does not call to the attention of this court any decision which would aid us in determining whether the alteration was or was not material. We think this proposition is ruled by statute (1921, C. O. S. § 5083, 1931 O. S. § 9504) as construed by this court in the second syllabus in *Bailey* v. *Evans*, supra, as follows: "An alteration of a written contract becomes material when it may have the effect to enlarge, extend, or diminish the duties, liabilities, or obligations of the obligor or promisor, in any manner not in contemplation of the parties at the time of execution, if done without the knowledge or consent of the party to be bound." An instrument so altered ceases to be the contract executed, and the law does not make new contracts nor enforce new and different liabilities, not in contemplation of the parties when they contract. This is the general rule, and it is made the rule in this state by legislative enactment.

Bisesi v. Farm & Home Savings & Loan Association of Missouri
231 Mo. App. 897, 78 S. W. (2d) 871 (1935)

This was an action by Mike Bisesi (plaintiff) against the Farm & Home Savings & Loan Association of Missouri (defendant). Judgment for defendant and plaintiff appealed. Judgment affirmed.

Mike Bisesi deposited $2,000 with the defendant and received the following writing:

$2000.00 Nevada, Mo., 12/20/1923

"Received of Mike Bisesi two thousand dollars for 20 shares fully paid.

"Farm and Home Savings and Loan
Association of Missouri
"By (*signed*) Vosburgh"

The shares of stock mentioned in the writing were never delivered. In March, 1931, plaintiff demanded the return of the $2,000 and payment was refused. This action was filed June 4, 1931, to recover a judgment for $2,000 on the theory that, the shares of stock not having been delivered within a reasonable time, plaintiff was entitled to the return of the amount paid for the stock. The defendant set up the running of the Statute of Limitations as a defense.

Becker, J. In light of the testimony in the case and the fact that plaintiff's action was begun over seven years and five months after the date of the purchase and sale of the stock, it is essential that we determine whether the character of plaintiff's action is such as to fall within the five-year or the ten-year statute of limitation.

Appellant insists that "the defense of the Statute of Limitations is never looked upon with favor by courts. Numerous cases so hold." To the contrary, statutes of limitations are favored in the law and cannot be avoided unless the party seeking to do so brings himself directly within some exception.

As numerous cases point out, statutes of limitations promote repose by giving security and stability to human affairs; they stimulate promptness and punish negligence; their object is to suppress fraudulent and stale claims from being asserted after long lapses of time when perhaps the necessary vouchers and evidence are lost, or when the facts have become obscure, or the memory of witnesses defective, or when witnesses may no longer be available either by reason of death or because their whereabouts have become unknown.

Section 861, Rev. St. Mo. 1929 (Mo. St. Ann. § 861, p. 1139) provides, among other things, that "an action upon any writing, whether sealed or unsealed, for the payment of money or property, ... (and) actions for relief, not herein otherwise provided for," shall be commenced within ten years; and section 862, Rev. St. Mo. 1929 (Mo. St. Ann. § 862, p. 1143) provides that "all actions upon contracts, obligations or liabilities, express or implied, except those mentioned in section 861 . . . ." shall be commenced within five years.

The action for money had and received has always been regarded as an action in assumpsit, based upon a promise to repay which the law implies, where one has possession of money which in equity and good conscience belongs to another.

"Having money that rightfully belongs to another, creates a debt; and wherever a debt exists without an express promise to pay, the law implies a promise; and the action always sounds in contract."

In actions for money had and received, "the law, operating on the act of the parties, creates the duty, establishes the privity and implies the promise and obligation, on which the action is founded."

With reference to the receipt relied on for the basis of plaintiff's action, unquestionably plaintiff could at his option have sued for the delivery of the stock, since the law implies a promise on the part of the defendant that it will deliver the stock mentioned therein, in which event the ten-years statute of limitation would have been controlling, for what the law implies in an express contract is as much a part of the contract as if it was stated in the contract in direct terms. But plaintiff elected to disaffirm the contract and chose as his remedy his present action as for money had and received, in which action the promise of payment arises only by proof of extrinsic facts and not from the instrument itself, namely, the receipt. But where evidence aliunde must be sought to establish such promise, namely, the implied assumpsit, the cause of action is governed by the five-year statute of limitation.

A statute of limitation begins to run when a cause of action has accrued to the person asserting it, and a cause of action accrues when a breach of duty has occurred or when a wrong has been sustained such as will give a right then to bring and sustain a suit.

In the case before us no definite time was set for the delivery of the certificate to plaintiff by defendant, and in this situation it is ordinarily presumed that a reasonable time is intended, and limitation begins to run after such reasonable time.

Since we rule that plaintiff's cause of action is subject to the five-year statute of limitation, and plaintiff did not file his suit until more than seven years and five months had elapsed from the date upon which plaintiff paid to the defendant the money herein sought to be recovered, and no facts are set up in the petition to bring the delay in filing the action within an exception of the statute, it becomes essential to determine when plaintiff's cause of action accrued to determine whether his action was barred by limitation prior to the filing thereof.

What, then, was a reasonable time beyond which, as a matter of law, the defendant must be held to have breached its agreement to deliver the twenty shares of stock to plaintiff, and thereby have given plaintiff an election of his cause of action?

Upon the conceded facts in this case, to rule that plaintiff had filed his suit within the five-year period of limitation we would have to hold that over two years and five months were available to defendant as a reasonable time within which to make delivery of the stock. So to hold is out of the question. The issuing of certificates of stock in a corporation, resident of the state, is a matter in the ordinary course of business that usually requires but a few days' time, and clearly a period of over two years and five months is so far beyond what in any event could be held to be reasonable time for the defendant to have issued the stock, that it needs neither argument nor authority to support a holding that as a matter of law defendant must be held to have breached its agreement to deliver the certificate of stock to plaintiff, and that plaintiff's right of action accrued much short of said period of time. It follows that plaintiff's cause of action was barred by the five-year statute of limitation long prior to the date upon which he filed his suit.

QUESTIONS AND PROBLEMS

1. Archer leased a building to Burch and they filled in and signed a printed form lease. One of the printed provisions of the lease stated that the lessee (Burch) was to make all repairs on the building during the term of the lease. In the blank space on the form, the parties had inserted a written provision stating that the lessor (Archer) was to make all repairs on the building during the term of the lease. Which one of the parties is bound to make the repairs on the building?
2. What is the difference between "usage of trade" and "course of dealing"?
3. Walls contracted to plaster Bailey's house for $1 per square yard. When Walls measured the house, he made no deduction for openings—doors, windows, etc. Bailey refused to pay the amount claimed and contended that allowance should be made for openings. Walls proved that it was established usage not to deduct openings in determining the number of square yards plastered. Bailey claimed that he knew nothing about the usage and was not bound by it. Is Bailey bound by the usage?
4. The Refrigerating Co. sold to Seitz, on a written contract, a refrigerating plant. There were no express warranties made in the written contract as to the temperature which could be maintained by the refrigerating plant. After the refrigerating plant was installed, Seitz refused to pay the purchase price. When sued he offered to prove that the Refrigerating Co. orally warranted that the plant would maintain a temperature of 40 degrees or below, and that the plant would not maintain such temperature. Should this evidence be admitted?
5. Johnson took out a policy of insurance with the Phoenix Insurance Co. insuring his house against fire. The policy provided that in the event of loss by fire Johnson must file with the Insurance Co. at its home office within sixty days a certificate of proof of loss, signed by a magistrate or notary public, stating the nature and the extent of the fire. Johnson suffered a loss but did not file the certificate of loss

until eighty days after the date of the loss. Can Johnson recover the amount of the loss from the Phoenix Insurance Co.?

6. Archer agreed to sell his automobile to Burch for $850 on July 1, 1945. Burch promised to pay Archer $850 for the latter's automobile on July 1, 1945. Archer did not tender delivery of the automobile and Burch did not tender the money on July 1, 1945. On July 5, 1945, Archer, without tendering the automobile to Burch, sued Burch to recover the purchase price of the automobile. Is Archer entitled to a judgment?
7. Nolan contracted to build a house for Whitney according to certain plans and specifications. Payments were to be made as the work progressed on the production of the architect's certificate, and the final payment was to be made thirty days after completion of the work. The architect refused to give a certificate for the final payment. The work was done according to plans and specifications except for a few trivial defects. Nolan sued to recover the final payment and Whitney set up Nolan's failure to produce the architect's certificate as a defense. Is the defense good?
8. The Bailey Co. contracted to make alterations of certain boilers for Gardner. The work was to be paid for as soon as Gardner was satisfied that the boilers as altered were successful and would not leak under a pressure of one hundred pounds of steam. The work was completed on May 10. After Gardner had had a reasonable time in which to test the boilers, the Boiler Co. demanded payment and Gardner refused to pay stating that he was not satisfied that the boilers were successful. Gardner had been using the boilers during the entire period. The Boiler Co. sued. Is the Boiler Co. entitled to a judgment?
9. Jacobs contracted to build a residence for Kent at a cost of $77,000. The contract provided that all pipe should be of Reading manufacture. Part of the pipe used was of the grade specified but was not of Reading manufacture. The substitution was not wilful on the part of the contractor but was the result of his failure to carefully inspect the pipe used. Kent refused to pay the final payment of $3,500. Is Jacobs entitled to payment either in part or in full?
10. Du Bois leased a filling station to Gentry for a term of five years beginning January 1, 1940. Gentry operated the filling station for a period of two years and abandoned the lease. Du Bois sued to recover the rent, and Gentry set up that as a result of the war he could not get gasoline, tires, or help and that it was impossible to operate the filling station. Gasoline and tires were rationed but could be obtained under the regulations set up. Help was scarce. Is the defense good?
11. Heaton sold a wagon at auction to Angier for $30.25. The same day, Angier sold the wagon to Chase for $31.25. Angier and Chase went to Heaton, who agreed to accept Chase as paymaster, and delivered the wagon to Chase. Chase did not pay and Heaton sued Angier for the purchase price of the wagon, $30.25. Is Heaton entitled to a judgment against Angier?
12. Kester sold Nelson a refrigerating plant and other meat market equipment for $1,000. Nelson paid $120 down and agreed to pay the balance in equal installments. This contract was in writing and signed by both parties. Later, Nelson was unable to make his payments, and Kester and Nelson orally agreed that Kester would accept the return of the refrigerating plant, which was the principal item sold, and that Nelson would store it free of charge until it could be disposed of, and that the $120 down payment would be accepted as payment in full for the other equipment. Later, Kester sued Nelson on the original written contract for the unpaid balance of the purchase price of the equipment. Is Kester entitled to a judgment?
13. Archer gave Burch his promissory note for $100 in payment for goods purchased. The note provided that it was payable $10 the first of each month. After the note was delivered, Burch wrote thereon "on failure to make any payment when due the entire balance shall become immediately due and payable." Archer did not

pay the first installment when due, and Burch brought suit to recover the entire unpaid balance of the note. Is Burch entitled to a judgment?

14. Archer purchased goods of Burch on open book account on October 1, 1939. Burch did not send Archer an invoice nor demand payment. On November 3, 1945, Burch started suit to recover on the claim. Archer set up the statute of limitations as a defense. The statute in force provided that suits on open accounts must be brought within five years after the cause of action accrued. Is Burch entitled to a judgment?

CHAPTER XIII

REMEDIES

Nature of Remedies

In deciding a case involving the breach of a contract the court must determine whether or not an enforceable contract was entered into, must determine the terms of the contract, must interpret the contract, and must determine whether or not the contract has been breached, and if it has been breached, must decide to what remedy the injured party is entitled.

We have considered the problems involved except as to what remedy the injured party is entitled. The usual remedy granted for the breach of a contract is compensatory damages. If no pecuniary loss can be shown, nominal damages may be all that the injured party can recover. The parties may have stipulated in the contract the amount which will be paid as damages for breach of the contract. Such a stipulation is termed liquidated damages.

If the remedy at law (damages) is inadequate, the party may be entitled to one of the equitable remedies. Under some circumstances the court may grant the remedy of specific performance, that is, decree the performance of the contract. In other instances the court may grant the remedy of reformation, that is, decree a change in the terms of the contract. This remedy is frequently granted when a mistake has been made in drafting a written contract. The court will decree that the terms of the contract be changed so that the error is corrected. Injunctive relief may be granted in special instances. The court will enjoin one of the parties from following a threatened course of action, thereby coercing him into the performance of the contract. If a contract has been induced by fraud, the court may decree a cancellation of the contract. This remedy is especially appropriate in case a negotiable instrument has been issued or a deed signed and delivered as the result of fraudulent representations.

A judgment or a decree would be an empty remedy if some means were not provided for enforcing the judgment or decree. If the remedy granted is a judgment for damages, the usual means of enforcing the judgment is by the issuing and levying of an execution. Under some circumstances one may attach the goods of the party defendant at the time the suit is brought. By writ of garnishment one can reach property or credits in the hands of third persons which belong to or are owing to the judgment creditor. If one does not comply with the decree of the judge, rendered in a case in equity, he will be in contempt of court, and the judge can impose whatever penalty the circumstances of the case justify.

Damages

In cases of breach of contract the remedy granted will be a judgment for damages unless the case is unusual. In granting a judgment for damages the court attempts to compensate the party for the injury he has suffered. In determining the amount of damages to which one is entitled the court attempts to determine how much the injured party has lost as the direct result of the breach of the contract. To be entitled to compensation in damages the injured party must prove, with a reasonable amount of certainty, the amount of money necessary to compensate him for his injury. If the plaintiff proves a breach of the contract but cannot prove that he suffered a loss as a result of the breach, he will be entitled to nominal damages but not to compensatory damages. The amount granted as nominal damages is not uniform throughout the United States; for example, in some states a judgment of 6 cents will be given, while in others the judgment will be for $1.00.

Recoverable damages must be the direct result of the breach of the contract and must have been within the contemplation of the parties at the time the contract was entered into.

Archer contracts to sell and deliver to Burch 100 bushels of No. 1 white wheat. Archer does not deliver the wheat as promised, thereby breaching his contract. Archer wishes to grind the wheat into a special flour to be used as a sample in bidding on a large contract. After Burch learns that Archer has breached his contract, he finds that Clark who lives at Kirk, fifty miles from Burch's mill, has 100 bushels of the same quality of wheat and Burch starts for Kirk with his truck to buy Clark's wheat. On the way to Kirk, Burch wrecks his truck. Burch does not obtain other wheat and as a result fails to get his bid in on the contract.

Burch sues Archer and claims as damages $25, the difference between the contract price of the wheat and the market price at the time and place of delivery, $560 for repairs to the truck, and $5,000 for loss of the contract for flour. Burch will be entitled to $25 damages. The $560 repairs to the truck is not the direct result of the breach of the contract to sell wheat. The claimed $5,000 loss as the result of not obtaining the contract for flour is speculative, is not the direct result of the breach of the contract, and was not within the contemplation of the parties when the contract was entered into.

Loss of profits may be allowed if the amount can be established with a reasonable degree of certainty. If the plaintiff has been in business for a period of time and has a fair set of books, he will be able to show loss of profits in most instances. However, if the contract involved a new and speculative venture, he will be unable to establish his loss of profits unless he has a good cost accounting system and in many cases not even then.

Weiss v. Revenue Building & Loan Ass'n.
116 N.J. Law 208, 182 Atl. 891 (1936)

This was an action by Samuel M. Weiss (plaintiff) against the Revenue Building & Loan Association (defendant). Judgment for plaintiff and defendant appealed. Judgment reversed and remanded.

Plaintiff leased from the defendant a building at 26-28 West Kinney Street for rooming-house purposes and at the same time entered into a contract with the defendant whereby the defendant agreed to lease to plaintiff the adjoining building, 22-24 West Kinney Street, for rooming-house purposes, for a period of three years from the ensuing February 1. The two buildings were alike in every respect. On February 1 the defendant refused to execute a lease for the building at 22-24 West Kinney Street. Plaintiff claims that as a result of the breach of contract to lease he suffered as damages loss of profits which he would have earned by the operation of a rooming-house. To establish the amount of loss he was permitted to prove the amount of profits earned in the operation of the rooming-house at 26-28 West Kinney Street during the past year.

Heher, J. The rule of damages applied by the trial judge was "the difference between the actual value of the leasehold estate that should have been enjoyed by the plaintiff, and the agreed rental." More specifically, the jury were instructed that the plaintiff was entitled to recover "the value of his term," and that, in the appraisement, it was proper to "consider the use to which the property may be most advantageously put," and that, while the plaintiff was not entitled to an award of "those profits that he would have earned for the entire term," they were permitted, if not indeed required, to "consider what it is probable that this property would earn in determining what the term was worth to him."

In these instructions, and, by the same reasoning, in the related rulings on evidence to be adverted to hereafter, the trial judge fell into error.

Ordinarily, the prima facie measure of damages for the breach of a contract is the quantum of loss consequent thereon. The injured party is entitled to the value of the contract to him. It was this that he lost by the default of the other. But this general rule is subject to two qualifications designed to confine within reasonable limits the appraisement of the consequences of the default, viz.: First, the damages shall be those arising naturally, i. e., according to the usual course of things, from the breach of the contract, or such as may fairly and reasonably be supposed to have been in the contemplation of the parties to the contract at the time it was made, as the probable result of the breach; and, second, they must be the reasonably certain and definite consequences of the breach, as distinguished from mere quantitative uncertainty. *Hadley* v. *Baxendale,* 9 Exch. 341, 23 L. J. Exch, 179, 18 Jur. 358, 5 Eng. Rul. Cas. 502. This general principle seems to have had its genesis in the last cited case. There Baron Alderson declared that if special circumstances attending the making of the contract were communicated by the party asserting the breach to the one charged therewith, the reasonably contemplated damages resulting from the breach "would be the amount of injury which would ordinarily follow from a breach of contract under these special circumstances so known and communicated"; per contra, if the special circumstances were wholly unknown to the party guilty of the breach, he "could only be supposed to have had in his contemplation the amount of injury which would arise generally, and in the great multitude of cases not affected by any special circumstances, from such a breach of contract." This doctrine is grounded upon the right of the parties to make special provision for the damages in the event of a breach of a contract made under exceptional circumstances.

This is likewise the formula for the assessment of the damages ensuing from a breach of a contract to lease. In *McCulloch* v. *Lake & Risley Co.,* 91 N.J. Law 381, 103 A. 1000, Mr. Justice Swayze, speaking for our Supreme Court, declared it to be the settled rule that "the lessee is entitled to recover at least the value of his term." He expressed approval of the principle enunciated in *Neal* v. *Jefferson,* 212 Mass. 517, 99 N.E. 334, 335, 41 L.R.A. (N.S.) 387, Ann. Cas. 1913D, 205: "Where a lessor has prevented the lessee from entering and occupying the leased premises, or where an owner of property has broken his agreement to give a lease thereof to a prospective tenant, the measure of damages in an action for this breach of contract, if no rent has been paid, and if nothing further appears, is the difference between the actual value of the leasehold estate that should have been enjoyed and the agreed rental that was to have been paid therefor." But, in the ascertainment of the value of the term, the apposite rule, in the absence of special circumstances, is the difference between the actual rental value and the rent reserved. This rule measures the damages naturally arising from the breach of such a contract.

The insistence is, however, that the deprivation of prospective profits was, under the known special circumstances, reasonably in the contemplation of the parties at the time of the making of the contract, as the probable consequence of the breach. It is pointed out that the lessee contemplated the operation of the two houses as one unit, and that this would permit of economies and other advantages translatable into pecuniary profit not possible if they were widely separated; and, further, that the contract called for a provision reserving to the lessor the right of cancellation of the lease, subject to the payment of $5,000 to the lessee if canceled during the first year of the term, $3,500 if terminated during the second year, and $2,500 during the third year. But, assuming arguendo that lost profits were within the contemplation of the parties as the measure of damage, the claimed anticipated profits were not so certain and definite as to be the legally deducible consequences of the breach.

There is a well-established distinction, in respect of the ascertainment of future probable profits, between a new business or venture and one in actual operation. In the first, the prospective profits are too remote, contingent, and speculative to meet the legal standard of reasonable certainty; while in the second, the provable data furnished by actual experience provides the basis for an estimation of the quantum of such profits with a satisfactory degree of definiteness. In the one case, the success of the business usually depends upon a variety of circumstances, and the outcome is therefore too uncertain to provide a tangible basis for computation; while in the other, past experience has demonstrated the success of the enterprise and provides a reasonably certain basis for the calculation of plaintiff's probable loss consequent upon the breach of the contract to lease.

The instant case falls into the former category. Respondent was permitted to testify, over objection, that he operated other rooming houses in the city of Newark during the period in question, and that, based upon his "knowledge and experience in the business in the City of Newark and in that locality," the "reasonable return on the same business conducted in 22-24 (West Kinney Street) would be . . . . $2,500 a year." He explained that that sum represented "the gross profits for one year"; and later he said that he was "testifying to the profits . . . . made in operating 26-28 West Kinney Street." The following question and answer make it quite clear that he was not estimating the anticipated profits from the operation of the building in question: "Q. You didn't make any estimate or any figure of what in your opinion the return on 22-24 would be, did you? A. I have not been operating 22-24." Moreover, there was no evidence of a need for additional housing facilities in the vicinity. The adjoining house was not operated to capacity. Respondent testified: "Our rooms are quite filled up, practically 90 per cent." This business was essentially transient in character, and fluctuated in volume.

In these circumstances, the anticipated profits were so remote, speculative, and problematical as to preclude their consideration in the appraisement of the loss. They obviously did not satisfy the legal standard. Profits anticipated from a bargain take this classification when "they have reference to dependent and collateral engagements, entered into on the faith and in expectation of the performance of the principal contract. . . . . But profits or advantages which are the direct and immediate fruits of the contract entered into between the parties stand upon a different footing," and are recoverable as the natural and proximate consequence of the breach.

Liquidated Damages

The parties may as a part of their agreement stipulate the amount of damages that will be paid in the event the contract is breached. It is a common practice to provide in a building contract that the contractor will pay as liquidated damages a stated sum per day for each day he is late in the completion of the building. The courts enforce liquidated damage agreements but they will not enforce a penalty provision in a contract. A penalty provision is an agreement that one of the parties will pay a stated sum as a penalty for breach of the contract. Often a penalty provision in a contract will be stated as a liquidated damage provision. Whether a provision for the payment of a stated sum on the breach of a contract is a liquidated damage provision or a penalty provision will depend entirely on the nature of the provision. If the amount stipulated is reasonable and it is clear that the parties intended it as a provision for liquidated damages, it will be enforced, but if the enforcement of the provision will in fact impose a penalty, the provision will not be enforced. The test is whether or not the damages stipulated are reasonable and would have resulted from a breach of the contract.

Archer contracts to build a house for Burch and to have it completed by July 1. The contract provides that Archer will pay as liquidated damages $1000 per day for each day he is late in the completion of the house. The contract price of the house is $10,000 and the reasonable rental value of the house is $150 per month. The provision is clearly a penalty provision. If the amount were $5 per day the courts would no doubt enforce it.

Suburban Gas Co. v. Mollica
131 N.J.L. 61, 34 A. (2d) 892 (1943)

This was an action by the Suburban Gas Company (plaintiff) against Phillip Mollica (defendant). Judgment for plaintiff and defendant appealed. Judgment affirmed.

Porter, J. Plaintiff sued for breach of contract and recovered the amount due together with liquidated damages as provided for in the contract. It is not disputed that the contract was breached by the defendant. The sole ground argued on appeal is that the trial court erred in awarding liquidated damages, the contention being that the contract should have been construed as providing for a penalty and not for liquidated damages.

The plaintiff is a distributor of liquefied petroleum product commonly known as "bottled gas." It is delivered to the consumer in metal cylinders which are refillable. On April 8, 1939, the parties entered into a written agreement under which the defendant agreed to purchase from the plaintiff exclusively all liquid petroleum gas required by him at the premises specified for a period of three years at a fixed price and to pay the regular charges for installation and servicing of necessary equipment. It was also provided that a monthly minimum charge would be $1.15. The clause of the contract concerning damages reads as follows: "(*f*) Inasmuch as any loss arising from a breach of this agreement would be difficult of determination it is agreed that liquidated damages for any such breach is agreed upon to be fixed at the rate of $2.00 per month for all unexpired months of the life of this agreement." At the time of the breach the contract had eight months to run.

Parties to a contract may not fix a penalty for its breach. The settled rule in this state is that such contract is unlawful. Liquidated damages, however, are enforceable, and the intention of the parties will be carried out. The distinction between penalty and liquidated damages is to be tested by the reasonableness of the amount stipulated by the parties in the contract. If unconscionable, exorbitant, or excessive under all the conditions and circumstances, they are a penalty and not recoverable because the law limits recovery to indemnity from loss.

It has also been held that where damages are uncertain in amount and not readily susceptible of proof and the parties have agreed upon a sum not disproportionate to the presumable loss it may be recovered as liquidated damages; "but where the agreement contains disconnected stipulations of various degrees of importance, the sum named . . . . will be considered as a penalty, unless the agreement specifies the particular stipulation or stipulations to which the liquidated damages are to be confined."

It is the contention of the appellant that under these rules the damages for the breach of the contract should have been found in a nominal amount, there having been no proof of actual damages sustained; that the contract should have been construed by the trial court as providing for a penalty and not for liquidated damages. We think not. It seems obvious that the plaintiff was unwilling to assume the expense of installing pipes, cabinets, and other equipment in defendant's premises without assurance of indemnity against loss by securing a contract for exclusive sales for a reasonable period and for some formula for fixing liquidated damages in case of breach by the defendant. It is true that the contract contains several covenants by the appellant, the failure of any one of which would, of course, constitute a breach. For instance he agrees to have the plaintiff install necessary connections and equipment and to pay for same, to permit removal of same upon the breach or expiration of the contract, to permit servicing of equipment, to purchase gas exclusively from plaintiff and to pay for same on demand, and to pay a monthly minimum charge. Nevertheless we do not think the contract contains stipulations of various degrees of importance but rather that the various covenants are not independent nor of varying degrees of importance. The object of the contract and of each of its covenants was to secure to plaintiff the trade of the defendant for a definite period of time. The breach of any of the covenants would violate the rights of the plaintiff under the contract, and the amount of the damage would in each case be precisely the same. The amount specified as liquidated damages considering the nature of the contract, the minimum monthly charge and the proofs of the quantity of gas sold during the life of the contract satisfies us that the amount of $2.00 per month is not exorbitant, excessive, or unconscionable. It seems to us rather to be a reasonable and fair amount to fix as indemnification and does not seem to be a penalty.

Executions, Garnishments, Attachments

After a judgment has been rendered, if the judgment debtor does not pay the judgment, the judgment creditor is entitled to a writ of execution. This writ is addressed to the sheriff and authorizes him to take into his possession and sell so much of the judgment debtor's property, that is not exempt from execution, as is necessary to satisfy the judgment and to sell the same according to law and apply the proceeds to the payment of the judgment. Both personal property and real estate are subject to execution. All the states have exemption laws which provide that certain property owned by the judgment debtor is not subject to levy of execution but these exemption statutes vary widely. The procedure to be followed in the levy of an execution and the sale of the property levied on is set out by statute and is not uniform.

Garnishment is also statutory and is supplemental to the execution. In general, it is used to reach property or credits of the judgment debtor which are in the hands of a third person, and the procedure varies with the different states. As a general rule, garnishments are used to reach bank accounts, wages due, or accounts receivable; however, under some statutes one can reach goods in storage, the redemption value of pawned goods, etc.

Archer has a judgment against Burch for $1,000. Archer learns that Burch has an account in the First Bank. Archer has a writ of garnishment issued to the First Bank. It will order the bank to pay any moneys Burch has due him from the bank into court to be applied on the payment of Archer's judgment.

Under some circumstances the plaintiff may have the sheriff seize property of the defendant at the time suit is started. The procedure is in the nature of the levy of an execution before trial and judgment. The goods cannot be sold, with the exception of perishable goods, until a judgment for the plaintiff is entered. This procedure is called an attachment. The grounds for attachment are generally set out by statute and are not uniform throughout the United States. Generally, if the debtor is a non-resident and has property within the jurisdiction of the court, the property may be attached. The remedy of attachment usually is available in tort cases, especially in fraud cases. If the debtor is about to remove or dispose of his property for the purpose of defeating, defrauding, or delaying his creditors, a creditor may start suit by attachment. As a general rule, one starting suit by attachment must give bond to protect the defendant in the event the plaintiff is unable to obtain a judgment and the defendant is injured as a result of the attachment.

Specific Performance

The remedy of specific performance had its origin in equity and is still equitable in its nature. The remedy of specific performance requires the defaulting party to perform the contract as promised. This is accomplished by the granting of a decree which requires the party to perform. However, the court is not confined in its decree to requiring the performance of the terms of the contract, but the decree in special cases may be so drawn as best to effectuate the purposes for which the contract was made, and the decree may be granted on such terms and conditions as justice requires.

The court will not grant a decree of specific performance in those cases in which a money judgment is adequate. It is within the province of the court to determine when a money judgment is inadequate. The courts have uniformly held that the parties to a contract for the sale of land are entitled to the remedy of specific performance. In other cases the courts have adopted rules to aid them in determining the adequacy of a money judgment, but within the scope of these rules its adequacy turns upon the opinion formed by the court after weighing all the factors that exist in the case which is being tried.

If it is very difficult to determine the effect of a breach of a contract or to estimate the damage which would result, the court may grant specific performance of the contract.

The court may decree specific performance of contracts to sell personal property if the property contracted for has a sentimental value or esthetic interests which cannot be measured in money or if it is very difficult or impossible to obtain a duplicate or the substantial equivalent. Also if it is improbable that a judgment for damages could be collected, the court may decree the specific performance of the contract.

As a general rule, the court will not decree specific performance of a contract for personal services, since it is against the policy of the law to require persons to continue a personal relation which is distasteful to them. However, in cases where the nature of the services is unique or extraordinary, the courts have enjoined the party from performing such services for others during the term of the contract, thus by a negative decree granting a remedy substantially equivalent to specific performance.

The courts will not grant the remedy of specific performance of a contract, the performance of which would require prolonged and detailed supervision by the court, such as a building contract; nor will they grant specific performance of a contract, the performance of which would result in undue hardship.

The remedy being equitable, the court has the power to withhold the remedy when the ends of justice will thus be best served.

Pope Manufacturing Company v. Gormully
144 U.S. 224, 12 S. Ct. 632, 36 L. Ed. 414 (1892)

This was an action by Pope Manufacturing Company (plaintiff) against R. Phillip Gormully (defendant). The bill was dismissed and plaintiff appealed. Judgment affirmed.

The plaintiff brought a bill in equity asking for an accounting on a contract and also asking for an injunction enjoining the further violation of the provisions of the contract. The contract was an agreement whereby the defendant was licensed to manufacture and sell bicycles and tricycles containing certain patented devices under patents held by the plaintiff. The contract contained many restrictive provisions, some of questionable legality. The contract in its entirety was a harsh, one-sided agreement.

Mr. Justice Brown delivered the opinion of the court.

Whether this contract be absolutely void as contravening public policy or not, we are clearly of the opinion that it does not belong to that class of contracts, the specific performance of which a court of equity can be called upon to enforce. To stay the arm of a court of equity from enforcing a contract it is by no means necessary to prove that it is invalid; from time to time immemorial it has been the recognized duty of such courts to exercise a discretion; to refuse their aid in the enforcement of unconscionable, oppressive or iniquitous contract; and to turn the party claiming the benefit of such contract over to a court of law. This distinction was recognized by this court in *Cathcart* v. *Robinson*, 5 Pet. 264, 276, wherein Chief Justice Marshall says: "The difference between that degree of unfairness which will induce a court of equity to interfere actively by setting aside a contract, and that which will induce a court to withhold its aid, is well settled. 10 Ves. 292; 2 Coxe's *Cases in Chancery*, 77. It is said that the plaintiff must come into court with clean hands, and that a defendant may resist a bill for specific performance, by showing that under the circumstances the plaintiff is not entitled to the relief he asks. Omission or mistake in the agreement, or that it is unconscientious or unreasonable, or that there has been concealment, misrepresentation or any unfairness, are enumerated among the causes which will induce the court to refuse its aid." This principle is reasserted in *Hennessy* v. *Woolworth*, 128 U.S. 438, 442, in which it was said that specific performance is not of absolute right, but one which rests entirely in judicial discretion, exercised, it is true, according to the settled principles of equity, and not arbitrarily or capriciously, and always with reference to the facts of the particular case.

These principles apply with great force to the contract under consideration in this case. Not only are the stipulations in paragraphs 9 and 11 unusual and oppressive, but there is much reason for saying that they were not understood by the defendant as importing any obligation on his part beyond the termination of his license. Indeed, the operation of these covenants upon his legitimate business was such that it is hardly possible he could have understood their legal purport. The testimony upon this point was fully reviewed by the court below in its opinion, and the conclusion reached that the contract "was an artfully contrived snare to bind the defendant in a manner which he did not comprehend at the time he became a party to it." We have not found it necessary to go into the details of this testimony. While we are not satisfied that his assent to this contract was obtained by any fraud or misrepresentation, or that the defendant should not be bound by it to the extent to which it is valid at law, we are clearly of the opinion that it is of such a character that the plaintiff has no right to call upon a court of equity to give it the relief it has sought to obtain in this suit.

First National Exchange Bank of Roanoke et al. v.
Roanoke Oil Co., Inc.
169 Va. 99, 192 S. E. 764 (1937)

This was an action by Roanoke Oil Company, Inc. (plaintiff) against First National Bank of Roanoke and R. H. Thomas, executors of the estate of Paul Massie, deceased (defendants). Decree was entered for plaintiff and defendants appealed. Decree affirmed.

The Roanoke Oil Co., Inc., leased a certain lot of land, part of a larger tract, from the First National Exchange Bank, executor of the estate of Paul Massie. The lease contained a provision giving the estate the right to cancel the lease in the event of a bona fide opportunity to sell. It then further provided that the Roanoke Oil Co., Inc., would be given an opportunity to purchase at the price offered. The Oil Co. was to have five days within which to purchase the property. The estate had an offer to purchase and so notified the oil company. The oil company exercised their right, under the lease, to purchase, but the estate refused to sell and convey the property. The oil company sued asking specific performance of the contract.

Spratley, J. It is settled by a long course of decisions, as a principle of equitable jurisprudence, that specific performance of a contract is not a matter of absolute or arbitrary right, but is addressed to the reasonable and sound judicial discretion of the court. There are general rules and principles, which govern its application, but relief is granted, or refused, according to the circumstances of each particular case. Therefore, no positive rule fitting all cases can be laid down. In general, it will be used to promote an exact measure of justice, as nearly as is possible, and will be refused when it will produce injustice. It is never granted unless it is entirely in accordance with equity and good conscience. When the contract sought to be enforced has been proven by competent and satisfactory evidence, and there is nothing to indicate that its enforcement would be inequitable to a defendant, but will work injury and damage to the other party if it should be refused, in the absence of fraud, misapprehension, or mistake, relief will be granted by specific enforcement.

Here the executors made a definite offer as to price, terms, and subject-matter. This offer, as we have seen, was accepted without modification or change. There is no evidence that the letter of July 6th, or any word therein, was written by mistake. Both parties, certainly, until the acceptance letter of July 9th, construed and treated the option clause as requiring notice of an acceptable offer for the entire property to be given to the lessee. The record shows no legal obligation on the part of the executors to Jones, nor any hardship to be inflicted on the latter. The Massie estate will receive $20,000 for the entire property, whether it be sold as a whole, or in parcels. There is nothing to render the performance of the contract inequitable against the estate of Massie. It is apparent, on the other hand, that the enforcement of the contract will be of considerable benefit to the oil company, and that it will suffer substantial damage should specific performance be refused. The contract is unobjectionable in its nature and in the circumstances connected with it. The remedy in equity is more beneficial than the remedy in law, since it would be difficult to establish the entire damages before a jury. All of the equities favor the oil company.

Injunctions

The injunction is an equitable remedy designed to protect property or other rights from irreparable injury by commanding acts to be done or prohibiting their commission. It is used in a multitude of situations and affords the court of equity a flexible remedy which may be resorted to in an unlimited variety of situations.

It may be used to prevent hardship and oppression in contract cases; however, it is a remedy which is used sparingly in contract situations because it is only in the exceptional case that some other adequate remedy is not available. The court may grant an injunction enjoining the negotiation of a negotiable instrument, the transfer of property essential to the performance of a contract, or the violation of a building restriction. If one sells his business and contracts not to enter into business in competition with the purchaser, the courts may enforce such a provision by injunction. If one having exceptional skills contracts to employ those skills exclusively for a party but threatens, in violation of the contract, to employ those skills for others, the court may enjoin the use of such skills for anyone except the one with whom he contracted.

O'Melia et al. v. Berghoff Brewing Corporation et al.
304 Mich. 471, 8 N. W. (2d) 141 (1943)

This was an action by O'Melia and others (plaintiffs) against Berghoff Brewing Corporation and others (defendants). Judgment for defendants and plaintiffs appealed. Judgment affirmed.

Plaintiffs and defendants entered into a written contract whereby defendants appointed plaintiffs as the "exclusive wholesale distributor of Berghoff beer" in certain designated territory for a "period of five years." The contract provided in part:

"Berghoff agrees: . . . .

"*b*. During the life of this contract to give to Distributor (plaintiffs) the exclusive right to wholesale Berghoff beer within said territory.

"*c*. To sell beer to no one else in said territory."

The plaintiffs claim that defendants have wrongfully terminated the contract and are selling beer to others in the territory and ask for an accounting and an injunction enjoining the defendants from selling beer to others in the territory.

Starr, J. In their bill plaintiffs asked the court to "order the defendant, Berghoff Brewing Company, to carry out the terms of its contract." This was, in effect, a request that the court compel the Berghoff Corporation to deliver beer to plaintiffs and otherwise to perform the contract. A court of equity will not enforce such affirmative provisions of the contract.

In the alternative, plaintiffs asked the court to enforce the negative provisions of the contract; that is, Berghoff Corporation's agreement not to sell its beer to anyone else in the specified territory. This raises the question as to whether a chancery court should enjoin the breach of such negative provisions.

In *White Star Refining Co.* v. *Hansen,* plaintiff entered into an agreement with defendant granting him a certain territory and the exclusive right to sell its products therein. Defendant agreed to buy his entire requirements of motor fuel from plaintiff and further agreed not to sell any other brands of motor fuel on his premises. Plaintiff filed bill of complaint to restrain defendant from selling other brands of motor fuel. In reversing an order dismissing such bill Mr. Justice Clark said:

"While the court of equity cannot enforce specifically the affirmative provisions of a contract such as this, it may, nevertheless, and it should in a proper case, prevent a breach of the negative covenant. A proper case for such equitable relief is one where the remedy at law is not adequate. . . . .

"The exceptional cases in which equity will grant injunctive relief are, as has been said, those in which the remedy at law is not adequate, as where the injury cannot be compensated in damages and as where a judgment for damages would be worthless.

"On the facts thus far stated the trial court, on the authority of the Hardy case, was right in dismissing the bill. But the court seems to have overlooked an allegation of the bill, here to be taken as true, that defendant is financially irresponsible, and that judgment could not be collected.

"The right to recover a worthless judgment is not an adequate remedy at law. So plaintiff stays in equity on its allegation that a judgment against defendant would be worthless."

In the White Star Company case we recognize the rule that equity will grant injunctive relief only where the remedy at law is not adequate. In that case we reversed the order dismissing plaintiff's bill, because the bill alleged that the defendant was financially irresponsible and that "the right to recover a worthless judgment" was not an adequate remedy at law. It should be noted that in the present case plaintiffs did not allege in their bill that defendants, or either of them, were financially irresponsible or that a judgment against them was worthless. Neither did plaintiffs in their reply deny the allegation in defendants' answers that they were financially responsible and able to respond in damages.

Philadelphia Ball Club, Limited, v. Lajoie et al.

202 Pa. 210, 51 Atl. 973, 58 L.R.A. 227, 90 Am. St. Rep. 627 (1902)

This was an action by the Philadelphia Ball Club, Limited (plaintiff) against Napolcon Lajoie and others (defendants). Judgment for defendants and plaintiff appealed. Judgment reversed.

Potter, J. The defendant in this case contracted to serve the plaintiff as a baseball player for a stipulated time. During that period he was not to play for any other club. He violated his agreement, however, during the term of his engagement, and, in disregard of his contract, arranged to play for another and a rival organization. The plaintiff, by means of this bill, sought to restrain him during the period covered by the contract. The court below refused an injunction, holding that to warrant the interference prayed for "the defendant's services must be unique, extraordinary, and of such a character as to render it impossible to replace him; so that his breach of contract would result in irreparable loss to the plaintiff." In the view of the court, the defendant's qualifications did not measure up to this high standard.

We think that in refusing relief unless the defendant's services were shown to be of such a character as to render it impossible to replace him he has taken extreme ground. It seems to us that a more just and equitable rule is laid down in Pom. Spec. Perf., p. 31, where the principle is thus declared: "Where one person agrees to render personal services to another, which require and presuppose a special knowledge, skill, and ability in the employee, so that in case of a default the same service could not easily be obtained from others, although the affirmative specific performance of the contract is beyond the power of the court, its performance will be negatively enforced by enjoining its breach. . . . . The damages for breach of such contract cannot be estimated with any certainty, and the employer cannot, by means of any damages, purchase the same service in the labor market." We have not found any case going to the length of requiring, as a condition of relief, proof of the impossibility of obtaining equivalent service. It is true that the injury must be irreparable; but, as observed by Mr. Justice Lowrie in *Com.* v. *Pittsburgh & C. R. Co.*, 24 Pa. 160, 62 Am. Dec. 372: "The argument that there is no 'irreparable damage' would not be so often used by wrongdoers if they would take the trouble to discover that the word 'irreparable' is a very unhappily chosen one, used in expressing the rule that an injunction may issue to prevent wrongs of a repeated and continuing character, or which occasion damages which are estimated only by conjecture, and not by any accurate standard." We are therefore within the term whenever it is shown that no certain pecuniary standard exists for the measurement of the damages. This principle is applied in *Vail* v. *Osburn*, 174 Pa. 580, 34 Atl. 315. That case is authority for the proposition that a court of equity will act where nothing can answer the justice of the case but the performance of the contract in specie, and this even where the subject of the contract is what, under ordinary circumstances, would be only an article of merchandise. In such a case, when, owing to special features, the contract involves peculiar convenience or advantage, or where the loss would be a matter of uncertainty, then the breach may be deemed to cause irreparable injury.

The court below finds from the testimony that "the defendant is an expert baseball player in any position; that he has a great reputation as a second baseman; that his place would be hard to fill with as good a player; that his withdrawal from the team would weaken it, as would the withdrawal of any good player, and would probably make a difference in the size of the audiences attending the game."

We feel that the evidence in this case justifies the conclusion that the services of the defendant are of such a unique character, and display such a special knowledge, skill, and ability, as render them of peculiar value to the plaintiff, and so difficult of substitution that their loss will produce "irreparable injury," in the legal significance of that term, to the plaintiff. The action of the defendant in violating his contract is a breach of good faith, for which there would be no adequate redress at law, and the case, therefore, properly calls for the aid of equity in negatively enforcing the performance of the contract by enjoining against its breach.

QUESTIONS AND PROBLEMS

1. What is the remedy which is usually granted for breach of contract?
2. If the remedy at law—compensatory damages—is inadequate, to what remedies may the party be entitled?
3. Goodman and McKinley entered into a contract whereby Goodman agreed to manage a lunch counter for McKinley for a term of one year beginning September 1, 1944. After Goodman had worked one month, she was discharged without cause. What remedy would Goodman have for the breach of the contract? What would be the measure of her damages?
4. In granting a judgment for damages, what is the basis of determining the amount of damages awarded for breach of contract?
5. Archer purchased a radio from Burch. Archer claimed that the radio was not as warranted and demanded that Burch make his warranty good. Burch claimed that the radio was as warranted. Archer, while driving to see his lawyer about his claim against Burch, drove off the road and damaged his automobile. Archer sued Burch claiming as damages: (1) loss resulting from breach of warranty, and (2) cost of repairing his automobile. To what damages, if any, is Archer entitled?
6. What are speculative profits?
7. Newbold was starting an elevator and farmer's supply business at Kinston. Newbold ordered a quantity of fertilizer from Meadows Co. which Meadows Co. contracted to ship. Meadows Co. later refused to ship the fertilizer, and Newbold sued claiming as damages loss of profits. Is Newbold entitled to recover loss of profits as damages?
8. What is the test of the validity of a liquidated damage provision in a contract?
9. Gay leased a factory to Camp for a period of two years at a rental of $10,000 per year. The lease provided that if Camp breached the lease, he would pay, in addition to back rent, $5,000 as liquidated damages. When the lease had 18 days to run, Camp was adjudged bankrupt and as a result the lease was breached. Is Gay entitled to a claim of $5,000 as liquidated damages?
10. Tracy contracted to assign to Corbin a patent right which had not been used. Tracy refused to assign the patent right, and Corbin brought a bill for specific performance. Should a decree of specific performance be granted?
11. Carnera entered into a contract with Madison Square Garden Corp. to box with the winner of the proposed Schmeling-Stribling contest. One of the provisions of the contract was that Carnera would not, pending the contest, box in any major contest. "A major contest is understood to be one with Sharkey, Baer, Campalo, Godfrey or like grade heavyweights." Carnera contracted to box with Sharkey without the consent of the Garden. The Garden brought suit, asking for an injunction enjoining Carnera from boxing Sharkey. Should the injunction be granted?

PART III

PROPERTY

CHAPTER XIV

NATURE AND CLASSIFICATION OF PROPERTY

Nature of Property

The conception of property is so ancient in its origin that some writers consider it a part of natural law. No one can know the true origin of property; it is a conception which is known to all people, however primitive their society may be. In fact, animals and birds exercise a dominion over their caverns and nests which is analogous to our conception of property.

Property is defined in Black's *Law Dictionary* as "That which is peculiar or proper to any person; that which belongs exclusively to one; in the strict legal sense, an aggregate of rights which are guaranteed and protected by the government. The term is said to extend to every species of valuable right and interest.

"More specifically, property is ownership; the unrestricted and exclusive right to a thing; the right to dispose of a thing in every legal way, to possess it, to use it, and to exclude every one else from interfering with it."

Ownership is defined as "The complete dominion, title or proprietary right in a thing or claim.

"The entirety of the powers of use and disposal allowed by law."

From these definitions of the two terms it is apparent that they are used with a similar meaning. Property is the more general term, including both the thing owned and the legal rights incident to ownership. The benefits arising from property are the legal rights incident to ownership. We do not know the origin of all these incidents, but they are well established in our society and are remarkably similar in all societies. The principal incident is the exclusive right to use. This carries with it the right to possess. The right to dispose of property is another important incident of ownership. There are some limitations on these rights. One is not permitted to use his property so that others are injured. There are some limitations on one's right to dispose of property. As a general rule, in the United States, a married man is not permitted to will all his property to strangers, leaving nothing to his widow. One's right to use and dispose of his property is limited only to the extent which is necessary to insure to others in society a similar property right and to protect society from burdens imposed by unwarranted use or disposal of property.

Wood v. Security Mutual Life Insurance Co.
112 Neb. 66, 198 N.W. 573 (1924)

This was an action by Edward A. Wood (plaintiff) against Mutual Life Insurance Company (defendant). Judgment for defendant and plaintiff appealed. Judgment affirmed.

Plaintiff leased a room in defendant's building for the purpose of operating a barber shop. The defendant wished to remodel the building. The plaintiff's lease had two and one-half years to run.

The defendant offered to allow the plaintiff to occupy another room in the building, rent free during the time the building was being remodeled. The plaintiff accepted this offer and signed the following release: ". . . . the undersigned hereby agree to hold the insurance company harmless from all liability for damages to the person or property of the undersigned. . . ." The plaintiff sued to recover for the damages to his business. The plaintiff contended the word property referred to his tools and equipment and did not include his business.

Dean, J. His argument is that the only damage which could have been reasonably contemplated thereunder was damage to visible, tangible property "which plaintiff had in his shop" and which was capable of physical custody. He insists that the contract had no reference to plaintiff's trade or business and did not therefore work a release of liability for damage thereto.

We do not think plaintiff's argument is tenable. He cites decisions to support his contention which do not seem to be in point and which, in view of the weight of authority, are not applicable to the facts before us.

It is to be noted that, by the language of the instrument in question, plaintiff agreed to hold defendant harmless "from all liability for damage to the person or property" of plaintiff. The inquiry then should be directed to what is meant, under the law, by this expression as used by the parties in their agreement.

Property, in a broad sense, is defined as any valuable right or interest considered primarily as a source or element of wealth, and includes in modern legal systems practically all valuable rights. In New Jersey it was held that "a calling, business or profession, chosen and followed, is property." It has also been held that the owner of a vessel has a property right, not only in the vessel itself, but in its use and the business in which it is employed. *Sailors' Union of the Pacific* v. *Hammond Lumber Co.*, 156 Fed. 450, at page 454, 85 C. C. A. 16, 20. In the case last cited, the court said:

"The appellee's property is not only its vessels, but the business of carrying freight and passengers, without which the vessels would lose their value. The right to operate vessels, and to conduct business is as much property as are the vessels themselves."

In Pennsylvania the court declared that the labor and skill of the workman, be it of high or low degree, the plant of the manufacturer, the equipment of the farmer, investments of commerce, are all in equal sense, property. In the Purvis Case the court held, in direct terms, that a person's business is property within the meaning of the law. In Illinois it has been held:

"The term 'property' includes every interest any one may have in any and everything that is the subject of ownership by man, together with the right to freely possess, use, enjoy and dispose of the same."

In the Bailey Case it was also held that the right to entertain lodgers in a lodging house is a property right.

Classification

Because of the variety of things which are subject to ownership and the varied incidents of ownership, property has been divided into various classes. These classes are not mutually exclusive; the same thing may, owing to its various characteristics, fall into more than one classification. Property may be classed as tangible or intangible—sometimes termed corporeal or incorporeal. The basis for classifying property as tangible or intangible is the physical nature of the property. Property which has a physical existence, such as land, buildings, furniture, etc., is tangible, and property which has no physical existence, such as patent rights, easements, bonds, etc., is intangible. This distinction is important in determining the right to tax, in the probating of estates, and in similar situations. As a general rule, tangible property is subject to taxation by the state in which it is located, while intangible property is taxable at the domicile (home) of the owner.

Property is also classed as public or private. The classification of property into public and private is based on the ownership of the property. If the government or a political division thereof is the title-owner, it is classed as public property; but if the property is owned by an individual, a group of individuals, a corporation, or some other business organization, it is classed as private property. The fact that property privately owned is devoted to a public use or is used to benefit a large class of persons does not change its nature so as to convert it into public property. Property owned by a municipal corporation, such as a city park, city hall, or municipal auditorium, is public property.

The most important classification is that of real and personal property. The earth's crust and all things firmly attached thereto are real property, while all other objects and rights capable of ownership are personal property, or, in other words, immovables are real property and movables are personal property. This classification is both historical and logical. That property which can accompany the person of the owner and is consumable is naturally distinguished from property which is fixed and which continues to exist for generation after generation. Although the distinction as stated is simple, the problems arising are frequently complex because that which was real property can be converted into personal property by severance and that which was personal property can be converted into real property by attachment. Stone in the ground is real property but when quarried it becomes personal property, and, if it is used in the construction of a building, it will again become real property. Perennial products, trees, grass, fruit trees, etc., which need not be seeded each year, are, as a general rule, treated as part of the land. Crops resulting from annual labor, potatoes, corn, oats, annual vegetables, etc., are in many cases treated as personal property, although, generally, they pass with the land. If perennial products are severed from the land, they become personal property. Some courts have held that an intent to sever and a dealing with the product as though severed is a legal severance and converts a product otherwise real property into personal property.

Klevmoen v. Farm Credit Administration
138 F. (2d) 609 (1943)

This action arose in a bankruptcy proceeding. Farm Credit Administration moved the local conciliation commissioner to require the bankrupt (Asmund Klevmoen) to schedule the growing crops of 1942 separately from the scheduled real estate. The commissioner denied the motion and the Farm Credit Administration filed a request for review by the district court. On review the district court granted the motion and Klevmoen appealed. Judgment of the district court reversed and remanded.

The crops in question were planted by the appellant in the spring of 1942, and were "all in by the middle of May on the bankrupt's land." He instituted his farm debtor proceeding on May 19, 1942, and with his petition filed schedules including among his assets his land, part of which only was his homestead, but not separately including the crops then very recently planted thereon.

The single question presented is whether or not these crops should be scheduled as chattel assets or should merely be included with, and constitute a part of, the land upon which they were growing.

Delehant, D. J. It is asserted by the appellant and acknowledged by the appellee that, under the law of North Dakota, those annual crops which are within the definition of fructus industriales are, during the period of their immaturity, and while they continue to derive sustenance from the soil, a part of the soil; that as such, their title is ordinarily in the owner of the land by virtue of such ownership, and passes upon his deed of the land to a purchaser or, upon involuntary alienation, to the grantee of the land at judicial sale.

The appellee directs our attention to the further unquestioned rule that the ownership of growing crops as an incident of the ownership of the soil in which they are growing is not invariable; that such crops may belong, in the first instance, to one not the owner of the land; and that even in the ownership of the proprietor of the land, they are susceptible of separate sale or encumbrance by him and subject to levy under judicial process. Such possibilities certainly exist; and when they transpire ordinarily result in the constructive severance from the soil of the growing crop and its treatment for the purposes of the particular transaction under scrutiny as chattel property, distinct from the soil. It will be noted that no such severance is disclosed in the record before us. No occasion arises, therefore, for determining whether a purely supposititious imposition by the appellant upon the growing crops of a valid lien before the institutiton of his farm debtor proceeding would have required the separate scheduling of the crops and their administration distinct from the land.

Acquisition of Personal Property

In most instances personal property is acquired by purchase. The law governing the acquisition of personal property is known as the law of sales and will be treated later under that title.

Personal property may also be acquired by gift. A gift is a voluntary transfer of property by one person to another without any consideration. To have a valid gift, the donor must presently deliver the property with the intent to vest ownership in the donee. From an early date the courts have held that without delivery there can be no gift. Delivery is a transfer of possession from one person to another. The delivery may be to the donee or to a third person for the donee. If the donee is already in possession of the property, a clear declaration by the donor that he gives the property to the donee is sufficient. In some instances the courts have recognized symbolic delivery; for example, the courts have held that the delivery of the key to a strong box is symbolic delivery of the contents of the strong box.

Unowned things become the property of the person who first reduces them to possession; for example, a wild animal will become the property of the person who first takes possession of it. A wild animal caught in a trap or a fish caught in a net becomes the property of the owner of the trap or net; however, if the animal or fish escapes, it again becomes unowned property. If one abandons his property, it becomes unowned property and, if someone takes possession of the abandoned property, he becomes owner of it. If Archer discards an old clock on the public dump and Burch takes it from the dump, the clock becomes the property of Burch.

Lost property becomes the property of the finder as against all persons except the original owner. If Archer loses his ring and Burch finds it and later loses the ring and Clark finds it, Burch can claim the ring from Clark but Archer, the original owner, has the superior right to the ring and can claim it from either Burch or Clark. If the finder of lost property knows who the owner is, yet appropriates it to his use, he is guilty of larceny. If he does not know who the owner is and does not have reasonable means of discovering the owner, yet appropriates the property to his own use, he will be guilty of conversion if the owner later proves his right to it. Some states have passed statutes which permit the finder of lost property to clear his title thereto by complying with the statutory procedure. The courts have made a distinction between lost goods and mislaid goods. If Archer while in Burch's store drops his purse in the aisle, it will generally be classed as lost property but, if he lays it on the counter and, forgetting it, leaves the store, the purse is mislaid. If the purse is mislaid, Burch will become bailee thereof. If Clark finds the purse in the aisle, Clark will have the right to take possession of it but, if Clark discovers the purse on the counter, Burch will have the right to take possession of it. It is very difficult to distinguish between lost property and mislaid property; consequently, the cases on the subject are not in accord.

Title to personal property may be acquired by confusion and by accession. Confusion is the mixing of goods so that the parts cannot be identified and separated. For example, crude oil belonging to several persons is mixed in one tank. If the mixing is by common consent or inevitable accident, each party will be deemed the owner of a proportionate part of the mass. If the mixing is by wilful, tortious act, the innocent party will be protected and the entire mass will become the property of the innocent party if such action is necessary to protect his interest. In case of accidental confusion, if one of the owners is guilty of negligence, he will have to suffer any loss resulting from the confusion.

Literally, accession means that something has been added, and as applied to property it means that new value has been added to existing property by labor or by the addition of other property. As a general rule the owner of the original property will become the owner of the improvements. If Burch repairs Archer's automobile by adding some new parts, Archer will be the owner of the automobile when repaired and he will also own the new parts which Burch has added.

Difficulties arise when one person improves another's property (1) by the addition of labor or (2) by the addition of labor and materials, when the owner has not contracted for or consented to the improvement. The decisions of the courts are not in accord and in many respects the decisions are confusing. As a general rule if one person has tortiously taken property of another and by his labor improved the property, the owner of the original property can recover the property in its improved state and will not have to compensate the tort feasor for his labors. In developing this rule the courts have applied the two following familiar principles of law: (1) one cannot benefit from his own wrong, and (2) a person who is not guilty of wrong cannot be made a debtor unless he consents. In a few decisions the courts have refused to follow this rule to its logical conclusion and have held that, if the value of the improved property is so out of proportion to the value of the original property that to allow the owner to claim the property in its improved state would shock the conscience of men, recovery will be denied. If the original property has been improved by the addition of the labor and materials of the wrongdoer, the improved property goes to the owner of the original property. If the person making the improvement honestly but mistakenly believes that he is the owner of the property at the time he makes the improvement, the courts will, as a general rule, permit a recovery for the benefits conferred on the true owner of the property as a result of the improvements.

If the owner of the property wishes, he may sue a wrongdoer in tort for the conversion of his property and recover a judgment for the damage he has suffered.

Michael v. Holland
111 Ind. App. 34, 40 N.E. (2d) 362 (1941)

This was an action by Joseph L. Michael (plaintiff) against Albert Holland (defendant). Judgment for defendant and plaintiff appealed. Judgment reversed and new trial ordered.

Plaintiff loaned defendant \$450. The defendant went to plaintiff's office to pay the loan and at that time plaintiff asked defendant for his check book. Defendant gave his check book to plaintiff who wrote out a check for \$150 and told defendant that \$150 was all he wanted on the loan. Defendant protested and said he wished to pay the full amount, but plaintiff refused to accept more than \$150. About three years later plaintiff demanded payment of the \$300 balance which defendant refused to pay. Plaintiff sued and defendant claimed that plaintiff had made him a gift of the \$300 balance of the debt.

Bedwell, P. J. Upon many occasions this court and the Supreme Court of this state have passed upon the requisites of a gift inter vivos, where the subject of the gift is a chattel or a chose in action that is evidenced by a written instrument such as a bank deposit, corporate stock, a negotiable instrument, a bond, or check; but as far as we have been able to ascertain, no case in this state has dealt with the question of what constitutes a good forgiveness of a simple debt due from the donee to his donor. It is well settled here, as well as in other jurisdictions, that the delivery of the written instrument evidencing an obligation to pay, such as a note or bond, with intent thereby to give the debt to the donee, is a good gift of the debt.

"A 'gift inter vivos' of personal property may be defined as the voluntary act of transferring the right to and the possession of a chattel, whereby one person renounces, and another acquires, immediate right and title thereto. It cannot be made to take effect in the future.

"An agreement or promise to make a gift, being without consideration, is void. . . . . There must be both an intention to give and a stripping of the donor of all dominion or control over the thing given. . . . . The change of the title is and must be irrevocable.

"The delivery must be of possession, of the dominion, and of the control of the property. The transfer must be so complete that, if the donor again assumes control over the property without the consent of the donee, he becomes liable as a trespasser. And so essential is delivery as a factor in the transaction that it has been said: 'Intention cannot supply it; words cannot supply it; actions cannot supply it. It is an indispensable requisite, without which the gift fails, regardless of the consequences.'"

In this case the subject of the claimed gift had no corporeal existence. It was a pure chose in action without palpable form, and there was no document, symbol, or token that was evidence of title to it. As far as the evidence indicates there was not even a book account kept by appellant evidencing the indebtedness of appellee. While there is authority to the effect that where there is no written evidence of a debt, since no delivery can be made, there can be no gift, the great weight of authority in other jurisdictions, and we think the better rule, is that a gift of a simple debt without palpable form by the creditor to the debtor cannot be made effective without the execution and delivery of some instrument or the performance of some act or acts placing the debt beyond the legal control of the creditor.

The only evidence of a gift herein was the oral testimony of appellee. The mere fact that appellant wrote a bank check for $150, and that same was signed by appellee, is of no aid as written evidence of a gift.

Liesner et al. v. Wanie
156 Wis. 16, 145 N.W. 374 (1914)

This was an action by Liesner and others (plaintiffs) against Wanie (defendant). Judgment for plaintiffs and defendant appealed. Judgment affirmed.

This action was to recover the body of a wolf said to have been mortally wounded by plaintiffs and reduced to possession thereafter by defendant. Plaintiffs mortally wounded the wolf and so followed up their attack on the animal as to substantially have it in their possession. They had it where and in such condition and circumstances that escape was improbable, if not impossible. The defendant came upon the scene and with his gun pointed so as to reach within some three feet of the animal delivered a finishing shot. He took the body as his property and retained it to the damage of the plaintiffs. The sum recoverable, in case of defendant being liable, was not in serious dispute.

Marshall, J. It is conceded that if the plaintiffs had substantially permanently deprived the wolf of his liberty—had him so in their power that escape was highly improbable, if not impossible, before defendant appeared on the scene and with his gun pointed so as to reach within some three feet of the animal delivered a finishing shot, it has become the property of plaintiffs and was wrongfully appropriated by appellant. Such is according to the prevailing rule. The instant a wild animal is brought under the control of a person so that actual possession is practically inevitable, a vested property interest in it accrues which cannot be divested by another's intervening and killing it. *The Law of Animals*, Ingham, 5. Such is the law of the chase by common law principles, differing from the more ancient civil law which postponed the point of vested interest to that of actual taking.

Bozeman Mortuary Ass'n. v. Fairchild et al.
253 Ky. 74, 68 S.W. (2d) 756 (1934)

This was an action by Bozeman Mortuary Association (plaintiff) against J. M. Fairchild and others (defendants) wherein defendants filed a counterclaim. Judgment for defendants on part of their counterclaim and plaintiff appealed. Judgment reversed and remanded.

A Buick automobile was stolen from plaintiff who was in business in Bozeman, Montana. The thief was arrested in Rockcastle county, Kentucky, for "shooting up a filling station" and at the time of his arrest the thief was in possession of the stolen automobile. The sheriff took possession of the automobile and later it was sold for storage and a garage bill. Fairchild purchased the automobile from the person who purchased it at the foreclosure sale. When the automobile was found by plaintiff, Fairchild refused to surrender it and when sued he asserted a counterclaim for $130.48 for a battery, muffler, tires, and a few minor parts, and for oil and grease furnished the car. The lower court allowed Fairchild $81.18 which the court determined to be the cost of "necessary improvements." The automobile was in good repair when stolen and had new tires. Fairchild drove the automobile 3,000 miles while he had it.

Stanley, Commissioner. The facts of the present case obviously place it under the classification where the rights are designated as by accession as distinguished from rights by specification, for there was no change in the form or transmutation in the species of the subject-matter. The consideration of relative values of the original and the new, which often has an important bearing in the adjustment of the title to chattels by accession, also supports this conclusion.

The new battery, tires, and other accessories put upon the automobile in substitution of those worn out—either by the defendants or others who had it after it was stolen—could yet be identified and be removed, which fact creates some difficulty and takes the case out of that line where there was such confusion or intermingling of properties as to make them inseparable. We do have some cases of this character, at least in respect to separability, to be noticed. Where the automobile or other chattel is subject to a conditional sale contract or mortgage, with respect to accessions the general rule is that title to the accessories will not pass with the principal chattel when reclaimed by the conditional vendor or on foreclosure of the mortgage where they can be readily identified and detached without injury to it. In those annotations are digested cases holding property to pass by accession and cases holding the contrary, the different conclusions depending upon whether the seller of the accessories (including specifically automobile tires and the like) had retained title to them. Berry, in his work on Automobiles, section 1806, shows that distinction, but couples with the matter of identity the important consideration of whether the accessory may be detached without injury to the principal chattel. The removal of these accessories (the cost of which apparently the trial court allowed) would destroy the machine's usefulness until the owner should replace them. It may be said, then, that these accessories were united to the principal thing so as to constitute an integral part of it and the owner of the greater acquired title to the lesser articles. The installation of these items is not far removed from repairs to a chattel, and it is the rule that ordinary repairs become a part of the thing repaired by accession. 1 C. J. 384, and notes.

But our decision in this case may not rest wholly upon any conclusion in respect to the nature of the accessions, for the relation of the parties always has a controlling influence. We may look again to the Lampton Case for guidance. It is there said that there are two comprehensive and fundamental rules pervading the authorities "from the first of which it is not known that there are any exceptions, and from the last of which, it is believed that there cannot be many. These rules are: 1st. That no trespasser, who takes property of another wantonly and without the owner's consent, can ever acquire a right to it, by any 'accession' or 'specification,' whatsoever. 2d. When the property of one comes to the possession of another, innocently, he may acquire the right to it, if by 'accession' or 'specification,' the species be changed." But it is pointed out that the various and indifferent characters of the cases which have been excepted from this last rule result in difficulties. This distinction between a willful and an involuntary wrongdoer or trespasser is uniformly recognized.

Upon the principle that a party can obtain no right by nor derive any advantage from his own wrong, the willful trespasser, as against the owner, can never acquire title to the thing itself and will never be allowed to reclaim the articles he has put upon it or commingled with it, or to receive their value, however great or small the change wrought in the original article may be, or however much or little the enhancement in value may be.

The second class of claimants, that is, those who come into possession of another's property innocently or under color of title and alter or add to it, are commonly referred to as unintentional trespassers. Their rights and the limitations upon those rights, upon the authority of a number of cases, including those we have cited, are thus stated in a general way in 1 C. J. 385: "One, although technically a trespasser, may, if he has acted under a mistake of right and without wrongful intent, acquire a right of property by accession. It is not, however, the policy of the law to offer any encouragement to trespassers, to put a premium upon carelessness in regard to the rights of others, or to make one person suffer for the mistake of another; and ordinarily a trespasser, although acting under a mistake of right, cannot acquire title to property by accession, as against the owner, where its identity is not lost and it has not been so increased in value as to make it obviously inequitable for the original owner to reclaim it."

Public welfare and public policy will not allow one to assert any rights to stolen property or to anything he spends or puts on it as against the owner. To hold otherwise would be to encourage the nefarious business of handling stolen automobiles which has grown to such amazing and alarming proportions.

Acquisition of Real Property

In the original thirteen states the title to the land vested in the commonwealth. The Northwest Territory was ceded by the states to the federal government, and title to this land vested in the federal government. In those instances in which the United States acquired territory by purchase or annexation, the title to the land vested in the federal government, subject to existing rights of individual owners.

From the earliest times certain formalities have been considered as essential to the transfer of ownership of real property. At the present time any contract affecting an interest in real property must be in writing and all conveyances of real property are required by statute to be in writing and certain definite formalities must be complied with in the execution of the written conveyance. Such written instruments are called "deeds."

Ownership in real property may be acquired by gift. The donor of real property must deliver to the donee, or to some third person for the benefit of the donee, a deed which complies with all the statutory requirements of the state in which the real property is located. It is not necessary for the donee, or some third person acting for the donee, to take actual physical possession of the real property. The essential element of the gift is the delivery of the deed. If the donor makes deeds to real property and leaves them in his safety deposit box to be delivered to the named donee after the death of the donor, the gift will fail for lack of delivery.

Title to real property may be acquired by adverse possession. The statutory law of the states provides that no action shall be brought for the recovery of the possession of land after a stated number of years, which may vary from five to twenty years. If a person holds land by open, continuous, and adverse possession for the statutory period, he can acquire title to the land by complying with certain statutory requirements. To acquire title by adverse possession there must be (1) actual occupancy; (2) which is hostile to the owner's title; (3) with open claim to title; (4) continuously for the statutory period. In some states the claimant must, in addition to the four requisites set out above, pay the taxes. One person need not occupy the land for the entire period, but the adverse possession must be continuous. Burch takes possession of land owned by Archer and claims title to the land and remains in possession for four years at which time Burch sells his interest to Clark who immediately takes possession and remains in possession for six years. If the statutory period is ten years, Clark can acquire title to the land at the end of his six-year occupancy. He acquired Burch's rights which, added to his rights, satisfy the statutory requirement.

If the taxes are not paid on real property, as a general rule, the unpaid taxes become a lien on the property which is prior to the claims of all persons having an interest in the property. After a stated time the state sells the land for taxes, and the purchaser at the tax sale acquires title to the property. The entire procedure is statutory, and there is no uniformity in the tax laws of the several states.

The owner of real property has the right, subject to some restrictions which will be discussed in a later section, to dispose of his real property by will. The will to be effective must be drawn and executed in accordance with the statutory requirements of the state in which the real property is located. If the owner of real property dies without having made a will, the land will descend to his heirs according to the laws of the state in which the real property is located.

Pepe v. Aceto

119 Conn. 282, 175 Atl. 775 (1934)

This was an action by Frank Pepe (plaintiff) against Tony Aceto (defendant). Judgment for defendant and plaintiff appealed. Judgment affirmed.

Plaintiff and defendant each claimed a triangular piece of land containing 2.07 acres which lay between land owned by plaintiff and land owned by defendant. The description in plaintiff's deed was such that it did not expressly include the disputed land. Plaintiff claimed the land by adverse possession.

Plaintiff bought a tract of land from the estate of Robert Holliner. The tract had a shack on it in which Holliner had lived. Part of the tract was enclosed by a stone wall which had an opening or gate in it. From this opening or gate a road led to the main road. The three cornered piece in dispute was bounded by the main road, the road leading from the opening in the stone wall to the main road and the stone wall which intersected the main road. The tract was grown up to brush and weeds but it had some timber on it. After he acquired the property in 1916, plaintiff cut some firewood and poles on the tract and cleared a portion of it and planted it to garden. In 1924 defendant acquired the adjoining tract and immediately claimed the tract in dispute. Defendant acquired the adjoining tract from some old people who did not live on the tract and seldom visited it. There is no showing that Holliner in his lifetime claimed the disputed tract or made any use of it. He did use the road leading from the gate in the stone fence to the main road.

Avery, J. The trial court further found that the plaintiff had failed to prove that either Robert Holliner, or any of his predecessors in title, laid claim to or occupied the disputed area, or were in exclusive, continuous, open, notorious, and adverse possession thereof. Neither the plaintiff's deed nor that of any of his predecessors in title in evidence located the southern boundary of the plaintiff's land other than being bounded south by land of heirs of Samuel Beach. While title to a particular tract of land, in the absence of any evidence to the contrary, draws possession with it, general possession of the tract will not avail as regards any particular piece of land, unless it is satisfactorily shown to have been a part of that tract. In view of the defendant's denial of the complaint, the burden was upon the plaintiff to prove the correct boundary line and his ownership of the tract in dispute.

To establish title by adverse possession, it must be of fifteen years' duration, Gen. St., § 6004, and the adverse user must be with the knowledge and acquiescence of the owner; to give this knowledge and obtain this acquiescence, the law requires that the owner shall be ousted of possession, that the ouster shall be continued uninterruptedly for the statutory period, and that the possession shall be open, visible, and exclusive in another. The finding clearly shows that the use, if any, by Holliner was not exclusive and hostile, nor were the defendant's predecessors in title on notice of the existence of any adverse holding. As to the possession of the plaintiff, even if it be considered adverse, it was in any event interrupted in 1924, and at most continued for about eight years. Upon the finding as made, the court correctly ruled that the plaintiff had failed to establish his cause by adverse possession.

QUESTIONS AND PROBLEMS

1. What is the nature of property rights?
2. What things may be owned?
3. What is the difference between tangible property and intangible property? Give some examples of each.
4. Tracy owned land to the center of a non-navigable river. Patts owned the land on the other side of the river. Patts cut ice on Tracy's side of the river, and Tracy sued Patts for damages for trespass on Tracy's land. Was the ice on Tracy's side of the river Tracy's real property?
5. Thom, a sculptor, built a home having spacious grounds. Thom placed a statue and sun-dial on the grounds. The statue and sun-dial were placed on a cement base but they were not clamped or bolted to the base. They weighed between three and four tons and were held firmly in place by their own weight. The house and grounds were sold on mortgage foreclosure sale. Thom claims that the statue and sun-dial are personal property and that they remain his property. Warring, the purchaser at the foreclosure sale, claims that they are a part of the real estate. Are the statue and sun-dial real or personal property?
6. Marshall delivered two promissory notes to Shoun and explained to Shoun that the notes were a gift to Marshall's wife and that Shoun was to collect the notes and turn the money over to Marshall's wife. Later at Marshall's request Shoun returned one of the notes to Marshall and Marshall gave the note to Russell. Mrs. Marshall sued Russell to recover the note claiming that it was her property. Does Mrs. Marshall own the note?
7. Post was hunting on the beach with his dogs when they started a fox. While the dogs were in pursuit of the fox, Pierson killed the fox and carried it away. Post sued Pierson for the value of the fox claiming it as his (Post's) property. Is the fox Post's property?
8. Sincoe entered upon the land of Pickering and cut timber and had it made into staves. The manufacture of the staves was done in good faith, and the expenditure of labor and money in so doing increased the value of the timber in the trees more than 500 per cent over the value of the standing trees. Pickering brought an action to recover the manufactured staves. Should Pickering be permitted to recover the manufactured staves?
9. Gay owned a tract of land. Gay's signature was forged to a deed from him to his wife, Beatrice. A subsequent deed was given by Beatrice to an innocent purchaser for value. Gay now claims the land. Can Gay recover the land?
10. Clare under a void deed took possession of a tract of land which he occupied for a period of several years. He could have secured title thereto by continuing his adverse possession for a period of ten years. It is contended that prior to the expiration of the ten-year period, Clare did not have an interest in the land which he could transfer by a conveyance. Do you agree with this contention?

CHAPTER XV

PERSONAL PROPERTY

Possession

The old saying, "possession is nine points in the law," contains an element of truth. Possession is a legal element incident to ownership which frequently plays an important role in determining the legal rights in property. This is especially true in regard to personal property. Possession is used with such a variety of meanings that it is futile to attempt to define it. In its simplest sense it signifies that one has complete physical control of an object; however, in law this concept is inadequate. Archer has a watch in his pocket—he has possession of the watch. He takes the watch out of his pocket and puts it in the drawer of his desk. Does he still have possession of the watch? To answer this question it is necessary to inquire into Archer's relation to the watch as compared with the relations of other persons who may have some interest in or connection with the watch. Ordinarily we would say that Archer does have possession of the watch.

As a general rule the person who takes "possession" of a wild animal becomes owner of the animal. Archer, while hunting, shoots and mortally wounds a fox. Archer is following the fox and in the normal course of events will overtake the fox and take actual physical possession of it. Before Archer reaches the fox, Burch shoots the fox and takes actual physical possession of it. Archer, while hunting with his dogs, starts a fox. While the fox is running free on an open beach, with Archer's dogs in pursuit, Burch shoots the fox and takes actual physical possession of it. In the above situations who owns the fox? If "possession" is limited in its meaning to actual physical possession, Burch will become the owner of the fox in both situations. However, the courts do not always interpret "possession" to mean actual physical possession. If we follow a decision of the Wisconsin court in which the facts were similar to those in the first illustration, and if we follow a decision of the New York court in which the facts were similar to those in the second illustration, we will decide that Archer became the owner of the fox in the first illustration and that Burch became the owner of the fox in the second illustration. In the rule of law stated above, the courts have interpreted "possession" as degree of control rather than actual physical possession.

In connection with personal property two elements are of general importance: (1) physical control and (2) intent to claim legal rights in the object. The courts recognize "legal possession" which is the legal right to control the physical object, but actual physical possession is not a necessary element of legal possession. In our first illustration if Archer is the owner of the watch which is in his pocket, he has both actual physical possession and legal possession. A servant or agent may have actual physical possession of an object which is the property of his master or principal, but he does not have legal possession—he has custody. In working out problems arising in the law of master and servant and principal and agent, courts consider the master or principal as the party in legal possession of property which has been intrusted to the servant or agent by his master or principal.

The term "possession," when used in the abstract, includes such a multiplicity of situations that it loses its significance. Possession may indicate one factual and legal situation when we say that "to have a valid levy of execution, the sheriff must take possession of the property," and another when we say that "to create a bailment of property, possession must be delivered to the bailee," and still another when we say that "the crime of larceny involves the felonious taking possession of and carrying away of another's property."

Bailments

In the abstract, the nature of a bailment is well settled, but it is frequently difficult to determine whether or not a particular contract will create a bailment. The intention of the parties plays an important part in determining the nature of the relation created by a given contract. There are several types of bailments possessing distinctive characteristics, but there are some general characteristics which may be referred to for the purpose of identifying a bailment. All of these characteristics need not be present, but one or more will be present in all bailments.

Usually both custody and service of some sort will be involved, for example, the storage of personal property, the repairing of a watch, and the renting of an automobile. Also, possession of the property bailed will be severed from ownership, and the bailee's possession will be more than mere custody; he will have such a right of possession that he may exclude the possession of others and, in some instances, even that of the bailor. The bailor has the right to the return of the property bailed either in its original or in an altered form. If the bailee cannot return the property, he must account for it.

The bailment is frequently confused with a sale in cases in which the original article is not to be returned, but an article of similar characteristics is to be returned in its place. If grain is stored in a common mass and the elevator is to return the same number of bushels of grain as was stored, is the relationship a bailment or a sale? A similar problem is the case in which stock is pledged in block and the same certificates are not to be returned, but certificates representing an equal number of shares of the same stock will suffice. In those cases involving the storage of grain, it is held that, if the purpose of the arrangement is simply the storage of the grain, it is a bailment; in those cases in which stock has been pledged, it is generally held that the contract creates a bailment. The share of stock is intangible property and the certificate is merely evidence of the property right, so it is immaterial that the exact certificate is not returned. Other relations which may be confused with a bailment are conditional sales, trusts, and agencies. In the conditional sale, the vendee has a property interest in the property in addition to possession and, if the conditional sale contract is fulfilled, the vendee will become owner and the property will not be returned to the vendor. In the trust, the trustee has both legal title and possession. His ownership and possession are for the benefit of the beneficiary of the trust. In the agency, the agent's duties may be much broader than the duties of the bailee. Bailment and agency are distinct concepts.

The modern courts and writers classify bailments into three general classes. The basis of the classifications is whether or not the bailee is compensated. In accordance with this idea, bailments are now generally classified as: (1) bailments for the sole benefit of the bailor, (2) bailments for the sole benefit of the bailee, and (3) bailments which benefit both the bailor and the bailee.

Another classification, which is based primarily on the liabilities imposed on the bailee, is (1) ordinary bailments and (2) extraordinary bailments. Ordinary bailments may include all three of the classes aforementioned and are the types of bailments which we shall treat in this chapter. Extraordinary bailments usually include bailments involving common carriers, innkeepers, and other similar public agents.

The bailor is the owner of the bailed property and as such assumes all the risks incident to ownership. The bailee is liable only in the event the property bailed is damaged as the result of the failure of the bailee to perform his duties as bailee. As a general rule the bailee must exercise ordinary care in the preservation of the bailed property. The parties may shift the risks involved by contract, that is, the bailee may assume greater duties than those imposed on him by law or he may be relieved of part, if not all, of his ordinary duties. In the case of extraordinary bailments, the liability of the bailee is that of an insurer of the bailor's goods. The bailee in an extraordinary bailment is not liable in every instance in which the bailor's property is damaged or destroyed, but he must protect the property from all ordinary hazards such as fire, theft, etc., or, as the liability is sometimes expressed, the extraordinary bailee is liable for all losses except those resulting from acts of God or the inherent propensities of the property bailed.

Wells v. West
212 N.C. 656, 194 S.E. 313 (1937)

This was an action by Nelson W. Wells (plaintiff) against Mrs. W. S. West (defendant). Judgment for defendant and plaintiff appealed. Judgment affirmed.

Plaintiff rented a room in the defendant's lodging-house. Plaintiff left an accordion in his room and told defendant not to let anyone have it. Sometime thereafter defendant permitted a man, calling himself Ward, to remove the accordion from the house on the fraudulent pretext that plaintiff had sent him for it. The suit was brought against defendant to recover the value of the accordion on the theory that defendant was bailee of the accordion and as such had not exercised reasonable care in the preservation of the property.

Devin, J. Plaintiff, however, contends that by virtue of having placed personal property, with defendant's consent, in his rented room in her house, the relationship of bailor and bailee resulted, and that an action for a breach of duty on the part of the bailee, though based on negligence, was one in which he could elect to waive the tort and sue on contract.

But the law of bailment is not applicable to the facts disclosed in this case. The property was not placed in possession of defendant nor was custody thereof accepted by her. It was at all times in the room rented by plaintiff in the house of defendant, and there was neither actual nor constructive possession of the accordion delivered to her. That defendant had access to the room, for the purpose of maid service, would not constitute possession of plaintiff's personal property placed by him in the room. Defendant was not an innkeeper and was not an insurer of plaintiff's property.

In *Hanes* v. *Shapiro*, 168 N.C. 24, 84 S.E. 33, will be found a full discussion of the law of bailment. The generally accepted definition of a bailment is that it is "a delivery of goods in trust upon a contract, express or implied, that the trust shall be duly executed and the goods restored by the bailee as soon as the purposes of the bailment shall be answered." 2 Kent Comm. 559. To constitute a bailment there must be a delivery by the bailor and acceptance by the bailee of the subject matter of the bailment. It must be placed in the bailee's possession, actual or constructive.

"There must be such a full transfer, actual or constructive, of the property to the bailee as to exclude the possession of the owner and all other persons and give the bailee for the time being the sole custody and control thereof."

The rental of a room, and the deposit therein by the tenant of certain personal property, though the landlord had access to the room for janitor or maid service, would not constitute such a delivery of the personal property as to constitute the landlord a bailee.

Peet v. Roth Hotel Co.
191 Minn. 151, 253 N.W. 546 (1934)

This was an action by Mrs. Charles L. Peet (plaintiff) against The Roth Hotel Company (defendant). Judgment for plaintiff and defendant appealed. Judgment affirmed.

Plaintiff's engagement ring, a platinum piece set with a large cabochon sapphire surrounded by diamonds, was made to order by Mr. Hotz, a manufacturing jeweler. One of the small diamonds had been lost and plaintiff arranged with Mr. Hotz to have it replaced. She was to leave the ring for him at the St. Paul Hotel which was owned and operated by defendant. Plaintiff went to the hotel and asked for Mr. Hotz and was told that he was not in. She had the ring on her finger. She went to the cashier, Miss Edwards, and told the cashier that she wished to leave the ring for Mr. Hotz. The cashier took the ring, placed it in an envelope, wrote "for Mr. Ferdinand Hotz" on the envelope and left it on her desk where it was within easy reach of anyone passing by her window. The ring was stolen or lost, but the loss was not reported to either Mr. Hotz or plaintiff for over a month. Plaintiff sued to recover the value of the ring, $2,500, on the theory that defendant was bailee and the loss was the result of defendant's failure to exercise ordinary care in the preservation of the ring.

Stone, J. The jury was instructed that defendant was a "nongratuitous" bailee. By that it is doubtless intended to say that the bailment was "reciprocally beneficial to both parties." Clearly, that was a correct interpretation of the proof. The ring was accepted in the ordinary course of business by defendant in rendering a usual service for a guest, and so, plainly, it was for defendant's advantage, enough so, at least, to make the bailment as matter of law one for the benefit of both bailor and bailee.

The jury was charged also that, the bailment being for the reciprocal benefit of the parties, defendant, as bailee, was under duty of exercising, in respect to the subject-matter, ordinary care, that is the degree of care which an ordinarily prudent man would have exercised in the same or similar circumstances. The instruction was correct. The former distinction between bailments for the sole benefit of the bailor; those for the mutual benefit of both bailor and bailee; and those for the sole benefit of the latter, in respect to the degree of care required of the bailee in order to protect him from liability for negligence, has long since been pretty much discarded here as elsewhere. "It is evident that the so-called distinctions between slight, ordinary, and gross negligence over which courts have perhaps somewhat quibbled for a hundred years can furnish no assistance."

Defendant's liability, if any, is for negligence. In that field generally, the legal norm is a care commensurate to the hazard, i.e., the amount and kind of care that would be exercised by an ordinary prudent person in the same or similar circumstances. The character and amount of risk go far, either to decrease or increase the degree of care required. The value of the property, its attractiveness to light fingered gentry, and the ease or difficulty of its theft, have much to say with triers of fact in determining whether there has been exercised a degree of care commensurate to the risk, whether the bailment be gratuitous or otherwise. However unsatisfactory it may be, until legal acumen has developed and formulated a more satisfactory criterion, that of ordinary care should be followed in every case without regard to former distinctions between slight, ordinary, and great care. Even the courts which adhere to the former distinctions will be found in most cases to be demanding no other degree of care than one commensurate to the risk and other relevant circumstances; e.g., in *Ridenour* v. *Woodward*, 132 Tenn. 620, 179 S. W. 148, 149, 4 A. L. R. 1192, it was held that a gratuitous bailee was answerable only for his gross negligence or bad faith. But, as the court proceeded to say, the care to be taken was "to be measured, however, with reference to the nature of the thing placed in the keeping." The defendant was relieved of liability because it was held as matter of law that he had "acted with a fairly commensurate discretion" in handling the bailed property.

The rule of our decision law puts upon the bailee the burden of proving that the loss did not result from his negligence. This burden, in the language of the late Mr. Justice Dibell, is "not merely the burden of going forward with proofs, nor a shifting burden, but a burden of establishing before the jury that its negligence did not cause the loss." That proposition we adopted as "the practical working rule." We are not disposed to depart from it.

Fixtures

A fixture is personal property which, because of its attachment to or its use with real property, is regarded as real property. There is no simple test which can be applied in determining when personal property has been converted into a fixture—real property. The early courts emphasized attachment and many cases have held that the mode of attachment is the controlling fact; however, in other cases—few in number—it has been held that certain property is a fixture although it is not attached to the land or building.

The better reasoned cases hold that, within limits, the intention of the parties is controlling and that mode of attachment, usefulness in connection with the real property, relation of the parties, etc., are but evidence of intention.

In determining the intention of the parties the court will apply an objective test. If the parties have expressly agreed that property shall become a fixture or shall not become a fixture, such expressed intention will be conclusive. However, parties cannot by express agreement convert a city lot into personal property, or convert personal property, which is in no way attached to nor used in association with real property, into a fixture. As a general rule attachment is essential and, if personal property is not attached to the real property, it is not a fixture. The few cases holding that unattached property is a fixture because of association in use with the real property have involved property which had been specially constructed for use with the real property and which would have been of little value for any other use. For example, it was held that storm windows, which had been specially built for a hotel building but which had been taken down and stored on the premises, were fixtures and, on the sale of the hotel, became the property of the purchaser.

The relation of the parties is also of outstanding importance. If the owner of real property improves his property by the addition of personal property, there is an all but conclusive presumption that he intended the improvement to become a part of the real property and, if he sells or mortgages the real property without reservation, the courts have held that the additions are fixtures and pass as real property to the purchaser or mortgagee.

If the owner purchases personal property on conditional sale or chattel mortgage and with the seller's consent attaches it to his real property, in nearly all instances the courts have held that the property will remain personal property. However, if, after the attachment of the personal property, the real property is sold to a buyer who has no knowledge of the existence of the conditional sales contract or chattel mortgage, the weight of authority is that the innocent purchaser takes the attached personal property as a fixture. Both the Uniform Conditional Sales Act and the Uniform Chattel Mortgage Act have provisions covering the foregoing situation.

As between landlord and tenant the earliest cases held that any improvement made by a tenant became a part of the real property, but the courts soon began to make a distinction between attachments made by tenants of business property for trade purposes and attachments made by ordinary tenants. This distinction is important today. The courts have generally held that personal property, brought onto premises, leased for business purposes, for use in the carrying on of the business for which the premises are leased, remains personal property irrespective of the mode of attachment. However, if the personal property is so built into the real property that its removal will weaken the structure, the courts have held that it becomes a part of the real property.

In domestic and agricultural tenancies the general rule of intention has been applied in the later cases. However, as a general rule, the courts have not indulged in the same strong presumption that the property attached to the real property is to remain personal property as they have done in the case of trade fixtures. In all tenancies if the tenancy is for a definite period, the tenant must remove the property which he has attached to the real property before the expiration of the lease and, if he fails to remove it before the lease expires, he loses his right to the property. If the tenancy is for an indefinite period, such as a life estate, the tenant has a reasonable time after the expiration of the lease in which to remove such property.

Fehleisen v. Quinn
182 Ia. 1283, 165 N.W. 213 (1917)

This was an action by Fehleisen (plaintiff) against Quinn, receiver of the New-Lite Manufacturing Company (defendant). Judgment for defendant and plaintiff appealed. Judgment affirmed.

New-Lite Manufacturing Company carried on its business of manufacturing certain automobile accessories at Newton, Iowa. It entered into an arrangement with the Boone Commercial Association, whereby it undertook to remove its plant to Boone. The association donated two lots to the company for the purpose of erecting a building thereon. These lots were in fact conveyed to plaintiff who erected on the lots, at a cost of $7,500, a building suitable for the company's purposes. The lots and building were sold by plaintiff to the company for $7,500 payable in installments of $100 per month. The contract contained a forfeiture provision, whereby the plaintiff was given the right to declare a forfeiture and repossess the property if the company defaulted. The company moved its machinery and equipment into the building. The machinery was bolted to the concrete floor or otherwise attached to the building. At the time the company entered into the contract with plaintiff, it was insolvent and it made no payments on the contract. The company moved into the building on May 15 and on July 1 a receiver was appointed. The receiver paid $100 to plaintiff as one month's rent. This suit was brought to prevent the receiver from selling and removing the machinery and equipment on the ground that, by attachment, it became fixtures and on forfeiture it became the property of plaintiff.

Evans, J. Property attached to buildings and which would be

deemed as a part of the realty as between vendor and vendee or as between an heir and an administrator may properly be deemed chattel property as between a landlord and a tenant. Whether in a given case property attached to a building upon real estate should be deemed as a part of the real estate is, in the last analysis, a question of intention. Such intention is usually implied from all the facts appearing in the case. The manner in which such property may be affixed to the soil or to the building is often an important consideration in determining the intention. Where an owner of realty affixes thereto fixtures that are appropriate to the use of the property, it is usually deemed as consistent with the interests of the owner to treat the same as a part of his realty. If it be to his interest to so treat it, the implication naturally arises that he so intended it. Under the earlier cases fixtures so attached were regarded almost uniformly as a part of the realty. Under the later decisions that rule has been relaxed, and the question of intention has been made the criterion of its application.

When the improvements under consideration have been attached to the realty by one not the owner of the realty, the implication of intention assumes a different color. This is so when a tenant for his own purpose of utilizing the leased premises attaches thereto such equipment as seems to him advantageous to the use of the leasehold by himself. Here again the earlier cases held grimly and with little reason that any equipment firmly affixed to the realty by the tenant became at once a part of the realty and the property of the landlord. That doctrine has been quite generally repudiated by the later cases.

As between landlord and tenant the doctrine of trade fixtures has been given practically universal recognition, and is generally applied with much liberality to the protection of the tenant in the ownership of such fixtures. Theoretically this is deemed as tending to encourage trade and industry. Manifestly a tenant would hesitate to incur large expense in equipping himself with the necessities of his trade or industry if the ownership of the equipment thus acquired is to pass at once by operation of law from him to his landlord. Nor would the landlord be easily induced to acquire such equipment for the tenant if by the operation of the rule referred to he could acquire the same at the expense of the tenant. In the case of *Ottumwa Woolen Mills Co.* v. *Hawley*, 44 Iowa, 57, 24 Am. Rep. 719, Grim, who affixed the equipment to the realty, was the absolute owner of the realty unincumbered. He therefore owned the equipment no less as a part of the realty than he would have owned it if it had been deemed chattel. Subsequently he mortgaged the realty to Hawley, and still later sold the same to the Ottumwa Woolen Mills Company. The controversy that arose was between the mortgagee and the vendee. The question at issue between them had to be determined, not by the act or interest or intention of either litigant, but by the implied intention of Grim, the common grantor. Grim's intention was fixed as of the time that the fixtures were attached.

The holding was that he intended the equipment to attach to the realty as a part thereof. In *Ray* v. *Young*, 160 Iowa, 613, 142 N.W.

393, the question arose as against a tenant who had built the improvement upon the leased property for trade purposes. It was held that the doctrine of trade fixtures applied, and that the tenant was entitled to hold the same as chattel and to remove the same without injury to the realty.

In its facts the case on trial appears to occupy a position somewhat midway between the two cited cases. The appellant contends that the manufacturing company which brought its equipment from Newton to Boone and installed the same in the new building had become the owner also of the realty, and that it should, for that reason alone, be deemed to have intended the installation as an improvement of the realty, and therefore to become a part thereof. On the other hand, the appellee contends that in practical effect the manufacturing company was a mere tenant, wholly unable to become an owner under its executory contract, and that its intention, therefore, should be ascertained and implied in a court of equity from that point of view. This latter was the view adopted by the trial court. The machinery in question, so far as it was attached at all, was so attached by bolts and nuts so far as the superstructure was concerned. The attachment to the cement floor was accomplished by drilling of holes for bolt attachments and the fastening of the same with sulphur cement. The sulphur cement was used in preference to other cement because it was softer and therefore more pliable and permitted the removal of the fixtures thus made with greater facility. If the manufacturing company should fairly be deemed practically a tenant rather than the owner of the property, it seems quite clear to us that the nature of the fixtures was such that they should be deemed as chattel and removable. Whether we should deem the manufacturing company as owner or as tenant, its actual relation to the title of the realty, and the condition which it was in as to solvency, is a very important consideration as bearing upon the question of its intention.

We reach the conclusion that the facts in evidence would not justify the finding of an intention, by implication or otherwise, on the part of the manufacturing company at the time it installed its equipment, to make the same as a part of the realty. Taking the case in all its facts, we think no different inferences of intention could be implied than would be implied as against a tenant occupying the same realty. The practical interest of the manufacturing company was substantially the same as that of a tenant, especially in view of its known insolvency, and therefore inability to perform its executory contract.

QUESTIONS AND PROBLEMS

1. What is meant when we say that one has legal possession of property?
2. Harris was in the business of selling trucks and delivered to Good a truck for trial pending negotiations for the purchase of the truck. Good used the truck for purposes other than those contemplated and negligently abused and misused the truck. Would Good be liable for having used the truck for purposes other than those contemplated?
3. Wentworth patronized a restaurant owned by Riggs. While in the restaurant,

Wentworth hung his coat on a hook which was about two feet from where he was sitting. There was no checkroom, but a place was provided by the cashier's desk where valuables could be checked. There were notices posted about the place, "not responsible for hats, overcoats, umbrellas, etc.," but Wentworth claimed that he did not see these. Wentworth's overcoat was stolen and he sued Riggs to recover its value. Should Wentworth recover?

4. Stephens loaned money to Reed and took a mortgage on the Altmont Apartments as security. The Altmont Apartments were "efficiency apartments" and were equipped with Murphy folding beds which had been built into the walls of the building. Reed defaulted and Stephens started foreclosure proceedings. Reed contends that he has the right to remove the Murphy beds from the building. Is Reed's contention correct?
5. Hillebrand purchased at a mortgage foreclosure sale the real estate of the Beatrice Brick Co. Later Nelson, the sheriff, undertook to seize fifteen wheelbarrows, one tool box, one sand box, a quantity of lumber, one oil tank and contents, three crowbars, and two shovels. Hillebrand claims these articles as fixtures because they are necessary in the operation of the business of the Beatrice Brick Co. Are Hillebrand's contentions correct?

CHAPTER XVI

REAL PROPERTY

Historical Development

In England the law of real property had its origin in the feudal system of land tenures, which was established following the Norman Conquest. Under the feudal system the title to all land was vested in the king who parcelled the land out in return for services and fealty. The king granted the land in large estates to the nobility who, in payment, rendered military service. The nobility in turn parcelled the land out either to lesser nobles who rendered military service or to villeins who worked the manor lands and who were given in return the crops which they raised on small tracts of land allotted to them.

At first each person held for life only, but later the right of succession was recognized; however, until a relatively late date estates tail and primogeniture were in force in England. Land held in estate tail, after 1285 A.D., was inalienable by the grantee as against his heirs and it descended only to the heirs of his body—his children—and the estate ceased when they failed. Under the rule of primogeniture the eldest son inherited the entire estate together with all rights accompanying it. Neither estates tail nor primogeniture are in force in the United States.

In the United States land is held free from all service and fealty; however, in one respect our law of real property follows the feudal system. We recognize that the original title to land rested in the government and, if the owner of land dies intestate leaving no heirs or next of kin, the land goes back to the state—escheats to the state.

Estates in Real Property

In the United States at the present time estates in real property are divided into freehold estates, less than freehold estates, and future estates. Freehold estates are estates in fee simple, life estates, and determinable fees. An estate in fee simple is the highest type of estate. It is not limited in time, and on the death of the holder the property descends to his heirs unless he has disposed of it by will. A life estate is

limited in time in that it terminates at the end of the life upon which it is based. A life estate may be for the life of the holder or for the life of another or others. The life tenant has the right to use the property but he does not have the right to do any act which will permanently injure the property. The life tenant cannot cut ornamental trees but he can cut ripe timber; he cannot open a mine but he can work a mine which has been opened; he cannot remove permanent buildings or permit them to decay for lack of care. A determinable fee is created when real property is granted for an indefinite period as "for 99 years renewable forever" or "as long as the property is used for educational purposes." The estate thus created is a freehold estate and is real property.

Estates less than freehold estates are estates for a term of years, estates from year to year, and estates at will and by sufferance. An estate for a term of years is created by a lease of the property to a tenant for a fixed period, as for ten years or fifty years. A lease for a fixed term is personal property irrespective of the length of the term. An estate from year to year may be created by agreement or by a holding over. If a tenant holds over after the expiration of his term and the landlord acquiesces in such holding over, an estate from year to year will be created providing the rent reserved in the lease is payable annually. Some courts have held that, if the rent reserved is payable monthly, the holding over creates an estate from month to month. Estates from month to month or week to week are basically the same as an estate from year to year. An estate from year to year continues until terminated by notice. At common law six months' notice was required to terminate such an estate. Many states have statutes which set the requisites for terminating periodic leases. As a general rule, if the period is less than a year, the notice must be given at the beginning of a period—a month's notice would be required to terminate an estate from month to month.

An estate at will is an estate which may be terminated at the option of either party. An estate at sufferance is created when one, having entered into possession rightfully, "holds over" wrongfully after his estate has terminated. One who refuses to surrender after mortgage foreclosure and the expiration of the redemption period would hold by sufferance.

Future estates are estates which will come into existence on the happening of some future event. If real property is willed to Archer to be held in trust for the benefit of Burch and on the death of Burch the property is to go to Clark, Clark has a future estate in the property.

Ralston Steel Car Co. v. Ralston
112 Ohio St. 306, 147 N.E. 513 (1925)

This was an action by Annie M. Ralston (plaintiff) against Ralston Steel Car Company (defendant). Judgment for plaintiff and defendant appealed. Judgment affirmed.

Joseph S. Ralston in his lifetime was the lessee of certain real estate in the city of Columbus, under an instrument called a permanent lease, sometimes called a perpetual lease, the tenure of which was for 99 years *renewable forever*. The estate was insolvent. The widow claimed the lease was real estate and that she was entitled to dower. The creditors claimed it was personal property and that the widow had no dower interest in it.

Marshall, C. J. Much of the law of real property of this present period is the outgrowth of principles established in England during the feudal period. Classifications and definitions which were applicable then are still employed to a large extent. The obsolete doctrines of the English laws of real property have become the foundations of modern rules, except in so far as their technicalities have been disregarded, and except as they have been modified or superseded by statutory provisions. Property is defined as the right and interest which a man has in lands and chattels to the exclusion of others.

Blackstone divided property into two classes: Personal, which consists in goods, money, and other movable chattels; and real, which consists of such things as are permanent, fixed, and immovable, as lands, tenements, and hereditaments of all kinds which are not annexed to the person, or cannot be moved from the place in which they subsist.

A hereditament comprehends anything which may be inherited, whether corporeal or incorporeal, and includes both lands and tenements.

These ancient classifications and definitions, which are yet applicable and potent when considered in conjunction with section 8597, General Code, would seem to leave no doubt that a permanent leasehold is real property.

Blackstone has again divided estates into freehold and less than freehold. He has further described a freehold estate as one which requires actual possession of the land; again, it is such an estate in lands as is conveyed by livery of seizin. His description is summed up in the following conclusion:

"As, therefore, estates of inheritance and estates for life could not by common law be conveyed without livery of seizin, these are properly estates of freehold."

Estates less than freehold include estates for years, at will, and by sufferance, and in 2 Blackstone, 143, the rule is declared that—

"Every estate which must expire at a period certain and prefixed, by whatever words created, is an estate for years."

All authorities agree that in the last analysis the true test of a freehold is indeterminate tenure. Measured by this standard, how can it be said that a so-called permanent leasehold is really a lease at all, and what possible reasons exist for classifying it as a chattel?

"A grant or lease in fee reserving rent operates as an assignment or sale and not as a lease, although, for some purposes, the relation of lord and tenant, or of landlord and tenant, may be assumed to exist between the parties. Properly speaking, a term of years or other certain period of time and a reversion seem to be indispensable to the idea of a lease."

Transfer by Deed

In transferring real property, certain formalities are necessary. Each state has jurisdiction over the land lying within its boundaries and has the right to set out the formalities which must be followed to transfer the ownership of such land. The several states have, by statute, set out the form of conveyance which is to be used in conveying title to real property. These statutes are not uniform in their provisions, but do follow a general pattern.

Two types of deeds are in general use in the United States, the quitclaim deed and the warranty deed. When one conveys by a quitclaim deed, he conveys whatever title he may have to the purchaser, but he does not, by the form of the deed, claim to have a good title or, in fact, any title; if the title proves defective or if the seller had no title, the purchaser has no cause of action under the deed.

A warranty deed contains covenants of warranty; that is, in addition to conveying the title to the property, the grantor binds himself by express warranties to make good any defects in the title he has conveyed. The grantee under a warranty deed gets only the title his grantor has, but if the title is not as warranted by the grantor, the grantee has a cause of action under the deed and can recover in damages for any injury he has suffered by reason of the defective title. If the property is mortgaged or the title is subject to some other encumbrance, it is customary to give a deed containing general covenants of warranty and then expressly except the known encumbrance from the operation of the warranty provisions.

The deed form in general use in the United States will name the grantor and grantee, will contain words of conveyance, will recite the consideration, will describe the property, will be signed, usually will be sealed, in some states will be witnessed, in some states will be acknowledged and, before the deed becomes operative, it must be delivered.

The grantor and grantee must be named or indicated with sufficient certainty so that they may be identified. No particular words of conveyance are necessary, but the phrases "give, grant, bargain, and sell" and "convey and warrant" are in common use. Any language which indicates the grantor's intention to transfer his ownership to the grantee is sufficient.

Although a deed is not a contract, it is standard practice to recite a consideration in the deed. At one time in England if the deed did not recite a consideration, the presumption was that the grantee held the land in trust. At this time it became standard practice to recite a consideration in a deed and the practice has not been abandoned. The description in the deed need not be technically accurate, but it must be such that the property can be identified. In cities descriptions are usually by plat, block, and lot, and in the country, if the land has been surveyed by the government, it is usually described by reference to the government survey, otherwise it is described by metes and bounds.

In the United States the several states have recording statutes which establish a system for the recording of all transactions which affect the ownership of real property. The statutes are not uniform in their provisions, but in general they provide for the recording of all deeds, mortgages, etc., and further provide that an unrecorded transfer is void as against an innocent purchaser or mortgagee for value. Under this system it is customary for the seller to give the buyer an abstract of title certified to date. The abstract is a history of the title of the real property according to the records and is not a guaranty of title. For his own protection the buyer should have the abstract examined by a competent attorney who will render an opinion as to the title held by the grantor. The opinion will state whether or not the grantor has a merchantable title to the property and, if the title is defective, the nature of the defects will be stated.

Several of the states have adopted the "Torrens System." Under this system the person who owns the land in fee will, through the procedure set up by the statute, obtain a certificate of title from the designated official and, when the real property is sold, the grantor will deliver a deed and his certificate of title to the grantee who delivers the deed and certificate of title to the designated official and receives a new certificate of title. All liens and encumbrances against the property will be noted on the certificate of title, and the purchaser is assured that his title is good except as to liens and encumbrances noted thereon. In some states some encumbrances, such as liens for taxes, short-term leases, and highways rights, are good against the purchaser even though they do not appear on the certificate.

Calhoun, Trustee v. Drass
319 Pa. 449, 179 Atl. 568 (1935)

This was an action by John C. Calhoun, trustee in bankruptcy of estate of John N. Drass, bankrupt (plaintiff) against John B. Drass (defendant). Judgment for defendant and plaintiff appealed. Judgment affirmed.

John N. Drass, a real estate agent, was indebted to his father, John B. Drass, in the amount of $7,500. The property in question was listed with John N. Drass for sale and John N. Drass advised his father that it was a "good buy" and the father authorized the purchase of the property for himself. John N. Drass arranged the deal and had the owners of the property execute a deed to the property, leaving the name of the grantee blank. John N. Drass paid the purchase price and John B. Drass gave him credit for the amount on the debt due to him (John B. Drass). John N. Drass held the deed for almost a year at which time the name "John B. Drass" was inserted as grantee. John B. Drass held the deed for about six months before he recorded it. The deed was recorded three days after John N. Drass was adjudged bankrupt. The trustee in bankruptcy contends that the deed is void and that the property is part of the estate of John N. Drass.

Opinion by Mr. Justice Kephart. Appellant's main contention is that the deed was not a valid deed, as it did not contain the name of a grantee when delivered to John N. Drass. Assuming then that creditors may contest such conveyance, where there is not sufficient evidence to support the allegation that the conveyance was made to delay, hinder, or defraud creditors, this position of the appellant is not well taken. That a deed cannot exist as such without a grantee is fundamental. But the law controlling such instrument is vastly different from that covering a deed without a grantee where authority is given to some one to insert the grantee's name. While there is a conflict of decisions as to whether that authority should be in writing, or whether it may be oral, express, or implied from the circumstances, a majority of jurisdictions do not require written authority to insert the grantee's name; Pennsylvania is one of the oldest in that class. An agent of the grantor may insert the name of the grantee, notwithstanding such direction is verbal, and many states recognize the doctrine of implied authority to insert the name of the grantee in the blank space left therefor.

Our statute of frauds (33 PS § 1) would seem not to require such written authority to insert the name of a grantee. That statute provides, in effect, that no estates shall be granted unless by a writing signed by the grantor "or their agents, thereunto lawfully authorized by writing." In *Bell* v. *Kennedy*, 100 Pa. 215, an action of assumpsit to recover back purchase money, as the result of a conveyance without the name of a grantee therein expressed, which was later filled in, we said: "It may be conceded, in case a deed, duly executed in other respects with a blank left therein for the name of the grantee, be put in that condition in the hands of a third person with verbal authority to fill up the blank in the absence of the grantor, and to deliver the deed to the person whose name is inserted as grantee, and the deed be so filled and delivered, it becomes a valid deed."

While this statement of law is urged as dictum, it has been followed and has had legal effect in this commonwealth for years, we have found no authority to the contrary. A valid deed may be signed, acknowledged, and delivered with the name of the grantee left blank, provided there is authority, oral or written, express or implied, in some one to fill in the blank. Assuming, as appellant contends, that John B. Drass' name was not in the deed when it was delivered and the space therefor was left blank, in view of the father's testimony that there was an agreement between his son and himself that the deed was to be for the father, John N. Drass being a real estate agent, having received a commission from the grantors for making the sale, and the grantors paying this commission, parting with title, under such circumstances John N. Drass was a competent person to fill in the name of his father.

Smith v. Federal Land Bank of Columbia et al.
181 Ga. 1, 181 S.E. 149 (1935)

This was an action by Will Smith (plaintiff) against Federal Land Bank of Columbia and others (defendants). Judgment for defendants and plaintiff appealed. Judgment reversed.

Hutcheson, J. The deed from Mary Merritt to Jacob Merritt, purporting to convey "all that tract or parcel of land lying and being in the County of Coffee, said State, and being all of 100 acres, situated in the northwest corner of lot of land No. 18 in the first land district of Coffee County, being bounded on the north and west by the original lot lines, on the east by lands of Louis Clayton, and on south by lands of Ava Cauley," was not void because of insufficient description, although the land in controversy was actually situated in the Fourth district, and not in the First district, as recited in this deed. In view of the particular statement that the tract conveyed was bounded on the east and south by lands of named owners, parol evidence was admissible for the purpose of applying the description to the intended subject-matter and to show that the statement as to the district number was a clerical error. Such extraneous evidence being sufficient in this case to apply the description to the land in controversy, the court erred in excluding the deed from evidence upon the ground that it contained no adequate description of the property.

The deed from Jake Merritt to Ida Smith and her children, conveying "all the tract of land lying and being in the 4th district of originally Irwin now Coffee County, containing one hundred acres in the northwest corner of lot of land No. 18, the survey to start at northwest corner of said lot and run the line south to the dividing corner," was not on its face void for uncertainty of description as applied to the land in controversy, and was not shown to be void for uncertainty by the testimony that "the dividing corner" was so located as to give to the tract as a parallelogram a greater dimension from north to south than from east to west, but that the witness did not know the exact location of such corner, where there was additional evidence to identify and locate this corner by reference to ownership of the lands south of and adjacent to such parallelogram. The statement in this deed that the survey was to start at the northwest corner of said lot and "run the line south to the dividing corner" was matter of particular description added to the words of general description, and could be explained by extraneous evidence to the end that the whole description might be accurately applied to the subject-matter of the conveyance. In view of such explanatory evidence, the court erred as against the plaintiff in ruling that this deed was void for uncertainty of description and in excluding it from evidence. "A deed to land will not be declared void for uncertainty of description, if the description is certain, or if it furnish the key to the identification of the land intended to be conveyed by the grantor." Where the description is sufficient to afford the key by which the land may be definitely located by the aid of extraneous evidence, the record of the deed is sufficient to put a subsequent purchaser "from the same grantor on notice as to what land was in fact conveyed by such deed."

Transfer by Will and Descent

In the early period of the development of the law of real property when one died his right in the land which he held reverted to his lord. Later the privileges of inheriting and of disposing of real property by will were recognized. Today the right to inherit property and the disposition of property by will are generally controlled by the state.

As a general rule the statutes of the states permit persons of full age and sound mind to dispose of their property by will, provided certain formalities are complied with in the execution of the will. The required formalities vary with the different states, and the laws of the states which may affect the will must be consulted before the will is executed. Formalities which are required by many states are: (1) the will must be in writing, (2) it must be signed and sealed by the testator, (3) it must be witnessed by two or three witnesses, (4) it must be published by the testator—as a general rule all that is required for publication is a declaration by the testator, at the time of signing, that the instrument is his will—and (5) the testator must sign in the presence of and in the sight of the witnesses and the witnesses must sign in the presence of and in the sight of the testator and in the presence of and in the sight of each other. If the statutory formalities are not all complied with, the will is not valid. As a general rule an attestation clause, stating the formalities which have been followed in the execution of the will, is written following the testator's signature.

The transfer of the ownership of real property is controlled by the laws of the state in which the real property is located; consequently, if real property is devised by will, to be effective the will must comply with all the statutory requirements of the state in which the real property is located. A will which complies with the laws of the domicile of the testator is sufficient to transfer the ownership of the testator's personal property.

Some states recognize the validity of holographic wills and some recognize the validity of nuncupative wills. A holographic will is a will which is wholly written, signed, and sealed in the testator's or testatrix's own hand. The statutes of a few states recognize these wills as valid without formal execution or attestation. A nuncupative will is an oral will. In many states the oral wills made by sailors at sea or soldiers in actual service are recognized as valid for the purpose of disposing of the personal estate in the actual possession of the testator at the time of the making of the will.

One distinguishing feature of a will is that it is not to take effect except upon the death of the maker; it has no binding effect during the lifetime of the maker. All wills are revocable at the option of the maker, and a will does not confer any present right in the property, devised or bequeathed, at the time of the execution of the will. One may revoke his will by destroying or cancelling it or by a later will duly executed in which he expressly states that he thereby revokes a former will. If the testator or testatrix is married, as a general rule, he or she will not be permitted to dispose of all of his or her property without reservation. Under the statutes of the several states the wife is given certain rights in the husband's estate which cannot be defeated by will, and also, as a general rule, the husband has certain rights in the wife's estate which cannot be defeated by will.

If one dies intestate—without having made a will—his property will descend according to the statutes of descent and distribution. His personal property will be distributed according to the statutes of the state of his domicile, and his real property will be distributed according to the statutes of the state in which it is located.

Hamlet et al. v. Hamlet
183 Va. 453, 32 S.E. (2d) 729 (1945)

This was an action by Dr. J. M. Hamlet and others for probate of the will of Dr. Robert Edward Hamlet, deceased, contested by John Chappell Hamlet. Judgment denying probate and Dr. J. M. Hamlet and others appealed. Judgment affirmed.

Dr. Robert Edward Hamlet died in November, 1943, leaving several instruments purporting to be wills or codicils to wills. One instrument was typewritten and concluded:

"Given under my hand this the 7 day of October, 1929.
(Signed) "Dr. Robert Edward Hamlet."
(Signed) "Mrs. Garland Wilkinson
"Gordon Paulette
"A. C. Paulette."

The probate of this writing was refused because the usual attestation clause is lacking, and it appeared from the testimony of the two surviving attesting witnesses that the instrument had not been signed or acknowledged by Dr. Hamlet in the presence of two witnesses, all being "present at the same time," as required by the statute. Code, § 5229. All of the parties agree that this ruling of the trial court was correct.

The main controversy concerns the action of the trial court in declining to admit to probate a two-page holographic writing, dated November 13, 1941. We quote so much of the instrument as is material to the issue before us. The first two paragraphs read as follows:

"Having had my other Wills examined by a Lawyer who stated that they contained some flaws, & at his suggestion & advice I am hereby writing this one in my own handwriting, that is my wish and Will to be carried out, on this Thirteenth (13th) day of November 1941.

"I, Dr. Robert Edward Hamlet, now of Pamplin, Va. being of sound & disposing mind do hereby make, Publish & declare this to be my last Will & Testament, hereby Revoking any other Will, by me at any time made."

Other writings testamentary in nature and in the handwriting of the deceased were found among the papers of the deceased. All of these writings were in pencil and none was signed at the end thereof by the deceased. The trial court took the view that none of the papers offered should be admitted to probate. This holding was based upon the view that the instruments dated November 13, 1941, July 8, 1943, and July 11, 1943, were not "signed" as required by the statute.

Eggleston, J. The material part of Code, § 5229, is as follows: "No will shall be valid unless it be in writing and signed by the testator, or by some other person in his presence and by his direction, in such manner as to make it manifest that the name is intended as a signature; . . . ."

This statute has been before this court in numerous cases, and correctly states the rule deducible from our decisions: "Under the statute it is essential that a holograph will, like any other, be signed by the testator 'in such a manner as to make it manifest that the name is intended as a signature'; and therefore in the absence of any affirmative evidence on the face of the paper that it is intended as a signature, the testator's name appearing at the commencement or in the body of the will is not a sufficient signature."

And as Judge Prentis pointed out in *Meany* v. *Priddy*, 127 Va.

84, 85, 102 S.E. 470: "No mere intention or effort to dispose of property by will, however clearly and definitely expressed in writing is sufficient. Such purpose must be executed in the only manner authorized by the statute; that is, the writing itself must be authenticated by the signature of the decedent. It is not sufficient to raise a doubt as to whether his name is intended to authenticate the paper which is propounded as a will, for, to use the explicit language of the statute, it must be signed 'in such manner as to make it manifest that the name is intended as his signature,' and unless so signed it is not valid."

The appellants do not dispute these principles, but their contention is that the writing of November 13, 1941, shows on its face that the name "Dr. Robert Edward Hamlet" was placed at the beginning of the second paragraph as a signature to the instrument. They stress the fact that the name is in the second and not in the opening paragraph. We are not impressed with this argument. The first paragraph is merely the author's explanation for rewriting his will. The second paragraph, in which the name is inserted, is that usually employed in the commencement of a will, and we have several times held that the placing of the name there does not of itself indicate that it was intended as a signature.

In our opinion, the trial court correctly held that the instrument of November 13, 1941, was not signed in the manner required by the statute. Code, § 5229. While the animus testandi (the intention to make a will) is clear, the necessary animus signandi (the intention to sign) the instrument relied on is lacking.

Trust Estates

A trust in real property exists when a person holds the legal title to the real property but is under an equitable obligation, by reason of a confidence reposed in him or a duty assumed by him, to use the real property for the benefit of another person. The law of trusts was developed in the courts of equity and, as a general rule, all disputes regarding trust estates are tried in equity. Today both real property and personal property may be held in trust. The person who creates the trust is the trustor or settlor; the person who holds the legal title to the property is the trustee; and the person having the beneficial interest is the beneficiary or cestui que trust.

No technical formalities are required to create a trust. All that is necessary is a declaration that certain property is to be held in trust for definite beneficiaries. In most instances the property will be conveyed to the trustee or trustees and the trustee or trustees will accept the title to the property, subject to the terms of the trust. If the trust estate is real property, the trust must be declared in writing—this requirement is statutory—but an oral trust of personal property is generally enforceable. If the named trustee refuses to act as trustee or is incapacitated, the trust will not fail for lack of a trustee. On application of the parties in interest, a court of equity will appoint a trustee. The owner of property may appoint himself trustee, in which event he ceases to hold the property as owner and thereafter holds it as trustee.

The trustee, if the trust is an active trust, owes a duty to the beneficiary to manage the property to the best of his ability and realize from the property the greatest income consistent with prudent management of the property. The trustee cannot benefit from the management of the property in any manner other than the compensation which he receives for his services as trustee. He is not permitted to buy the trust property, sell to the trust estate, borrow the trust money, nor in any way place himself in such a position that his personal interests conflict with the performance of his duties as trustee. As a general rule, the trust agreement will define the trustee's power and the rights of the beneficiary. In case of doubt the trustee can petition the court of equity for instructions. If the trustee has power to sell trust property, he can pass good title to third persons but, if he does not have the power to sell, a third person purchaser having notice or knowledge of the trust will take the property subject to the rights of the beneficiary. If an innocent purchaser for value purchases from the trustee, as a general rule, the third person will acquire good title to the property. The trustee is personally liable on all contracts entered into in connection with the management of the trust estate; however, he is entitled to reimbursement out of the trust property for all legitimate expenditures.

The beneficiary must be named or indicated with reasonable certainty. A trust cannot exist without a beneficiary. Trusts are divided into private trusts and public or charitable trusts. In a private trust the beneficiaries are individuals or a group as, for example, the children of Archer. In a public or charitable trust the beneficiary is a group or class as, for example, the poor of Wales County, Trinity Church, a named school, etc. The rights of the beneficiaries will be set out in the trust agreement. If the trustee does not fulfill his duty, the beneficiary can bring suit in a court of equity, and he will be granted whatever relief the situation demands.

Golstein v. Handley et al.

390 Ill. 118, 60 N.E.(2d) 851 (1945)

This was an action by Morris A. Golstein (plaintiff) against Anne Golstein Handley and others (defendants). Judgment for defendants and plaintiff appealed. Judgment affirmed.

This suit is brought for the construction of the will of Peretz A. Golstein, deceased. In the first three paragraphs the testator made certain specific gifts. The fourth paragraph was as follows:

"Fourth: Balance to be divided as follows:
25% to Sister, Sima Golstein
10% to Sister, Clara Fishman . . . .
25% to Brother, Morris A. Golstein"

etc., until the residue of the estate was disposed of.

Paragraphs fifth, sixth, seventh, and eighth were similar in wording. Paragraph sixth read as follows: "Sixth: The 25% specified above, for brother Morris A. Golstein, should be placed in trust and be paid to him in the sum of Two Hundred ($200.00) Dollars per month." The plaintiff contends that, by paragraph fourth, outright gifts were made and that paragraph fifth, sixth, seventh, and eighth are not sufficient to create a trust.

Smith, J. It is argued by appellant that the fifth, sixth, and seventh paragraphs are not legally sufficient to create a trust. It is not necessary to the validity of a trust that every element necessary to constitute it must be so clearly expressed in detail in the instrument creating it that nothing can be left to inference or implication. No particular form or words are necessary, but wherever an intention to create a trust can be fairly collected from the language of the instrument and the terms employed, such intention will be supported by the courts. In *Orr* v. *Yates*, 209 Ill. 222, 70 N.E. 731, 737, we said: "Conceding that the trust provisions of this will are not altogether explicit and absolutely certain, yet these uncertainties are such as a court of equity will aid by construction, and not such as will defeat the intention of the testator. . . . ."

By the will here in question, the subject matter of the trust is clearly expressed. The beneficiaries of each share are named. The nature and quantity of the interests are certain. Each of the beneficiaries named in the fifth, sixth, seventh, and eighth paragraphs is given an interest which vested upon the death of the testator. The interest of Morris A. Golstein under the sixth paragraph, and the interest of Sam A. Golstein under the seventh paragraph, are the entire beneficial interests of their respective shares. The interest of Clara Fishman under the fifth paragraph is the entire beneficial interest, subject only to the condition that if her share is not exhausted at the time of her death, the remainder goes in equal shares to her sons, Edward and Joseph Fishman, to be paid to them when they reach the age of twenty-seven years. The interests of Edward and Joseph Fishman, under the eighth paragraph of the will, are the entire beneficial interest, payable one-half at once, and the remainder at the end of five years. The manner and method in which the trust is to be performed is specifically provided for in paragraphs five, six, and seven of the will—the payment of specified sums to the various beneficiaries monthly. By paragraph eight, one-half is to be distributed at once and the remaining one-half at the end of five years. As to the investment of the trust property, this is controlled by section 1 of

"An Act concerning powers of trustees." Ill. Rev. Stat. 1943, chap. 148, par. 32. It is true the testator here did not name a trustee. But it is elementary that courts of equity will not permit a trust to fail because no trustee is designated. In such cases, the court will appoint a trustee for the purpose of carrying out the trust.

No particular form of words or language is necessary in a gift of property to create a trust. It is sufficient, particularly in the case of wills, that such intention is apparent from the whole will when considered in all its parts, under the circumstances of the particular case. In our opinion the will contained all the requirements for the creation of a trust and must be so construed.

Co-ownership

Co-ownership of real property exists when two or more persons own an undivided interest in the real property. There are five kinds of co-ownership of real property recognized in the United States today: (1) joint tenancy; (2) tenancy in common; (3) tenancy by entireties; (4) community property; and (5) partnership property.

The common characteristic of co-ownership is that the owners of the real property have no separate rights in any portion of it, but each shares in every part of the whole. In a joint tenancy the parties have equal shares in the property. The property must have been deeded to them by one deed which named all of the joint tenants as grantees. The outstanding characteristic of a joint tenancy is that of survivorship. If one joint tenant dies, his share of the property passes to his joint tenant or tenants. If Archer, Burch, and Clark own real property as joint tenants and Archer dies, his share passes to Burch and Clark and, if Burch then dies, his share passes to Clark. On Clark's death the property passes to Clark's heirs at law—Archer's and Burch's heirs would acquire no interest in the property. A joint tenant cannot dispose of his share of joint real property by will because, under the rule of survivorship, on death the interest passes to the survivor, and nothing remains which can be disposed of by will. A joint tenancy can be destroyed during the lifetime of the joint tenants either by partition proceedings in court or by a conveyance of one of the joint tenants. If Archer, Burch, and Clark own real property as joint tenants and Archer deeds his share to Drew, Drew will hold with Burch and Clark as a tenant in common, but, as between Burch and Clark, they hold as joint tenants. If Burch deeded his share to Fox, then Clark, Drew, and Fox would hold as tenants in common. Each joint tenant has the right to use the property but he has no right to exclude his co-tenants from an equal right to use. Joint tenancies are not favored in the United States. In some states the legislatures have abolished survivorship and in others it has entirely abolished joint tenancies, making what would have been a joint tenancy a tenancy in common.

Tenants in common own undivided shares in the real property. Their shares need not be equal, and on the death of a tenant in common his interest in the real property passes to his heirs or devisees. A tenant in common may dispose of his interest in the real property either by deed or will without affecting the interests of his co-tenants. The right to possess and use are the same as in a joint tenancy.

Tenants by the entireties must be husband and wife. It is fundamentally a joint tenancy with rights of survivorship. It can be created only by a conveyance to persons who are husband and wife at the time of the conveyance. A tenancy by the entireties cannot be destroyed by the acts of either party. Real property owned by the entireties cannot be sold under execution issued on a judgment rendered against either the husband or wife individually, but it can be sold on execution issued on a judgment rendered against them on a joint obligation. Neither can convey the real property by deed unless the other joins and neither can dispose of the property by will. Tenancies by the entireties are not recognized in all of the states.

In eight states [1] what is known as the system of community property prevails. The principal characteristic of the system is that whatever property is acquired by the efforts of either the husband or wife during marriage becomes a common fund or as it is called community property. Either the husband or the wife may own, in addition to his or her interest in the community property, "separate property." Generally "separate property" includes property owned prior to marriage and property acquired after marriage by gift, devise, descent, or in exchange for property owned as separate property. The details of the system are set out by the statutes of each state which has adopted the system.

Partnership ownership of real property is discussed under the heading of "Partnership."

Divorce does not break up a tenancy by entireties

Andrews v. Andrews
— Fla. —, 21 S. (2d) 205 (1945)

This was an action by Rachael Andrews (plaintiff) against Owen Andrews (defendant). From that portion of the decree of divorce determining the rights of the parties to certain realty purchased jointly and deeded to them as husband and wife, Rachael Andrews appeals. Decree affirmed in part and reversed in part with directions.

---

[1] Arizona, California, Idaho, Louisiana, Nevada, New Mexico, Texas, and Washington.

Thomas, J. Appellant and appellee were divorced, and neither challenges that part of the decree severing the marriage tie, there being presented now only the matter of the correctness of the chancellor's determination of the rights of the parties to a certain piece of property purchased jointly and deeded to them as husband and wife, thereby creating an estate by the entirety. Both parties eventually defaulted in the payment of taxes, and the title became vested in the state of Florida. The property was subsequently sold at auction, and the appellant was the successful bidder, whereupon the property was conveyed to her individually by the trustees of the internal improvement fund. This all occurred while the marriage relation existed.

So, to summarize, one holder of an unseverable interest, whose duty to pay the tax was the same as her co-holder, obtained a deed conveying the whole title, hence took advantage of her own failure as well as that of her co-owner. The question arises whether a husband or a wife could eliminate the interest of the other spouse in such an estate via the process of recapturing the property under the provisions of the Murphy Act.

In the case of *Strauss* v. *Strauss*, it was further said that upon divorce the husband and wife who held an estate by the entirety became "joint tenants or tenants in common." Of course by Section 3, Chapter 20954, Laws of Florida, it is now expressly provided that "in cases of estates by entirety, the tenants, upon divorce, shall become tenants in common."

From the authorities we have examined it appears that there is one distinguishing feature of an estate in common; namely, "unity" of possession. In joint tenancy there are three additional "unities"; that is, the interests must be the same, must have originated in the identical conveyance, and must, therefore, have commenced simultaneously. There is the added characteristic of survivorship. In tenancy by the entirety all of these "unities" of joint tenancy are present and also that additional "unity" of person, springing from the relationship of husband and wife, and, too, neither holder may alone sever the estate.

We think the effect of the action of the wife, appellant, may be tested by the elements peculiar to estates by the entirety, which, we repeat, are unity of person and the concomitant, unity of estate. As we stated at the outset, it was written in *Strauss* v. *Strauss* that the estate is not severable, and in *Bailey* v. *Smith* in reiterating this pronouncement the court clearly demonstrated the connection between the indivisibility of estate and oneness of person. It was expressed thus: "The essential characteristic of an estate by the entirety is that each spouse is seized of the whole or the entirety and not of a share, moiety, or divisible part. There is but one estate, and, in contemplation of law, it is held by but one person." A like statement of the law on the subject may be found in 26 Am. Jur., *Husband and Wife*, page 697; also in Thompson's *Commentaries on Real Property*, Vol. 4, page 333, where we learn that the singleness of person is traceable to the common law conception of man and wife as one.

If, then, in such a situation there is but one person and but one indivisible estate, which could pass from one to the other only by death and from them to a third party only by joint deed, how could either eliminate the other's interest by failing to pay a tax and then purchasing the whole title as a result of the default? If they are but one, then his default was hers as well, and her act in purchasing the property was his also.

An attempt by one spouse to take advantage of the other by the purchase of property held by the entirety cannot be sanctioned. If a tenant purchases the joint property at a tax sale, his act benefits all the co-tenants and discharges the lien.

Each tenant by the entirety owes to the other the highest degree of confidence and trust. We repeat, if a tenant in common may not take advantage of his co-tenant by purchasing a tax deed on the property they hold, there is all the more reason why the rule should be applied in the case of estates by the entirety.

The cause is reversed with directions to revise the final decree so it will provide that upon the divorce appellant and appellee became tenants in common.

Easements and Licenses

An easement is a right or privilege to do a certain class of acts which are detrimental to the land of another person, or the right to compel another person to refrain from making certain uses of his land. An easement is more or less permanent in its nature, and, as a general rule, an easement is accessory to adjoining land. Archer and Burch own adjoining lots and they have a joint driveway; each has an easement of right of way over that portion of the other's lot over which the driveway passes. Common easements are the right to run a sewer across another's land, and the right to run telephone or electric light wires across another's land. A negative easement is the right to have another refrain from erecting a structure on his land which will cut off the light and air from the adjoining land. An easement is created by a deed, a reservation in a deed, or by prescription. It, being an interest in real property, is required by the Statute of Frauds to be in writing. An easement which is not accessory to adjoining land may be granted, but such an easement will be personal to the grantee and cannot be transferred to another and will terminate with the death of the holder.

A license is similar in some respects to an easement; however, a license is not an interest in land and may be created orally and, unless it is coupled with an interest, is revocable at the will of the licensor. Permission to cross another's land or to hunt or fish on his land is a license. One entering on to the land of another for the purpose of transacting business is a licensee. If one purchases trees from another which are to be cut by the purchaser and hauled away, the purchaser would have an irrevocable license to go onto the land for the purpose of cutting and hauling the logs. There are innumerable situations in which one person has a license to go upon the land of another. As a general rule a license creates a temporary right to use another's land in a limited and specific manner.

Eastman v. Piper

68 Cal. App. 554, 229 Pac. 1002 (1924)

This was an action by Stanley Eastman (plaintiff) against Anita Piper (defendant). Judgment for plaintiff and defendant appealed. Judgment affirmed.

Moffit owned Lot G block 12, Monrovia Tract. He conveyed the east one-half of this lot to Belden who conveyed to defendant. When defendant purchased the east one-half of the lot he executed to Moffit an instrument in writing as follows: "The undersigned, owner of the within described property, hereby grants the privilege of a temporary roadway 10 feet wide along the south boundary of the East one-half of Lot G, block 12, Monrovia Tract, to Samuel F. Moffit, his heirs and assigns, until such time as the extension of Alta Vista street is completed past the west one-half of said lot G, block 12, Monrovia Tract. Anita Piper Owner." Moffit conveyed the West one-half of the lot to Caldwell who conveyed to plaintiff. Defendant now threatens to put a fence across the roadway to prevent plaintiff from using it, claiming that the instrument in question granted a license to Moffit and that the license terminated when Moffit conveyed the land.

Finlayson, P. J. The distinction between a license and an easement is often subtle and difficult to discern. The former is defined as a personal, revocable, and unassignable permission or authority to do one or more acts on the land of another without possessing any interest therein. "It is a distinguishing characteristic of a license that it gives no interest in the land, and that it may rest in parol. It is clear, of course, that this must necessarily be so, for if by a license an interest in the land could be created within the meaning of the statute of frauds, under that statute it could not be created by parol, and, if created by grant and an interest in the land thereby passes, the distinctive feature of the transaction as a license vanishes at once. And so the fact that a valid license to enter on land may be given by parol rests on the distinction that a license is only an authority to do an act or series of acts on the land of another, and passes no estate or interest therein." A license, because it is personal, is incapable of being assigned by the licensee. "Being a mere personal privilege it is never extended to the heirs or assigns of the licensee, and ordinarily, as to the licensee himself, a parol license is regarded as destroyed by an attempt to assign it."

An easement, unlike a license, creates an interest in the land—an incorporeal interest. It is a liberty, privilege, or advantage, without profit, which the owner of one parcel of land may have in the lands of another. "While the distinction between an easement . . . . and a license is sometimes difficult of discernment, in theory, at least, the distinction is clear, for an easement creates an interest in the land." Though a license may be created by parol or by any act of the licensor sufficient to show his assent thereto, an easement can be created only by grant, or by implication or prescription, each of which presupposes a grant. This is necessarily so, because, under a well-established principle, an interest in or arising out of land lies in grant only.

The grant of the privilege of a roadway to Moffit, "his heirs, or assigns" was an express recognition that the privilege was to be inheritable and assignable. But as the qualities of inheritability and assignability are inconsistent with a license, we must conclude that something more than a license was intended to be granted; that it was intended to create an inheritable interest in a servient estate,—in short, an easement.

Landlord and Tenant

A lease is, technically, a conveyance by which a lesser estate than that held by the lessor is vested in another; it is a conveyance of an interest in real property less than a freehold estate. The term "lease" is commonly used in a broader sense which includes not only the conveyance of an interest in real property but also the contractual obligations created by the covenants entered into by the lessor and lessee. Although at common law no formalities were required to create a lease in real property, under the provisions of the Statute of Frauds a lease, being a conveyance of an interest in land, was required to be in writing. As a general rule short-time leases—less than one year under some statutes, less than three years under others—are expressly exempted from the operation of the statute.

In the absence of covenants to the contrary, the landlord guarantees that he will give the tenant possession of the premises and that the tenant's possession shall not be interfered with as a result of any acts, or omissions on the part of the landlord, or defects in the landlord's title. The landlord does not warrant the conditions of the premises. The tenant takes the premises as he finds them except that the landlord owes a duty to disclose to the tenant any hidden defects which may prove injurious to the tenant, such as the existence of a hidden cesspool.

The tenant has the right to use the premises as he wishes; however, his use must be such that it does not result in permanent injury to the premises. The landlord owes no duty to keep the premises in repair and, if the buildings burn, he is not bound to rebuild. If the tenant or an invitee or licensee of the tenant is injured because of the defective condition of the premises, the landlord is not liable. However, if the premises are leased to two or more tenants and portions of the premises, such as the halls and stairs of an apartment house, are retained by the landlord for the common use of the tenants, the landlord will be held liable for injuries resulting from the defective condition of such portions of the premises, providing the existence of the defects result from the negligence of the landlord. As a general rule, without the consent of the tenant the landlord has no right to enter the premises during the term of the lease.

Some of the rules stated above have been changed by statute and others have become obsolete. New rules, usually imposing a greater liability on the landlord, have been developed by usage. In leasing real property the parties should define their respective rights and liabilities. The rules stated were developed at an early period and in many respects are not in accord with modern practices. The parties have the right to change the rules by express stipulation in their lease agreement; consequently, it is important that the lease contain covenants covering such essential matters as the use permitted by the tenant, who shall make repairs, the landlord's right to enter the premises and the purposes for which he may enter, the rent reserved, warranty as to condition of the premises, whether or not the lease may be assigned, and whether or not the premises, or any part thereof, may be sublet.

In the absence of a covenant to the contrary, the tenant may assign his lease to another. When the tenant assigns the lease he does not relieve himself from the contractual obligations—covenants in the lease—but he does divest himself of his interest in the property. If the tenant subleases the premises or any part of them, he retains an interest in the property and is liable to the landlord on all the covenants in the lease. He is, however, a landlord as to the sublessee. He cannot grant to the sublessee greater rights than he has under the original lease.

Richard Paul, Inc., v. Union Improvement Co.
59 F. Supp. 252 (1945)

This was an action by Richard Paul, Inc. (plaintiff) against Union Improvement Company (defendant). Judgment for plaintiff for $565.63.

On May 11, 1942, defendant leased the basement, first, and second floors, together with an areaway, necessary stairways, etc., of a building located in Wilmington to plaintiff for a period of three years. The lease was in writing and provided that defendant would make certain stipulated repairs. The defendant did not make all of the agreed repairs and plaintiff made certain of the repairs stipulated in the lease. Plaintiff contends that the premises were not suitable for its business, that as a result of delay in making repairs it was unable to make full use of the building and that it paid three months' rent under protest and that this rent should be returned to it. Plaintiff claims damages in the sum of $17,050.

Leahy, D. J. There was a breach of covenant on the part of defendant. It is clear from the evidence that defendant failed to make the minor repairs contemplated in the lease. This is shown by the nature of the repairs made and paid for by plaintiff, which included cleaning the demised premises. It is equally apparent there was no collateral agreement that the building met the requirements of the various building ordinances of the city of Wilmington. There is no implied warranty that the premises are fit for the particular purpose to which they are to be put.

The basis of this result is that the rule of caveat emptor ordinarily applies between landlord and tenant and, in the absence of fraud, there is no liability on the part of the landlord even in situations where the premises are so unsafe or unhealthy that habitation is impossible. The case of *Leech* v. *Husbands*, 4 W.W. Harr. 362, 152 A. 729, 731, while not directly in point, holds that the rule of caveat emptor applies between landlord and tenant in the absence of fraud. In that case the court said: "It, therefore, necessarily follows that in the absence of fraud, there is no implied covenant or representation of any character that a house or apartment is free from vermin, bugs, or disease germs, and that such conditions should usually be guarded against by express covenants." The landlord, here, did not covenant that the premises satisfied any particular requirements. Paragraph 4 of the agreement which provides that "the Lessee shall use . . . . premises for the purpose of carrying on its business of manufacturing and dealing in textile products or other products the manufacture of which will not be detrimental to the aforesaid premises and for no other purpose whatsoever" obviously is for the protection of the landlord and is not an implied promise that the premises meet any definite standard of requirements. The landlord did not covenant, then, that the premises satisfy any particular requirements. Liability can be imposed upon the landlord by express contract, but in the absence of this there is no implied warranty that the building is fit for the purpose for which it is intended to be used, or that it complies with the requirements of public regulatory bodies. The conclusion, therefore, is that there has been a violation of the written lease through failure to make the necessary minor repairs, but that this is the sole breach committed by defendant.

QUESTIONS AND PROBLEMS

1. What is a freehold estate?
2. John Busby was the title owner of a house and lot. John executed a deed to the property in which he named his wife, Mary Busby, as grantee. John showed the deed to Mary and told her that he would put the deed in his safety deposit box and that on his death the property was to be hers. John died and Mary claimed the house and lot. Was the house and lot transferred to Mary by the deed?
3. In Problem 2 if John had, after executing the deed, left it with his attorney

with instructions that the attorney was to hold the deed for Mary and that on John's death the attorney was to record the deed and see that Mary got possession of the house and lot, would the house and lot have been transferred to Mary?

4. Mary Tyrrell, a resident and property owner of Arizona, died at Phoenix. After her death an envelope containing a writing on a piece of stationery was found. On the envelope was written, "The will of Mary Tyrrell." The writing contained in the envelope purported to be Mary Tyrrell's will and disposed of all her property. This writing and the notation on the envelope were entirely in the handwriting of Mary Tyrrell; however, the writing was not signed by Mary Tyrrell nor did her name appear in the writing. The statutes of Arizona recognize the validity of holographic wills but require that the instrument be authenticated by the signature of the testator. Is this purported will valid?
5. If a person dies intestate leaving both personal and real property, how will such property be distributed?
6. Burch, trustee for Archer, has charge of $100,000 worth of Archer's property. Through special sources of information Burch is able to invest the funds in corporate stocks and realize a 30 per cent profit. The average income from trust funds is 4 per cent. Burch credits the estate with 10 per cent of the profits and takes 20 per cent as his compensation as trustee. May he do so?
7. L. S. Phillips, deceased, by his will bequeathed to his wife all of his property, amounting to about $100,000. The will named the wife executrix and added, "If she (the wife) finds it always convenient, she is to pay my sister, Caroline Buck, the sum of $300 a year. I wish this to be done." Did the will create a trust for the benefit of Caroline Buck?
8. Martha and George West inherited a store building from their father and owned the building as tenants in common. Martha owned and operated a business which occupied, with George's consent, the first floor of the building. The second floor was finished into apartments which were rented and the income divided. George claims that Martha owes him rent for the use of the first floor of the building. Is George's claim correct?
9. Sewell owned lot one, block 122, and Reilly owned lot two, block 122, in Miami. Sewell and Reilly entered into a written agreement whereby each agreed to allow the other to use the south ten feet of his lot for alley purposes "for so long as the alley" over the other party's lot remained open. Did this agreement create an easement or a license?
10. Sullivan leased a three-story brick building to Pearson to be used as a hotel. Thereafter Pearson decided to tear out the front and replace it with a new tile front. He also intended to put in new granolithic floors, tile walls, and metal ceilings on the first floor and planned to change certain stairways and inclose a back porch. Sullivan objected to the making of these alterations. Does Pearson have the right to make the alterations?

CHAPTER XVII

SECURITY TRANSACTIONS

Nature of Security

In the United States a large percentage of business is transacted on credit. Property of all kinds is sold, the ownership passing to the buyer on the buyer's promise to pay the purchase price some time in the future. Money is loaned, the borrower promising to repay at a future date. Often the seller or the lender wishes something more than the buyer's or borrower's promise to pay. He may be uncertain about the honesty of the buyer or borrower or, owing to the uncertainties of life, he may feel that the buyer or borrower, although honest, may not be able to pay when the debt falls due. In such instances the seller or lender will ask for security. Security may be of two kinds, *in rem*, in which case property may be charged with the payment of the obligations, and *in personam*, in which case some third party may agree to pay if the buyer or borrower defaults. When property is charged with the payment of a debt, the creditor is said to have a lien on the property. When one agrees to pay if another does not, he is a surety or guarantor, depending on the nature of his undertaking.

If property is used as security, the lienee acquires an ownership interest in the property put up as security. The terms of the security contract will define the nature of the interest acquired by the lienee. A debt or other obligation is essential to the existence of a lien and, whenever the debt or obligation secured by the lien is discharged, the property interest of the lienee automatically ceases to exist—the lien is discharged.

The common types of security transactions are real estate mortgages, trust deeds, and land contracts in which real property is used as security; pledges (collateral security), chattel mortgages, conditional sales, and trust receipts in which personal property is used as security; guaranty and surety in which the surety or guarantor pledges his personal credit as security; and liens created by operation of law in which either at common law or by statute certain liens are created for the protection of persons rendering special services.

Real Estate Mortgage

The early real estate mortgage was a deed, conveying the title to the property to the mortgagee. The deed contained a defeasance clause, that is, a provision that, if the mortgagor paid the debt when due or performed the obligation stated, the conveyance would become null and void and of no effect. The common law courts enforced these provisions strictly, and, as a consequence, any default on the part of the mortgagor resulted in the loss of all claim to the mortgaged land. At an early date the courts of equity began to relieve from these harsh results and allowed the mortgagor to redeem from the forfeiture. Now we have two theories of mortgages, the lien theory and the title theory. The lien theory was developed in the courts of equity. The mortgagee is regarded as having a lien on the land, title remaining in the mortgagor. The mortgagor is recognized as the owner of the land, subject to the mortgagee's interest. The mortgagor has the right of possession and is entitled to the rents and profits accruing. The only limitation on his rights as an owner is that he cannot so use the property as to injure the mortgagee's security. The title theory is the common law mortgage modified. The title passes to the mortgagee, carrying with it ownership and the right of possession. The mortgagee must account to the mortgagor for the rents and profits and in addition owes a duty to use reasonable care and diligence in the handling of the property. He cannot commit waste, that is, do anything that will injure the property, such as cut timber or remove buildings. It is customary, even in states recognizing the title theory, to provide in the mortgage that the mortgagor shall have possession until default. In some states where the title theory is in force, by statute, the mortgagor is entitled to possession unless the mortgage contains a clause expressly providing that the mortgagee shall have possession.

The statutes of all the states require that certain formalities be followed in drafting a mortgage. In the title theory states the mortgage is in form a deed with a defeasance clause, and the same formal requirements are followed in executing a mortgage as are followed in executing a deed. In the lien theory states the mortgage does not follow the form of a deed, but it is executed with the same formalities as are required in the executing of a deed. As between the parties, the validity of the mortgage does not depend on the fulfillment of the formal requirements. If the transaction is intended as a loan and security for the repayment of the loan, the courts will declare it a mortgage, irrespective of the form of the conveyance. The courts jealously guard the mortgagor's right to redeem and will not enforce any contract or agreement cutting off this right. Even though the conveyance is in the form of a warranty deed, the courts will declare it a mortgage if it was given as security.

However, if a deed is given as security for the payment of a loan and the real property is sold by the owner of record—the mortgagee—to an innocent purchaser for value, the innocent purchaser for value acquires good title. The lender will be liable to the borrower for any damages which the borrower has suffered as a result of the sale of the property.

The owner—the mortgagor—may sell the property without the consent of the mortgagee, but such a sale in no way affects the mortgagee's interest in the property nor his claim against the mortgagor on the debt. In case there is a default, the mortgagee may foreclose the mortgage, have the mortgaged property sold, and, if on foreclosure sale the property does not bring enough to pay the costs, interest, and the principal, the mortgagee is entitled to a deficiency judgment against the original debtor—the mortgagor. If the property should sell for more than enough to pay the costs, interest, and principal, the surplus will go to the transferee. The transferee may buy the mortgage property "subject to the mortgage" or he may "assume" the mortgage. If the transferee has purchased "subject to the mortgage" and there is a default and foreclosure, he is not liable for a deficiency but, if he "assumes" the mortgage, he is liable for any deficiency. The property is always liable and may be sold to pay the mortgage debt and the mortgagor is always liable to the mortgagee because he cannot assign his liability; however, if the transferee "assumes the mortgage," he is liable to the mortgagor for the mortgage debt and, if the mortgagor is forced to pay a deficiency, the mortgagor can recover from the transferee.

The mortgagee may assign his interest in the mortgaged property. To do this the mortgagee must assign the debt and, if the debt is evidenced by a negotiable note, the assignment is usually made by the negotiation of the note plus an assignment of the mortgage; however, in most jurisdictions the negotiation of the note carries with it the right to the security, and the holder of the note is entitled to the benefits of the mortgage.

On default the mortgagee has the right to foreclose the mortgage. As a general rule, the procedure to be followed in foreclosure will be set out by statute, and the statutes of the state in which the property is located will have to be complied with. Generally, the court determines that the mortgagor is in default, finds the amount due, and orders the property sold. The sale is made by the sheriff or a commissioner after the property has been advertised, and the purchaser receives a sheriff's certificate.

All states give the mortgagor or any other person who has an ownership right in the property, which will be cut off by the foreclosure, the right to redeem by paying the purchaser at the foreclosure sale the amount of the sale price plus interest. The period within which the property may be redeemed is one year in most states. The person who wishes to redeem from a mortgage foreclosure sale must redeem the entire mortgaged interest; he cannot redeem a partial interest by paying a proportionate amount of the price bid at the foreclosure sale.

The proceeds of the foreclosure sale are distributed first, to pay the costs, second, to pay interest due, and third, to pay the principal, and any surplus is paid to the mortgagor unless there is a second mortgage on the property in which event it will be paid to the second mortgagee.

Combs et al. v. Jett.
299 Ky. 17, 183 S.W. (2d) 826 (1944)

This was an action by Oscar Combs and others (plaintiffs) against Zeke Jett (defendant). Judgment for defendant and plaintiff appealed. Judgment affirmed.

During his lifetime Granville Spencer executed a mortgage on a tract of land to G. B. Stamper and in an action to enforce the mortgage the land was sold. A. J. Creech became the purchaser at the price of $130, and the master conveyed the land to him. On January 5, 1935, Granville Spencer and A. J. Creech entered into a written contract whereby Creech agreed to convey the land to Spencer within thirty days thereafter upon the payment to Creech of $130. On February 5, 1935, Creech and wife conveyed the land to defendant for a cash consideration of $130. Defendant is a nephew of Spencer. On December 7, 1939, plaintiffs, heirs at law of Granville Spencer, brought this action to have the deed from A. J. Creech to defendant declared a mortgage. The plaintiffs contend that defendant, at the time the land was deeded to him, agreed to convey the land to Granville Spencer upon payment to defendant of $130 and interest; that shortly thereafter defendant collected from the county $173 for a right of way through the land for a state highway. The plaintiffs contend that this payment discharged Spencer's debt to defendant and that they are entitled to the land as heirs of Spencer.

Rees, J. The deed from A. J. Creech to Jett is absolute on its face. In order to have such a deed declared a mortgage, the relation of debtor and creditor must exist between the grantee and the one who seeks to have it declared a mortgage. Spencer was not indebted to Jett prior to the execution of the deed, and the evidence fails to show any agreement enforceable by the latter. At most, the alleged agreement was an option to purchase. Under a somewhat similar state of facts, the court said in *Spicer* v. *Elmore*, where the agreement was in writing:

"In the case before us the relation of debtor and creditor is clearly non-existent. By the terms of the contract between the parties appellants were merely given an option to pay the money and receive a conveyance of the property. Nothing in the contract bound them to pay. Were the situation reversed and appellee seeking judgment for the purchase money paid out by her, we would clearly be called on to hold that no obligation of payment was contained in the contract or to be implied in the circumstances."

Flynn et al. v. Kenrick et al.
285 Mass. 446, 189 N.E. 207 (1934)

This was an action by Nellie T. Flynn and others (plaintiffs) against William A. Kenrick and others (defendants). Judgment for plaintiffs and defendants appealed. Judgment affirmed.

Property was sold under an agreement of purchase and sale, containing the following recital: "Said premises are to be conveyed on or before September 1, 1930, by good and sufficient warranty deed of the party of the first part, conveying a good and clear title to the same, free from all incumbrances except a first mortgage of $5,000 . . . . and for such deed and conveyance the party of the second part is to pay the sum of $6,500 of which $100 has been paid this day, balance above mortgage, are to be paid in cash upon delivery of said deed." According to the contract the property was deeded to the purchasers. The mortgage debt was not paid and on foreclosure the property was sold for $4,500 and a deficiency decree was entered against the mortgagor, which he has paid. Suit is brought against the purchaser by the mortgagor to recover the amount paid on the ground that the purchaser agreed to pay the mortgage debt. The deed was drawn subject to the mortgage.

Crosby, J. It has long been held in this commonwealth that where land is conveyed subject to a mortgage the grantee does not become bound by mere acceptance of a deed to pay the mortgage debt. In the absence of other evidence, the deed shows that the grantee merely purchased the equity of redemption. If a deed contains a stipulation that the land is subject to a mortgage which the grantee assumes or agrees to pay, by his acceptance of the deed the law implies a promise to perform his promise. The contention of the defendants that they purchased merely the plaintiffs' equity of redemption and did not assume and agree to pay the mortgage cannot be sustained in view of the agreement, the deed, and the agreed facts. The agreement recites that the defendants for such conveyance are to pay "the sum of Sixty-five Hundred dollars of which One Hundred dollars have been paid this day, balance above mortgage, are to be paid in cash upon delivery of said deed." It thus appears that for the deed and conveyance the defendants agreed to pay the sum of $6,500; that $100 was paid on the date of the agreement, and on delivery of the deed $1,400 was to be paid. The words "balance above mortgage" properly construed mean that the defendants having paid $100 obligated themselves to assume and pay the mortgage, and that the balance above the mortgage of $1,400 is to be paid upon the delivery of the deed.

The words of the deed "for consideration paid" interpreted in the light of the agreement mean that the defendants under the terms of the agreement are to pay $6,500 as the entire consideration. This seems to have been the construction put upon the agreement and the deed by the parties, as it is agreed that after the defendants entered into possession of the property they paid the interest installments on the mortgage until July 7, 1932. The agreement of the defendants to pay $6,500 for the property is equivalent to a stipulation that they assumed or agreed to pay the mortgage.

Fagan v. People's Savings & Loan Association
55 Minn. 437, 57 N.W. 142 (1893)

This was an action by James A. Fagan (plaintiff) against the People's Savings & Loan Association (defendant). Judgment for plaintiff and defendant appealed. Judgment affirmed.

One Haugen executed to the defendant a first mortgage on a piece of real property and at a later date executed a second mortgage on the same property to the plaintiff. Haugen defaulted on the first mortgage and defendant foreclosed its mortgage. On the foreclosure sale the defendant purchased the property for an amount in excess of costs, interest, and principal of the first mortgage. The plaintiff contends that he is entitled to the surplus even though his mortgage debt is not yet due.

Mitchell, J. It is further contended that plaintiff is not entitled to recover this surplus, because, by its terms, the debt secured by his mortgage is not yet due. But he is not suing on the debt, but to recover the proceeds of his mortgage security. When land is sold on a first mortgage, which is subject to a subsequent lien, the lien is transferred from the land to the surplus money. The proceeds of the sale, after satisfying the first mortgage, stand in place of the equity of redemption to those who had title to or lien upon it. The right to this surplus passes to the grantee or assignee of the mortgagor by a conveyance of or mortgage upon the equity of redemption; and the court will always direct the application of the money according to the rights of the parties as they existed previous to the alteration of the estate. In case of future installments to become due on the first mortgage; or, in case of a second mortgage, not due, the mortgagees would be entitled to the surplus to the extent necessary to pay their mortgages in full.

Trust Deed

There are three parties to a trust deed transaction: the trustor who borrows the money, the trustee who holds legal title to the real property put up as security, and the lender who is beneficiary of the trust.

The purpose of a trust deed transaction is to facilitate the liquidation of the security in the event of default. Most of the states have declared a trust deed to be a mortgage and have required court foreclosure, thereby defeating the purpose of the arrangement. In a trust deed transaction the borrower deeds the real property, which is to be put up as security, to the trustee. By the terms of the trust agreement the trustee is given the power to sell the property in the event the borrower fails to make the required payments on the debt. Usually the trustee does not sell until the beneficiary—the lender—notifies the trustee that the debt is in default and demands that the security be sold. The trustee sells the property, usually at public sale, and applies the proceeds to the payment of costs, interest, and principal. If there is a surplus, it is paid to the trustor. The lender will have to sue on the debt and recover a judgment if he wishes to collect any deficiency.

Land Contracts

The land contract, as a security device, is limited in its use to the securing of the payment of the balance of the purchase price of real property. The seller of the property agrees to sell, and the buyer agrees to buy and pay the stipulated purchase price set out in the contract. Usually the purchaser takes possession of the property, pays all taxes and assessments, keeps the property insured, etc. In fact the purchaser is the equitable owner, but the seller holds the legal title and does not deed the property to the buyer until the purchase price is paid in full. In the event the buyer defaults, the seller has the right to declare a forfeiture and take possession of the property, thereby cutting off all of the buyer's rights in the property. The laws of the states vary in regard to the rights of the parties to a land contract. In some states, statutory procedure has been set up which is to be followed in the event of default and forfeiture, while in other states the courts of equity have developed the procedure to be followed in the event of default and forfeiture. If the buyer, after default, voluntarily surrenders possession to the seller, no court procedure is necessary; the seller's title will become absolute and the buyer's equity will be cut off.

Pledge

When personal property is pledged as security for a debt, the property must be delivered to the pledgee or his agent. Ownership of the property remains in the pledgor, but on default of the pledgor the pledgee has the right to sell the pledged property and can pass as good title to the purchaser as the pledgor could have passed at the time the property was pledged. The pledgor has the right to redeem the property any time before its sale by paying the debt or discharging the obligation.

The pledge, being a security transaction, must be founded on a debt or obligation. The property pledged must be delivered to the pledgee or someone acting for him—there must be change of possession. This does not mean that there must be an actual change of physical possession but does require some change which will serve to put third persons on notice. In some instances, the pledgor has held the property as agent for the pledgee, but as a general rule such holding does not create a pledge good as against third persons; it is, however, good as between the parties.

The pledge is a bailment for the purpose of securing an obligation. As in all bailments, the ownership of the property remains in the pledgor and the right of possession is in the pledgee. In the absence of special provisions in the pledge agreement, the pledgor has the right to vote stock pledged. He owes a duty to pay taxes levied on pledged property, and, if the pledged property is damaged or destroyed without the fault of the pledgee, the pledgor must stand the loss. In fact all the benefits and risks of ownership rest in the pledgor, subject to the pledgee's special interest in the pledged property.

The pledgor has the right to redeem the pledged property at any time before it has been sold. The ownership of the pledgor is not cut off until the pledgee has sold the property in accordance with the pledge contract, or, if the contract does not specifically provide for the sale of the property, until it has been sold at public auction after notice to the pledgor and reasonable notice of the sale to the public. The ownership in the property does not pass to the pledgee on the pledgor's default. However, the pledge contract may give the pledgee the right to purchase either at private or public sale and without notice, but the courts will not permit the pledgee to take an unfair advantage of the pledgor. If the pledgee purchases at private sale and without notice to the pledgor, the sale must be fair, open, and aboveboard, and the purchase price must be reasonable or the pledgor can have the sale set aside.

The pledgee may, in the absence of agreement, exercise his own judgment as to when he will sell. He does not have to sell on the pledgor's request. The pledgor's remedy is to redeem. If he does not redeem, the pledgee is free to exercise his own judgment as to when he will sell. The pledgee is not legally bound to sell the pledged property. He may sue on the debt and satisfy the judgment out of other property belonging to the debtor. If he does proceed in this manner, he can retain the pledged property until the debt is satisfied in full. He does not lose his lien when he brings suit.

Manufacturers Acceptance Corporation v. Hale et al.
65 Fed. (2d) 76 (1933)

This was an action by Manufacturers Acceptance Corporation (plaintiff) against Will Hale and others, trustees in bankruptcy of the estate of Dixie Chair Company, bankrupt (defendants). Judgment for defendants and plaintiff appealed. Judgment affirmed in part and reversed in part.

The plaintiff loaned $12,000 to the bankrupt and claims that as security the bankrupt pledged certain lumber and ply-wood. The trustee in bankruptcy—defendant in this case—claims that the pledge was void because of lack of delivery.

When the $12,000 loan was made by the appellant to the bankrupt upon the security of the lumber and ply-wood, there was no physical delivery of the chattels, but upon receipt of the assignment and accompanying inventory, the appellant leased from the bankrupt by written contract a room in the bankrupt's plant in which the ply-wood was stored, and a portion of the ground outside of the building on which the lumber stood. The room in the plant was shut off from the rest of the factory by a separate door. Both of the leased spaces were marked by signs indicating that they were warehouses of the appellant. Such signs remained until after the trustees took possession. At the time of the assignment the appellant executed to the bankrupt its warehouse receipt for the lumber and ply-wood, indicating that the chattels had been delivered to the appellant and were being held by it in its warehouse subject to a claim for $12,000. The assignment agreement permitted the bankrupt to use the lumber and ply-wood in its manufacture of chairs, but provided for substitution of new material purchased, or in the alternative, for payment.

Simons, C. J. It seems clear to us that what the parties intended, and in fact accomplished, by the assignment of the lumber and ply-wood, the lease of the premises upon which the material was stored, the execution of the warehouse receipt, the segregation and marking of the property as belonging to the appellant, was a pledge of chattels for a present consideration passing from pledgee to pledgor, and that there was sufficient delivery to consummate the pledge. That which distinguishes a pledge from a chattel mortgage, conditional sale, or other form of chattel security, is possession by the party secured, and when possession is lost so is the security. We have, then, presented the narrow question as to whether the pledge originally made was later destroyed by the surrender of the pledged property by the pledgee to the pledgor.

It is the general rule that a pledge will be deemed to be waived or lost by the voluntary and unconditional surrender of the pledged property. It has been held, however, that if pledged property is returned to the pledgor for a limited or specific purpose, the pledgee's lien is not lost. This is true where the pledgor becomes a bailee for the pledgee, where pledged property is delivered to the pledgor for purposes of sale, or for collection for the account of the pledgee, or for exchange, the substituted property to become security instead. There are many cases upholding the validity of the so-called "field storage" system for the warehousing of heavy or bulky material, the actual moving of which is inexpedient. In such cases it has been held that if the warehouseman fully discharges his duty to negative ostensible ownership by the pledgor, withdrawal and substitution will not destroy the lien. We are of the opinion that under the circumstances of this case there was no such unqualified surrender of possession back to the pledgor as to invalidate the security. The indicia of ownership of the pledged property were maintained throughout. The lease of that portion of the premises upon which the property was stored was never surrendered or canceled. The subsequent inventory taken by the appellant was inconsistent with surrender of possession. The record kept by the bankrupt of material removed, and its replacement by subsequent purchases so that the inventory remained substantially constant, was clearly recognition of the adverse possession of the pledged chattels by the pledgee. No creditor is shown to have been deceived, or to have extended credit in reliance upon the pledged property being the property of the bankrupt. It must be remembered also that the appellant does not claim a lien upon any of the property removed. It asks to have its security applied only to that which remains. We think it is entitled to its security for the $12,000, and that the court below erred in disallowing it.

Coleman v. Solomon et al.
225 Ala. 407, 143 So. 576 (1932)

This was an action by James Coleman (plaintiff) against David R. Solomon, Madeline Solomon, and James R. Smith (defendants). Judgment for defendants and plaintiff appealed. Judgment reversed and remanded.

Plaintiff borrowed $400 from Madeline Solomon and pledged as security eight promissory notes of $500 each, secured by a real estate mortgage on real property of the value of $9,000. Plaintiff did not pay the debt when due and the collateral notes were sold shortly after the maturity of the $400 debt and were bid in by the payee and pledgee Madeline Solomon for $442.15. Plaintiff shortly after learning of the sale of the pledged notes tendered the full amount of the debt, interest, and costs and demanded the return of the pledged notes. Madeline Solomon refused the tender and plaintiff brought this suit to recover the collateral notes.

Anderson, C. J. Sales of pledges and the right to redeem therefrom are generally controlled by the rules of law applicable to mortgages, and the equity of redemption arises under like circumstances.

In our recent case of *Persons* v. *Russell*, 212 Ala. 506, 103 So. 543, we held that when the pledgee purchased at his own sale without the consent of the pledgor, the pledgor could avoid the sale, without regard to the question of fairness in conducting the same or the adequacy of the price. Here, however, we have a case where the pledgor, in the note given, consented for the pledgee to become the purchaser at the sale of the collateral, and which she did at a grossly inadequate price, and the question arises, will this fact alone create a presumption of fraud and give the pledgor a right to cancel the sale and redeem the collateral upon seasonable application and tendering or paying the debt due the pledgee?

A mortgagee purchasing at a grossly inadequate price, obtains only a colorable title, and is accountable to the owner for the fair value of the property at the time of appropriation. The owner may disregard the sale and redeem the property. The burden is upon the mortgagee purchasing at his own sale under a power to show that the sale was fairly and openly made, in strict compliance with the power, and that the price paid was not so clearly and grossly inadequate as to raise a presumption of bad faith.

We think, and so hold, that the consideration for the sale of these collateral notes was so grossly inadequate as to shock the conscience and raise a presumption of fraud and thus authorize the pledgor to avoid same upon seasonable action, which was done within a few months after said sale by an offer or tender to the pledgee of the full amount due her; in fact a few dollars in excess.

First National Bank of Blakely v. Hattaway
172 Ga. 731, 158 S.E. 565 (1931)

This was an action by J. F. Hattaway (plaintiff) against First National Bank of Blakely (defendant). Judgment for plaintiff and defendant appealed. Judgment reversed.

In 1920 Hattaway was indebted to the First National Bank and pledged to them as security fifty bales of cotton. The cotton was in a warehouse.

The notes were renewed from time to time. On November 15, 1923, after the maturity of the notes, Hattaway demanded that the bank sell the cotton; it was worth 37 cents a pound at that time. The bank did not sell but held the cotton for about a year and a half and during this time the price of cotton steadily declined. The cotton was sold March 3, 1925, for $24\frac{15}{16}$ cents. The proceeds from the sale were not sufficient to discharge the indebtedness. Hattaway sued to recover the difference between the market value of the cotton when he demanded the bank to sell and the amount received when the bank did sell.

Beck, P. J. Neither at common law nor under the statutes of this state, in the absence of contract, is the holder of collateral bound to sell it, though he may have the right to sell it, under certain conditions, by giving notice as required by the statute. As a matter of law, a pledge of chattels is a mere security for the obligation that the pledgor would pay the debt. The pledgee may sell the collateral in order to protect himself, if he deems it wise to do so, after compliance with the statute as to notice, etc., or in the exercise of special contractual power. But he is not obliged to sell the collateral to satisfy the debt in whole or in part, even upon the demand of the pledgor. The pledgee may look solely to the promisor, and may proceed against him on his promise, without exhausting the collateral. The creditor may sue on the note and obtain an ordinary common-law judgment without exhausting the security. The property pledged, the chattel in the present case, is merely security for the debt. Where the creditor holds a promissory note given him by his debtor and holds other promissory notes or other collateral for the principal obligation, he is bound to use ordinary diligence in collecting the collateral; but as regards other pledges, such as cotton, stocks of corporations, and the like, the obligation of the creditor is to exercise ordinary care in the preservation of the collateral, to the end that it may be delivered to the debtor when he pays the debt in substantially as good a condition as it was when received. "A pledge, or pawn, is property deposited with another as security for the payment of a debt." "The pawnee is bound for ordinary care and diligence." The doctrine is thus stated in 21 R. C. L. 689, § 49: "It is the well-settled general rule that pledgee though entitled to do so, it is not bound to sell the pledge at the maturity of the debt, but may sell or not at his option, and in the absence of any agreement requiring the pledgee of property to sell it on the maturity of the debt he cannot be held liable for a depreciation in the value of the property occurring after the maturity of the debt secured by the pledge. The pledgor having the right of redemption, he must redeem and sell the pledged property himself if he wishes to avoid loss by depreciation."

Chattel Mortgage

Originally, when one mortgaged chattels, he passed the title to the property to the mortgagee, the title to revert if the mortgagor performed as required in the mortgage agreement. If he failed to perform his obligation, the title to the property became absolute in the mortgagee. The form of the mortgage was that of a bill of sale containing a defeasance clause. The idea of a sale with a defeasance provision is still the basis of our mortgage law. In some jurisdictions the title to the property passes to the mortgagee, while in others title does not pass—the mortgagee is given a lien on the property.

With few exceptions it is immaterial, in working out the rights of the parties, whether the courts follow the title theory or the lien theory.

In most instances the mortgaged property is left in the possession of the mortgagor.

Third parties dealing with the mortgagor would not know of the outstanding interest. Such a situation, if not remedied, would, under modern methods of buying, selling, and exchanging of chattels, result in unwarranted hardship to third persons dealing with the mortgagor and having no knowledge of the mortgagee's interest in the chattels mortgaged. To remedy this defect, all the states [1] and the District of Columbia have passed statutes requiring the filing or recording of chattel mortgages. These statutes are not uniform, but in the majority of jurisdictions they provide for certain formal requirements, as acknowledgment, affidavits of good faith, witnesses, etc. The formal requirement of acknowledgment is the most common. Substantially all the statutes state that the chattel mortgage shall be void as to third parties unless the giving of the mortgage is "accompanied by an immediate delivery and actual and continued change of possession" or the provisions of the statute are complied with. The purpose of the statutes is to give third persons notice of the mortgagee's interest in mortgaged property which is in the possession of the mortgagor. The results of failure to comply with the statute vary in the different states. In some jurisdictions, failure to comply with the statute renders the chattel mortgage void as to all persons except the parties to the chattel mortgage. In other jurisdictions, the chattel mortgage is valid as to all persons having notice of it and void as to creditors, purchasers, and lien holders taking without notice. Between these extremes we have almost all conceivable combinations, such as void as against subsequent lien holders, prima facie void as to third persons regardless of actual or constructive notice, and void as to creditors and subsequent purchasers and mortgagees in good faith. The place of recording or filing also varies. Some jurisdictions require filing or recording with the county official in charge of the recording of deeds to real estate, while others require filing or recording with a designated city or township official. When the mortgagor is not a resident of the state in which the mortgaged property is located, usually the mortgage must be recorded or filed where the chattel is located; when he is a resident of the state, usually it must be recorded or filed where the mortgagor resides, but several jurisdictions require the mortgage to be recorded or filed in both the county of the mortgagor's residence and the county where the goods are located. A mortgage should be filed or recorded immediately on its execution. A few jurisdictions require recording or filing within a stated time. In some jurisdictions, chattel mortgages must be refiled

[1] Chattel mortgages are not generally in force in Pennsylvaina. However, there are a few specified exceptions.

or an affidavit of renewal be filed periodically, usually every year or every three years; if the recording or filing is not renewed, the mortgagee is no longer protected against third party claimants.

As a general rule, property not in existence cannot be mortgaged, and any attempt to mortgage future property is interpreted as a contract to mortgage. Such a contract creates rights between the parties but does not create a lien valid against third persons. One exception recognized in most of the states is a mortgage on a stock of goods for resale at retail which expressly provides that it shall be a lien on all replacements and additions to the stock. Some courts have held that in cases of this nature a chattel mortgage properly drawn and recorded protects the mortgagee against the claims of third parties. Other courts have followed the general rule of sales of personal property to its logical conclusion and have held that such a transaction cannot give rise to a property interest in goods not in existence or not owned by the mortgagor at the time the mortgage is given.

On default the mortgagee has the right to take possession of and sell the mortgaged property and from the proceeds pay costs, interest, and principal and turn any surplus over to the mortgagor. Foreclosure proceedings in the foreclosure of chattel mortgages are usually easily complied with. There is no redemption period. A common practice is to include a power of sale in the mortgage which gives the mortgagee the right to sell on default without court action. If the property is sold under a power of sale, the sale must be an open, honest, and above-board sale, and if it is not, the court will grant the mortgagor relief.

In re Herkimer Mills Co., Inc.
39 F. (2d) 625 (1930)

This was an action by Nathan Stabbins brought in the matter of the Herkimer Mills Company, Inc., bankrupt, petitioning for the review of a decision by the Referee in Bankruptcy, declaring certain assignments to Stabbins invalid as against creditors. Decision affirmed.

Herkimer Mills Co., Inc., bankrupt, filed its voluntary petition June 9, 1923. It was indebted to Nathan Stabbins and, after the indebtedness arose, it made two assignments to secure the indebtedness. Both assignments were of a quantity of cotton sweater coats in the possession of Tatum, Pinkham and Gray, who held warehouse receipts therefor, and who had made advances thereon to the bankrupt to cover the cost of manufacture. The first assignment provided that the Herkimer Mills "hereby sell and assign all our interest and right"; the second provided that the Herkimer Mills "hereby assigns our equity" to Nathan Stabbins "with the right of payment direct to him." Neither assignment was recorded as provided in the statute requiring the filing of chattel mortgages. Stabbins claims the transaction is a pledge and the instruments need not be filed.

Cooper, D. J. The claimant concedes that, if these assignments were chattel mortgages, they were void because not filed before bankruptcy. The essence of claimant's contention is that these assignments are in legal effect pledges, that filing was not necessary; that actually delivery of possession could not be made because of the prior right of possession of Tatum, Pinkham and Gray, but that the assignments were constructive delivery of possession of the goods; that the assignments were given pursuant to an agreement to give them, made prior to the four-month period, were effective as of the date of the agreement, and that claimant's rights are superior to those of the trustee in bankruptcy.

In re People v. *Remington*, 59 Hun. 287, 12 N.Y.S. 824, 826, 14 N.Y.S. 98, affirmed without opinion in 126 N.Y. 654, 27 N.E. 853, the court distinguished pledges from chattel mortgages as follows:

" 'A "pledge" differs from a "chattel mortgage" in three essential characteristics: (1) It may be constituted, without any contract in writing, merely by delivery of the thing pledged. (2) It is constituted by a delivery of the thing pledged, and is continued only so long as the possession remains with the creditor. (3) It does not generally pass the title to the thing pledged, but gives only a lien to the proprietor while the debtor retains the general property.' Jones, Pledges, § 4. 'Whenever there is a conveyance of the legal title to personal property upon an expressed condition subsequent, whether contained in the conveyance or in a separate instrument, the transaction is a mortgage.' Id. § 8. 'A delivery must always accompany a pledge, while a mortgage may be valid without delivery.' Jones, Chat. Mortg., § 7. 'A decisive test of a legal mortgage of personal property is the use of language which makes the instrument one of sale conveying the title to the property to the creditor conditionally, so that the sale is defeated by the debtor's performance of his agreement.' Id. § 8."

The transactions involved here fail to meet the requirements of a pledge in the following respects: (*a*) There was no actual delivery of the things pledged; (*b*) there was a writing which purported to pass the title rather than a special interest or to create a lien; (*c*) while claimants contend that the assignments were constructive delivery of the possession, the possession was already in a third person, and there is no proof that such third person knew of such constructive delivery or consented to accept the obligation thereof and hold the goods for claimant.

The writing rather satisfies the definition of the chattel mortgage, for there was a conveyance of a legal title to personal property or at least of all the bankrupt's interest therein, and, while the transfer of title was not stated in the instrument to be defeasible upon performance of an express condition subsequent, claimants necessarily contend, in calling the transaction a pledge, that there was such a definite condition subsequent.

These assignments are chattel mortgages rather than pledges, and so void for the reasons above stated.

Dexter v. Curtis et al.
51 Me. 505, 40 Atl. 549 (1898)

This was an action by Charles W. Dexter (plaintiff) against Milford A. Curtis and others (defendants). Judgment for plaintiff and defendants appealed. Judgment affirmed.

One Edward F. Goss gave plaintiff a chattel mortgage on his stock of goods and fixtures as security for a debt. The mortgage contained the following descriptions of the property: "All my stock in trade, consisting principally of confectionery, fruit, and cigars, and all my store furniture, fixtures, and appliances, excepting my soda fountain and appliances, and including all machinery and appliances for making ice cream, now contained and used in the store and basement occupied by me, situated in said Auburn, on the southerly side of Court street, and known as No. 50 on said street."

The mortgage also contained the following provisions: "It is mutually agreed and understood by the parties to this mortgage that the said Edwin F. Goss shall be allowed to barter, sell, and exchange the above-named stock, and with the proceeds purchase other goods of a like kind, which, together with all additions to said stock, shall be equally subject to the lien of this mortgage."

Goss turned over to defendants, in payment of a past due debt, goods which were part of his stock at the time the mortgage was executed or which were subsequently purchased by him for the purpose of replenishing his stock. The plaintiff claims that this was a conversion of the property mortgaged.

Wiswell, J. It has been frequently decided in this state that a chattel mortgage does not ordinarily pass the legal title to after-acquired-property, without some new act sufficient for the purpose, like a delivery to the mortgagee, and retention of the same by him, or a confirmatory writing properly recorded. But the rule is subject to this exception. That if the mortgage contains a stipulation authorizing the mortgagor to sell any portion of the mortgaged property, and requiring him to replace that sold by purchasing with the proceeds other articles of a like kind, which are to be subject to the lien of the mortgage, then the mortgage will have that effect, and will pass to the mortgagee the legal title to the property so acquired.

Are the defendants liable for a conversion of these goods? They were creditors of Goss. They had both constructive and actual notice of the mortgage. They obtained these goods from Goss for the purpose of reducing his indebtedness to them, and credit was given him for the goods upon their account. The title to goods thus obtained did not pass to them. While the mortgagor had the right to sell or to exchange any portion of his stock, he did not have the right to sell these goods to his creditors in payment of past indebtedness. Any person who obtained these goods of the mortgagor for this purpose did not acquire title to them, as against the mortgagee. The refusal to deliver the goods thus obtained, upon demand by the plaintiff, was a conversion.

Conditional Sales

A conditional sales agreement is the opposite of a chattel mortgage in that the conditional vendor (seller) retains the title and the conditional vendee (buyer) has possession. When selling goods, the seller may pass title to the buyer and then take back a chattel mortgage to secure the purchase price, or he may retain the title, giving the buyer possession and reserving the right to repossess the goods if the buyer defaults. The latter transaction is a conditional sales agreement. Under a conditional sales agreement, the buyer agrees to purchase the goods. He is absolutely bound to pay the purchase price and accept the title, and in the majority of jurisdictions he accepts all the risks of ownership. The seller retains the title as security for the payment of the purchase price and has the right, on the buyer's failure to fulfill his obligations under the contract, either to repossess the goods or to pass title and sue for the purchase price. The majority of the states have passed statutes restricting the operation of the conditional sales contract. Many of the states require recording or filing, and failure to comply renders the contract void as to third persons. A Uniform Conditional Sales Act has been drafted and adopted by ten states, Alaska, and Hawaii (1945).

To determine the rights of third persons, it is necessary to consult the statutes of the state having jurisdiction of the case. However, there have been developed general rules which apply in the absence of statutory provisions determining the rights of third parties and which also help in interpreting the statutes. The conditional vendor's title is good as against third parties, and, in case of default by the conditional vendee, he can retake the goods wherever he finds them. One generally recognized exception to this rule is that when the conditional vendor sells to one operating a retail business, his title is not good as against one purchasing from the conditional vendee in the regular course of the latter's business. The conditional vendor's title is good against subsequent lien holders. In some states, by statute, a mechanic's lien is given priority over the conditional vendor's title.

At common law, in the event the conditional vendee defaults, the seller can declare a forfeiture, and, if the conditional vendee does not pay, the conditional vendor is under no obligation to refund any part of the purchase price paid, nor is he entitled to a deficiency judgment if the value of the goods, when repossessed, is less than the unpaid balance of the purchase price. If the conditional vendor does not wish to repossess the goods, he has the right to pass title to the conditional vendee and sue for the unpaid balance of the purchase price. The Uniform Conditional Sales Act and the statutes of approximately one half of the states make some provision for the sale of the goods and the recovery by the seller of the unpaid balance or the payment to the buyer of the balance received over and above the unpaid balance of the purchase price together with costs.

Mills Novelty Co. v. Morett et al.
266 Mich. 451, 254 N.W. 163 (1934)

This was an action by Mills Novelty Company (plaintiff) against Frank O. Morett and another (defendants). Judgment for defendants and plaintiff appealed. Judgment affirmed.

Eight automatic phonographs were purchased on five separate contracts, identical except as to amounts and dates. The contracts were filed in compliance with the statute requiring filing of chattel mortgages and an affidavit of renewal also was filed. On default the phonographs were repossessed and sold; the sale price was $2,775 less than the unpaid balance of the purchase price. Suit is brought to recover this deficiency. Defendant claims that the contract is a conditional sales contract and repossession exhausts plaintiff's remedies.

Edward M. Sharpe, J. The sole question for decision is whether the instrument in question is a chattel mortgage or a conditional sale. A conditional sale is an agreement for the sale of a chattel in which the vendee undertakes to pay the price, and possession of the chattel is immediately given to the vendee, but the title to the same is retained by the vendor until the purchase price is paid, when it passes to the vendee. But if the contract of the parties imports that title is retained as security merely, and the vendor is given the right to reclaim and resell the property, the taking and holding additional security and the enforcement of statutory liens are not inconsistent with the reservation. The right to resell and recover any balance of the purchase price which may be unpaid evidences a retention of title by way of security only.

This court has consistently followed the rule laid down in the Atkinson Case, that the distinction between the two types of transaction lies in the rights and remedies of the vendor: In the conditional sale, the seller may retake the goods on default and rescind the sale or may sue for the price and elect to pass the property to the buyer; in the chattel mortgage, the vendor has a lien on the property with the right to reclaim and resell the res and sue for a deficiency.

The instant instrument has some aspects of a chattel mortgage and some of a conditional sales contract. The determination of the nature of the transaction (at least where rights of third persons are not involved) depends upon the intention of the parties making the contract under consideration, as ascertained by the correct construction of its terms. If the intent is not clear, ambiguities will be resolved against the party who was relied upon to, and who did, select the language of the contract. Doubts should be resolved against the vendor when there is a purposeful ambiguity adopted in the hope of construing the contract later as a chattel mortgage or a conditional sale as may best serve the vendor's purpose.

Plaintiff asserts that the instrument is a chattel mortgage, yet it is not in the form nor does it use terms that are ordinarily found in a chattel mortgage. The use of the words "chattel mortgage" in the renewal affidavit could not make the instrument a chattel mortgage. The framer of the instrument seems studiously to have avoided using the term "security" or any similar expression. The contract in the instant case is certainly not explicit as to the remedies available to the vendor. It is worthy of notice that it is nowhere specifically provided that the vendor, after reclaiming the phonographs, may have an action for the deficiency in the purchase price. The reference to "any other remedy which law or equity may permit" and the provision that "remedies shall be cumulative and not alternative" are more than overbalanced by the explicit provision that in case of repossession "payments shall be retained to cover expense of taking possession and to recover usage and wear and tear on same." Such application of payments would not be permissible in the case of a chattel mortgage. It is readily apparent from the record and the surrounding circumstances that the defendants never considered the instrument as a chattel mortgage.

Trapani v. Universal Credit Co.

151 Kan. 715, 100 P. (2d) 735 (1940)

This was an action by Louis A. Trapani (plaintiff) against Universal Credit Company (defendant). Judgment for plaintiff and defendant appealed. Judgment affirmed.

The Palmer Company, in effect, purchased a Lincoln Zephyr car from the Universal Credit Co., giving its note in payment and a conditional sales contract on the car to secure the balance due. The car was kept for several weeks on display by the Palmer Company at its show rooms and was sold to plaintiff on February 15, 1938, for $1,318. The Universal Credit Co. knew that the Palmer Company purchased the car for resale and that it had the car on display at its show rooms. Palmer Company did not pay its note to Universal Credit Co. and Universal Credit Co. repossessed the car from plaintiff. This suit is brought to recover the value of the car on the theory that Universal Credit Co. in repossessing the car is guilty of conversion.

Smith, J. Defendant argues that under the facts in this case under the conditional sales contract the Palmer Motor Company never had any title to the Lincoln Zephyr automobile and therefore could not pass any title to plaintiff. In connection with this argument it should be noted that the findings of the court show that the Universal Credit Company knew that the Palmer Company was buying the car for the purpose of resale. Its agents knew it was being demonstrated and knew that the Palmer Company bought it for no other purpose than to sell it. Under such circumstances it would not do to hold that the Palmer Company did not have sufficient title in this car so as to pass title to a purchaser in good faith. To do so would open the door to fraud. The case of *National Cash Register Co.* v. *Pfeifer*, 149 Kan. 582, 88 P. 2d 1032, is relied upon by defendant in this connection. However, that was a case where the conditional sales contract was for an article not to be resold in the regular course of trade and was properly on record and there was no mistake as to the description. In Estrich on Instalment Sales, Sec. 151, the rule is laid down as follows: "Where there is a sale of property in which the seller reserves title, but expressly or impliedly authorizes a resale, it seems clear that the seller has no rights as against the purchaser from the conditional buyer, who purchased in accordance with the authority to sell. Nor does there seem to be any necessity for insisting upon the condition that the subsequent purchaser be a bona fide purchaser. Where, however, the seller has not authorized a resale, but has intrusted the goods to a dealer in such goods, or has laid down certain conditions in the sale, it may be necessary to condition the purchaser's superior rights upon his being a bona fide purchaser. Authority to sell may be implied, as well as express. The broad proposition has been announced that the seller of property cannot, as against subsequent purchasers, reserve his title and authorize his vendee to sell; his authorization of a sale by his vendee is inconsistent with the reservation of title in himself; accordingly, a purchaser from the vendee has a good title as against the conditional seller. Where the sale is to a retailer or dealer in the articles sold, the rights of a purchaser from such retailer or dealer in the ordinary course of trade are superior to those of the seller; as to such purchasers from the retailer the reservation is invalid. Or, as expressed in some cases, the seller is estopped to claim the goods as against such a purchaser from the retailer."

Trust Receipts

The trust receipt is of recent origin. It was used in the United States as early as 1875, but it has attained its position of importance since 1900. Originally it was used in import transactions, but it is now used extensively in the financing of automobile dealers. The trust receipt is a three-party transaction. The trust receipt in general use in the import trade provides (1) that the ownership of the goods shall remain in the lenders, (2) that the lender has the right to repossess the goods at any time, and (3) that the buyer-trustee has the right to warehouse the goods, immediately returning the warehouse receipts to the lender, or that he has the right to process the goods, immediately turning the documents of ownership over to the lender, or that he can sell the goods, immediately paying the proceeds of the sale over to the lender.

In a typical trust receipt transaction, as used in financing automobile dealers, the dealer will arrange with a finance company or bank to lend him sufficient money to purchase the new cars which he wishes to buy. Then he will arrange to have the manufacturer ship the cars to the finance company or bank. The cars will be shipped, bill of lading draft attached, to the finance company or bank, and on the arrival of the bill of lading the finance company or bank will pay the draft, obtain the bill of lading, and deliver the automobiles to the dealer on trust receipt. One form of trust receipt in common use provides that the dealer will hold the automobiles as the property of the finance company or bank, will store them, etc., and will return them on demand, and then provides that the dealer may sell the automobiles and immediately pay over to the finance company or bank the proceeds of sale. Another form of trust receipt in common use contains substantially the same provisions except that it prohibits the sale of the automobiles unless the amount stipulated in the trust receipt is first paid and a release obtained.

In a valid trust receipt transaction the title to the goods must pass from the seller to the lender. If title passes from the seller to the buyer and from the buyer to the lender, the transaction is a chattel mortgage. Archer wishes to purchase automobiles from Burch Co., and Clark is willing to lend to Archer the money needed to complete the deal if the automobiles are put up as security for the loan. If a trust receipt is to be used as security, the automobiles will be sold by Burch Co. to Clark and title will vest in Clark. When the automobiles are delivered they will be delivered to Archer but, before the automobiles are delivered to Archer, he will be required to execute to Clark a note for the amount advanced by Clark secured by a trust receipt. Clark is the title owner of the automobiles and Archer has possession as trustee under the trust receipt. A bona fide purchaser for value in the regular course of trade gets good title to goods financed under a trust receipt, but the lender's title is good as against creditors of the trustee and purchasers other than bona fide purchasers for value in the regular course of trade.

The Uniform Trust Receipt Act, which was recently drafted and has been adopted by several of the states,[2] has recognized the trust receipt as a new type of security device. The court decisions are not in accord in regard to the nature of a trust receipt. The prevailing holding of the state courts is that the trust receipt is a chattel mortgage. The federal courts have held it to be a new type of security de-

---

[2] Twenty-one states have adopted the Act (1945).

vice. Some state courts have held the trust receipt to be a conditional sale, and some have held it to be a bailment. In business it is employed as a short-term security device, used to aid in the marketing of goods. The Uniform Trust Receipt Act is based on this view of the trust receipt.

In re James, Inc.
30 F. (2d) 555 (1929)

This was an action in the matter of the bankruptcy of James, Incorporated, bankrupt, wherein by order of the District Court, offering the report of a special master, Sidney S. MacComber and another, trustees in bankruptcy, were awarded certain motor cars. Commercial Investment Trust and others appeal. Decree reversed.

When James, Incorporated, was adjudged bankrupt, it had in its possession twenty-seven cars which it held on trust receipt. The trust receipts were not filed or recorded. The special master held that the trust receipts were in effect chattel mortgages and, not having been filed or recorded as required by the statutes, they were void as against the creditors of the bankrupt and ordered the trustees in bankruptcy to dispose of the cars as part of the bankrupt's estate. Commercial Investment Trust and General Motors Acceptance Corporation contend that the trust receipts are not chattel mortgages and that they are valid without recording or filing.

Manton, C. J. The holder of a trust receipt, if he derives his security title from a person other than one responsible for the satisfaction of the obligation which the property secures, is not obliged to file his security as is required in the case of a chattel mortgage. In such case only can he deliver the property to the obligor to act as his fiduciary.

There are various forms of chattel security, as a pledge, conditional sale, or mortgage. But the trust receipt does not, on its face or by its name, purport to conform to any of these types. It is not a pledge, for a pledge depends upon possession of the parties secured, and, when possession is lost, so is the security. While the title in the case of a pledge is in the pledgor, or in another than the pledgee, such is not true in a trust receipt, where the title is intended to remain in the party secured while the possession is intrusted to one who has a certain interest as yet indefinite in the property. The practice of a conditional sale bears some resemblance to a trust receipt. Possession cannot be retaken until there is a default; whereas in a trust receipt, it can be retaken at any time. The holder of the trust receipt is not interested in the sale of the property or its commercial or market value. If he retakes the goods, and sells them for an amount in excess of the sum, this excess belongs to the buyer or importer; whereas, in a conditional sale, the buyer is interested only in such amount as he has paid on account of his contract. In any event, the holder of the trust receipt does not sell the goods to the importer or domestic trader, and whether or not the bank, finance company, or individual has an intention of selling goods to him, it lends him credit and advances the money for the buyer's account.

In the case of a mortgage, whether of chattels or realty, the security is dependent upon the title, as distinguished from a pledge, which rests upon possession. Title is given to the person, while possession may be given to the mortgagor, or the debtor, or his representative. The title thus conveyed to the mortgagee is as security for the performance of his obligation, and, in the case of a trust receipt, title has never been in the importer or domestic buyer, and he consequently cannot convey such title back to the holder of the trust receipt. If the mortgagor conveys this title to the mortgagee as security for the performance of an obligation of a third person, the equity of redemption belongs to him, and not to the third person, and the property reverts to him upon performance of the obligation by the third person. In a trust receipt, under no circumstances does title revert to the manufacturer or seller. It has been recognized that there are sound business reasons why it is unnecessary to record trust receipts, and also that they should have superior protection as compared with an unrecorded chattel mortgage, when they are given to a lender of money by some one other than the debtor, and where either the delivery or possession against trust receipts is made to the debtor.

The trust receipts held by the General Motors Acceptance Corporation and the Commercial Investment Trust are valid and they are a first lien against the funds now held by the trustee.

Common Law and Statutory Liens

The common law lien was first recognized as the right of an innkeeper to hold the effects of his guest until the guest paid for his food and lodging, and as the right of a common carrier to hold the goods carried until the charge for the carriage was paid. This rule was an exception to the early rule that one should contract for protection if he wished it. The justification for the exception was that innkeepers and common carriers were by law bound to serve the public, and if this duty was imposed on them, they were entitled to the protection of a lien for their charges. Later, the right to a common law lien was extended to artisans. If an owner delivered his property into the possession of an artisan who improved it by his labor and by the addition of his material, the artisan was given a lien on the property for his proper charges.

The common law lien gives the lien holder the right to retain possession of the property until the debt or obligation has been discharged. The right of possession does not carry with it the right to sell the chattel on default. Before the lien holder can sell he must sue, obtain judgment, levy an execution or attachment, and sell at execution or attachment sale. The two essentials of the common law lien are the existence of a debt or obligation and possession. If possession is surrendered intentionally, the lien is lost. If the debtor obtains possession through artifice or fraud, it does not extinguish the lien. If the debt or obligation is discharged, the lien is automatically discharged because the foundation of the right is the existence of the debt or obligation, and a lien right cannot exist separate and apart from the debt or obligation. However, the discharge of the lien does not affect the right to recover on the debt or obligation.

Statutory liens on personal property are, in large part, an enactment of the existing common law with added provisions providing for a sale of the property held. It is true that the lien right has been given a much larger scope by statutory enactments. To determine the scope of statutory liens, one must consult the statutes of the various states.

Each state has its own lien statutes creating such liens as the needs of the people in the states suggest to the legislators. These statutes will also set up the procedure to be followed in the foreclosure of the liens.

Carrier's liens and warehouseman's liens are provided for in the Uniform Bill of Lading Act and the Uniform Warehouse Receipt Act.

If the lien created by statute was not recognized at common law, the statute creating the lien is said to be in derogation of the common law. The same is true of a statute which provides for a lien which was recognized at common law but which gives to one of the parties rights which were not recognized under the common law lien. The courts have developed a rule of statutory construction which is generally applied in interpreting and applying such statutes. If the statute is in derogation of the common law, it will be strictly construed. By that the courts mean that all the provisions of the statute must be complied with before the party can claim benefits under the statute and that the courts will not enlarge the scope of the statute by implications. If one claims a lien on property and refuses to surrender possession when demand is made by the owner and he is not entitled to a lien at common law or under some statute, he will be liable to the owner for the conversion of the property or for damages for the unlawful detention of the property.

There is no common law lien on real estate. The mechanics' lien is a creature of statute and has been created by law for the purpose of securing the payment of the price of erecting or improving buildings or making other improvements which increase the value of real property. There is no uniformity in the statutes, but for the purpose of general discussion they may be divided into two systems, the New

York system and the Pennsylvania system. Under the New York system the subcontractor, materialman, or laborer cannot recover more than is owing to the general contractor, while under the Pennsylvania system the subcontractor, materialman, or laborer is given a direct lien on the property improved for the amount of his claim. The general scheme of mechanics' liens is to require the filing or recording of a notice of lien within a definitely stated time. On the filing of this notice the lien attaches and usually dates from the time the first labor or material was furnished by the lien claimant. The lien must then be foreclosed within a stated period. The foreclosure procedure is similar to the procedure for the foreclosure in equity of a real estate mortgage. Since the lien is statutory, the material provisions of the statute must be complied with. In the majority of states, strict compliance is required, but even in these states, the courts have not been technical in their requirements.

The theory of mechanics' lien is that one has added to the value of the property and should have a lien on the property to secure the payment of the cost of the improvement. Hence, one is not entitled to a lien for materials or labor unless such became a part of the real estate. To determine definitely what will become a part of the real estate and what will remain personal property, one must refer to the law of property. There is some conflict, owing in a large part to the differences in the wording of the statutes, as to what are materials and when they are furnished. The materials furnished must be furnished for a specified building. As a general rule, materials are furnished when they are delivered on the premises and accepted, irrespective of when they may be incorporated in the building. This rule has been adopted to prevent fraud. To require a materialman to prove conclusively that the materials delivered on the premises for use in a building or other construction work were actually incorporated into the building or other construction work would impose an unwarranted burden on him. To relieve the materialman of this unwarranted burden, the courts have held that, if the materials are delivered on the premises and accepted, it is conclusively presumed that they are incorporated into the building.

A majority of the mechanics' lien statutes provide that the claim for a mechanic's lien must be filed within 60 days "after performing such labor or furnishing such materials." This phrase has been interpreted as being equivalent to a requirement that the claim for a lien must be filed within 60 days after the last work is performed or the last material is furnished.

O'Brien v. Buxton
9 N.J. Misc. 876, 156 Atl. 17 (1931)

This was an action by Mary A. O'Brien, administratrix of the estate of James O'Brien, deceased (plaintiff) against William P. Buxton (defendant). Judgment for plaintiff.

James O'Brien in his lifetime owned an ice boat named "Jack Frost." Defendant, a boat builder, stored the boat and also acted as its sailing master. Plaintiff tendered the amount claimed as storage, but not the amount claimed for services as sailing master, and demanded possession of the boat. Defendant refused the tender and demand and later sold the boat in compliance with the terms of a statute providing for the sale of property held under a common law lien. The defendant purchased the boat at the sale and later plaintiff replevined the boat, claiming that defendant had no lien on the boat and that the sale was void.

Lawrence, C. C., Judge. The primary question, therefore, is whether the boat was subject to a common-law lien merely for defendant's services as sailing master or for storage. It may be said that he was given permission to amend the stipulation of facts by submitting to the court an itemized statement of his account, showing, if he could, any service involving labor performed or materials provided in conditioning or repairing the iceboat, but apparently had no such account susceptible of proof. Such proof, consequently, as disclosed by the stipulation of facts, remained confined to the statement of services as sailing master and for storage. That these services do not come within the definition of a common-law lien, or indeed within the provision of the statute resorted to to enforce it, seems apparent. They were not for work, labor, or materials employed in repairing, conditioning, or constructing the boat.

At common law the debt must have been incurred for some service or work rendered by claimant on the property against which the lien is asserted. It is entirely distinct from the debt or obligation which it secures; it is but an incident of the debt or obligation and a remedy therefor. The debt or obligation itself may be enforced with or without the aid of the lien; further proceedings on the lien may be barred, but not on the debt or obligation, and the payment of the debt extinguishes the lien. The term "lien" is sometimes used in a broad sense as being equivalent to "claim or demand," but in a technical sense a lien is in the nature of security and is distinct from a "claim or demand," as a person may have a claim and yet not be entitled to a lien to secure the payment thereof.

A workman who by his skill and labor has enhanced the value of a chattel, under an employment to render the service by the consent, express or implied, of the owner, has a lien on the chattel for his reasonable charge.

In *Lanterman* v. *Luby*, 96 N.J. Law, 255, 257, 114 A. 325, a lien is defined as neither a right of property in a thing nor a right of action for a thing, but simply a right of detainer. It differs from a mortgage, in that a mortgage is a transfer of title as security; whereas, a lien confers no title; it differs from a pledge, in that a pledge is a transfer of possession as security; whereas, in the case of lien the transfer of possession is not for the purpose of security, but in order that the service may be rendered to the chattel in question, and the lien arises from the rendering of that service, if such service be not paid for. It is essentially a right to detain. It is the natural outcome of the transaction wherein one takes his chattel to another with whom he contracts for the performance by the latter of some service upon it for its betterment. The owner does not pay for the service before it is performed, because he has the right to see that it is right before he pays for it; on the other hand, the one who performs the service, having performed it well, has the right to be paid for it before the owner may take away his property so benefited by the service. At common law, bailees, other than innkeepers, common carriers, and warehousemen, were not recognized as having a lien on the property for mere storage, or for other services that did not enhance the value of the property, while, in the absence of statute or special contract securing a lien, a servant or employee has no lien upon the property of his master or employer for his wages or compensation. Even though it has appeared that defendant has been engaged in the business of storing ice boats and would be entitled to a lien for such storage while it remained unpaid, it did not arise in the present case, because it is stipulated that plaintiff tendered the storage charge, included as an item in the bill rendered, and that it was refused by defendant.

In the circumstances, the proofs fail to show that defendant has a common-law lien on the ice boat in question, and the result is that plaintiff must be held entitled to it.

Puritan Engineering Corporation v. Robinson et al.
207 Ind. 58, 191 N.E. 141 (1934)

This was an action by Puritan Engineering Corporation (plaintiff) against Chester L. Robinson, as trustee for Robert H. Shelhorn and others (defendant). Judgment for defendant and plaintiff appealed. Judgment affirmed.

Shelhorn was a building contractor. He built houses on lots which he owned and sold them and also built for others. He maintained a central depot or warehouse and carried a line of building materials and engaged to some extent in selling to the public. He purchased fifty water softeners from the plaintiff on title retaining contract. Thirty-five were delivered, ten paid for, and the other twenty-five were installed in houses built by Shelhorn on lots owned by him. Plaintiff filed a mechanic's lien upon the twenty-five separate lots upon which Shelhorn had constructed houses and installed twenty-five of the water softeners.

Fansler, J. The mechanic's lien statute (Burns' Ann. St. 1926, § 9831 et seq.), being in derogation of the common law, will be strictly construed to ascertain who are within its provisions, and the burden is upon one asserting a lien to bring himself within its provisions.

As pointed out above, the written contract, by express provision, contained all of the agreements and understandings of the parties concerning the subject-matter. There is no provision of any kind indicating the purposes to which the water softeners were to be put, or the manner in which they were to be used. Under the contract, the purchaser was at perfect liberty to sell them at retail, or to other building contractors, or to use them himself in buildings of his own, or in buildings which he may have been constructing for others. There is nothing in the contract to indicate that appellant contemplated the possibility of a mechanic's lien as security for the contract price of the water softeners. In the contract, appellant reserved title to the softeners until they were paid for. This seems inconsistent with an intention that they were to be used in specific buildings, on specific lots, against which appellant had the assurance of a lien by filing notice within sixty days.

"A materialman claiming a lien must ordinarily show that his materials were furnished for and were actually used in the erection, alteration, or repair of the building against which the lien is asserted." *Potter Mfg. Co.* v. *A. B. Meyer & Co.*

It is not sufficient to show that the material was furnished to the contractor or owner and used in the building.

Appellant failed to show that the water softeners were furnished for the property against which the liens are claimed. The court correctly held that it was not entitled to a lien.

Guaranty or Suretyship

The distinction between a guaranty and suretyship is technical and is of minor importance. In both the guaranty and surety the guarantor's or surety's obligation is secondary, that is, their obligation is to perform an act in the event the primary obligor does not perform. The distinction is that the guarantor's duty to perform does not arise until the happening of some event, while the surety's duty arises at the same time as that of the primary obligor and is co-extensive with that of the primary obligor. Unless notice of default is waived in the guaranty contract, as a general rule, a guarantor is entitled to notice of the primary obligor's default, and failure to give notice of default within a reasonable time after the default will release the guarantor of liability. A surety is not entitled to notice of default. Otherwise, the laws of guaranty and suretyship are substantially the same, and we shall not attempt to distinguish between the two types of contracts in our discussions except in instances where the distinction is of basic importance.

The party primarily liable on a contract is called the principal, the party secondarily liable is called the surety, and the party entitled to performance is called the obligee or creditor; we shall use the latter term. A suretyship contract must be in writing under the Statute of

Frauds; it is an obligation to answer for the debt or default of another. Suretyship contracts are used in a variety of situations ranging from a simple agreement to guarantee the repayment of a loan to a bond guaranteeing that one contracting with the federal government to build a federal building at a cost of several millions of dollars will fulfill all the terms of his contracts. Bonds posted by employees intrusted with the handling of money, and bonds posted by treasurers of organizations are common examples of surety contracts.

A suretyship agreement is a contract and, as a general rule, any party having capacity to contract can enter into a contract of suretyship. In some states the married women statutes are so drafted that a married woman does not have the capacity to bind herself as surety, while in other states her incapacity goes only to contract as surety for her husband. As a general rule, a corporation has either no power or limited power to contract as a surety; however, a corporation may be granted the power to carry on the business of writing surety bonds.

As a general rule, if the principal is not bound, the surety is not bound; however, this general rule must be qualified in several respects. A more accurate statement would be that, if the principal has a defense which goes to the merits of the primary contract, such defense is available to the surety. Such defenses as infancy, insanity, discharge in bankruptcy, etc., which do not go to the merits of the contract, although available to the principal, are not available to a surety.

The surety contracts to be responsible for the performance of his principal's obligation. If the principal and the creditor by mutual agreement alter the terms of the primary contract and the surety does not consent thereto, the alteration will operate to relieve the surety of his liability. The surety undertakes to assume the risks incident to the performance of a particular contract, and his obligation cannot be altered without his consent.

Under this rule an agreement between the principal and the creditor, by which the principal is given an extension of time for the performance of the contract, releases the surety unless the surety consents thereto. However, mere indulgence on the part of the creditor does not release the surety. If a debt is due and the creditor tells the principal that he can have additional time in which to pay, the surety is not released because there is not a valid agreement to extend the time of payment. To have a valid extension of time, the promise to extend the time of payment must be supported by consideration.

The creditor owes certain duties to the surety. The creditor cannot induce the surety to assume the risk by fraudulent representations as to the nature of the risk; also, if the creditor has knowledge of facts which would materially increase the risk, he owes a duty to disclose such facts to the surety. In the bonding of employees if the employer (creditor) knows that an employee (principal) has been guilty of fraudulent or criminal misconduct, the creditor must disclose this information to the surety. If a bonded employee is guilty of a defalcation covered by the bond, but the employer decides to give the employee another chance and does not report the defalcation to the bonding company (surety), the bonding company will be released from liability on the bond. If the creditor holds security for the performance of the principal's obligation, which the creditor has received from the principal, and the creditor surrenders such security to the principal without the consent of the surety, as a general rule, the surety will be released to the extent by which the surrender of the security has injured him. Some states have held that the surety is completely discharged.

If the surety has to perform the obligation of his principal, the surety acquires, by operation of law, all the rights which the creditor had against the principal. This is known as the surety's right of subrogation. If Archer borrows $1,000 from Burch and Clark signs the contract as surety and Archer defaults and Clark pays Burch, Clark will acquire all of the rights Burch had against Archer. If Archer had pledged stocks or bonds as security or had given Burch a chattel mortgage or other security, Clark would be entitled to such security when he paid Burch. A surety's right of subrogation does not arise until the creditor has been paid in full.

If two or more persons become sureties for the same principal on the same obligation and on the principal's default one surety pays the obligation in full or pays more than his share of the obligation, he is entitled to reimbursement from his co-sureties for the amount paid over and above his share. This is known as a surety's right of contribution. If one or more of the co-sureties is insolvent, the loss will be distributed equally among the solvent sureties. If a surety discharges the obligation for less than the principal sum due, he is entitled to contribution of the amount actually paid in discharge of the obligation. Co-sureties may enter into an express agreement which provides that the risks of the suretyship shall be distributed in unequal portions. Archer, Burch, and Clark may sign as sureties for Drew. At the time the suretyship contract is entered into, Archer, Burch, and Clark may agree that, if Drew defaults, Archer will pay one-half of the loss and that Burch and Clark will each pay one-fourth.

J. R. Watkins Co. v. Jennings, et al.
131 Okla. 295, 269 P. 265 (1928)

This was an action by J. R. Watkins Company (plaintiff) against Lewis F. Jennings and others (defendants). Judgment for plaintiff for less than it asked. Plaintiff appealed. Judgment affirmed.

On the 25th of April, 1922, Jennings entered into a contract with the plaintiff whereby Jennings was to sell plaintiff's products. By the terms of the contract plaintiff was to sell and deliver to Jennings, at wholesale prices, goods and other articles manufactured by it. Jennings was to pay cash for said goods and, if he did not pay cash, he was to make a weekly report to plaintiff; however, the contract provided that the weekly reports might be waived by plaintiff.

The defendants, Oliver, Snowden, and Hagen, signed the contract as sureties or guarantors.

The first shipment of goods, amounting to about $300, was shipped in July, 1922, and in August and September, 1922, Jennings sent plaintiff checks in the sum of $5, $18.50, and $10.50 which were protested and dishonored, and regardless of the bad checks plaintiff continued to ship goods to Jennings until the termination of the contract in June, 1923. During the life of the contract Jennings made small payments which were always less than the price of goods shipped. This suit is brought to recover an unpaid balance of $760.07. The defendants, Oliver, Snowden, and Hagen, claim that the plaintiff's failure to notify them of the delinquency of their principal, Jennings, releases them from liability. The court gave the plaintiff a judgment for $157.61, the unpaid balance of the first shipment of $300.

Foster, C. As a general rule, a surety is bound to perform the obligation of its principal, and cannot complain when the creditor does not notify him of the default of his principal, or of the state of the accounts between himself and the principal, for whom the surety is liable. Mere inaction of the creditor will not discharge the surety, and the fact that the principal is delinquent in payments of sums due does not affect the liability of a surety.

But this rule does not apply where there is a question of moral turpitude involved, or where the principal is guilty of conduct indicating dishonesty, or bad faith, or utter unfitness for trust, after the knowledge of such conduct has come to the obligee's attention.

"If, however, the obligation of the surety is a continuing one, and the extent of the liability of the principal rests entirely within the knowledge of the obligee, notice of the principal's default must be given to the sureties within a reasonable time or they will be discharged." 32 Cyc. p. 109.

In 20 Cyc. p. 336, it is stated, as follows:

"And it has been held that where there is no limit, either as to time or amount of the creditor's liability, the amount of credit which may be extended must be reasonable, taking into consideration the language of the guaranty and of the circumstances of the case."

In the case of *Lehigh Coal & Iron Co.* v. *Scallen*, 61 Minn. 63, 63 N.W. 245, it is held that where a guaranty provided, "I agree to become responsible for any amount of credit you may give him," that this language must be given weight. But, even under this language an unreasonable amount of credit might be given and, where there was evidence tending to show that a reasonable line of credit in the business of the principal debtor was from $300 to $400, it was a question for the jury whether it was unreasonable, on the faith of the guaranty, to extend to him a line of credit amounting to over $3,000.

It seems to us that the giving of the three bogus checks, soon after the first shipment of more than $300 was made to the defendant Jennings, is a sufficient indication that the party is guilty of a moral delinquency and unfit for trust, where it also appears that the payments thereafter made were very small in proportion to the amount of goods shipped; that such conduct within the knowledge of the plaintiff, under a contract which is continuing, was sufficient under all the other facts and circumstances in this case to present a question to the court or jury as to whether or not notice should have been given. And since this case was tried by the court, and the court found that the sureties were released because of want of notice, we believe the evidence is sufficient under the rules above stated that said judgment will not be disturbed by this court.

Carpenter et al. v. Hogan et al.
50 N.Y.S. (2d) 123 (1943)

This was an action by Harriet A. Carpenter and Crescens Hubbard, as executors of the last will and testament of Hattie A. Pinchbeck, deceased (plaintiffs) against Walter V. Hogan and Catherine A. Hogan (defendants). Judgment for plaintiff.

Hattie A. Pinchbeck, in her lifetime, sold to Walter V. Hogan certain premises, taking in payment of the balance of the purchase price a note (bond) for $8,000 secured by a real property mortgage on the premises. Later Walter V. Hogan sold the property, subject to the mortgage, to his mother, Catherine A. Hogan. (The court held that as a result of this sale the mother became primarily liable for the payment of the $8,000 debt and that Walter was secondarily liable.—The mother was principal and Walter V. Hogan was surety.)

Catherine A. Hogan, after she purchased the property, wished to refinance the debt with the Home Owners Loan Corporation. The corporation would not make a loan which was sufficient to discharge the $8,000 mortgage. It was agreed that plaintiffs' testatrix would accept the amount loaned by the corporation in part payment of the debt and that she would extend the time of payment of the balance, $1,150. The refinancing transaction was closed on August 8, 1934. On September 7, 1934, Walter V. Hogan signed an agreement in which he approved the extension of time for the payment of the $1,150 balance. This balance has never been paid and, when sued, Walter V. Hogan claimed that the extension of time released him as surety and that the agreement signed on September 7, 1934, was unenforceable because it was not supported by consideration.

Aldrich, J. The right of surety to claim a discharge by a legal extension of time of payment given to the principal without the consent of the surety, is personal to the surety and may be waived by him. His consent may be given after the transaction. He may ratify the extension by a subsequent affirmative act. He may waive his defense. If, with full knowledge of the facts, he does any affirmative act which contemplates the continued existence of his status as a surety, he thereby waives the right to claim that he is discharged. If he makes a new promise to pay the debt or acknowledges its continued existence, he thereby waives such a defense. This particular subject of the release of the surety has been under extensive consideration by the Law Revision Commission. In its 1937 report, the rule on the precise point here was stated as follows (pp. 912, 913, note 133):

"A subsequent promise by a surety, who has knowledge that he has been discharged by an extension of time, nevertheless to answer for the debt, will be binding upon the surety without other consideration. The right of action in such case is based, however, upon the original obligation, and not upon the subsequent promise. Extension of time is treated as a defense personal to the surety, which he may waive. This situation has been described as one of the exceptional cases in which a promise is binding without consideration."

There are numerous decisions to the same effect. These authorities lead to the conclusion that Walter V. Hogan, by virtue of the instrument dated on September 7, 1934, is still liable for the balance unpaid on the amount secured by his original bond as reduced and extended.

QUESTIONS AND PROBLEMS

1. Can a security right in property continue to exist after the debt which it secures has been discharged?
2. What rights are acquired by the mortgagee of real property?
3. Willis and wife owned a house and lot which they mortgaged to the Loan Association to secure a loan of $800. They were in default and, fearing that they would lose the property, they conveyed it to Holladay who paid the mortgage debt. Holladay gave a written option to Mrs. R. A. Willis—Willis' mother—to purchase the property within a period of two years at the price paid by him with interest. After the expiration of the two years, Mrs. Willis not having exercised the option, Holladay sold the property to Mann for $1,600. Willis and wife brought suit against Holladay to require him to account for the proceeds of the sale over and above the amount he paid, contending that the conveyance to Holladay was a mortgage. Was the conveyance to Holladay a mortgage?
4. What is the difference between a real estate mortgage and a trust deed?
5. The Empire Sales Agency owned and operated an automobile salesroom. Fletcher American National Bank, a banking corporation, loaned Empire Sales Agency $500 and took as security a note, containing a pledge agreement, whereby Empire Sales Agency pledged an Empire automobile as security for the note. Empire Sales Agency retained possession of the automobile, but the following written agreement was given to the bank:

"Indianapolis, Ind., May 29, 1935.

"Received from Fletcher American National Bank, new Empire car No. 332408 in trust, to be handled by me, Fletcher American National Bank's agent and accounted for to its satisfaction.

"Signed: Empire Sales Agency."

McDermid, a judgment creditor of the Empire Sales Agency, seized the car on an execution. The bank claimed the car as pledgee. What are the bank's rights in the car?

6. Allen was indebted to Scruggs for rent. Allen delivered a quantity of tobacco to Scruggs on the condition that Scruggs would sell the tobacco and apply the proceeds to the payment of the debt, and if there was a surplus, Scruggs would turn the surplus over to Allen. Previously, Allen had mortgaged the tobacco to Moody, but Moody had not recorded the mortgage before Allen delivered the tobacco to Scruggs. Who is entitled to the tobacco, Scruggs or Moody?
7. White sold Perkins an electric refrigerator for $300. The contract provided that White was to retain the title to the refrigerator until the full purchase price was paid. After paying $150, Perkins made no further payments and White sent his truck to Perkins' house and demanded the refrigerator. It was surrendered, and White later sold it for only $50, which was the best price obtainable. White sued Perkins for $100. Is White entitled to a judgment?
8. What are the essential characteristics of a trust receipt?
9. Maxwell owned the timber on a certain tract of land and hired Fitzgerald to cut the timber into logs and put them in the mill pond. Fitzgerald had the logs cut and put on the bank of the mill pond where they were levied on by a judgment creditor of Maxwell. Fitzgerald claimed a common law lien on the logs for his labor in cutting and hauling the logs. Does Fitzgerald have a common law lien on the logs?
10. Freed contracted with Sexton to furnish materials and perform labor in plastering his building. Sexton purchased the mortar and other plastering materials for the job from the Materials Co. Sexton did not pay for the mortar and other plastering materials, and the Materials Co. filed a mechanic's lien and foreclosed thereon. The sales price was less than the amount of the lien. Is Freed personally liable for the deficiency?
11. The National Bank loaned Stewart $450 and Morse, Heath, and Braly signed the note as sureties. The note was not paid when due. Braly offered to pay the amount of the note but the National Bank refused to accept payment because its president did not want Morse and Heath sued. Braly paid one-third of the amount due. Later Morse and Heath became insolvent. Thereafter O'Connor, as receiver of the National Bank, brought a suit against the sureties to recover the unpaid balance of the note. Is O'Connor entitled to a judgment against Braly?

PART IV

SALES

CHAPTER XVIII

TRANSFER OF PROPERTY IN GOODS

Introduction

One of the primary functions of business is the distribution of goods. This function is carried on primarily through the sale of personal property; consequently, the law of sales is an important division of the law from the standpoint of the merchant.

In determining the rights of the parties in a sales transaction, the basic principles of contract law and of the law of personal property are applied. However, many usages and practices are followed by merchants in the buying and selling of goods which have resulted in the development of special rules or presumptions that apply to sales and are not of general application. Throughout the law of sales great weight has been given to established practices of merchants, and, in a large measure, the law of sales is made up of a judicial determination of those established practices. This does not mean that the courts have attempted to force all buyers and sellers to follow a standard practice. The courts, in the absence of a declaration of intention by the parties, have presumed that the parties intended to follow standard practices and, in determining the rights of the parties, have read into their sales contracts such standard practices unless the agreement or other circumstances show a contrary intent.

In buying and selling goods, merchants generally agree on only a few important points. Such an agreement, tested by strict legal principles of contract law, would be unenforceable for uncertainty, yet, tested by the law of sales, it may be a complete contract because the courts will fill in the gaps by presuming that, as to the matters not mentioned in the express agreement, the parties intended to follow the standard practice of merchants. If a sales agreement is silent on a material point and there is no standard practice in regard to the omitted matter, the agreement will be unenforceable for uncertainty. It is important to remember, in dealing with sales problems and in carrying out a sales transaction, that the parties can define their rights and liabilities in their agreement, but as to those matters on which the agreement is silent, the courts will presume, in the absence of strong evidence to the contrary, that the parties intended the standard practices of merchants to control.

Uniform Sales Act

The National Conference of Commissioners on Uniform State Laws drafted a Uniform Sales Act which was adopted by three states in 1907 and which is now in force in thirty-four states, Alaska, the District of Columbia, and Hawaii (1945). The drafters of the Uniform Sales Act used the English Sale of Goods Act as their pattern. The objective of the drafters in drafting the act was to state, in concise form, the law of sales as it existed in the United States in so far as the law was uniform throughout the states, and to formulate a workable rule as to those matters on which there was an existing conflict.

The Uniform Sales Act has been revised and rewritten by the joint committee of the American Law Institute and the National Conference of Commissioners on Uniform State Laws. The Revised Uniform Sales Act is in final form and has been approved by the American Law Institute and has been tentatively approved by the Commissioners on Uniform State Laws, but has not been adopted by any state (1945). The Revised Uniform Sales Act does not follow the organization of the original act, nor does it adhere to the philosophy of the original act; however, no attempt is made in the Revised Uniform Sales Act to reform our law of sales. The drafters of the Revised Uniform Sales Act have, in drafting the act, emphasized the standard practices of merchants and minimized the technical legal aspects of sales. The organization of the original Uniform Sales Act is followed in this discussion.[1]

Sale and Contract To Sell

A sale is defined in the Uniform Sales Act as "an agreement whereby the seller transfers the property in goods to the buyer for a consideration called the price." [2] This definition limits the scope of the meaning of sale to a situation in which the property in the goods is passed immediately to the buyer. If the property in the goods is passed to the buyer at the time of the agreement, it logically follows that the goods sold must be in existence and identified at the time of the sale. The courts have arrived at this conclusion and have adopted it as the general rule.

The contract to sell is so closely related to a sale that the average

[1] Uniform Sales Act, appendix, pp. 889-905.

[2] Sec. 1 (2).

merchant does not realize the difference and makes no distinction between the two in his everyday transactions. Technically, the difference is material and is the basis for the determination of the rights of the parties in many cases. A sale is the transfer of the property in the goods, while a contract to sell "is a contract whereby the seller agrees to transfer the property in goods to the buyer for a consideration called the price."[3] Frequently, business men will enter into a contract which by its terms purports to transfer the property in goods not in existence. Such an agreement cannot operate as a sale because one cannot transfer the property in non-existent goods, and such an agreement will be interpreted by the courts as a contract to sell. Usually, it is of little practical importance whether an agreement is a present sale or a contract to sell. The transaction will be completed in the regular course of the parties' business and neither party is interested in the technical question—At what instant of time did the property in the goods pass to the buyer?—but if the goods are damaged or destroyed, the answer to this question becomes all important, because the owner of the goods must stand the loss. If the parties have entered into a contract to sell and the contract is still executory, the seller owns the goods and must bear the risks of ownership, but if the contract is a contract of sale, the property in the goods passes immediately to the buyer, and the buyer bears the risks of ownership. This distinction is also important in determining the remedies to which the parties are entitled in the event of a breach of the contract of sale or to sell.

Alfred Low & another v. William A. Pew & another
108 Mass. 347 (1871)

This was an action by Alfred Low and Company (plaintiff) against William A. Pew, assignee in bankruptcy of the firm of John Low & Son (defendant). Judgment for defendant.

John Low & Son purported to sell to Alfred Low & Company all the fish caught by the master and crew of the schooner "Florence Reed" which was owned by John Low & Son and which was then sailing for the Grand Banks. Alfred Low & Company paid John Low & Son $1,500 as part payment for the fish to be caught. Before the schooner returned to port, John Low & Son were adjudged bankrupt and an assignee in bankruptcy was appointed. When the schooner "Florence Reed" returned to port, the assignee in bankruptcy had the United States marshall seize the schooner and cargo of fish as part of the assets of the bankrupt. Alfred Low & Company claimed the fish as their property, and, on the assignee's refusal to deliver the fish, Alfred Low & Company replevined them.

Morton, J. By the decree adjudging John Low & Son bankrupts

[3] Uniform Sales Act, sec. 1 (2).

all their property, except such as is exempted by the bankrupt law, was brought within the custody of the law, and by the subsequent assignment passed to their assignees. The firm could not by a subsequent sale and delivery transfer any of such property to the plaintiffs. The schooner which contained the halibut in suit arrived in Gloucester August 14, 1869, which was after the decree of bankruptcy. If there had been then a sale and delivery to the plaintiffs of the property replevined, it would have been invalid. The plaintiffs therefore show no title to the halibut replevined, unless the effect of the contract of April 17, 1869, was to vest in them the property in the halibut before the bankruptcy. It seems to us clear, as claimed by both parties, that this was a contract of sale, and not a mere executory agreement to sell at some future day. The plaintiffs cannot maintain their suit upon any other construction, because, if it is an executory agreement to sell, the property in the halibut remained in the bankrupts, and, there being no delivery before the bankruptcy, passed to the assignees. The question in the case therefore is, whether a sale of halibut afterwards to be caught is valid, so as to pass to the purchaser the property in them when caught.

It is an elementary principle of the law of sales that a man cannot grant personal property in which he has no interest or title. To be able to sell property, he must have a vested right in it at the time of the sale. Thus it has been held that a mortgage of goods which the mortgagor does not own at the time the mortgage is made, though he afterwards acquires them, is void. The same principle is applicable to all sales of personal property.

In the case at bar, the sellers, at the time of the sale, had no interest in the thing sold. There was a possibility that they might catch halibut; but it was a mere possibility and expectancy, coupled with no interest. We are of the opinion that they had no actual or potential possession of, or interests in, the fish; and that the sale to the plaintiffs was void.

Presumptions

The Uniform Sales Act has adopted, as the basis for determining the rights and liabilities of the buyer and seller, the rule of property law that the risks of ownership follow the title to the goods. In the buying and selling of goods merchants have, as a general rule, given little consideration as to when legal title to the goods passes from the seller to the buyer; consequently, the time that title passes has been worked out by adopting rules of presumption which apply in the absence of an agreement or circumstances which indicate that the parties intended the title to the goods to pass at a particular time.

If the goods are specific and identified, title passes to the buyer when the contract is completed, even though the time of delivery or the time of payment or both are postponed. If the goods are not specific and identified, the title to the goods does not pass to the buyer until there has been an unconditional appropriation of the goods to the contract, either by the seller with the buyer's consent, or by the buyer with the seller's consent.

If Archer has fifty chairs and Burch agrees to buy them at the price stated, the property in the goods will pass immediately unless the parties agree that the property in the goods shall not pass until some agreed time. The chairs being in existence and definitely identified are specific goods.

If Archer has a large number of chairs in his warehouse and Burch agrees to buy fifty of them, the property in the chairs will not pass. The goods are unascertained. Although they are in existence they have not been definitely identified as the subject matter of the sale, and property in the goods will not pass until fifty of the chairs have been selected from the larger number and unconditionally appropriated as Burch's chairs.

One exception to this rule is generally recognized by the courts of the United States. There may be a present sale of an undivided share of a specific mass of fungible goods. Fungible goods are defined as: "goods of which any unit is from its nature or by mercantile usage treated as the equivalent of any other unit." [4] If parties intend a sale of an undivided share of fungible goods, the property in the goods passes at once, and the parties become owners in common of the mass.

If Archer shows Burch a sample chair and agrees to acquire or manufacture chairs like the sample and Burch contracts to buy fifty such chairs to be acquired or manufactured by Archer, the property in the goods will not pass until the goods have been acquired or manufactured and have been unconditionally appropriated to the contract. Such a sale would be a sale of future goods.[5] At the time the contract is entered into, the goods are neither in existence nor are they identified.

Even though the goods are specific and identified, if the seller is bound to do something to put the goods in a deliverable state, the title does not pass until such thing is done. Also, if the seller agrees to deliver the goods, title does not pass to the buyer until the goods are delivered to the designated place.

As an aid in determining when goods have been unconditionally appropriated to the contract, the courts have adopted the presumption that there is an unconditional appropriation when the goods have been delivered to the carrier. However, the paramount idea is that some

[4] Uniform Sales Act, sec. 76, appendix, p. 904.

[5] *Ibid.*, sec. 76, appendix, p. 904.

overt act has been done which unconditionally indicates that certain goods have been irrevocably earmarked for a particular buyer. If the goods remain within the control of the seller, and may be used by him as he wishes, there is no unconditional appropriation, even though he may have stated or indicated an intention to appropriate the goods to a particular contract.

Merchants have adopted special mercantile terms and when such terms are used in a contract, the foregoing presumptions give way to the mercantile meaning of the terms used. Such special mercantile terms will be discussed in subsequent sections.

United States v. Amalgamated Sugar Co.
72 F. (2d) 755 (1934)

This was an action by the United States of America (plaintiff) against the Amalgamated Sugar Company (defendant). Judgment for defendant and plaintiff appealed. Judgment affirmed.

During the last month of its fiscal year, the defendant entered into contracts for the sale of 190,374 bags of sugar. The sugar was carried on the books of the defendant as the property of the buyers. Under the contracts with the buyers of the sugar, no definite date of payment was stated. It is the uniform custom in the sugar industry, in regard to such sales, for the buyers to have sugar delivered to such places and in such quantities as their needs might require. There was no attempt made to separate the sugar in the warehouse and, when a request for delivery came in, the defendant shipped from the mass of sugar. When defendant filed its 1917 income tax report, it included the profit on the 190,374 bags of sugar which were contracted for but were still in the warehouse. The United States contends that the profits on this sugar should have been included in the defendant's 1918 income tax report because title to the sugar did not pass to the buyer until segregation and delivery of the sugar; that there was no segregation and delivery until 1918, and consequently the sale of the sugar was business transacted in 1918 and taxable as such. The tax deficiency claimed by the United States was $210,810.56.

Bratton, C. J. It is and has been the uniform custom existing in the sugar industry and in the conduct of the company's business for the purchaser to have sugar delivered at such places and in such quantities as his needs may require, and if not delivered within thirty days from the date of the contract, invoice is sent and payment made despite the fact that some or all of it remains in the warehouse of the seller. Oftentimes it is resold repeatedly before delivery and payment. Such a contract is regarded generally throughout the industry as an outright sale with the right of the purchaser to resell and direct immediate or deferred delivery according to his wishes, but the transaction is treated as one of sale with title presently vested in the purchaser.

After an extended hearing at which oral testimony and documentary evidence were submitted, the Board found in effect that the parties in each instance in question intended to make a sale with immediate passage of title and that such was the effect of the transaction. Is the finding supported by evidence? In the first place, each contract refers to the transaction as a sale, not an agreement to sell at a future time. That is persuasive. The company filed and preserved such contracts as an original record. It kept a record in the form of a memorandum purporting to show the total amount of sugar manufactured and the quantity sold. That record was posted from day to day, thereby indicating currently the amount of sugar manufactured, the amount sold and the amount on hand subject to sale. Sugar embraced in contracts but not paid for nor shipped was included along with that paid for and delivered. That suggests that the company regarded such contracts as constituting present sales. Furthermore, on February 28, 1917, at the close of the fiscal year and prior to the time the controversy presented here arose, the company made the following entry in its general journal: "Charge to inventory cost of sugar sold $1,132,744.25. Credit sugar inventory $1,132,744.25. 411,907 bags at $2.75. This entry leaves 512,609 bags of sugar, consisting of 190,374 bags of sugar sold under contract which will net approximately $6.25 per bag and 322,235 bags of unsold sugar at $6.25, the fair market net at this date." That entry points strongly to an understanding on the part of the company that the sugar in question had been sold during that fiscal year. The fact that it remained in the warehouse subject to shipping instructions does not argue that title had not passed. Nor is the date on which invoice was sent decisive because under the system employed by the company, an invoice was a mere statement of account due. If a broker made a sale, his commission was appropriately entered on the books of the company and settlement currently made regardless of the time payment of the purchase price was received or the sugar delivered. The insurance carried by the company contained a provision that it covered sugar sold but not delivered, again indicating that such sugar was regarded as the property of the purchaser. And the fact that the purchase price was paid thirty days after the contract was executed, whether the sugar had been delivered or not, and that a resale was often made during that time indicates that the purchaser understood he acquired the property upon execution of the contract. In fact, all the testimony was to the effect that the parties intended that title should pass concurrently with the execution of the contract.

Whether a contract is one of sale or one to sell depends very largely upon the intention of the parties. If they intend a present transfer of title it is a contract of sale; otherwise, it is a contract to sell. As between contracting parties, if the statute of frauds or the rights of third persons are not involved, neither immediate delivery of the chattels nor payment of the purchase price is essential to effect a present sale with immediate transfer of title.

But it is contended that the contracts were executory and that title remained in the company on February 28, 1917, because the property had not been segregated and identified in separate form.

Beet sugar of a standard and uniform grade, in bags of one hundred pounds each, is fungible property. In that respect it falls within the same class as flour, grain, or oil. The title to an unseparated part or unit of a larger quantity of fungible property passes under a valid contract of sale without separation, or segregation, if that is the intention of the parties. Segregation is not essential to the validity of a sale of chattels of that kind. The owners of respective interests are tenants in common. And that doctrine should apply in the absence of some forbidding circumstance, although the property may be in two or more parts or parcels if it is a part of a common stock or supply. The contracts in question were to be filled with sugar manufactured by the company during the previous refining season and stored as a common stock in its warehouses in Utah and Idaho, for sale to its various customers. The sugar was one entity or mass although geographically separated and located in different places. The fact that it was stored in different warehouses used in the operation of the business did not render inapplicable the ordinary rules respecting the sale and passage of title to a part of fungible property without separation or segregation. It should be noted that through adoption of two pertinent sections of the uniform sales act, community of interest in fungible property stored in a warehouse has been recognized in Utah since 1917.

Radloff v. Bragmus et al.
214 Minn. 130, 7 N.W. (2d) 491 (1943)

This was an action by John Radloff (plaintiff) against George Bragmus and others (defendant). Judgment for defendant and plaintiff appealed. Judgment reversed.

Plaintiff owned a flock of about 100 turkey hens and 600 Toms. Plaintiff and defendant entered into an agreement whereby plaintiff agreed to sell and defendant agreed to buy the turkeys at a stated price per pound for the number one turkeys and the number two turkeys were to be 3 cents less. The defendant was to remove all the turkeys on November 13, 1940. On November 11, 1940, a blizzard killed 330 of the turkeys and those not destroyed were damaged. Defendant refused to accept and pay for any of the turkeys. The lower court held that the turkeys were at the risk of the plaintiff.

Julius J. Olson, J. We have here a simply worded contract, easily understood, which was prepared by defendants for use in their everyday business transactions. We can see nothing ambiguous about it. Plainly, by its terms, there was an immediate transfer of title to the buyer. In plain language, selected and used by defendants, they confirmed the sale made to them that day by plaintiff. Upon the strength of it they paid $50 as a part of the purchase money. Defendants concede as much by their answer. They were to take the turkeys at plaintiff's farm not later than the 13th. That the turkeys were "in a deliverable state" on November 9 is not denied. There was nothing further for plaintiff to do "for the purpose of putting them into a deliverable state." The counting, weighing, and grading of the turkeys were purely matters of routine and of simple computation, as much so as if so many steers had been involved to be paid for at so much per pound.

In respect to grading, a matter considered by the trial judge as presenting considerable difficulty because of the possibility of a dispute over it between the parties, we think this furnishes no more opportunity for disagreement than counting or weighing. After all, grading of poultry is as well defined and established by rules and regulations as is grading of grains, hay, eggs, and many other farm products. By L. 1931, c. 394, § 7, Minn. St. 1941, § 27.07, the commissioner of agriculture, dairy and food is given "power to establish grades on all produce" as therein defined. And by § 2 Id., "produce" as used in this act shall mean and include "poultry and poultry products." The commissioner, instead of making and promulgating such rules, has adopted and made operative those of the Federal Agricultural Marketing Administration, effective since July, 1940.

Furthermore, defendants cannot deny that they had knowledge of such rules and regulations, for in their answer they say that "plaintiff was unable to furnish or deliver to defendants any . . . . turkeys, suitable for grading, and suitable for dressing, packing and resale by defendants for public use to conform with the laws of this State under which they operate."

Shipler et al. v. New Castle Paper Products Corporation
293 Pa. 412, 143 Atl. 182 (1928)

This was an action by W. H. Shipler and others (plaintiffs) against New Castle Paper Products Corporation (defendant). The Hygienic Fibre Company filed a petition requesting that certain property be delivered to it. The petition was dismissed and Hygienic Fiber Company appealed. Judgment affirmed.

The defendant entered into a contract with Hygienic Fiber Company whereby it sold its entire output of absorbent paper to the Hygienic Fiber Company. Under the terms of the contract, as the paper was manufactured it was to be warehoused by the defendant on the premises of the defendant. The paper came off the machines in 90-inch rolls and was to be warehoused in the roll. Before delivery defendant was to cut the paper into sizes as directed by Hygienic Fibre Company, pack it into appropriate cartons, and ship it as directed. The Hygienic Fibre Company had advanced to defendant $36,000 in all and about $5,000 worth of paper had been packed and shipped when a receiver was appointed for defendant. Hygienic Fibre Company in its petition claimed the paper which was in the warehouse in the roll. The receiver claimed that the defendant was the owner of the paper.

Sadler, J. If the receiver is to be considered, under the facts, as having the standing of an execution creditor, then his rights are to be determined as of the date of his appointment, and he is entitled to possession of all of the property and assets of the insolvent corporation for the benefit of the creditors as their interests may appear. In determining whether title to the paper passed, there having been no actual delivery though paid for, it is first to be noticed that the sale was not here complete, even as between the parties themselves, for the buyer could not have been compelled to accept it in satisfaction of the contract obligation until it had been cut and packed in accordance with directions given. The Uniform Sales Act, § 19, rule 2, provides:

"Where there is a contract to sell specific goods and the seller is bound to do something to the goods, for the purpose of putting them into a deliverable state, the property does not pass until such thing be done."

With this clause, section 76 must be read. It says, in part:

"Fourth. Goods are in a 'deliverable state' within the meaning of this act when they are in such a state that the buyer would, under the contract, be bound to take delivery of them."

In other jurisdictions, where the like Uniform Sales Act is in force, it has been held that the transaction is not consummated so as to pass title until all acts engaged to be performed have been completed, for example, where the seller agreed to bottle liquor purchased (*Kahn* v. *Rosenstiel* (D.C.) 298 F. 656), to bale hay (*Shultz & Co.* v. *De Nood*, 185 N.Y.S. 785), to cut and float logs (*Barton & Co.* v. *Turnbull*, 226 Mich. 685, 198 N.W. 186), or dismantle machinery bought (*Pulkrabek* v. *Bankers' Mtg. Corp.*, 115 Or. 379, 238 P. 347).

"It is not necessary that the work to be done by the seller shall be such as to change the character of the goods. An obligation to pack or load them will make the presumption (that title has not passed) applicable if the seller's undertaking was to sell the goods packed or loaded." 1 Williston on Sales, 532.

In the present case, the transaction was not complete, in so far as the corporation was concerned, until the 90-inch rolls in storage had been reduced to the desired sizes, packed, and shipped. This was an obligation which the buyer could waive, having paid in full for the paper, but it could not do so after the rights of the receiver had attached, so as to withdraw the property from his grasp.

Louis F. Dow Co. v. Bittner et al.
187 Minn. 143, 244 N.W. 556 (1932)

This was an action by Louis F. Dow Company (plaintiff) against Herman Bittner and others (defendants). Judgment for plaintiff and defendants appealed. Judgment affirmed.

Stone, J. Defendants were copartners who, January 16, 1930, contracted with plaintiff for the purchase of 400 calendars, upon which, according to the contract, certain indicated advertising of defendants and their business was to be printed. After that printing was done, but before delivery of the calendars "f.o.b. cars, St. Paul," as the contract required, defendants attempted to repudiate. Their one defense now is that, while they might be liable for damages for breach of contract, they are not so for the contract price, their assertion being that, when repudiated, the contract was wholly executory, that the goods had not been appropriated to the contract, and so title had not passed.

Defendants' law is good, but their view of the facts all wrong. The contract had been performed, executed to a substantial extent by plaintiff when defendants attempted to repudiate. The calendars had been printed, manufactured specially for defendants. By plaintiff's performance of the contract, they had been rendered unsuitable for the general trade, and had been set aside for shipment to defendants pursuant to the contract. Clearly, therefore, the goods had been appropriated to the contract, title had passed, and plaintiff had so far performed that defendants are liable for the purchase price.

There are many cases where goods have been sold for delivery f.o.b. cars at the shipping point, and it has been held that until such delivery the property did not pass. But that conclusion is not tenable where the process of special manufacture for the buyer has gone so far as irretrievably to allocate the goods to him under the contract. Delivery is not the essential thing, but only one, and quite a usual way of effecting it. What is essential to the passing of title is an unconditional appropriation of the goods to the contract by one party with the assent of the other. 1 Uniform Laws Ann. (Sales) 161. "There may be appropriation without either delivery or payment." Here, for example, the calendars were printed or embossed with defendants' name and their special advertising matter. That, and their setting aside for shipment to defendants, certainly made irrevocable their appropriation to the contract, passed title to defendants, and made them liable for the purchase price.

The property passes when the parties intend that it shall pass. Section 8394, Mason's Minn. St. 1927 (section 19, Uniform Sales Act) enunciates certain rules for determining the intention of the parties, "unless a different intention appears." Here, the parties could not have intended otherwise than that the property should pass not later than the moment when the calendars had put upon them the name and advertising matter of defendants, for thereafter they would be of no further use to plaintiff or anybody other than defendants.

Possibly it should be added by way of explanation that defendants attempted to cancel because of the sale of their business. Plaintiff offered to add to the printing matter on the calendar the name of the purchaser, that he was successor to defendants, and to do the work at cost. That certainly was fair enough, but defendants declined the offer.

F.O.B., F.A.S., C.I.F., C.A.F. Sales

Through mercantile practices certain shipping terms have become standardized and when such terms are used in the sales contract the rights and duties of the parties have become fixed. If the delivery terms of the contract of sale are F.O.B. or F.A.S., the seller is obligated to put the goods in the possession of the carrier (F.O.B.) or alongside the vessel (F.A.S.). The delivery terms might be F.O.B. destination or some named place, in which event the seller would be obligated to deliver the goods at the place named at his own expense. F.A.S. terms require the seller to deliver the goods at his own expense alongside the vessel in the manner usual in the port from which shipment is to be made.

The terms C.I.F. ("cost" of the goods, "insurance," and "freight" to the named destination) and C.A.F. or C. and F. or C.F. ("cost" and "freight") are similar to F.O.B. and F.A.S. terms in that the seller is obligated to deliver the goods to the carrier in the manner which is customary at the place of shipment. In addition, the seller must obtain a negotiable bill of lading covering the entire transportation, pay the freight to destination, and also insure the goods against those risks customarily covered during transportation, in the name of the buyer or to the account of whom it may concern. The amount of the premium, except the premium on war risk insurance, is paid by the seller. If the terms are C.A.F., the seller's obligations are as stated above except he is not obligated to insure the goods.

Occasionally the parties to a sale will mark the sale agreement F.O.B. or C.I.F. or some similar designation of delivery terms. They will then add express terms in the agreement which are in direct conflict with the standard mercantile practices under the designated delivery terms. In such cases the courts hold that the express terms control.

Madeirense do Brasil S/A v. Stulman-Emrick Lumber Co.
147 F. (2d) 399 (1945)

This was an action by Madeirense do Brasil S/A (plaintiff) against Stulman-Emrick Lumber Co. (defendant). Judgment for defendant and plaintiff appealed. Judgment affirmed.

Plaintiff contracted to sell to defendant a quantity of lumber. By the terms of the contract dated October 15, 1940, plaintiff sold to defendant 140,000′ of Brazilian pine lumber, kiln dried, and 310,000′ (later increased to 360,000′) of naturally dried lumber, at a price of $40 for the former and $38 for the latter "per 1,000 feet c & f New York," for "immediate shipment up to the 31st day of October at the latest," with inspection "upon arrival of the steamer in New York" and terms of "Letter of credit for 90% of the f.o.b. value, and the balance of 10% after arrival of the shipment in New York, the freight charges of $12.00 per 1,000′ to be paid in New York for your account."

Plaintiff had trouble obtaining a ship and later cabled defendant that it could obtain a ship if it (plaintiff) could ship 1,000 tons or

710,000′ of lumber. Defendant agreed to purchase the additional lumber required to make up this quantity. It was also agreed that defendant would compute the freight on this additional lumber at the rate of $14 per 1,000′ instead of $12 per 1,000′. Plaintiff was unable to obtain the ship, but offered to ship the lumber "above decks" at defendant's risk. Defendant refused to permit such shipment. Finally plaintiff shipped the lumber originally contracted for, but did not ship the lumber called for under the second contract. The freight rate was $33.13 per 1,000′. Plaintiff sues to recover an unpaid balance of $1,078.98 and defendant files a counterclaim for $2,490 "excess freight" and for damages for breach of the second contract. The court granted the defendant a judgment on its counterclaim for $5,282.50 less $1,078.98 making a total of $4,203.52.

Clark, C. J. Plaintiff argues that it has duly performed because a c. & f. contract requires it only to deliver, or to tender delivery of, the lumber to a carrier in Brazil. The term "c. & f." means that the price includes in a lump sum "cost" and "freight" to the named destination. Uniform Revised Sales Act, Proposed Final Draft No. 1, 1944, § 45, with comments by Professor Llewellyn, the Reporter, and his advisers, pp. 177-179, citing and discussing the authorities. The term "c. & f." thus either requires the seller to prepay the freight or permits the buyer after having paid the actual charges to deduct them from the price, in either case putting the seller under an ultimate obligation to pay for the transportation. Ordinarily where the seller pays the freight, there is an inference under Rule 5 of § 19 of the Uniform Sales Act, that the parties intend no passage of title until the goods reach the destination to which the freight is paid. But commercial usage, recognized by the courts and text writers, is that under a c. & f. contract the seller fulfills his duty on shipment of the goods, and that the risk thereafter is on the buyer unless other terms of the contract indicate a contrary intention. In *Pittsburgh Provision & Packing Co.* v. *Cudahy Packing Co.*, 260 Pa. 135, 103 A. 548, 549, a case criticized in the comments to the proposed Uniform Revised Sales Act, "c. a. f." was erroneously translated as "cash and freight" and as "having apparently the same significance as f.o.b." destination. Unlike the latter, however, the general understanding is that the freight figures substantially only as a part of the purchase price, not as a reservation of title, and that the situation is similiar to that of a c.i.f. contract, that is, one for "cost, insurance, and freight" to the designated destination.

Indeed, here the necessary inference is the same as that for a c.i.f. contract, since the documents showed that insurance was to be effected by the buyer. Hence the risk during transit is upon the buyer, thus indicating an intention that title is to pass upon shipment and, as in the c.i.f. contracts, requiring delivery to a carrier only. Moreover, the transaction by its terms was for 90 per cent of the f.o.b. value of the lumber at the mill in Brazil, with only the freight and balance of 10 per cent remaining to be paid after the arrival of the lumber in New York. Delivery of goods at destination thus is not made a condition precedent to the obligation of the buyer for the price, a contract provision which serves as further evidence of an intention on the part of the contracting parties not to obligate the seller beyond shipment. And this intention is not contradicted, as defendant contends, by the fact that under the agreement it is entitled to inspect the lumber upon arrival.

But even though the plaintiff is correct that under the contract title passes upon delivery to the carrier, it is not excused from making at least adequate delivery to such carrier; and according to section 46 of the Uniform Sales Act, the seller is required to make such contract with the carrier "as may be reasonable, having regard to the nature of the goods and the other circumstances of the case." Consequently even this limited obligation of plaintiff required it to make a contract with the steamship company, by which the latter would agree to carry the lumber below deck. Though plaintiff appears to intimate that it had such a contract with the carrier, it has shown nothing of the kind and obviously had nothing with the shipping company of a binding nature, for it immediately gave way when only limited facilities were supplied and was ready to take whatever was offered. It is clear, therefore, that plaintiff had not fulfilled its obligation to deliver under the contract.

C.O.D. and Bill of Lading Draft Attached Sales

As a general rule, if the terms of payment are either C.O.D. (cash on delivery) or order bill of lading draft attached, the seller is retaining the control of the goods until he is paid the purchase price. From the standpoint of mercantile practice, the retention of the control of the goods is for security purposes and does not alter the general rules relative to the assumption of the risks of ownership of the goods. Unless the circumstances show a contrary intent, the seller has performed all his obligations when he has delivered the goods to the carrier, and thereafter the goods are at the risk of the buyer.

If the shipment is a C.O.D. shipment, the carrier is considered as acting for the buyer in carrying the goods to destination, but the carrier acts for the seller in collecting the purchase price and returning it to the seller. If the goods are damaged or lost in transit, the buyer must stand the loss but, if the goods are delivered and the purchase price is collected but remittance is not made to the seller, the seller must stand the loss.

In an order bill of lading draft attached sale, the carrier acts for the buyer in carrying the goods to destination but, under the terms of the bill of lading, the carrier is bound to hold the goods and deliver them to the person who presents the order bill of lading properly indorsed. The bank acts for the seller in collecting the purchase price and delivering the bill of lading to the buyer. When the goods are shipped, the seller gets the order bill of lading which he indorses and to which he attaches a draft for the purchase price of the goods. The seller takes the bill of lading with draft attached to his bank, and his bank sends the bill of lading to a bank in the buyer's city. When the bill of lading and draft are received at the bank in the buyer's city, the buyer is given notice. The buyer then goes to the bank, pays or accepts the draft, obtains the bill of lading, and then goes to the carrier where he presents the bill of lading and receives the goods. In either C.O.D. or order bill of lading draft attached sales, the buyer may be allowed to inspect the goods before paying but, if this privilege is not contracted for, the buyer must pay first and inspect after receiving the goods. If, on inspecting the goods, the buyer finds they do not comply with the contract, he may reject them and, if he has paid the purchase price, he can recover the purchase price from the seller.

American Ry. Express Co. v. Ready
232 Mich. 624, 206 N.W. 344 (1925)

This was an action by the American Railway Express Company (plaintiff) against T. Willard Ready (defendant). Judgment for defendant and plaintiff appealed. Judgment affirmed.

The defendant purchased large quantities of glue from Armour & Co. Many shipments to defendant were on open account but considerable amount was sent by C.O.D. shipments. Armour & Co. claimed that some of the C.O.D. shipments had not been paid for. The plaintiff satisfied itself as to the merits of Armour & Co.'s claims, paid the claims, took an assignment from Armour & Co. of its account against defendant, and brought this suit to recover thereon. NOTE.—The principal question discussed on the appeal was whether or not the trial judge erred in charging the jury that the plaintiff must bear the burden of proving that the goods were not paid for on delivery. The part of the opinion which refers to this point has been omitted.

Fellows, J. (dissenting). We should first consider the relations of the parties on a C.O.D. shipment. Plaintiff is a common carrier. A delivery to it by the consignor of goods for shipment is a delivery to the consignee. By the weight of authority this was the rule as to C.O.D. shipments before the adoption of the Uniform Sales Act. By delivery of the goods to the carrier for shipment the right of property in the goods passed to the consignee, although the right of possession did not pass until payment, and the consignor retained a lien for the purchase price. The carrier was the agent of the consignee to transport the goods, and the agent of the consignor to transport the money received on their delivery. In Corpus Juris it is said:

"There is a square conflict in the authorities as to whether the attaching of this condition to the delivery affects the ordinary presumptions as to the title to the goods while in transit. By the decided weight of authority, delivery C.O.D., like an ordinary delivery to a carrier, presumptively passes title to the consignee, the only difference being that the carrier is to retain possession of the goods as agent for the shipper until payment is made by the consignee, and on receiving money in payment is, as carrier for the consignor, to transport back such money. In other words, under this view, the title to the goods passes to the consignee on delivery to the carrier, but right to possession in the nature of a vendor's lien remains with the consignor while the goods are in the carrier's possession, and terminates only when the condition is performed and the money paid by the consignee to the carrier, whereupon the title to, and possession of, the money vests in the consignor."

Alderman Bros. Co. v. Westinghouse Air Brake Co.
92 Conn. 419, 103 Atl. 267 (1918)

This was an action by Alderman Bros. Company (plaintiff) against Westinghouse Air Brake Company (defendant). Judgment for plaintiff and defendant appealed. Judgment reversed and new trial ordered.

Defendants sold to Jacob Swirsky three carloads of brass chips containing 244,160 pounds at the rate of 15½ cents per pound. The contract was assigned to the plaintiff. By the terms of the contract, the brass was to be shipped order bill of lading draft attached. The defendant had the order bill of lading drawn to the order of himself. He indorsed it in blank, attached a draft for the purchase price of the brass and sent it to defendant's agent in New Haven—the destination of the brass. Plaintiffs paid the draft, obtained the brass and, when it was reweighed, found there was a shortage of 39,625 pounds. Plaintiff sued to recover $6,141.25, the value of the shortage. The loss occurred while the brass was in transit. The defendant (seller) claims that the brass, while in transit, was at the plaintiff's (buyer's) risk.

Beach, J. If it should appear that the goods were sold by description or were not ascertained, the question of subsequent appropriation would come up, and under rule 4 of section 19, a presumption of unconditional appropriation would arise from the delivery of the goods to the carrier f.o.b. at Wilmerding, subject, however, to the provisions of section 20. If it should appear that at the time of the contract something remained to be done by the seller to put the goods in a deliverable condition, the title would not pass until that was done. Section 19, rule 2. Presumably they were in a deliverable condition when shipped, and if that is so a presumption arises that the title passed on or before delivery to the carrier f.o.b. Wilmerding, subject again to the provisions of section 20. Section 20 deals with the reservation of the right of possession of, or the property in, goods shipped to the buyer. It makes the distinction that if the bill of lading is drawn to the order of the buyer or his agent, and is retained by the seller or his agent to secure payment of the price, the seller reserves only the right of possession of the goods; but if the bill of lading is drawn to the order of the seller or his agent "the seller reserves the property in the goods." This last statement is, however, qualified by the next succeeding words, "but if, except for the form of the bill of lading, the property would have passed to the buyer on the shipment of the goods, the seller's property in the goods shall be deemed to be only for the purpose of securing performance by the buyer of his obligations under the contract." Manifestly, the intention is to make some kind of a distinction between a reservation of title with intent to remain the owner of the goods for all purposes, and a reservation of title for the sole purpose of securing payment of the price.

The legal effect of this distinction is pointed out in section 22: "Unless otherwise agreed, the goods remain at the seller's risk until the property therein is transferred to the buyer . . . . except that (a) where delivery of the goods has been made to the buyer, or to a bailee for the buyer, in pursuance of the contract, and the property in the goods has been retained by the seller merely to secure performance by the buyer of his obligations under the contract, the goods are at the buyer's risk from the time of the delivery."

In this case the delivery of the goods to the carrier f.o.b. at Wilmerding was authorized by the buyer, and section 46 provides that:

"Where, in pursuance of a contract to sell or a sale, the seller is authorized . . . . to send the goods to the buyer, delivery of the goods to a carrier, whether named by the buyer or not, for the purpose of transmission to the buyer, is deemed to be a delivery of the goods to the buyer, except in the cases provided for in section 19, rule 5 (where the seller contracts to deliver the goods to the buyer or at a certain place, etc.), or unless a contrary intent appears."

A delivery to a carrier in accordance with section 46 is a delivery to the buyer within the meaning of section 22, notwithstanding the fact that the buyer cannot have possession of the goods until the seller is paid, because the Sales Act contemplates that the seller may at his option reserve the jus disponendi.

It makes no difference to a buyer who has agreed to pay the freight whether a sight draft is presented to him attached to a bill of lading drawn to his own order, or to a bill of lading drawn to the order of the seller and indorsed in blank. In either case he must pay his draft in order to get possession of the goods, and in either case his rights on paying the draft are the same. The risk of loss unquestionably passes to the buyer in the former case as soon as the goods are delivered to the carrier, and section 22 of the Sales Act provides that it shall pass to the buyer at the same time in the latter case, provided the seller's purpose in drawing the bill of lading to his own order was merely to secure payment of the draft. This resolves for us any conflict of opinion on the point, and gives to the maxim res periit domino an interpretation which makes the risk follow the beneficial interest according to the intent of the parties and not the legal title held merely as security for the payment of the price.

Cash Sales

If a contract of sale is entered into and the contract does not provide for credit, the presumption is that the terms are cash and that the delivery of and payment for goods must take place concurrently. The general rights of the parties under such a contract are discussed under the heading of concurrent conditions in contracts.

If the terms of the contract are expressly stated to be cash, the ownership of the goods does not vest in the buyer until the purchase price is paid. A cash sale should not be confused with a conditional sale. In a cash sale, the buyer is to have neither the title nor the use and enjoyment of the goods until the price is paid. In a conditional sale the buyer has the use and enjoyment of the goods, but the seller retains the title as security for the payment of the purchase price.

The principal problems arising in regard to cash sales involve the rights of third parties to the goods sold. If the terms of the sale are cash and the seller delivers the goods to the buyer, temporarily and for a special purpose, such as inspection, weighing, testing, etc., and the buyer sells the goods to a subpurchaser, the seller can, as a general rule, claim the goods from the subpurchaser. If the seller delivers the goods to the buyer and permits the buyer to retain possession of the goods for an unreasonable time, or permits him to use and enjoy the goods, or permits him to display the goods for resale, an innocent purchaser for value will get good title as against the seller.

If the terms of the sale are cash, and the buyer gives a worthless check in payment, an innocent purchaser from the buyer will get good title to the goods. A few cases have taken a contrary view.

Harbert et al. v. Ft. Smith Canning Co. et al.
134 Kan. 240, 5 P. (2d) 849 (1931)

This was an action by Homer Harbert and another (plaintiffs) against the Fort Smith Canning Company and others (defendants). Judgment for defendants and plaintiffs appealed. Judgment affirmed in part and reversed in part and remanded with instructions.

Harbert and Walker, plaintiffs (appellants), were partners in the business of canning tomatoes. The Fort Smith Canning Company was not a corporation. It was a trade name for one Wampler whose business was that of selling canned tomatoes to jobbers. After taking the orders from the jobbers, he would then purchase the tomatoes from the canners. S. E. Lux, Jr., Mercantile Company was a corporation engaged in the business of wholesale buying and selling of groceries.

On March 30, 1927, Lux contracted with Wampler for five thousand cases of tomatoes and gave Wampler two trade acceptances in payment which were due June 9th and July 9th. The acceptances when due were paid in cash.

On May 14th, Wampler contracted with plaintiffs for the purchase of a carload of tomatoes and on May 16th he gave plaintiffs his check for $1,653.80 in payment for the tomatoes. The tomatoes were shipped May 16th to Lux in the name of Fort Smith Canning Co. This transaction took place after banking hours. Next morning, May 17th, plaintiffs telegraphed the bank on which the check was drawn and the bank replied that the check was no good. The check was presented to the bank later and payment was refused. On May 18th, plaintiffs ordered the railroad to stop and hold the car of tomatoes. The railroad stopped the car of tomatoes but refused to deliver it to plaintiffs. Lux claims the car of tomatoes.

Smith, J. The questions pressed here by appellants are as follows:

First. Was the transaction between the plaintiffs and the defendant Wampler one for cash on delivery of the goods, and upon failure of the buyer to pay were the plaintiffs entitled to the immediate possession of the goods from him?

Second. Does the Lux Company stand in the position of an innocent purchaser for value without notice?

As to the question whether the transaction is one for cash, this must be answered in the affirmative. The agreed statement of facts provides that, and the trial court so treated it in the memoranda of opinion. Also, this court has held that where goods are sold under a bargain that payment is to be cash and payment is made by check at the time the goods are delivered, which check turns out to be bad for want of funds in the bank on which it is drawn, then the parties are in the same position as though no check had been given. *People's State Bank* v. *Brown*, 80 Kan. 520, 103 P. 102, 103.

We will discuss this case with that point settled. The case of *People's State Bank* v. *Brown* was one where a farmer had sold wheat to an elevator company for cash and had taken its check in payment therefor. Before the check was cashed the company failed and the check was not paid. This court held that the farmer still owned the wheat. The court quoted from Williston on Sales, 346, as follows: "If after bargaining for a cash sale the seller subsequently voluntarily delivers to the buyer the goods, with the intent that the buyer may immediately use them as his own (i.e., not for inspection or a similar purpose), and without insisting upon contemporaneous payment, this action is absolutely inconsistent with the original bargain. Such a delivery is not only evidence of the waiver of the condition of cash payment; it should be conclusive evidence." This court then said: "But as a practical necessity, to avoid the inconvenience of requiring the seller of an article to keep one hand upon it until with the other he grasps the currency tendered in payment, there must be some relaxation of this rule. Delivery and payment as a practical matter cannot be absolutely simultaneous. Some slight interval between the two acts is inevitable, and the criterion upon which the courts have agreed with substantial unanimity is that such interval does not conclusively prove a total abandonment of title and the right of possession by the seller, unless under all the circumstances of the case it in fact shows that result to have been intended."

The question of the respective rights of buyer and seller, where the bargain was for a cash sale and a bad check is given in payment therefor, is well settled by the above case.

In *Kemper Grain Co.* v. *Harbour*, 89 Kan. 824, 133 P. 565, 567, this court spoke with approval of the decisions in *People's State Bank* v. *Brown*, supra, but said: "If the property had reached an innocent purchaser, a very different question would have been presented."

In the case at bar the Lux Company argues that it is an innocent purchaser, that the tomatoes had been turned over to it by appellees, and that all right of appellees to possession of them was gone. The case of *Kemper Grain Co.* v. *Harbour*, supra, is relied on to sustain this position. In that case a grain company had sold grain to Harbour. It had possession of the bills of lading. Those were delivered to the railroad company. The grain company and Harbour were both in the same town, but notwithstanding this a draft was drawn by it upon Harbour for the amount of the purchase price and sent to Kansas City for collection. During the time that the draft was making the trip to Kansas City and back, Harbour obtained possession of the cars and the bill of lading for them. He sold them to Christopher & Co. and drew a draft upon that company for the price, attaching the bill of lading. In the meantime the draft drawn by Harbour to the Kemper Company had been presented to the bank upon which it was drawn and payment refused. The Kemper Company brought an action for possession of the wheat. The court held that title to grain had passed to Christopher & Co.

In the memoranda of decision the trial court in the case at bar stated that the case of *Kemper Grain Co.* v. *Harbour* was controlling. There is a distinction between the two cases. In the Harbour Case the trial court held, and this court approved, that the sale by Kemper Grain Company to Harbour was on credit. In the case at bar we conclude that the sale was for cash.

In the Harbour Case the Christopher Grain Company, which stood in the same position that the Lux Company stands in, had paid out money on the particular transaction, relying on bills of lading which Harbour had in his possession. It satisfied all the requirements of an innocent purchaser for value. In the case at bar the Lux Company parted with nothing as a result of the transaction at Green Forest on May 16th. As far as the record shows, the trade acceptances had been drawn by Wampler in April. The record was silent as to when they were paid by the Lux Company. They were not due till June and July. The agreed statement of facts says that it is presumed that they were paid. It is a fair inference that they had reached the hands of an innocent purchaser.

There is no evidence, however, that the Lux Company parted with anything as a result of the transaction between Wampler and Harbert and Walker. The Lux Company paid appellants nothing for the tomatoes, but received whatever title to them it had in consideration of advances previously made Wampler. It was not an innocent purchaser of the tomatoes. In *Henderson* v. *Gibbs*, 39 Kan. 679, 18 P. 926, 930, this court said: "But even with these views, which are liberal as towards the second purchaser, it must be held that where the second purchaser has taken the property only in payment or part payment of a pre-existing debt, and has not paid or parted with or surrendered anything of value in consideration therefor, he takes nothing but the fraudulent vendee's title, and the original owner may rescind his contract with his fraudulent vendee, and retake the property."

"Sale or Return" and "Sale on Approval"

Frequently a prospective buyer will hesitate to purchase goods not wanting to take the property in the goods without reservation. To overcome this reluctance on the part of the buyer, sellers have pursued two courses differing materially in their legal aspects, yet accomplishing substantially the same results from a practical standpoint. These two sales devices are (1) the sale or return and (2) sale on approval. In the sale or return the buyer takes the goods but has the right to return them to the seller within a stipulated time, or if no time is stated he must return the goods within a reasonable time. In the sale on approval the buyer takes the goods on trial. If the goods prove satisfactory, he keeps them; if they prove unsatisfactory, he indicates his dissatisfaction. If the goods are sent on trial for a definite time, such as 10 days' trial, the buyer must indicate his dissatisfaction within the time allotted; if no time is stated, he must express his dissatisfaction within a reasonable time. In both of these transactions the buyer is given an opportunity to try the goods before he is bound to keep them.

In the sale or return the property in the goods passes to the buyer, and while the buyer has the goods they are at his risk. The buyer has the right to pass the property in the goods back to the seller by returning the goods to the seller within the time allowed. In the sale on approval the property in the goods does not pass to the buyer until he has indicated his approval. If the buyer retains the goods beyond the time allowed, the property in the goods will pass to him. The act of keeping the goods beyond the time allowed is accepted in law as equivalent to an expression of approval.

Goebel Brewing Co. v. Brown, Auditor General, et al.
306 Mich. 222, 10 N.W. (2d) 835 (1943)

This was an action by Goebel Brewing Company (plaintiff) against Vernon J. Brown, as Auditor General of the State of Michigan and others (defendants). Judgment for plaintiff and defendants appealed. Judgment affirmed.

The State of Michigan imposed a use tax on the plaintiff on the theory that the bottles and cartons, in which its beer was packed, were delivered to purchasers with the privilege of using such cartons and bottles. It was expressly provided that the tax did not apply to "Property sold to a buyer for consumption or use in industrial processing." The plaintiff contends that the cartons and bottles used by it in the distribution of its beer come under this exception. In the sale of its beer the plaintiff had handled all of its sales in the same manner. When a carton of beer was sold, a charge was made for the beer and a deposit was required for the cartons and bottles. The return of the bottles and cartons was optional upon the part of the purchaser, but when returned the purchaser was entitled to and did receive his deposit.

The trial court found as a fact that: "Consideration of all the factors indicate conclusively to the court that title to the bottles and cases passes unreservedly from the brewery to the purchaser."

Sharpe, J. In cases which involve containers for which a deposit is taken, the general rule is that there is a sale thereof. It is also the general rule that there is a sale when the goods are packed in the container and the cost of the container and packing is included in the price of the finished product.

In *Dewey Portland Cement Co.* v. *Crooks*, the contract of sale contained the following provision: "Sacks. The price named includes the sacks in which the cement is to be shipped. Cloth sacks of Dewey Brand delivered hereunder will be repurchased subject to the seller's inspection and count, at twenty-five cents each if returned promptly in serviceable condition at Dewey, Oklahoma. Sacks that have been wet or are worthless will not be repurchased."

Plaintiff's method of entering the contracts on its books was as follows: "Plaintiff recorded the transactions upon its books by charging its customer with the price of the 'cement including sack,' crediting ten cents to 'Sack Inventory' account and crediting the balance to 'Cement Sales' account. When sacks were returned an entry was made debiting 'Sack Inventory' account with ten cents for each sack and crediting the customer a like amount."

The court there said: "It is to be noted that the title to the sacks passed to the purchaser of the cement, and that he was under no obligation to return them; and that plaintiff's liability to repurchase the sacks was subject to two contingencies: First, that the purchaser of the cement saw fit to return the sacks; second, that the sacks were usable and acceptable."

In 24 R.C.L. pp. 425, 426, it is said: "A very common form of contract is that known as 'sale or return,' by which property is sold, but is liable to be returned to the seller at the option of the buyer. In this class of cases the transaction vests title immediately in the buyer, who has the privilege of rescinding the sale, and until this is exercised, the title remains in him. . . . . So where beer, mineral waters or the like are sold in bottles by the manufacturer and a so-called deposit is taken for the value of the bottles which the buyer is to receive back upon a return of the bottles, but there is no duty imposed on him to return the same, this has been considered a sale of the bottles transferring the title."

The facts in the case at bar show that after the sale was made, the seller (Goebel Brewing Company) had no control over the bottles and cartons. The purchaser could return them and claim his deposit or he could keep them and forfeit his deposit. We are in accord with the finding of the trial court that: "There is undoubtedly a second contract between the brewery and the purchasers of its beer. By that contract the purchaser has the option to resell the bottles or cases to the brewery for the amount which he paid for them, and the brewery commits itself to repurchase them. But the compulsion implicit in such agreement is unilateral. The purchaser, as has been stated, is under no obligation to exercise his option to resell, even though the brewery is under obligation to repurchase upon demand."

In our opinion, the transactions involved herein were sales and, as such, were not subject to the tax sought to be imposed.

Sale by Person Other Than Owner

There are three well-established exceptions to the rule that the buyer acquires no better title to goods than the seller had. If the owner of the goods has by his conduct led the buyer to deal with the seller as the owner of the goods or as one authorized to sell the goods, the true owner will be precluded from denying the seller's authority to sell.[6] Just what acts on the part of the owner will be sufficient to preclude him from denying the seller's authority to sell is a question of fact, and each case arising will present a separate problem. It is established that the putting of a third person in possession of the goods, without additional acts, will not be sufficient to preclude the owner from recovering the goods from one buying from the party in possession.

If one buys goods but leaves them in the possession of the seller and the seller resells the goods, the second purchaser will get good title.[7] This situation is included in the above discussion but is treated separately in the Uniform Sales Act owing to its importance in the field of sales. It definitely establishes that the leaving of goods, which

[6] Uniform Sales Act, sec. 23, appendix, p. 894.
[7] *Ibid.*, sec. 25, appendix, p. 894.

one has purchased, in the possession of the original owner is sufficient to preclude the first buyer from denying the original owner's authority to sell.

Under the law of contracts, if one is induced by fraudulent representations to enter into a contract, he has the right, on discovery of the fraud, to rescind the contract. This rule applies with equal force in the field of sales. If one is induced by fraudulent representations to sell his goods, he has the right, on discovery of the fraud, to rescind the sale and recover the goods, but, if, before he has acted, the goods are sold to a buyer who buys in good faith, for value, and without notice of the defect in the seller's title, the original owner cannot recover the goods.[8]

Coburn v. Drown
— Vt. —, 40 A. (2d) 528 (1945)

This was an action by Homer B. Coburn (plaintiff) against Warran B. Drown (defendant). Judgment for defendant and plaintiff appealed. Judgment reversed and cause remanded.

In August, 1943, the plaintiff purchased 25 cattle from Leon Regan and gave the latter a check for $1,500 as the purchase price. The plaintiff was not in a position to take the cattle at the time of the purchase, so Regan agreed to keep them for a few days. During the time that Regan kept the cattle for the plaintiff no steps were taken to indicate any change in their ownership. The day before the plaintiff was to come to the Regan farm to take the cattle, the defendant purchased the same cattle from Regan and gave a check for $1,550 for them. Within a few minutes of the time he received the check Regan told the defendant that Coburn had bought the cattle. After the receipt of this information the defendant took the animals from the Regan farm. The fair value of the cattle at the time they were so taken exceeded the amount for which they were sold to the plaintiff.

Jeffords, J. The plaintiff in order to maintain this action was required to prove that at the time the defendant took the cattle he (the plaintiff) had the right to the immediate possession of the animals. Whether the plaintiff had such a right depends on whether the transaction between Regan and the defendant conveyed a valid title to the cattle to the latter.

Under our law the retention of possession of the cattle by Regan, the vendor, made the sale to Coburn fraudulent in law, or per se, as to creditors of Regan or as to bona fide purchasers without notice. This rule of law is so well settled as to require no citation of authorities.

It is apparent that the trial court and counsel for the defendant took the position that the giving of the check for the cattle before

---

[8] *Ibid.*, sec. 24, appendix, p. 894.

notice of the prior sale made Drown a bona fide purchaser of the animals so that it was immaterial that he received such notice before the cattle had been delivered to him.

The plaintiff's position was, and is, that Drown is not entitled to the rights of a bona fide purchaser as he had notice of the prior sale before he had received possession of the cattle. The plaintiff in support of his position relies on P.L. 7950 (sec. 25 of the Uniform Sales Act).

Our search of the cases reveals none which has directly construed this section of the Sales Act on this point. This may be due to the fact that the language of the section is so plain and unambiguous in meaning as to leave no room for construction. Moreover, as this statute is not susceptible of two meanings, there is no occasion to examine it in the light of common law principles. It follows that P.L. 7950 is to be given the meaning that its words clearly import. Thus, in order for one to be a bona fide purchaser entitled to the protection of the statute, the subsequent purchaser must both receive possession of and pay value for the goods before notice of the prior sale.

P.L. 7950 governs the case and if it changed in any way our common law rule in respect to the essentials necessary to constitute this defendant a bona fide purchaser, a matter which we do not in any way decide, the change was brought about by the clear and unambiguous language required to make changes by statute in the common law.

The defendant in his brief claims that the case is governed by P.L. 7951 (sec. 26 of the Sales Act). This section pertains to the rights of creditors of a vendor who has retained possession of the goods which he has sold. As far as it appears from the record Drown was not a creditor of Regan. The cattle were taken by Drown as a purchaser and not as a creditor. Consequently P.L. 7951 does not here apply.

The trial court in its discussion with counsel of P.L. 7950 indicated it believed that P.L. 8474 which relates to fraudulent transfers made to avoid a right, debt or duty had some bearing in the case. A reading of this section and the cases construing the same discloses that it does not apply to the facts in the present case.

It is not questioned that the parties intended in both instances that the title to the cattle should pass to the respective vendees when the contracts were made. Thus as between Regan and the plaintiff title to the animals vested in the latter when their contract was entered into. Inasmuch as the defendant was not entitled to protection as a bona fide purchaser of the cattle under P.L. 7950 it follows that he did not acquire title to the property from Regan, as the title which the latter purported to give was not in him at that time but in the plaintiff. As far as the facts show, title gave the plaintiff the right to immediate possession of the cattle. Thus the court erred in directing a verdict for the defendant on the ground which we have considered. For the same reasons, there was error in excluding the offered evidence.

QUESTIONS AND PROBLEMS

1. Why is it important to determine when the property in goods sold passes from the seller to the buyer? What is the fundamental test of when the property in the goods passes?
2. What are the essential elements of a present sale of goods?
3. When are the "rules of presumption," developed by the courts, applied in determining when the property in the goods passes from the seller to the buyer?
4. Archer purchases from Burch a lot of hay in a barn, paying a part of the price and receiving credit for the balance. The hay was to remain in the barn until fall, and the quantity of hay was to be determined by weighing when the hay was removed. Before the hay was removed the barn burned and the hay was entirely destroyed. Who must stand the loss, Archer or Burch?
5. Andrews purchased goods from Cheney. Cheney did not have the goods in stock, and Andrews selected the goods from samples. Cheney was to obtain the goods within two weeks at which time Andrews was to call for them; if they were ready before that time, Cheney was to notify Andrews. Within the stipulated time Cheney got the goods into his store, set them apart, and marked them with Andrews' name. The goods, together with the stock, were destroyed by fire. The goods were ordered October 28 and were destroyed November 21. Andrews was not notified that the goods had arrived. Who stands the loss, Cheney or Andrews?
6. McNeal contracted with Braun for a quantity of coal of specific quality to be delivered to McNeal at Burlington at $4.10 a ton delivered. The coal was shipped by Braun in a barge selected by him. The barge was alongside McNeal's wharf and ready for unloading when it sank and the coal was lost. Who stands the loss, McNeal or Braun?
7. Fleming, being a wholesale liquor dealer licensed and carrying on business in Allegheny County, sold and sent from his place of business, C.O.D. to Mercer County, where he had no license to sell, liquor ordered by persons in Mercer County. Fleming was indicted for selling liquor in Mercer County without a license. If the property in the goods passed in Allegheny County, he is not guilty. Is Fleming guilty?
8. Pence, a jeweler, sent two diamond rings to Carney with the agreement and understanding that, if Carney was pleased with the rings, she would keep them and pay to Pence an agreed price, and if she was not pleased with the rings, she would return them to Pence within a reasonable time. The rings were lost without fault of Carney, before the lapse of reasonable time, and before she had indicated in any way that she was satisfied with the rings. Who stands the loss, Pence or Carney?
9. Joseph shipped to Van Buren a small stock of watches. The agreement provided that Van Buren was to remit for all watches sold between January 1 and January 5, and that if he wished he could retain the unsold watches for an additional period of 60 days, and at the end of, or during, that period he had the privilege of returning the unsold watches. All watches returned were to be in as good shape as when shipped. While the watches were in Van Buren's possession they were stolen, without fault on his part. Who stands the loss, Joseph or Van Buren?
10. Song gave a diamond to Stein to show to a prospective customer. It was not given to Stein to sell. Stein was to return the diamond to Song before 2:00 P.M., but instead of returning the diamond Stein pawned it to Evans as security for a $100 loan. Song demanded the diamond but Evans refused to return it. Is Song entitled to the return of the diamond without paying the loan?

CHAPTER XIX

WARRANTIES

Representations and Warranties

In the sale of goods, it is a common practice on the part of the seller to guarantee or warrant the goods. These terms are used synonymously in the business world, but they are not synonymous in their technical meaning. A warranty is a promise or affirmation on the part of the seller of goods that the goods have certain characteristics or are of a stated quality. This promise or affirmation, although a part of the general contract of sale, is not essential to the passing of the property in the goods; it is a collateral contract. A contract of sale containing a warranty is composed of two parts: (1) the agreement whereby the property in the goods and possession are passed from the seller to the buyer, and (2) an agreement that the goods have certain characteristics and qualities. The first part may stand alone, but the second cannot. One may make a sale without a warranty, but cannot make a warranty which does not relate to a sale. Technically, a guaranty is a contract by which one person is bound to another for the performance of a promise or obligation of a third person.

When the seller is negotiating a sale, it is customary for him to make representations concerning the goods. Such representations may fall into one of three classes. If the representations are false and the seller knows or should know that they are false and the seller makes them to induce the buyer to buy and the buyer does buy relying on the false representations, the seller is guilty of fraud. If the representations are stated as the opinion of the seller or are vague and general in nature, as that the goods are "a good buy," or "a bargain," or similar expressions, they are "sales talk" or "puffing." It is impossible to state a general rule which will adequately distinguish fraudulent representations from sales talk; each case must be decided on its own facts. If the seller makes representations as to existing facts and these representations are promissory in their nature, the representations are warranties. In the early history of the law of sales, the rule of *caveat emptor*, "the buyer beware," was in force. The general conception was that it was poor policy to disturb a closed transaction; the buyer should know that he could not rely on the seller's statements and should satisfy himself that the goods were as represented before he bought. Unless there was a clearly expressed promise on the part of the seller to stand back of the goods, the buyer had no remedy, and in interpreting the promise the courts would not enlarge its scope to cover any qualities other than those clearly stated in the promise. The trend has been away from this view toward the other extreme, "the buyer is always right" or *caveat vendor*.

Express Warranties

An express warranty is defined in the Uniform Sales Act as follows: "Any affirmation of fact or any promise by the seller relating to the goods is an express warranty if the natural tendency of such affirmation or promise is to induce the buyer to purchase the goods, and if the buyer purchases the goods relying thereon. No affirmation of the value of the goods, nor any statement purporting to be a statement of the seller's opinion only shall be construed as a warranty."[1]

This definition is broad enough in its terms to include all representations which could be classed as fraudulent and to include in addition thereto all representations of existing facts which have tended to induce the buyer to purchase the goods. It does not include ordinary "sales talk" or "puffing," but the seller, in making his sales talk, must make his statements as his opinion or make vague, general statements; otherwise, he will be held responsible.

The distinction between fraud and warranty is that fraud is based on deceit while warranty is based on contract. To have a deceit there must be a misrepresentation knowingly made; consequently, if the misrepresentation is innocently made, the seller cannot be held for tort damages. A warranty is contractual and, consequently, misrepresentation of an existing fact is not an essential to liability. When the seller warrants the goods, he contracts to assume a risk, incident to the transaction, which would otherwise fall on the buyer. If the goods are not as warranted, the seller has contracted to make good the resulting loss.

In those cases in which the seller has made fraudulent misrepresentations, the buyer may elect to pursue either his remedy in tort or his remedy for breach of warranty.

---

[1] Uniform Sales Act, sec. 12, appendix, p. 891.

Lentz v. Omar Baking Co.
125 Neb. 861, 252 N.W. 410 (1934)

This was an action by Charles Lentz (plaintiff) against the Omar Baking Company (defendant). Judgment for plaintiff and the defendant appealed. Judgment affirmed.

The plaintiff was a cripple and walked slowly, awkwardly, and with difficulty. He wished to purchase a horse to drive. His daughter contacted the defendant, who had a horse for sale, and explained her father's condition to the defendant and his need for a gentle horse. The defendant assured the daughter that the horse was gentle in every respect and, relying on the statements of the defendant, the daughter purchased the horse as agent of plaintiff.

When the plaintiff with the help of others first hitched the horse to a buggy and got in, the horse without warning ran away, broke the side of the barn and a part of the fence, caught the buggy on a heavy post and broke loose from it and ran away.

Both of the plaintiff's legs were broken in this event. Thereafter, the horse was sold by the plaintiff to a man who used him upon a garbage wagon, where he walked over his route without being tied while the driver was calling at various houses. So far as the record discloses, the incident when the horse ran away with the plaintiff is this horse's only deviation from the character of a safe and gentle horse. It is difficult to understand, but the fact is undisputed that upon this one occasion he did not behave as a gentle horse suitable for the plaintiff to drive. There is no explanation in the record as to the cause of the runaway except that he was not gentle. It seems he ran away without apparent cause.

The defendant contends that it is not liable because the horse was always gentle while it owned the horse and because it had no knowledge that the horse was not gentle.

Day, J. There was much conversation between the daughter of the plaintiff and employees of defendant in negotiating the sale. It was thoroughly understood that plaintiff was a cripple and his necessity required a horse of unquestioned gentleness. It is apparent under the circumstances that the plaintiff must have been induced to purchase the horse by the express warranty of the defendant. The evidence supports a finding that there was an express warranty as to this horse. The horse so warranted did not prove to be gentle and as a result the plaintiff was injured.

Where the seller makes an affirmation of fact or promise the natural tendency of which induces buyer to purchase relying thereon, it is an express warranty. The defendant was not entitled to a directed verdict in this case, as contended.

It is not necessary to prove seller's knowledge of the evil propensities of a horse where there is an express warranty, to recover for breach. This is not a tortious action but contractual, and negligence is not involved. Therefore the common-law rule of scienter is not applicable. In *Cameron* v. *Mount*, 86 Wis. 477, 56 N.W. 1094, 22 L.R.A. 512, the court held that, where prospective purchaser was induced to drive a horse by an absolute warranty that the horse was gentle, the action sounded in tort, but that it was not necessary to prove knowledge of its falsity. The opinions of the Wisconsin court cite many authorities to which we refer by reference. The appellant does not cite any, nor have we found any, to the contrary, which would support the theory upon which it seems to have tried the case.

Since we have determined that this is a contractual action arising from a breach of warranty and that it was not necessary to prove the seller's knowledge that the horse was not gentle when it ran away without apparent cause, the assignments of error relating to the refusal to give instructions on this point need not be considered because they do not state the law applicable to the facts in this case.

United States Pipe & Foundry Co. et al. v. City of Waco et al.
Supreme Court of Texas, 108 S.W. (2d) 432 (1937)

This was an action by the city of Waco and others (plaintiffs) against the United States Pipe & Foundry Co. and others (defendants). Judgment for plaintiffs and defendants appealed to Court of Civil Appeals which affirmed the judgment. Defendants appealed to the Supreme Court. Judgment for plaintiffs affirmed.

The City of Waco wished to install an underground pipe line from its storage lake to the city, a distance of about five miles. Cast-iron pipe and concrete were competitive materials, and the latter was favored because of its low original cost. To meet the competition it was necessary to have some material cheaper than cast-iron pipe. Defendants represented Hi-tensile pipe to be such. It was of comparatively recent origin and little known to users of pipeline materials.

The defendants sent to the plaintiffs the results of certain tests that it made which, according to the report of the test, showed that the pipe was suitable for the plaintiffs' purposes. As a result of the tests and other statements of the defendants, the plaintiffs specified Hi-tensile pipe for the job. Within a comparatively short time after the pipe was installed, about seventy breaks appeared in the line which rendered it practically worthless except as a temporary line.

Martin, C. It is vigorously denied that any warranty was given for the reason that the statements relied on to show warranty were at most but the expressions of an opinion or judgment only.

"Any covenant, promise, or assertion of the vendor concerning the quality of the article sold, if relied upon by the vendee and understood by both parties as an absolute promise or assertion, and not a mere expression of opinion, will amount to a warranty. Any representation as to quality made by the vendor on a sale for the purpose of inducing the vendee to purchase, and which did induce him to purchase, amounts to a warranty." 37 Tex. Jur. p. 250, § 103.

"Another circumstance which is treated as indicating whether a statement is a mere expression of opinion is whether or not its correctness is a matter of which either of the parties can judge as well as the other, upon which the buyer can, and may, reasonably be expected, in the exercise of ordinary diligence, to have formed his own opinion. According to some statements, the decisive test of whether there is a warranty is whether the seller assumes to assert a fact of which the buyer is ignorant, or whether he merely declares his belief with reference to a matter on which he has no special knowledge and on which the buyer may be expected also to have an opinion, and to exercise his judgment; the former situation constituting a warranty while the latter does not. Where the fact affirmed is one whose nature is such that the seller is likely to be acquainted with the truth or falsity of his statement, that circumstance indicates the affirmation to be a warranty rather than a mere opinion, although knowledge of falsity is not an essential to a warranty, while if the subject is one outside the seller's knowledge, that indicates an expression of opinion only. Although the seller's statement coincides only with his opinion or belief, nevertheless, if the manner of his expression is that of an assurance of fact on which the buyer relies, the statement is a warranty."

"Superior knowledge of seller, in conjunction with the buyer's relative ignorance, operates to make the slightest divergence from mere praise into representations of fact effective as a warranty."

"There is another class of actions which I must refer to also for the purpose of putting it aside. I mean those cases where a person within whose special province it lay to know a particular fact, has given an erroneous answer to an inquiry made with regard to it by a person desirous of ascertaining the fact for the purpose of determining his course accordingly, and has been held bound to make good the assurance he has given."

Implied Warranties

When no representations or warranties are made at the time of the sale, certain warranties attach by operation of law unless it is expressly agreed that such warranties shall not attach. Such warranties are termed implied warranties.

The seller of goods impliedly warrants that he has title to the goods, or that he will have title to the goods, and that the buyer shall have title free from incumbrances, and that he shall have quiet possession of the goods as against any lawful claims existing at the time of the sale. This warranty covers all sales except sales which are made by a sheriff, auctioneer, mortgagee, or other persons professing to sell, by virtue of authority in fact or law, goods in which a third person has a legal or equitable interest.

The other implied warranties attach only under stated circumstances and, consequently, are not of general application. If goods are sold by description or by sample, or by description and sample, there is an implied warranty that the goods delivered shall correspond to the description and also that the bulk of the goods shall correspond to the sample. In sales by description or by sample, or by description and sample, there is also an additional warranty that the goods delivered shall be of merchantable quality. This means that the goods must be of the fair average quality of such goods as are generally sold on the market.

If the buyer makes known to the seller his need and the seller selects goods to fill that need, the buyer relying on the seller's judgment in the selection of the goods, there is an implied warranty that the goods selected shall be reasonably suitable for the buyer's purpose. If the buyer orders goods by trade name, by catalogue description, or by specification and the seller delivers the specified goods, there is no implied warranty that the goods will be suitable for the buyer's purpose even though the seller knows the buyer's purpose and knows that the goods are not suitable for such purpose.

Other implied warranties may attach by usage of trade, or the scope of the application of the implied warranties stated above may be enlarged by usage of trade.

Bekkevold v. Potts et al.
173 Minn. 87, 216 N.W. 790 (1927)

This was an action by John Bekkevold (plaintiff) against William J. Potts and others (defendants). Judgment for plaintiff and defendant appealed. Judgment affirmed.

The plaintiff purchased from the defendants a Fordson tractor, a two-wheel truck used as a trailer, a connecting hitch, and a hydraulic hoist for unloading.

The contract of sale contained a printed provision:

"No warranties have been made in reference to said motor vehicle by the seller to the buyer unless expressly written hereon at the date of purchase."

None were written thereon.

The buyer made his needs known and relied on the seller's judgment as to the suitability of the outfit for his purposes. There was, therefore, an implied warranty, unless excluded by the provision of the contract quoted above.

Wilson, C. J. Such an implied warranty of the fitness of an article sold, under such circumstances, for the purpose for which it is to be used, is superseded by an express warranty covering the same matter only if inconsistent therewith. G. S. 1923, § 8390, subd. 6. If there be an inconsistent express warranty that covers only a part of the matters covered by an implied warranty, the purchaser may avail himself of as much of the implied warranty as is not covered by such express warranty. It is only when an implied warranty is inconsistent with an express provision of the contract that all implied warranties are merged in, or superseded by, the express provisions of the contract. In other words, warranties are not implied in conflict with the express terms of the contract. It has always been competent for the parties to put their entire agreement in writing and to expressly stipulate that no obligation arising out of an oral agreement, imposition of law, or otherwise, shall rest upon either, save as defined by their written agreement. If the parties wish to avoid the implied warranty, they must in form, or in substance, contract against it.

An implied warranty is not one of the contractual elements of an agreement. It is not one of the essential elements to be stated in the contract, nor does its application or effective existence rest or depend upon the affirmative intention of the parties. It is a child of the law. It, because of the acts of the parties, is imposed by the law. It arises independently and outside of the contract. The law annexes it to the contract. It writes it, by implication, into the contract which the parties have made. Its origin and use are to promote high standards in business and to discourage sharp dealings. It rests upon the principle that "honesty is the best policy," and it contemplates business transactions in which both parties may profit. Defendants' claim does not commend itself to us as consistent with the honesty of purpose with which they are entitled to be credited in their dealings with their customers. The doctrine of implied warranty should be extended rather than restricted.

In the case at bar the parties say:

"No warranties have been made . . . . by the seller to the buyer unless written hereon."

None were written thereon. We are of the opinion that the parties intended to say that no contractual warranties had been made; that the seller had not spoken or written any warranty in reference to the outfit. There was no other way by which such warranties could have been "made." No action of the parties was necessary to "make" that implied warranty which the law writes into it. We must conclude that the parties did not intend to exclude the implied warranty which could easily have been done in unmistakable terms had they so chosen. Hence there was no error in receiving the evidence to prove the breach thereof. This conclusion is consistent with the Uniform Sales Act.

C. D. Brown & Co., Inc. v. Standard Hide Company
301 Pa. 543, 152 Atl. 557 (1930)

This was an action by C. D. Brown & Company, Incorporated (plaintiff) against Standard Hide Company (defendant). Judgment for plaintiff and defendant appealed. Judgment affirmed.

Defendant sold to plaintiff three carloads of "first salted" selected skins at 22 cents a pound. The words "first salted," under the custom of the trade, meant hides properly salted to prevent decay. If hides are not properly salted, the fiber in the hide deteriorates, and when the hide is put through the tanning process, "salt rust" will appear. Such leather is of inferior quality. When the hides were put through the tanning process, "salt rust" was discovered, making the finished product useless for the purpose intended. Plaintiff sued claiming breach of implied warranty.

Sadler, J. It is first urged that there was no warranty of quality. The telegram and telephone conversation called for "first salted" skins, which arrangement was referred to in the following letters, and became necessarily incorporated therein. This was a description of a trade article, and an expert testified that, if in this condition, and not resalted, rust or further decay in the skins, which actually occurred, rendering them useless for the manufacture of grain leather, would not appear. Even if not an express warranty that the hides were properly "first salted," as the term was understood by the trade, the words used would impose responsibility on the seller, under Section 14 (69 PS § 123), which provides that, "where there is a contract to sell or a sale of goods by description, there is an implied warranty that the goods shall correspond with the description." Under such circumstances a recovery can be had if a breach occurs.

J. W. Anderson Co., Inc. v. Tomlinson Chair Mfg. Co., Inc. 206 N.C. 42, 172 S.E. 538 (1934)

This was an action by J. W. Anderson Company, Inc. (plaintiff) against the Tomlinson Chair Manufacturing Company, Inc. (defendant). Judgment for plaintiff and defendant appeals. Judgment reversed and new trial granted.

Defendant ordered from the plaintiff certain tapestries which were to be used in manufacturing furniture. The defendant gave the agent of the plaintiff samples of tapestries which he wanted duplicated. The tapestries delivered had some threads in the background which varied from the samples by a shade, and there was a variation in the size of the design. The tulip in the design on the sample was two and five-eighths inches high, and on the manufactured tapestries it was two and one-half inches high.

Defendant refused to accept and pay for the tapestries and plaintiff sued. Defendant set up breach of implied warranty as a defense.

Brogden, J. What duty is imposed upon the manufacturer of an article for sale by sample?

The judge of the municipal court charged the jury as follows:

(1) "Now, the court charges you in a case of this nature where a contract is entered into between a buyer and a seller, where the goods must be manufactured, and where there is a sample presented for the manufacture of the goods, that the manufacturer of the goods who contracts to manufacture the goods in accordance with the sample presented, warrants that the goods that he manufactures will

be in a reasonable compliance or will be reasonably similar to the sample that is presented to him, that there will be a substantial duplication of the sample.

(3) "That there was a duty on the plaintiff Company to manufacture a fair specimen; that is, that it was a substantial duplication, a reasonable duplication in design, color, and quality of the sample furnished to it.

(4) "And if you find that the goods were capable of being used as a substantial duplicate of the goods from which the samples came, and that there was not a material difference or variation in the goods made and shipped by the plaintiff and that represented by the samples, then the court charges you that would be a compliance with the contract and a refusal on the part of the defendant to accept the goods would be a breach of the contract."

The Supreme Court of North Carolina has spoken upon the subject in *Main* v. *Griffin*, 141 N.C. 43, 53 S.E. 727, and *Pickrell* v. *Wholesale Co.*, 169 N.C. 381, 86 S.E. 187. Quoting with approval from another jurisdiction, this court said in the Pickrell Case, supra: "Strictly speaking, a contract of sale by sample is not a warranty of quality, but an agreement of the seller to deliver, and of the buyer to accept, goods of the same kind and quality as the sample. The identity of the goods sold in kind, condition, and quality with that of the sample is of the essence of the contract; and where the goods sold do not correspond with the sample, there would seem to be no performance of the contract. . . . . The rule recognized in the cases as governing sales by sample seems to be founded on, or to be a simple application of, the principle that to fulfill a contract of sale the seller must deliver that which he has agreed to sell, and that if he does not the purchaser may rescind the contract, or receive the goods and claim a deduction for their relative inferiority in value." Consequently the standard prescribed in this jurisdiction in sales by sample is that the seller must furnish "goods of the same kind and quality as the sample. The identity of the goods sold in kind, condition and quality with that of the sample is of the essence of the contract." Obviously, if color was of the essence of the contract, the same rule would require that articles of the same kind, quality, condition, and color should be furnished in order to discharge the obligation of the contract.

The municipal judge used the expressions "reasonable compliance" or "reasonably similar," "reasonable and substantial similarity," "a fair specimen," "substantial duplication," or "reasonable duplication in design, color and quality." These instructions, tested by the standard prescribed in our decisions, are too broad. It is apprehended that the correct rule as pronounced by this court is that in sales by sample the seller must deliver goods of the same kind, condition, quality, design, and color where any or all of these elements are of the essence of the contract.

Iron Fireman Coal Stoker Co. v. Brown et ux.
183 Minn. 399, 234 N.W. 685 (1931)

This was an action by the Iron Fireman Coal Stoker Company (plaintiff) against H. Rowatt Brown and wife (defendants). Judgment for plaintiff and defendants appealed. Judgment reversed.

Defendants purchased an "Iron Fireman" stoker from the plaintiff. The "Iron Fireman" was not known to defendants. They were entirely ignorant as to its ability or capacity or the work which it would do. Plaintiff was in possession of all the facts. Defendants did not even know it had a trade-name. It then had a limited use in their community. Plaintiff sought to sell them the equipment, and assured them that they would not have to go to the furnace room the last thing at night nor the first thing in the morning. They were willing to buy something that would accomplish that purpose. They had no knowledge of the "Iron Fireman" by reputation or otherwise. They made their desires known to plaintiff. One of the reasons that caused them to buy was that plaintiff repeatedly told them they would take the equipment out if not satisfactory. Defendants unsuccessfully attempted to make it work. Plaintiff knew defendants had no knowledge of the equipment or its operation.

Defendants claim that there was an implied warranty of suitability, and plaintiffs claim that this was a sale by trade-name and that no implied warranty attached.

Wilson, C. J. "In the case of a contract to sell or a sale of a specified article under its patent or other trade name, there is no implied warranty as to its fitness for any particular purpose."

If a person requests a dealer to deliver to him a specifically designated article, known to the buyer and the trade by its trade-name, and it is done, it is obvious that the article would be sold under its trade-name within the meaning of the statute. Such negotiation indicates that the article is known by both parties and the buyer has designated just what he wants. He knows what he wants. The theory of the statute is that, since he knows what he wants, and gets it, after having so designated it, it must be supposed that the trade-name carries such qualities as to cause the purchase.

The spirit and intent of subdivision 4 of the statute is that the seller is not held to an implied warranty because the buyer gets the distinct thing selected by him, an exact article, for which he bargains. So, acting upon his own desires, he takes his own chances as to the fitness of the article, and should not be permitted to complain of the seller who has supplied him with the very thing he sought. In such cases it is not important that the buyer discloses to the seller his intentions as to the use of the article. It is usually helpful to determine upon whose judgment and responsibility the purchase was made. Or, to state it another way, if the thing is itself specifically selected and ordered, the buyer takes upon himself the risk of its effecting the desired purpose. Under such circumstances, the law does not impose an implied warranty; nor should it. The situation is quite different where the buyer yields to the trade talk of a salesman who sells him something that is wholly unknown to him. Perhaps it might be said that, where the buyer selects the article, subdivision 4 applies, and, where the seller selects the article suitable for the purposes needed, subdivision 1, hereinafter mentioned, applies. We are of the opinion that, where the buyer fully informs the seller of his particular needs, and the seller undertakes to select or supply an article suitable for the purpose involved, subdivision 1 applies even though the article may be described in the contract of sale by its trade-name.

There are authorities that seem to put a strict construction upon this provision of the Uniform Sales Act and hold that, if the contract describes an article by the trade-name, there is no implied warranty, but such authorities apparently involve cases where the contract discloses the article sold under a trade-name and the record fails to disclose any circumstances such as are involved in this case. It would seem that such a contract, in the absence of evidence of circumstances to the contrary, should be construed under the statute as if the purchaser had selected the article purchased.

The mere fact that an article sold is described in the contract by its trade-name does not necessarily make the sale a sale under or by a trade-name. Whether it is so or not depends upon the circumstances. *Baldry* v. *Marshall* (1925) L.R. 1 K.B. 260.

This provision of the statute is merely a restatement of the common-law rule that, where there is a sale of a known, described, and defined article, and if that article is in fact supplied, there is no implied warranty. But we think the rule at common law and now under such a statute means articles known in the market, and among those familiar with that kind of trade, by that description.

Defendants' reliance upon plaintiff's judgment as to the suitability of the equipment to meet their requirements is evident from all the circumstances.

G. S. 1923 (2 Mason, 1927) § 8390, subd. 1, reads:

"Where the buyer, expressly or by implication, makes known to the seller the particular purpose for which the goods are required, and it appears that the buyer relies on the seller's skill or judgment (whether he be the grower or manufacturer or not), there is an implied warranty that the goods shall be reasonably fit for such purpose."

The fact that the article has a trade-name does not do away with the implied warranty arising out of the circumstances indicated.

Under the circumstances, we are of the opinion that under this subdivision of the statute there was an implied warranty that the equipment was reasonably fit for the purpose for which it was sold.

The doctrine of implied warranty is to be liberally construed. The rule is an equitable one.

Agoos Kid Co., Inc., v. Blumenthal Import Corporation et al.
282 Mass. 1, 184 N.E. 279 (1932)

This was an action by Agoos Kid Company, Incorporated (plaintiff) against the Blumenthal Import Corporation and others (defendants). Judgment for plaintiff and defendants appealed. Judgment reversed and remanded with directions.

This suit was brought to recover damages arising from the alleged breaches of two contracts for the purchase and sale of certain goat skins. Under the first contract, dated September 9, 1930, the defendants agreed to sell and the plaintiff to buy four thousand dozen Bagdad goat skins dry salted; and under the second contract, dated September 25, 1930, to buy three thousand dozen of the same kind of skins. The skins arrived in two shipments, each containing a part of the goods purchased under each contract. The plaintiff received, paid for, and used the entire first shipment, but refused to accept or pay for the second. The claim of the plaintiff is for breach of warranties as to the skins delivered under the first shipment, and it contends that it was lawfully entitled to refuse to receive or pay for the second shipment. The defendants claim damages for the plaintiff's failure to accept and pay for the second shipment. Both contracts involve the purchase and sale of "Bagdad goat skins dry salted" of various weights and at different prices, and provided that the skins were "to be of the good season." It was agreed that the skins were in fact "of the good season."

"Bagdad goat skins dry salted" are well known in the trade. As a general rule, such skins are purchased in various places in Asia Minor and India from local butchers. If the skins are properly cured, the texture is preserved, but if the skins are cured too quickly, the inside is likely to rot. The defect cannot be detected by ordinary inspection and will not appear until the skin is tanned. Normally, from one and one-half to three per cent of the skins in a large shipment will be defective. In the first shipment, when tanned, it was found that nearly one-half of the skins were defective.

Crosby, J. The contracts in question were for a sale of goods by description and there was an implied warranty that they would correspond with the description. G. L. c. 106, § 16. "The goods are merchantable when they are of the general kind which they are described or supposed to be when bought." Williston on Sales (2d Ed.) § 243. "Where goods of a character commonly known in trade are ordered by description, and there is no inspection, there is an implied warranty that those furnished will be such as are merchantable under the descriptive term used by the parties. The purchaser is entitled to get what he ordered." The plaintiff did not contract to buy seven thousand dozen goat skins, one half of which were to be rotten and worthless. It agreed to buy that number of skins dry salted, and there was an implied warranty that, with the exception of not more than three per cent thereof, they should be of merchantable quality. Although it was found that a lot of dry salted goat skins is deemed of merchantable quality and reasonably fit for the purpose of making it into leather if the defect here existing is limited to not more than three per cent of the lot, it was found that the first shipment was not merchantable throughout "within this definition, and was not reasonably fit throughout within this definition for the purpose of being made into leather." If the skins had been inspected by the plaintiff before they were subjected to the process of making them into leather, it is found that defects in many of the skins were latent and could not be discovered by inspection. The judge accordingly ruled as follows: "Upon the facts hereinbefore stated, I rule that there was an implied warranty of merchantability as to the goods included in the first shipment. The goods were sold by description. There was no inspection in fact; and inspection would have been not only useless, because the defect was latent, but also impracticable, because the price was to be paid upon delivery of the documents, before delivery of the goods. The defendant was a dealer in goods of the same description. The goods were not sold by any 'patent or other trade name' so as to relieve the seller from implied warranties provided he delivered goods corresponding to the name. . . . . Goods are not merchantable simply because their defect is latent and an unsuspecting buyer might be found. . . . . Neither are goods merchantable because a fragment of a large lot may be free from defect." It is plain that the evidence warranted these findings, and that the rulings were correct. In *Inter-State Grocer Co.* v. *George William Bentley Co.*, 214 Mass. 227, 231, 233, 101 N.E. 147, 149, it was said: "Upon the sale of goods, by name or description, in the absence of some other controlling stipulation in the contract, a condition is implied that the goods shall be merchantable under that name. . . . . This is not a warranty of quality. . . . . It is a requirement of identity between the thing which is described as the subject of the trade and the thing proffered in performance of it. The buyer is entitled to receive goods fairly answerable to the description contained in his contract of sale. . . . . The jury must have understood that the plaintiff, in order to prevail, was bound to prove that the goods were not merchantable at the time they were delivered to the buyer." Where, as here, one half of the skins comprising the first shipment are found to have been defective, it is obvious that they were not of merchantable quality.

NOTE.—New trial was granted because of errors on other matters.

Who Benefits from a Warranty

In theory, a warranty is a contractual obligation which is either expressly assumed (express warranties) or imposed by operation of law (implied warranties) as a part of, and yet collateral to, a contract of sale. Proceeding from this accepted theory, it logically follows that one not a party to the contract cannot benefit from the contract. When one who has purchased an article sells it to another, he has not assigned the original contract of sale to the buyer but has entered into a new contract of sale. As a result, the general rule is that the immediate purchaser is the only one who can recover for the breach of a warranty. There have been some exceptions to this rule, notably in food cases in which a recovery has been granted against the one who originally prepared and packed the food. This may be justified on the basis of public policy.

Cotton v. John Deere Plow Co.
— Ala. —, 18 So. (2d) 727 (1944)

This was an action by John Deere Plow Company (plaintiff) against E. C. Cotton (defendant). Judgment for plaintiff and defendant appealed. Judgment affirmed.

One Jordan sold defendant a mill and motor which had been manufactured by the plaintiff. Defendant gave Jordan two negotiable promissory notes payable to Jordan in payment for the mill and motor. Jordan indorsed the notes to plaintiff who took the notes as a holder in due course. When the notes fell due, defendant refused to pay and, when sued, set up breach of warranty of the mill and motor made by plaintiff to Jordan.

Simpson, J. The defendant bought from Jordan, not from the plaintiff. There was no privity of contract between the present suit parties. So, conceding the assertion that the plow company was the manufacturer of the articles sold defendant by Jordan, such a defense is not available against the plaintiff, under the general rule of nonliability of a manufacturer for a warranty as to third persons in no way a party to the contract. "It is well settled as a common-law rule that the benefit of a warranty does not run with the chattel on its resale so as to give the subpurchaser any right of action thereon as against the original seller."

Haut v. Kleene et al.
320 Ill. App. 273, 50 N.E. (2d) 855 (1943)

This was an action by Charles Haut, administrator of the estate of Estelle Haut, deceased (plaintiff) against A. F. Kleene, Amy Slad and others (defendants). Judgment for plaintiff and defendant Amy Slad appealed. Judgment reversed and remanded.

Charles Haut purchased four rabbits from defendant Amy Slad, who operated a small retail market. Estelle Haut, his wife, washed the rabbits, cut them up, and cooked them. A short time thereafter she became ill and the doctor was called. She died about two weeks later. The doctors who treated her gave as their opinion that she died of tularemia or rabbit poisoning. This suit was brought to recover damages on the ground that in the sale of the rabbits there was an implied warranty that the rabbits were "free from injurious defects in the handling and consumption" of them. Defendant contends that the sale was to Charles Haut and that, if there was an implied warranty, he is the only one who can recover for its breach.

O'Connor, P. J. Counsel for defendant Slad say that the decided weight of authority in the United States holds that there is an implied warranty that meats sold for immediate consumption are wholesome and that this implied warranty cannot be extended to the handling and preparation of meats. There is also some argument that the implied warranty, if any, extended only to Charles Haut and not to his wife or family. There are a number of cases from jurisdictions that hold that the implied warranty in such cases does not extend beyond the immediate purchaser, but we think they are unsound. To say that in the case at bar there was an implied warranty to Charles Haut who purchased the rabbits for food but that it did not extend to his wife and children, in our opinion, does not make sense. This question has recently been given careful consideration by another division of this court in *Welter* v. *Bowman Dairy Co.*, 318 Ill. App. 305, 47 N.E. (2d) 739, in which the conflicting authorities on this question are analyzed and discussed. The court speaking by Mr. Presiding Justice Burke said: "Apparently, this question has never been presented directly to a court of review in this State" and it was held that the implied warranty of fitness of food for human consumption extends to one although not the purchaser. We agree with this holding.

NOTE.—The case was reversed and remanded because of errors not included in this extract.

Seller's Tort Liability

A seller of defective goods may be held liable in tort not only to the immediate purchaser but also to anyone who may reasonably be expected to be endangered as the direct result of the defect. The basis of the seller's liability is negligence, and, as a general rule, no recovery has been allowed unless it can be shown that the seller has failed to exercise that degree of care which a reasonable person in the same or similar circumstances would have exercised. This standard leaves the question of seller's liability primarily a question of fact.

In the cases involving the sale of defective foods or drugs, the majority of the courts have held the manufacturer liable without affirmative proof of negligence. The fact that defective foods or drugs are marketed is accepted as conclusive proof of negligence. This theory of strict liability has been extended in some jurisdictions to cases involving cosmetics and clothing in which substances injurious to the health of the user have been used in the manufacture, coloring, or dyeing of the product.

Manufacturers of other products which are classed as inherently dangerous have been held liable under certain circumstances. If it is reasonably forseeable that the user of defectively manufactured goods may be injured, and if the manufacturer has not used reasonable care in inspecting and testing the goods before they are marketed, the manufacturer, as a general rule, will be liable to a user of the goods if he is injured as a result of the defect in the goods.

As to jobbers and retailers their duties are less extensive than those of the manufacturer. They owe a duty to make a reasonable inspection of goods before they sell them and to warn the buyer of any discoverable defects. The extent of the duty to inspect depends on the nature of the goods and the probability of injury from their use.

If the buyer is guilty of contributory negligence, he cannot recover damages from the seller. Under some circumstances, the user of the goods may owe a duty to inspect or, under other circumstances, the defect may be so obvious that the buyer's failure to detect it will amount to contributory negligence. Also, the buyer must have used the goods in the usual manner in which such goods are used. The seller is not liable unless the goods have been put to a normal use by a normal user.

This rule of seller's liability has not been confined to personal injury cases, but has been extended to injury to property resulting from defects in goods sold to be used with such property.

Corum v. R. J. Reynolds Tobacco Co., Inc.
205 N.C. 213, 171 S.E. 78 (1933)

This was an action by James C. Corum (plaintiff) against R. J. Reynolds Tobacco Company, Inc. (defendant). Judgment for plaintiff and defendant appealed. Judgment affirmed.

The defendant manufactures a brand of plug or chewing tobacco known as "Apple Sun-cured." It sold some of this tobacco to J. W. Smitherman, a wholesale merchant in Winston-Salem, who in turn sold it to Norman Brothers at Eastbend. On June 4, 1931, the plaintiff bought a plug of it from Norman Brothers and returned to his home. The plaintiff claims that while going back to Eastbend he put a part of the plug in his mouth to bite off a chew, and "jerked the tobacco," when a fishhook which was embedded in the plug "stuck on the inner side of his lip and came out on the outside"; that with the fishhook and the tobacco he went to a physician who removed the hook; that after its removal, the plaintiff "prized the tobacco open" and found a mark inside "where the fishhook had been lying"; that on the end of the hook there was a piece of string about two inches long; that he suffered pain, was given antitoxin to prevent tetanus, had difficulty in opening and closing his mouth, and complained of stiffness in his jaw and neck.

Adams, J. The defendant contends that the record contains no adequate evidence of negligence which is actionable. We have repeatedly held, in accord with the general principle, that the fact of personal injury is not regarded as proof either of negligence or of proximate cause, and that a mere conjecture will not support an action for damages. The plaintiff, however, is not required to make out his case by direct proof, but may rely upon circumstances from which a reasonable inference of negligence may be drawn, in which event the evidence must be interpreted most favorably for the plaintiff, and if it is of such character that reasonable men may form divergent opinions of its import, it is customary to leave the issue to the ultimate award of the jury.

There are many decisions to the effect that one who prepares in bottles or packages foods, medicines, drugs, or beverages, and puts them on the market, is charged with the duty of exercising due care in the preparation of these commodities, and under certain circumstances may be liable in damages to the ultimate consumer.

In this case the plaintiff adduced evidences tending to show that the defendant is the sole manufacturer of "Apple Sun-cured Tobacco"; that the tobacco in question was of this brand and had the appearance of having recently come from the store; that it was protected by a wrapper; that all the wrapper had not been removed at the time of the injury; that when a part of it was torn away the imprint of a fishhook and a string which had been embedded in the plug of tobacco was discovered; that some other foreign substance had been found in the same brand of tobacco within two months preceding the injury; and that the foreman of the machine room had previously had complaints that other foreign substances had been left in the manufactured product. The plaintiff introduced independent evidence which called for a verdict.

Without antagonizing the stated principle, the defendant takes the position that tobacco is not a food or within the category of any of the articles numerated above, and is hence beyond the scope of the cited cases. The word "food" has been variously defined by lexicographers as nutritive material taken into the body for the purpose of growth, repair, or maintenance; that which is eaten or drunk for nourishment; whatever supplies nourishment to organic bodies. It may be conceded for the present purpose that tobacco is not a food; but it does not necessarily follow that the defendant is exempt from liability.

In *Pillars* v. *R. J. Reynolds Tobacco Co.*, 117 Miss. 490, 78 So. 365, 366, the plaintiff sued the defendant for damages resulting from the chewing of a piece of Brown Mule tobacco in which a decomposed human toe was concealed. After referring to the general rule and its exceptions together with the contention that the limit has been reached by the courts and that the facts did not warrant an exception in favor of the plaintiff, the court observed: "We know that chewing tobacco is taken into the mouth, that a certain proportion will be absorbed by the mucous membrane of the mouth, and that some, at least, of the juice or pulp will and does find its way into the alimentary canal, there to be digested and ultimately to become a part of the blood. Tobacco may be relatively harmless, but decaying flesh, we are advised, develops poisonous ptomaines, which are certainly dangerous and often fatal. Anything taken into the mouth there to be masticated should be free of those elements which may endanger the life or health of the user. . . . The fact that the courts have at this time made only the exceptions mentioned to the general rule does not prevent a step forward for the health and life of the public. The principle announced in the cases which recognize the exceptions, in our opinion, apply, with equal force, to this case."

Upon the merits of the present case we entertain a similar opinion. A fishhook embedded and concealed in a plug of tobacco, though not a poison, is no less capable of inflicting serious physical injury. The trial court was correct in denying the motion for non-suit.

Dempsey v. Virginia Dare Stores, Inc., et al.
— Mo. App. —, 186 S.W. (2d) 217 (1945)

This was an action by Otto Dempsey (plaintiff) against the Virginia Dare Stores, Inc., and another (defendants). Judgment for defendants and plaintiff appealed. Judgment affirmed.

Plaintiff purchased from the defendants, at one of their retail stores in Kansas City, a lounging robe called a "Fuzzy Wuzzy." The robe was made of viscose rayon. The base was of jersey and the outside was like brushed wool. The outside surface was composed of very fine fibers. The plaintiff had taken a bath, put on her gown and the "Fuzzy Wuzzy" robe over it, and was sitting on her bed smoking a cigarette when the "Fuzzy Wuzzy" caught fire. The robe burned rapidly and plaintiff was burned seriously.

Plaintiff contends that the defendants were negligent in not warning her of the highly inflammable nature of the "Fuzzy Wuzzy." The proof established that viscose rayon had been in use since 1890 and that, although the robe was inflammable, it was no more inflammable than other similar material such as cotton.

Bland, P. J. It is well settled that a person who sells an article, which he knows or should know, is inherently dangerous to human life, limb or health, to another person who has no knowledge or notice of its dangerous character, and fails to give notice thereof to the purchaser, is liable in damages to a third person who, while exercising due care, is injured by its use, or which should have been contemplated by the seller and that the danger is nonetheless inherent because it was brought into action by some external force.

Defendants insist that there was no duty upon them to notify plaintiff of the inflammability of the robe, for the reason, that the fuzz was on the outside of the fabric and was plainly visible; that she testified that she saw it and knew it was there at the time she purchased and wore the robe; that there is no evidence that the material in the robe was any more inflammable than any other material used in clothing; that all persons know that material such as "fuzzy wuzzy" is highly inflammable; that, therefore, there was no latent dangerous condition shown, and that, aside from this, there is no evidence that defendants knew or could have known anything more about the construction or inflammability of the robe than plaintiff knew.

Plaintiff admitted that this "open" fuzz was on the outside and was plainly visible to her, but she testified that she did not know that the qualities of the fuzz were such as to make the robe highly inflammable, and that no one told her that it was.

However, plaintiff cannot claim that she did not know what any ordinarily intelligent person would know by observing the material. It is not necessary for one selling dynamite or matches to notify the purchaser that the dynamite will explode or that the matches will take fire, for every one knows of these qualities inherent in these objects. Persons of ordinary intelligence also know that openly woven, fluffy and "fuzzy wuzzy" materials will ignite and burn more readily than ordinary cloth. There is no duty on the part of the seller of such material to notify the buyer of its inflammable qualities. While counsel for defendants, in his opening statement, admitted, in effect, that defendants knew that the material in question was highly inflammable, the word "highly" is a relative term. "Highly inflammable" ordinarily is taken to mean material that will more readily ignite and burn than ordinary inflammable material. The evidence shows, as everyone knows, that even ordinary cloth is inflammable. The reference of counsel to the material in the "Fuzzy Wuzzy" robe, as being highly inflammable meant that it was of higher inflammability than ordinary cloth.

There is no question but that the robe in question was highly inflammable, in the light of this understanding of the term, and persons of ordinary intelligence would know of such quality inherent in the material upon observation. Therefore, plaintiff is in no position to claim that she did not know that the robe in question was more likely to ignite and burn than ordinary cloth and, therefore, of higher inflammability.

It will thus be seen that plaintiff was confronted with a very difficult problem of making a case of a duty to warn on the part of the defendants. We do not say that, under no circumstances, would the seller of such an article of the general character as the robe in question, be excused from warning the buyer of its inflammable qualities if it is made of some latently inflammable material; but it would appear that there would be no duty to warn unless it was composed of material that was almost explosive in character. There is no evidence tending to show that it was of that quality.

QUESTIONS AND PROBLEMS

1. What is the difference between a warranty and a misrepresentation which constitutes a fraud?
2. Smith purchased a buggy from Hale. Before purchasing the buggy Smith examined it and expressed a doubt that it was strong enough to carry her and her husband. Hale stated that the buggy was well built and that it would carry Smith, her husband, and a hundred pounds of meal. Three days after the purchase of the buggy a spring broke. Hale claims that he is not liable because Smith examined the buggy before purchasing it. Is Hale liable for breach of an express warranty?
3. What is the nature of an implied warranty?

4. Archer purchased a quantity of leather from Burch. Burch had purchased the leather from Clark who operated a tannery. Clark had embezzled the leather from Drew, a customer of Clark's. Drew recovered the leather from Archer. Archer sued Burch and Burch claims that he bought and sold the leather in good faith and is not liable. Is Burch liable?
5. Keystone ordered from Norman a carload of lumber to be "No. 1 and No. 2 common, soft, yellow poplar." When the car arrived it was found that part of the lumber was "hard white, hickory poplar." Keystone refused to accept the lumber and Norman sued. Keystone set up as a defense breach of warranty. Was there a breach of warranty?
6. Collins wished to buy some low-grade cotton. Burton had such cotton for sale. Collins went with Burton to the warehouse where the cotton was stored. Samples of cotton were drawn from the bales and examined by Collins. Collins purchased the cotton, but when the bales were opened it was found that they contained foreign substances and that the cotton in the center of the bale was not of the same grade as the samples. Collins sued Burton for breach of warranty. Is Collins entitled to a judgment?
7. Narzisenfeld sold to Cudahy Packing Co. a carload, 400 cases, of eggs. The eggs were in cold storage. Before purchasing the eggs an agent of Cudahy went to the warehouse and inspected 10 cases of the lot and found them satisfactory, and on the basis of this inspection purchased the entire lot. There was no limit placed on the number of cases the buyer inspected, and the buyer selected the cases to be inspected, not the seller. The eggs, when delivered, were moldy and were sold by Cudahy Packing Co. at a reduction in price. Cudahy Packing Co. refused to pay for the eggs claiming that the sale was a sale by sample and there was an implied warranty that the bulk would correspond to the sample. Is Cudahy Packing Co.'s claim correct?
8. Perry purchased from Cornell 360 tons of ice to be shipped from Pembroke, Maine, to New Bedford. The ice delivered was impure and not fit for use. Perry refused to pay for the ice and when sued set up breach of warranty as a defense. Was there an implied warranty that the ice would be merchantable?
9. The Hotel Co. ordered from Wharton two "Harrison Safety Boilers" of 150 horse-power each. The only water available for use in the boilers was Missouri river water. On account of the sediment in the water the boilers did not operate satisfactorily. The boilers were of good material and well made. The Hotel Co. refused to pay for the boilers and when sued set up a breach of warranty as a defense, contending that Wharton knew to what use the Hotel Co. intended to put the boilers. Was there any implied warranty of suitability?
10. Land ordered a barrel of cod liver oil from the Drug Co. The Drug Co. negligently shipped linseed oil and Land sold some of the oil to Ellis as cod liver oil. At the time of the sale Ellis stated that he did not think that the oil was good cod liver oil but was assured that it was. Ellis used the oil in his chick feed and as a result his chicks were damaged. Is the Drug Co. liable to Ellis for the resulting damage?

CHAPTER XX

PERFORMANCE AND REMEDIES FOR BREACH

Delivery

A contract of sale does not differ in its basic aspects from any other type of contract. If a contract of sale is breached, the remedies of the injured party are fundamentally the same as those granted in cases of breach of other types of contracts. However, owing to the nature of the contract of sale, certain rights and duties arise which are individual to the sales contract.

When the parties have entered into a contract to sell and the time to perform arrives, the seller owes a duty to deliver the goods and the buyer owes a duty to accept and pay for them in accordance with the terms of the contract. In the absence of a provision to the contrary, the place of delivery is the seller's place of business or, if he has no place of business, at his residence. However, if the goods are ascertained and to the knowledge of the parties are in some other place at the time the contract to sell or the sale was made, then that place is the place of delivery.[1]

If the seller is to send the goods to the buyer, the seller must select the carrier and deliver the goods to the carrier. The seller must use reasonable care in selecting the carrier and must make a reasonable contract with the carrier, protecting the buyer's rights. If it is customary to insure the goods while in transit, the seller must insure the goods or give the buyer notice so that he can have them insured.[2]

If, at the time of the sale, the goods are in the possession of a bailee for the seller, the bailee's consent to hold the goods for the buyer is equivalent to delivery. If a negotiable bill of lading or negotiable warehouse receipt has been issued by the bailee to the seller, the indorsement by the seller and delivery of such negotiable bill of lading or negotiable warehouse receipt to the buyer is equivalent to delivery.

If no time of delivery is stated in the contract, delivery must be made within a reasonable time. If no contract for credit has been entered into, delivery and payment are concurrent conditions.

---

[1] Uniform Sales Act, sec. 43, appendix, p. 897.

[2] *Ibid.*, sec. 46, appendix, p. 898.

To perform his contract the seller must deliver goods of the kind, quality, and quantity stipulated.

If the seller delivers less than he contracted to sell, the buyer may reject them, or if he wishes he may accept them and pay for them at the contract rate. If the buyer accepts and uses a lesser quantity of goods not knowing that the seller is not going to perform his contract in full, the buyer shall not be liable to pay more than the value of the goods to him. If the seller delivers more than he contracted to sell, the buyer may reject all, accept all, paying the contract rate for the excess, or select the quantity contracted for and reject the balance. If the seller delivers the goods mixed with others, the buyer may select the goods which are in accordance with the contract and reject the rest or he may reject the whole.[3]

Minor variations in quantity, unless the seller is intentionally attempting to pad the contract or make short delivery, will not, as a general rule, justify the buyer's refusal to accept the goods.

Wilson & Co., Inc. v. State
45 N.Y.S. (2d) 610 (1943)

This was an action by Wilson & Co., Inc. (plaintiff) against the State of New York (defendant). Judgment for plaintiff. (Note.—The case was appealed to the Supreme Court, Appellate Division, where the judgment was affirmed without opinion. 48 N.Y.S. (2d) 19, 267 App. Div. 1028. May 10, 1944.)

The plaintiff sold a quantity of butter to the State. At the time the contract of sale was entered into, plaintiff had a large quantity of butter stored in the Gotham-Harrison Cold Storage Corporation's warehouse. The plaintiff issued a delivery order to the Storage Corporation instructing them to transfer to the State 84 tubs of butter, Lot No. 11300 describing the butter. This order was dated December 21, 1942, and, pursuant to this order, the Storage Corporation issued its nonnegotiable warehouse receipt, dated December 23, 1942, to the State and mailed it to the proper state official on that date.

In December, 1942, the Christmas holiday fell on Friday, and the state offices were not open and mail was not received until Monday, December 28th. The storage warehouse was likewise closed, and when it opened for business on Monday, the 28th, it was discovered that the butter covered by the warehouse receipt issued to the State on December 23rd had been stolen. The Storage Company notified the Commissioner of the loss.

Under the circumstances, does the seller or the buyer bear the loss?

Dye, J. This transaction was handled in the regular course of trade. The title to goods passes when the contract is made. This we

[3] *Ibid.*, sec. 44, appendix, p. 897.

hold occurred here when the claimant, acting on the inquiry of the Division of Standards and Purchase, directed its warehouseman to transfer the 84 tubs of butter, Lot No. 11300, to the State Department, which direction the warehouseman recognized by issuing its nonnegotiable warehouse receipt to the order of the State Commissioner, dated December 23, 1942, and on the same day deposited same duly addressed to the Commissioner in the United States mail. From then on, as between the seller and the buyer, the risk of loss was on the latter, except for such remedy as might exist against the warehouseman.

The State contends that the warehouseman had not acknowledged to the buyer that it held the butter on the buyer's behalf, because it was the receipt by the buyer of the warehouse receipt, and not the mailing thereof, that constituted the acknowledgement referred to in the statute.

Words to express intent are not always happily chosen, but in this transaction at least we hold that the warehouse receipt was an effective acknowledgment that the merchandise was being held for the account of the State, and no one else and that the mailing of the warehouse receipt in due course was sufficient as a notification. The fact that the theft of the butter occurred before the State received the letter containing the warehouse receipt cannot change the fact that title had previously passed.

Shpetner v. Hollywood Credit Clothing Co., Inc.
— D.C. —, 42 A. (2d) 522 (1945)

This was an action by Oscar L. Shpetner (plaintiff) against Hollywood Credit Clothing Co., Inc. (defendant). Judgment for defendant and plaintiff appealed. Judgment affirmed.

Defendant gave an order for two dozen ladies' hats to a salesman employed by plaintiff. Defendant's order was subject to confirmation by plaintiff; but without further notice or communication, plaintiff eight days later shipped to defendant by express four boxes, each containing two dozen hats.

One box was received by defendant, accepted, and the contents placed in stock for sale. Two days later, a Sunday having intervened, the other three boxes were delivered to defendant by the express company and immediately returned with the statement that the articles had not been ordered. Plaintiff was also notified by letter of defendant's refusal to accept the three boxes.

Plaintiff claimed that the shipment of eight dozen hats, upon receipt of the order for two dozen, was in legal effect a counter-offer. requiring defendant to elect whether to accept or return the entire lot; that acceptance of the part bound defendant to accept and pay for all. The trial judge rejected this theory and entered judgment for defendant. Plaintiff has appealed, reasserting here the same contention made in the trial court.

Richardson, C. J. Had defendant's order been accepted by confirmation, as was contemplated when it was given, thereby completing a contract, a right to retain the goods ordered and to return the excess is expressly recognized under Section 44 of the Uniform Sales Act. Plaintiff says, correctly we think, that the section does not apply unless the delivery is made under contract wherein the quantity has been fixed by agreement of the parties.

Prior to the adoption of the Uniform Sales Act in New York, it was held that one ordering articles at a unit price was entitled to retain the quantity ordered and return the surplus. This, however, is too general a statement unless it be regarded as applicable to facts of that case not disclosed in the reported decision. The reasonable and we think the correct rule to be applied in such cases is that one receiving an order to supply merchandise may submit a counter-offer by shipping different goods or a greater quantity of the goods ordered. This is but a tender which the purchaser may accept, thereby becoming bound for the whole, or reject without incurring liability. But if he retains part and rejects part, no contract is created requiring him to pay for the whole unless delivery was expressly made subject to that condition or other circumstances exist from which it may be found as a fact that he assented to a delivery not conforming to the terms of his order.

This was the rule followed in *American Lumber & Mfg. Co.* v. *Atlantic Mill & Lumber Co.*, 3 Cir., 290 F. 632, 635, where it was said:

"Where one makes an offer and assents to an acceptance which is not responsive to the proposal, a contract is made and he is, of course, bound by it. . . . .

"Having in mind the defendant's conduct in accepting and paying for twelve cars of lumber after the plaintiff had conditionally accepted its orders, the trial court submitted to the jury the question whether the defendant had, as evidenced by its conduct, assented to the plaintiff's terms and thereby had brought their minds together. The defendant assigns this as error on the ground that the question of the existence of the contracts was one of law for the court to decide. In this contention we do not concur for here the existence, not the construction, of the contracts was the point in issue. When the evidence is conflicting it is for the jury to determine whether a contract does in fact exist, and, if so, what are its terms?"

Here the judge, hearing the case without a jury, had before him, in addition to the facts we have stated, the shipping receipt, a copy of which was delivered to defendant with the first box, which bore the notation "No. Pieces 4." He had the invoice plaintiff had mailed defendant when the shipment was made, billing defendant for eight dozen hats. He found on all the evidence that defendant did not assent to the purchase of eight dozen hats; that he might logically have regarded the billing of eight dozen hats as a bookkeeping error. He, therefore, properly denied a recovery for the six dozen hats which defendant had not ordered and refused to accept, limiting plaintiff's recovery to the goods ordered and accepted, payment for which at the unit price had been tendered and refused.

Inspection and Acceptance

As a general rule, the right to inspect goods is a condition precedent to the buyer's obligation to pay for the goods. However, the buyer may contract to pay before inspection. Such a provision is common in C.O.D. and bill of lading draft attached sales. If it is necessary to test the goods for the purpose of determining whether or not the goods tendered comply with the contract, the buyer will be permitted to take a reasonable sample for testing purposes. The buyer will be given a reasonable time in which to make a test, but the buyer will have to stand all the expense of the test unless the contract expressly relieves him of this expense. By its terms the contract of sale may make inspection by the buyer a condition precedent to the passing of the property in the goods to the buyer. If the contract does not cover this point, the courts have generally held that, after the seller has unconditionally appropriated goods to the contract, the goods are at the risk of the buyer unless the goods appropriated to the contract are obviously not in compliance with the contract, in which case the shipping of the goods is considered a counter-offer on the part of the seller, and the property in the goods will not pass to the buyer until he has inspected and accepted the goods. If the goods appropriated to the contract are not in conformity with the contract, on inspection, the buyer has the right to reject the goods, and thereafter the goods are at the risk of the seller even though the goods were at the risk of the buyer during transit.

As a general rule, the place of inspection is at the place of delivery, but if the goods are to be shipped by the seller to the buyer, the place of inspection is at the destination of the goods unless the parties have agreed that inspection shall be at the point of shipment. If the buyer does not inspect the goods within a reasonable time, he will have waived his right to inspect.

A buyer accepts the goods when he states that he accepts the goods or when he exercises rights of ownership over the goods which are inconsistent with ownership of the seller. An acceptance of goods by the buyer does not amount to a waiver of rights against the seller for defects in the goods or for other breaches of the seller's contract, but if the buyer accepts goods, he must give notice of defects to the seller within a reasonable time after the buyer knows or should know of the defects, or the buyer will be held to have waived his rights against the seller.

Inland Seed Co. v. Washington-Idaho Seed Co.
160 Wash. 244, 294 Pac. 991 (1931)

This was an action by the Inland Seed Company (plaintiff) against Washington-Idaho Seed Company (defendant). Judgment for plaintiff and defendant appealed. Judgment affirmed.

The plaintiff brought action to recover against the defendant a balance claimed to be due on a carload of peas alleged to have been sold by the plaintiff to the defendant and destroyed by a fire which burned the warehouse in which the peas were stored.

The written order of defendant verbally accepted by plaintiff December 13, 1927, for twelve hundred sacks of Blue Bell peas at $2.95 a hundred f.o.b. Spokane, specified: "Shipment to be made when ready, peas to contain not more than one per cent bleached or white peas. These peas are to be shipped to C. B. Pyle, Harrisville, Mich., using shipper's order bill of lading with arrival draft attached. . . . . Inspection allowed."

This agreement was later modified and the shipment was consigned by the plaintiff to himself. They were stored in a warehouse at destination and plaintiff kept the warehouse receipts. The defendants paid part of the price but never paid the rest. The peas burned in the warehouse where they were stored. The defendant contends that peas were never offered for inspection. The question arises whether title to the peas rested in defendant prior to their destruction.

Millard, J. Appellant contends that the order was to ship the goods subject to inspection; that the opportunity was not afforded to make such inspection to ascertain whether the percentage of weevil and white peas exceeded a stated percentage as prescribed by the contract; and that the goods could not be appropriated to the contract with the assent of the buyer until the buyer has so manifested his approval of the quality of the goods as to preclude him from subsequently giving notice of rescission.

The place of inspection, where no agreement has been made to the contrary, is the destination of the goods. Under the contract the destination of the peas, the place of delivery, was Palouse, Washington, and the place of inspection under the contract and under the statute was Palouse. There the goods remained in storage for two months prior to their destruction by fire awaiting payment by the appellant buyer of the balance due on the purchase price. Delivery to the bailee under the facts of this case was delivery to the buyer. Of course, the appellant buyer had the right, though the contract contained no provision therefor, to inspect within a reasonable time the goods before acceptance of and payment for the same.

Surely two months afforded a reasonable opportunity to appellant to examine the peas to ascertain whether they were in conformity with the contract. Appellant's unqualified assent to the delivery to the warehouse, under the conditions herein recited, was an acceptance of the title.

". . . . The defendant insists the goods are not appropriated to a contract with the assent of the buyer until the buyer has so manifested his approval of their quality as to preclude him thereafter from giving notice of rescission. In that view, the passage of title may be indefinitely postponed for the reasonable time within which a buyer is privileged to return goods found to be defective will vary with many circumstances, as, for instance, the nature of the defects, whether patent or concealed. We think assent to appropriation is something more immediate and certain. It does not signify an acceptance so definitive and deliberate as to bar rescission for defects. It signifies the buyer's willingness to take as his own the goods appropriated by the seller, subject to rescission and return if defects are afterwards discovered. . . . . This does not mean that a buyer is helpless if the goods when they reach their destination are found to be defective. His assent to the appropriation of goods in a deliverable state is not assent to the appropriation of any goods, though of a kind or a quality at variance with the contract. On the other hand, his assent will stand, and may not be retracted, if the variance is pretended. There is no distinction in this respect between delivery to the buyer through a carrier or other intermediary and delivery to the buyer personally. The question in each case is whether delivery is made in such circumstances as to indicate assent to the appropriation by the seller. . . . .

"When we speak of delivery, we must be on our guard, nonetheless, against misleading ambiguities. Delivery to be operative as a transfer of the property must be assented to by the buyer. . . . . The examination is waived, however, in so far as it is a condition precedent to the transfer of the property, when there is an assent to delivery without reservation or condition accompanying the receipt and qualifying or postponing or neutralizing its effect. Examination prior to such acceptance is indeed, as we have seen, to be permitted 'on request,' yet even when requested, it is immediate and summary, closing, at least in ordinary conditions, with the close of the day, for which reason tender must be made at a seasonable hour.

"Undoubtedly, a right survives to examine and reject thereafter, but it survives as a condition subsequent, and its exercise does not bar an action for the price if the goods rejected were in truth in a deliverable state. When we speak of the condition as subsequent, we mean that assent to the appropriation stands unless revoked for a sufficient cause. It is a different question whether in the event of revocation, the seller is relieved of the burden of proving as a condition precedent to recovery that the goods, though appropriated with assent, conform in kind and quality to those called for by the contract. Enough for present purpose that the effect of receipt without reservation or disclaimer is to defer the examination indefinitely for the convenience of the buyer. True, a dissent must be announced within a reasonable time, but a reasonable time is without determinate limits and varies with the facts. If title does not pass when there is assent to a consummated delivery, the seller will have to bear the risk of the destruction of the goods during a period of indeterminate duration, though he has complied with his contract and the grounds of rejection are capricious or pretended. There can be little doubt that the announcement of such a rule will be a shock to the average merchant who believes that he is through with the transaction upon delivery accepted by the buyer, unless indeed he has made delivery of goods that are defective. If conflicting interpretations of the statute are reasonably possible, our preference should be for the one that keeps it in accord with mercantile practice.

Rheinstrom et al. v. Steiner et al.
69 Ohio St. 452, 69 N.E. 745 (1904)

This was an action by Wm. Steiner Sons & Co. (plaintiffs) against Rheinstrom Bros. (defendants). Judgment for plaintiffs and defendant appealed. Judgment reversed.

Defendants ordered a quantity of labels to be manufactured by the plaintiffs. The labels were to be manufactured according to sketches furnished the plaintiffs by the defendants. When the labels were delivered, they were not according to the sketches, and defendants wrote plaintiffs that the labels were not satisfactory. A few days later a representative of the plaintiffs called at the defendants' place of business, and defendants told the representative that they could not use the labels. They also requested the representative to take the labels but he refused to do so. The defendants did not return the labels nor did they use any of them. Plaintiffs claim that defendants' failure to return the labels amounted to an acceptance.

Spear, J. The burden was upon plaintiffs below to prove a compliance with their contract. The effect of the finding and judgment of the common pleas on the issues is that the goods furnished were not the goods ordered. The finding and judgment in this respect not having been found erroneous by the circuit court, but the judgment in respect thereto having been affirmed, the only ground on which a recovery could have been predicated was that the goods had been accepted by the buyers, and hence they were liable for the price. Here, too, the burden was on the sellers. Their own evidence shows conclusively that the buyers did not accept, unless a failure to manually return the rejected goods is, in law, an acceptance. Is it? From the standpoint of ordinary fairness, how is it? The buyers had ordered labels of a specified kind. The sellers had delivered labels of a different kind, not conforming to the agreement, of which facts the sellers were at once, by letter, fully apprised, to which they responded that, by the time their letter should reach the buyers, one of their firm would call, and matters could be explained. He did call, and was distinctly notified that the labels were wholly useless to the buyers, and as distinctly informed that they were rejected. On what principle of commercial dealing could they ask the buyers to take further trouble in the matter, at the peril of being compelled to pay for a wholly useless article, and one which they had not purchased? We can conceive of no rule of business comity which would justify such a claim. If maintainable at all, it must be by force of some rigid rule of law.

Numerous authorities are cited by counsel for defendants in error which bear on the subject of sales, and afford general rules which should govern the conduct of the buyer where the goods are not satisfactory. Without doubt, the rule is well settled that the buyer's retention of the goods beyond a reasonable time for examination and communication with the seller, standing alone, will be regarded as warranting the conclusion that he has accepted, and thus become liable, especially if the delay has worked prejudice to the seller. But we find no case, either among those cited or elsewhere, analogous to the case at bar on its facts, and none in which mere failure to make manual return of the goods after a timely and explicit rejection of them, and where it appears that no prejudice to the seller has been caused by the delay, is held to make the buyer liable under the contract. On the contrary, there is abundant authority for the proposition that, unless otherwise agreed, where goods are delivered to the buyer, and he refuses to accept them, having the right so to do, he is not bound to return them to the seller, but it is sufficient if he informs the seller that he refuses to accept them.

Unpaid Seller's Lien and Stoppage in Transitu

If the property in the goods has passed to the buyer but the seller retains possession, the seller may retain such possession until the purchase price has been paid unless the goods have been sold on credit. However, if goods have been sold on credit and before delivery the seller learns that the buyer is insolvent, he may retain possession until the purchase price is paid or secured. When the seller retains possession of the goods, property being in the buyer, the seller is said to have an unpaid seller's lien. If he surrenders the goods to the buyer or waives his lien rights, he thereby loses his lien. When the seller has an "unpaid seller's lien" on the goods, if the buyer does not accept and pay for the goods within a reasonable time, the seller may sell the goods and hold the buyer for the resulting loss. The seller may sell at public or private sale but must make a reasonable sale.

The seller is not required to give the buyer notice of his intention to sell nor is he required to give the buyer notice of the time or place of sale, but it is good practice for the seller to give the buyer such notice. Under the provisions of the Uniform Sales Act, the giving of such notice is evidence of the lapse of reasonable time and is also evidence of the seller's good faith.

When the seller delivers the goods to the carrier and the property passes to the buyer, the seller under certain conditions may recall the goods and retain his seller's lien. This right is known as stoppage in transitu. To entitle the seller to exercise this right, the buyer must be insolvent and the goods must be in transit. The goods are in transit from the time they are delivered to the carrier for the purpose of transmission to the buyer until the buyer takes delivery of them from the carrier. If the buyer obtains possession of the goods or if on their arrival the carrier acknowledges that he holds the goods for the buyer, the transit is terminated. Where part delivery has been made, the right of stoppage in transitu may be exercised as to the remainder unless the part delivery was such as to show an agreement with the buyer to give up possession of the whole of the goods. If a negotiable document of title representing the goods has been issued by the carrier or other bailee, the seller is not entitled to the return of the goods until he first surrenders such document. This requirement requires the seller to recover from the buyer, or other persons who might have such document of title, the negotiable document of title before he is entitled to the return of the goods. If such document of title has been properly negotiated to a bona fide purchaser, his claim to the goods is paramount to that of the seller.

To exercise the right of stoppage in transitu, the seller must obtain actual possession of the goods or give notice of his claim to the carrier or bailee who has possession of the goods or to an agent of such carrier or bailee. The notice must be given at such time and under such circumstances that, by the exercise of reasonable diligence, delivery of the goods to the buyer may be prevented.

In exercising his right of stoppage in transitu, the seller should carefully check on the solvency of the buyer. The right is based on the buyer's insolvency; consequently, if the seller stops the goods while in transit and reclaims them and the buyer is not insolvent, the seller is liable for failure to deliver the goods. In those instances in which the buyer has been adjudged a bankrupt, a receiver has been appointed, or an assignment for the benefit of creditors has been made, the seller is safe in exercising this right, but if the seller exercises the right on the strength of a credit report or similar information, he will be assuming a substantial risk.

Ellis v. Greenbaum Sons Inv. Co.
307 Pa. 77, 160 Atl. 702 (1932)

This was an action by Abraham M. Ellis (plaintiff) against Greenbaum Sons Investment Company (defendant). Judgment for plaintiff and defendant appealed. Judgment affirmed.

Plaintiff purchased certain bonds from the defendant and, at the time of the purchase, the defendant contracted to repurchase the bonds at the sale price less 1 per cent. The plaintiff tendered the bonds to the defendant and demanded that the defendant repurchase the bonds in accordance with its contract of repurchase, but the defendant refused to do so. The defendant was the only market for the bonds, but the plaintiff had an opportunity to and did resell part of the bonds. The plaintiff tendered the unsold bonds to defendant and brought this suit to recover the agreed repurchase price of the bonds less the sum received from the sale of the bonds which had been resold before suit was brought. Defendant claims that it is entitled to the return of all the bonds, and if plaintiff cannot return all the bonds, he is not entitled to recover.

Kephart, J. Appellee's rights are fixed by section 63, subd. 3 of the Sales Act which provides that, if the goods cannot be readily resold for a reasonable price, the seller may offer to deliver the goods to the buyer, and, if the buyer refuses to receive them, may notify the buyer that the goods are thereafter held by the seller as bailee for the buyer, and may thereafter treat the goods as the buyer's and may maintain an action for the price. Section 54 of the Sales Act provides that an unpaid seller of goods who is in possession of them is entitled to retain possession of them until payment or tender of the price, and that he may exercise his right of lien, notwithstanding that he is in possession of the goods as agent or bailee for the buyer. While appellee held the bonds, as he was entitled to do, he retained his lien on them; this even after he had obtained judgment for the purchase price (see Section 56 of the act). But he is not required to hold the goods indefinitely; if the buyer has been in default an unreasonable time, and, if he has an opportunity to sell, he may do so under Section 60 of the act and credit the proceeds of such sale against any loss that may have been occasioned by the breach of the contract of sale. The appellee, under such circumstances, had the right to sell any of the property in his hands and on which he had a lien without releasing the company from liability for breach of contract. Where part of the goods are sold as here, the measure of damages is the difference between the repurchase price and the price realized from sale. There is no allegation that the bonds could have brought a better price. Appellant's contention that the latter part of Section 63 of the Sales Act should apply is groundless, for the reason that it is applicable only where "the price is payable on a day certain, irrespective of delivery or of transfer of title." This is not our case. On the other hand, Sections 56 and 60 of the above act cover it, and provide for the retention of the seller's lien and his right of sale elsewhere. Greenbaum Company was the only market for these bonds, and, after the tender and refusal under the contract to repurchase, appellee was entitled to maintain his action for the purchase price.

In re Nesto
Appeal of Ellis
270 Fed. 503 (1921)

This action was a bankruptcy proceeding against R. Nesto. From an order requiring the payment of the proceeds from the sale of certain property to Connellsville Macaroni Company, A. C. Ellis, receiver, appealed. Order affirmed.

Connellsville Macaroni Company sold to R. Nesto a carload of macaroni on credit and consigned it to him at Pittsburgh. The car arrived at Pittsburgh on November 12, 1919. Nesto immediately reconsigned the car to R. Ferri at New York where it arrived on November 20. On the same day an involuntary petition in bankruptcy was filed against R. Nesto, and A. C. Ellis was appointed receiver. R. Nesto and R. Ferri were the same person. Nesto was doing business in New York under the name of Ferri and was making purchases under the name of Nesto of Pittsburgh and was immediately reconsigning the goods to Ferri in New York and thereby attempting to defraud his creditors.

The Macaroni Company issued a stoppage in transitu order after the macaroni was reconsigned by Nesto to Ferri but before the car was actually delivered to A. C. Ellis, the receiver in bankruptcy proceedings. A. C. Ellis contends that the original transit terminated when the car was reconsigned to Ferri; the Macaroni Company contends that the reconsignment was a continuation of the original transit and that they are entitled to the goods. (By agreement the macaroni was resold and the respective claims attached to the proceeds of the sale.)

Woolley, C. J. On these facts alone there can be no dispute as to what the law is or what the decision should be. The law briefly stated is this: In the sale of goods to one becoming insolvent, the vendor's right to stop them is restricted to their transit. After their arrival at the appointed destination and their delivery to the purchaser the transit is at an end; and if later, the goods are moved toward another destination under fresh directions by the purchaser a new transit is begun, which is no part of the original transit, and the vendor's right to stop is gone. .

In aid of the exercise of this right, the statute defines affirmatively when the goods are in transit and negatively when they are not. Of these several provisions, the only ones pertinent to this issue are the following:

"First. Goods are in transit, within the meaning of section fifty-seven—

"(a) From the time when they are delivered to a carrier by land or water, or other bailee, for the purpose of transmission to the buyer, until the buyer, or his agent in that behalf, takes delivery of them from such carrier or other bailee.

"Second. Goods are no longer in transit, within the meaning of section fifty-seven—

"(b) If, after the arrival of the goods at the appointed destination, the carrier or other bailee acknowledges to the buyer or his agent that he holds the goods on his behalf and continues in possession of them as bailee for the buyer or his agent; and it is immaterial that further destination for the goods may have been indicated by the buyer;

"(c) If the carrier or other bailee wrongfully refuses to deliver the goods to the buyer, or his agent in that behalf."

In a word it appears from both the general rule and its statutory embodiment that a seller's right of stoppage in transitu upon discovery of the buyer's insolvency rests on the fact that the goods are in transit; and the fact of transit turns on the question whether or not delivery has been made to the buyer. Applying this test to the surface facts of this case (which show that Nesto, the buyer at Pittsburgh, although he never assumed actual possession and therefore never took actual delivery of the goods, rebilled the goods to an ostensibly new purchaser at a new destination), it would seem that Nesto had acquired such dominion and had exercised such control over the goods as to establish a new transit and defeat the seller's right to stoppage therein. If the reconsignment of the goods by Nesto at Pittsburgh to Ferri at New York was made pursuant to a bona fide resale thereof by Nesto to Ferri, obviously Nesto's Receiver in bankruptcy could have no right to them. In order, we apprehend, to show that the goods belonged to the bankrupt and therefore to establish a receiver's right to their possession, the Receiver, in his petition to the court for leave to execute the bond in question, averred the following fact:

"The said Romeo Nesto (the bankrupt) consigned to himself as R. Ferri, the following cars of merchandise (eight in number) via the Pennsylvania Railroad and are now held by said Pennsylvania Railroad at New York City and said cars contain macaroni, olive oil and other groceries."

The car in controversy was one of the number. At this juncture Nesto absconded.

Assuming it to be a fact on the Receiver's admission that Ferri, the consignee in what purported to be the second transit, was no other than Nesto, the consignee in the first transit, and that the two nominal consignees were one and the same person (but for which we surmise, the Receiver could not have made a valid claim to possession of the bankrupt's property) there at once arose the question whether Nesto ever took delivery of the goods at Pittsburgh, and whether, accordingly, the seller's right to stoppage in transitu was lost at Pittsburgh or continued to New York. This question, as in every case of stoppage in transitu, turns on the fact of delivery.

Delivery in the law of sales may be either actual or constructive. Actual delivery consists in giving the buyer, or his accredited agent, the real possession of the goods sold. Constructive delivery comprehends those acts which, although not truly conferring real possession of the goods sold, are held constructione juris equivalent to acts of real delivery. In this sense it includes symbolical or substituted delivery. Both actual and constructive delivery, however, contemplate the absolute giving up of control and custody of the goods on the part of the seller and the assumption of the same by the buyer. Applying this unquestioned rule to the facts in this case, as completed by the Receiver's admission that Ferri and Nesto were but different names for the same person, what do we find as to the fact of delivery?

That there was no actual delivery is not seriously disputed. When the car reached Pittsburgh the carrier notified Nesto of its arrival. Without assuming possession of the same, and, so far as we are shown, without seeing the car, Nesto immediately reconsigned it to himself under a new name at a new destination. From the very nature of the transaction there was no actual delivery to Nesto at Pittsburgh. His reconsignment of the car to himself, although under an assumed name, was a declination by him to accept delivery at Pittsburgh and an affirmation of his intention to accept delivery at New York. Was there constructive delivery? While ordinarily the law would raise a delivery by construction under circumstances which brings the goods within the dominion of the purchaser, where he has exercised full control over them by bona fide reconsigning them, the law will not hold a delivery as constructive—that is, the law will not construe as done that which was really not done—in aid of an obviously fraudulent transaction.

Therefore we hold that at the time the Macaroni Company notified the carrier at New York of its right to stop the shipment in transitu, delivery, either actual or constructive, had not been made to the buyer, under either his real or fictitious name, and therefore, as against Nesto, the Macaroni Company's right to stoppage in transitu was preserved.

Hunter v. [illegible] Director General of Railroads
184 N.Y.S. 433 (1920)

This was an action by Martha E. Hunter (plaintiff) against John Barton Payne, Director General of Railroads (defendant). Judgment for defendant.

The Viking Corporation, a manufacturer of spark plugs, borrowed about $3,000 from plaintiff and, as security, pledged and delivered to plaintiff about 5,000 spark plugs. Viking Corporation received from Burd-Ring Sales Co. of Chicago an order for spark plugs. It was unable to fill the order from its own stock and made arrangements with the plaintiff to ship the plugs held by her. It agreed to turn over to her the money that would be received on the sale thereof to apply on the loan. The terms of the sale to Burd-Ring Sales Co. was to be cash on receipt of bill of lading and invoice. Burd-Ring Sales Co. had no knowledge of plaintiff's interest in the spark plugs. Viking Corporation owed Burd-Ring Sales Co. about $3,000 which was overdue. After the plugs were shipped, Burd-Ring Sales Co. notified Viking Corporation that they would give Viking credit on account for the purchase price of the plugs. Plaintiff was notified and notice of stoppage in transitu was given to the carrier. The carrier delivered the plugs in violation of the notice given and this suit is to recover for the resulting damages.

Davis, J. It is apparent that the plaintiff's claim to recover must fail, if she is relying upon the rights of a shipper of stoppage in transitu. There is no claim or evidence that the consignee was insolvent. The right of stoppage in transitu arises solely when an unpaid seller has shipped goods to an insolvent buyer.

The case upon which plaintiff's counsel strongly relies to establish the liability of the defendant is a case where the buyers became insolvent, and the seller, learning of it, gave notice to the carrier to stop the shipment, and thereafter, through the negligence of the carrier, the merchandise was delivered to the buyers, and it was held that the plaintiff could recover damages of the carrier to the extent of the value of the goods, by reason of its negligent failure to obey the instructions of the plaintiffs and return the goods. The difference between that case and the one at bar is the vital one—that in the case cited the buyers were insolvent, and the right of stoppage in transitu had arisen, while in the case here the buyer was solvent, and that right had not arisen.

Plaintiff's counsel urges, however, that a property interest in the goods remained in the plaintiff, even after delivery to the carrier, so long as the consignee failed to make payment in cash or by its check; that she had a right to stop or divert the shipment; that when the agent of the defendant at Fulton was given such instruction, and was furnished an indemnity bond, such as he required, the defendant was charged with the absolute duty of returning the goods to her, and his negligent failure to act according to instructions fixes the defendant's liability.

I cannot follow the reasoning of the learned counsel to this conclusion. Undoubtedly, on a sale without credit, a failure to pay cash contemporaneously with the receipt of goods on the part of the buyer nullifies the sale, and gives to the seller the right to retake or replevy the goods. But if the goods are sold to a buyer, who is a creditor of the seller in a larger amount than the purchase price, I can find no authority holding that the rule just stated is then operative. It seems to me that in such a case, unless there was a special, definite agreement expressly forbidding the buyer to apply the debt to the payment of the goods, the buyer would be entitled to treat the existing debt as equivalent to a cash payment, and could successfully interpose defenses of offset, counterclaim, and payment, in an action to recover damages or for replevin.

The delivery to the carrier constituted a delivery to the purchaser, subject to the right of stoppage in transitu, and the unpaid seller loses his lien on the goods by such delivery.

Refusal to Deliver

If the seller has entered into a contract to sell or has made a sale and refuses to deliver the goods according to the contract, the buyer's remedies will depend on the terms of the contract and the circumstances of the case.

If the property in the goods has passed to the buyer and the seller refuses to deliver the goods, the buyer has an election of remedies. He may sue for breach of the contract and recover damages, or he may bring an action in tort based on the conversion of the goods by the seller and recover damages in tort, or he may replevin the goods from the seller. The buyer is given the fullest possible relief.[4]

If title has not passed and the seller wrongfully refuses to deliver the goods, the buyer may bring an action for damages for non-delivery. The measure of damages is substantially the same as in other cases of breach of contract. If the goods can be purchased in the market, in the absence of special circumstances, it will be the difference between the contract price and the market price at the time and place of delivery. If no specific time is fixed for delivery, the damages will be the difference between the contract price and the market price at the time of refusal to deliver. In some cases a court of equity will grant specific performance of a contract to sell, but such remedy will not be allowed unless a money judgment would be an inadequate remedy.

O'Kane v. North American Distilling Co.
171 N.Y.S. 275 (1918)

This was an action by Francis O'Kane (plaintiff) against the North American Distilling Company (defendant). Judgment for plaintiff for \$69.82 and plaintiff appealed. Judgment reversed and new trial ordered.

The plaintiff, in October, 1911, purchased from the defendant fifteen barrels of whisky in bond and paid therefor \$156 in cash and gave ten notes of \$31.10 each, payable monthly. The whisky was stored in defendant's bonded United States warehouse under a standard warehouse agreement. In 1914, the defendant sold the whisky to a third person for the net sum of \$213.07. This sale was wrongful and the trial court allowed the plaintiff to recover \$69.82 which was the \$213.07 less a sum due defendant for the unpaid balance of the purchase price, storage, etc. Plaintiff contends that he is entitled to recover the value of the whisky at the time of the conversion—\$311.50.

Lehman, J. There can be no doubt but that the sale was a sale of specific goods set aside for delivery to the plaintiff, and that the delivery of the warehouse receipts constituted a symbolic delivery of title to the plaintiff, and that thereby he became the owner of the goods, subject only to a reserved right of possession by the seller until the amount of the purchase price was paid. If the defendant thereafter wrongfully sold these goods, the plaintiff was not obliged to make a useless demand for the goods and tender of their price; but he could sue in conversion for the value of the goods, or he could disregard the tort and bring a suit for money had and received, upon the theory that the defendant by its action had rescinded the contract

[4] Uniform Sales Act, sec. 66, appendix, p. 903.

of sale and revested title in itself, and was therefore bound to return to the plaintiff the consideration paid by him. The rescission in such case would be made not by the plaintiff, but by the defendant, and the plaintiff would not be required to tender back to the defendant the warehouse receipts delivered to him, for these warehouse receipts were at that time nothing more than waste paper.

Bowman v. Adams et al.
45 Idaho, 200, 261 Pac. 679 (1927)

This was an action by R. A. Bowman (plaintiff) against L. R. Adams and others (defendants). Judgment for plaintiff and defendants appealed. Judgment reversed and remanded.

Plaintiff agreed to sell and deliver to defendants 5,500 ewes (later the number was increased to 13,002) on or before September 25, 1922. Defendants were to pay five cents a pound. $2,500 was to be paid in cash and the balance on delivery. At the same time the parties entered into another contract by the terms of which the defendants agreed to resell the ewes to plaintiff. Defendants were to fatten the ewes, were to begin redelivery after 90 days, and were to complete the delivery before February 23, 1923. The plaintiff credited $2 per head on the purchase price paid by the defendants and agreed to pay seven cents per pound. All ewes redelivered were to be "strictly fat ewes." Defendants borrowed money from Western Bond and Mortgage Co. to pay for the sheep and buy feed and gave the Western Bond and Mortgage Co. a mortgage on the sheep. After 90 days defendants cut out of the flock 3,200 ewes and tendered them to plaintiff, who refused to accept them as "strictly fat ewes," and demanded that they be allowed to cut out the ewes that they did not consider as "strictly fat ewes." Defendants refused. Later defendants shipped 2,200 of the ewes and turned the proceeds over to the Western Bond and Mortgage Co. Plaintiff brings this suit asking that the defendants be enjoined from selling the remaining ewes and asking specific performance of the contract.

Brinck, C. The only theory upon which respondent cites any authorities in support of his contention (that he is entitled to specific performance of the contract) is the rule applied in cases of executory contracts of sale of real estate that a vendor of real estate holds the title in trust for the vendee. This rule is not in general applied to sales of personal property, but is merely a right recognized under contracts of sale of real estate by reason of the peculiar nature of real property whereby equity has come to recognize a right to the specific performance of such contract. Where a contract is susceptible of specific performance in equity, the vendee has an equitable interest in the property to be conveyed, and it is considered that the vendor's title is burdened with a trust in favor of the vendee. The same doctrine is applicable in sales of personal property where goods are of a peculiar nature and value to the vendee of the property, so that pecuniary damages at law are inadequate. In such cases, it is considered that the purchaser, having a right to the very thing itself, has an equitable interest in it. But in the sale of ordinary chattels, which have a market value, the legal remedy of damages is adequate, and there is no necessity for equitable interference, and for such specific performance. In such case, where no lien is expressly granted to the vendee by the contract, the vendee has no equitable interest in the thing itself.

Plaintiff seeks to bring himself within a familiar exception to the general rule against the specific performance of a contract for the sale of chattels by alleging and testifying that the time when defendants refused to deliver the sheep, there was not available a like number and kind of sheep which plaintiff might have bought. A contract for the sale and delivery of chattels which are essential in specie to the plaintiff, and which defendant can supply, while no one else can, can be specifically enforced. But in the present case, the only sheep which plaintiff was to receive were strictly fat sheep, ready for market, and intended by him to be immediately resold. They were in no wise indispensable to him, since he sought only to resell them and reap a profit, the amount of which was alleged and determinable. In his complaint, he alleges the actual value of the sheep to be $90,000. Even when a chattel is special and unique, if its pecuniary value can be readily ascertained, so that the remedy of damages is adequate, specific performance will not be granted. So, where the plaintiff has contracted to sell the article to a third person, or alleges the actual value of the article, thus putting an exact estimate upon the amount of damage, he will suffer by breach of the contract, specific performance will not be awarded. We think, therefore, that under the allegations in this case, damages at law are shown to be adequate.

Purchase Price or Damages

If the buyer refuses to accept the goods when tendered or notifies the seller that he cancels the contract, the seller is entitled to recover damages which he has suffered as the result of the breach of the contract. If title to the goods has passed to the buyer, the seller may hold the goods as bailee for the buyer and recover a judgment for the purchase price of the goods.

As a general rule, if title to the goods has not passed to the buyer, the seller's only remedy is an action for damages for breach of the contract. However, if the goods contracted for cannot be readily resold for a reasonable price, the seller may offer to deliver the goods to the buyer, and if the buyer refuses to accept the goods, the seller may notify the buyer that the goods are thereafter held as bailee for the buyer and maintain an action for the purchase price. If the seller does not notify the buyer, within a reasonable time, that he is holding the goods as bailee for the buyer, the seller will lose his right to recover the purchase price of the goods.

If the contract of sale expressly provides that the buyer will pay the purchase price at a stated date, which is before the date of delivery, and the buyer does not pay as agreed, the seller can maintain an action for the purchase price unless the buyer can show that the seller will be unable to deliver the goods as required by the contract.

If title has passed to the buyer and the buyer is in default, the seller may hold the goods a reasonable time, and if the buyer has not accepted the goods, the seller may sell the goods for the account of the buyer and recover from the buyer as damages the difference between the contract price and the sale price plus reasonable costs. On such a resale the seller is not bound to give the buyer notice that he intends to resell the goods, nor does he have to give the buyer notice of the time and place of such resale; however, it is good business practice to give the buyer timely notice of the intent to resell and also of the time and place of the resale. If such notice is given, it is strong evidence of the seller's good faith.

Cohen v. La France Workshop, Inc.
112 Pa. Super. Ct. 309, 171 Atl. 90 (1934)

This was an action by Benjamin Cohen (plaintiff) against the La France Workshop, Incorporated (defendant). Judgment for plaintiff and defendant appealed. Judgment reversed and remanded.

The defendant, a manufacturer of lamp shades, placed an order with the plaintiff, a manufacturer of wire frames for lamp shades, for fifty thousand such wire frames. Forty thousand were manufactured, delivered, accepted, and paid for. This suit was brought to recover the purchase price of the remaining ten thousand. Plaintiff claimed they were manufactured and tendered but defendant refused to accept and pay for them. Defendant claimed the frames did not comply with the contract.

Parker, J. This action, as shown by the pleadings and proofs, is for the purchase price agreed upon and not for damages sustained by reason of breach of contract by the vendee. Considering section 63 of the Sales Act, the first and pertinent inquiry is whether the ownership and title to the goods had passed. In our opinion, the contract was executory. In other words, it was not a purchase of existing specific property, but an agreement to purchase unascertained and nonexistent goods to be thereafter produced. The order for the goods was by a catalogue number of which the following is a typical example: "1000 31-10 Frames at .06 $60.00." The plaintiff testified that he manufactured the goods after the order was placed. "An agreement to sell future goods is executory and does not pass the title, although couched in the present tense." In cases where personal property of a certain description is purchased but not identified or selected from a mass of the property of the vendor, the contract is executory and incomplete and the title to it remains in the vendor.

The third paragraph of section 63 of the Sales Act is as follows: "Although the property in the goods has not passed, if they cannot readily be resold for a reasonable price, and if the provisions of section sixty-four are not applicable, the seller may offer to deliver the goods to the buyer, and, if the buyer refuses to receive them, may notify the buyer that the goods are thereafter held by the seller as bailee for the buyer. Thereafter the seller may treat the goods as the buyer's, and may maintain an action for the price."

The appellant contends very earnestly that the trial court should have said as a matter of law that the lamp shade wires could readily be resold for a reasonable price. There was not any direct evidence on this subject. We are dependent alone upon the fact that the purchase was made of an article described by a catalogue number. Under such circumstances we cannot say as a matter of law that the goods could or could not be readily sold for a reasonable price. These are not articles the nature and use of which are matters of common knowledge, or where it is a matter of common knowledge that such articles have a ready sale for a reasonable price, such as sauerkraut. Neither does it appear that these goods, although manufactured, were only useful to the buyer, such as a suit of clothes, structural steel cut to special sizes, etc. It did not, however, affirmatively appear that the goods did not have a ready sale for a reasonable price.

There is a more serious difficulty. There is neither an averment in the pleadings nor any proof that the seller notified the buyer "that the goods are (were) thereafter held by the seller as bailee for the buyer." Such being the case, the seller has failed to bring himself within the provisions of this section of the Sales Act and his remedy, if any, is by an action for damages for nonacceptance. We cannot regard this provision as anything else than mandatory. It was the apparent purpose of the Legislature to require the seller to take a definite position in this respect before starting suit by declaring himself bailee for the buyer. The failure of the plaintiff to offer proof of such notice was fatal to his case. "It is essential to bring a case within the rule that the goods cannot be readily resold, and that the seller has notified the buyer that the goods are held as a bailment for him."

Knight & Bostwick v. Moore
203 Wis. 540, 234 N.W. 902 (1931)

This was an action by Knight & Bostwick (plaintiff) against E. C. Moore (defendant). Judgment for the defendant and plaintiff appealed. Judgment reversed and remanded. (The judgment of the trial court was reversed because of errors on points of law not included in this extract.)

Moore ordered nursery stock from plaintiff. Before it was selected and packed for shipment, Moore cancelled the order, claiming fraud. Plaintiff shipped the stock and now sues to recover the purchase price.

Fowler, J. The plaintiff claims that it is entitled to judgment for the full purchase price of the goods ordered. This claim cannot be upheld. The plaintiff received the countermand of the order before the goods were shipped or packed. The defendant might breach his promise not to countermand, just as he might breach his promise to pay. His breach entitled the plaintiff to recover the damages consequent on the breach, but did not entitle it to ship the goods and recover the purchase price. Its damages were the expense, if any, that it had undergone pursuant to fulfillment of the order up to the time of the cancellation and the profits of its bargain.

Breach of Warranty

In the event of a breach of warranty, the buyer is entitled to alternative remedies. The buyer may accept or keep the goods and set up against the seller the breach of warranty by way of recoupment in diminution or extinction of the purchase price. The practical result of this remedy is that the buyer is permitted to keep the goods and pay the seller the reasonable value of the goods. If the buyer wishes to pursue this remedy, he must give the seller notice of his intent within a reasonable time after he receives the goods.

When the goods are not as warranted, the buyer may pursue his remedy for breach of contract. The buyer may refuse to receive the goods and maintain an action for damages, or he may receive the goods and set up the breach of warranty by way of set-off. If he elects to pursue the latter remedy, in many instances, the result will be substantially the same as though the first remedy discussed were pursued.

If title to the goods has not passed to the buyer, or if title has passed to the buyer but the goods remain in the possession of the seller, the buyer may rescind the contract for the seller's breach of warranty and get restitution of any payments already made. If the title to the goods has passed to the buyer and the goods are in the buyer's possession, the buyer may return the goods or offer to return the goods to the seller and get restitution of any payments already made. If the buyer is in possession of the goods and rescinds the contract for breach of warranty, the buyer may claim a lien on the goods as security for payments made on account. In such cases the rights of the buyer in the goods is the same as that of an unpaid seller who has an unpaid seller's lien on goods. If the buyer wishes to rescind, he must give the seller timely notice. As a general rule, if the parties cannot be put in status quo, the buyer cannot rescind the contract. Also the majority of courts hold that, if the buyer elects to rescind, he is not entitled to damages.

Holcomb & Hoke Mfg. Co. et al. v. Osterberg
181 Minn. 547, 233 N.W. 302 (1930)

This was an action by Holcomb & Hoke Manufacturing Company and another (plaintiffs) against Osterberg (defendant). Judgment for defendant and plaintiffs appealed. Judgment reversed and new trial ordered.

Osterberg purchased, on conditional sales contract, a corn-popping and peanut-roasting machine. The machine was delivered about January 20, 1927. February 1, the defendant wrote the company complaining about the machine and stating he thought it was not a new machine but a rebuilt machine. The first part of April the defendant told the plaintiffs' agent that he did not want the machine. April 23, he consulted an attorney who wrote demanding the company remedy the defects in the machine. Suit was brought by the seller to recover the purchase price some eleven months after delivery. At this time defendant set up rescission of the contract as a defense.

Loring, J. In discussing the question of the defendant's alleged rescission, we shall approach it from the standpoint of the effect of the letter of April 23 upon the conversation which the defendant had had with Vollmer, assuming for the present, but not deciding, that an offer of the character defendant described was as effective as if made directly to the company. The conversation as related by defendant was an unqualified demand that the company take back the machine, but, before the demand was acted upon and before many days had passed, the defendant's legal representatives, not his present counsel, wrote the letter of April 23, which stated defendant's position as being that of unwillingness to pay "unless you can make this machine fulfill its guarantee and work satisfactorily as your contract provides." In effect it was a demand to put the machine in condition to fulfill the warranty, and consequently it was inconsistent with and an abandonment of the previous attempt to rescind. In our opinion it superseded and nullified any offer to turn back the machine. It indicated a purpose to refuse to accept only in case it was established that the machine was rebuilt. This last matter is now outside the issues, because it was not established to be a rebuilt machine, and the trial court so held. Therefore the letter for our present purposes can be construed as if that clause had been omitted. Without it the letter amounts to a request to make the warranty good, not an attempt to rescind. As before stated herein, the company replied to this letter with instructions about how to adjust and operate the machine. After this nothing further was done by defendant looking toward a rescission until this suit was brought and his answer was interposed in January of 1928.

On the trial of the action, the defendant relied upon the conversation of early April as a rescission, and the trial court submitted the case to the jury upon the question as to whether or not this conversation amounted to a rescission. In the light of the letter of April 23, this was error. That disposes of the defendant's claim to a rescission in April. Was his answer a rescission, and if so, was it timely? We are of the opinion that it was not timely. The Uniform Sales Act provides, that the buyer must "notify the seller within a reasonable time of the election to rescind." This was the rule prior to the statute. In 2 Black on Rescission and Cancellation, § 536, the author has selected, in a comprehensive note, the latest and most important from the multitude of cases which support this doctrine of the necessity of reasonable promptness in making a rescission. In commenting thereon in the text he says: "The true doctrine is that, after discovering the facts justifying rescission the party is entitled to a reasonable time in which to decide upon the course he will take. But this does not mean that he will be indulged in a vacillating or hesitating course of conduct, but that he must act with such a measure of promptness as can fairly be called 'reasonable' with reference to all the circumstances of the particular case." The reasonable time begins to run from the time of discovery of the facts on which the right to rescission is based. 2 Black on Rescission and Cancellation, § 538. In the case at bar this discovery was made not more than a month after the receipt of the machine. From this time the reasonable time for defendant to rescind would begin to run, unless he was led by promises or other inducement from the company to delay the exercise of the right. Had he adhered to his intention as announced to Vollmer early in April, he might have been held to be within a reasonable time, owing to the peculiar circumstances of the case. But when he consulted a firm of lawyers of high standing and instructed them to write the letter of April 23 without any inducement from the company to reconsider his course, he deliberately abandoned his efforts at rescission and never resumed them until he put in his answer in January, 1928, eleven months after he admits discovery of the defects and discovery of his inability to remedy them by change in method of operation. We can find no case in the books where, in such a case, indulgence has been extended so far as to allow the assertion of the right of rescission so long after discovery of the right.

In commenting on rescission of sales of personal property, Black, in section 542 of the work above cited, says: "It is of course impossible to fix an absolute limit of time within which such action must be taken, as each case must be governed by its own circumstances. But from an examination of the authorities it would appear that thirty days is about the utmost length of time which the courts are disposed to allow to the purchaser for this purpose, unless there are unusual circumstances in the case excusing a longer delay. At any rate periods of time ranging from one month to a year have been held too great to save the party attempting to rescind from the imputation of laches, while, on the other hand, purchasers who have rescinded within periods extending from one day to thirty days have been held to have acted with reasonable promptness." We do not attempt to fix any arbitrary limit, but the right of rescission must be exercised with reasonable promptness.

We are constrained to hold that the lapse of time from the discovery by defendant of the machine's defects until he set up a rescission was laches as a matter of law. It appears, however, that the defendant may have cause of action or counterclaim for damages upon appropriate amendment of his pleadings. Such amendment is within the discretion of the trial court. It is therefore not a case for judgment notwithstanding the verdict.

Dunck Tank Works, Inc. v. Sutherland
236 Wis. 83, 294 N.W. 510 (1940)

This was an action by Dunck Tank Works, Inc. (plaintiff) against Frank Sutherland, trustee of the City Beverage Company, a bankrupt (defendant). Judgment for defendant and plaintiff appealed. Judgment modified and affirmed.

The City Beverage Company purchased from the plaintiff four pressure tanks, to be used in the former's brewery, for the sum of $1,500. When the tanks were installed and tested, it was found that they were porous and could not be used as pressure tanks. City Beverage Company communicated this fact to plaintiff and plaintiff suggested a treatment to the heads of the tanks in the hope that the seepage would stop, but the treatment was unsuccessful. City Beverage Company purchased pressure tanks from other manufacturers and used the tanks purchased from plaintiff as storage tanks. During the summer plaintiff sent its representative to the City Beverage Company's plant to repair the tanks, but the circumstances were such that the City Beverage Company's operations would have been seriously interrupted and loss might have ensued had repairs been made during the time of the visit of plaintiff's representative. Plaintiff sued to recover the unpaid balance of the purchase price, and defendant set up breach of warranty as a defense.

Fairchild, J. The buyer had no duty to request the seller to make good the breach of warranty before being entitled to damages. A defect which amounted to a breach of warranty places upon the seller the duty to remedy without constant requests on the part of the buyer. Where there is a breach of warranty by the seller, the buyer may at his election accept and keep the goods and maintain an action against the seller for damages for the breach of warranty. The tanks were installed in 1933 and they are still in respondent's brewery. They were useful as storage tanks; they were used as such; and in that capacity were worth $200 apiece. No other or special damages were pleaded or shown to have resulted from a breach of the warranty. Damages resulted only because the tanks had less value as storage tanks than they would have had as pressure tanks. The correct measure of damages is the difference between the contract price and the actual value of the tanks at the time of delivery.

Judgment was granted in favor of respondent on its counterclaim and the $850 paid was returned as damages. The findings of the trial court that the warranty was made and that the tanks failed to meet the requirement of that warranty is amply supported by the testimony. But the evidence also showed that the tanks were retained and used as storage tanks and that they are suitable for that purpose.

Rescission is not involved. No attempt was made by the brewery to rescind the contract. The counterclaim for breach of warranty and the fact that use was made of the tanks shows an intention not to rescind. Respondent failed to comply with one of the essential requirements of rescission which is that an unconditional offer to return the property be made.

The result of the dealings and exchanges between the parties is that the property in the goods passed to the buyer with the seller liable to the buyer for the breach of warranty. Although there was a failure on the part of the seller to deliver goods of the character ordered, the retention and use of the goods by the buyer results in an acceptance of the goods as delivered and creates an obligation to pay a reasonable value therefor.

Cause remanded, with directions to modify the judgment by reducing the amount thereof to $50, and when so modified the judgment is affirmed.

QUESTIONS AND PROBLEMS

1. Potter ordered four pieces of goods suitable to be manufactured into cloaks. Each piece was priced separately. When the goods arrived Potter accepted two of the pieces of goods and tendered the amount due for them, $311.19. The remaining two pieces he rejected as not in accordance with the order. Rubin sued to recover the full purchase price of the four pieces, $638.99, claiming that Potter must either accept or reject all of the order. Is Rubin's contention correct?
2. If the sale price of the four pieces of goods had been stated in one sum—$638.99—and the nature of the goods had been such that the value of the separate pieces could not be determined with a reasonable degree of accuracy, would Potter be permitted to retain part of the goods and reject the remainder?
3. Bowen called at Whiting's store at Chicago and ordered a quantity of clothing from samples. The clothing was to be shipped to Bowen at Detroit. Whiting contends that he is entitled to payment for the clothing before Bowen inspects it. Is Whiting's contention correct?
4. Cole purchased from Bartel a quantity of plush coats. The coats reached Cole on August 17 and were unpacked, inspected, tagged, priced, and put in stock. At the time the coats arrived Miss McGuinn, the clerk in charge of the coat department, was in the hospital. She did not return to the store until September 11. Cole and employees in the store inspected the coats and found that some were defective and that three extra coats had been shipped. An attempt was made to remedy the defects. On August 18, Cole wrote Bartel acknowledging receipt of the coats and asking a reduction in price, but he did not object to the quality of the merchandise or mention the extra coats. On September 11, when Miss McGuinn returned to the store, the defective coats and the three extra coats were returned to Bartel together with a check for the purchase price of the coats retained. Did Cole have a right to return the coats?
5. Newman sold Dale ten barrels of oil. Dale paid part down and gave his note for the balance. There was no agreement as to the time of delivery. The oil was left in Newman's warehouse. Three days after the note matured, Dale demanded delivery of the oil but he did not tender the amount due on the note. Is Dale entitled to the oil?
6. Arctic Stores ordered from Douglas a car of tomato pulp which was shipped, consigned to "Arctic Stores, Cussein's Siding, Marion, N.J." The car arrived at Marion and was placed on the siding, which was alongside the warehouse of

Arctic Stores, at 7:00 A.M. At noon the same day Arctic Stores were adjudged bankrupt. Douglas issued a stoppage in transitu order the next day. Is Douglas entitled to the car of tomato pulp?

7. Ray agreed to sell Manton twenty-five shares of the capital stock of the Home Co. Ray refused to deliver the stock. Manton sued asking specific performance of the contract. Manton proved that the Home Co. was a small corporation, that its stock was not sold on the stock market, that its shares did not have an established value, that Ray had the stock, and that twenty-five shares of the stock could not be acquired elsewhere. Should specific performance of the contract be granted?
8. Holt gave the Post Card Co. an order for Christmas cards to be printed specially. The cards were to be shipped August 1. On July 16, Holt cancelled the order but at that time the cards were printed and ready for shipment. In the trade there is no sale for such cards after July 1. Can the Post Card Co. recover the purchase price of the cards?
9. Morris, a manufacturer of axes, purchased from Parks a quantity of steel to be used in the manufacture of axes. The steel was expressly warranted to be equal to the best English ax steel. After the steel was manufactured into axes, it was found to be of inferior quality, and the axes manufactured from it were worth $1.50 per dozen less than they would have been if the quality of the steel had been as warranted. Morris manufactured 2,000 dozen axes from the steel and now sues for $3,000 damages. Is Morris entitled to a $3,000 judgment?
10. Levy purchased a stove from Chonavitz. The stove was warranted but was not as warranted. Levy offered to return the stove and demanded the return of the money he had paid. Chonavitz came for the stove but refused to return the money Levy had paid. Levy refused to allow Chonavitz to take the stove. Is Chonavitz entitled to the return of the stove without returning the down payment to Levy?

PART V

NEGOTIABLE INSTRUMENTS

CHAPTER XXI

INTRODUCTION

Historical Background

A negotiable instrument is a simple contract for the payment of money so drawn that it fulfills definite formal requirements and which, because of its form, is given special characteristics not attributed to contracts in general. It has been used by every society which has developed a commercial system. Its primary function is to facilitate the transaction of business by providing a simple means of extending credit and also by providing a safe and adequate medium which can be used in lieu of money for the payment of debts.

Just when the negotiable instrument was first used is uncertain. There is reliable evidence that negotiable instruments were used by the Egyptians, Babylonians, Greeks, and Romans. The bill of exchange was introduced into England from the continent in the twelfth or thirteenth century and at one time was used among merchants as a substitute for money. When first introduced into England, the bill of exchange was used only by merchants. Cases involving negotiable instruments did not begin to appear in the decisions of the common law courts until the sixteenth and seventeenth centuries and were not common until the beginning of the eighteenth century. The law of negotiable instruments was developed in the merchant courts and was gradually absorbed into the common law of England. This process of absorption was substantially completed when the American colonies gained their independence.

Uniform Negotiable Instruments Law

During the early development of the United States, trade was local in nature, and many usages were developed which were local in their scope. These local usages had their effect on the development of the law in the various sections of the country. This was especially true of the law of negotiable instruments. As trade expanded, the need for greater uniformity became increasingly apparent. In 1895 a conference was held in Detroit, Michigan, at which a resolution was adopted requesting the drafting of a bill to make uniform the law of negotiable instruments. The following year a bill was drafted, and the draft of the proposed law was adopted by the commissioners on uniform state laws and has since been adopted by all the states and by the District of Columbia, Alaska, Hawaii, Puerto Rico, and the Philippine Islands.

Nature of Uniform Law

In drafting the Uniform Negotiable Instruments Law, the commissioners made no attempt to reform the existing law. The law of the majority of the states was in accord in respect to the basic principles; the differences were in matter of details rather than in fundamentals. In drafting the Uniform Law the drafters used the English Bills of Exchange Act as their pattern. If a rule of law was followed by all or substantially all of the states, the drafters of the Uniform Law merely stated the existing law in statutory form. If the law of the states was in conflict as to a rule of law, the drafters of the Uniform Law studied the various decisions and after careful study formulated a rule which in their opinion would best serve the needs of the people. The law was comprehensive in its scope, yet the drafters of the law realized that some points might have been omitted. To cover possible omissions the act expressly provides, "In any case not provided for in this act the rules of the law merchant shall govern." In interpreting and applying the act the court looks to the common law of negotiable instruments, which is essentially the law merchant, as background; consequently, it is necessary to know the common law in order to fully understand the act.

Types of Negotiable Instruments

At common law and by the provisions of the Uniform Negotiable Instruments Law, only those instruments which are payable in money are classed as negotiable. By trade usage and by statute, instruments other than instruments payable in money are given certain characteristics of negotiability. The order bill of lading, the order warehouse receipt, and the certificate of corporate stock are the most widely used of these instruments. The order bill of lading and the order warehouse receipt call for the delivery of goods instead of the payment of money. By statute they are given most of the characteristics of the negotiable instrument. The certificate of corporate stock is evidence of ownership in a corporation and is given many of the characteristics of the negotiable instrument by the Uniform Stock Transfer Act. Other instruments, which are not negotiable under the terms of the Uniform Negotiable Instruments Law but which, either by statute or by usage, are given certain characteristics of negotiability, are registered corporate bonds, municipal warrants, and interim certificates.

Negotiable instruments are divided into three classes in the Uniform Negotiable Instruments Law—promissory notes, bills of exchange, and checks. The promissory note is a promise to pay, and the parties to the promissory note are the maker, who issues the instrument and who makes the promise to pay, and the payee to whom the promise is made.

$ 460.00 July 15 19 46

Sixty days *after date* I *promise to pay to*

the order of James Smith

Four hundred sixty and no/100 *Dollars*

at American National Bank, Chicago, Illinois

Value received.

No. 143 *Due* 9/13/46 Henry Jenkins

PROMISSORY NOTE

The bill of exchange is an order to pay, and the parties to the bill of exchange are the drawer, who draws the instrument, and the drawee, to whom the instrument is addressed, and the payee, who is to receive the money. The check is a bill of exchange drawn on a bank. The

$ 133.47 July 15 1946

On sight *Pay to*

the order of John Doe

One hundred thirty-three and 47/100 WITH EXCHANGE *Dollars*

Value received and charge the same to account of

To American National Bank

Chicago, Illinois Richard Thompson

BILL OF EXCHANGE OR DRAFT

parties to the check are the same as those to a bill of exchange; however, the drawee on a check must be a bank.

Many variations of promissory notes are in common use. A collateral note is a promissory note, combined with a pledge agreement, whereby the maker pledges securities to the payee to secure the payment of the debt. A chattel mortgage note is a combination of a promissory note and a chattel mortgage whereby the maker of the note gives the payee a chattel mortgage on certain personal property as security.

A title-retaining note is a combination of a promissory note and a conditional sales contract whereby the maker promises to pay the purchase price of goods purchased from the payee, but agrees that title to the goods shall remain in the payee until the purchase price is paid in

No. 1046

CHICAGO, July 15 1946

PAY TO THE ORDER OF Harry J. Johnson $298.00

THE SUM 298 DOLS 00 CTS DOLLARS

THE TERMINAL NATIONAL BANK OF CHICAGO

2-83 / 7

MEMBER FEDERAL RESERVE SYSTEM

Robert Clark

CHECK

full. Cognovit notes, which, in addition to the maker's promise to pay, give the payee permission to take judgment against him without trial if the maker fails to pay on the due date, are used in a limited number of states.[1]

The draft is the most common form of bill of exchange in use today. The trade acceptance, which is a draft drawn by the seller of goods on the buyer of goods for the purchase price of the goods, is used extensively in some lines of business. It is a common practice for the drawer of a trade acceptance to name himself as payee. A bank acceptance is a draft drawn on and accepted by a bank. A cashier's check is a bill of exchange drawn by a bank upon itself, and accepted by the act of issuance.

Terms of Negotiable Instruments

On its face a negotiable instrument is a contract for the payment of money, and in many respects the rights of the parties are determined by the application of general contract law. In addition to the terms which are expressed on the face of the instrument, many terms are added by usage. The contract between the maker and payee of a promissory note is expressed with some fullness, but the obligations of the drawer of a bill of exchange to the payee or other holder are not expressed. The same is true of the liabilities assumed by one who indorses a negotiable instrument. The form of the indorsement is also important in determining the contract of the indorser. A negotiable

[1] Judgment notes may be used in Colorado, Delaware, Illinois, Maryland, Ohio, Pennslvania, Tennessee, Virginia, and Wisconsin. In Indiana it is a misdemeanor to induce a person to sign such a note. Burns Anno. Stat., 1933, 2-2906.

instrument has aptly been called a contract in shorthand. The law of negotiable instruments defines the rights and liabilities of the parties. It is to a large extent a statement of the usages which were followed by merchants in their use of negotiable instruments and which crystallized into law.

Benefits of Negotiability

As stated above, a negotiable instrument is fundamentally a simple contract for the payment of money. If it remains in the hands of the original parties to the instrument, the advantages of having the promise negotiable in form are mostly procedural. If a promise to pay money were non-negotiable in form and suit were brought on the contract, the payee-plaintiff would have to prove consideration, but if the promise to pay were negotiable in form, the payee-plaintiff would not have to prove consideration. If no consideration were given or if the consideration had failed, the maker-defendant would have to allege and prove as matter of defense the lack or failure of consideration. However, if the instrument is negotiable in form and has been negotiated to one who can qualify as a holder in due course, the holder in due course acquires greater rights than the party from whom he acquired the instrument.

Archer purchases an automobile from Burch and signs a non-negotiable contract whereby Archer agrees to pay Burch $100. Burch assigns the contract to Fox. When the $100 is due, Fox requests Archer to pay but Archer refuses, claiming that Burch warranted the automobile and that it was not as warranted. This defense is good against Fox. If Archer had given Burch his negotiable promissory note for the $100 and Burch had negotiated it to Fox so that Fox became a holder in due course, Fox could recover from Archer. The defense of breach of warranty is not good against the negotiable note in the hands of a holder in due course.

QUESTIONS AND PROBLEMS

1. What was the form of the negotiable instruments first used in England?
2. Why was the Uniform Negotiable Instruments Law drafted and what is its purpose?
3. How many states have adopted the Uniform Negotiable Instruments Law?
4. What is the form of a note?
5. What is the form of a bill of exchange?
6. What is the form of a check?
7. What is the distinction between the assignment of a contract and the negotiation of a negotiable instrument?

CHAPTER XXII

FORM OF NEGOTIABLE INSTRUMENTS

Importance of Form

Whether or not a contract is a negotiable instrument is a matter of form. A negotiable instrument is a formal contract, that is, it acquires its characteristics of negotiability because of its form. The requirements for negotiability are set out in the Uniform Negotiable Instruments Law as follows:

"1. It must be in writing and signed by the maker or drawer;

"2. Must contain an unconditional promise or order to pay a sum certain in money;

"3. Must be payable on demand, or at a fixed or determinable future time;

"4. Must be payable to order or to bearer; and,

"5. Where the instrument is addressed to a drawee, he must be named or otherwise indicated therein with reasonable certainty."

If the instrument fulfills these requirements, it is a negotiable instrument; if it does not, it is a non-negotiable instrument.

One should not confuse negotiability with validity or collectibility. An instrument signed by an infant, if it complies with the foregoing requirements, is a negotiable instrument. The fact that the defense of infancy would be available if suit were brought against the infant is immaterial. Negotiability depends on form, not on the enforceability of the contract. The same is true of a negotiable instrument given in payment of a gambling debt in a state which has a statute that declares negotiable instruments given in payments of gambling debts to be illegal and void. The instrument may be void, yet, if it is in proper form, it is a negotiable instrument.

To be negotiable the instrument need not follow any particular pattern nor need it follow the language of the statute. Section 10 of the Uniform Negotiable Instruments Law expressly provides, "The instrument need not follow the language of this act, but any terms are sufficient which clearly indicate an intention to conform to the requirements hereof." In the business world printed forms are usually used in drawing negotiable instruments. This is a good business practice in that it helps standardize the forms of negotiable instruments used and also aids in avoiding errors in the drawing of negotiable instruments; yet, an inartistically drawn instrument which fulfills the requirements set out above is negotiable.

"I promise to pay bearer one hundred dollars.

"Albert Archer"

is a negotiable promissory note. Many provisions customarily included in the familiar forms used in business, such as the place and date, the time the instrument is payable, the words "for value received," the rate of interest to be paid, etc., are omitted. However, all of the provisions of the Uniform Negotiable Instruments Law have been satisfied; consequently, the instrument is negotiable.

In Writing and Signed

The requirement that the instrument be in writing is framed in general language. No particular type of writing is required, no particular material is designated on which the writing shall appear; all that is required is that the instrument be in writing. Writing has been defined as "the giving of an outward and objective form to a contract, will, etc., by means of letter or marks placed on paper, parchment or other material substance." [1]

One could draw a valid negotiable instrument on wrapping paper in lead pencil. It would be poor business practice, but it would fulfill the requirement that the instrument be in writing.

It is customary for one to sign a negotiable instrument, subscribing his name in script. The Uniform Negotiable Instruments Law provides that the instrument must be signed by the maker or drawer; it does not define "signed." Anything which can be designated as a signing will satisfy this requirement. "Sign" has been defined as "To make any mark, as upon a document, in token of knowledge, approval, acceptance, or obligation." [2]

An "X" or any other mark may serve as a signature if it is affixed to the instrument for the purpose of authenticating it. To be negotiable the instrument need not be signed in any particular place; however, it is customary to sign negotiable instruments in the lower right hand corner. The Uniform Negotiable Instruments Law does provide [Section 17 (6)]: "Where a signature is so placed upon the instrument that

[1] Black's *Law Dictionary*, 3d ed.
[2] Black's *Law Dictionary*, 3d ed.

it is not clear in what capacity the person making the same intended to sign, he is to be deemed an indorser."

Field et al. v. Lukowiak et al.
114 N.J. Law 268, 176 Atl. 319 (1935)

This was an action by Jerome T. Field and Helen Grace Kearney, administrators of Edwin J. Field, deceased (plaintiffs) against Edward Lukowiak and others (defendants). Judgment for plaintiffs and defendants appealed. Judgment affirmed.

The defendants' signatures on the note in question were in the upper left-hand corner of an ordinary, printed form. The note read as follows:

"$1,600 August 15, 1931

"Edward Lukowiak, Joseph M. Lukowiak,
Anna Lukowiak, Helen Lukowiak

"On demand after date promise to pay to the order of E. J. Field, Sixteen Hundred Dollars at 5%

"Payable to E. J. Field personally.

"Value received Sixteen Hundred Dollars

"No. 1 Due on Demand."

The defendants contended that the signatures were so irregular as to constitute the signers indorsers and not liable as makers.

Lloyd, J. No contention seems to have been made that the paper did not import an obligation, nor could there be. The position of the signature on the paper is immaterial if it clearly appears to have been intended as such. 8 Corp. Jur., p. 108, and cases there cited. While the signatures in the present instance are at the top rather than at the lower right-hand corner of the paper, as is usually the case, it clearly imports an intention to be bound thereby, and it is equally clear that it must have been as makers; otherwise there are no makers and consequently no indorsers. They were the persons primarily liable and absolutely required to pay the note.

In re Donohoe's Estate
271 Pa. 554, 115 Atl. 878 (1922)

Richard Donohoe filed certain claims in his mother's estate. Part of the claims were allowed and part were rejected. Richard Donohoe and others interested in the estate appealed. The appeals were dismissed.

The following promissory note was given by Cecelia Donohoe to her son Richard. The *italicized* portions were in Mrs. Donohoe's handwriting.

"August 30th, 1910

"*$13,070.86.*

"*I, Cecelia W. Donohoe*, after date, *August 30th*, promise to pay to the order of *Richard Donohoe, thirteen thousand and seventy dollars and 86/100* dollars without defalcation, value received, *with interest at 6%*. . . . Witness *my* hand and seal.

"(Seal.) Hester Johnson,
"Notary Public."

It is contended that the note is not signed by Cecelia Donohoe and therefore is not enforceable.

Walling, J. That Mrs. Donohoe's signature appears in the body of the note and not at the end is unimportant, so long as she intended thereby to obligate herself for its payment. There is no law requiring a note to be signed at the end thereof, as in the case of a will; hence, whenever it can be found that a signature, wherever it appears, was intended as an execution of the note it is sufficient. For example to write, "On demand, I, John Smith, promise to pay Thomas Brown, one hundred dollars," is, in form, a good obligation and that is essentially this case.

"It is not necessary that the signature of a party to a contract should appear at the end thereof. If his name is written by him in any part of the contract, or at the top, or the right or left hand, with intention to sign or for the purpose of authenticating the instrument, it is sufficient to bind him." 9 Cyc. 301.

"When a signature is essential to the validity of an instrument it is not necessary that the signature appear at the end of the instrument. If the name of the party whose signature is required is written by him in any part of the instrument, for the purpose of authenticating it, it is sufficient signature." 36 Cyc. 449.

The same rule applies to commercial paper. The fact that for greater solemnity Mrs. Donohoe called in a notary public who was a stranger to the instrument and mistakenly wrote her name in the wrong place, is unimportant; the obligation remained that of Cecelia W. Donohoe, and being perfected by delivery, is unassailable.

An Unconditional Promise or Order

The requirement that to be negotiable the instrument must contain an unconditional promise to pay a sum certain in money gives rise to three questions: (1) when is the promise or order unconditional? (2) what is a sum certain? and (3) what is money?

The first of these questions has presented many problems for the courts to solve. Fundamentally, the problem is one of interpretation of language. If a note contains a clear promise to pay or a bill of exchange contains a clear order to pay, no difficulty will arise; but if terms are added to the instrument, the added terms may condition the promise or order, and if they do the instrument is not negotiable. If the instrument contains any provision which requires one to refer to something outside the instrument for the purpose of determining his rights on the instrument, the promise or order will be conditional irrespective of the nature of that to which reference is made. Archer gives Burch an instrument which reads, "I promise to pay to Burch or order $100 according to the terms of a contract entered into this day." The instrument is not negotiable because Archer's promise is conditioned on the provisions of the contract referred to in the instrument.

The Uniform Negotiable Instruments Law expressly provides that: "An unqualified order or promise to pay is unconditional within the meaning of this act, though coupled with—

"1. An indication of a particular fund out of which reimbursement is to be made, or a particular account to be debited with the amount; or

"2. A statement of the transaction which gives rise to the instrument.

"But an order or promise to pay out of a particular fund is not unconditional."

These provisions permit the drawer or maker of the instrument to make notations on the instrument which will aid in keeping records of the business transaction. If Archer draws a bill of exchange on Drew and notes on the instrument that Drew, when he pays or accepts the instrument, is authorized to reimburse himself out of particular moneys or credits over which he has control, or if Archer notes on the instrument instructions to Drew that on the payment of or the acceptance of the instrument Drew is to charge the amount to a stated account, the notations will not affect the negotiability of the instrument; but if Archer notes on the instrument that Drew is to pay the instrument out of a stated fund, the instrument will not be negotiable because Drew is not to pay unless there is enough in the fund to cover the amount of the bill of exchange. The order is conditional. It is in effect an order to pay "if" there is enough in the fund to cover the bill of exchange. It is immaterial whether or not there is enough in the fund to cover the bill of exchange. To be negotiable, the instrument must show on its face what are the rights of the holder. If the instrument is payable out of a particular fund, one cannot know that it will be paid unless he investigates the fund to determine how much there is in the fund.

If Archer notes on the instrument the transaction which gives rise to the instrument, it will not affect its negotiability. Such a notation can be treated as surplusage.

The sum is certain if one can compute the amount which will be required to pay the instrument at any given time without going outside the instrument. An instrument which provides for the payment of a stated amount plus taxes is not negotiable because the amount of the tax cannot be determined from what is on the instrument nor can one determine from what is on the instrument whether or not there is a tax to be paid. The Uniform Negotiable Instruments Law expressly provides that certain additions will not affect the negotiability of the instrument. (See N.I.L., Sec. 2.)

The requirement that to be negotiable the instrument must be payable in money distinguishes negotiable instruments from negotiable warehouse receipts, negotiable bills of lading, and similar instruments which have many characteristics of negotiability. If the instrument is payable in the legal tender of the country in which it is made payable, it is payable in money.

An instrument drawn in New York payable in London in English pounds is payable in money, but if the instrument were payable in New York in English pounds, it would not be payable in money and would not be negotiable.

If the holder has the option of accepting something other than money, the negotiability of the instrument is not affected, but if the party obligated to pay the instrument has the option of doing something other than paying money, the instrument is not negotiable. Section 5 of the Uniform Negotiable Instruments Law sets out certain permissible provisions which may be included in the instrument without affecting its negotiability.

First National Bank of Hutchinson v. Lightner
74 Kan. 736, 88 Pac. 59, 8 L.R.A. (N.S.) 231 (1906)

This was an action by the First National Bank of Hutchinson (plaintiff) against George W. Lightner (defendant). Judgment for defendant and plaintiff appealed. Judgment reversed and remanded.

The Snyder Planing Mill Company entered into a contract with defendant Lightner for the erection of a barn at the contract price of $3,500. Before the barn was completed the Snyder Planing Mill Co. was adjudged bankrupt and Lightner was compelled to and did complete the barn at his own expense.

Prior to the time the Snyder Planing Mill Co. was adjudged bankrupt, Lightner accepted two orders, one for $1,000 and one for $1,500, which were drawn on him by the Snyder Planing Mill Co. These orders were discounted with the First National Bank of Hutchinson. Lightner refused to pay the orders to the bank claiming that the orders were non-negotiable and nothing more than an assignment of the rights of the Snyder Planing Mill Co., that the Snyder Planing Mill Co. had failed to complete their contract and that the balance due on the contract was considerably less than the amount of the two orders. If the orders are negotiable Lightner must pay the bank the amount of the orders; if they are not negotiable the bank can recover only the amount due the Snyder Planing Mill Co.

The orders and acceptances were identical with the exceptions of the amounts and dates. The one for $1,500 read as follows:

"'Hutchinson, Kansas, Aug. 10, 1903.

"'G. W. Lightner, Offerle, Kansas—Dear Sir: Pay to the order of the First National Bank of Hutchinson, Kansas, on account of contract between you and the Snyder Planing Mill Co. $1,500.

"'The Snyder Planing Mill Co.,
"'Per J. F. Donnell, Treas.

"'Accepted. G. W. Lightner.'"

Porter, J. The main controversy is whether the orders given by the planing mill company to the bank, and accepted by defendant, are negotiable instruments. It is true that no specific time of payment is mentioned, but that does not affect their validity as such instruments, and, where no date is mentioned, they are payable on demand. Each of them, therefore, possesses all the essential elements of a bill of exchange unless the words "on account of contract between you and the Snyder Planing Mill Co." make them payable out of a particular fund and conditionally so that the acceptance is thereby qualified. The law is well settled that a bill or note is not negotiable if made payable out of a particular fund. But a distinction is recognized where the instrument is simply chargeable to a particular account. In such a case it is beyond question negotiable; payment is not made to depend upon the sufficiency of the fund mentioned, and it is mentioned only for the purpose of informing the drawee as to his means of reimbursement. In *Ridgely Bank* v. *Patton et al.*, 109 Ill. 479, it is said: "A bill or note, without affecting its character as such, may state the transaction out of which it arose, or the consideration for which it was given." "So, also, the insertion into a bill or note of memoranda, explaining the nature of the business or debt, for which the instrument is given, will not make it non-negotiable, for such a memorandum does not make the payment conditional."

The test in every case is said to be: "Does the instrument carry the general personal credit of the drawer or maker, or only the credit of a particular fund?" In *Pierson* v. *Dunlop*, 2 Cowp. 571, an order which was to be charged "to freight" was held negotiable. A note expressed to be in payment of certain tracts of land was held negotiable. Likewise a note which stated that it was given in consideration of certain personal property, the title of which was not to pass unless the note was paid. This court held in *Clark* v. *Skeen*, 61 Kan. 526, 60 Pac. 327, 49 L.R.A. 190, 78 Am. St. Rep. 337, that "a note for the payment of a certain sum at a fixed date is not rendered non-negotiable by a stipulation that, upon default in the payment of interest, the whole amount shall become due at the option of the holder, and then draw a greater rate of interest." In *Corbett* v. *Clark and another*, 45 Wis. 403, 30 Am. Rep. 763, an order to pay a certain sum "and take the same out of our share of the grain," referring to grain harvested or growing on certain farms, accepted by the drawee, was said to be a valid bill of exchange, and the order and acceptance absolute, the words above quoted merely indicating the means of disbursement."

In *Redman* v. *Adams*, 51 Me. 429, a bill directing the drawee to charge the amount against the drawer's share of fish caught on a certain schooner is held valid and negotiable. One of the leading cases is *Macleed* v. *Snee*, 2 Strange, 765. There a bill of exchange was dated May 25th for the payment of a certain sum one month after date, "as my quarterly half-pay to be due from 24th of June to 27th of September next, by advance." This was held a negotiable bill of exchange.

In *Whitney* v. *Eliot National Bank*, 137 Mass. 351, 50 Am. Rep. 316, the drafts or bills of exchange were in the ordinary form except that they contained the direction to "charge the same to account of 250 bbls. meal ex schooner Aurora Borealis." The court said: "This direction to charge the amount of the bills to a particular account, we think, does not make them payable conditionally, or out of a particular fund; they are still payable absolutely, and are negotiable, and do not constitute an assignment of a particular fund, or of a part of a particular fund. . . . . The rule with regard to words which refer to the consideration is well stated in *Siegel et al.* v. *Chicago Trust & Savings Bank*, 131 Ill. 569, 23 N.E. 417, 7 L.R.A. 537, 19 Am. St. Rep. 51, as follows: "The mere fact that the consideration for which a promissory note is given is recited in it, although it may appear thereby that it was given for or in consideration of an executory contract, or promise on the part of the payee, will not destroy the negotiability of the note, unless it appears through the recital that it qualifies the promise to pay, and renders it conditional or uncertain, either as to the time of payment or the sum to be paid."

Plaintiff and defendant agree upon the abstract proposition of law involved in the controversy. Counsel for defendant concedes that an instrument, negotiable in itself, is not changed in character, or rendered non-negotiable "by a recital of the consideration or a direction as to how the drawee shall reimburse himself"; but insists that the insertion of the words "on account of" has the same effect as the words "out of the proceeds of." The controversy is thus narrowed down to whether the words "on account of contract between you and the Snyder Planing Mill Co." amount to a direction to pay out of a particular fund, or, on the other hand, are to be considered as simply indicating the fund from which the drawee, Lightner, might reimburse himself. Many of the cases attach but little importance to the words "account of," and give the same effect to them as to the words "out of."

The weight of authority and reason supports the proposition that the words amount to no more than an indication of the fund from which the drawee is to reimburse himself. The words used are substantially the same as though the orders read "and charge to account of contract with Snyder Planing Mill Company," or "credit to account of contract," etc.

Davis et ux. v. Union Planters National Bank & Trust Co. et al.
171 Tenn. 383, 103 S.W. (2d) 579 (1937)

This was an action by W. M. Davis and wife (plaintiffs) against the Union Planters National Bank & Trust Company (defendant). Judgment for defendant and plaintiffs appealed. Judgment affirmed.

Davis and wife executed their promissory note to Turley Mortgage Company, Incorporated, a mortgage broker, for $4,000, payable in installments over a period of years and secured the same by executing a deed of trust on their home in Memphis. The agreement was that Turley was to sell the note to the New York Life Insurance Company and turn the proceeds over to Davis and wife. In violation of the agreement, Turley negotiated the note to the defendant and paid Davis and wife nothing. Shortly thereafter Turley died. On learning what had happened, Davis and wife brought this action asking that the bank be enjoined from foreclosing the trust deed. Davis and wife contend that the note was not a negotiable instrument.

McKinney, J. The question before us is whether a certain note is negotiable. If not, the assignee thereof takes it subject to all equities and defenses available between the original parties.

Plaintiffs insist that the following provision in the note destroys its negotiability:

"Upon breach of any promise made in this note or in the deed of trust securing it, at the option of the holder the entire indebtedness hereby evidenced shall become due then or thereafter as the holder may elect regardless of the date of maturity. Notice of the exercise of such option is hereby expressly waived."

Section 7325 of the Code defines a negotiable instrument, providing, among other things, that the sum to be paid and the time of payment must be certain and unconditional.

The weight of authority, as well as the better-reasoned cases, holds that the form of the note determines its negotiability. The note alone must be looked to in considering its negotiability. The annotator of 75 A.L.R. p. 1211, upon this question says:

"The weight of authority supports the doctrine of the reported case that, notwithstanding the rule that two or more instruments executed by the same parties at the same time and referring to each other must be construed together, the form of a note or bond may alone be considered in determining its negotiability, although it is secured by a mortgage or trust agreement, and that, unless the terms of the latter are referred to in a way to incorporate their provisions into the note or bond, the mortgage or trust agreement is but an incident thereto and is to be regarded as a security only, the provisions of which will not render the bond or note non-negotiable if it is otherwise a negotiable instrument."

By section 7326 of the Code the negotiability of a note is not destroyed by the fact that it is payable in installments, with a provision that, upon default in payment of any installment or of interest, the whole shall become due.

A review of the numerous cases to which we have been referred satisfies us that the text found in 3 R.C.L. 909, 910, is supported by the weight of authority, as well as upon reason, and is as follows:

"The fact that the date of payment may be accelerated by the default of the debtor in failing to comply with specified conditions does not affect the negotiability of the paper. Accordingly, a note secured by a real estate mortgage is negotiable, although it provides that on default in the payment of interest, or failure to comply with any conditions of the mortgage, the whole principal shall, at the option of the mortgagee, become due and payable. This conclusion has been reached under the Negotiable Instruments Law, which declares in effect that the negotiability of an instrument shall not be affected by a 'provision that upon default in payment of any installment or interest the whole shall become due.' "

The holder can ignore the acceleration clause if he so desires, because it does not affect the note if it is otherwise negotiable. And the holder of the note, by virtue of the statute, can only mature it before its due date upon the breach of some provision by the maker.

Counsel for plaintiffs have referred us to a number of cases supporting the well-recognized rule clearly and succinctly stated in 3 R.C.L. 883, 884, as follows:

"It may be stated as the general rule that wherever a bill of exchange or promissory note contains a reference to some extrinsic contract, as distinguished from a reference importing merely that the extrinsic agreement was the origin of the transaction, or constitutes the consideration of the bill or note, the negotiability of the paper is destroyed."

There is considerable conflict in the authorities as to whether the presence of words in a note "as per contract of even date herewith" would be sufficient to render the paper non-negotiable.

As illustrative of the foregoing text, in *American Exchange Bank* v. *Blanchard*, 7 Allen (Mass.) 333, it was held that the note was non-negotiable because it was payable "subject to the policy."

The Court of Appeals of New York, in *Enoch* v. *Brandon*, makes this very clear statement of the rule invoked by plaintiffs: "If in the bond or note anything appears requiring reference to another document to determine whether in fact the unconditional promise to pay a fixed sum at a future date is modified or subject to some contingency, then the promise is no longer unconditional. What that document may provide is immaterial. Reference to the paper itself said to be negotiable determines its character."

The note in question contains no such reference and does not provide that it is subject to the deed of trust. The holder is at liberty to examine the deed of trust to see what promise, if breached, would authorize him to accelerate the maturity of the note. Or he can ignore the acceleration clause and defer action until the due date of the note.

In 9 C.J. 49, it is said: "But where a bond contains special stipulations and its payment is subject to contingencies not within the control of the holder, it is deprived of the character of a negotiable instrument and becomes exposed to any defense existing thereto, as between the original parties to the instrument."

The payment of the note in controversy is subject to no contingencies not within the control of the maker, which distinguishes this cause from those cited by plaintiffs. There is no uncertainty as to the amount or the time of payment; hence it is unnecessary to refer to any other instrument to ascertain these facts.

This is a cause where one of two innocent parties must suffer, and the loss will have to be borne by plaintiffs, due to their misplaced confidence in Mr. Turley.

Persky v. Bank of America Nat. Ass'n.
261 N.Y. 212, 185 N.E. 77 (1933)

This was an action by Simon Persky (plaintiff) against the Bank of America National Association (defendant). Judgment for defendant in trial court was reversed on appeal to the Appellate Division and plaintiff appealed to the Court of Appeals. Judgment of Appellate Division reversed and judgment of trial court affirmed.

Lehman, J. Summary judgment in the sum of $46,000, together with interest of over $10,000, has been entered in favor of the plaintiff for the unpaid balance of a promissory note made by one Maria di Francesco to the order of one Alexander Capasso. The note is annexed to the complaint. It is dated June 14, 1926. It contains a promise to pay the sum of $50,000 "in successive semi-annual payments of not less than One Thousand Dollars each . . . . for a period of eight years from date, and the balance then due to be payable on demand thereafter, with interest on the principal unpaid at the rate of six per cent. per annum, payable semi-annually, together with all taxes assessed upon said sum against said payee or the holder of this note."

The maker of the instrument promises to pay not only the sum of $50,000, with interest, which is a "sum certain," but also "all taxes assessed upon said sum" against the payee or holder of the note, and the amount of the taxes which may be assessed thereafter is not a sum certain. *Mechanics' Bank of New Haven* v. *Johnson*, 104 Conn. 696, 134 A. 231, and the cases there cited. For that reason, the promissory note is not a negotiable instrument.

Citizens State Bank v. Pauly
152 Kan. 152, 102 P. (2d) 966, 134 A.L.R. 941 (1940)

This was an action by Citizens State Bank (plaintiff) against Ben Pauly (defendant). Judgment for defendant and plaintiff appealed. Judgment affirmed.

Defendant gave a note payable to Sowers Plan Crop Insurance Mutual Company in payment of the premium on a policy of crop insurance. The note was negotiated to the plaintiff. Defendant suffered a loss which was covered by the policy of insurance and which has not been paid. The Sowers Plan Crop Insurance Company is in receivership. The plaintiff sued on the note and the defendant set up the unpaid claim as a set-off, claiming that the note was not negotiable because the assignment clause required the maker to do something in addition to paying money.

Hoch, J. First, is the note at issue a negotiable instrument, under the statute? There can be no dispute that the first paragraph of the note is an unconditional promise to pay a certain sum, and otherwise meets the requirements of Sec. 52-201. The controversy centers about two later paragraphs in the note, hereinafter referred to as "the mortgage clause" and the "assignment clause," and which read as follows:

"To secure the payment of this note, I, or we, do hereby mortgage and convey unto the payee, or its assigns, the crops described, and this mortgage extends to and covers said crops, whether standing and growing, or when cut and in shock or stack, and/or when threshed and in the bin, granary or otherwise.

"In the event of crop failure, I, or we, do hereby assign that portion of any insurance collected from Sowers Plan Crop Insurance Mutual Company necessary to pay this note to Sowers Plan Crop Insurance Mutual Company."

The arguments urged for non-negotiability are that the promise to pay is not unconditional because it is a promise to pay out of a particular fund; and that the instrument "contains an order or promise to do any act in addition to the payment of money," which destroys negotiability.

What then is the meaning and effect of the assignment clause? We agree with appellant that whatever it meant, it was *a present assignment*. But what did the maker assign? In effect, he said, "I now agree and promise that if I suffer a crop loss and collect for it from the company, I will hold such collection for the benefit of the holder of this note—to whatever extent that may be necessary to pay the note." As to subsequent holders, the clause does have real significance. To illustrate:—let us assume that the company has transferred the note for value and no longer has any interest in it. A loss is suffered before maturity of the note and the company pays the loss. The insured has thus "*collected*" for the loss. What now is the effect of the assignment clause? Its plain significance is that having "*collected*" for the loss and his note being unpaid, the maker has agreed to keep intact for the benefit of the holder of the note, whoever he may be, the amount he has "*collected*." In the absence of such a clause, the holder of the note, in the circumstances stated, could only look to the general credit of the maker to enforce payment. But with this assignment clause in the note, he has the additional promise of the maker that if he does collect insurance while the note is unpaid, he will not spend the amount collected, or commingle it with other assets, but will retain it intact in so far as necessary to protect his obligation on the note. Whatever it may be called, this assignment constitutes in substance the imposition of a trust upon any future collections for losses as long as the note is unpaid. If it be said that such a trust would afford little additional security for the note, the answer is that the question here is not one of *security* but of *negotiability*. Although the breaking of such a promise might leave the holder with little more recourse in case of default on the note, the fact remains that the note contains the promise; and such an additional promise clearly makes the note non-negotiable under the provisions of G.S. 1935, 52-205. (Some illustrative examples of additional promises in a note which have been held to render it non-negotiable: a promise to pay expenses on repossessing the article for which the note was given, and to finance its reconditioning, reselling, etc., a promise that "no part of the crop shall be mortgaged (or) sold," a promise that the maker will "pay any taxes assessed upon the note or its mortgage security," a promise to insure the property pledged, a promise to "hold all fertilizers . . . . bought for us in trust," a promise to keep the machine, in payment for which it was given, in repair.)

Louisa National Bank v. Paintsville National Bank et al.
260 Ky. 327, 85 S.W. (2d) 668, 100 A.L.R. 819 (1935)

This was an action by the Louisa National Bank (plaintiff) against the Paintsville National Bank and another (defendants). Judgment for the defendants and plaintiff appealed. Judgment affirmed.

Mrs. Alice Mayo loaned certain bonds to the Paintsville National Bank and the bank executed the following writing: "Paintsville, Ky. Nov. 18, 1910. Received of Alice Mayo, Seventy five hundred ($7500.00) Dollars of U.S. Bonds, deliverable to her order six months from date of notice, in bonds of same issue in her name or to her order, or cash equal to the par value of the bonds, at our option, for which we agree to pay her 2% in addition to the Government rate, bonds being 2% Consols of the issue of 1930. Paintsville National Bank by Jno. E. Buckingham, Cashier." Thereafter the bank paid Mrs. Mayo the 4 per cent on the $7,500 as it agreed. On February 27, 1920, Mrs. Mayo issued her demand note to the Louisa National Bank and pledged as security the above obligation of the Paintsville National Bank. The Louisa National Bank did not give the Paintsville National Bank notice that the obligation had been pledged to them. The Paintsville National Bank had made loans to Mrs. Mayo and, when the Louisa National Bank demanded payment of the Paintsville National Bank, Mrs. Mayo was indebted to the latter in the sum of $12,200. Paintsville National Bank claimed their right to offset this claim against the obligation evidenced by the above writing. If the writing is a negotiable instrument, Paintsville National Bank must pay Louisa National Bank; if it is not negotiable, they may set the amount off against the amount which Mrs. Mayo owes them.

Thomas, J. Having said this much concerning the right of an

obligor in a chose in action to interpose the defense of set-off in an action thereon by a transferee when the obligation is a negotiable instrument, and also when it is not so, we will now proceed to determine the nature and characteristics of the instrument executed by defendant on November 18, 1910, to Mrs. Alice Mayo. We have but little trouble in doing so, since it is clearly what has come to be called and designated as a "non-negotiable instrument," i.e., one not embraced by or subject to the rights and privileges conferred upon parties to a commercial instrument of the characteristics of a bill of exchange and embraced by the negotiable instrument statute. The essentials of such latter obligations are set forth in the first section of the act, which is section 3720b-1 of our present Statutes. The second requisite therein is, that the instrument in order to be a negotiable one within the purview of the act "must contain an unconditional promise or order to pay a sum certain in money." The promise made by defendant to Mrs. Mayo, as contained in the writing it executed to her (and which as we have seen is the foundation of plaintiff's cause of action against defendant), does not meet the requirements of that subsection. It is true that under the provisions of section 5 of the Negotiable Instruments Statute, the negotiability of the instrument is not destroyed where it "gives the *holder* an election to require something to be done in lieu of payment of money" (our italics), but the instrument with which we are dealing confers no such privilege on the *holder* (Mrs. Mayo or plaintiff as assignee thereof). It does, however, confer such a privilege on defendant as the maker thereof, in that it is given the option to discharge the obligation thereby assumed by, (a) returning to Mrs. Mayo the identical bonds at any time within six months after notice from her, or (b) the return to her within such time of similar bonds of the same value, or (c) paying her the cash value of such bonds at the time.

There is no law, statutory or otherwise, so far as we have been able to discover that allows such an alternative promise by the maker of the instrument in strictly commercial or negotiable paper, since to do so would violate the inserted requirement, supra, that the promise must be unconditional (i.e., by the promisor), and when not so the instrument becomes an ordinary chose in action with all the rights and privileges attached to them by the law; one of which is assignability so as to vest the assignee with the right to maintain an action thereon in his own name, and with the right of the maker to interpose in defense of such an action any offset claim that he may have acquired as against the original obligee up to the time that he receives notice of the assignment.

Time Payable

This provision is intended to give certainty as to the time of payment. As interpreted and applied by the courts, absolute certainty is not obtained. However, an instrument which will not mature at some time is not negotiable.

An instrument payable on demand is expressly declared to be negotiable. An instrument drawn payable "at sight" or "on presentation" is a demand instrument. These terms are commonly used in bills of exchange instead of the term "on demand." If no time of payment is stated in the instrument, it is payable on demand. (See N.I.L., Sec. 7.) A check is an example of such an instrument.

An instrument is payable at a fixed time when it is payable at a stated time as July 5, 1946. The time of payment of such instruments is certain in all respects.

There is considerable confusion in regard to what provisions are permissible in regard to the time of payment of an instrument, payable at a determinable future time. The courts are in accord in holding that an instrument made payable thirty days after date or after sight is payable at a determinable future time. The Negotiable Instruments Law provides that an instrument is payable at a determinable future time if it is payable on or before a fixed or determinable future time specified in the instrument or if it is payable on or at a fixed period after the occurrence of an event specified therein, providing the event is certain to happen; but if the instrument is made payable on a contingency, it is not negotiable and the happening of the event does not cure the defect.

If an instrument is payable "on or before five years after date," the time is determinable; also, if an instrument is payable "at the death of my father" or "one year after my death," the time of payment is determinable; but if the instrument is made payable "when you reach your twenty-first birthday," it is payable on a contingency and is not negotiable, and the fact that *you* reach your twenty-first birthday will not cure the defect and make the instrument negotiable.

Business men frequently include in an instrument a provision which may hasten the maturity date of the instrument. Such provisions are called acceleration clauses. It is customary to state a maturity date and then provide that on the happening of a stated event either the maturity date will automatically be hastened or the holder may at his option hasten the maturity date. The effect of such a provision on the negotiability of the instrument is not easily determined. In installment notes or notes of a series it is a common practice to provide that on the maker's failure to pay any installment or any note when due the entire unpaid balance shall become immediately due and payable. The courts are in accord in holding that such a clause does not render the instrument non-negotiable. The majority of courts hold that, if the right to accelerate the maturity date is based on some default on the part of the party primarily liable, the clause does not render the instrument non-negotiable. However, the majority of courts have held that, if the holder is given the right to demand payment "if he deems himself insecure," the instrument is not negotiable. This holding is difficult to justify.

Another common practice is to combine the promise to pay with a chattel mortgage, title-retaining contract, or pledge agreement. The instrument is a combination of a promise to pay, secured by the security agreement. Some security agreements contain a provision that, in the event the security decreases in value, the holder may declare the debt due and payable. Others provide that, in the event the security decreases in value, the holder may demand additional security and, if additional security is not given, the holder may declare the debt due and payable. Sometimes the security agreement is more extensive and gives the holder additional rights. The courts are not in accord in their holdings in regard to the effect of such provisions on the negotiability of the instrument. From a business point of view, there is no objection to holding such instruments to be negotiable and several courts have so held. From a technical point of view, the requirements in the security contract violate the requirements of the Negotiable Instruments Law. The acceleration provision is based on the happening of an uncertain event. The requirement that, on depreciation in value of the security, the party primarily liable shall give additional security requires the party primarily liable to do something in addition to the payment of money. The majority of the courts have held that the title-retaining contract note is negotiable. However, it has been held that the title retaining provisions render the instrument non-negotiable. Lack of uniformity in security provisions in instruments adds to the uncertainty in the law.

McClenathan v. Davis

243 Ill. 87, 90 N.E. 265, 27 L.R.A. (N.S.) 1017 (1909)

This was an action by C. V. McClenathan (plaintiff) against Emmons Davis and another (defendants). Judgment for plaintiff in trial court and defendants appealed to Appellate Division where judgment was affirmed and defendant Davis appealed to Supreme Court. Judgment for plaintiff affirmed.

Suit was brought on a promissory note given in the settlement of a dispute over an estate. The note was as follows:

"For value received I promise to pay Elizabeth Gamble, or order, the sum of fifteen hundred dollars in twelve months after I shall become the legal owner of one hundred and fifteen acres of land conveyed to me by my father, H. V. Davis, reserving to him, H. V. Davis, a life estate in said land, by which at his death I am to become possessed of and the owner in fee of said one hundred and fifteen acres, situated in the southeast corner of section 30, in township 18 north, range 11 east of the third P.M., Champaign county, Illinois.

Emmons Davis."

Farmer, C. J. Appellant states in his brief that the vital question in the case is, Was the instrument sued on a negotiable instrument? and that the decision of that question will be decisive of the case.

Appellant's contention is that the instrument sued on is not a promissory note, because it is not payable at a specified time which must certainly arrive, but is payable upon a contingency, which may or may not happen. The contingency upon which it is argued the payment depends is the actual ownership and possession of the land by appellant, and it is said this may never happen, because it may be that the grantor in the deed had no title to the land, or that appellant might fail to record his deed, and the grantor make another deed to an innocent purchaser, or that appellant might before the death of his father have joined with him in a conveyance to a third person, thereby destroying appellant's estate and interest in the land before the life estate of his father was terminated. We think there is no merit in this position of appellant. It is not claimed that there is any basis for the contention that it might possibly turn out appellant's father had no title to the land conveyed, and as to the other alleged contingencies it was in the power of appellant to prevent them happening. Besides, we do not consider them contingencies, within the meaning of the law, that could affect the certainty of the time for the payment of the instrument sued on. Properly analyzed and understood, that instrument recites that H. V. Davis had conveyed to appellant 115 acres of land, reserving a life estate therein; that appellant was to become the owner in fee and possessed of said land upon his father's death, and he promised to pay Elizabeth Gamble $1,500 within 12 months after he became such owner of said land—i.e., within 12 months after his father's death. The payment was not dependent upon a contingency that might never happen. The death of H. V. Davis would entitle appellant to the possession of the land, and his death was certain to happen. It seems to us it would be an absurd and unreasonable construction of this instrument to say that the parties did not understand or intend that the money was to be paid absolutely and within a definite, certain, and fixed time.

McCornick & Co., Bankers v. Gem State Oil & Products Co.
38 Id. 470, 222 Pac. 286 (1923)

This was an action by McCornick & Co., Bankers (plaintiff) against Gem State Oil and Products Company (defendant). Judgment for the plaintiff and defendant appealed. Judgment for plaintiff affirmed.

Defendant gave certain trade acceptances to the Utah Rubber

Company in payment of goods. The trade acceptances were negotiated to the plaintiff. The goods were later returned by the defendant to the seller. Defendant refused to pay the trade acceptances when due and when sued set up the failure of consideration as a defense. Defendant contends that the trade acceptances are not negotiable. The trade acceptances were in regular form but contained the following provision:

"The obligation of the acceptor of this bill arises out of the purchase of goods from the drawer. Upon the acceptor hereof suspending payment, giving a chattel mortgage, suffering a fire loss, disposing of his business or failing to meet at maturity any prior trade acceptance, this trade acceptance, at the option of the holder, shall immediately become due and payable."

Adair, D. J. If it was a negotiable instrument, the payment thereof to the original payee, Utah Rubber Company, before maturity, and without notice of its assignment, would not discharge it as against the holder in due course, the respondent herein. If, on the other hand, the instrument is non-negotiable, the appellant could set up the defense of payment against the assignee thereof, the respondent herein, and, since the payment and discharge of the instrument was made without notice of its assignment, and before maturity, it would be a valid and complete defense to said action.

We are concerned, therefore, only with the one question as to the negotiability of said instrument. Aside from the printed matter on the margin, the paper is purely an ordinary bill of exchange, properly drawn and accepted, and complying in all respects with the requirements of the statute and the law merchant as to negotiable paper. There is obviously no doubt but that it would be negotiable, except for such marginal matter, and to that, and that alone, we will direct our attention.

The law of bills and notes and other means of trade, like all other substantive law, is the creature of growth. Founded on the custom and needs of merchants it is the combined result of reason and experience, and should keep pace with and respond to commercial usage.

"The tendency of modern jurisprudence is to get away from the rigid rules of interpretation which seem to have prevailed when the famous expression of Chief Justice Gibson that 'a negotiable bill or note is a courier without luggage' . . . . was coined. The law of negotiable instruments, as a part of the law merchant, is based upon the necessities, usages, and customs of business, and must develop with it. Whenever the additional stipulations are merely in aid of the collection of the note, and do not constitute an undertaking to give or do something else foreign to that end, they do not destroy negotiability."

In the modern commercial world, trade acceptances are fast becoming an important form of contract, ranking with notes, checks, drafts, and other mediums of trade. The matter contained therein, aside from the direct order to pay money, is often valuable and intended to facilitate its transfer, and an option similar to that inserted in the margin of the instrument in question might tend to assist the holder in its transfer or sale to another. The fact that it does contain matter other than an order for the payment of money does not in itself render it non-negotiable. The first sentence in the margin, to the effect that "the obligation of the acceptor of this bill arises out of the purchase of goods from the drawer," does not affect nor deprive the instrument of its negotiability.

The last sentence, providing for accelerating the time of payment upon the happening of certain contingencies or events which may or may not take place, is the provision in the paper which appellant contends renders it non-negotiable. Does this clause render the time of payment undeterminable or indefinite?

The Uniform Negotiable Instruments Act, adopted by Idaho, as well as all the states of the Union makes definiteness in the time of payment one of the controlling factors in determining the question of negotiability. If the clause in question does not render the due date indefinite, the instrument is negotiable. It is generally held that it is the duty of the courts to have in mind the purpose of securing uniformity in the law of commercial paper. That was the motive which actuated the various state Legislatures when they adopted and passed the Uniform Negotiable Instruments Act.

The precise question involved in the instant case has never been before this court for determination. This court has held that a recital in a title-retaining note that the title to the property for which it was given shall remain in the payee, and that he shall have the right to take possession of it whenever he may deem himself insecure, even before the maturity of the note, renders such instrument non-negotiable. In that case, however, the issue was determined on the theory that the contract contained a covenant and promise to do certain acts in addition to the payment of money, as well as leaving the time of payment uncertain. It was held that the clause accelerating the time of payment gave the holder the right to declare the debt due, thus placing the right of declaring the date of maturity wholly under the control of the holder, and completely dependent upon his whim or caprice, and independent of any act of the maker.

The paper involved here provides for the acceleration of the time of payment upon the happening of any one of five events, four of which, viz., suspending payment, giving a chattel mortgage, disposing of his business, or failing to meet at maturity any prior trade acceptance, are wholly within the control of the acceptor or maker, and the other contingency, that is, suffering a fire loss, is an event over which no party to the paper has any control. None of the contingencies named are within the control of the holder.

Each of the clauses in this instrument providing for accelerating the time of payment is a contingency definitely stated therein, and having a well-known and recognized meaning incapable of misconstruction. The phrases "suffering a fire loss," "disposing of his business," and "failing to meet at maturity any prior trade acceptance" could not be misunderstood nor be more accurately and concisely stated. The "giving of a chattel mortgage" means the signing and delivery thereof, or, in other words, its execution in such a manner as to make it a valid lien upon the property of the maker described in such mortgage.

It has been suggested that the phrase "suspending payment" creates some doubt as to the intended meaning, and thereby renders the time of payment uncertain. An examination of the authorities removes this objection.

The overwhelming trend of modern authority is to the effect that, where an instrument is made payable on a definite day, and also contains a conditional promise to pay at an earlier date, the instrument is not necessarily rendered non-negotiable by such acceleration clause.

The most common cases involving this principle which have arisen are those which provide for accelerating the due date, at the option of the holder, for default in the payment of interest, and those where several notes maturing at different times belong to a single transaction and form a connective series; the negotiability thereof is not affected by a provision that, on the failure of the maker to pay any one of the series, the rest shall become due and payable at the option of the holder.

The general rule is that, where instruments are payable at a day certain, or sooner, if some specific event shall happen, they shall be construed to be due at all events at the day limited, and to be negotiable.

We think this general rule should be, and the same is, adopted in this state, and, applying it to the paper here in question, we hold that the same is negotiable. None of the conditions in the acceleration clause depend upon any act of the holder, nor are they within his control, but all of such contingencies depend either upon some act or omission of the maker, upon an event indicated in the paper not within the control of either party.

Guio et al. v. Lutes
97 Ind. App. 157, 184 N.E. 416 (1933)

This was an action by Albert Lutes (plaintiff) against Oliver Guio and another (defendants). Judgment for plaintiff and defendants appealed. Judgment reversed and new trial ordered.

This was a suit against the defendants as indorsers of a promissory note. The defendants contend that the note was not negotiable. The note is a title-retaining contract note, containing the following provision:

"*Guio and Mumma has full power to declare this note due, and take possession of said property at any time they may deem this note insecure, even before the maturity of the same.*" (Our italics.)

Dudine, J. The reasons given by appellants for their contentions are that the clause in the note, which is italicized in this opinion, made said note non-negotiable, and that the evidence shows that the assignee (appellee) did not exercise due diligence against the maker. No other objections to the content of the note are raised on appeal.

"An instrument to be negotiable must conform to the following requirements: . . . .

"3. Must be payable on demand, or at a fixed or determinable future time."

It is clear that the note in suit does not come within either of the classes of the notes which are payable on demand.

"An instrument is payable at a determinable future time, within the meaning of this (Neg. Inst.) act, which is expressed to be payable: 1. At a fixed period after date or sight; or 2. On or before a fixed or determinable future time specified therein; or 3. On or at a fixed period after the occurrence of a specified event, which is certain to happen."

The note in suit does not expressly provide that it is payable "At a fixed period after date or sight." On the contrary, it expressly provides that the payees may declare it due at any time they may deem it insecure. The date of maturity is uncertain and remains uncertain until the payees "deem themselves insecure." Hence this note does not fall in that class of notes covered by subsection 1 of section 11363, Burns' 1926.

The note in suit does not expressly provide that the note is payable "on or at a fixed period after the occurrence of a specified event which is certain to happen." The maturity of this note does not depend upon, nor relate to, any "occurrence of a specified event," unless it be agreed that it relates to the "deeming," by the payees, that they are insecure, and that such "deeming" is an "occurrence of a specified event" within the meaning of said subsection 3 of section 11363, Burns' 1926. Even though it be assumed that the "deeming" by the payees that they are insecure, be an "occurrence of a specified event" within the meaning of said subsection, still it cannot be seriously contended that it is an occurrence of a specified event which is certain to happen. Hence the note in suit does not belong to the class of notes covered by subsection 3 of section 11363, Burns' 1926.

The great weight of authority in the courts of appeal of the several states, both before and since the adoption of the Uniform Negotiable Instruments Law, is to the effect that a provision which gives the holder of the note unlimited authority to accelerate the maturity of the note, "when he deems himself insecure," makes the time of payment uncertain and indefinite, hence renders the note non-negotiable.

Holliday State Bank v. Hoffman
85 Kan. 71, 116 Pac. 239, 35 L.R.A. (N.S.) 390,
Ann. Cas 1912D 1 (1911)

This was an action by Holliday State Bank (plaintiff) against C. B. Hoffman (defendant). Judgment for plaintiff and defendant appealed. Judgment reversed and remanded.

Defendant gave his promissory note in payment of corporate stock. The note was negotiated to the plaintiff who claimed to be a holder in due course. Defendant sets up as a defense that he was induced to purchase the stock by false and fraudulent representation and that the note is not negotiable.

Porter, J. The case turns upon the question whether the note is negotiable. It reads as follows:

"$4,500.00 No. ...... Kansas City, Mo., Sept. 18th, 190.... Due ...... Six months ...... after date for value received ...... I promise to pay to the order of Merchants' Refrigerating Company, Kansas City, Missouri ...... forty five hundred and no/100 ...... dollars at the office of the Merchants' Refrigerating Company, Kansas City, Mo., with interest from maturity until paid at the rate of six per cent. per annum. To secure the payment of this note and of any and all other indebtedness which .... I .... now owe to the holder hereof, or may owe him at any time before the payment of this note ..... I have hereto attached, as collateral security the following: Stock certificate No. 137 of the capital stock of the Merchants' Refrigerating Company, calling for 50 shares of the stock; par value $5,000. The above collateral has a market value of $6,250.00. If, in the judgment of the holder of this note, said collateral depreciates in value, the undersigned agrees to deliver when demanded additional security to the satisfaction of said holder; otherwise this note shall mature at once. Any assignment or transfer of this note, or obligations herein provided for, shall carry with it the said collateral securities and all rights under this agreement. And I hereby authorize the holder hereof on default of this note, or any part thereof, according to the terms hereof, to sell said collateral or any part thereof, at public or private sale and with or without notice, and by such sale the pledgor's right of redemption shall be extinguished. C. B. Hoffman."

The provisions of the negotiable instruments law, which it is claimed are applicable to the note, are as follows:

"An instrument to be negotiable must conform to the following requirements: (1) It must contain an unconditional promise or order to pay a sum certain in money; (2) must be payable on demand or at a fixed or determinable future time.

"An instrument is payable at a determinable future time, within the meaning of this act, which is expressed to be payable: (1) on or before a fixed or determinable future time specified therein; or (2) on or at a fixed period after the occurrence of a specified event which is certain to happen, though the time of happening be uncertain. An instrument payable upon a contingency is not negotiable, and the happening of the event does not cure the defect.

"An instrument which contains an order or promise to do any act in addition to the payment of money is not negotiable. But the negotiable character of an instrument otherwise negotiable is not affected by a provision which: (1) authorizes the sale of collateral securities in case the instrument be not paid at maturity."

The defendant contends that under these provisions of the statute the note is non-negotiable for three reasons: (1) It is not for a sum certain; (2) it is not due at a fixed or determinable future time; (3) it contains promises to do acts in addition to the payment of money.

In our opinion the most serious objection to the form of the note, the particular provision which most clearly destroys the negotiable character of the instrument, is the agreement as to matters other than the payment of money. This is the stipulation by which the maker agrees to deliver, when demanded, additional collateral security to the satisfaction of the holder, in default of which the note shall mature at once. It would hardly be different if the note recited that it was secured by a chattel mortgage upon certain live stock, and contained an agreement that in case their value should depreciate, and the holder should deem the security insufficient, the maker would, on demand, execute and deliver to the holder a mortgage upon certain real estate for such amount as would satisfy the holder, and that otherwise the note should mature at once. Such an instrument would not be an unconditional promise to pay money, but would be a promise to do something in addition thereto.

The negotiable instruments law, which is merely declaratory of the mercantile law on the subject, contains a provision which, as we construe it, makes the note in the instant case non-negotiable. Section 5258 of the General Statutes of 1909 reads: "An instrument which contains an order or promise to do any act in addition to the payment of money is not negotiable." The section then enumerates certain things which are not to be regarded as falling within the inhibition. None of these exceptions cover such a promise as the one under consideration.

The note is non-negotiable for the further reason that the same provision renders doubtful and uncertain the time at which it shall become due. If the maker shall fail when demanded to furnish additional security to the satisfaction of the holder, the note shall mature at once. It is argued that this is no different in principle from the provision that default in the payment of any installment shall accelerate the maturity of the note, and cases are cited in which we have held that a similar provision will not render the note non-negotiable. The negotiable instruments law itself expressly declares that a negotiable instrument may contain provisions of this kind. The distinction between such a stipulation and the one in question lies in the fact that in the one instance the maturity is accelerated by the default of the maker alone, and the default is to consist in his failure to pay money. Here the maturity of the note is to be accelerated by the failure of the maker to do something in addition to the payment of money, and both contingencies are made to depend upon something over which he has not the absolute control. It is within the power of the holder, by refusing assent to what the maker has done, arbitrarily to make the note due at any time between the date of its execution and six months thereafter. If the holder is not satisfied with the additional security, the note matures at once, and thus the time at which it may mature would depend upon the time at which the holder declared himself dissatisfied with the security delivered by the maker. The effect of this stipulation is to leave the time when payable uncertain and indefinite.

Payable to Order or Bearer

Unless the person issuing an instrument intends it to be a negotiable instrument, it is not negotiable. It is customary to indicate the intention that the instrument be negotiable by the use of the words "order" or "bearer"; however, it is not necessary to use either of these words. Any language used in the instrument which indicates such intention is sufficient. If no words of negotiability are used in the instrument, it is not negotiable.

Instruments are generally made payable "to Burch or order," "to the order of Burch," "to Burch or bearer," or "to bearer." An instrument drawn payable "to bearer Burch" is not negotiable because it indicates that payment is to be made to Burch who is bearer of the instrument and to no one else.

Haggard v. Mutual Oil & Refining Co.
204 Ky. 209, 263 S.W. 745 (1924)

This was an action by Rodney Haggard (plaintiff) against Mutual Oil & Refining Company (defendant). Judgment for defendant and plaintiff appealed. Judgment affirmed.

Clarke, J. The single question presented by this appeal is whether or not the following check is a negotiable instrument:

"$2,500.00. Winchester, Ky., July 10, 1920.

"The Winchester Bank, of Winchester, Ky.:

Pay to Arco Refinery Construction Company twenty-five hundred and no/100 dollars, for a/c constructing refinery, switch, and loading racks, Win. Ky.

"Mutual Oil & Refining Co.,

"By C. L. Bell, Pres."

Subdivision 4 of section 3720b, which is the Negotiable Instruments Act (Acts 1913, p. 213), § 1, provides that:

"An instrument to be negotiable must conform to the following requirements: . . . .

(4) Must be payable to the order of a specified person or to bearer."

Since, as the check itself shows, and as is admittedly true, the maker, in issuing the check, drew a line through the printed words "or bearer," we need only to examine it to ascertain whether or not it was "payable to the order of a specified person," for unless so, it lacked one of the essentials prescribed for negotiability.

Section 8 of the act (section 3720b8 of the Statutes) defines when an instrument is payable to order as follows:

> "The instrument is payable to order where it is drawn payable to the order of a specified person or to him or his order."

It will be noticed that the above check is not payable to the order of the payee, nor to the payee or its order, but is payable simply to the payee. It therefore seems to us too clear for dispute that this check is not payable to order, and is therefore, as the lower court held, not negotiable.

In other words, we think it is clear that subsection 8 means, as it says, that the instrument must be payable either (1) to the order of the payee, or (2) to the payee or order, and that it does not permit of the construction that the instrument may be payable (1) to the order of the payee, (2) or to the payee, or (3) to his order.

To give the section the latter of these two constructions rather than the former makes the first and third alternatives identical, and this plainly was never intended. Not only is this conclusion unavoidable from a consideration simply of the language of the section, but it has uniformly been so construed by this and other courts.

QUESTIONS AND PROBLEMS

1. Why is the form of an instrument important?
2. A hand-written note reads as follows:
   "I, Adam Archer, promise to pay, on demand, to Burt Burch or order $100.00."
   Is it a negotiable instrument?
3. A bill of exchange is issued without the signature of the drawer. The bill is presented to the drawee who accepts it by signing his name across the face of the instrument. After the drawee has signed his name across the face of the instrument, is the instrument negotiable?
4. A promissory note which complied with all the formal requirements of the statute contained the following notations: "This note is given for the purchase money of stocks and the same is not transferrable or assignable without the said certificate attached thereto. Said stock is to be delivered to the makers hereof upon payment of this note." Does this notation render the instrument non-negotiable?
5. Is the following instrument negotiable?
   "At sight pay to the order of Elliott National Bank $795.
   Value received and charge the same to account of 250 bbls. of meal ex schooner Aurora Borealis.
   "To Ralph Whitney. Signed Hatborey & Co."
6. A promissory note which complied with all the formal requirements of the statute contained the following notation: "Subject to the purchase of the Cuba Elevator." Is the note negotiable?
7. A note negotiable in form contained the following: "This note covers the deferred installments under a conditional sales contract made this day between the payee and the maker hereof." Is the instrument negotiable?
8. A bill of exchange is drawn payable "at the first frost in the fall of 1918." Is it payable at a fixed or determinable time?
9. The American Telephone and Telegraph Company issued bearer bonds containing a provision that the holder of the bond would receive the face of the bond in

money or, at his option, an equivalent in stock of the corporation. Does the option destroy the negotiability of the bond?

10. A note, otherwise negotiable, contains the following provision: "With interest at the rate of 7 per cent per annum payable annually, together with all taxes assessed upon said sum, against payee or holder of this note." Is the instrument negotiable?
11. Is a note, payable "one day after my death," negotiable?
12. A draft was drawn payable "on completion of brick apartment." Is it negotiable?
13. A note given in payment of the purchase price of a machine provides that the maker shall keep the machine in repair and also that he shall keep the machine insured for the benefit of the holder of the note. Is the note negotiable?
14. Is the following instrument negotiable?
"I. O. U., E. A. Gay, the sum of seventeen 5/100 dollars, for value received.
"John R. Rooke"
15. A promissory note negotiable in form is signed by a maker who is an infant. Does the fact that the maker is an infant destroy the negotiability of the instrument?

CHAPTER XXIII

NEGOTIATION AND HOLDER IN DUE COURSE

Negotiation

The concept of negotiation is confined to negotiable instruments. One may assign a contract which is not negotiable, but he cannot negotiate it. Negotiation is the transfer of a negotiable instrument from one person to another in such a manner as to constitute the transferee the holder of the instrument. To constitute the transferee the holder of the instrument one must in transferring the instrument comply with the requirements of the Uniform Negotiable Instruments Law. If the instrument is payable to order, it is negotiated by the indorsement of the payee completed by delivery. If the instrument is payable to bearer, it is negotiated by delivery. This raises three questions: (1) when is an instrument payable to order? (2) when is an instrument payable to bearer? and (3) what constitutes delivery?

An instrument is payable to order when it is drawn payable to the order of a specified person, or to him or his order. An instrument drawn "Pay to the order of Burch" or an instrument drawn "Pay to Burch or order" complies with this requirement and is an instrument payable to order. The instrument need not be drawn payable to a named individual, but may be drawn payable to the order of two or more persons, as "Pay to the order of Burch, Sinn, and Rank" or "Pay to the order of Burch or Sinn or Rank." Also an instrument drawn "Pay to the order of the Treasurer of the United States" is drawn payable to order. When the instrument is payable to order, the payee must be named or otherwise indicated therein with reasonable certainty. To negotiate an instrument payable to order, a person must indorse and deliver it. If the payee is not named or indicated therein, one taking the instrument could not know whether or not it was properly indorsed.

An instrument is payable to bearer when it is expressed to be payable to bearer, as "Pay to bearer" or when it is payable to a named payee or bearer, as "Pay to Burch or bearer." When an instrument is drawn payable to a fictitious or nonexisting person, and such fact is known to the person making it so payable, or when the name of the payee does not purport to be the name of any person, the instrument is payable to bearer. To hold otherwise would make it impossible to negotiate such instruments because they, being drawn payable to the order of a named payee, if treated as instruments drawn payable to order, would have to be indorsed and delivered to be negotiated, and if the payee is a fictitious or nonexisting person or does not purport to be a person, there would be no one who could indorse the instrument; consequently, it could not be negotiated. Such instruments, therefore, are treated as payable to bearer and are negotiated by delivery. An instrument drawn "Pay to the order of David Copperfield" if the person drawing the instrument used the name as the name of a fictitious person is drawn payable to bearer. Also an instrument drawn "Pay to the order of Cash" is drawn payable to bearer. An instrument drawn "Pay to bearer Burch" is not payable to bearer; nor is it a negotiable instrument.

Delivery is the physical handing over of the instrument to another person with the intent that such person shall become owner of the instrument. The delivery may be contingent; for example, Archer may deliver a note to Burch on Burch's promise to hold the instrument and return it to Archer on the happening of some stated event. If a negotiable instrument is given by the drawer, maker, or indorser to his own agent to be given to a named person, there will be no delivery until the instrument is given to the named person or his agent.

Security-First National Bank of Los Angeles v. Bank of America National Trust & Savings Ass'n.
22 Cal. (2d) 154, 137 P. (2d) 452 (1943)

This was an action by the Security-First National Bank of Los Angeles (plaintiff) against the Bank of America National Trust & Savings Association (defendant). Judgment for plaintiff and defendant appealed. Judgment affirmed.

Dee L. Ellis, Jr., was head of the accounting division of plaintiff's trust department. A. M. Hadley was one of plaintiff's officers and as such signed checks. Ellis prepared checks for the trust department and Hadley signed them. Ellis prepared a number of checks for Hadley's signature, drawn to the order of L. W. Bobbitt, presented them to Hadley in the regular course of the business, and Hadley signed the checks. There was such a person as L. W. Bobbitt, but he knew nothing of the transaction and Ellis did not intend that he receive any of the checks. Ellis indorsed the checks as agent of L. W. Bobbitt and the defendant cashed the checks for Ellis. The checks were presented to the drawee bank and paid by it. When the fraud was discovered plaintiff sued defendant to recover the amount of the checks

If the checks were drawn payable to order they were not negotiated because not properly indorsed; however, if they were drawn to bearer they were negotiable by delivery and plaintiff cannot recover.

Traynor, J. Defendant invokes section 9 (3) of the Uniform Negotiable Instruments Act providing: "The instrument is payable to bearer . . . . (3) when it is payable to the order of a fictitious or nonexistent person, and such fact was known to the person making it so payable. . . . " If these checks are payable to a fictitious payee, and are therefore bearer paper, defendant's guarantee of the indorsements imposes no liability. The fact that Bobbitt was an actual person does not prevent his name from being that of a fictitious payee, for it is settled that an instrument is drawn to the order of a fictitious payee if it is not intended that the person named on its face have any interest in it. Such a check, however, is not payable to bearer unless the fact that the payee is fictitious is known by "the person making it so payable."

This condition limits the extent to which the fictitious payee rule qualifies the usual rules governing the effect of forged indorsements. A forged indorsement is ordinarily a nullity. It does not pass title to a check, and a bank may not charge to the account of its depositor a check paid on the basis of such an indorsement. Where the drawer intentionally makes a check payable to a fictitious payee, he knows that it will be indorsed in the name of the payee by someone bearing another name and he thus cannot obtain the benefit of these rules. Similarly, when he intrusts an employee with the responsibility of signing his checks, the signer takes the place of the drawer. His signature creates the check and his knowledge binds the drawer. When the drawer or his signer is the victim of the fraud of the bookkeeper who is charged with examining the drawer's accounts and informing him of his liabilities, the person buying or paying the check has no right to a release at the expense of the innocent drawer from the responsibility of determining the authenticity of the indorsements.

Hadley, not Ellis, was the signer of plaintiff's checks. Defendant, however, asserts that Hadley acted as a mere automaton, and that Ellis's authorization was in effect an order to him to execute the checks. While Hadley ordinarily signed in reliance on vouchers executed by Ellis, the record shows that he refused on at least one occasion to sign a check authorized by Ellis. In many large businesses, it is necessary for the officer authorized to sign checks to do so in reliance on the vouchers of another employee, although that employee has no authority over him. In this situation, as in the execution of plaintiff's checks, the fraud of the employee preparing the vouchers automatically leads to the unwitting execution by the signer of checks to fictitious payees. Since this severance of the function of investigating disbursements from that of executing checks creates the only situation in which checks can be commonly executed to a fictitious payee without the knowledge of the person making them so payable, it is probable that the requirement of knowledge was included in the section to prevent such checks from becoming payable to bearer.

Cartwright v. Coppersmith et al.
222 N.C. 573, 24 S.E. (2d) 246 (1943)

This was an action by J. Milton Cartwright as executor of Sarah E. Elliott, deceased (plaintiff) against W. B. Coppersmith, Sr., and wife (defendants). Lydia Mae Whitehurst was made a party defendant on the request of the defendants. Judgment for plaintiff against defendants Coppersmith and defendant Whitehurst appealed. Judgment affirmed.

In 1935 and 1936 defendants Coppersmith and wife executed four negotiable promissory notes payable to Sarah E. Elliott in the sum of $2,500. When suit was brought by plaintiff the defendants Coppersmith admitted the execution of the notes and the obligation on them but denied that the notes were the property of Sarah E. Elliott and alleged that they were the property of Lydia Mae Whitehurst. Whitehurst was made a party defendant and filed a separate answer in which she alleged she was the sole owner of the notes by virtue of indorsement and delivery of the notes to her by Sarah E. Elliott.

In 1937 while Coppersmith was on a visit to Sarah E. Elliott, she told him that she wanted Mrs. Whitehurst to have the Coppersmith notes after her death, and that the only thing she wanted was the interest as long as she lived. Coppersmith advised Miss Elliott that the only way she could accomplish that without making a will was to indorse the notes and make them payable to Mrs. Whitehurst. Not having a pen convenient, Coppersmith wrote on each in lead pencil, "Pay within note to Lydia Mae Whitehurst without recourse" and Sarah E. Elliott signed the indorsement on each note and retained possession of the notes. In 1940 when Coppersmith paid the interest on the notes, he saw the notes and noticed that the indorsement had been erased but that it still showed dimly. There was no evidence as to who erased the indorsement. When Sarah E. Elliott died the notes were in the possession of her agent. The agent had no instructions to hold the notes for Mrs. Whitehurst.

Devin, J. The burden of proof was upon Mrs. Whitehurst to show not only the indorsement of the notes by Sarah E. Elliott, but also that the intention to give or assign them to her was completed by delivery, actual or constructive. In this we think she has failed, even if the entire evidence of Mr. Coppersmith had been admitted.

It is provided by C.S. § 3010 that if a negotiable instrument is made payable to order (as were these notes) the transfer from one person to another is "by the indorsement of the holder, and completed by delivery." To constitute delivery there must be a parting with the possession and with power and control over it by the maker or indorser for the benefit of the payee or indorsee. To constitute delivery it must be put out of possession of the indorser. An actual delivery, however, is not essential, and a constructive delivery will be held sufficient if made with the intention of transferring the title, but there must be some unequivocal act, more than the mere expression of an intention or desire.

The general rule is stated in 7 Am. Jur., p. 809, as follows: "While it is not indispensable that there should have been an actual manual transfer of the instrument from the maker to the payee, yet, to constitute a delivery, it must appear that the maker in some way evinced an intention to make it an enforceable obligation against himself, according to its terms, by surrendering control over it and intentionally placing it under the power of the payee or of some third person for his use."

It is true the fact of retention of possession by the indorser is not always fatal to a claim of constructive delivery. It is said in 10 C.J.S., Bills and Notes, § 78, p. 513: "There may be a delivery notwithstanding the maker keeps the note in his possession, where it is apparent that he intended to hold it for the benefit and as the agent of the payee."

But here the proffered testimony falls short of coming within that principle. According to the evidence no word was ever spoken by Sarah E. Elliott to Mrs. Whitehurst. The notes were retained in possession by the indorser, after signing the indorsement, without any declaration of agency or purpose other than that she wished the indorsee to have them after her death. The notes continued in her exclusive possession until some two years later when they came into the possession of J. M. Cartwright for her, with the indorsements erased. There was no parting of control over them either to the indorsee or to any other person for her benefit. The expressed intention did not contemplate a present transfer but a prospective donation. The intention not having been completed by delivery, title did not vest in the indorsee.

Indorsement

A negotiable instrument may be indorsed for two distinct and separate reasons. It may be indorsed because the indorsement is necessary to the negotiation of the instrument or it may be indorsed to lend credit to the instrument. When a person indorses a negotiable instrument, he assumes definite obligations. These obligations of an indorser will be discussed later under a separate heading. There are five types of indorsements generally recognized but only three of these have a direct bearing on the negotiation of negotiable instruments; consequently, we shall confine our present discussion to these three types of indorsements.

An order instrument when indorsed with a special indorsement continues as order paper and must be again indorsed before it can be further negotiated. If an instrument drawn "Pay to the order of Burch" is indorsed "Pay to Fox, Burch" and is delivered to Fox, the indorsement is a special indorsement and if Fox wishes to negotiate the instrument he must indorse it.

The most common indorsement is the indorsement in blank. The indorsement in blank specifies no indorsee, and an instrument so indorsed is payable to bearer and may be thereafter negotiated by delivery. If an instrument drawn "Pay to the order of Burch" is indorsed "Burch" and delivered to Fox, the instrument is indorsed in blank and is converted to a bearer instrument. Fox can negotiate the instrument by delivery.

If an order negotiable instrument is indorsed in blank and delivered to a holder, the holder may convert the blank indorsement into a special indorsement by writing over the signature of the indorser in blank any contract which will not in any way alter the obligations imposed by the blank indorsement. One cannot convert an instrument payable to bearer to order paper by indorsing it with a special indorsement. Although the courts are not in complete accord, the majority of courts hold that a special indorsement following a blank indorsement will not reconvert the instrument to order paper. If a negotiable instrument drawn "Pay to the order of Burch" is indorsed "Burch" and delivered to Fox, Fox has the right to write over Burch's indorsement "Pay to Fox," thereby converting the blank indorsement into a special indorsement, and the instrument would have to be again indorsed before it could be further negotiated; but if the instrument is indorsed "Burch" and delivered to Fox and thereafter Fox indorses it "Pay to Grew, Fox," the majority of the courts hold that the instrument continues as bearer paper and can be negotiated by delivery. If a negotiable instrument drawn "Pay to Burch or bearer" is indorsed "Pay to Fox, Burch," it continues to be bearer paper and can be negotiated by delivery.

The third type of indorsement which we wish to discuss is the restrictive indorsement. No particular pattern is followed in making a restrictive indorsement, but any indorsement which prohibits or restricts further negotiation of the instrument, or which in effect appoints the indorsee the indorser's agent, or which vests the title to the instrument in the indorsee as trustee for the benefit of some other person, is a restrictive indorsement. To be a restrictive indorsement the restriction must be expressly set out in the indorsement. If there are no restrictive words in the indorsement, it is held that the indorsement is not restrictive. A restrictive indorsement confers on the indorsee the right to receive payment of the instrument, the right to bring any action on the instrument which the indorser could bring, and to transfer any right which he has acquired in the instrument where the form of the indorsement permits him to do so. Any holder taking an instrument bearing a restrictive indorsement takes with notice of the restrictions and acquires only the title of the first indorsee under the restrictive indorsement.

Two common restrictive indorsements are "Pay to First Bank for collection only" and "Pay to First Bank for deposit only." These indorsements constitute the First Bank the agent of the indorser for the purpose of collection, and anyone taking the instrument from the First Bank would acquire no title to the instrument. An indorsement "Pay to Fox only" would prohibit the further negotiation of the instrument. A restrictive indorsement is equally effective on order or bearer paper. Such an indorsement restricts the further negotiation of the paper according to the terms of the restriction and is notice to all subsequent holders of the instrument; consequently, it is immaterial whether the instrument is bearer or order paper.

Edgecombe Bonded Warehouse Company v. Security National Bank
216 N.C. 246, 4 S.E. (2d) 863 (1939)

This was an action by Edgecombe Bonded Warehouse Company (plaintiff) against Security National Bank (defendant). Judgment for plaintiff and defendant appealed. Judgment reversed and a new trial was ordered.

Plaintiff transacted its banking business with the defendant. Between November 14, 1936, and May 12, 1939, the plaintiff claims that the defendant paid 49 checks totaling $4,862.77 which were payable to the order of plaintiff and indorsed "Pay to the order of any bank, banker or trust company. All prior indorsements guaranteed. Edgecombe Bonded Warehouse Company, by A. B. Bass, Sec.-Treas." to persons other than a bank, banker, or trust company, and that plaintiff did not receive the proceeds from the collection of the checks. It further claims that the indorsement is a special indorsement and that the defendant having paid the check to persons other than the indorsee the defendant is liable to the plaintiff for the loss. Defendant contends that the money representing the proceeds from the collection of the checks was paid to officers or employees of plaintiff, pursuant to one of the customary methods adopted by the plaintiff in handling checks received by it. The trial judge ruled that the indorsement was a special indorsement and that the defendant offered no evidence of facts which would justify the defendant in paying the checks to anyone other than the named indorsee and directed a verdict for the plaintiff. On appeal two questions were raised (1) was the indorsement a special indorsement? and (2) did the defendant offer sufficient evidence, to have the evidence submitted to the jury, of an established custom or course of dealing between the plaintiff and defendant which would relieve the defendant of liability to the plaintiff for having paid the checks to others than the named indorsee?

The Supreme Court reversed the decision and ordered a new trial on the ground that the case should have been submitted to the jury.

Barnhill, J. Our statute provides that an indorsement may be either in blank or special, and it may also be either restricted, or qualified or conditional. A special indorsement specifies the person to whom, or to whose order, the instrument is to be payable; and the indorsement of such indorsee is necessary to the further negotiation of the instrument. If payable to the bearer, it is negotiated by delivery; if payable to order, it is negotiated by the indorsement of the holder and completed by delivery. For convenience, indorsements might well be put into two general classes; unqualified—in blank; and qualified—all indorsements not in blank.

The requirement that an indorsement shall specify the person to whom, or to whose order, the instrument is payable is necessary to make it a special indorsement is fully met when a particular class is designated. Thus, an indorsement to "any bank, banker or trust company" is a sufficient designation of a person to make the indorsement special and to require the indorsement of one within that class as a prerequisite to the further negotiation of the instrument. Nothing else appearing, a check indorsed in the manner adopted by the plaintiff in the hands of someone who had found it upon the street or by a person other than the plaintiff or its agent would not be negotiable in the hands of such person and he could not pass title thereto. Any one accepting the same would do so at his own risk unprotected by the Negotiable Instruments Law. Under these circumstances, by reason of the limitations of the indorsement, neither the person cashing the check nor the bank receiving it could have or acquire any title to the same.

Doucette v. Old National Bank & Union Trust Co.
161 Wash. 159, 296 Pac. 570 (1931)

This was an action by Pricia Doucette, formerly Mrs. E. D. Tamas (plaintiff) against the Old National Bank & Union Trust Company (defendant). Judgment for defendant and plaintiff appealed. Judgment affirmed.

Mr. & Mrs. E. D. Tamas had a joint account with the defendant and E. D. Tamas had an individual account with it. On October 17, 1927, Mrs. Tamas had a check for $2,120 drawn payable to Mrs. E. D. Tamas. The check was indorsed in blank by Mrs. Tamas, the indorsement reading "Mrs. E. D. Tamas" and given to E. D. Tamas. At the time Mrs. Tamas gave the check to her husband she instructed him to deposit it in their joint account, but Tamas indorsed the check "Mr. E. D. Tamas, Martin Hotel" and deposited it in his individual account. He has since withdrawn the money. The balance of his account on April 4, 1928, was $176.79. On April 3, 1928, Mrs. E. D. Tamas got a statement of the joint account and at this time learned that the check had not been deposited to the joint account. Before this suit was brought, Mrs. Tamas obtained a divorce and had her former name restored. In this suit she contends that the defendant is liable because it knowingly participated in the diversion of the money.

Millard, J. The check in controversy was indorsed by the appellant payee in blank. So indorsed, a check passes by delivery as fully and freely as a bank note.

"An indorsement in blank, which is the simplest and most common form of indorsement, is one which does not mention the person in whose favor it is made, and consists generally simply of the name of the indorser written on the back of the instrument . . . . an indorsement in which no indorsee is named is a blank indorsement, although it contains a guaranty of payment." § 536, p. 357, Vol. 8, C.J.

Appellant indorsed the check in blank—she simply wrote her name on the back of the check and did not mention the person in whose favor it was made—thus clothing her husband with the full indicia of ownership. The bank had no notice nor was it put upon notice that the check was to be deposited to a joint account. Had she placed a restrictive indorsement upon the check her rights would have been fully protected. On the day Tamas deposited this check he also deposited to his personal account $100.22, the proceeds from the hotel he and his wife were operating. Appellant knew that her husband had a personal checking account and that he was frequently drawing on same account in respondent bank. Though appellant made or her husband made one deposit for her to their joint account, it does not follow that the bank would thereafter be charged with notice that each and every check indorsed in blank presented by the appellant's husband should be placed to the credit of the joint account. There is no more reason for such presumption than that the bank would be presumed to know that whenever the appellant's husband deposited cash same should be placed to the credit of the joint account. Having indorsed the check in blank, the bank was not placed upon notice that same was to be placed to the credit of the joint account. If a bank pays a check indorsed in blank upon presentment to the holder thereof having at the time no reasonable cause for suspecting any irregularity or any cause for refusing such payment, the bank will be protected in doing so, no matter what facts unknown to it may have occurred prior to the presentment.

First National Bank of Sioux City, Iowa v. John Morrell & Co.
53 S.D. 496, 221 N.W. 95, 60 A.L.R. 863 (1928)

This was an action by the First National Bank of Sioux City, Iowa (plaintiff) against John Morrell & Co. (defendant). Judgment for defendant and plaintiff appealed. Judgment affirmed.

Defendant had an account with the Sioux Falls National Bank and deposited checks received from its customers drawn on banks in their respective localities. It indorsed the checks which it deposited as follows: "Pay to the order of Sioux Falls National Bank, for deposit only. John Morrell & Co." In the early part of January, 1924, defendant deposited in Sioux Falls National Bank twenty checks aggregating about $3,900, all bearing the indorsement hereinbefore quoted. The Sioux Falls National Bank on January 8th, 9th, and 10th, transmitted these checks to plaintiff at Sioux City, indorsed "Pay to the order of the First National Bank of Sioux City, Iowa. Sioux Falls National Bank 98-1. Thomas A. Wadden, Vice President and Cashier."

Plaintiff credited the Sioux Falls National Bank conditionally with the amount of the checks and forwarded them for collection to banks in the localities on which they were drawn. On January 11th the Sioux Falls National Bank failed. John Morrell & Co. telegraphed its customers, the drawers of the checks, and had them have the payment of the checks stopped. The dishonored checks were returned to the plaintiff and plaintiff brought this action claiming that defendant is liable to it as indorser of the checks.

Brown, J. Appellant contends that, because defendant received credit in his account in the Sioux Falls National Bank for the amount of the checks, the relation of debtor and creditor existed between defendant and the bank; that the bank became the owner of the checks, and that, by its indorsement of them to plaintiff, plaintiff became the owner of the checks, with a right of recourse, in the event of their dishonor, against any prior indorser. But this contention entirely ignores the contract between defendant and the Sioux Falls bank, created by the indorsement on the checks. The indorsement "for deposit only" is a restrictive indorsement and clearly vests title in the indorsee in trust for the indorser. Such an indorsement confers upon the indorsee the right to transfer its rights as indorsee, because the indorsement authorized payment "to the order of Sioux Falls National Bank"; but the subsequent indorsee (in this case, plaintiff) acquires only the title of the first indorsee under the restrictive indorsement, and, plaintiff could only have the rights of an agent or trustee for the defendant, clothed with authority to collect the checks. Appellant says that:

"It is frankly conceded that the sole and only purpose of stopping payment of these checks was to enable defendant to reduce its balance in the Sioux Falls bank when the same closed, and, by collection of the items through other channels, thus to realize 100 cents on the dollar, instead of taking the proportion of loss, if any, which other depositors may sustain through failure of the bank."

But this is just what defendant had a lawful right to do. It had a right at any time to revoke the agency of plaintiff for collection of the checks, and to avoid loss by collecting through other channels the accounts due from the makers of the checks. Had the checks been collected through the medium of the banks, and the money had reached the Sioux Falls National, the relation of debtor and creditor between the bank and defendant would then, and not until then, have arisen.

The right of an indorsee under a restrictive indorsement are not those mentioned in section 1770 of the Code, but only those enumerated in section 1741, among which is not the right to recover from the indorser on dishonor of the instrument.

Holder in Due Course

To qualify as a holder in due course one must have taken the instrument under four specific conditions. (1) The instrument must be complete and regular on its face. (2) The holder must have become such before it was overdue and without notice that it had been previously dishonored if such was a fact. (3) The holder must have taken the instrument in good faith and for value. (4) At the time the instrument is negotiated to him the holder must have had no notice of any infirmity in the instrument or defects in the title of the person negotiating it. If the holder cannot comply with these requirements, he is not a holder in due course.

Complete and Regular on Its Face

If an instrument at the time the holder takes it has unfilled blanks in it, it may or it may not be incomplete. Whether or not it will be held to be incomplete will depend on what has been omitted from the instrument as the result of the failure to fill the blanks. If the omission is material, the instrument is incomplete and the holder is not a holder in due course. The holder of an instrument which is wanting in any material respect has prima facie authority to complete the instrument by filling up the blanks. In order, however, that any such instrument when completed may be enforced against any person who became a party thereto prior to completion, it must be filled up strictly in accordance with the authority given and within a reasonable time. If any such instrument, after completion, is negotiated to one who can qualify as a holder in due course, he can recover on it. The courts have held that an instrument is incomplete if it is payable to order and the name of the payee is left blank. An instrument which was drawn "——— after date, etc," and one drawn "ten ——— after date" were held to be incomplete. Failure to fill in a pronoun does not make the instrument incomplete as "——— promise to pay." Also the omission of "or" in order paper does not make the instrument incomplete as "Pay to Burch order."

Anything on the instrument which would put the holder on notice that something was wrong with the instrument is an irregularity and makes the instrument irregular on its face. Any noticeable alteration would make the instrument irregular on its face. The courts have held that the following do not make the instrument irregular on its face: (1) Post dating, (2) omission of revenue stamps when revenue stamps are required by statute, (3) difference between the handwriting in the body of the instrument and the signature, (4) difference in the handwriting in the body of the instrument, and (5) the amount in figures and not in writing. It has also been held that an instrument which had been detached from a contract is not irregular on its face.

An instrument which is stamped "paid" or "payment refused," or one made out to an officer of a corporation and signed by the same officer as agent of the corporation, or an instrument which provides for a usurious rate of interest has been held to be irregular on its face.

A draft, trade acceptance, or check which has not been accepted by the drawee is regular on its face.

Moore v. Vaughn et al.
167 Miss. 758, 150 So. 372 (1933)

This was an action by J. H. Moore (plaintiff) against D. F. Vaughn and others (defendants). Judgment for defendants and plaintiff appealed. Judgment affirmed.

Plaintiff sued on three notes which were the same except as to due date. A copy of one of the notes is as follows:

"$50.00 Sept. 16th, 1931

"February 1st, 1932, after date.........promise to pay to the order..........Fifty..........Dollars. For value received with interest at the rate of........per cent per annum from..........and if the interest be not paid annually to become as principal, and bear the same rate of interest. This note is negotiable and payable without defalcation or discount and without any relief or benefit whatever from stay, valuation, appraisement or homestead exemption laws.

"D. F. Vaughn.

"No. 4. Due............."

Indorsed on back: "W. F. Cullinane, Katherine C. Hansen." Moore sued Vaughn et al., on the note. Vaughn set up failure of consideration as a defense. Moore purchased the note from Anderson paying full value for it.

McGowen, J. The appellant, Moore, contends that he is the holder, for value, in due course, of said notes, that the notes with the blanks therein were delivered to Anderson with implied authority to fill in the blanks, and that the words "This note is negotiable" render the notes bearer notes and negotiable instruments; and that therefore any evidence offered as a defense on behalf of the maker of the notes is incompetent.

Before discussing the question thus sharply presented as to whether or not these instruments were negotiable under the Negotiable Instruments Law, let it be noted that no effort to fill in the blanks by any holder, or the payee, appears therein. It appears that suit is brought and recovery sought on the face of the notes without amendment, alteration, or without any proof as to how the blanks should be filled in.

By section 2657, Code 1930, notes must be payable to order or bearer, and it is not subject to dispute that, when a note is payable to order, the payee must be named.

By section 2708, Code 1930, a holder in due course is a holder who has taken the instrument upon the condition that it is complete and regular upon its face.

The defense of failure of consideration is not available where the instrument is in the hands of a holder in due course. Of course, however, if a person seeking a recovery is not a holder in due course, the instrument is subject to the same defenses as if it were a non-negotiable instrument.

The appellant, J. H. Moore, seeks to avoid the effect of failure to fill in the blanks in the instruments here being considered by putting his reliance upon section 2670, Code 1930, which permits a person in possession of an instrument wanting in any material particular to fill in the blanks therein. It provides, however, that they be filled in accordance with the authority given and within a reasonable time, and, if the party in possession is to be the holder thereof, in due course.

In the case at bar, the notes are payable to the order of........ and interest is to begin on.........

In disposing of the contention that the recital in the instruments, "This note is negotiable," cures the defects, we will say that such recital does not render the notes negotiable, and that the words "pay to the order of" must be construed to require a named, specific person as payee. For illustration, if A undertakes to sell B a horse, and puts a label on a cow reading, "This is a horse," such label does not change the character, or name, of the animal. These words alone would not be sufficient to make an order note a bearer note. The contract here to the effect that the notes were negotiable did not supply the requirement mandatorily fixed by the statute, and does not avail to render them complete and regular on their face, so that Moore can now be declared to be a holder in due course.

We are therefore clearly of the opinion that Moore, the appellant here, took the notes with the infirmity thereon, and was put upon inquiry of Anderson, who sold them to him. If Anderson, to whom the notes were delivered by the maker, had filled in the blanks, and Moore had paid value therefor, without notice, the defense here probably could not have interposed.

We are not unmindful of the great value to the commercial world of removing obstacles in order to facilitate the transfer of negotiable instruments. Ninety per cent of the great volume of the business of this country is conducted by the medium of negotiable instruments. Negotiable instruments, of one kind or another, are absolutely essential, in this day, to business of all kinds; but, where a person buys paper with patent defects thereon, with unfilled blanks, and his transferor does not fill same, nor does he do so himself, he stands charged with knowledge of such defects and irregularities apparent on the face of the paper, and he is not a holder in due course.

Dunbar et al. v. Iowa State Bank
221 Mo. App. 979, 295 S.W. 835 (1927)

This was an action by Phillip E. Dunbar and another (plaintiffs) against Iowa State Bank (defendant). Judgment for plaintiffs and defendant appealed. Judgment reversed.

A person representing himself to be B. W. Miller deposited a check for $800 payable to his order and drawn on the First National Bank of Englewood, Colorado, in the Iowa State Bank. This deposit was made on March 5, 1925. At the same time the Iowa State Bank issued two cashier checks for $100 each payable to B. W. Miller and post dated them. One was dated March 14, 1925, and the other was dated March 24, 1925. On March 9, B. W. Miller telegraphed the Iowa State Bank that he had lost the checks and to stop payment on them. The checks were indorsed "B. W. Miller" and negotiated. When presented for payment the dates had been altered; the numerals before the 4 on the dates being blotted out. The ink used was of a different color than that used in writing the dates. The $800 check deposited by Miller was protested and never paid. The Iowa State Bank refused payment on the cashier's checks. Plaintiff sued the Iowa State Bank claiming he was a holder in due course.

Williams, C. Plaintiff submitted his case on the theory that he did not discern any alteration on the face of the check.

Under the evidence of the witnesses, the exhibits, and the stipulation, the change was such as to be apparent upon the face of the paper and was easily discernible by inspection.

It is not an answer in a case where a material alteration is patent upon the face of the instrument to say that the one purchasing did not see the alteration, and therefore becomes a holder in due course.

Respondent relies upon the case of *Ivan Link* v. *J. W. Jackson, et al.*, 158 Mo. App. loc. cit. 63, 139 S.W. 588. However, this case does not discuss an altered instrument, but only discusses the rights of innocent parties, the paper being regular upon its face. What the court said in discussing an innocent purchaser for value of paper regular upon its face can have no application to facts such as presented by this record.

It is next contended by respondent, one of two innocent parties must suffer, and the one who made the wrong possible is the one to suffer the loss. While this is a correct principle of law, it cannot apply to a material alteration discernible upon the face of the paper. To apply that principle to the law of negotiable instruments would repeal many of our statutes upon that question.

Overdue and Dishonored Paper

A negotiable instrument which bears a fixed due date is overdue after that date, and an instrument which is payable a stated time after date or after it is issued is due when the time stated has elapsed. One who takes an instrument when it is overdue takes it subject to defenses to the instrument. The fact that the instrument is overdue and has not been paid puts anyone taking the instrument on notice, and he cannot take as a holder in due course.

If the instrument is a demand instrument, one taking the instrument an unreasonable time after its issue cannot take as a holder in due course. The Uniform Negotiable Instruments Law provides as follows: "In determining what is a 'reasonable time' or an 'unreasonable time' regard is to be had to the nature of the instrument, the usage of trade or business (if any) with respect to such instruments, and the facts of the particular case" (Sec. 193). Whether or not a demand instrument has been negotiated before it is overdue will depend on the facts and circumstances of the particular case. Georgia, by statute, has declared that a demand instrument is immediately due. Under this statute anyone taking a demand instrument would take after the due date and could not qualify as a holder in due course. In the other states each case must be decided according to the facts of the case. Other facts being the same, a check would become overdue in a shorter time than a demand note or sight draft because the nature of a check is such that it is presented for payment within a relatively short period of time.

An instrument has been dishonored when it has been presented either for payment or acceptance, and payment or acceptance has been refused. Archer draws a check on the First Bank payable to Burch. Burch presents the check at the First Bank and payment is refused because Archer does not have sufficient funds on deposit to pay the check. If Burch negotiates the check to Fox who knows that payment has been refused, Fox does not take as a holder in due course; however, if Fox has no knowledge of the dishonor of the instrument, he could take as a holder in due course. If Archer draws a draft on Drew payable to Burch thirty days after date and Burch presents it to Drew for acceptance and Drew refuses to accept and thereafter Burch negotiates the draft to Fox who has knowledge of the presentment and dishonor, Fox is not a holder in due course.

Louisiana Mortgage Corporation, Inc. v. Pickens et al.
La. App. Ct. of App. of La., 182 So. 385 (1938)

This was an action by Louisiana Mortgage Corporation, Inc. (plaintiff) against Thomas G. Trotti, Wilmer J. Boudreaux, and others (defendants). Judgment for defendants and plaintiff appealed. Judgment affirmed.

Plaintiff brought this action to recover possession of a note which it claims was acquired by fraudulent and illegal means. The note was a demand note in the sum of $680.53, dated April 24, 1928. The interest and installments on the principal had been paid with a reasonable degree of regularity from the date of issue until the time defendant Boudreaux acquired it in June, 1934. The note was given to the plaintiff on a loan. The note was seized by the sheriff on an execution and sold at sheriff's sale to the execution creditor and was negotiated by the execution creditor to Trotti. Trotti borrowed money from Boudreaux and negotiated the note to him as security for the loan. The plaintiff contends that Boudreaux is not a holder in due course because he took the note when it was overdue.

Ott, J. The evidence clearly shows that when Boudreaux acquired the note as a pledge in June, 1934, he had no knowledge of the methods used by Trotti in acquiring it, nor did he have any actual knowledge of any infirmities or defects in the note other than appeared on its face. He made a bona fide loan to Trotti of $325 and took this note as security. Of course, if the Pickens note, originally payable on demand, was then overdue for an unreasonable length of time, Boudreaux was not a holder in due course, and took the note subject to the equities existing between plaintiff and Trotti.

Section 53 of Act No. 64 of 1904, the Negotiable Instruments Law, provides that where an instrument payable on demand is negotiated an unreasonable length of time after its issue, the holder is not deemed a holder in due course. As to what constitutes a reasonable time for the negotiation of a demand note so as to make the transferee a holder in due course, we quote the following from 8 American Jurisprudence, p. 172, Section 428:

"A holder is not deemed a holder in due course where he takes an instrument, payable on demand, an unreasonable time after its issuance, whether the instrument is payable with or without interest; but where he is otherwise qualified, he is a holder in due course where he takes it within a reasonable time after its issuance. What is a reasonable time within this rule is not necessarily the same as what is a reasonable time in which such an instrument must be presented for payment, and it is not to be arbitrarily stated for it depends upon the nature of the instrument, the usage of the trade or business (if any) with respect to such instrument, and the facts of the particular case, including the payment of interest. It has been said by some cases to be a question of fact for the jury, by others to be a question of law for the court, and by others to be a mixed question of law and fact depending on circumstances. The negotiation of such an instrument on the day of its date, the next day, two days after date, or at various intervals, even to the extent of two years after date and, in an English case, where interest payments were three years in default, eight years after date, has, under varying circumstances, been held to be before the maturity of the instrument so as to give the holder taking it the status of a holder in due course or its equivalent."

While the Pickens note was some six years old when Boudreaux took it in pledge from Trotti, yet the indorsements thereon show that regular installments of ten dollars each were paid thereon more or less regularly monthly for some ten months after the note was given, which amounts were applied to the payment of the interest and small amounts on the principal. Other payments were made thereafter as a notation on the note shows that there was a balance due of $498.52 on April 7, 1931, indicating that more than one hundred dollars had been paid on the principal in addition to the interest since the last ten dollar payment on February 1, 1929. The interest was paid and payments were made on the principal to October 18, 1932, and, as before stated, the interest was paid to February 10, 1933, while Trotti had the note, and three regular monthly payments had been made thereon just before Boudreaux acquired the note.

Considering that the note evidently represented a loan and was secured by a mortgage with the interest payable semi-annually, it is reasonable to assume that it was the intention of the parties that the maker was to pay the note in installments. The relation of the maker and the payee was not such that the note would be expected to be paid in full on demand. No demand was ever made for the payment of the note, so far as the record shows, and we think in this particular case that there was nothing in the situation or on the face of the note to indicate to Boudreaux that this demand note was overdue to the extent of taking him out of the category of a holder in due course, and as such, entitled to the protection given such a holder.

Anderson v. Elem
111 Kan. 713, 208 Pac. 573 (1922)

This was an action by J. Anderson (plaintiff) against J. H. Elem (defendant). Judgment for plaintiff and defendant appealed. Judgment affirmed.

Plaintiff sued defendant as the drawer of a check. The defendant gave the check to the payee in a transaction concluded at night. The next day the defendant stopped payment because of failure of consideration. The check was not presented for payment by the payee. He remained in the city for several days and was accessible to the drawer (defendant) who knew where he was but who took no steps to obtain possession of the check.

The check was given at Wichita October 20, 1919, and was cashed at Salina November 14, 1919, by a purchaser who had no knowledge of the failure of consideration. The defendant contends that plaintiff is not a holder in due course because he took the check when it was overdue.

Burch, J. If a check be negotiated to an innocent purchaser, it stands on the same footing as other negotiable paper with respect to defenses the drawer may interpose when sued on the instrument. For purpose of negotiation, a check is not "due" until presented for payment, and one who acquires an unpresented check a considerable time after it was issued may nevertheless be a holder in due course. Section 60 of the Negotiable Instruments Act requires that the time shall not be unreasonable. What is a reasonable time depends on a variety of facts and circumstances.

The payee, W. B. Lynch, was a patron of the plaintiff's hotel in Salina. The plaintiff was in the habit of cashing checks for his guests, and had cashed a $50 check for Lynch two weeks before he was asked to cash the check sued on.

Did the lapse of 24 days from the date the check was issued, without more, necessarily give to it, in the eyes of the plaintiff, or in law, the same appearance as that of a dishonored draft or of an overdue and unpaid promissory note?

No question arises with reference to solvency of the bank, or liability of parties other than the maker, or the statute of limitations. It is perfectly true that a check is ordinarily to be regarded as an instrument for present use; but the Negotiable Instruments Act did not declare that a check is due at once, or that it must be presented, or put in course of collection, by the close of business on the next business day after issue. A check is not overdue, for purpose of negotiation, unless there has been unreasonable delay in presenting it, and unreasonable delay must be interpreted to mean such delay as to make the check obviously stale.

The facts are all before the court. It is essential to uniformity that the court itself should determine questions of this character, and the court holds that the time elapsing between the issuing of the check and its negotiation did not deprive the plaintiff of the rights of a holder in due course.

The proof was uncontradicted that the plaintiff had no notice of infirmity in the instrument, and the circumstances under which he acquired it had no tendency to indicate bad faith.

For Value

Value is defined in the Uniform Negotiable Instruments Law as "any consideration sufficient to support a simple contract. An antecedent or pre-existing debt constitutes value" (Sec. 25). To be a holder in due course one must give value for the instrument. A promise to give value is not sufficient. If one promises to give value for an instrument but before he has paid the full amount agreed to be paid he learns of an infirmity in the instrument or a defect in the title of the person who negotiated it to him, he will be deemed to be a holder in due course only to the extent of the amount he has paid at the time he learns of the infirmity or defect.

If Burch owes Fox a past due debt and gives Fox Archer's negotiable note in payment, Fox has given value for the note. Burch agrees to sell Archer's negotiable note to Fox for $300, and Fox pays Burch $100 at the time the note is negotiated to him and agrees to pay Burch the $200 balance in two weeks. Before Fox pays the $200 he learns that Archer has a defense to the note, and even though he has knowledge of the defense, he pays Burch the $200. Fox is a holder in due course for $100 but not for the $200 paid after he learned of the defense.

A note or bill of exchange given as the renewal of a prior note or bill of exchange is given for value. Also, if a negotiable instrument is given as security for a loan, it is given for value to the extent of the amount of the loan secured. If Burch borrows $100 from the bank and pledges Archer's negotiable note for $300 as security, the bank will be a holder for value for $100.

Allen-Wright Furniture Co. v. Spoor
33 Idaho 411, 195 Pac. 632 (1921)

This was an action by the Allen-Wright Furniture Company (plaintiff) against Jacob Spoor (defendant). Judgment for plaintiff and defendant appealed. Judgment affirmed.

Plaintiff sued defendant on two negotiable promissory notes which had been indorsed and negotiated to it by the payee Empire Home Company. The Empire Home Company had purchased furniture from plaintiff giving a title-retaining note payable in installments in payment. Later the Empire Home Company defaulted the payment of several installments and indorsed the notes in suit in blank and gave them to the plaintiff in payment of the past-due installments. The Empire Home Company defaulted on later installments, and finally the plaintiff repossessed the furniture and sold it and applied the proceeds on the payment of the unpaid balance of the title note. Defendant contends that having repossessed the furniture the plaintiff is not a holder for value of the notes sued on, that there was a failure of consideration, and that he is not liable.

Lee, J. At the time these notes were indorsed and transferred to plaintiff, there was a valid and subsisting indebtedness due it from the Empire Home Company. These notes are set forth, by copy, in the record, and they are negotiable instruments.

The indorsement and transfer of these notes in due course, before maturity, by the Empire Home Company, in part payment of its indebtedness to plaintiff, was sufficient consideration to support such transfer. The fact that this indebtedness was evidenced by a title-retaining note, and that plaintiff subsequently repossessed the property for which it had been given in order to recover the balance of the account, does not result in such a failure of consideration as will defeat plaintiff's right to recover upon these notes, in the absence of a showing that by the terms of the title note such retaking of the property rescinded the sale and entitled the vendor to a return of the previous payments made. The record is silent as to the terms of this title note.

First National Bank of Appleton v. Court
183 Wis. 203, 197 N.W. 798 (1924)

This was an action by the First National Bank of Appleton (plaintiff) against E. H. Court (defendant). Judgment for plaintiff and defendant appealed. Judgment affirmed.

Defendant purchased common stock of the N. Simon Cheese Company through Havorka & Co., stock brokers, and gave his negotiable promissory note payable to Havorka & Co. for $1,000 in payment. Havorka & Co. indorsed the note "without recourse" and delivered it to N. Simon Cheese Company. The cheese company indorsed the note to the plaintiff and the plaintiff thereupon gave the cheese company credit on its open checking account for the note. On the date of the indorsement of the note, August 19, 1921, at the opening of business that day the cheese company had to its credit with the plaintiff bank a balance of $20,739.26. On the same day the bank honored and paid checks of the cheese company aggregating $90,959.50, leaving a balance at the close of business on that day to the credit of the cheese company of $14,289.20. During the course of the day the cheese company had made deposits aggregating $84,509.47.

The note matured February 16, 1922, and it appeared that the cheese company's balance with the bank exceeded the amount of the note at all times between August 19, 1921, and February 16, 1922, except on the date of maturity of the note when the cheese company's balance was $899.15. The plaintiff bank took the note in the regular course of its business. Defendant contends that the note was obtained by fraud, that the plaintiff is not a holder for value and that he is not liable on the note.

Doerfler, J. A vital, concrete proposition here presented is whether a bank in discounting a note of one of its depositors, and crediting the amount to the checking account of such depositor, becomes the bona fide owner of such note for value, where it appears from the evidence that on the date of the discount the depositor added largely to his balance by additional deposits, but withdrew from his account by checks actually paid an amount sufficiently large so as to leave to his credit at the close of business on that day a sum considerably less than the amount to his credit at the opening of business on that day, but leaving a balance at the close of business largely in excess of the amount credited by the discount of the note.

It has been firmly established in this state and throughout the country that a bank is not a holder in due course of a negotiable instrument in its possession, unless it has honored and paid checks of the depositor, or has given value for the note, or has assumed an obligation of the depositor on account of the discount of the note. Under such circumstances the mere relationship of debtor and creditor is created between the bank and the depositor, and so long as that relation continues and the deposit is not drawn out, the bank is held subject to the equities of the prior parties, notwithstanding the note was taken before maturity and without notice of any infirmity therein.

In *Mann* v. *Second Nat. Bank*, 30 Kan. 412, 1 Pac. 579, the court said:

"The proposition rests on the plainest principles of justice, and in no manner impairs the desired negotiability and security of commercial paper. Whenever the holder is a bona fide holder, he has the right to claim protection, but protection only to the extent he has lost or been injured by the acquisition of the paper. If he has parted with value, either by a cash payment or the cancellation of a debt, or giving time on the debt, or in any other manner, to that extent he has a right to claim protection; but when he has parted with nothing, there is nothing to protect. A mere promise to pay is no payment. He may rightfully say to the party from whom he purchased: 'The paper you have given me is valueless, and therefore I am under no obligation to pay'; and if the paper be in fact valueless, payment cannot be compelled."

When the note proves valueless, or the bank receives notice of infirmity of the note, it can return the note to the depositor, and debit his account for the amount thereof.

There is thus raised the question in this case whether, after the discount of a note, the amount being placed to the credit of the depositor in his checking account in the bank, and he subsequently withdraws from such checking account an amount equal to his credit at the time of the deposit, and including the amount of the discounted note, the bank becomes a bona fide holder for value of the note, notwithstanding there may remain thereafter at all times between the date of the discount of the note and the maturity of the note a balance in excess of the amount of the note.

We have examined the cases, the textbooks, and the reference books upon this subject, and we find the rule firmly established by overwhelming authority, that in such case the bank becomes a holder for value of the note. Under such circumstances the authorities hold that the doctrine of the presumption of the application of payment applies; the maxim being stated as follows: "The first money in is the first money out."

The rule of the presumption of the application of payments is founded upon principles of equity and justice. Where it can be said that the bank still has in its possession the proceeds of the discounted note, and where an infirmity appears in the note on account of fraud of which the bank has notice, and where the bank is in a position where by cross entry or set-off it can make itself whole and also protect such maker, the money so deposited should be applicable for the benefit of such bank and maker. Such a ruling redounds to the benefit of the defrauded party, and works no injury to the bank. Where a note is executed to a depositor, and the note is indorsed to a bank, and the amount credited to the depositor's account, the rights of the maker are referable to the amount so credited, and vanish when the bank honors the checks of the depositor whereby the amount is withdrawn. Upon the transfer to the bank by the depositor of the notes of subsequent makers, there springs up and exists in each of such makers a similar right, which is defeated when the respective amounts are drawn out by the depositor. So that each maker is accorded a special right or interest in the fund created by his note, and it is upon this basis only that substantial justice can be done.

Notice of Infirmities

If at the time one takes a negotiable instrument he knows of the existence of defenses to the instrument or has knowledge of such facts so that his action in taking the instrument amounts to bad faith, he cannot take as a holder in due course. The fact that the holder learns of defenses to the instrument after he has acquired it will not defeat his rights as a holder in due course. Just when the holder will be held to have knowledge of facts which will make his taking the instrument amount to bad faith is difficult to determine. It is something less than actual knowledge of the existence of defenses, yet more than mere suspicion. If the taking of the instrument is not a breach of business ethics, the courts have held that the holder's taking does not amount to bad faith.

If one has obtained the instrument or any signature to the instrument by fraud, duress, illegality, breach of faith, or other fraudulent or unlawful means, his title is defective, and if the holder had notice or knowledge of the defects in the title at the time he took the instrument, he cannot take as a holder in due course.

In determining whether or not one has taken an instrument without knowledge or notice of infirmities or defects in the title and in good faith, the question is whether the holder has acted honestly, not whether he has acted prudently. One inexperienced in the handling of negotiable instruments might take as a holder in due course whereas the cashier of a bank, under like circumstances, would not.

Edelen et al. v. First National Bank of Hagerstown
139 Md. 413, 115 Atl. 599 (1921)

This was an action by the First National Bank of Hagerstown (plaintiff) against Edward J. Edelen and others (defendants). Judgment for plaintiff and defendants appealed. Judgment affirmed.

The notes in question were given in substitution of two notes given in payment of shares of stock in an oil producing and refining company. The stock was never delivered. The notes were indorsed to the bank as security for a loan. The person borrowing the money from the bank was a depositor of the bank and borrowed the money for the purpose of purchasing a business.

Urner, J. In this case the plaintiff unquestionably acquired the notes before maturity and for value. The only inquiry is whether it accepted them without knowledge of the fraud in their origin, or of such facts as would subject it to the imputation of bad faith in the transaction.

The circumstances under which the notes were presented to the bank were not such as to create a doubt as to their validity. They were offered by a known patron of the bank as part of the collateral security for moderate loans made in the customary way, and intended and used for the purpose of an investment in a local enterprise. The fact that they were truthfully said to have been given for stock in an oil producing and refining company was certainly not sufficient to raise an inference that they were obtained by fraud. In their testimony as to the fraud actually committed the defendants did not refer to the value of the stock, but complained of its nondelivery. It is suggested that inquiry in reference to the notes should have been made of the Leonardtown Bank, where by their terms they were made payable. But the omission to make such an inquiry could hardly be held to affect the position of the plaintiff as a holder in due course. The designation in a promissory note of a bank at which it is to be presented for payment at maturity does not indicate that information will be available there as to the circumstances under which the note was executed. There is nothing in the record to support the theory that the plaintiff's officers designedly refrained from seeking independent information as to the origin of the notes offered in this instance. The proof wholly fails to prove the existence of conditions which might have imposed the duty upon the bank to make such an investigation. Under the plain terms of the law it is entitled to the rights of a holder in due course, unless it had "actual knowledge of the infirmity" in the notes, or "knowledge of such facts that its action in taking the notes amounted to bad faith." There is no reason in the evidence for the conclusion that the plaintiff was possessed of such knowledge. No rational inference can be drawn from the record that the plaintiff actually knew of any fraud or failure of consideration affecting the notes, or was cognizant of any facts on account of which its good faith in the transaction could be denied.

Canajoharie National Bank v. Diefendorf
123 N.Y. 191, 25 N.E. 402, 10 L.R.A. 676 (1890)

This was an action by the Canajoharie National Bank (plaintiff) against Diefendorf (defendant). Judgment for defendant in the trial court and plaintiff appealed to the general term where judgment was reversed. Defendant appealed to the Court of Appeals. The order of the general term was reversed and judgment for defendant entered.

Henderson and Van Balkenburgh procured, by fraud and misrepresentation, eight promissory notes of $1,000 each, payable to Henderson or bearer at various times from 3 to 12 months from date. They agreed that the notes would be retained in their possession, and that the notes would be paid out of the profits from a business which was to be carried on by the parties.

Two of these notes were purchased by the plaintiff under the following circumstances. Henderson was introduced to plaintiff's cashier by one Vosburg. Henderson offered the two notes for sale and asked the cashier what he would give for them. The cashier offered 85 per cent of their face value, and the offer was accepted without objection or bargaining. Vosburg was asked to indorse the notes but refused. At the time the plaintiff purchased the notes he knew that the maker —Diefendorf, the defendant in this suit—was a farmer living at Root, a town about six miles from Canajoharie, that he was about 60 years old, that he had never used negotiable paper to any great extent, and that the notes were for a greater amount than defendant's financial transactions of the past. The cashier asked Henderson no questions about the notes; he knew nothing about Henderson and made no inquiries concerning him. On the trial the cashier admitted that Henderson was a "perfect stranger," that the notes were drawn in Rochester which was 200 miles distant, and that he knew that the defendant seldom travelled. The plaintiff took the notes before they were overdue and for value. At the time it took the notes it had no knowledge of any infirmity in the instrument or defect in the title of the party transferring the instrument. Defendant claims that the plaintiff did not take the notes in good faith.

Ruger, C.J. The history of the negotiation is best described by negatives, and is more significant from what was omitted than what was avowed. Greater caution in avoiding the most natural information could not have been exhibited by the plaintiff if the cashier had known the notes were obtained by fraud or crime, and desired to remain in ignorance of those facts. His conduct indicated something more than negligence. He exhibited a studious desire to avoid any information which might throw light upon the origin of the notes, or the existence of equities in favor of their maker. Henderson, a "perfect stranger" to the plaintiff, coming red-handed from the perpetration of his fraud, and desiring to realize its fruits, while his confederate kept Diefendorf employed at a distance from his residence, could not have discovered a less scrupulous or more accommodating instrument than this national bank, if he had sought the customary agencies for the negotiation of feloniously acquired securities. Henderson displayed a cautious reticence in recommending the paper he had to dispose of; and the cashier, with a delicacy as novel as it was considerate, appreciated his situation and refrained from putting any questions which might embarrass his vendor in negotiating a successful sale. Without being called upon to make the explanation usually required by banking institutions, in respect to the most ordinary transactions of every-day customers, this stranger, it is claimed, walked into a national bank and converted his feloniously acquired property into money without difficulty or delay. Common prudence, and a decent regard for the rights of those who might be injured by his conduct, required more than this from the least scrupulous of men, and much more, it would seem, from the managers of a chartered financial institution. Such institutions have no right to advertise the purchase by them of unlawfully acquired notes, bonds, or negotiable paper, without inquiry or question, neither have they the right to deal in such securities in defiance of the salutary rules regulating the acquisition of title to personal property. It cannot be seriously contended that a business carried on in such a manner is conducted according to the usual and ordinary course of such institutions, within the meaning of those words as used in relation to transfers of personal property.

The plaintiff claims that the proof showing it purchased the notes before maturity, paying value therefor, conclusively establishes its character as a *bona fide* holder, and entitles it to recover, in the absence of proof showing that it had notice, or knowledge of facts constituting a defense to the action. The plaintiff's contention eliminates the element of good faith from the transaction, and assumes that the language, "a holder for value," as used in the authorities, is satisfied by proof that the notes were purchased before maturity, and value paid therefor. We think this contention is contrary to the weight of authority in this state, even if it is not wholly unsupported by it. The payment of value for negotiable paper is a circumstance to be taken into account, with other facts, in determining the question of the *bona fides* of the transaction, and, when full value is paid, is entitled to great weight; but that fact is never conclusive, except in the absence of evidence tending to show notice of bad faith. Those who seek to secure the advantages which the commercial law confers upon the holders of bankbills and negotiable paper must bring themselves within the conditions which that law prescribes to establish the character of a *bona fide* holder. They are entitled to the benefits of that rule only when they have purchased such paper in good faith, in the usual course of business, before maturity, for full value, and without notice of any facts affecting the validity of the paper.

What constitutes good faith in such transactions has been the subject of frequent discussion in the books; and, while differences of opinion may exist on some points, there is perfect uniformity among them upon the point that a want of good faith in the transaction is fatal to the title of the holder, and that gross carelessness, although not of itself sufficient, as a question of law, to defeat title, constitutes evidence of bad faith. The requirement of good faith is expressed in the very term by which a holder is protected, and is fundamental in the maintenance of the character claimed to be protected.

Justice Swayne, in the case of *Murray* v. *Lardner*, 2 Wall. 121, says: "The rule may be said to resolve itself into a question of honesty or dishonesty, for guilty knowledge and willful ignorance alike involve the result of bad faith."

Special Problems

Two situations have arisen which present special problems. One is the position of a holder who has taken a negotiable instrument from a holder in due course, and the other is the question of whether or not the named payee can hold a negotiable instrument as a holder in due course.

The Uniform Negotiable Instruments Law expressly provides ". . . a holder who derives his title through a holder in due course, and who is not himself a party to any fraud or illegality affecting the instrument, has all the rights of such former holder in respect to all parties prior to the latter." If Archer makes a negotiable promissory note payable to Burch and Burch negotiates the instrument to Fox who takes as a holder in due course and Fox makes a gift of the instrument to Grew, Grew would acquire Fox's rights as a holder in due course. Grew could not qualify as a holder in due course in his own right because he has not given value for the instrument, but by gift Fox, who is a holder in due course, can transfer to Grew his (Fox's) rights as a holder in due course. If Grew were a party to some fraud or illegality affecting the instrument, he could not acquire the rights of a holder in due course. If Burch and Grew had acquired the instrument from Archer by fraudulent representations, Grew could not at a later time acquire the rights of a holder in due course by taking the instrument from a holder in due course.

As a general rule a payee cannot comply with the requirements set up for a holder in due course, and a minority of the courts hold that the payee of a negotiable instrument cannot hold the instrument as a holder in due course. However, the majority of the courts hold that under some circumstances the named payee may hold as a holder in due course. Burch wishes to borrow money from the First Bank but the bank refuses to make the loan. At Burch's request Archer agrees to accommodate Burch, and Archer makes a promissory note payable to the order of the First Bank and delivers it to Burch, leaving the amount blank. Burch agrees to fill in an amount for not more than $300. Burch fills in the amount for $500 and takes it to the First Bank who pays Burch $500 on the note. When the note falls due the First Bank presents the note to Archer and demands payment, and Archer refuses to pay the note because it is for a larger amount than authorized. If the First Bank is a holder in due course, it can recover $500 from Archer, but if it is not a holder in due course, it cannot. The majority of courts would allow the First Bank to recover $500.

United States v. O'Hara et ux.
46 Fed. Supp. 780 (1942)

This was an action by the United States of America (plaintiff) against John P. O'Hara and another (defendants). Judgment for plaintiff.

The note on which this suit was brought was negotiable in form, was payable to the order of Maxwell Construction Company, and was negotiated to the Morris Plan Bank of Detroit which took as holder in due course. The note was signed by the defendants as makers. The note was payable in installments, and when the first installment fell due, the defendants refused to pay claiming that the note was given on Sunday, May 8, 1938, rather than on Friday, May 13, 1938, the date on the note, and that the note was given in payment for modernization work at defendants' home and that the work had not been performed.

The note was guaranteed by the Federal Housing Administration, and upon notice of the defendants' default, the total amount due on the note was paid to the bank by the Government and the note was negotiated to the Government. The defendants contend that they are not liable to the Government on the note.

Lederle, D. J. The Morris Plan Bank of Detroit was a holder in due course of the note in suit.

Sunday contracts are void in Michigan; however, if a negotiable instrument, in fact executed on Sunday, but bearing a secular date, reaches the hands of a holder in due course, the maker of such note is estopped to repudiate the apparent date, and the note is a valid and enforceable obligation to the same extent as if it had been executed on a secular date.

Where a holder of a negotiable instrument, not a party to any fraud or illegality affecting the instrument, derives title through a holder in due course, as did plaintiff here, such holder has all the rights of such former holder in due course in respect to all parties.

A holder in due course holds the instrument free from any defect of title of prior parties and free from defenses available to prior parties among themselves, and may enforce payment of the instrument for the full amount thereof against any party liable thereon, and plaintiff, by virtue of taking from a holder in due course, has like rights against the defendants herein.

Howard National Bank v. Wilson
96 Vt. 438, 120 Atl. 889 (1923)

This was an action by Howard National Bank (plaintiff) against Graham Wilson and another (defendants). Judgment for plaintiff and Wilson appealed. Judgment affirmed.

Elliott induced defendant Wilson to make a negotiable promissory note payable to the plaintiff. Elliott, who was connected with the plaintiff, but who did not act for it in this transaction, took the note to the cashier of the plaintiff bank and had the cashier draw a cashier's check payable to Wilson for the amount of the note. Elliott took the cashier's check to Wilson who indorsed it in blank and turned it over to Elliott who deposited it in Waterbury Bank & Trust Company to the credit of Elliott's account with that bank. Elliott obtained the note from Wilson by making false and fraudulent representations. Before payment of the note was demanded Elliott died, insolvent. When demand was made for payment defendant Wilson refused to pay, setting up the fraud as a defense. Plaintiff claims to be a holder in due course and that the defense of fraud is not available against it. Wilson contends that plaintiff is payee and cannot hold as a holder in due course.

Taylor, J. It is insisted that the plaintiff, being the payee of the note, is not a holder in due course as a matter of law. As we shall see, this position is neither wholly right nor wholly wrong.

It is at once apparent that the delivery of the note to the plaintiff made it a "holder" thereof in contemplation of the Negotiable Instruments Act. It is insisted, however, that the payee of a negotiable instrument is not "a holder in due course" under the act and certain decisions in other states are relied upon in support of the claim. The theory of these decisions is that, under the Uniform Negotiable Instruments Act, a holder in due course is a person to whom, after completion and delivery, an instrument has been "negotiated"—one who has taken by negotiation and not as an original party. "Negotiated" is construed as meaning "transferred from one holder to another." *Vander Ploeg* v. *Van Zuuk* is frequently cited to the general proposition that the protection accorded a holder in due course does not extend to the payee of a negotiable instrument. However, in deciding the question presented, the court said: "We do not mean to say that in no case can the person named as payee in a negotiable instrument be the holder thereof in due course," assuming by way of illustration a case very similar to the case at bar.

The case is supported by decisions in Missouri, South Dakota, Oregon, and Washington; but the weight of authority is against the decision, at least so far as it may be considered as deciding that the term "negotiated," as used in the act, does not include a transfer to the payee of a negotiable instrument.

That a payee is capable of being a holder in due course at common law has been held almost without dissent. This is the well-recognized doctrine of our own cases. The cardinal purpose of the principles developed in the law merchant has been the protection of a bona fide holder for value who has acquired a negotiable instrument in the due course of trade or business. Commercial paper serves as common currency. Its unhampered use is indispensable to the business of the modern world. Any medium of exchange cannot have free currency without confidence; and experience has taught that it is dangerous to cast doubt even upon a payee's right to recover when he has taken commercial paper complete and regular on its face, honestly and for value. The codification of commercial law into a uniform negotiable instruments act has been accomplished, not for the purpose of changing any of its essential principles, certainly not for weakening or destroying the cardinal principle, but for the purpose of harmonizing certain minor differences existing in the various jurisdictions. The only provision of the act even suggesting that it was intended to exclude a payee in every case from the status of a holder in due course is found in section 52, subd. 4, but such is not its necessary implication. The question turns on the meaning of "negotiated" as employed in this section. Its common legal significance is "concluded by bargain or agreement." So, a promissory note, complete as to form and payable to a named person, may be negotiated to that person by being sold to him or taken by him for value. Such was the sense in which the term was used in the law merchant, and its meaning has not been changed by the Negotiable Instruments Act.

Rights of Holder in Due Course

The holder in due course holds the instrument free from any defects of title of prior parties and free from defenses available to prior parties among themselves. In discussing the rights of a holder in due course it is customary to classify defenses to a negotiable instrument into two classes—real defenses and personal defenses. A real defense goes to the existence of the instrument as a legally enforceable obligation, to the capacity of the parties, and to the title to the instrument. A personal defense does not go to the existence of the instrument or the title of the holder, but sets up some reason why the party to the instrument should not be held liable on the instrument.

Real defenses are forgery, unauthorized signature, non-delivery of an incomplete instrument, illegality where the illegality operates to make the instrument absolutely void, lack of title, and incapacity. If one forges your signature to a negotiable instrument, you have made no promise and you should not be held liable. The Uniform Negotiable Instruments Law expressly provides that a forged signature is inoperative. The same is true if an agent not authorized to sign negotiable instruments signs an instrument in his principal's name (Sec. 23). However, if the person whose name is forged has by his conduct led the party taking the instrument to believe that the signature is genuine, or if the principal has by his conduct led the party taking the instrument to believe that the agent has authority to sign, he will be bound.

The Uniform Negotiable Instruments Law expressly provides that the non-delivery of an incomplete instrument shall be a good defense against any holder (Sec. 15). The courts have held that, if an incomplete instrument gets into the channels of commerce as a result of the negligence of the party sued, he will be held liable. In theory the party is liable for the damages resulting from his negligence, not on the instrument, but the courts have held that this liability is the amount of the instrument.

Fraud may be either a personal or a real defense. If the party is induced to sign a paper which is fraudulently represented to him to be an autograph album but which is in fact a negotiable instrument, he will not be liable to any holder. He did not intend to sign a negotiable instrument and will not be held liable. If a stock salesman through fraudulent representations induces one to purchase worthless stock and to give his negotiable promissory note in part payment, the instrument is enforceable in the hands of a holder in due course. In the first instance the party did not know he was signing a negotiable instrument and did not intend to issue a negotiable instrument. In the second instance the party knew he was issuing a negotiable instrument and intended to issue it. The fact that he was induced to issue it as a result of fraudulent representations would be a good defense among the parties to the instrument, but is not good against a holder in due course.

Illegality may be either a real or personal defense. As a general rule the rights of a holder in due course are not affected by any illegality in the transaction between prior parties. If Archer purchases liquor from Burch in violation of the revenue laws and Archer gives Burch his negotiable promissory note in payment, Archer could set up the defense of illegality if Burch sued on the instrument; but if Burch negotiates the note to Fox who takes as a holder in due course, the defense of illegality will not be good against Fox. Some statutes expressly declare that negotiable instruments given in violation of the statute are void. In such instances the defense of illegality is good against the holder in due course because the instrument has no legal standing. In some states the usury statutes make the entire instrument void if the interest charged is usurious. Some states, by statute, provide that a negotiable instrument given in payment of a gambling debt is void. The effect of such statutes on the validity of the instrument depends on the wording of the statute.

If the holder never acquired title to the instrument, he can claim no rights under it. If the payee's indorsement is forged on an order instrument, title to the instrument does not pass, and anyone who takes the instrument through this forged indorsement acquires no title to the instrument. Such a defense is good against a holder in due course. A holder in due course takes free from defects in title. One's title is defective when he obtained the instrument, or any signature thereto, by fraud, duress, or force and fear, or other unlawful means, or for an illegal consideration, or when he negotiates it in breach of faith, or under such circumstances as amount to fraud (Sec. 55).

The defense of incapacity is not cut off by negotiating the instrument to a holder in due course. The defense of incapacity is available in a suit on a negotiable instrument the same as it would be if the instrument were non-negotiable.

Personal defenses include such defenses as failure or lack of consideration, fraud, duress (unless extreme in nature), undue influence, set-off, payment, lack of delivery, breach of faith, illegality (unless instrument is declared void by statute), etc. In many of the cases which we have studied, the party defendant has set up a personal defense to the instrument.

The holder in due course may enforce the instrument for the full amount of the instrument. Archer gives Burch his negotiable promissory note for $100. Burch negotiates the note to Fox who takes as a holder in due course, paying Burch $75 for the note. Burch obtained the note by fraud. When sued by Fox, Archer sets up the fraud as a defense. Fox can recover a judgment for $100, the full amount of the note.

Whitaker et al. v. Smith

255 Ky. 339, 73 S.W. (2d) 1105, 95 A.L.R. 727 (1934)

This was an action by Emily Smith (plaintiff) against Laura Whitaker and husband (defendants). Judgment for plaintiff and defendants appealed. Judgment reversed, with directions in accordance with opinion.

On January 21, 1924, defendants executed to the Hargis Bank & Trust Co. their promissory note for $3,000. They agreed to pay and did pay a usurious rate of interest on the loan, but the usury did not appear on the face of the instrument. Plaintiff took the note as holder in due course. Defendants did not pay the note and when sued claimed that they were entitled to credit for the usurious interest paid. Plaintiff contends that she is a holder in due course and that the defense of usury is not good against her.

Thomas, J. We thus see that the only questions for determination are: (1) Whether or not plaintiff, under the facts presented by the record, became and is the holder of the note in due course, and, if so, then (2) whether our negotiable instruments statute protects her as such holder from the defense of usury made and relied on by defendants? In determining the latter question, it becomes necessary to consider the condition of the law as it has been declared in this jurisdiction with reference to contracts which are declared by statute to be "void." It will be perceived that the question as we have so propounded it does not embrace contracts which are void at common law, although in treating the obligatory effect of void contracts in the hands of innocent parties (including notes and obligations for the payment of money) most of the decisions and text-writers draw no distinction between a contract declared to be void by statute and one so declared by the common law.

The almost universal rule regarding such contracts is that they are void and may not be enforced, not only as between the original parties thereto, but likewise are they prohibited from enforcement by one who may become the holder of them in due course, and which is upon the ground that being void they never had any obligatory force and are no more binding upon the maker than if he had never executed them. The theory upon which that conclusion was reached is that the Legislature in so providing (i.e., that the particular contract should be void) did so in furtherance of what it conceived to be a wholesome public policy, and that to prevent that policy from being thwarted through the act of an assignment of the instrument (or contract) would put it into the hands of the parties to it to defeat such declared public policy. The latest text, embodying such court conclusions, will be found commencing on page 556 of Brannan's Negotiable Instruments Law (5th Ed.), and which is thus stated by the author: "It has sometimes been held that illegality ceases to be a real defense under the N.I.L. unless made so by a subsequent statute, and that the statutes previously in force declaring void instruments for gaming or upon usurious interest or other forbidden transactions are impliedly repealed by the N.I.L. The weight of authority however seems contra."

The text in 3 R.C.L. 1020, § 228, clearly states that under a statute, making void a contract made contrary thereto, is void even in the hands of an innocent holder, and which rule is applicable to usurious contracts to the extent that the statute against usury makes them void. Part of that text, specifically applicable here, says: "Under this statute (12 Anne, Ch. 16, relating to negotiable instruments) and the subsequent enactments that have been modeled thereon, it has generally been held that a note or bill is void for usury even in the hands of an innocent purchaser. This class of cases comes within the exception to the rule—that a bona fide purchaser may enforce a negotiable instrument although as between the original parties it is unenforceable because originating in an illegal transaction—which exists generally when a statute declares a contract void. The contract gathers no vitality by its circulation in respect to the parties executing it, but it and the instrument evidencing it are void in the hands of every holder."

The same conclusion was reached in the Alexander Case, 123 Ky. 677, 97 S.W. 353, 29 Ky. Law Rep. 1214, where the note in contest was given in consideration of what is commonly referred to as a "gambling" debt, which is inhibited by section 1955 of our present statutes, and which says that all such contracts based upon the consideration therein named "shall be void." This court held in that opinion, applying the rule hereinbefore stated, that our Negotiable Instruments Law "does not authorize one holding in due course a note given for a gambling debt to enforce such note."

Our statute denouncing the taking of usury is section 2219 of the 1930 edition of Carroll's Kentucky Statutes, and it says: "All contracts and assurances made, directly or indirectly, for the loan or forbearance of money, or other thing of value, at a greater rate than legal interest, shall be void for the excess over the legal interest." It will be noted that the statute says that "all contracts and assurances made, directly or indirectly, for the loan or forbearance of money," and which is leveled against the *transaction* and does not confine its denunciation to any writing that may be executed in evidence thereof. So that the defense is available in favor of the maker, notwithstanding the note evidencing the agreement may be fair on its face and to thereby submerge the vice in the transaction.

Thompson v. C. I. T. Corporation
Ct. of Civ. App. Texas, 157 S.W. (2d) 961 (1941)

This was an action by C. I. T. Corporation (plaintiff) against Lula M. Thompson (defendant). Judgment for plaintiff and defendant appealed. Judgment affirmed.

Murray, J. C. I. T. Corporation instituted this suit against Mrs. Lula M. Thompson, seeking to recover the amount of principal, interest and attorney's fees alleged to be due upon a certain negotiable promissory note payable to the order of the Herweck's Paint & Wall Paper Company, in the principal sum of $689.87, payable in monthly installments, signed by Mrs. Lula M. Thompson, indorsed and delivered to C. I. T. Corporation by Herweck's Paint & Wall Paper Company for a valuable consideration of $600.

The C. I. T. Corporation is a holder in due course of this note, and the signature of Mrs. Thompson to the note is a genuine signature. Mrs. Thompson's only defense is that she was induced to sign the note by the fraud of her son-in-law I. S. (Jack) Kahn, Jr.

It is clear that before Mrs. Thompson can prevail against a holder in due course upon her plea of fraud, she must show that, being herself free from negligence, she was induced by some fraudulent trick or device to execute the note under the belief that the instrument she signed was one of a different character. Unless it is affirmatively shown that Mrs. Thompson is herself free from negligence her plea of fraud cannot be upheld.

We are of the opinion that if Mrs. Thompson did not know that she was signing a note then, under the undisputed facts, she was guilty, as a matter of law, of the grossest negligence in signing her name to such instrument and cannot escape liability on her plea of fraud.

Mrs. Thompson admitted that she was a graduate of both a high school and a business college; that she could read without glasses. Her son-in-law never attempted to prevent her from reading the instrument before she signed it. She noticed the blank spaces in the instrument were not filled out and called this matter to the attention of her son-in-law. She signed three instruments at the time, to-wit: the promissory note, a completion certificate, and a credit statement.

A most casual glance at the note would have disclosed its true nature.

Under all the facts, we hold that she was guilty of negligence as a matter of law in signing the blank note without reading it.

Mrs. Thompson was bound to know that she might be misled as to the contents of the instrument by Kahn. She could have easily read the instrument and ascertained its true nature. Rather than do this she chose to put confidence in Kahn and rely upon his representations. Her confidence thus reposed in Kahn is now bound to result in injury either to herself or to the C. I. T. Corporation. It was her act that enabled Kahn to occasion the injury, therefore she should bear the loss rather than the C. I. T. Corporation.

QUESTIONS AND PROBLEMS

1. Archer drew his check on the First Bank payable to the order of Burch and delivered it to Burch in payment of services rendered. Burch lost the check and Drew found it. The check was not indorsed by Burch. Drew presented the check at the First Bank and requested payment. Should the First Bank pay the check?
2. Would the situation be the same in the foregoing case if the check had been drawn payable to Burch or bearer?
3. Greenfield, as agent of Snyder, was given power of attorney to draw checks on Snyder's account. Greenfield drew four checks payable to Charles Niemann aggregating $18,387.50. Niemann was a customer of Snyder's, but the checks were delivered by Greenfield to a friend who forged Niemann's indorsement and negotiated the checks. When they were presented to the bank, the bank honored the checks and charged them to Snyder's account. Did the bank have a right to charge the checks to Snyder's account?
4. A note drawn payable to the order of J. A. Wheeler had the following written on the back of the note: "I hereby assign this note over to E. H. Farnsworth this Nov. 1st, 1910." Was this a special indorsement?
5. A check drawn payable to the order of F. M. Rounds was indorsed:
   "Pay to the order of ————."

   "F. M. Rounds."

   Was the indorsement a special indorsement or an indorsement in blank?
6. A note is indorsed: "Pay to the order of Maude Y. Shingler, executrix." Is the indorsement a restrictive indorsement?
7. A creamery company supplied its agent with blank checks. The form had printed on it: "Not good for more than $15." The creamery company's agent issued a check for $37.98 and crossed out the above-quoted provision. Marshall and Co. took the check from the payee and paid the payee the full face value of the check. Is Marshall and Co. a holder in due course of the check?
8. Archer holds a note which is due July 1. On July 1, Archer indorses and transfers the note to Burch for value. Is Burch a holder in due course?
9. The payee of a check transfers it thirty days after the date of issue. Is the holder a holder in due course?
10. Kehoe indorsed a note and negotiated it to the Central National Bank in exchange for a certificate of deposit issued by the bank to Kehoe. On the certificate of deposit the cashier of the bank wrote: "This certificate of deposit is issued for a note and is subject to the final payment of the note." Is the Central National Bank a holder in due course of the note?
11. The First Bank took a negotiable promissory note without making inquiry as to its issue. The note was issued as an accommodation note, and the maker had a valid defense which would have been revealed if inquiry had been made. Did the bank's failure to make inquiry prevent it from being a holder in due course?

12. The Gin Co. issued a note in payment for a cotton baling machine which was to be delivered at a future date. Jones took the note before overdue and for value; however, at the time Jones took the note he knew the cotton baling machine had not been delivered. Jones took the note before the delivery date of the cotton baling machine. Is Jones a holder in due course?
13. Archer took a note as a holder in due course. Archer sold the note to Burch after maturity. The maker has a good defense of fraud against the payee. Can Burch enforce the note?
14. Hurly gave his negotiable promissory note payable to the order of Manning in payment of shares of stock in a corporation which was to be organized by Manning. Manning negotiated the note to Goolsby who took as a holder in due course. When the note matured Hurly refused to pay it and, when sued by Goolsby, set up that the note was given in payment of stock in a corporation to be organized and that the corporation was never organized. Is the defense valid?
15. Archer issued his negotiable promissory note payable to the order of Burch. Before the due date Archer paid the amount of the note to Burch and Burch gave Archer a receipt in full. At the time Archer paid Burch, Burch told Archer that the note was in his safety deposit box and that he would mail the cancelled note to him. On the due date Clark, who had acquired the note as a holder in due course, presented the note to Archer and demanded payment. Is Archer liable on the note?

CHAPTER XXIV

LIABILITY OF THE PARTIES

Nature of Liability

The liability of a party to a negotiable instrument may be either a primary liability to pay the instrument or it may be secondary; that is, the duty to pay does not arise until the party primarily liable has defaulted. Also, a party to an instrument may, by signing the instrument, assume liabilities which are closely analogous to the liability of a seller of goods on implied warranties.

The maker of a note and the acceptor of a bill of exchange are primarily liable for the payment of the instrument. If a bank certifies a check, it becomes primarily liable for the payment of the check. The drawer of a bill of exchange or check and the indorsers of any negotiable instrument are secondarily liable. The drawee of a bill of exchange or check is not liable on the instrument until he has accepted it and then he becomes primarily liable. To hold one secondarily liable, the holder of the instrument owes a duty to present the instrument for payment or acceptance, as the case may be, and, if the instrument is dishonored, to give notice of dishonor to all parties who are secondarily liable. Failure to present the instrument and to give notice if it is dishonored, in accordance with the provisions of the Uniform Negotiable Instruments Law, will relieve the party secondarily liable from his obligations on the instrument unless the party secondarily liable has waived presentment and notice. Presentment and notice may be waived either at the time one becomes a party to the instrument or afterwards.

Presentment and Notice

Presentment and notice are necessary to fix the liability of a secondary party to pay the instrument in the event the party primarily liable does not, but presentment and notice are not required to fix the liability of a party to a negotiable instrument on his implied warranties. The Uniform Negotiable Instruments Law provides in respect to the liability of the drawer and of an unqualified indorser: "and the necessary proceedings on dishonor be duly taken, he will pay the amount thereof to the holder, or to any subsequent indorser who may be compelled to pay it" (N.I.L. Secs. 61, 66).

An instrument may be presented either for payment or for acceptance, depending on the nature and terms of the instrument. If the instrument is a note, it must be presented for payment when due. If the instrument is a bill of exchange, it may be necessary to present it for acceptance, and it will be necessary to present it for payment on its due date if parties secondarily liable are to be held. Presentment for payment is not necessary in order to charge the person primarily liable on the instrument (N.I.L., Sec. 70).

In general the requirements for presentment for payment are:

How—The instrument must be exhibited to the person from whom payment is demanded, and if paid the instrument must be delivered up to the party paying it. This requirement cannot be complied with unless presentment is made in person.

When—Presentment must be made on the due date. If the instrument is a demand instrument, not having a due date, it must be presented for payment within a reasonable time after the date of issue. However, if the instrument is a bill of exchange, presentment within a reasonable time after the last negotiation thereof is sufficient.

Where—Presentment must be made at the usual place of business or residence of the person primarily liable if no address or place of payment is given on the instrument. If an address is given on the instrument or if a place of payment is stated on the instrument, presentment should be made at such address or stated place of payment.

Time of Day—Presentment must be made at any reasonable hour. If a bank is named as the place of payment, the instrument should be presented during banking hours. However, if the party to make payment has no funds in the bank, presentment before the bank closes is sufficient.

By Whom—Presentment may be made by the holder or anyone authorized by him to receive payment in his behalf.

To Whom—Presentment must be made to the party primarily liable on the instrument, or if he cannot be found or is inaccessible, to any person found at the place where the presentment is made.

It is not always possible to comply strictly with the rules set out above; consequently, special rules have been adopted to cover the more common situations like the death or insanity of the party primarily liable. In all events the holder of the instrument must make an honest effort to comply with these rules, but if he cannot comply with them, he will be excused. The law does not require the impossible but it does require an effort in good faith and, if one does not comply with the rules, he has the burden of justifying his failure to do so.[1]

The formalities to be followed in presenting a bill of exchange for acceptance are substantially the same as those set out for presentment for payment. The acceptance of the bill is the signification by the drawee of his assent to the order of the drawer. The acceptance must be in writing, must be a promise to pay in money and, if the holder requests it, acceptance must be on the instrument. The usual manner of accepting a bill is for the drawee to write "accepted" and sign his name across the face of the instrument; however, any other form which fulfills the requirements of the Uniform Negotiable Instruments Law will be binding. If the holder consents, the acceptance may be on a separate piece of paper, but such an acceptance does not bind the acceptor except in favor of persons to whom it is shown and who, on the faith thereof, receive the bill for value.

Not all bills will be presented for acceptance. If the bill is drawn payable at sight, it is payable on presentment and will not be presented for acceptance. Time bills may be so drawn that they must be presented for acceptance. If a bill is drawn payable at a stated time after sight, it is necessary to present the bill for acceptance in order to fix the date of maturity. The bill may expressly stipulate that it must be presented for acceptance, in which case the stipulation must be complied with. If the bill is drawn payable at a place other than at the residence or place of business of the drawee, it must be presented for acceptance. For example, if Archer draws a bill payable to Burch naming Drew as drawee and makes the bill payable at First Bank, Burch, if he wishes to hold parties secondarily liable on the bill, must present it to Drew for acceptance.

When a bill is presented to the drawee for acceptance, he may take twenty-four hours to investigate and determine whether or not he will accept the bill. If the bill is left with the drawee for acceptance and he destroys the bill or refuses within twenty-four hours, or such additional time as may be agreed upon, to return the bill accepted or non-accepted, he will be deemed to have accepted the same.[2]

When a negotiable instrument has been dishonored by non-acceptance or non-payment, notice must be given to the drawer and to each indorser. If notice is not given, the party to whom notice is not given is discharged.

---

[1] For a detailed statement of the requirements for presentment for payment see Uniform Negotiable Instruments Law, Title I, Article VI: "Presentment for Payment."

[2] For a detailed statement of the requirements for acceptance see Uniform Negotiable Instruments Law, Title II, Article II, Acceptance.

In general the requirements for notice are:

How—No particular form or method of giving notice is specified. If the party entitled to notice is notified of the dishonor, he will be bound.

When—As a general rule notice must be given the day following the dishonor. However, if the party entitled to notice does not live at the same place as the party giving notice, the depositing of the notice in the mails on the day following is sufficient.

Where—If an address is given, notice should be sent to such address. If no address is given, the notice should be sent either to the party's place of business or residence if the address is known. If the address is unknown, notice must be sent to the post-office nearest to the party's place of residence or to the post-office where he is accustomed to receive his letters. However, if notice is actually received by the party within the time allowed, it will be sufficient.

By Whom—Notice may be sent by the holder or his agent, or by or on behalf of any party to the instrument who might be compelled to pay it to the holder.

To whom—Notice must be sent to the party secondarily liable or his agent.[3]

If a foreign bill is dishonored, in addition to presentment and notice, the bill must be protested. A foreign bill is a bill drawn in one state or country and payable in another state or country. A bill drawn in Chicago payable in New York is a foreign bill, but a bill drawn in Chicago payable in Illinois is a domestic bill. If a Chicago merchant draws a draft in Chicago on a Chicago bank and sends it to New York in payment of a bill which he owes to a New York wholesaler, the bill is a domestic bill and not a foreign bill.

Protest is a formal statement of the presentment and dishonor of the bill. It is made under the hand and seal of the notary making it (under oath) and must contain the facts necessary to identify the bill and show that it was duly presented and dishonored. Banks customarily protest both domestic and foreign bills if the amount involved warrants the expense. Protesting a bill does not dispense with the necessity of giving notice.

Cairo National Bank of Cairo, Illinois v. Blanton Co.
— Mo. App. —, 287 S.W. 839 (1926)

This was an action by the Cairo National Bank of Cairo, Ill. (plaintiff) against the Blanton Company and another (defendants).

[3] There are many special situations provided for in the Uniform Negotiable Instruments Law. See Title I, Article VII, "Notice of Dishonor."

Judgment for plaintiff and defendant Blanton Company appealed. Judgment affirmed.

This was a suit against defendant as the drawer of a bill of exchange. The plaintiff claims that it presented the bill for payment and payment was refused. The defendant contends that the bill was not duly presented and that it is discharged from its liability as drawer.

The bill was drawn by defendant as drawer on the Cairo Cotton Oil Mill, Inc., as drawee, payable to the Liberty Central Trust Company at sight. The Liberty Central Trust Company indorsed the bill and sent it to plaintiff. The bill was drawn on September 19, 1923, and on the same day the drawer (defendant) deposited the bill with the Liberty Central Trust Company and received credit thereon. On September 19, 1923, the Liberty Central Trust Company indorsed the bill and sent it to plaintiff. Plaintiff received the bill in the regular course of mail on Friday morning, September 21, 1923, and called the drawee over the telephone and was informed that the bill would be paid. Friday had been declared by the mayor of Cairo to be a holiday and plaintiff bank closed at noon on Friday. The bank was also closed at noon on Saturday, which was a half-holiday. On Monday, September 24, 1923, plaintiff, not having received a remittance from the drawee, called again over the telephone and was informed by the drawee that it would not pay the bill. The plaintiff caused the bill to be presented by a notary at the office of the drawee. Payment was refused, the bill was regularly protested and notice thereof was duly given.

Bennick, C. Defendant argues most earnestly that the act of plaintiff in calling the drawee over the telephone on Friday constituted an election on its part to make presentment in such manner and at such time; that such presentment was insufficient; that thereby defendant was discharged; and that, having been discharged, defendant's liability could not be reinstated by any subsequent acts of plaintiff. In this connection plaintiff frankly concedes that the communication over the telephone was not a legal presentment. It insists, however, that it was entitled to a reasonable time after the negotiation of the draft to it within which to make presentment (as defined by the statutes of Illinois, duly pleaded and proven), and that defendant was not discharged until after plaintiff had failed to make such presentment within a reasonable time.

There is no question but that the manner of presentment, demand, and protest made on Monday conformed to the requirements of the law. Accordingly, disregarding the telephone conversation of Friday (concededly insufficient), was the presentment on Monday made within a reasonable time? What is a reasonable time depends upon the peculiar circumstances of each case. Plaintiff obtained the draft on Friday. While not a legal holiday, this particular Friday had been declared as such by the mayor of the city of Cairo, and plaintiff's bank was closed on the afternoon of such day. The statute made it optional with plaintiff whether the draft should be presented on Saturday. Of course, no presentment was required on Sunday. The question as to whether the presentment by plaintiff on Monday was made within a reasonable time thus became one of fact for the jury under proper instructions. Upon this issue the jury found for plaintiff. Consequently the liability of defendant as drawer of the bill of exchange was established.

Legal Discount Corporation v. Martin Hardware Co. et al.
199 Wash. 476, 91 P. (2d) 1010, 129 A.L.R. 420 (1939)

This was an action by Legal Discount Corporation (plaintiff) against Martin Hardware Company and another (defendants). Judgment for plaintiff and defendants appealed. Judgment reversed and case dismissed.

Suit was brought on four trade acceptances drawn on the Capital Park Building Company, as drawee, by defendant Martin Hardware Company payable to "ourselves." When presented the drawee accepted the trade acceptances. The Martin Hardware Co. indorsed the trade acceptances in blank and transferred them to the Olympia National Bank. The bank failed on January 22, 1932—before the due date of the trade acceptances—and its affairs were taken over by the comptroller of the currency. The trade acceptances were never paid and late in 1937 or early in 1938 they were sold to plaintiff. Defendant Martin Hardware Company sets up as a defense that it was never served with any notice of protest, or of the failure of the acceptor, Capital Park Building Company, to pay the acceptance on the due date thereof.

Robinson, J. The court found only the facts alleged in the complaint; that is to say, there is no finding that the instruments were ever presented for payment to the acceptor or notice of dishonor ever given to the indorser. The defendant relied, and now relies, primarily upon § 89 of the uniform negotiable instruments law:

"*Except as herein otherwise provided*, when a negotiable instrument has been dishonored by non-acceptance or non-payment, *notice of dishonor must be given* to the drawer and *to each indorser, and any* drawer or *indorser to whom such notice is not given is discharged*" (Italics ours).

The first indorser of a negotiable instrument does not unconditionally engage to pay it if the person primarily liable does not, but only to do so if it be dishonored and the necessary proceedings on dishonor be duly taken. If the necessary proceedings on dishonor are not taken, as we have already seen, the indorser is discharged. This means that, in order to hold the indorser, the holder must present the note or bill to the maker or acceptor, as the case may be, and, if he refuses to make payment, give the indorser immediate notice of dishonor. When the holder and indorser live in the same town, immediately means not later than the next day.

When a holder of a negotiable instrument seeks to charge an indorser, he must allege and prove that he gave him due notice of dishonor, or that such notice was waived, and, when not waived, proof of the giving of the notice is absolutely necessary to establish his cause of action. It has been held that, in a case where a complaint in such an action did not aver presentment and notice of dishonor or a legal excuse for failure, and even though the point was not raised by answer or demurrer, proof thereof was, nevertheless, required in order to allow a recovery, since, in the absence of such proof, the right to recover does not affirmatively appear.

Liability of the Maker or Acceptor

The maker of a note and the acceptor of a bill are primarily liable. In addition to their promise to pay the instrument, they assume certain additional obligations. The maker of the note admits the existence of the payee and his then capacity to indorse. The obligations of the acceptor of a bill are even more extensive. The acceptor, by accepting the instrument, not only promises to pay the instrument according to the tenor of his acceptance but also admits the existence of the drawer, the genuineness of his signature, and his capacity and authority to draw the instrument, and further he admits the existence of the payee and his capacity to indorse.

The liabilities of the maker and acceptor are alike in that both promise to pay the instrument according to its tenor and both admit the existence of the payee and his then capacity to indorse. The acceptor of a bill in addition to these liabilities guarantees the genuineness of the instrument in that he admits the existence of the drawer, the genuineness of his signature, and his capacity and authority to draw the instrument.

If the drawer is a fictitious person, if the signature of the drawer is forged, if the drawer is an infant or insane person, or if the drawer's name is signed by an agent who does not have authority to issue negotiable instruments, the instrument is not enforceable against the drawer. However, if the drawee accepts the instrument when it is presented to him, he will be liable to the holder of the instrument and cannot set up any of the defects enumerated above as a defense when sued on the instrument.

Fried v. Holloran et al.
272 Ky. 323, 114 S.W. (2d) 121 (1938)

This was an action by Emanuel F. Fried (plaintiff) against Thomas Holloran and another (defendants). Judgment for defendants and plaintiff appealed. Judgment reversed and remanded.

This was a suit on a note drawn by the defendants payable to "Atlas Construction Company" and indorsed "Atlas Construction Company by Aaron Klein Partner" and negotiated to the plaintiff who took as a holder in due course. Plaintiff, Emanuel F. Fried, was doing business under the trade name of Colonial Finance Company. The lower court held: "This indorsement was ineffective to pass title to the paper to the Colonial Finance Company, or Fried, or any one else; and, if the Atlas Construction Company was a partnership, all the partners should have been named and made payees of the note."

Ratliff, J. It is thus seen that the statute does not prohibit the assignment of a negotiable instrument in a trade or assumed name, but by implication recognizes such right, and provides that the person who makes such an assignment will be liable to the same extent as if he had signed it in his own name.

Section 3720b-60 of the statutes reads as follows: "*Maker's liabilities.*—The maker of a negotiable instrument by making it engages that he will pay it according to its tenor, and admits the existence of the payee and his then capacity to indorse."

Measuring the note here involved to the last-quoted statute, appellees engaged that they would pay the note according to its tenor (the face of the note) and admitted the existence of the payee, Atlas Construction Company, and admitted the capacity of the Atlas Construction Company to indorse the note.

Ocean Accident & Guarantee Corporation, Limited
v. Lincoln National Bank
112 N.J.L. 550, 172 Atl. 45 (1934)

This was an action by Ocean Accident & Guarantee Corporation, Limited (plaintiff) against Lincoln National Bank (defendant). Judgment for defendant and plaintiff appealed. Judgment reversed.

An agent of plaintiff who was authorized to draw drafts on plaintiff drew a draft on plaintiff, as drawee, payable to Joseph Johnson for $600. The agent forged Johnson's indorsement on the draft and sold it to defendant. Defendant presented the draft to plaintiff who accepted and paid the draft. Later plaintiff discovered the forgery and sued defendant to recover the $600 paid on the draft. Several questions were raised which are not included in this abstract. The lower court held that the acceptance and payment of the draft on which the payee's indorsement had been forged cured the defect.

Perskie, J. The learned trial judge held, and again that holding is urged on this appeal, that section 62 of our Negotiable Instruments Act justified the nonsuit.

This section is as follows:

"The acceptor by accepting the instrument engages that he will pay it according to the tenor of his acceptance; and admits: I. The existence of the drawer, the genuineness of his signature, and his capacity and authority to draw the instrument; and

"II. The existence of the payee and his then capacity to indorse."

The plain language of the section clearly indicates that the acceptance of a draft does not admit the genuineness of the payee's signature. It merely admits the existence of the payee and his then capacity to indorse. There was a payee who had capacity to indorse, and, since it is clear that he did not indorse, hence his purported indorsement necessarily was a forgery. In a fairly recent and similar case, the Supreme Court of Pennsylvania, in *National Union Fire Insurance Co.* v. *Mellon National Bank*, in a learned opinion by Justice Schaffer, considered the same sections of the Negotiable Instruments Act involved on this appeal, and disposed adversely of like contentions to this made by the defendant in this case. In that case it was held, inter alia:

" 'The drawee of a bill of exchange is conclusively presumed to know the signature of the drawer, and if he accepts or pays, in the usual course of business, a bill whereon the signature of the drawer is a forgery, he will be estopped after to deny the genuineness of such signature. But the drawee is not chargeable with knowledge of any other signature on the bill of exchange, and by accepting or paying the bill does not admit the genuineness of any indorsement on it. The acceptor is not deemed to admit the signature of the payee.' 3 Ruling Case Law, p. 1145.

" 'Acceptance does not admit the genuineness of the signature of the payee or of any subsequent indorser, but the signatures of all indorsers necessary to transfer title to the holder must be proved in order to obtain judgment against the acceptor.' 8 Corpus Juris, 332."

Commercial & Savings Bank Co. of Bellefontaine, Ohio
v. Citizens' National Bank of Franklin
68 Ind. App. 417, 120 N.E. 670 (1918)

This was an action by the Commercial & Savings Bank Company of Bellefontaine, Ohio (plaintiff) against the Citizens' National Bank of Franklin, Indiana (defendant). Judgment for defendant and plaintiff appealed. Judgment affirmed.

A check drawn on the plaintiff bank as drawee and with the name W. H. Kellison signed as drawer was presented to the defendant bank for payment. The check was for $320.00, payable "to the order of myself" and indorsed on the back thereof "W. H. Kellison." The defendant bank refused to pay the check but took it for collection. The check was thereupon sent direct to plaintiff for collection, was accepted by it as genuine, and a draft was sent defendant for the amount less charges for collection. Defendant on receipt of the draft paid the money over to the presenter of the check.

Felt, P. J. Appellant asserts that it is entitled to recover in this case under the general proposition of law that money paid under a mistake of fact may be recovered by the person making such payment.

It is universally held that an exception to the general rule aforesaid obtains as to drawees of bills by which they are charged with knowledge of the signatures of the drawers of such instruments, and as a general rule must bear the loss, if any, resulting from a failure on their part to detect forgeries until after payment has been made. The principle underlying such rule or exception is applied to banks of deposit, and they are charged with the responsibility of knowing the signatures of their depositors. Where a check purporting to have been drawn by one of such depositors is presented to the bank by a bona fide holder thereof for value, and is paid by the bank, the latter cannot compel such holder to whom payment has been so made to repay the amount to it, if it subsequently discovers the check to have been forged.

It has frequently been announced that this rule is founded on the supposed negligence of the bank in failing to detect the forgery and refuse payment. But there are several important reasons which have led to the adoption and application of the rule. Banks of deposit have superior advantages and facilities for knowing the signatures of their depositors and detecting forgeries. For this reason it has generally been recognized that the rule is especially applicable where the drawee is a bank of deposit, and the check purports to have been drawn upon it by one of its depositors. The question of public policy is also taken into account, and it is held that, as between a good-faith holder for value of a check purporting to have been drawn upon such bank by one of its depositors, the bank should be made the place of final settlement, where all prior mistakes or forgeries should be detected, settled, or corrected, once for all, and, if not then and there detected, payment by such bank to such holder should be treated as final, without recourse upon any such holder by the bank making payment under such circumstances.

The rule also tends to promote the security of depositors and the stability of banks, and should not be relaxed or ignored for trivial reasons or minor considerations, but should be applied unless the facts and circumstances of the involved transaction bring it clearly within some established rule adopted and enforced to promote the ends of justice.

Liability of Drawer

The drawer of a bill admits the existence of the payee and his then capacity to indorse and engages that the bill will be accepted or paid or both.

The first liability is unconditional. If the payee is a fictitious person, a corporation which is not granted the power to indorse negotiable instruments, an infant, or an insane person who is insane at the time the instrument is issued, the drawer will be liable and cannot set such fact up as a defense. The drawer does not guarantee the genuineness of the payee's indorsement and can set up the forgery of the payee's indorsement as a defense.

The drawer's liability for non-acceptance and non-payment is a secondary liability and, if the requirements of presentment and notice are not complied with, the drawer will be relieved from this liability.

The drawer may limit his liability by inserting in the instrument an express stipulation limiting or negativing his own liability to the holder.

Selected Kentucky Distillers, Inc., v. Foloway
124 W.Va. 72, 19 S.E. (2d) 94, 139 A.L.R. 1377 (1942)

This was an action by Selected Kentucky Distillers, Incorporated (plaintiff) against B. B. Foloway (defendant). Judgment for defendant and plaintiff appealed. Judgment reversed and remanded.

On May 1, 1935, defendant gave plaintiff his check in the sum of $253 payable to the order of plaintiff and drawn on the First National Bank of Williamson, West Virginia. When presented for payment the check was dishonored because defendant did not have funds on deposit with the drawee bank sufficient to pay the check. Notice of dishonor was given, and later defendant paid $25 on the check which was credited on the back of the check. Suit was started on the check more than five years after it was issued.

The defendant set up the running of the statute of limitations as a defense. Under the statutes governing the action, if the contract is in writing, suit must be brought within ten years, but if the promise is an implied promise, suit must be brought within five years. The question presented was what was the nature of the liability of the drawer of the check.

Riley, J. Our next inquiry is whether the present action is barred under the provisions of our statute of limitations, which requires that an action upon a contract in writing be instituted within ten years after the right to bring the same shall have accrued, and if "upon any other contract, express or implied, within five years." Initially, we observe that while the claim sought to be recovered represented money due for merchandise, the right of action was on the check and not on the indebtedness evidenced thereby. Courts in other jurisdictions have adjudicated that a check is a written contract. Under Code, 46-5-2, the drawer of a negotiable instrument engages that, on due presentment of the instrument, it will be accepted or paid, or both, according to its tenor, and that, if it be dishonored, and the necessary proceedings on dishonor be duly taken, he will pay the amount of the instrument to the holder. The issuance of the check is itself rooted in the negotiable instruments law and the obligation resulting from such issuance is a statutory obligation, the legal effect of which attaches immediately upon delivery to a holder of a check. The engagement is then absolute and express. Hence, the signature of the drawer carries with it the statutory engagement as if it were written on the check. Therefore, we are of opinion that a check is a written contract within the meaning of Code, 55-2-6, and an action thereon is barred only after the lapse of ten years from the time when a cause of action thereon accrues.

Liability of Qualified Indorser

A negotiable instrument may be negotiated by delivery without indorsement, and it may be indorsed with a qualified indorsement, an unqualified indorsement, or a restrictive indorsement. A qualified indorsement is a "without recourse" indorsement. It may be a qualified blank indorsement as "Without recourse, Burch" or it may be a qualified special indorsement as "Pay to Fox, without recourse, Burch." If the words "without recourse" or words of similar import are not added to the indorsement, it will be unqualified.

The liability of one negotiating a negotiable instrument without indorsement and the liability of the qualified indorser are the same with one exception. The qualified indorser is liable to *all subsequent holders* of the instrument, while one who negotiates the instrument by delivery is liable only to the *immediate transferee*. The liability of an unqualified indorser is more extensive than that of the qualified indorser. The liability of a restrictive indorser will depend on the restrictive terms of his indorsement.

The liability of one who negotiates the instrument by delivery and the qualified indorser is primary. It is in the nature of a warranty of the instrument. He warrants (1) that the instrument is genuine and in all respects what it purports to be; (2) that he has good title to it; (3) that all prior parties had capacity to contract; and (4) that he has no knowledge of any facts which would impair the validity of the instrument or render it valueless. An exception is made in that one negotiating public or corporation securities, other than bills and notes, does not warrant the capacity of the parties.

Under (1) the warranty would include any defect which would go to the validity of the instrument such as forgery of the maker's or acceptor's signature, the non-delivery of an incomplete instrument, etc. Under (2) the warranty would go to the validity of the payee's indorsement, if such indorsement is essential to the negotiation of the instrument, or to any other defect which would prevent the qualified indorsee from acquiring title to the instrument. An infant's indorsement passes title to the instrument; however, the infant cannot be held liable on his indorsement. Under (3) the qualified indorser warrants that the parties to the instrument have capacity to contract. This warranty does not include the capacity of the drawer of a bill which has been accepted by the drawee. Under (4) the warranty is limited to those defects of which the qualified indorser has knowledge. The courts have held that this warranty includes knowledge of the insolvency of the maker of a note, knowledge of want of consideration, and knowledge of a usurious rate of interest charged for the loan.

Leekley v. Short et al.
216 Iowa, 376, 249 N.W. 363, 91 A.L.R. 394 (1933)

This was an action by Eleanor H. Leekley (plaintiff) against I. E. and Erma Short and Ella B. Ward (defendants). Judgment for defendant Ella B. Ward and plaintiff appealed. Judgment affirmed.

On the 5th day of June, 1931, the defendants I. E. and Erma Short executed and delivered to Ella B. Ward a promissory note for $10,000 due March 1, 1936. The note was secured by a real estate mortgage upon 270 acres of farm land. On August 1, 1931, Ella B. Ward indorsed the note "Without recourse on me pay to the order of Eleanor H. Leekley" and negotiated the note to the plaintiff. September 1, 1931, the makers defaulted in the payment of an installment due and in the payment of interest. Plaintiff declared the entire amount due and payable and brought this suit. The plaintiff contends that the note was not worth more than $6,500 when sold to her and that this fact was known to the defendant Ella B. Ward and that the defendant Ella B. Ward is liable on her implied warranty as a qualified indorser.

Anderson, J. The appellant's claim is that even though a note is transferred by a qualified indorsement, if the indorser knew that the note was of no value and that the person could not collect it, such indorser thereby perpetrated fraud upon the purchaser and obtained the money upon false pretense. The appellant contends in argument that the appellee knew she was selling a worthless note to the plaintiff, and she cannot limit plaintiff's recovery against fraud by a qualified indorsement of the note. The plaintiff's petition is a complete answer to this contention. The petition alleging that this particular note was not worth more than $6,500 and "will not sell at sheriff's sale for an amount in excess of $6,500.00." The conclusion necessarily follows that the note was not valueless and that the defendant had "no knowledge of any fact which would impair the validity of the instrument or render it valueless." It also follows that there was no breach of an implied warranty that the note was not "valueless." The fact that the note was not worth par does not render it valueless or impair its validity.

The section of the statute under consideration is a part of the Negotiable Instruments Law and the question here presented is one of first impression in this court.

The warranties implied by the statute, accompanying an indorsement without recourse, do not include the solvency of the maker, but are restricted to matters affecting the legal enforceability of the paper; and, without an allegation of fraud or deceit, there can be no recovery thereon based upon the insolvency of the maker or his inability to pay.

We hold that the Iowa statute under consideration creates no implied warranty, under a restricted indorsement, as to the solvency of the maker of a negotiable instrument, or that the instrument is worth par. An indorsement without recourse impliedly warrants that the instrument is genuine and in all respects what it purports to be; that the transferor has a good title to it; that all prior parties had capacity to contract; and that the instrument is legally enforceable. There is the additional implication that the indorser knows of no fact which would impair the validity of the instrument or render it valueless, but this provision or implication can only arise when the indorser has such knowledge and fraudulently conceals or withholds the same from the transferee. All of the cases, except the early ones, arose under the Negotiable Instruments Law and hold that the word "valueless" does not refer to the value of the security nor to the solvency of the maker, but simply to some legal insufficiency.

"The legal effect of the words, 'without recourse,' . . . . is to clearly indicate that the one so signing . . . does not intend to assume the position of an unconditional indorser, or to incur any liability if the note is not paid . . . . even if the parties to the paper should prove to be wholly insolvent." *Cameron* v. *Ham.* He, the indorser without recourse, assumed no liability "except for a breach of the warranties which by statute accompanied his qualified indorsement. He made no warranty as to the value of the security for the payment of the notes." *Walter* v. *Kilpatrick.*

Armstrong v. McCluskey et al.
188 Ark. 1093, 65 S.W. (2d) 558 (1933)

This was an action by J. W. Armstrong as receiver of the Planters' National Bank (plaintiff) against J. A. McCluskey, D. D. Allison, and others (defendants). Decree for defendants Allison and another and plaintiff appealed. Decree affirmed in part and reversed in part and remanded.

The holder of a negotiable promissory note brought suit against the makers and indorsers on the note. The payee J. M. Whitlow had indorsed the note "Endorsed to Clarence Whitlow without recourse J. M. Whitlow." One of the makers set up as a defense that the note was usurious. J. M. Whitlow claimed that his qualified indorsement relieved him from all liability on the note. It was established that the note was usurious and that J. M. Whitlow had knowledge, at the time he transferred the note, that it was usurious.

Kirby, J. The trial court was of the opinion that because of J. M. Whitlow's indorsement on the note without recourse, coupled with the fact that the appellant accepted the same as collateral for a past-due note of Clarence Whitlow, he was not liable therefore for its payment. In this the court was mistaken. An assignment of a note without recourse is equivalent to a mere sale without an express warranty, but there remains the implied warranty, among others, that there is no legal defense growing out of the assignor's own connection with its origin (*Smith* v. *Corege*, 53 Ark. 295, 14 S.W. 93), and that the assignor has no knowledge which would impair the validity of the instrument or render it valueless. Therefore, since the validity of the note is warranted by the indorser where the note is not valid because of usury, because of the implied warranty the indorser becomes liable for its payment.

It follows that J. M. Whitlow is liable for the payment of the note by reason of the implied warranty contained in his indorsement and that the court erred in contrary judgment.

Liability of Unqualified Indorser

The unqualified indorser by his indorsement makes all the warranties made by the qualified indorser. The warranties made by the unqualified indorser are more extensive than those made by the qualified indorser in one important respect. The qualified indorser warrants that he has no knowledge of any facts which would impair the validity of the instrument or render it valueless, while the unqualified indorser warrants that the instrument is at the time of his indorsement valid and subsisting. In a state which has a statute that declares all negotiable instruments given in payment of gambling debts to be void, Archer gives Burch his negotiable note in payment of a gambling debt. Burch negotiates the note to Fox who takes without knowledge of the origin of the instrument. If Fox indorses the note "Without recourse, Fox" and negotiates it to Grew, Fox cannot be held liable on his indorsement on the ground that the note is void because given in payment of a gambling debt. Fox is a qualified indorser and has no knowledge of the fact that the instrument was given in payment of a gambling debt. But, if Fox had indorsed without qualifying his indorsement, he would be liable because as an unqualified indorser he warrants that the instrument is valid and subsisting.

In addition to warranting the instrument, the unqualified indorser guarantees the acceptance or payment of the instrument. This liability is a secondary liability. If the instrument is not presented for payment or for acceptance, in case acceptance is required, or if presented and dishonored and notice of dishonor is not given, the unqualified indorser will be released from his liability to pay the instrument on the default of the party primarily liable.

An unqualified indorser may waive presentment, protest, and notice either at the time he indorses the instrument or subsequently. If the waiver is embodied in the instrument itself, it is binding upon all the parties, but where it is written above the signature of the indorser, it binds him only (N.I.L. Sec. 110).

Blucher v. Eubank et al.
Comm. of App. of Texas, 5 S.W. (2d) 972 (1928)

This was an action by George A. Blucher (plaintiff) against B. A. Eubank, R. D. Sands, and others (defendants). Judgment for plaintiff in the trial court was reversed, as to defendant R. D. Sands, in the Court of Civil Appeals and plaintiff appealed to Commission of Appeals. Judgment of the Court of Civil Appeals reversed and judgment of trial court for plaintiff affirmed.

On March 16, 1915, B. A. Eubank and wife executed a promissory note for the sum of $1050 payable to the order of R. D. Sands, due three years after date. The note contained the following provision: "All sureties, indorsers, and guarantors hereof hereby severally waive presentment for payment, notice of non-payment, protest and notice of protest and diligence in bringing suit against any party hereto."

Sands indorsed the note in blank by writing his name on the back thereof and delivered the note to the cashier of the bank, who said he was acting for a "customer of the bank." George A. Blucher, the plaintiff, subsequently became holder of the note. On November 3, 1920, plaintiff filed this suit against the Eubanks, R. D. Sands and others, wherein he seeks to recover of the Eubanks, as makers, and Sands, as indorser. Sands set up as a defense that in indorsing the note and delivering it to the cashier he intended his indorsement as a receipt for the money received and that he did not intend to incur any liability. Sands also set up the four-year statute of limitations as a defense.

Harvey, P. J. An unqualified indorsement of a note by the payee constitutes a new and substantive contract, embodying all the terms of the note. By indorsing the note in blank, the payee engages, among other things, that the note will be paid according to its purport. This engagement is assumed by him, under his indorsement in blank, in all respects the same as if it were written in the indorsement. The law attaches this meaning and effect, among others, to the indorsement, and parol evidence is incompetent to vary the contract thus made. The trial court properly disregarded oral testimony purporting to show that the indorsement was not intended to have this meaning and effect which the law ascribes to it.

When, as here, the note contains a stipulation to the effect that all indorsers of the note waive performance of all acts preliminary to the fixing of their liability, the liability of an indorser becomes fixed by the fact of non-payment of the note by the maker in accordance with the terms of the indorsement contract.

In the instant case, the terms of the note as written therein entered into and became part of the contract which Sands made by his indorsement and delivery of the note. When, therefore, the note was not paid three years after its date in accordance with those terms, the indorsement contract of Sands matured, and he thereupon became absolutely liable for the payment of the note. The holder of the note not having elected to mature the liability of Sands, as indorser, prior to the date of maturity specified in the note, no cause of action against the latter arose until that time. For this reason, the statute of limitation did not begin to run in favor of Sands until the cause of action against him accrued by the failure of the makers to pay the note on March 16, 1918, in accordance with the indorsement contract.

Clearfield Trust Co. et al. v. United States
318 U.S. 363, 63 S.Ct. 573, 87 L. Ed. 838 (1943)

This was an action by the United States (plaintiff) against Clearfield Trust Co. (defendant). J. C. Penney Co. intervened. Judgment for defendant and plaintiff appealed to the Circuit Court of Appeals. Judgment reversed and an appeal to the United States Supreme Court was granted. Judgment of the Circuit Court of Appeals for the United States affirmed.

The United States issued a check dated April 28, 1936, in the sum of $24.20 payable to the order of Barner. The check never reached Barner. An unknown person obtained the check, forged Barner's indorsement on the check and transferred it to J. C. Penney Co. in exchange for goods and cash. J. C. Penney Co. indorsed the check over to the Clearfield Trust Co. for collection. The check was presented through the Federal Reserve Bank, and paid on November 30, 1936. The United States knew that the payee's indorsement on the check had been forged. No notice was given the Clearfield Trust Co. or J. C. Penney Co. until January 12, 1937. Clearfield Trust Co. and J. C. Penney Co. claim that they are not liable to the United States on their indorsement because of its failure to give notice of the forgery.

Mr. Justice Douglas delivered the opinion of the Court.

The Court held that the United States could recover as drawee from one who presented for payment a pension check on which the name of the payee had been forged, in spite of a protracted delay on the part of the United States in giving notice of the forgery. The Court followed *Leather Manufacturers Bank* v. *Merchants Bank*, 128 U.S. 26, which held that the right of the drawee against one who presented a check with a forged indorsement of the payee's name accrued at the date of payment and was not dependent on notice or demand. The theory of the National Exchange Bank case is that he who presents a check for payment warrants that he has title to it and the right to receive payment. If he has acquired the check through a forged indorsement, the warranty is breached at the time the check is cashed. It has been urged that "the right to recover is a quasi contractual right, resting upon the doctrine that one who confers a benefit in misreliance upon a right or duty is entitled to restitution." But whatever theory is taken, we adhere to the conclusion of the National Exchange Bank case that the drawee's right to recover accrues when the payment is made. There is no other barrier to the maintenance of the cause of action. The theory of the drawee's responsibility where the drawer's signature is forged is inapplicable here. The drawee, whether it be the United States or another, is not chargeable with the knowledge of the signature of the payee.

The National Exchange Bank case went no further than to hold that prompt notice of the discovery of the forgery was not a condition precedent to suit. It did not reach the question whether lack of prompt notice might be a defense. We think it may. If it is shown that the drawee on learning of the forgery did not give prompt notice of it and that damage resulted, recovery by the drawee is barred. The facts that the drawee is the United States and the laches those of its employees are not material. The United States as drawee of commercial paper stands in no different light than any other drawee. "The United States does business on business terms." It is not excepted from the general rules governing the rights and duties of drawees "by the largeness of its dealings and its having to employ agents to do what if done by a principal in person would leave no room for doubt." But the damage occasioned by the delay must be established and not left to conjecture. We do not think that he who accepts a forged signature of a payee deserves that preferred treatment. It is his neglect or error in accepting the forger's signature which occasions the loss. He should be allowed to shift that loss to the drawee only on a clear showing that the drawee's delay in notifying him of the forgery caused him damage. No such damage has been shown by Clearfield Trust Co. who so far as appears can still recover from J. C. Penney Co. The only showing on the part of the latter is contained in the stipulation to the effect that if a check cashed for a customer is returned unpaid or for reclamation a short time after the date on which it is cashed, the employees can often locate the person who cashed it. It is further stipulated that when J. C. Penney Co. was notified of the forgery in the present case none of its employees was able to remember anything about the transaction or check in question. The inference is that the more prompt the notice the more likely the detection of the forger. But that falls short of showing that the delay caused a manifest loss.

Liability of Accommodation Parties

A person may sign a negotiable instrument for the sole purpose of giving credit to the instrument and without receiving value therefor. Such a person is an accommodation party. Burch wishes to borrow $100 from the First Bank but his credit standing does not justify the loan. Archer, Burch's friend, has a good credit rating and is willing to help him obtain the loan and agrees to sign a note for the accommodation of Burch.

Archer may sign the note either as maker or indorser. If he wishes to sign as maker, he will draw the note payable either to the First Bank or to Burch and sign it, and Burch will take it to the First Bank and discount it. If he wishes to sign as indorser, Burch will draw the note payable to the First Bank, Archer will indorse it, and Burch will take it to the First Bank and discount it. In the first situation Archer is liable as maker to all holders for value and in the second situation Archer is liable as indorser to all holders for value who become such subsequent to his indorsement. The fact that the holder knows that Archer signed without receiving value and for the accommodation of Burch is immaterial.

Archer and Burch might use a bill of exchange instead of a note in which case Archer might sign as drawer, acceptor, or indorser. Archer has a credit balance with Drew. Archer draws a draft on Drew naming Burch as payee and delivers it to Burch without receiving value.

Archer is an accommodation drawer. Archer may authorize Burch to draw a draft on him as drawee. When the draft is presented Archer accepts the draft without receiving value. Archer is an accommodation acceptor. Burch holds a draft in which he is named payee and which has been accepted. Burch wishes to discount the draft, but the parties to the draft are unknown to the First Bank and it refuses to discount it. Archer, who is known to the First Bank, indorses the draft without receiving value. Archer is an accommodation indorser.

An instrument may be indorsed for the accommodation of a holder other than the payee. Archer issues his negotiable promissory note payable to Burch. Burch indorses the instrument and negotiates it to Fox. Fox wishes to discount the note at the First Bank but Fox, Burch, and Archer are not known by the First Bank and it requests an additional indorser. Grew indorses the note without receiving value and the bank discounts it. Grew indorses for the accommodation of Fox.

As a general rule payment by the person accommodated discharges the instrument. In our first example, if Burch pays the instrument, it is discharged even though on the face of the instrument Archer appears as maker. Also, on the bill of exchange accepted for the accommodation of Burch, if Burch pays the instrument, it is discharged even though on the face of the instrument Archer is the party primarily liable. In our last example, Grew would be liable to persons who become holders for value subsequent to his indorsement, but would not be liable to prior parties.

In the first example, in which Burch, the person accommodated, indorses the instrument, Burch is not discharged from liability if the instrument is not presented for payment or if notice of dishonor is not given, but in the example in which Archer indorsed for the accommodation of Burch, Archer is discharged from his liability if the instrument is not presented or if notice of dishonor is not given.

Brinker v. First National Bank of Cleveland
Ct. of Civ. App. Texas, 16 S.W. (2d) 965 (1929)

This was an action by the First National Bank of Cleveland (plaintiff) against P. M. Brinker and another (defendants). Judgment for plaintiff and defendant Brinker appealed. Judgment affirmed.

Brinker sold his interest in a mercantile business in Cleveland, Oklahoma, to Turley for $2,500. Turley wished to borrow the money from plaintiff to pay Brinker. A negotiable promissory note was executed, payable to the plaintiff and signed by Turley and Wear, but plaintiff bank refused to make the loan unless Brinker also signed the note as maker. Brinker did so and the note was not paid and plaintiff sued Turley and Brinker as makers of the note. Wear died and was not made a party to the suit. Brinker set up as a defense that he was an accommodation maker for, and not liable to, the payee.

McClendon, C. J. The legal principles applicable to accommodation paper which control the question here may be summarized as follows:

An accommodation maker is one who signs an instrument without receiving value and "for the purpose of lending his name to some other person." "Accommodation" so employed is the loan of credit without consideration by one party to another, "who undertakes to pay the paper and indemnify the lender (of credit) against loss on its account," the purpose being that the party accommodated "shall obtain money or credit upon it of some third party."

The fact that a party who signs a note as maker himself receives no consideration does not necessarily constitute him an accommodation maker for the payee. In legal acceptation, accommodation as applied to notes and other paper has a technical meaning and is not used in its broadest popular sense. The fact that the payee may receive benefit or be accommodated by or may solicit the signature of a party who receives no consideration therefor does not constitute such party an accommodation maker for the payee. It is only in those cases where the note is executed for the sole purpose of its negotiation by the payee in order that he may obtain credit thereby, and under an agreement that he is to provide for payment at maturity and indemnify the maker, that the instrument becomes in law accommodation paper for the payee.

It is clear that Brinker under the above evidence was not an accommodation maker for the bank, and this defense is unavailing.

Sandler v. Scullen et al.
290 Mass. 106, 194 N.E. 827 (1935)

This was an action by Betty R. Sandler (plaintiff) against Charles F. Scullen and one Smith and one Arnold (defendants). Judgment for plaintiff and defendants Smith and Arnold appealed. Judgment against Smith affirmed and judgment against Arnold reversed.

Plaintiff loaned Smith $11,500 and took a negotiable promissory note signed by Charles F. Scullen as maker and indorsed by Smith and Arnold. Scullen, an employee of Smith, signed the note as a "straw" and was of no financial ability. Smith and Arnold indorsed the note before delivery to plaintiff, the payee. The note was not presented for payment on the due date. Smith and Arnold set up the failure to present the note and give notice of non-payment as a defense.

Lummus, J. Where the maker of a note signs it for the accommodation of an indorser, the latter is not entitled to presentment of the note for payment, nor to notice of dishonor, for he has no reason to expect that he will not be required to pay such a note at maturity, or that the maker will pay it. No presentment for payment was made of the note in question, and no notice of dishonor was given to Smith or Arnold. Smith was not thereby freed from liability, for he was the party accommodated, and in reality the principal debtor. But we find no evidence to justify the finding that the note was made for the accommodation of Arnold also. The liability of Arnold ended upon the failure to make presentment and give notice. He was entitled to the ruling which he requested, that against him the plaintiff was not entitled to recover.

Order of Liability

The party primarily liable on an instrument is liable to all holders of the instrument. Those who are secondarily liable are, as a general rule, liable in the order in which they became a party to the instrument. The drawer of a bill is liable to all persons who became holders subsequent to his signing. Each indorser is liable to all subsequent indorsers, but is not liable to prior parties. The courts presume that the parties became parties to the instrument in the order of their indorsements.

In most jurisdictions the holder of a negotiable instrument can bring suit against the party primarily liable and all parties secondarily liable in one suit. Judgment will be rendered against all parties and the holder can enforce the judgment against any of the parties liable, but when the judgment is once satisfied he has exhausted his rights on the judgment. Under the laws of some states the holders cannot join the party primarily liable and parties secondarily liable in one suit. Archer issues his negotiable promissory note for $500 payable to Burch. Burch indorses the note and negotiates it to Fox who indorses it and negotiates it to Hall. On the due date Hall presents the note for payment and payment is refused. Hall gives notice to Burch and Fox. Hall can sue Archer, Burch, and Fox in one suit and get a judgment against all of the parties. However, when he has collected $500 he has exhausted his rights under the judgment. He might collect $100 from Fox, $300 from Burch, and $100 from Archer. In the foregoing example Fox, having paid $100, could recover this amount from prior parties, i.e., Archer or Burch. If Hall collected the entire $500 from Archer, the instrument would be discharged.

Discharge

If all the parties to a negotiable instrument fulfill their obligations, the instrument will be paid by the principal debtor. The principal debtor may be the party primarily liable on the instrument or he may be the party accommodated where the instrument is made or accepted for accommodation. Such a payment will discharge the instrument. Also the instrument may be discharged by payment in behalf of the principal debtor.

Payment need not be in money; however, in the normal course of business negotiable instruments are discharged by payment in money. The payment must be made to the holder of the instrument or to his duly authorized agent. The stamping of an instrument "paid" is not payment and does not discharge the instrument. A check presented to the teller for payment is not paid by the drawee bank until the money is paid to the holder, or if presented for deposit, the check is not paid until it is credited to the holder's account. If the drawee bank gives its own check or draft for the check, it is paid. When a party not a party to the instrument pays it, the intention of the party paying is controlling. If he pays in behalf of the obligor, the instrument is paid and discharged, but if he is purchasing the instrument, it is not discharged.

The holder of the instrument may discharge the instrument by cancellation. Any destruction or mutilation of the instrument with the intent that the instrument will no longer evidence an obligation is a cancellation. Also, delivery of the instrument to the obligor with the intention that the obligation be terminated is a cancellation.

If the principal debtor acquires the instrument in his own right at or after the date of maturity, the instrument is discharged. This is substantially the same as the payment of the instrument.

In addition to these specific means of discharging a negotiable instrument it may be discharged by any other act which will discharge a simple contract for the payment of money. The discharge of contracts was treated in an earlier chapter.

Persons secondarily liable on a negotiable instrument are discharged by the discharge of the instrument, by the cancellation of their signature by the holder, by the discharge of a prior party, or by a valid tender of payment made by a prior party. The liability of a party secondarily liable is analogous to that of a surety, and any change in the relations of the parties which will affect the liability of the party secondarily liable and which is made without his consent will discharge him. A release of the principal debtor without reservation of the holder's rights against the party secondarily liable will discharge the latter. Also, any binding agreement to extend the time of payment or postpone the holder's right to enforce the instrument, made without the consent of the party secondarily liable, will discharge him unless right of recourse against the party secondarily liable is expressly reserved.

Any material alteration of the instrument will discharge the instrument as to all parties who are not parties to the alteration or who have not consented thereto. A holder in due course who became a holder after the alteration and who is not a party to the alteration may enforce payment of the instrument as it was originally drawn.

Dewey v. Metropolitan Life Ins. Co.
256 Mass. 281, 152 N.E. 82 (1926)

This was an action by Mary Dewey (plaintiff) against the Metropolitan Life Insurance Company (defendant). Judgment for defendant and plaintiff appealed. Judgment affirmed.

Defendant drew its check on the Metropolitan Bank of New York as drawee, payable to the order of John F. Ryan and Mary Dewey (plaintiff). It was agreed between Ryan and plaintiff that the check was to be cashed by them jointly and that Ryan was to get $175 and plaintiff the balance. Ryan received the check and cashed it at the Union Trust Company in Springfield, Massachusetts. When deposited the check bore on its back the name of John F. Ryan as indorser and the name of Mary Dewey, by mark, as indorser. The genuineness of the signature of the name of Mary Dewey by mark was denied by the plaintiff and the jury found that she did not indorse the check. The check was presented to and paid by the drawee bank in the regular course of business. Plaintiff received nothing from the proceeds of the check and claims that the check is not discharged.

Pierce, J. A check is a bill of exchange drawn on a bank. As such it is a negotiable instrument. The rule deducible from the cases is that if payment of a bill at maturity, in full, by the acceptor or other party liable, to a person having a legal title in himself, and having the custody and possession of the bill ready to surrender, and the party paying has no notice of any defect of title or authority to receive, the payment will be good.

". . . . Faith is given to the holder, mainly on the ground of his possession of the bill, ready to be surrendered or delivered, and the actual surrender and delivery of it upon the payment or transfer."

It is a general principle that one of several joint obligees may discharge an entire claim by the receipt of payment of such claim and that payment of a bill or note payable to two or more persons jointly may be made to either of them and the debt be thereby extinguished.

The provisions of G. L. c. 107, § 64, that, "where an instrument is payable to the order of two or more payees or indorsees who are not partners, all must indorse, unless the one indorsing has authority to indorse for the others," is but a statement of the common law as it was understood in this commonwealth before the passage of the Negotiable Instruments Law, and has no application to the effect of a payment to one of several joint obligees or payees.

It follows that, by the payment to Ryan, by the bank, of the full amount called for by the check, it was discharged and canceled; and that the contractual rights against the insurance company, which were created by the delivery of the check to the authorized agent of the plaintiff, were extinguished on the delivery of the check to the bank, when it cashed it without notice of any limitation on the right of Ryan to receive the proceeds of it.

Mackey et al. v. Lefeber.
172 Okl. 99, 45 P. (2d) 148 (1935)

This was an action by Mrs. G. W. Lefeber (plaintiff) against R. M. Mackey and others (defendants). Judgment for plaintiff and defendants appealed. Judgment reversed with directions.

Virgil Davis and Belle Davis, his wife, executed their negotiable promissory note in the sum of $2,000 payable to J. C. Culbertson and secured it by a real estate mortgage on a tract of land. The land, subject to the Davis mortgage, was acquired by defendant R. M. Mackey. The note and mortgage were negotiated to Mrs. G. W. Lefeber who made extensive loans on real estate through Culbertson & Tomm, a copartnership composed of J. C. Culbertson and L. M. Tomm. During the life of the Davis mortgage the interest was paid to Culbertson and Tomm and in their dealings with the plaintiff Culbertson & Tomm collected both the principal and interest on loans made by them for the plaintiff. The Davis note and mortgage were made payable at the office of Culbertson and Tomm. Culbertson and Tomm became insolvent in April, 1926. On March 24, 1926, Mackey paid the amount of the note to Culbertson & Tomm, but the note was not cancelled and the mortgage was not released. Culbertson & Tomm did not turn the money over to plaintiff and at the time the payment was made Culbertson & Tomm did not have possession of the note and mortgage. Plaintiff brings suit to foreclose the mortgage and defendant Mackey sets up payment as a defense.

McNeill, C. J. We believe that the rule applicable to the issue here presented is well stated in *Sherrill* v. *Cole et al.*, 144 Okl. 301, 291 P. 54, as follows: "It is the universal rule that one who is bound to pay a negotiable promissory note is not protected if he pays it to the payee thereof, and at the place of payment named in the note, without the production of the paper by the person receiving the money, unless (1) the payee or the person receiving the payment is the authorized agent, express or implied, of the rightful holder; (2) or unless the conduct and course of dealings of the holder are such as to engender in the mind of the payee a justifiable belief that the payee or the party receiving the money is the agent of the holder for that purpose."

Where the question of agency is made an issue in a case of equitable cognizance, it becomes a question of fact to be determined by the court; and where a note is payable at payee's office, it is a circumstance tending to show that the payee was the holder's agent to collect. From a consideration of all the facts and circumstances, we are of the opinion that Culbertson and Tomm acted as the agents of Mrs. Lefeber in making collection upon the note in question, and that the judgment of the trial court was against the clear weight of the evidence.

QUESTIONS AND PROBLEMS

1. How does the liability of the maker of a note or the acceptor of a bill of exchange differ from that of indorser or the drawer of the bill of exchange?
2. Archer issues his negotiable promissory note payable to the order of Burch and payable at the First Bank on November 1, 1945. On November 1, 1945, Archer deposits sufficient money with the First Bank to pay the note and instructs the bank to pay the note when presented. Burch does not present the note for payment until November 15, 1945. Before the note is presented, Archer has withdrawn the money from the bank. Can Burch recover on the note?
3. Archer drew a bill of exchange on Burch payable to the order of Clark and delivered it to Clark on October 15. On October 16, Clark presented the bill of exchange to Burch for acceptance and Burch told Clark to bring it back in two or three days. Clark presented the bill a second time, on October 20, and was put off by Burch. Clark presented the bill a third time, on October 25, when Burch refused to accept it. On October 27, Clark gave Archer notice that the bill had been dishonored. Is Archer liable to Clark on the bill of exchange?
4. Hough issued his negotiable promissory note payable to the order of Partin Company, Incorporated. The note was indorsed, "Partin Company, Incorporated. Pay C. H. Partin, Manager," and negotiated to one who could qualify as a holder in due course. When sued on the note, Hough set up as a defense that Partin Company, Incorporated, had no corporate existence because it had not filed its charter and, consequently, could not indorse the note. Is the defense valid?
5. A draft drawn on the National City Bank of Chicago as drawee and payable to the American Sheet and Tin Plate Co. was stolen and the name of the payee was changed to Andrew H. Manning. Manning negotiated the draft thus altered to Barnett Bros. who took it for value and in good faith. Barnett Bros. presented the draft to the drawee who accepted the draft by writing across its face: "Accepted, payable through the Chicago clearing house, Jan. 9, 1915. The National City Bank of Chicago, per G. D. Grim, Paying Teller." When the draft was presented for payment, the acceptor refused to pay and set up the alteration of the payee's name as a defense. Is the acceptor liable on the draft?
6. Cooper contracted to sell goods to Morcott and drew a draft on Morcott for the purchase price of the goods payable to the order of International Banking Corporation. The payee presented the draft to Morcott who accepted it. On the due date International Banking Co. presented the draft for payment and payment was refused. When sued, Morcott set up as a defense Cooper's failure to ship the goods. Is the defense valid?
7. The Gainsville News issued its check payable to the order of Mrs. C. M. Harrison. Mrs. Harrison did not present the check to the drawee bank until more than six months after its date of issue. The drawee bank refused to honor the check and Mrs. Harrison brought suit against the drawer. Did the delay in presenting the check relieve the drawer from liability?
8. Archer issued his negotiable promissory note payable to the order of Burch. Burch indorsed the note, "Without recourse, Burch," and negotiated it to the First Bank. At the time Burch negotiated the note to the First Bank, Archer was insolvent but this was unknown to Burch. The note was not paid. Is Burch liable to the First Bank on his indorsement?
9. A check was issued payable to the order of E. H. Walden. Walden's indorsement was forged on the check and the check was negotiated to J. W. Edwards who took for value, in good faith, and without knowledge of the forgery. Edwards indorsed the check, "Without recourse, J. W. Edwards," and negotiated it to A. L. Roth. Roth presented the check for payment and payment was refused. Is Edwards liable to Roth on the check?
10. What is the nature of an unqualified indorser's liability to pay the instrument?

CHAPTER XXV

VARIOUS NEGOTIABLE AND QUASI NEGOTIABLE INSTRUMENTS

Introduction

Various instruments used in the commercial world are negotiable in varying degrees depending on their use. We have thus far limited our consideration to negotiable instruments as defined in the Negotiable Instruments Law and have considered only the legal relations created by the issuing or negotiation of such instruments. In this chapter we shall consider some relationships closely connected with the use of negotiable instruments and shall also consider some instruments that are not payable in money but which are negotiable in character.

Checks

A check is defined by the Negotiable Instruments Law as "a bill of exchange drawn on a bank payable on demand." In most respects the law applicable to bills of exchange is also applicable to checks; however, they differ in some important respects.

The relation between the drawer of a check and the drawee bank is both that of debtor and creditor, and principal and agent. When money is deposited in a commercial account, the bank becomes the debtor of the customer for the amount deposited and, either expressly or by implication, agrees to honor all checks properly drawn if the depositor has sufficient funds to cover the check. The drawing of a check does not assign any part of the funds on deposit with the bank, and the bank is not liable on the check unless it certifies it.

If, after the drawer has issued a check and before the check has been paid or certified, the drawer orders the bank not to pay the check when presented—issues a stop payment order—the bank must refuse payment of the check when presented and, if the bank does pay the check, it will be liable to the drawer for any injury resulting from such payment. The bank may reduce its liability to the drawer for the payment of a check after a stop payment order by special contract.

The liability of the drawer of a check is the same as that of the drawer of a bill of exchange. However, the majority of the American courts hold that the failure of the holder to give the drawer notice of the dishonor of a check does not relieve him of his liability. All courts hold that, if the drawee bank dishonors the check because the drawer has issued a stop payment order or because the drawer does not have an account with the drawee bank, notice is not necessary. If the check is dishonored for other reasons, the American rule is that failure to give the drawer notice will relieve him from liability only to the extent of injury actually suffered. The majority of the courts follow the American rule. The various states have statutes which declare the drawing of a check on a bank in which the drawer has no funds or insufficient funds to cover the check to be punishable either by a fine or imprisonment or both.

Three distinct situations arise in the use of checks in regard to the time within which one must act to protect his interests. (1) The Uniform Negotiable Instruments Law provides (Sec. 186): "A check must be presented for payment within a reasonable time after its issue or the drawer will be discharged from liability thereon to the extent of the loss caused by the delay." The courts have held, in the absence of special circumstances justifying the delay, that, if the holder and the drawee live in the same city, the check should be presented for payment within 24 hours, Sundays and holidays excluded. If the holder and the drawee are not in the same city, the holder must put the checks in the channels for collection within 24 hours. (2) To take as a holder in due course one must take the instrument before it is overdue. A check is payable on demand. The time within which a demand instrument becomes overdue has been discussed. (3) A check becomes stale when it has been out such a length of time that the drawee bank would be negligent in paying the check without inquiry. Some banks consider a check which has been out six months as a stale check while others do not consider a check as stale unless it has been out a year.

Certification of a check by the drawee bank creates the same liabilities on the part of the bank as the acceptance of a bill of exchange by the drawee. The bank becomes primarily liable. The check may be certified at the request of the drawer, the payee, or any holder. If the check is certified at the request of the drawer, he will be secondarily liable to the same extent as the drawer of a bill of exchange. If the check is certified at the request of the payee, the drawer is discharged from liability and, if the check is certified at the request of a holder, the drawer and all indorsers are discharged from liability thereon. The certification to be valid must be made at the bank by an officer authorized to certify checks. It is made by stamping or writing "certified" together with the name of the certifying bank and is signed or initialed by the certifying officer. At the time the check is certified the drawer's account is debited and the certified check account is credited. The bank becomes the debtor of the holder of the certified check. The certification of a check makes it more marketable in that the credit of the certifying bank is back of the instrument.

The drawee bank is not liable to the holder of a check which has not been certified and will incur no obligation to the holder of the check by its refusal to pay the check. However, if it wrongfully refuses to pay a check, it will be liable to the drawer. If the drawee bank pays a forged check, it cannot charge the amount to the drawer's account nor can it recover from the holder or indorsers on the check. If the bank pays a check drawn payable to the order of a named payee on which the payee's indorsement is forged, the bank cannot charge the amount to the drawer's account but it can recover from the holder and indorsers. If the bank pays an altered check, the bank can charge the amount of the check as originally drawn to the drawer's account, and the majority rule is that the bank can recover the difference from the holder and indorsers. Before the bank pays a check it can require the holder to identify himself. If the bank pays a check issued by a drawer in payment of a gambling debt and under the laws of the state the check is void, the bank can charge the check to the drawer's account.

The drawer of a check owes certain duties of care to the drawee bank. In the drawing of the check, if the drawer negligently leaves unfilled blanks and this results in the alteration of the check, the drawer will be liable to the bank for the amount of the check as altered. If the bank returns the drawer's cancelled checks to him, the drawer owes the bank a duty to examine the checks within a reasonable time after their return and to notify the bank of any forgeries. Any loss suffered as a result of the drawer's failure to fulfill this duty must be borne by the drawer.

State Bank of Siloam Springs v. Marshall.
163 Ark. 566, 260 S.W. 431, 34 A.L.R. 202 (1924)

This was an action by Charlotte Marshall (plaintiff) against State Bank of Siloam Springs (defendant). Judgment for plaintiff and defendant appealed. Judgment reversed. (Damages awarded were excessive.)

Plaintiff had a checking account with defendant and drew certain checks on it which defendant refused to pay. Defendant had wrongfully applied the amount which plaintiff had in her checking account on a note held by the defendant which was not yet due.

Hart, J. At the time the plaintiff drew the checks in question on the defendant bank she had on deposit there a sum subject to her check which was greater than the amount of the four checks drawn by her upon which the bank refused payment. The ground upon which the bank dishonored the checks was that it had applied the deposit of the plaintiff towards the payment of a debt which she owed the bank, but which was not then due. It was also shown by the plaintiff that she was not at the time insolvent, and that the bank had no lien on her deposit.

The general rule is that a bank is bound to honor checks drawn on it by a depositor, if it has sufficient funds belonging to the depositor when the check is presented, and the funds are not subject to any lien or claim; and for its refusal or neglect to do so it is liable in an action by the depositor. This rule is so well settled in this state as well as elsewhere that a citation of authorities in support of it is not necessary.

Hodnick v. Fidelity Trust Company
96 Ind. App. 342, 183 N.E. 488 (1932)

This was an action by Louis J. Hodnick (plaintiff) against the Fidelity Trust Company (defendant). Judgment for defendant and the plaintiff appealed. Judgment affirmed.

Plaintiff issued a check drawn on the defendant as drawee. Before the check was presented for payment the plaintiff signed a stop payment order which provided as follows: "x x the undersigned agrees . . . . not to hold said bank liable on account of payment contrary to this request if made through inadvertence or accident." The check was presented for payment through the clearing house on a Saturday which was a half holiday. The check was paid by the defendant. The circumstances were such that it was clear that the defendant had not willfully ignored the stop payment order. The plaintiff contends that the quoted provision is illegal because it relieves the defendant from the results of his own negligent acts.

Curtis, C. J. In the absence of a showing that any particular contract brought before the court is contrary to what the Constitution, the Legislature, or the judiciary have declared to be the public policy, it is necessary in order to have the court hold it void on the ground of public policy, to show clearly that such contract has a tendency to injure the public, or is against the public good, or is inconsistent with sound policy and good morals as to the consideration or as to the thing to be done or not to be done. Whether or not a contract is against public policy is a question of law for the court to determine from all of the circumstances in a particular case. The courts will keep in mind the principle that it is to the best interest of the public that persons should not be unnecessarily restricted in their freedom of contract and that their agreements are not to be held void as against public policy, unless they are clearly contrary to what the

Constitution, the Legislature, or the judiciary have declared to be the public policy, or unless they clearly tend to the injury of the public in some way.

Applying the principles of law announced in this opinion and in the cases and text above cited, we conclude that the "stop payment order" in this case was based upon a sufficient consideration and that it is not in Indiana void as against public policy, and that the finding of the court should not be disturbed upon these two grounds.

National Plumbing & Heating Supply Company v. B. Stevenson
213 Ill. App. 49 (1918)

This was an action by the National Plumbing & Heating Company (plaintiff) against B. Stevenson (defendant). Judgment for defendant and plaintiff appealed. Judgment affirmed.

Defendant gave plaintiff his check drawn on the Auburn State Bank. The check was given to the plaintiff's salesman at about 9 A.M., May 21. The following morning, May 22, the salesman turned the check in to the plaintiff's cashier. Plaintiff had two bank accounts, one being in the Citizens' Trust & Savings Bank, located a few blocks from the plaintiff's place of business and also near the defendant's place of business, and the other in the Lake View State Bank, located on the opposite side of the city, 10 or 15 miles away. On the evening of May 22, the plaintiff's cashier made up a deposit consisting of a number of checks, including the defendant's check, and sent it by mail to the Lake View State Bank. The record does not show when it was received, but when received the check was sent to the First National Bank of Englewood through which the Lake View State Bank cleared. The First National Bank of Englewood did not send the check through the clearing house but sent it by messenger to the Auburn State Bank for presentment. When the messenger arrived he found the Auburn State Bank had closed its doors at 5 P.M., May 22. The check was returned to the plaintiff on May 25. The defendant at all times had sufficient funds on deposit to cover the check.

Mr. Justice Thomas delivered the opinion of the court.

The trial court ruled that under the evidence the plaintiff was shown to have failed to present the check within a reasonable time and that had it done so the check would have been paid and that therefore the loss was the plaintiff's and it could not recover.

In contending that the court was in error and that the judgment should be reversed, the plaintiff urges that, upon receipt of the check, it proceeded to collect it in the customary manner by depositing it in its bank, and second, that even if its presentment of the check be held insufficient under the law, the defendant should not be relieved of liability as the drawer of the check, unless he is shown to have suffered some loss or injury thereby, and that no such loss or injury is shown by the evidence. The defendant has not filed an appearance nor presented a brief in this court.

The Negotiable Instruments Act (Rev. St. Ill. ch. 98, sec. 185,

J. & A. ¶ 7825) provides that: "A check must be presented for payment within a reasonable time after its issue, and notice of dishonor given to the drawer as provided for in the case of bills of exchange, or the drawer will be discharged from liability thereon to the extent of the loss caused by delay." As to what is a reasonable time for the presentment of a check, it has been held that where the bank on which the check is drawn, and all the parties interested reside in the same city, it is the duty of the holder of the check to present it to the bank for payment on the day the check is received or, at furthest, the next day.

The plaintiff urges that this rule should not be held to apply in the case of a large city like Chicago, which is composed of widely separated portions which were separate towns before they came to be part of the City of Chicago by annexation. This argument, applied to the facts here involved, works against the plaintiff rather than in its favor. All parties in interest, including one of plaintiff's banks of deposit and the bank on which the check was drawn, were located in the same general part of or "town" in the City of Chicago, but instead of depositing this check in its bank located there, plaintiff sees fit to deposit it by mail in a bank located 10 or 15 miles away in a distant part of or "town" in the City of Chicago. The holder of a check cannot be considered to have presented it for payment to the drawee within a reasonable time, where, 2 days after coming into his possession, he deposits it by mail in a bank in a distant part of the city and not in a bank in the same general neighborhood as the drawee, in both of which he regularly keeps accounts.

As to the other point urged by the plaintiff, it may be said that the want of due presentment of a check does not discharge the drawer unless he has suffered some loss or injury thereby, and then only *pro tanto*. In contending that the defendant in the case at bar suffered no loss as a result of the delay in presenting the check in question, the plaintiff argues that the Auburn State Bank could not operate unless it had a capital stock of $200,000, and that the stockholders were liable in a further sum of $200,000 over and above the capital stock, and that the State auditor called for a report of the bank's resources and liabilities every 3 months, citing the statutory provisions on those matters, and it was further urged that with a strict supervision of the State auditor it could be safely assumed that at the very lowest the bank's creditors would get 25 per cent of their claims. All these matters are presumptions in which the court cannot indulge. There is no evidence whatever in the record concerning them. While it is true that in case of an unwarranted delay in the presentment of a check, resulting in its nonpayment, the drawer of the check will not be relieved unless he has suffered some loss or injury by reason of the delay in the presentment of the check, and then only to the extent of such loss or injury, it is also true that the holder of the check has the burden of proving that his delay in presenting it has not resulted in loss or injury on the part of the drawer.

Welch v. Bank of Manhattan Co.
35 N.Y.S. (2d) 894 (1942)

This was an action by David J. Welch (plaintiff) against Bank of Manhattan Company (defendant). The defendant made a motion to interplead Ernest J. Pirman as a party defendant. Motion to interplead denied and judgment entered for plaintiff. Defendant appealed. Judgment and order reversed.

Ernest J. Pirman drew two checks totalling $2,750 on defendant bank payable to the order of plaintiff and had them certified by the defendant bank. The checks were delivered by Pirman to plaintiff as part payment for the purchase and sale of a parcel of real estate. When the checks were presented to the bank, the bank refused payment. The refusal was at the request of Pirman who claimed that plaintiff had breached the contract of purchase and sale and had committed serious waste on the property. The defendant admitted it held the money and made a motion that Pirman be added as a party defendant and that the court determine which party was entitled to the money, plaintiff or Pirman.

Memorandum by the court.

Where, as in the instant case, the certification was at the request of the drawer, the drawer was not discharged from liability. The certification merely operated as an assurance that the check is genuine and that the certifying bank becomes bound with the drawer. Under the circumstances, defendant should be permitted to interplead Pirman as a party-defendant so that he may interpose a defense based upon his claim of fraud and waste and thereby compel plaintiff and Pirman to litigate on the trial which of the two is entitled to the moneys set aside and being held by the bank for the payment of the checks. It is only where a check is certified at the request of the payee or holder that a bank may not resist the enforcement of its contract of certification in order to make a set-off or counterclaim available to its depositor. Obviously the reason for this is that under such circumstances the drawer is discharged from any further liability on the check since the certification is equivalent to an acceptance (Negotiable Instruments Law, § 324) and a complete novation occurs, creating the relation of debtor and creditor between the payee or holder and the bank.

McCarty v. First National Bank of Birmingham
204 Ala. 424, 85 So. 754 (1920)

This was an action by W. C. McCarty (plaintiff) against the First National Bank of Birmingham (defendant). Judgment for defendant and plaintiff appealed. Judgment reversed and remanded.

Plaintiff had a reserve account with the defendant in which he made substantial deposits and from which he made substantial withdrawals. Plaintiff's bank book was balanced and returned to him with his cancelled checks on February 24, 1917. He kept the book from then until July 3, 1917, when it was sent to the bank to be balanced.

It was balanced and ready for delivery to the plaintiff along with the cancelled checks on July 5, 1917. The bank book was left at the bank until September 4, 1917, when plaintiff's agent called for it. Plaintiff put the bank book together with the cancelled checks in the safe and did not examine them until after September 24, 1917. The bank had no rules regarding the balancing of bank books and the return of cancelled checks. Customers left their books when they wished and called for the balanced book and cancelled checks whenever they desired. Beginning on March 5, 1917, one Carney began a series of forgeries on plaintiff's account. He drew one or more checks on the account each month. The checks drawn prior to July, 1917, aggregated $2,400 and checks drawn after July up to the discovery of the forgery on September 24, 1917, aggregated $7,290. A check for $800 was drawn September 1, 1917, one for $500 was drawn September 10, and one for $500 was drawn on September 24. This last check overdrew the account and led to the discovery of the forgeries. The defendant contends that it is not liable for the forged checks paid after July, 1917, because of the plaintiff's negligence in not calling for his bank book and cancelled checks and the resulting failure to examine the cancelled checks and discover the forgeries.

Somerville, J. In the case of *First National Bank* v. *Allen*, 100 Ala. 476, 14 South. 335, it was said:

"The correct principles by which the respective liabilities of the bank and depositor are determined are these: The bank is bound to know the signature of its depositors, and the payment of a forged check, however skillfully executed, cannot be debited against the depositor. From the relations the depositor and the bank bear towards each other, there is a duty also upon the depositor to examine his accounts and vouchers, and to make known to the bank any improper vouchers or charges returned, and where injury results to the bank from the failure of the depositor to do his duty in this respect, the law holds the depositor liable for such injury, the result of the depositor's omission."

In all of the reported cases, this duty of diligence was imposed upon the depositor by reason of the fact that his passbook and canceled checks had actually been returned to him, so that notice of the forgeries was placed in his possession, and knowledge of them thereby made immediately accessible. The rationale of the rule is that, having been furnished with the means of knowledge, it is the depositor's duty to know; and, knowing, he is under the further duty of informing the bank of whatever he finds to be wrong.

It is clear that a depositor is not required to anticipate errors or irregularities in his account, and particularly the payment by the bank of forged checks; and hence the law imposes upon him no duty to initiate an inquiry with respect to such matters, and, in the absence of an agreement, express or implied, between him and the bank, he is not bound to ask for a statement of his account at any time, but may rely upon the bank's observance of all of its obligations in the premises. There was no such agreement here, and the question is whether merely leaving his passbook to be balanced by the bank imposed upon plaintiff the duty of calling for the book, and the canceled checks customarily returned therewith, in a reasonable time, or, indeed, at any time, under the penalty of releasing the bank from liability for the repetition of errors already committed.

We are satisfied that the law, operating upon the mere relation of the parties, imposed no such duty upon the depositor, and, so far as we are advised, no court has ever so held. A statement of account, though prepared and ready for delivery, does not become a stated account, with legal consequences, until it is actually placed in the hands of the party to be charged, and, with knowledge of its purport, he has acquiesced in its correctness.

Promissory Notes, etc.

Corporation and government bonds, certificates of deposits, and municipal warrants are promises to pay money and are basically promissory notes.

Government, state, and municipal bonds, as a general rule, contain a promise to pay to the bearer a stated sum of money on a named day; therefore, they qualify as negotiable instruments. Debentures are, as a general rule, of the same nature and are negotiable.

Sometimes such bonds provide that they are transferrable only on the books of the issuer, or, especially in the case of municipal bonds, that payment is to be made out of a special fund or from the proceeds of a special assessment.

Corporate bonds are, as a general rule, secured by a mortgage on the assets of the issuing corporation. The mortgage is usually a single mortgage given to a trustee for the benefit of all bond holders. The bond secured by such a mortgage will contain some reference to the trust mortgage. Unless this reference clause is carefully drafted it may make the promise to pay conditional and thus make the bond non-negotiable. If a non-negotiable bond is stolen and sold to an innocent purchaser for value, the owner from whom the bond was stolen can recover the bond from the innocent purchaser. If the bond is negotiable, the innocent purchaser acquires good title.

Bonds differ from promissory notes in one important respect. The transferor of a bond warrants that it is (1) genuine, (2) that he has good title, and (3) that he has no knowledge of any fact which would impair the validity of the instrument or render it valueless, but he does not warrant that all prior parties have capacity to contract as he would in the transfer of a promissory note.

A bank may issue certificates of deposit to its time depositors. Such certificates are not uniform in their terms, but generally they are so drawn that they are negotiable bearer promissory notes payable on demand, and the majority of the courts have treated them as notes.

Counties and municipalities frequently issue warrants in payment of debts. These warrants are usually negotiable in form; however, the majority of courts have held that one taking a warrant, even though he can qualify as a holder in due course, takes it subject to defenses which the issuing municipality or county may have to the warrant. This holding is based on the argument that to invest such instruments with all the characteristics of negotiable instruments would put into the hands of corrupt officials the power to bankrupt the municipality or county. The later decisions tend to repudiate this reasoning and hold such instruments to be negotiable if they are in the proper form.

Merchants' National Bank v. Detroit Trust Company
258 Mich. 526, 242 N.W. 739 (1932)

This was an action by the Merchants' National Bank (plaintiff) against the Detroit Trust Company (defendant). Judgment for plaintiff and defendant appealed. Judgment reversed and remanded with directions.

Certain corporate bonds were stolen and pledged by a bandit with the defendant as security for a loan. The plaintiff, as assignee of the owners from whom the bonds were stolen, brought this suit in replevin to recover the bonds.

McDonald, J. As to the disputed bonds, the question is, Do they contain an unconditional promise or order to pay at a certain time, and, at all events, a certain sum of money? If negotiable, the unconditional promise must appear on the face of the bond. In *Paepcke* v. *Paine* it is said: "The instrument itself determines its character. It must, of course, conform to the requirements of the Negotiable Instruments Law. But the statute deals with its form—with what an inspection of its face discloses."

In the Negotiable Instruments Law it is said: "An unqualified order or promise to pay is unconditional within the meaning of this act, though coupled with . . . . a statement of the transaction which gives rise to the instrument."

In applying these tests to the bonds in question, we will first consider the Butte, Anaconda & Pacific Railway bond.

This bond is negotiable unless the promise to pay is modified and rendered uncertain by the following provision: "This bond is entitled to the benefits and subject to the provisions of an indenture of mortgage dated February 1, 1914, made by the company to Guaranty Trust Company of New York as trustee, to which mortgage reference is hereby made for a description of the property and franchises mortgaged, the nature and extent of the security, the rights of the holders of the said bonds under the same, and the terms and conditions upon which said bonds are issued, received and held."

If the words "subject to the provisions of an indenture of mortgage" and the words "received and held" were eliminated from the above reference, the bond would be negotiable under the holding in *Paepcke* v. *Paine*. If the words "received and held" were eliminated, it would be negotiable under the holding in *Enoch* v. *Brandon*, 249 N.Y. 263, 164 N.E. 45, 47. In the latter case, the court held that the words "subject to the provisions of an indenture of mortgage" did not impair the negotiability of the bonds. It was said that a purchaser scanning the bonds "would interpret the statement that the bonds were secured by, and entitled to the benefits and subject to the provisions of, the mortgage, as meaning that a foreclosure or other relief might be had thereunder only subject to its provisions. He would see that reference to it is also made to determine the terms and conditions under which the bonds are issued and secured. Again, it would mean to him, as it means to us, that only by turning to the mortgage might he discover the precise nature of the lien he is to obtain. He would see that the bonds were to be issued, not only upon the general credit of the corporation, but upon the faith of some collateral mortgage. To it he must go, if further knowledge as to this security is desired."

In regard to this bond, its negotiability depends on the effect of the words "received and held." A reference in the bond to a mortgage to determine upon what conditions it was issued does not impair its negotiability. *Enoch* v. *Brandon*, supra. The words "received and held" add nothing to "issued" because the terms and conditions on which the bond is issued show how it was received and held. There is nothing in the words themselves indicating that there may be some condition in the mortgage qualifying the unconditional promise of the bond. They refer to the security.

It is our conclusion that the Butte, Anaconda & Pacific Railway Company bond is negotiable under authority of *Enoch* v. *Brandon*, supra.

The Ogden Gas Company bond contains the following recital: "This bond and the coupons thereto attached are expressly made subject to and shall be bound by all of the provisions in the said mortgage or deed of trust contained, the same as though all of said provisions were herein expressly set forth and the holder hereof expressly acknowledge notice of all such provisions."

The negotiability of this bond cannot be determined by its face. It incorporates by reference all of the provisions of the mortgage. Under all decisions of the court, it is not negotiable.

Trade Acceptances, etc.

Trade acceptances, bank acceptances, and drafts are bills of exchange and if in proper form they are negotiable instruments. The trade acceptance is a bill drawn on the buyer of goods by the seller of goods for the purchase price of the goods, and such fact is usually stated on the face of the instrument. A trade acceptance may be rediscounted at a Federal Reserve bank; consequently, the seller can get a better discount rate on it than he can on his own single-name paper.

A bank acceptance is a bill drawn on and accepted by a bank. Thus the bank is primarily liable on the paper and this makes the paper readily salable on the market. Bank acceptances can be rediscounted at a Federal Reserve bank.

Traveler's checks are orders to pay in which the name of the payee is left blank and the acceptor accepts the order before it is signed by the drawer. Traveler's checks are sold to the public at face value plus a commission. They are issued in convenient denominations ranging from $10 to $200. At the time the check is issued to the purchaser he signs his name on each check. When he cashes a check he writes in the name of the payee and signs the check in the presence of the payee. The payee can compare this signature with the signature already on the check and be assured that the countersignature is not a forgery. Such checks carry the credit of the issuer of the check. As a general rule traveler's checks are negotiable in form; however, some are so drawn that their negotiability is questionable.

The letter of credit is not a negotiable instrument, but its entire character depends on the law of negotiable instruments since it is concerned with the drawing and honoring of bills of exchange.

There are several types of letters of credit in common use, but these types are not uniform in their terms. Although the letter of credit has been in use in the commercial world since the sixteenth century, its form is not crystallized to the extent of the form of the bill of exchange.

A simple form of letter of credit is the traveler's letter of credit. One wishing to travel abroad who does not desire to carry sufficient cash to defray the expenses of his trip may purchase a traveler's letter of credit. He will deposit with his bank a sum of money which he deems sufficient for his needs plus the charges for the letter of credit. The bank will issue a letter of credit addressed to its correspondents abroad authorizing them to pay such drafts as are drawn in compliance with the letter of credit not exceeding the amount for which the letter of credit is drawn. The bank honoring the letter of credit by paying the draft will indorse the amount of the draft on the letter of credit, and the bank paying the draft which exhausts the letter of credit will forward it together with the draft to the issuing bank. The position of the issuing bank is substantially that of a person who has made an unconditional promise in writing to accept a bill before it is drawn.[1]

[1] Uniform Negotiable Instruments Law, sec. 135, appendix, p. 918.

A commercial letter of credit is a contract whereby the issuing bank opens a credit in favor of a seller who usually is a merchant or manufacturer in a foreign country. Commercial letters of credit may be (1) special or general and (2) revocable or irrevocable. A special letter of credit is addressed to a named person; a general letter of credit is addressed to whom it may concern. A revocable letter of credit may be revoked at any time before the honoring of drafts drawn under it. An irrevocable letter of credit cannot be revoked. Commercial letters of credit set out in detail the terms on which the issuing bank will accept drafts drawn under the letter of credit, and, if all these terms are not complied with, the issuer of the letter of credit is not legally bound to accept or pay the draft.

The relation between the buyer and the bank issuing a letter of credit is contractual. It is, in many respects, similar to the relation between the drawer of a draft and the drawee, or the drawer of a check and the drawee bank. The buyer establishes credit with the issuing bank, and the issuing bank agrees to accept or pay drafts drawn by sellers who have sold goods to the buyer. If the issuing bank refuses to accept or pay such drafts, it will have breached its contract with the buyer and must answer in damages.

By the terms of commercial letters of credit, the issuing bank agrees to accept or pay drafts properly drawn under the terms of the letter of credit. If the draft is properly drawn and accompanied by the proper shipping documents and the bank accepts or pays the drafts, the buyer must reimburse the bank, even though the shipping documents were forged or the goods shipped are of inferior quality. The liability of the issuing bank to accept or pay drafts drawn under the authority of the letter of credit depends on the terms of the letter of credit and not on the sales contract.

The duty of the issuing bank is to examine the draft and accompanying documents and, if they are in proper form and comply with the terms of the letter of credit, to accept or pay the draft. The issuing bank cannot refuse to accept or pay the draft on the ground that the goods shipped are of inferior quality unless the letter of credit provides that goods shipped must be of a designated quality.

Laudisi v. American Exchange National Bank
239 N.Y. 234, 146 N.E. 347 (1924)

This was an action by Lawrence Laudisi (plaintiff) against the American Exchange National Bank (defendant). Judgment for plaintiff and defendant appealed. Judgment was affirmed by the Appellate

Division and defendant appealed to the Court of Appeals. Judgment reversed with directions.

Plaintiff made a contract with Grande-Di Paola, Incorporated, which was doing business in New York City, for a quantity of Alicante Bouchez grapes which were shipped from California to plaintiff at Long Island City. Plaintiff made a contract with the defendant for the issuing to Grande-Di Paola, Incorporated, of a letter of credit under which its draft for the purchase price of the grapes was to be paid by defendant on presentation when accompanied by certain documents. The documents required under the terms of the letter of credit were "Invoice and negotiable railroad bill of lading showing destination to Eighth street yard Long Island City, to accompany drafts."

When the vendor presented its draft for the purchase price of the grapes, it presented therewith a negotiable railroad bill of lading duly issued at the point of shipment in California describing the article shipped, not as Alicante Bouchez grapes but as "grapes." The invoice was made out by the vendor in New York instead of by the shipper at the shipping point. The invoice fully described the grapes as complying with the contract between plaintiff and his vendor.

Plaintiff claims that the grapes shipped were of an inferior quality. He contends that the defendant should have refused to pay the draft because the description in the bill of lading was not complete and because the invoice was not made out by the shipper at point of shipment but by the vendor in New York.

Hiscock, C. J. The relation which arises between a customer and a bank in respect of a letter of credit issued by the latter for the account of the former is a familiar one and in its general aspects well understood. As a convenient method of paying for goods which he may purchase, the customer authorizes the bank to issue a letter of credit providing for the payment of drafts drawn by the vendor on such conditions as he may elect. He may authorize the bank to pay drafts without any accompanying document; he may authorize payment on a bill of lading and invoice, as in this case; he may prescribe much more stringent limitations upon the power of the bank. But in any case the bank has the power and is subject to the limitations which are given and imposed by this authority. If it keeps within the powers conferred it is protected in the payment of the draft. If it transgresses those limitations it pays at its peril. A customer having the right to prescribe and phrase limitations as he desires, it is our duty to give to language its ordinary and sensible meaning which will neither destroy the protection which the customer has exacted, nor, on the other hand, impose upon the bank some obligation not fairly warranted by the language which has been adopted by the parties.

Following these principles we find nothing in the description of the documents which were to accompany the drafts when presented for payment which, in our judgment, places upon the bill of lading the requirement of so describing all of the characteristics of the article shipped that it alone will show that such article is the one described in the letter of credit. The paramount purpose of a bill of lading is to show the shipment of goods which, so far as appears, conform to necessary requirements as stated in the letter of credit. If it affirmatively shows the shipment of goods which do not comply with the requirements of a letter of credit, a bank would not be justified in acting upon it. If it describes the goods shipped by a nomenclature different than that employed in the letter of credit, a bank would be justified in refusing to make payments on the strength of it and thereby incurring the possible burden of establishing in litigation that the different terms meant the same thing. Such, in the case of a guaranty, was our decision in *Bank of Italy* v. *Merchants' National Bank*, 236 N.Y. 106, 140 N.E. 211. If a customer in his contract with the bank and by the letter of credit requires that the bill of lading shall by itself and on its face show that certain described goods have been shipped, a bank will not be protected which pays on the faith of a bill which does not comply with this requirement.

But when we pass these particular cases and others which perhaps might be cited we think that a bank permitted to pay drafts on "invoice and negotiable bill of lading showing destination" to a certain point is justified in acting on a bill of lading which, so far as its description goes, shows the shipment of required goods, and is then supplemented by a proper invoice which completes the description and shows that the goods are the ones mentioned in the letter of credit. Such seems to us to be the natural and compelling interpretation of the clause which was used in this case. Even if we could be justified in straining the natural meaning of words in such a letter of credit so as to meet some call of policy or to secure some element of greater and proper safety to the one on whose account the draft is being paid, we do not see how we could find those conditions existent here. A bill of lading in this case, even if it specified the shipment of the particular kind of grapes ordered by the plaintiff would be no guaranty of the fact of such shipment. Of course nobody would expect a railroad company to open and examine the contents of 1,240 boxes of grapes and see that they all complied with the description in the letter of credit. In such a case it inevitably would take from the shipper the description of the goods which were being transported as indicated by the marks on the packages or by other statements and would then protect itself from inaccuracy or mistake by the clause ordinarily found in bills of lading and included in this particular one, "contents and condition of contents of packages unknown," and which, we have held, does protect a railroad company from inaccuracy in its description of goods being transported.

Then, passing to the contention made by defendant that the indeterminate description employed by the bill of lading in this particular case was so supplemented by the description of the invoice that the defendant was authorized to find a conformity of the shipment with the letter of credit, the plaintiff urges that the invoice was made in

New York instead of California, that its correctness was not authenticated or certified by any outside party, and that it was, therefore, merely a self-serving declaration of the vendor which furnished no authority for payment by the defendant. Again we find nothing which justifies these criticisms of the plaintiff or prevents the invoice from being regarded as a proper and sufficient supplement to the bill of lading. We certainly should not feel authorized in the absence of sufficient provision to that effect, or of facts not appearing on this motion, to hold that an invoice may not be made out by the vendor at the place where he is doing business rather than at the point from which he procures the goods to be shipped. Nobody can foresee the results to which any such requirement as that would lead. Neither is the invoice to be dismissed for the purpose claimed by defendant because it was made out by the vendor and was, as stated, a self-serving statement. Invoices ordinarily are made out by the vendor and contain its version of the transaction under review. A vendee apprehensive of the results which may flow from such action can very easily guard against them by requiring an invoice certified by some designated person or authority. This plaintiff might have made various provisions in his contract with the defendant to the end of securing a true, fair, and accurate invoice which should accompany the bill of lading and which would protect him from the misfortune which he now says has befallen him of having the purchase price paid for goods which were much inferior to those which he had ordered. The trouble is that he did not do it, and the courts have no right to interpolate in his contract provisions, guaranties, and safeguards which he himself did not deem it necessary to put there.

There remains one feature to be briefly considered. Before the defendant paid the draft it was notified by the plaintiff that the grapes did not comply with the requirements of the contract but were much inferior thereto, and it was notified or requested not to pay the draft. We do not think that it is very earnestly urged by the plaintiff that this fact changed the relations and rights of the parties. It did not. The contract between the customer and the bank, under which the latter issues an irrevocable letter of credit, is entirely distinct and apart from the contract between such customer and, as in this case, his vendor under which goods are to be shipped. The question between the customer and the vendor is the one whether the goods comply with the contract, and if they do not the former has his appropriate right of action. The question between the customer and the bank which issues the letter of credit is whether the documents presented with the draft fulfill the specific requirements, and if they do, speaking of such facts as exist in this case, the bank has the right to pay the draft no matter what may be the defects in the goods which have been shipped. The bank is not obliged to assume the burdens of a controversy between the vendor and vendee and incur the responsibility of establishing as an excuse for not paying a draft that the vendee's version is the correct one.

Negotiable Bills of Lading, etc.

Bills of lading and warehouse receipts are the same in their basic aspects. Both are receipts for goods and agreements to deliver goods—they are contracts of bailment. In our discussion of negotiable bills of lading and negotiable warehouse receipts we shall discuss the bill of lading and indicate in what respects the warehouse receipt differs from the bill of lading.

A bill of lading may be either a straight bill or an order bill. The straight bill provides that the goods will be delivered to a named person. The order bill provides that the goods will be delivered to a named person or his order. If the carrier has issued an order bill, he is under obligation to demand surrender of the bill when he delivers the goods. If he does not take the order bill up when he delivers the goods and the order bill subsequently comes into the hands of a bona fide purchaser for value, the carrier will be liable to him for the value of the goods.

The order bill is (1) a receipt for the goods shipped, (2) evidence of the contract of carriage, and (3) an order for the delivery of the goods to the designated person or his order.

An order bill is negotiated in the same manner as a negotiable instrument. It may be indorsed to a named person in which event it must be again indorsed before it can be further negotiated, or it may be indorsed in blank in which event it can be thereafter negotiated by delivery. One indorsing an order bill of lading warrants that it is genuine, that he has a right to transfer it, and that he has no knowledge of any facts which would impair its validity. These warranties go to the order bill of lading. In addition he also warrants that he has a right to transfer the title to the goods represented by the order bill of lading, but he assumes no secondary liability comparable to the unqualified indorser's liability for non-payment of a negotiable instrument. If the carrier defaults, the holder of an indorsed order bill of lading cannot hold the indorser.

One taking an order bill cannot acquire a better title to the goods represented than the consignor had. One may acquire good title to the bill of lading yet acquire no property interest in goods, or the goods delivered may be different than represented by the party negotiating the order bill of lading. The carrier in issuing the order bill of lading does not warrant the goods described in the bill of lading. The goods may be described in the bill of lading as boxes or barrels, contents unknown, or boxes labeled clothing, etc.

If the order bill of lading is forged, the person taking it acquires no rights against the carrier; however, if the agent of the carrier issues an order bill of lading without receiving goods, the carrier is liable to a bona fide purchaser for value. A forged indorsement on an order bill of lading, if the indorsement is necessary to the negotiation of the bill, transfers no rights to the bill. An altered order bill of lading is void to the extent of the alteration. The bona fide holder for value can enforce the altered bill as originally drawn and can hold his indorser for the injury suffered as a result of the alteration. One taking an order bill of lading as a bona fide purchaser for value takes it free from such defenses as fraud, duress, and breach of trust. In this respect the bona fide purchaser's rights are equivalent to the rights of a holder in due course of a negotiable instrument.

Order bills of lading have no due date, but one taking a bill of lading an unreasonable length of time after the date of issue is put on notice that it must be "spent" because carriers do not hold goods for long periods of time.

An order warehouse receipt is a receipt for the goods, a contract of storage, and an order for the delivery of goods to a designated person or his order. In many respects it is simpler than a bill of lading because it does not contain the many special stipulations which are customarily included in a contract of carriage. A warehouse receipt does not become "spent" or stale because the purpose of a warehouse receipt is to facilitate storage and frequently goods are stored for long periods of time. One taking an order warehouse receipt after a considerable length of time should make inquiry of the warehouseman issuing the order warehouse receipt as to his possession of the goods.

Southern Pacific Co. v. Bank of America
23 F. (2d) 939 (1928)

This was an action by the Southern Pacific Company (plaintiff) against the Bank of America (defendant). Judgment for defendant.

Ono & Co. shipped crab meat to Chicago on an order bill of lading. The order bill of lading was issued by the plaintiff to the order of Ono & Co. and was marked "notify the vendee." Ono & Co. indorsed the bill of lading in blank, attached a draft for the purchase price of the crab meat and sold the bill of lading and draft to the Pacific National Bank who forwarded them to a bank in Chicago for collection. Upon arrival of the bill of lading and draft, the Chicago bank notified the vendee who said the goods had not arrived, and that it would not honor the draft until the arrival of the goods.

The goods arrived immediately thereafter and by fraudulent representations the vendee obtained possession of the goods without surrendering the bill of lading. The vendee at once deposited the goods in a public warehouse and took a negotiable warehouse receipt therefor. The defendant, Bank of America, loaned the vendee $34,000 and took the negotiable warehouse receipt as security. At the time the defendant took the warehouse receipt it had no notice of the defects in the vendee's title and took as a bona fide purchaser for value.

The plaintiff, Southern Pacific Company, recognized its liability for the value of the crab meat, having delivered it without requiring the delivery of the bill of lading, and paid Pacific National Bank the value of the crab meat and took an assignment of their rights. Plaintiff claims that the original vendor's title has never passed to defendant, either by its consent or by estoppel, and that as successor to that title plaintiff is the present owner as against the fraudulent vendee and the defendant, even though the latter made its advancement in good faith upon the warehouse receipts. Defendant asserts that plaintiff, having by its agent's wrongful delivery made possible the negotiation of the warehouse receipts, is estopped to assert its title as against defendant, for the reason that, where one of two innocent persons must lose, he who made the loss possible should suffer.

Lindley, D. J. The first question presented is as to the position of defendant. Section 58 of the Uniform Warehouse Receipts Act, in force in Illinois, provides that "to purchase includes to take as mortgagee or as pledgee"; "value is any consideration sufficient to support a simple contract"; and "a thing is done 'in good faith,' within the meaning of this act, when it is in fact done honestly, whether it be done negligently or not." Defendant had no knowledge whatever of the outstanding order bill of lading, or of any other facts or circumstances affecting the invalidity of the title of the original vendee. It relied upon the apparent title of the warehouse receipts, and upon that reliance advanced the sum of $34,000. The fact that the borrower was then heavily indebted to the bank is not important, in view of the fact that the loan was made upon the goods and not the credit of the borrower.

In *Commercial National Bank* v. *Canal-Louisiana Bank*, 239 U.S. 520, 36 S. Ct. 194, 60 L. Ed. 417, the court said: "The negotiation of the receipt to a purchaser for value without notice is not impaired by the fact that it is a breach of duty or that the owner of the receipt was induced 'by fraud, mistake or duress' to intrust the receipt to the person who negotiated it. And, under section 41, one to whom the negotiable receipt has been duly negotiated acquires such title to the goods as the person negotiating the receipt to him, or the depositor or person to whose order the goods were deliverable by the terms of the receipt, either had or 'had ability to convey to a purchaser in good faith for value.' The clear import of these provisions is that if the owner of the goods permits another to have the possession or custody of negotiable warehouse receipts running to the order of the latter, or to bearer, it is a representation of title upon which bona fide purchasers for value are entitled to rely, despite breaches of trust or violations of agreement on the part of the apparent owner." Defendant, therefore, should be treated as a bona fide purchaser for value of the warehouse receipts, without notice of infirmity.

Plaintiff succeeded to the title of the Pacific National Bank under the bill of lading. It did so, however, after its agent had wrongfully delivered the goods to the vendee, and the latter had assigned the warehouse receipts to defendant for value, and with full knowledge of those facts. It now contends that its title, thus acquired, is superior to that of defendant. No owner of merchandise may be deprived of the title thereto, except by his consent, or by the existence of such facts as will create an estoppel against him to assert his title. A thief can convey no title to a bona fide purchaser, nor can a trespasser, or other tortious taker of merchandise, convey a good title thereto. However, one who secures title to property by fraudulent representations may convey good title to a bona fide purchaser. The vendor is there estopped to assert its rights.

Here, by its fraudulent representations, the vendee persuaded the delivering carrier to surrender the goods. That delivery was a conscious, voluntary delivery, induced by fraud, true it is, but none the less a delivery consciously, voluntarily made, a delivery within the apparent scope of the plaintiff's agent's authority. The goods were not stolen; they were not received by the vendee as a result of a trespass, but consent to delivery was fraudulently procured. It follows that the purchaser from the vendee stands in the position of the purchaser from any fraudulent vendee, whose rights by virtue of the doctrine of estoppel are well recognized as being superior to those of the vendor or parties in privity with him. In this situation it would be contrary to the established law to allow the plaintiff, who has purchased its title with full knowledge of the facts, to prevail against the bona fide purchaser, for its act, through its agent, made possible the procurement of the negotiable warehouse receipts and the sale thereof by the vendee.

Stock Certificate

A stock certificate is evidence of the ownership of corporate stock. The owner of corporate stock does not directly own any of the property of the corporation. A share of stock represents the owner's right to share in the profits of the corporation and to share in the assets of the corporation on liquidation. To have a complete transfer of a stock certificate the owner must transfer the stock certificate to the purchaser. The purchaser must then send the stock certificate to the designated corporate official or agent and have it transferred to him. A new stock certificate is then issued in his name. We are interested primarily in the first step.

If Archer owns a certificate for ten shares of stock in the American Corporation and wishes to transfer them to Burch, he can indorse the stock certificate and deliver it to Burch. The indorsement may be in blank or it may be indorsed specifically to Burch. Another method which is permitted is to deliver the certificate without indorsement but with an assignment of the transferor's rights executed on a separate document and attached to the certificate. This latter method is not recommended because, if the transferor should obtain possession of the certificate, he could transfer a good title to a bona fide purchaser for value by indorsing and delivering the certificate to him.

One who takes as a bona fide purchaser for value a stock certificate which has been indorsed by the person appearing by the certificate to be the owner of the shares represented thereby takes free from outstanding equities. His position is analogous to that of a holder in due course of a negotiable instrument.

One indorsing and transferring a stock certificate warrants that the certificate is genuine, that he has a legal right to transfer it, and that he has no knowledge of any fact which would impair the validity of the certificate. Like the indorser of a negotiable bill of lading and a negotiable warehouse receipt, the indorser of a stock certificate is not secondarily liable.

If the stock certificate is forged, it is of no validity and, if the indorsement is forged or made without authority, it does not pass title to the certificate. If a forged certificate or a certificate bearing a forged indorsement is presented to the issuing corporation for transfer and the corporation, not detecting the forgery, issues a new certificate, the corporation will be liable to one who purchases the new certificate as a bona fide purchaser for value.

A certificate indorsed in blank is known as a "street certificate" and can be transferred by delivery. It is analogous to a bearer negotiable instrument.

Peckinpaugh v. H. W. Noble & Co.
238 Mich. 464, 213 N.W. 859, 52 A.L.R. 941 (1927)

This was an action of replevin by Laura W. Peckinpaugh (plaintiff) against H. W. Noble & Co. (defendant). Judgment for plaintiff and defendant appealed. Judgment reversed and new trial granted.

E. A. Kemp, husband of plaintiff's daughter Hazel, borrowed $1,100 from defendant and pledged as security five stock certificates covering 3,000 shares preferred stock of Gladys Belle Oil Company. Laura W. Peckinpaugh, the plaintiff, appeared by the certificates to be the owner and each certificate was indorsed in blank by plaintiff.

Wiest, J. Disposition of the case involves the provisions of the

Uniform Stock Transfer Act. Sections of that chapter will be cited in the course of the opinion. Plaintiff claims she never sold the certificates, did not borrow money from defendant, and the pledge was without her consent or knowledge. The certificates were not indorsed by reason of any fraud or duress or under such mistake as to make the indorsement inequitable.

Defendant stands in the position of a purchaser for value in good faith, without notice of any fact making the transfer wrongful, and therefore, even if the certificates were delivered to defendant without authority from the owner, the protection afforded defendant by the mentioned section of the act bars this action by plaintiff. It may appear like a hard rule, looking at it from the standpoint of the owner of the certificates, but, from the standpoint of the good-faith purchaser, it has appealing equities, long recognized by the courts as a rule of the common law. These certificates, when indorsed in blank by plaintiff, possessed sufficient negotiability to pass title upon delivery to a purchaser.

According her testimony every intendment, it shows no more than that the certificates were delivered to defendant without authority from the owner. But this was not enough, for the statute expressly provides the certificates may not be reclaimed if, with indorsement, they were transferred without authority of the owner to a purchaser for value in good faith, without notice of any facts making the transfer wrongful. The evidence was undisputed that defendant took the certificates in pledge for a loan actually made, and later extended time of payment, and acted in good faith without notice of any fact making the transfer wrongful.

If larceny, by trick or felonious appropriation, was claimed, the burden rested on plaintiff to make some proof thereof. A purchaser in good faith of certificates of stock, indorsed in blank, is protected although they may have been stolen by the prior holder. This is the rule applied by this court with reference to negotiable bonds and we see no reason, giving due consideration to the provisions of the Stock Transfer Act, to make any different holding with reference to certificates of stock indorsed in blank. The purchaser of certificates of stock, made negotiable by signature in blank of the person to whom issued, owes no duty to such person to inquire into the title of the party in possession. The question of legal right never turns upon diligence or want of diligence in making inquiry into the right of the possessor, but is resolved by good or bad faith. The statute declares this rule: "A thing is done 'in good faith' within the meaning of this act, when it is in fact done honestly, whether it be done negligently or not" (Sec. 22).

Bad faith may, of course, be predicated upon actual notice demanding inquiry. But good faith, in a transaction arising in the usual course of business, demands no *sua sponte* questioning of the title of the possessor of certificates of stock indorsed in blank. Such indorsed certificates do not travel with the earmark *caveat emptor*, but possess *veritas nuda*. The rule, let the purchaser beware, and the doctrine of suspicion impugning rights of the possessor of indorsed certificates until the contrary is made to appear, would not only unduly retard negotiability demanded in the commercial world, but, in all except extremely rare instances, be considered a gratuitous insult.

The Uniform Stock Transfer Act accepts common honesty as a concept reasonably safe as a basis of everyday action in the commercial world, and leaves the few instances of "fraud, duress, mistake, revocation, death, incapacity and lack of consideration or authority" to be worked out under rules of law and equity, including the law merchant, principal and agent, executors, administrators and trustees, unless the certificate has been transferred to a purchaser for value in good faith without notice of any fact making the transaction wrongful. Upon indorsement in blank by the owner a stock certificate becomes a "courier without luggage, whose countenance is its passport."

We are not unmindful of the holdings at common law that stock certificates are not negotiable instruments and also that they are not made such by the Negotiable Instruments Law, for the certificates are but evidence of the shares and their ownership. While this is well settled, the certificates, when indorsed in blank, possess a quasi negotiable character, so closely allied to true negotiable instruments that the law sanctions their passing from hand to hand free from antecedent equities and the Uniform Stock Transfer Act protects them in the hands of a good-faith purchaser because of such quasi negotiable character and in recognition of the long-established and quite universal practice in transferring title thereto.

QUESTIONS AND PROBLEMS

1. Between 11:00 and 12:00 o'clock, November 6, Turner gave Kimble a check drawn upon a bank located in the city. It was presented for payment the next morning, and the bank upon which it was drawn was closed. Kimble sues Turner on the check. Can he recover?
2. Cass had $379.57 on deposit in the City Bank. Two checks drawn by him, one for $300 and one for $100, were simultaneously presented for payment. The bank refused to pay either of them. Is the bank liable to Cass for not paying one of the checks?
3. Cook had a checking account with the American Bank. He delivered his check for $2,000 to Light on Saturday, September 7, 1929. Before banking hours Monday morning, Cook telephoned the bank and ordered the payment of the check stopped. Later in the day the bank certified the check and subsequently paid it. When sued the bank set up as a defense (1) that the stop payment order was not given during banking hours, and (2) that the stop payment order was not in writing. Is either of these defenses valid?
4. A bank certified a check at the request of the drawer. At his request, has the bank the right to cancel the certification?
5. Archer had a personal checking account with the First Bank. The First Bank balanced the accounts of its depositors and returned their cancelled checks only when the depositors left their bank books and requested that they be balanced. Archer did not leave his bank book to be balanced between June 1, 1944, and September 6, 1945. During this period an associate of Archer's forged fifteen

checks aggregating $5,468. The bank contends that, since Archer had not left his bank book to be balanced at reasonable periods, it is not liable for the amount of the forged checks. Is the bank's contention correct?

6. Corporate bearer bonds provide that the obligation assumed by the corporation is subject to the terms of a certain mortgage given by the corporation to a trustee. The trust mortgage provides that, on the corporation's default in the payment of interest on the bonds, the holders of the bonds may declare them due. Are the bonds negotiable?
7. Frey & Sons entered into a written contract in New York with Sherburne Co. under which Frey & Sons bought 350 tons of Java sugar. Payment for the sugar was to be made in cash in New York, and Frey & Sons were to furnish irrevocable letters of credit. The contract gave Frey & Sons the right to cancel a portion of the contract under certain circumstances. An irrevocable letter of credit was obtained from City National Bank authorizing Sherburne Co. to draw on that bank. The letter of credit is irrevocable in form and requires shipping documents to be attached to the draft but is silent as to the provision in the sales contract, permitting Frey & Sons to cancel the contract. After 100 tons of sugar have been shipped, Frey & Sons cancel the contract. Sherburne Co. makes further shipments, draws a draft against City National Bank, and discounts this draft, with proper shipping documents attached, at its bank. Can City National Bank be compelled to pay the draft?
8. Archer owned and operated a flour mill. Archer placed a quantity of flour in his warehouse and issued to himself a warehouse receipt for the flour which was negotiable in form. Archer indorsed and delivered the warehouse receipt to the First Bank as security for a loan. Archer has been adjudged bankrupt. What are the First Bank's rights in the flour represented by the warehouse receipt?
9. The Southwest Grain Co. shipped a quantity of hay to Tchula Co., order bill of lading, draft attached. The First National Bank purchased the draft and bill of lading from the Southwest Grain Co., and the Tchula Co. paid the draft when the bank presented it. On weighing the hay it was found to be short weight. Tchula Co. sued Southwest Grain Co. and garnisheed the bank on the theory that the bank held the proceeds of the draft as trustee of the Southwest Grain Co. Is this theory of the transaction correct?
10. Archer, who owned certain shares of stock in the American Corporation, indorsed the stock certificates in blank and pledged them to Burch, who later converted them by selling them to Clark, a bona fide purchaser for value. Archer paid the debt to Burch and demanded the stock certificates. On learning that Clark had purchased the certificates from Burch, Archer sued Clark to recover the certificates. Who is entitled to the certificates, Archer or Clark?

PART VI

AGENCY

CHAPTER XXVI

CREATION OF THE RELATION

Introduction

The law of agency, as a separate division of the law, is of recent origin. When industry was carried on in the home, the head of the house transacted all the business; his helpers became members of the household, and the relationship between the head of the house and his helpers was that of master and servant. With the growth of industry, it outgrew the home and the factory was established. The old master and servant relationship gave way to that of employer and employee. The owner of the business found that he could not transact all of his business personally, so he began to delegate some of it to trusted employees or servants. With the centralization of industry, individual ownership gave way, to a marked degree, to partnerships and joint stock companies and later to corporations. These various types of business organizations are dependent on the principal and agency relationship for their existence. Agency grew with industry and is in many respects the outgrowth of the master and servant relationship.

Agency, in its broadest sense, includes all situations in which one person is employed to act for another. To aid in the analysis of legal problems it is customary to distinguish between the relation of master and servant, employer and employee, principal and agent, and employer and independent contractor.

From a legal standpoint there is, as a general rule, no distinction between the relation of master and servant and employer and employee. The term servant is commonly used in legal literature and court decisions to include an employee. Historically the term "servant" referred to one who lived in the master's household and performed manual duties for the master, while the term "employee" referred to one who lived apart from his employer's household and went to the employer's premises for the purpose of performing his duties. The housemaid living with the family is the nearest to the master and servant relation which exists today and a factory worker is a typical example of the employer and employee relation.

The relation of principal and agent arises when one person engages another to negotiate business transactions for him. The agent is authorized by the principal to contract with third persons in the principal's name. An independent contractor contracts to produce a result. In one respect he works for another, but his legal position differs from that of the employee or agent in that the employee or agent is obligated to follow the instructions of his employer or principal in the performance of his work, while the independent contractor is free to follow his own course in performing the work. His only obligation is to produce the agreed result.

Frequently, a person will act in a dual capacity. He will act as an employee in the performance of some of his duties and as an agent in the performance of others. A clerk in a general store in sweeping, dusting, arranging stock, etc., acts as an employee, but in selling goods, ordering goods, etc., he acts as an agent. The dividing line between an employee and an agent is not clearly drawn. Likewise, it is difficult to distinguish between an employee or agent and an independent contractor. The degree of control which the employer has reserved over the methods followed in the performance of the work will determine whether the relationship is that of employer and employee or employer and independent contractor.

Kruse v. Weigand and another
204 Wis. 195, 235 N.W. 426 (1931)

This was an action brought by Anna Kruse (plaintiff) against Wilcox and Weigand (defendants). Judgment for plaintiff against defendant Wilcox and the complaint against Weigand was dismissed. From so much of the judgment as dismissed the complaint and action as to defendant Weigand, plaintiff appealed. Judgment affirmed.

Wilcox, while demonstrating a Nash car, collided with a car in which Anna Kruse, the plaintiff, was riding, and injured her. Suit was brought against Wilcox and Weigand, owner of the Nash agency. It was claimed that Wilcox was the employee or agent of Weigand and that Weigand was liable as employer or principal. The lower court held that Wilcox was an independent contractor. Further facts are stated in the opinion.

Nelson, J. The errors assigned raise but a single question: Was Wilcox, at the time of the action, an independent contractor or was he an employee of Weigand, acting as such within the scope of his employment? Upon the answer to this question depends our decision. This court has, in several well considered cases, carefully pointed out the difference between a relationship of master and servant and one of employer and independent contractor. Both a servant and an independent contractor, engaged in performing services for another, may, in a sense, be considered agents of the master, or of the employer of the independent contractor. As to the act of a servant acting for his master and within the scope of his authority, the master is liable, while as to the acts of an independent contractor the employer is not liable. This is elementary and needs no citation of authority. Whether a person is a servant of another or an independent contractor depends, in large measure and almost always, upon the degree or power of control which the employer has retained as to the manner in which the details of the work are to be carried out or performed. In *Madix* v. *Hochgreve B. Co.*, 154 Wis. 448, 451, 143 N.W. 189, it was said:

"The most significant indicium of an independent contractor, however, is his right to control the details of the work. . . . . If such right remains in the employer, whether exercised or not, the relation will be held, in the absence of other controlling circumstances, to be that of master and servant or principal and agent, and not of employer and independent contractor."

In *Badger F. Co.* v. *Industrial Comm.*, 200 Wis. 127, 227 N.W. 288, it was held (p. 129):

"Whether or not a person is an independent contractor or a servant depends upon the right of control by the principal over the person engaged to do the work. The mere fact that the principal exercises such control is not significant if he has no right of control. The test is to be determined by the contract, not by the course of conduct. However, when the terms of the contract are in doubt, the course of conduct of the parties in the execution of the contract may be considered as an aid in construing the contract, but when the contract is determined, the right of control by the principal over the person doing the work is generally considered the important test. (Citing many cases.) In reaching a conclusion, of course there are other things to be considered besides the question of control, to wit: the nature of the business or occupation; which party furnishes the instrumentalities and tools; the place of work; the time of employment; the method of payment; and the intent of the parties to the contract."

At the expense of brevity, which is greatly to be desired in judicial opinions, we have quoted from several opinions of this court dealing with independent contractors to the end that these well established principles may now be applied to the facts of this case. There is not the slightest dispute as to the contract arrangement with Weigand under which Wilcox worked. Defendant Weigand had been handling Nash cars for many years. He had an agency in Chippewa Falls, an office and garage in Eau Claire, and sub-dealers in other places. The automobile business was his own. Defendant Wilcox came to him in the fall of 1928 and asked for a job of trying to sell Nash cars. Weigand inquired what Wilcox was then doing and was told that he had a farm out in the country. Weigand told him that if he would buy a Nash car and use it as a demonstrator and try to sell cars he would give him seven per cent commission on the cash that was brought in on such sales as were accepted, and also allow him $20 a month for gas, oil, and maintenance of his car. Weigand told him that he could come and go as he pleased. He was not required to report at the office at any particular time. He received no salary. Wilcox purchased a car and started trying to sell cars. Weigand, from time to time, gave him the names of prospects whom Wilcox called on as he conveniently saw fit. Wilcox obtained the names of certain prospects through his own efforts. Wilcox was permitted to sell cars in Eau Claire and Chippewa Falls and in other cities and villages where there were no dealers. In making sales Weigand had no control over Wilcox as to where he went, or when he went, or what he did to promote or bring about a sale. Weigand did not command him where to go, or when to go, or attempt to control the amount of time to be spent by Wilcox in trying to sell cars. The details of selling cars, meeting with and soliciting prospects, were all under the control of Wilcox, who could and did pursue his work when and as he saw fit. Wilcox was under no obligation to go anywhere pursuant to directions from Weigand. Wilcox was wholly free under the arrangement to work when and where and as much or little as he pleased so far as the details of selling cars were concerned. When he sold a car he received the seven per cent commission. Whenever a second-hand car was to be taken in on a deal Weigand had the right to determine the amount of the credit to be given for such used car. Whenever credit or part credit was to be extended it had to be approved by Weigand. The foregoing statement of the contract arrangement and the execution thereof is nowise in dispute.

There is no doubt that the relationship which existed between Weigand and Wilcox was that of employer and independent contractor. Weigand clearly had no right to control Wilcox as to the details of selling cars. The fact that at different times Weigand gave Wilcox names of prospects whom he expected Wilcox would call on; that he passed upon credit customers; that he reserved the right to pass upon the amounts to be allowed on trade-in cars, has no significant bearing upon the clear-cut and well-defined arrangement existing between Weigand and Wilcox. Clearly Weigand did not furnish the instrumentality—the car—to be used by Wilcox in promoting or effecting sales. Wilcox did not work in any particular place. He was free to work where and when he pleased. The nature of the business of selling cars was such as is quite generally performed by persons working as independent contractors. The method of payment which existed is consistent with the theory that Wilcox was an independent contractor. He received no salary. Weigand knew the difference between an independent contractor and a servant or employee and generally had in his employ three independent contractor salesmen and two regular salaried salesmen.

Saums v. Parfet et al.
270 Mich. 165, 258 N.W. 235 (1935)

This was an action by Mary L. Saums, as guardian of the estate of Mildred L. Chambers, a minor (plaintiff), against Ray T. Parfet and Deal (defendants). Judgment for plaintiff and defendants appealed. Judgment against Deal affirmed and judgment against Parfet reversed.

Parfet was a dealer in automobiles. Deal was a prospective purchaser. Parfet sent an automobile to Deal's home so that Deal could try the automobile out. While Deal was driving the automobile he injured Mildred L. Chambers, age 11 years. The judge in the trial court instructed the jury that Deal in driving the automobile was acting as Parfet's agent and that, if they found Deal liable, they should also find liability on the part of Parfet. Defendant Parfet contends that this instruction is erroneous.

Nelson Sharpe, C. J. " 'Agency' in its broadest sense includes every relation in which one person acts for or represents another by his authority." 2 C. J., p. 419.

"Whether an agency has been created is to be determined by the relations of the parties as they in fact exist under their agreements or acts." 21 R. C. L., p. 819.

"The characteristic of the agent is that he is a business representative. His function is to bring about, modify, affect, accept performance of, or terminate contractual obligations between his principal and third persons. To the proper performance of his functions, therefore, it is absolutely essential that there shall be third persons in contemplation between whom and the principal legal obligations are to be thus created, modified or otherwise affected by the acts of the agent." 1 Mechem on Agency (2d Ed.), p. 21.

"The word servant, in our legal nomenclature, has a broad significance, and embraces all persons of whatever rank or position who are in the employ and subject to the direction or control of another in any department of labor or business." Wood, Mast. & Serv., §1.

The distinction between an agent and a servant is that the former represents his principal in business dealings with another person, and the latter is in the employ of his master and subject to his direction and control in the work intrusted to him to perform.

No agency was created by the request of Parfet that Deal should try out the car sent to him. In doing so, he performed no act or service in which third persons were interested. Neither can it be said that he was at that time in the employ of Parfet as his servant, as no duty was imposed on him to do so. In our opinion the facts did not justify a holding that Deal was acting as the agent or servant of Parfet when driving the car at the time of the collision.

Creation of the Relation

As between the principal and agent, an agency is created by the consent of the parties. If the principal, either expressly or impliedly, indicates that he is willing to be represented as principal by another person and that person, either expressly or impliedly, indicates his willingness to act as agent, the relation of principal and agent is created. In the majority of instances the relation will be created by a contract, but the fact that the agent is acting gratuitously and that no contract is entered into will in no way affect the validity of the contracts negotiated by the agent in the name of the principal. If the agency is not created by a binding contract, the relationship may be terminated by either party at will, but if a contract does exist and either party terminates the relationship in violation of the contract, he will be liable in damages for breach of the contract.

Although, as a general rule, no formality is necessary in the appointment of an agent, in some situations a formal appointment, such as a power of attorney, is required. If one authorizes an agent to sign a mortgage or deed to real estate, the authorization must be in writing and is usually required to be in a certain form. Such authorization is recorded together with the deed or mortgage for the purpose of making a complete record of the transaction.

The relation of husband and wife does not create an agency nor does that of parent and child. The wife may, if the husband refuses to furnish her the necessities of life, purchase such necessities and bind the husband for their reasonable value and likewise one who furnishes an infant the necessities of life, when the parent has failed to furnish them, may hold the parent for the reasonable value of necessities furnished. However, in neither case is liability based on the existence of an agency between the husband and wife or between the parent and child. It is the husband's duty to support his wife and family, and his liability for necessities furnished his family is based on a breach of this duty.

Georgeson v. Nielsen et al.
214 Wis. 191, 252 N.W. 576 (1934)

This was an action by Earl Georgeson and others (plaintiffs) against N. R. Nielsen and others (defendants). From a judgment dismissing Georgeson's suit Georgeson appealed. Judgment reversed with directions.

Georgeson had purchased some cattle and borrowed a trailer to haul them in. He did not have a "hitch" for the trailer so went to a blacksmith shop to have his car equipped with a "hitch." Dennis, a friend of Georgeson's, was at the blacksmith shop and offered to use his car which was already equipped with a "hitch." Dennis and Georgeson went after the cattle in Dennis' car and on the return trip had a collision. On suit Georgeson claimed he was a guest of Dennis and Dennis' negligence is not imputable to him.

Nelson, J. Georgeson contends that the court erred in denying his motion for judgment on the verdict it rendered. In support of this contention it is argued that the undisputed facts show that the relationship existing between Dennis and Georgeson was that of host and guest and it was therefore improper to impute the negligence of Dennis to Georgeson. While there is some basis for the argument if only the conversation between Georgeson and Dennis at the blacksmith shop, as testified to by them, is considered, the undisputed fact is that Dennis was engaged in performing Georgeson's job namely, transporting cattle for him. It was clearly Georgeson's enterprise which Dennis and Georgeson were furthering. What was done was done for the benefit of Georgeson. Although, according to the testimony, Dennis was not to receive any compensation, it is our opinion that, while he was engaged in transporting the cattle for Georgeson, he was a gratuitous agent of Georgeson and the relationship of agency, not that of host and guest, existed between them.

"Agency is the relationship which results from the manifestation of consent by one person to another that the other shall act on his behalf and subject to his control, and consent by the other so to act. . . . .

"(a) The relationship of agency is created as the result of conduct by the parties manifesting that one of them is willing for the other to act for him subject to his control, and that the other consents so to act. The principal must in some manner indicate that the agent is to act for him, and the agent must act or agree to act on his behalf and subject to his control.

"(b) It is not necessary that the parties intend to create the legal relationship or to subject themselves to the liabilities which the law imposes upon them as a result of it. On the other hand, there is not necessarily an agency relationship because the parties to a transaction say that there is, or contract that the relationship shall exist, or believe it does exist. Agency results only if there is an agreement for the creation of a fiduciary relationship with control by the fiduciary." Restatement, Agency, § 1, p. 8.

Since the agency was gratuitous, neither party was under any obligation to continue the relationship. Sec. 16, *Restatement of the Law of Agency*. But so long as Dennis continued in Georgeson's enterprise, the agency continued. As before stated, it was Georgeson's work or enterprise that was being performed. He directed Dennis where to go to get the cattle and directed him where to transport them. While Dennis could have terminated the relationship at any time and was not under the control of Georgeson as to just how he should operate his automobile, he was, in our opinion, the agent of Georgeson while engaged in transporting the cattle.

Capacity of Parties

As a general rule, every person who has capacity to contract may appoint an agent for any purpose. The principal may be either a natural or an artificial person, but must be recognized by the law as a legal person. A voluntary association cannot act as a principal because it has no legal existence; it cannot sue and be sued. An infant may appoint an agent, but such an appointment is voidable at the election of the infant. Some early English cases held that an infant's appointment of an agent or attorney was void, not merely voidable. These decisions have been followed in a few courts, but now the clear weight of authority is that an infant may appoint an agent but that the appointment and also the contracts negotiated by the agent are voidable at the election of the infant.

The same capacity is not required to act as an agent as is required to appoint an agent. It is clear that a person of legal age and of sane mind can act as an agent and that a corporation may act as an agent if it acts within its corporate powers.

However, to act as an agent one need not have legal capacity to contract. If a principal appoints one who does not have full legal capacity to contract as his agent, the principal will be bound by the acts of his agent in the same manner and to the same extent as he would be bound if the agent had full legal capacity to contract. The principal is the party to the contract, the agent is the instrumentality through which the negotiations are carried on. It is the capacity of the principal which is essential, not the capacity of the agent.

Cousin v. Taylor et al.
115 Or. 472, 239 Pac. 96 (1925)

This was an action by Edward M. Cousin (plaintiff) against Walter K. Taylor and others (defendants). Judgment for plaintiff against part of the defendants and judgment for the remainder of the defendants. The judgment was reversed and sent back for new trial as to some of the defendants; affirmed as to others.

The Public Service Commission of Oregon fixed telephone rates which were unsatisfactory to the telephone users of Benton County and surrounding counties. The telephone users held mass meetings and organized themselves into the Oregon Telephone Federation which was a voluntary, unincorporated association whose purpose was to obtain a rehearing before the commission and a reduction of rates. Officers were elected and Walter K. Taylor and E. W. Zumwalt were authorized to engage a rate expert to represent the members of the Oregon Telephone Federation at such rate hearings. Taylor and Zumwalt employed the plaintiff and promised to pay him $2,000 for his services. Plaintiff was not paid and brought suit against Walter K. Taylor and fifteen others. The trial court dismissed the suit as to all the defendants except Taylor and one S. S. Harrelson. In the charge to the jury the trial judge instructed the jury that if the defendants Taylor and Harrelson, in employing the plaintiff, were acting as agents of the Oregon Telephone Federation, they would not be personally liable. The plaintiff assigns as error the dismissal of the case against the other defendants and the giving of the above instruction.

Rand, J. From the recitals contained in the bill of exceptions and other parts of the record, it appears that the Oregon Telephone Federation was a mere voluntary, unincorporated association, which was not organized to conduct business for a pecuniary profit and possessed none of the elements of a partnership. Its members therefore were not liable as partners. The association was not a legal entity and had no legal existence distinct from its membership. So far as the record shows, no articles of association were adopted by the members of the association, and it had no constitution, by-laws, or contract between its members. A record was kept of the transactions had at the various mass meetings referred to, and this record shows that at one of said meetings the persons present, by a resolution or motion, which was passed without dissent, declared themselves to be members of the Oregon Telephone Federation, and elected Taylor and Zumwalt as agents of the federation, and authorized them to employ a rate expert to assist them in obtaining a rehearing upon the order of the commission and a reduction of the rates fixed by the order. Evidence was offered tending to show that pursuant to this authority Taylor employed plaintiff, and plaintiff performed the service contracted for.

Since this association was not a legal entity and there is no statute in this state authorizing such an organization, or defining the duties, powers, and liabilities of the members of such an association when voluntarily formed, the association could neither sue nor be sued, and as such it had no capacity to enter into a contract, or to appoint an agent for any purpose. Therefore a contract entered into in the name of the association, or in its behalf, by any of the officers or members of the association would not be binding upon the association or enforceable against it. But no such a limitation exists upon the powers and liabilities of the individual members who compose such an association. As individuals they are free to contract, and to appoint agents or committees to enter into contracts for them, and any such contract, when thus entered into by such agent or committee, if within the scope of the authority conferred, is binding upon them as principals. It is true that no person can be charged upon a contract alleged to have been made upon his responsibility, unless it can be shown that to the making of that contract upon his responsibility he has given his express or implied consent. While under this principle no member of the association would be directly responsible as principal upon a contract made by Taylor, unless it was first shown that to the making of the contract by Taylor such member gave his assent, expressly or impliedly, but when it was shown that any member of the association present at the meeting assented to the appointment of Taylor for the purpose of employing plaintiff, or assented to the making of the contract by Taylor, or ratified and approved the contract after it was made, then under this principle such person would be directly responsible as principal. There was evidence tending to show that some of the defendants in whose favor a judgment of nonsuit was entered were present at the meeting and assented to the appointment of Taylor and Zumwalt as a special committee to employ plaintiff. And there was evidence tending to show that they ratified and approved the contract as made by Taylor, and received the benefits resulting from plaintiff's performance of the contract made with Taylor. For this reason it was error for the court to give judgment of nonsuit against plaintiff as to such defendants.

Talbot v. Bowen
1 A. K. Marsh. (8 Ky.) 436 (1819)

This was an action by Bowen (plaintiff) brought in chancery against Talbot (defendant) asking a decree of specific performance of a contract to convey an interest in a lot. Decree for plaintiff and defendant appealed. Decree affirmed with directions.

Talbot admitted that a contract to sell the lot was entered into with one Featherston and that Bowen had acquired Featherston's rights, but set up as a defense that the contract was negotiated by his son, an infant, as his agent, and it was contended by Talbot that owing to the son's infancy specific performance ought not to have been decreed.

Judge Owsley delivered the opinion of the court: And that the son was authorized either verbally or in writing to make the sale, from the circumstances detailed in evidence, there is no room for a moment to doubt.

And if authorized, according to the settled doctrine of law, his being an infant can afford no objection against the liability of Talbot; for although the contracts of infants are not, in all cases, binding upon them, there is no doubt but, as they may act as agents, their contracts, made in that character, if otherwise unexceptionable, will be binding upon their principal.

Authority of Agent

The source of the agent's power to bind his principal to a contractual obligation is the consent of the principal. This requirement is analogous to the fundamental concept in contract law that contractual obligations are obligations voluntarily assumed by the parties. In other words one cannot become bound by a contract unless he has given his consent to be so bound. To prove consent it is not necessary to show that a party expressly consented to the relation. The consent of the principal or, as it is more commonly expressed, the authority of the agent may be established by showing (1) that he had express authority to act for his principal, (2) that he had implied authority to act for his principal, and (3) that he had apparent authority to act for his principal.

In the first instance it is clear that the agent's authority is derived through the consent of the principal. In the second instance it is generally conceded that the agent's authority is derived through the consent of the principal, although it is not always clear that such is the case. In the third instance the agent's authority is not derived through the actual consent of the principal. It arises as a result of the acts of the principal, but may be contrary to his wishes. The agent's authority is based on the theory of estoppel—i.e., the principal has so acted that he is estopped from denying that he has authorized the agent to act for him.

There is a close relation between the express and the implied authority of an agent and it is impossible to determine with exactness where the one leaves off and the other begins. The principal may set out in minute detail the course which the agent is to pursue in negotiating a deal, yet some detail may arise in the course of negotiations which is not covered by the express authority given the agent. In such a situation the agent would have implied authority to complete the negotiation of the contemplated contract.

The agent's express authority is that authority which the principal expressly confers on the agent; the implied authority is such authority as is necessary, usual, and proper to carry through to completion the main authority conferred. The scope of the agent's implied authority must be determined from the nature of the business to be transacted. These powers will be broad if the agent is acting as a general agent as, for example, the manager of a store or branch office. They will be comparatively narrow if the agent is acting as a special agent as, for example, if the agent is appointed to transact one isolated deal. Usage of trade is important in determining the scope of the agent's implied authority. If Peters appoints Archer as his agent to sell Peters' house, Archer's implied authority to bind Peters will be limited by established usages. As a general rule, a real estate agent is not authorized to sign a contract of sale or a deed in the name of his principal. The agent usually finds a buyer and negotiates for the sale of the listed property, but the principal personally signs the contract of sale or the deed to the property. If Archer finds a buyer and signs, in Peters' name, a contract of sale or a deed to the property, Peters will not be bound by Archer's act unless he has expressly authorized him to sign the contract of sale or deed. However, if in negotiating the sale of the property Archer makes representations such as are customarily made by real estate agents in selling property, Peters will be bound by such representations even though Peters had instructed Archer not to make representations in the course of the sale of the property.

When one has, by his acts, made it appear that another is acting as his agent, or that his agent has been granted certain powers when such is not actually a fact, he will be bound as principal for the acts of such person or agent. It will be noted that the essential elements of apparent authority are (1) acts of the principal sufficient to lead a third person to reasonably believe that an agency exists or that the agent has certain authority, (2) knowledge of such acts on the part of the third person, and (3) action by the third person in reliance thereon.

In establishing the authority of the agent the third person must prove that the agent has authority to bind the principal. This does not mean that the third person must prove that the principal authorized the agent to negotiate the contract in suit, but must prove that as a result of the acts of the principal he, acting as a reasonably prudent person, was justified in believing that the agent was authorized to negotiate the contract. The statements of the agent are not admissible in evidence for the purpose of proving the scope of the agent's authority. The authority of the agent is based on the consent of the principal; therefore, that consent must be shown by proving that the words and acts of the principal were such that an ordinarily prudent person would believe that the principal had authorized the agent to act in his behalf.

Claflin et al. v. Continental Jersey Works
85 Ga. 27, 11 S.E. 721 (1890)

This was an action by Weisbein doing business as Continental Jersey Co. (plaintiff) against Claflin doing business as Claflin & Co. and others (defendants). Judgment for plaintiff in part and for defendants in part. Defendants appealed and judgment was reversed. The reversal was based on points of law not included in this extract.

Weisbein appointed Lichtenstein his agent to continue Weisbein's business during his absence. The appointment was in the form of a written power of attorney. Claflin and others contended that Weisbein had obtained goods through fraud and demanded a return of the goods and a settlement of the account. Lichtenstein returned the goods still in stock and settled the balances by delivering additional goods at a discount of 24 per cent off cost. Before making the settlement Lichtenstein showed his written power of attorney to the creditors involved in the deal.

The settlement entered into was outside the scope of his express authority. It is claimed that the principal is bound.

Simmons, J. The errors assigned go to the refusal of the court to give in charge to the jury certain principles of the law of agency which bear upon the question of the extent of Lichtenstein's authority. Where an agent's authority is conferred and defined in writing, the scope or extent of such authority is a question for determination by the court. *Dobbins* v. *Manufacturing Co.*, 75 Ga. 238, 243. As said by this court in the case above cited (page 243): "That it was the duty of the court to construe both the charter and the letter of attorney, and to determine the extent of power conferred by both and each of them upon the agent, we think, is a plain proposition. Taken alone, and without proof of other circumstances to which it was necessary to resort to clear ambiguities or to explain doubtful intention, there was nothing for the jury to find. The question was purely and simply one of law, to which it was the exclusive right and duty of the judge to respond." In requesting charges upon the extent and nature of a general agency, there seems to have been an attempt by the plaintiffs in error to enlarge the authority of Lichtenstein beyond the limits of his power, or at least to establish the construction that the instrument created a general agency. If there was any such effort, the court did not err in defeating it. It is not allowable, by the adduction of extrinsic oral evidence, to add to the powers expressly given in the writing. The authority must be proved by the instrument itself. The very purpose of a power of attorney is to prescribe and publish the limits within which the agent shall act, so as not to leave him to the uncertainty of memory, and those who deal with him to the risk of misrepresentation or misconception, as to the extent of his authority. To confer express authority is to withhold implied authority. There can be no parol enlargement of a written authority. Besides, the power of attorney was relied upon throughout the whole transaction. The plaintiffs in error believed Lichtenstein's acts to be within the letter of his authority, having taken the advice of counsel in reference thereto, so that they cannot claim to have been misled by any appearance of authority other than that which the writing gives.

Babicora Development Co., Inc. v. Edelman
Ct. of Civ. App. of Tex., 54 S.W. (2d) 552 (1932)

This was an action by Lee Edelman (plaintiff) against Babicora Development Company, Incorporated (defendant). Judgment for plaintiff and defendant appealed. Judgment reversed and remanded.

Edelman was thrown from his horse and injured while in the employ of the Babicora Development Co., Inc. He threatened to sue the company. W. M. Farris, the ranch superintendent, agreed to give him employment for life at a salary of $75 per month and board if he would not sue. Edelman was discharged and sued for breach of the contract. The company claimed the ranch superintendent had no authority to make such a contract.

Pelphrey, C. J. The authority of Farris having been specially denied by appellant, the burden was on appellee to introduce evidence establishing it. Appellee's pleading as to the authority of Farris reads: "That said contract of settlement was made with one Farris, who was the general manager in charge and control of the company's affairs and of its ranch in Mexico, and had authority to make said contract and said contract was made shortly after July 7th, 1925, and was communicated to the Executive Officers of the Company, whose mail (main) office is in San Francisco, California, and whose names to this plaintiff are unknown, and said contract was accepted by them, and became and was a binding contract upon said defendant."

Therefore, if appellee is to recover, it must be by showing that Farris had either the express or implied power to make the contract sued upon; or that his act in so doing was ratified by appellant.

From an examination of the statement of facts we find no evidence showing either an express authority or ratification. Consequently, the question we are called upon to decide is: Did the making of the contract fall within the implied powers of Farris as general manager or superintendent of appellant's ranches?

We think it may be conceded that Farris was the general agent of appellant, and if the implied powers of a general agent are sufficient to cover this character of act, or if the facts surrounding the agency are sufficient to raise an issue as to the act being within his implied powers, then appellant's assignment should be overruled. A decision of the question will depend upon a proper understanding of implied or incidental powers of a general agent.

As to such powers, we find in 2 C. J. § 219, p. 578, the following: "Implied authority is limited to the purposes for which the agency was created and to the acts and duties ordinarily entrusted to such an agent. It is also limited by the usual course of dealing in the business in which he is employed and as agent has no implied power to do acts that are unusual, extraordinary or unnecessary, however advantageous to the principal's interests the agent may believe them to be; for such acts he should secure special authority from the principal."

And, again, in section 222, we find: "A general agency, however, does not import unqualified authority; and the implied power of an agent, however general, must be limited to such acts as are proper for an agent to do, and cannot extend to acts clearly adverse to the interests of the principal, or for the benefit of the agent personally; and an agent has no implied authority to do acts not usually done by agents in that sort of transaction . . . . ; the most general authority is limited to the business or purpose for which the agency was created and it is not sufficient that the agent's act or conduct merely relates to the business of his agency."

In 1 Mechem on Agency, § 715, it is said:

"It is a fundamental principle in the law of agency that every delegation of authority 'general' or 'special,' carries with it, unless the contrary be expressed, implied authority to do all those acts, naturally and ordinarily done in such cases, which are reasonably necessary and proper to be done in the case in order to carry into effect the main authority conferred. . . . .

"The acts which are deemed authorized under this rule are those which are naturally and ordinarily necessary, which therefore are the usual incidents of the act in question, the acts which the principal presumptively would have included without question if his attention had been called to them,—the acts which the ordinary competent person already familiar with the situation and with the ordinary methods of business, or a similar person having the situation made clear to him,—like a juror,—and considering the matter in the light of everyday experience, would say without serious hesitation formed a natural and ordinary part of the main act authorized."

The facts here show that Farris was either the general manager or superintendent of appellant's ranches in Mexico and that he employed and discharged the help on such ranches. Are such facts sufficient to raise an issue as to his implied authority to employ appellee for life under the above-quoted rules? We think not. There is nothing in the record to show that the owners of ranches ordinarily give their injured employees employment for life; therefore, the making of this contract was not such an act as was ordinarily intrusted to the managers of ranches, nor was it in the usual course of dealing in the ranching business.

Neither do we think it can be said that the making of this contract was necessary and proper to be done in order to carry into effect the main authority conferred in Farris. There is no evidence which would have justified an ordinary competent person, familiar with the situation and with the ordinary methods of business, considering the matter in the light of everyday experience, to say without serious hesitation that the making of this contract by Farris formed a natural and ordinary part of the management of appellant's ranches.

It is true that the record here reflects that Farris had authority to employ the help needed on the ranches of appellant, but the authority to employ embodies only the right to make contracts of a usual and reasonable sort.

General Motors Truck Co. v. Texas Supply Company
64 F. (2d) 527 (1933)

This was an action by the Texas Supply Company (plaintiff) against the General Motors Truck Company (defendant). Judgment for plaintiff and defendant appealed. Judgment affirmed.

The Texas Supply Company purchased ten General Motors Trucks from Brooks-Price Company of Towson, Md. The Brooks-Price Company were not agents of the General Motors Truck Company, but were dealers in General Motors Trucks. The trucks carried a ninety day guarantee against defective material and workmanship. The trucks proved defective. After considerable negotiation between the Supply Company, the Brooks-Price Company, and the General Motors Truck Company, the president of the Supply Company, Mr. Brooks of the Brooks-Price Company, the branch manager of the General Motors Truck Company, and Pat E. O'Connor, the Eastern regional manager of the General Motors Truck Company, had a meeting at the office of the president of the Supply Company. At this meeting O'Connor, as agent of the General Motors Truck Co., agreed to accept the return of the trucks and pay the Supply Company $7,823.06. The General Motors Truck Co. refused to perform, claiming O'Connor had no authority to bind them.

Soper, C. J. We have then a case for the application of the rule that the act of an agent within the apparent but not within the real scope of his authority is binding upon the principal where a loss would otherwise result to one who has in good faith relied on such apparent authority; an act being within the apparent scope of an agent's authority when a reasonably prudent person, having knowledge of the usages of the business, would be justified in supposing the agent is authorized to perform the act from the character of his known duties. *Richmond Guano Co.* v. *E. I. Du Pont de Nemours & Co.* (C. C. A.) 284. F. 803, 807. In the application of this rule, the courts have held that the circumstance that an agent has been given apparent authority to manage or represent the principal's business in a particular locality or section or the country may be taken into consideration in determining whether it is reasonable for one dealing with the agent to assume that he has power to make settlements or to rescind or modify contracts.

The appellant contends that the rule of apparent authority does not apply in the pending case because the evidence shows that there is a custom in the automobile industry that a branch manager has no authority to rescind a sale and to take back vehicles alleged by the purchaser to be defective. The evidence, however, does not indicate that such an official as a regional manager of a manufacturing corporation is denied authority to make such settlements by an established custom of the industry; so that we have merely to consider whether there was sufficient evidence to go to the jury to establish an apparent authority upon which a reasonably prudent man would be entitled to rely. We think that there was such evidence in this case. O'Connor was not merely the manager of a local branch. He was held out as the manufacturer's representative in a large part of the United States, clothed with the title of "Eastern Regional Manager," and with the special duty of supervising sales in the territory assigned him. He was called in by the local agents of the company to adjust a bona fide complaint arising under a contract of sale of goods which the company had guaranteed. It was for the jury to say, under these circumstances, whether a person of ordinary care and prudence would have had reasonable grounds to believe that the regional manager, who had made the agreement of settlement set out in the evidence, was authorized so to act. There was no error in submitting this issue to the decision of the jury.

Ratification

An agent in negotiating a transaction may exceed his authority and his acts will not bind his principal, or a stranger may represent that he is acting as agent for another in which case the purported principal will not be bound. In either of these situations the lack of authority may be supplied by ratification. To ratify an unauthorized act, a person must fulfill certain essential requirements. (1) There must be a principal in existence at the time the act is done. (2) The act must be done by one who purports to act as an agent. (3) The principal must have knowledge of all the material facts when he ratifies. (4) The principal must intend to ratify.

Ratification cures the defect of lack of authority, and upon ratification the result is the same as though the agent had had authority to do the act at the time of its performance. If at the time the act was performed the purported principal was not in existence, the act cannot be ratified. Archer represents that he is agent of the Peters Corporation and negotiates a contract with Trent in the name of the Peters Corporation as principal, but the Peters Corporation has not been incorporated and has no legal existence. If the Peters Corporation is incorporated later, it cannot ratify the contract, because the ratification will be retroactive and the contract will be treated as made on the date Archer closed the deal with Trent. The Peters Corporation having no existence at that time cannot be a contracting party, and to have a valid contract there must be two contracting parties.

If a person, who is not acting as an agent, enters into a contract, a stranger to the transaction cannot acquire the rights of a principal in the contract by attempting to ratify it. If Archer, who is not acting as Peters' agent, contracts with Trent, Peters cannot acquire Archer's rights in the contract by ratifying it.

The ratification will not bind the principal unless he has knowledge of all the material facts. If one expressly ratifies the unauthorized acts of his agent without making any effort to learn the facts, he will be bound, but if the ratification is implied from the conduct of the principal, he will not be bound unless he has knowledge of the material facts.

The principal in order to be bound must have acted with the intent to ratify the unauthorized acts. As in contract law, there must be some act on the part of the principal which reasonably tends to show intent.

The ratification may be either express or implied. It need not be in writing unless the act is such that authority to perform the act would have to be in writing or under seal, in which event the ratification will have to be in writing or under seal. If the ratification is implied, it is necessary to show facts which establish with reasonable certainty the intent of the principal to ratify the unauthorized acts. The acceptance of benefits with knowledge of the facts and circumstances surrounding the unauthorized acts, as a general rule, is sufficient to show an intent to ratify.

The principal cannot ratify the illegal acts of his agent; however, he may ratify his torts. If the tort also involves a crime, the ratification of the unauthorized act will not relieve the agent from criminal liability even though it renders the principal liable for the tort. The same rule is generally applied to contracts. If Archer forges Peters' name to a negotiable promissory note drawn payable to Trent and Trent takes the note paying the amount of the note to Archer, Peters might ratify Archer's unauthorized act and render himself liable to Trent on the note, but such ratification will not bar criminal prosecution of Archer for the forgery.

If the principal wishes to ratify, he must ratify the entire transaction. He cannot ratify those portions of the contract which are beneficial and repudiate those parts which are detrimental. On ratification the principal will be bound in the same manner and to the same extent as he would have been if the agent had had full authority in the first instance. Ratification relieves the agent from personal liability to the third party. After ratification the third party is bound. The better view is that before ratification the third party may withdraw from the transaction; however, the states are not in accord on this point.

Strader v. Haley et al.
216 Minn. 315, 12 N.W. (2d) 608 (1943)

Four separate actions were brought by Marjorie T. Strader (plaintiff) against Dan Haley, etc., and others (defendants). The actions were tried together. Judgment for defendants and plaintiff appealed. Judgment affirmed.

Dan Haley and wife lived with Marjorie T. Strader, plaintiff. They paid no board or rent, but served as companions and did some work for her. Between July, 1936, and October, 1941, Haley cashed 66 checks totaling $1787.55. All of the checks were either signed or indorsed by Haley in the plaintiff's name. Haley had no authority to sign negotiable paper as plaintiff's agent. The court found that plaintiff received from Haley all the proceeds of the checks in the form of cash and merchandise, and that all cash and merchandise was received by plaintiff under such circumstances that she was charged with notice and knowledge that the same were the proceeds of the checks in question.

The court found as a conclusion of law that the plaintiff had ratified Haley's actions and conduct in cashing the checks. From this finding plaintiff appealed.

Peterson, J. There is no finding that plaintiff authorized Haley to sign her name to any check. No particular form of authorization is necessary. ". . . . the authority of the agent may be established as in other cases of agency." Plaintiff's ratification of Haley's acts is a substitute for precedent authority. Ratification by a party of another's unauthorized acts occurs where the party with full knowledge of all material facts confirms, approves, or sanctions the other's acts. Ratification is equivalent to prior authority. Although an act may be done without precedent authority, ratification creates the relation of principal and agent, and the former becomes bound by the act to the same extent as if it had been done under a previous authorization.

By ratification, the principal absolves the agent from any liability to the principal which otherwise would result from the fact that the agent acted without authority.

There is a conflict in the authorities as to whether or not a forgery may be ratified. By a forgery is meant an unauthorized signature on an instrument or a material alteration thereof in violation of a criminal statute. Where the unauthorized signing of another's name to an instrument does not constitute the crime of forgery, all the authorities agree that the party whose name was so signed may ratify the signature and become bound thereby.

An unauthorized signature on a note, check, or other instrument under circumstances not constituting the crime of forgery may be ratified.

Where a principal accepts and retains the benefits of an unauthorized act of an agent with full knowledge of all the facts, he thereby ratifies the act. The rule applies to unauthorized signatures. A party who with full knowledge of the facts receives and retains the proceeds or the benefits of his unauthorized signature upon an instrument ratifies the signature.

Here the evidence sustains the finding that plaintiff received the proceeds of the checks in cash and merchandise with full knowledge of all the facts. The finding is supported by Haley's testimony that he cashed the checks and delivered the cash and merchandise to her pursuant to her directions.

Our conclusion is that plaintiff ratified all the unauthorized signatures in these cases; that by reason of such ratification she is precluded from setting up the fact that her signatures were unauthorized in the actions against Haley and the other defendants.

Evans v. Ruth
129 Pa. Super. Ct. 192, 195 Atl. 163 (1937)

This was an action by James S. Evans (plaintiff) against Homer Ruth trading as Ruth Lumber Company (defendant). Judgment for plaintiff and defendant appealed. Judgment affirmed.

A state contract for stone was awarded to defendant. Plaintiff learned of the award and went to defendant's quarry and applied there to an unidentified foreman and was employed to haul stone. Each load of stone was weighed and slips bearing the name of Ruth Lumber Co., admittedly furnished by Ruth, were made out in triplicate, containing the weight and other necessary data. Plaintiff was to get 40 cents per ton for hauling.

On December 5th, after the work was completed, the plaintiff, together with four or five other truckers, went to Ruth's place of business in Scottdale and presented him with their bills. After examining these accounts, Ruth said: "Well, I see you finish the work for me. . . . . If you will have a sworn affidavit to that statement, I will pay you. I have the money right in the safe there." Ruth was furnished this affidavit, but Evans was not paid. Later, at a squire's office in Warrendale, Ruth offered to pay, and did pay 53 per cent of the claims to some of the claimants, but Evans refused to accept that proposition.

Ruth denied any liability to Evans, alleging that he had never entered into a contract of employment with him. He offered in evidence a written contract between himself and George Darr, subletting all the work allotted to him under the purchase orders to Darr as an independent contractor. He stated that he, personally, was never on the job, or had anything to do with it, other than to furnish two trucks on one occasion to hasten delivery of the stone. Darr testified to the existence of the contract, that he had two foremen on the job who kept the records, and that he was in complete control of the work. There was no evidence that Evans knew or had any way of knowing that Darr had this subcontract. Darr got into financial difficulty, and whatever money may have been due him from Ruth was attached by one of Darr's creditors.

Baldridge, J. The plaintiff relied primarily upon an oral contract with an agent, subsequently ratified by the principal. Affirming agency, the burden rested upon him to prove it. The agency could not be established by the declaration of the agent alone. If plaintiff's case depended solely on the statements of the unidentified foreman, admitted in evidence without objection, the position of the appellant that the agent's authority was not shown would be well taken. But the proof that Ruth furnished the weigh slips and received a copy after each load of stone hauled by the plaintiff had been weighed, which was the basis upon which Ruth was paid by the state, and Ruth's failure to disavow the contract, instead of affirming it by stating that the work was done for him and that he would pay for it provided an affidavit was furnished, were sufficient for the jury's consideration.

It is a well-recognized rule of law that, if A assumes to act for B without precedent authority, and B subsequently affirms A's act, it is a ratification which relates back and supplies original authority for the act. B is bound then to the same extent as if previous authority had been granted A.

Ruth could have previously authorized the plaintiff's employment, and it follows that he could subsequently ratify it. "Ratification is the affirmance by a person of a prior act which did not bind him but which was done or professedly done on his account, whereby the act, as to some or all persons, is given effect as if originally authorized by him." Restatement, Agency, § 82, page 197. "Affirmance is a manifestation of an election by the one on whose account an unauthorized act has been performed to treat the act as authorized, or conduct by him justifiable only if there is such an election." Restatement, Agency, § 83, p. 198. Our own cases are in accord with this pronouncement of the law.

The verbal agreement of Ruth to pay Evans did not fail for consideration, as appellant argues, as ratification does not require a new consideration.

QUESTIONS AND PROBLEMS

1. Mrs. Bertrand was injured when an automobile which she was driving collided with an automobile, owned by Mutual Motor Co. and driven by a prospective purchaser who was alone in the automobile at the time of the collision. Mrs. Bertrand sued the Mutual Motor Co. on the theory that the prospective purchaser was the agent of the Mutual Motor Co. Is this theory correct?
2. Archer operated a pool room and sold lottery tickets, which was a violation of the statutes of the state. Archer hired Burch to manage the sale of the lottery tickets. Was a valid agency created?
3. Webb owned and operated a hotel. He hired Binford to repair the cornice. The manner and means to be employed was left entirely to Binford. While working on the building, Binford negligently dropped a plank which struck and injured Hexamer. Hexamer sued Webb for damages. Should he recover?
4. Echols, a tailor, agreed to make a suit of clothes for a customer. The customer paid Echols $10.00, the price of the suit, at the time the suit was ordered. Echols never made the suit nor did he return the money. Echols was charged with having embezzled, as agent or servant, money belonging to his employer. Is Echols an agent or employee of his customer?
5. Clark, Smart, and Clark were partners engaged in business under the firm name Clark, Smart and Co. The firm appointed Ball as their agent. Ball transacted business in the firm name with the Railroad Co. The Railroad Co. claims that they are not bound by the contracts because a partnership cannot act through an agent. May a partnership act through an agent?
6. Must an agent have authority in writing to execute a contract in writing? Must an agent have authority under seal to execute a contract under seal?
7. Harte was the manager of the branch office of Nichols and Shepard Co. at Peoria. Harte collected money due the company and paid all the bills of the Peoria office. Harte opened a checking account with the National Bank and deposited all moneys received in the account and paid all bills with checks drawn on the account. The account was in the name of the company. Harte drew twenty-four checks aggregating $1023.60 which created an overdraft for that amount. Harte absconded with the proceeds of the checks. The National Bank sued Nichols and

Shepard Co. to recover the amount of the overdraft. Is the bank entitled to a judgment?

8. McMurray, a physician, was engaged by the conductor of a train to attend a brakeman injured while on duty. The conductor was the highest in authority of any of the employees of the railroad present at the time of the accident. The railroad refused to pay McMurray for his services and he sued. Is McMurray entitled to a judgment against the railroad?
9. F. H. Fleer, who lived in Philadelphia, owned a farm in North Carolina. He placed his brother in complete control of the farm. His brother directed all the work on the farm, kept the time of the employees, and paid the employees wages by checks signed in the name of F. H. Fleer. The brother employed Troll for a period of twelve months. Before the expiration of the period, Troll was discharged without cause. Troll sued F. H. Fleer who set up lack of authority in his brother to make the contract as a defense. Is F. H. Fleer bound by the contract?
10. Day, as agent for Short, sold a piano to Peabody, a stockbroker. The agreement provided that the purchase price of the piano was to be paid out of commissions which might become due Peabody in connection with stock transactions handled by Peabody for Day. Short sued Peabody to recover the price of the piano, contending that Day had no authority to sell the piano on the credit terms stipulated in the contract. May Short affirm the sale and yet repudiate the credit terms in the sales contract?

CHAPTER XXVII

RELATION OF PRINCIPAL AND THIRD PERSONS

Introduction

The fundamental rule of agency is that the acts of the agent bind the principal when the agent acts within the scope of his authority, whether that authority is express, implied, or apparent, or when the acts of the agent are ratified by the principal.

Under this rule the liability of the third party to the principal and of the principal to the third party will depend upon the authority of the agent to negotiate the transaction or upon the principal's ratification of unauthorized acts. Consequently, the discussion and cases herein will complement the earlier discussion of the authority of the agent.

The agent, in dealing with third persons, may disclose the existence of the agency and the identity of his principal; he may disclose the existence of the agency but not disclose the identity of his principal, or he may conceal both the existence of the agency and the identity of the principal. As a general rule, if the existence of the agency is disclosed and the agent acts within the scope of his authority, the principal and the third persons are the ones bound by the contract. The agent acts for the principal, and his acts are considered as the acts of the principal; consequently, the agent is in no way a party to the contract. If the existence of the agency and the identity of the principal are concealed, the contract purports to be between the agent and the third person, and of necessity the agent is a party to the contract and is bound by it. However, the undisclosed principal is also bound if the agent acts within the scope of his authority.

Disclosed Principal

When the principal is disclosed and the business is transacted in his name, the principal is bound if the agent is acting within the scope of his authority. If the contract is in writing and the principal is named as the contracting party, he will be the only one bound even though the agent signs his own name to the contract. If the transaction is negotiated by oral negotiations but in the name of the principal, the principal will be the only one bound even though the agent in the course of the negotiations uses such expressions as "I will buy." If the contract is a negotiable instrument or an instrument under seal, in a jurisdiction where the efficacy of the seal is recognized, it must be drawn in the name of the principal and the principal's name must be signed to the instrument or the principal will not be bound. It is a rule that one not a party to a negotiable instrument or an instrument under seal cannot be bound by it. In the past, there was considerable controversy as to what form the signing of the instrument must take in order that the principal, and not the agent, would be bound. As to negotiable instruments, if the identity of the principal is disclosed and words are added to the agent's signature indicating that he signs in behalf of a principal, the agent is not bound.[1] A somewhat similar situation exists in regard to sealed instruments.[2]

From the standpoint of good business practice a written contract should be drawn in the principal's name and signed in such a manner that it is clear that the agent does not become a party to the agreement. For example, "I Peters hereby promise. . . .

"Signed Peters
"By Archer his agent."

Whitney v. Wyman
101 U.S. 392 (1879)

This was an action brought by Baxter Whitney (plaintiff) against Charles Wyman and others (defendants). Judgment for defendants and plaintiff appealed. Judgment affirmed.

Plaintiff sued defendants to recover the value of certain machinery which he contended he manufactured and sold to the defendants. The defendants claimed that the machinery was sold to the Grand Haven Fruit-Basket Co., a corporation, and that they were not liable. Several letters were exchanged between the parties which were material:

---

[1] N. I. L.; sec. 20. Where the instrument contains or a person adds to his signature words indicating that he signs for or on behalf of a principal, or in a representative capacity, he is not liable on the instrument if he was duly authorized; but the mere addition of words describing him as an agent, or as filling a representative character, without disclosing his principal, does not exempt him from personal liability.

[2] Agency, Restatement; sec. 325. An agent is not liable as a party to a sealed instrument unless he is named in the instrument as the covenantor and it also purports to be sealed by him. If this appears unambiguously, extrinsic evidence is not admissible to show that it was agreed that he should not be a party, except for the purpose of reforming the instrument.

The first letter was addressed to "Baxter Whitney, Esq." and was signed

"Charles Wyman
"Edward P. Ferry
"Carlton L. Storrs
"Prudential Committee Grand Haven Fruit-Basket Co."

A reply was addressed to "Grand Haven Fruit-Basket Co." and was signed "Baxter D. Whitney." A letter in which a bill for the machinery was inclosed was addressed "Messrs. C. E. Wyman, E. P. Ferry, C. L. Storrs," and was signed "Baxter D. Whitney." The machinery was charged to defendants individually on the plaintiff's books and the plaintiff drew a draft for the purchase price of the machinery on the defendants individually which was refused when presented for payment.

Mr. Justice Swayne. Where the question of agency in making a contract arises there is a broad line of distinction between instruments under seal and stipulations in writing not under seal, or by parol. In the former case the contract must be in the name of the principal, must be under seal, and must purport to be his deed and not the deed of the agent covenanting for him.

In the latter cases the question is always one of intent; and the court, being untrammelled by any other consideration, is bound to give it effect. As the meaning of the law-maker is the law, so the meaning of the contracting parties is the agreement. Words are merely the symbols they employ to manifest their purpose that it may be carried into execution. If the contract be unsealed and the meaning clear, it matters not how it is phrased, nor how it is signed, whether by the agent for the principal or with the name of the principal by the agent or otherwise.

The intent developed is alone material, and when that is ascertained it is conclusive. Where the principal is disclosed, and the agent is known to be acting as such, the latter cannot be made personally liable unless he agreed to be so.

Looking at the letter of the defendants of the 1st of February, 1869, and the answer of the plaintiff of the 10th of that month, we cannot doubt as to the understanding and meaning of both parties with respect to the point in question.

The former advised the latter of the progress made in organizing the corporation; that the order was given by the direction of its officers, and the letter is signed by the writers as the "Prudential Committee of the Grand Haven Fruit-Basket Co.," which was the name in full of the corporation. The plaintiff addressed his reply to the "Grand Haven Fruit-Basket Company," thus using the name of the corporation as the party with whom he knew he was dealing, and omitting the names of the defendants, and their designation as a committee, according to the style they gave themselves in their letter.

It seems to us entirely clear that both parties understood and meant that the contract was to be, and in fact was, with the corporation, and not with the defendants individually.

The agreement thus made could not be afterwards changed by either of the parties without the consent of the other. *Utley* v. *Donaldson,* 94 U.S. 29.

Liability for Agent's Acts

The liability of the principal for the acts of his agent can be traced back to the early idea of status. Only certain persons had full legal rights and such persons were answerable for the acts of those over whom they had control. The master was liable for the acts of his slave and this idea was applied at a later date to the master and servant relation; the master was liable for the acts of his servant. We no longer recognize the archaic concept of status but have substituted for it the concept of intent; yet the responsibility of the principal for the acts of his agent does not depend entirely on the consent of the principal. In many instances the principal will be bound by the acts of the agent if the agent acts within the scope of and in the course of the principal's business even though the agent violates positive instructions of the principal, acts fraudulently without the knowledge or consent of the principal, is negligent in the performance of his duties, or makes mistakes in carrying out his instructions. However, in all instances if the third person is permitted to hold the principal liable for the acts of the agent, the third person has the burden of proving that he, believing that the agent was acting within the scope of his authority, acted in good faith. If the third person knew or, in the exercise of reasonable care, should have known that the agent exceeded his authority, the principal will not be bound; nor will the principal be bound unless he is responsible for the appearance of the authority exercised by the agent. These rules are based on broad principles of public policy. If one of two innocent persons must suffer a loss, the one most at fault should bear the loss. The principal selects the agent, clothes him with authority and benefits by his acts. If the agent does not follow instructions, act honestly, exercise reasonable care or possess reasonable skill, the principal, not an innocent third person, should answer for the results.

Chicago, St. P., M. & O. Ry. Co. v. Bryant
65 F. 969 (1895)

This was an action by Forest E. Bryant, administrator of James Davidson, deceased (plaintiff) against the Chicago, St. Paul, Minneapolis & Omaha Railway Company (defendant). Judgment for plaintiff and defendant appealed. Judgment reversed.

At the direction of the "day yard master" the engineer of a switch engine drew a passenger coach filled with employees of the defendant from the shops to the Union Depot where the employees attended a meeting. On the return trip the coach collided with some freight cars and Davidson was killed in the accident. The defendant contended that the yard master had no authority to run this train and that it was not liable.

The point near the shops between which and the Union Depot this train moved on the night of the accident was not within the limits of the company's yard, but was about three-fourths of a mile west of its westerly limit, and was connected with it by but a single track. The company operated no passenger cars or trains between these points, and never had operated any, except that, by special order of the superintendent or train dispatcher, an excursion train, with a regular conductor, engineer, and brakeman, was once or twice operated from the shops to Hudson, Wis., five or six years before this accident, to carry the employees to a picnic. The yard through which this train passed was a freight yard, was used to switch freight cars and to make up freight trains, and the yard master who ran this train had nothing to do with making up, switching, or running passenger cars or trains, unless directed to do so in a specific case by a special order of his proper superior, save that, when such trains came through his yard, it was his duty to see that they had a clear track, and to direct engineers who were not familiar with the yard on what tracks they should run their engines; and, save that he occasionally switched an extra passenger coach in the yard, this yard master never had any authority to receive or carry passengers for this company, except in one instance, when, by special order of his superiors, he was directed to take the superintendent of the company, on an engine, to Shakopee, a distance of about 25 miles, and except that occasionally, by the special orders of his superiors, he acted as conductor of a regular passenger train between St. Paul and Merriam Junction, a distance of about 40 miles, when the regular conductors were for some reason unable to act. With these exceptions, he had never carried any passengers for this company before the night of the accident. He was the "day yard master" in this freight yard. He had no duties to discharge for this company after 6 P.M. At that time he went off duty, and from that time until the next morning the yard was in charge of, and the duties of the yard master were discharged by, another, who was termed the "night yard master." These duties were so discharged by the night yard master on the night of this accident. Nevertheless, this day yard master operated this train between 7 and 11 o'clock at night, for the purpose of enabling himself and his fellow servants to ride free to a meeting of their own. He had no authority to run passenger trains or coaches over this railroad from the company or any of its officers, and none of the officers of the company that had the right to permit such trains to run between the depot and these shops knew that he intended to operate this train until after the accident occurred.

Sanborn, C. J. The relation of a common carrier to its passenger is a contract relation. Whether or not such a relation existed between the company and the deceased depends primarily upon the question, whether this yard master must be held to have been the agent of the company when he was operating this fatal train, for the company made no contract to carry the deceased, unless it made it through this man. That this yard master had no actual authority to operate this train or make this contract is not denied, but counsel for the defendant in error, in support of their view, invoke the rule that as against third persons the principal is bound by the acts of the agent done in the course of his employment, not only when these acts are within the scope of his actual, but when they are within the scope of his apparent, authority. This rule, in our opinion, has no application to this case, for two reasons: First, the company never invested this yard master with any apparent authority to carry passengers on or to run this passenger train for it; and, second, he did not run this train in the course of his employment for the company, but for his own ends, when he was not engaged in serving his company. There is no doubt that a principal who holds his agent out to the world as the possessor of certain authority may be bound by the latter's acts within the scope of that authority, although he has secretly restricted it to narrower limits. The reason for the rule that the principal is bound by the acts of the agent within the scope of his apparent authority is that it is inequitable for a principal to induce strangers to enter into contracts with one that he gives the appearance of his agent, and to change their actions and relations on the faith of such agency, and then to deny that the agency was what he made it appear to be. The rule rests upon the principle of estoppel. It follows that the principal is bound only to the extent of the appearance he gives, or knowingly permits the agent to give, or might reasonably expect the agent to give, to the agency, and not by any appearance of agency beyond this that the agent himself wrongfully produces without the knowledge or consent of his principal. It is only acts within the scope of the apparent authority with which the principal clothes the agent, not those within the scope of the apparent authority with which the agent wrongfully clothes himself, without the assent or knowledge of his principal, that are binding upon the latter. Undoubtedly, the principal in conferring the authority upon his agent must be held to the rule of reasonable foresight, prudence, and care, and may be bound by such acts of the agent as a reasonably prudent man would expect that his agent might appear to have the right to do, from the authority actually given. Tested by this rule, this yard master never had any apparent authority to carry passengers for this company on a wild train in the night, or in any other way, over any part of this railroad, without orders from or notice to the train dispatcher or some other superior who had the authority to permit and provide for it. The possession and control of the passenger coach gave him the only appearance of authority to carry passengers that he had, and that coach he took, according to this record, without notice to and without the knowledge of any of the employees of the company who had the authority to permit it to run upon this road. Whatever appearance of authority the possession of this coach conferred upon him, then, was not bestowed upon him by the company, but was produced by his own act, without its knowledge or assent. Nor was there any act or permission of this company that any reasonably prudent man could have foreseen would be likely to confer any apparent authority upon this agent to carry passengers for this company. The general authority of a freight yard master did not confer it. The specific authority of this yard master did not bestow it. The course of business and custom of years had never produced a single instance of its exercise by this employee without a special order from a superior officer who had the proper authority to direct it. How could this company judge of the future but by the past? And who could have anticipated that a servant who had never had any authority to carry passengers, and who in a service of years had never carried one without a special order to do so from his proper superior, would seize a passenger coach and a switch engine, and run them, loaded with his fellow servants, over the busiest and most dangerous part of this railroad, in the night, without notice to train dispatcher, superintendent, or general manager, or any other officer that had authority to permit the passage of such a train or to clear the way for it? In our opinion, no one could have anticipated an act so foolhardy and unusual, and this was not an act within the scope of the apparent authority with which this company clothed this agent.

Liability for Agent's Representations

The principal is liable for the statements of the agent made in the course of a transaction, whether or not the agent is expressly authorized to make such statements, if the statements are such as would ordinarily be made under the circumstances and the third person does not have notice that the agent is not authorized to make the statements. When one appoints an agent authorizing him to transact business, it is a known fact that, during the negotiations, statements and representations will be made. In making statements and representations, if the agent does not exceed his apparent authority, the principal is bound. If the principal has falsely instructed the agent or has negligently failed to instruct the agent and as a result the agent makes untrue or misleading statements, it is obvious that the principal is bound. If the agent knowingly makes false or misleading statements, even though he has been correctly instructed and expressly instructed to make only true statements, the principal will be bound if under the circumstances the third person is justified in relying on the statements made. The courts have held that the principal is not bound by the agent's statements of his authority. The third party must prove the agent's authority; the agent's statements as to his authority are not admissible as proof of his authority. Even in cases where the third person is not justified in relying on the agent's statements, if he has relied on them and they are fraudulent, the third person is given the privilege of returning what he has received and recovering that with which he has parted.

A third person has the right to rescind a contract which he has entered into in reliance on false representations made by the agent. This right is absolute and can be exercised even though the principal is in no way connected with the making of the false representations and even though the representations are in excess of the agent's authority. This rule is based on the plainest dictates of justice. It would be unjust and inequitable to permit the principal to enjoy the benefits of the misrepresentations of his agent yet disclaim the responsibility therefor.

Whether or not the principal can be held liable in damages in a tort action of deceit for the misrepresentations of the agent depends on the facts and circumstances of the case. The courts are not in accord in their holdings; however, if the principal has participated in the fraudulent representations, it is clear that he is liable in a tort action. To bind the principal it must appear that the fraudulent acts of the agent were done during the existence of the agency in the course of the transaction and within the scope of the agent's actual or apparent authority, or the principal must have ratified the acts of the agent. Some courts have held the principal liable in deceit if there is something in the business being transacted or in the terms of the employment or in the powers conferred on the agent which includes the making of representations and if under the circumstances the principal, in justice and good morals, should be bound.

Janeczko et al. v. Manheimer et al.
77 F. (2d) 205 (1935)

This was an action by Adam Janeczko and wife (plaintiffs) against Edward A. Manheimer and others (defendants). Judgment for defendants and plaintiffs appealed. Judgment affirmed.

The defendants owned a block of unimproved lots which were a part of a wild undeveloped section a mile or more in length in the eastern suburbs of Hammond, lying on the north and south side of a paved boulevard known as Summer Boulevard. The section of this large tract in which defendants' lots were located was bounded by Summer Boulevard on the north, Tenth Street on the south, Michigan Avenue on the east, and Indiana Avenue on the west. Excepting Summer Boulevard there was nothing but unmarked stakes on the land to indicate where the streets, lot lines or blocks were, and they could be determined accurately only by a survey.

The defendants listed the property for sale with McGarry, a real estate broker, and authorized him to sell the property for $125 per lot. At the time the property was listed the defendants sent McGarry a small blueprint showing the location of the property. They told McGarry that they had never seen the property and that they would not authorize a survey. McGarry advertised the lots and plaintiffs made inquiry. McGarry told plaintiffs that he did not know the exact location of the lots and that the owners would not authorize a survey. McGarry did check the plot in the city engineer's office and from the information there decided that the lots were three blocks east of Parrish Avenue, the closest landmark. McGarry and plaintiffs went to what McGarry thought was the intersection of Parrish Avenue and Summer Boulevard and attempted to calculate the distance of three city blocks by using the speedometer on the car. McGarry had the blueprint with him at this time and showed it to plaintiffs. Plaintiffs purchased the lots and about a year and a half afterwards it was first discovered by the parties that the land described in the deed was about a half mile east of the plat which was shown to the plaintiffs and was of much less value.

Plaintiffs bring this action to recover damages on account of the deceit of McGarry, defendants' agent.

Sparks, C. J. The only contested issue is whether the court erred in directing a verdict for defendants. The determination of that issue is based entirely on the narrower issue of the legal liability of appellees for the mistake of their agent in attempting to definitely locate the land. Under the facts disclosed it was conceded that appellants had a choice of two remedies, either rescission in equity or an action at law in tort for deceit. Under the first they could have tendered back the property and recovered from the principals the price paid therefor, upon a showing that the agent committed fraud, or that a mutual mistake was made by the agent and the purchasers. Under that remedy a court of equity would have placed appellants in status quo.

Appellants, however, elected the legal remedy of retaining the property and seeking damages from the principals on account of the deceit of the agent. Appellants had a perfect right to pursue the legal remedy, but recovery could be had against only the party or parties who were personally liable therefor. A principal will not be held personally liable for his agent's deceit unless he has authorized the deceit or participated in it or has knowingly permitted the agent to commit it.

Appellants contend, however, that the agent here was presumed to have authority to designate the land. That contention under the facts stated cannot be sustained. The doctrine of presumed, implied or apparent authority will not operate to hold an innocent principal for the tort of his agent. A broker who merely has property listed to sell at a certain price is not a general but a special agent of limited authority, which limitations the purchaser must ascertain at his peril. The broker has no power to bind his principal beyond the express authority conferred upon him.

Whatever might be said concerning the apparent authority of a real estate broker to point out a clearly defined parcel of real estate, such as a house and lot, is beside the question now presented. Here the land, though plotted of record, was a part of a wild, uncultivated, and unoccupied tract which appellees had never seen and could not physically designate, of which facts appellants had knowledge. The only information appellees had of its location was the blueprint, which they delivered to their agent who, in turn, delivered it to appellants. It correctly disclosed the precise location of the lots. From it, the agent in the presence of appellants, attempted to locate the land by means of measurement with an automobile speedometer, aided by information previously acquired by the agent from the recorded plot in the office of the city engineer at Hammond, which subsequently proved to have been incorrectly obtained by the agent. Appellants knew the character of this land, and the difficulty of precisely locating it with the naked eye. They had access to the only means of identification which the sellers had, and they had all the information concerning its precise location that the sellers ever possessed. Furthermore, the official plot of the entire addition, including the sub-divisions, was on file in the office of the engineer of the city in which appellants resided, and yet they made no effort to verify the alleged statements of the agent, nor did they inquire further as to the exact location, but they chose to rely upon the agent's statement as to the location, which the undisputed evidence discloses was ascertained in a very crude and uncertain manner, and within the knowledge of appellants.

Several conferences were had in the office of appellants' attorney prior to receiving from the Chicago Title & Trust Company its letter of opinion as to the sellers' title, and before the deed was made. At one of those conferences appellants' attorney asked the agent if he could show him (the attorney) where the property was, to which the agent replied: "I told him to the best of my ability I would, and the question came up in his office about the owners showing me the property. I told Mr. Sevald (the attorney) that the owners had never been out so they didn't really know where the property lay."

Under these circumstances we think the agent was not authorized by his principals to locate the land in question for appellants, and that the appellants had no right to rely upon his statements in that respect. It is true there are cases which have held that the designation of location of real estate to a purchaser was within the scope of the agent's authority, but those rulings were not under any such state of facts as are present here. Even though such authority of a real estate agent be presumed as a general principle, that presumption may be rebutted and dissipated by the facts, and we think that has been done in this case. We accept as true all of appellants' statements on all controverted questions of fact, and yet we think the evidence falls far short of establishing the fact, by presumption or otherwise, that appellees authorized the deceit, or participated in it, or knowingly permitted the agent to commit it.

Taylor et al. v. Wilson
44 Ohio App. 100, 183 N.E. 541 (1932)

This was an action by Martha W. Wilson (plaintiff) against Earl D. Taylor and another (defendants). Judgment for plaintiff and the defendants appealed. Judgment affirmed.

Defendants owned a house and lot which they listed with Feezel and Bordner, real estate brokers, for sale. While negotiating a sale of the property to plaintiff, Feezel and Bordner represented that the premises had thereon a good cesspool, a mighty good one. Plaintiff purchased the property relying on the representations. The representations proved false and untrue. The cesspool was wholly inadequate for the needs of the premises in that the waters from rains and waste backed up into the cellar making the house damp, giving off nauseating odors and causing the plaintiff and her family to suffer severe colds and causing other inconveniences. The plaintiff claimed damages in the amount of $2,000.

Lemert, J. The principal question at issue in the lower court was an issue of fact, namely, was there a good cesspool, such as alleged and described in plaintiff's petition, and were the defendants bound by their agents' representations about the same?

The question of whether there was a good cesspool or a good drainage system on the premises conveyed at the time of sale was a question of fact for the jury, and the jury must have found that there was not. An examination of the record clearly shows that the cesspool or drainage was faulty.

We note that the premises in question were located in a suburban section which had no public sewer. It would therefore follow that whatever sewage system the premises did have was solely within the personal knowledge of the defendants, and it was physically impossible for plaintiff below to ascertain same by personal observation. Hence, she was obliged to make inquiry. She was on the premises and in the home of the defendants below with defendant's agents, and it was from defendant's agents that plaintiff was informed as to the kind and character of sewage the property had.

We are of the opinion that the agents of defendants had implied authority to do more than just find a buyer and make the representations about the cesspool described in the petition. Defendants admit that their agents negotiated the transaction between the plaintiff and the defendants. In other words, they do not claim that said agents were employed merely to find a buyer or to bring the parties together.

For a proper determination of the first-claimed ground of error, we believe the true test to be a determination of the exact extent the principal permitted the agent to hold himself out as such, and what a prudent person in good faith, under the circumstances, would reasonably believe such authority to be.

"The rule in civil cases, which holds the principal, as to third persons, liable for the acts of his agent done within the general scope of his authority, irrespective of actual instructions that were unknown to the person dealing with the agent. In such case, as between the principal and a third person dealing with the agent on the faith of his apparent authority, the law conclusively presumes the actual authority of the agent to be what it openly appears to be; while, as between the principal and agent, the extent of the actual authority may be shown." *Anderson* v. *State*, 22 Ohio St. 305, 307.

The general rule is, that as to third persons the principal is liable for the acts of his agent done within the general scope of his authority, and that such authority may be general, though limited to a particular business.

"The extent of the agent's authority may be shown by the terms of the appointment, if they are explicit, or it may be shown by a course of dealing by which the agent is held out as having an authority which would include the act in question."

"False and fraudulent representations by an agent may affect the principal because he has expressly or impliedly authorized representations to be made by the agent and the latter made false and fraudulent ones."

So that after all, the question of whether the agent acted within the scope (implied or apparent) of his employment is to be gathered from all the facts and circumstances in evidence and is a question of fact for the jury.

It has been held that a vendor of real estate, seeking to enforce contract made by his agent, is bound by representations to purchaser made by his agent, though not himself having knowledge thereof.

Where, in the sale of real estate, certain facts are accessible to the vendor only, and he knows that such facts cannot, by reasonable diligence, observation, and judgment, exercised by the vendee, be ascertained, the vendor is bound to disclose the facts.

As a general proposition a principal is not responsible for the deceit practiced by his agent, unless there is something in the nature of the engagement, the terms of employment, or the powers conferred, broad enough to include a power on the part of the agent to deal with the property in such manner that the principal, in good morals and equity, ought to be bound by what the agent may have said.

Liability for Agent's Warranties

The courts are not in complete accord as to the scope of a selling agent's implied authority to warrant the goods sold. If the warranty made by the agent does not go beyond the warranty implied by law in such sales, the courts are unanimous in holding that the principal will be bound by the express warranty of the agent. If Peters appoints Archer his agent and authorizes Archer to sell Peters' horse and Archer sells the horse to Trent expressly warranting that the title to the horse is clear and free from liens, Peters will be bound by the warranty. The law implies a warranty of title in any sale unless such warranty is expressly excluded. The same rule applies to the implied warranties in sales by description, sales by samples, implied warranty of suitability, and implied warranty of merchantability.

The principal will not be bound by an extraordinary warranty made by the agent without authority. In the foregoing case if Archer warranted that the horse would win not less than $60,000 in purses during the racing season, Peters would not be bound by the warranty. The warranty does not go to the quality of the horse and is extraordinary in nature.

Between these two extremes the courts are not in complete accord. The test generally applied is whether or not it is customary to make similar warranties in the sale of such goods in the market in which the goods are sold. In effect the test is one of usage of trade. If it is customary, in the market in which the goods are sold, to make the warranty made by the agent, the principal will be bound by it, otherwise, he will not. The third person will not be bound by secret limitations on the agent's authority or secret instructions given to the agent. However, the third person will be bound by such limitations or instructions if he has notice or knowledge of them.

Fulwiler v. Lawrence et al.
Ct. of Civ. App. of Tex. 7 S.W. (2d) 636 (1928)

This was an action by W. J. Fulwiler (plaintiff) against G. N. Lawrence and another (defendants) in which defendants filed a cross action. Judgment for defendants and plaintiff appealed. Judgment affirmed.

Fulwiler's agent, King, sold Lawrence and Craig a Fordson tractor. Lawrence and Craig wished to use the tractor to break new land. King warranted the tractor to do the work in a satisfactory manner. The tractor did not do the work satisfactorily. Fulwiler claimed King had no authority to warrant the tractor.

Hickman, C. J. The other group of propositions present in various ways the question of the authority of an agent employed by a dealer to sell personal property manufactured for a particular purpose to bind his principal by representations and warranties that the article to be sold is suitable for the purpose for which it is purchased. It is the contention of appellant that his agent had no authority, either express or implied to bind him in the manner alleged by appellees. Appellant offered evidence, which was excluded by the court, but which, if admitted, would have established the want of any express authority on the part of the agent thus to bind him. The question, thus narrowed down, is whether appellant's agent, King, had the implied authority to bind him by the representations and warranties made by the agent to appellees.

In the case of *Norvell-Wilder Hdwe. Co.* v. *McCamey*, 290 S.W. 772, this court reviewed the authorities upon this question, and announced the conclusion that, where goods are purchased for a particular purpose known to the seller at the time of the sale, a warranty of soundness and suitability will be implied. We need not again cite the authorities therein cited. The same rule is announced and applied by the Commission in *Turner et al.* v. *Shackelford,* 288 S.W. 815. Applying this rule to the instant case, it is our opinion that, since appellant had knowledge through his agent of the particular use for which the tractor was purchased, he impliedly contracted that the tractor was suitable for that particular use. That implication would have arisen in the absence of an express representation. Certain it is that an agent has the implied authority to make a warranty which does not impose any greater liability upon his principal than that which would have been imposed by law in the absence of an express warranty. This proposition is self-evident, but, if any authority is desired, reference may be held to the case of *H. B. Smith Co.* v. *Williams et al.*, 29 Ind. App. 363, 63 N.E. 318.

Even though it may be said that the express warranty of the agent exceeded in some degree the implied warranty which would have existed in the absence of such express warranty, still we are of the opinion that the agent was impliedly authorized to make such express warranty. When an article is manufactured for a particular purpose, a dealer naturally expects his agent to make known that purpose, and to make known to prospective purchasers that the article can be safely used for that purpose. It follows that, where the agent does that which is expected to be done, and without which sales could not be made, the principal impliedly authorizes him so to do. This rule has particular application to manufactured articles and machinery about which the purchaser is not informed and the dealer is presumed to have superior information.

Johnson v. City Company of New York, Inc.
78 F. (2d) 782 (1935)

This was an action by A. E. Johnson (plaintiff) against the City Company of New York (defendant). Judgment for defendant and plaintiff appealed. Judgment affirmed.

November 1, 1929, the manager of defendant's Denver office sold plaintiff 200 shares of capital stock of the National City Bank of New York at $450 per share and as a part of the sale warranted that by November 4—three days thereafter—the market price of the stock would be $650. The price of the stock dropped and on November 6 plaintiff sold 100 shares for $295 a share and on the next day sold the remaining shares at $270 a share.

Plaintiff brings suit for damages for breach of warranty. Defendant claims that it is not liable on the ground that it was not bound by the warranty because its agent had no authority to make the warranty.

Bratton, C. J. The warranty in suit was given by the manager in charge of defendant's office in Denver. He was a general agent, but there was no proof that he had authority to give a warranty of that kind and the burden was on plaintiff to establish such authority. A general agent may not transcend the scope of the usual course of the business intrusted to him. Authority to warrant that stock can be sold at a specified price on a fixed day in the future cannot be implied from a general agency to conduct a brokerage business and there was no evidence tending to show that it was the custom for the manager to do so; in fact, it was not shown that he had ever done so on any other occasion. But plaintiff urges that defendant cannot retain the benefits of the transaction and at the same time repudiate the authority of its agent to make it. That general doctrine applies where the principal has not changed his position between the time he receives the benefits and the time he acquires knowledge of the unauthorized act. Of course, if a principal receives benefits and before changing his position learns of the unauthorized collateral provision in the contract, his retention of the benefits constitutes ratification of the ultra vires act, but there is nothing here to indicate that defendant acquired knowledge of the agent's unauthorized act intermediate receipt of the benefits and a change of its position; and it was incumbent upon plaintiff to establish those facts in order to avail himself of the principle of law upon which he depends.

Payment of Debt to Agent

The fact that an agent has negotiated a transaction does not, as a matter of law, confer on the agent the authority to collect. Such authority arises when it is the usual and reasonable incident of the business to be transacted. As in other cases, it may be shown that the agent has express, implied, or apparent authority to collect, but as a general rule authority to sell does not confer on the agent authority to collect or receive payment. A sales agent who has authority to solicit orders for future delivery does not thereby have the authority to collect the purchase price of the goods. However, it is generally held that, if the selling agent has possession of the goods, he has implied authority to collect the purchase price of goods sold. Also, it is generally held that an agent making over-the-counter sales has authority to collect. Usage of trade, course of dealing, or the acts of the principal may confer on the agent authority to collect.

Possession of an instrument, evidencing the debt, is strong, yet not conclusive evidence of authority to collect. Archer is acting as selling agent for Peters. Peters gives Archer a statement of Trent's account which is due. The fact that Archer has, and presents to Trent, a statement of his account is evidence of Archer's authority to collect. This evidence could be overcome by showing facts which would clearly indicate that Archer was not authorized to collect, but in the absence of such facts payment to Archer will discharge the debt.

As a general rule, if an agent has negotiated a loan, a sale of property, or other similar business and the agent is allowed to retain the possession of the written security, which fact is known to the debtor, the agent has apparent authority to collect. Conversely, if the written security is not left in the possession of the agent, he does not have apparent authority to collect. Also, the receipt of interest payments tends to establish the agent's authority to collect. If the debtor is paying a debt before due, he should make careful inquiry as to an agent's authority to collect. Payment before the due date is the exception in most business transactions and the debtor does not have the advantage of having made payment in the usual course of business.

Schaeffer Bros. & Powell Mfg. Co. v. Williams
St. Louis Ct. of App. Mo. 52 S.W. (2d) 457 (1932)

This was an action by Schaeffer Bros. & Powell Manufacturing Company (plaintiff) against A. L. Williams (defendant). Judgment for defendant and plaintiff appealed. Judgment reversed and remanded.

Plaintiff was a manufacturer of motor oils, greases, and the like. Defendant was engaged in retailing oils and greases to the general public. Defendant had purchased oils and greases from plaintiff for several months and, in accordance with the agreed credit terms, paid before the 10th of each month for the goods purchased during the preceding month. Defendant made payment to plaintiff by mailing his check to plaintiff's office. Both plaintiff and defendant were doing business in St. Louis. With a few exceptions, all of the goods purchased by defendant were purchased through one Chappell, plaintiff's city salesman.

There was an error in the June statement and defendant called plaintiff's office over the telephone and plaintiff's credit manager told defendant that he would have Mr. Chappell or one of their representatives call and adjust the matter. Mr. Chappell called, adjusted the error, and requested defendant to draw the check payable to him instead of making it payable to Schaeffer Bros. & Powell Mfg. Co. Defendant drew the check payable to "A. R. Chappell for Schaeffer Bros. & Powell Mfg. Co." Chappell cashed the check and appropriated the funds to his own use. Shortly thereafter Chappell died. On defendant's refusal to pay, plaintiff brought this suit.

Bennick, C. The fact of Chappell's agency to sell is of course admitted; and there is no dispute about his acceptance of the check from defendant and his subsequent appropriation of the proceeds thereof. In the final analysis, therefore, the vital issue between the parties is one of the implied or apparent authority of Chappell to have received payment on plaintiff's account so as to have warranted defendant, acting in good faith and with reasonable prudence, in having drawn the check in favor of Chappell personally, and in having turned the same over to him. We say the issue is one of Chappell's implied or apparent authority, for defendant admits in his brief that there was no evidence of his express authority to have made collection.

The general rule of law is that a sales agent, who sells goods on credit, and is not intrusted by his principal with the possession of the goods to be sold, has no implied authority to receive payment from the mere fact of his power to sell; and that, if the purchaser of the goods makes payment to the agent, he does so at his peril, and it will devolve upon him, in an action by the principal for the purchase price, to prove that the agent was clothed with authority, either direct or apparent, to have received payment on the part of his principal.

Defendant testified that on two occasions prior to the submission of the statement of the June, 1929, account, he had bought certain small orders of oil from Chappell, and had paid him for the purchases. However, on both such occasions, Chappell had the oils in his actual possession, and the transactions were on a cash rather than a credit basis; and consequently defendant was warranted in paying Chappell personally under such circumstances, as we have heretofore pointed out, though those transactions could not be regarded as the basis of any estoppel on the part of plaintiff to dispute Chappell's authority to accept payment by check or otherwise on purchases on credit for which defendant was to be billed at the 1st of the following month.

Indeed, plaintiff's evidence was that the particular oils were Chappell's own property which he sold in the course of his own private business which he conducted aside from his agency for plaintiff, to all of which defendant's answer was that he was under the impression that the oils came from plaintiff, since they were in the same sort of containers as in the case of other shipments in the past.

Plaintiff's own evidence admitted the fact that Chappell possessed the same authority as its other salesmen, and that the salesmen sometimes picked up customers' checks made payable to plaintiff itself and turned them in to the office; but there was no showing whatsoever that Chappell, or any other salesman, ever took a check made payable to himself in payment of an account for merchandise sold by plaintiff on a credit basis.

For an agent's authority to do a given thing to be inferred or implied from the agent's previous conduct and the principal's acquiescence therein, the acts relied upon as establishing the scope of the agency by implication must be of like character to that which gives rise to the controversy.

In view of such limitation upon the length to which the doctrine of implied agency may be extended, it cannot be said that the occasional practice of plaintiff's agents in picking up checks made payable to plaintiff warranted defendant in believing that Chappell possessed the authority to bind his principal by accepting a check on a credit transaction made payable to himself and subject to be cashed by him. Consequently it follows that, for want of evidence upon this feature of the case, defendant's plea of payment must be held to have failed as a matter of law, leaving him liable to plaintiff on the account notwithstanding the fact of his payment to Chappell.

If the result seems harsh, it is to be remembered that defendant was fully aware that he was proceeding out of the ordinary; that he admitted that Chappell requested the payment to be made to him in this particular instance because of difficulties he was having with his principal; that defendant did not see fit to call plaintiff's office, as he might easily have done, to ascertain if payment to Chappell would be accepted by plaintiff; and that he himself was doubtful of the propriety of what he was about to do, and did not make out the check in Chappell's favor until he had first consulted with an acquaintance of his relative to the legal effect of payment made in that manner.

Pledging of Principal's Credit

The agent, in the absence of express authority, will not have authority to purchase on the principal's credit. This rule is not absolute. If the agency is general and if in order to carry out the purposes of the agency it becomes necessary for the agent to borrow money or purchase goods on the principal's credit, the principal will be bound. If the principal has held the agent out as having authority to borrow money or purchase goods on his credit or has knowingly permitted the agent to borrow money or purchase goods on his credit, the principal will be bound.

If the agent is authorized to purchase goods and is furnished money by the principal with which to make the purchase, and if the third person accepts the personal check of the agent in payment of the goods, the third person cannot recover from the principal if the check is not honored. If the agent is authorized to purchase goods, but is not furnished the money with which to pay for the goods, the agent will have implied authority to purchase on the credit of the principal.

C. L. Gray Lumber Co. v. Shubuta Motor Co.
169 Miss. 393, 153 So. 155 (1934)

This was an action by the Shubuta Motor Company (plaintiff) against the C. L. Gray Lumber Company (defendant). Judgment for plaintiff and defendant appealed. Judgment reversed.

This was a suit on a promissory note and open account. The defendant's main office was at Meridian, Miss., and it owned and operated a planing mill and commissary at Hiwanee, Miss. It also owned standing timber near Hiwanee. The defendant entered into a contract with E. L. Wetherbee to manage and operate its planing mill and commissary; to cut its timber, saw it into lumber at a mill owned by Wetherbee, to deliver the lumber so sawed to the planing mill, where it would be planed and disposed of as the defendant should direct. The expense of operating the planing mill was to be paid by the defendant, but the expense of cutting, sawing, and delivering the lumber to the planing mill was to be borne by Wetherbee. For this Wetherbee's compensation was to be $100 per month and "so much per thousand feet" (the amount of which does not appear) for the lumber delivered at the planing mill. There was a sign at the commissary reading "Wayne Lumber Company."

Wetherbee purchased an automobile truck for use in hauling timber to his mill and lumber therefrom to the planing mill, and gave a promissory note therefor, the signature to which was "Wayne Lumber Company, by E. L. Wetherbee." He also purchased a lot of automobile supplies and parts which constitute the account sued on. Wetherbee had no express, and defendant did not hold him out as having, authority to purchase trucks and accessories therefor on its credit, unless such a holding out can be inferred from the facts hereinbefore stated. Wetherbee died before the trial, and the defendant did not know that the plaintiff looked to it for payment for the automobile and supplies therefor until after his death.

Smith, C. J. Under his contract Wetherbee was the defendant's agent for the management and control of its commissary and planing mill. The commissary may be left out of view as the debts sued on were not contracted in connection therewith. As to the cutting and delivering of the timber to the mill, he was an independent contractor, but we will assume that persons dealing with him under the circumstances had the right to assume that his agency covered the latter as well as the former. In other words, that he was the apparent agent of the defendant as to the cutting and hauling of the timber. He had no express authority to contract debts, of the character here sued on, on the credit of the defendant, and the only manifestation of assent by the defendant to exercise authority in excess of that expressly conferred is such as is implied by his appointment to manage and control the planing mill, which we will assume apparently included the cutting of the timber and its delivery to the planing mill. There being no evidence of any custom or usage to the contrary, Wetherbee's apparent authority was such only as can be implied from his real and apparent appointment as the defendant's manager for the above-stated purpose. "The words 'manage' and 'manager' are not of precise legal import. It is consistent with the idea of management that some one else shall determine plans and policies which the manager is to execute." Whether a manager of a business has implied authority to purchase supplies and equipment therefor on the owner's credit depends on the character of the business and custom and usage relative thereto. In the absence of custom and usage, the line of demarcation between when such authority will be implied and when it will not is frequently close.

The successful management of a planing mill for another does not necessarily require authority in the manager to purchase—leaving emergencies out of view—supplies and equipment therefor. So to do may properly rest with the owner. The manager of a retail store, as such, may or may not have such authority, although he may be expressly authorized to purchase for cash. The answer to the question depends on the character of the business. The manager of a plantation, employed "to manage and control it as their (the owner's) agent and to cultivate it for their account," has no such implied authority.

The court below should have granted the defendant's request for a directed verdict.

Liability on Negotiable Instruments

The negotiable instrument is given a separate and distinct place in the business world. This situation results in the creation of some problems in the law of agency which warrant special consideration. The nature of a negotiable instrument and the liabilities of the parties to a negotiable instrument are such that the authority to sign or indorse negotiable instruments is granted sparingly. The courts hold that the express authority to sign or indorse negotiable instruments must be strictly pursued and, if an agent is expressly authorized to sign or indorse negotiable instruments, the authority must be confined to those transactions which benefit the principal. Peters authorizes Archer to sign and indorse negotiable instruments as his agent. Archer draws a negotiable promissory note for $100 making it payable to himself (Archer) and negotiates it to Trent and absconds with the money. In the absence of special circumstances Peters will not be bound. Trent is put on notice by the form of the instrument that Archer is exceeding his authority. An agent authorized to sign or indorse negotiable instruments is not authorized to sign or indorse a negotiable instrument as surety.

An agent may have implied authority to sign or indorse negotiable instruments in his principal's name, but such authority is not lightly implied. It must appear that the signing or indorsing of negotiable instruments is necessary to the transaction of the business intrusted to the agent. If the agent can perform his duties without signing or indorsing negotiable instruments, no authority to sign or indorse will be implied. Possession of the instrument does not imply authority to indorse, and authority to collect does not imply authority to indorse negotiable instruments given in payment. An authorization "to transact any and all business" does not imply authority to sign or indorse negotiable instruments unless such acts are essential to the carrying on of the business intrusted to the agent.

An agent may have apparent authority to sign or indorse negotiable instruments; however, it must be clearly shown that the principal had knowledge of the acts of the agent which gave rise to the appearance of authority. It has been held that the fact that the agent had signed or indorsed negotiable instruments in the past, that this was known to the principal and that the principal honored the signature without objection, is sufficient to establish apparent authority to sign or indorse negotiable instruments.

The fact that the agent is given a special title is not sufficient in and of itself to create apparent authority to sign or indorse negotiable instruments. The fact that one is president, manager, secretary, treasurer, or cashier of a corporation does not establish authority to sign or indorse negotiable instruments in the name of the corporation. Usage of trade or course of dealing may be sufficient to establish such authority. It is generally held that a partner has apparent authority to sign or indorse negotiable instruments in the firm name.

Merchants' & Manufacturers' Ass'n. v. First National Bank of Mesa
40 Ariz. 531, 14 P. (2d) 717 (1932)

This was an action by the Merchants' & Manufacturers' Association (plaintiff) against First National Bank of Mesa, Arizona (defendant). Judgment for defendant and plaintiff appealed. Judgment reversed and remanded with directions.

The plaintiff was engaged in the general collection and credit and mercantile reporting business with its principal office in Phoenix. Nachtweih was local manager of plaintiff's office in Mesa and was authorized to solicit business, make collections, to accept checks therefor, and to indorse the checks for deposit with defendant for plaintiff's account. Before opening the Mesa office plaintiff wrote defendant confirming an earlier telephone conversation in which arrangements were made for opening an account with defendant, inclosing a signature card, and notifying defendant that all checks drawn on the account would be signed "Merchants' & Manufacturers' Association By D. M. Gillan Secretary," and stating that no one else was authorized to sign checks or do anything with the funds. The letter stated that Nachtweih "will not handle the finances."

Nachtweih deposited checks drawn payable to plaintiff which he indorsed for deposit in the plaintiff's name. Three checks indorsed by Nachtweih in plaintiff's name were deposited in Nachtweih's personal account and the proceeds were used by Nachtweih. During the trial of the case defendant's cashier testified that he never received the letter referred to above.

Ross, J. If the drawee of the check pays it, or anyone else, bank or individual, in the course of business takes it with an unauthorized or forged indorsement, it is at the risk of having to make it good to the payee. If the payee, as was the case here, is a corporation, the check can be indorsed only by an authorized agent of the corporation. The business world, and more especially the banking world, knows that corporations can act only by and through agents, and it also knows, or should know, that the mere fact that a person is in possession of a check payable to the order of a corporation is not proof of his right to indorse it. On the contrary, it is put upon notice that the check and its proceeds belong to the corporation and that the possessor may or may not have authority to indorse it. In such circumstances, common prudence would dictate an inquiry and investigation into the authority of such person to indorse the check before paying it or accepting it in trade. "The well-settled rule" is "that authority to collect does not imply authority to indorse negotiable paper received in payment." It is also a "well-established rule that the authority of an agent to indorse negotiable paper is a very responsible power, not lightly to be presumed or implied."

Mechem, in his learned work on Agency, says the power to indorse negotiable paper "can exist only when it has been directly conferred or is warranted by necessary implication."

In 2 Corpus Juris, 636, § 280, the rule is stated as follows: "Commercial paper, such as bills, notes, and checks, passes current to a limited extent like money, and accordingly power to an agent to execute or indorse it is to be strictly limited, and will never be lightly inferred, but ordinarily must be conferred expressly."

In view of the information conveyed to defendant in a letter as to limits of Nachtweih's right to indorse paper for plaintiff, the indiscriminate cashing of plaintiff's checks on the indorsement of Nachtweih was a reckless disregard of the bank's duty to the plaintiff, for which under the law it should be made to account as for money had and received. The rule is that one who accepts in good faith a check from an agent who has authority to make in form a general indorsement, but is required to deposit the proceeds to the credit of the principal, obtains a good title to the check although the agent misappropriates the proceeds. But if the limited authority to indorse for deposit to the principal's account is known to one accepting paper, he is bound by such knowledge. It is said in 2 Corpus Juris 569, § 210: "Instructions modifying or limiting the authority of the agent, which are known to a person dealing with him, are as binding upon such person as they are upon the agent, and he can acquire no rights against the principal by dealing with the agent contrary thereto. . . . . If specific instructions are brought home to the knowledge of a third person dealing with the agent it cannot matter whether he is a general or a special agent; in either case his power to bind his principal will be limited by these known instructions or limitations."

Notice to or Knowledge of Agent

As a general rule, the knowledge of an agent is binding on the principal in so far as it concerns the business which is being transacted by the agent. Two reasons are given for this rule. Some courts base it on the conception of the legal identity of the principal and agent, while others prefer to base it on the duty of the agent to communicate to the principal all material matters connected with business transacted for the principal. The rule is also supported by public policy. If a contrary rule were adopted, the failure of the agent to communicate knowledge to the principal would result in injury to the innocent third person. If one wishes to employ an agent, the one employing the agent should bear the burden of the agent's negligence, not the innocent third person.

Under this rule the knowledge of the agent is imputed to the principal; hence, the principal's knowledge is constructive, not actual. The principal could not be held criminally liable if knowledge is an essential element of the crime and the agent has not communicated the fact to the principal and the principal does not have actual knowledge.

The rule does not apply in those situations in which it is clear that the agent would not communicate the knowledge to his principal. The courts have held that if the agent's interests conflict with the interests of the principal and the agent's interests will be furthered by not communicating a fact to the principal, the principal will not be bound by the knowledge of the agent. If, however, an innocent third person will be injured if the principal is not bound by the uncommunicated knowledge of the agent, the courts will hold that the principal is bound. If the agent and the third person collusively or fraudulently withhold knowledge from the principal, the principal will not be bound.

The principal will not be bound by the knowledge of the agent unless the matters known to the agent are material and come to the agent from a reliable source. The agent is not expected to carry to his principal every idle rumor and every detailed fact coming to his notice. Neither is the principal bound by knowledge of the agent of matters entirely outside the scope of the agent's authority and in no way related to business transacted by the agent. This rule includes knowledge coming to an employee hired to perform ministerial acts. Peters hires Elder to drive a delivery truck for him. Elder knows that there is an unrecorded chattel mortgage in favor of Martin on a truck which Peters is purchasing from Trent. If Peters purchases the truck, he will be an innocent purchaser for value; Elder's knowledge of the existence of the unrecorded chattel mortgage will not be imputed to Peters.

Knowledge of the agent includes those things of which he has been given notice during the course of the negotiation of a transaction and those things which, by the exercise of reasonable prudence, he would have learned. Whether or not knowledge gained by the agent in prior transactions not transacted for the principal will be imputed to the principal depends entirely on the circumstances of the case. If it appears that knowledge of certain material facts, learned during the transaction of earlier unrelated business, were present in the mind of the agent and were used to the advantage of the principal, the principal will be bound by such knowledge. Substantially the same rule applies to knowledge gained in earlier business transacted for the principal. If the agency is a continuous agency—for example, the manager of a store—knowledge of the agent gained in earlier transactions will be imputed to the principal if under the circumstances the agent should have such knowledge in mind at a later time when he negotiates business for his principal. Knowledge gained by an agent after the agency has been terminated is not imputed to the principal unless the agency is a continuing agency. In such a case the principal will be bound by notice given to the agent by a third person who has customarily dealt with the agent and who, at the time of giving the notice, had no notice or knowledge of the termination of the agency.

People ex rel. Carr, County Collector v. Gullborg.
324 Ill. 538, 155 N.E. 324 (1927)

This was a tax proceeding brought by the people on the relation of P. J. Carr, County Collector (plaintiff) against John S. Gullborg (defendant). Judgment for plaintiff and defendant appealed. Judgment reversed.

Thompson, J. This appeal is from a judgment of the county court of Cook County overruling objections to taxes extended against an apartment building at 1549 Fargo Avenue, Chicago, and ordering a sale of the property.

The property was valued by the board of assessors in 1924 at $103,750, but the board of review reduced the valuation to $80,250. In 1925 the board of assessors continued the valuation of $80,250, but the board of review raised it to $110,250. Appellant paid the taxes based on a full valuation of $80,250 and filed objections to the balance on the ground that he had not received notice of the hearing before the board of review and that it was without jurisdiction to increase the valuation. The records of the board of review show that notice of the hearing was sent to George P. Adams. Appellant testified that he is a manufacturer and that Adams is employed in his office; that in 1925 Adams occupied one of the apartments in his building at 1549 Fargo Avenue and was authorized to receive the rent from the other tenants; that Adams was not a leasing agent nor an agent having general supervision of his property; and that his authority to represent him was limited to receiving the rent and delivering it to him at his office. Appellant lived at 4628 Beacon Street, Chicago, and his tax bill was mailed to him at that address. Notice of the hearing was not received by him through the mail nor was it delivered to him by Adams or any one else.

The law is well settled that, when notice to an agent is relied upon to bind a principal, the nature of the agency must be such that the law will presume that the agent carried the notice to his principal, or it must be established as a fact that the agent did communicate to his principal such notice. Notice to or knowledge of an agent while acting within the scope of his authority and in reference to a matter over which his authority extends is notice to or knowledge of the principal, but, in order to be binding upon the principal, the knowledge must be acquired while his agent is acting within the scope of his authority and in reference to a matter over which his authority extends. Conceding that Adams received the notice of the hearing before the board of review, it was not binding upon appellant because it was not a matter over which Adams' authority extended.

Ohio Millers' Mutual Insurance Co. v. Artesia State Bank.
39 F. (2d) 400 (1930)

This was an action by the Ohio Millers' Mutual Insurance Company (plaintiff) against Artesia State Bank (defendant). Judgment for defendant and plaintiff appealed. Judgment reversed and remanded.

The plaintiff sued the defendant upon a certificate of deposit issued by the defendant and purchased by the plaintiff. When sued the defendant set up as a defense that it had been induced by fraud to purchase $5,000 of the bonds of the Integrity Mutual Casualty Company and that the certificate of deposit was given in payment. The principal defense of the defendant was that at the time the plaintiff purchased the certificate of deposit it had knowledge or notice of the fraud.

The bonds were purchased by the defendant from J. C. Adderly, Inc., an insurance management corporation. J. C. Adderly, Inc., sold the certificate of deposit before its maturity and for face value plus interest to the plaintiff. At the time of the transaction J. C. Adderly was president of all three corporations—J. C. Adderly, Inc., which sold the bonds; Integrity Mutual Casualty Co., which issued the bonds; and Ohio Millers' Mutual Insurance Company (plaintiff), which purchased the certificate of deposit. The three corporations also had the same vice-president, secretary-treasurer, and general counsel. The two insurance companies had different boards of directors and different policy holders.

Adderly had no knowledge of the fraud committed in the sale of the bonds to the defendant. The plaintiff had nothing to do with the sale of the bonds to the defendant or with any representations made by Adderly or his company. Adderly as president of plaintiff approved of the purchase of the certificate of deposit. The record does not show that plaintiff's treasurer or any of its directors had knowledge of the fraud.

Grubb, D. J. If notice is charged to plaintiff, it must be through the undoubted knowledge that its president Adderly had of any such fraud at the time he participated in the purchase of the certificate of deposit by the plaintiff from his company, at least to the extent of approving it. Knowledge of an agent is ordinarily notice to his principal. The exceptions to this general rule are two-fold. When the interest of the agent is adverse to that of his principal in such a way as that the agent will be presumed to conceal his knowledge from his principal and not to disclose it to him, the rule does not apply. Also, when the knowledge of the agent is not acquired while acting in the course of his employment for his principal, it does not bind the principal. The principal is not chargeable with notice of facts within the knowledge of his agent, when the latter acquired such knowledge while acting as agent for another. The two exceptions are so well settled as not to require citation of authority.

Applying them to the facts of this case, Adderly's interest in the transaction of the sale of the certificate of deposit to plaintiff was adverse to it. If he knew his title to the investment was infected by its fraudulent acquisition, it was to his interest to conceal this knowledge from the plaintiff, since disclosing it would defeat a sale of the instrument to plaintiff, which Adderly desired to make for his company. It would be presumed, and the fact was, that he would make no disclosure of the fraudulent acquisition of the instrument by him to the plaintiff, though he was its president, since this would defeat his attempt to sell it to plaintiff. Again, the knowledge that Adderly acquired of the fraud was acquired while he was acting as president of the Adderly Company, which owned and sold the bonds to defendant, and not as president of the plaintiff, which had no connection with or interest in the sale of the bonds.

The defendant contends that there are exceptions to the exceptions which bring this case back to the general rule.

First, that as between two innocent parties, he must suffer who clothed the guilty party with power to commit the fraud. The plaintiff in this case did not clothe Adderly with the power to defraud the defendant. It had nothing to do with the bonds of the Integrity Company or their sale to the defendant. It only bought the defendant's certificate of deposit, and in that transaction there was no fraud. It was the Integrity Company and the Adderly Company, either or both, that clothed Adderly with the power to defraud defendant, and not the plaintiff.

Second. Nor did the plaintiff and defendant consent that Adderly should be their mutual agent. The plaintiff had nothing to do with the defendant's purchase of the Integrity bonds, the transaction in which the alleged fraud was committed, and Adderly was not an agent of plaintiff in that transaction. Knowledge of the fraud, then acquired, would not be notice to plaintiff in the subsequent transaction, relating to the purchase of the certificate of deposit, in which Adderly did represent both the buyer and seller of the certificate of deposit. The defendant was not a party to the subsequent transaction, and Adderly was not its agent therein.

Third. Adderly's interest was not balanced between his company and the plaintiff. His endeavor to pass to the plaintiff the certificate of deposit, without disclosing the infirmity of his title to it, is conclusive of where he regarded his interest to lie.

Fourth. Nor was Adderly the sole representative of the plaintiff in acquiring the certificate of deposit for it. His function was limited to approval of Ott's act by the very terms of the resolution of plaintiff's directors. It was Ott who had the authority to make the investment, and it was Ott who did so by signing the check that paid for the certificate. Ott testified that a finance committee also approved the investment, probably in advance, and the minutes of a later meeting of the directors show that Ott reported the investment as having been made by him and approved by Adderly, and the directors approved it by acquiescence in the report. The evidence tended to show that Ott, the finance committee, and the directors, as well as Adderly, represented plaintiff in the acquisition of the certificate.

Fifth. The defendant also relies upon the identity in interest of the three corporations, all of which it asserts were controlled by Adderly, to impute to all three the knowledge of Adderly, regardless of in whose business it was acquired.

In this case, the ownership in the three corporations was entirely different. While the insurance features were conducted by the same management corporation, and all the corporations had the same officers, the corporate business and financing were conducted by different and apparently independent directors at different localities, and the ownership in all three corporations was entirely distinct, the dominant person having no beneficial interest in either of the mutual insurance companies.

Our conclusion is that the District Court erred in charging the jury that Adderly's knowledge of the fraud alleged to have been committed upon the defendant by him was notice to the plaintiff of the infirmity in the title of the Adderly Company to the certificate of deposit.

Torts of the Agent

The rule that the principal is liable for the torts of his agent or employee which are committed in the course of and within the scope of the employment is universally recognized by the courts. This rule is based on the ancient theory of respondant superior, and the only question is whether or not at the time the agent or employee committed the tort was he acting within the scope of and in the course of his employment. The principal cannot escape liability by showing that the agent or employee was acting contrary to express instructions at the time he committed the tort. If the principal is sued in tort for the fraud or deceit of his agent, he can escape liability if he can show that the third person knew that the agent was not authorized to make the representations on which the suit is based.

The principal is liable for the wilful and malicious torts of an agent or employee if the acts are within the scope of and in the course of the employment.

Peters employs Archer to drive Peters' delivery truck and make deliveries for Peters. While making a delivery Archer sees Trent, against whom Archer holds a grudge. Archer drives the delivery truck against Trent and injures him. Peters is liable to Trent. If, instead of driving the truck against Trent, Archer had parked the truck and accosted and injured Trent by striking him, Peters would not be liable to Trent. Archer, in parking the truck and leaving it for the purpose of striking Trent, has abandoned his employment and his acts are not in the course of or within the scope of his employment.

The principal may ratify the torts of the agent either expressly or by implication. If the principal ratifies an unauthorized transaction in which a tortious act occurred, the principal will be liable for the tort. The rule that, if the principal ratifies an unauthorized transaction, he must ratify it in its entirety is broad enough in its application to include torts committed in the course of the transaction.

Snow v. De Butts et al.
212 N.C. 120, 193 S.E. 224 (1937)

This was an action by Joe A. Snow (plaintiff) against Sydnor De Butts and another (defendants). Judgment for plaintiff and defendant, the Atlantic & Yadkin Railway Company, appealed. Judgment as against the Atlantic & Yadkin Railway Company reversed.

Plaintiff was a mail carrier on the line of the corporate defendant and defendant De Butts was its general manager.

In May, 1931, the corporate defendant petitioned the Corporation Commission of North Carolina to be allowed to discontinue certain passenger trains, then being operated by it. There were a number of hearings before the commission, and the plaintiff as a citizen of Mt. Airy appeared and opposed the petition.

On the evening of May 16, 1933, plaintiff went to the station of the corporate defendant to meet a friend, and, while waiting for the arrival of the train, a controversy arose between him and the defendant De Butts, and the plaintiff was abused, insulted, and assaulted by said defendant. There was ample evidence to sustain the verdict against the defendant De Butts, and he did not appeal.

The jury having found by its verdict that the defendant De Butts at time of said assault was acting within the scope of his employment as general manager of the Atlantic & Yadkin Railway Company, judgment was entered against said defendant and the Atlantic & Yadkin Railway Company appealed.

Barnhill, J. The one question we need to discuss on this appeal is the liability of the appealing defendant on the judgment rendered against the individual defendant. If De Butts was not acting within the scope of his employment and in furtherance of his master's business at the time of his assault upon the plaintiff, this question must be answered in the negative and the other exceptive assignments of error become immaterial.

The plaintiff described the setting of the assault in substance as follows: "I was standing right near the mail wagon; others were present; I was waiting there for Mr. Brower. Someone said in a humorous way, that perhaps the train had been discontinued. The defendant De Butts was present. Someone asked the question: 'Do you think the trains will be taken off?' I replied, that I did not think they would, because it was too important to the public from the standpoint of mail, express and passenger service. About that time De Butts approached me and said: 'Mr. Snow, when are you going to get your promotion?' I said: I am not going to get it. He said: 'You said you were going to be made chief clerk; you said it, didn't you?' I said: Yes, I thought I was going to get it, but another man got it. He said: 'Why didn't you get it?' I said: Another man got it. He says: 'I know why you didn't get it; you lied to the Corporation Commission; you lied to the Legislature.' I said: Mr. De Butts, there is no reason why we should have any personal ill-will towards each other. I have nothing against you. I did what I did simply because I thought it was my duty and I presume you did the same. He replied: 'You are a G. D. liar. You are interfering with my business. I am trying to save money for the company and it is none of your business. . . . .'" The plaintiff then outlined the abusive language and conduct of the defendant De Butts, which amounted to an assault.

There is no hard and fast rule governing the application of the doctrine of respondeat superior. The application of the doctrine depends upon the facts in the case under consideration. There are, however, certain general rules established by the decisions of this and other courts which govern its application.

A principal is liable for the torts of his agent (1) when expressly authorized; (2) when committed within the scope of his employment and in furtherance of his master's business—when the act comes within his implied authority; (3) when ratified by the principal.

There is no contention in this case that the conduct of De Butts was expressly authorized, or that it was thereafter ratified by his employer. If the corporate defendant is liable at all, it is by reason of the fact that De Butts was acting within the line of his duty and exercising functions necessarily implied by the general nature of his employment; that is, he was acting within the range of his employment.

The principles requiring the application of the doctrine are variously expressed.

It is elementary that the principal is liable for the acts of his agent, whether malicious or negligent, and the master for similar acts of his servant, which result in injury to third persons, when the agent or servant is acting within the line of his duty and exercising the functions of his employment.

If the wrongdoer, while acting in the range of his authority, does an act which injures another, the principal or master is liable therefor without reference to whether the intent of the agent or servant was good or bad, innocent or malicious.

Liability exists as against the master for wrongful or negligent acts of his servant only when the agent is acting within the scope of his employment and is about his master's business, attempting to do what he was employed to do.

"A servant is acting in the course of his employment when he is engaged in that which he was employed to do and is at the time about his master's business. He is not acting in the course of his employment if he is engaged in some pursuit of his own. Not every deviation from the strict execution of his duty is such an interruption of the course of employment as to suspend the master's responsibility, but if there is a total departure from the course of the master's business the master is no longer answerable for the servant's conduct."

A principal is liable for assaults committed by its agent or servant only when the assault is committed while the agent or servant is about his master's business and acting within the range of his employment, unless his conduct was thereafter ratified by the principal.

On the other hand, there are pertinent decisions holding that the principal under certain conditions is not liable.

The principal is not liable when the agent is about his own business, or is acting beyond the scope and range of his employment. This is true irrespective of the intent of the agent.

A master is not responsible for the torts of his servant committed wholly for the servant's own purpose and in consummation of his personal desire.

A master cannot be held liable for the unauthorized act of a servant on the ground that the servant did the act with the intent to benefit or serve the master.

Nor is a master liable when his servant steps aside from the master's business to commit a wrong not connected with his employment.

If an assault is committed by the servant, not as a means or for the purpose of performing the work he was employed to do, but in a spirit of vindictiveness or to gratify his personal animosity or to carry out an independent purpose of his own, then the master is not liable.

It is a well-established rule that the master is not responsible for the tort of his servant when done without his authority and not for the purpose of executing his orders or doing his work, but wholly for the servant's own purpose and in pursuit of his private and personal ends.

Ordinarily the intent of the agent, or his purpose to promote the interest, or protect the property of his principal, is not a determining factor.

It is immaterial that the employee intended by such act to

secure a benefit for the employer. Liability of the principal, or the master, depends not upon the motive of the agent, or the servant, such as his intent to benefit his employer, or to protect his property, but upon the question whether in the performance of the act which gave rise to the injury the agent or the servant was at the time engaged in the service of his employer. It is not sufficient that the act shows that he did it with the intent to benefit or serve the master. It must be something done in attempting to do what the master has employed the servant to do. Nor does the question of liability depend on the quality of the act, but rather upon the question whether it has been performed in the line of duty and within the scope of authority conferred by the master. There is a marked distinction between an act done for the purpose of protecting the property by preventing a felony, or recovering it back, and an act done for the purpose of punishing the offender for that which has already been done. This view is expressed in *Kelly* v. *Shoe Company*, 190 N.C. 406, 130 S.E. 32, 34, by Varser, J., as follows: "Liability does not flow from the employee's intent to benefit or serve the master, but it does flow from the acts of the servant or employee in attempting to do what he was employed to do; that is, the acts complained of must have been done in the line of his duty and within the scope of his employment."

The general scope of the authority of the defendant De Butts was very broad. The term "General Manager" implies the right to exercise judgment and skill, and the idea that the management of the affairs of the company has been committed to him with respect to the property and business of the corporation. It implies general power and permits a reasonable inference that he was invested with the general conduct and control of the defendant's business committed to his charge. The term carries with it the implied authority to act in emergencies, or, generally, as the principal officer of the corporation in reference to the ordinary business and purposes of the corporation in the conduct of its affairs within his charge. It does not, however, include the implied authority to punish for past offenses or to assaults committed outside the scope of employment and not in the range of the servant's duties, prompted by the personal ill will or malice of the employee.

Applying the principles enumerated in these decisions to the testimony in the instant case, we are constrained to hold that the evidence fails to show that De Butts was acting within the range of his employment and was about his master's business in assaulting the plaintiff, but rather that he was acting in a spirit of vindictiveness to gratify his personal animosity. The wrong was not committed under such conditions as would invoke the doctrine of respondeat superior and no liability attaches to his principal for the resulting injury.

McClung v. Dearborne

134 Pa. 396, 19 Am. St. Rep. 708, 8 L.R.A. 204 (1890)

This was an action by William McClung (plaintiff) against George E. Dearborne (defendant). Judgment for defendant and plaintiff appealed. Judgment reversed and new trial ordered.

Dearborne was a dealer in cabinet organs and other musical instruments which he sold on the instalment plan. Fox was an employee of Dearborne and his business was to hunt up instruments upon which instalments were unpaid and collect the unpaid instalments or repossess the instrument. Fox discovered that McClung had an organ which had been sold by Dearborne to a customer and on which unpaid instalments were due. Fox with two helpers went to McClung's house to repossess the organ. Before they set out they were instructed by Dearborne not to commit an assault and battery on any person and not to break the law. While repossessing the organ, Fox and his helpers committed an assault and battery.

Opinion by Mr. Justice Williams: This action was brought by McClung to recover damages for this high-handed and hostile invasion of his home. On the trial, the learned judge of the court below told the jury that the conduct of Fox "was without mitigation, and deserving of the severest condemnation," but that whether Dearborne was responsible for it or not, depended on the instructions he gave him when he started out on the expedition. The correctness of this instruction is the point on which this appeal depends.

The general doctrine laid down by the learned judge, that every man is liable for his own trespass only, must not be taken too literally; for one must be held to do that which he procures or directs another to do for him, as well as that which he does in his own person. Servants and employees are often without the means to respond in damages for the injuries they may inflict on others by the ignorant, negligent, or wanton manner in which they conduct the business of their employer. The loss must be borne in such cases by the innocent sufferer, or by him whose employment of an ignorant, careless, or wanton servant has been the occasion of the injury, and, under such circumstances, it is just that the latter should bear the loss. But the master is not liable for the independent trespass of his servant.

An excellent illustration is afforded by the case of *Garretzen* v. *Duenckel*, 50 Mo. 104. The defendant was a gunsmith. In his absence from his store a clerk was waiting upon a customer who wanted to buy a rifle. The customer desired to see it loaded, and would not buy unless this was done. The orders of the defendant to his clerk were that he should not load a rifle in the store. The customer was so earnest in desiring it that the clerk loaded it, and by accident it was discharged, the ball injuring the plaintiff, who was sitting at a window on the opposite side of the street. The defendant set up his orders to his clerk as a defense, but it did not prevail. The court said: "There is no pretence that he (the clerk) was endeavoring to do anything for himself. He was acting in pursuance of authority, and trying to sell a gun, to make a bargain for his master; and, in his eagerness to subserve his master's interests, he acted injudiciously and negligently."

In the case now before us, Dearborne sent Fox and his helpers to the house of McClung for the purpose of seizing and bringing away the organ. He says: "I told him to take the men and team when he was ready, and to bring the organ in, but to be careful and not have any row about it." Black, who drove the team, testifies: "Mr. Dearborne told Fox to go down and get this organ on South Sixteenth street; to get it as peaceably as possible, and not to have any assault and battery, or any disturbance whatever." These directions show that Dearborne knew that the errand on which he sent his employees was one that was likely to result in trouble, and would require to be managed with great coolness and care, in order to avoid collision and a breach of the peace. But, however, the rule may be held in regard to the criminal liability of the master, under such circumstances, it is very clear that he cannot escape liability civilly by virtue of his instructions to his servant as to the manner of doing an act which the servant is to undertake on his behalf. He knew that the invasion of McClung's house, in the manner contemplated, was likely to excite indignation and resistance on the part of the inmates, and that what ought to be done might have to be determined under excitement, and without time for consultation or reflection by his employees. Under such circumstances, he puts them in his own stead, and he is bound by what they do in the effort to do the thing which was committed to them.

The defendant was bound not only to give proper instructions to his servants when sending them on such an errand, but he was bound to see that his instructions were obeyed.

Undisclosed Principal

In transacting the business of his principal, the agent may conceal the existence of the agency, also the identity of his principal, and transact the business in his own name. In such cases the undisclosed principal can take over and enforce the contract unless it is so drawn that the agent is dealt with exclusively. If the undisclosed principal does take over the contract, he takes it subject to all the equities of the third person against the agent. It would be unfair to allow the agent to deal in his own right and then permit the undisclosed principal to step in and acquire rights under the contract to which the agent would not have been entitled. The converse is also generally true. The undisclosed principal is liable on the contract to third persons. This rule is contrary to our general rules of contract in that one not a party to a contract is not bound by it, but it can be justified on the grounds that the undisclosed principal will reap the benefits, so should be held on the contract. The agent is also liable; hence the third party can hold either the principal or the agent, but he cannot hold both. It is not a joint obligation. If the third party wishes to recognize the existence of the agency and hold the undisclosed principal, he is given that privilege, but when he elects to recognize the agency, he must be bound by the rules of agency, that is, that it is the principal and not the agent who is bound. On the other hand, if the third person wishes to enforce the contract as drawn and hold the agent, he may do so. The agent of the undisclosed principal can bind the principal by acts which he has express, implied or apparent authority to perform. If the agent operates a business in his own name but for an undisclosed principal, any act of the agent done in the conducting of the business will bind the principal.

Contracts under seal and negotiable instruments are generally held to be exceptions to the rule stated. At common law one not a party to a contract under seal could not be held on the contract. This rule is in force in some states. Two special situations arise in regard to sealed contracts: (1) where a seal is attached but is not necessary to the validity of the contract and (2) where a seal is attached but by the statutes of the state the seal has been declared to be of no force or effect. In each of these situations the courts disagree. Some courts hold that the rule applies if the instrument is sealed; other courts hold that if the seal is unnecessary or ineffective the rule does not apply.

When the third person discovers the existence of the principal, he may elect to hold either the principal or the agent. To make an election the third person must know of the existence of the agency and the identity of the principal. Just what acts will amount to an election cannot be stated with certainty. The third person must clearly and unequivocally indicate that he intends to hold either the principal or the agent to the exclusion of the other before he will be held to have made an election.

If the principal is led to believe that the third person intends to hold the agent and in reliance on the acts of the third person settles accounts with the agent, the principal will be discharged from liability.

Hollywood Holding & Development Corporation v. Oswald
119 Cal. App. 21, 5 P. (2d) 963 (1931)

This was an action by the Hollywood Holding & Development Corporation (plaintiff) against George H. Oswald (defendant). Judgment for plaintiff and defendant appealed. Judgment affirmed.

Defendant wished to purchase a tract of land owned by the plaintiff and attempted to make the purchase through his brother M. E. Oswald, a real estate broker, but the plaintiff refused to sell to defendant. Later defendant induced G. S. Chapin to purchase the land for him. The purchase was made in Chapin's name. Defendant authorized Chapin to pay $51,000 for the land. Chapin contracted to pay $51,000 for the land, $25,000 payable in cash and the $26,000 balance to be secured by a mortgage on the land. Chapin also contracted to pay, in addition to the $51,000, the cost of certain street improvements to be made by plaintiff. Before this deal was closed, E. O. Earle was substituted for Chapin who signed over to Earle all of his rights and the deal was finally closed with Earle. The plaintiff issued a deed to Earle and Earle executed his note secured by a mortgage for the $26,000 balance. M. E. Oswald handled the negotiations for the purchase, in behalf of his brother, the defendant. Plaintiff did not learn that defendant was the real purchaser until October 1, 1927. The contract of purchase was signed by Chapin February 9, 1925. The improvements were made by plaintiff but were not paid for at the time this suit was brought. This suit was brought to recover the cost of the improvements. Defendant claims that he did not authorize Chapin to contract to pay for the improvements.

Mr. Justice pro tem. Jamison delivered the opinion of the court.

Plaintiff believed, and under the facts of this case had the right to believe, that he was dealing with the actual purchaser when it contracted to sell the property to Chapin, and that he had authority to enter into the contract to pay for the improvements. The rule is well established that the contract of an agent who deals in his own name without disclosing that of his principal, is the contract of the principal. The theory upon which the actual purchaser is held liable is based upon the fact that, by permitting the agent to hold himself out as the principal with full power to contract, and thereby innocent third parties are thus led into dealing with such apparent principal, they will be protected. Their rights under such circumstances do not depend upon the actual authority of the party with whom they directly deal, but are derived from the act of the real principal, which precludes him from disputing, as against them, the existence of authority, which through negligence or mistaken confidence he has allowed to be vested in the party with whom they are dealing.

As was said by the Supreme Court in *Hicks* v. *Wilson*, 197 Cal. 269, 240 P. 289, 290: "It is equally well settled, however, that a principal is bound, not only by the acts which he has actually authorized an agent to perform, but also by those which he has allowed third persons to believe him to be authorized to do." When an agent, on behalf of his principal, performs an unauthorized act, yet if the principal has put the agent in a position to mislead innocent parties, he is responsible to them. We are of the opinion that the agreement of Chapin to pay for the improvements is binding upon defendant.

Defendant claims that if plaintiff's contention is correct that the contract with Chapin is not canceled, its remedy is against Chapin. This claim is without merit. Where one deals with another, believing him to be the principal, on subsequently learning that he was dealing with an agent of an undisclosed principal, he may recover either from the person he dealt with or from the undisclosed principal.

In the action under consideration, while defendant denied authorizing Chapin to make any agreement to pay for said improvements, he clothed him with apparent authority so to do by concealing the fact that Chapin was merely an agent, and having him appear as the bona fide buyer.

Where one of two innocent persons must suffer by the act of the third, he by whose negligence it happened must be the sufferer. A loss through the trust and confidence placed by a principal in his agent should not be borne by those who were led to deal with the agent through the acts of the principal. Where one of two innocent persons must suffer, the loss should be borne by him whose acts made the loss possible.

Pittsburgh Terminal Coal Corp. v. Williams
70 F. (2d) 65 (1934)

This was an action by S. A. Williams (plaintiff) against Pittsburgh Terminal Coal Corporation (defendant). Judgment for plaintiff and defendant appealed. Judgment affirmed.

This suit was brought against the Pittsburgh Terminal Coal Corporation, the undisclosed principal of one Hoffacker. The contract sued on was a written and sealed contract. At an earlier date Hoffacker had been sued on the contract but at that time the existence of an undisclosed principal was unknown. It is claimed that: (1) The contract being under seal, the alleged agent is the only person that can be sued upon it. (2) The plaintiff by electing to proceed to judgment against Hoffacker, abandoned his right, if any, against the defendant.

Davis, C. J. The fact that the contract was under seal had no effect in West Virginia where the contract was signed and where the lands in question lie. The statute of West Virginia provides that: "The affixing of what has been known as a private seal, or scroll in lieu thereof, or the word 'seal' by any natural person hereafter to any deed, trust deed, mortgage, lease, bond, or other writing, conveying, selling or agreeing to sell, leasing, renting or encumbering any real estate, shall not give thereto any additional force or effect; and the omission of any such seal, word or scroll, shall in no way detract from the legal effect of any such deed." Acts of West Virginia, 1920, c. 71, § 2 p. 187.

The statute of West Virginia, which in effect abolished distinctions between contracts under seal and those not under seal, controls.

In Pennsylvania, the forum of this suit, the same rule prevails as in West Virginia. "Where a simple contract other than a bill or note is made by an agent in his own name, his undisclosed principal may maintain an action or be sued upon it; and an unauthorized and unnecessary addition of a seal to such a contract may be treated as surplusage." *Lancaster* v. *Knickerbocker Ice Company*, 153 Pa. 427, 26 A. 251.

Consequently, whether the contract in this case was or was not under seal is immaterial.

The plaintiff sued Hoffacker, defendant's agent, and secured judgment against him. Did this fact, as defendant contends, bar him from proceeding against the defendant itself in this case? When the case was here before, we held that the plaintiff did not know until April 13, 1928, that the defendant was Hoffacker's principal and that he could not by reasonable diligence have discovered that fact before that time.

Election to sue Hoffacker which defendant says bars subsequent suits against it involved a choice, and choice presupposes knowledge of the alternatives and freedom and ability to choose between them. A plaintiff cannot choose between principal and agent if he does not know who is the principal. Hoffacker was described as the agent in the contract, but the name and identity of the principal was not known to the plaintiff until long after suit had been brought against Hoffacker. Therefore the doctrine of election is inapplicable here, and plaintiff is not on that account barred from proceeding against the defendant.

QUESTIONS AND PROBLEMS

1. A written contract which reads, "Adam Archer hereby agrees, etc.," is signed, "Bert Burch, his agent." Is Bert Burch personally liable on the contract?
2. The Metropolitan Insurance Co. made certain loans to its policyholders. Checks for the amounts of the loans, payable to the policyholders, were sent to O'Day, the company's agent. O'Day forged the names of the payees and cashed the checks at the Star Restaurant. The Star Restaurant sued the Metropolitan Insurance Co. to recover the amount of checks on the theory that the principal is liable for the fraudulent conduct of the agent. Is the Metropolitan Insurance Co. liable on the checks?
3. Annis owned a farm. Her son, acting as her agent, sold the farm to Rhoda. The son in making the sale misrepresented the farm, and Rhoda purchased the farm relying on the misrepresentations. The misrepresentations were made without Annis' knowledge or consent. Rhoda sued Annis to recover damages for the deceit. Annis sets up as a defense that the son had no authority to make the misrepresentations. Is the defense good?
4. Howard, agent of Johns, sold Jaycox 200 talking machines. The machines were purchased by Jaycox to give away to his customers. When the sale was made, Howard, in the name of his principal Johns, made a warranty in writing that Jaycox would sell twenty-five records for each machine given away. Howard had no express authority to make the warranty. Is Johns bound by the warranty?
5. Shaw was employed by Hand as a salesman. Shaw had authority to solicit orders from customers but he did not have authority to make sales. Orders for goods, solicited by Shaw, were sent to Hand who accepted and filled the orders or rejected them. Grims gave Shaw an order for goods and the goods were shipped by Hand. Later, Grims paid Shaw for the goods. Shaw did not turn the money over to Hand. Hand sued Grims for the purchase price of the goods. Grims set up payment to Shaw as a defense. Is the defense good?
6. New was employed by Call as chauffeur. While driving Call's automobile, it

broke down and New employed Gage, who operated a garage, to make temporary repairs. The automobile broke down again, and New called Gage to come and get the automobile and to make all repairs on it necessary to put it in first-class condition. Gage got the car but before making repairs he wrote Call telling him what had been done and asking if he should carry out the instructions. Call did not answer Gage's letter. Gage proceeded to completely overhaul the automobile. Is Call bound by the contract for repairs?

7. Barnes made Purdy the general manager of his drugstore. It was expressly agreed between Barnes and Purdy that Purdy should buy goods for the store only for cash and that he should not run up any account for any goods or supplies of any kind whatever. Purdy made a contract with the Telephone Co. for telephone service. Barnes refused to pay for the telephone service and the Telephone Co. sued Barnes. Is Barnes liable on the contract for telephone service?
8. Dixon was authorized by Graham to make collections. Dixon accepted two checks drawn payable to the order of Graham in payment of accounts. Dixon indorsed the checks as agent of Graham and presented them to the drawee bank —The Savings Institute—who gave Dixon the money on the checks. Dixon appropriated the money to his own use. Graham sued the bank to recover the amount of the checks. Can Graham recover a judgment?
9. Jenkins Bros. sued White Co., as partners, to recover the amount due for goods sold. Fred White was made a party defendant. Fred White contends he is not liable on the ground that before the sale he withdrew from the partnership and that when the order, on which suit is brought, was given to Jenkins Bros.' salesman, notice was given to the salesman that Fred White had withdrawn from the partnership. The salesman did not communicate this notice to his principal. Is the principal bound by the notice given to the salesman?
10. The employees of Adams Co., while attempting to collect past-due payments on a clock sold to Stein, committed assault and battery upon her. The employees attempted forcibly to take the clock from Stein's home, and she tried to prevent them from taking it. One of the employees struck Stein, seriously injuring her. Stein sued Adams Co. to recover damages for the assault and battery. Can she recover?
11. Bishop purchased certain property ostensibly for himself, but Barnett directed every step taken by Bishop in his negotiations with Kayton. The property was immediately turned over to Barnett and he still holds it. Kayton sues Barnett for the unpaid balance of the purchase price. Is Kayton entitled to a judgment?

CHAPTER XXVIII

RELATION OF AGENT TO THIRD PERSONS

Liability on Authorized Contracts

It is an accepted rule that an agent is not liable to a third person on contracts which he negotiates for a disclosed principal while acting within the scope of his authority.[1] However, the agent may make himself liable by becoming a party to the contract either as a co-promisor or as surety for the principal. Under certain circumstances the agent will become a party to the contract. If the agent acts for a disclosed principal, the contract will ordinarily be made in the name of the principal, and the agent will not be a party to the contract. If there is no agreement which negates the agent's liability to the third person, the agent will be liable if he is acting for a partially disclosed principal.[2] If the third person has notice that the agent is or may be acting for a principal but has no notice of the principal's identity, the principal for whom the agent is acting is partially disclosed.[3] If the principal is only partially disclosed, in that his identity is unknown, there is an almost irresistible inference that the agent intends to become a party to the contract, and this inference will prevail in the absence of an express agreement to the contrary. If the agent is acting for an undisclosed principal, he is of necessity a party to the contract and, being a party to the contract, will be bound by it.

If the agent is authorized to sign negotiable instruments or sealed contracts and the principal is disclosed, yet the principal's name does not appear in the instrument and the agent signs in his own name, the agent will be held liable.

However, if the principal's name appears in the instrument and the agent indicates that he is signing in a representative capacity, parol evidence will be admitted to establish the intent of the parties. Archer is treasurer of the Peters Corporation. Archer uses a printed negotiable instrument form which has "Peters Corporation" printed on the face. Archer signs the instrument "Archer, Treas." In the majority of courts

[1] See *Restatement of the Law of Agency*, sec. 321, p. 712.

[2] *Ibid.*, sec. 4 (2), p. 15.

[3] *Ibid.*, sec. 322, p. 714.

Archer will be permitted to prove by parol evidence that the note was intended as a corporation note and not as his individual note.

If the contract is not under seal or is not negotiable, the agent will be bound if he contracts in his own name and not in the name of the principal. However, if the contract is informal in nature, such as letters or telegrams or letters and telegrams, the court will determine from all the negotiations the intention of the parties and, if it is clear that the parties intended to contract in the name of the principal, the agent will not be bound even though letters or telegrams may have been signed by the agent without adding words to indicate that he signed as agent.

Zehr et al. v. Wardall et al.
134 F. (2d) 805 (1943)

This was an action by Joseph Zehr and another (plaintiffs) against William J. Wardall, as trustee of McKesson & Robbins, Incorporated (defendant). Judgment for defendant and plaintiffs appealed. Judgment affirmed.

McKesson & Robbins, Inc., was United States agent for British Cod Liver Oil Producers, Ltd. McKesson & Robbins, Inc., wrote plaintiffs stating that they were agents for British Cod Liver Oil Producers, Ltd., and solicited an order from them. After the exchange of several letters and telegrams, plaintiffs sent an order for two cars of cod liver oil. McKesson & Robbins, Inc., accepted the order signing the acceptance in its name without indicating that it signed as agent. The agency and the identity of the principal were fully disclosed in several of the letters of negotiation which preceded the placing of the order. As a result of the war the British firm was unable to make shipment. Plaintiffs sued defendant to recover damages for breach of contract, contending that McKesson & Robbins, Inc., was liable on the contract.

McAllister, C. J. It must be assumed that appellee was acting, not for itself in the transaction, but as agent for the British company, its principal. Furthermore, an examination of the correspondence does not indicate that there was any other evidence from which the court, or the jury, could draw inferences that appellee was not acting as agent, merely because appellee, in its letters, used such language as "We are pleased to quote British Cod Liver Oil . . . . as follows" and "We . . . . confirm having entered your order. . . . ." "One who purports to contract on behalf of a designated person does not manifest by this that he is making a contract on his own account, and only where he so manifests does the agent become a party to the transaction which he makes. In the absence of other facts, the inference is that the parties have agreed that the principal is and the agent is not a party. This is true, although the agent uses such an expression as, 'I will sell.' "

But it is contended that where an agent executes a contract in his own name, he is personally bound. While this is the general rule with regard to formal contracts, including deeds, instruments under seal, and promissory notes, yet where the parties are negotiating informally, such rule is not controlling. This would be especially so where the informality of a contract is characterized by letters and other correspondence. It cannot be concluded that appellee was personally bound because in a letter replying to appellants' telegram, it did not sign as an agent, in view of the fact that three previous letters had informed appellants that appellee was the agent for the British company.

Liability on Unauthorized Contracts

The courts are in accord in holding that, if the agent exceeds his authority, that is, if the principal is not bound because the agent has acted beyond the scope of his authority, the agent will be held answerable to the third person. The courts are not in accord as to the nature of the agent's liability. A minority view is that the agent is liable on the contract on the theory that there must be two parties to a contract and, if the principal is not bound, the agent must be held to be the other contracting party. The majority of courts hold that the agent is not liable on the contract. The agent may be held liable in tort on the theory that he has misrepresented the scope of his authority and thereby induced the third person to act to the latter's injury, or he may be held liable on the theory that in negotiating the contract he impliedly warranted that he had authority to so act. As a general rule, the former theory is applied if it appears that the agent knowingly misrepresents either the existence of the agency or the scope of his authority with the intent of defrauding the third party. However, if the agent innocently exceeds the scope of his authority, the majority of the courts will hold the agent liable on the theory of breach of implied warranty. If the agent knowingly exceeds his authority but does it with the expectation that the principal will ratify the unauthorized act, he is clearly guilty of misrepresentation but an intent to defraud is lacking. In some instances the tort theory of liability has been applied, while in other instances the breach of warranty theory has been applied. In all cases in which the third person justifiedly relies on the authority of the agent when the agent does not bind the principal, the agent will be held liable for the resulting injury to the third person.

If the principal ratifies the unauthorized act of his agent, it operates to cure the defect in the contract, thereby binding the principal and releasing the agent from his liability. If the third person knows the agent is exceeding his authority or if the agent discloses all the facts of his appointment and the third person deals with him with full knowledge, the agent is not liable even though he has exceeded his authority. If the agent's liability to the third person is based on the theory of a breach of warranty, and if the third person has full knowledge, he does not rely on a representation, either actual or implied, made by the agent as to his authority, and the agent cannot be held for breach of warranty.

The courts have also held that, if the principal would not have been bound had the agent been authorized to negotiate the contract, the agent cannot be held liable. Archer, acting without authority, enters into an oral contract in the name of Peters as principal to purchase a tract of land from Trent. Trent cannot hold Archer liable for Peters' refusal to carry out the contract. The contract is unenforceable under the Statute of Frauds because there is no note or memorandum of the agreement and, if Archer had had authority to purchase for Peters, Peters would not have been bound.

Clements v. Citizens' Bank of Booneville
177 Ark. 1085, 9 S.W. (2d) 569 (1928)

This was an action by Charles Clements (plaintiff) against Citizens' Bank of Booneville and Charles X. Williams (defendants). Judgment for defendants and plaintiff appealed. Judgment affirmed.

Williams was cashier of the defendant bank. As agent for the bank Williams signed a contract of guaranty in the name of the bank. The court held in a former case that the bank was not liable on the contract because under its charter the bank was not authorized to give a contract of guaranty. Plaintiff contends that, if the bank is not liable, Williams who signed as agent is liable. The suit is based on the contract.

Mehaffy, J. When an agent makes a contract for a principal which he has no authority to make, or a contract in excess of his authority, and, because of either not having authority or exceeding his authority, does not bind the principal, he is bound himself. Some courts have held that an action may be maintained against him on the contract, on the theory that he intended to bind some one by the contract, and, if he did not bind the principal, he would bind himself. But the great weight of authority is to the effect that, while the agent is liable, he is not liable on the contract. It is said by a text-writer:

"Whether the agent can be held liable upon the contract itself, which he has, without authority, assumed to make, is a question which has been much discussed, and upon which the cases cannot be entirely reconciled. It would seem, however, that this question is one which must be determined largely by the circumstances of each case. Where the promise is made in the name of a principal, who might have authorized it, and as his contract, the better opinion is that the agent cannot be held liable upon it, but only in an action based upon the deceit, or upon the contract of warranty or indemnity, even in the case of a written contract, where the assumed relation of agency appears upon the face of it. Some courts have, indeed, manifested a disposition in this latter case to reject the words referring to the alleged principal as mere surplusage, and to hold the agent liable upon the remainder as upon his own contract. This however, as has been well said, is rather to make a new contract for the parties than to construe the one which they have made for themselves." 1 Mechem on Agency (2d Ed.) 1023, 1024.

"The proper remedy against an agent by a third party, with whom the agent has dealt, where the agent acts without, or in excess of, his authority, is an action of assumpsit upon his expressed or implied warranty of authority, or, in a proper case, an action of trespass on the case for fraud and deceit, and in some jurisdictions the latter is held to be the only remedy in such cases." 2 C. J. 892.

In discussing the liability of agents under circumstances like this, the Wisconsin court said:

" 'This whole doctrine proceeds upon a plain principle of justice; for every person so acting for another, by a natural, if not a necessary, implication, holds himself out as having competent authority to do the act; and he thereby draws the other party into a reciprocal engagement. If he has no such authority, and acts bona fide, still he does a wrong to the other party; and if that wrong produces injury to the latter owing to his confidence in the truth of an express or implied assertion of authority by the agent, it is perfectly just that he who makes such assertion should be personally responsible for the consequences, rather than that the injury should be borne by the other party who has been misled by it.' . . . . Later and better considered opinion seems to be that the liability, when the contract is made in the name of his principal, rests upon implied warranty of authority to make it, and the remedy is by an action for its breach." *Oliver* v. *Morawetz*, 97 Wis. 332, 72 N.W. 877.

The authorities seem to be unanimous in holding that the agent, under such circumstances, is liable, and almost unanimous in holding that an action cannot be maintained on the contract itself, but on an implied promise on the part of the agent that he has the authority to make the contract. If suit could have been maintained on the contract itself, the cause of action would not have been barred, because it could have been begun any time within five years. But this is a suit on an implied contract not in writing, and it was barred within three years.

First State Bank of Roby v. Hilbun
Ct. of Civ. App. Tex., 61 S.W. (2d) 521 (1933)

This was an action by the First State Bank of Roby (plaintiff) against J. C. Hilbun (defendant). Judgment for defendant and plaintiff appealed. Judgment affirmed.

The First National Bank of Roby, Texas, was being liquidated. Hilbun was appointed liquidating agent. He was, at the time, cashier of the First State Bank of Roby. The First National Bank owed the Federal Government $1,600 for taxes. Hilbun had only $1,200 on hand; so he proposed to the directors of the First State Bank of Roby that they make a loan of $400 so that he could pay the government claim. Hilbun gave a note signed "J. C. Hilbun, Liquidating Agent, First National Bank, Roby, Texas, by J. C. Hilbun." The First State Bank of Roby sued Hilbun on the note.

Hickman, C. J. It has been many times announced that an agent acting without, or in excess of authority, incurs a personal liability, but probably more cases can be found following exceptions to the general rule than can be found which apply the rule. For at least two reasons it cannot be applied in the instant case, even if it be conceded that the agent was acting without authority. In the first place, liability incurred by an agent thus exceeding his authority arises either upon his express or implied warranty of authority or from deceit practiced by him. A suit to enforce such liability should not be brought upon the contract itself, but should be for breach of warranty or deceit. Plaintiff's suit was based upon the contract itself, which did not purport to be the contract of the defendant, and clearly it was not entitled to a judgment thereon.

Another all-sufficient reason why the rule relied upon by plaintiff is not applicable to the facts of this case is afforded by this well-established exception to that general rule: "The rule that an agent acting without or in excess of authority is personally liable is subject to the qualification that the person dealing with him must have acted on the faith of the representation, express or implied, that the agent had the authority assumed and without knowledge of any want of authority on the agent's part. If therefore the agent fully discloses to the third person the facts concerning his authority, so that the latter may have the same opportunity of judging of the sufficiency thereof as the agent himself, or if the third person himself has actual or presumptive knowledge of those facts, the agent cannot be held personally liable even though the principal is not bound." 2 C. J. pp. 809, 810.

This rule is well supported by the decisions from many jurisdictions. An exhaustive case note will be found in 34 L. R. A. (N.S.) 518. It is the rule in Texas.

Non-Existent or Incompetent Principal

If the agent acts in the name of a non-existent or incompetent principal and the third person does not know that the purported principal is non-existent or incompetent, the agent is personally liable on the contract. However, if the third person knows that the purported principal is non-existent or incompetent, the agent will not be bound unless he agrees to be bound. One who contracts in the name of a corporation which is not yet organized or who contracts in the name of an unincorporated association is liable under the rule stated above.

An agent does not guarantee the capacity of his principal. If the contract which the agent negotiates is within the scope of his authority and for his principal, but is not enforceable against the principal because of lack of capacity, the agent is not liable to the third person unless the agent has misrepresented the capacity of his principal.

Hagan v. Asa G. Candler, Inc.
189 Ga. 250, 5 S.E. (2d) 739, 126 A.L.R. 108 (1939)

This was an action by Asa G. Candler, Inc. (plaintiff) against H. T. Hagan (defendant). Judgment for plaintiff and defendant appealed. Judgment affirmed.

On November 28, 1933, plaintiff leased the premises located at 60 Peachtree Street in Atlanta to Food Shops, Inc. The lease was signed in the name of Food Shops, Inc., by defendant as its president. At the time the lease was negotiated and signed defendant represented that Food Shops, Inc., was a corporation, that he was its president and that he had been authorized to sign the lease by the board of directors. It is now admitted that no corporation existed and that defendant acted for a non-existent principal. This suit was brought on the lease. Defendant contends that he is not personally liable on the contract and that, if he is liable to plaintiff, the liability is damages for deceit or for breach of implied warranty.

Gordon Knox, J. The question whether or not an agent who executes a contract on behalf of a non-existent principal is himself liable on the contract has provoked considerable discussion and created a wide diversity of opinion in the different jurisdictions of the country. In some States, notably North Dakota, the liability of the agent on the contract has been established by statute. In Florida, South Carolina, and some other jurisdictions the general rule of law fixing the liability of the agent on the contract is recognized and approved, although it is not embodied in the statute law of these States. This general rule of law is expressed in 2 American Jurisprudence, 248, § 316, in the following language: "It is a general rule that one who assumes to act as agent for a principal who has no legal status or existence renders himself individually liable on contracts so made." However, it appears that the general rule has been definitely repudiated in New York, Massachusetts, and a number of other jurisdictions. In these States the opposite party to the contract, in seeking redress, is limited to the action arising in tort. Georgia has no statute fixing the liability of the agent on the contract; so it must be determined if the general rule of law above stated is recognized and approved in this State. The Court of Appeals in this case based its decision upon the general rule of law, stating it as follows (59 Ga. App. 587, 1 S.E. 2d 695): "The general rule relative to non-existent principals, is that one who professes to contract as agent is personally liable on the contract if, unknown to the other party, his purported principal is actually non-existent, however, the agent is not liable where the third person has knowledge of the non-existence of the principal or where there is an agreement or understanding to the contrary. It is to be remembered, however, that 'if an agent, although purporting to be acting for a principal, is in fact acting for himself, he will be personally liable on the contract.' 3 C. J. S. Agency, § 213, page 118."

Liability for Torts

An agent is liable to third persons for injuries resulting from the agent's torts. Usually the tort liability is a joint liability, that is, both the principal and agent are liable. The principal is liable if the tort is committed by the agent in the course and within the scope of the agency and the agent is liable because his tortious conduct is the cause of the injury. If the act of the agent is not a breach of a duty owed by the agent to the third person, the agent is not liable even though the act of the agent may render the principal liable in tort to the third person. An agent is personally liable to the third person for injuries resulting from his fraud and misrepresentations even though the agent reaps no personal benefit as a result of the fraud or misrepresentation. However, the agent is not personally liable for representations made innocently and in good faith even though later the representations prove to be false.

An agent is not liable to third persons for a breach of duty which he owes to his principal. However, the circumstances may be such that the agent's failure to perform a duty owed to his principal will result in such an injury to a third person that the agent will be liable to the third person.

A problem closely related to the tort liability of an agent to third persons is the liability of a certified public accountant to third persons who rely on a certified balance sheet to their injury. Peters engages Archer, a C.P.A., to audit his books. At the time the audit is made Archer knows that the certified balance sheet will be used as the basis of obtaining credit. Archer is negligent in making the audit and the balance sheet shows that Peters is solvent when in fact he is insolvent. Peters shows the balance sheet to Trent who, in reliance on the balance sheet, makes a loan to Peters. Shortly after the loan is made Peters is adjudged bankrupt and the loan is discharged. Is Archer liable to Trent because of his negligence in making the audit? The answer to this question depends on the facts of the case. In most instances Archer will not be liable, but if his negligence is absolutely inexcusable, he will be held liable on a constructive fraud theory.

State Street Trust Co. v. Ernst et al.
278 N.Y. 104, 15 N.E. (2d) 416 (1938)

This was an action by State Street Trust Company (plaintiff) against Alwin C. Ernst and another (defendants). In the trial court the jury found for the plaintiff, but the judge rendered a judgment in favor of the defendants notwithstanding the verdict. On appeal the appellate division affirmed the judgment. The case was appealed to the Court of Appeals where the judgment was reversed and a new trial ordered.

Pelz-Greenstein Company was engaged in the business of financing wholesalers or mills. On January 19, 1928, Pelz-Greenstein Company applied to the plaintiff for a $300,000 loan. At the time the application for the loan was made an estimated balance sheet was presented and Pelz-Greenstein Company told plaintiff that defendants were making an audit. The loan was refused. Later a certified balance sheet dated April 2, 1929, showing the condition of Pelz-Greenstein Company as of December 31, 1928, was presented and relying on this balance sheet plaintiff made the loan. On April 26, 1930, Pelz-Greenstein Company was petitioned into bankruptcy. Plaintiff received only a small portion of the loan. On the trial it was established that Pelz-Greenstein Company made old and probably uncollectible accounts appear good by causing payments to be made to it by another corporation which it owned, which payments, credited to such old accounts, made it appear as though the debtors had been paying their debts. False inventories of goods supposedly subject to liens to Pelz-Greenstein Company were made by one Saqui who was working for Pelz-Greenstein Company. Saqui also assigned false accounts to Pelz-Greenstein Company. In one account of $800,000, there were $300,000 of wholly fictitious sales. None of the discrepancies were detected in making the audit because of the negligence of defendants and their employees.

Finch, J. To what extent may accountants be held liable for their failure to reveal this condition? We have held that in the absence of a contractual relationship or its equivalent, accountants cannot be held liable for ordinary negligence in preparing a certified balance sheet even though they are aware that the balance sheet will be used to obtain credit. Accountants, however, may be liable to third parties, even where there is lacking deliberate or active fraud. A representation certified as true to the knowledge of the accountants when knowledge there is none, a reckless misstatement, or an opinion based on grounds so flimsy as to lead to the conclusion that there was no genuine belief in its truth, are all sufficient upon which to base liability. A refusal to see the obvious, a failure to investigate the doubtful, if sufficiently gross, may furnish evidence leading to an inference of fraud so as to impose liability for losses suffered by those who rely on the balance sheet. In other words, heedlessness and reckless disregard of consequence may take the place of deliberate intention.

In *Ultramares Corporation* v. *Touche*, 255 N.Y. 170, 174 N.E. 441, 74 A.L.R. 1139, we said with no uncertainty that negligence, if gross, or blindness, even though not equivalent to fraud, was sufficient to sustain an inference of fraud. Our exact words were: "In this connection we are to bear in mind the principle already stated in the course of this opinion that negligence or blindness, even when not equivalent to fraud, is none the less evidence to sustain an inference of fraud. At least this is so if the negligence is gross."

The defendants, however, contend that they may escape all liability by insisting that the balance sheet merely purported to reflect the condition of the books and that it did this correctly. The balance sheet, however, did not correctly reflect the condition of the company even as shown by the books, as will later appear. Nor is the duty of an accountant in preparing a balance sheet confined to a mere setting up of the items from the books. Such duties have been defined.

"His (the auditor's) business is to ascertain and state the true financial position of the company at the time of the audit, and his duty is confined to that. But then comes the question, How is he to ascertain that position? The answer is, By examining the books of the company. But he does not discharge his duty by doing this without inquiry and without taking any trouble to see that the books themselves show the company's true position. He must take reasonable care to ascertain that they do so. Unless he does this his audit would be worse than an idle farce. Assuming the books to be so kept as to show the true position of a company, the auditor has to frame a balance showing that position according to the books and to certify that the balance sheet presented is correct in that sense. But his first duty is to examine the books, not merely for the purpose of ascertaining what they do show, but also for the purpose of satisfying himself that they show the true financial position of the company." *Matter of London and General Bank* (1895) 2 Ch. 673.

The record is, indeed, replete with evidence, both oral and documentary, to make a prima facie case against the defendants.

Third Person's Liability to Agent

Under the generally accepted theory that the agent is not a party to or liable on a contract negotiated in the name of his principal and within the scope of his authority, it follows that an agent would have no right to sue the third person for damages for the breach of such a contract. Also, if the agent is acting for an undisclosed principal, the agent is generally a party to the contract and is liable to the third person if the contract is breached. However, the third person may elect to hold the principal. The agent being a party to the contract may sue the third person and recover damages for breach of the contract, but this right is secondary to the principal's rights in the contract and, if the principal wishes to bring suit, his rights will be superior to those of the agent. In any event the third person is subject to only one suit.

If the agent sues in his own name and recovers, the principal cannot at a later date bring another suit in the name of the principal. The one suit exhausts the remedies for the breach of the contract. In the event of suit by the agent, recovery of a judgment, and payment to the agent, the obligation will be discharged, and the agent will hold the money as trustee for the principal.

If the agent has negotiated a contract in the name of his principal and the agent has a special interest or property in the contract, the agent may bring a suit in the latter's name for damages suffered as a result of a breach of the contract. Peters Insurance Co. appoints Archer as its agent authorizing him to issue fire insurance policies. Archer issues a fire insurance policy to Trent. Trent does not pay the premium at the time the policy is issued. When Archer remits premiums collected to Peters Insurance Co., his principal, Archer includes the premium on the policy issued to Trent, paying the amount of the premium out of Archer's own funds. Archer may sue in his own name and recover a judgment against Trent for the amount of the unpaid premium. If the principal transfers a contract negotiated by the agent in the name of the principal to the agent, the agent may sue on the contract in his own name unless the laws of the state require that suit on an assigned contract must be brought in the name of the original parties to the contract.

In some situations an agent, by custom or usage, is permitted to bring suit in his own name. It is customary for commission merchants or factors to make sales, extend credit, and bring suits in the name of the agent.

If an agent pays out money of his principal by mistake or in reliance on fraudulent representations, the agent may recover from the third person in a suit brought in the name of the agent.

The agent may also sue in his own name and recover damages from the third person for torts committed against the agent.

Scott v. Louisville & N. R. Co.
170 Tenn. 563, 98 S.W. (2d) 90 (1936)

This was an action by Frank R. Scott (plaintiff) against the Louisville & Nashville Railroad Company (defendant). Judgment for defendant and plaintiff appealed. Judgment affirmed.

Scott as agent for the Rex-Jellico Coal Company contracted in the name of his principal to sell to defendant 34,500 tons of coal. The contract was in writing and was drawn and signed in the name of Rex-Jellico Coal Co. by Scott as agent. Defendant refused to accept and pay for 22,210 tons of the coal contracted for. Scott was to receive a commission of 10 cents per ton of coal sold to the railroad company under the contract. Scott's contention is that by reason of this commission he had, and was the owner of, a property right and interest in the contract.

De Haven, J. In the Restatement of the Law of Agency the rule is thus stated:

"Sec. 320. Unless otherwise agreed, a person making or purporting to make a contract with another as agent for a disclosed principal does not become a party to the contract."

In the comment on this rule it is stated: ". . . . One who purports to contract on behalf of a designated person does not manifest by this that he is making a contract on his own account, and only where he so manifests does the agent become a party to the transaction which he makes. In the absence of other facts, the inference is that the parties have agreed that the principal is and the agent is not a party."

The general rule is that one who contracts as agent cannot maintain an action in his own name and right upon the contract. However, there are exceptions to this rule. In *Herron* v. *Bullitt & Fairthorne*, 35 Tenn. (3 Sneed) 497, 500, 501, the court said:

"The cases in which agents acquire rights against third persons, founded upon contracts made by them, are said to be resolvable into four classes.

"First, where the contract is made in writing, expressly with the agent, and imports to be a contract personally with him, although he may be known to act as an agent.

"Secondly, where the agent is the only known or ostensible principal, and therefore is, in contemplation of law, the real contracting party.

"Thirdly, where, by the usage of trade, or the general course of business, the agent is authorized to act as the owner, or as a principal contracting party, although his character as agent is known.

"Fourthly, where the agent has made a contract, in the subject matter of which he has a special interest or property, whether he professed, at the time, to be acting for himself or not.—Story on Agency, § 393."

It is obvious that Scott could not maintain this suit under either one of the first three of the above rules. Can he maintain his suit under the fourth rule? We think not. He had no special interest, or property, in the subject-matter of the contract. His only claim is for commission for making the sale of the coal. His power as agent was not coupled with an interest in the subject-matter of the contract. His interest was in the proceeds which arose from the exercise of his power as agent in making the sale.

In the Restatement of the Law of Agency, § 372, par. 2, it is stated:

"An agent does not have such an interest in a contract as to entitle him to maintain an action at law upon it in his own name merely because he is entitled to a portion of the proceeds as compensation for making it or because he is liable for its breach."

For lack of a special interest, or property, in the subject-matter of the contract, it must be held that the plaintiff has no right of action thereon.

QUESTIONS AND PROBLEMS

1. A reward was offered in the following terms: "Two thousand dollars reward will be paid to any person furnishing evidence that will lead to the arrest and conviction of the person who shot Edward Cunningham, November 21, 1945.

   "J. Walter Bradlee
   "T. Edward Ruggles
   "J. Albert Simpson
   "Selectmen of Milton"

   Are the signers of the offer of the reward personally liable?
2. Lewis sold and shipped to the Paper-Bag Co. a carload of paper. The paper was shipped under a contract with the Paper-Bag Co., the performance of which was guaranteed by a guaranty agreement which was signed: "Iowa National Bank,
   "By William Daggett, V. P."

   A bank has no power to bind itself as guarantor for third persons. Is William Daggett personally liable on the guaranty contract?
3. Pitcairn was acting as agent for a fire insurance company and represented to Kroeger that the company, notwithstanding the terms of the policy, would allow Kroeger to keep petroleum. Kroeger did keep petroleum, and his stock was destroyed by fire. The insurance company was not liable; the keeping of petroleum on the premises invalidated the policy. Kroeger sued Pitcairn to recover the loss. Is Pitcairn personally liable to Kroeger for the loss suffered?
4. Graham, the head of an unincorporated association, engaged Comfort as attorney to represent the interests of the association. The association did not pay Comfort for his services, and he sued Graham. Is Graham personally liable to Comfort for services rendered?
5. Hicks was the agent of Mott, an infant. Hicks negotiated a contract in the name of his principal—Mott—with Patterson. At the time the contract was negotiated, Hicks disclosed the infancy of his principal. Mott breached the contract and Patterson sued Hicks on the theory that Hicks was liable because of the incapacity of his principal. Is Hicks liable to Patterson for Mott's breach of the contract?
6. Byers, Winner, Perkins, and Bunker were the officers of the Investment Co. While acting for the Investment Co., they caused to be printed on bonds, issued by the Investment Co., a statement that such bonds were first-mortgage bonds. This was a false and fraudulent statement. In reliance on the statement the bank purchased some of the bonds. Are the officers (agents of the Investment Co.) personally liable for the fraud?
7. Camp, acting as agent for an undisclosed principal, entered into a contract with Barber. After Camp had performed his part of the contract in full, Barber defaulted. Camp brought suit in his own name to recover damages. Barber set up as a defense that Camp was acting as agent and could not sue in his own name. Is this contention correct?

CHAPTER XXIX

RELATION OF PRINCIPAL AND AGENT

Agent's Duty of Loyalty

The relation between the principal and agent is fiduciary; that is, it is a relation involving trust and confidence, and, consequently, the agent is held to the highest standards of loyalty and honesty in the transacting of business for his principal. This rule of loyalty does not apply when the relation is that of master and servant, or employer and employee and the servant or employee is performing ministerial services and no agency exists.

Under this rule, the agent owes a duty to his principal to use his best efforts to further the interests of his principal and is not permitted to put himself in such a position that the agent's personal interests are in conflict with the interests of the principal, nor will the agent be permitted to represent interests which are adverse to the interests of the principal. However, if the principal is fully informed that the agent has adverse interests or is representing adverse interests and, after full disclosure of all material facts, the principal consents to the contract negotiated, the principal cannot at a later date attack the contract on the ground that the agent had or represented adverse interests. However, if it can be shown that the agent did not act fairly and honestly, the courts will grant relief to the principal.

Under this rule, any contract between the third person and the agent, whereby the third person either directly or indirectly agrees to pay the agent a secret commission or bonus, is illegal because it is against public policy. This rule applies whether or not the agent is to receive compensation from his principal. An agent authorized to buy or sell property is not permitted to buy for himself or sell to himself unless he makes a full disclosure to the principal and the principal gives his consent. Any interest acquired by an agent in his own name, which should have been acquired for the principal or the acquisition of which is a breach of the duty owed by the agent to the principal, will be declared to be held by the agent in trust for the principal. An agent will not be permitted to contract in the name of his principal with himself as the other contracting party. Peters Insurance Company appoints Archer as its agent with authority to issue fire insurance policies. Archer issues a fire insurance policy on his house to himself. The policy is voidable at the election of the Peters Insurance Co. If the agent discloses his wish to contract with the principal and the principal consents, the contract will be enforceable providing the agent discloses to the principal all facts material to the transaction of which he, the agent, has knowledge.

Lybarger v. Lieblong et al.
186 Ark. 913, 56 S.W. (2d) 760 (1933)

This was an action by R. J. Lybarger (plaintiff) against J. S. Lieblong and the Faulkner County Bank & Trust Company (defendants). Judgment for the defendants and the plaintiff appealed. Judgment reversed and remanded with directions.

Plaintiff had for several years been a customer of the Faulkner County Bank & Trust Company and the bank had acted as agent for the plaintiff in making loans and collections. It made a loan in plaintiff's behalf to Lieblong, taking a mortgage on a farm owned by Lieblong as security. At the time this loan was in existence, the bank obtained from Lieblong a mortgage on the same farm as security for a pre-existing debt due it. The bank recorded its mortgage first, thereby obtaining a first lien on the farm. This suit was brought by plaintiff to have his mortgage declared to be a first lien on the farm.

Kirby, J. Every one, whether designated agent, trustee, servant, or what not, under contract or other legal obligation to represent and act for another in any particular business or line of business or for any valuable purpose, must be loyal and faithful to the interests of such other person in respect to such business or purpose. He cannot lawfully serve or acquire any private interest of his own in opposition to that of his principal. "This is a rule of common sense and honesty, as well as of law." In 21 R.C.L. 825, it is also said: "He may not use any information that he may have acquired by reason of his employment, either for the purpose of acquiring property or doing any other act which is in opposition to his principal's interest." See *Dudney* v. *Wilson*, 180 Ark. 416, 21 S.W. (2) 615, 616, where the court quoted with approval from *Trice* v. *Comstock*, (C.C.A.) 121 F. 620, 61 L.R.A. 176, the following: "Every agency creates a fiduciary relation, and every agent, however limited his authority, is disabled from using any information or advantage he acquires through his agency, either to acquire property or to do any other act which defeats or hinders the efforts of his principals to accomplish the purpose for which the agency was established."

The fact that the agency is gratuitous does not affect the rule requiring good faith and loyalty on the part of the agent if he has entered upon or assumed the performance of his duties.

Ready v. National State Bank of Newark
117 N.J. L. 554, 190 Atl. 76 (1937)

This was an action by Matthew J. Ready (plaintiff) against the National State Bank of Newark, New Jersey, executor of the will of Thomas S. Henry, deceased (defendant). Judgment for defendant and plaintiff appealed. Judgment affirmed.

Plaintiff was acting as agent for one Brokaw and was authorized to employ an attorney to represent Brokaw in certain condemnation proceedings. Plaintiff as agent for Brokaw engaged Thomas S. Henry to represent Brokaw in the proceedings. Henry was to receive 10 per cent of the recovery as compensation. Henry entered into a contract with plaintiff whereby Henry was to pay plaintiff 5 per cent of the recovery. Plaintiff was to assist Henry in the preparation of the law and the facts in the case. Henry received $6,000 for his services. Henry paid plaintiff $100 on account. Henry has since died and this suit was brought against Henry's estate to recover $2,900, the unpaid balance of the sum Henry agreed to pay plaintiff.

Brogan, C. J. Assuming that the plaintiff was authorized to make a contract in behalf of Brokaw for legal services to be rendered by the attorney, he could not, by secret arrangement, profit by his agency to employ counsel. An agent must not profit by the trust and confidence reposed in him. If it be true that the client instructed the plaintiff to select counsel for him, the plaintiff cannot ask the sanction of a court for the enforcement of a claim on a contingent fee paid to counsel by the client unless there was a full disclosure to the client of the fact that the agent expected to participate in the compensation to be paid for the attorney's services and the client agreed.

"A contract by an agent, even though acting as such without compensation, to receive without his principal's consent compensation for the performance of the agency is invalid."

The trust and confidence of the principal accompanies the agency and the agent may not profit from his selection or recommendation of the attorney without the consent and knowledge of his principal. His choice of counsel cannot be disinterested if it was infected with self-interest.

Cicurel v. Plaza Service Corporation of Canada
20 Cal. App. (2d) 211, 66 P. (2d) 706 (1937)

This was an action by William Cicurel (plaintiff) against Plaza Service Corporation of Canada (defendant). Defendant filed a counterclaim and cross-complaint. Judgment for plaintiff and defendant appealed. Judgment affirmed.

Defendant was engaged in the business of conducting hat and valet concessions in hotels. It held a contract with Crocker Hotel Company by which it conducted such concessions in the St. Francis Hotel and the Palace Hotel in San Francisco. Plaintiff was employed by defendant as its San Francisco manager at a weekly salary and a percentage of the profit from the concessions. When plaintiff's employment terminated he claimed the defendant owed him for salary and percentage of profits the sum of $4,945.40. The defendant set up by way of counterclaim that on the expiration of their contract with the Crocker Hotel Corporation, plaintiff, in violation of his duties to it, solicited the contract for himself to the damage of the defendant. The facts established on the trial of the case were as follows: The entire capital stock of the defendant was held by one Crespi who died sometime before the expiration of the contract. After the death of Crespi the defendant became in arrears on its payments and the Crocker Hotel Company became dissatisfied with the way the new manager of the defendant conducted its business. The plaintiff used his best efforts to negotiate a renewal of the contract but, as a result of the dissatisfaction with the way the old contract had been handled by the new manager, the Crocker Hotel Company refused to renew it. It was only after all possibilities of the defendants obtaining a renewal were exhausted that plaintiff entered into a contract with the Crocker Hotel Company.

Per Curiam. Testimony, which the trial court believed, was clearly sufficient to support the finding of plaintiff's good faith, that there was no previous solicitation on his own behalf, and that the renewals could not have been obtained by the defendant.

It is well settled that an agent must use the utmost good faith and must not postpone his principal's interest to his own or use information acquired in the course of his agency as a means of acquiring an advantage for himself; but where there is no breach of duty in these respects, and a lease is obtained upon information which is not secret or confidential, or by reason of or in the course of an employment, the rule has no application. Here the evidence shows, and the court found, there was no breach of faith; and it is clear that defendant's conduct and not that of plaintiff caused the refusal to renew with the defendant.

Agent's Duty To Act for Only One Party

An ancient and universally accepted rule is that one cannot serve two masters. This rule applies to an agent. Three situations may arise in regard to an agent representing both parties to a transaction.

1. Transactions in which the agent acts for both parties to the transaction and neither party to the transaction knows that the agent is also acting as the agent of the other party. In this situation neither party is bound by the contract, since it is voidable at the election of either party.[1] The agent is not entitled to compensation from either party.

2. Transactions in which the agent acts for both parties to the transaction and one party knows that the agent is acting for both parties but the other party does not. In this situation the party who did not know that the agent was acting for both parties is not bound

[1] See Restatement of the Law of Agency, sec. 313 (2), p. 697.

by the contract; it is voidable at his election. The failure to disclose that the agent is also acting for the other party to the transaction is a fraud. The decisions are not uniform as to the agent's right to compensation. Some courts hold that the agent is entitled to the agreed compensation from the party who consented that he act for both. The courts are uniform in holding that he is not entitled to compensation from the party who did not know that he was acting for both.

3. Transactions in which the agent acts for both parties to the transaction and both parties know that the agent is acting for both. In this situation both parties are bound unless the agent in breach of his duty favors one of the parties. The agent would be entitled to the agreed compensation from both parties unless he is guilty of a breach of his duty to one of the parties.

Ledirk Amusement Co., Inc., et al. v. Schechner et al.
133 N.J. Eq. 602, 33 A. (2d) 894 (1943)

This was an action by Ledirk Amusement Company, Inc., and others (plaintiffs) against Samuel Schechner and R. L. S. Corporation (defendants). Suit dismissed.

The Mutual Theater Company owned two theaters which it sold to the R. L. S. Corporation. Schechner was one of the principal stockholders of the R. L. S. Corporation. The plaintiffs brought this suit in equity asking that R. L. S. Corporation be compelled to convey the theaters to plaintiffs at the price it paid for them. They base their claim on the following facts: The Ledirk Amusement Company, Inc., and the Colonial Theater, Inc., plaintiffs, are corporations the stock of which was owned by Moe Kridel and his two sons. The Mutual Theater Company owned the theaters in question. Kridel was a close friend of defendant Schechner who was a real estate broker. Brothers owned the controlling stock in the Mutual Theater Company. The theater property was heavily mortgaged to the Reconstruction Finance Corporation and payments on the mortgage were in arrears. Schechner represented to Kridel that he had the exclusive right to sell the theater properties for the Mutual Theater Company and agreed to work out a deal with Kridel. Schechner was to negotiate a new mortgage with Connecticut Mutual Life Insurance Company which Schechner represented, and, when the mortgage deal was cleared up, was to purchase the property for Kridel. Kridel knew Brothers and the others interested in the theater property and Schechner warned Kridel not to mention the deal to anyone. Instead of working a deal out for Kridel, Schechner effected a purchase for the R. L. S. Corporation, his own company.

Bigelow, V. C. If we accept the Kridels' evidence at face value, it is clear that they believed they were dealing with the man who had been engaged by the Mutual Theater Company as exclusive agent or broker to effect the sale of the property. Moe Kridel testified that he so understood. Again, asked if he had agreed to compensate Schechner for his services, he replied: "A broker gets his commission from the seller. I didn't hire him. He gave his word and he had the exclusive sale and he is working on it." The proofs are susceptible of the interpretation that plaintiffs were all the time dealing with Schechner as agent of the Theater Company, and that they never employed him or accepted his services as their own broker. "As a general rule, though subject to many exceptions, the same person may not represent opposite parties. An agent employed by one party is presumed, throughout the transaction, to be acting for that principal and not for the opposite party. . . . . The fact that one party puts faith in the agent of another does not shift the agency." I think plaintiffs failed to show that they ever employed Schechner or authorized him to act as their agent. But let us assume that plaintiffs' view of the proofs is correct.

If Schechner, to plaintiffs' knowledge, owed a duty to the Mutual Theater Company which was incompatible with the service they expected of him, they cannot recover. The doctrine of unclean hands is based upon conscience and good faith; it repels a suitor whose conduct has been morally reprehensible. It does not apply if he acted in ignorance of the facts which supply the basis of the charge. And conversely the maxim operates if what plaintiffs mistakenly believed to be the fact, brings his conduct within the condemnation of equity.

The plaintiffs rely on *Rogers* v. *Genung*, 76 N.J. Eq. 306, 74 A. 473, as authority for the proposition that Schechner's engagement by them was permissible though they knew he was agent for the owner. The defendant in that case was a real estate broker with whom property had been "listed" by the owner and whom the owner had promised to pay a commission if he produced a purchaser and the purchaser and the owner could agree upon terms. All that was expected of him was a person ready to enter into negotiations. The court held that he was at liberty to accept employment from a prospective purchaser and to represent the purchaser in negotiations with the owner.

But the situation as plaintiffs saw it was very different. Schechner was the exclusive agent, the sole person on whom Brothers was relying to bring about a sale. Even though Schechner was not empowered to fix a price and to agree upon terms of sale, he was under a duty to Brothers to exert his best efforts to accomplish results most advantageous to the owner.

In some instances, there is no legal or practical impediment to one person acting as broker for both parties, but there must be the fullest disclosure to each principal that the broker is acting for both, in order that the principals may deal at arm's length. Plaintiffs do not bring themselves within the exception. Certainly they did not expect Schechner to tell Brothers he was acting for them or even that they were eager to buy. Though the Kridels had long been on friendly terms with Brothers and saw him frequently, they obeyed Schechner's injunction, "Don't mention it to Brothers."

Agent's Duty of Obedience

The agent owes a duty to follow faithfully all instructions given him by his principal. If the agent refuses or fails to follow his principal's instructions, he must answer in damages to the principal for any injury which the principal has suffered. The agent's refusal or failure to follow instructions is a breach of the agency contract, and, if such action on the part of the agent is a material breach of the agency contract, the principal has the right to terminate the agency. There are some situations in which the agent may be justified in not following instructions. If an emergency arises and the agent cannot consult with his principal, he may be justified in using his own judgment, especially if following instructions would clearly result in injury to the principal; but, if no emergency has arisen, the agent must follow instructions, even though he deems the course of action designated by the principal to be clearly injurious to the principal. If the principal instructs the agent to do an illegal or criminal act, the agent is not bound to follow instructions. If the agency is general in its nature and the principal has not given the agent detailed instructions, the agent must use his own judgment and follow that course of action which in his judgment will best further his principal's interests.

Washington et al. v. Mechanics & Traders Insurance Co.
174 Okl. 478, 50 P. (2d) 621 (1935)

This was an action by Mechanics & Traders Insurance Company (plaintiff) against J. Wilson Washington and others (defendants). Judgment for plaintiff and defendants appealed. Judgment affirmed.

One of the defendants, Joe H. Edmondson, was the local policy writing agent of the plaintiff. The other defendants, J. Wilson Washington and Virgil D. Carlile, were sureties on Edmondson's bond given to plaintiff to secure faithful performance of his duty and the remittance of moneys collected.

Edmondson issued a fire insurance policy in the sum of $1,500 insuring the property of Sallie Young. The plaintiff ordered Edmondson to cancel the policy, but Edmondson did not carry out the plaintiff's instructions.

The undisputed testimony in the record shows that the plaintiff instructed the said Edmondson on October 21, 1927, to cancel the policy issued to Sallie Young, and said instruction was repeated on November 1, 1927, November 15, 1927, and November 29, 1927; yet, in view of these instructions, the agent, Edmondson, failed, neglected, or refused to cancel said policy. The further fact was undisputed that the house of the assured was destroyed by fire, and that the husband of the assured, John Young, was in the agent's office the day before the fire, and that the cancellation of this policy was discussed and the agent, Edmondson, at that time did not cancel the policy when he had sufficient funds on hand to return the premiums, but instead of this he continued the policy in effect in direct conflict with his instructions and refused to talk the matter over with the general agent, Kline, of the insurance company when he came to his office the next week, and the property was destroyed the next night and plaintiff company had to pay the loss.

Per Curiam. "Where an agent, whose powers extend to the cancellation of policies, is directed by the company to cancel a policy, and he neglects to do so within a reasonable time, and in the meantime there has been a loss, he is liable to the company for the amount which the latter is compelled to pay on such loss, unless he can show some valid reason for his failure to follow the company's direction. His delay or failure to cancel the policy will not be excused by the fact that he believed that the company was mistaken as to the safety or danger of the risk, or as to the wisdom of retaining it, or by the fact that he gave notice of the cancellation to the broker who negotiated the insurance and directed him to cancel it."

In the case of *Kraber's Ex'rs* v. *Union Ins. Co.*, 129 Pa. 8, 18 A. 491, 492, it is said: "When the principal gives instructions, they are binding on the agent, and he must follow them. He has no legal right to sit in judgment on the wisdom or the expediency of the directions that are given him. His duty as agent is to execute the orders of his principal with reasonable promptness, and with fidelity."

In the case of *St. Paul Fire & Marine Ins. Co.* v. *Laubenstein*, 162 Wis. 165, 155 N.W. 918, it was held:

"An agent is bound to exercise good faith and diligence in his relations with his principal and in following the instructions of his principal.

"An agent in the discharge of his duties as such must exercise ordinary care, and for negligence in failing to do so he will be liable to his principal."

The neglect and failure of the agent, Edmondson, to carry out the instructions of plaintiff company, to cancel the Sallie Young policy, for more than five weeks, was not the exercise of good faith and reasonable diligence, as to which reasonable men could differ, and the fact that the plaintiff company had the same authority to cancel the policy would not excuse or justify the agent, Edmondson, in failing or refusing to follow its instructions.

In *Westchester Fire Ins. Co.* v. *Bollin*, 106 S.C. 45, 90 S.E. 327, it was held: "It is no defense to an action for an insurance agent's failure to cancel a policy that the special agent who directed its cancellation had power to cancel it." At page 328 of 90 S.E., 106 S.C. 45, the court said: "A man has the right to transact his own business. He has the right to employ as many agents and give them as much power as he pleases. When one agent undertakes to do a certain piece of work, he cannot relieve himself of responsibility by showing that there were other agents who had the same power."

Agent's Duty of Care and Skill

An agent owes a duty to exercise ordinary care and skill in the transaction of his principal's business. The general standard applied in determining whether or not an agent has exercised ordinary care and skill is the ordinarily prudent man test. Has the agent exercised that degree of care and skill that an ordinarily prudent man would exercise under like circumstances? If an agent has been guilty of negligence, he must answer to his principal in damages for any injury which is the direct result of the agent's negligence.

Under this general rule the courts have held that the failure of the agent to disclose facts within his knowledge or to communicate to his principal notice which has been given to the agent in the course of the transaction of the principal's business is negligence and the agent will be held liable for any injury which results from such negligence. If the agent is authorized to collect, he is negligent in accepting payment in anything other than money unless authorized to do so. The agent owes a duty to follow instructions as to the method of remitting money and, if no special instructions are given, he owes a duty to use ordinary means of remittance. If the agent uses an extra hazardous means of remitting and as a result the funds are lost, the agent is liable. If an agent is authorized to collect on negotiable paper, the agent must present the instrument and give notice to indorsers if such is necessary to preserve the value of the paper.

An agent authorized to sell property on credit owes a duty to use ordinary care in checking the credit standing of the buyer. In a like manner an agent authorized to make loans for the principal must investigate the credit standing of the borrower and, if it is customary to require security, it is the duty of the agent to require adequate security. The agent is not an insurer of his acts, but must exercise ordinary care, skill, and diligence in the performance of his duties. The agent may by contract assume greater responsibility than that imposed on him by law and, conversely, the agent may by contract relieve himself from such liability.

The agent may hold himself out as possessing special skills and may contract to perform duties requiring special skills. In such cases the agent must possess and exercise that degree of special skill which is possessed and exercised by persons in the community performing such skilled services. If Peters engages Archer, a C.P.A., to make an audit, Archer must possess and exercise that degree of skill which is possessed and exercised by C.P.A.'s practicing in that locality. If Archer does not possess and exercise that degree of skill and, as a result of Archer's lack of skill or his failure to exercise skill in the performance of his duties, Peters is injured, Archer will be liable. A C.P.A. does not insure his work; that is, he is not liable for honest errors of judgment, but he must bring to the job and exercise the trained judgment of a C.P.A.

Mason Produce Co. v. Harry C. Gilbert Co.
194 Ind. 462, 141 N.E. 613 (1924)

This was an action by the Mason Produce Company (plaintiff) against Harry C. Gilbert Company (defendant). Judgment for defendant and plaintiff appealed. Judgment reversed and new trial ordered.

Defendant, acting as broker for plaintiff, took an order for a car load of beans from the Lexington Company. The Lexington Company cancelled the order by giving notice of the cancellation to defendant. At the time the notice of cancellation was given to defendant, the beans had not been shipped. Defendant failed to inform plaintiff that the order had been cancelled and plaintiff shipped the beans from Colorado to Kentucky. The beans could not be disposed of on their arrival in Kentucky and had to be reshipped to Colorado. The resulting loss was $500.

Ewbank, C. J. But even if the telegrams had made a complete and binding contract, the evidence shows that defendant was remiss in the performance of its duty as a broker, and that much of the loss resulting from the refusal of the purchaser to perform such contract resulted from its failure to do what the law required of it. A broker owes to his principal the duty to act with the utmost good faith in all their dealings with each other, and is under the legal obligation to disclose to a person by whom he is employed as broker all facts within his knowledge or which he may learn in the course of a transaction in behalf of such person that are or may be material to the matter in which he is employed, or which might influence the action of his principal in relation thereto. And, where the broker, at a time when its employer's property was still in his warehouse in Colorado, where it was of the full market value for which a sale had been negotiated, learned that the purchaser to whom it was to be shipped had repudiated his order and bought elsewhere and denied liability on the order given to such broker, claiming that it was not accepted in time, and without communicating those facts to the employer, permitted such employer, at an expense of more than $500, to ship a carload of beans 1,000 miles away to a customer in a small city who had fully supplied his needs by purchasing from others, where they arrived more than three weeks later, when there was little demand for them, is liable in damages for any resulting loss sustained by the employer. If the facts known to the broker had been communicated to the employer, he might have sold the beans to others at the place where they were, or diverted the car, while in transit, to some other city where the demand for beans had not been met by purchases from others, or have kept the beans in the warehouse, and thus have minimized, if not wholly prevented, the alleged loss.

The amount of loss sustained by plaintiff of which defendant's negligence was the proximate cause was not agreed upon, but must depend, in part, upon inferences to be drawn from the facts proved. Drawing such inferences is a function of the jury or of the trial judge sitting as a jury, and not of an appellate tribunal.

Bashford v. A. Levy & J. Zentner Co. et al.
123 Cal. App. 204, 11 P. (2d) 51 (1932)

This was an action by W. L. Bashford (plaintiff) against A. Levy & J. Zentner Co. and others (defendants). Judgment for plaintiff and defendants appealed. Judgment affirmed.

Plaintiff entered into a written contract with defendant A. Levy & J. Zentner Co. whereby he agreed to purchase, pack, and ship fruit as agent for the defendant and was to receive a stated commission on all fruit handled. Plaintiff claims that he has commissions due him in the total sum of $6,632.38. Defendant claims that plaintiff did not properly pack part of the fruit shipped and that, as a result of the improper packing, the fruit was damaged and sets up as a counterclaim the loss suffered as a result of the damage to the fruit.

Marks, J. The defendant maintains that there was poor packing of grapes, plums, and peaches, and that the piling of boxes of peaches on top of each other caused damage to the fruit, the exact extent of which does not appear. It should be observed that all the fruit packed by Bashford passes official inspection. The defendant's witnesses testified that in perfect packing of fruit the defects complained of would not occur. They also testified that a perfect pack was never obtained in the best regulated houses and that similar defects in packing and handling fruits were apparent in all packs. The plaintiff was required to use ordinary care, skill, and prudence in handling and packing the fruit, but was not required to produce a perfect pack where such results were not obtained in the district by the best and most careful and skillful packers. The jury was justified in concluding from the evidence that Bashford packed and handled the fruit with due care and skill; that the results obtained by him were equal to those of the best packers of fresh fruit in the district; and that the few defects in his packing and handling of the fruit shown by the evidence furnished no sufficient ground for the defendant discharging him and terminating the contract.

City of East Grand Forks v. Steele et al.
121 Minn. 296, 141 N.W. 181 (1913)

This was an action by the City of East Grand Forks (plaintiff) against J. Gordon Steele and others (defendants). A motion was made to dismiss the case on the ground that plaintiff's complaint did not state a cause of action. From a ruling on the motion both parties appealed. The ruling was affirmed in part and reversed in part.

Defendants, representing themselves to be expert accountants and able to detect irregularities in the transactions of the city officers, contracted to audit the books of the city officers, especially the books of the clerk who collected money due the city for electric lights, water and sewer assessments, and license fees. An audit and investigation was made in 1908 for which the city paid defendants $150 and a second audit and investigation was made in December, 1909, which covered both the years 1908 and 1909 for which the city paid the defendants $500. The defendants after each audit and investigation certified that the accounts had been correctly kept and all funds properly accounted for. Shortly after the December, 1909, audit and investigation, the state examiner made an examination of the city clerk's books and discovered that the clerk embezzled the sum of $1,984.28 prior to the 1908 audit and investigation and the additional sum of $5,339 in 1909. Defendants' failure to discover these defalcations was the result of their incompetence and negligence. The clerk had given surety bond for the faithful performance of his duties. Had the 1908 audit and investigation revealed the embezzlement, the money could have been recovered at that time, but the surety on the clerk's bond became insolvent after the audit.

The plaintiff seeks to recover the following items, and states each as a separate cause of action: (1) The sum of $5,339, embezzled by the clerk after the first audit and before the second audit. (2) The sum of $1,984.26, embezzled by the clerk prior to the first audit. (3) The compensation paid the defendants for making the first audit. (4) The compensation paid the defendants for making the second audit.

Taylor, C. The rule governing liability for breach of contract is given in the syllabus to *Sargent* v. *Mason*, 101 Minn. 319, 112 N.W. 255, as follows: "In an action for damages for breach of contract, the defaulting party is liable only for the direct consequences of the breach, such as usually occur from the infraction of like contracts, and within the contemplation of the parties when the contract was entered into as likely to result from its nonperformance."

To recover damages, not naturally and necessarily resulting from a breach of the contract, on the ground that such damages were within the contemplation of the parties when making the contract, it is said in *Liljengren F. & L. Co.* v. *Mead*, 42 Minn. 420, 44 N.W. 306, that "there must be some special facts and circumstances, out of which they naturally proceed, known to the person sought to be held liable, under such circumstances that it can be inferred from the whole transaction that such damage was in the contemplation of the parties, at the time of making the contract, as the result of its breach, and that the party sought to be charged consented to become liable for it." This rule is well established.

The damages claimed on account of the losses resulting from the defalcations of the clerk and the insolvency of his surety are too remote to be recovered, without showing the existence of special circumstances, known to defendants, from which they ought to have known that such losses were likely to result from a failure to disclose the true condition of affairs. Such losses are neither the natural nor the proximate consequences of the failure of defendants to make a proper audit. Neither are any facts shown from which it may be inferred that a loss from either of these causes was or ought to have been contemplated, when the contract was made, as likely to result from a breach of duty on the part of defendants.

If, at the making of the contract and in the light of the knowledge then possessed by them, the parties had taken thought as to what consequences might reasonably be expected to result from its breach, there is nothing set forth in the complaint from which we can say that they ought to have foreseen or to have contemplated that the clerk was likely to commit a crime, or that his surety was likely to become bankrupt, and thereby entail financial loss upon the city. There may be circumstances under which the negligence of an expert accountant may make him liable for losses, as where he is employed to determine the amount that should be exacted from a surety for the default of his principal; but the facts alleged in the complaint do not bring this case within any such rule.

Defendants represented themselves as expert accountants, which implied that they were skilled in that class of work. In accepting employment as expert accountants, they undertook, and the plaintiff had the right to expect, that in the performance of their duties they would exercise the average ability and skill of those engaged in that branch of skilled labor. They were employed to ascertain, among other things, whether any irregularities had occurred in the financial transactions of the city clerk, and, if so, the nature and extent of such irregularities. If, from want of proper skill, or from negligence, they did not disclose the true situation, they failed to perform the duty which they had assumed, and failed to earn the compensation which plaintiff had agreed to pay them for the proper performance of such duty.

The work of an expert accountant is of such technical character and requires such peculiar skill that the ordinary person cannot be expected to know whether he performs his duties properly or otherwise, but must rely upon his report as to the thoroughness and accuracy of his work. The full contract price having been paid in the belief, induced by defendants' report, that such report disclosed fully and accurately the condition of the city's accounts, the city is entitled to recover back the amounts so paid, upon proving that, through the incompetence or the negligence of defendants, the report was in substance misleading and false.

Agent's Duty To Account

It is the agent's duty to keep a true and accurate account of the business transacted for the principal and to be ready to render to his principal a complete account of all business transacted for the principal. The agent owes a duty to account for and turn over to the principal all moneys and property of the principal coming into the agent's possession. In the event the agent receives property other than money, the agent must turn the property received over to the principal. If the agent disposes of the property and turns over to the principal other similar property or an amount of money equal to the value placed on the property at the time the agent acquired it, the agent will be guilty of a breach of duty unless the contract of agency permits such substitution.

The agent owes a duty to keep the property of his principal separate from his own. If he commingles the principal's property with his own, he will be liable for any resulting loss. If the property of the principal is commingled with that of the agent and the property cannot be separated, the agent must satisfy every legitimate claim of the principal. If it is necessary in order to protect the interests of the principal, the courts will grant the entire mass of commingled property to the principal.

If the agent has used the principal's property or money or has failed to keep it separate, the principal can follow his property or property purchased with the principal's money and recover it, or he can hold the agent for the conversion of the property. Archer acting as agent for Peters collects $5,000 for Peters. Instead of turning the money over to Peters, Archer purchases corporate stock with it. Peters, if he can show that Archer purchased the stock with his money, can claim the stock even though it has increased in value since the purchase or he may hold Archer accountable for the money collected.

An agent may deposit moneys collected for his principal in a bank unless the agent has been given contrary instructions. However, if the agent deposits his principal's money in a bank, he must choose a bank of good standing and must deposit the money in the name of the principal or under some mark to indicate that the money is that of the principal and not the money of the agent. If the agent deposits the principal's money in his own name or in his own personal account, he will ordinarily be held for any loss.

Bills v. Hyde
49 S.D. 18, 205 N.W. 708 (1925)

This was an action by Emma J. Bills (plaintiff) against Charles L. Hyde (defendant). Judgment for plaintiff and defendant appealed. Judgment affirmed.

Defendant acting as plaintiff's agent promised plaintiff that he would invest funds, furnished by plaintiff to defendant, in securities bearing interest at not less than 8 per cent per annum. Defendant further promised that he would make the investments in such a manner that plaintiff should receive therefrom interest in monthly installments and that he (the defendant) would guarantee the safety of the investments and the payment of the principal and interest thereon.

Plaintiff remitted to the defendant $1,500 on the 6th of February, 1920, $1,600 on the 12th of April, 1920, $1,700 on the 11th of March, 1921, $1,650 on the 14th of September, 1921, and $350 on the 9th of November, 1921, in all the sum of $6,800; thereafter defendant represented to plaintiff that he had invested and loaned the said money for her and held securities for the same. Plaintiff demanded of defendant that he account to her for the said sum and deliver the securities purchased therewith, but the defendant failed and refused to account to plaintiff in any manner whatever. No part of said sum or securities purchased has ever been paid to plaintiff. Defendant has paid interest at 8 per cent per annum monthly thereon, up to and including the 1st of October, 1922. Plaintiff is informed and believes that defendant has not invested said sums in securities, but has converted the same to his own use, and has mingled them with his own money, and intends to keep and withhold the same from the plaintiff.

This suit is brought for an accounting and to recover the securities purchased, if any were purchased, or to recover a judgment for the money paid over to the defendant.

Burch, C. It is argued by defendant that there is no intimation in the pleading that the defendant was obliged, as a matter of contract or law, to deliver over any such securities, and, if he guaranteed the interest and the safety of the investment, that he has the right to retain the securities. The relation between the plaintiff and defendant is one of agency creating a trust relation. The plaintiff cannot allege more than the truth, or state the time when the securities were to be delivered, if in fact no time was mentioned as a part of the contract. We assume that the complaint states the truth, and that all the facts relative to the contract have been pleaded. Are such facts sufficient to create a contract upon which an action may be based and maintained? It is a well-recognized duty of an agent to account for money of his principal received by him. The principal has the right to assure himself that the accounts are proper and correct. Measures taken in good faith by the principal to secure a proper accounting and to assure himself of its propriety are therefore not in violation of the contract, although they may not be in its expressed terms. As a rule, the funds are to be applied to the purposes of the agency, and the least turning aside of funds held in trust by the agent is legally a wrongful act. Upon the contention that the agent is entitled to retain the securities because of his guaranty, he has no such right unless by express terms of the contract he is empowered to do so. A guarantor's contract is independent of the contract between the holder of securities and the obligors thereon. We are satisfied that the complaint states a cause of action for an accounting.

Wangsness v. Berdahl
— S.D. —, 13 N.W. (2d) 293 (1944)

This was an action by Ole M. Wangsness (plaintiff) against James O. Berdahl (defendant). Judgment for plaintiff and defendant appealed. Judgment affirmed.

Defendant, an attorney, recovered a judgment for the plaintiff in a suit brought by defendant as attorney for the plaintiff. The amount of the judgment was paid by the judgment debtor to defendant as attorney and agent for plaintiff. The defendant deposited the money thus collected in his personal account in the First State Bank of Sioux Falls, South Dakota, and drew his personal check payable to plaintiff for the sum collected. Before the check cleared, the First State Bank of Sioux Falls failed and the check was not paid.

Plaintiff gave no instructions to defendant as to the manner in which remittance should be made of the proceeds of said collection, and defendant himself decided in what manner he should receive such proceeds, and handle same, and attempt remittance to plaintiff.

Roberts, J. Defendant cites authorities in support of the principle that where an attorney acts with a proper degree of attention, with reasonable care, and to the best of his skill and knowledge, he is not responsible for loss sustained by his client. It is argued that the failure of the plaintiff to receive payment resulted solely from the failure of the bank and not from the neglect of defendant to discharge some duty which was fairly within the purview of his employment. This case involves no claim of negligence. An attorney who has collected money for his client holds the same as trustee, and the circumstances under which he is liable are much the same as any other trustee. It is often stated to be the rule that where a trustee deposits trust funds in his own name, thereby vesting himself with title, he is liable for any loss of the funds. In *Naltner* v. *Dolan*, 108 Ind. 500, 8 N.E. 289, 291, 58 Am. Rep. 61, attorneys who deposited money collected for their client in a bank in the firm name were held liable to the client for loss resulting from failure of the bank. The court said:

"In case it becomes the duty of an agent or trustee to deposit money belonging to his principal, he can escape the risk only by making the deposit in his principal's name, or by so distinguishing it on the books of the bank as to indicate, in some way, that it is the principal's money. If he deposit in his own name, he will not, in case of loss, be permitted to throw such loss on his principal. . . . . In such a case the good faith or intention of the trustee is in no way involved. Having, for his personal convenience, or from whatever motive, deposited the money in his own name, thereby vesting himself with a legal title, it follows, as a necessary consequence, when loss occurs, he will not be permitted to say, as against his cestui que trust, that the fact is not as he voluntarily made it appear."

We think that the rule is applicable to the facts found in the case at bar. It is entirely immaterial that defendant acted in good faith and that the loss would have occurred though defendant had made the deposit in the name of his client. Many of the cases hold that the rule is inflexibly applicable because of the likelihood that where funds are deposited in the individual name of the trustee a mingling of funds may result and because of the right which the bank and others dealing with the funds would have to treat the same as the individual property of the trustee.

Principal's Duties to Agent

Usually the relation of principal and agent is created by contract and the contract will stipulate the compensation which the agent is to receive for his services. In such cases the amount of compensation due the agent will be determined by interpreting the contract. If there is no express agreement creating the agency or if the agreement does not stipulate the amount of compensation to be paid to the agent, whether or not the agent is to be compensated will be determined from the relation of the parties and the surrounding circumstances. In such cases, if the agent is to be compensated, he is entitled to the reasonable value of the services rendered.

The courts have generally held that the agent is not entitled to compensation if the agent is also representing interests adverse to those of the principal without the principal's knowledge or consent; if the agent is guilty of fraud or misrepresentation; if the agent is negligent and the agent's negligence results in serious injury to his principal; or if the business transacted by the agent is illegal.

Frequently the agent's compensation is contingent. In such cases the agent is not entitled to compensation until he has fulfilled his contract. Selling agents may be paid a commission on orders accepted and approved. In such cases the principal must act in good faith in the acceptance and approval of orders. If an order has been accepted and approved, the agent is entitled to his commission even though the order is never shipped or the goods are never paid for. Whether or not an agent has earned a contingent commission will depend on an interpretation of the agency contract. If the principal, by his acts, prevents the agent from completing the transaction, the agent will be entitled to the stipulated compensation.

If the agent has made advancements, in behalf of the principal, in the transaction of the principal's business and within the scope of the agent's authority, the agent is entitled to reimbursement for all such advancements. Also, if the agent has suffered losses in the conduct of the principal's business, the principal is legally bound to indemnify the agent for such losses, providing the agent has acted within the scope of his authority.

Harris v. McPherson et al.
97 Conn. 164, 115 Atl. 723 (1921)

This was an action by Morton S. Harris (plaintiff) against Minnietta S. McPherson and another (defendants). Judgment for plaintiff and defendants appealed. Judgment affirmed.

Defendants owned a tract of land and the buildings thereon which they listed with plaintiff, a real estate broker, for sale. The listing was as follows:

"Contract.

"Suffield, Conn., 3/11/1918

"This is to certify that on this date I have given to Morton S. Harris the exclusive sale of my property, viz: Six acres land more or less with all standing buildings thereon, for the sum of $8,000 (8,-000.00) and do agree to pay the said M. S. Harris 5 per cent of the purchase price at transfer of deed.

"F. B. McPherson.
"Minnietta S. McPherson."

Plaintiff advertised the place for sale and expended time and money in showing the place and interviewing prospective buyers. On April 20, 1918, defendants sold the place and notified plaintiff that they cancelled the listing. The plaintiff demanded a commission on the sale which defendants refused to pay.

Curtis, J. The defendants claimed that, if a mutual contract arose by the plaintiff's acceptance, through acts, of the offer contained in this agreement, yet that such contract did not preclude the sale of the property by the defendants to a purchaser of their own procuring, without obligation to pay a commission to the plaintiff as damages for a breach of contract. In other words, that the giving of the exclusive sale of property by an owner to a broker, at the most, gave him merely an exclusive agency.

In the law relating to the relations between the owner of real estate and a broker employed to procure a purchaser, there is a difference in the cases in interpreting a contract in which the owner gives the broker the exclusive sale of property. There appears to be no diversity of view in interpreting a contract whereby the owner gives the broker an exclusive agency. Such a contract may be defined as follows: A contract employing a broker as an exclusive agent is an agreement on the part of the owner that during the life of the contract he will not sell the property to a purchaser procured through another agent. This does not preclude the owner from selling to a purchaser of his own procuring. There are cases which define a contract by the owner giving a broker the exclusive sale of property, as giving him merely an exclusive agency as defined above. We are satisfied that the weight of reason and authority support the following definition of such a contract: A contract of the owner giving a broker the exclusive sale of property is an agreement on the part of the owner that he will not sell the property during the life of the contract to any purchaser not procured by the broker in question. In the instant case, the contract with the broker gave him the exclusive sale of the property. Therefore a sale by the owner to a purchaser of his own procuring was a breach of contract if made while the contract was in force.

Applying the foregoing principles of law to the instant case, we have a contract whereby the defendants (owners) give the plaintiff (agent) the exclusive sale of a particular piece of property for a reasonable time. The trial court by its judgment found that the reasonable time which this contract was to endure had not expired in April, 1918, at the time of the sale by the owner. That finding was as definite as the court was required to be under the circumstances, although under the facts found, it would seem that it could reasonably have been found that the reasonable time involved would have extended a considerable period beyond April, 1918. Under the law as stated above, the owners in this case had the power to revoke the plaintiff's agency by notice, or by the sale of the property on April 20th, 1918, but, under the facts, they did not have the right to terminate the contract by such revocation, as the reasonable time for its duration had not expired. The owners, therefore, by their conduct breached their contract with the plaintiff, and he has a right of action against them. In this action by the broker against the owners, he is entitled to recover his commission as damages for breach of the contract, if during the reasonable time that was the life of the contract the owners sell the property to a purchaser procured by their own efforts, or by other agents, or if the plaintiff during such period produced a customer ready, able and willing to buy the property. The owners sold the property during the life of the contract, thereby breaching the contract, therefore the plaintiff was entitled to recover his commission as damages for the breach.

Termination of the Agency

The principal and agent relationship is a personal relationship; thus, it can be terminated at the will of either party. It may be terminated by the mutual agreement of the parties, by the accomplishment of the object of the agency, by its expiration under the terms of the contract, by the death of either party, by the insanity or bankruptcy of the principal, by a change in the law rendering the object of the agency illegal, or by the destruction of the subject matter of the agency. There is no set method of terminating the relationship. If the agent wishes to terminate it, he may cease to represent the principal or in any other manner he chooses express his intention to quit. If the principal wishes to terminate the relationship, he may revoke the agent's authority by giving the agent notice that his authority has been revoked. If either party in terminating the relationship has breached the contract of agency, he will have to answer in damages to the other party. The courts recognize an agency coupled with an interest as an exception to the rule that the agency relationship may be terminated at the will of either party. In such cases, the agency being created for the benefit of the agent, the principal cannot terminate it.

To have an agency coupled with an interest, the agent must have an ownership or equity in the subject matter of the agency. Peters borrows $1,000 from Archer and as security gives Archer a chattel mortgage on Peters' personal property. The chattel mortgage contains a clause appointing Archer as Peters' agent and authorizing Archer, in the event Peters defaults in his payments, to sell the mortgaged property and pay himself out of the proceeds of the sale. Peters cannot terminate this agency and the agency would not be terminated by Peters' death.

McCallum v. Grier
86 S.C. 162, 68 S.E. 466 (1910)

This was an action by J. L. McCallum (plaintiff) against Kate B. Grier (defendant). Judgment for defendant and plaintiff appealed. Judgment affirmed.

Kate B. Grier gave the McCallum Realty and Insurance Co. written power of attorney to sell certain property for her. Before a sale was consummated she orally revoked the authority. After such revocation the company contracted to sell the property to its president, McCallum. This suit is for specific performance of the contract. The question is whether Grier could revoke the agent's authority by oral notice.

Gary, A. J. The next question that will be considered is whether the defendant had the power to revoke the authority of her agent during the time fixed for the continuance of her contract with the agent. "As between principal and agent, authority is revocable at any time, if not coupled with an interest. The authority of an agent to represent the principal depends upon the will and license of the latter. It is the act of the principal which creates the authority; it is for his benefit, and to subserve his purposes, that it is called into being; and unless the agent has acquired with the authority an interest in the subject-matter, it is in the principal's interest alone that the authority is to be exercised. The agent, obviously, except in the instance mentioned, can have no right to insist upon a further execution of the authority, if the principal himself desires it to terminate. It is the general rule of law, therefore, that as between the agent and his principal, the authority of the agent may be revoked by the principal at his will at any time, and with or without good reason therefor, except in those cases where the authority is coupled with sufficient interest in the agent. And this is true, even though the authority be in express terms, declared to be 'exclusive' or 'irrevocable.' But although the principal has the power thus to revoke the authority, he may subject himself to a claim for damages, if he exercises it, contrary to his express or implied agreement in the matter. An agency is sometimes said to be irrevocable, when it is conferred for a valuable consideration. It is believed, however, that this is only another form of stating the general rule, that it must be coupled with an interest." Mechem on Agency, § 204.

"A power of attorney constituting a mere agency, is always revocable. It is only when coupled with an interest in the thing itself, or the estate which is the subject of the power, it is deemed to be irrevocable, as where it is a security for money advanced, or is to be used as a means of effectuating a purpose necessary to protect the rights of the agent or others. A mere power, like a will, is in its very nature revocable, when it concerns the interest of the principal alone, and, in such case, even an express declaration of irrevocability will not prevent revocation. An interest in the proceeds, to arise as mere compensation for the service of executing the power, will not make the power irrevocable. Therefore, it has been held, that a mere employment to transact the business of the principal is not irrevocable without an express covenant founded on sufficient consideration, notwithstanding the compensation of the agent is to result from the business to be performed, and to be measured by its extent. In order to make an agreement for irrevocability, contained in a power to transact business for the benefit of the principal, binding on him, there must be a consideration for it, independent of the compensation to be rendered, for the services to be performed." *Blackstone* v. *Buttermore*, 53 Pa. 266.

"It is not denied by the plaintiff that, in this case, it was within the power of the defendant to put an end to his agency by revoking his authority. Indeed, this is a doctrine so consonant with justice and common sense, that it requires no reasoning to prove it. But he contends that it is a maxim of common law that every instrumentality must be revoked by one of equal dignity. It is true an instrument under seal cannot be released or discharged by an instrument not under seal or by parol, but we do not consider the rule as applicable to the revocation of powers of attorney. The authority of an agent is conferred at the mere will of the principal, and is to be executed for his benefit; the principal, therefore, has the right to put an end to the agency, when the confidence at first reposed in him is withdrawn."

As a broker is a special agent a third party deals with him at his peril. Therefore, after the defendant revoked the authority of her agent, D. R. McCallum, Jr., could not enter into a contract binding on her for the sale of the land, even though the plaintiff was not then aware that the agent's authority had been revoked. The foregoing authorities dispose of all the exceptions, relative to the power of revocation.

Duty To Notify Third Persons

If the agency is general and the agent has been dealing with third persons for a period of time, the principal, if he revokes the agent's authority, owes a duty to notify third persons that the agency has been terminated. The facts and circumstances surrounding each case will be determinative of the principal's duty to notify third persons of the termination of the agency. If the relationship between the agent and the third persons has been such that they are justified in assuming his authority is a continuing authority, the principal will owe a duty to notify them of the termination of the relationship.

If the agency is terminated by the death of the principal, the agent will not have the power to bind the estate of the principal, and, as a general rule, any act of the agent will not bind the estate of the principal even though at the time of the transaction neither the agent nor the third person had knowledge of the principal's death.

Union Bank & Trust Co. v. Long Pole Lumber Co.
70 W.Va. 558, 74 S.E. 674 (1912)

This was an action by the Union Bank & Trust Company (plaintiff) against the Long Pole Lumber Company (defendant). Judgment for plaintiff and defendant appealed. Judgment affirmed.

One W. J. Newenham was president of the Long Pole Lumber Co. and had during his presidency indorsed notes to the Union Bank & Trust Co. After his resignation as president of the company, he indorsed the note in question to the Bank. The company claimed they were not bound by the indorsement because the agency had been terminated.

Poffenbarger, J. The only evidence adduced to prove notice of the termination of such authority as Newenham had was oral testimony to the publication of a notice of the resignation in a newspaper. That is wholly insufficient, in the absence of proof that it was seen and read by the agents of the bank, who deny that they ever saw it. On the termination of an agency, persons who have dealt with the principal through the agent may continue to do so, in the absence of knowledge of the fact, and the principal will be bound by the acts of the former agent as fully as if his authority had not ceased. The duty of the principal to notify third persons of the termination of the agency is of the same character and requires the same degree of certainty as that which the law imposes upon the members of a copartnership in the case of dissolution as a measure of protection from liability by reason of subsequent acts of the former members of the dissolved firm.

In all such cases, persons who have dealt with the principal through the agent will be protected in continuing to do so, unless and until they have in some way obtained actual notice of the termination of the relation, and, as to them, mere publication of notice in a newspaper and local notoriety of the fact are not sufficient.

QUESTIONS AND PROBLEMS

1. McCabe and the Lake View State Bank had made a loan, and as security all the capital stock of the Bel-Pine Apartment Corp. had been pledged to McCabe and

the bank. The assets of the Bel-Pine Apartment Corp. consisted of an apartment building known as the Bel-Pine Apartments. Acting as agents for Mary Lerk, McCabe and the bank purchased the Bel-Pine Apartments for Mary Lerk and, as part of the transaction, Mary Lerk assumed all the indebtedness of the Bel-Pine Apartment Corp. Mary Lerk asks to have the transaction set aside on the ground that McCabe and the bank have an interest in the transactions. Should the transaction be set aside?

2. Wright was employed by the Lynn Publishing Co. as a reporter. Wright learned, in the course of his employment, that the Publishing Co.'s lease on the premises occupied by it was about to expire and that the premises had a peculiar value to his employer or to one carrying on a publishing business, and he also learned the name of the landlord. Wright, without the knowledge or consent of his employer, leased the premises in his (Wright's) own name for a period of years. The Lynn Publishing Co. brought an action to have Wright assign the lease to it. Should Wright be forced to assign the lease to the Lynn Publishing Co.?
3. Blake listed certain real estate with Tracey, a real estate broker, for sale. Nye listed certain real estate with Jones, a real estate broker, for sale. Tracey, without the knowledge or consent of Blake, agreed to pay Jones one-half of his commissions if Jones would negotiate a deal whereby Nye exchanged his real estate for Blake's real estate. The exchange was negotiated. Blake refused to pay Tracey his commissions and when sued set up the secret deal between Tracey and Jones as a defense. Is Tracey entitled to a commission?
4. Sparkman, whose wife was sick, sent his brother John to Bedford for the purpose of employing Dr. McCowan. John was unable to employ Dr. McCowan but did obtain the services of Dr. Bartlett. Did John violate his duty as an agent?
5. Mann was an importer of silk and Heard was a commission merchant in Hong Kong. Mann engaged Heard to represent him as agent in the purchase of silk. Mann instructed Heard to purchase a cargo of silk and furnished Heard with funds. Heard did not purchase the silk as instructed although there was an ample supply of such silk on the market. As the result of Heard's failure to purchase the silk, Mann suffered substantial losses. Is Heard liable to Mann for such losses?
6. Sargeant employed Downey to sell cheese the latter had made from milk supplied by Sargeant. Downey deposited the proceeds from the sale of the cheese in the Exchange Bank in his (Downey's) name. At the time the deposits were made, the bank was in good repute. The bank became insolvent and the money deposited by Downey was lost. Was Downey liable to Sargeant for the sum lost?
7. Ross requested Clifton to purchase a mill for him. Clifton purchased the mill, and after it was purchased Ross decided it was too small and refused to accept it. No price was fixed which Clifton was to pay for the mill. Clifton sues Ross to recover the amount he paid for the mill. Can Clifton recover?
8. Cuddy engaged Millar as his agent to perform certain services and agreed to pay him what "he thought the services were worth to him." Millar performed the services and on Cuddy's refusal to pay for the services Millar brought suit. Cuddy claims that the services were of no value to him. Is Millar entitled to a judgment?
9. Rogers appointed Cloe as his agent to survey, plot into lots, and sell a certain tract of land. Cloe was to receive as compensation a commission on each lot sold. Cloe surveyed the land, plotted it into lots, and advertised the lots for sale but had sold no lots when Rogers notified Cloe that the agency was revoked. Does Rogers have the power to terminate the agency? If the agency is terminated what, if any, are Cloe's rights?
10. J. B. Burch owned a store in a logging settlement. Mike Burch had been employed by him as clerk and was in general charge of the store. Mike Burch was discharged. The salesman of the grocery company came to the store about two months after Mike had been discharged and asked for Mike. He was told that

Mike was at the mill but was not told that Mike was no longer employed at the store. The salesman went to the mill and asked Mike if he needed anything for the store, and Mike gave an order for a shipment of tobacco. Mike intercepted the tobacco, so it was never delivered to the store. The grocery company was never notified that Mike had been discharged. Is J. B. Burch liable for the tobacco?

PART VII

PARTNERSHIPS

CHAPTER XXX

CREATION OF PARTNERSHIP

Introduction

A partnership is defined in the Uniform Partnership Act as an association of two or more persons to carry on as co-owners a business for profit. The origin of the partnership dates back to the earliest days of commercial activity. It is a natural outgrowth of the social relationship. One would naturally expect two or more persons to unite their possessions and skill to accomplish ends which neither could attain working alone. In discussing the partnership relation we shall confine ourselves to the partnership as defined above, that is, to the partnership organized to carry on a business for profit. This will eliminate all social, charitable, political, and educational associations and all other clubs and groups, not incorporated, whose objective is other than carrying on a business for profit.

As a business organization, the partnership holds a position midway between a sole proprietorship and a corporation. The present theory of a partnership is that it has no existence separate and apart from the members who compose it. This is the theory on which the Uniform Partnership Act is based. In the business world, the partnership is treated as a separate entity. Although the courts do not look upon a partnership as an entity, they do treat it as an entity under certain circumstances. In determining the rights of partnership creditors to partnership assets, the partnership is treated as an entity. This view is recognized in the Federal Bankruptcy Act.

The law of partnership had its origin in the Law Merchant. When the Law Merchant was absorbed into and became a part of the common law, the merchants' conception of the law of partnership was altered to a greater extent than the merchant law of negotiable instruments, insurance, and sales. The law of property was well developed and crystallized under the common law, and the common law judges applied the rules of common law to the partnership even though they were not suited to the partnership relation. As a result of this development, our partnership law became a fusion of the merchant law, the common law, and, to some extent, civil law.

The Uniform Partnership Act,[1] as drafted, for the most part follows the law of partnerships, but it does clear up some of the more confused phases of the law.

Intention of Parties

No particular formalities are necessary in the creation of a partnership. If two or more persons enter into an agreement to form a partnership or to do those acts which are characteristic of a partnership, the relationship will arise. The intent to become partners is essential. Intent as used means legal intent, not subjective intent, or, as it is often stated, their intention will be gathered from their contracts and acts, not from their declarations of intention. Where there is a definite declaration of intention to enter into a partnership and such declaration of intention is reduced to writing, usually there is no question as to the existence of the relationship; yet the use of the word partnership or the declaration of intention is not controlling. If the contract of the parties and their acts do not disclose an intention to carry on a business as co-owners for profit, no partnership will be formed. In the absence of expressed intention and in the absence of written articles of copartnership, it is often difficult to determine whether or not the partnership relation exists. Certain basic tests, not absolutely controlling, are applied. If the parties share the profits of the enterprise, it is strong evidence of the existence of a partnership. However, often rent is paid, the manager is paid, or interest on money borrowed is paid on the basis of the profits made in the conduct of the business. Parties receiving a share of the profit as payment for such services are not partners. If the parties share both profits and losses, it is not conclusive evidence of a partnership but is evidence of the strongest kind. The existence of a partnership is a combined question of fact and law.[2]

Kennedy v. Mullins
155 Va. 166, 154 S.E. 568 (1930)

This was an action by Dallas Mullins (plaintiff) against B. F. Kennedy (defendant). Judgment for plaintiff and defendant appealed. Judgment affirmed.

The plaintiff, knowing that the Chemical Wood Corporation owned a tract of timber in the county, wrote them and asked them to give him a contract to cut the timber. They replied that they wished to let the cutting, logging, hauling, and loading on railway

[1] Adopted by 24 states and Alaska (1946).
[2] Uniform Partnership Act, Section 7, appendix, p. 926.

cars all under one contract. Plaintiff proposed to the defendant that he (the plaintiff) cut and log the timber and that the defendant haul and load it in cars.

Later plaintiff and defendant had a conference with representatives of the Chemical Wood Corporation in which the cutting, logging, hauling, and loading of the timber was discussed, but no agreement was reached because they did not agree on the price to be paid.

After this conference the plaintiff and defendant discussed the deal and decided to take the contract at the price offered by the Chemical Wood Corporation if they could not get a better price. The price offered by the Chemical Wood Corporation was $17 per thousand. Mullins was to cut and skid the logs for $8 per thousand and Kennedy was to do the hauling and loading for $9 per thousand and they were to split equally anything over the $17 which they could get. Defendant called on the Chemical Wood Corporation and signed a contract in his own name in which he was to get $18 per thousand for the work. Defendant refused to permit plaintiff to participate in the contract. Plaintiff sued to recover damages for breach of the contract to form a partnership. The lower court rendered a judgment for plaintiff for $500. On appeal the Supreme Court held that the plaintiff failed to prove the partnership, but that the plaintiff did establish the existence of a contract and the breach thereof.

Hudgins, J. His own evidence shows that the only thing the plaintiff ever agreed to become responisble for was the cutting and logging, or, as he termed it, the cutting and skidding. The above evidence establishes the fact that the parties were working together for separate and distinct parts of the proposed contract, each party assuming a different responsibility, the responsibility and benefit separate and distinct from the other. Because the plaintiff termed their relationship a partnership does not make it such.

"If the terms of the contract existing between the parties do not constitute a partnership, none will be declared, even though the parties in words call the arrangement one." 20 R. C. L. 832.

The test as to whether or not the agreement of the parties constituted a partnership, certainly as between themselves, is governed largely by their intention.

"The particular test as to the existence of the partnership relation which is most widely accepted today and which is applicable especially as between the parties themselves irrespective of the rights of third persons is that a partnership is formed and exists only when it was the intention of the parties that they should be partners. Partnership contracts, like other contracts, are governed by the intention of the parties. Every partnership rests on the mutual consent of the members. This intent may be manifested by the terms of their agreement, the conduct of the parties to each other under it, or by the circumstances generally surrounding the transaction." 20 R. C. L. 831.

That the plaintiff did not intend to form a partnership, or consider any agreement binding on him, is further shown by the fact that after the conference with the representatives of the Chemical Wood Corporation at Clintwood he stated to the defendant that he was going back to accept the offer made him by Mr. White to take the cutting and logging at $8 per thousand.

Who May Form a Partnership

The formation of a partnership requires the exercise of two legal capacities—(1) the capacity to contract and (2) the capacity to own property. Whether or not a person may become a member of a partnership depends on his capacity to enter into the contract which creates the partnership and his capacity to own an interest in a partnership. Few restrictions are placed on the capacity to own property; consequently, the lack of capacity to own an interest in a partnership is such a rarity that the question of one's capacity to own partnership property is of no practical importance.

The capacity to enter into the contract of partnership is for all practical purposes the same as the capacity to enter into contracts in general. An infant may be a member of a partnership. The infant's contract is voidable and the infant has the right to disaffirm the contract of partnership and withdraw from the partnership at any time. The courts are in accord in holding that the infant may disaffirm his individual liability on partnership contracts, but the courts are divided on whether or not, on disaffirmance of the contract of partnership, the infant can recover from the adult partners the amount of his investment less moneys withdrawn from the business. Some courts hold that, if the partnership has suffered losses, the infant will have to bear his proportionate share of losses up to but not to exceed the amount of his capital investment. The fact that a member of a partnership is an infant does not make the contracts of the partnership voidable.

At common law, a married woman was without legal capacity and could not become a partner, but modern legislation has removed the married woman's disability, and in most jurisdictions a married woman may be a member of a partnership. In some jurisdictions she may become a partner with her husband. Under the Uniform Partnership Act a corporation may become a partner, but the courts have held that such an act is *ultra vires* unless the corporation's charter expressly gives it the power to become a partner. An argument against a corporation becoming a partner is that a corporation's business should be managed by a board of directors, and, if the corporation became a partner, the board of directors would surrender a portion of the management to the other partner or partners. Under existing corporation statutes it is doubtful if a corporation could legally enter into a partnership.

Carrying on a Business

To have a partnership two or more persons must be co-owners of the business carried on by the partnership. It is possible to have a partnership which owns no property, yet satisfies this requirement. Archer, a doctor, has an established practice and a fully equipped office. Archer enters into a partnership with Burch, a young doctor, to engage in the practice of medicine. Burch has no equipment. It is agreed that all the office equipment, etc., shall remain the individual property of Archer. Archer and Burch are co-owners of the business—practice of medicine—but the partnership of Archer and Burch owns no property.

Persons may be co-owners of property and not be partners. Frequently, two or more persons will own property as tenants in common. For example, Archer, Burch, and Clark may own an apartment building as tenants in common and not be partners. They may rent the building as a unit and divide the net proceeds, or they may rent each apartment separately and divide the net proceeds and not be held to be partners. The renting of the apartment building or the separate apartments is not operating a business for profit. The owner of a farm and his tenant who own stock and equipment as tenants in common and who divide the proceeds of the farm are not, as a general rule, partners. Neither are farmers who organize an association to purchase a threshing machine for their several uses. The same would be true of business or professional men who organize an association to further or protect their common interests and purchase property for the use of the association. In each instance the parties are co-owners of property but not partners. The carrying on of a business has been defined as "the conduct of a business for a substantial period for the purposes of livelihood or profit, and not merely the carrying on of some single transaction." [3] Joint ventures, syndicates, drilling for oil or gas, opening of a mine, and similar undertakings, as a general rule, are not held to be the carrying on of a business. Although they involve the transaction of some business, they lack that continuity of acts usually associated with the carrying on of a business.

The carrying on of a business for profit is an essential element of a partnership. At one time the sharing of profits was the sole test of the existence of a partnership, but this is no longer true. Many charita-

---

[3] *Mosby & Calvert,* Inc. v. *Burgess,* 153 Va. 779, 787, 151 S.E. 165.

ble organizations engage in business transactions for a profit, but not for the benefit of the members, and such associations are not held to be partnerships. Also, many trade associations engage in the transaction of business not for profit, but for the purpose of furthering the business interests of the associates. Many non-profit associations transact business, but they do not carry on a business *for profit* and are not partnerships. Section 7 of the Uniform Partnership Act (p. 926) sets out the rules for determining the existence of a partnership.

Florence v. Fox
193 Iowa, 1174, 188 N.W. 966 (1922)

This was an action by Florence (plaintiff) against Fox (defendant). Judgment for defendant and plaintiff appealed. Judgment affirmed.

While working on a farm owned by defendant and operated by Beason, the plaintiff injured his hand in a cane mill. The plaintiff sued the defendant on the theory that the defendant and Beason operated the farm as partners. The agreement between Beason and the defendant was in writing and was in the nature of a "share crop" lease. Fox furnished the farm and cows; Beason and Fox were to furnish "share and share alike" hogs and chickens. They were to share equally the cost of threshing. Fox was to furnish the gasoline engine and Beason was to furnish the cane mill and each was to pay one-half of the expense of operation. Fox was to get one-half of the proceeds as rent and Beason was to get one-half of the proceeds for his work. If the parties are not partners Fox is not liable to plaintiff.

Preston, J. The courts hold quite generally that there are obvious reasons for holding that farm contracts or agricultural agreements, by which the owner of land contracts with another that such land shall be occupied and cultivated by the latter, each party furnishing a certain portion of the seed, implements, and stock, and that the products shall be divided at the end of a given term, or sold and the proceeds divided, shall not be construed as creating a partnership between the parties.

Another test of the existence of a partnership is founded on the answer to the question whether the supposed partners acquired any control as owner, over the profits, while they remained undivided. There is nothing in the record in the instant case to show that defendant had any control, as owner, over the profits, had there been any, while they were undivided, or that he had anything to do with the management of the farm, including the sorghum mill.

Another test is that of community of interest. Doubtless every partnership is founded on a community of interest, but every community of interest does not necessarily constitute a partnership. It has been held that the salient features of an ordinary partnership are a community of interest in profits and losses, a community of interest in the capital employed, and a community of power in administration; that there must be such community of interest as enables each party to make contracts, manage the business, and dispose of the whole property.

It is true, of course, that there may be exceptions to some of these rules; for instance, one may agree to furnish all the capital or define the specific duties of each in regard to the management, etc. There is nothing in the instant case to indicate that defendant would have any right to dispose of the property on the farm.

Another test is that there must be an agreement to share in losses as well as profits. It seems to be now well settled that participation in the profits does not constitute a partnership in respect to the adventure from which the profits arise, and this court is committed to the doctrine that there must be a share in the losses. It may be that cases may arise where it may be inferred that the agreement was to share the losses from all the circumstances, such as the character of the business, the relation of the parties thereto, other provisions of the contract, and so on. But here we have a written contract, and there is nothing therein to show that there was any well-defined business in the manufacture of sorghum contemplated. It may be conceded for the purpose of the argument that, as contended by appellant, there may be cases where one transaction or one venture may be a partnership. In the instant case the grinding of cane was a mere incident to the farming operations under the lease. Other cases are cited, holding that one's receiving a share in the profits of an enterprise as compensation for services with property or opportunity furnished by him in aid of the business does not constitute a partnership; that he must share in the profits as such.

Person Represented To Be a Partner

Some of the earlier cases held that a partnership could be created by operation of law, but this theory has been abandoned. Unless a partnership exists as between the parties, there is no partnership. It is true that one may, under certain conditions, become liable to third persons as a partner, when he is not a member of the partnership or when no partnership exists. If one holds himself out as a member of a partnership or permits himself to be held out as a member of a partnership, he will be held liable as a partner to third persons dealing with the partnership in reliance on such holding out. The same is true when one represents that a partnership exists and that he is a member of it or permits such representations on the part of others. The liability is based on the theory of estoppel. The only persons who can hold one liable as a partner are those persons who know of the holding out and have dealt with the partnership or supposed partnership, in reliance on such holding out, to their injury. One does not become a partner solely because he has held himself out as a partner or because he has allowed others to hold him out as a partner.

The cases are not in accord as to what acts, on the part of a person who has been held out to be a partner, will amount to permission. Some of the earlier cases have held that, if one is held out to be a partner and knows that he is being so held out, yet does not take affirmative action to stop the holding out and also takes no action to notify the public that he is not a partner, he will have permitted himself to be held out as a partner. The later cases and the Uniform Partnership Act take the view that to be held liable as a partner one must consent to the holding out. Under this view knowledge that one is being held out as a partner, without other facts, will not amount to consent. Archer advertises in the local paper that Archer and Burch are partners and are operating a garage. No partnership actually exists. Burch will not have to run a notice in the local paper denying that he is Archer's partner in the garage business to protect himself from liability as Archer's partner.

Hartford Accident & Indemnity Co. v. Oles et al.
247 N.Y.S. 349 (1934)

This was an action by the Hartford Accident and Indemnity Company (plaintiff) against Wilbur S. Oles and Daniel Franklin as copartners doing business under the name and style of W. S. Oles & Co. (defendants). The case was dismissed as to defendant Franklin and judgment was rendered for the plaintiff against defendant Oles.

In 1919 the defendant Oles married the defendant Franklin's niece. At this time Franklin loaned Oles $1,000 for the purpose of purchasing the insurance agency of Thompson & Co. The agency was operated in offices adjoining Franklin's office. About a year after Oles purchased the Thompson Co. agency, Franklin moved his office to a near-by city. Oles, after he purchased the agency, operated it under the name of W. S. Oles & Co. The agency's contract with plaintiff was signed "W. S. Oles Co. By W. S. Oles" and recited in the body thereof that W. S. Oles & Co. was a copartnership composed of Oles and Franklin. Oles also represented in his application to the State Insurance Department for an agent's certificate of authority that W. S. Oles & Co. was a copartnership composed of Oles and Franklin. It is conceded that no partnership existed. There was no evidence that Franklin knew about the representation until W. S. Oles & Co. became insolvent in 1931, owing plaintiff $4,010.20 in premiums collected but not remitted. At this time plaintiffs contacted Franklin and Franklin denied the existence of the partnership and his liability as a partner.

McNaught, J. Under certain conditions a recovery may be allowed against a defendant where in truth the partnership relation is absent. This is because of the circumstances the alleged debtor may not deny the claim and is based upon estoppel. In substance, the statute provides that when a person by spoken or written words, or by conduct, represents himself, or consents to another representing him, as a partner, he is liable to any person to whom the representation has been made who has on the faith of it given credit to the actual or apparent partnership, and if the representation or consent to its being made has been in a public manner, he is liable to the person who has extended credit, whether the representation was communicated to such person extending credit or not. This statutory enactment is but a reiteration of what has long been the law. It is based upon the doctrine of estoppel. When estoppel is sought to be enforced in a case of this character, it may be classified as an "equitable estoppel" or "estoppel in pais," a term which is applied to a situation where, because of something which he has done or omitted to do, a party is denied the right to plead or prove an otherwise important fact. Courts from an early day have been disposed to consider the rule a harsh one. It was and still is a somewhat common expression that "estoppels are odious." "An estoppel in pais is a moral question. It can only exist where the party is attempting to do that which casuists would decide to be a wrong; something which is against good conscience and honest dealing." *Delaplaine* v. *Hitchcock*, 6 Hill, 14, 17.

Estoppel in pais is applicable only where the conduct or words of the party estopped are intended, or are of such character that under the circumstances shown they will be presumed to have been intended, to influence the other party to act thereon, and did in fact so influence him.

To constitute an equitable estoppel there must have been some act or admission by the parties sought to be estopped inconsistent with the claim he now makes and done or made with the intention of influencing the conduct of another, which he had reason to believe would, and which did in fact, have that effect. Silence will not estop unless there is not only a right but a duty to speak. The doctrine is to be strictly guarded and carefully applied and only when the grounds for its application are clearly and satisfactorily established.

The liability attaches to one who holds himself out, or knowingly allows another to hold him out, as a partner. Any act, representation, or conduct on the part of a person responsible calculated to induce the belief that he is a partner constitutes a holding out. The act of representation, however, must be that of the party sought to be charged, or with his knowledge.

Persons not partners inter se can be subjected to liability because of a holding out, only when the person seeking to hold them to liability dealt with the ostensible partnership in the belief that the parties were partners. It must appear that plaintiff was injured or influenced by the omission, word, or act of the defendant. If plaintiff relied solely on the statement of another, such statement would in no wise be binding upon the defendant without proof either of authority therefor, or that it was made with the knowledge of the defendant.

A plaintiff who never considered defendant liable, except as an afterthought when recovery from his original debtor necessarily failed because of insolvency, cannot create a retroactive estoppel. The cause must precede the result. Representation or conduct relied on must be concurrent with or prior to the action they are alleged to have influenced.

QUESTIONS AND PROBLEMS

1. What is the nature of a partnership?
2. Fischer and Schwartz orally agreed upon all the terms of a partnership, intending later to put the agreement in writing. Fischer put in his portion of the capital, and for fourteen weeks the partnership was conducted upon the basis of the oral agreement. Schwartz refused to sign the partnership agreement and Fischer demanded the return of his investment. Was a partnership formed?
3. John Phillips owned a business. His sons worked with him making a success of the business. The father paid them from time to time, out of the profits of the business, such sums as they needed. The business was operated under the name of John Phillips and Sons, but no definite partnership agreement was entered into, and when the father on one occasion was requested to organize the business into a partnership, he refused. Was there a partnership between Phillips and his sons?
4. Clark owned a vacant lot. Bird was engaged in building houses. A verbal arrangement was entered into between Clark and Bird whereby Bird was to erect a house on the lot. Upon the sale of the house and lot, Bird was to have his money first, Clark was then to have the agreed value of the lot, and the profits were to be equally divided. Did a partnership exist?
5. Elliott, Trowbridge, and Jennings entered into an agreement to operate a business as partners. Trowbridge and Jennings were infants at the time the agreement was entered into. Did a partnership result from the agreement and the operation of the business?
6. A number of dentists formed an association, each paying a $5.00 membership fee and agreeing to pay such assessments as should be made from time to time. The purpose of the association was to combat claims to a patent on certain hard rubber material used in dentistry. Burt, an attorney, was engaged by the officers of the association to defend the patent suits. Burt sues the members of the association as partners. Did a partnership exist?
7. Two hundred members of a masonic lodge formed an unincorporated association for the purpose of operating a golf course. It was to be operated as a private course, each member paying an agreed amount and agreeing to pay his share of any deficit incurred in operating the golf course. Have these members organized a partnership?
8. The following item appeared in a newspaper: "Charles M. Beckwith, who has managed the grain and hay business of M. L. Sweet and Co. since the death of the late D. M. Rutherford, has concluded to embark in the same business on his own account, having formed a partnership with Mrs. D. M. Rutherford for that purpose." Afterward, Mrs. Rutherford was informed of the article but did not see it. She asked Beckwith to contradict it but it was not contradicted in the paper. Munton sold merchandise to Charles M. Beckwith and Co., relying on Mrs. Rutherford's credit standing. Is Mrs. Rutherford liable to Munton?
9. J. W. Thomas was doing business under the name of J. W. Thomas and Co. In a financial statement of the condition of the firm of J. W. Thomas and Co., Hobbs signed the statement as a partner. Thomas showed the statement to the bank and obtained a loan from the bank. The bank brought suit against Thomas and Hobbs to recover the amount of the loan. Hobbs admits signing the statement but denies the existence of a partnership and denies that he authorized Thomas to use the statement to obtain credit from the bank. Is Hobbs liable to the bank?

CHAPTER XXXI

RELATION OF PARTNERS BETWEEN THEMSELVES

Introduction

As stated earlier, the partnership relation is created by the acts and agreement of the parties. Since the relationship is created by contract, the rights of the parties may be defined by contract. A well-organized partnership will be created by written articles of copartnership. Well-drawn articles of copartnership will define the major rights of the partners. Usually, the articles of copartnership will give the name of the firm, the business to be carried on, the place at which the business is to be conducted, term of the partnership, capital investment of each partner, how the profits and losses will be shared, how the business will be managed, how books, etc., are to be kept, wages or drawing account of each partner, definition of the authority of the partners to bind the firm, provisions for withdrawal of partners, provision for dissolution and winding up of the business, and often provisions for continuing the business after the death of one of the partners. Even in the most carefully drawn articles of copartnership it is impossible to anticipate all the contingencies which may arise in conducting the business. A body of law has been developed governing the rights of the partners in the event the situation is not provided for in the partnership agreement.

Partnership Property

A partnership may exist although it owns no partnership property but, as a general rule, when a partnership is organized the partners contribute either property or money, and such contributions are partnership property. After the partnership is created, it may purchase property with partnership funds for partnership purposes. Such property is generally held to be partnership property, but in final analysis whether certain property is partnership property or the property of the partners as individuals will depend on the intentions of the partners.

If Archer, Burch, and Clark own a store building as tenants in common and decide to organize a partnership to carry on a retail shoe store in the store building, the use of the store building by the partnership will not make it partnership property unless they agree that it shall be partnership property. If they indicate that they intend to continue to own the store building as tenants in common, it will remain the property of the partners as individuals.

Whether or not property is partnership property will depend on the intention of the partners. Their intention will be determined by their declarations and acts. The manner of carrying the property on the books, the way in which the property was acquired, the way the property is used, and other similar facts will all be evidence of the ownership of the property.

Azevedo et al. v. Sequeria et al.
132 Cal. App. 439, 22 P. (2d) 745 (1933)

This was an action by A. J. Azevedo and others (plaintiffs) against M. E. Sequeria and others (defendants). Judgment for defendants and plaintiffs appealed. Judgment affirmed.

The plantiffs, A. J. and M. J. Azevedo, and the defendants, Sequeria, Silveira, and another, organized a partnership and operated, as partners, a dairy business under the name of A. J. Azevedo & Co. Six shares of the capital stock of the Gustine Creamery, Inc., were purchased with partnership funds and the shares were issued in the name of A. J. Azevedo & Co. Later an additional share was purchased so that each partner could have one share. About a year later the partnership "split up." The assets of the partnership were purchased by plaintiffs together with persons other than the defendants. A. J. Azevedo claimed that he and his brother purchased the creamery stock as their individual property subsequent to the reorganization of the partnership and brought this suit to quiet title to the shares in themselves. The defendants claimed that at the time the creamery stock was purchased each partner became the individual owner of one share of creamery stock.

Mr. Sequeria testified that seven shares of the creamery stock were purchased so that each of the original seven partners might separately own one share. He said that the original seven partners had a conversation about the shares of stock when an accounting of the business was had at the time of the reorganization of the partnership. He testified: "Antone Azevedo said that they (the Gustine Creamery) were selling stocks in the creamery at Gustine . . . . and (asked) if we wanted to buy some, and all of us said yes. . . . . And afterwards he bought it, $300 worth of shares, six shares. . . . . We had seven partners in that business and we all agreed to buy one more share so that each of us would have a share. . . . . At that time I don't know whether he bought it in the (name of the) company, or for each one individually, ... but I know now that the shares were all in the name of A. J.

Azevedo." At the time this last conversation occurred regarding the stock, it was agreed the seventh share would be purchased "so that each one of us would have one share. . . . . It was all agreed and understood between all of us . . . . that he would buy one more share so each one of us would have one share in the creamery. . . . . I did not know whether he had it in A. J. Azevedo and Company or in each one of us individually." Azevedo was the manager of the dairy business. There is evidence to indicate that he acted as the agent for the respective members of the partnership in the purchase of the stock, and that the purchase price of the stock was originally taken from the proceeds of the business and subsequently charged to each in the final accounting. Sequeria testified that in a subsequent conversation A. J. Azevedo "told me I would get my share without any trouble, ... that he knew it was mine."

Mr. Justice R. L. Thompson. This evidence is sufficient to support the findings of court to the effect that the original stock was purchased by A. J. Azevedo as the agent of each individual member of the original partnership for their private ownership, and that he wrongfully procured the issuing of the stock in the name of the partnership; that each member owned one share of the stock which earned by means of stock dividends two additional shares, and that the defendants Sequeria, Avila, and Pereira are the owners of three shares each of said stock. The judgment is therefore amply supported by the evidence.

It is true that, "unless the contrary intention appears property acquired with partnership funds is partnership property." Almost any kind of property may be acquired and owned as partnership property. The intention with which the property is acquired and used will usually determine the question as to whether it is partnership or individual property. The intention of the parties with respect to the ownership of property acquired at the time of the organization of the partnership or subsequently may be determined by the acts or oral declarations of the parties. In the absence of evidence to the contrary, it will be presumed from the fact that if the stock is purchased in the name of the partnership and with its funds that it belongs to the partnership, and that the interest of each member therein extends jointly and not separately to the whole thereof. But it is not unusual that real or personal property may be acquired and used for the benefit of the partnership and still be owned individually by one or more of the partners. Indeed, in the present case the plaintiffs are contending that the very stock which is involved in this suit is their individual property and not that of the partnership to which they succeeded in association with other members. From the fact that this stock was purchased from the funds of the partnership business in the name of the firm, there is a presumption that it belongs to the partnership. But that presumption has been dispelled by substantial evidence that it was the intention of the parties that the creamery stock was to be purchased and owned individually by the respective partners in equal shares. The fact that one additional share was subsequently purchased so that each of the seven members might own a share is a strong circumstance supporting the finding of the court that it was the intention of the partners that the stock should become their individual property. This was agreed to by all the partners according to Sequeria, at the settlement of their interests after the original partnership was dissolved.

Klingstein v. Rockingham National Bank of Harrisonburg et al.
165 Va. 275, 182 S.E. 115 (1935)

This was a suit in equity by Rockingham National Bank of Harrisonburg (plaintiff) against E. L. Klingstein and others (defendants). Judgment for plaintiff and defendant Klingstein appealed. Judgment reversed in part.

B. J. Dean and W. S. Clemmer formed a partnership under the name of "Dairy Lunch" for the purpose of operating a restaurant. Dean owned an unimproved lot across the street from the building in which the partners were operating their restaurant. The partners agreed that Dean would convey an undivided one-half interest in the lot to Clemmer and that they would erect a building on the lot suitable for the partnership business. Dean conveyed an undivided one-half interest in the lot to Clemmer and a building was erected on the lot at a cost of between $7,000 and $8,000. After the building was erected, the partnership occupied and used the building. The cost of erecting the building, the taxes and the insurance on the building were paid out of partnership funds. Rents collected from a part of the building not used by the partnership were paid to and used by the partnership. In a statement made to the bank Dean did not list this property as a part of his individual property. On Dean's death the lot and building were sold, as partnership property, to Klingstein. The plaintiff had a claim against Dean and brought this suit asking that the sale to Klingstein be set aside and the property be declared to be held by Dean and Clemmer as tenants in common. The lower court held that the form of the deed indicated that the property was held by Dean and Clemmer as tenants in common and that the property was not partnership property. Klingstein appealed from this holding.

Eggleston, J. The principles of law applicable to this situation are well settled. When the title to real estate is held by partners individually, the presumption is that the partners hold the property as tenants in common. Therefore, the introduction in evidence by the complainant of the title deeds showing that Dean and Clemmer each owned an undivided one-half interest in the property made out a prima facie case that it was held by the partners as tenants in common.

But this presumption may be rebutted in equity. And whether the land, in fact, belongs to the partnership or to the individuals composing it, depends upon the intention of the parties.

In 20 R.C.L., p. 831, § 36, it is said: "Partnership contracts, like other contracts, are governed by the intention of the parties. Every partnership rests on the mutual consent of the members. This intent may be manifested by the terms of their agreement, the conduct of the parties to each other under it, or by the circumstances generally surrounding the transaction." This principle applies with equal force to a contract for holding partnership real estate as it does to an agreement for operating a partnership business.

It is likewise well settled that the agreement, showing the intent of the parties with reference to the partnership real estate, need not be in writing, but may be oral or implied.

Among the circumstances (in addition to an express agreement) which may show the intention of the parties are: The acts and declarations of the partners; the acquisition of the property for partnership purposes; its use by the partnership; the payment for improvements thereon out of firm assets; and the payment of taxes and insurance thereon by the partnership.

We think the combination of facts and circumstances here, established by undisputed testimony, show that the parties intended that this real estate should be partnership property. We have (1) the agreement of the partners established by Clemmer's testimony and corroborated by Dean's statements to the banks; (2) the borrowing of money by the firm on the property as a partnership asset; (3) the payment out of partnership funds of the cost of improvements, which contributed more than 60 per cent of the total cost price of the property; (4) the acquisition and use of the property for partnership purposes; (5) the payment of taxes, insurance, and repairs out of partnership funds; and (6) the collection by the partnership, as such, of the rents on that part of the building not used for the partnership business.

Individual Partner's Rights in Partnership Property

The nature of the interest of the individual partner in the partnership property is difficult to define. At the time the common law courts began to hear and determine business controversies, much confusion arose in regard to the nature of the interest of the individual partner in the partnership property, especially his interest in partnership real estate. At common law, the only types of co-ownership known, which were in any respect similar to the mercantile conception of partnership ownership, were joint tenancy and tenancy in common. Neither type of co-ownership was adequate; so, in determining partnership controversies, the courts resorted to an inexplainable mixture of the two conceptions of co-ownership. The result was much confusion and little consistency in the holdings of the courts. In the drafting of the Uniform Partnership Act, this situation was recognized, and the act was so drawn as to clear up the situation in so far as possible. The mercantile conception was adopted, and the act declares that a partner's interest in the partnership property is that of a tenant in partnership. The incidents of this tenancy are set out in the Uniform Partnership Act.[1]

Even though the Uniform Partnership Act is drafted on the theory that the partnership is not an entity, existing separate and apart from the members that organized it, and even though the provisions relative to the partner's right in specific partnership property are drafted in accordance with this concept of the partnership, the practical result is analogous to the mercantile concept of partnership property; that is, that partnership property is owned by the partnership as an entity. The individual partner does not own any definite proportion of a particular item of property. His ownership is the right to have the property used for partnership purposes, the right to his share of profits arising from such use, the right to have the property applied in payment of partnership debts, and, on dissolution, the right to participate in the distribution of the property in accordance with the articles of partnership.

Dobson v. Whitker
242 Mich. 308, 218 N.W. 770 (1928)

This was an action by Russell T. Dobson, Jr. (plaintiff) against Henry A. Whitker (defendant). Judgment for plaintiff and defendant appealed. Judgment reversed and remanded.

Plaintiff, defendant, and one Kyer operated as partners a wholesale grocery business. The business was profitable but the personal relations of the partners were not agreeable; consequently, Kyer and Whitker wished to purchase Dobson's interest in the partnership. They offered Dobson $38,000 for his interest which he refused to accept. Whitker entered into a side agrement with Dobson whereby it was agreed that Dobson would sell his interest in the partnership to Kyer and Whitker for $38,000, that thereafter the business would be incorporated and that Whitker would transfer to Dobson 400 shares of the capital stock, par value $10 per share. Kyer was not a party to this agreement and had no knowledge of it. Dobson brought this suit asking a partnership accounting. The lower court granted the acounting on the theory that, as a result of Whitker's agreement, Dobson acquired an interest in the partnership and was entitled to equitable relief.

McDonald, J. Counsel says that after the plaintiff had withdrawn from the partnership and the business was being continued by Kyer and Whitker that, in so far as Whitker was concerned, it was conducted on joint account with the plaintiff. This claim is apparently based upon a misconception of partnership relations and interests.

---

[1] Section 25, appendix, p. 929.

Whitker could have no secret partner whose interest could be enforced against the partnership property of Kyer and Whitker. As copartner with Kyer, he had no separate interest in the property of the going partnership business. "The assets are held in a sort of community, but the partners do not hold as common tenants or joint tenants. The property is distinctly separated from that belonging to the individual members and it constitutes an identical and entire interest." By its terms the secret agreement gave the plaintiff no right to a joint interest with Whitker in the partnership business. It merely provided that certain shares of Whitker's stock in a corporation thereafter to be formed should be assigned to the plaintiff.

Creditors of Individual Partners

The nature of the interest of the individual partner in the partnership property is the basis of the rights of the individual partner's creditors against the partnership property. It is well settled that the creditor of a partner can acquire no greater rights in the partnership property than the debtor partner has. The problem has been, by what manner of process can the partner's interest be reached so that it may be applied to the discharge of his individual debts. Prior to the adoption of the Uniform Partnership Act there was almost no consistency in the holdings of the courts.

In some jurisdictions the interest of a partner in the partnership could not be reached by legal process. In other jurisdictions the theory of community of ownership of partnership property was recognized and the courts held that levy could not be made on particular items of partnership property in satisfaction of a judgment against an individual partner but the sheriff could levy on the entire assets of the partnership, take possession of them, and sell the debtor partner's interest in the assets. Technically, this procedure was in accord with the prevailing theory of the individual partner's interest in partnership assets, but the procedure was objectionable from a practical standpoint because of the interference with the operation of the partnership business during the period the partnership assets were in the possession of the sheriff. Also, one wishing to purchase the debtor partner's interest would have no way of determining the value of the interest. In several states statutes have been passed defining the rights and duties of the parties. The objective of this legislation is to provide a procedure whereby the interest of the debtor partner can be reached by his creditors with a minimum of injury to the other partners. This objective is substantially accomplished under the provisions of the Uniform Partnership Act.[2]

[2] Section 28, appendix, p. 930.

Management of the Business

Presumably all partners have a right to participate in the management of the partnership business and the exclusion of a partner from a voice in the management of the business has been held to be grounds for dissolution. The partners may by agreement vest the right to manage the business or certain divisions of the business in one or more of the partners, yet such an agreement will not operate to exclude the other partners from all participation or from their right to an accounting. If, in the conduct of the partnership business, the partners disagree on what course to pursue, the decision of the majority will bind the minority. However, if the decision involves fundamental change in the nature of the business, the unanimous consent of the partners is necessary. As a general rule the partners cannot resort to the courts for the settlement of disputes arising in the course of the operation of the business. The partnership relation is a personal relation and the success of the business depends on the co-operative action of the partners. If the partners cannot agree on matters of business policy, their course is to dissolve the partnership and wind up the business. In some instances a court of equity has granted an equitable remedy and decreed the continuation of the partnership business, but, before a partner is entitled to this extraordinary remedy, he must show that the only way his interests can be protected is by the continuation of the partnership. The usual action in case of disagreement is to petition for an accounting, for the appointment of a receiver, and for a winding up of the partnership business.

Katz v. Brewington
71 Md. 79, 20 Atl. 139 (1889)

This was an action by Charles Brewington (plaintiff) against Louis Katz (defendant). Judgment for plaintiff and defendant appealed. Judgment affirmed.

Plaintiff and defendant were partners carrying on the fruit-packing business. The defendant had possession of the books and was in the control of the assets of the business. Defendant concealed the books and refused the plaintiff access to them and also excluded the plaintiff from all control of the business and refused to give him any information in regard to the business of the firm. Plaintiff brought this suit asking for the appointment of a receiver.

Bryan, J. Each partner has an equal right to take part in the management of the business of the firm. Although one of them may have an interest only in the profits, and not in the capital, yet his rights are involved in the proper conduct of the affairs of the firm, so that profits may be made. So each partner has an equal right to information about the partnership affairs, and to free access to its books. The complainant had a right to learn from the books whether there were profits, and whether there were debts. If he were denied this information, as charged in his bill of complaint, a sufficient reason appears for not alleging that profits had been earned, and that debts existed. In *Const.* v. *Harris*, 1 Turn, & R., 496, Lord Eldon said: "The most prominent point, in which the court acts, in appointing a receiver of a partnership concern, is the circumstance of one partner having taken upon himself the power to exclude another partner from as full a share in the management of the partnership as he who assumes that power himself enjoys." This principle seems to be universally approved by the authorities. It is decisive of the present question.

Johnston & Co. v. Dutton's Administrator
27 Ala. 245 (1855)

This was an action by Charles W. Dorrance, administrator of the estate of William Dutton, deceased (plaintiff) against William Johnston and Samuel Fogg, partners doing business as Wm. Johnston & Co. (defendants). Judgment for plaintiff and defendant William Johnston appealed. Judgment affirmed.

Wm. Johnston & Co. was a partnership composed of William Johnston, Samuel Fogg, and one Vanderslice who was not a party to this suit. The partnership operated a sawmill. Dutton furnished supplies to the mill. Johnston gave Dutton notice that he would not be liable for goods furnished to the mill. Thereafter Dutton furnished supplies to the mill at the request of Fogg and Vanderslice. Notes signed by Fogg in the name of the partnership were given to Dutton in payment for the supplies furnished. This suit is brought to recover on said notes and Johnston set up his notice to Dutton as a defense.

Goldthwaite, J. The evidence in this case tended to show that appellants and one Vanderslice carried on in copartnership a steam saw-mill, which, by the articles of copartnership, was to continue at least five years; that the note sued on was given with the concurrence of two of the partners, Fogg and Vanderslice, for supplies necessary for the hands engaged in carrying on the mill, which had been ordered by one of them. Upon these facts alone, there can be no doubt that the firm would be bound. The furnishing of supplies to those engaged in the immediate direction of the business was essential to the conducting of it, and within the scope of the purpose for which the individuals had associated; and the authority of either of the partners to purchase such supplies, and give the note of the firm, cannot be questioned.

The principal ground of objection, however, is, that the evidence proved that, before the goods were furnished and the note given, the appellant, Johnston, gave notice to the public that he would not be responsible for any future debt contracted on account of the copartnership, and that this notice was brought home to the party with whom the debt was contracted; and it is insisted that its effect was to revoke the authority of the other partners, so far as he was concerned, to bind the firm from that time.

It is to be observed, that in the present case the contract was concurred in by two members of the firm; and the question, therefore, is as to the right of the majority to bind the other partners, against their dissent, as to matters appertaining to the common business, and in the absence of any stipulation conferring that power in the articles of copartnership. This question is a new one in this court, and, indeed, we have found no case in which it has been expressly decided. Both in England and the United States there are cases which assert the general proposition that a partner may protect himself against the consequences of a future contract, by giving notice of his dissent to the party with whom it is about to be made. . . . . And where the firm consists of but two persons, and there is nothing in the articles to prevent each from having an equal voice in the direction and control of the common business, the correctness of the proposition cannot be questioned. In such case the duty of each partner would require him not to enter into any contract from which the other in good faith dissented; and, if he did, it would be a violation of the obligations which were imposed by the nature of the partnership. It would not, in fact, be the contract of the firm; and the party with whom it was made, having notice, could not enforce it as such. So, if the firm was composed of more than two persons, and one of them dissented, the party with whom the contract is made acts at his peril, and cannot hold the dissenting partner liable, unless his liability results from the articles or from the nature of the partnership contract. All the cases can be sustained on this principle; and it is in strict analogy with the civil law, which holds, where the stipulations of the partnership expressly intrust the direction and control of the business to one of the partners, that the dissent of the other would not avail, if the contract were made in good faith. Were it otherwise it would be denying to parties the right to make their own contracts. If our views as to the governing force of express stipulations are correct, the effect of such terms or conditions as result by clear implication from the articles, or arise out of the nature of the partnership, must be the same. It is as if they had been expressly provided.

Now, whenever a partnership is formed by more than two persons, we think that in the absence of any express provision to the contrary there is always an implied understanding that the acts of the majority are to prevail over those of the minority as to all matters within the scope of the common business; and such we understand to be the doctrine asserted by Lord Eldon in *Const.* v. *Harris*, and such was the opinion of Judge Story. Story on Part. § 123; 3 Kent's com. (5th Ed.) 45. The rule as thus laid down is certainly more reasonable and just than to allow the minority to stop the operations of the concern against the views of the majority.

We do not say that it would be deemed a bona fide transaction, so as to bind the firm, if the majority choose wantonly to act without information to or consultation with the minority. . . . . But when, as in the present case, the one partner has given notice, and expressed his dissent in advance, there could be no reason or propriety in requiring him to be consulted by the other two.

Our conclusion is that the act, being concurred in by two of the partners, was, under the circumstances, the act of the firm; and that the charge, asserting the proposition that the dissent of one partner against the other two would necessarily exonerate him, was properly refused.

Profits and Losses

In the absence of an agreement defining the partners' rights in the profits and declaring how the losses will be borne, the profits are distributed equally and the losses are borne equally by the solvent partners. Usually, the articles of copartnership will set out the method of distributing the profits and, also, how the losses will be borne. If the articles set out the manner of distributing profits but are silent as to the losses, the losses will be borne according to the partners' share in the profits.

Harris v. Flournoy & Flournoy
Waller v. Same
238 Ky. 329, 38 S.W. (2d) 10 (1931)

Separate actions were brought by W. T. Harris and by T. S. Waller (plaintiff) against Flournoy & Flournoy (defendants). Judgment for defendants and plaintiffs appealed. The cases were consolidated on the appeal. Judgment affirmed.

Flournoy & Flournoy, attorneys practicing as partners, were engaged as defense attorneys in a will contest case. At the request of parties in interest, they employed Harris and Waller to assist them. Harris and Waller were each practicing individually. When employed nothing was said about fees. The court allowed $6,000 fees. Flournoy & Flournoy each retained one-fourth and gave Harris one-fourth and Waller one-fourth. Harris and Waller contend they are each entitled to one-third and the partnership of Flournoy & Flournoy is entitled to one-third.

Logan, C. J. The case of *Underwood* v. *Overstreet*, 188 Ky. 562, 223 S.W. 152, 10 A. L. R. 1352, was another case where the employing client by contract employed both of the attorneys, and there was no agreement as to the division of the fee. The court held, in the absence of an agreement as to the division of the fee, it must be divided equally between the two attorneys. There are statements in the opinion in *Underwood* v. *Overstreet* indicating that in such cases this court treats the attorneys who are parties to such agreements as constituting a special partnership. It is true that it is well settled under the law governing partnerships that, when the question is one of the divisions of profits, the presumption is that the profits are to be divided equally.

It is unfortunate that there should be a disagreement between good attorneys over the division of fees. It would be a safer and more businesslike method to have an agreement in advance where an attorney, or firm, employs other firms or attorneys, to assist in legal matters. It is a sound rule that, where an attorney, or firm, employs other attorneys, or firms, in the absence of an agreement, the employed attorneys should receive only reasonable compensation from the attorneys employing them. But in this case the firm employing Harris and Waller treated their firm as having opened for the admission into it of Harris and Waller for the conduct and trial of the particular case, and the fee was divided among the special partners equally. Under the facts and circumstances, all admitted by the reputable attorneys connected with this litigation, we are impelled to hold that the two individual attorneys were entitled to one-fourth each, which was reasonable compensation.

Relation between the Partners

When two or more persons enter into a partnership for the purpose of operating a business, each is a principal and each an agent. Each person has the power to bind the other in contracts within the scope of the partnership business. In the exercise of this power, each owes a duty of good faith. Each owes a duty not to exceed the powers given in the articles of copartnership, and each owes a duty of care and skill in the transaction of the partnership business. In the absence of an agreement to the contrary, each owes a duty to devote his entire time and energy to the business, and no partner is entitled to wages; his compensation is his share of the profits. A partner has no right to conduct a business as an individual, if it will in any manner compete with the partnership business or interfere with the duty owed to the partnership, without the consent of his partners. Each partner should consult with the other partners concerning partnership matters as each partner has an equal voice in the management of the business. No partner has a right to make a secret profit from the relationship. The courts demand the highest type of good faith and fair dealing between partners. In all transactions between partners, each owes the other a duty of full disclosure. If a partner takes a secret profit, exceeds his authority in transacting the partnership business, breaches, in any manner, the partnership agreement, causes a loss due to his negligent or unskillful transacting of the partnership business, or in any other manner fails to fulfill his duties to the other partners, he will have to answer in damages to his partners. Each partner has free access to the books of account of the partnership, and, under some circumstances, a partner may be entitled to a formal accounting. Partners cannot sue each other or the firm, nor can the firm sue the individual partners on partnership claims. As a general rule, a partnership accounting, usually together with a dissolution and winding-up proceedings, is the only court action open to the partners to settle internal disputes.

Any right of a partner against the partnership or any duty of the partner to the partnership ordinarily must be adjusted in the course of accounting of partnership affairs, and no judicial remedy is available other than the dissolution, accounting, and winding up of the partnership affairs. If Archer, Burch, and Clark organize a partnership and, in the distribution of profits, Archer claims that he is entitled to more than he has received, Archer cannot recover a judgment against the partnership for profits which have not been paid to him. In such a situation the only judicial remedy available to Archer is an accounting on the dissolution and winding up of the partnership business.

Bracht v. Connell et al.
313 Pa. 397, 170 Atl. 297 (1933)

This was an action by O. B. Bracht (plaintiff) against W. L. Connell and another (defendants). Judgment for plaintiff and defendants appealed. Judgment modified and case remitted.

Connell, Lamb, and Bracht formed a partnership for the purpose of carrying on a road construction business. The partnership was organized in 1921 and carried on business until 1925 when disagreements began to arise. August 1, 1925, defendants, without the knowledge of the plaintiff but with the use of firm funds, bid upon and obtained a large contract in West Virginia for building a hard-surfaced road. The partnership was dissolved on August 10, 1925, but the West Virginia contract was not included in the assets of the partnership when the partnership assets were divided. Later, defendants refused to permit plaintiff to share in the West Virginia contract and plaintiff brought this suit for an accounting.

Kephart, J. Partners stand in a fiduciary relationship to copartners; each is under a duty to act for the benefit of all and not to gain individual advantage at the expense or to the detriment of other partners. When a partnership has terminated, for whatever reason or by whatever means, the assets of the partnership must still be handled in accordance with this fiduciary principle.

Defendants considered the contract for the construction of the West Virginia road their own. They made it in good faith and the court below was unable to discover bad faith or fraudulent intent in their actions, and we concur in that finding. Defendants were led to the conclusion that they had a right to make this contract, by their conduct in other prior instances when they made similar contracts which had the apparent assent of plaintiff, though he denied knowing anything about them. Defendants were under the impression they might perform the West Virginia contract as their own. They were mistaken as to the legal aspect of their action in making this contract with the aid of partnership funds as Judge Parker finds. The result is that the law imposes on the contract a partnership status at dissolution and gives plaintiff the right at dissolution either to have the contract distributed, that is, lawfully appraised, so that plaintiff could receive the value of his interest, or, plaintiff, being denied this, could require defendants to account for his proportion of the profit. See Partnership Act, § 42 (59 PS § 104). When defendants took over the asset, i.e., the contract, they were using a property right of plaintiff. The section does not refer merely to physical property; it includes just such assets as this, or a leasehold as in *McCollum* v. *Carlucci*, 206 Pa. 312, 55 A. 979, 98 Am. St. Rep. 780. We repeat, the action is not for breach of the partnership contract, but for the value of plaintiff's interest in that asset as it was administered by defendants who had wrongfully refused plaintiff any right therein. Defendants' authorities do not apply. Whether plaintiff's right is assessed as damages, the value of the contract at dissolution, or, as profits on an accounting for the administration of a partnership asset, the result is the same in this case because the value of the contract was determined when the contract was completed. The question of value was not then one for speculation. Plaintiff generally has the option of taking the right which is most beneficial.

United Brokers' Co. v. Dose
143 Or. 283, 22 P. (2d) 204 (1933)

This was an action by the United Brokers' Co. (plaintiff) against Fred Dose who filed a counterclaim (defendant). Judgment for plaintiff and defendant appealed. Judgment affirmed.

Plaintiff and defendant entered into a joint venture with one Luther Harrel in producing a crop of potatoes. Harrel was to receive one-half of the profits and the other half was to be divided equally between plaintiff and defendant. The crop netted a profit of $36,772.16, one-half of which was paid over to defendant. Defendant paid plaintiff $8,263.13. Also the plaintiff advanced $1,009.06 to the defendant, one-half of which amount the defendant agreed to pay. Defendant set up as counterclaim that he was entitled to $1,155 compensation for his services as general manager of the business.

Defendant also, as a part of his counterclaim, demanded contribution from plaintiff by reason of money which defendant expended in settlement of an automobile accident which occurred while acting within the scope of the partnership business.

Plaintiff in its reply denied the new matter alleged by way of counterclaim.

Belt, J. The trial court denied the counterclaims, and, on the first cause of action, entered a decree in favor of plaintiff for $929.91, together with interest thereon at rate of 6 per cent per annum until paid, and, on the second cause of action, entered a decree in favor of plaintiff for $504.33, together with interest thereon at rate of 6 per cent per annum from April 25, 1930, until paid. Defendant appeals.

Relative to the claim of compensation for services rendered by defendant, it is clear that the court was right in denying the same. There is no evidence of any express agreement that defendant was to receive compensation for his services. The rule applicable is thus stated in 20 R.C.L. 877: "The general rule is that a partner is not entitled to compensation for services in conducting the partnership business beyond his share of the profits unless there is a stipulation to that effect, and that he has no right by implication to claim anything extra by reason of any inequality of services rendered by him, as compared with those rendered by his copartners."

The second counterclaim arose out of an automobile accident which occurred while defendant, Dose, was driving to Washington to inspect some potatoes. The trip was made with the knowledge and consent of the plaintiff. Dan Schuler, who accompanied Dose, was injured as a result of the latter's negligence. Schuler threatened to bring an action. Dose thereupon, without the knowledge or consent of the plaintiff, paid to Schuler, in settlement of his claim, the sum of $2,000. The further sum of $1,214.60 was paid by Dose to cover hospital bills for Schuler and himself. The liability of the partnership to a third person for the negligence of one of the partners while acting within the scope of the partnership business is not involved. Neither is this a case where the injury was caused by the negligence of an employee of the partnership.

The law of partnership is the law of agency. Each partner is the agent of the other, and impliedly agrees that he will exercise reasonable care and diligence in the operation of the partnership business. When a loss is paid by a partnership, there is a right of indemnity against the partner whose negligence caused the loss. It is the same rule where the principal is held liable for the negligent act of his agent. Upon payment of the loss, the principal may bring action against his agent to be indemnified for the loss sustained: "Losses caused wholly by the negligence or misconduct of one party must be borne by him." "A partner has no right to charge the firm with losses or expenses caused by his own negligence or want of skill. . . . ."

In *Carlin* v. *Donegan*, 15 Kan. 495, Mr. Justice Brewer, speaking for the court in an action brought by one partner against his copartner for an accounting, approved an instruction that each partner would be " 'held responsible for fraud, negligence, etc.' and that 'the degree of care and diligence that partners are generally held to between themselves is such care and diligence about any transaction as men generally of common or average care and prudence would exercise.' " It was also declared by the court that "the omission of such ordinary care and prudence is ordinary negligence; and a partner is responsible for losses resulting from ordinary negligence."

In *Kiffer* v. *Bienstock*, 128 Misc. 451, 218 N.Y.S. 526, it was held that, where a judgment was recovered against a partner individually by a person injured by a partner's sole negligence in operating partnership automobile in firm business, partner was not entitled to contribution by copartner on dissolution of partnership.

QUESTIONS AND PROBLEMS

1. Price and Brown organized a partnership to operate a hotel. The partnership was operating a rooming house in an apartment building which was leased by the partnership. Brown purchased, with his own funds and without Price's knowledge, the apartment building in which the partnership was operating the rooming house, and he also purchased the adjacent apartment building. Is Price entitled to a partnership interest in the property purchased by Brown?
2. Nathan G. Bagley and John R. Bagley were copartners doing business as Bagley Bros. Twenty-two shares of the capital stock of the Service Filling Station Company were purchased with partnership funds. The title to the stock stood: ten shares in the name of John R. Bagley and twelve shares in the name of Nathan G. Bagley. The stock was pledged to the State Bank as security for a loan to the partnership. The books of the partnership show that the stock was purchased with partnership funds but do not show a distribution to the individual partners. Is the stock partnership property?
3. Eugene Kraus, Albert Kraus, and Leo Kraus were copartners. The firm owned and operated a farm. After the dissolution of the partnership, Albert Kraus took possession of the farm and operated it for his own profit, to the exclusion of his copartners. What are the rights of Eugene and Leo?
4. The laws of Massachusetts provide that "the owner" of an automobile shall make application for the registration of an automobile. An automobile was owned by the Sea Food Shops, a partnership. The automobile was registered in the name of George Kilduff, one of the partners. Was the automobile registered by "the owners"?
5. Brown had a judgment against Case, individually. Case, Parker, and Barney were copartners doing business as the Construction Co. A writ of attachment was issued on the judgment against Case, and the sheriff levied the writ on certain machinery which was the property of the partnership. The Uniform Partnership Act is in force in the state. Is the attachment valid?
6. Wilke and Wright were copartners engaged in farming and stock-raising. The partnership agreement stipulated that Wilke was "to have control and management of said business." Thereafter, Wright sold some cattle to Gross, a cattle buyer. In the absence of an agreement between the partners, would Wright have a right to sell cattle? Under the agreement between Wilke and Wright did Wright have a right to sell cattle?
7. The articles of partnership of the firm of Whitcomb & Co. provided: "J. C. Converse to contribute $50,000; to receive interest at 7 per cent and devote such time as he may be able to give and to receive 25 per cent of the profits. J. M. Whitcomb to contribute $50,000, receive 7 per cent interest on the same, to give all his time to the business and to receive 25 per cent of the net profits. E. R. Blagden to contribute all his time to the business and receive 25 per cent of the net profits. Walter Stanton to contribute all his time to the business and receive 25 per cent of the net profits." There was no provision for distribution of losses. On dissolution and winding up of the business, it appeared that the business had been operated at a loss of $25,000.00. How should this loss be distributed?
8. Lofgren, Bloom, and others formed a partnership for the purpose of buying and owning a certain stallion. Lofgren had already purchased the stallion for $1,200.00, but the other partners were ignorant of that fact. Lofgren represented to the

other partners that he paid $1,800.00 for the stallion and produced a receipt from the pretended owner. The partnership paid Lofgren $1,800.00 to reimburse him for the money paid for the stallion. On dissolution and winding up of the partnership, it is claimed that Lofgren is indebted to the partnership in the sum of $600.00 and interest. Is this claim correct?

9. Ball and Wise were partners in the operation of a mine. The partnership had a lease on certain mining lands. The partnership adventure was not very successful and operations were discontinued for a period. During this period Ball intentionally permitted the payments on the lease to become in arrears which gave the lessors the right to declare a forfeiture of the lease. Ball, without the knowledge of Wise and while the lease was in default, purchased the mining claims from the owners. Ball now refuses to permit Wise to share in the mining claims. Does Wise have a right to a share in the mining claims?

10. Levy and Kahn, as partners, purchased a large quantity of bacon from the United States government which they expected to resell within a short time. Kahn contributed $50,000 as capital and was to receive 20 per cent of the profits. Levy was to manage the undertaking. The venture did not progress as expected and Levy devoted his entire time to the venture for more than a year. When the bacon was finally disposed of and the accounts of the partnership were being settled, Levy claimed that he was entitled to compensation for his services. Is Levy entitled to compensation for his services?

CHAPTER XXXII

RELATION OF PARTNERS TO THIRD PERSONS

Partner as General Agent of Firm

In a partnership, each partner is the agent of the other partners, or, if one regards the partnership as an entity, each partner is the agent of the firm. As between themselves, as in the law of agency, their authority will be defined by the articles of partnership or by subsequent agreement. If no articles of partnership have been agreed to and if there is no agreement as to the authority of the partners, their authority will be implied from the nature of the business. Each will have the authority to do those things which are ordinarily done in the conduct of the business in which the partnership is engaged.

As to third persons, substantially the same rules apply as in the agency relationship. The third person cannot, with safety, blindly assume that a partner has unlimited authority to bind the firm or his partners. He must ascertain whether or not a partnership exists and take notice of apparent limitations of the partner's authority. Unless the third person has notice or knowledge of restrictions on a partner's authority, he may safely assume that the partner's authority is that of a general agent and that the partner has authority to bind his partners in all matters falling within the scope of the partnership business. This authority may be enlarged by the express agreement of the partners. Sometimes a distinction is made between a trading and non-trading partnership, but such distinction is not recognized by the Uniform Partnership Act. Under the general rule there is little need for such a distinction, because the difference in the nature of the business, conducted by a trading and a non-trading partnership, would account for the limitations on the authority of the partner of the non-trading partnership. As a general rule, the partner does not have authority to dispose of all the partnership assets, nor does he have authority to dispose of assets essential to the carrying on of the partnership business. He cannot make an assignment for the benefit of creditors, sign sealed instruments, confess judgment, especially if such confession would bind the partners individually, nor can he bind the partnership as surety or guarantor for a third person. However, under special circumstances and in particular situations, a partner may bind his partners in the matters stated above. The partner, if he is acting within the scope of the business, may borrow money, mortgage or pledge assets of the firm, sign negotiable instruments, make sales, receive payments, pay debts of the firm, bring suits at law, engage attorneys to defend suits, insure the property of the firm, engage agents, and perform all other acts customarily performed in the conduct of a business. In fact, the partner is a general agent with a proprietory interest in the business and the scope of the business conducted is the limitation of his authority. The partner's authority can be limited in any manner by agreement of the partners, and such limitation will be binding on third persons having notice or knowledge of it.

Caswell v. Maplewood Garage.
84 N.H. 241, 149 Atl. 746, 73 A.L.R. 433 (1930)

This was an action by Burton C. Caswell (plaintiff) against the Maplewood Garage, a partnership (defendants). Judgment for defendants and plaintiff appealed. Judgment affirmed.

The Maplewood Garage was a partnership in which Charles A. Badger and Ira Brown were partners. While Orville C. Badger, son of Charles A. Badger, was driving an automobile which was the property of the partnership, the plaintiff was injured. The partnership was sued on the theory that at the time of the accident Orville was acting as agent for the partnership and was engaged in partnership business. On the trial the direct evidence was to the effect that at the time of the accident Orville was not engaged in partnership business, but was engaged upon business of his own. The only evidence offered to prove that Orville was acting for the firm was a statement made by Badger to the effect that on the trip to Boston Orville was to get some parts for the garage and a statement alleged to have been made by Brown, but denied by him, to the effect that the partnership was liable. To be admissible in evidence it must appear that admissions were made in the course of and within the scope of the business of the partnership.

Peaslee, C. J. The issue, how far the statements of one are evidence against another who was his partner, or against the firm, involves questions of the law of partnership rather than that of evidence. "A partner charges the partnership by virtue of an agency to act for it; how far his admissions are receivable depends therefore on the doctrines of agency as applied to a partnership." 2 Wig. Ev. § 1078 (3).

In general, it may fairly be said that the rule is that the power of a partner to act for the firm extends only to the transaction of partnership business.

"In truth, 'the law as to partnership is undoubtedly a branch of the law of principal and agent; and it would tend to simplify and make more easy of solution the questions which arise on this subject, if this true principle were more constantly kept in view.' . . . . 'All questions between partners are no more than illustrations of the same questions as between principal and agent. . . . .' The real and ultimate question in all cases like the present is one of agency."

It is the accepted law everywhere that one partner is not the agent of the firm to admit the existence of the partnership.

By a parity of reasoning the conclusion is reached that he is not such agent to admit that a transaction was a part of the firm's business. The rule was stated by Judge Cooley as follows: "A partner's declarations may bind his associates in partnership matters, but not in concerns foreign to the partnership; and he cannot by his mere admission or declaration bring a transaction within the scope of the business when upon the facts in proof it appears to have no connection."

Judged by this test, neither the admission made by Badger, nor the one alleged to have been made by Brown, would be evidence against the partnership. Neither was transacting or undertaking to transact partnership business. Each definitely declared that he spoke for himself. . . . .

The issue presented here is one of agency to act for and bind the firm. And this, in turn, involves the inquiry whether when a partner acts or speaks he does so as a principal and agent of his partners, or rather as the agent of the firm.

"Everybody knows that a partnership is a sort of agency, but a very peculiar one. You cannot grasp the notion of agency, properly speaking, unless you grasp the notion of the existence of the firm as a separate entity from the existence of the partners; a notion which was well grasped by the old Roman lawyers, and which was partly understood in the courts of equity before it was a part of the whole law of the land, as it is now. But when you get the idea clearly, you will see at once what sort of agency it is. It is the one person acting on behalf of the firm. He does not act as agent, in the ordinary sense of the word, for the others so as to bind the others; he acts on behalf of the firm of which they are members; and as he binds the firm and acts on the part of the firm, he is properly treated as the agent of the firm. If you cannot grasp the notion of a separate entity for the firm, then you are reduced to this, that inasmuch as he acts partly for himself and partly for the others, to the extent that he acts for the others he must be an agent, and in that way you get him to be an agent for the other partners, but only in that way, because you insist upon ignoring the existence of the firm as a separate entity." Jessel, M. R., *Pooley* v. *Driver*, 5 Ch. Div. 458, 476.

"Almost the whole law on this subject resolves itself into the rule, that the representations or misrepresentations of a partner are binding on the firm, provided they are made in the course of, and relate to, and are material to, the transaction of the business of the firm."

That which is evidence against one partner, but not against the firm as a whole, cannot be admitted to prove the existence of facts not concerning the existence and extent of the compact between the partners. The ground for receiving admissions of a party in evidence is not because the statement was against the interest of the speaker, but because one is accountable for his words. As the firm is not accountable for the unauthorized sayings of a partner, so they are not evidence against the firm.

In *Pierce* v. *Wood*, 23 N.H. 519, the decision is well stated in the headnote. "The acts and sayings of one member of a firm, in the general partnership business, done or said within the scope of that business, will govern the firm, whether honestly, or dishonestly transacted." A single quotation from the opinion shows the correctness of the conclusion. "At the time the compromise was effected, the defendants were in partnership. The debts to be settled were partnership debts. The compromise was for the benefit of the firm. It was an act done by and for the firm, and the defendants were jointly interested in it. It was strictly partnership business."

Borrowing on Firm's Credit

Whether or not a partner has the power to borrow money on the firm's credit depends on the nature of the firm's business. If the firm is a trading partnership, as a general rule, the borrowing of money will be necessary to carry on the business, and a partner will have the power to borrow money on the firm's credit. The fact that the partnership does not need the money or that the partnership has never borrowed money in carrying on its businesss will not be controlling. If the business carried on by the partnership is such that it is customary, in carrying on such a business, to borrow money, a partner will have the power to borrow money in the firm name. If a partnership is a non-trading partnership, a partner, as a general rule, does not have the power to borrow money in the firm name. A non-trading partnership will have no occasion to borrow money in the operation of its business, and such an act will be without the scope of the partnership business. If the third person has notice of or knowledge of limitations placed on a partner's power to borrow money in the firm name, he will be bound by such notice or knowledge. Likewise, if a member of a non-trading partnership is authorized to borrow money in the firm name, the firm will be bound. Closely related to the borrowing of money in the firm name is the partner's authority to sign negotiable instruments or other instruments in the firm name. Archer, Burch, and Clark are partners operating a trading partnership. Clark borrows

$100 from Trent in the regular course of the firm's business, and gives Trent a negotiable promissory note signed in the firm name and secured by a chattel mortgage on the firm assets which was also signed in the firm name. The firm will be bound by Clark's acts. If, after borrowing the money, Clark converts it to his own use, the firm will be bound. If Clark borrows the money in his own name giving Trent a promissory note signed by Clark secured by a chattel mortgage on Clark's individual assets which is also signed by Clark, Trent cannot hold the firm liable by showing that the money was used for firm purposes. If the borrowing of the money and the signing of the instruments are within the scope of the firm's business and in the firm name, the firm is liable irrespective of what use is made of the money borrowed, unless the third person knows that the partner borrowing the money intends to misappropriate it and the third person so acts that he aids in the misappropriation.

Reid v. Linder et al.
77 Mont. 406, 251 Pac. 157 (1926)

This was an action by Edgar P. Reid as receiver of the Bank of Twin Bridges (plaintiff) against A. A. Linder and others, copartners doing business under the firm name of Trout Creek Land Company (defendants). Judgment for plaintiff, and defendants, except Wilcomb, appealed. Judgment affirmed.

The Trout Creek Land Company, a partnership, was organized by A. J. Wilcomb, A. A. Linder, James P. Darnutzer, and Carl Darnutzer and at various times during its existence rented land and raised wheat, purchased land and raised cattle, and speculated on the wheat market. The firm had no capital but borrowed money from the bank to finance its operations. It seems that substantially all of its undertakings resulted in losses which were absorbed by the bank. A. J. Wilcomb was cashier of the bank and handled the finances of the firm. In June, 1921, Wilcomb borrowed a total of $16,828.26 from the bank upon four promissory notes signed "Trout Creek Land Company by A. J. Wilcomb." The money was used by Wilcomb to speculate in the grain market and was lost. The bank closed its doors on May 28, 1923, and this suit was brought by the receiver on the four notes. The partners, except Wilcomb, appeared and set up as a defense (1) that the firm was a non-trading partnership and that the making of the notes was not within the scope of the firm's business, and not necessary to the transaction of such business, (2) that the power to borrow money and execute notes was vested only in the members acting together and that no one member had authority to execute a note in the firm name, (3) that no one of the defendants nor the firm received anything of value paid for the notes, and (4) that the bank had knowledge of the limitations on the authority of a partner to act for the firm because Wilcomb was cashier of the bank and a member of its board of directors.

Matthews, J. The evidence does not establish a custom of the firm known to the bank, requiring that all notes of the firm be signed by all of the members, for the record discloses notes, acknowledged as firm notes and paid or renewed as such, signed only by one or more members of the firm, or signed as were the notes in question and indorsed on the back by the individuals constituting the firm.

It is contended that the firm was a non-trading copartnership. The question is important, as in such a partnership a partner has no implied power to borrow money and give firm mercantile paper therefor.

"The test of the character of the partnership is buying and selling. If it buys and sells, it is commercial or trading; if it does not buy or sell, it is one of employment or occupation." *Lee* v. *Bank*, 45 Kan. 8, 25 P. 196, 11 L.R.A. 238.

"The partnership must be in a trade or concern to which the issuing or transfer of bills is necessary or usual." Chitty on Bills (13th Ed.) 58.

And although a firm may ordinarily come within the definition of a non-trading partnership, where the partnership engages in trading requiring capital and the use of credit, the rule as to non-trading partnerships does not apply.

Here no question of fact arises; the facts are undisputed. They show that the firm engaged in buying and selling cattle, as well as in farming and selling grain, and that it required capital and the use of credit; in fact, it operated from the beginning on credit alone, and established a custom within itself long prior to the issuance of the notes in question. Whether the firm was a trading or non-trading partnership was but a question of law for the court. It appears that the issuance of negotiable paper was justified by custom and necessity of the firm as well as by the fact that the firm engaged in trading.

As the notes were traced back on the books of the bank as renewals of notes, the proceeds of which were credited to the checking account of the firm, it is apparent that the bald statement made by the appellants, that neither as individuals nor as members of the firm did they receive any consideration for the notes, presents no issue requiring determination by the jury.

As the firm was a trading partnership, each member of the firm was the agent for the partnership in the transaction of its business and had authority to do whatever was necessary to carry on such business in the ordinary manner, and for that purpose could bind the partnership by an agreement in writing, and notes executed by one of the partners for the benefit of the firm became partnership obligations, binding upon all of the members of the firm, in the absence of bad faith on the part of the contracting partner and knowledge thereof on the part of the payee.

But it is contended that Wilcomb used the firm credit for the purpose of playing the wheat market, without authority from the other members of the firm, and, in this, acted with bad faith toward his copartners. Even though this be admitted to be true, the borrowing was ostensibly authorized, and, if the bank was a bona fide lender, it was entitled to recover on the notes, even though the partner borrowing was actually obtaining the money for his own use.

It is contended, however, that the bank was not a bona fide lender as Wilcomb had full knowledge of all the facts regarding the notes and their purpose, and, as Wilcomb acted as agent for the bank in the transaction, his knowledge was imputed to the bank. In passing, it may be said that the record clearly discloses that Wilcomb was superseded as managing agent of the bank three days before the notes were given, but, as the notes were renewals of other notes issued as far back as 1919, this fact may be disregarded.

It is the general rule that knowledge obtained by an officer of a bank while acting for the bank is imputed to the bank, but knowledge obtained by such officer while acting, not on behalf of the corporation but for himself, or in a manner antagonistic to the corporation, is not imputable to it.

Limitations on Partner's Power

In general, a partner cannot bind the partnership unless the contract negotiated in the name of the partnership is within the scope of the partnership business. Certain transactions are generally considered as being beyond the scope of a partner's power to bind the partnership. It is generally held that the unanimous consent of all the partners is necessary to bind the firm on an agreement to make an assignment for the benefit of creditors, sell the good will of the partnership, or do any act which will make it impossible to carry on the ordinary business of the partnership.

Two other acts which, as a general rule, will require the consent of all the partners are the confession of a judgment and the submission of a claim or liability to arbitration or reference. Such acts are extraordinary in their nature and will come within the scope of the general rule. In addition, the right to have a dispute decided by a court of competent jurisdiction is jealously guarded and the confession of judgment, or the submission of a claim or liability to arbitration or reference, amounts to a waiver of this right. If one or more but less than all of the partners were permitted to bind the partnership by such action, the partner or partners who did not consent would lose their right to resort to the court without having voluntarily waived such right.

Another act which is generally held to be outside the scope of the partnership business is a contract of guaranty or suretyship signed in the firm name by one of the partners as an accommodation to a third person. As a general rule, if a contract will not tend to benefit the partnership, it is not within the scope of the partnership business. If the circumstances are such that the interests of the partnership will be furthered by the guaranty or surety contract, the partnership will be bound; but, if the partnership will not benefit from the transaction, as a general rule, the partnership will not be bound. If all the partners consent to the signing of the guaranty or surety contract or if the signing of such contracts is part of the ordinary business of the partnership, the partnership will be bound.

Jamestown Banking Co. v. Conneaut Lake Dock and Dredge Co. et al.
339 Pa. 26, 14 A. (2d) 325 (1940)

This was an action by Jamestown Banking Co. (plaintiff) against the Conneaut Lake Dock & Dredge Company, a partnership (defendant). A judgment was entered against defendant by confession. On the petition of Scott A. Harshaw (a member of the partnership) the judgment was opened and plaintiff appealed from the order opening the judgment. The order was affirmed.

Holcomb, Ehrhart, McMasters, and Harshaw were partners doing business as Conneaut Lake Dock and Dredge Co. Holcomb, Ehrhart, and McMasters were partners in another venture doing business as the Conneaut Lake Improvement Co. The Conneaut Lake Improvement Co. was the maker of two notes on which the judgment in this case was rendered. The Improvement Co. gave the two notes to the Dock and Dredge Company in 1922 and 1924 respectively. The notes were assigned in the name of Conneaut Lake Dock and Dredge Co. to the plaintiff. The assignment contained a guaranty of payment and a confession of judgment and was signed, "Conneaut Dock & Dredge Co., H. O. Holcomb, Pres., J. P. Ehrhart, Sec." The Improvement Co. received the proceeds from the notes. The Improvement Co. did not make payment; consequently, judgment was entered on the assignment and guaranty against the Conneaut Lake Dock and Dredge Co. Later, executions were issued against the individual assets of the partners. At this time Harshaw petitioned that the judgment be opened and set aside as to him on the ground that he had no notice or knowledge of the guaranty and confession of judgment, had not ratified it, and was not bound by it.

Maxey, J. We find no error in the action of the court. Although appellee did not sign the warrants of attorney, he was a member of the firm whose signature by other partners necessarily included him as prima facie bound on the obligations. The authorization to enter judgment is not limited to the parties who placed their signatures on the instruments. The prothonotary may look beyond the instrument itself and enter judgment against "the person or persons who executed the same," but this does not mean signatories alone; it includes partners and principals, whose agents have signed for them. It follows that the judgment entered against appellee in the present instance was on its face regular. It was not void but voidable.

Since Harshaw did not sign the guaranties and warrants of attorney to confess judgment, the burden was on appellants to prove facts sufficient to show either that the instruments forming the basis of the judgment were signed by Holcomb and Ehrhart for the partnership with Harshaw's express authority or consent, or that he subsequently ratified its execution by acquiescence or otherwise. A partner has implied authority only to bind his firm by transactions in the ordinary course of business. As expressed in the Uniform Partnership Act, "Every partner is an agent of the partnership for the purpose of its business, and the act of every partner, including the execution in the partnership name of any instrument, for apparently carrying on in the usual way the business of the partnership of which he is a member, binds the partnership. . . . ." But for a transaction not in the ordinary course of business a partner has no implied authority to bind his firm. Such a transaction is a confession of judgment. The same section of the Partnership Act provides: "Unless authorized by the other partners, or unless they have abandoned the business, one or more but less than all the partners have no authority to . . . . (*d*) Confess a judgment. . . . ." Hence if the instruments on which judgment was entered are considered merely as confessions of judgment, Holcomb and Ehrhart had no implied authority to bind the partnership or its property, much less the individual assets or estate of the appellee Harshaw. Prior to the Uniform Partnership Act it was held that such a confession of judgment would bind the partnership assets and likewise the individual assets of the partners who confessed judgment, but not the estate of those who did not. Even if the warrants of attorney to confess judgment are disregarded, the assignments remain guaranties executed by only two of the four partners. They had no implied authority to bind the firm or appellee, for fewer than all the partners cannot bind the firm as guarantor to a third person without express authority from the remaining partners or without such conduct on their part as amounts to ratification. This is because a guaranty is usually not given in the ordinary course of a partnership business.

It follows that upon Harshaw's denial of having given Holcomb or Ehrhart authority to execute the assignments, the burden was on the plaintiff in the judgment to prove express authority on their part or facts indicating ratification of their acts by Harshaw. There is here no evidence of such express authority. On the question of ratification a conflict arose which could be resolved only by a jury trial.

First National Bank v. Farson et al.
226 N.Y. 218, 123 N.E. 490 (1919)

This was an action by the First National Bank of Ann Arbor, Michigan (plaintiff) against John Farson, Jr., and William Farson (defendants). From a judgment of the Appellate Division, affirming a judgment for plaintiff, defendant appealed. Judgment reversed and new trial ordered.

John Farson, Sr., and the defendant John Farson, Jr., were members of a partnership carrying on the business of buying and selling bonds under the firm name of Farson, Son & Co. A salesman sold five $1,000 bonds to plaintiff. At the time the sale was made the agent making the sale told the plaintiff that Farson, Son & Co. would guarantee the payment of the principal and interest on the bonds. In fulfillment of this promise John Farson, Sr., signed in the name of the firm and sent to the plaintiff a written guaranty which contained among other things the following: "For value received, we hereby guarantee payment of principal and interest promptly at maturity of the following bonds, namely: (Followed by a designation of the five bonds.)"

The acts of John Farson, Sr., were performed by him purporting to act as a member of the firm. The bonds were not paid nor was the interest on the bonds paid as it became due. Plaintiff sued on the guaranty. The defendants contend that the guaranty was outside the scope of the business and did not bind the partnership.

Collins, J. The power or authority of a partner in a commercial partnership is to be tested and measured, when the actual agreements between the partners are unknown, by the ordinary usages of and the methods customarily used in partnerships conducting a business like unto, or by the usages and methods of, his own partnership. Each partner is impliedly empowered to conduct the business in the way usual to that class of business, or to his partnership.

The instant case does not involve, through the findings or evidence or the briefs or argument of counsel, a method or course of dealing peculiar to Farson, Son & Co., or a ratification of or acquiescence in the guaranty by John Farson, or an express or actual authorization to John Farson, Sr., to execute it. The findings present us with the facts: The existence of the partnership; the nature of its business; the sale and the attendant circumstances; the execution of the guaranty; and the consequent liability. Those findings do not directly or by just and reasonable inference beget the conclusion that persons engaged in the business of buying and selling bonds and other securities in the cities of New York and Chicago, customarily and as an ordinary usage in selling bonds owned by them, guaranteed the payment of the principal and interest of the bonds. The law has known and recognized certain transactions and contract of one partner as binding upon the other partners and the partnership, because they were manifestly within the scope or objects of the partnership; they were directly and reasonably, if not necessarily, incident to or connected with the business of the partnership. Thus a member of a trading or commercial partnership has, through implication, the power to buy and sell the articles dealt in, to borrow money for the business, and to give notes and checks of the partnership, to transfer and indorse by the partnership the notes and checks given the partnership, or enforce their payment by actions at law, or hire and discharge employees. Those acts and others are within the general usages and methods of those partnerships.

The only base upholding the implied authority of John Farson, Sr., to execute the guaranty must, under the findings of fact, arise from the general usages and methods of partnerships of its class. The guaranty executed by John Farson, Sr., to the plaintiff has two elements: The one, it guaranteed the payment of the debts of a third party, namely, the Eden Irrigation & Land Company; the other, the debts or bonds were the property of the partnership and the guaranty was made as a part of and presumably to effect a sale of them. The first element need not detain us, because it is a thoroughly established rule of law that a partner has not implied authority to bind his partner or the partnership by contracts of guaranty or suretyship, either for himself individually or for third persons. The second element requires more consideration. The law does not know, and the courts cannot know or take notice, that a general agent or a partner in making sales of the property of the principal or partnership is impliedly authorized by mere force of the agency to make any guaranty or warranty in relation to the article. Generally speaking, his implied authority, if he has it, springs from the usage of the business in which the principal or partnership is engaged. If in that business it is usual to give the guaranty in making the sale, the authority to sell carries with it the power to guarantee. It is a general rule that the power of an agent to bind the principal in contracts of guaranty or suretyship can only be charged against the principal by necessary implication, where the duties to be performed cannot be discharged without the exercise of such a power, or where the power is a manifestly necessary and customary incident of the authority bestowed upon the agent, and where the power is practically indispensable to accomplish the object in view.

Liability for Partner's Wrongful Acts

The agency rule, that the principal is liable for the torts of the agent committed in the course of and in the scope of the employment, applies in determining the liability of the partnership for the torts of a partner. The cases involving the liability of the partnership for injuries resulting from the negligence of a partner are most numerous. If the negligent act is performed by the partner while engaged in partnership business, the partnership is liable; but, if the negligent act is not within the scope of the business, the partnership is not liable. Archer and Burch are partners in the operation of a retail store. The partnership owns an automobile. It is agreed that the partners shall use the automobile for their own pleasure on alternate Sundays. Burch, while using the automobile on Sunday to drive to a wedding, negligently injures Trent. Trent cannot hold the partnership or Archer for damages.

As a general rule, if a partner is guilty of fraud or misrepresentations in the transaction of partnership business, the partnership is liable.

If the partnership accepts the benefits of the fraud or misrepresentations, it is clearly liable.

Whether or not the partnership can be held liable for the wilful torts of a partner depends on the circumstances of the case. It is generally held that, if the tortious act is a partnership act, the partnership will be liable; but, if the act is wilful and malicious and done by one partner without the knowledge and consent of the others and not for the benefit or purposes of the partnership, the partnership will not be bound. Archer and Burch are partners in the lumber business. Trent has asked for an estimate on lumber needed on a job. Archer learns that Trent placed his order with another firm. Archer sees Trent and asks him why he did not place his order with Archer & Burch. In an altercation which follows, Archer without provocation strikes Trent. Neither the partnership nor Burch will be liable. If a partnership is liable for a tort committed by a member of the partnership, the liability is a joint and several liability. It is similar in this respect to the tort liability in agency. The partner committing the tort is liable because he is guilty of the tort and each partner is liable as a principal. Also, the partnership is liable in that the injured person would be considered as a creditor of the partnership.

If a partner commits a crime in connection with the carrying on of the partnership business, the other members of the partnership cannot be held criminally liable unless they participated in the criminal act.

Roux v. Lawand
131 Me. 215, 160 Atl. 756 (1932)

This was an action by John Roux (plaintiff) against Simon Lawand (defendant). Judgment for plaintiff and defendant appealed. Judgment affirmed.

This action is against one Simon Lawand as the surviving partner of a partnership, alleged to have consisted of himself and his since deceased son, to recover damages for personal injuries from a tort, committed in his life time by the decedent, acting in the scope of the partnership business, on the plaintiff, then an employee of the firm.

The referees found the proximate cause of the injury to the plaintiff (that is, the cause which, in natural and continuous sequence unbroken by any efficient intervening cause produced the injury, and without which the result would not have occurred) to have been the negligence of the copartner, in the usual course of the concern's business.

The copartner, while cleaning a hat in the back part of the hat cleaning and shoe shining shop of the firm, struck a match to light a cigarette, and got the hat afire. He threw the burning hat to the floor; then picked it up, and flung it toward the sink, where it fell into a pail of inflammable fluid, which burst into flames. He took up the pail of blazing liquid and hurled the contents through a doorway, or opening, into a small compartment between the hat cleaning room and the shoe shining stands. The plaintiff, who had changed to working clothes, was in this compartment, standing before a mirror and combing his hair, previous to beginning his usual daily work shining shoes. Seeing the act of his employer, plaintiff started to run, but did not escape the flames; he was severely burned about the back and legs.

Dunn, J. Partners are liable jointly, and also severally, for the tortious acts of a copartner done in the line of, or reasonable scope of, the partnership business, whether they personally participate therein, or have knowledge thereof, or not.

If a partnership is liable for a tort, each member thereof is individually liable, and an action may be maintained against a member of the partnership as a joint tort-feasor. The theory is that of agency. The test as to the liability of the firm for the tort of a partner is the question of agency; and generally the firm is liable if it would have been liable had the same act been committed by an agent intrusted with the management of the business.

Philips et al. v. United States
United States v. Stevens et al.
59 F. (2d) 881 (1932)

This was an action by the United States of America (plaintiff) against John Philips and others (defendants). (Two suits were consolidated in this action.) Judgment for plaintiff in the first action and defendant appealed. Judgment for defendant in the second action and plaintiff appealed. Judgment for plaintiff in first action affirmed and judgment in second action reversed.

At the close of World War I the United States had on hand a large quantity of unused lumber. Both the government and the lumber industry realized that it would be undesirable to dump this lumber on the market.

Various lumber associations entered into a contract whereby they became the joint purchasers of the surplus lumber. The contract set up standards for the determination of the price to be paid to the United States.

Philips and Stevens agreed to handle the sale and distribution of the lumber for the associations. The partnership was to receive a commission on the lumber handled. Chambers was the agent of the United States with the authority to determine prices to be paid for the lumber. Philips acted as agent for the association. Chambers and Philips set the price to be paid for the lumber without the intervention of a third person. Philips handled the field work and Stevens had charge of the office and clerical part of the work. Under the contract, whenever any of this lumber was sold, an invoice showing the sales price was sent to the United States. Of the invoice price 12 per cent was deposited to the account of Philips and Stevens and 88 per cent was deposited in a special account from which the United States was paid the agreed price it was to receive for the lumber. In almost no instance was the lumber invoiced to the United States at the true sales price paid by the purchaser to Philips and Stevens. It was invoiced at the base price fixed by Philips and Chambers, but Philips secretly received large sums from the purchasers from Philips and Stevens. These sums were frequently paid in cash and not by check. In addition to this method of receiving profits, defendant Philips in some instances became a secret partner of the purchaser of this lumber.

Philips and Chambers fixed the base price below the real sale price so that they could deceive the government and make a secret profit on the deals. Chambers received a share of the secret profits from Philips. Stevens was not a party to these secret deals and had no knowledge of them. This suit is brought to recover from the partnership and from Philips and Stevens a judgment for the secret profits. Stevens defends on the ground that he was not a party to the illegal transactions, knew nothing about them, and derived no benefit from them.

Van Orsdel, A. J. The theory upon which the court below distinguished between the liability of Philips and Stevens was based upon the liability of Philips for the frauds perpetrated, and as Stevens did not participate in the frauds his liability would only arise through breach of contract. We are not impressed with this conclusion. The liability of both Philips and Stevens is based upon the contract, and the suit is for a violation of the government's rights under that contract. Indeed, the suit is for a breach of the contract, and the fraud alleged and proved is material as showing and establishing that fact. In the last analysis the question is whether Stevens is liable for Philips' breach, which in law is the breach of both.

The agreement between Stevens and Philips was in the nature of a partnership agreement. It provided for an apportionment of the work, a division of the profits, and a common undertaking. These constitute the elements of a partnership. Each of the partners was not only an agent for the partnership but an agent for the other partner. They were, therefore, liable for the default or fraud of each within the scope of the common undertaking.

It follows, therefore, that, Philips having been held liable to the United States for the profits realized under this contract which accrued to him in fraud of the rights of the United States, Stevens' liability as a partner follows as a matter of law by reason of the joint responsibility which he assumed with Philips under the contract.

Partner's Individual Liability

At common law a partnership obligation was generally held to be a joint obligation; that is, the partners were obligated on a group promise and not on the individual promise of each partner. The Uniform Partnership Act provides that the partners are jointly liable on partnership obligations. At common law if one wished to sue and recover a judgment against joint obligors, it was, with few exceptions, necessary to get personal service on each of the joint obligors, an act which was often difficult if not impossible. The common law rule as to the procedure to be followed in enforcing a joint obligation has been changed by state statutes. These statutes are not uniform; consequently, one, if he wishes to determine the procedure to be followed in enforcing a partnership obligation, must consult the statutes of the state having jurisdiction of the case. In some states all joint obligations are by statute made joint and several; that is, suit may be brought against the partners jointly or against each individual partner. Several states have statutes which permit the party plaintiff to proceed to judgment if he serves one or more of the joint obligors even though he has not served all. The judgment when obtained is enforceable against joint assets of the obligors and against the individual assets of the parties served with process, but is not enforceable against the individual assets of the parties not served with process. If a plaintiff serves all of the joint obligors with process, the judgment when rendered may be enforced against the joint property of the obligors or against their individual property. In all jurisdictions partners are jointly and severally liable for damages for the torts of the partnership. The foregoing discussion of the nature of partner's liability is from the standpoint of his liability for contract obligations.

Mason v. Eldred et al.
73 U.S. 231 (1867)

This was an action by Mason (plaintiff) against Anson Eldred (defendant). The judges of the Circuit Court were not in accord as to the judgment which should be rendered. The case was certified to the United States Supreme Court for decision. Judgment for plaintiff.

Anson Eldred, Elisha Eldred, and one Balcom were trading as partners and issued to Mason a partnership note. Mason sued on the note in the Michigan Court, and Elisha Eldred was the only party served, but Mason proceeded to judgment. In this suit Anson Eldred claims that he cannot be sued on the note because the note is a joint obligation and the Michigan judgment exhausts Mason's remedies on the note. The rights of the parties were controlled by the joint debtor statute then in force in Michigan.

Mr. Justice Field. The plaintiff contends that a copartnership note is the several obligation of each copartner, as well as the joint obligation of all, and that a judgment recovered upon the note against one copartner is not a bar to a suit upon the same note against another copartner; and the latter position is insisted upon as the rule of the common law, independent of the joint debtor act of Michigan.

It is true that each copartner is bound for the entire amount due on copartnership contract; and that this obligation is so far several that if he is sued alone, and does not plead the non-joinder of his copartners, a recovery may be had against him for the whole amount due upon the contract, and a joint judgment against the copartners may be enforced against the property of each. But this is a different thing from the liability which arises from a joint and several contract. There the contract contains distinct engagements, that of each contractor individually, and that of all jointly, and different remedies may be pursued upon each. The contractors may be sued separately on their several engagements or together on their joint undertaking. But in copartnerships there is no such several liability of the copartners. The copartnerships are formed for joint purposes. The members undertake joint enterprises, they assume joint risks, and they incur in all cases joint liabilities. In all copartnership transactions this common risk and liability exist. Therefore it is that in suits upon these transactions all the copartners must be brought in, except when there is some ground of personal release from liability, as infancy or a discharge in bankruptcy; and if not brought in, the omission may be pleaded in abatement. The plea in abatement avers that the alleged promises, upon which the action is brought, were made jointly with another and not with the defendant alone, a plea which would be without meaning, if the copartnership contract was the several contract of each copartner.

The general doctrine maintained in England and the United States may be briefly stated. A judgment against one upon a joint contract of several persons bars an action against the others, though the latter were dormant partners of the defendant in the original action, and this fact was unknown to the plaintiff when that action was commenced. When the contract is joint, and not joint and several, the entire cause of action is merged in the judgment. The joint liability of the parties not sued with those against whom the judgment is recovered, being extinguished, their entire liability is gone. They cannot be sued separately, for they have incurred no several obligation; they cannot be sued jointly with the others, because judgment has been already recovered against the latter, who would otherwise be subjected to two suits for the same cause.

In *Oakley* v. *Aspinwall*, the Court of Appeals of New York had occasion to consider the effect of a judgment recovered under the joint debtor act of that State, which is the same as the Michigan statute, upon the original demand. Mr. Justice Bronson, speaking for the court, says: "It is said that the original demand was merged in, and extinguished by the judgment, and consequently, that the plaintiff must sue upon the judgment, if he sues at all. That would undoubtedly be so if both the defendants had been before the court in the original action. But the joint debtor act creates an anomaly in the law. And for the purpose of giving effect to the statute, and at the same time preserving the rights of all parties, the plaintiff must be allowed to sue on the original demand. There is no difficulty in pursuing such a course; it can work no injury to any one, and it will avoid the absurdity of allowing a party to sue on a pretended cause of action, which is, in truth, no cause of action at all, and then to recover on proof of a different demand."

QUESTIONS AND PROBLEMS

1. Harvey, an employee of J. P. Morgan & Co., a partnership, was injured in the course of his employment. The personnel manager, who was a member of the firm, promised Harvey a pension for life in settlement of his claim against the firm. The pension was paid for seven years and then the firm refused to make further payment. When sued, the firm set up lack of authority on the part of the partner. Is this a valid defense?
2. Williams and Williams was a partnership operating a mine. William J. Williams, one of the partners, employed Smith to drive his car as chauffeur while he, Williams, was incapacitated as the result of an injury, and later to drive a truck at the mine. While driving William J. Williams' car on a business trip, the car collided with another car and Smith was injured. The firm of Williams and Williams denied liability on the ground that William J. Williams had no authority to hire employees for the firm. Is the firm liable?
3. Marks and James operated a creamery as partners. Beers, at the request of Marks, loaned money to the firm. James did not participate in the negotiations for the loan and he made no promise to repay the loan. Is the firm liable to Beers?
4. In the foregoing case if the money had been loaned to Marks on his individual note, would the use of the money for firm purposes render the firm liable for the amount of the loan?
5. Austin and Smith were attorneys and practiced law as partners. Austin borrowed money from Bayes and gave Bayes a note signed in the name of the law firm—Austin and Smith. The money was not used for firm purposes. Was the firm liable on the note?
6. Allen issued his negotiable promissory note payable to the order of Bennett & Co. The note was indorsed, "Bennett & Co. by N. E. Watson," and negotiated to the Trust Co. for value and before maturity. N. E. Watson and James V. Bennett were partners doing business as Bennett & Co. Allen claims that the Trust Co. is not a holder in due course of the note because it was not indorsed by both of the partners. Is this claim correct?
7. Claxton, Briggs, and Bogle operated an electrical appliance business as partners. The partnership was organized primarily to help Bogle. Claxton and Briggs did not actively participate in the business. Bogle purchased the majority of the merchandise from Savory, Inc. Through mismanagement, the store became overstocked. Savory, Inc., accepted the return of part of the goods and agreed not to ship goods in the future unless the order was signed either by Claxton or Briggs. A letter was written to Savory, Inc., stating that the firm would not be liable for orders unless the orders were signed either by Claxton or Briggs. Thereafter, Savory, Inc., shipped goods to the firm on orders signed by Bogle. Is the firm liable on such orders?
8. Barnes, Koppel, and Post were partners operating a junk business under the name of Idaho Junk House. Koppel told one Gums that there was a tractor frame on Klam's ranch and asked him to get it. Gums got the tractor frame and broke it up, and Koppel purchased the junk from Gums for $8. Klam missed the tractor frame and on investigation found the pieces in the possession of the Idaho Junk House. The tractor frame was stolen by Gums and purchased in the course of the partnership business by Koppel. This was a conversion of Klam's property. Can the partnership be held liable in tort for the conversion?
9. Thomas and Patrick Connolly were partners in the sheep and livestock business. Thomas was trustee of a trust fund. Thomas, without the knowledge or consent

of Patrick, used trust funds to purchase sheep for the partnership. Is the partnership liable to the beneficiary of the trust?

10. A judgment was recovered against the partnership of Stout and Wingut for $90 and costs of suit. When suit was brought both partners were served with process. An execution was issued and the execution was levied on the individual property of Stout. Stout claimed that the sheriff had no right to levy an execution, which had been issued on a judgment rendered on a partnership debt, on his (Stout's) individual property. Is Stout's contention correct?

CHAPTER XXXIII

DISSOLUTION AND WINDING UP

Dissolution

Dissolution is defined in the Uniform Partnership Act as follows: "The dissolution of a partnership is the change in the relation of the partners caused by any partner ceasing to be associated in the carrying on as distinguished from the winding up of the business." The term is sometimes used to designate the termination of the relation together with those acts incident to the final settlement of the partnership affairs. The dissolution may be caused by the accomplishment of the object of the partnership, by the agreement of the partners, by the will of any partner, by the expulsion of a partner, by the death of a partner, or by the bankruptcy of a partner. A dissolution will result if the business of the partnership is declared unlawful. The partnership is not terminated on dissolution but continues until the winding up of the affairs of the partnership is completed.

The partnership relation is personal, and, as a general rule, the court will not force the partners to continue the partnership relation against the will of any one of the partners. It is only in very rare cases and only when such action is necessary to protect the interests of a partner that the court will force the partners to continue the relationship by granting a decree of specific performance. If the term of the partnership is not set out in the articles of copartnership, any partner may, as a matter of right, dissolve the partnership at will. If the partnership was created to continue for a definite time, it may be dissolved at the will of any partner; but, if in dissolving the partnership the partner has breached the articles of copartnership, he must answer in damages to the other partners. No particular acts are necessary to dissolve a partnership. Any definite expression of intention to withdraw from the partnership is sufficient. The dissolution of the partnership does not, of necessity, require a discontinuance of the partnership business. The business may be continued by a new partnership composed of succeeding partners without interruption. The rights of the partners will be adjusted either by amicable settlement or by appropriate court action.

McCollum et al. v. McCollum

Ct. of Civ. App. Tex., 67 S.W. (2d) 1055 (1934)

This was an action by Lorance L. McCollum (plaintiff) against B. E. McCollum and others (defendants). Temporary injunction granted plaintiff and defendants appealed. Temporary injunction dissolved and case dismissed.

Murray, J. Appellee, Lorance L. McCollum, instituted this proceeding against appellants, B. E. McCollum, Graham McCollum, Mozzelle Murray and her husband, Pete Murray, Mattie W. Goulding and her husband Willard R. Goulding, and E. D. Henry, seeking a temporary mandatory injunction restoring him to the position of partner in the firm of Hagy-McCollum Funeral Home, and also restoring him to the position of manager of the firm. He also asked for the payment of his salary of $300 per month.

It appears from appellee's petition for injunction that Mrs. Mattie W. Goulding, who is the mother of the appellee, on the 26th day of July, 1933, conveyed to her four children, Lorance L. McCollum, B. E. McCollum, Graham McCollum, and Mrs. Mozzelle Murray, all of the land, buildings, and equipment used in the business of Hagy-McCollum Funeral Home, each to own a one-fourth undivided interest in the business.

The above four named children of Mrs. Goulding, in July, 1933, entered into a contract of partnership for the conduct of this business, in which it was provided that the compensation to each of the partners should be as follows: Lorance L. McCollum $300 per month; B. E. McCollum $200 per month; Graham McCollum $150 per month; and Pete Murray, who is the husband of Mozzelle Murray, $150 per month. The partnership was to continue for many years, but there were also a number of provisions for a dissolution.

On November 1, 1933, appellee, Lorance L. McCollum, received notice that he was no longer a member of the firm and that his salary had been discontinued. On January 5, 1934, this injunction proceeding was instituted by him.

This injunction, in effect, attempts to prevent the dissolution of a partnership. Under the law a partnership calling for the personal services of the partners can always be dissolved, even though it constitutes a breach of contract. The right to dissolve may not exist but the power to dissolve always exists. If the dissolution constitutes a breach of the contract, there may be a suit for damages for the breach, but the power to dissolve nevertheless exists.

There can be no such thing as an indissoluble partnership.

Appellee contends that he was entitled to the relief sought because he was a one-fourth owner of the business. We cannot agree with this contention. If joint owners of a business are unable to agree upon the management of the business, one of such joint owners might have the right to require the appointing of a receiver upon a proper showing, but he would, under no circumstances, be permitted to compel the maintaining of a partnership by mandatory injunction.

Change in Membership

Any change in the membership of a partnership causes its dissolution; however, it is not necessary to discontinue and liquidate the business operated by the partnership. Archer, Burch, and Clark operate a retail business as partners. Clark wishes to withdraw from the partnership. Archer and Burch purchase Clark's interest in the partnership. The old partnership of Archer, Burch, and Clark will be dissolved by Clark's withdrawal, but the new partnership of Archer and Burch will continue to operate the business without interruption. Clark will continue to be personally liable on the debts of the Archer, Burch, and Clark partnership; but, if proper notice is given, he will not be personally liable on the debts of the Archer and Burch partnership. Instead of selling to Archer and Burch, Clark might sell his interest to Drew. If such a sale were contemplated, it would be necessary to obtain Archer's and Burch's consent, because one cannot become a member of a partnership without the consent of all of the members. The Archer, Burch, and Clark partnership will be dissolved; but the Archer, Burch, and Drew partnership will continue the business without interruption. Clark will continue personally liable on the debts of the old partnership; but, if proper notice is given, Clark will not be liable for the debts of the Archer, Burch, and Drew partnership. If the Archer, Burch, and Clark partnership is in need of additional capital and they agree that, if Drew will pay $3,000 into the partnership, they will take him in as an equal partner and Drew pays in $3,000 and becomes an equal partner, the Archer, Burch, and Clark partnership is dissolved but the Archer, Burch, Clark, and Drew partnership will continue the business without interruption. Drew is not personally liable to the creditors of the Archer, Burch, and Clark partnership; but such creditors, in most states, will be treated as creditors of the Archer, Burch, Clark, and Drew partnership, and the assets of the new partnership including Drew's contribution may be applied to the payment of the partnership debts of the old partnership. The creditors of the old partnership and the creditors of the new partnership will have equal rights in the assets of the Archer, Burch, Clark, and Drew partnership.

When a new member is taken into a partnership he may contract to pay the debts of the old partnership and by such an agreement make himself personally liable for the existing obligations of the old partnership. If a partner sells his interest in the partnership, either to his partners or to another, and the continuing partnership agrees to assume and pay all the debts of the old partnership, the retiring partner is not discharged from his personal obligation on partnership debts. If, however, the creditors of the old partnership agree to accept the new partnership as their debtor in the place of the old partnership and agree to discharge the retiring partner, as a general rule, the retiring partner will be discharged of his personal liability.

Money Corporation v. Wolfis
269 Mich. 601, 257 N.W. 749 (1935)

This was an action by Money Corporation (plaintiff) against Dirk Wolfis (defendant). Judgment for plaintiff and defendant appealed. Judgment reversed and new trial ordered.

The plaintiff is the owner of all indebtedness once owing Muskegon Citizens' Loan & Investment Company (hereafter referred to as the Loan Co.). The defendant guaranteed the credit of Claude Wolfis to the Loan Co.

Claude Wolfis and Joe Snyder were partners operating the East End Auto Market. The partnership sold automobiles on title-retaining contracts, conditional sales notes, and ordinary promissory notes. These conditional sales contracts and notes were indorsed by the partnership and discounted by the Loan Co. In the event a conditional sales contract or note was not paid, the partnership was liable to the Loan Co. for the unpaid balance. In September, 1926, Claude Wolfis retired from the partnership, at which time both Wolfis and Snyder notified the Loan Co. that Wolfis had retired. Snyder continued the business and continued to discount conditional sales contracts and notes with the Loan Co. More than a year after Wolfis retired, Snyder went out of business. At the time Snyder went out of business all the conditional sales contracts and notes which had been discounted by the partnership prior to Wolfis' withdrawal had either been paid out or taken up by Snyder. The entire indebtedness sued on arose out of conditional sales contracts and notes discounted subsequent to Wolfis' retirement.

Potter, J. The average date of all the conditional sales contracts and notes in the hands of plaintiff, assignee of Muskegon Citizens' Loan & Investment Company, is more than a year after Claude Wolfis retired from the business of the East End Auto Market. The liability of Claude Wolfis upon the conditional sales contracts and notes indorsed by the copartnership while he was a partner did not cease upon his retiral from the partnership, but continued until he was legally discharged therefrom. The conditional sales contracts and promissory notes indorsed and discounted by Snyder were not substitutions or extensions. The record shows such contracts and notes were indorsed and discounted and the proceeds credited to him on open account. Snyder then drew his checks against that account for the amount due on the notes upon which Claude Wolfis was liable, and these checks were paid, canceled, and returned, and the notes paid thereby were paid, canceled, and returned. This constituted payment of the notes.

Subsequently Snyder failed, owing around $600 or $700 to the Muskegon Citizens' Loan & Investment Company; and it is sought to extend defendant's guaranty of the credit of Claude Wolfis to cover the ultimate liability after failure of Snyder. It may not be so extended. Plaintiff has the conditional sales contracts and notes discounted by Snyder, five in number, in its possession. It seeks to sustain a judgment on the guaranty against defendant for the full amount due from Snyder, and keep these conditional sales contracts and notes; and, if it were able to collect on this judgment and upon the conditional sales contracts and notes, it might be able to collect the indebtedness twice. This it cannot do.

Wood v. Waterman et al.
102 Cal. App. 516, 283 Pac. 143 (1929)

This was an action by Carrie D. Wood (plaintiff) against G. A. Waterman and others, copartners doing business as California Fruit Land Association (defendants). Judgment for defendants and plaintiff appealed. Judgment reversed and remanded.

John H. Wood and G. A. Waterman were partners doing business as the California Fruit Land Co. The partnership owned a tract of land which it divided into small tracts. These small tracts were sold on contract to various individuals including the plaintiff. These contracts provided that the California Fruit Land Co. would plant the tracts to fig trees and grape vines and at the end of three years turn the tract over to the purchaser as a producing vineyard and orchard. John A. Wood withdrew from the partnership on the 11th of June, 1923, and Waterman purchased Wood's interest in the partnership. Later the same month Waterman sold Charles F. Hill a one-half interest in the project, making him an equal partner. At the time Hill purchased an interest in the project, he and Waterman called on all the parties having contracts, including the plaintiff, and Hill told each contract holder that he would, in partnership with Waterman, carry out the contracts. Subsequently, Hill spent time and money in the performance of the contracts. The fall of 1923 was a dry fall and the project could not be carried to a successful completion without irrigation. In September, 1923, the contracts were abandoned and notice given that the partnership could not perform. Installment payments were made on the contracts by the purchasers, but no such payments were made after January, 1924. This suit was brought by Carrie D. Wood in her own behalf and as assignee of the other contracting parties to recover installments paid on the contracts. The lower court held that Hill was not personally liable.

Sloane, P. J. The original partnership doing business as the California Fruit Land Association consisted of G. A. Waterman and John H. Wood. When Wood withdrew and transferred his interest to Waterman in June, 1923, this partnership was dissolved.

If Waterman and the defendant Hill entered into an agreement to associate themselves together to continue the business under the same name, it nevertheless created a new legal entity, in which the incoming partner would not be liable for the obligations of the old partnership, unless he definitely assumed such obligations in a way to create a legal liability. The fact that he may have held himself out as a partner with Waterman for carrying on this contractual business, and even orally assured the vendees that it was the intention of the new concern to carry out the terms of the agreements, or that he actually contributed of his time and means to that end, will not bind him in the absence of a new consideration, or some prejudice suffered by the contract holders induced by his representations.

It is the recognized rule that, where an obligation of an incoming partner to be responsible for the debts of the old partnership is alleged, such obligation must be evidence in writing under the statute of frauds, unless the assumption of liability grows out of and is part of the consideration of the new partnership agreement.

The case of *Freeman* v. *Badgley*, 105 Cal. 372, 38 P. 955, lays down this latter rule that an agreement made after the partnership is formed, whereby the new partner agrees to assume the debts of the old firm, is an agreement to pay the debt of another, and must be established in compliance with the provisions of the statute of frauds. But this same decision holds that, if the assumption of liability for the obligations of the old firm is part of the consideration given for an interest in the business, it is supported by the consideration of the original contracts.

The evidence relating to the partnership agreement between Waterman and Hill, and the assumption of the obligations of the old firm, is somewhat meager and indefinite, but it must be borne in mind that the judgment here is one of nonsuit, given at the close of plaintiff's case, and with no rebutting evidence on the part of defendant.

Under such condition, every inference and presumption that can be drawn from the evidence of plaintiff must be drawn in his favor. And it cannot be said in this case that the evidence of the defendant Waterman does not tend to support the contention that defendant Hill, subsequent to the execution of the sales contracts, entered into a partnership with Waterman for the express purpose of taking over and carrying out these sales agreements, and that as part of the consideration for the partnership agreement he assumed obligation on the part of the new firm to carry out the terms of these sales contracts.

Powers after Dissolution

After the dissolution of a partnership, as a general rule, the next step is to wind up the affairs of the partnership. On dissolution the partnership ceases to be a going concern, but its existence is not terminated; however, its powers are limited to those acts which are reasonably necessary to the winding up of its affairs. Winding up involves the orderly liquidation of the assets of the partnership, payment of partnership creditors, and distribution of the remaining funds to the partners, or, in the case of the bankruptcy or death of a partner, to his estate in accordance with his rights therein.

If the dissolution is brought about amiably during the life of the partners, they have the right to wind up the business. If the dissolution is due to the death or bankruptcy of a partner, the surviving partners or partners not bankrupt have the right to wind up the business. If the dissolution is by court decree, usually, although not necessarily, a receiver is appointed who winds up the business. If a partner sells his interest in the business to his partner or partners or to a third person whom the other partners have agreed to accept as a partner, the business is continued, but the affairs of the old partnership are wound up usually in accordance with an agreement into which the parties entered at the time of the sale.

The partner or partners who have charge of winding up the partnership business have the power to bind the partnership in any transaction necessary to the liquidation of the partnership assets. They can collect on negotiable paper held by the partnership, collect moneys due, sell partnership property, sue to enforce partnership rights, and do such other acts as the nature of the business and the circumstances dictate. As a general rule, a partner who is winding up a partnership business cannot borrow money in the name of the partnership. However, if, by borrowing money and using it to pay partnership obligations, he can preserve the assets of the partnership, he will have such power. The majority of jurisdictions hold that he has no authority to make, renew, or indorse negotiable instruments. His power to bind the partnership on contracts will depend on the nature of the contract. If the contract is in furtherance of the orderly liquidation of the assets, he can bind the partnership but, if it is "new business," the partnership will not be bound.

Rosenberg et al. v. J. C. Penney Co. et al.
30 Cal. App. (2d) 609, 86 P. (2d) 696 (1939)

This was an action by Ira H. Rosenberg and another, surviving partners of a partnership firm, doing business under the firm name and style of Rosenberg & Bush (plaintiffs) against J. C. Penney Co. and others (defendants). Judgment for plaintiffs and defendants appealed. Judgment reversed as to defendant Bowen and modified and affirmed as to defendant J. C. Penney Co.

Bowen was manager of J. C. Penney Co.'s store in Healdsburg. The firm of Rosenberg & Bush was composed of Esther C. Rosenberg, Ira H. Rosenberg, and Harold B. Rosenberg. Esther C. Rosenberg died and the business had since then been conducted by Ira H. and Harold B. Rosenberg as surviving partners.

On September 27, 1924, Bowen displayed in the window of the J. C. Penney Co. store a sample of "gym pants." The display consisted of a pair of "gym pants" sold by J. C. Penney Co. and a pair of "gym pants" sold by Rosenberg & Bush, together with placards pointing out the superior quality of the "gym pants" sold by J. C. Penney Co. and stating that the garment sold by Rosenberg & Bush was of inferior quality, poorly made and of shoddy material.

This suit was brought in the name of the partnership by the surviving partners. On appeal J. C. Penney Co. contended that it was necessary to join the estate of the deceased partner, Esther C. Rosenberg, as a party plaintiff.

Mr. Presiding Justice Pullen delivered the opinion of the court.

Section 2435 et seq. of the Civil Code provided that the death of a partner brought about the dissolution of the partnership and made it the duty of the surviving partner to account to the personal representative for the assets thereof. By these sections therefore, the surviving partners were entitled to continue in control of the business for the purpose of liquidation, subject to an obligation to account to the personal representative of Esther C. Rosenberg, the deceased partner. The fact that the business had been carried on by the surviving partners for some considerable length of time is not of itself material. If such delay was a matter of loss to the personal representative, that would be a matter of which such representative could complain, but none other. The only interest of defendants would be to insure their protection against future liability for the same tort.

While in *Berson* v. *Ewing*, 84 Cal. 89, 23 P. 1112, the tort affecting the partnership business was committed prior to the death of the partner, the court considered the question generally. That action was for the malicious prosecution of a civil action. It was there contended that inasmuch as a partner in liquidation was authorized to collect debts only, the surviving partner had no right to sue for damages for a tort. The court held, however, that by virtue of section 1585 of the Code of Civil Procedure providing that a "surviving partner has the right to continue in possession of the partnership, and to settle its business . . . . without delay," the surviving partner had the right to maintain the action, for "the power to settle gives full authority to the surviving partner to do everything that may be necessary to wind up the affairs of the partnership . . . . ," and also construing section 2461 of the Civil Code, which provided that a surviving partner could collect debts, but could only release and compromise claims, the court holding debts and claims were there synonymous, said: "It would indeed be strange if a surviving partner could compromise any claim against the firm, but could neither compromise nor enforce one in favor of it."

This rule is also recognized generally in Corpus Juris and in Ruling Case Law, as follows: "It is a well established general rule that an action at law to enforce rights, claims or choses in action of a partnership which has been dissolved by the death of a partner is properly brought by the surviving partners, and it is neither necessary nor proper to join the representatives of the deceased partner as plaintiffs, although by virtue of statute a different rule sometimes exists."

"In all matters connected with a partnership dissolved by the death of a partner the surviving partner is the proper party to bring suit."

Froess v. Froess
284 Pa. 369, 131 Atl. 276 (1925)

This was an action by Sarah L. Froess, administratrix of the estate of Philip J. Froess, deceased (plaintiff) against Jacob Froess (defendant) for an accounting. From decrees below both parties appealed. Decree in favor of plaintiff affirmed.

Philip J. Froess and Jacob Froess were equal partners, engaged in the sale of pianos and other musical instruments. Philip J. Froess died on January 29, 1920, and Jacob continued to operate the business. There was no provision in the partnership agreement permitting the continuation of the business after the death of a partner and the representative of Philip's estate did not agree to the continuation of the business. The court found that at the time of Philip's death the net worth of the partnership assets was \$91,977.71. On August 3, 1921, a bill was filed by plaintiff asking for the appointment of a receiver, an accounting by the liquidating partner, and for a decree that the share found to be due be paid to her. Jacob Froess lost money in the operation of the business after the death of Philip. The plaintiff claims that she is entitled to one-half of the value of the partnership assets at the date of Philip's death (\$45,988.85) plus interest until the sum is paid. Defendant claims that Philip's estate must bear its share of the loss resulting from the continued operation of the business.

Sadler, J. Admittedly, the partnership was dissolved by the death of the copartner. That this result followed appears by the Uniform Partnership Act and it was equally true before that legislation became effective. After the death it became the duty of the survivor to settle the partnership affairs, and all authority on his part ceased, except such as was necessary for the winding up of the business, or completing transactions then begun, but not yet finished. Of course, an agreement to continue the firm may be made by the parties interested, and thus new liabilities be assumed. But to so bind the purpose to authorize a further carrying on must clearly appear, and it does not in this case, as found by the court. It is the duty of the liquidating partner to account as trustee for assets which come into his hands, and on cause shown, as here, the court may direct that this be done.

The interest of the decedent is fixed by a valuation as of the time of the dissolution, and all members of the firm are entitled to a part of the surplus of assets over the amount necessary to pay the creditors of the firm.

"The plain duty of the surviving partner is to collect the assets of the partnership, receive and receipt for payments, pay and settle partnership debts, settle and wind up the partnership business and distribute the net surplus among the parties entitled to it." *Herron* v. *Wampler*, 194 Pa. 277, 286, 45 A. 81, 82.

The determination of the right of the deceased partner, where there has been no agreement to continue the business or dispose of the estate's interest for a fixed sum—facts found by the court in the present case—may be controlled by an election of the personal representative of the decedent to take a share of the assets and profits which have been gained by the use of the property prior to actual settlement. Or, in lieu of the latter, interest may be demanded on the value of the property, estimated as of the date of dissolution.

"The legal rule is fixed on this subject. If the survivors of a partnership carry on the concern, and enter into new transactions with the partnership funds, they do so at their peril, and the representatives of the deceased may elect to call on them for the capital, with a share of the profits, or with interest. If no profits are made, or even if a loss is incurred, they must be charged with interest on the funds they use, and the whole loss will be theirs." *Brown's Appeal*, 89 Pa. 139, 147.

"The representatives of the dead partner have not only been allowed to elect between interest and the profits, but an inquiry has been directed to ascertain which would be the more advantageous." *Beatty* v. *Wray*, 19 Pa. 516, 519, 57 Am. Dec. 677.

Notice of Dissolution

Ordinarily, third persons dealing with a partnership are justified in assuming that the partnership will continue in business. Consequently, unless the third person has knowledge or notice that the partnership has been dissolved, he is justified in continuing to deal with it as he has been accustomed to do. The partners owe third persons a duty to give some form of notice in the event of a dissolution of the partnership. The type of notice required will depend on the cause of dissolution and the relation between the partnership and the third party. At common law, if dissolution was brought about by operation of law, that is, by death or bankruptcy of a partner, by war or by declaring the business illegal, no formal notice was necessary. The act was held to be a public act and everyone was held to have notice. In the event the dissolution has been brought about by the expiration of the term, by agreement of the partners, by the expulsion or withdrawal of a partner or by any other similar act, the partners or one or more of them must give notice of the dissolution in order to escape liability to the third persons. If the third person has extended credit to the partnership, he must be given actual notice. This may be given by communicating notice to him personally or by mailing a notice to him, or any other method of giving notice may be used. If notice is mailed, properly addressed and postage prepaid, the presumption is that it will be received; but, if it is not received, the third person is not bound. As to others not having extended credit to the partnership but knowing of it, notice published in a paper having a general circulation in the community or communities where the partnership carried on its business is sufficient. If one has knowledge of the dissolution, it is equivalent to actual notice.

Modern Appliance & Supply Co., Inc. v. B. F. Ibos & Sons
— La. App. —, 16 So. (2d) 552 (1944)

This was an action by Modern Appliance & Supply Co., Inc. (plaintiff) against B. F. Ibos & Sons, a copartnership and Bertrand F. Ibos and others individually as composing the copartnership (defendants). Judgment for plaintiff and Emile Ibos, copartner, appealed. Judgment affirmed.

B. F. Ibos & Sons, a copartnership, was engaged in the business of plumbing contractors. When the partnership was organized its members were Bertrand F. Ibos, Bertrand Joseph Ibos, and Emile Ibos, but Emile withdrew prior to October, 1941. This suit was brought to recover judgment for the purchase price of supplies sold to the partnership during October, November, and December, 1941. Emile claims that at the time he withdrew he went to the office of plaintiff and personally notified Max Pastel, plaintiff's manager, and T. A. Shaw, plaintiff's credit manager, that he was no longer connected with B. F. Ibos & Sons. Both Pastel and Shaw deny that Emile ever notified them that he had withdrawn from the partnership and both deny that they had any knowledge of Emile's withdrawal from the partnership.

McCaleb, J. The law of the case is not in dispute. In order for a partner who has withdrawn from a firm to relieve himself from responsibility for the debts of the firm, contracted after his withdrawal, to a creditor who has been doing business with the firm prior thereto, actual notice to such creditor must be given. Accordingly, the partner, who seeks to be exonerated and who (as in this case) has filed a special defense to that effect, assumes the burden of showing by a preponderance of evidence that actual notice to the creditor was given. The usual mode in which such notices are sent is (as pointed out by the Supreme Court in *Reilly* v. *Smith*) by circular letters addressed to the creditors and customers of the firm. This is particularly true in instances where the remaining partners continue the business of the firm in the same or a similar name. Of course, the retiring partner has the right to show, if he can, that verbal notice of his withdrawal had been given or that the creditor had actual knowledge; but, in such cases, he encounters difficulty in sustaining his defense where the creditor denies his testimony. Thus, in the case at bar, we are unable to say from a reading of the record that the evidence of appellant preponderates over the denials of plaintiff's witnesses. The trial judge, who saw the witnesses and heard their testimony, did not think so and we cannot say that his conclusion on this question of fact was obviously wrong.

Distribution of Assets

The order of distribution of the assets of a partnership is well settled. If the partnership has been operated without losses which impair its capital, few problems are presented in the distribution of assets. Partnership creditors are paid first. (All partnership debts will be paid in full; consequently, problems involving the rights of different classes of creditors will not arise.) Advances made by partners, plus interest thereon, will be paid second. Capital investment of each partner will be returned and whatever remains will be distributed as profits.

If the partnership is insolvent, the same order of distribution will be followed, but the additional problem of distribution of losses arises. If the individual estates of the partners are solvent, each partner will contribute according to his share of the profits if there is no provision in the partnership agreement to the contrary. In the event the partnership is insolvent and some or all of the partners are insolvent, the partnership creditors will have first claim on partnership assets and individual creditors will have first claim on individual assets. Archer, Burch, and Clark organize a partnership. Archer contributes $25,000, Burch contributes $15,000, and Clark contributes $10,000. After operating for several years, the firm suffers losses and is insolvent. The assets of the partnership, when liquidated, total $30,000. The partnership owes to partnership creditors $40,000. The accounts of the individual partners are as follows:

	Contributed to Capital of Partnership	Individual Assets	Individual Liabilities
Archer	$25,000	$75,000	$5,000
Burch	15,000	10,000	2,000
Clark	10,000	2,000	6,000

The $30,000 will be distributed to partnership creditors pro rata leaving $10,000 of partnership debts unpaid. Archer's individual creditors will be paid in full leaving a $70,000 balance in Archer's individual estate. Burch's individual creditors will be paid in full leaving $8,000 balance in Burch's individual estate. Clark is insolvent; his creditors will receive 33⅓ per cent of their claims.

The losses of the partnership total $60,000 (capital investment, $50,000 plus unpaid debts after distribution of assets, $10,000). In the absence of a provision in the partnership agreement as to distribution of profits and losses, they are distributed equally. Each partner would be liable for $20,000 losses.

	Capital	Loss	
Archer	$25,000	$20,000	+$ 5,000
Burch	15,000	20,000	− 5,000
Clark	10,000	20,000	− 10,000

In this case Burch is legally liable to contribute $5,000 and Clark $10,000. This sum would be distributed, $10,000 to partnership creditors and $5,000 to Archer. In our illustration Clark is insolvent and can contribute nothing; consequently, his share of losses over and above his capital investment will be redistributed between the solvent partners. However, Burch has only $3,000 in his estate and the final result will be Burch will pay $3,000 of this loss and Archer will pay $7,000. Burch will have a claim against Clark for the $3,000 he pays and Archer will have a claim against Clark for $7,000. If one of the partners is an infant, that fact will alter the distribution of the assets accordingly.

Edelman v. Schwartz et al.
178 N.Y.S. 587 (1919)

This was an action by Benjamin Edelman (plaintiff) against Harry Schwartz and others (defendants). Judgment for defendants.

The plaintiff has a judgment against Harry Schwartz who is insolvent. The partnership of Schwartz and Schwartz of which Harry Schwartz is a member has a judgment against the partnership of Edelman and Levine of which plaintiff is a member. In this action Edelman seeks to have his judgment against Harry Schwartz set off against the judgment which the partnership of Schwartz and Schwartz has against the partnership of Edelman and Levine.

Cropsey, J. The liability of partners is joint and several, but "in marshalling the joint assets of persons composing a partnership and the assets of the individuals composing such partnership it is well established in equity that the partnership assets must first be used in the payment of partnership liabilities and the individual assets in the payment of individual liabilities."

The only possible basis for a set-off here is the insolvency of Harry Schwartz. But that cannot justify the relief sought, for to do so would be inequitable. The creditors of the firm composed of the two defendants Schwartz are entitled to have preserved unimpaired their right to collect their judgment against the plaintiff and his partner, because the collection of that judgment will increase the fund available for the satisfaction of their claims; and as the cases cited show, their equity in this fund is superior to that of the creditors of the individual members of the partnership, one of whom is the plaintiff. To permit the sought set-off would result practically in the application of partnership funds to the payment of one partner's individual debts to the exclusion and prejudice of the partnership creditors. This cannot be permitted at law or in equity.

Parry and Jones v. Lackawanna Grange Produce Association et al.
72 Pa. Super. Ct. 603 (1919)

This action was a bill in equity by the creditors of an unincorporated association asking for a receiver and an assessment to pay indebtedness claimed to be due plaintiffs. The court entered the following decree: "that the Lackawanna Grange Produce Association is insolvent and Everett S. Ross, Esq., is appointed receiver to wind up the affairs of the association with authority to assess upon and collect from each and every of the members named in the bill the sum of fifty ($50) dollars in order to raise a fund out of which to pay the claims of the plaintiffs together with the cost incident to the action. . . . ."

An appeal has been taken to that portion of the decree which authorizes the assessment.

Opinion by Williams, J. The findings and evidence clearly show that plaintiffs are members of defendant organization, and, therefore, have the status of partners with the individual defendants, and not, as stated by the court below in its second conclusion of law "creditors of the association." The liability for the repayment of advances to a partnership by individuals, as between the partners is quite different from the liability of the separate partners to make good to "creditors of the association," who are not partners, both in regard to priority and the nature of the liability. The right of a partner here is to contribution from his copartners in proportion to the amount in which they were to share in the profits, while the right of a creditor is to payment of his claim irrespective of how the money is raised. We need but refer to "An Act Relating to and regulating partnerships," which follows, in most of its provisions, the general law of partnerships as previously expounded, as a guide in working out the relative rights and duties of the parties to this suit.

Limited Partnership

A limited partnership is a partnership in which one or more of the partners have contributed capital, and their liability is limited to the capital invested. The other partner or partners are general partners and their liability is unlimited. Unless such partnerships are permitted by state statute, a partner cannot limit his liability except by contract with each person dealing with the partnership. To form a limited partnership, there must be a statute under which it can be formed, and the provisions of the statute must be substantially complied with.

QUESTIONS AND PROBLEMS

1. French and Mulholland, as copartners, were engaged in conducting an amusement park. They desired to sever the relation by one purchasing the interest of the other. Mulholland stated that he would either sell to French for a stated amount or that he would buy French's interest for the same amount. French purchased Mulholland's interest. Later, French sued Mulholland for damages for deceit on the ground that Mulholland had misrepresented the condition of the business to him. Mulholland contends that French's only remedy is a partnership accounting. Is Mulholland's contention correct?
2. Crews and Sweet were partners engaged in business under the name of Standard Milk Co. Sweet became insolvent and was adjudged bankrupt. Was the firm dissolved by the bankruptcy of Sweet?

3. Wood, Catron, and Lewis, as partners, operated a trading post at Ft. Wingate. Wood, without the knowledge or consent of Catron and Lewis, sold his interest in the partnership to Mann. Was the partnership dissolved?
4. Walsh and O'Connor, a partnership, leased certain premises in the firm name. Later, Barnes purchased an interest in the firm and became a member of the partnership, and all the rights in the original lease were assigned to the firm of Walsh, O'Connor, and Barnes. About a year later Barnes sold his interest in the partnership. During the time Barnes was a member of the firm, the firm defaulted in the payment of the rent. Suit was brought against the firm including Barnes. Barnes contends that the lessees were Walsh and O'Connor and that he is not liable. Is Barnes' contention correct?
5. Quarles and Hunter operated a business as partners. The firm borrowed money from the bank in the firm name and for firm purposes, giving a note signed in the firm name. Quarles died. After the death of Quarles, whose death was known to the bank, the note to the bank fell due. Hunter gave a renewal note to the bank signed in the firm name. Is the estate of Quarles liable on the renewal note?
6. Thompson and Ford were partners, doing business as Tomford Tire Co. The firm became indebted to the Hewitt Rubber Co. Subsequently, the partnership was dissolved and Ford continued to operate the business. Hewitt Rubber Co. sued the firm to recover the price of certain tires sold to the firm before Thompson withdrew. Thompson claims that he is not liable because, at the time he withdrew, the firm had sufficient assets to pay all firm debts in full. Is Thompson liable?
7. Harry Wilson and Fred Wilson were partners and were engaged in the brokerage business under the name of Wilson and Wilson in Charleston, South Carolina. In 1917, Harry Wilson sold his interest in the firm to Fred and joined the army. Fred Wilson continued the business under the name of Wilson and Wilson. However, Harry's name was dropped from the stationery and Dun & Bradstreet, Inc., were notified of the dissolution and the change was noted in its reports. No other notice of the dissolution was given the public but it was generally known in Charleston that the firm was dissolved. In 1918, Simmel sold Wilson & Wilson a carload of tomatoes. This was the first transaction Simmel had ever had with Wilson & Wilson and he made no investigation as to who composed the firm of Wilson & Wilson. The tomatoes were not paid for and Simmel sued both Harry Wilson and Fred Wilson as partners. Is Harry Wilson liable?
8. Holland was a member of the firm of Dillon, Beebe & Co., a partnership. Loveland was employed by the firm to purchase lumber in the western states and Canada. Holland withdrew from the firm and notice of his withdrawal was published in a Toledo, Ohio, paper. The firm's office was located in Toledo. Thereafter, Loveland performed services for the firm and in payment accepted a note signed in the firm name. There is no evidence that Loveland saw the notice in the paper. No other notice of Holland's withdrawal was given Loveland. Is Holland liable to Loveland on the note?
9. Simmons, Hoffman, and Murray were partners doing business under the firm name of Simmons & Co. The firm borrowed money from the bank and gave the bank the firm's note for the loan. In addition, each partner guaranteed the note individually. The firm became insolvent and a receiver was appointed. The bank claims that it has a right to file its claim as a firm debt and also that it has a right to participate in the distribution of the assets of the individual partners before partnership creditors receive any payments from such assets. Is the bank's claim correct?
10. What is the order of distribution of partnership assets under the Uniform Partnership Act?

PART VIII

CORPORATIONS

CHAPTER XXXIV

NATURE AND INCORPORATION

Historical Background

The corporate form of organization has been in existence from an early date. It was recognized in England as early as the sixteenth century, but the sixteenth-century corporation differed greatly from our present-day business corporation. These early corporations were for the most part ecclesiastical, municipal, educational, or eleemosynary corporations. The trading corporation usually was organized to exercise some monopolistic privilege. The early trading corporations were granted a monopoly of the trade with a certain colony. The corporation was quasi governmental in that it was granted the right to colonize, govern the colony, and exercise other functions of a governmental nature. At the time the United States had its inception, the general conception of the corporation was a vast trading company possessing many special privileges.

It was not until the nineteenth century that the business corporation, as it is known today, had its inception. It is a natural outgrowth of the industrial period. The outstanding advantages of the corporate form are the limited liability, continuous existence, and the method of administration of the business. After the American colonies won their independence from England, business began to develop rapidly. There were many business opportunities, but each was accompanied by a risk. The outcome of any venture in the new world was uncertain; yet, if the venture proved successful, the profits were proportionally great. Many were willing to risk capital in a venture, but they were not willing to assume full liability for the outcome of the venture. The corporate form protected the investor from a loss exceeding his investment. It also afforded him an opportunity to have some control over the policies of the business, yet relieved him from the responsibilities of the everyday management of the business. Under the corporate form, people could share in the assumption of a risk they would not assume individually, and as a result many business ventures were entered into that would not have been undertaken under any other form of organization.

At first, in the United States, a corporation was granted its charter by the state legislature. The early corporations were organized to operate tollroads, tollbridges, and other types of business in the nature of public callings which were basically monopolistic. In granting a charter, the legislature was careful to limit the powers of the corporation to the needs of the business to be undertaken. The idea of special privilege still dominated, and in the United States at that time special privileges were not freely granted.

In the case of *Dartmouth College* v. *Woodward*,[1] which involved a corporation created by special charter for the purpose of establishing a college, Chief Justice Marshall defined a corporation as "an artificial being, invisible, intangible, and existing only in contemplation of law. Being a mere creature of law, it possesses only those properties which the charter of its creation confers upon it, either expressly, or as incidental to its very existence." This definition is often quoted as the definition of a modern business corporation; however, the modern business corporation differs in many important respects from the corporation defined by Marshall. We recognize the modern business corporation as a separate legal person, owing its existence to the state and being subject to state regulation. The corporate charter imposes limitations on the powers of the corporations; however, the limitations are far less rigid than those imposed in the earlier day. The idea of special privilege which furnishes the background for Marshall's definition is lacking today. As early as 1811, general corporation statutes were passed which set up the procedure to be followed in organizing a business corporation, and which provided that any persons who complied with the requirements of the statute would be granted a corporate charter. The early statutes restricted the types of business which could be engaged in by a corporation organized under the general corporation law and also imposed other restrictions on the corporation. Today the same general procedure is followed in the organization of a business corporation. We have liberalized and broadened the general business corporation statutes and have also classified businesses and enacted special statutes under which certain types of business must be incorporated. The business corporation acts now in force generally provide that ". . . . may form a corporation under this act for any lawful purpose except. . . . ." The common exceptions are banks, railroads, insurance, building and loan, and similar corporations, and special statutes have been enacted permitting the organization of such

---

[1] 4 Wheat. 518

corporations. In some instances under special regulatory statutes one must obtain a certificate of convenience and necessity before entering into certain quasi-public businesses such as transportation and banking.

The law of modern business corporations is in its infancy. The statutes of the various states are not uniform, and the decisions of the courts are not in accord on all points of law; however, this does not mean that the law relative to business corporations is chaotic. The general principles of law are well defined, but, as new situations arise, the application of these general principles to the new situations must be worked out, and the courts do not always agree as to which principle applies or as to the conclusions to be drawn from the application of the principle. These differences account for the uncertainty which exists in any developing body of law. The scope of this study does not permit a detailed discussion of these points of difference; consequently, it is necessary to confine our discussion to general principles and to a statement of the majority rule.

Nature of a Corporation

The outstanding characteristic of a corporation, which distinguishes it from other business organizations, is its legal personality. In contemplation of law the corporation has a legal existence separate and apart from the physical persons who are its members. Another characteristic, which contributes to the desirability of the corporate form of business organization, is its continuous existence. The corporation, being a legal person existing separate and apart from its members, is not affected by a change in its membership. The death or bankruptcy of a stockholder or the transfer of shares of stock in no way affects the existence of the corporation. Under many of the existing statutes the corporation may have perpetual existence.

As a legal person the corporation is vested with certain legal capacities. It can own, purchase, sell, and incumber property in the name of the corporation. This capacity greatly simplifies the transaction of business. It can sue and be sued in the corporate name and, in fact, under the general corporation statutes of many of the states, the corporation can carry on any legitimate business. The corporate business is conducted by agents. In carrying on its business the corporation is the principal and its directors and officers are agents. In determining the extent of the agent's power to bind his corporate principal, the general principles of the law of agency are followed. However, because of the nature of the corporate principal, the implied or apparent authority of the corporate agent may vary in some respects from the implied or apparent authority which the agent of a natural person would have under like circumstances. After a corporation has been brought into existence, it will continue to exist as a legal person even though all of its outstanding stock is owned by one man. The courts recognize the separateness of the corporation and its members as long as the corporate entity is not used for illegitimate purposes. The right to do business as a corporation is a privilege granted to the members of the corporation; it is not a special privilege because under the existing general corporation laws any person may organize the corporation by complying with the requirements of the statute. If the members of a corporation abuse the privilege granted them, the members may be held liable by the state or other injured parties. The nature of this liability depends on the circumstances of the case. This holding of the members liable when they have abused their privilege of doing business as a corporation and have used the corporate form in a manner which is detrimental to society is referred to by the courts as "disregarding the corporate entity." In the earlier cases the idea of the corporate entity—separateness of corporation and its members—was emphasized to such an extent that the corporate entity was disregarded only in extreme cases. Today, if the members have used the corporate form as a shield for "shady" transactions, the court will disregard the corporate entity and hold the members liable.

Since it has become a common practice of corporations to organize and hold the stock of subsidiary corporations for the purpose of operating some special branch of the business of the parent corporations or for some other special purpose, cases involving the liability of a parent corporation for the acts and debts of its subsidiary are not uncommon. If the subsidiary is used in an open and above board manner and for legitimate purposes, the courts recognize the separateness of the two corporations. However, if the subsidiary is organized as a screen behind which the parent is attempting to gain some unfair advantage, the parent will be held responsible for the acts and debts of the subsidiary.

Under existing corporation statutes, corporations may be divided into three classes: (1) corporations for profit, (2) non-profit corporations, and (3) governmental corporations. Many other classifications are followed by writers and legislators.

A corporation for profit is a business corporation operated for the purpose of making a profit which may be distributed to the stockholders in dividends. Many states subdivide corporations for profit into railroad, banking, insurance, building and loan, farm co-operative marketing, and general corporations for profit, and enact special statutes under which the railroad, banking, insurance, building and loan, etc., corporations must be incorporated, leaving all corporations for profit which do not fall within these special classes to be organized under the general corporation for profit act.

The non-profit corporations include incorporated churches, lodges, schools (which are not operated for the profit of the owners), fraternities, etc. The object of the non-profit corporation is generally charitable, social, or educational. In most states a separate statute has been enacted under which non-profit corporations are organized.

Governmental corporations are corporations organized for governmental purposes. Incorporated municipalities, the T.V.A., the R.F.C., etc., are examples of governmental corporations.

We shall confine our discussion to corporations for profit, emphasizing the general corporation for profit.

North v. The Higbee Co.
131 Ohio St. 507, 3 N.E. (2d) 391 (1936)

This was an action by Amanda C. North (plaintiff) against the Higbee Company and others (defendants). From a judgment of the Court of Appeals affirming a judgment for plaintiff, defendants appealed. Judgment of Court of Appeals and trial court reversed and judgment entered in favor of Higbee Co.

The Cleveland Trust Co. owned, in trust, a tract of land in Cleveland fronting on Chester Ave. which it leased to Crowell & Little Securities Company on a 99-year lease. Higbee Co. was a corporation operating a department store in Cleveland and was doing a large mercantile business throughout northern Ohio. In 1919 Higbee Co. caused the Higbee Realty Co. to be organized. The stock ownership of the subsidiary was in the parent company (Higbee Co.), the officers and directors of which were also the officers and directors of the subsidiary. Separate books and records were kept at all times.

The Higbee Realty Co. subleased from Crowell & Little Securities Co. the Chester Avenue land for a period of time expiring December 31, 2007. The Higbee Realty Co. agreed to pay as rental $170,000 per year plus taxes and assessments and agreed to erect a building on the land at a cost of $700,000, the building to be completed by July 1, 1923. Higbee Realty Co. leased the property to Higbee Co. for a term of 10 years. Later Crowell & Little Securities Company sold the Higbee Realty Co. lease to Union Trust Co. as trustee, and the latter issued and sold to the public leasehold trust certificates which entitled the holder to a proportionate ownership in the lease and a corresponding right in the rent collected. Before the expiration of the 10-year lease, Higbee Co. vacated the building but it paid rent for the period. After the expiration of the 10-year lease, Higbee Realty Co. was unable to find a new tenant and defaulted in its payments on the lease.

Day, J. Plaintiff relies for recovery upon the doctrine of disregarding the separate entities of the parent and subsidiary corporation and of holding the parent liable for the obligations of the subsidiary upon the theory that the latter was controlled by stock ownership in the former.

In the opinion of the trial court, no fraud appeared to have been shown on the part of either subsidiary or parent. The legal proposition involved was stated by that court as follows: "Can the court disregard the fiction of separate corporate entity of the subsidiary corporation when the facts disclose that a wrong and an injustice has been perpetrated upon innocent third persons *in the absence of fraud or illegality* and hold the parent company liable for the obligations of its subsidiary?"

The case of *Richmond & I. Const. Co.* v. *Richmond*, 68 F. 105, was decided by the Court of Appeals of the Sixth District, and was heard before Judges Taft, Lurton and Severens. The first proposition of the syllabus reads:

"The fact that the stockholders in two corporations are the same, or that one corporation exercises a control over the other, through ownership of its stock, or through the identity of the stockholders, such corporation being separately organized under distinct charters, does not make either the agent of the other, nor merge them into one, so as to make a contract of one corporation binding upon the other."

While this case was brought against a railroad as the parent company, it did not involve a transaction which affected the public. In the course of the opinions, on page 108, Mr. Lurton, circuit judge, said:

"It contends that under the evidence in this case the contract company was, in legal effect, the railroad company, and that engagements made by it were, in legal effect, engagements made by the railroad company. In support of this, appellant has endeavored to show that the stockholders in each corporation were the same, and that the contract company dominated and controlled the railroad company. . . . . The contract company was a legal corporation, wholly distinct and separate from the railroad company. The fact that the stockholders in each may have been the same persons does not operate to destroy the legal identity of either corporation. Neither does the fact that the one corporation exercised a controlling influence over the other through the ownership of its stock or through the identity of stockholders, operate to make either the agent of the other, or to merge the two corporations into one. There is no pretense of any fraudulent concealment of the interest of the one corporation in the other, or of the fact that the persons controlling the one corporation likewise controlled the other."

What was said by the learned judge of the federal Court of Appeals can be applied to the instant case. The Higbee Company and the realty company were distinct and separate corporations. There was no concealment of the fact that the parent company owned substantially all the stock of the subsidiary. There was no concealment of the fact that the lessee, the realty company, entered into an obligation to pay the rentals as they accrued. That lease is on record and was constructive notice to all who dealt with the property. Nor was there any fraudulent concealment of the fact that the lessor looked to the realty company for its rentals. Practically all the evidence contained in this record relates to conversation, letters or exhibits concerning transactions which occurred two years or more before the certificate holders acquired any interest in this property. Moreover, not one of the certificate holders testified that he was misled or that he had ever heard of any of the instances which the plaintiffs now rely upon as showing bad faith upon the part of the parent company.

The organization of a corporation for the avowed purpose of avoiding personal responsibility does not in itself constitute fraud justifying the disregard of the corporate entity. In *Elenkrieg* v. *Siebrecht*, 238 N.Y. 254, (144 N.E. 519, 34 A.L.R. 592), the court stated:

"Whether or not the corporation is the creature of Siebrecht is not a determining feature. Whether it be a subterfuge is misleading. Many a man incorporates his business or his property and is the dominant and controlling feature of the corporation. He may do so for the very purpose of escaping personal liability."

Williams, J., dissenting. To avoid fallacious reasoning, it must be kept in mind that the parent corporation desired for its own use in its business a department store building, which it was already occupying, and employed the wholly owned and controlled subsidiary to get the lease thereon. The subsidiary had no use for the building and did not profit by the getting of the leasehold. All the negotiations and the transaction itself were managed and controlled from beginning to end by the parent. True the subsidiary had been used before in a similar way, but that circumstance cannot alter the case. In such a situation the subsidiary serves, not its own purposes, but those of the parent.

If these facts in evidence are ignored, the result will be a conclusion based on erroneous premises. Of course a corporation is organized to afford limited liability, and its stockholders, natural or artificial, are not, merely as such, liable for its debts. But to regard this principle as controlling the instant case is to disregard the main issue.

What is the law applicable to a case of this character? The rule that ordinarily a parent corporation is not liable for debts contracted in the name of its incorporated subsidiary is subject to exceptions. Where the subsidiary is a scheme or device to enable the parent to avoid its own obligation as distinguished from the bona fide obligations of the subsidiary, the law will pierce the corporate entity of the latter to reach the parent as the real debtor. Fraud of the parent is not an indispensable ingredient of the creditor's right of action but, if existent and relevant, it may be shown as an aid to recovery. If the subsidiary is a mere agent, arm, instrumentality or department of the parent in the transaction in which the debt is incurred, such debt is that of the parent regardless of the existence of fraud. The subsidiary is often spoken of as a "dummy" where it merely serves the parent's purposes and the obligation is, in fact, that of the parent itself.

In 1 Fletcher *Cyclopedia of Corporations*, Section 43, page 154, the author and compiler summarizes the law from cited authorities in this language: "A very numerous and growing class of cases wherein the corporate entity is disregarded is that wherein it is so organized and controlled, and its affairs are so conducted, as to make it merely an instrumentality, agency, conduit or adjunct of another corporation."

The Corporation and the State

A partnership may be created at the pleasure of the members and without taking any formal action, but the law does not recognize the rights of individuals to do business as a corporation without the consent of the state.

Under our form of government each state has the power to authorize the organization of corporations and to regulate the corporation after it is organized. This power is exercised through the state legislature and the scope of the legislative power is determined by the state and federal constitutions.

The power to create a corporation gives the state, which grants the corporation its charter, the right to regulate the corporation. The corporation under the regulatory powers of the state may be required to file special reports, may be required to pay special franchise fees, is subject to special taxes, and may be regulated in other respects. One of the principal advantages of the partnership over the corporation is that the partnership is not subject to special fees, taxes, and regulations.

If the business to be carried on by the corporation is local in nature, it will ordinarily be most advantageous to incorporate under the laws of that state, but if the business of the corporation will be carried on in several states, the incorporators will wish to organize it under the laws of the state whose laws prove to be most advantageous to the corporation. The statutes of the several states vary in several important respects. The matter of fees and taxes is always important. What is the initial expense of incorporation? What annual taxes or franchise fees are imposed? Does the state impose a stock transfer tax? Does the state have a corporate income tax? The possibilities of working out a desirable capital structure is also important. Can no-par or non-voting stock be issued? Are certain special provisions required in preferred stock? Can common stock having a par value be issued at less than par? The corporation statutes usually contain some provisions regulating the management of the corporation. What are the limitations placed on the powers of the directors? Can the directors adopt and amend by-laws? Can they mortgage the assets of the corporation? What liabilities are imposed on the directors? The marketing of corporate securities is often an important matter. What regulations are imposed on the issue and sale of corporate stock? Other things being equal it is, as a general rule, more advantageous to incorporate in a state in which the laws relative to corporations have become stabilized. The state may change its laws at will and after incorporation the corporation may sometimes lose expected advantages as the result of these changes.

The state's power to regulate a corporation is not without limitation. The state cannot pass laws which will impair the obligation of contract between the corporation and its stockholders or between the corporation and its creditors; nor can it pass laws which will result in the taking of corporate property without due process of law. Under the present general corporation laws or by provisions in the state constitution, the state may reserve the right to repeal, alter, or amend the corporate charter but such power cannot be exercised in an arbitrary, unreasonable, and oppressive manner.

Standard Pipe Line Co. v. Burnett
188 Ark. 491, 66 S.W. (2d) 637 (1934)

This was an action by W. M. Burnett (plaintiff) against the Standard Pipe Line Company, Inc. (defendant). Judgment for the plaintiff and defendant appealed. Judgment affirmed.

Burnett was employed by the defendant and while cleaning out a pumping station was permanently injured. The defendant set up as a defense a contract in writing by the terms of which the parties agreed that in the event of personal injuries the rights of the parties would be adjusted according to the provisions of the Workman's Compensation Act of Louisiana. The plaintiff was a resident of Arkansas and was injured while working in Arkansas. The Arkansas Workman's Compensation Act expressly denied corporations the right to enter into any contracts which would relieve them from the provisions of the act. Plaintiff contends that he is not bound by the contract. The defendant claims that the provision of the statute relied on by the plaintiff is unconstitutional because it impairs the right to contract.

Butler, J. This argument is advanced because section 7147 limits its application to corporations, except those engaged in interstate commerce, and does not apply to individuals or partnerships. To sustain its contention, the appellant cites *Chicago, etc., Ry. Co.* v. *State*, 86 Ark. 412, 111 S.W. 456, and *Prudential Insurance Co.* v. *Cheek*, 259 U.S. 530, 42 S. Ct. 516, but those cases recognize the fundamental difference between natural and artificial persons and that those provisions in our own Constitution and the Constitution of the

United States, by which laws are forbidden denying any person equal protection, or which do not secure equal privileges and immunities, do not relate to corporations, because these do not exist naturally, but are the creatures of law, possessing only such powers as are granted them, and making only such contracts as they are authorized to enter into, and that, wherever an act is general and uniform in its operation upon all persons coming within the class to which it applies, it does not come within the prohibition of the Constitution. We have many times upheld the validity of acts relating to corporations, limiting their rights beyond those of natural persons for the reason that a citizen or natural person has the inherent right, independent of any legislation, to contract, while the corporation is clothed only with such power as may be given it by the legislative will, and this may be altered, revoked, or annulled at the pleasure of the Legislature, and terms prescribed under which they may conduct their business; the only limitation upon its power being that it may not interfere with any vested right of the corporation or its incorporators, or violate any fundamental principle of natural justice. On this principle, the Supreme Court of the United States and this court have often upheld the validity of such legislation.

Incorporators

The state sets up the procedure which must be followed to obtain a corporate charter. In our discussion of formal statutory requirements we shall confine our discussion to business corporations and shall, in stating statutory requirements, follow the provisions of the Model Business Corporation Act which was approved by the National Conference of Commissioners of Uniform State Laws in 1928. It has been adopted by Idaho, Louisiana, and Washington. Under existing general corporation statutes it is a simple matter to obtain a corporate charter; consequently, it is a common practice to obtain the charter first and then proceed to set up the permanent corporate structure.

The charter is obtained by persons designated as incorporators. A common statutory provision is: "three or more natural persons of full age, at least two-thirds of whom are citizens of the United States, its territories or possessions, may obtain a corporate charter as incorporators." To obtain a charter the incorporators must file articles of incorporation with the Secretary of State. The articles must be in triplicate and must state the name of the corporation; its purpose; its duration; the location and post-office address of its registered office in the state; its capital structure (number of shares of stock and classes of stock); its paid-in capital; the first directors, their post-office address, and duration of office; name and post-office address of the incorporators and the number of shares of stock subscribed by each. The statutes require that a minimum amount, usually $500 to

$1000, must be paid in "in cash or other property taken at a fair valuation." When these formalities are complied with, the corporate charter will be issued and the corporation will have legal existence; however, certain additional conditions must be fulfilled before the corporation is permitted to transact business. The conditions precedent to beginning business will be discussed later.

After the corporation is brought into existence, the shares of stock may be issued to anyone who has the legal capacity to own stock. A corporation, under the provisions of the statute cited, cannot act as an incorporator, but a corporation, having power to own corporate stock, can purchase all the shares of stock of a corporation. (Under the laws of some states directors must be stockholders and in such states one person or corporation could not purchase all the stock but all the stock except "qualifying shares" could be held by one owner.)

Schwab v. E. G. Potter Co. et al.
194 N.Y. 409, 87 N.E. 670 (1909)

This was an action by Joseph E. Schwab (plaintiff) against E. G. Potter Company and others (defendants). Judgment for plaintiff and defendants appealed to Appellate Division where the judgment was reversed and plaintiff appealed to the Court of Appeals. Judgment of trial court for plaintiff affirmed.

Defendant corporation owned in the city of New York a lot and office building known as 477 Fifth Avenue. At a stockholders' meeting the directors of the defendant were authorized, by a vote of the majority of the stock having voting power, to organize a new corporation with capital stock of the par value of $100,000. They were further authorized to convey the equity in the Fifth Avenue real estate to the new corporation in exchange for all of the stock of the new corporation. Plaintiff brought this action to prevent the directors from carrying the plan into execution claiming that the entire plan was illegal.

Vann, J. Corporations are created by statute and have no powers except those conferred by statute, directly or indirectly. There is no statute in this state which directly authorizes one corporation to organize another, and, as we think, such action is not indirectly authorized by any reasonable inference from the most extensive powers committed to any class of corporations known to our law. Corporations are organized by natural persons, acting under the direction of a statute, and they only can become corporators, directors, or officers. "Artificial persons," without brain or body, existing only on paper through legislative command, and incapable of thought or action except through natural persons, cannot create other "artificial persons" and those, others still, until the line is so extended and the capital stock so duplicated and reduplicated, as to result in confusion and fraud. If, in the case before us, the proposed plan is carried into effect, the old corporation will be the only stockholder of the new corporation when it comes into being, which is the time to test its legality, and the entire capital stock of the latter will have been taken from the assets of the former. After the old corporation has thus split itself into two corporations, both together will have only the capital that the old corporation had before. Not a dollar of new capital will have been contributed either in money or property, and only when the old corporation sells to subscribers or outsiders—and it is not alleged that it will be able to sell to either—all or a part of the shares of stock, issued to it by the new, can any money come from the transaction.

Section 40 of the stock corporation law does not aid the defendants. That statute authorizes a stock corporation, if permitted by its charter, to acquire, hold, and dispose of shares of stock issued by another corporation, and in any case to acquire, hold, and dispose of shares of stock issued by certain classes of corporations, including those engaged in a similar business and those with which it might be consolidated. It does not permit one corporation to create another, endow it with capital from its own assets, and take all its shares of stock in exchange.

Domicile of Corporation

Although a corporation is an artificial person and cannot vote, get married, commit a common law crime, or enjoy those special privileges reserved to natural persons, it does exercise legal rights and it is under legal duties which require that it have a domicile—a home. Although some confusion has resulted from the attempt to apply the legal concept of domicile to the corporation, certain basic principles have been worked out. The state, under whose laws the corporation is incorporated, is the domicile of the corporation, and the place within the state where it has its principal office is its domicile within the state. The federal corporations which have been organized by special act of congress have no domicile unless the incorporating act assigns a domicile to the corporation. Several of the existing federal corporations have been incorporated under the laws of one of the states and their domicile is the state of incorporation.

The rights and powers of the corporation are determined by the constitution and statutes of the state of incorporation. For example, the Model Business Corporation Act provides that the power to make by-laws may be expressly vested in the board of directors, but it denies the board of directors the right to make or alter any by-law fixing their qualifications, classification, term of office, or compensation. The Delaware General Corporation statutes provide that any corporation may, in its certificate of incorporation, confer the power to make by-laws on the board of directors. If the corporation is incorporated under the laws of Delaware, the board of directors might be granted greater power to make or alter the by-laws than could be granted to the board of directors of a corporation incorporated under the laws of Idaho. The federal courts have jurisdiction of actions between citizens of different states. In determining jurisdiction of the federal courts, the United States Supreme Court has in effect held that a corporation is a citizen of the state under whose laws it is incorporated. Likewise in questions of taxation it has been held that the corporation will be considered as being domiciled in the state of its incorporation.

Fisher & Van Gilder v. First Trust Joint-Stock Land Bank of Chicago
210 Iowa, 531, 231 N.W. 671, 69 A. L. R. 1340 (1930)

This was an action by Fisher & Van Gilder (plaintiff) against First Trust Joint-Stock Land Bank of Chicago (defendant). Defendant filed a special appearance objecting to the service of notice. The trial court overruled the special appearance (held that the court had acquired jurisdiction over the defendant). Defendant appealed and the Supreme Court of Iowa reversed the trial court's ruling.

De Graff, J. The sole question presented for decision is whether the jurisdiction of the defendant was acquired by the service of the original notice on the vice president of the defendant federal corporation in Chicago, Ill., the domicile of the corporation under its charter granted by an act of Congress. It is admitted that the defendant joint-stock land bank had its principal place of business in Chicago, had no agent, representative, or office in the state of Iowa, had been engaged and had the right to be engaged in business, under the provisions of its charter, in the state of Iowa.

The respective contentions of the plaintiff-appellee and of the defendant-appellant may be briefly stated. The plaintiff claims that the defendant corporation, although federal in origin, is a domestic corporation and a resident of any state in which it transacts business. The claim of the defendant is that a federal corporation, unless specifically made so by statute—as for example, a national banking association—is not a citizen or resident of the states (other than its domicile) in which it transacts its business. The defendant corporation is by statute a national or federal corporation. The defendant joint-stock land bank was organized under the Federal Farm Loan Act of July 17, 1916, with its principal place of business in Chicago, Ill. Confessedly, the defendant federal corporation, while doing business in Iowa, was not a foreign corporation, within the ordinary meaning of that term. May it be viewed as a domestic corporation, which connotes a corporation organized under the law of this state, and therefore under the jurisdiction of the courts of this state, as defined by the state statute? Clearly not, as it was created by an act of Congress. The appellee affirms that the defendant corporation did have a residence in Iowa because it transacted business in Iowa. The words "citizenship," "residence," and "domicile" express, as a general rule, distinct legal concepts. A domicile is the place with which a person has a settled connection for legal purposes; either because his home is there or because it is assigned to him by the law. Every person has at all times one domicile, but no person has more than one domicile at a time.

Clearly, the domicile of the defendant corporation, as defined by charter, is Chicago, Ill. If the domicile of the defendant was not fixed by its charter, there may be some merit in the contention of appellee that the defendant has a residence in every state wherein it did business and was privileged by its charter to do business.

The domicile of a corporation is the place considered by law to be the center of its affairs and the place where its functions are discharged.

Service on a non-resident outside the state confers no jurisdiction to render a personal judgment against such defendant. A personal judgment cannot be rendered against a non-resident corporation by a service of notice outside the state.

What is the domicile of a corporation created by an act of Congress? It is the place where its principal office is located. A federal corporation, other than a national bank, is not a citizen or resident of the states in which it transacts its business. Doing business by a non-resident defendant in a state other than its domicile does not imply consent to be reached by process of the courts in that state.

A corporation cannot change at will its residence or its citizenship. It can have its legal home only at the place where it is located by or under the authority of its charter.

In the instant case the federal corporation had its domicile defined by Congress, and "in a sense, it was always at home" at Chicago, Ill. It is said in *State ex rel.* v. *District Court of Winnebago County et al.*, 191 Iowa, 244, 182 N.W. 211, 213: "A corporation is not ambulatory. . . . . A corporation, unlike a natural person, has a stationary legal domicile in the state and county of its creation, which may not be changed at will, but only as authorized by statute. It is not migratory."

The residence of the defendant federal corporation, as alleged by plaintiff, is bottomed on the fact that the defendant did business in the state of Iowa. It was privileged by its charter to do so. This, however, does not under the admitted facts change a non-resident to a resident and subject it to process, as claimed by plaintiff in the instant case.

Name, Seal, etc.

In addition to the selection of the state under whose laws they wish to incorporate, those who are responsible for the incorporation must make several important decisions. A corporation must have a name and also a seal. Both the name and the form of the seal must be selected by the incorporators. Certain restrictions are placed on the name which may be selected for the corporation. In some states the name selected for a business must indicate that the business is incorporated. The word "corporation" or "incorporated" or some abbreviations thereof will be sufficient to satisfy such a requirement. Also, the statute of the state of incorporation may prohibit the use of certain words. For example, the use of such words as "Bank," "Trust," "Insurance," "Co-operative," etc., is frequently prohibited, especially if the type of corporation which would be indicated by the use of the word is regulated by special statute. The name selected for the corporation must be different from the names of corporations doing business in the state at the time of the organization of the corporation. The name selected must be such that the general public, in the exercise of ordinary care, will not confuse it with the name of another corporation doing business in the state. The name of the corporation may be changed by complying with the pertinent statutory provisions. In some states a corporation may transact business under a name acquired by use or reputation, and hence a corporation may be known by more than one name.

Under the general corporation laws now in force, a corporation may adopt and use a common seal. In general, the statutory provisions are permissive—not mandatory. In the United States the majority of courts have held that a corporation can contract without the use of its corporate seal in all transactions in which an individual may bind himself without the use of a seal. No form of seal is prescribed and a scroll or the word "seal" or the letters "L.S." may be used. The seal in common use is an impression made in the paper of the contract or deed or other instrument. The corporate seal is usually in the custody and possession of the secretary, and it is a common practice to have the secretary affix the seal to the instrument and have it attested by his signature.

The general structure of the corporation is set out in the articles of incorporation, and many of the details of the corporate structure are left to the choice of those organizing the corporation. The articles must state the purpose of the corporation, but the organizers may set out the purpose of the corporation in broad general terms thereby imposing almost no limitations on the business conducted by the corporation, or they may restrict the purpose of the corporation to narrow limits. The organizers also are free to state the classes of stock to be issued, the number of shares in each class, and the rights of shareholders in each class. They can state the amount of capital over and above the minimum, if any, which must be paid in before the corporation shall start business. In some states, if it is so provided in the articles of incorporation, the capital stock may be sold below par. Also by so stating in the articles, the directors may be given the power to adopt and amend by-laws.

In what other respects the organizers of the corporation may, by special provisions in the charter, shape the structure of the corporation will depend, primarily, on the laws of the state of incorporation.

Universal Credit Co. et al. v. Dearborn Universal Underwriters Credit Corporation et al.
309 Mich. 608, 16 N.W. (2d) 91 (1944)

This was an action by Universal Credit Co. and others (plaintiffs) against Dearborn Universal Underwriters Credit Corporation and others (defendants). Decree for plaintiffs and defendants appealed. Decree affirmed.

Plaintiff, a Delaware corporation, had been doing business in the state of Michigan under the corporate name of Universal Credit Company since 1928. It engaged in the business of financing automobiles by furnishing capital to automobile dealers and discounting commercial paper arising from the sale of automobiles. Its business which was nation-wide required automobile insurance, both casualty and fire, on a large scale. For many years prior to the commencement of this suit, defendant David F. Broderick had been associated with plaintiff's business and particularly had charge of the insurance phase of its transactions covering loss by fire. The plaintiff used the name "Universal Credit Company" in contracts distributed to dealers and had expended about $25,000 annually advertising its name and business.

Defendant Broderick caused the defendant Dearborn Universal Underwriters Credit Corporation to be incorporated for the purpose of carrying on the same general type of business carried on by the plaintiff. The defendant corporation engaged office space in the same building in Detroit that housed the plaintiff's Detroit office.

North, C. J. The corporate powers of the defendant Dearborn Universal Underwriters Credit Corporation are amply broad enough to permit it to engage in the automobile finance business in competition with plaintiffs. The corporate name sought to be used by this defendant is the same as one of the plaintiffs with the addition of "Dearborn" and "Underwriters." This attempted adoption of a similar corporate name, especially using the word "Universal" in connection with "Credit" is plainly indicative of a studied attempt on the part of defendants to indulge in unfair competition with plaintiffs and to appropriate the good will of their established business. As noted above, the business of defendants is carried on in the same office building in Detroit as that in which plaintiffs for years have had local business offices. The business of the defendant corporations is in the same field as that of plaintiff corporations. For years preceding the organization by Broderick of the Dearborn Universal Underwriters Credit Corporation he had been intimately associated with the business of plaintiff corporations in the same field in which Broderick proposes to carry on. Under the facts hereinbefore noted it is well established that plaintiffs are entitled to have defendants restrained from using the word "Universal" as part of a corporate name, and from using the abbreviation "U. C. C.," which by use in plaintiffs' business has come to denote "Universal Credit Company" or "Universal Credit Corporation." We arrive at this conclusion notwithstanding various reasons urged by appellants in opposition thereto.

Appellants urge that there is no showing of actual confusion or deception. However "Actual confusion need not be shown, but it is sufficient that confusion is probable or likely to occur."

Corporations De jure and De facto

To organize a legally valid corporation it is necessary that the incorporators substantially comply with the mandatory provisions of the statute under which a corporation, such as the incorporators are attempting to organize, may be organized. If the incorporators do substantially comply with the mandatory provisions of the statute, a de jure corporation—corporation in law—is brought into existence. However, failure to comply with all the mandatory provisions of the statute does not prevent the members of the attempted corporation from carrying on business as a corporation. If the incorporators fail to comply substantially with all the mandatory provisions of the statute and as a result do not form a corporation de jure, they may nevertheless bring into existence what is usually called a corporation de facto—a corporation in fact. The majority of the courts have held that, (1) if a valid statute is in force under which the corporation could be incorporated, and (2) a good faith attempt has been made to organize a corporation under the statute, and (3) business has been transacted as a corporation, a de facto corporation exists. The doctrine of de facto corporation is based on public policy. The majority of the courts have held that, if an honest attempt has been made to organize a corporation under an existing valid statute, practical convenience and the security of business transactions demand that neither the members of the corporation nor persons dealing with the corporation should be permitted to raise technical questions as to the legal existence of the corporation as a means of escaping from the obligations of their transactions. If a de facto corporation sues or is sued, neither the corporation nor the other party to the suit will be permitted to collaterally attack the existence of the corporation.

The state can attack the corporation's existence in a direct attack by bringing quo warranto proceedings. The transaction of business as a corporation is a privilege granted by the state to those who comply with the conditions set out in the statute permitting incorporation. If these conditions are not complied with, the members of the attempted corporation have not earned the privileges granted by the statute, and the state can oust the association from the exercise of corporate powers. However, the state cannot oust an association from the exercise of corporate powers by a collateral attack. If a de facto corporation brings a suit against the state on a claim, the state is not permitted as a defense to attack the corporation's existence as a de jure corporation.

If a domestic corporation sues or is sued and it becomes necessary to establish its existence as a corporation, all that is necessary to establish corporate existence is the introduction in evidence of the duly issued charter of the corporation. The opposing party cannot defeat the corporation's right to recover by showing that the corporation did not comply with all the provisions of the corporation statute.

The doctrine of de facto corporations is made a part of the Model Business Corporation Act[3] and similar provisions are found in the corporation statutes of several of the states.[4]

Thies v. Weible et al.
(Farmers' Union Live Stock Credit Association, Intervener)
126 Neb. 720, 254 N.W. 420 (1934)

This was an action by Louis Thies (plaintiff) against Fred W. Weible and others (defendants) wherein the Farmers' Union Live Stock Credit Association intervened. Judgment for plaintiff and Farmers' Union Live Stock Credit Association appealed. Judgment reversed and case remanded with directions.

Weible, his wife, and two minor children organized as incorporators the Weible Mercantile Company. The Weible Mercantile Company purchased of the Farmers' Union Live Stock Credit Ass'n 58 cattle, giving a chattel mortgage back on the cattle to secure the payment of the purchase price. Louis Thies obtained a judgment against Weible, his wife, and Fred Thies for the sum of $650. The sheriff levied on 26 of the cattle delivered to the Weible Mercantile Company by the Farmers' Union Live Stock Credit Ass'n to satisfy the judgment against Weible, his wife, and Thies.

Hastings, D. J. It is claimed by the appellee that the chattel mortgage was void between the parties for the following reason: (1) That the Weible Mercantile Company never had any existence as a corporation. It is urged by appellee that the Weible Mercantile Com-

---

[3] Business Corporation Act Sec. 9

[4] Arizona, California, Louisiana, Maryland, Montana, Nevada, Oklahoma, Oregon, South Carolina, South Dakota, Tennessee, and Vermont.

pany never had any existence as a corporation, for the reason that some of the incorporators and others, who are stockholders therein, are infants. The answer, in effect, admits a colorable attempt on the part of the alleged incorporators to organize a corporation. The record shows that articles of incorporation, duly signed and acknowledged by the corporators, were adopted by the Weible Mercantile Company on December 3, 1927, and filed and recorded in the office of the county clerk of Wayne county on December 7, 1927, and also that such articles were filed and recorded in the office of the secretary of state on December 9, 1927. The Weible Mercantile Company, since the filing of its articles of incorporation, has continuously carried on and transacted the business of buying and selling live stock, grain and feed, and groceries, as provided for in its articles of incorporation. It has elected officers to carry on the said business, adopted and used a corporate seal, and during all of said time the judgment debtor, Fred W. Weible, has been the managing officer and secretary thereof. Furthermore, it has made and published statements as to its financial condition.

Section 24-201, Comp. St. 1929, provides that any number of persons may be associated and incorporated for the transaction of any lawful business, and infants are not expressly excluded by the statute as persons who may not associate themselves with others in forming corporations. We do not find it necessary in this case to decide whether they may do so or not. Although a de jure corporation may not have been formed, owing to the incapacity of some of the corporators, we are convinced that there was a corporation de facto whose existence cannot be questioned by appellee in this action. The general rule is: "When persons assume to act as a body, and are permitted by the acquiescence of the public and the state to act as if they were legally a particular kind of corporation, for the organization, existence, and continuance of which there is express recognition by the general law, such a body of persons is a corporation de facto, although the particular persons thus exercising the franchise of being a corporation may have been ineligible and incapacitated by the law to do so. This is on the same principle on which it is held that a person may be a de facto officer, although ineligible."

We have frequently held that where the law authorizes a corporation and there has been an attempt in good faith to organize, and the requirements of the statute have been colorably complied with and corporate functions thereunder exercised, there exists a corporation de facto which ordinarily cannot be called into question collaterally.

The reason a collateral attack by a third person will not avail against a corporation de facto, is that, if the rights and franchises have been usurped, they are the rights and franchises of the state, and it alone can challenge the validity of the franchise. Until such interposition, the public may treat those in possession and exercising corporate powers under color of law as doing so rightfully. The rule is in the interest of the public and is essential to the safety of business transactions with corporations. It would produce disorder and confusion, embarrass and endanger the rights and interests of all dealing with the association, if the legality of its existence could be drawn into question in every suit in which it is a party or in which rights were involved springing out of its corporate existence.

Speaking of an attempt to question the legal existence of a corporation, this court has said in *Haas* v. *Bank of Commerce*: "It would be intolerable to permit, in any civil action to which such a body was a party, an inquiry into the legal right to exercise corporate functions,—a right which it is for the state alone to question in appropriate proceedings for that purpose. On this there is a substantial unanimity in the authorities."

In this case the appellant dealt with the Weible Mercantile Company in good faith, believing that it was a corporation, and was entitled to assume that the corporation rightfully possessed corporate powers. The appellee, having acquired no right or interest in the mortgage property by reason of the levy, will not be permitted to make a collateral attack on the existence of the Weible Mercantile Company as a corporation.

Liability on Failure to Organize Corporation

If those associating themselves together as a corporation or other type of association which, under the laws of the state, would be declared a corporation, have made no attempt to comply with the general corporation laws of the state or have attempted to incorporate under a law which does not provide for a corporation such as the incorporators intended to organize, or, if they did attempt to organize, and their effort was so defective that the court would hold that a de facto corporation did not come into existence, the courts will hold the parties individually liable as partners.

Weber Engine Co. v. Alter et al.
120 Kan. 557, 245 Pac. 143 (1926)

This was an action by the Weber Engine Company (plaintiff) against D. S. Alter and others (defendants). Judgment for defendants, and plaintiff appealed. Judgment reversed and remanded, with directions.

Hopkins, J. This controversy presents two questions: First, whether a "Massachusetts trust" or "business trust" may transact business in this state without corporate license; and, second, whether failure to secure corporate license renders those composing such a "trust" liable as individuals for its debts. The action was one to recover from certain of the individuals composing such a trust the purchase price of a gas engine and accessories. The defendants prevailed, and plaintiff appeals.

As compensation for their privileges, corporations have substantial burdens to bear. For instance, they are subject to supervision by the state; they pay fees for incorporation; they make detailed reports to the state, and pay special taxes. In return, the state has given to their shareholders the privilege to engage in business without personal liability, provided they comply with the corporate law in the organization and conduct of the business. The law is strict concerning them. It requires an accurate statement of the capital, the recording of the articles, and safeguarding of the public in its dealings with them in various ways. It requires proof that the capital of the corporation has been paid in before it is permitted to do business. It provides means by which those who purchase stock therein may know that the proceeds of the purchase go into the capital of the company. It discloses a policy designed to protect the public against loss in the transaction of business with them. These purposes of the law may be circumvented if associations of the kind under consideration are permitted to secure exemption from personal liability for their membership without compliance with the provisions of law. Such a situation was never contemplated. It is contrary to the intent of our Constitution and laws.

Marshall, J. (concurring specially). I concur in the conclusion reached for the following reasons: D. S. Alter & Co. is not a corporation, because it has not been organized as such. The defendants did not attempt to organize a corporation. For that reason, the law governing corporations in their dealings with third parties cannot be applied to the transaction involved in this action. D. S. Alter & Co. is an association of individuals. The only applicable laws governing the business transactions of the associations of men are those which concern partnerships. Under the "declaration of trust" now being considered, "the trustees shall hold all money and property, real, personal or mixed, which they shall in any manner acquire as such trustees, together with the proceeds thereof, in trust, to manage and dispose of the same for the benefit of the holders from time to time of the certificates for shares issued and to be issued hereunder as hereinafter provided." The trustees are named by those beneficially interested in the trust to act for them in the management of the trust property and business; in other words, the trustees are agents. If this association of persons is a partnership, it is what is called a "limited partnership." Such a partnership may be organized under the laws of this state. R. S. § 56-101 to § 56-121, inc. It is not shown that the declaration of trust under consideration was filed with the county clerk of Sedgwick county. By the failure to file the declaration of trust with the county clerk, the association became a general partnership. The trustees, being partners, had power under the law to contract, and all the members are liable thereunder.[5]

QUESTIONS AND PROBLEMS

1. What was the nature of the earliest English corporations?
2. When did the industrial corporation, as it is known today, have its inception?

[5] Massachusetts trusts are recognized in those states which do not have legislation prohibiting them or declaring them corporations. See Magruder, "The Position of Shareholder in Business Trusts," 23 *Columbia Law Review* 423; Cook, "The Mysterious Massachusetts Trust," 9 *American Bar Association Journal* 763.

3. What is the nature of a corporation?
4. Bresserman, personally, bought land of Mosson and paid for it with checks signed: "Bresserman, Inc., by Bresserman, President." The corporation sued to recover the amount of the checks on the theory that Mosson had notice that Bresserman was misusing corporate funds. Bresserman, Inc., was organized with $500.00 capitalization to make butcher fixtures. There had never been a directors' meeting, no dividends had ever been paid, the stock certificates had never been issued, no financial statements had ever been made, and the only checks drawn out of the corporation were by the president for family expenses, the checks being made payable to Bresserman's wife. B. Bresserman and Frank Bresserman were the only stockholders. Can Bresserman, Inc., recover?
5. Felsenthal Co. was a corporation organized to deal in tailor's clippings. Fox owned one-half of the outstanding stock and the balance was pledged to Fox as security for a loan to the corporation. Fox was president and manager of the corporation. The property of the corporation was insured by the corporation against fire. Fox hired a "fire-bug" to set fire to the corporate property. The entire corporate assets were destroyed by the fire. The insurance company refused to pay and the Felsenthal Co. brought suit. Is the corporation entitled to a judgment?
6. Would the judgment be the same if Fox owned only a portion of the stock and there were also creditors of the corporation?
7. Can a valid corporation be organized without the consent, expressed or implied, of the state?
8. The Los Lugos Consolidated Gold Mine, a corporation, organized the Los Lugos Gold Mines and acted as incorporator. It took all the capital stock of the Los Lugos Gold Mines. The Los Lugos Consolidated Gold Mine gave its property in exchange for the stock of the Los Lugos Gold Mines. Is the Los Lugos Gold Mines legally organized?
9. Application was made to the Secretary of State for a certificate of organization of a corporation under the name of "National Liberty League." The Secretary of State refused the certificate on the ground that there was a duly incorporated organization doing business in the state bearing the name, "National Liberty Legions." Should the Secretary of State be compelled to issue the certificate?
10. The general incorporation laws required the insertion in the articles of incorporation of the number and names of the directors. These were omitted in the articles filed. Would this omission prevent the corporation from having de jure existence?
11. J. W. Butler Paper Company sold $1,305.80 worth of merchandise to the C & C Company. B. Chamberline, H. Cleveland, and F. Cleveland were directors and owned all of the stock of the C & C Company. The act under which the C & C Company was incorporated provided that notice of directors' meetings should be given ten days before the meeting. When the C & C Company was organized, no formal notice of the first directors' meeting was given, but all the directors were present and signed a formal waiver of notice. The paper company sued B. Chamberline, H. Cleveland, and F. Cleveland, personally, claiming that the statute had not been complied with, that no corporation was organized, and that B. Chamberline, H. Cleveland, and F. Cleveland were liable as partners. Can the paper company recover?

CHAPTER XXXV

ORGANIZING AND FINANCING THE CORPORATION'S BUSINESS

Promoters

In organizing a corporation, some individual or group of individuals called *promoters* must assume the task of getting the business incorporated and in operation. In the organization of a small corporation or in the incorporation of a partnership business, the parties in interest will assume this task and carry the organization of the corporation through to completion without the aid of promoters.

If the corporation is organized by a promoter, the promoter's task is to get the proposed enterprise started and operating. He promotes the proposition. He usually starts by getting prospective investors interested in the proposition, and when he has sufficient capital interested to warrant further steps, he makes arrangements for the acquisition of the necessary property for the carrying on of the business by taking options for the leases or purchase of property and enters into such other preliminary contracts as are warranted by the nature of the proposed enterprise. When these preliminary arrangements have been made, the promoter then organizes the corporation; usually, the promoter, together with interested parties, acts as the incorporators.

The promoter may be paid a salary for his services, he may take stock in the new enterprise, he may be given a position in the corporation, or he may be compensated in some other manner. The unscrupulous promoter may turn options, etc., over to the corporation at a price higher than he actually paid, concealing the increase by having an amount in excess of that actually paid inserted in the agreement, or by some other method make a secret profit out of the promotion of the corporation. The status of subscription agreements, promoters' contracts, and other transactions entered into in the course of the organization of a corporation present some interesting problems.

Promoters' contracts, entered into in behalf of a proposed corporation not yet organized, cannot bind the corporation at the time the contracts are made and do not bind the corporation when it comes into existence unless the corporation by its acts renders itself liable. The corporation cannot ratify the contract in the sense that a principal ratifies the unauthorized acts of his agent because, under the law of agency, to have a ratification, there must be an existing principal at the time the contract is made. In most jurisdictions, the corporation may adopt the contract. No set formality is necessary to do this. If the corporation clearly shows its intention to be bound, it is sufficient unless the contract is of such a nature that formal action by the board of directors or stockholders is required before the corporation can make such a contract. In some jurisdictions, the courts have held that there is a novation; that the third party contracted with the promoter for a novation at the time the contract was made. It is generally held that the promoter is individually liable on the contract even after its adoption by the corporation unless he has been released from liability by the third party. In those jurisdictions adhering to the novation theory, the promoter will be relieved from liability as soon as the novation is complete. The contract may expressly relieve the promoter from all personal liability; such a provision will be enforced.

The promoter's relation to the corporation which he is promoting is unique. He is not an agent, because he is self-appointed, and he has no principal in existence. It is generally accepted that the promoter's relation to the corporation in the process of formation is fiduciary. If the promoter has taken options or purchased property in the process of the organization of the corporation, he is not permitted to turn the options or property over to the corporation and take a secret profit on the transaction. The promoter owes a duty to deal with the corporation in an open and honest manner and will be held liable for any secret or unfair advantage he takes of the corporation. The promoter may sell his property to the new corporation at a profit, but unless it is a fair, open and aboveboard transaction, the corporation will be permitted to avoid the transfer.

Wheeler & Motter Mercantile Co. v. Lamerton et al.
8 F. (2d) 957 (1925)

This was an action by the Wheeler Motter Mercantile Co. (plaintiff) against W. E. Lamerton and others (defendants). Judgment for plaintiff against one defendant only and plaintiff appealed. Judgment affirmed.

J. E. Reed decided to organize a corporation for the purpose of carrying on a general mercantile business. Reed induced W. E.

Lamerton, a physician, and F. B. Buzzard, a farmer and real estate broker, to sign the articles of incorporation. Lamerton subscribed for $200 stock but Buzzard took no stock. These men signed the articles of incorporation to enable Reed to obtain a corporate charter for his proposed corporation. Between June 20 and June 24, 1922, Reed ordered merchandise from plaintiff for the agreed price of $9,300.97. Neither Lamerton nor Buzzard knew about the purchase of the goods. The goods were delivered about July 20, 1922. The corporate charter was issued by the Secretary of State August 8, 1922. This suit was brought against Reed, Lamerton, and Buzzard, as promotors of the corporation, to obtain a judgment for $5,636.70, the unpaid balance of the purchase price of the goods. Judgment was rendered against Reed but not against Lamerton or Buzzard.

Sanborn, C. J. In the absence of statutes to the contrary, the signer of articles of incorporation thereby gives no authority to his cosigners, and does not constitute them, or any of them, his agent or agents, prior to the conclusion of the incorporation, to purchase for the proposed corporation, for him or them, or to make him or them liable for goods, merchandise, or other property requisite or convenient for the expected business of the proposed corporation. The rule, caveat emptor, governs vendors under such circumstances. The authority or agency granted to the cosigners is limited to the performance of the acts necessary to perfect the organization of the corporation. Nor does the fact that one signs and verifies the articles of incorporation and subscribes for capital stock in a proposed corporation make him a promoter thereof, within the legal significance of that equivocal and ambiguous term in cases of this character.

Folse v. Loreauville Sugar Factory, Inc., et al.
Builders' Supply Co., Inc. v. Same
— La. App. —, 156 So. 667 (1934)

Actions were brought by E. P. Folse and by the Builders' Supply Co. (plaintiffs) against Loreauville Sugar Factory, Inc., and others (defendants). The suits were consolidated and tried together. From separate judgments in favor of each of the plaintiffs, the defendants appealed. Judgments affirmed.

The promotors and organizers of a proposed corporation purchased certain equipment and materials from the plaintiffs in the name of the proposed corporation. The contracts were entered into prior to the time a charter was granted to the proposed corporation. The equipment and materials were not paid for, and this suit was brought against the promotors to recover the purchase price of the equipment and material.

Le Blanc, J. The reasons, handed down by the trial judge, in a written opinion, we find to be sound and logical, and we adopt them as our own. They are as follows:

"I must conclude that these individual defendants are liable for the debt herein sued on. The fact that this debt was contracted for in the name of the corporation through a trustee, which at that time was not organized, but purely projected, a fact unknown to plaintiff, cannot defeat their individual liability. They must be held bound for their plans of organizing a corporation, which they expected would enjoy the benefits thereof, and in turn discharge the obligation created by them. There is no evidence of a novation of the debt or any intention of that fact expressed.

"In Corpus Juris, p. 269, we find: 'Of course promoters of a corporation are personally liable on contract which they have entered into personally, even though they have contracted for the benefit of the projected corporation, and although the corporation has been formed and has received the benefit of the contract; and they are not discharged from liability by the subsequent adoption of the contract by the corporation when formed, unless there is a novation or other agreement to such effect.'

"There is no evidence to show that plaintiff had any knowledge of the projection of the corporation by these individual defendants. Undoubtedly, not being placed on its guard, plaintiff rightfully assumed that it was dealing with a factory in the name of an individual authorized and representing persons engaged in commercial pursuits.

"There was therefore neither express nor implied understanding that plaintiff would look to any other but the persons actively engaged in operating this factory as a joint commercial enterprise. Plaintiff was certainly not called upon to anticipate the assumption of this debt by the contemplated corporation. The record is barren of any proof to show that the plaintiff ever subsequently consented to the assumption of this debt by the corporation and the release of the promoters from their individual liability."

Arn et al. v. Dunnett et al.
93 F. (2d) 634 (1937)

This was an action by W. G. Arn (plaintiff) against Operators Royalty & Producing Company, Ray M. Dunnett and his associates and others (defendants). Judgment for defendants and plaintiff appealed. Judgment affirmed.

Arn was a stockholder in Operators Oil Company, organized in 1926 and domiciled at Tulsa, Oklahoma. It was a producing company engaged in the acquisition and development of land for oil and gas. It had forty-three stockholders. Plaintiff, a resident of Chicago, and Dunnett and associates residents of Oklahoma and others were owners of stock, and Dunnett and associates managed the corporation's affairs.

Dunnett and associates promoted and caused Operators Royalty & Producing Company to be incorporated under the laws of Delaware with an authorized capital stock of 200,000 shares of no-par value stock. Dunnett acquired two separate royalty interests paying $18,000 for one and $2,500 for the other. The purchase money was borrowed from a Tulsa bank and Dunnett and his associates gave their personal notes for the amount of the loan. The titles to the royalties were taken in the name of Dunnett. Dunnett transferred both of such royalties to the corporation on May 10th; the entire authorized capital stock of 200,000 shares was thereupon issued to him; and a complete record of the transaction was entered upon the books of the corporation. The corporation owned no assets at that time except the royalties thus transferred to it. Dunnett donated 80,000 shares of the stock back to the corporation; 10,000 shares were specially set apart for sale to owners of stock in the oil company; and the remaining 110,000 shares were divided among Dunnett and his associates.

Plaintiff and other stockholders in the oil company purchased 9,450 shares of stock paying $3.50 per share. The indebtedness to the Tulsa bank, incurred in the purchase of the royalties, was paid out of the proceeds from the sale of this stock. Later the price of oil dropped and the company became financially embarrassed. Plaintiff attacked the transaction in which the royalties were transferred to the corporation and the stock issued therefor. They sought cancellation of the stock still retained by Dunnett and his associates, an accounting, and the appointment of a receiver.

Bratton, C. J. Promoters occupy a relation of trust to the corporation which they caused to be organized. They may make a sale of their property to the corporation, but they may be required to disgorge a secret or unlawful profit resulting from such a sale. A profit is not secret or unlawful, however, if all persons having a present interest in the transaction know the facts and give assent to it. And owners of all of the stock of a corporation are the persons having an interest in a transaction so far as the rights of the corporation extend. Further, the duty of full disclosure in a transaction of that kind is confined to persons having an interest in the corporation at the time. It does not extend to those subsequently acquiring shares of stock. Here the promoters of the corporation owned the royalties. They transferred such royalties to the corporation, and the stock was issued in exchange or in payment for them. They had given their personal notes for the royalties in the first instance, and the corporation never became liable for the purchase price, either by assumption of the notes or otherwise. The effect of the transaction was that the corporation acquired and became owner of the property free of obligation, and the promoters owned the stock; and the value of the stock was measured by the value of the royalties. All parties having any interest whatever in the corporation knew the facts and assented to the transaction. There were no other stockholders; there was no secrecy; and no facts were withheld from the promoters or any one having an interest in the corporation. The corporation was not injured through fraud, secrecy, or otherwise; and it could not complain. Plaintiffs acquired their stock after the transaction had been consummated. They cannot assert in a derivative action of this kind that the stock now in the hands of the promoters should be canceled and restored to the corporation.

It is urged that *Davis* v. *Las Ovas Company*, 227 U.S. 80, *McCandless* v. *Furlaud*, 296 U.S. 140, and *Yeiser* v. *United States Board & Paper Co.*, 107 F. 340, 52 L.R.A. 724, are decisive; but they are distinguishable on considerations of logic and analogy. In the first, certain members of the syndicate which promoted the corporation made a secret profit on the land being acquired for the corporation. They withheld knowledge of that fact from their associates. The innocent associates subscribed for stock and the money paid for it was used to pay the exaggerated price for the property. In the second, the corporation was reduced to hopeless insolvency as result of the transaction. Aside from its obligation to owners of stock, it had outstanding notes and bonds which exceeded the value of its assets by more than $2,000,000. The effect of the promoters' conduct was to paralyze the corporation from the very outset. The action was by a receiver for the benefit of creditors and stockholders. In the third, the fact that the promoters were making a secret profit was withheld from stockholders and directors. One stockholder and one director had knowledge of such profit, and they were induced to silence by illicit considerations. No analogous facts are present here.

By-Laws

After the formalities of incorporation have been complied with, and the charter has been granted and filed or recorded as required by the statute, the corporation has a legal existence, but it is not a completed organization ready to carry on a business. The constitution and the statute of the state of incorporation provide the foundation for the corporation; the articles of incorporation give us the framework of the corporation but it remains for the by-laws to complete the structure.

If the articles of incorporation and the state statute do not contain a special provision in regard to who may make and amend the by-laws of the corporation, this power rests with the stockholders. In the majority of the states the statutes provide that the power to make by-laws may, by express provision in the articles of incorporation, be vested in the board of directors. In some states the power of the directors to make and amend by-laws is subject to the power of the stockholders to repeal or amend the by-laws adopted by the board of directors. The lack of uniformity in the laws in this respect makes it necessary to examine the statutes of the state of incorporation and the articles of incorporation to determine who has the power to make and amend by-laws.

The by-laws will usually state the time and place at which the annual stockholders' meeting shall be held; how special meetings of stockholders may be called; define a quorum; state how stockholders' meetings shall be organized; and regulate how the voting shall be carried on and how elections shall be conducted. They will also provide for the organization of the board of directors; state the place and time for the regular meetings of the board of directors; how special meetings shall be called; officers to be elected or appointed and the duties of the officers; and who shall be authorized to sign contracts, etc., in behalf of the corporation. The by-laws may make provision for special committees defining the scope of their activities, the membership of the committee, etc. They will set up the machinery for the transfer of shares of stock, keeping of stock records, etc., and will also make provision for the declaring of and the paying of dividends.

Any by-law is void and unenforceable which (1) violates the statutes of the state of incorporation, (2) is contrary to the express provisions of the articles of incorporation, or (3) violates vested rights of the stockholders. Stockholders are bound by all valid by-laws properly adopted whether they approve of them or not. It is not necessary that a stockholder have notice or knowledge of a by-law to be bound by it. As a general rule a by-law which would deprive a stockholder of voting rights or other contractual rights arising out of his membership in the corporation is not valid; however, such a by-law may be valid if it is adopted by the unanimous consent of the stockholders and does not violate the laws of the state or the express provisions of the articles of incorporation. All by-laws must be reasonable and must conform to the general law of the land.

Third persons are bound by by-laws which are, in express terms, authorized by the articles of incorporation and they are also bound by by-laws of which they have notice. Otherwise, third persons are not bound by the by-laws of a corporation. Stockholders are bound by the by-laws in respect to their rights as stockholders, but in respect to general contracts entered into with the corporation, the stockholder is considered as a stranger to the corporation, and his rights would be the same as any third person dealing with the corporation.

Hueftle et. al. v. Farmers Elevator et al.
— Neb. —, 16 N.W. (2d) 855 (1944)

This was an action by Gotthill C. Hueftle and others (plaintiffs) against Farmers Elevator and others (defendants). Judgment for plaintiffs and defendants appealed. Judgment affirmed.

Plaintiffs were stockholders in Farmers Elevator, a corporation organized under the general corporation statute of Nebraska to carry on the business of buying and selling grain, hay, livestock, and other agriculture products. On March 4, 1943, at a stockholders' meeting it was voted by a majority of the stockholders to convert the corporation into a co-operative corporation and to distribute dividends upon a patronage basis. The articles were amended and subsequently the directors adopted by-laws authorizing the distribution of profits on a patronage basis. At the time the change was made, the corporation had undistributed profits which could have been distributed to stockholders.

Carter, J. The purpose of this suit is to prevent the distribution of the profits of the corporation in the manner provided by the amended articles and by-laws. It is self-evident that stockholders under the original articles will be deprived of dividends to which they were entitled thereunder. By their purchase of stock they acquired a contractual right to share in the net profits in the form of dividends on stock. An attempt to make a distribution of net profits on a patronage basis constitutes a violation of plaintiffs' contract rights.

"It is settled law that a corporation has no power to adopt by-laws which impair or destroy the obligations of contracts or rights thereunder or vested rights, and that by-laws which have that effect are invalid and unenforceable against a person whose rights are impaired or destroyed thereby." 8 Fletcher, Private Corporations (Perm. ed.) sec. 4188. The foregoing rule applies with equal force to amendments to the by-laws.

In a case very similar on fact and principle this court said: "In 1916 there was an attempt to amend the articles of incorporation by changing the Farmers Elevator Company to a co-operative association within the meaning of the statute cited. Later defendants planned to distribute profits under the amendment. Such a course, if pursued, would deprive plaintiffs of dividends to which they were entitled under their contracts as original stockholders and would destroy their contractual rights. This neither the legislature nor the defendants can lawfully do." *Allen* v. *White*, 103 Neb. 256, 171 N.W. 52.

The amendments change the fundamental arrangement and plans of the corporation as it was organized when plaintiffs became stockholders and impair the contractual rights which they then acquired. It follows that the amendments and the proceedings of the defendants taken thereunder are void.

Defendants urge that plaintiffs are estopped to question the validity of the amended articles and by-laws for the reason that they permitted defendants to advertise and solicit business for approximately seven months without objection thereto, that the articles and by-laws provided for their own amendment at the time plaintiffs purchased their stock and they are bound thereby, and that previous amendments to the articles and by-laws had been made to which plaintiffs had acquiesced. We find no merit in these contentions. A delay of seven months cannot be deemed unreasonable where, as here, no effort was made to distribute dividends on a patronage basis until shortly before the suit was brought.

While it is true that the right to amend the articles and by-laws was reserved at the time plaintiffs became stockholders, the right to amend was not absolute. The power to amend articles and by-laws is an incident of the power to adopt them and a general reservation of the right to amend ordinarily creates no different situation than if it were not reserved at all. In either event, the fact that a stockholder may purchase stock at a time when the right to amend the articles and by-laws is reserved does not operate to confer authority to make an amendment which will amount to the destruction or impairment of the vested or contract rights of the member. Neither does the fact that a stockholder acquiesces in previous amendments estop him from asserting his rights when a subsequent article or by-law is amended which materially affects his interests.

Organization Meetings

The general corporation laws of some states require, either expressly or by implication, the holding of an organization meeting. However, even though the statutes of the state do not require such a meeting, it is common practice to hold one. There is considerable doubt as to the persons who are entitled to participate in such a meeting. Under the statutes of some states the incorporators signing the articles of incorporation are the only ones who participate in the first organization meeting, while in other states the subscribers to the stock of the corporation are the participants. Those who are entitled to participate must be given notice of the time and place of the meeting unless such notice is waived. The incorporators, or one to whom such authority is delegated, gives the notice. The best practice is to give written notice. If the first board of directors is named in the articles of incorporation and the board of directors is given authority to adopt by-laws, an organization meeting of the incorporators, subscribers or stockholders, as the case may be, may be dispensed with.

The first step taken at such a meeting is the organization of the meeting. An incorporator will act as temporary chairman until the meeting is organized. The business to be transacted will depend almost entirely on the nature of the corporation, the laws of the state of incorporation, and the provisions of the articles of incorporation. As a general rule, a board of directors will be elected, but if the directors are named in the articles of incorporation, a resolution will be passed approving the board named. By-laws may be approved and adopted. Such other matters necessary to the completion of the organization of the corporation, which are reserved for stockholder action by statute or by the articles of incorporation, will be disposed of at the meeting.

The details of the completion of the organization of the corporation are customarily left to the directors. The directors, as a general rule, will hold a directors' meeting immediately after the adjournment of the first organization meeting. The meeting is usually held upon consent and waiver of notice of all the directors. The following matters of business are usually transacted at the first meeting of the directors: (1) officers are elected, (2) a corporate seal is adopted, (3) the form of the stock certificate is approved, (4) payment of expenses of organization, including compensation to promotors, is authorized, (5) promoters' contracts, entered into in the course of the promotion of the corporation, are adopted, (6) the signing of checks is authorized, etc., and (7) the principal office, and the time and place of future board meetings are designated. If the adoption of by-laws is delegated to the board of directors, one of the first matters of business will be the adoption of by-laws. If the corporation is to do business in other states or intends to sell its stock or bonds to the general public, the directors will take the steps necessary to accomplish this. No detailed statement can be made of the business which will come before the first meeting of the board of directors.

Minutes of all meetings held by stockholders or directors should be kept by the secretary.

Issuing Stock

Part if not all of the money or property needed to operate the business of the corporation is obtained by issuing capital stock. The stockholders are, in effect, the owners of the corporation and are not creditors, irrespective of the class of stock which they may own.

As a general rule stock having a par value cannot be issued for less than par. After stock has been issued it may be sold at whatever price it will bring. Under the statutes of some states par value stock may be issued for less than par if the articles of incorporation expressly provide that such stock may be sold below par. The principal problems regarding the issue of par value stock arise when it is issued for property, for services, or for notes, checks, or other evidence of indebtedness of the purchasers. Three methods of appraising property, given in exchange for shares of stock, are followed in the several states. In some states the value of the property, given in exchange for par value stock, must be taken at its fair value. In other states, if the directors, incorporators, or stockholders who appraise the property act in good faith in making the appraisal, the appraisal is not subject to attack even though such property is greatly over-valued. A few states make some provision for state appraisal of such property. Par value stock issued for services rendered presents a similar problem—are the services rendered a fair exchange for the stock issued? In several states it is expressly provided that stock shall not be issued except for services actually rendered, thus making it illegal to issue stock in exchange for future services. In some states it is not permissible to accept a note, draft, or uncertified check in payment for stock issued, and as a general rule, if a note, draft, or uncertified check is accepted in payment of stock issued, the stock is not considered as fully paid until the note, draft, or check is paid. In all instances in which par value stock is issued for property or services, the board of directors should make a careful and detailed record of the property received and a statement of its value.

No-par value shares may be issued, and their value will be determined either by the stockholders or by the board of directors, providing such authority has been vested in the board of directors. It may be issued at different prices from time to time depending on the market. It may be issued in payment of promotors' services or in payment for property without placing a definite value thereon. It may also be issued in connection with the sale of bonds or preferred stock. Under the statutes of some states even no-par stock cannot be given away as a pure bonus. In fixing the price of no-par stock the board of directors must observe those equitable limitations on the discretion of directors and fix a price which is not fraudulent or discriminatory.

If stock is to be issued to the general public, it may be necessary to qualify the stock with the state securities commission or with some other state body. The "Blue Sky" laws of the states are not uniform in their requirements, and the laws of the state in which the issue is to be sold will have to be consulted to determine whether or not the stock is exempt from the provisions of the law, and if not, what procedure is necessary to qualify the shares. If the stock is to be sold interstate, or through the mails, the Federal Securities Act must be complied with.

Bodell et al. v. General Gas & Electric Corporation
15 Del. Ch. 420, 140 Atl. 264 (1927)

This was an action by Joseph J. Bodell and others (plaintiffs) against the General Gas & Electric Corporation (defendant). Judgment for defendant and plaintiffs appealed. Judgment affirmed.

The defendant corporation was organized in July, 1925. The capital stock consists of both preferred and common shares, all without nominal or par value. In this case we are concerned with the common stock only, which is divided into 800,000 shares of Class A common and 400,000 shares of Class B common.

The complainants are holders of both Class A and Class B common stock. The rights of the common stocks are as follows:

After the preferred dividends are provided for, the Class A common stock shall receive a dividend (non-cumulative) at the rate of $1.50 per annum; then, the common stock Class B is entitled to receive a like dividend of $1.50 per annum, and in case dividends are further declared from surplus or net profits, Class A common and Class B common are entitled to share equally therein.

Upon liquidation, subject to the preference of the preferred stocks, Class A common is preferred over Class B common to the extent of $25 per share, then Class B common receives $25 per share, and threafter any remaining assets are distributable between Classes A and B common in equal amounts.

The holders of Class A stock (which was no-par stock) were given the privilege of purchasing additional Class A stock, to the extent of their dividends, at $25 per share.

Class A stock sold on the market at from $50 to $64 per share and was issued by the corporation in large blocks for $45 per share. The average price received by the corporation for Class A stock issued (including Class A sold at $25 per share) was $41.77. The book value of Class A stock was in excess of $25 per share. The plaintiff contends that it was illegal to issue Class A stock to a selected group—"Class A stockholders"—at less than its true value. The directors contend that the price at which Class A stock can be sold to the public has been substantially increased by the scheme and that the corporation has benefited thereby in that it has been able to provide for all the financial needs of the corporation at low cost and without creating fixed charges.

Pennewill, C. J. The Chancellor says: "The controversy has solely to do with the right of the directors to issue no-par common stock A to present holders of that stock, for the consideration of $25 per share to the extent of their dividends while at practically the same time they offer to sell and succeed in selling to all other classes of stockholders, or in the alternative to underwriting bankers, a much larger number of shares of the same kind of stock at $45 per share."

After all, that is the real and sole question in the case. The defendant, under its Certificate of Incorporation, had a right to sell the stock in question; did it have a right to sell it to Class A stockholders only at the price they paid?

It is argued by the defendant that the power now given to a corporation in this state to sell no-par value stock and fix the consideration therefore is broad and unlimited in its terms and should not be restrained in any case except for fraud. We are not required in this case to go so far, but we do say that the broad and general language of the statute, embodied in the Certificate of Incorporation, should be liberally construed in favor of the directors. The Legislature, in enacting the statute, meant to clothe the directors of a corporation with exceptionally large powers in the sale of its no-par value stock. If in the particular case there is nothing to show that the directors did not exercise their discretion for what they believed to be the best interest of the corporation, certainly an honest mistake of business judgment should not be reviewable by the Court.

It may be impossible to lay down a general rule on this subject, but we think the discretion of a board of directors in the sale of its no-par value stock should not be interfered with, except for fraud, actual or constructive, such as improper motive or personal gain or arbitrary action or conscious disregard of the interests of the corporation and the rights of its stockholders.

The complainants, B stockholders, say that A stockholders have received for $25 per share, stock immediately resalable at $45 and there has been a conscious sale of A stock to the A stockholders at a price at least $20 per share below the sales value. Their position is that the practice complained of constitutes a conscious offer of no-par value stock below its fair sales value, and like all such offers, is illegal; and even if a conscious offer of no-par value stock below its fair sales value may be legal if made to certain persons, it is illegal if made to the A stockholders alone in addition to their quarterly cash dividends of 37½ cents per share and before the B stockholders have received $1.50 per share.

The complainants say the Chancellor agreed with the rule that a conscious offer of no-par value stock below its fair sales value is illegal, and that both he and counsel for the defendant conceded that there was a conscious sale for less than fair sales value.

The Chancellor says in his opinion: "The mere showing of the two prices would without satisfactory explanation undoubtedly entitle the complainants to relief. But if these two prices are justified by a showing of fairness in the light of all the circumstances so that what appears to be an injury turns out to be a benefit to those complaining, there can be no ground for interference. . . . . It would be highly unreasonable to point to sales at $45 as showing the inadequacy of sales at $25 if the latter was what in fact made the former possible. . . . . If, as a result of the policy thus grounded, the corporation is able to secure funds from stock sales greatly in excess of the amount they otherwise could hope to realize, it is manifest that an advantage has been secured for the corporation and for all its stockholders."

It is impossible, of course, to tell to what extent the policy was successful, or whether a like stock sale privilege given to B stockholders might not have been effective, but judging from the affidavits filed, we cannot escape the belief that the plan pursued was very successful. Nor do we know what would have happened to the company if the policy complained of had not been adopted. It does clearly appear that the success of the company and the interests of all its stockholders depended upon the ability of the directors to raise a large amount of money at a low cost, and who can say that the plan adopted was not the best? Certainly no one can say the directors did not use their honest and best judgment in meeting a pressing emergency, and in solving a problem that meant much to the success of the corporation. It seems to us to be a case that comes clearly within the language and meaning of the statute which gives the directors a large discretion in selling no-par value stock and fixing the consideration therefor.

Issuing Bonds

The principal question arising in regard to an issue of bonds is who has the power to authorize the issue. Bonds may be unsecured or secured and, if secured, the security given may be a portion of the assets of the corporation, may be all the assets of the corporation, or may be all the real estate of the corporation. The bond issue may require stockholder action or it may be within the powers of the board of directors to authorize the issue. In determining whether or not a bond issue has been legally authorized, it will be necessary to analyze the bond issue and determine the nature of the obligations imposed on the corporation by the issue; then it will be necessary to examine the statutes of the state of incorporation, the articles of incorporation, and the by-laws to determine the extent of the powers of the corporation and to determine who has the power to authorize the issue. No general statement can be made which will serve as a test of the validity of a bond issue. The validity of the issue will depend on the combination of the nature of the issue, the provisions of the statutes of the state of incorporation, the provisions of the articles of incorporation, the provisions of the by-laws, and the action which has been taken in authorizing and issuing the bonds. As a general rule a corporation has the power to borrow money for the purpose of carrying on its business, and it has the implied power, as an incident thereto, to execute and issue bonds.

Orme v. Salt River Valley Water Users' Association.
25 Ariz. 324, 217 Pac. 935 (1923)

This was an action by John P. Orme (plaintiff) against Salt River Valley Water Users' Association (defendant). Judgment for defendant and plaintiff appealed. Judgment affirmed.

Defendant was a corporation organized under the laws of Arizona for the purpose of providing an adequate supply of irrigation water for a 250,000 acre tract of land known as the Salt river project. The articles provide that revenue for corporate purposes shall be raised by levying assessments upon the shareholders, and that such assessments when levied shall become, be, and remain until paid a lien on the lands of the shareholders against which they are levied and the stock appurtenant thereto, but that an indebtedness to exceed $50,000 (later raised by amendment to $100,000), except for ordinary operation, maintenance, and repair, may not be incurred in any one year unless it be ratified by at least two-thirds of the votes cast at an election called for that purpose, and in no event may the corporate indebtedness exceed two-thirds of the capital stock.

At a stockholders' meeting at which less than one-half of the outstanding stock was voted, the directors were authorized to issue bonds of the corporation in the sum of $1,800,000 to finance the construction of an improvement designated as Mormon Flat development No. 1. After the authorization of the bond issue, the state legislature passed a bill which validated the bond issue in so far as the state statutes were concerned. Plaintiff, a stockholder, brought this action to enjoin the bond issue. Several questions were raised in the case in addition to the question of the validity of the bond issue.

McAlister, C. J. It is contended that the judgment is erroneous for the reason that the articles of incorporation do not authorize the issuance of bonds. There is no provision specifically conferring this authority but the articles contemplate the incurrence of an indebtedness, for it is provided in section 7 thereof that an indebtedness exceeding $100,000 (as amended) for other than ordinary operation, maintenance, and repair purposes, may not be incurred in any one year unless two-thirds of the votes cast at an election called for that purpose ratify it. But even though the articles did not confer this authority, the power to incur an indebtedness for corporate purposes would exist as an implied one, for—

"The power to contract includes the power to borrow money for legitimate purposes; and the power to purchase includes power to borrow money to pay for the thing purchased. In fact, it may be laid down as a general rule that whenever the charter of a corporation gives it the power, expressly or impliedly, to purchase property or otherwise incur a debt, it has the implied power, in the absence of restrictions in its charter, to borrow money to pay for the property or to pay the debt." 2 Fletcher on Corporations, par. 939, p. 1891.

The power of a corporation to issue bonds for corporate indebtedness is likewise implied where there are no restrictions in its articles of incorporation or the statute. It is a necessary result or incident of the power to contract a debt. "There seems to be no reason," said Judge Hoar in *Com.* v. *Smith*, 10 Allen (Mass.) 448, 87 Am. Dec. 672, "why a railroad corporation should not be considered as having power to make a bond for any purpose for which it may lawfully contract a debt, without any special authority to that effect, unless restrained by some restrictions, express or implied, in its charter, or in some other legislative act."

QUESTIONS AND PROBLEMS

1. The promoters of the Ravenna Creamery Co. agreed to pay Davis & Rankin $6,850 for the construction of a factory for the proposed corporation. Thereafter, the creamery company was incorporated, but the corporation refused to accept and pay for the factory. Davis & Rankin sued the Ravenna Creamery Co. to recover the contract price of the factory. Are they entitled to a judgment against the corporation?
2. Johnson had a patent on a cushion heel shoe. He proposed the organization of a shoe factory. Hartt, on Johnson's promise to make him foreman of the factory and compensate him for his time, helped in getting subscriptions and in getting the corporation organized. After the corporation was organized, the directors refused to give Hartt a job and also refused to compensate him for his time in assisting in the organization of the corporation. One director said he thought

Hartt ought to be paid something, but no board action was taken. Can Hartt recover from the corporation?

3. Davis proposed the organization of a corporation to purchase land in Cuba and formed a syndicate for that purpose. The syndicate was to purchase certain lands for $35,000, organize a corporation with a capital stock of $150,000, take 40 per cent of the stock for services as promoters, and the remaining stock was to be subscribed for by the promoters. They were to pay $40,000 for it, $35,000 to go for the land and $5,000 for expense money. Davis had previously taken an option on the land for $20,000. He had the original vendor deed it to Escalante and then had Escalante deed it to the syndicate to cover up the secret profit. The corporation sued Davis and the other promoters to recover the secret profits on the land and to cancel the stock which was issued to them in payment of their services as promoters. Can the corporation recover?
4. The articles of incorporation of the Richardson Dry Goods Co. provided that: "Said preferred stock shall be entitled to a dividend of six per cent per annum out of the net yearly income earned in any one year before any dividend shall be made and paid on any of the common stock." The by-laws provide that dividends on preferred stock shall be cumulative. What effect would the by-laws have on the rights of the holders of preferred stock?
5. Who has the power to adopt and amend by-laws?
6. Is a meeting of the incorporators, subscribers, or stockholders a prerequisite to the doing of business by a corporation?
7. By its articles of incorporation, the Pioneer Realty Co. was authorized to issue $125,000 preferred stock. It issued $75,000 of preferred stock in 1920, and in 1923 it issued the remaining $50,000. Elliott, a holder of shares of preferred stock first issued, brought an action to enjoin the corporation from issuing the remaining stock. Should an injunction be granted?
8. Measel purchased shares of the capital stock of Demott Bank & Trust Co. and gave the corporation his note in payment for the stock. On the due date the corporation demanded payment and Measel refused to pay. The corporation brought suit on the note. Is the corporation entitled to a judgment?
9. The Warrior Corporation issued twenty thousand shares of its no-par value stock to Deer. In payment Deer contracted to render future services to the corporation. An action was brought to secure the cancellation of the stock. Should the stock be cancelled?
10. Does a corporation, as a general rule, have the power to issue bonds?

CHAPTER XXXVI

OPERATING THE CORPORATE BUSINESS

Scope of the Business

The power or authority of a corporation is determined by the statutes of the state in which it is incorporated and its articles of incorporation. The stereotyped expression is that a corporation has only those powers which are granted to it by the state. At the time when a corporation was granted a charter by a special act of the legislature, this conception was more accurate than it is today. Under the general corporation statutes which are in force in the various states, a corporation may be organized to carry on almost any type of legitimate business. Consequently, the statement of the purposes for which the corporation is organized is a self-imposed limitation rather than one imposed by the state. A corporation organized to carry on a stated type of business is legally bound to confine its activities to the ordinary scope of the business selected. This limitation is similar to the limitations on a partnership. If the corporation wishes to enlarge its field of activity, it should amend its articles of incorporation, and to amend the articles of incorporation, certain formalities must be observed.

The purpose for which the corporation is organized will be stated in its articles of incorporation. Such a statement of purpose will be enlarged and supplemented by the statute under which the corporation is incorporated. Such a statute customarily grants to the corporation the power to sue and be sued, to enter into contracts, to own property, and such other powers as are fundamental to the existence of a corporation for profit. In determining the scope of the powers of a corporation, the courts will look to the statement of the purpose of the corporation as set out in the articles of incorporation and will accept it as a statement of the express powers of the corporation.

In addition to these express powers, the corporation will have such other implied powers as are reasonably necessary for the corporation to accomplish the object for which it was incorporated. The rules for determining the implied powers of a corporation are, in theory, the same as those for determining the implied powers of a general agent. The limits of the powers of a corporation are, primarily, questions of fact and interpretation of language.

Certain situations have given rise to some special questions in regard to the powers of a corporation. In the absence of express provision, either in the statute under which the corporation is incorporated or in the articles of incorporation, does the corporation have the power to hold property in trust; give its property away; dispose of all its assets by sale or otherwise; act as surety or guarantor; become a member of a partnership; own property in common with others; be a joint obligor on a contract; take and hold the stock of another corporation; or acquire and hold its own stock? As a general proposition if the doing of any of the enumerated acts will contribute to the accomplishment of the objectives of the corporation as stated in its articles of incorporation, it will have the power to so act.

As a general rule a corporation will have the power to hold property in trust; however, under the statutes of some states "trust companies" must be incorporated under special statutes, and a corporation incorporated under the general corporation act will not have such power. The making of gifts, as a general rule, will not further the objectives of a corporation, but the courts have been liberal in finding that contributions to civic projects, gifts for the benefit of employees such as gifts to hospitals at which employees will be cared for or the establishment of hospital benefit funds for employees, and similar gifts, further the objectives of the corporation and are within its power.

If the corporation is being operated at a loss, if its business is becoming obsolete, or if the exigencies of the business demand it, the corporation has the power to sell its entire assets, but, if the business is profitable, it will not, as a general rule, have such power. Many states have statutes defining the rights of a corporation to dispose of all of its assets and providing protection for minority stockholders in the event of such a sale.

As a general rule a corporation has no power to act as a surety or guarantor because by such a contract the corporation assumes a risk without expectation of a compensating benefit. It does have the power to indorse negotiable paper, thereby assuming a secondary liability, and it would have the power to act as surety or guarantor for a customer if by so doing it could further its business interests. As a general rule, a corporation cannot be a member of a partnership, but it may own property with others as tenants in common and it may enter into contracts jointly with others.

The power of a corporation to acquire and hold the stock of another corporation has presented a variety of questions. The majority of the courts now hold that a corporation may acquire and hold stock in another corporation. Some courts have held that the right is limited to the holding of stock in a corporation when such holding will further the objects of the corporation; for example, a railroad owning stock in a coal mining corporation and thereby assuring itself a supply of coal. The holding of stock in a subsidiary corporation is a common practice. A corporation may acquire and hold stock in another corporation as an investment, but the courts have generally held that a corporation has no power to speculate in corporate stocks. The majority of courts now hold that a corporation may acquire and hold its own stock, but all the courts hold that such stock must be paid for out of surplus and that, if the acquisition of its own stock will injure creditors, the transaction will be set aside as a fraud on the creditors. In drafting the articles of incorporation it is desirable to state expressly that the corporation shall have the power to purchase stock in other corporations, etc., thus removing any existing doubt on these controversial points.

State v. San Antonio Public Service Co.
Tex. Comm. App., 69 S.W. (2d) 38 (1934)

This was an action by the State of Texas (plaintiff) against San Antonio Public Service Company (defendant). To review a judgment of the Court of Civil Appeals, affirming in part and reversing in part a judgment of the District Court, the State appeals. Judgment of the Court of Civil Appeals affirmed.

This action was brought by the state to enjoin the defendant from transacting business in excess of its charter powers.

The state alleged that appellant was incorporated "for the purpose of constructing, acquiring, maintaining and operating lines of electric motor railway," and "for the manufacture, supplying and selling of electricity and gas (artificial, natural, or both), for light, heat and power to the public and to municipalities"; and that in violation of article 1349, R.S. 1925, inhibiting a corporation from employing "its stock, means, assets or other property, directly or indirectly for any purpose whatever other than to accomplish the legitimate business of its creation, or those purposes otherwise permitted by law"; and as ultra vires of its corporate powers, appellant was employing its means and assets: (1) In the purchase for sale and the sale of all kinds and character of electric and gas appliances, maintaining a department, salesrooms, and salesmen therefor, and employing in excess of $150,000 of its means and assets for such purposes.

Blair, J. It is manifest that article 1349, supra, authorizes a corporation to do whatever may "accomplish the legitimate business of its creation, or those purposes otherwise permitted by law." The statute does not necessarily add to or take from the general rule of implied powers of a corporation, but rather restates the rule by other appropriate language. That is, the rule of implied powers would authorize appellant to do those things which are incident to and reasonably necessary to the carrying out of the powers expressly granted. No distinction can be made between this rule and the provisions of the statute authorizing a corporation to do whatever may "accomplish the legitimate business of its creation." Implied powers of a corporation are necessarily "those purposes otherwise permitted by law"; and we are clear in the view that the evidence detailed shows that the sale of gas and electric appliances tends directly to increase the use and consumption by the public of gas and electricity, and therefore tends directly to "accomplish the legitimate business" of appellant, to wit, the manufacturing, supplying, and selling of gas and electricity to the public.

There is no important disagreement as to the general rule of law involved; but the disagreement arises with respect to the proper application of the rules to the facts of this case, which, as the authorities point out, is the chief difficulty in determining what are the implied powers of a corporation. It is agreed in this case that the power to sell gas and electric appliances to its customers using gas and electricity for lighting, heating, and power purposes is not expressly granted by the charter of appellant, or by specific statute; but that if appellant has such power, it is by implication of law, as being incident to and as reasonably necessary to accomplish the legitimate business of its creation. The authorities cited by both parties agree that the implied powers of a corporation, such as are necessary to effectuate or carry out the powers expressly granted, or to accomplish the legitimate business of its creation, are not limited to such as are indispensable for those purposes, but comprise all that are necessary in the sense of appropriate and suitable, including the right of reasonable choice of means to be employed. And the authorities further agree that the question presented is one of mixed law and fact; and that whether an act of a corporation comes within its implied powers must be determined in each case from all its facts and circumstances.

As above stated, the question presented is one of first impression in Texas. The authorities from other jurisdictions sustain our above conclusion, and no authority dealing directly with the question presented has been cited or found, holding to the contrary. The leading case sustaining our view is the case of *Malone* v. *Lancaster Gas Light & Fuel Co.*, 182 Pa. 309, 37 A. 932, 933, by the Supreme Court of Pennsylvania, wherein the stockholders sought to enjoin the issuance of new stock and increase the corporation's bonded indebtedness on the ground that the money so acquired was for operating a department for the sale of gas consuming appliances; the court holding as follows: "It is argued for plaintiff that the charter purpose of the gas company is limited by the words 'manufacturing and supplying illuminating and heating gas,' and that nothing can be included which is not a necessary part or appliance for manufacturing or supplying. This is too narrow and literal a construction, and overlooks the fundamental object of the corporation,—the manufacture and supply of gas to customers for profit. It would be of no use to manufacture gas if there were no customers to buy, and hence the company may fairly supply, not only the gas itself, but, incidentally, such appliances and conveniences as will induce new customers to use gas, or old ones to use more. This is a legitimate mode of extending the company's business, in direct furtherance of its charter object. In considering such questions, much weight must be allowed to the judgment of the parties most interested,—the officers and stockholders of the corporation itself; and while they will not be permitted, as against the commonwealth or a dissenting stockholder, to go outside of their legitimate corporate business, yet, where the act questioned is of a nature to be fairly considered incidental or auxiliary to such business, it will not be unlawful because not within the literal terms of the corporate grant. This is the general rule even where corporate privileges are most strictly construed. 'Corporations may transact, in addition to their main undertaking, all such subordinate and connected matters as are, if not essential, as least very convenient, to the due prosecution of the former.'"

Hayman et al. v. Morris et al.
36 N.Y.S. (2d) 756 (1942)

This was an action by Seymour Hayman and others in behalf of all stockholders (plaintiffs) against Arthur J. Morris and others (defendants). Judgment for defendants.

Plaintiffs and defendants were stockholders in Industrial Finance Corporation, a Virginia corporation licensed and doing business in the state of New York. The corporation was a holding company and owned substantially all the stock of the Morris Plan Banks doing business in the United States.

Prior to the stock market collapse in October, 1929, the Industrial Finance Corporation, for the purpose of stimulating trading in its stocks and thereby creating a better market for its stocks, began to purchase, with corporation money, both its preferred and common stock. It expended $779,580.52 purchasing 6600½ shares of preferred and 2459½ shares of common stock. This action is brought to compel the defendants (the sellers of the stock) to restore this sum to the corporation. After the stock market collapse the stock declined materially in value.

Eder, J. Both our civil and penal laws require dividends to be paid out of surplus, and this applies to both domestic and foreign corporations; the penal law makes it a misdemeanor for a domestic or foreign corporation to purchase its own stock except out of surplus.

There appears to be no statutory prohibition in our civil law against a corporation purchasing its own stock out of capital, nor was there in this state any such inhibitory rule at common law, and while our penal law does contain such a denouncement, its violation does not give rise to a civil action for any redress because of such violation.

The underlying reason for judicial or statutory prohibition against the use or allocation of capital for the acquisition by a corporation of its own stock, or for the payment of dividends, is that it results in depletion of the fund upon which creditors rely in extending credit to the corporation and which they resort to for payment. If there are no creditors, neither the statute nor judicial rule in that regard has any application, and the prohibition is without effect.

Under the civil law of New York and Virginia the creditor feature is an element of prime importance, and it is so also under the penal law of New York; apparently there is no penal provision in Virginia. In the instant case there are no creditors' rights involved, so these statutes of New York are without application or effect even if New York law was held to be applicable or controlling. Under Virginia law a corporation may purchase its own stock out of capital in the absence of statutory or charter restraint and provided the rights of creditors are not prejudiced and there is no fraudulent invasion of the rights of other stockholders.

Nor is there anything in the law of Virginia or in the charter of the corporation which restricts the purchase and acquisition of the company's capital stock to the sole purpose of its retirement, as plaintiffs maintain. Retirement of the stock is one of the purposes authorized; it is not exclusive. The provision in the charter, that the corporation may otherwise deal in stocks of any kind and description to the same extent as a natural person is permitted to do, intends and contemplates that such stock so acquired may in addition be utilized for any other lawful purpose and the purchase and acquisition thereof for trading purposes or to aid in obtaining additional capital is a valid act and within the corporate powers conferred.

Ultra Vires Transactions

As stated above a corporation has no power to enter into a transaction unless such transaction is in the furtherance of the objects of the corporation as set out in its articles of incorporation. However, corporations do enter into transactions which are beyond the powers of the corporation. What is the legal status of such transactions? The answer to this question and the theories on which such answers are based differ so widely that it is impossible to state a rule or principle which will control in such a situation. Any act in excess of the powers of the corporation is ultra vires the corporation. In the early decisions the courts held that a corporation, being an artificial person, had only those powers conferred on it by the state and any transaction entered into in excess of such powers was a nullity. Under existing corporation statutes, especially those which permit any legitimate business to be carried on by corporations, the limits on the powers of the corporation are imposed by the incorporators for the protection of stockholders and others in interest rather than by the state.

There is so much confusion and inconsistency in the holdings of the courts in regard to ultra vires contracts that one cannot classify the decisions with any degree of certainty. However, for the purpose of discussion, they may be roughly classified into three groups. If the ultra vires contract has been fully performed by both parties to the contract, as a general rule the courts will not interfere but will allow each party to retain what he has received. If the contract is wholly executory, the majority of courts will not permit either party to maintain an action on the contract. If the contract is fully performed on one side but the other party has not performed, the courts are divided. Some courts allow a recovery on the contract, while others declare the contract void but allow a recovery in quasi contract for the benefits conferred. The courts holding ultra vires contracts void base their decisions on the ground that the corporation derives its power to act from the state, and if it is not given the power to enter into the contract, no contract obligation arises; its act is a nullity.

Much of the confusion in the cases is the result of the courts' failure to distinguish between illegal contracts and contracts in excess of the powers of the corporation which are not contrary to public policy. To hold that ultra vires contracts are not binding on a corporation gives the stockholders protection at the expense of third persons. Had the courts treated a corporation as analogous to a partnership, the problem would have been simplified and the results more satisfactory, because the power of the directors to bind the corporation would then be determined on the basis of the apparent scope of the business instead of on the basis of an interpretation of the powers granted in the articles of incorporation. The third person would be bound by notice or knowledge of limitations on the powers of the board of directors. In regard to agents of the corporation the general rules of agency law would apply. If the contract entered into was illegal because it was against public policy or because it was expressly forbidden by law, the courts would apply the accepted legal principles which apply to illegal contracts. If the ultra vires act were ratified by the stockholders, it would be binding on the corporation even though, when entered into, the third party knew it was in excess of the powers of the corporation.

Under the existing state of the law the courts have held that, if the contract is within the apparent power of the corporation although it is rendered ultra vires by extrinsic facts which are unknown to the third person, the corporation will be held liable on the contract. For example, if the Archer Corporation draws a bill of exchange on the Burch Corporation which the Burch Corporation accepts for the accommodation of the Archer Corporation, and the draft is negotiated to Fox who takes as a holder in due course, Fox can hold the Burch Corporation if the Burch Corporation has the power to issue negotiable paper. The fact that issuing accommodation negotiable paper is ultra vires is not a defense to accommodation paper in the hands of a holder in due course.

Temple Lumber Co. v. Miller
Ct. of Civ. App. Tex., 169 S.W. (2d) 256 (1943)

This was an action by A. A. Miller (plaintiff) against Temple Lumber Company (defendant). Judgment for plaintiff and defendant appealed. Judgment affirmed.

Plaintiff entered into a contract with defendant whereby the defendant agreed to furnish all the materials and construct a house for plaintiff according to certain plans and specifications. The corporate charter of defendant set out the purposes of the corporation as "manufacturing lumber and the purchase and sale of materials used in such business and doing all things necessary and incident to such lumber business." The defendant completed the house and the plaintiff paid the defendant the agreed contract price but did not pay $180.56 which was due for extras. The materials and workmanship were defective and plaintiff sued to recover damages resulting from such defective materials and workmanship. It is insistently urged that since defendant's charter only authorized it to buy and sell lumber and building materials, it could not be held to have made a contract to construct a building, as contended by plaintiff.

Speer, J. We will forego the historical background of the policy of our law for which our statutes have been enacted for the creation of corporations with specific powers and authority and their business relation to the public as a body politic. It appears that the early English cases, as well as some by federal courts, and even the early cases decided by our state courts, are not in complete harmony with respect to the extent a corporation may go and bind itself. But the trend seems to be that even though the charter provisions do not, in so many words, authorize an act, the corporation may bind itself to do many things, when not against public policy and are not forbidden by law. There is a clear distinction between acts which are void because of legal inhibitions, and those which are not prohibited but are those which are not enumerated in the purpose clause of the charter. In the latter class are to be found instances which include acts which are appropriate, convenient and suitable in carrying out the purposes for which the charter was expressly granted. These are termed implied powers and authority.

To our minds, the contract involved here was one not prohibited by law nor by any principle of public policy. No good reason exists why defendant could not contract with plaintiff to sell him the materials to go into his house. We think it would logically follow that as an inducement to plaintiff to buy the materials from it, defendant could agree and bind itself to deliver the materials at its own expense, although its charter did not expressly authorize it to haul building materials. If it could deliver, then could it not even cut the lumber into desired lengths? Carrying the thought further, it could with propriety obligate itself to do many things not expressly mentioned in its charter, when "appropriate," "convenient" and "suitable" in the prosecution of the line of business expressly mentioned in the charter. An act of a corporation is said to be ultra vires when beyond the scope either of the express or implied powers of its charter. If the acts are within the scope of the implied powers of the corporation, they cannot be said to be ultra vires, yet some of our courts deem them such if they are not within the express terms of the charter. We think that if the act is not one prohibited by law or public policy, and it inures to the direct benefit of the corporation, and is executed, it is not, strictly speaking, ultra vires, and this is apparently the view taken by the trial court.

We need not speculate upon whether plaintiff believed Mr. Graham, whom he says he thought was manager of the business, had the authority to enter into the kind of contract before us, for the testimony shows that, irrespective of who was its manager at Denton, it had for some time carried advertising matter in the local newspaper to the effect that the Company would look after all details and construct homes for those desiring to build. One especially of such advertisements reads: "Where The Home Begins, Build your home with the complete assistance of Temple Lumber Single Unit Building System. . . . . All the details of building are taken care of in one simple complete transaction. The Planning, Financing and Construction is carefully supervised from one office. . . . ."

The court found as a fact (and there is an abundance of evidence to support it) that the house was in fact erected by defendant, and that plaintiff had paid to defendant the entire original contract price —the contract was fully executed on both sides; the controversy here being over defective workmanship and materials. It would appear that in such circumstances, defendant would be estopped to plead and rely upon ultra vires, and at the same time receive and retain the direct benefits of the contract it seeks to avoid. Such contention does not appeal to our sense of justice and equity. Estoppel was pleaded by plaintiff; court found the facts as indicated, and concluded that defendant was estopped to rely upon its plea of ultra vires. In this we think he was correct.

Brinson et al. v. Mill Supply Co., Inc.
219 N.C. 499, 14 S.E. (2d) 505, (1941)

This was an action by W. T. Brinson, in behalf of himself and all other stockholders and creditors (plaintiffs) against the Mill Supply Company, Incorporated (defendant) asking the appointment of a receiver. A receiver was appointed and Laura J. Harvey, executrix of the estate of Mrs. Harriet L. Hyman, filed a claim. From a judgment rejecting the claim claimant appealed. Judgment affirmed.

On March 14, 1931, Albert F. Patterson borrowed from Harriet L. Hyman the sum of $5,000 evidenced by a note. The payment of the note was guaranteed by the Mill Supply Company. Patterson was president of the corporation and the contract of guaranty was executed in accordance with a resolution adopted by the executive committee of the corporation. The executive committee was vested with all the powers of the board of directors and any act of the committee taken between meetings of the board of directors was as binding on the corporation as though authorized by action of the board. At the time the receiver was appointed there was an unpaid balance due on the note of $2,318.97. A claim for this amount was filed with the receiver, the claim being based on the guaranty contract.

Barnhill, J. The contract of guaranty was no part of a transaction in which the corporation was borrowing or raising money for the purposes of its incorporation. It was clearly and exclusively an act in aid and for the accommodation of its president as an individual. From it the corporation received no benefit.

Hence, it appears that the undertaking of the corporation was not directly "necessary, suitable, convenient or proper for the accomplishment of" either of these or of any other purpose authorized by the charter.

Was the contract of guaranty incidental to or in furtherance of the powers expressly granted? If not, it was ultra vires and unenforceable.

A corporation is an artificial being, created by the State, for the attainment of certain defined purposes, and, therefore, vested with certain specific powers and others fairly and reasonably to be inferred or implied from the express powers and the object of the creation. Acts falling without that boundary are unwarranted—ultra vires.

"A corporation . . . . being the mere creature of law, ... possesses only those properties which the charter of its creation confers upon it, either expressly, or as incidental to its very existence." Marshall, C. J., in *Dartmouth College Case*, 4 Wheat. 518, 636, 4 L. Ed. 629. "An incidental power exists only for the purpose of enabling a corporation to carry out the purposes expressly granted to it—that is to say, the powers necessary to accomplish the purposes of its existence—and can in no case avail to enlarge the express powers and thereby warrant it to devote its efforts or capital to other purposes than such as its charter expressly authorizes, or to engage in collateral enterprises, not directly, but only remotely, connected with its specific corporate purposes."

Ordinarily, the power to endorse or guarantee the payment of negotiable instruments for the benefit of a third party is not within the implied powers conferred upon a private business corporation.

The general rule is that no corporation has the power, by any form of contract or endorsement, to become a guarantor or surety or otherwise lend its credit to another person or corporation.

In the absence of express statutory authorization, a corporation has no implied power to lend its credit to another by issuing or endorsing bills or notes for his accommodation, where the transaction is not related to the business activity authorized by its charter as a necessary or usual incident thereto.

A corporation is without implied power to guarantee for accommodation the contract of its customers with third persons on the ground that it may thus stimulate its own business. Such use of its credit is clearly beyond the power of an ordinary business corporation. It has no authority to use its credit for the benefit of a stockholder or officer.

A claim of the holder of promissory notes made by an officer of a corporation against the corporation as accommodation endorser thereon, which endorsement was authorized by the stockholders, is not provable against the corporation in subsequent bankruptcy proceedings.

Trustees of Charlotte Tp. v. *Piedmont Realty Co.*, 134 N.C. 41, 46 S.E. 723, and other cases to the same effect, holding that where the contract is executed by the other party to the contract and the corporation has received the benefit thereof it is estopped from setting up the defense that it was ultra vires, are not in point.

The question here presented is not whether there was sufficient consideration to support the note. The question is, Was there sufficient consideration moving to the corporation to support the contract of guaranty? The liability of the individual upon the note (which was not signed by the corporation) is not contested. It is the liability of the corporation which is at issue. Hence, the rule that where the corporation has received the benefits under a contract which is not incidental, it will be held liable under the doctrine of estoppel, for the reason that it should not be permitted to accept and retain the benefits and at the same time disavow the contract on the plea of ultra vires, has no application. It is when the corporation has received the full benefit of the contract that it will not be relieved of liability because the contract was ultra vires.

The contract of guaranty was executed for the benefit of an individual. No part of the consideration moved to the defendant corporation. It was not either expressly or impliedly authorized by its charter to enter into contracts for the accommodation of a third party. To permit the payment of the claim would clearly result in an invasion of the assets of the defendant corporation in the hands of the receiver as a trust fund for the payment of legitimate creditors. The defendant's plea of ultra vires must be sustained.

Torts and Crimes

Under the early conception of the powers of a corporation—that it could not do acts not authorized by its charter—it was thought that by the nature of things a corporation could not commit a tort or a crime. The present view is that a corporation is a principal, and that it is liable for the torts of its employees and agents to the same extent and in the same respect that a natural person acting as principal would be liable for the torts of his employees and agents.

As to a corporation's liability for crime, a similar rule applies. Clearly, a corporation cannot commit a crime which requires criminal intent, and a corporation cannot be punished by imprisonment, but a corporation is criminally responsible for public nuisances and for the violation of police regulations, and a corporation may be made criminally liable by the express provisions of statutes. As a punishment, the corporation may be fined or its charter may be canceled.

Vowles v. Yakish et al.

191 Ia. 396, 179 N.W. 117, 13 A.L.R. 1132 (1920)

This was an action by Vowles (plaintiff) against Yakish and Security Fire Insurance Company (defendants). Judgment for plaintiff and defendants appealed. Judgment reversed.

Plaintiff owned a grocery store which was insured against fire with the defendant insurance company. The whole was totally destroyed by fire. A dispute arose over the amount of the loss suffered. Yakish was state agent of the insurance company and carried on negotiations with plaintiff for the adjustment of the disputed amounts. During the course of the negotiations the plaintiff met Yakish in a bank in Cedar Rapids and while discussing the disputed items, Yakish, in the presence of others, accused Vowles of having burned his store so that he could collect the insurance and also threatened to have him arrested for arson. Yakish said, "I will make you go some. I have the goods on you for burning it up." Vowles sued to recover damages for slander and recovered a judgment of $5,000 against both defendants. On appeal by a three to two decision the court held that the slanderous words were not uttered in the course of and within the scope of the agent's employment.

Stevens, J. It is not claimed by counsel that a corporation is never liable for damages on account of slanderous utterances of its agent, but that liability is imposed only when the slander charged was uttered by the agent within the scope of his authority, express or implied. This question has been frequently discussed and passed upon by the courts of other jurisdictions, but with considerable diversity of holding. While a few courts and text-writers have announced the doctrine that a corporation is never liable for slanderous words uttered by its agent, the overwhelming weight of authority is to the contrary. The majority rule seems to be that, if the agent, acting within the scope of his employment and in the actual performance of the duties thereof, touching the matter in question, utter a slander, though without the knowledge of the corporation or with its approval, liability attaches.

Management

The management of the business of the corporation is vested in a board of directors, or as it is sometimes called, the board of trustees. In some respects they are the agents of the corporation while in other respects they function as principals. Their position in respect to the operation of the corporate business is, in many respects, analogous to that of the members of a partnership. They have implied authority to authorize any act or contract which falls properly within the scope of the ordinary business of the corporation. They cannot make any fundamental changes in the organization of the corporation; that is, they cannot amend the articles of incorporation or make any changes which would result in violating a provision of the articles of incorporation, and if the stockholders have retained the power to make and amend the by-laws, the directors cannot authorize contracts or acts which are contrary to the by-laws.

Johnson v. Radio Station WOW, Inc.
144 Neb. 406, 13 N.W. (2d) 556 (1944)

This was an action by Homer H. Johnson, on behalf of himself and all other members of the Woodmen of the World Life Insurance Society (plaintiff) against Radio Station WOW, Inc., and others (defendants). Judgment for defendants and plaintiff appealed. Judgment reversed with directions.

The Woodmen of the World Life Insurance Society owned and operated radio station WOW. The board of directors leased the station to defendant for a period of 15 years. The plaintiffs brought this action to have the lease cancelled and set aside.

Wenke, J. Section 3 of the Constitution, Laws and By-Laws as amended in 1941 provides: "The objects of this Society shall be . . . . own, maintain and operate radio broadcasting stations. . . . ." While it is true, as stated in 2 Fletcher, Cyclopedia Corporations (Perm. Ed.) 399, § 511: ". . . . the directors of a corporation have no authority to make or authorize contracts or do other acts which are beyond the powers conferred upon the corporation by its charter." However, tested by the provisions of the statute, the Articles of Incorporation and the Constitution, Laws and By-Laws of the Society, we determine that the board of directors had the power and authority to enter into and authorize the execution of the 15-year lease of its radio station.

The next question is, should a court of equity modify the lease? After the conclusion of the trial the plaintiff moved to amend the prayer of his petition by including therein conditions for modification of the lease. The prayer of plaintiff's petition includes the following: ". . . . and for such other, further and different relief as equity and justice may require." If we were inclined to consider the question of modification this part of the prayer would be broad enough to permit us to do so. However, as stated in 19 C.J.S., Corporations, p. 83, § 743: "Within the limits of their authority directors or trustees possess full discretionary power, and in the honest and reasonable exercise of such power they are not subject to control by the stockholders or by the courts at the instance of a stockholder, ... in the absence of usurpation, of fraud, or of gross negligence, courts of equity will not interfere at the suit of a dissatisfied minority of stockholders, merely to overrule and control the discretion of the directors on questions of corporate management, policy, or business." And as stated in *Royal Highlanders* v. *Wiseman*, 140 Neb. 28, 299 N.W. 459, 460: "The accepted principle is that the wisdom and expediency of corporate business policies and the methods of executing them are left to the discretion and decision of the board of directors. In the absence of usurpation, or fraud, or gross negligence, or transgression of statutory limitations, courts of equity will not interfere at the suit of dissatisfied stockholders merely to overrule the discretion of directors on questions of corporate management, policy or business." Therefore, in the absence of usurpation, fraud, gross negligence or transgression of statutory limitations this court will not interfere with the discretionary powers of directors on questions of corporate management, policy or business.

Directors

Directors are elected by the stockholders and, as a general rule, the board must be composed of at least three directors. In some states the directors must be stockholders; however, this is not a requirement in all states. The term of office of the directors may be stated in the articles of incorporation or in the by-laws, but a director will continue in office until his successor is elected. A director may resign before the expiration of his term. In the event of a vacancy in the board of directors, as a general rule, the remaining directors may fill the vacancy until a successor is elected by the stockholders. The successor may be elected at the next annual meeting or at a special meeting duly called for that purpose.

In the larger corporations the directors are compensated; however, in many small corporations no separate compensation is paid to them, especially if the directors are actively engaged in the conduct of the business. As a matter of law the officers and directors are not entitled to compensation for performing the ordinary duties of their offices.

In order that a director may legally demand compensation for services as a director, it must appear that a by-law or resolution, fixing the compensation to be paid, was adopted before the services were rendered. If an officer or director performs services as an employee or acts as a ministerial officer of the corporation, such as manager, superintendent, etc., he will be entitled to compensation. Under the laws of some states the compensation of the directors is fixed by a vote of the stockholders. As a general rule, the directors cannot fix their own salaries unless expressly authorized by the charter or by the stockholders to do so.

A director may be removed for cause before the expiration of his term by vote of the stockholders. It has been held, on the theory that a director is an agent of the corporation, that a director may be arbitrarily removed by unanimous vote of the stockholders; however, if such a removal results in breach of contract between the director and the corporation, the corporation will have to answer in damages. As a general rule, the directors cannot remove a fellow-director, but this power may be conferred on them.

Directors' Meetings

It has generally been held that the directors must act as a board, and that action taken by polling the members of the board without a board meeting will not bind the corporation. This rule has not been followed strictly. In theory, board action is required as a protection of the interests of the stockholders. If the stockholders do not object to action taken by the directors without their having met as a board, they will be held by such action. In small corporations in which all the stock is held by the directors or by one or two persons, formalities are frequently dispensed with—a practice which it is not advisable to follow.

The general corporation laws of the state usually provide that meetings of the board of directors shall be held but make no further provision for such meetings. The statutes commonly provide that the meetings may be held at such time and place and upon such notice as may be provided in the articles of incorporation or in the by-laws, or they may provide that the meetings shall be held at such place as the majority of the directors may appoint. Under the provisions of present-day statutes it is not, as a general rule, necessary to hold the directors' meetings within the state of incorporation.

Meetings of the board of directors will ordinarily be held at short intervals—once each month or every two weeks—and if a time or place is stated in the articles of incorporation or in the by-laws or has been established by custom, it will not be necessary to give notice of such meetings; however, it is necessary to give notice of special meetings unless notice is waived by the members of the board. The notice must be given a reasonable time before the date of the meeting and must state the purpose of the meeting. The number of directors will, in almost all instances, be relatively small; consequently, a meeting of the directors may be called with less formality than would ordinarily be required in the calling of a stockholders' meeting. If all the directors are present and participate, without objection, in the business transacted, the action of the directors cannot be attacked later because of lack of or irregularity in the giving of notice of the meeting. It has been held that failure to give notice to directors who live outside the state and who could not attend the meeting, if notice had been given, does not render invalid action taken at such meeting.

A majority of the directors, qualified to vote on the matters before the board, usually constitute a quorum and the directors must be present in person—a director cannot act by proxy.

The president of the board presides at the meeting of the board and the secretary keeps minutes of the meetings. A permanent record of the minutes should be kept and the minutes should show the time and place of the meeting, the number of directors present, the resolutions passed, and such other matters of importance which were considered by the members of the board.

Lycette v. Green River Gorge, Inc., et al.
Trethewey et ux. v. Same.
21 Wn. (2d) 859, 153 P. (2d) 873 (1944)

This was an action by John P. Lycette (plaintiff) against Green River Gorge, Inc., and others (defendants) to foreclose a mortgage, which was consolidated with an action of W. J. Trethewey and his wife (plaintiffs) against Green River Gorge, Inc., and others (defendants) to set aside the mortgage and an easement. Decree for plaintiff in first action and defendants appealed. Decree for defendants in second action and plaintiffs appealed. Decree reversed and remanded with directions in each instance.

Green River Gorge, Inc., is a domestic corporation operating a resort. Elmer P. Campbell and wife owned seventy-five per cent of the stock and W. J. Trethewey and wife owned twenty-five per cent of the stock. Mr. Campbell was president of the corporation, Mrs. Campbell was vice-president, Mrs. Trethewey was treasurer, and Mrs. Campbell, Mrs. Trethewey, and Mr. Lycette, an attorney who owned no stock, were the directors of the corporation. For seventeen years the Tretheweys had operated the resort owned by the corporation.

On March 31, 1943, the Tretheweys brought suit against the corporation to recover wages due for services rendered and recovered a judgment of $10,373.52. At the time the suit was brought Campbell employed Lycette to defend the corporation. Also a note signed in the name of the corporation payable to Lycette for the amount of his fees, $1,250, secured by a mortgage on the real estate of the corporation was signed and issued to Lycette. Mrs. Trethewey was not present at the meeting of the board of directors at which this action was taken. The meeting was a special meeting and no notice of the meeting was given and no records or minutes were kept. The Tretheweys claim that the business transacted at this meeting does not bind the corporation.

Millard, J. The president (E. B. Campbell) of respondent corporation retained counsel (Mr. Lycette) to defend an action brought by two creditors (Tretheweys), who were also minority stockholders of the corporation, to recover back salary for an amount in excess of all of the assets of the corporation. The president was the managing officer of the corporation and as such had authority to employ counsel without any express delegation of power to do so. Having accepted the services rendered by counsel retained by its president, the corporation is obligated to pay the reasonable value of such services. It does not follow, however, that whether they acted in good or bad faith in so doing, two of the corporation's three directors, Mr. Campbell and Mr. Lycette were authorized to encumber or dispose of all of the corporate property to secure payment of Mr. Lycette's fee. Whatever the motives of the two directors the mortgaging of all of the corporation's property was constructively fraudulent and void.

Only two directors, Mr. Campbell, who was also a stockholder, and Mr. Lycette, who was not a stockholder, were present at the office of one of the directors at the time of the execution of the mortgage and note. Mrs. Campbell, a stockholder, was present. Mrs. Trethewey, who is a director and stockholder of the corporation, and her husband who is a stockholder were not afforded an opportunity to object to dissipation of the assets of the corporation by Mr. Lycette and the Campbells.

No meeting of the board of directors was called or held. Mrs. Trethewey was one of the directors of the corporation, therefore she was entitled to notice of meeting of the board. The other two directors (Mr. Campbell and Mr. Lycette), as stated above, acted informally and no record was made of their action other than the execution of the instruments mentioned. A meeting of a board of directors of a corporation is not legally constituted without notice to all of the directors.

The excuse urged by respondents, for failure to give notice to Mrs. Trethewey of the meeting, that the giving of the notice would have been fruitless and would have prevented carrying out of the business that Mr. Lycette and Mr. Campbell intended is without merit. The fact that a director might dissent from the action of the board cannot be successfully urged in excuse of deprivation of his legal right to know what action is being taken so that he may proceed in a manner which he deems proper respecting it. He is entitled to be present and make himself heard.

Mr. Lycette and Mr. Campbell never met as a board of directors and acted as a board to authorize the execution of the mortgage and easement. The great weight of authority is to the effect that notice of a special meeting—in the case at bar there was not a regular nor was there a special meeting of the directors as a board—must be given to each director unless there is some express provision in the charter or by-laws, or established usage to the contrary, or unless it is impossible or impractical to do so. Except in those cases, even a special meeting held in the absence of some of the directors, and without any notice to them, is illegal and the action at such a meeting, although by a majority of the directors is invalid unless subsequently ratified (there was no ratification) or unless rights have been acquired by innocent third persons (no innocent third persons in the case at bar) as against whom the corporation must be held estopped, and their full knowledge of the time, place, and fact of such meeting will not do away with this requirement.

Authority of Officers and Agents

The board of directors cannot carry on the day-to-day business of the corporation by board action but must delegate the authority to transact that business to officers and agents of the corporation. The by-laws usually provide for certain officers and, as a general rule, define in general terms their powers. The board of directors must determine the general policies of the corporation and they cannot delegate this duty to the officers and agents of the corporation. They may, however, delegate to them the power to do any act which is necessary and proper in the carrying on of the corporate business even though the act may require the officer or agent to exercise his independent judgment.

Like the agents of a natural person, the officers and agents of a corporation have only the authority which has been conferred on them by their principal. In the case of a corporation the authority is conferred by the by-laws or the board of directors. The officers and agents of the corporation may bind their corporate principal in the same manner and to the same extent as the agent of an individual may bind his principal under like circumstances. The corporate officer or agent may bind his principal by any act which is within his express, implied, or apparent power.

Although there is some authority to the contrary, the majority of the courts hold that the mere fact that a person is an officer of a corporation does not imply that he has any power to bind the corporation in any particular type of transaction. A director of a corporation, by virtue of the fact that he is a director, has no power individually to bind the corporation by any transaction. Also, the officers have only the powers conferred on them by the by-laws or by the directors and, unless they are clothed with apparent authority, all persons dealing with them are bound to ascertain their authority.

Established business usage may confer implied or apparent authority on an officer of a corporation. Although the by-laws or directors may confer as little or as much authority on an officer as they wish, unless the limitations or the powers of the officer are known to the third person, he will be justified in assuming that the officer has those powers which are commonly conferred on like officers of corporations operating similar business in the locality. The corporation cannot escape liability by placing secret limitations on the authority of its agents. A person dealing with the officers of the corporation is chargeable with notice of limitations imposed upon the authority of corporate officers by the articles of incorporation or statutes, but he is not chargeable with notice of limitations imposed upon the officers by the by-laws which are not known to him. A corporation may ratify the unauthorized acts of its officers and agents.

The compensation of officers and agents, who are not directors of the corporation, may be fixed by the board of directors, but if the officers and agents are also directors, the better rule is that their compensation must be fixed by stockholder action or have stockholder approval. Officers and agents performing general services for the corporation, in the absence of a contract for compensation, are entitled to the reasonable value of the services rendered.

Stevens Davis Co. v. Sid's Petroleum Corporation.
St. Louis Ct. of App. Mo., 157 S.W. (2d) 246 (1942)

This was an action by the Stevens Davis Company (plaintiff) against Sid's Petroleum Corporation (defendant). Judgment for plaintiff and defendant appealed. Judgment reversed.

The stock of the defendant was owned by Fred Dubinsky and his two sons, Irven and Sidney. Fred was president of the corporation and had sole charge of its business. Irven was vice-president and Sidney was secretary-treasurer. The defendant supplied gasoline to service stations. Irven operated, for his own account, a retail service station at DeBaliviere and Waterman streets in St. Louis. Irven signed a contract with the plaintiff and in the name of the defendant corporation for "Service Station Builder" for 78 weeks which was a sales promotion plan consisting of weekly bulletins and other services. Fred Dubinsky refused to accept the material when it was tendered. When sued the defendant set up as a defense that Irven had no authority to bind the defendant on the contract.

Sutton, C. As a general rule the president of a corporation, merely by virtue of his office, has no greater power than a director other than the power to preside at meetings of directors and of stockholders. Whatever additional authority he possesses is conferred by statute, charter, by-law, or the board of directors, or is implied from an express grant, usage, custom, or the nature of the business of the corporation. The authority of directors to bind the corporation belongs to them collectively and not individually. The mere fact that a person is a director gives him no authority to act individually for the corporation as its agent, even though he owns or controls a majority of the stock. Authority to so act may be specifically conferred on him, but does not exist unless it is so conferred. Usually the vice-president of an ordinary corporation has little or nothing to do with the conduct of its business, except in case of the absence, disability, or death of the president, when, usually, he may act in his stead, presiding at the meetings of the board of directors and performing the other functions of the office. He has only such authority to represent or bind the corporation as has been properly conferred upon him. However, if he acts as the agent of the corporation, and is by it so recognized and treated, or held out to the world, his acts within the scope of the authority given to him are binding on the corporation, and where he acts as president and general manager his powers are accordingly enlarged, but even as acting president and general manager he is without power to do anything unusual or extraordinary. It is well settled that, when, in the usual course of the business of a corporation, the president has been allowed to manage its affairs, his authority to represent the corporation may be implied from the manner in which he has been permitted by its directors to transact its business. The powers habitually exercised by him, with its knowledge and acquiescence, defines and establishes as to the public, those powers, provided that they be such as the directors may, without violation of its charter, confer on him. In other words, he may, without any special authority from the directors, perform all acts of an ordinary nature which by usage or necessity are incident to his office, and may bind the corporation by contracts in matters arising in the usual course of business. The corporation cannot clothe him with apparent authority, and, as to third persons, object to the exercise of such authority. But agency cannot be established by proof of acts, declarations, and conduct of the alleged agent, unless such acts, declarations, and conduct are known to the principal, or are so often repeated that knowledge on the part of the principal is implied.

Liability of Directors, Officers, and Agents

The directors are the managing agents of the business. They must acquaint themselves with the business of the corporation, its by-laws, and its charter so that they are capable of directing its policies in a reasonably skillful manner. The directors are not responsible for honest errors in judgment or the shortcomings of agents appointed by them if they exercised reasonable care in selecting the agents. They are liable for injury resulting from their neglect of duty or their negligence in the performance of their duty. Whether or not they have exercised reasonable care and skill must be determined from the facts of the individual case.

However, if the directors knowingly and intentionally enter into an ultra vires transaction and the corporation suffers a loss, the directors will be personally liable to the corporation for the loss. As managing agents of the corporation they owe a duty to keep within their authority and the scope of their authority is the scope of the corporate business as set out in the articles of incorporation. If the directors honestly believe that the transaction is within the powers of the corporation and they are justified in that belief, they will not be held personally liable. Also, if their acts are ratified by the stockholders, they will be relieved of personal liability to the corporation. In some instances they may be liable to creditors if their acts have resulted in injury to the creditors of the corporation. The general corporation statutes impose personal liability on the directors in some situations.

If a director has a personal interest in a contract or transaction which is being negotiated in behalf of the corporation, his personal interest will disqualify him.

As a general rule, he must not act as a director when the proposed contract is being considered by the board of directors and he cannot be counted to make a quorum. If he does take a part as a member of the board, and especially if his is the deciding vote, the contract is voidable at the election of the corporation. Such a transaction would be, in fact, a situation in which the director would be acting for both parties to the transaction and would be evidence of bad faith.

The majority rule is that if the director takes no part in the board's consideration of the contract and the contract is fair, it will be held to bind the corporation. Under these circumstances, each party is adequately represented, and in the absence of evidence of unfair dealing there is no objection to the contract.

The liability of the officers and agents of the corporation is no different than that of any agent both in respect to their liability to the corporation and to third persons.

Spiegel v. Beacon Participations, Inc., et al.
297 Mass. 398, 8 N.E. (2d) 895 (1937)

This was an action by Edward Spiegel (plaintiff) against Beacon Participations, Incorporated, and others (defendants). The defendants appealed from certain orders and decrees and the plaintiff appealed as to other portions of the decree. The final decree of the trial court was reversed and the case was sent back for further proceedings.

This suit was brought by the plaintiff, a stockholder in defendant corporation, in behalf of the corporation and other stockholders, against the present and former directors of the defendant. The defendant was organized to buy, sell, and deal generally in stocks, bonds, and securities. The defendant was organized by the active directors of the Beacon Trust Company. The plaintiff claims that the directors of the defendant, on June 4, 1928, caused the defendant to buy from Beacon Trust Company a note for the price of its face value, $520,000, the maker of which was Beacon Building Trust, Inc. (an affiliate of Beacon Trust Co.) and which was payable to Beacon Trust Co. and indorsed by it without recourse. At the time the note was purchased it was of no value, a fact which was known to the directors. The plaintiff sets out other transactions authorized by the directors wherein defendant suffered losses which the plaintiff claims could have been avoided by the exercise of reasonable care and judgment.

Rugg, C. J. The standard of duty established by the law for directors of a corporation such as the defendant is settled. The defendant was a business corporation organized for the purpose of trading in stocks, bonds, and securities. It involved none of the special incidents attaching to banking corporations. The directors of an ordinary business corporation often have been called trustees and their relation to the corporation is at least fiduciary. They are bound to act with absolute fidelity and must place their duties to the corporation above every other financial or business obligation. They must act, also, with reasonable intelligence, although they cannot be held responsible for mere errors of judgment or want of prudence. They cannot be permitted to serve two masters whose interests are antagonistic. They are liable if, through their bad faith, financial loss to the corporation results. They are responsible if they unlawfully divert the assets of the corporation. If directors, acting in good faith, nevertheless act imprudently, they cannot ordinarily be held to personal responsibility for loss unless there is "clear and gross negligence" in their conduct.

An individual director cannot be held liable except for the results of his own misconduct. He is not responsible for the consequences of the wrongful conduct of other directors in which he did not participate.

Simon v. Socony-Vacuum Oil Co., Inc., et al.
38 N.Y.S. (2d) 270 (1942)

This was an action by Carl N. Simon, in behalf of stockholders (plaintiff) against Socony-Vacuum Oil Company, Incorporated, and others (defendants). Judgment for defendants.

Defendant corporation entered into a buying program agreement with other large oil companies whereby the companies purchased "distress" gasoline from small refiners in the Mid-Western areas and thereby prevented such gasoline from being sold at forced sale and thus depressing the market.

These transactions were made the basis of an indictment charging an unlawful combination and conspiracy in restraint of trade and commerce by raising and fixing the prices for gasoline in violation of the Sherman Anti-Trust Act.

Upon the trial, defendants were convicted by a jury. The conviction was reversed by the Circuit Court of Appeals for alleged errors in instructions to the jury. The United States Supreme Court, by a divided court, reinstated the verdict. As a result of the conviction the corporation was fined. This action was brought to charge the directors personally with the loss which the corporation suffered as a result of having entered into the illegal transaction.

Benvenga, J. That the defendant corporation participated in the unlawful buying program is not disputed. Nor is it questioned that defendants, as directors, participated therein in behalf of the corporation. But it is asserted that, in so doing, defendants did not violate any duty which they owed the corporation; that they acted honestly and reasonably and for what they believed to be the best interests of the company. The evidence supports this conclusion. It does not show that defendants acted fraudulently, negligently, corruptly or in bad faith. Nor does it show that they knew, or had reason to believe, that the buying program violated the Sherman Act. Neither does it show that they made any personal profit or gained any personal advantage at the expense of the corporation or otherwise. Accordingly, defendants are entitled to the presumption or inference that their actions were fair and honest.

The question here presented is whether, under the circumstances, the defendants should be held personally liable to the corporation for damages resulting from participation in the buying program.

It is elementary that directors owe a corporation the duty to exercise reasonable care in managing its affairs; that is, the same degree of care which a business man of ordinary prudence generally exercises in the management of his own affairs. If the directors fail to use such care, they are liable to the corporation for damages. However, if the directors act in good faith and exercise reasonable care in the performance of their duties, they are not liable for mistakes or errors of judgment, either of law or of fact. "It is too well settled to admit of controversy that ordinarily neither the directors nor the other officers of a corporation are liable for mere mistake or errors of judgment, either of law or fact, when they act without corrupt motive and in good faith." 3 Fletcher Cyclopedia Corporation, Perm. Ed., § 1039. "Where directors act honestly, and for what they regard as the best interests of the corporation and do not wilfully pervert or exceed their powers but only misjudge the same, on the plainest principles of justice, as well as under the adjudicated cases, they cannot be held liable." 2 Thompson, Corporations, 3d Ed., § 1404.

Applying these principles, it would seem that defendants did not fail in their duty of reasonable care. At most, they made an honest and reasonable mistake or error of judgment or of law.

But it is argued that defendants are liable because they committed acts prohibited by statute; that when the defendants, as directors, participated in the buying program in behalf of the defendant company, they failed in their duty to the corporation, even though they acted in good faith and with reasonable care.

The rule for which plaintiff contends is too broadly stated. Whether directors are personally liable for committing acts prohibited by statute depends upon the nature of the prohibited act; whether the statute is plain and unambiguous, and whether it contains a limitation or restriction on the powers of the corporation or the powers or duties of the directors themselves. Moreover, the rule is the same whether the act is ultra vires or prohibited by statute.

Nor do the cases upon which plaintiff relies lay down the rule for which plaintiff contends. They merely hold that directors are liable for losses sustained by the corporation on an illegal loan or investment, if they participated in the transactions or were negligent in permitting them. Thus, in the *Broderick* v. *Marcus* case, the statute prohibited loans in excess of ten per cent of the capital and surplus of the bank. The statute is plain and unambiguous. It clearly lays down the rule governing the duty of directors in respect of loans. Therefore, when the directors made or participated in the making of the prohibited loans, there was no error or mistake of judgment, or any error or mistake of law or fact. On the contrary, in making the loans, the directors must have done so "with the knowledge of the extent and limitations of the powers of the corporations for which they act, and of their own authority as the agents of these corporations." In short, the directors must have known when they made the loans that they were ultra vires and illegal. Obviously, no such knowledge can be imputed to the defendants when they, in behalf of the defendant corporation, entered into the buying programs which were later held to be in violation of law.

The decisions upon which plaintiff relies are in accordance with the general rule laid down by Fletcher: "If the liability of a corporate officer is based on the alleged fact that he has acted beyond his powers or beyond the powers of the corporation, or in violation of a statute or the charter or by-laws, the test of reasonable care which applies when he acts within his powers has nothing to do with the question of liability except in so far as such care bears on whether he should have known that the acts in question were ultra vires or expressly forbidden or beyond his powers. If he knowingly exceed his authority or the authority of the corporation, he is liable without regard to exercise of reasonable care." 3 Fletcher, supra, § 1023.

Duffy v. Omaha Merchants' Express & Transfer Co.
127 Neb. 273, 255 N.W. 1 (1934)

This was an action by Arthur W. Duffy and others (plaintiffs) against the Omaha Merchants' Express and Transfer Co. and others (defendants). Judgment for defendants and plaintiffs appealed. Judgment affirmed in part and reversed in part and cause remanded with directions.

Johnson, Baker, and Condit were the directors and controlling stockholders of the corporation. They used funds of the corporation to discharge their own individual indebtednesses and then sold to the corporation 40 shares of stock for $15,000, deducting from the purchase price their indebtedness to the corporation and issuing to themselves corporate notes for the balance of the purchase price. The stock had no market value. Its book value was eighty cents on a dollar.

Hastings, D. J. The directors of a corporation are the trustees of the corporate property for the corporation and the stockholders, and as such are charged with the highest degree of responsibility in dealing with the corporation in their own behalf. The accountability of the defendants, as managing officers and directors, is to be determined by the strict standards of rectitude that bind a fiduciary.

The defendants, as officers of the corporation, had no lawful right or authority to take the property of the corporation to settle their own private indebtedness. In doing so they betrayed the trust imposed upon them as officers and directors. In the instant case all the directors, except one, and the managing officers of the corporation, were interested in the transaction. In the sale of the stock the defendant stockholders, acting for themselves, fixed the price they were to be paid for the stock and the terms of payment, then, as directors and managing officers of the corporation, approved and consummated the sale. The sale under such circumstances is, at least, voidable.

In 4 Fletcher, Cyclopedia Corporations, 3588, § 2339, it is said: "One of the reasons for holding this class of transactions to be voidable is that a person cannot, as a director or other officer of a corporation, enter into a valid contract on behalf of the corporation with himself in his individual capacity, or be both vendor and purchaser, since two persons are a necessary element in the formation of a contract. The fact that he acts as an officer of the corporation on one side, and for himself on the other, can make no difference.

"No principle in the law of corporations, therefore, is founded on sounder reasons, or more surely settled, than the principle that the directors, trustees or other officers of a corporation, who are entrusted with its interests, and who occupy a fiduciary relation towards it, will not be allowed to contract with the corporation. directly or indirectly or to sell property to it, or purchase property from it, where they act both for the corporation and for themselves. In such a case, the transaction is, at least, voidable at the option of the corporation, and it may be avoided and set aside, or affirmed and any profits recovered, without proof of actual fraud, or of actual injury to the corporation. Generally, this rule is applied in case of directors but it is equally applicable to other officers."

At the time of the sale of the stock to the corporation it had approximately $8,700 of cash on hand and was not in debt. The effect of the sale of the stock was to absorb the greater part of its cash and to leave it indebted to the defendant stockholders in the sum of $4,500. Owing to the financial depression then existing and the credit stringency, the money in its treasury was needed to successfully carry on and conduct its business, and was essential to the enjoyment and realization of the full value of its other property. The effect of the transaction was to postpone payment of dividends and to impair the value of the remainder of the property. The evidence is convincing that the transaction complained of was injurious and prejudicial to the corporation and the minority stockholders. It is manifest that the entire transaction was conceived and manipulated by the defendant stockholders, as the sole officers of the corporation, for their own benefit. They sought profit at the expense of other nonparticipating stockholders, and in so doing were unfaithful to the relation they had assumed, and were guilty, at least, of constructive fraud. The sale of the stock to the corporation cannot be upheld as a valid sale, and should have been set aside by the trial court and the parties restored to their former position as nearly as possible.

QUESTIONS AND PROBLEMS

1. The Radiator Co. entered into an agreement with Harris to buy from him a certain amount of its own stock. Before the contract was performed, a receiver was appointed for the corporation. Harris filed a claim with the receiver for damages based upon the corporation's failure to fulfill the contract. Should Harris' claim be allowed?
2. The People's Bank, a banking corporation, pledged part of its assets as security for a loan. The bank became insolvent and ceased doing business, and a receiver was appointed. The receiver brought an action to recover the pledged assets without paying the debts secured thereby. The receiver claimed that the corporation had no power to pledge its assets as security for a loan. Did the corporation have this power?
3. The Todd & Stanley Co. was a corporation operating a foundry; Todd Pulley Works was a corporation engaged in a similar business; and both corporations had common stockholders and officers. The Todd Pulley Works purchased belting from the Jewell Belting Co., and Todd & Stanley Co. signed the notes given in payment for the belting as surety. Todd & Stanley Co. made a voluntary assignment for the benefit of creditors. Jewell Belting Co. filed a claim for the amount of the notes which had been given by Todd Pulley Works and which were overdue and unpaid. A creditor of Todd & Stanley Co. objected to the allowance of the claim on the ground that the surety contract was ultra vires. Should the claim be allowed?
4. Bowman Dairy Co., a corporation, was organized to "buy and sell dairy products, especially milk, butter, cheese, and ice cream." It purchased a wholesale and retail oyster business. It entered into a written contract with Mooney, employing him to drive an oyster wagon for two years and binding Mooney not to sell oysters in competition with Bowman Dairy Co. after the termination of the employment. Mooney worked two days, quit and started selling oysters on his own account

to Bowman Dairy Co.'s customers. Bowman Dairy Co. brought an action asking an injunction against Mooney. Mooney sets up that the contract was ultra vires and unenforceable. Is Mooney's contention correct?

5. Russell, the store manager for J. J. Newberry Co., a corporation, accused Mrs. Judd of stealing a pair of gloves and caused her to be detained four or five hours. The court found that Russell's acts were sufficient to make out a case of "false imprisonment." Mrs. Judd sued J. J. Newberry Co. to recover damages. Is the corporation liable for the tort of Russell?
6. Mrs. Orloff was a director and secretary of the board of directors of the Stott Realty Co., a corporation. The board of directors, by vote of the majority, contracted to build an office building on land owned by the corporation. To accomplish this it was necessary to give a mortgage on the building. Mrs. Orloff refused to sign the necessary papers. The signature of the secretary of the corporation was essential to the validity of the transaction. The board of directors removed Mrs. Orloff as secretary. Suit was brought to enjoin the action of the board. Did the board have the power to remove Mrs. Orloff as secretary?
7. The city of Springfield owned stock in a corporation. Wight, the mayor of the city, was authorized to represent the city and vote the stock at stockholders' meetings. Wight was elected a director but the other directors refused to recognize him as such, claiming that he was not a stockholder and therefore could not act as a director. The general corporation statute did not expressly provide that the directors must be stockholders. Can Wight be a director of the corporation?
8. The Compress Co. was incorporated by Lake, Alphin, Smith, and Walker. Walker was named in the articles of incorporation as a director but he was named as a stockholder and director only for the purpose of completing the organization. At a directors' meeting, at which Walker was not present and of which he had no knowledge or notice, the three directors present voted to mortgage the assets of the corporation. It is contended that the mortgage given pursuant to this action is void because Walker was not given notice of the meeting. Is this contention correct?
9. Gass and three other directors voted to convey certain real estate to Gass on the performance of certain acts by him. Three directors were less than a quorum. The corporation brought an action to have the deeds canceled. Should the deeds be canceled?
10. The charter of the National Car Coupler Co. was about to expire, and the corporation was about to wind up its business. Nowak, a director of the corporation, purchased all its assets, paying fair value for them. Suit to set the sale aside was brought on the ground that a sale to a director is void. Is this contention correct?
11. Abercrombie and others were members of the investment committee of a savings bank. They made loans to individuals and corporations in excess of the limit imposed by statute, and losses were incurred as a result of these loans. The bank sued the members of the committee to recover the losses. Can it recover?

CHAPTER XXXVII

STOCK AND TRANSFER OF STOCK

Share of Stock, Capital Stock, etc.

The owners of a corporation are the stockholders or shareholders; these terms are synonymous. The articles of incorporation state the kinds of stock and the number of shares of stock of each kind which the corporation is authorized to issue or the method whereby the kind and number of shares of stock to be issued shall be determined. When one purchases a share of stock, he does not acquire a property interest in the assets of the corporation; that is, the stockholders are not owners of the corporate assets as tenants in common but they acquire intangible property or legal rights. The rights acquired are determined by the terms of the contract between the corporation and the stockholders. This contract is not a formal contract but consists of the provisions of the state statute, if any, the provisions of the articles of incorporation, and, in some instances, the by-laws of the corporation. Usually the rights which the stockholder acquires when he purchases a share of stock will be printed on the face of the stock certificate which is issued to him.

Unfortunately certain terms are used to express different meanings, and one must determine from the content of the writing in which the term is used the meaning the author has attributed to the term. A share of stock is intangible and is not capable of manual delivery. It is a right to participate in the corporate business. A certificate of stock is a certificate issued by the corporation under the seal of the corporation and signed by the authorized officers and shows that the person named therein is the owner of the number of shares therein specified. It is not the "shares of stock" but is the evidence of the ownership of the stated number of "shares of stock."

The "capital stock" of the corporation when used in its technical meaning signifies the amount paid in or secured to be paid in by the stockholders of the corporation, either in money, property, or services. A distinction should be made between "authorized capital stock," "issued stock," and "treasury stock." The "authorized capital stock" is the amount of stock which the corporation is authorized, by its articles of incorporation, to issue. The "issued stock" of a corporation is the amount of stock actually issued to the stockholders of the corporation and is the "capital stock" of the corporation. The Archer Corporation may, by its articles of incorporation, be authorized to issue 100,000 shares of $100 par value common stock but only 10,000 shares may be actually issued. The Archer Corporation would have $1,000,000 of stock authorized but only $100,000 of stock issued. It would have $900,000 of unissued stock. "Treasury stock" is stock which has been issued and later acquired by the corporation and not cancelled. It is dormant in that the corporation cannot vote the stock at stockholders' meetings or claim other similar rights as holders of the stock. The corporation can sell the stock in the same manner as any stockholder can sell his stock.

Frequently the "capital stock," the "authorized capital stock," and the "capital" of a corporation are confused. The "capital" of a corporation is the net worth of the corporation. The "capital" varies from day to day. As stated above, the "capital stock" represents the value paid in by the stockholders. The "authorized capital stock" is the maximum amount of stock the corporation is authorized to issue under the provisions of its articles of incorporation. A corporation having a "capital" of $126,532 might have "capital stock" outstanding of the par value of $100,000 and might have "authorized capital stock" of $1,000,000.

United States Radiator Corporation v. State
208 N.Y. 144, 101 N.E. 783, 46 L.R.A. (N.S.) 585 (1913)

This was an action by the United States Radiator Company (plaintiff) against the State of New York (defendant). From a judgment of the Appellate Division affirming a judgment of the Court of Claims dismissing the claim, plaintiff appealed. Judgment affirmed.

The plaintiff purchased certain property from each of four corporations, paying for the property by issuing to the corporations shares of stock in the plaintiff corporation. However, instead of transferring the stock to each of the corporations, the stock was transferred to the stockholders of the corporation, each stockholder receiving stock in proportion to the number of shares he owned in the selling corporation. The state assessed a tax on the transfer from each corporation to its stockholders on the theory that it was a transfer of stock. Plaintiff corporation paid the tax under protest contending that the transfer of the stock to the stockholders of the corporation was a distribution of the shares (corporate assets) to the true owners and not a taxable transfer under the provisions of the statute.

Collins, J. A share of corporate stock is the right which the shareholder has to participate according to the number of shares in the surplus profits of the corporation on a division, and in the assets or capital stock remaining after payment of its debts on its dissolution or the termination of its active existence and operation. It is created by the joint action of the corporation and the shareholder. It imports a contribution to the capital stock made by the shareholder and accepted by the corporation. When a corporation has agreed that a person shall be entitled to a certain number of shares for a consideration permitted by law and executed by the person, those shares come into existence and are owned by him.

The statement in the certificate of incorporation or charter of the corporation that the capital stock is a designated amount divided into a certain number of shares, each of a named value, creates neither shares nor capital stock. It expresses the power of the corporation to acquire a capital stock. It creates potential shares which, transferred into actual shares by the acquisition of members and their payments, produce the money or property which, put into a single corporate fund, is the actual capital or capital stock on which the corporate business is undertaken and in which are the shares. It also fixes the sum of the payment necessary to create a share.

The certificate of the corporation for the shares, or the stock certificate, is not necessary to the existence of the shares or their ownership. It is merely the written evidence of those facts. It expresses the contract between the shareholder and the corporation and his co-shareholders. But it is the payment, or the obligation to pay for shares of stock, accepted by the corporation, that creates both the shares and their ownership.

Each of the four corporations became, upon the transfer of its assets to the plaintiff, the owner of the shares of the capital stock of the plaintiff, which were the consideration for it.

The appellant urges, with ability and earnestness, that if the four corporations did in the first instance own the shares, the transfer of them to the shareholders was a division among the true owners of their own property, and therefore not a taxable transfer. While conditions may exist under which equity will consider the shareholders as the proprietors and the ultimate beneficiaries of the corporate interests, the fact is that a corporation is an individual being capacitated through statutory powers to acquire the title to, own, and dispose of real and personal property, enter into contracts, engage in business, sue and be sued and taxed. It is the owner of all the corporate property, real and personal, and within the powers conferred upon it by the charter can deal with it as absolutely as a private individual can with his own. The whole title to it is in the corporation, and the shareholders are neither tenants in common nor in any legal sense the owners of it.

Kinds of Stock

Three kinds of stock are generally recognized. They are common stock, preferred stock, and no-par stock. Common stock entitles the owner of the stock to share in the profits and assets of the corporation in proportion to the amount of the stock he owns. He has no priorities or preference over other stockholders. There may be more than one class of common stock as it is not unusual for a corporation to issue voting and non-voting common stock.

Preferred stock gives the owner certain preferences over the common stockholders. The nature of the preferences is set forth in the articles of incorporation and on the face of the stock certificate. It is the duty of those who are working out the financial structure of the corporation to determine the nature and extent of the preferences granted to the owners of the preferred stock. With few exceptions the owners of preferred stock are given preference as to dividends and are preferred as to the return of capital on the winding up of the corporation. Frequently, protective provisions are included which provide that the corporation shall not issue securities having prior claims on the earnings or assets of the corporation, such as bonds or notes, without the consent of a stated proportion of the owners of the outstanding shares of preferred stock. The preferred stock may be made redeemable and provision may be made for the setting up of a sinking fund for the redemption of the preferred stock. It may be made convertible into common stock or into other securities of the corporation. Preferred stock may be given voting rights, especially in the event of default in the payment of dividends. All preferences and restrictions as between the different classes of stock should be clearly and fully set forth in the articles of incorporation. As a general rule, unless the preferences are stated in the articles of incorporation, they do not exist. In a few states the directors may be given the power to fix the preferences from time to time by resolution.

Preferred stock may be "cumulative" or "non-cumulative." The dividends cannot be paid on preferred stock unless the corporation has earned a surplus out of which it can legally pay dividends. If the preferred stock is cumulative and the stipulated dividend is not paid in any year, it will accumulate and will be a charge on the earnings of the corporation in subsequent years, and if at a later time the corporation has a surplus out of which it may legally pay dividends, it will not be permitted to pay a dividend to the common stockholders until it has first paid all passed dividends and also the dividends for the current year on the preferred stock. If the preferred stock is non-cumulative, the dividends must be paid out of current profit. If there is no provision stating whether or not dividends are cumulative or non-cumulative, the majority of courts have held that they will be cumulative.

Preferred stock may be "participating" or "non-participating." Participating preferred stock shares in the profits of the corporation with the common stock after the common stock has been paid the same dividend as the preferred. If a corporation has surplus sufficient to pay 25 per cent on all its outstanding stock and has outstanding 7 per cent participating preferred and common stock, it will pay 7 per cent dividend to the preferred stockholders and 7 per cent to the common stockholders and will then pay a 5½ per cent dividend to both preferred and common stockholders. If the preferred were non-participating, the preferred stockholders would receive 7 per cent and no more. The common stockholders would receive 18 per cent.

The statutes of some states provide that a corporation may issue stock having no-par value. Such stock does not state any value on its face but does state on its face what proportionate ownership the owner of the stock has in the corporation. Under the statutes of some states no-par stock cannot be issued for less than a stated minimum price, for example, $5.00 per share, but other states permit such stock to be issued for any amount which the incorporators or directors may fix. The value of outstanding no-par stock, if the corporation has issued no other kind of stock, is determined by dividing the net worth of the corporation by the number of shares of stock outstanding.

Elko Lamoille Power Co. v. Commissioner of Internal Revenue
50 F. (2d) 595 (1931)

This was an action by Elko Lamoille Power Co. (plaintiff) against the Commissioner of Internal Revenue (defendant). Judgment for defendant and plaintiff appealed. Judgment affirmed.

The plaintiff issued $80,000 preferred stock, bearing 7 per cent dividends, payable semiannually, preferred as to income and assets, and callable after three years at 110. In its tax returns the plaintiff treated this issue of preferred stock as an indebtedness and deducted the dividends from its tax return as interest. The stock was sold on the representation that the owner could return it to the corporation at any time he wished and receive the amount paid together with accumulated dividends. Later the board of directors passed a resolution which ratified and approved the representations made at the time the stock was sold. The only issue before the court was whether the preferred stockholders could be treated as creditors.

Neterer, D. J. The distinction between common stockholders and preferred stockholders may be said to be that the common stockholder is an owner of the enterprise in the proportion that his stock bears to the entire sock, and is entitled to participate in the management, profit, and ultimate assets of the corporation. A stock certificate is evidence of the shares owned.

A preferred stockholder is a mode by which a corporation obtains funds for its enterprise without borrowing money or contracting a debt, the stockholder being preferred as to principal and interest, but having no voice in the management. It differs only from other stocks in that it is given preference and has no voting right. A preferred stockholder is not a creditor of the company.

On the books, the preferred "stock was carried as preferred stockholders interest account." Neither the resolution passed long after the sale of the preferred stock nor the method of bookkeeping have any probative value; nor have the representations of the president and secretary as stock salesmen. They had no power to bind the corporation, except as conferred by law or by-law, and there is no law or by-law cited to the court. The assets of a corporation are a trust fund, and the directors may not arbitrarily change the status of stockholders into that of general creditors. The status of the tax liability between the corporation and the United States was fixed on the issuance of the preferred stock. The agreement of the salesmen officers was a collateral agreement between the officers and the stockholders. The evidence presented establishes that the stock was purchased by the stockholders upon the representation that they could bring it back at any time and get their money and dividends. Several testified that they considered it a loan. This evidence can have no probative value. The sale was effected with a collateral understanding that they would be redeemed on demand. "The rights of the holders of preferred stock in this case must be determined by the language of the stock certificate."

Stock Subscriptions

A stock subscription is an offer to purchase, when issued, a stated number of shares of the original unissued stock of a corporation. The offer becomes a contract when accepted by the corporation.

A stock subscription agreement may be entered into with the corporation after its organization. In fact, the more common practice is to organize the corporation, pay in the nominal sum required as paid in capital, or turn over to the corporation property in payment for stock sufficient to satisfy the statutory requirements, and sell the major part of the stock after the corporation has been organized. If the stock subscription is with an organized corporation, the relationship is that of any two persons negotiating for or entering into a contract, and their rights will be governed accordingly. If the corporation has not been organized, a different problem presents itself. The negotiation or contract cannot be between the subscriber and the corporation because the corporation does not, as yet, have any existence. Some courts have enforced subscription agreements between the various subscribers, holding that they are supported by the consideration of a promise for a promise, the promise of each subscriber being in exchange for the promise of every other subscriber. The more generally accepted rule is that such stock subscriptions are offers to buy and that they may be revoked at any time before they are accepted by the corporation. In other words, they may be revoked at any time before the corporation is organized and before it, in some manner, communicates to the subscriber its intention to accept the offer. Under some corporate statutes those subscribing, as incorporators, cannot withdraw their subscriptions. The wording of the subscription is always an important factor in determining the rights of the subscriber.

A stock subscription does not differ in its fundamental aspects from any other offer or contract, and the courts have applied general contract law in determining the rights of the parties. From the nature of the transaction it is implied that a de jure corporation will be organized having the powers set out in the subscription agreement and that the stock will be legally issued. The subscription agreement may contain such special terms as are not illegal. As a general rule the subscription agreement will state the time of payment, but if the time of payment is not stipulated, the general rule is that payment must be made on call of the board of directors.

L. E. Fosgate Co. et al. v. Boston Market Terminal Co. et al.
275 Mass. 99, 175 N.E. 86 (1931)

This was an action by L. E. Fosgate Company and others (plaintiffs) against Boston Market Terminal Company and others (defendants). Judgment for plaintiffs and defendants appealed. Judgment affirmed.

In 1922 the wholesale fruit merchants in Boston, after many meetings, decided to establish a wholesale market terminal and on July 27, 1922, organized a corporation—Boston Market Terminal Co.—with the intention of putting their plans in operation. At first it was agreed that each firm or dealer would purchase one share of stock and that no establishment could have more than one membership. Later the twenty-nine wholesale dealers, who were the original organizers of the corporation, each subscribed for nineteen additional shares, $100 par value. These subscription agreements were to be held and the money called in if needed. Five years later, since the terminal market had been successful and profitable beyond the expectations of the parties, the directors decided to pay a large dividend. At this time it was agreed that the subscriptions would be called. This would give the original twenty-nine merchants a material advantage because they would each receive dividends on twenty shares whereas other members held only one share. This suit was brought to prevent this action.

Crosby, J. The "subscription agreement" of August 16, 1922, whereby the individual defendants subscribed for nineteen additional shares of stock, was a mere voluntary offer until acted on and accepted by the corporation. Since no definite time was specified in the instrument, the offer was open for a reasonable length of time. As all the facts appear in the master's report, it is a question of law as to what was a reasonable time for the acceptance of the offer. What is a reasonable time depends upon the facts and circumstances of the case. The subscription agreement properly construed does not import perpetuity, it means that the stock to be issued must be issued within a reasonable time. The offer was not to continue forever, and upon the facts found by the master the judge rightly ruled that it was not accepted by the defendant corporation within a reasonable time.

It is argued by the defendants that "The purpose of the subscriptions was to provide for a fund which could be raised immediately and be at the disposal of the corporation for the purposes for which it was organized." The findings of the master support this argument. But he also found that the corporation in 1928, because of its great success, "did not need the money which would result from calling the subscriptions."

The individual defendants who were directors of the corporation were acting in a fiduciary capacity and were required to exercise their authority in the utmost good faith. They could not "rightly manipulate the affairs of the corporation primarily with the design of securing the control of the corporation to one particular group of stockholders, or of excluding another group from the exercise of its corporate rights." From the master's findings and the reasonable inferences to be drawn therefrom, it is manifest that the conduct of the defendants was in violation of the duty they owed the plaintiffs. Their sole purpose in voting to accept the lifeless offer of August 16, 1922, over five years after it had been made, was to secure for themselves and their associate subscribers a large and disproportionate share of the corporate assets at the expense of the minority stockholders. The honesty of purpose of the defendants is not a decisive test of the propriety of their conduct. The right of the plaintiffs to prevent an issue of stock by the defendants to themselves for their own gain does not rest on fraud but on the fiduciary duty of the directors. A necessary and obvious consequence of the issuance of the nineteen additional shares to the individual defendants and the other subscribers would have resulted in destroying the equality of stock ownership which had obtained since the organization of the corporation. It is settled that the directors of a corporation cannot lawfully issue treasury stock to themselves or to a confederate for the purpose of gaining control of the corporation without giving the other stockholders an opportunity to subscribe. The attempt by the defendants to obtain for themselves a larger share of the assets and control of the corporation cannot be justified.

Issuing Stock

The basis on which the original stock of the corporation can be issued has been discussed in an earlier chapter. If stock is issued in violation of these rules, the stock is not void; however, the person to whom the stock is issued and any transferee who takes the stock with knowledge or notice that it was issued in violation of the statute may be liable. The nature of the stockholder's liability is discussed in a subsequent chapter.

If the corporation attempts to issue stock in excess of the amount authorized by its articles of incorporation, all stock issued in excess of the amount authorized is void, and the holders of such stock acquire no rights as stockholders. Their remedy would be against the corporation for damages which resulted from the issuing of void stock to them.

If stock is issued as the result of a fraud practiced on the corporation, such stock is not void but it is voidable. The corporation can, in a proper action, have such stock cancelled unless it has been transferred to an innocent purchaser for value, in which event the corporation could sue in tort and recover as damages the value of the stock less any value actually paid to the corporation for the stock.

Woodson et al. v. McAllister et al.
119 F. (2d) 924 (1941)

This was an action by Merle Young Woodson on behalf of herself and all other stockholders similarly situated (plaintiffs) against W. W. McAllister and others (defendants). Judgment for defendants and plaintiff appealed. Judgment reversed and remanded for further proceedings.

W. W. McAllister was president and manager of San Antonio Building & Loan Association, a Texas corporation. As manager he had a contract with the corporation whereby he received as compensation for his services all the profits of the corporation after payment of certain expenses and dividends. The San Antonio Building & Loan Association up until 1931 was operated at a profit but during 1931 its income dropped materially. It had outstanding 3,000 shares of $100 par value stock. McAllister had an option to purchase this stock for $300,000. The Southern Associated Companies, a Texas corporation, of which McAllister was also president, issued to McAllister $400,000 of its stock in payment for McAllister's option to purchase the stock of San Antonio Building & Loan Association. The directors of Southern Associated Companies valued this stock at $750,000 but its actual value was not more than par. This suit was brought to have the stock, issued to McAllister, cancelled.

Holmes, C. J. The provisions relied upon by her provide that no corporation shall issue stock except for money paid, labor done, or property actually received and that all fictitious increase of stock shall be void. Even the note of a solvent person, though property in a literal sense, is not property of a nature that may constitute the capital of a corporation. Under the Texas law, the term "means property readily capable of being applied to the debts of the corporation."

Even if the option was property in the hands of McAllister, the San Antonio Building & Loan Association legally could not have received it for its permanent stock or for any part thereof. The constitution and laws of Texas are not so easily evaded as to permit the officers and directors to do indirectly what they may not do directly; and yet nothing is clearer than that one of the immediate purposes of organizing Southern Associated was to carry out the scheme of enabling McAllister to receive stock for his contract, his option, or his good will, whichever you choose to call it. The entry, as first put on the books of the Associated Companies, recited that $400,000 of stock had been issued to W. W. McAllister "to record the purchase of good will of the San Antonio Building & Loan Association from W. W. McAllister."

It is contended that the directors valued the 3,000 shares of permanent stock at $750,000, and McAllister's good will or option at $400,000. These valuations are too fanciful and speculative to constitute the capital of a Texas corporation.

The facts in the record are undisputed. We do not have here a question merely of overvaluation of the permanent stock. McAllister did not purchase the permanent stock; he never owned it; he did not exchange it for Southern Associated stock at an agreed valuation. McAllister did not transfer to Southern Associated any good will of San Antonio Building & Loan Association. He paid no money of his own for the permanent stock. He gave nothing which may legally constitute the capital of a corporation to Southern Associated for the $400,000 of stock in controversy, and Southern Associated received nothing of such nature for it from any one else. He did not even transfer the option, as is now claimed. What he did was to fail to exercise the option for himself; he exercised it for and in the name of Southern Associated, and bought the stock for Southern Associated with the money and in the name of Southern Associated. It is clear enough now, and should have been clear at the time, that Southern Associated paid in cash full value for the 3,000 shares of permanent stock it received from San Antonio Building & Loan Association.

The stock in controversy should be cancelled, and the dividends paid thereon refunded. This will be adequate relief upon the record before us. No innocent purchasers are parties hereto, and it does not appear that any of the stock has passed beyond the control of McAllister. Relief by cancellation, of course, precludes any recovery of damages against McAllister for failure to pay his stock subscription, and such relief is denied.

Commercial Bank of Spanish Fork v. Spanish Fork South Irrigation
— Utah, —, 153 P. (2d) 547 (1944)

This was an action by the Commercial Bank of Spanish Fork (plaintiff) against Spanish Fork South Irrigation Company (defendant). Judgment for plaintiff and defendant appealed. Judgment affirmed.

Prior to June 16, 1923, Perry A. Thomas was owner of ten and one-half shares of stock in the defendant company, evidenced by certificate number 534. About June 16, 1923, Perry A. Thomas, who was then president of defendant corporation, falsely represented that he had lost certificate number 534, and upon such representations and his furnishing an indemnity bond, the defendant issued to Perry A. Thomas certificate number 1176 for ten and one-half shares of stock in lieu of certificate 534. At the time certificate 1176 was issued defendant's stock had all been issued and was all outstanding. Plaintiff later acquired the certificate of stock as a bona fide purchaser for value. This suit was brought to recover for the loss sustained by plaintiff because the stock was an overissue and void.

Henderson, D. J. Plaintiff's recovery rests upon the generally recognized rule that a corporation is liable for damages proximately caused to a bona fide holder for value of a certificate for its shares of stock where the certificate, although regular on its face, is void because it represents an overissue procured through fraud but has been issued by officers of the corporation having the apparent authority to do so. The decisions have based liability in such cases upon various grounds such as negligence, breach of warranty or estoppel. It is said that while the certificate of stock is not the stock itself but merely evidence thereof, it is nevertheless a continuing representation that the stock therein described is valid and genuine and that the person therein named is the owner of the stock represented thereby and has the capacity to transfer the same. Under this theory recovery is allowed a bona fide holder of a spurious certificate, because he has suffered damages by relying on such representations.

It is probable that the underlying reason for the protection afforded a bona fide holder in such cases is that ordinary stock certificates are muniments of title which have gained the confidence of business men and have been widely dealt with in the open market much the same as negotiable securities. Although stock certificates are not strictly negotiable, in the sense of negotiable instruments, the tendency has been to treat and refer to them as quasi negotiable. Defendant apparently does not seriously challenge the general rule above stated.

Transfer of Stock

A share of stock, the ownership of which is customarily evidenced by a stock certificate, is intangible property. The stock certificate is regarded as a quasi-negotiable instrument and like negotiable instruments the rights of the owner may be conveyed to another party. Such a conveyance is called a transfer. The transfer of stock from one person to another involves two steps. First, there is the transfer of the certificate from the transferor to the transferee, and second, the transferee must deliver the certificate to the corporation, which will enter the transfer upon its books and issue a new certificate in the name of the transferee.

A common requirement of the corporation is that stock shall be transferable only on the books of the corporation. To make such a transfer the owner of the share of stock indorses an assignment on the certificate (stock certificates in general use have such an assignment printed on the back of the certificate) or on a separate paper and delivers the certificate of stock and the assignment to the buyer who sends the certificate and assignment to the transfer agent of the corporation. It is the duty of the transfer agent to see that the certificate and assignment are in proper form, and if they are he issues to the buyer a new certificate for the number of shares of stock transferred and cancels the old certificate. An unregistered transfer gives the buyer the equitable ownership of the stock, but, as a general rule, it gives him no rights against the corporation, that is, he would not be entitled to dividends, to vote at stockholders' meetings, etc.

Restriction on the right of a stockholder to transfer his stock may be imposed by statute, by the articles of incorporation, by by-laws, or by agreement between the stockholder and the corporation. The transfer of stock may be prohibited altogether by provisions in the articles of incorporation making the stock of the corporation non-transferable and such a provision would be binding on all persons who become stockholders. Usually restrictions on the transfer of stock provide that a stockholder must first offer his stock to the corporation or to the other stockholders, or that the person to whom the stock is transferred must be first approved by the directors.

As a general rule restrictions placed on the transfer of stock by the by-laws are limited to such regulations as are reasonably necessary to protect the corporation against colorable or fraudulent transfers, and to enable the corporation to know who its stockholders are and as such entitled to dividends, etc. A by-law which would attempt to make the stock of the corporation non-transferable or impose unreasonable restrictions on its transfer would not be upheld.

By an agreement between the corporation and its stockholders the transfer of its stock may be restricted but the courts have held that, if such agreement makes the stock non-transferable or imposes unreasonable restrictions on the transfer of the stock, it is void. Such an agreement would be in restraint of trade and against public policy.

The corporation owes a duty to the transferee of stock to make the transfer on the books of the corporation and issue to the transferee a new certificate in his name. If the corporation refuses to do so, it is liable to the transferee. The nature of the action which the transferee may maintain against the corporation will depend on the jurisdiction and the circumstances of the case. Transferees have recovered the value of the stock in suits in conversion and have been granted specific performance by courts of equity. The corporation has the right to make reasonable inquiry and investigation before it transfers the stock. It will not be liable for any delay which is reasonably necessary to make whatever investigation the circumstances of the case warrant.

If the owner of a certificate of stock dies, the ownership of the stock passes to his estate, and his administrator or executor has the right to transfer the stock. The procedure followed will depend on the probate laws of the state of domicile of the deceased. If the certificate of stock is held by one acting in the capacity of a trustee, the trustee is the legal owner of the stock, but such trustee may not have the power to sell. Before the corporation transfers stock which it knows is held in trust, it should, for its own protection, require proof that at the time of the sale the trustee was actually the trustee, that he had power to sell, and that the sale was within the scope of his power as trustee because the corporation will be liable if the trustee does not have power to transfer the stock.

The rights acquired by one taking a certificate of stock as a bona fide purchaser were discussed in the chapter on "Various Negotiable and Quasi Negotiable Instruments," page 524.

Penthouse Properties, Inc. v. 1158 Fifth Avenue, Inc., et al.
11 N.Y.S. (2d) 417 (1939)

This was an action by Penthouse Properties, Incorporated (plaintiff) against 1158 Fifth Avenue, Incorporated, and others (defendants). Judgment for defendants.

Mrs. Harriss owned 777 shares of stock and in connection therewith held a proprietary lease to an apartment and two maid's rooms in an apartment house owned by the defendant. The defendant corporation was organized for the purpose of building and operating a co-operative apartment house. If one wished to obtain an apartment, he would purchase a stipulated number of shares of stock in the corporation and in connection therewith would enter into a 99-year proprietary lease for the apartment. There was no provision in the defendant's articles restricting the transfer of its stock, but the directors adopted a resolution which did restrict the transfer of its stock. The resolution provided that the stock and accompanying lease could not be transferred unless notice of the transfer was given to the board of directors, and unless the transfer was approved by the holders of two-thirds of the outstanding capital stock. Notice of the restriction was stamped on the stock certificate and the restriction was set out in the proprietary lease. Mrs. Harriss transferred her shares and lease to the plaintiff corporation which was organized by Mr. Harriss for the sole purpose of acquiring the stock and lease. Mr. Harriss was the sole stockholder of plaintiff. At the time of the transfer no notice was given to the directors and the restrictions on the transfer were not complied with. Plaintiff claimed that the restrictions were invalid and unenforceable and brought this suit to force the defendant to transfer the stock and lease to it.

Untermyer, J. The question now presented, apparently never decided in this State, is the validity of the restrictive plan under which co-operative apartment houses have been constructed and the stock sold. The validity of such a plan is challenged by the plaintiff and by Mrs. Harriss on the ground that restraints against the alienation of the corporate stock imposed by the limitations contained in the lease, prohibiting any sale without the consent of the directors or two-thirds of the stockholders, are against public policy and therefore unenforceable.

The general rule that ownership of property cannot exist in one person and the right of alienation in another has in this State been frequently applied to shares of corporate stock and cognizance has been taken of the principle that "the right of transfer is a right of property, and if another has the arbitrary power to forbid a transfer of property by the owner, that amounts to an annihilation of property." The same rule has been applied in other States. But restrictions against the sale of shares of stock, unless other stockholders or the corporation have first been accorded an opportunity to buy, are not repugnant to that principle. The weight of authority elsewhere is to the same effect. Likewise, restrictions against the assignment by the tenant of a leasehold, or against subletting, without the consent of the landlord first obtained, have frequently been sustained.

We are now required to decide within which of these divergent principles the co-operative apartment house restrictive plan is to be classified. In the consideration of that question the residential nature of the enterprise, the privilege of selecting neighbors and the needs of the community are not to be ignored. The tenant stockholders in a co-operative apartment building are concerned in the purchase of a home. Necessarily, therefore, the permanency of the individual occupants as tenant owners is an essential element in the general plan and their financial responsibility an inducement to the corporation in accepting them as stockholders. Under the "Plan of Organization" each stockholder is entitled to vote upon the choice of neighbors and their financial responsibility. The latter consideration becomes important when it is remembered that the failure of any tenant to pay his proportion of operating expenses increases the liability of other tenant stockholders. Thus, in a very real sense the tenant stockholders enter into a relation not unlike a partnership, though expressed in corporate form. Holmes, C. J., in *Barrett* v. *King*, 181 Mass. 476, 63 N.E. 934, 935, said of this: "Furthermore, looking at the stock merely as property, it might be said that, so far as appears and probably in fact, it was called into existence with this restriction inherent in it, by the consent of all concerned. . . . . There seems to be no greater objection to retaining the right of choosing one's associates in a corporation than in a firm." Although it is true that the corporation which holds title to the real estate is not organized in co-operative form, it is manifest from the conceded facts that it was organized as a vehicle for the establishment of a community of homes rather than for the purpose of pecuniary profit to the stockholders. The primary interest of every stockholder was in the long term proprietary lease alienation of which the corporation had the power to restrain. The stock was incidental to that purpose and afforded the practical means of combining an ownership interest with a method for sharing proportionately the assessments for maintenance and taxes.

From all these considerations it follows that if restraint on alienation of the stock may be said to be imposed at all, it is a restraint which in every respect is reasonable and appropriate to the lawful purposes to be attained. We are unwilling to declare that arrangement to be illegal and unenforceable, particularly since such a declaration would invalidate a form of enterprise to which the legislature has accorded implied recognition. We conclude, therefore, that the special nature of the ownership of co-operative apartment houses by tenant owners requires that they be not included in the general rule against restraint on the sale of stock in corporations organized for profit.

QUESTIONS AND PROBLEMS

1. Does a share of stock give a stockholder ownership in any portion of the assets of the corporation?
2. Under a statute which imposed a tax on "money at interest" the assessor taxed certain corporate stocks owned by C. Chandler. Were the stocks taxable as "money at interest"?
3. The Foundry Co. issued non-cumulative 7% preferred stock. In the years 1902, 1903, 1904, and 1909, the corporation made a surplus net profit sufficient to pay the dividends on the preferred stock in full. The board of directors failed to pay the dividends in full but transferred a substantial amount of the surplus net profits to a special account. Later, the board of directors voted to pay the passed dividends to the preferred stockholders. Bassett, a common stockholder, brought an action to enjoin the payment of the dividend on the ground that the profits of any year, not distributed in dividends declared in that year, belong to the common stockholders. Is Bassett entitled to an injunction?
4. The corporation issued 6% preferred stock which was "entitled to a preference over all other stock of said company in every future dividend of profits declared." No profits were made and no dividends paid on the preferred stock for the years 1940, 1941, 1942, and 1943. In the year 1944, the corporation made a profit and declared a 6% dividend on the preferred stock and a 3% dividend on the common stock. The holders of the preferred stock claim that no dividends may be paid on the common stock until back dividends for the years 1940 to 1943 are paid on the preferred stock. Is this contention correct?
5. Carey signed a stock subscription agreement whereby he agreed to purchase one share of the capital stock of the Athol Music Hall Co. when the proposed corporation was organized. The corporation was organized, and the share of stock was tendered to Carey who refused to accept. Carey was carried on the books

of the corporation as a stockholder and notice of all stockholders' meetings was sent to him, but he never attended the meetings. Suit was brought to recover the purchase price of the stock, and Carey contended that, inasmuch as he never attended meetings and had never taken any part in the affairs of the corporation since its organization, he had not ratified his subscription agreement and was not bound by it. Is Carey's contention correct?

6. Certain business men undertook to organize a packet company for the purpose of plying a steamboat on the Yazoo river. Wright agreed to help and said he would state, at a later date, the amount of stock he would subscribe. Later, at a preliminary meeting, Wright voted $500 worth of stock. Before the corporation was completely organized, Wright advised those in charge of the subscription list that he withdrew his subscription. Wright refused to pay his subscription, and the corporation sued. Can the corporation recover?
7. A corporation was organized with an authorized capital stock of 100 shares, par value of $100 a share. By action of the board of directors, an additional 50 shares were issued and sold for $100 a share. The articles of incorporation were not amended to increase the authorized capital of the corporation. What rights do the holders of the additional 50 shares of stock have as stockholders?
8. The stockholders of a corporation issued to themselves stock, par value $100, as fully paid and nonassessable. They turned over to the corporation, in payment of the stock, property of nominal value. The corporation is insolvent. Can the unpaid general creditors recover anything from the stockholders?
9. The Blanke Company issued to Parchman a certificate for 40 shares of its common stock. Parchman sold the stock to Chandler, signed the assignment of the certificate, and delivered it to Chandler. The company refused to transfer the shares on the books of the company claiming a lien on them for $980, the unpaid balance of the purchase price of certain merchandise, which had been sold to Parchman. The certificate provided on its face that it was transferable only upon the books of the company in accordance with the by-laws. The by-laws created a lien in favor of the company for debts owed the company by its stockholders. Is the company correct in its refusal to transfer the stock?

CHAPTER XXXVIII

STOCKHOLDERS' RIGHTS AND LIABILITIES

Dividends

A dividend (except a liquidating dividend) is a distribution of profits ordered by the directors of the corporation or, in some instances, by the stockholders. The declaration of a dividend rests in the sound discretion of the directors, and the courts will not force the payment of a dividend unless there is a clear showing that the corporation has a surplus which is not needed in the operation of the business and that the failure to distribute the surplus is an abuse of discretion on the part of the directors.

A dividend is declared by formal action of the board of directors, and when a dividend is fully declared, it becomes a debt owing to the stockholders, and if not paid, a stockholder can sue the corporation and recover a judgment for the amount of the unpaid dividend. The courts are not in complete accord as to when a dividend has been fully declared, but the majority of the courts hold that the mere vote of the directors to pay a dividend may be rescinded, but when the declaration of a dividend has been made public by notice to stockholders or by any other means, the directors cannot rescind their action. Inasmuch as a dividend when declared becomes a debt payable to the stockholder, the courts have held that if a dividend has been legally declared, and after such declaration, but before payment, the corporation becomes insolvent, the stockholders will have a right to file a claim for the unpaid dividend and share with general creditors in the distribution of the assets of the corporation. If the directors have declared a dividend and have set aside a fund for the payment of the dividend, that fund becomes a trust fund held for the benefit of the stockholders which they will be entitled to as against other creditors.

Under the laws of the various states, it is unlawful to pay a dividend unless the corporation has a surplus. Considerable controversy has arisen as to when a corporation has a surplus out of which it is lawful to pay a dividend. The majority rule is that if the corporation has made a profit in excess of expenses for the year, it may pay a dividend. Each year is regarded as a separate unit. Whether or not a profit has been made is primarily an accounting problem. It has been held that a corporation will not have to have assets equal to the par value of its outstanding capital stock before paying a dividend; that it is not necessary that all losses suffered in prior years be recouped before paying a dividend; and that it is not necessary to pay the bonded indebtedness before paying a dividend. However, it has been held that interest on the bonded indebtedness must be provided for, and that a sinking fund for the payment of bonds should be provided. If the payment of a dividend is clearly an attempt to distribute the assets of the corporation to the stockholders to the injury of creditors, the payment is illegal. If the corporation, such as a mining company, has wasting assets, a portion of the capital assets may be returned as dividends.

Dividends may be paid in money, property, bonds, or stocks. Usually dividends are paid in money, but if the directors wish, they will be permitted to distribute property of the corporation as a dividend. If it is desirable to use the profits of the corporation in the expansion of the business, yet the directors wish to pay a dividend, the dividend may be paid by issuing bonds to the stockholders for the amount of the dividend. If the corporation has unissued stock, it may distribute such stock as a dividend, or if it does not have unissued stock, it may amend its articles and increase its stock and use the increase for the payment of a stock dividend. The payment of a stock dividend is no more than a bookkeeping transaction. The effect of the declaration and payment of a stock dividend is to capitalize surplus; that which was surplus becomes capital.

As between the corporation and the stockholder, the stockholder of record at the time the dividend is declared is entitled to the dividend. The New York Stock Exchange rule is that the owner of the stock at the time the dividend is paid is entitled to the dividend. The courts in reaching their decisions follow the rule that the dividend, when declared, becomes a debt owing to the stockholder of record and hold further that a transfer of the stock does not include an assignment of this debt. The courts are not in accord as to the rights to a dividend declared to be payable to those who are stockholders of record on a specific future date. Some cases hold that the declaration is prospective and is payable to those who are stockholders of record at the specified future date, while other cases adhere to the rule that the dividend becomes the property of those who own the stock at the time the dividend is declared. If, at the time the stock is transferred, it is agreed that the transferee shall be entitled to the declared dividend, such an agreement is an assignment of the debt which will be enforced by the courts. If the corporation is given notice after the declaration, but before the payment of a dividend, that the dividend is payable to the transferee of the stock, the corporation is obligated to pay the dividend to such transferee.

Fundamentally, there is no difference between a preferred stockholder's and a common stockholder's rights to dividends. The difference in their respective rights is based in the contract each has with the corporation. The directors cannot pay dividends on preferred stock unless there is a surplus out of which dividends may lawfully be paid, but they are not bound to pay dividends if there is a surplus. The courts have held that if the preferred stock is non-cumulative and the corporation has made a profit but the directors have not declared and paid the dividend on the preferred stock for that year, the dividend is not lost to the preferred stockholder, but it is payable in subsequent years when funds are available for the payment of dividends. The directors will not be permitted to benefit the common stockholders by refusing to declare and pay the dividends on non-cumulative preferred stock when profits have been earned by the corporation.

Dodge et al. v. Ford Motor Co. et al.
204 Mich. 459, 170 N.W. 668 (1919)

This was a suit by John F. Dodge and Horace E. Dodge (plaintiffs) against Ford Motor Company and others (defendants). Decree for plaintiffs and defendants appealed. Affirmed in part and reversed in part.

The plaintiffs were stockholders in the Ford Motor Company. From the beginning in 1903 to July 31, 1916, the corporate business had been profitable. The capital stock had been increased from $150,000 in 1903 to $2,000,000 in 1908. A regular dividend of 5 per cent per month on its capital stock of $2,000,000 had been paid since 1911, and in addition thereto special dividends had been paid which ranged from $1,000,000 to $10,000,000 per year and which totaled $41,000,000 for the years 1911 to 1915 inclusive. In 1916, the directors decided to continue to pay the regular dividend of 5 per cent per month on the corporation's capital stock of $2,000,000 but to discontinue all special dividends. At this time the corporation had a surplus of $112,000,000; its yearly profits were $60,000,000; its total liabilities including capital stock were less than $20,000,000; it had cash on hand of $54,000,000, and all planned improvements would cost approximately $24,000,000. This action was brought to force the directors to pay a special dividend.

Ostrander, C. J. The rule which will govern courts in deciding these questions is not in dispute. It is, of course, differently phrased by judges and by authors, and, as the phrasing in a particular instance may seem to lean for or against the exercise of the right of judicial interference with the actions of corporate directors, the context, or the facts before the court must be considered. This court, in *Hunter* v. *Roberts, Throp & Co.*, 83 Mich. 63, 71, 47 N.W. 131, 134, recognized the rule in the following language:

"It is a well-recognized principle of law that the directors of a corporation, and they alone, have the power to declare a dividend of the earnings of the corporation, and to determine its amount. Courts of equity will not interfere in the management of the directors unless it is clearly made to appear that they are guilty of fraud or misappropriation of the corporate funds, or refuse to declare a dividend when the corporation has a surplus of net profits which it can, without detriment to the business, divide among its stockholders, and when a refusal to do so would amount to such an abuse of discretion as would constitute a fraud, or breach of that good faith which they are bound to exercise towards the stockholders."

In Morawetz on Corporations (2d Ed.) § 447, it is stated:

"Profits earned by a corporation may be divided among its shareholders, but it is not a violation of the charter if they are allowed to accumulate and remain invested in the company's business. The managing agents of a corporation are impliedly invested with a discretionary power with regard to the time and manner of distributing its profits. They may apply profits in payment of floating or funded debts, or in development of the company's business; and so long as they do not abuse their discretionary powers, or violate the company's charter, the courts cannot interfere.

"But it is clear that the agents of a corporation, and even the majority, cannot arbitrarily withhold profits earned by the company, or apply them to any use which is not authorized by the company's charter. The nominal capital of the company does not necessarily limit the scope of its operations; a corporation may borrow money for the purpose of enlarging its business, and in many instances it may use profits for the same purpose. But the amount of the capital contributed by the shareholders is an important element in determining the limit beyond which the company's business cannot be extended by the investment of profits. If a corporation is formed with a capital of $100,000 in order to carry on a certain business, no one would hesitate to say that it would be a departure from the intention of the founders to withhold profits, in order to develop the company's business, until the sum of $500,000 had been amassed, unless the company was formed mainly for the purpose of accumulating the profits from year to year. The question in each case depends upon the use to which the capital is put and the meaning of the company's charter. If a majority of the shareholders or the directors of a corporation wrongfully refuse to declare a dividend and distribute profits earned by the company, any shareholder feeling aggrieved may obtain relief in a court of equity."

The record, and especially the testimony of Mr. Ford, convinces that he has to some extent the attitude towards shareholders of one who has dispensed and distributed to them large gains and that they should be content to take what he chooses to give. His testimony creates the impression, also, that he thinks the Ford Motor Company has made too much money, has had too large profits, and that, although large profits might be still earned, a sharing of them with the public, by reducing the price of the output of the company, ought to be undertaken. We have no doubt that certain sentiments, philanthropic and altruistic, creditable to Mr. Ford, had large influence in determining the policy to be pursued by the Ford Motor Company—the policy which has been herein referred to.

It is said by his counsel that—

"Although a manufacturing corporation cannot engage in humanitarian works as its principal business, the fact that it is organized for profit does not prevent the existence of implied powers to carry on with humanitarian motives such charitable works as are incidental to the main business of the corporation."

And again:

"As the expenditures complained of are being made in an expansion of the business which the company is organized to carry on, and for purposes within the powers of the corporation as hereinbefore shown, the question is as to whether such expenditures are rendered illegal because influenced to some extent by humanitarian motives and purposes on the part of the members of the board of directors."

In discussing this proposition, counsel have referred to decisions such as *Hawes* v. *Oakland*, 104 U.S. 450, 26 L.Ed. 827; *Taunton* v. *Royal Ins. Co.*, 2 Hem. & Miller, 135; *Henderson* v. *Bank of Australia*, L.R. 40 Ch. Div. 170; *Steinway* v. *Steinway & Sons*, 17 Misc. Rep. 43, 40 N.Y. Supp. 718; *People* v. *Hotchkiss*, 136 App. Div. 150, 120 N.Y. Supp. 629. These cases, after all, like all others in which the subject is treated, turn finally upon the point, the question, whether it appears that the directors were not acting for the best interests of the corporation. We do not draw in question, nor do counsel for the plaintiffs do so, the validity of the general proposition stated by counsel nor the soundness of the opinions delivered in the cases cited. The case presented here is not like any of them. The difference between an incidental humanitarian expenditure of corporate funds for the benefit of the employes, like the building of a hospital for their use and the employment of agencies for the betterment of their condition, and a general purpose and plan to benefit mankind at the expense of others, is obvious. There should be no confusion (of which there is evidence) of the duties which Mr. Ford conceives that he and the stockholders owe to the general public and the duties which in law he and his codirectors owe to protesting, minority stockholders. A business corporation is organized and carried on primarily for the profit of the stockholders. The powers of the directors are to be employed for that end. The discretion of directors is to be exercised in the choice of means to attain that end, and does not extend to a change in the end itself, to the reduction of profits, or to the non-distribution of profits among stockholders in order to devote them to other purposes.

There is committed to the discretion of directors, a discretion to be exercised in good faith, the infinite details of business, including the wages which shall be paid to employes, the number of hours they shall work, the conditions under which labor shall be carried on, and the price for which products shall be offered to the public.

It is said by appellants that the motives of the board members are not material and will not be inquired into by the court so long as their acts are within their lawful powers. As we have pointed out, and the proposition does not require argument to sustain it, it is not within the lawful powers of a board of directors to shape and conduct the affairs of a corporation for the merely incidental benefit of shareholders and for the primary purpose of benefiting others, and no one will contend that, if the avowed purpose of the defendant directors was to sacrifice the interests of shareholders, it would not be the duty of the courts to interfere.

Defendants say, and it is true, that a considerable cash balance must be at all times carried by such a concern. But, as has been stated, there was a large daily, weekly, monthly, receipt of cash. The output was practically continuous and was continuously, and within a few days, turned into cash. Moreover, the contemplated expenditures were not to be immediately made. The large sum appropriated for the smelter plant was payable over a considerable period of time. So that, without going further, it would appear that, accepting and approving the plan of the directors, it was their duty to distribute on or near the 1st of August, 1916, a very large sum of money to stockholders.

People of Colorado ex rel. Fraser v. Great Western Sugar Co.
29 F. (2d) 810 (1928)

This was an action by the people of the State of Colorado on the relation of Robert W. Fraser (plaintiff) against the Great Western Sugar Company (defendant). Decree for the defendant and plaintiff appealed. Decree affirmed.

This originally was a suit for mandamus but was transferred to the Federal District Court and was tried as a suit for the recovery of money.

The Great Western Sugar Company was organized in 1905 under the laws of the State of New Jersey with an authorized capital stock of $20,000,000 of which $10,000,000 was common. In 1906, the capital was increased to $30,000,000; $15,000,000 thereof was preferred and $15,000,000 common. In 1922, the par value of the common stock was changed from $100 par value to $25 par value, and in 1927, the common stock was changed to no-par value stock. The preferred remained $100 par value cumulative, non-participating. The articles of incorporation provided: "in case of liquidation or distribution of assets of the corporation the holders of preferred stock shall be paid the par amount of their preferred shares before any amount shall be payable to the holders of the common stock, and after the payment of an equal amount to be distributed pro rata among the holders of the common stock the remainder of the assets and funds shall be distributed one-half (½) thereof ratably among all the preferred shareholders and the remaining one-half (½) thereof ratably among all the common shareholders, without preference."

A 7 per cent dividend was paid to preferred stockholders each year and dividends were also paid on the common stock. The net income of the corporation for the fiscal year ending February 28, 1927, was $3,365,713.27. At this time the corporation in addition thereto had an accumulated surplus of $39,001,342.77 in excess of all liabilities, including its liability on its capital stock. It paid a 7 per cent dividend to the preferred stockholders and it paid out the balance of its earnings for the year ending February 28, 1927, in dividends to the holders of the common stock. In addition thereto the board of directors voted and paid to the holders of the common stock as dividends $2,484,286.73 and at a later date $3,660,000 or a total of $6,144,286.73, which was paid out of the accumulated surplus. Plaintiff claims that this payment was made out of capital and was a violation of the provision of the articles of incorporation which is set out above.

Van Valkenburgh, C. J. It is apparent that the company had through past years earned this considerable sum of money in excess of what it had paid out in dividends, taxes, operating expenses, and fixed charges. It was retained for the purpose of being used as working capital, or otherwise for the purpose of increasing the company's earning capacity, if needed, and for creating a greater security for the payment of dividends and for the protection of the credit of the corporation. It had never been dedicated to corporate uses, whereby it became capital, within the meaning of that term pertinent to this discussion. The distinction between fixed capital and surplus net profits or earnings is obvious.

"Undistributed profits, or surplus in any form, may be invested or employed in the businesss of the corporation without thereby becoming 'capital' . . . . and until such profits are effectually and irrevocably dedicated to corporate uses through the processes of a stock dividend, they do not pass beyond the control of the directors nor cease to be available for distribution to those to whom they might have been originally allotted as cash dividends."

It is further held that, where the profits so employed for a time in the business of the corporation have finally been converted into money and made payable to stockholders in the form of a cash dividend, such a transaction by a solvent and prosperous corporation is in no proper sense a liquidation or surrender of a portion of its capital.

"Money earned by a corporation remains the property of the

corporation, and does not become the property of the stockholders, unless and until it is distributed among them by the corporation. The corporation may treat it and deal with it either as profits of its business, or as an addition to its capital. Acting in good faith and for the best interests of all concerned, the corporation may distribute its earnings at once to the stockholders as income; or it may reserve part of the earnings of a prosperous year to make up for a possible lack of profits in future years; or it may retain portions of its earnings and allow them to accumulate, and then invest them in its own works and plant, so as to secure and increase the permanent value of its property." *Gibbons* v. *Mahon*, 136 U.S. 558, 10 S. Ct. 1058.

The power of directors is absolute if they act in the exercise of an honest judgment, and earnings of prosperous years may help out the deficiencies of other years. And dividends may be declared where there are profits above the actual assets with which the corporation began business and this is true although the total assets may not exceed the debts and the nominal share of capital. In the granting of dividends the directors are vested with a wide discretion, subject to intervention for improper refusal. Such dividends need not be declared out of the profits for the current year. A surplus not dedicated to corporate uses as capital is carried as the property of the corporation, until such time as the directors may decide as to its disposition by way of distribution or otherwise. And when the property of a corporation exceeds the sum limited for its capital in its charter, the excess is surplus, which may be divided among the stockholders.

The general rule is thus well summarized in 14 Corpus Juris, 802:

"The terms 'net profits' or 'surplus profits' may be defined as what remains after deducting from the present value of all the assets of a corporation the amount of all liabilities, including the capital stock, in other words, that which remains as the clear gain of a corporation, after deducting from its income all the expenses incurred and losses sustained in the conduct and prosecution of its business. Hence a dividend is lawful, if, at the time of its declaration and payment, the corporation is solvent or has assets in excess of the amount of its debts and capital stock. And it makes no difference whether such surplus assets have been carried on the books of the corporation as surplus, or as segregated assets, or in a special fund account, or otherwise. Dividends may be paid from surplus accumulated out of profits of previous years, although there have been no actual profits for the year in which dividends are paid. The actual value of the assets with which the corporation began business is to be deducted and not the nominal share capital, and the business of a corporation is to be viewed as a unit in determining whether or not there are net profits."

It is evident from the foregoing citations, and from many others which might be adduced to the same effect, that the sum accumulated by appellee in the way of surplus or undivided profits was subject to the control of the directors and might be applied to the payment of dividends at any time when such payment would not impair the capital of the corporation.

Stockholders' Meetings

The general corporation statutes usually provide that at least one meeting of the stockholders shall be held in each calendar year, and further provide for the calling of a stockholders' meeting by any stockholder if the directors do not hold the annual stockholders' meeting within a stipulated time, such as within eighteen months. Provision is also made for the calling of such special meetings as may be desirable.

Under many of the earlier corporation statutes it was necessary to hold all stockholders' meetings within the state of incorporation, but under the statutes now in force the majority of state statutes permit the holding of stockholders' meetings within or without the state of incorporation unless otherwise provided in the articles of incorporation. The place of holding the annual meeting may be stated in the articles of incorporation or in the by-laws, or it may be set by action of the board of directors. Special meetings of the stockholders may be called at any time by the board of directors and, as a general rule, a special meeting may be called by a stated percentage of the stockholders. The number of stockholders required to call a special meeting and the procedure to be followed vary widely.

With few exceptions it is necessary to send out special notice of stockholders' meetings, and failure to send such notice will render any action taken at the meeting a nullity unless such action is ratified by stockholders who did not receive notice and were not present. Any stockholder may object to action taken at a stockholders' meeting which has not been properly called. It is impossible to state in detail the procedure to be followed in calling a stockholders' meeting, but in general, notice of the time, place, and the matters to come before the meeting must be sent to each stockholder of record at least ten days before the meeting. In calling a special meeting it is of outstanding importance that the notice state the purpose of the meeting, and any action taken at the meeting which is not within the scope of the purposes stated in the notice may be declared a nullity if attacked by stockholders who have not acquiesced in the action. The stockholders may waive notice of meetings, and if all the stockholders are present at a meeting and participate in the meeting, they will be held to have waived irregularities in the calling of the meeting. If certain classes of stockholders are not entitled to vote, they do not take part in stockholders' meetings and are not entitled to notice of such meetings.

In all instances in which stockholders' action must be taken, the action must be the collective action of the stockholders; individual action is insufficient. If Archer, Burch, and Clark own all the voting stock of the A.B.C. Corporation, and without holding a stockholders' meeting each signs a contract which requires stockholders' action to execute, the contract would not be properly executed. The powers of the stockholders are vested in them collectively.

In the absence of a provision of the statute, charter, or by-laws, any number who may be present, provided there are at least two, may transact business at a legally called stockholders' meeting. Sometimes, by an express provision, the statute, charter, or by-laws set out the number of stockholders which is necessary to constitute a quorum. In determining whether a quorum is present it is customary to count as present shares represented by person and by proxy. Less than a quorum usually has the power to adjourn the meeting.

It is customary for the president of the corporation to preside at the meeting and for the secretary to keep minutes of all business transacted at the meeting.

Bryan et al. v. Western Pacific Railroad Corporation
— Del. Ch. —, 35 A. (2d) 909 (1944)

This was an action by Thomas H. Bryan and others (plaintiffs) against the Western Pacific Railroad Corporation (defendant). Order was entered which advised the granting of preliminary injunction asked by plaintiffs.

The defendant was a holding company and the plaintiffs were preferred stockholders in the defendant. The defendant was in the process of reorganization under the provisions of the Bankruptcy Act. During the course of the reorganization it became necessary to have stockholder approval of a proposed contract. Notices were sent out, but plaintiffs did not receive notice of the meeting. The defendant declined continuously after April 29, 1943, to accept for transfer on its books certificates for shares of its capital stock. Plaintiffs acquired their stock after April 29, 1943, and presented it for transfer and transfer was refused. In giving notice of the stockholders' meeting, which was to be held December 28, 1943, notice was given to stockholders of record April 29, 1943. The Delaware statutes require the transfer of stock on the records of the corporation and also provide that the books can be closed for the purpose of giving notice of stockholders' meetings, etc., not more than fifty days before the date of the meeting. In this case the books were closed eight months before the date of the meeting.

The Vice Chancellor. In November, 1943, a special meeting of stockholders was called for December 28. A notice of the meeting, prepared by order of the board of directors, sets forth that the meeting was called for the purpose of considering and voting upon a resolution approving the directors' agreement above discussed, and of electing directors and transacting such other business as might come before an annual meeting of stockholders. Copies of the notice, dated November 24, were sent to the persons appearing on defendant's list of registered shareholders. Since the corporation had declined to register transfers after April 29, the persons thus notified were the stockholders of record on April 29.

The problem here will be approached from the standpoint of notice of the meeting. No provisions of the charter or by-laws concerning notice have been mentioned. However, it is elementary that in the absence of waiver, consent or estoppel, reasonable notice to stockholders entitled to vote is a prerequisite to the validity of a special meeting of stockholders. Ordinarily, the requirement of notice is met if the shareholders registered on the corporate books are given some appropriate form of notification.

A corporation owes a duty to register transfers of shares of its stock, and the board of directors may properly close the transfer books only for limited purposes and for a limited period. It seems to me that the adequacy of a list of registered shareholders as a circumscription of the persons to be notified must depend upon whether, in a particular case, the provisions of these two statutes have been observed. Defendant's directors did not observe them, for they refused to register transfers, and their refusal was not authorized by the provisions of Section 17.

One of the manifest purposes of Section 17 is to permit and facilitate reasonable methods of notification. The statute gives recognition to the practical necessity of dispensing with notice to persons who attempt to become registered shareholders shortly before a meeting. Thus, if the transfer books are closed (or a "record date" is fixed) pursuant to Section 17, persons presenting stock certificates for transfer within a period preceding a meeting (or registered shareholders who become such within a period preceding a meeting) may be properly excluded from the group of persons to be notified. If either of these devices is employed, the maximum duration of such a period of exclusion is 50 days. It is a reasonable and logical corollary of the statutory provisions that whether or not resort is had to one of these devices, at least no persons should be excluded from the group to be notified who would not have been excluded if either of the devices had in fact been employed. Defendant's use, for the purpose of notification, of the stockholders' list in which the last entry was almost 8 months before the meeting, had the effect of omitting notification to persons who could not have been excluded if defendant had properly employed either of the devices of the statute. Hence, at least these persons were wrongfully denied notice.

The only method of notification attempted, in addition to the sending of notices to persons appearing on the stockholders' list, is described by defendant's president as follows:

". . . a substantial amount of the stock of the defendant corporation stands of record in the name of brokers or their nominees and deponent verily believes that most, if not all of the bona fide owners of such stock, who are not owners of record, hold stock certificates registered in the name of such brokers or nominees. Many of these brokers, in accordance with the custom under the rules of the New York Stock Exchange requested additional copies of the notice of the special meeting of December 28, 1943, and the other documents mailed therewith to stockholders of record for the purpose of forwarding to their customers and obtaining voting instructions. In each such case the additional copies requested were furnished by the defendant corporation which also supplied such brokers with the amount requested to cover expenses for forwarding the material to their customers and your deponent verily believes that the customers of such brokers in that manner received notice of said meeting and were in a position to have their stock voted in accordance with their instructions. Proxies for the meeting of December 28, 1943, received from brokers, which invariably covered only a portion of the stock registered in their respective names, would indicate this to be a fact."

By this, it does not seem to me that defendant has demonstrated that supplying brokers with copies of the notice was an adequate or appropriate means of notifying the particular group of shareholders to whom the defendant wrongfully failed to give notice.

The means of notification here were patently insufficient to fulfill the requirement of notice of the meeting. In order to enforce, and to afford adequate protection to, the right to notice of those to whom notice was wrongfully denied, any action of persons assembled pursuant to the notification given should not be accorded the legal significance and consequences which are attendant upon action of stockholders at a meeting validly called and held. Of course, this would not follow if it affirmatively appeared that the persons denied notice had consented to the holding of the meeting, or waived or otherwise given up their right to object. Consequently, at this point in the proceeding, a preliminary injunction to prevent the corporation from recognizing as valid action taken at any assemblage pursuant to the notice dated November 24, 1943, is a proper and suitable form of relief.

Voting Rights

At common law each stockholder was entitled to one vote irrespective of the number of shares of stock he held, but this rule is no longer in effect. The voting rights of stockholders are defined by the laws of the state of incorporation, by the articles of incorporation, and by the by-laws of the corporation. Usually, voting rights are based on the number of shares a stockholder holds. Under the laws of some states it is permissible to issue non-voting common stock and thereby confine voting rights to a small block of closely held shares. Voting rights may be, and frequently are, given only to the holders of the common stock of the corporation. In issues of preferred stock it is a common practice to give the holders of such stock voting rights only in the event that dividends are not paid. Voting rights have also been given to bondholders in the event of default in the payment of interest. The right to vote will be defined by the contract between the corporation and the stockholder, providing the contract is not contrary to the existing laws of the state of incorporation.

As a general rule only stockholders of record will have the right to vote at a stockholders' meeting. The by-laws of the corporation may provide that the transfer books shall be closed a stated number of days before the meeting, and may impose such other reasonable regulations on voting as are expedient, but a stockholder cannot be deprived of his right to vote by a by-law unless he consents thereto. In the absence of regulations either in the state laws, articles of incorporation, or by-laws, the person who has legal title to the stock has the right to vote the stock. The courts have generally held that under this rule the pledgor of stock has the right to vote the stock, and if the stock is registered in the name of the pledgee, the pledgee will, in the absence of an agreement to the contrary, be forced to give the pledgor a proxy so that he can vote the stock.

A corporation cannot vote its own stock which is unissued or which is held as treasury stock, but it can vote stock which it holds in other corporations unless its holding of the stock is ultra vires or unless, for some other reason, the voting of the stock would be against public policy. The fact that a stockholder has a personal interest in the matters being voted on will not deprive him of his right to vote his stock.

Cumulative voting for directors is a common practice, but the right to cumulate votes does not exist unless expressly authorized. Cumulative voting is the privilege, where several directors are to be elected at one time, of casting all of one's votes for one director or distributing them as he wishes. For example, if a stockholder holds ten shares of stock and three directors are to be elected, he may cast ten votes for each director, thirty votes for one director, or fifteen votes for each of two directors.

As a general rule a stockholder can vote by proxy. At common law all stockholders were required to vote in person but now the right to vote by proxy is generally given either by statute, by the articles of incorporation, or by a by-law. Since the right to vote by proxy is an agency, it is revocable at will unless the agency is coupled with an interest.

Sometimes, stockholders will enter into a voting trust agreement for the purpose of controlling the policies of the corporation. They will transfer their shares to a trustee, taking back certificates entitling them to all the beneficial interests in the stock and leaving the voting rights in the trustee. Such arrangements have been held legal and not open to attack so long as the device is not used for the purpose of injuring the stockholders who are not parties to the arrangement.

In re Giant Portland Cement Co.
— Del. Ch. —, 21 A (2d) 697 (1941)

This action was brought by William H. Brown and another and was a petition to review the validity of the election of directors of the Giant Portland Cement Company, a Delaware corporation.

The petitioners claimed that certain shares were improperly counted. The corporation had outstanding 282,543 shares of common stock with voting rights; 214,823 of these shares were voted for the election of directors. Nine directors were to be elected. There were two tickets in the field, one called the "Management" ticket and the other the "Opposition" ticket. Four of the persons nominated for directors were on both tickets and their election was not questioned. The other five who were on the "Opposition" ticket were elected by small pluralities. The leader of the ticket had a plurality of 611 votes; each of the other five had a plurality of 91 votes. By a resolution of the board of directors, stockholders of record as of February 4, 1941, were permitted to vote at the meeting which was held February 24, 1941. The laws of Delaware expressly give the directors the power to close the stock transfer books of a corporation for a period not exceeding fifty days preceding the date of any meeting of stockholders. After February 4, 1941, and before the meeting of February 24, 1941, 6,856 shares of common stock were sold and transferred to new owners, but this stock was voted by the stockholders who were stockholders of record on February 4, 1941. Of these shares 5,472 were voted for the "Opposition" ticket and 1,384 for the "Management" ticket. Petitioners contend that since the stockholders of record were not owners of this stock at the date of the meeting, they had no right to vote it. If these shares are not counted, the "Management" ticket will have a plurality of votes.

The Chancellor. The right to vote shares of corporate stock, having voting powers, has always been incident to its legal ownership. Nor is the first part of Section 17 anything more than declaratory of that common law rule. Moreover, whatever the rights of the mere unrecorded assignee of the stock certificate might be in the absence of a by-law or other contract provision requiring all transfers of shares to be recorded on the books of the corporation, it is not contended that such a provision is not authorized or is not binding as between stockholders and the corporation.

Under the rule in this State, and in numerous other jurisdictions, notwithstanding such a by-law, as between the transferor and the unrecorded transferee of the stock certificates, the legal title, apparently, passes to the latter. Practical reasons may, perhaps, justify that rule.

But a very different rule applies between the corporation and the mere unrecorded assignee of the certificate of stock. That is because limited contract restrictions, relating to stock transfers, are for the benefit of the corporation, and to enable it to ascertain from its records who its members or stockholders are. So far as the corporation is concerned, until such a by-law is complied with, the record owner must, therefore, be regarded as the real owner of the stock, with the consequent general right to vote it by proxy, or otherwise. When considered from a legal standpoint, there is no privity of contract between the mere holder of the certificate and the corporation, and he is not a real member of that organization until the transfer is recorded. Until that time, the possible legal rights of the holder of the certificate are of an inchoate nature. In other words, a real novation, whereby a new contract between the mere holder of the certificate and the corporation is substituted for the prior contract of the record owner, can only be brought about by complying with the corporate regulation relating to transfers of stock. The record owner may, therefore, be the mere nominal owner, or technically, a trustee for the holder of the certificate but legally he is still a stockholder in the corporation, and so far as the corporation is concerned, like the usual trustee, ordinarily has the right to vote the stock standing in his name. In cases of this nature, when nothing more than a mere dry trust is involved the owners of the certificates can usually protect their rights by recording the transfers and having new certificates issued; but, even though that could not be done in this case because the corporate transfer books were closed at the time of the assignments, they could have compelled the record owners to give them proxies to vote the stock standing in their names. A mere nominal owner naturally owes some duties to the real beneficial or equitable owner of the stock; and even if the right to demand a proxy is not exercised, if the vendor exercises his legal right to vote in such a manner as to materially and injuriously affect the rights of the vendee, he is, perhaps, answerable in damages in some cases. The real scope of that rule, as between the parties, need not be considered; but, even in this proceeding, it can hardly be contended that the actual consent of the holder of the certificate is ordinarily essential to the right of the record owners to vote stock standing in their names. At any rate, in cases of this nature, in the absence of an objection, consent would ordinarily be presumed.

Section 29 of the General Corporation Law, is, also, in general accord with these established principles. It provides a limited, but practical statutory rule of evidence, whereby the persons entitled to notice of and to vote at a stockholders' meeting can be readily ascertained by an inspection of the corporate records; but it is in no sense the real origin of the stockholder's right to vote.

Ordinarily, the inspectors conducting an election for the selection of directors for the corporation are bound by that section, and cannot question the right of a registered owner to vote stock standing in his name on the books of the corporation. But when Section 29 is read in connection with Section 31, it is apparent that it is not necessarily controlling on this Court, if inequitable circumstances appear making it improper for the record owner, having the bare legal title, to vote the stock standing in his name.

All of the persons nominated on the "Opposition" ticket were, therefore, legally elected directors of the defendant corporation.

Trefethen v. Amazeen et al.
—N.H.—, 36A (2d) 266 (1944)

This was an action by E. T. Trefethen (plaintiff) against Nancy Amazeen, trustee and others (defendants). The case was transferred from the trial court to the Supreme Court. The case was discharged because of errors in the form of the petition; however, the court held the voting agreement to be valid.

April 7, 1933, the plaintiff and George B. Chadwick each owned 50 shares of the common stock of the defendant Atlantic Terminal Corporation, organized under the laws of this state. Stanley O. Holden owned 270 shares and other persons 26 shares. In order to secure additional funds for the corporation, the three individuals, named on the date stated, agreed in writing that in consideration of Chadwick and Trefethen each buying 52 shares of the preferred stock entitling them to 52 shares each of the common stock, Holden would not vote 92 shares of his common stock without their consent so long as either of them personally owned any stock, preferred or common, in said corporation. The result was that Holden even with the votes of the 26 shares held by others would have no greater voting power than Chadwick and Trefethen. The stock was purchased and the plaintiff Trefethen later acquired Chadwick's shares of common stock so that he now owns 204 shares of the common stock. Holden's stock was transferred to defendant Amazeen as trustee, who claims the right to vote all the Holden common stock regardless of the voting agreement.

Johnston, J. The validity of a contract between stockholders is to be determined by the effects of its provisions. In *Bowditch* v. *Jackson Company*, 76 N.H. 351, 82 A. 1014, this Court upheld a stockholders' agreement for a voting trust applying as a test the conclusions that there was no wrong to the corporation, no special benefit to the parties to the contract and no turning over of management to strangers. The Court did not leave out of consideration other stockholders individually and creditors. Briefly, the present stockholders' agreement was for the purpose of securing additional working capital for the corporation and provided that Mr. Holden would waive his right to vote certain shares so long as either of the other two contracting stockholders should own stock in the company, so that these two would be able to vote at least 50 per cent of the voting stock. The effect of this upon other interests no one can say. "It is not in violation of any rule or principle of law nor contrary to public policy for stockholders who own a majority of the stock of a corporation to cause its affairs to be managed in such a way as they may think best calculated to further the ends of the corporation, ..." See also 71 A.L.R. 1290 for a statement that voting trust agreements and so-called pooling agreements are valid if beneficial to the corporation, "as, for instance, for the purpose of financing it." The trial Court has found that there was no fraud in fact.

"Prima facie the right to vote accompanies the legal title, but when the title is divided, and an equity exists, as between pledgor and pledgee, trustee and cestui que trust, or, as in the present case, between vendor and (a) vendee with a title inchoate until payment, the right to vote is subject to the agreement of the parties. This is the rule . . . . of the common law."

Certainly the party to the contract so assenting cannot complain of the loss of the right to vote. There is no unreasonable restraint on alienation of the stock where the stock may still be transferred although possibly less attractive because of a waiver of voting rights for a definite time made in an agreement otherwise valid. The defendant trustee acquired the stock in question subject to and with full knowledge of the agreement of April 7, 1933, and has no greater rights with respect thereto than Stanley O. Holden.

Right To Inspect

In the United States the courts have held that a stockholder has the right to inspect the books, papers, and property of the corporation at a reasonable time and place providing he does so for legitimate purposes. The stockholder may employ an attorney, accountant, or other agent to aid him in his inspection and may make copies of such portions of the books and papers as he wishes. In many states this rule has been broadened by statute. The statutes generally provide that the stockholders of private corporations shall "have the right of access to, inspection and examination of books, records, and papers of the corporation, at reasonable and proper times"; however, the court will deny a stockholder the right to inspect the books and papers of the corporation if it can be shown that he wishes to use the information for illegal purposes or for the benefit of a competitor to the detriment of the corporation.

Sanders v. Neely et al.
— Miss. —, 19 So. (2d) 424 (1944)

This was an action by R. D. Sanders (plaintiff) against W. H. Neely and others, executive officers of the Standard Life Insurance Company of the South (defendants). Judgment for defendants and plaintiff appealed. Judgment reversed and remanded.

Plaintiff was a stockholder in the Standard Life Insurance Company of the South and requested permission of its officers to examine the books and records of the company "at such times and under conditions that would not interfere with the operation or conduct of the affairs" thereof. This request was refused and plaintiff filed a petition for a writ of mandamus ordering the officers to permit such inspection.

McGehee, J. The common law right of a stockholder to inspect the books and records of his corporation is stated in 13 Am. Jur. 480, as follows: "A stockholder in a corporation has, in the very nature of things and upon principles of equity, good faith, and fair dealing, the right to know how the affairs of the company are conducted and whether the capital of which he has contributed a share is being prudently and profitably employed. In order to obtain this information he has . . . . a common law right, at proper and seasonable times, to inspect all the books and records of the corporation." And, it is not contended by counsel for the appellees herein that this is not an accurate statement of the rule, but it is stated by them, and correctly so, that this common law right can be exercised by the stockholder only in good faith and for a just, useful or reasonable purpose germane to his interest as a stockholder; and that such right will not be enforced by the courts for speculative purpose or to gratify idle curiosity, and particularly when the purpose of the inspection is hostile to the corporation. In other words, the appellees contend that to this extent the right is not absolute, but is a qualified one.

It may be conceded that such right as a stockholder may have in this State to inspect and examine the books and records of his corporation is governed by the common law, since we have no statute providing therefor, and also that the same is qualified to the extent above stated.

Altering Capital Structure

An increase or reduction in the capital stock of a corporation involves a change in the fundamental structure of the corporation, and such change will require stockholder consent. An increase or reduction cannot be made merely by a vote of the stockholders, but in making such a change in the capital structure, the laws of the state of incorporation must be complied with. Such change usually is made by amending the articles of incorporation. If the power to increase or reduce the capital stock of the corporation is expressly given to the board of directors, either by statute or by the articles of incorporation, stockholder action is dispensed with; however, as a general rule, the statutes provide that no such change shall be made unless it is authorized by the stockholders, and many of the statutes provide that it will require the affirmative vote of two-thirds of the voting power of all stockholders.

If a corporation purchases its own stock and holds it as treasury stock, the corporation has not reduced its capital stock.

In the event of a reduction of the capital stock of a corporation, each stockholder has the right to have his holdings reduced pro rata; however, this right may be waived by the stockholders whose interests are affected by the reduction. A corporation will not be permitted to reduce its capital stock and distribute its assets to stockholders if such distribution will injure the rights of creditors.

In the event of an increase in the capital stock, each stockholder is entitled to purchase his proportionate share of the increase. Each stockholder has a proportionate control over the corporate business through his voting rights, and he also is entitled, on dissolution and distribution, to his proportionate share of the profits and assets. These rights cannot be taken away from him without his consent. This right to purchase a proportionate share in the increase of the capital stock of the corporation is known as a stockholder's pre-emptive right. By statute some states provide that unless this pre-emptive right is expressly provided for when the increase in capital stock is authorized, the right is waived.

A common device used to protect this right of the stockholders is the issue of stock rights. When the increase in the capital stock is authorized, the corporation will issue to each stockholder rights which entitle him to his proportionate share of the increase. These stock rights, which are transferable, enable the stockholder to sell the rights and realize any benefits which might accompany the right to purchase shares of the new issue.

The courts have also applied the principle of pre-emptive rights to the distribution of unissued stock in cases where the results of the distribution of the unissued stock are similar to the distribution of a new issue. The Archer Corporation is organized in 1910 with an authorized capital stock of $2,000,000 of which $1,000,000 is issued. In 1940, after the corporation has been operated successfully for thirty years, it is decided that the $1,000,000 of unissued stock will be distributed. Some courts have held that in such a situation the old stockholders will have pre-emptive rights in the unissued stock.

In re Watkins' Will
In re Lincoln Alliance Bank & Trust Co.
51 N.Y.S. (2d) 46 (1944)

This action was a petition by the Lincoln Alliance Bank & Trust Company as executor of the will of Carrie P. Watkins, deceased, for the construction of the will and distribution of two shares of stock.

By her will Carrie P. Watkins bequeathed to her daughter 22 shares of Eastman Kodak stock "together with any stock dividends which hereafter increase the number of shares so held by me." No stock dividends were declared but the capital stock was increased, and the testatrix purchased and held at the time of her death two shares of stock which she was entitled to purchase under her pre-emptive rights. The court was requested to determine the nature of and the ownership of the two shares of stock.

Feely, Surrogate. Although a "right" to purchase stock differs to this extent that it is designed to bring new capital into the corporation, with a corresponding increase in the number of shares, it otherwise rests on the same recognition that such an offer by the company is also an appurtenant to the ownership of stock, inasmuch as the offer must be made first to the existing stockholders before it can be available to outsiders. So, such a right has been declared to be one that is preferential, or pre-emptive, having the "first call," because it is an equity inherent in stock ownership, as a quality inseparable from the capital interest represented by the old stock. Where the stockholder exercises the right, he does so to protect as far as possible the existing principal in a disadvantageous situation; and the new stock is an addition to principal. Where the right is sold, the proceeds are "an increment to principal," and the original holding then has relatively less participation in the company. The act of this testatrix in exercising the right inherent in her 22 shares necessarily changed their value and effectiveness. By the purchase the quality of her first holding was somewhat impaired or "diluted"; but not as much as if the rights had been sold. The purchase put the old shares on the same level with the two new ones. The purchase was not an entirely independent matter; but was partly a modification of the original shares, made possible by the capital attribute known as a stock right. When she had adjusted her position by that means, she carried both lots together until her death.

The right, as an appurtenant to stock, while not literally a source of increase, is yet an original inherent means to prevent a decrease in its value, or to minimize the loss, and thus provides a sort of protection. When advantage is taken of this provision, the old stock and the new develop into a relation to each other that is real and mutual for some purposes. In this respect the right resembles a specific piece of productive property that necessarily carries with it, or in its train, as the subject of a bequest, all its natural or constructive appurtenances, increments or increases, unless the testator expresses a different intention in bequeathing the property.

Here the testatrix clearly bequeathed a lot of specified stock, with some of its future increase. Thereafter the benefit or protection that accrued to it through her use of the right was partly the development of an attribute that was inherent in the original stock itself, and both lots were kept by her together until her death, and should pass in the same way.

Stockholders' Suits, Minority Stockholders' Rights

A stockholder has the right to sue the corporation to enforce his personal rights against the corporation. A stockholder cannot maintain an action at law against third persons or against the directors or officers of the corporation to enforce a right belonging to the corporation. However, under certain conditions, a stockholder may bring an action in equity in behalf of the corporation or in behalf of himself and other stockholders for the purpose of enforcing rights of the corporation. Before a court of equity will accept jurisdiction of such a case, the stockholder must show that he has made a good-faith effort to induce the directors or officers to bring suit in behalf of the corporation, and that they have refused to act, and that such refusal is a breach of their fiduciary duty to the corporation. If the refusal to sue is properly within the discretionary powers of the directors, a stockholder will not be permitted to sue.

The general rule of majority control applies in the affairs of a corporation. Unless a greater proportion than a majority is expressly required, the vote of the majority is controlling. Under this rule the minority stockholders have no control over the affairs of the corporation. As long as the majority act in good faith, the minority stockholders must abide by the decisions of the majority; if the business is not managed to their liking, they can sell their stock. However, if the majority of stockholders pursue a course which will operate as a fraud on the minority stockholders, a court of equity will interfere in behalf of the minority stockholders.

Green v. Victor Talking Machine Co.
24 F. (2d) 378 (1928)

This was an action by Lydia M. Green (plaintiff) against Victor Talking Machine Company (defendant). Judgment for defendant and plaintiff appealed. Judgment affirmed.

The plaintiff owns all the stock of the Pearsall Company, a corporation, having acquired the same under the will of her deceased husband. The Pearsall Company's business was to resell products purchased by it from the defendant. The corporation had an agency contract with the defendant which gave it the right to sell defendant's products "as long as said corporation should remain financially sound and successful in the sale of defendant's products." Plaintiff claims that after the death of her husband the defendant and its directors entered into a malicious scheme and conspiracy to secure for itself or its nominee the assets and good will of the Pearsall Company, and in furtherance of such scheme sought to induce plaintiff to sell her stock, by falsely pretending to give her disinterested advice to sell, and by attempting to intimidate her into selling by notifying her that, unless she would do so, defendant would cease to deal with Pearsall Company after December 14, 1924, although Pearsall Company had remained financially sound and a successful distributor of defendant's products; that defendant sought to cause employees of Pearsall Company to leave it, gave its competitors confidential information concerning its business and finances, damaged its credit, and by secret and unfair means interfered with its business; that defendant offered to withdraw its refusal to sell its products to Pearsall Company after December 14, 1924, if plaintiff would sell her stock, and, upon her declination, defendant did cease to sell to Pearsall Company after said date; and that by reason of the unlawful and malicious acts of defendant the value of Pearsall Company as a going concern was destroyed, and all the benefits accruing to plaintiff through her ownership of its stock were lost, to her damage in the sum of $500,000.

Swan, C. J. The essence of her complaint is that defendant, after inducing her testator to purchase certain shares in the Pearsall Company, impaired the value of them (1) by affirmative interference with its business; and (2) by refusing to continue to deal with it; and did these things with the purpose of inducing her to sell her stock to the defendant's nominee, and, failing in that, with the purpose of destroying the value of her shares.

Considering first the affirmative interference with the corporation's business: The attempt to induce employees to leave the Pearsall Company, not only is nowhere alleged to have been successful, but, if so, would have given rise to a cause of action to the corporation, rather than to its shareholders. The allegations of disclosure of confidential information, damage to credit, and unfair interference with business are mere conclusions of the pleader; but, even if they were treated as adequately pleaded, they would be subject to the same objection that they charge a breach of duty owing to the corporation rather than to its shareholders. The shareholders' rights are derivative, and, except through the corporation, the shareholders have no relation with one who commits a tort against the corporation's rights.

When there are numerous shareholders, it is apparent that each suffers relatively, depending upon the number of shares he owns, the same damage as all the others, and that each will be made whole if the corporation obtains restitution or compensation from the wrongdoer. Obviously it is sound policy to require a single action to be brought by the corporation, rather than to permit separate suits by each shareholder. In logic the result is justified, because the only right of the shareholder which has been infringed is what may be called his derivative or corporate right. Having elected to conduct their business in a corporate form, the men behind the corporation have, in the phrase of Justice Holmes, "interposed a nonconductor" between themselves and those who deal with them in their corporate enterprise. Even when all the stock is owned by a sole shareholder, there seems no adequate reason to depart from the general rule that the corporation and its shareholders are to be treated as distinct legal persons. Therefore even a sole shareholder has no independent right which is violated by trespass upon or conversion of the corporation's property. Only his "corporate rights" have been invaded, and consequently he cannot sue the tort-feasor in an action at law.

Allied Chemical & Dye Corporation v. Steel & Tube Co. of America et al.
14 Del. Ch. 1, 120 Atl. 486 (1923)

This was an action by Allied Chemical & Dye Corporation (By-Products Cook Corporation, intervener) (plaintiffs) against Steel and Tube Company of America, Clayton Marks and others (defendants). Preliminary injunction was granted and defendants appealed. Decree affirmed.

Plaintiffs and the intervener are minority stockholders in defendant corporation. They own 20 per cent of the entire common stock issued. The majority of the stockholders authorized the sale of the entire assets of the defendant corporation to the Youngstown Sheet & Tube Company. If the sale is completed, the common stockholders will realize only 40.5 per cent of the book value of their stock. Preferred stockholders will be paid in full. The plaintiffs claim that the sale of the assets is a fraud on the minority stockholders and ask that the sale be enjoined.

The Chancellor. Before examining the facts adduced by the complainants for the purpose of showing fraud, it will be in order first to define the relations which equity will regard as subsisting between the controlling majority members of the corporation and the minority. That under certain circumstances these relations are of a fiduciary character is clear.

No one, of course, questions the fiduciary character of the relationship which the directors bear to the corporation. The same considerations of fundamental justice which impose a fiduciary character upon the relationship of the directors to the stockholders will also impose, in a proper case, a like character upon the relationship which the majority of the stockholders bear to the minority. When, in the conduct of the corporate business, a majority of the voting power in the corporation join hands in imposing their policy upon all, it is beyond all reason and contrary, it seems to me, to the plainest dictates of what is just and right, to take any view other than that they are to be regarded as having placed upon themselves the same sort of fiduciary character which the law impresses upon the directors in their relation to all the stockholders. Ordinarily the directors speak for and determine the policy of the corporation. When the majority of stockholders do this, they are, for the moment, the corporation. Unless the majority in such case are to be regarded as owing a duty to the minority such as is owed by the directors to all, then the minority are in a situation that exposes them to the grossest frauds and subjects them to most outrageous wrongs.

When a number of stockholders combine to constitute themselves a majority in order to control the corporation as they see fit, they become, for all practical purposes, the corporation itself, and assume the trust relation occupied by the corporation towards its stockholders. Although stockholders are not partners, nor strictly tenants in common, they are the beneficial joint owners of the corporate property, having an interest and power of legal control in exact proportion to their respective amounts of stock. The corporation itself holds its property as a trust fund for the stockholders, who have a joint interest in all its property and effects, and the relation between it and its several members, is for all practical purposes, that of trustee and cestui que trust. When several persons have a common interest in property, equity will not allow one to appropriate it exclusively to himself, or to impair its value to the others. Community of interest involves mutual obligation. Persons occupying this relation towards each other are under an obligation to make the property or fund productive of the most that can be obtained from it for all who are interested in it; and those who seek to make a profit out of it, at the expense of those whose rights in it are the same as their own, are unfaithful to the relation they have assumed, and are guilty, at least, of constructive fraud. In *Dodge* v. *Woolsey*, 18 How. (59 U.S.) 331, (15 L. Ed. 401), Wayne, J., says: "It is now no longer doubted, either in England or the United States, that courts of equity in both have a jurisdiction over corporations, at the instance of one or more of their members, to apply preventive remedies by injunction, to restrain those who administer them from doing acts which would amount to a violation of charters, or to prevent any misapplication of their capital or profits, which might result in lessening the dividends of stockholders or the value of their shares, as either may be protected by the franchises of a corporation, if the acts intended to be done create what is in the law denominated a breach of trust. And the jurisdiction extends to inquire into, and to enjoin, as the case may require that to be done, any proceedings by individuals, in whatever character they may profess to act, if the subject of complaint is an imputed violation of a corporate franchise, or the denial of a right growing out of it, for which there is not an adequate remedy at law. . . . . It is not only illegal for a corporation to apply its capital to objects not contemplated by its character, but also to apply its profits. . . . ."

The present case furnishes an instance of gross abuse of trust. Must the cestui que trust be committed to the domination of a trustee who has for seven years continued to violate the trust? The law requires of the majority the utmost good faith in the control and management of the corporation as to the minority. It is of the essence of this trust that it shall be so managed as to produce for each stockholder the best possible return for his investment. The trustee has so far absorbed all returns. What is the outlook for the future? This court, in view of the past, can give no assurances. It can make no order that can prevent some other method of bleeding this corporation, if it is allowed to continue. I think a court of equity, under the circumstances of this case, in the exercise of its general equity jurisdiction, has the power to grant to this complainant ample relief, even to the dissolution of the trust relations. Complainant is therefore entitled to the relief prayed.

Stockholder Liability

If stock has been issued to the stockholders of the corporation as fully paid and non-assessable, and the full agreed purchase price has been paid at the time of issue, the corporation cannot assess and collect from the stockholder any additional amount. If at the time of issue the full agreed purchase price of the stock is not paid, the unpaid balance becomes a debt owing to the corporation and can be collected in the same manner as any other debt owing to the corporation. If the stock is issued as assessable stock, the holder of the stock at the time any assessment is made is liable for the assessment. As a general rule the transferee of stock is liable for any unpaid balance of the purchase price of the stock or assessment on the stock, but if the transfer is made to one who cannot be held liable or who is insolvent, the transferor will be held.

The creditor of a corporation has all the rights of a creditor of a natural person. The creditor can reduce his claim to judgment and, by process, enforce its payment out of the assets of the corporation. On dissolution and winding up of the corporation, the creditors must be paid out of the assets of the corporation before any part of the assets is distributed to the stockholders. Although the stockholder's liability is limited to his investment, if he has received a dividend out of capital or has not paid his subscription in full, he is considered as a debtor of the corporation, and in an appropriate action, usually a creditor's bill, he can be made to pay what he owes to the corporation for the benefit of corporate creditors. The creditor cannot sue the stockholder in a direct action but must bring the action in a court of equity in behalf of the creditors of the corporation. As a general rule, the action can be brought against one or more of the stockholders, and judgment for the entire amount of the unlawfully paid dividend which they have received or the entire amount of the unpaid balance of the subscription can be recovered. A similar situation arises when stock is issued for less than par, as fully paid and non-assessable, or for labor or for property of a value less than the par value of the stock. If we consider the relationship of the corporation and the stockholders, the stockholder does not owe the corporation anything. However, the courts in the majority of jurisdictions allow the creditors of an insolvent corporation to recover from the stockholder. The various jurisdictions are not in accord as to the basis of the right or the amount of the recovery. Some hold the stockholder liable on the ground that the transaction is a fraud on the creditor, while others hold the stockholder liable on the ground that the capital of the corporation is a trust fund for the benefit of the creditors, and it cannot be distributed among the stockholders without provisions first being made for the payment of creditors. A third view is that there is an obligation on the stockholder to contribute to the capital of the corporation for the benefit of creditors as an incident to membership in the corporation. In some states, by statute, stockholders are made liable if they purchased their stock from the corporation for less than par or exchanged property or labor for stock at a value less than par.

G. Loewus & Co., Inc. v. Highland Queen Packing Co.
125 N.J. Eq. 534, 6 A. (2d) 545 (1939)

This was an action by G. Loewus & Co. (plaintiff) against Highland Queen Packing Company (defendant) wherein a receiver was appointed. The receiver seeks to have three stockholders in the Highland Queen Packing Company assessed a sum sufficient to pay creditors and administration expenses on the theory that their stock is not fully paid.

Decree for the stockholders.

The Highland Queen Packing Company's articles of incorporation authorized the issue of no-par stock at a price to be fixed by the board of directors. Jessie B. Triplett and Boise E. Triplett sold their business to the corporation, the corporation agreeing to assume and pay all outstanding obligations of the business, and they received in payment 200 shares of the capital stock of the corporation. Edgar H. Lackey paid $1,050 and cancelled a note for $950 which he held, the payment of which was expressly assumed by the corporation as part payment for the business conveyed to it by the Tripletts, and 100 shares of the capital stock of the corporation were issued to him. The following statement was included in the corporation records in connection with these transactions: "It is understood that the said shares of stock shall be issued at the price of $20 per share and representing a total value of $6,000." The books of the corporation show that it is indebted to Lackey in the sum of $2,000, but Lackey denies that the company is indebted to him and claims that the $2,000 was paid to the corporation for his stock.

The assets and good will of the business turned over by the Tripletts to the corporation were worth only $1,500, so it is alleged. The receiver takes the position that the consideration for the stock fixed by the directors was $20 per share, or a total of $6,000, of which only $1,500, or $1,500 plus $1,050, has been paid, and that there is owing by the stockholders the difference or so much thereof as may be necessary to satisfy creditors.

Bigelow, Vice Chancellor. The duty of holders of par value stock—as distinguished from non-par stock—to contribute toward the payment of creditors finds three supports: One is the contract of the subscriber to pay a certain amount for his shares. Upon the insolvency of the company and the abandonment of its business, he is relieved of his obligation except so far as may be necessary to satisfy creditors. But his contractual debt to that extent remains enforceable at the suit of creditors or receiver. Second comes the trust fund or fraud theory which rests liability upon the representation or holding out to persons extending credit to the company, that its capital, in a certain sum, has been paid in full. The third basis for liability is statutory. "It depends upon the stockholder's voluntary acceptance, for considerations touching his own interest, of a statutory scheme to which watered stock, under whatever device issued, is absolutely alien, and which requires stock subscriptions to be made good for the benefit of creditors of insolvent companies."

The statutory plan on which stockholders' liability depends is found principally in three sections of our corporation act, which provides that where the capital shall not have been paid in full, and the capital paid shall be insufficient to satisfy debts, each stockholder shall be bound to pay the sum necessary to complete the amount of each share held by him or such proportion thereof as shall be required to satisfy the creditors. In the event less than the full amount of the stock is paid and the company becomes insolvent, the stockholders are liable to pay in the balance regardless of any contract or understanding which they had with the corporation, for any agreement by the company to accept less than par is void as to creditors. Liability does not depend on a "holding out" to creditors.

Par value stock has a definite value, fixed by the certificate of incorporation, stated in terms of dollars, but it may be issued for money or property or services. Stock without par value is issued for a "consideration" prescribed by the certificate of incorporation or by directors or stockholders. The consideration fixed may be money or property, or anything that constitutes a good and valuable consideration.

In *Smith* v. *General Motors Corp.*, 6 Cir., 289 F. 205, a suit by a solvent corporation on a subscription to its stock, the circuit court of appeals said that a subscription for stock of a definite par value and one for no-par value stock at a fixed and definite price seemed to depend upon the same principles and affirmed a judgment for the amount due on the subscription to non-par stock.

Likewise, in the case of insolvency, pretty much the same principles determine the obligations of subscribers and holders of either class of stock. If the consideration for non-par stock is duly fixed at $20 a share, and only $10 a share is paid in, then R.S. 14:8-13, N.J.S.A. 14:8-13, becomes effective and the stockholders may be assessed. Or if the consideration be certain property and the stock is issued though only a part of the property is transferred to the corporation, the stockholders must answer to the call of creditors.

Counsel for respondents direct attention to the provision in R.S. 14:8-6, N.J.S.A. 14:8-6, that "shares without nominal or par value issued as permitted by this article shall be deemed fully paid and non-assessable, and the holder of such shares shall not be liable to the corporation or its creditors in respect thereof." A similar provision relating to par value stock issued for property is found in R.S. 14:3-9, N.J.S.A. 14:3-9, and has been part of our statute law many years. The question remains whether there was delivered to the corporation in exchange for the stock the full consideration as fixed by the directors. Careful examination of the minutes satisfies me that the only consideration which the Tripletts offered to give and the directors agreed to accept was the transfer of the business conducted by the Tripletts. The directors, by accepting the offer, fixed the consideration for the stock within the intent of R.S. 14:8-13, N.J.S.A. 14:8-13. The meaning of the statement in the minutes that the stock should be issued at the price of $20 per share, or a total value of $6,000, is not clear. Certainly the parties did not intend that $6,000 should be paid in, additional to the transfer of the business, or even that the difference between $6,000 and the value of the business should be paid in. Probably the sentence has some relation to the deal with Lackey, who was paying $2,000 for a third interest in the enterprise.

The duly fixed consideration for the stock was fully satisfied and the stockholders are not assessable.

QUESTIONS AND PROBLEMS

1. In 1877, the Manufacturing Co. became insolvent and Harlin took over its affairs and made a compromise settlement with its creditors. The Manufacturing Co. prospered, and creditors were paid in full. A surplus of about $150,000 was built up, all debts were paid, and a 25% dividend had been paid for several years. The yearly earnings had been $100,000 or more. McNab brought a bill in equity to force the distribution of the surplus as dividends. The directors answered that the surplus was used as working capital and was necessary to the efficient operation of the business. Should the payment of a dividend be ordered?
2. The Mill Co., a corporation, being solvent and possessing ample surplus funds, at a regular meeting of its board of directors, unanimously adopted the following resolution: "Moved and seconded that the company declare a dividend of six per cent, payable February 15, April 1, July 1, and October 1, 1903." No further resolution was passed, nor were funds set aside out of which the dividend was to be paid. The first installment was paid, but thereafter the company rescinded its action. A stockholder sued to recover the installment due April 1. Can he recover?
3. The president of the Atlantic Co. published in one newspaper a notice of a special meeting of stockholders to be held at Newborn, N.C. The stockholders present at the meeting adjourned to Moorehead, N.C., on the same day. The stockholders present voted to authorize a lease. Suit was brought to annul the lease on the ground that the stockholders' meeting was not properly called and held. Is this contention correct?
4. At an annual meeting of its stockholders, the by-laws of the Reno Oil Co. were

amended whereby the number of directors was increased from nine to eleven. Thereafter, the stockholders present proceeded to elect two more directors than was necessary to fill existing vacancies. Were the extra directors legally elected?

5. At an election of directors, stock which was pledged to Watson and which stood on the books in the name of "Watson, trustee" was denied the right to vote because Watson was pledgee and not title owner. The state statute, the charter, and the by-laws provided that: "the certificate of stock and the transfer books of the corporation shall be prima facie evidence of the right to vote thereon at any election." Did Watson have the right to vote the stock?
6. Varney owned 80 shares of the capital stock of a corporation, the whole number of shares being 350. Varney had been told that the corporation had lost several thousand dollars. Varney demanded permission to examine the books of the corporation, and his demand was refused on the ground that the corporation was solvent and prosperous. Varney brought an action to obtain permission to examine the books. Should he be permitted to examine the books?
7. The directors of the City Railway Co., without calling a meeting of the stockholders, resolved to increase the capital stock of the company from $1,250,000 to $1,500,000. Allerton, a stockholder, objected and filed a suit asking for an injunction to prevent the increase. Should the injunction be granted?
8. The Trust Co. increased its capital stock from $500,000 to $1,000,000. The directors agreed to sell the entire increase, without giving the stockholders an opportunity to purchase any portion of it, to an investment banker. This agreement was approved by a majority vote of the stockholders. Stokes, a stockholder, voted against the sale of the new issue. Stokes brought an action to compel the corporation to issue to him a proportionate number of shares of the new issue. Is Stokes entitled to an opportunity to purchase a proportionate number of shares of the increase?
9. The Copper Co. issued its shares of common stock as fully paid and nonassessable at 33% of its par value. Harley and others purchased the stock. The corporation gave Sherman its note for $10,000. The corporation is insolvent. Sherman sued Harley and others to recover on the corporate note. Is Sherman entitled to a judgment?
10. The Hardware Co., while doing business at a loss, paid a dividend on its outstanding capital stock. Two months thereafter it made an assignment for the benefit of its creditors. The assignee paid 55% of the debts, which exhausted the assets. The Wire Co., a creditor, sued Eddy, a stockholder, to recover the amount paid to Eddy as dividends. Must Eddy refund the dividend?

CHAPTER XXXIX

MERGER, CONSOLIDATION, REORGANIZATION, AND DISSOLUTION

Merger and Consolidation

Mergers and consolidations are the union of two or more corporations under legislative authority. Frequently, the terms are used synonymously, but technically there is a distinction between a merger and a consolidation. In a merger one of the corporations retains its charter, franchises, privileges, and property—it absorbs the other corporation—while in a consolidation all the consolidating corporations are consolidated into a new corporation. The procedure to be followed in effecting a merger or consolidation will be set out in the statutes of the state under which the merger or consolidation is to be effected. In the event of a consolidation, as a general rule, the consolidating corporations are dissolved and cease to exist, while in a merger only the merging corporation is dissolved.

By a merger or a consolidation the creditors of the merging or consolidating corporations cannot be deprived of their right to have access to the property of such corporations for the payment of their claims. In some states the statutes will define the rights of creditors and the procedure to be followed in enforcing such rights. In the absence of statutory provisions the merged or the consolidated corporation may be held liable for the debts and contracts of the merging or consolidating corporations. This is true if all the liabilities of the merging and consolidating corporations are expressly assumed by the merged or consolidated corporation. In any event the assets of the merging or consolidating corporations can be followed in equity and be applied to the payment of claims. If all liabilities are assumed by the merged or consolidated corporation, the liability of the merged or consolidated corporation for the debts and contracts of the merging or consolidating corporations is unlimited. If the assets are followed in equity, as a general rule, recovery will not exceed the value of the assets which the merging or consolidating corporations had at the time of the merger or consolidation.

If one corporation purchases all the assets or all the stock of another corporation, the corporations are not merged or consolidated—each corporation will continue to exist. To have a merger or consolidation there must be a statute which permits the merger or consolidation, and the requirements of the statute must be complied with.

Freeman, Secretary of Banking v. Hiznay et al.
349 Pa. 89, 36 A. (2d) 509 (1944)

This was an action by William C. Freeman, Secretary of Banking (plaintiff) against Joseph M. Hiznay and Victor Lee Dodson (defendants). From a judgment against Hiznay for the sum of $17,500 and from a judgment in favor of defendant Dodson, the plaintiff appealed. Judgment reversed and remanded with directions.

The Pennsylvania Bank and Trust Company of Wilkes-Barre was incorporated in 1912 to carry on the business of banking, and Liberty State Bank and Trust Company was incorporated in 1923 to carry on the business of insuring titles to real estate. In 1929, the two corporations, both of which were solvent, consolidated under the name of Pennsylvania Liberty Bank and Trust Company.

At the time of consolidation, Pennsylvania Bank and Trust Company of Wilkes-Barre had a capital stock of $200,000 divided into 2,000 shares of a par value of $100 each, and Liberty State Bank and Trust Company had a capital stock of $250,000 divided into 5,000 shares of a par value of $50 each. Pennsylvania Liberty Bank and Trust Company, the consolidated corporation, was organized with a capital stock of $325,000, divided into 13,000 shares of a par value of $25 each, of which 8,000 were exchanged and distributed to the shareholders of Pennsylvania Bank and Trust Company of Wilkes-Barre in the proportion of four shares of new stock for one share of old stock, and 5,000 shares were exchanged and distributed to the shareholders of Liberty State Bank and Trust Company in the proportion of one share of new stock for one share of old stock. The statute under which the Pennsylvania Bank and Trust Company of Wilkes-Barre was incorporated imposed a double liability on the stockholder, but the law under which Liberty State Bank and Trust Company was organized imposed no additional liability on its stockholders.

The Secretary of Banking took over the Pennsylvania Liberty Bank and Trust Company in September, 1931. One of the shareholders was Joseph M. Hiznay, who had originally owned 175 shares of Pennsylvania Bank and Trust Company of Wilkes-Barre of the aggregate par value of $17,500, which he had exchanged in the consolidation for 700 shares of Pennsylvania Liberty Bank and Trust Company of the same aggregate par value, and had thereafter purchased 606 additional shares of Pennsylvania Liberty Bank and Trust Company of the aggregate par value of $15,150; he thus owned, at the time of the assessment, 1,306 shares of the aggregate par value of $32,650. Another shareholder was Victor Lee Dodson, who had owned 61 shares of Liberty State Bank and Trust Company of the aggregate par value of $3,050, which he had exchanged in the consolidation for an equal number of shares of Pennsylvania Liberty Bank and Trust Company of the aggregate par value of $1,525.

The present litigation is a test suit to determine the liability of these two shareholders and thereby that of all the others. The court below entered judgment against Hiznay for the sum of $17,500 (the par value of the stock he had owned in Pennsylvania Bank and Trust Company of Wilkes-Barre), with interest from February 26, 1937, the date when the assessment was payable. As to Dodson the Court entered judgment for defendant.

Horace Stern, J. If the consolidation which resulted in the formation of Pennsylvania Liberty Bank and Trust Company had been that of two banks incorporated under the Act of 1876 there would be no question but that the individual liability imposed by that act on the shareholders of each of the constituent corporations would have continued for the benefit of the creditors of the consolidated corporation. Here, however, we have a union of two companies the shareholders of only one of which were subject to individual liability, and the perplexing question thus arises as to the effect of the consolidation upon the liability or non-liability of the shareholders of the constituent corporations. Was all individual liability destroyed by the consolidation? Or did the shareholders of the consolidated corporation become subject to liability in the full amount, $325,000, of the par value of its capital stock? Or should individual liability be confined to the sum of $200,000, which was the aggregate par value of the stock exchanged for that of Pennsylvania Bank and Trust Company of Wilkes-Barre, and, if so, should the liability in that amount be borne wholly by the holders of the shares which were exchanged for the stock of that company or should it be distributed equally and ratably among all the shareholders of the consolidated corporation? The problem is obviously one that does not lend itself to solution by the application of any particular rules of logic, but calls rather for an answer dictated by practical considerations so far as consistent with legal principles.

The Act of 1876 established the then policy of the State that, in the case of banks, creditors should have the benefit of individual liability of the shareholders in addition to the assets of the corporation itself; why then, should they be deprived of that benefit, or why should the shareholders be allowed to escape such liability, merely because of the consolidation of the bank with another corporation? It is true that while, in the case of a merger, one of the combining corporations continues in existence and absorbs the others, in a consolidation all the combining corporations are deemed to be dissolved and to lose their identity in a new corporate entity which takes over the properties, powers and privileges, as well as the liabilities, of the constituent companies: *Buist's Estate*, 297 Pa. 537, 541, 147 A. 606, 607. But Pennsylvania Liberty Bank and Trust Company, the consolidated corporation, continued to conduct the business of banking, and as its power to do so was derived from the Act of 1876 under which its constituent, Pennsylvania Bank and Trust Company of Wilkes-Barre, had been incorporated, its creditors were entitled to the protection afforded by the liability imposed by that act. Section 3 of the Act of May 3, 1909, under which the consolidation was effected, provided that "all rights of creditors . . . . shall continue unimpaired. . . . ." The general intendment of that act and of the decisions dealing with the consolidation of corporations is to the effect that a consolidation does not work any change in the assets, rights and liabilities of the constituent corporations or in the status of creditors and shareholders; it rather resembles the flowing together of two rivers the waters of which become mingled in a common stream. Therefore the individual liability which existed to the extent of $200,000 when the constituent corporations combined was continued as an attribute of the new corporate organization. On the other hand, just as the consolidation could not impair, so also it could not increase the total amount of that liability, and the Attorney General, conceding this, does not ask that the shareholders of the consolidated corporation be held individually liable to the extent of $325,000, the aggregate par value of the capital stock of the new corporation, but only in the amount of $200,000, since the entire liability of all the shareholders who joined in the formation of the consolidated corporation did not exceed that sum.

We are of opinion that all the shareholders of Pennsylvania Liberty Bank and Trust Company are equally and ratably liable in the aggregate amount of $200,000, which, there being 13,000 shares, constitutes a liability of $15.38 plus per share. The fund raised by the assessment will be for the benefit of all creditors of the consolidated corporation existing at the time of the receivership, whether they had been creditors of either of the constituent corporations or had become creditors only after the consolidation.

Reorganization

The reorganization of a corporation is the scaling down of the debt and share structure of the corporation. It may be accomplished by mutual agreement, but this is difficult to accomplish because each claimant and stockholder will have to agree to relinquish some rights, and unless all, or substantially all, parties in interest agree to the reorganization plan, it will not succeed.

Reorganizations through equitable receiverships were used extensively prior to 1933. In a reorganization through an equity court receivership, a receiver is appointed who takes possession of all the assets of the corporation. Committees are organized which represent the various classes of creditors and stockholders. A new corporation is organized and the assets of the old corporation are sold by the receiver to the new corporation. The new corporation pays for the assets of the old corporation by cancelling the outstanding obligations of the old corporation which have been transferred to it by the committees which represented the various classes of creditors and stockholders. The securities of the new corporation are turned over to the committees in exchange for the obligations of the old corporation, and these securities are distributed by the committee, to the person whom they represent, on a pro rata basis. The reorganization plan is worked out by the committees before the new corporation is organized and before the assets of the old corporation are sold. The details of a reorganization through court procedure vary, but the foregoing plan gives the procedure generally followed.

This procedure proved to be cumbersome, expensive, and in some respects inadequate. By amendments to the national Bankruptcy Act the federal courts have been given jurisdiction over corporate reorganizations. Reorganizations under the bankruptcy act have been simplified, and most of the difficulties encountered in equitable receivership reorganizations have been overcome. The entire reorganization plan is under the supervision of the court. The appointment of the committees, the proposals for the reorganization, and all other details are carried out through the court as a centralizing agency, and the court has the power to force minority creditors and stockholders to accept the plan of reorganization which is finally adopted. The necessity of organizing a new corporation, selling the assets of the old corporation, and other similar procedures of the equitable receivership reorganization have been eliminated. Also a reorganization under the bankruptcy act is less expensive for two reasons—it is simpler and therefore involves less work, and all fees and expenses must be approved by the court.

Dissolution

A corporation is dissolved when its franchise is extinguished and its existence is terminated. A corporation may be dissolved voluntarily by the action of the stockholders with the consent of the state. It may be dissolved by the expiration of the time limited in its charter or by the happening of a contingency prescribed in its charter. If the state has reserved the right, a corporation may be dissolved by statutory action, and if the corporation has violated its charter, the state may dissolve the corporation by court action. Insolvency, discontinuation of the business, or bankruptcy does not ipso facto dissolve a corporation but may furnish the basis of dissolution either by voluntary action or by court action.

After dissolution the corporation is no longer in existence and cannot sue or be sued or function in any other manner. At common law this legal concept of dissolution was followed, and the courts held that on dissolution the corporation's real estate reverted to the persons who granted the property to the corporation and that its personal property went to the state. Claimants lost all rights which they had had against the corporation, and any claims which the corporation had against others were automatically extinguished. Modern courts have not followed this rule. On the dissolution of the corporation, its assets, after the payment of debts, become the property of the stockholders as tenants in common. In the event of voluntary dissolution, the statutes of some states require the winding up of the corporate business as a prerequisite to final dissolution. In most states the court of equity will take jurisdiction of the affairs of the corporation and distribute the assets in accordance with the rights of the various parties in interest. In all states the rights of creditors and stockholders are protected on the dissolution of the corporation.

United States v. Safeway Stores, Inc. (Texas) et al.
140 F. (2d) 834 (1944)

This was an action by the United States (plaintiff) against Safeway Stores, Incorporated (Texas) and others (defendants). From a judgment ordering the proceedings abated, the United States appealed. Judgment affirmed.

Safeway Stores, Inc., was organized under the laws of Maryland. It caused seven subsidiary corporations to be organized. Each of the subsidiary corporations was duly dissolved pursuant to the laws of the state in which it was organized and created. Thereafter, indictments were returned against each subsidiary, charging violation of the Sherman Act. The lower court held that the defendants could not be prosecuted for the reason that their corporate existence had terminated prior to the return of the indictment.

Vaught, D. J. It is well settled at common law and in the federal courts that a corporation which has been dissolved is as if it did not exist. The result of dissolution cannot be distinguished from the death of a natural person in its effect. As the death of a natural person abates all pending litigation to which he is a party, dissolution of a corporation at common law abates all litigation to which the corporation is a party, unless it is continued by the law of the state where it is dissolved for the purpose of prosecuting or defending civil suits or criminal actions. Thus the question, as to whether a corporation is continued for the purpose of prosecuting or defending civil suits or criminal actions, depends upon the law of the state of its incorporation.

If the statutes of the state where the corporation is incorporated and dissolved do not give authority to maintain such a prosecution, it does not exist.

The death of an individual and the administration of his estate, and the dissolution of a corporation and the winding up of its affairs, are the same in principle.

In *State* v. *Arkansas Cotton Oil Co.*, 116 Ark. 74, 171 S.W. 1192, 1193, a suit to recover from a dissolved corporation penalties for violation of the state anti-trust laws, the court said:

"We have here no action for the payment of debts. This is one by the state to recover a penalty; the purpose being not to recover a debt, but to punish for alleged infractions of the law. The statute makes no provision for the continuance or survival of any such action against a dissolved corporation.

"It is insisted that the suit cannot be abated as against the state, and for ground of that contention it is said that the state would be without a remedy. But we inquire: Why cannot the action be abated, if there is nothing in the statute which authorizes its continuance? The legislative will is supreme, and the unqualified right of dissolution is declared in the statute. The statute does, as before stated, contain a provision for the payment of debts and distribution of assets, but this does not, for obvious reasons, apply to the recovery of a penalty."

In the case at bar, no debt or claim is sought to be recovered. At the time of the dissolution of the appellees no actions were pending. There is, as we view it, nothing in the statutes of the various states that authorizes the prosecution against the dissolved corporations.

QUESTIONS AND PROBLEMS

1. What is the difference between a merger and a consolidation?
2. The American Malt Co. was organized to hold the stock of the American Malting Co. The statutes authorized the merger of corporations engaged in businesses of similar nature. The stockholders voted to merge the American Malting Co. into the American Malt Co. Is this permissible under the statute?
3. The Missouri Pacific Railway Co. entered into a contract with the Pullman Co. to haul the Pullman cars on its passenger trains. The Missouri Pacific Railway Co. consolidated with itself certain other companies. The consolidated corporation discontinued hauling Pullman cars. Is the consolidated corporation liable for breach of the contract?
4. If a corporation is reorganized, is it necessary to organize a new corporation to take over the assets of the old corporation?
5. Do the stockholders of a corporation have the power to dissolve the corporation without court action?

CHAPTER XL

FOREIGN CORPORATIONS

Right To Do Business

A corporation created under the laws of a state or country is called a domestic corporation in the state or country of its creation but is called a foreign corporation by states or countries other than that of its creation. Under the rule of comity between states a foreign corporation could do business in another state; however, it has no legal right to do business in any state other than the state creating it. The right to do business as a corporation is a privilege granted by the state creating the corporation, and a state cannot grant privileges to be exercised beyond the territorial jurisdiction of the state which has granted the privilege. Consequently, a corporation cannot do business in any state other than the state creating it without the consent of the other state. Under the rule of comity, consent is implied unless such consent is expressly denied. In the United States it is the universal practice of the states to deny a foreign corporation the right to do business in the state unless certain formalities are complied with.

The early cases held that the state had the right to deny a foreign corporation the right to do business in the state; consequently, the state could impose any restrictions it wished on the foreign corporation as a condition precedent to its doing business in the state. This theory has been repudiated. It is true that the state can impose restrictions on a foreign corporation, but the restrictions imposed must not be in violation of constitutional rights.

When a state grants a corporation permission to do business in the state, it usually imposes some restrictions on that corporation. These restrictions are imposed by state statutes; consequently, they vary in their nature. Usually the foreign corporation must, by complying with statutory requirements, obtain a license to do business in the state. A fee for the license is charged. The corporation must submit to the jurisdiction of the courts of the state, pay taxes on its property in the state, and, in the case of insurance companies, make a deposit with a state official as security for policyholders in the state.

The penalties imposed for doing business in the state without permission are defined by statutes. There is almost no uniformity in such statutes, and in order to learn what penalties are imposed one will have to consult the statutes of the various states. The penalties range from declaring all contracts void to imposing an added percentage to fees. Some states refuse the foreign corporation the use of the courts to enforce their rights; others impose heavy fines.

H. K. Mulford Co. v. Curry
163 Cal. 276, 125 Pac. 236 (1912)

This was an action by H. K. Mulford Company (plaintiff) against C. F. Curry, Secretary of State (defendant). Judgment for plaintiff.

The plaintiff, a foreign corporation, petitioned the court for a writ of mandate ordering the defendant (Secretary of State) to accept and file its petition for a license to do business in the state. The defendant refused to accept and file the petition because it was not accompanied by the fee required by statute. The license tax imposed by the statute was based on the total authorized capital stock of the corporation. Petitioner's contention is that as to it, a foreign corporation, the exaction of these license taxes is the imposition of a direct burden upon its interstate commerce, in violation of the commerce clause of the Constitution of the United States.

Henshaw, J. The principle of the decisions may be briefly stated. The admitted power of the state to regulate and prescribe terms under which a foreign corporation may engage in intrastate or domestic business is subject to this limitation that, where such foreign corporation is engaged in interstate, as well as intrastate, business, no such term, condition, or requirement will be constitutional, if it imposes any burden upon the interstate business of such corporation, whatever be its name or form. A license or privilege tax for the conduct of such intrastate business, based upon the total capital or the total capital stock of such corporation, without just relation to the proportion which the capital or the capital stock used in the state bears to the whole capital or capital stock, though in terms declared to be directed solely to the intrastate business of such corporation, is unconstitutional and void, (a) as being in violation of the commerce clause of the Constitution by the imposition of an illegal burden upon interstate commerce, and (b) because violative of the fourteenth amendment of the Constitution and its equal protection and due process of law clause, as an effort to tax the property of citizens of the United States, which property is situated beyond the jurisdiction of the taxing state, and is not amenable to its revenue laws.

The limitations upon the power of the state to forbid a corporation from doing a domestic business within its borders, or to regulate the conduct of that business, may be thus summarized: A corporation, unless expressly forbidden so to do, may acquire rights of contract and property in a foreign jurisdiction. A state, however, may exclude absolutely a foreign corporation not engaged in interstate commerce, but which proposes solely to engage in domestic business, from doing such business within its limits, and so may, of course, impose terms and conditions upon which alone such business may be commenced within its limits, provided no unconstitutional condition is made a part of any actual agreement. When a foreign corporation has once engaged in domestic business within the state, the state may not exercise its powers of exclusion or regulation to the destruction of the property of the corporation or of its vested constitutional rights. And, finally, when such corporation is engaged both in interstate, as well as intrastate, business, no fee or regulation, though expressly directed to intrastate business, will be upheld, if in the view of the Supreme Court of the United States, such exaction or requirement imposes a burden upon the interstate business of such corporation.

Washington ex rel. Bond & Goodwin & Tucker, Inc. v. Superior Court of Washington for Spokane County et al.
289 U.S. 361, 53 S. Ct. 624 (1933)

This was an action by Bond & Goodwin & Tucker, Incorporated (plaintiff) against the Supreme Court of Washington, for Spokane County (defendant). Judgment for defendant and plaintiff appealed. Judgment affirmed.

In 1926, plaintiff qualified to do business in the state of Washington pursuant to the statutes of the state. Duncan Shaw of Seattle was appointed resident agent for the acceptance of service of process. In 1929, the plaintiff withdrew from the state, ceased to do business there, and filed formal notice of withdrawal with the Secretary of State. The appointment of Shaw as resident agent was never revoked. In 1929, he moved to California. In 1932, suit was started against plaintiff, and the sheriff served the summons and complaint upon the Secretary of State. Plaintiff was never given notice that suit had been commenced. Plaintiff appeared specially in that suit and moved to quash the service. The motion was overruled. Thereupon application was made to the Supreme Court of the State for a writ of prohibition. The present appeal is from the judgment refusing the writ.

Mr. Justice Roberts delivered the opinion of the court.

The appellant urges that the statute denies the due process and equal protection guaranteed by the Fourteenth Amendment. The first contention rests upon the fact that substituted service upon the Secretary of State is validated without any requirement that he shall give the defendant notice of the pendency of the action; the second is bottomed upon the circumstance that a different procedure requiring the Secretary of State to send notice to defendants is prescribed as respects suits against domestic corporations having no office within the State, and foreign insurance companies.

The statute requires a foreign corporation to appoint and register a resident agent empowered to accept service of process in any action or suit pertaining to the property, business or transactions of such corporation within the State. The agent may be changed by filing with the Secretary of State a new appointment. The portion of the Act which gives rise to the present controversy is:

". . . . in the event such foreign corporation shall withdraw from this state and cease to transact business therein it shall continue to keep and maintain such agent within this state upon whom service of process, pleadings and papers may be made, until the statute of limitations shall have run against anyone bringing an action against said corporation, which accrued prior to its withdrawal from this state. In case said corporation shall revoke the authority of its designated agent after its withdrawal from this state and prior to the time when the statutes of limitations would have run against causes of action accruing against it, then in that event service of process, pleadings and papers in such actions may be made upon the secretary of state of the State of Washington, and the same shall be held as due and sufficient service upon such corporation."

The State need not have admitted the corporation to do business within its borders. Admission might be conditioned upon the requirement of substituted service upon a person to be designated either by the corporation, or by the State itself, or might, as here, be upon the terms that if the corporation had failed to appoint or maintain an agent service should be made upon a state officer. The provision that the liability thus to be served should continue after withdrawal from the State afforded a lawful and constitutional protection of persons who had there transacted business with the appellant.

It has repeatedly been said that qualification of a foreign corporation in accordance with the statutes permitting its entry into the State constitutes an assent on its part to all the reasonable conditions imposed. It is true that the corporation's entry may not be conditioned upon surrender of constitutional rights, as was attempted in the cases on which the appellant relies. And for this reason a State may not exact arbitrary and unreasonable terms respecting suits against foreign corporations as the price of admission. But the statute here challenged has no such operation. It goes no further than to require that the corporation may be made to answer just claims asserted against it according to law. By appointing a new agent when Shaw ceased to be a resident of the State the appellant could have assured itself of notice of any action. The statute informed the company that if it elected not to appoint a successor to Shaw the Secretary of State would by law become its agent for the purpose of service. The burden lay upon the appellant to make such arrangement for notice as was thought desirable. There is no denial of due process in the omission to require the corporation's agent to give it such notice.

Doing Business

If the corporation transacts some part of its ordinary business within the state, it has been held that it is "doing business" within the state. Just what acts amount to the "doing of business" and whether a series of such acts is necessary to amount to "doing business," is not definitely settled; the cases are to some extent conflicting. The corporation can engage in interstate commerce without obtaining permission from the state. It can buy goods in another state to be shipped into the state of its domicile, and it can sell goods in the state of its domicile to be shipped into another state. It can solicit business in another state either by mail or by resident salesmen so long as the contract to sell or the sale is made in the state of its domicile. It can send goods into another state on consignment or to be sold on commission. Such transactions are considered as interstate commerce, and the state has no authority to interfere with such commerce. However, in some states consigning goods to an agent for sale, allowing an agent to deliver goods, collecting money, employing labor for the installation of machinery sold, and purchasing materials have been held to be "doing business" within the state. If the state statutes expressly prohibit a foreign corporation from doing business in the state without complying with statutory requirements, the majority of the courts have held that any contract entered into by a foreign corporation which is in violation of such a statute is illegal. Under the majority rule the contracts of a foreign corporation doing business in the state without having qualified are not enforceable by the corporation but are enforceable against the corporation. The statutes are for the protection of the public, and if the corporation were to set up illegality as a defense to such contracts, it would be taking advantage of its own wrong, and the statutes would be a fraud on the public instead of protecting the public.

Mandel Bros., Inc. v. Henry A. O'Neil, Inc., et. al.
69 F. (2d) 452 (1934)

This was a suit by Mandel Bros., Inc. (plaintiff) against Henry A. O'Neil, Inc., and another (defendants). Judgment for defendants and plaintiff appealed. Judgment affirmed.

Mandel Bros., Inc., a Delaware corporation, with its principal office at Chicago sold to Henry A. O'Neil, Inc., a corporation organized under the laws of South Dakota, the furnishings for a hotel. The furnishings included lighting fixtures, kitchen equipment and utensils, shades, floor coverings of every sort, linens, glassware, silverware, chinaware, blankets, lamps, and various miscellaneous items—in short a complete furnishing of the entire hotel. The articles of merchandise were to be delivered at Belle Fourche, South Dakota, and were to be installed by and at the expense of the seller, to the end that, when the contract was fully executed, the hotel should be completely furnished and equipped.

Part of the purchase price was paid when the contracts were executed, part when furnishings and equipment were delivered and installed; the balance was evidenced by a series of eighteen promissory notes. Suit is brought on unpaid notes. The defense is that the notes are void because Mandel Bros., Inc., is a foreign corporation and was doing business in South Dakota without a license.

Section 8909, Revised Code, South Dakota reads thus: "Contracts, When Void. Every contract made by or on behalf of any foreign corporation, subject to the provisions of this chapter, affecting the personal liability thereof or relating to property within this state, before it shall have complied with the provisions of this chapter, shall be wholly void, on its behalf and on behalf of its assigns, but shall be enforceable against it or them."

Van Valkenburgh, C. J. Whether there is substantial evidence to support the findings makes necessary a consideration of what may constitute intrastate business as within the meaning of the South Dakota Statutes invoked. Merely soliciting orders for goods to be shipped in the course of interstate commerce does not constitute doing business in the state to which the goods are shipped, and therefore does not subject such property to police regulation.

The test is whether the business done in the state of destination involves a "question of the delivery of property shipped in interstate commerce, or of the right to complete an interstate commerce transaction," or whether it concerns "merely the doing of a local act after interstate commerce had completely terminated." *Browning* v. *Waycross*, loc. cit. pages 22 and 23 of 233 U.S., 34 S. Ct. 578, 580. In the case last cited the Supreme Court held that: "Parties may not by the form of a non-essential contract convert an exclusively local business subject to state control into an interstate commerce business protected by the commerce clause so as to remove it from the taxing power of the State."

By the contract in that case the price paid for lightning rods included the duty to erect them without further charge. Concerning this the court said: "It is true that it was shown that the contract under which the rods were shipped bound the seller, at his own expense, to attach the rods to the houses of the persons who ordered rods, but it was not within the power of the parties by the form of their contract to convert what was exclusively a local business, subject to state control, into an interstate commerce business, protected by the commerce clause. It is manifest that if the right here asserted were recognized, or the power to accomplish by contract what is here claimed were to be upheld, all lines of demarkation between national and state authority would become obliterated, since it would necessarily follow that every kind or form of material shipped from one state to the other, and intended to be used after delivery in the construction of buildings or in the making of improvements in any form, would or could be made interstate commerce."

The distinction between what is inherently intrastate and what is inherently and necessarily connected with interstate commerce is clearly pointed out by the Supreme Court in the cases cited, to which may be added *York Manufacturing Company* v. *Colley*, 247 U.S. 21, 38 S. Ct. 430, 62 L. Ed. 963, 11 A.L.R. 611, and the decision of this court in *Palmer* v. *Aeolian Co.* (C.C.A.) 46 F. (2d) 746, 752. The York Case involved the sale of an ice-making plant, which required the supervision of an expert in assembling and erecting it as necessary to complete delivery in interstate commerce. *Palmer* v. *Aeolian Company* concerned the manufacture and sale of a pipe organ, the installation of which required "not only the highest mechanical skill, but a thorough understanding of the methods employed by the manufacturer in the arrangement of mechanical and electrical connections." The installation was held to be inherently connected with interstate commerce.

In *General Railway Signal Company* v. *Virginia*, 246 U.S. 500, 38 S. Ct. 360, 62 L. Ed. 854, the contract was to furnish completed automatic railway signal systems. It was held that, in the installation, local business was involved, separate and distinct from interstate commerce, and subject to the licensing power of the state. In all cases bearing upon the subject the distinction is carefully drawn between situations requiring local work as essential to a complete delivery in interstate commerce, because of the peculiar nature of the subject-matter of the contract, and those in which the local work done is inherently and intrinsically intrastate. In our judgment, the installation of these furnishings in the hotel at Belle Fourche, S.D., falls within the latter classification.

It is contended that the statute of South Dakota does not forbid the doing of a single act of business in the state. In *Walters Co.* v. *Hahn*, 43 S.D. 153, 178 N.W. 448, it was stated generally that a single transaction does not constitute the doing of business under such a statute. However, in the later case of *Tripp State Bank* v. *Jerke*, 45 S.D. 448, 188 N.W. 314, *Walters Co.* v. *Hahn* was held not to be decisive of the question. Acts done in connection with a single transaction were recognized, under certain circumstances, as constituting more than an isolated transaction. We may readily conceive of a situation where the corporation has done but a single act of business and purposes to do no more; but we think the decisive test is that outlined clearly in the late cases of the Supreme Court of the United States, namely, whether or not the local work done is essential to a complete delivery in interstate commerce, is intrinsically interstate, and immediately and inherently connected with interstate commerce. However, in the instant case, Mandel Bros., Inc., clearly evinced a purpose to do many acts of business.

It is further urged in the alternative that, if certain parts of the work done be deemed intrastate in character, the cost thereof may be segregated, and the balance of the notes allowed. This contention is without merit in any view. While the various items were furnished at different times, and were charged separately, the contract was for the entire installation, and the transaction was a unit.

Mayer v. Wright et al.
234 Iowa, 1158, 15 N.W. (2d) 268 (1944)

This was an action by Albert C. Mayer (plaintiff) against Gary Wright doing business as Dr. Pepper Bottling Company of Des Moines, Iowa, and Dr. Pepper Company, a foreign corporation (defendants). Defendant Dr. Pepper Company appeared specially and moved to quash the claim on the ground that the service of process was insufficient. The motion was granted and plaintiff appealed. Judgment affirmed.

Plaintiff was employed by Gary Wright who carried on a business of bottling carbonated beverages under the assumed name of Dr. Pepper Bottling Company. Dr. Pepper Company furnished the syrups for the manufacture of Dr. Pepper, and, under their franchise, retained a certain amount of supervision over the manufacturing of the finished product, and also gave advice in regard to the manufacture and sale of the finished product. Dr. Pepper Company is incorporated under the laws of the state of Colorado. Its principal place of business is in Dallas, Texas. It sells its product, a syrup made under a secret process, only to licensed bottlers, who in turn manufacture the finished product therefrom as a part of the licensee's private business. It has not applied for and does not have a foreign corporation permit to do business in the state of Iowa. It has no office, and claims that it has no agent or place of business which it operates in the state. If Dr. Pepper Company was doing business in the state of Iowa at the time the process was served, the service of process was legal, otherwise not.

Wennerstrum, J. It has been the holding of the courts that the question whether a corporation or company is "doing business" within a state, must be decided upon the facts as disclosed by the record presented in each particular case. However, our prior holdings provide a guide to us in our consideration of the facts presented in this case. The principal question that we must decide is whether the Dr. Pepper Company was "doing business" within this state in such a manner as to justify our holding that the courts of this state could obtain jurisdiction of it in the present litigation.

In the case of *American Asphalt Roof Corporation* v. *Shankland*, 205 Iowa, 862, 865, 866, 219 N.W. 28, 29, 60 A.L.R. 986, this court, speaking through Stevens, C. J., said:

"The term 'doing business' within a state foreign to the one in which the corporation is organized and has its principal place of business is substantially defined by the Supreme Court as follows:

" 'The general rule deducible from all our decisions is that the business must be of such nature and character as to warrant the inference that the corporation has subjected itself to the local jurisdiction, and is by its duly authorized officers or agents present within the state or district where service is attempted.' . . . .

"Two elements are always involved; namely, Was the foreign corporation doing business, within the meaning of that term, as defined by the Supreme Court, within the state? and Was service had upon a proper or duly authorized agent thereof? Many cases involving these questions have been decided by both state and federal courts. Except for the general rules established or recognized thereby, they are, however, of aid only to the extent that they present analogous questions of fact."

As previously stated the facts in each case must disclose circumstances from which an inference must be drawn that the foreign corporation is doing business within the state where the suit is brought and jurisdiction is sought to be obtained. We do not see how this inference can be drawn from the facts disclosed in the record of the present case. Dr. Pepper Co. has no interest in Dr. Pepper Bottling Company of Des Moines, Iowa. The bottling company is a separate entity. Dr. Pepper Company has no selling agent in the State of Iowa and has no display room. It maintained no office within the state and has no control over the bottling company. It did act in an advisory capacity in connection with the sale and promotion of the manufactured product made from the syrup furnished by it but this activity when carried on within the state was only temporary and at infrequent intervals. Such activities do not constitute doing business within the state. It is therefore our conclusion that Dr. Pepper Company was not doing business within the State of Iowa so as to warrant a holding that jurisdiction might be obtained of it by service of an original notice upon a claimed agent within this state.

QUESTIONS AND PROBLEMS

1. What is the difference between a domestic and a foreign corporation?
2. The Life Insurance Co. was incorporated under the laws of Indiana. It issued a policy of insurance on the life of C. B. Thompson in favor of his wife. The Thompsons then resided in Texas and the Life Insurance Co. had a license to do business in Texas. The Life Insurance Co. was also licensed to transact business in South Dakota and had agreed to accept service of summons in an action against the company served upon the insurance commissioner. After the death of Mr. Thompson, his wife, who then lived in Nebraska, brought suit on the policy in South Dakota and served summons on the insurance commissioner. The Insurance Co. contends that the state legislature has no power to bring a foreign corporation within the jurisdiction of the state courts for claims of nonresidents arising in other states. Is this contention correct?
3. The Kimberlite Co., a Missouri corporation, was duly licensed to do business in Arkansas. The Arkansas Foreign Corporation law provided that, if a foreign corporation on being sued in a state court removed the suit to the Federal Courts, it should thereby forfeit its authority to do business in Arkansas. The corporation contends that this restriction on its right to remove cases to the Federal Court is unconstitutional. Is this contention correct?
4. The packing company was organized under the laws of the State of Washington. It had its principal place of business outside the state, and the majority of its capital stock was held by aliens. The laws of the state prohibited foreign corporations from holding real estate within the state. Can the packing company hold real estate in the State of Washington?
5. Haddam Granite Co., a Connecticut corporation, sold paving blocks to Brooklyn Heights R. Co., a New York corporation, to be used in Brooklyn, New York. The contract was negotiated in writing, and the blocks were to be delivered over

a period of 10 months. Was Haddam Granite Co. "doing business" in New York State?

6. An agent of the International Text Book Co., a Pennsylvania corporation, solicited business in Kansas. The agent took applications for scholarships and sent them to Scranton, Pennsylvania, where they were accepted or rejected. Correspondence lessons and materials were then mailed to the student, who returned the lessons to Scranton for correction and grading. Was the International Text Book Co. "doing business" in Kansas?
7. Imperial Curtain Co., a Pennsylvania corporation, sent a salesman into Detroit, Michigan, who took an order from a Detroit resident and sent the order to the Imperial Curtain Co. at Philadelphia, where it was accepted. Later, the goods ordered were shipped from Philadelphia to Detroit. Payment was refused, and on suit the purchaser set up as a defense that the Imperial Curtain Co. was a foreign corporation, had not complied with the requirements of the State of Michigan to do business in the state and was therefore barred from bringing the action. Is the defense good?

PART IX

MISCELLANEOUS

CHAPTER XLI

INSURANCE

The Contract

The contract of insurance is a risk-bearing contract but is not a wagering contract. The purpose of the insurance contract is to distribute an existing risk so that the losses resulting from the risk do not fall on any one person or on a limited number of persons. The wagering contract creates a risk which would not otherwise exist.

It is often difficult to distinguish between an insurance contract and other contracts of contingent obligation, such as contracts of guaranty or contracts for services to be rendered on the happening of some future event which is not certain to happen. Owing to the present regulation of insurers by the state, it is frequently important to distinguish insurance contracts from other contracts of contingent obligation.

The different kinds of insurance contracts written at the present time are as numerous and varied as the human undertakings which are subject to the risks of future events. For convenience, insurance contracts may be divided into two large classes—property and personal insurance. The property insurance contract is a contract of indemnity. Any contract of property insurance whereby the insured expects to gain by the happening of the event insured against is in the nature of a wagering contract and is not allowed. The purpose of property insurance is to indemnify a person against a loss actually suffered, not to wager on the happening of the event.

The ordinary life insurance contract is not an indemnity contract. It is an arrangement whereby the insured pays an annuity and the insurer agrees to pay a certain sum at an uncertain time. The amount to be paid is based on the amount of the periodic payment and not on the value of the insured's life. We do not attempt to put a monetary value on human life. The life insurance contract differs from the property insurance contract in another respect. The payment contracted for in the property insurance contract is conditioned on the happening of an uncertain future event, and the time within which the event is to happen is expressly limited; the payment contracted for in the life insurance contract is conditioned upon an event which is certain to happen, but the time at which it will happen is uncertain. In both types of contracts, in order that the contract of insurance shall be valid, it must possess the essential elements which are requisite to the validity of all contracts—offer, acceptance, consideration, parties having capacity to contract, and legality of the contract.

Ollendorff Watch Co., Inc., et al. v. Pink
300 N.Y.S. 1175 (1937)

This was an action by the Ollendorff Watch Company, Incorporated, and another (plaintiffs) against Louis H. Pink, as superintendent of insurance of the state of New York (defendant). Judgment for plaintiffs.

The single question presented is whether plaintiff Ollendorff Watch Company, Inc., is transacting insurance business in violation of section 9 of the Insurance Law. That section prohibits the transaction of insurance within the state without a certificate of authority issued by the superintendent of insurance.

Plaintiff is a domestic corporation engaged in manufacturing and selling watches. Since October, 1930, that plaintiff has been delivering a certificate to purchasers of its watches whereby it contracts with each owner as follows:

"To replace such watch with a new Ollendorff watch of like quality and value and selling for the same retail price, provided the first watch aforesaid is lost in the United States of America or the Dominion of Canada through Burglary or Robbery as herein defined, within one year from the date of its purchase. This Agreement, however, shall not apply to the replacing watch."

Since the inception of this plan, plaintiff has delivered more than 60,000 of these certificates throughout the United States, including owners in the state of New York. The certificates are forwarded by plaintiff from its New York office directly to the owners. In the stipulation of facts it is agreed that the plaintiff adds no charge to the sale price of its watches for the aforesaid certificates and agreements.

The coplaintiff, the Travelers Indemnity Company, is a Connecticut corporation authorized to transact the business of casualty insurance in the state of New York. That plaintiff has agreed to indemnify the Ollendorff Company for all losses sustained under the certificate.

Defendant contends that these certificates are insurance contracts. Plaintiffs insist that the certificate is more in the nature of a guaranty made in connection with the sale of Ollendorff products. The question submitted to this court is: "Does the delivery of said certificates and agreements by the plaintiff Ollendorff Watch Co., Inc., to the owners of its watches violate Section 9 of the Insurance Law of the State of New York?"

It is important to note that the undertaking of the plaintiff with a purchaser is not to pay money for the lost watch, but merely to replace it with a new one.

Hefferman, J. Our statute contains no declaration as to what constitutes an insurance contract and hence we must resort to the common-law definition of that term. Whether a contract is one of insurance is determined from its contents and not merely from its terminology. The principal ingredients of such a contract are the consideration, the risk, and the indemnity. The consideration is the premium for the insurer's undertaking; the risk may be said to be the perils or contingencies against which the assured is protected; and the indemnity is the stipulated desideratum to be paid to the assured in case he has suffered loss or damage through the perils and contingencies specified. Perhaps the best definition of a policy of insurance is that it is an agreement by which one person for a consideration promises to pay money or its equivalent, or to do some act of value to another, on the destruction or injury of something by specified perils. Broadly defined, insurance is a contract by which one party, for a compensation called the premium, assumes particular risks of the other party and promises to pay to him or his nominee a certain or ascertainable sum of money on a specified contingency. As regards property and liability insurance, it is a contract by which one party promises on a consideration to compensate or reimburse the other if he shall suffer loss from a specified cause, or to guarantee or indemnify or secure him against loss from that cause.

In Vance on Insurance, 2d Ed., 2, an insurance contract is thus defined:

"The contract of insurance, made between parties called the insured and the insurer, is distinguished by the presence of five elements:

"(a) The insured possesses an interest of some kind susceptible of pecuniary estimation, known as an insurable interest.

"(b) The insured is subject to a risk of loss through the destruction or impairment of that interest by the happening of designated perils.

"(c) The insurer assumes that risk of loss.

"(d) Such assumption is part of a general scheme to distribute actual losses among a large group of persons bearing similar risks.

"(e) As consideration for the insurer's promise, the insured makes a ratable contribution to a general insurance fund, called a premium.

"A contract possessing only the three elements first named is a risk-shifting device, but not a contract of insurance, which is a risk-distributing device; but, if it possesses the other two as well, it is a contract of insurance, whatever be its name or its form."

Courts and text-writers have emphasized the necessity of a premium exaction in order to constitute a contract of insurance. That important feature is absent in the certificates before us, for concededly the purchaser parts with no consideration whatsoever for the issuance of that certificate. We are convinced that the certificate issued by the Ollendorff Watch Company is not a contract of insurance, but simply an agreement on its part, for which it receives no additional consideration, to replace a purchaser's watch lost through burglary or robbery. Obviously, it is a mode of advertising to which the Ollendorff Company resorts for the purpose of increasing its sales and not an attempt on its part to engage in a new business.

The Application

In discussing insurance it is often convenient and helpful to distinguish personal insurance—life, sickness and accident insurance—from property insurance—fire, theft, hail, casualty insurance. These two types of insurance differ in many practical respects. There are some important differences in the methods of writing personal and property insurance. These differences are reflected to some extent in insurance law, but for the most part both types of insurance transactions come under the same general rules.

To have a contract, there must be an offer made by one of the contracting parties, and the offer must be accepted by the other contracting party. In the field of insurance, the insured is usually the offeror. Most insurance is solicited by insurance agents, who do not have the authority to bind the insurance company. The person who desires the insurance signs a written application which contains such information concerning the subject of the proposed insurance as may be desired by the insurer. If the application is for personal insurance, it will contain information concerning the age, health, family history, etc., of the person on whom the insurance is to be issued. If the application is for property insurance, it will contain information concerning the property to be insured as to value, location, nature of surrounding property, etc. Usually the application will be sent to the home office of the insurer where it will be considered and either accepted or rejected. If this procedure is followed, the insurance will not become effective until the application has been accepted.

The application may be so drafted that the insurance becomes effective on the signing of the application. This is a more common practice in the field of property insurance than in the field of personal insurance. When the insurance becomes effective on the signing of the application, the courts have generally held that the parties are bound by the terms of the general policy of insurance for which the application is made. The application may bind the insurer until the insurance is terminated by rejection of the application, or the duration of the temporary insurance may be expressly limited by the terms of the application.

It is customary to make applications in writing on forms furnished by the insurer, but in the field of property insurance, an application may be in the form of an informal memorandum, called "binding slip," or it may be oral. If the insurance is to become effective on the signing of the application or on the making of the memorandum, the application or memorandum must be sufficiently complete so that the court will be able to determine with a reasonable degree of certainty the terms of the insurance. Owing to the fact that there are many established usages in the field of insurance, a very meager application or memorandum may be sufficient.

An application, which is a mere offer, is not accepted by the delay of the insurer in rejecting it, and the fact that the insured has paid his first premium does not alter the rule. It has, however, been held by a few courts that retention of the premium, paid with the application, for an unreasonable time constitutes an acceptance. In some states, statutes have been passed requiring that the insurer, in emergency insurance such as hail, must give notice of rejection within a stated time or he will be bound.

Several courts have allowed a recovery in tort for the insurer's negligent delay in acting upon the application. Such holdings are based on the theory that an insurance company is licensed by the state and owes a duty to the public to insure those who are qualified, and that an unreasonable delay in acting on the application delays the party in obtaining protection. The theory has been accepted by several courts and appears to be growing in favor.

Western & Southern Life Ins. Co. v. Vale
213 Ind. 601, 12 N.E. (2d) 350 (1938)

This was an action by Lon Vale (plaintiff) against Western & Southern Life Insurance Company (defendant). Judgment for plaintiff and defendant appealed. Judgment affirmed.

On August 15, 1932, defendant's local agent and district superintendent called upon plaintiff and solicited him to purchase a policy of industrial insurance. Plaintiff signed an application for a policy for $761 for which the premium was $1.29 a week and paid two weeks' premium in advance. At the time of signing this application, plaintiff had a small policy with the defendant upon which the premium was 35 cents per week.

Vale answered the questions contained in the defendant's standard application and signed it. A receipt was issued to plaintiff which, among other provisions, contained the following: "Provided the insured is in sound health and over six months of age at the date of said application, the company's liability under such policy, if and as issued, shall commence as of the date of said application." The plaintiff, on examination, was found to be in good health and insurable.

The papers were sent to the defendant's home office and were received at the home office August 22, 1932. On August 18, 1932, plaintiff's left hand was cut off just above the wrist in the mine where he was working.

At the time the application was received at the home office of defendant, the accident had not been reported to that office. The policy was not issued on receipt of the application because the defendant's officer in charge of issuing industrial policies was uncertain as to plaintiff's ability to pay the weekly premium, and he wished to investigate the plaintiff's financial standing. Before a policy was issued, the accident was reported to the defendant's home office and no policy was issued. The industrial policy issued by defendant contained a provision to the effect that the company assumed no obligation unless, on the date of the delivery of the policy, "the insured is alive and in sound health."

The defendant denied all liability and plaintiff brought suit on the theory that the defendant was bound until the company rejected the application.

Fansler, J. In most jurisdictions it is held that a receipt, stating that the insurance shall be in force from its date, provided the application is approved and accepted at the home office of the insurer, is ineffectual in providing protection to the applicant until the application is approved, and that it is wholly in the power of the company to reject the application, after death or injury insured against, arbitrarily and without giving any reason for the rejection. An examination discloses that these cases are founded upon the authority of *Mutual Life Insurance Company* v. *Young's Administrator*, 1874, 23 Wall. 85, 106, 23 L. Ed. 152, 154. They are based upon the theory that the application is an initial step; that the absolute right to accept or reject is with the company; that, until there is an acceptance, there is no contract. But it is said: "The acceptance was a qualified one, and there was none other."

But there are cases to the contrary, which hold that the insurance is effective as of the date of the receipt, subject to the right of the company to reject as of the date of the application, if, upon reasonable grounds, the applicant was not insurable upon that date. In *Gardner* v. *North State Mutual Life Ins. Co.*, 1913, 163 N.C. 367, 79 S.E. 806, 808, doubt is indicated as to whether the company "can arbitrarily or even unreasonably" reject the application or withhold its approval. In *Starr* v. *Mutual Life Ins. Co.*, 1905, 41 Wash. 228, 232, 83 P. 116, 117, it is pointed out that, if the company has the right to arbitrarily reject the application in the event of death of the applicant before the policy is issued, no benefit is derived from that portion of the premium which covers the time between the application and the acceptance and issuance of the policy. This is undoubtedly true, since, if the company is not bound to pay a loss occurring in the period, there is no insurance for the period. It is said: "The chief object of the provision would, therefore, seem to be to enable the insurance company to collect the premiums for a period during which there was in fact no insurance, and consequently no risk."

The cases stating the view that the company may arbitrarily elect not to accept if death occurs are based upon the assumption that there is no contract between the parties until the company elects to accept or reject the application; that the application is but an offer; and, still, in the leading case, it is said: "The acceptance was a qualified one, and there was none other." We cannot escape the view that where the facts are as in the case at bar, and an agent of the company is authorized to solicit business and is equipped with printed forms of receipts, prepared by the company and intended to be delivered to applicants for insurance upon the payment of a premium in advance, which say to the applicant that, under some circumstances at least, the company's liability shall commence from the date of the application, and the applicant pays the premium, and the receipt is executed by the company's agent having authority to execute it, and delivered to the applicant, a contract is then and there created between the company and the applicant. It may be that the acceptance of the application and of his money is a "qualified one," but it cannot be doubted that the company has represented to the applicant that it has become conditionally liable under the policy for which he has applied, and that the ordinary person, and especially the ordinary applicant for industrial insurance, would be led to believe that he is conditionally insured. It would be unconscionable to permit an insurance company, issuing such a receipt and receiving a premium from an applicant, part of which was to pay for protection under its policy from the date of the application to the date of acceptance, to say that it had not bound itself to give anything whatever for that portion of the premium; that it deliberately intended to accept the premium for that period, but that it never intended to, and that it had not insured the applicant for that period. In construing the language of a contract, the primary purpose is to discover the mutual intention of the parties, and the intent of one party only does not suffice. Where there is doubt, the contract will be interpreted in the sense that the promisor knew or had reason to know, the promisee understood it. A construction that works a forfeiture will be avoided, as well as a construction that is inequitable and gives an unfair or unreasonable advantage to one of the parties. The court will consider the situation and condition of the parties and the purpose of the contract. Where printed forms are used, the words will be construed most strongly against the one preparing them; and it will not be supposed that, in preparing the form, the words were used for the purpose of inducing the other to act or part with a consideration on the supposition that his words mean one thing while he secretly harbors the intention to contend that they mean something quite different. A construction will be avoided that imputes bad faith or fraud to one of the parties. Appellee did not solicit appellant to insure him. On the contrary, appellant, through its agent, solicited appellee to purchase insurance. He was solicited to fill out the application form, by which the company sought certain specified information, and, by answering the questions, he made certain representations, binding upon him in so far as they were material. Among other things, he represented himself to be physically sound and in good health. He paid the amount of the premium requested, and it was represented to him, not only by the agents, but by the terms of the receipt, that he was then insured. The terms and conditions, the inquiries, and the representation that insurance began immediately, were all dictated by the company. It is inconceivable, in the face of all of the circumstances, that appellee could have understood and believed that under no circumstances was he insured until after the acceptance of the application. The contract to insure for the period before acceptance of the application may have been qualified or conditioned, but the company cannot be permitted to say that under no conditions or circumstances was it liable, for the receipt did not say that the applicant was not insured, but that he was insured. If the company was bound only if it chose to be bound, or if it could disclaim liability for some arbitrary reason of its own choosing, it was not bound at all.

Delivery of Policy

The time at which insurance becomes operative depends on the terms of the agreement. In some instances insurance may be effected by an oral agreement and the insurance becomes operative as soon as the agreement is completed.

The prevailing practice in all types of insurance is for the insurer to issue a written policy of insurance to the insured. As a general rule, in such cases the insurance becomes operative when the policy is delivered. Delivery is primarily a question of the intention of the parties. The party issuing the policy must intend to give it effect as a completed instrument. As in other cases of contracts, this intention must be indicated by some act on the part of the insurer which puts the policy beyond the legal control of the insurer. To accomplish this, it is not necessary that the policy be put beyond the physical control of the insurer.

The courts are not in accord as to just what acts on the part of the insurer will amount to delivery. The majority of courts have held that when the insurer has executed and mailed the policy, it is delivered, and any loss suffered after the policy has been mailed is covered. Under some circumstances, the courts have held that the policy is delivered and the insurance is operative when the policy has been completely executed although the policy remains in the physical possession of the insurer. In some instances, the insurer sends the policy to its local agent for delivery to the insured. If the agent is vested with some discretionary power in regard to delivery, as a general rule, the insurance is not operative until the agent has delivered the policy. However, in the field of life insurance if the application provides that the insurance will not be operative unless the insured is in good health at the time of the delivery of the policy, the courts have held that the insurance becomes operative at the time of the mailing of the policy if the insured is in good health at that time, even though the policy has been mailed to the local agent for personal delivery to the insured. In these cases the courts have held that the agent's duty is merely to explain the policy to the insured and not to determine the "good health" of the insured.

Mutual Life Insurance Co. v. Otto
153 Md. 179, 138 Atl. 16, 53 A.L.R. 487 (1927)

This was an action by Margie Otto (plaintiff) against Mutual Life Insurance Company of Baltimore (defendant). Judgment for plaintiff and defendant appealed. Judgment affirmed.

The appellant in this case conducts a life insurance business in Baltimore City. On or about April 20th, 1925, Clarence W. Foxwell, its soliciting agent, received from Earl W. Otto, an infant, an application for a five hundred dollar twenty year endowment insurance policy on his life in favor of his mother Margie Otto, and at the same time received from him fifty-eight cents in payment of the first week's premium to become due on the policy when issued. The application was accepted, and, on April 25th, 1925, the policy was issued and delivered by the appellant to Foxwell, to be by him delivered to Otto. Otto was injured in an automobile accident on April 28th, 1925, before Foxwell had manually delivered the policy to him, and on the same day he died. Thereupon Mrs. Otto demanded of the appellant the amount of the policy, and upon its refusal to pay the same she brought this suit.

Offutt, J. The appellant's defense below, and its contention in this Court, is that, since the policy had not been manually delivered to Otto in person before his death, it never became effective, and it bases that contention on this clause of the policy: "Second. This policy shall become void, if upon date of actual delivery, the insured is not alive and in sound health. . . ."

The only questions before us are whether at the time of Otto's death there had been an "actual delivery" of the policy to him, within the meaning of the clause above referred to, or if not, whether such delivery was waived by the appellant.

The case really turns on the meaning to be given the words "actual delivery" used in the policy. Appellant contends that they mean a physical delivery to Otto in person, while the appellee says that they mean delivery either to Otto or to any other person authorized to receive it for him. In construing the words "actual delivery" as used in the policy, no assistance is to be had by reference to the notice in the receipt that "no obligation is incurred by the company by reason of" the payment of the first premium "unless . . . . a policy is delivered," first, because the word "delivery" is broader than the phrase "actual delivery"; second, because the notice was no part of any contract and, whatever it amounted to, it was merged in the completed contract, to wit, the policy; third, because the agent had no power to limit the right of his principal to vary any or all of the terms found in the notice; and finally, because the action is not upon any supposed contract evidenced by the notice but upon the policy. So that the question is, was there "a delivery" within the meaning of the policy?

Where an insurance policy, expressly or by implication, provides that it shall not bind the insurer until it is actually delivered, manifestly such delivery is necessary to complete the contract. The question then is, What, under such circumstances, do the words "actually delivered" as used in the policy mean? Delivery can only mean delivery to the insured, or to some person acting for him and expressly or by fair implication authorized to receive it for him. The policy does not expressly require that the "actual delivery" shall be to the insured in person, so that delivery to his agent or any person authorized to receive it for him would completely gratify the letter as well as the spirit of the contract.

It appears, as has been said, that on April 25th, 1925, the company had received and accepted the insured's application and accepted from him a premium fully paying for insurance under a policy to be issued on such application for one week from the date thereof, and had actually executed and issued such a policy and delivered it to the soliciting agent, to be by him manually delivered to the insured. The insurer had therefore done everything it could to complete the contract, and had actually issued, and had delivered to its soliciting agent for unconditional delivery to the assured on April 25th, 1925, the very policy No. 771,226 for which the insured had applied. That it was not manually delivered. to the insured on that day was purely fortuitous, and due to reason which had nothing to do with the completion of the contract of insurance, but concerned only the personal convenience of the agent. After the policy had actually been issued, and the company had accepted payment for insurance for one week from the date of its issue, it certainly could not have intended that the protection which the policy afforded the insured should depend upon the casual impulses or convenience of the agent whom it had instructed to deliver it to the insured.

So that the question is narrowed to this, Was Foxwell so far authorized to receive the policy for Otto that a delivery to him was a delivery to Otto? There was evidence from which the jury could have inferred that the policy was executed, issued, and delivered to Foxwell for unconditional delivery to Otto. Under such circumstances, while there is some authority to the contrary, the great weight of authority supports the view that delivery to Foxwell was delivery to Otto. In fact the rule supported by the weight of authority goes even farther than that, for it is that delivery under such circumstances to one in the relation of Foxwell to the insurer was delivery to the insured, even though the policy stipulated that delivery should be made to the insured before the policy became effective, and was therefore a condition precedent, while here such delivery is not a condition precedent. That conclusion has been supported on a variety of grounds, that the insurer's agent is a trustee for the insured, that he is the agent of the insured, and that delivery to him is "equivalent to delivery to the applicant." But running through all of these cases is the principle that, where the minds of the insurer and insured have met upon a definite contract, which has been accepted by both, and evidenced by the execution and issuance of a policy by the insurer, where the application has been accepted and the premium paid, and where it is the intention of both that the proposed contract of insurance shall be in force from its issue, and nothing further remains to be done but its manual traduction to the insured, and it is delivered to the soliciting agent to effect that traduction, and he has no discretion or authority to do anything other than deliver it, that delivery to him is delivery to the insured, because in such a case the agent is but a minister or vehicle to transmit the written evidence of the contract, just as the mails or any other public messenger would be.

Bond, C. J., filed the following dissenting opinion.

There are undoubtedly authorities in support of the conclusion which the court has reached in this case, but I question whether the weight of authority is in agreement with it. The author of the special study on "Delivery of a Life Insurance Policy," in 33 *Harvard Law Review*, 198, 221, concluded that, "These stipulations requiring a delivery of the policy to the applicant have been literally construed in most instances, and it has accordingly been held by most of the courts which have passed upon the question that if the applicant dies before the delivery of the policy to him, no recovery on the policy can be had. . . . . Adopting the traditional attitude toward 'freedom of contract,' a majority of the courts have strictly enforced such stipulations."

My view is that the intention, in the drafting of the present stipulations for "delivery" or "actual delivery" as a prerequisite to the effectiveness or validity of the insurance, can have been only that there must be a transfer of possession or control of the policy to the insured. That is the common, ordinary meaning of delivery of an instrument and there seems to be no ground for supposing that the words were used in the stipulations with any meaning out of the ordinary. And in this view of the intention of the stipulations, there can be little, if any, question, I take it, that it would have to be held that the present policy did not become effective. There was no such transfer of possession or custody of it to the insured. We may say it was nearly so delivered and that only fortuitous circumstances prevented such delivery, but it was not so delivered, and could not, as I see it, be called delivered except by putting an unauthentic meaning into the word. And if this is correct, the beginning point fixed in the policy was not reached. And, of course, the court would not be authorized to substitute something which it thinks ought to suffice, for that which the instrument being enforced fixes for itself. The difference between custody by the insurance agent, and delivery by him as he intended, may be small in one aspect, but in another it is large, if my construction of the intention is correct, for, being the difference between what was intended and what was not, it may lead to just the difference between following the rule of the intention of the instrument and following no rule at all. There is no rule of law for the case except that which was intended by the words used.

The agent who had custody of the policy here seems to me to have been, clearly enough in fact, only the agent of the insurer, and finding a delivery to the insured by characterizing him as an agent or trustee of the insured, as suggested in some of the cases cited, would, I think, be a resort to fictions which would rather transparently cloak a departure from the principle of carrying out the intention of the instrument.

Representations and Warranties

If one wishes to insure against a risk, it is the duty of the applicant to state to the insurer the nature of the risk so that the insurer can determine whether or not he wishes to insure it and, if willing to accept the risk, on what terms he will insure. In marine insurance the insurer generally relies on the statements of the applicant, but in other types of insurance, especially in the United States, the insurer makes an independent investigation; e.g., if one wishes to insure his life, a doctor in the employ of the insurer will examine the applicant to determine whether or not he is an insurable risk; however, the applicant is required to describe the risk. This description of the risk may be an oral statement, a written application, or the filling out of a blank form furnished by the insurer.

The applicant owes a duty to make an honest statement of all the material facts relating to the risk. If the application is informal and the applicant fails to state material facts, such concealment may render the insurance contract voidable. The better rule in force in the United States is that failure to state a material fact will not render the insurance contract voidable unless the fact was concealed with fraudulent intent. This rule does not apply to marine insurance. If the application is made on a form furnished by the insurer, the presumption is that all the information desired is requested; however, if the applicant fraudulently conceals material facts, the insurance contract is voidable.

The statements made in the application which do not become a part of the contract of insurance are representations. If the applicant makes false representations of material facts, the insurance contract is rendered voidable. It is immaterial that the false representation is made in the honest belief that it is true. It is the duty of the applicant to give the insurer the information he requests concerning the risk. If this information is incorrect and the insurer accepts the risk in reliance on such incorrect information, his injury is as great as though the incorrect statement had been made fraudulently. If the representation is immaterial, it will have no effect.

Warranties are statements or promises which are a part of the insurance contract. They may be written into the contract or they may be incorporated by reference. The application may be made a part of the insurance contract by incorporation. A warranty may be a statement that certain conditions or facts exist—an affirmative warranty—or it may relate to the existence or non-existence of a future condition—a promissory warranty.

The parties to the insurance contract, by including the warranties in the contract, agree that they are essential. The warranty is conclusively presumed to be material to the risk assumed by the insurer, and, if the statement is not true in every respect, the insured cannot recover in the event of loss.

In construing representations and warranties, the courts have favored the insured. If a representation is substantially true and there is no evidence of bad faith, the courts as a general rule will declare the insurance contract enforceable. In determining whether or not certain statements are warranties, the courts have held the statements to be representations unless it is clear that the parties intended them as warranties. The practice of inserting warranties in contracts of insurance often works hardship on the insured. For example, if the statement that one is of good health and free from disease is included in a life insurance contract as a warranty, and it can be shown that the insured was not free from disease at the time the insurance contract was entered into, the insurer can escape liability even though the insured honestly thought he was free from disease and even though an ordinary medical examination would not have revealed the presence of the disease. To avoid such undesirable results, some courts have held that all the insured warranted was his good faith. Some states have remedied the situation by passing statutes which either abolish or modify the doctrine of warranties.

Pilot Life Ins. Co. v. Dickinson
93 F. (2d) 765 (1938)

This was an action by Eloise Scarborough Dickinson (plaintiff) against Pilot Life Insurance Company (defendant). Judgment for plaintiff and defendant appealed. Judgment affirmed.

The defendant claims that the insured made false answers to questions contained in his application and failed to disclose a diseased condition for which he had been treated. Plaintiff contends that the insured had answered the questions truthfully and had made full disclosure in light of his knowledge at the time of the application.

The questions and answers upon which the company relies for its defense are 7-A, 7-K, and 8-B. With these must be considered also the answer to 7-J. These questions and answers are as follows:

"7-A: Have you ever suffered any disease of the brain or nervous system? Answer, No.

"7-J: Have you ever been a patient in any sanitorium, hospital or asylum? Answer, Yes: (Under name of ailment, disease or injury) Bad teeth: (Under number of attacks, date, duration, severity, results, name and address of attending physician) teeth all removed.

"7-K: Have you consulted a doctor for any cause not included in above? Answer, No.

"8-B: Are you aware of any physical defect or have you had any complaint not mentioned above? Answer, No."

There was testimony that at the time insured's teeth were removed, which was more than two years before the application for the policy, he was admitted to a hospital suffering from a general toxic condition resulting in attacks of vertigo, temporary lapses of consciousness, loss of speech, and temporary attacks of weakness in his extremities. A careful diagnosis of his condition was made, and the diagnostician reported that his condition might be due to one of three sources: extensive infection of the teeth, obesity, or excessive use of tobacco. The extraction of the teeth was advised, and after they had been extracted, insured recovered his health and attended to his extensive business enterprises as usual. He was apparently in good health when he was examined for this insurance two years later by the same physician who treated him when his teeth were removed.

Insured died from cerebral thrombosis a few months after the issuance of the policy, and there was testimony of medical experts tending to show that he must have been suffering from the disease that resulted in his death at the time he was admitted to the hospital more than two years prior thereto. On the other hand, the evidence is that the physician who treated him at that time advised that his teeth were the cause of the trouble; that this was the opinion also of the diagnostician who examined him; that recovery followed the extraction of the teeth; that insured believed himself to be sound and well following their extraction; that this belief was shared by the physician who treated him; that he and that physician discussed his hospitalization at the time of the application for insurance; and that the physician himself directed the answer that was given. Collusion between the insured and the physician is not suggested, and the insured is shown to have been a man of high character and standing in his community. Any attempt to defraud the company is negatived by the fact that when a policy for $10,000, double the amount applied for, was offered the insured, he declined to accept it and delayed acceptance of any policy until one in the amount for which he had applied could be written.

Parker, C. J. Under these circumstances we think that the court properly denied the motion for directed verdict. It is well settled that, for the purposes of such a motion, the evidence must be viewed in the light most favorable to plaintiff; and when the evidence here is so viewed, there is no ground upon which the verdict could have been directed. While there was evidence that insured may have suffered from a disease of the brain or nervous system prior to his application, as inquired about in question 7-A, there was evidence also from which a contrary conclusion might reasonably have been drawn; and certainly there was ample evidence to justify a finding that he did not know that he had suffered from such a disease. The negative answers to questions 7-K and 8-B are true when there is read into them the exception for which they provide and which is contained in the answer to 7-J. The insured in answer to that question truthfully stated what his attending physician had told him was the "ailment or disease" which had sent him to the hospital. No inquiry was made of him as to the symptoms attending the disease, and no reason is suggested why he should have disbelieved what the physician had told him.

The questions contained in the application here, as in the case of *Moulor* v. *American Life Ins. Co.*, 111 U.S. 335, 4 S. Ct. 466, 469, 28 L. Ed. 447, show clearly that good faith in answering them was all that was required of the applicant; and this is emphasized by the statement required of him as a part of his application to the effect that the answers made were true to the best of his "knowledge, information and belief." If the company intended to rely upon the answers as warranties against the existence of diseases with which the applicant did not know or believe himself to be afflicted, specific provision to that effect should have been made either in the policy or in the application. As was said in the Moulor Case, supra: "In the absence of explicit, unequivocal stipulations requiring such an interpretation, it should not be inferred that a person took a life policy with the distinct understanding that it should be void, and all premiums paid thereon forfeited, if at any time in the past, however remote, he was, whether conscious of the fact or not, afflicted with some one of the diseases mentioned in the question to which he was required to make a categorical answer. If those who organize and control life insurance companies wish to exact from the applicant, as a condition precedent to a valid contract, a guaranty against the existence of diseases, of the presence of which in his system he has and can have no knowledge, and which even skilful physicians are often unable, after the most careful examination, to detect, the terms of the contract to that effect must be so clear as to exclude any other conclusion."

Insurable Interest

The law requires the person entering into a contract of insurance to have an "insurable interest" in order that the contract may escape condemnation on the grounds that it is a wagering contract. In discussing insurable interest we must distinguish between property insurance and personal insurance. In the field of property insurance the purpose of the insurance is to indemnify against a loss suffered. The loss is of such a nature that it can be expressed in terms of dollar values. In personal insurance there is an element of indemnity, especially in sick and accident insurance, but the indemnity element is of minor importance. We do not attempt to value human life. Life insurance is more of an investment than indemnification against loss. In the field of property insurance, if one has such an interest in the thing insured that he will suffer a loss if it is destroyed or injured, he can insure against the loss, the amount of the insurance being limited by the value of the interest to be protected.

The problem of determining when one has an insurable interest in a human life is more complex. The courts have not been in accord and no definite rule can be extracted from the decided cases. It is primarily a question of public policy to be determined in accordance with the facts in the case. Some general rules which aid the courts in deciding cases have been established, and in some states statutes have been passed which guide the courts, but owing to the complexity of the problem, no one simple solution is possible or advisable.

Another important difference between property insurance and personal insurance concerns the time at which the insurable interest must exist. The insurable interest in property must exist at the time of the loss, while the insurable interest in personal insurance must exist at the time the insurance contract is entered into. This difference is due to the difference in the nature of the insurance. Property insurance is indemnity insurance, and if the insured has no interest in the property at the time of its injury or destruction, he has suffered no loss. Life insurance is an investment; the event, especially with regard to life insurance, is certain to happen, so it is logical to determine the insurable interest at the time the contract of insurance is entered into.

One who has the legal title to property has an insurable interest in the property. It is not necessary that the title carry with it the right to present possession and enjoyment. One who has a reversionary interest in property has an insurable interest, but an heir who has only an expectancy does not have an insurable interest irrespective of how certain it may be that he will not be cut off. One who has an equitable title or a lien on property such as a mortgage, a mechanic's lien, or an execution lien has an insurable interest, but a general creditor does not. A bailee or one holding property in trust or a sheriff who has levied execution on property and has it in his possession has an insurable interest. It has been held that a mortgagor who has sold the mortgaged property to a purchaser who has assumed and agreed to pay the mortgage debt still has an insurable interest in the property, because in the event that the purchaser defaults and the property will not sell for the amount of the mortgage debt, he will be personally liable. The property insured need not be in existence at the time the insurance contract is entered into, but the insurance will not be valid until the property is acquired. The insuring of stocks of goods for resale when the value of the stock fluctuates is a typical example of the insurance of goods not in existence at the time the insurance contract is entered into.

Losses of profits and interests closely akin to profits may be insured. Football games, fairs, etc., are insured against rain and similar hazards which affect the profits of the venture. Swarthmore College insured its expedition to Durango, Mexico, for the purpose of taking solar eclipse pictures, against clouds obstructing the face of the sun.

Life insurance contracts may be divided into two groups—those taken out by the insured on his own life for his own benefit or for the benefit of named beneficiary, and those taken out on the life of another. One has an insurable interest in his own life, and the generally accepted rule is that the beneficiary need have no insurable interest in the life of the insured. With regard to an insurable interest in the life of another, one test is whether the party who takes out the insurance has a bona fide desire and interest that the life insured shall continue to its natural end. Under this test, pecuniary interest has played an important part. If the party who takes out the insurance is dependent on the insured for support and care, it is strong evidence of an insurable interest. Relationship is another test. Close blood relationship is held by some courts to be sufficient, while other courts have required some interest in addition to mere relationship. Relationship by marriage, except husband and wife, will not, standing alone, create an insurable interest. A creditor may insure his debtor's life for the purpose of protecting his debt, the principal question in such cases being the amount of insurance allowable. No satisfactory test has been adopted, the courts being content with the rule that the amount of the insurance must not greatly exceed the amount of the debt. A corporation may insure the life of its officers, and a partner may insure the life of his partner. In these commercial cases, the element of indemnity is more prominent and the amount of the insurance must not greatly exceed the interest insured.

Block v. Mylish et al.
351 Pa. 611, 41 A. (2d) 731 (1945)

This was an action by Gordon A. Block (plaintiff) against Isaac D. Mylish and Jerome J. Drucker (defendants). Judgment for plaintiff and defendants appealed. Judgment affirmed.

Isaac D. Mylish, Alfred Mann, and Jerome J. Drucker were partners. By agreement, policies of insurance, aggregating $60,000, were taken out on the life of each partner. The partnership was named beneficiary in all the policies and at all times paid the premiums thereon with partnership funds. The sums paid were carried on the books of the partnership as a business expense. The partnership agreement provided that on the death of a partner the survivors would have an option to purchase the deceased partner's interest in the business upon a basis and terms as provided in the agreement. Alfred Mann died June 4, 1943, and the surviving partners gave notice to Gordon A. Block, executor of the estate of Alfred Mann, that they elected to exercise their option. The insurers paid the $60,000 to the partnership. In appraising the value of the deceased partner's interest in the partnership business, the plaintiff contends that the $60,000 should be included as an asset of the partnership. The defendants contend that only the cash surrender value of the policies on the life of Alfred Mann should be included as a partnership asset. In the course of the trial the question of the partnership's insurable interest in the life of a partner was raised and decided by the court. If the partnership had no insurable interest in the life of the partners, it could not take the $60,000; it could take only the cash surrender value of the policies.

Jones, J. The element of wager, based upon the fortuity of survivorship, which the appellants' construction of the agreement would introduce, could serve to deny the right of the partners to a reciprocal insurable interest in the life of each other. This is, by no means, intended to suggest that partners do not have an insurable interest in the life of one another. Undoubtedly, they have such an interest, but, as the Supreme Court of the United States said in *Connecticut Mutual Life Insurance Company* v. *Luchs*, 108 U.S. 498, 505, 2 S. Ct. 949, 952, in quoting with approval from one of its earlier decisions, *Warnock* v. *Davis*, 104 U.S. 775, ". . . in all cases (involving the right to insure) there must be a reasonable ground, founded upon the relations of the parties to each other, either pecuniary or of blood or affinity, to expect some benefit or advantage from the continuance of the life of the assured." Under the present appellants' contention, a partner's expectation of benefit or advantage could lie not in the continuance of the lives of his partners but rather in the possibility of their deaths prior to his own. The impeachment of the basis for the insurance which the appellants' construction would thus inject would require that the contention be discountenanced. In interpreting a contract, a construction which would effect an unreasonable or unlawful end is to be avoided.

Le Doux et al. v. Dettmering et al.
Niagara Fire Insurance Co. v. Le Doux et al.
316 Ill. App. 98, 43 N.E. (2d) 862 (1942)

This was an action by Joseph Le Doux and others (plaintiffs) against Henry D. Dettmering and others (defendants) and a cross-complaint by Niagara Fire Insurance Company against Joseph Le Doux and others. From an adverse judgment, Niagara Fire Insurance Company appealed. Judgment reversed and remanded with directions.

Joseph Le Doux and Thomas Frankiewicz owned a lot on which there was a five-room house. They borrowed $1,000 from Henry D. Dettmering and gave Dettmering their promissory note for the amount of the debt, secured by a trust deed to the house and lot. The trust deed provided that Le Doux and Frankiewicz would keep the property insured against loss by fire and tornado and that the insurance would be made payable to Dettmering. The trust deed further provided that, in the event that Le Doux and Frankiewicz failed or refused to insure, Dettmering could insure the buildings and charge the premium to Le Doux and Frankiewicz. Le Doux and Frankiewicz refused to insure the buildings. Thereupon, Dettmering, at his own expense and without the knowledge or consent of Le Doux and Frankiewicz, procured a policy insuring him (Dettmering) as "legal holder of the note" against loss by fire and tornado. Dettmering did not bill Le Doux and Frankiewicz for the premium on the policy nor charge it to them nor seek to collect it from them. The policy was issued by Niagara Fire Insurance Company, was for $2,000, and was issued May 16, 1936. A fire occurred on August 2, 1936. The insurance company paid Dettmering $1,340.12, the full amount due on the note, and Dettmering assigned the note and trust deed to the insurance company. The insurance company, after the note fell due, demanded payment and payment was refused. Le Doux and Frankiewicz asked that the note be cancelled and that the trust deed be discharged on the theory that they were owners of the insured premises, that the insurance was for their benefit, and that the payment by the insurance company to Dettmering discharged the debt. They also claimed that Dettmering had no insurable interest in the buildings and that he had no right to insure the buildings without their knowledge and consent.

Dove, J. A contract of insurance is one of indemnity merely and any person having an interest in property may, through an insurance contract, indemnify himself against loss by fire or other insurable casualty. Mortgagors and mortgagees each have an insurable interest in the mortgaged property and the interests of both may be covered in one policy, or each may take out a separate policy and where the mortgagee does insure at his own cost, without privity with the mortgagor, the insurer which pays the mortgagee a loss is entitled to be subrogated to his claim, and the mortgagor cannot claim any benefit of the insurance. If, however, insurance has been effected at the request or by the authority of the mortgagor, or under circumstances that would make him chargeable with the premium, the mortgagor, in case of a loss, is entitled to have the proceeds of the insurance applied in liquidation of the mortgage debt pro tanto.

From these and other authorities it is apparent that the question here to be determined resolves itself into one of privity. In cases like the instant one the insurance is considered as a further security of the debt; and on the familiar principle that a surety who pays the debt may resort to the principal debtor for payment, the insurer is permitted to recover from the mortgagor.

Appellees here refused to procure insurance in compliance with their covenant in the trust deed and Dettmering having obtained insurance without their knowledge or consent, for his own benefit exclusively and at his own expense, there is no privity between appellees and him, nor between them and appellant. They stand as strangers to the insurance transaction, as much so as if the trust deed had not contained any insurance clause.

While the insurance clause in the trust deed authorized Dettmering to insure at the expense of appellees, it was at his option, and he was not thereby denied the privilege of insuring for his own exclusive benefit. He did so, and appellees cannot bring the provision in the trust deed into force against him by their own default. They are in no different or worse situation than if Dettmering had never insured his interest. If he had not done so the only difference would be that his security would have been impaired to the extent of the loss occasioned by fire, and appellees would still owe the debt. They have not paid it and they carried no insurance. The fire loss is naturally theirs, and as observed above, the only effect is that there has been a change of creditors.

Notice and Proof of Loss

Notice of loss, damage, injury, or death is required by the insurer for his protection. The requirement for such notice is stated in the policy in the form of conditions precedent, but are in fact conditions subsequent, because the liability of the insurer arises at the time of the loss, and failure to give the notice required terminates the liability. By the terms of the insurance contract, "immediate notice" is required. The courts have given this and similar terms a liberal construction. The length of time which may elapse between the event causing the loss and the giving of the notice depends on the nature of the thing insured and the circumstances of the particular case. In personal injury cases covered by automobile liability insurance, theft of small yet valuable articles, and similar cases, it is important that the insurer have notice in order that he may seasonably take steps to protect his interests.

Proof of loss or death are also required. In the standard fire insurance policy the proof of loss must be made within 60 days. Under the terms of some policies, the rendering of a proof of loss within the time stated is a condition, and failure to comply will render the insurance void, while under the terms of other types of policies, the failure to render proof of loss suspends the right to recover on the policy.

If the party can show that he was prevented from rendering proof of loss by circumstances beyond his control, and can show that he used due diligence in rendering the proof of loss, the courts will hold that he is excused from prompt performance.

Jellico Grocery Co. v. Sun Indemnity Co. of New York
272 Ky. 276, 114 S.W. (2d) 83 (1938)

This was an action by the Jellico Grocery Company (plantiff) against Sun Indemnity Company of New York (defendant). Judgment for defendant and plaintiff appealed. Judgment affirmed.

Defendant issued to plaintiff on August 1, 1928, an insurance policy of indemnity by the terms of which plaintiff was indemnified against loss which it might sustain through the fraud, dishonesty, forgery, theft, embezzlement, and wrongful abstraction by any of its employees. Robert W. Easley, the manager of one of plaintiff's branch stores, was included as one of its employees, and the indemnity insurance covered him to the amount of $1,000.

Plaintiff instructed Easley not to extend credit to M. I. Thompson Coal Co., but Easley, in violation of his instructions, extended credit to M. I. Thompson and to M. I. Thompson Coal Co. and falsified his records to conceal his acts. In March, 1934, plaintiff learned that Easley had extended credit to M. I. Thompson and to M. I. Thompson Coal Co. Both M. I. Thompson and M. I. Thompson Coal Co. were insolvent and the account was not paid. Plaintiff did not notify defendant of the loss until April, 1936.

The policy of indemnity contained the following provisions:

"Upon the discovery by the Employer of any dishonest act on the part of any Employee the Employer shall, at the earliest practicable moment, and at all events not later than five days after such discovery, give written notice thereof addressed to the Surety at its home office."

Defendant set up the failure to give notice as required by the policy as a defense.

Baird, J. In the case of *Home Owned Store, Incorporated* v. *Standard Accident Insurance Company*, the claim of appellant in that case was considered and disposed of in opposition to the contention of appellant this far: In that case no notice was given at all as provided by the policy, and for that reason we decided that no cause of action could be maintained. In the instant case a notice was given more than two years after the discovery, but in direct violation of the plain terms of the policy so far as time was concerned. The policy provided that the notice should be given as soon as practicable and not later than five days after discovery of the wrong. It requires little thinking to reach a just conclusion that it would be unreasonable and unfair as well as unjust to the indemnity company to defer the giving of the notice for more than two years. This provision of the policy should be construed according to the intention of the parties. The contract like any other should be given a practicable and reasonable interpretation consistent with its language in expressing the intention of the parties.

The notice given in the present case was equivalent to no notice at all. It is contended, however, that the delay in giving the notice was attributable to the effort on the part of the grocery company to ascertain the extent of the loss before giving the notice. Such delay cannot be justified on the contention that appellant did not have sufficient information as to the losses it had sustained. If that should be the rule, the insurer would be kept long in the dark while wrongdoings and dishonest acts of the employee were possibly going on. Its liability might be increased by leaps and bounds. The purpose of the notice to be given as soon as practicable was to give the insurer a reasonable opportunity to protect its rights. No other construction would be reasonable or fair, or would reasonably comport with the plain terms of the bond of indemnity. We are supported in this conclusion, in the main, by numerous decisions of this court as well as by courts of foreign jurisdiction.

Termination and Lapse

As a general rule, a policy of life insurance cannot be terminated by the insurer except for fraud or misrepresentation at the time of its procurement. The time within which an insurer may terminate a life insurance policy for fraud or misrepresentation is fixed by statute in most states. Also, it is a common practice of insurers in the field of life insurance to put an "incontestable clause" in the policy which provides that the policy may not be contested after a stated period of time except for non-payment of premiums. The time limit for contesting a policy for fraud or misrepresentation is, in most instances, two years.

If the insured wishes, he may terminate the insurance at any time by surrendering the policy to the insurer. On the surrender of the policy, the insured is entitled to the "cash surrender value" of his policy. As a general rule, the insured has the privilege under the terms of his policy to take either paid-up insurance or extended insurance. If he takes paid-up insurance, he will be issued a paid-up policy of life insurance for such amount of insurance as the cash surrender value of his policy will purchase at his age. If he takes extended insurance, he will be issued a term policy for the original amount, the length of the term being determined by the cash surrender value of his policy.

If the insured fails to pay the premiums on his policy, the policy will lapse. By statute, the insured is given thirty days after the premium falls due in which to pay. The mailing of a check for the premium on the thirtieth day after the due date has been held to be sufficient to satisfy the requirements. However, if the check is not honored when presented for payment, the policy will lapse. If the insured permits his policy to lapse for non-payment of premiums, he will have the same privilege of election as when he surrenders his policy. He may elect to take either the cash surrender value, paid-up insurance, or extended insurance. As a general rule, life insurance policies provide that, in the event the policy is permitted to lapse for non-payment of premiums, and the insured does not make an election within a stated time, the provision for extended insurance shall be effective.

Policies of property and casualty insurance are issued for a definite term and terminate at the expiration of the term. It is customary to define the term of the policy with a high degree of definiteness. For example, a fire insurance policy would provide that the policy terminates at noon C.S.T. June 15, 1948. Either party may terminate a property or casualty policy by giving the other party notice. Under existing statutes if the insurer elects to terminate a policy, he must give the insured five days' notice. Under the terms of the revised New York standard policy, the notice must be in writing. If the insurer terminates the policy, he must return the unearned portion of the premium. The insured may terminate the policy at any time by surrendering his policy. If the insured terminates the policy, he is entitled to the return of premiums paid on the "short rate" basis, i.e., the premiums for the time the policy has been in force is computed at a rate slightly higher than that for the full term of the policy, and the overplus is returned to the insured.

Also, in property and casualty insurance, the policy customarily provides that if the insured by his acts materially increases the risk, the insurer's liability shall terminate. The policy will, in addition to such general clause, contain clauses which state specifically that certain acts on the part of the insured shall terminate the insurer's liability. Acts which are customarily prohibited by such clauses are: generating illuminating gas on the premises, keeping on the premises explosives and inflammable substances, and allowing the premises to remain vacant or unoccupied for a stated period. Also, if any portion of the building collapses, the insurance terminates.

If the property insured is a stock of goods for resale, the policy will contain an "iron safe clause" which provides that the insured must take an inventory once a year, that he must keep a set of books showing all sales, both cash and credit, and that the inventory and books must be kept in a fireproof safe or other place not exposed to danger. The courts are not in accord as to the effect of the violation of such a provision of the policy. A minority of the courts hold that the violation of such a provision terminates the policy in toto. The majority of the courts hold that the liability of the insurer is suspended during such time as the prohibited condition exists. Archer insures his house against fire in the Burch Insurance Co. The policy provides that if the house is vacant or unoccupied beyond a period of ten days, the insurer shall not be liable for loss occurring. Archer's house is vacant and unoccupied for a period of fifteen days. Thereafter it is again occupied and while occupied it is damaged by fire. Under the minority rule, Archer could not recover because the house had been vacant and unoccupied for a period in excess of that permitted by the policy and this caused the policy to lapse. Under the majority rule, the policy would be in effect during the first ten days that the house remained vacant and unoccupied, but would not be in effect during the succeeding five days. However, the policy would again become effective as soon as the house was again occupied. In order to take care of such a situation, it is customary to attach a rider, known as a "vacancy rider," on a policy during the time a building is vacant. Any other provision of an insurance policy may be waived by the attachment of a rider or by any other act of the insurer which indicates his intention to relinquish the benefits of the provision.

Mittet et al. v. Home Insurance Co.
49 S.D. 319, 207 N.W. 49 (1926)

This was an action by Andrew Mittet and another (plaintiffs) against Home Insurance Company (defendant). Judgment for plaintiffs and defendant appealed. Judgment reversed and judgment entered for defendant.

On May 12, 1921, the defendant issued a policy of automobile theft insurance in the sum of $1,500 on a certain automobile owned by the plaintiff Andrew Mittet. The insurance policy contained the following provision:

"Exclusions:

"(2) It is a condition of this policy that it shall be null and void:

"(a) If the automobile described herein shall be used for carrying passengers for compensation, or rented or leased, or operated in any race or speed contest, during the term of this policy.

"This policy is made and accepted subject to the provisions, exclusions, conditions, and warranties set forth or endorsed hereon.

"Conditions:

"(4) The uses to which the automobile described is and will be put are private use and business calls, excluding commercial delivery."

On August 21, 1921, the automobile covered by the policy was taken by an adult son of Andrew Mittet to be used for conveying a passenger from Andrew Mittet's farm near Stamford, S.D., to Martin, S.D. The transportation of this passenger was undertaken for hire, although no compensation therefor was ever actually collected. While on the trip from Stamford to Martin, O. A. Mittet, who was driving, stopped the car and went back a short distance to get some water for the radiator, leaving the passenger seated in the car. About the time the driver was dipping the water the passenger started up the car and drove away. Neither the car nor the passenger was seen again by any one interested in the recovery of the car.

Moriarty, C. In dealing with warranties such as that now under consideration the courts have devoted most of their attention to the force of the word use, using or used, as found in policies of insurance. What treatment of property is sufficient to constitute using it in a manner prohibited by the terms of the policy?

Upon the question there is great divergence of authority. With reference to their position on this question the decisions may be classified under three distinct heads:

First, those which hold that a single instance of the property being treated contrary to the strict wording of the prohibition is sufficient to constitute a breach of the warranty.

Second, those which hold that single, occasional, or incidental treatment of the property is not sufficient to constitute a breach; that using, keeping, storing, allowing, etc., mean repeated, usual or customary treatment of the property or of the prohibited substance.

Third, those holding that single, occasional, or unusual treatment of the property, or of the prohibited substance, merely suspends the liability while such treatment continues; that if no loss results from the prohibited treatment the insurance is revived by the cessation of the treatment, but, if loss is occasioned by the prohibited treatment, the insurer is not liable for such loss.

This court has never had occasion to pass directly upon this question as it is presented in the instant case. Perhaps the decision in *Farmers' State Bank of Parker* v. *Tri-State Fire Ins. Co.*, 41 S.D. 398, 170 N.W. 638, upon casual reading, might be considered to have done so. It is true that the decision in that case cites with approval authorities holding that:

"What is intended to be prohibited is the habitual use of such articles, not their exceptional use upon some emergency."

In that case the provision was that the policy should become void if gasoline " 'be kept, used, or allowed' on the insured premises." The court held that a single instance of using a mixture of kerosene and gasoline to remove rust from the machinery in the insured building did not avoid the liability of the insurer. But it is evident that the court did not intend to pass upon the effect of the prohibition where the loss is admittedly due to the presence of the prohibited substance, for the court says:

"Whether the presence of the above mixture of gasoline and kerosene was the cause of the fire or not is by no means clear."

This language would be entirely unnecessary had the court intended to hold that the question whether the prohibited substance caused the loss was immaterial. The use of the language indicates that the court recognized the existence of the distinction, and did not wish to be understood as passing upon it.

In commenting upon the contention that, in order to constitute use there must be proof of habitual use, the Supreme Court of New York says:

"We cannot concur in this construction. In the nature of things, if the use of kerosene oil occasioned the loss, the result must have been caused by such use on some particular occasion, and it would be of very little moment whether or not the oil had been habitually used previously without doing injury. It is impossible to conceive how such previous habitual use of the article could have caused the fire. If immediately after taking out the policy, kerosene oil was used, and on the very first occasion it set fire to the barn, according to the construction claimed the loss would have been recoverable, because there must have been a previous habitual harmless use of the oil to entitle the insurance company to the benefit of the stipulated exemption. Such could not have been the intent of the stipulation." *Matson v. Farm Buildings Ins. Co.*, 73 N.Y. 313, 29 Am. Rep. 149.

The logic of this opinion seems to be unanswerable. To hold that a prohibited use must have become usual or habitual to avoid the liability is equivalent to saying that, if an insurer seeks to exempt itself from liability for a loss occasioned by a use so perilous that loss is almost certain to result from the first occasion of such use, the insurer's effort to escape liability must fail, because there is no possibility of the use being repeated frequently enough to make it habitual or usual use. In other words, the more glaring and certain the peril the more nearly impossible becomes the effort to avoid liability for loss occasioned by it.

To do this is to destroy the right to make a binding contract. The only escape from such fallacious doctrine is either to hold with those courts which construe the words of the contract strictly and say that a single instance of the prohibited act absolutely terminates the contract beyond revival, and those which, seeking to avoid inequitable forfeitures, hold that even a single instance of a prohibited use or condition suspends the liability while the prohibited use or condition continues, but the insurance is revived when such use or condition ceases.

This theory is indicated by the language of Judge McCoy in *Edmonds* v. *Insurance Co.*, 33 S.D. 55, 144 N.W. 718, where he says:

"If the death of insured had occurred prior to November 21, 1911, by reason of and while he was engaged in the prohibited occupation then there is but little question, but what a recovery on this policy would have been improper. . . . . There is absolutely nothing in the circumstances of this case that would, to the least degree, indicate that the death of the insured was in any manner whatsoever due to or connected with the one month's employment in violation of the contract."

Although there is no express declaration of the adoption of the doctrine, these expressions imply the adoption by this court of the doctrine established by the weight of authority, viz., that occasional or incidental violations of the strict terms of a promissory warranty merely suspend the liability of the insurer, and, if no loss occurs during such violation, the policy is revived when the violation ceases. The doctrine necessarily requires release from liability where the loss occurs during the violation and is caused by such violation.

The general rule as to the suspension of liability is thus stated in Elliott on Insurance, § 205.

"The weight of authority seems to support the view that a violation of a condition that works a forfeiture of the policy merely suspends the insurance during the violation, and if the violation is discontinued during the life of the policy, and does not exist at the time of the loss, the policy revives and the company is liable."

As the car involved in the instant case was being used in violation of the provisions of the policy at the time of the loss, and the loss would not have occurred but for the excepted peril, the insurance was suspended at the time of the loss, and the learned trial court erred in denying the defendant's motion for the direction of a verdict in its favor.

Assignment of Policy

As a general rule, a fire insurance policy is not assignable. One of the important risk elements in fire insurance, and similar insurance, is the character of the insured. To allow an assignment of such a policy would be to permit a change of the risk insured without the consent of the insurer. This is not permissible. If the owner of property on which a fire insurance policy has been issued sells the property, the purchaser acquires no interest in the policy. If the insurer is notified of the sale and consents to the transfer of the insurance policy to the purchaser, the majority of the courts treat the transaction as a novation, that is, a new contract results between the purchaser and the insurer.

After a loss has been suffered, the insured can assign the contract as freely as any other choses in action. After loss, the insurer is indebted to the insured for a fixed sum of money. It has also been held that the insured can assign a fire policy as security for a debt. Such an assignment gives the assignee the right to any money due as the result of a loss suffered. There is no change in the ownership of the insured property and, consequently, no change in the risk. The same rule is generally applied when the insured property is mortgaged and the fire policy is assigned to the mortgagee as his interest may appear.

The effect of the assignment of a life insurance policy by the insured depends on the terms of the policy, the relation of the parties, and the laws of the state. The life insurance policy is basically a contract to pay a sum certain on the death of the insured in consideration of the insured having paid the premiums. Such a contract is assignable. The courts have held that the insured cannot assign a life insurance policy without the consent of the beneficiary named in the policy unless the power to do so is reserved. Where the power to assign is not reserved, an assignment without the consent of the beneficiary and without notice to, and the consent of, the insurer is inoperative against the claim of the beneficiary; but even though the power to assign is not reserved, an assignment on forms furnished by the insurer has been held, by a majority of the courts, to be valid against the claim of the beneficiary.

As a general rule, the insured may assign a life insurance policy to whomsoever he wishes. However, if the assignment is made to one who does not have an insurable interest in the insured's life, and if the assignment is made for the purpose of evading the law forbidding wagering insurance, the assignment is void.

Swaine v. Teutonia Fire Ins. Co.
222 Mass. 108, 109 N.E. 825 (1915)

This was an action by John Swaine (plaintiff) against the Teutonia Fire Insurance Company (defendant). Judgment for defendant and plaintiff appealed. Judgment affirmed.

The plaintiff's predecessor in title, Ellen Kennedy, on January 1, 1910, purchased from the Teutonia Fire Insurance Company a policy of fire insurance, in the Massachusetts standard form, on a certain house which she then owned, for a term of three years. There was a mortgage upon the property, and the loss in case of fire was made payable to the mortgagee, Charles E. Hitchcock, as his interest might appear.

Before any loss by fire the owner, Mrs. Kennedy, conveyed her title to one Johnson, and Johnson in turn conveyed his title on December 6, 1911, to the plaintiff. Both conveyances were executed and delivered without the assent in writing or in print of the insurer. In any aspect of the testimony it does not appear that before any loss by fire the insurer or its agent, Lyman, knew of a conveyance of the title by Johnson to the plaintiff Swaine, or had other than a general information that the title was to be or had been transferred.

The property was destroyed by fire on December 19, 1911, and plaintiff claims that he is entitled to the benefits of the policy of insurance issued by defendant to Mrs. Kennedy.

Pierce, J. The policy is not incident to the estate nor does it run with the land. Its assignment, when accepted by the insurer, operates by way of novation to discharge the rights and obligations incident to the original parties, and by agreement of parties and operation of law gives birth to a new contract between the insurer and the assignee upon the old terms. In the case at bar there was no assignment actual or implied.

The transfer of title from the owner to Johnson and from Johnson to the plaintiff was without the assent in writing or in print of the insurer and rendered the policy void as to all persons other than the mortgagee unless the insurer be estopped to make use of this weapon of defence, or has waived this condition of the policy. There is nothing in the record to justify an argument that any act of word or of conduct of the insurer or its agent led Johnson or the plaintiff to neglect to have the Kennedy policy assigned to him, or that either of them in consequence thereof failed as owner to insure his interest upon a new policy.

The plaintiff at the time of loss had neither title to a policy of insurance issued by the defendant company nor an equitable right to have as against the defendant the benefit of such. Had he had such, the unexplained and unexcused delay of three months in furnishing a sworn statement of loss would prevent recovery in this action.

Minnesota Mutual Life Ins. Co. v. Manthei et al.
— Mo. App. —, 189 S.W. (2d) 144 (1945)

This was a suit in interpleader by the Minnesota Mutual Life Insurance Company (plaintiff) against Edna Manthei and Joseph H. Dreher (defendants) for adjudication of defendants' conflicting claims to the proceeds of a life insurance policy. Judgment for defendant Dreher and defendant Manthei appealed. Judgment affirmed.

The insured Richard Manthei and defendant Joseph H. Dreher owned the capital stock of a corporation which operated a grocery store. Manthei owned 134 shares of the stock, Dreher owned 65 shares, and Charles Vogel owned one qualifying share.

From time to time Dreher and Manthei advanced money to the corporation, and in the summer of 1939 it was agreed between Dreher and Manthei that a summary should be made of their respective accounts with the corporation. As a result of this summary it was agreed that Manthei was indebted to Dreher in the amount of $7,-289.65. Manthei gave a promissory note signed by himself and his wife, defendant Edna Manthei, for this amount payable to Dreher, and due six months from date. When the note fell due, January 2, 1940, a renewal note was given payable in six months. May 22, 1940, Richard Manthei assigned a $5,000 policy of life insurance, issued by plaintiff on his life, to Dreher as security for the note. The assignment was made on forms furnished by the plaintiff and it was executed by Richard Manthei and Edna Manthei who was named in the policy as beneficiary. On August 16, 1940, Richard Manthei notified the plaintiff that he revoked the assignment.

Richard Manthei died September 20, 1940. Both Edna Manthei and Joseph Dreher claimed the proceeds of the policy. Plaintiff paid the amount due on the policy into court and filed a bill of interpleader asking the court to determine which of the two claimants was entitled to the money.

Bennick, C. In reaching our ultimate decision in the case, there are certain fundamental considerations about which there can be no reasonable basis for dispute.

For instance, if the assignment of the policy was valid, the assignment could not thereafter have been revoked at the mere pleasure of the insured as assignor, after the rights of the parties had become fixed. The court was therefore undoubtedly correct in determining the case from the standpoint of whether the assignment had been made for value, in denying any legal significance to the insured's purported revocation of the assignment under date of August 16, 1940, which he attempted to bring about without regard to the lack of Dreher's consent thereto.

Moreover, so far as concerns the question of consideration for the assignment which was made on May 22, 1940, as security for the note which had been theretofore executed on January 2, 1940, it is enough to say that an antecedent or pre-existing debt will constitute sufficient consideration for the subsequent assignment of something of value as collateral security for its payment.

There is still the further question of whether, irrespective of any question of consideration, the assignment of the policy should be held void upon the ground that Dreher had no insurable interest in the life of the insured. Where a policy is assigned in good faith and without any intention that the assignment is to be used as a cloak for a mere wager or gambling transaction, the assignment is not against public policy, and the policy may be assigned by the insured. The only qualification is that where the assignment is made to a creditor of the insured as security for a debt, it is only valid to the extent of the debt it secures, and the creditor must thereafter account to the beneficiary, or to the insured's estate as the case may be, for any excess in the amount of the proceeds. In this case the assignment was based upon the fact that Dreher was the creditor of the insured, and as a matter of fact contained the express provision that the proceeds of the policy should only be payable to Dreher "as his interest may appear."

QUESTIONS AND PROBLEMS

1. Towle was soliciting agent for the Single Men's Endowment Association. The contract provided that each member was to pay $10.00 initiation fee, $2.00 dues each year, and $1.25 on the marriage of each member. He promised, on the penalty of forfeiture of the benefits, that he would not himself marry for two years. If he married after two years, he was to receive as many dollars as there were associates in the order, not exceeding $1,000.00. Towle was indicted for soliciting insurance without a license. Was this scheme insurance?
2. Lucas made an application for a $5,000 policy of preferred risk life insurance. The application was submitted to the company which sent a policy to the agent together with an amended application with directions that the policy was not to be delivered until the amended application had been signed. Lucas refused to sign the amended application; however, Lucas did authorize the agent to request the company to issue to him a $3,000 policy of ordinary life insurance. Before this request was acted upon Lucas died. Five days elapsed from the time the request was made for the $3,000 policy and the death of Lucas. Was the company liable on the $3,000 policy?
3. Bobb signed an application for fire insurance on farm buildings in the Farm Mutual Co. The premium was not paid at the time the application was filed. The by-laws of the company provided that the application would not be binding upon the company until the premiums had been paid and the application had been approved by the secretary. The company's secretary did approve the application. The buildings covered by the application were destroyed by fire the same afternoon the application was signed and before the premiums were paid or a policy issued. Is the company liable?
4. Hallock made application for a fire insurance policy on his buildings on March 10. The application was mailed to the home office, and the policy was issued and mailed to Hallock on March 13. After the policy was mailed, but before Hallock received it, the buildings burned. Were Hallock's buildings insured?
5. On August 7, West made an application for a policy of insurance on his life and the policy was issued on August 13. In the application West answered the question: "What illness, injury, or accident have you ever had? Give details. (A) None except children's diseases in infancy." West had had a serious gall bladder attack which confined him to his bed most of the time from June 25 to July 23. He died September 11, but his death was not the result of the gall bladder attack. Is the insurance company liable on the policy it issued?
6. Mendenhall insured the buildings on a farm he was occupying against fire. The farm had been purchased by Mendenhall's father and the deed was in the father's name, but the father, in his will, had devised the farm to Mendenhall who operated it as his own, and it was understood that the farm would go to Mendenhall on his father's death. The buildings burned, and the insurance company refused to pay the insurance on the ground that Mendenhall had no insurable interest in the property. Did Mendenhall have an insurable interest in the property?
7. Mason insured a yacht in the Marine Insurance Company for the sum of $1,000, the policy of insurance being in the form of a standard policy. The yacht was totally destroyed by fire on August 22, and proof of loss was served upon the insurance company on October 10. The policy provided that proof of loss should be made forthwith and that payment of loss was to be made within 60 days after proof of loss. The policy did not provide that failure to make proof of loss would void the policy. Did the failure to make proof of loss within a reasonable time after the loss prevent recovery on the policy?

8. Letts had insured his factory with the Royal Assurance Co. The company desired to cancel the policy. The policy provided that the company could cancel the policy by giving five days' notice in writing. The agent of the company discussed the cancellation of the policy and the substitution of another policy with Letts but no definite agreement was reached. On March 2, the agent wrote Letts giving him notice of the cancellation of the policy and enclosing a proposed substituted policy. The letter was received the morning of March 4. The insured buildings were destroyed the morning of March 4. Is the insurance company liable on the original policy?
9. Berg insured his life for $500 and the policy was payable to his "administrator, or assigns." Berg delivered the policy to Ellis as a gift but it was later returned to him for safe-keeping, whereupon Berg gave Ellis a written statement indicating that the policy was to be paid to her. On Berg's death his administrator claimed the proceeds of the policy contending that inasmuch as there was no change of beneficiary the policy was payable to Berg's administrator. Is this contention correct?
10. If Archer owns a house and lot and has the house insured against fire in the Burch Insurance Co. and Archer sells the house and lot to Clark, is Clark entitled to the benefits of the policy of insurance?

CHAPTER XLII

BANKRUPTCY

Introduction

The idea of bankruptcy is not modern in its origin. One aspect of the idea was present in the Jewish sabbatical year of release, practiced more than three thousand years ago. The Cessio Bonarum of Julius Caesar's time included another aspect of bankruptcy. Our present American bankruptcy acts had their origin in the English bankruptcy acts which were originally quasi criminal in their nature. The first English bankruptcy act was passed in 1542 (34 Henry VIII). A second English act was passed in 1570 (13 Elizabeth). In these early acts there was no provision for discharge. The first provision for the discharge of the bankrupt was included in Queen Anne's Act, 1705 (4th Anne). All of these early bankruptcy acts were acts providing better protection to creditors against the dishonest practices of debtors. This was the general aim of bankruptcy acts at the time the Constitution of the United States was drafted.

The framers of the Constitution gave the federal government the right to regulate and control bankruptcies. This power was first exercised in 1800. This act followed the general plan of the English bankruptcy acts. It was limited by its own terms to five years but was repealed in 1803. The country was without a Federal Bankruptcy Act until 1841, when a second bankruptcy act was passed. This act was constructed along broad lines and included all the basic elements of a true bankruptcy act, but it was short-lived, being repealed in 1843 primarily for political reasons. A third act was passed in 1867 which was in force for eleven years. This act proved to have many weaknesses. Under the act it was far too easy to throw a debtor into bankruptcy, and, once in bankruptcy, it was exceedingly difficult for the bankrupt to obtain a discharge.

It was in the light of the shortcomings of the act of 1867 that the present act was drafted. Our present act was passed in 1898, and although it has been amended many times, the general plan of bankruptcy procedure has been maintained. Many new features have been added since 1929, such as Railroad Reorganizations, Corporate Reorganizations, Municipal Debt Readjustments, Agricultural Compositions and Extensions, and Compositions and Extensions. As a result of the many amendments, which altered and added to the original text of the 1898 act, our bankruptcy act became disorganized in its structure, and due to the passage of time, it became obsolete in some of its features. To remedy this situation the Chandler Bill was passed June 22, 1938, and became effective September 21, 1938. The Chandler Bill states the law accurately, scientifically, and comprehensively. It eliminates overlapping and discards cumbersome phrasing. Although the Chandler Bill is in form an amendment of the act of 1898, it is so comprehensive in its scope that it is equivalent to a complete redrafting of the act.

The purpose of the bankruptcy act is (1) to protect creditors from one another, (2) to protect creditors from their debtor, and (3) to protect the honest debtor from his creditors. To accomplish these objectives the debtor is required to make a full disclosure of all his property and to surrender it to the trustee. Provisions are made for examination of the debtor and for punishment of the debtor who refuses to make an honest disclosure and surrender of his property. The trustee of the bankrupt's estate administers, liquidates, and distributes the proceeds of the estate to the creditors. Provisions are made for the determination of creditors' rights, the recovery of preferential payments, and the disallowance of preferential liens and encumbrances. If the bankrupt has been honest in his business transactions and in his bankruptcy proceedings, he is granted a discharge.

Bankrupts

The earlier bankruptcy acts were drafted on the theory that only those engaged in business should be declared bankrupt and that no one could on his own motion be declared bankrupt. The proceedings were primarily for the benefit of the creditors. Under our present act a debtor may be adjudged bankrupt on his own petition, or he may be adjudged bankrupt on the petition of his creditors. In the former case he is a voluntary bankrupt, while in the latter case he is an involuntary bankrupt. The bankruptcy act makes a distinction between voluntary bankrupts and involuntary bankrupts. Substantially any person, partnership, or corporation may become a voluntary bankrupt, the exceptions being a municipal, railroad insurance, or banking corporation, or a building and loan association. These are excepted from the operation of the bankruptcy acts because other provisions have been made for the handling of the affairs of such corporations in the event they become insolvent.

Not everyone who may become a voluntary bankrupt may be adjudged an involuntary bankrupt. Wage earners and farmers cannot be adjudged involuntary bankrupts. Any natural person, except a municipal, railroad, insurance, or banking corporation, or a building and loan association may be adjudged bankrupt upon default or impartial trial if they owe debts to the amount of $1,000 or over, providing they have committed an act of bankruptcy. Acts of bankruptcy are defined in the bankruptcy act as follows:

Acts of bankruptcy by a person shall consist of his having (1) conveyed, transferred, concealed, removed, or permitted to be concealed or removed any part of his property, with intent to hinder, delay, or defraud his creditors or any of them; or (2) transferred, while insolvent, any portion of his property to one or more of his creditors with intent to prefer such creditors over his other creditors; or (3) suffered or permitted, while insolvent, any creditor to obtain a lien upon any of his property through legal proceedings and not having vacated or discharged such lien within thirty days from the date thereof or at least five days before the date set for any sale or other disposition of such property; or (4) made a general assignment for the benefit of his creditors; or (5) while insolvent or unable to pay his debts as they mature, procured, permitted, or suffered voluntarily or involuntarily the appointment of a receiver or trustee to take charge of his property; or (6) admitted in writing his inability to pay his debts and his willingness to be adjudged a bankrupt.

Three or more creditors, having fixed and liquidated claims in the amount of $500 over and above the value of any security held by them, may file a petition to have their debtor adjudged bankrupt. If the debtor owes less than twelve persons, one creditor whose claim is $500 or over may file a petition. The act of bankruptcy on which the petition is based must have been committed within four months of the filing of the petition.

In re Adams et al.
53 F. Supp. 982 (1944)

This was a proceeding in the matter of the bankruptcy of Calvin J. Adams and Raymond F. Schramm, partners, trading and doing business as Susquehanna Engineering Company. A motion was made by the alleged bankrupts to dismiss the involuntary petition. Motion granted.

After alleging the usual formal allegations, the creditors' petition sets forth the following allegations respecting the petitioning creditors and the act of bankruptcy relied on:

"That your petitioners are creditors or representatives of creditors of the said Susquehanna Engineering Company, having provable claims amounting in the aggregate, in the excess of securities held by them, to the sum of $500.00. That the nature and amount of your petitioners' claims are as follows:

"Vulcan Stoker Corporation, $3,824.75, representing amounts due the petitioner for royalties and parts and equipment furnished.

"Mills Electrical Company, $324.32, representing parts and equipment furnished, sold and delivered.

"Pennsylvania Foundry Supply & Sand Company, $115.38, for goods sold and delivered as set forth in the petitioner's books of original entry.

"And your petitioners further represent that the said Susquehanna Engineering Company is insolvent; and that within four months next preceding the date of this petition the said Susquehanna Engineering Company committed an act of bankruptcy, in that the partners conveyed or transferred certain realty situate at the southeast corner of Ninth and Iron Streets in the Town of Bloomsburg, Columbia County, Pennsylvania, said property being used for the sole purpose and benefit of the said partnership, with intent to hinder, delay or defraud its creditors, or any of them."

The bankrupt contends that the petition of the creditors is insufficient in that it does not allege facts sufficient to justify an adjudication of involuntary bankruptcy.

Watson, D. J. In my opinion the creditors' petition must be dismissed because it does not properly state a cause of action against the alleged bankrupt. The essential conditions for a creditor to qualify as a petitioning creditor are that his claim against the debtor be provable in bankruptcy, fixed as to liability, and liquidated in amount. That the claims of the petitioning creditors conform to these general requirements should be alleged in the petition, preferably in the language of the Act.

The allegations respecting the claims of the petitioning creditors in this case do not set forth that the claims are fixed as to liability and liquidated in amount and, from the information respecting such claims contained in the petition it cannot be inferred that all of the claims set forth are of the required nature.

A more serious defect in the petition and one which requires the dismissal thereof is that the allegation of the Act of Bankruptcy charged against the alleged bankrupt is not set forth with sufficient particularity to inform the respondent of the charge made against it. The facts relied upon to establish an alleged fraudulent transfer must be set forth with such fullness as to apprise the alleged bankrupt of what he will be required to meet. An allegation in the language of the statute alone stating that the bankrupt disposed of his property intending to hinder, delay, or defraud creditors is not sufficient. A petition should describe the property alleged to have been transferred, the time of the alleged transfer, and to whom it was made.

In the present case, the petition does not allege the person to whom the alleged fraudulent transfer was made or the date upon which it was made. The result is that the alleged bankrupt is not sufficiently informed as to the charge he will be required to meet. To this extent the petition does not set forth a statement of the petitioners' claims showing that they are entitled to relief as required by the rules of pleading of this Court.

For the foregoing reasons, the creditors' petition filed in this case must be dismissed.

Administration of Bankrupt's Estate

Petitions for both voluntary and involuntary bankruptcy are filed in the federal district court. After adjudication, the estate of the bankrupt is referred to the referee for the purpose of administration.

The referee calls the first meeting of creditors not less than ten days nor more than thirty days after the adjudication. At this first meeting of creditors, the judge or referee presides, and the business is usually taken up in the following order. First, the claims are allowed. After the claims are allowed the trustee is elected. The trustee is elected by a vote of the claims which have been allowed, and the person who receives the majority vote in number and amount is elected. In determining the number of claims voted, claims of $50 or less are not counted, but such claims are counted in computing the amount. The judge or referee is not bound to appoint the person elected by the creditors as trustee. If the person elected is not qualified or for some other reason would not be desirable as trustee, the judge or referee may appoint someone of his own selection.

The next step is the public examination of the bankrupt. He is examined by the judge or referee who presides at the meeting, and, in addition, any creditor has the right to examine the bankrupt. This may be done by the creditor himself or by an attorney whom the creditor has employed to conduct the examination in his behalf. The purpose of the examination of the bankrupt is to bring out all the facts relating to his bankruptcy, to determine whether he has made a full and complete disclosure of all his property, to determine whether he has been guilty of any acts which would bar his discharge, and to clear up any questions arising as to claims, etc.

The trustee, as soon as he has qualified, takes possession of all the property of the bankrupt, inventories it, has it appraised, and sets aside the bankrupt's exemptions. He also examines the claims filed, and objects to any claims which are not allowable or which for any reason are improper. The trustee reduces the estate to money as expeditiously as is compatible with the best interests of the parties.

Title to all the bankrupt's estate vests in the trustee; consequently, in the administration of the estate, the trustee acts as owner. He has the right to sue in any court in which an owner could sue, and such suits are brought in the name of the trustee. All suits are brought under the direction of the court.

The trustee must keep an accurate account of all property and money coming into his hands, deposit all moneys in the authorized depositories, pay by check or draft all dividends within ten days after they are declared by the referee, and lay before the final meeting of the creditors a detailed statement of the administration of the estate.

In re Austin Resort & Land Co.
12 Fed. Supp. 459 (1935)

This was a proceeding in bankruptcy in the matter of Austin Resort and Land Company, bankrupt. Certain creditors filed a petition asking the District Court to review orders of the referee. The orders of the referee were approved and confirmed.

On the 22d day of June, 1935, the first meeting of creditors was held before the referee. Three persons were nominated for the office of trustee: J. A. Ratchford, who claimed he was entitled to vote sixteen claims, aggregating $3,899.89; Walter Reichert, supported by the votes of four claims, aggregating $1,692.87; and F. H. Boggs, supported by the votes of four claims, aggregating $1,295.09. Among the claims which were voted by the nominee Ratchford was that of Rauer's Law & Collection Company, a corporation, in the sum of $2,040.64, voted by the attorney for the collection company, who stated to the referee that claimant would waive all security under said claim. The referee, believing that the nominee Ratchford had the support of the majority of claims voted, both in number and amount, announced and confirmed his election as trustee and fixed his bond at $10,000. The first meeting of creditors then adjourned and the persons interested left the court.

Thereafter, on the 24th day of June, 1935, the referee sent to the attorney for the collection company a telegram which read, "Serra claim of Rauer's Collection Agency not permitted to vote for trustee." The collection company replied: "Undersigned waives right to security or preference by reason of abstract of judgment formal waiver follows." On the same day, the referee telephoned to Ratchford that he (referee) had withdrawn the claim of the collection company; that said claim could not be counted as being voted for Ratchford; that as a result no election of trustee had been had; and that he (referee) would forthwith appoint a trustee for the bankrupt estate. Forthwith the referee made the orders which are subject of review, the first, rescinding, vacating, and setting aside the confirmation of the election of Ratchford as trustee, and the second, appointing Williams as trustee.

St. Sure, D. J. It is contended that the order appointing Williams trustee was erroneous for the reasons that Ratchford was, and is, the duly elected trustee of the bankrupt estate; that at the first meeting of creditors Ratchford received a majority in both number and amounts of claims present and voting; that at the first meeting of creditors Ratchford was declared by the referee to be the duly elected, appointed, and acting trustee of the bankrupt estate.

The referee erred when he allowed the collection company's claim to be voted for the trustee, but he immediately corrected his error. It thus appears that there was no election of trustee because no one received a majority of votes in number and amount. Had the referee appreciated the true situation during the meeting, and had there been no request on the part of the creditors that they be given a further opportunity to vote for a trustee, the referee unquestionably could have appointed a trustee and no one could have been heard to complain.

Under the facts and circumstances disclosed by the record, the most that can be said against the acts of the referee is that they were improvident and irregular.

It is the law that before the entry of an order, a referee has the right to set it aside, if improvidently made. He may do this upon his own motion, particularly when the order relates to the allowance of a claim. As said in *International Agr. Corporation* v. *Cary*, 240 F. 101, at page 105, "There may or may not have been good reason for proceeding sua sponte, but the presence or absence of such reason is not fatal to jurisdiction. A court of bankruptcy is a court of equity; the proceedings therein are more summary than in ordinary suits and it cannot be that an equity court, acting under such summary practice, is powerless, in the interests of justice, on its own motion to take steps to correct what it believes to have been an erroneous action had upon insufficient knowledge."

There is nothing in the Bankruptcy Act making the selection of a trustee by the creditors absolute at all events. Proceedings in bankruptcy are flexible and liberal and in their major aspects administrative. Such proceedings are intended to be and usually are carried out informally. "The whole matter of appointing trustees is subject to the power and superintendence of the court. If the court ought to have summoned the creditors to elect a trustee, its failure to do so was a mere irregularity." *Scofield* v. *United States* (C.C.A.) 174 F. 1, 3.

Undoubtedly, it would have been better practice for the referee to have called another meeting of the creditors and given them an opportunity to appoint a trustee of their own selection. But it is the settled practice of this court not to disturb the acts of the referee "in administrative matters—of which the election of a trustee is a typical example—unless a plain and injurious error of law or abuse of discretion is shown." No such error of law or abuse of discretion has been shown.

The fundamental purpose of the Bankruptcy Act "is to reduce the assets to cash as speedily as practicable for equitable distribution to the creditors." The trustee appointed by the referee has long since qualified and entered upon the discharge of his duties. To grant the prayers of petitioners would subserve no useful purpose, but would cause confusion, delay, and probably loss in the administration of the estate.

Nothing has arisen subsequent to the appointment and qualification of Williams as trustee which would warrant his removal. Furthermore, "Proceedings for the removal of the trustee must be carried on pursuant to the Bankruptcy Act and the general orders adopted by the Supreme Court and the forms for complaint by a creditor or creditors."

Debts

For the purpose of the administration of a bankrupt's estate, his debts have been classified as provable debts, allowable debts, dischargeable debts, and debts having priority. If a debt is provable, it is the basis of its owner's right to share in the estate of the bankrupt. Provable debts include all debts founded on judgments or on instruments in writing absolutely owing at the time of the filing of the petition whether payable or not, taxable costs, open accounts, contracts express or implied, and also claims reduced to judgment after the filing of the petition and before consideration of the bankrupt's discharge. An award made under workmen's compensation acts for injury or death occurring prior to the filing of the petition is a provable debt. Unliquidated tort claims are not provable, but if an action has been brought on the claim before the filing of the petition, it is a provable debt. Contingent claims arising on contracts such as contracts of guaranty and surety, damages for anticipatory breach of contract, and damages for breach of a lease are provable debts. In the lease case the damages are limited to the amount of the rent reserved by the lease for the year next succeeding the date of the surrender of the premises, or the date of re-entry by the landlord.

The fact that a debt is classed as a provable debt does not assure its owner's participation in the distribution of the assets. Before a creditor can participate in the bankrupt proceedings, he must prove his claim and the claim must be allowed. The proof of claim is a sworn statement of the amount of the claim, the consideration therefor, security held, etc., and if it is based on a written instrument, such instrument must be filed with the proof. Claims, which are not filed within six months after the first date set for the first meeting of creditors, will not be allowed. If the bankrupt had any defense to the debt, such defense will be set up by the trustee, and, if established, the claim will not be allowed, or if the defense goes to only part of the claim, the amount of the claim will be reduced. All the defenses which would have been available to the bankrupt will be available to the trustee.

Debts having priority should not be confused with secured debts. Certain debts are declared by the Bankruptcy Act to have priority over other classes of debts. Costs of preserving the assets of the bankrupt, administration expenses, etc., wages due workmen, servants, clerks, etc., which have been earned within three months and not exceeding $600 in amount, costs of successfully opposing bankrupt's discharge, costs of convicting any person of an offence under the act, taxes due the United States or any state or any subdivision thereof are the principal debts given priority.

Certain debts are not affected by the bankrupt's discharge. Section 17 of the Bankruptcy Act provides that a discharge in bankruptcy shall release a bankrupt from all of his provable debts, whether allowable in full or in part, except such as (1) are due as a tax levied by the United States, or any state, county, district, or municipality; or (2) are liabilities for obtaining money or property by false pretenses or false representations, or for willful and malicious injuries to the person or property of another, or for alimony due or to become due, or for maintenance or support of wife or child, or for seduction of an unmarried female, or for breach of promise of marriage accompanied by seduction, or for criminal conversation; or (3) have not been duly scheduled in time for proof and an allowance, with the name of the creditor, if known to the bankrupt, unless such creditor had notice or actual knowledge of the proceedings in bankruptcy; or (4) were created by his fraud, embezzlement, misappropriation or defalcation while acting as an officer or in any fiduciary capacity; or (5) are for wages which have been earned within three months before the date of commencement of the proceedings in bankruptcy due to workmen, servants, clerks, or traveling or city salesmen, on salary or commission basis, whole or part time, whether or not selling exclusively for the bankrupt; or (6) are due for moneys of an employee received or retained by his employer to secure the faithful performance by such employee of the terms of a contract of employment.

These debts are provable debts and the owner of such a debt has the right to participate in the distribution of the bankrupt's estate, but his right to recover the unpaid balance of the debt is not cut off by the bankrupt's discharge. All provable debts except those listed above are dischargeable debts; that is, the right to recover the unpaid balance is cut off by the bankrupt's discharge.

Reaugh v. Hadley
93 F. (2d) 29 (1937)

This was an action by Ernest O. Reaugh, receiver of the First National Bank of Cambridge, Illinois (plaintiff) against Mae B. Hadley (defendant). Judgment for defendant and plaintiff appealed. Judgment affirmed.

The bank closed its doors voluntarily on November 15, 1930. At that time, defendant was a shareholder and there is no evidence of transfer of her stock thereafter. On January 5, 1931, defendant was adjudged bankrupt upon her voluntary petition filed that day. Eight days later, the bank, through its shareholders, voted to enter upon voluntary liquidation, and this it proceeded to do. Subsequently, on the 8th day of January, 1932, the Comptroller of the Currency declared the bank insolvent, appointed the receiver, and on February 5, 1932, levied an assessment upon the shareholders for the sum of $100 per share, due and payable on the 12th day of March, 1932. The bankrupt was discharged on June 30, 1933.

Plaintiff contends that the liability was not discharged, as there is no showing that it was scheduled or that the receiver had notice of the bankruptcy, while the defendant contends that the order of discharge is a complete defense.

Lindley, D. J. The assessment liability, always existing under the banking act, became fixed in a definite amount on the 15th day of February, 1932, some fourteen months before the bankrupt was discharged. The claim, quasi contractual in its origin and basis, an incident affixed by law to the contract of membership between shareholder and bank, was provable in bankruptcy even before fixed in amount. Whether the debtor listed the debt in her original schedules or by amendment thereto, whether any claim was filed in the bankruptcy court, whether plaintiff had knowledge of the proceedings in apt time, and whether the trustee administered upon the shares as an asset, the agreed facts do not disclose.

By section 17 of the Bankruptcy Act it is provided that the bankrupt's discharge shall release him from all of his provable debts, except, among others, those which "have not been duly scheduled in time for proof and allowance." In *Kreitlein* v. *Ferger*, 238 U.S. 21, Mr. Justice Lamar said: "There are only a few cases dealing with the subject, but they almost uniformly hold that where the bankrupt is sued on a debt existing at the time of filing the petition, the introduction of the order makes out a prima facie defense, the burden being then cast upon the plaintiff to show that, because of the nature of the claim, failure to give notice, or other statutory reason, the debt sued on was by law excepted from the operation of the discharge." In the later case of *Hill* v. *Smith*, 260 U.S. 592, Mr. Justice Holmes added: "By the very form of the law the debtor is discharged subject to an exception, and one who would bring himself within the exception must offer evidence to do so." It follows that, inasmuch as the cause of action to recover the assessment came into existence while the bankruptcy case was pending and prior to the bankrupt's discharge, when the debtor pleaded and proved the discharge, if the plaintiff had any evidence to bring himself within the exception, it was incumbent upon him to produce the same and, having failed to do so, his action failed.

In re Boggess
21 Fed. Supp. 905 (1937-1938)

This was a proceeding in the matter of Charles Dudley Boggess, Jr., bankrupt. Certain creditors filed a petition for permission to file proofs of claims. Petition denied.

On January 11, 1936, Charles Dudley Boggess, Jr., was adjudged a bankrupt on his voluntary petition. The first meeting of the creditors was held the 23d day of January, 1936. The bankrupt listed as his only asset a one-half interest in a note in the amount of $16,000.

At the first meeting of the creditors, this note was discussed and the bankrupt stated that it was secured by a mortgage on a small tract of land. Eventually, the trustee realized $1,600 on the bankrupt's interest in the note. The bankrupt filed, with his schedule of liabilities, a list of his creditors, with claims aggregating approximately $1,091.03.

Swinford, D. J. The Bankruptcy Act contains the following provisions:

Section 57n. "Claims shall not be proved against a bankrupt estate subsequent to six months after the adjudication."

Section 66b. "(b) Dividends remaining unclaimed for one year shall, under the direction of the court, be distributed to the creditors whose claims have been allowed but not paid in full, and after such claims have been paid in full the balance shall be paid to the bankrupt."

Two of the creditors, with claims aggregating approximately $258.69, filed their claims, duly proven, within six months from the date of the adjudication of bankruptcy.

No other claims were filed or presented within six months after the adjudication, but in June, 1937, which was after the expiration of the six-month period, creditors with claims approximating the aggregate amount of $700 presented to the referee their respective proofs of claims and asked that they be filed and allowed. The bankrupt objected on the ground that the claims were not properly proven or tendered for filing within six months of the date of adjudication. The referee entered an order denying the creditors' motion to file the claims and disallowing the claims.

The creditors, whose claims were disallowed, filed a petition alleging either fraud or mistake on the part of the bankrupt in filing his schedule and prayed that a notice be given to all the creditors and that they be given an opportunity to file proofs of claims; prayed for an order allowing and directing payment of all lawful and just debts. The bankrupt filed a demurrer to this petition. The referee treated the demurrer as the bankrupt's motion to dismiss the petition.

The court is called upon to pass upon the following question: Should dilatory creditors be permitted to prove their claims after the expiration of six months from date of adjudication and participate in the distribution where the trustee has sufficient money to pay the costs of administration and all creditors in full where only the bankrupt objects?

The allegation of fraud in the claimants' petition is pleading a conclusion.

The record in the case shows that the bankrupt did nothing to conceal his assets or in any way mislead the claimants. No facts are alleged which would constitute fraud.

To hold that the claimants should be permitted to file their claims requires a forced construction of a statute which is not open to construction. There is no ambiguity in the language of this section of the Bankruptcy Act and the clause applicable is plain and unequivocal. For this particular case it would seem that Congress might have with wisdom made an exception, but the fact remains that it did not. Congress undoubtedly had the right to fix this limitation and the court can assume no power to extend the period of limitation or to interpolate an exception which Congress expressly declined to do.

The fact that it is the bankrupt's objection to the filing of the claim adds nothing to the petitioners' contention. With such a fixed limitation giving no exception the court cannot extend the time.

As is said in the case of *In re Silk*, 2 Cir., 55 F. 2d 917, 918, "the assets of the bankrupt (are) not for the benefit of all his creditors, but only for those whose claims are proved and allowed as specified in the Act." And, as further pointed out in the Silk Case, contemplates a return of any surplusage to the bankrupt.

It is therefore the opinion of the court that those creditors not having filed and proven their claims against the bankrupt estate within six months of the adjudication are not entitled to an allowance of their claims.

Preferences, Liens, and Fraudulent Transfers

One of the principal objectives of the Bankruptcy Act is the protection of the creditors. Under the common law, the creditor, who first attached or obtained a lien on the debtor's property or who was able to induce the debtor to pay his claim, could retain the advantage which he had gained, irrespective of the fact that such advantage might deplete the debtor's estate to such an extent that other creditors could recover nothing. Under the Bankruptcy Act such preferences may be avoided.

That a business man should be permitted to carry on his business in the regular course, even though he may be in stringent financial circumstances, is recognized, and the Bankruptcy Act is so drafted that it does not interfere with one if his transactions are in the regular course of business. If, however, while insolvent, one attempts to prefer one or more of his creditors, the Bankruptcy Act affords the other creditors protection providing they act seasonably.

If one, while insolvent, makes a preferential payment, it is an act of bankruptcy, and if the debtor is adjudged bankrupt, the trustee may recover the preferential payment for the benefit of the estate. In order to be a recoverable preference, the transfer must have been made within four months of the filing of the petition in bankruptcy and must have been made while the debtor was insolvent. The effect of such transfer must enable the creditor to obtain a greater percentage of his debt than other creditors in the same class. Such a transfer may be avoided by the trustee if the creditor receiving it had, at the time the transfer was made, reasonable grounds to believe that the debtor was insolvent.

A creditor may attempt to obtain a preference by obtaining a lien on the debtor's property. The lien may be obtained either by legal or equitable process or by contract with the debtor. Any lien which is obtained within four months of the filing of the petition is null and void if the lien is to secure a pre-existing debt, and if the debtor was insolvent at the time the lien was obtained. If a person loans money or sells goods to an insolvent debtor and takes a lien as security, such a lien is valid.

Transfers for the purpose of hindering, delaying, or defrauding creditors are null and void. This rule is applied generally throughout the United States. Transfers made by a debtor and every obligation incurred by him within one year of the filing of the petition in bankruptcy are void as to creditors, if made or incurred without fair consideration and while insolvent, or if the transfer or obligation will render him insolvent. If one makes a transfer of property or incurs obligations without fair consideration in contemplation of incurring debts beyond his ability to pay, the transaction is fraudulent to both existing and future creditors. In all the foregoing situations the transfer or obligation may be declared void if made within one year from the date of the filing of the petition in bankruptcy. A transfer made or an obligation incurred within four months of the filing of the petition is fraudulent as to existing and future creditors if made with the intent to use the consideration obtained to effect a preference which is voidable under the act.

In addition to the above, any transfer made or suffered or any obligation incurred by a debtor, who has been adjudged a bankrupt, which under any federal or state law applicable thereto is voidable by any creditor having a provable claim, shall be void as against the trustee. Such property remains a part of the bankrupt's estate and passes to the trustee, and the trustee owes a duty to reclaim the property or collect its value for the benefit of the estate.

All of these safeguards are set up to prevent the debtor from concealing or disposing of his property in fraud of his creditors or to prevent him from favoring one creditor at the expense of his other creditors; yet they are so framed that the honest but hard-pressed debtor is not unduly handicapped in continuing the operation of his business. If he "plays fair," he is protected, but if he does not "play fair," the creditors are protected.

In re Gill
First National Bank of Huntsville et al. v. Ford
92 F. (2d) 810 (1937)

This was a proceeding in the matter of Eugene R. Gill, bankrupt, on the claim of First National Bank of Huntsville. The claim was disallowed as a secured claim. The order of the referee was sustained by the District Judge and claimant appealed. Order affirmed.

Holmes, C. J. Eugene R. Gill was adjudicated a bankrupt on April 25, 1936. The mortgage in question bears date April 18, 1930, and was filed for record January 4, 1936. On May 22, 1936, appellant filed its claim as a secured creditor and attached thereto a statement of the indebtedness and the evidence thereof, together with the mortgage. The trustee objected to the allowance of the claim as a secured one, and the matter was set down for hearing before the referee. The hearing was held, and resulted in the order, the affirmance of which resulted in this appeal.

On the hearing it appeared that, prior to giving the mortgage in 1930, the bankrupt was heavily indebted to appellant, as well as other creditors; that a director of appellant approached him with a request for the mortgage, saying that the bank examiners had taken exceptions to the loans to the bankrupt; and that, unless the security of the mortgage could be given, the credit of the bank would be seriously impaired. The bankrupt became offended, and said that he was then solvent, but that the giving of such a mortgage and the subsequent recording thereof would destroy his credit, and precipitate his bankruptcy. Thereafter, the president of appellant, who was the uncle of the bankrupt's wife and had his full confidence, approached him in an effort to obtain the mortgage. The bankrupt persisted in his previous objections, but consented to execute the mortgage in favor of appellant and deliver it into the hands of his wife's uncle on assurance from him that it would not be placed on record by the bank, but that, if recording became necessary, the unrecorded document would be returned to the bankrupt.

The foregoing facts are not contradicted, nor is it denied that the mortgage passed into the hands of the bank and was frequently discussed by its directors without their being informed as to the manner in which it was obtained. It is claimed that the mortgage was withheld from the record in the interest of the bank rather than for the benefit of the bankrupt, but that is a matter as to which reasonable minds might differ. Without regard to what the directors knew either individually or as a board, the bank, as a corporate entity, had knowledge of the agreement to withhold the mortgage from the record so as to avoid destroying the bankrupt's credit, because the knowledge of the president, acquired while acting for the bank within the scope of his authority, was imputed to the bank. There is no claim that the president was acting against the interest of the bank in securing the mortgage and making the agreement.

It is well settled that, where a mortgage is withheld from record under an agreement between the mortgagee and the bankrupt, in order that the bankrupt may obtain credit which otherwise would not be available, the mortgage is rendered fraudulent and void, not only as to subsequent creditors, but as to all those interested in the bankrupt's estate.

Appellant cannot be heard to say that, since the agreement to withhold was not brought to the attention of the directors, it was not its agreement. The mortgage was obtained by its president on the agreement, without which it would not have been given. Appellant is estopped to repudiate the agreement not to record and at the same time to claim the benefit of the mortgage obtained pursuant to that agreement. Actions speak louder than words, and, in ascertaining what the parties intended, it is permissible to look to what the parties did, as well as what they said. The giving of this mortgage, followed by withholding it from record, naturally and probably operated to hinder, delay, and defraud the bankrupt's creditors. Subsequent facts have proven that it actually had that effect. Parties are presumed to intend the natural and probable consequences of their own acts. The District Court found that the mortgage was given and withheld from record for the purpose of hindering, delaying, and defrauding creditors of the bankrupt. We see no reason to disturb this finding.

Discharge

Under the earlier bankruptcy acts the debtor was not granted a discharge, but under modern bankruptcy acts the bankrupt is granted a discharge unless he has been guilty of serious infractions of the code of business ethics or has failed to fulfill his duties as a bankrupt. His adjudication operates as an application for his discharge. The party may waive his right to a discharge by filing a written waiver with the court before the time set for a hearing on the discharge.

The time for the filing of objections to the bankrupt's discharge is fixed after the bankrupt has been examined either at the first meeting of creditors or at a special meeting called for that purpose. Notice of the time fixed for filing objections to the discharge is given to all interested parties. If objections have been filed within the time fixed or within any extension of time which may have been granted by the court, the court will hear proofs of the objections at such time as will give the parties a reasonable opportunity to be fully heard. If the court is satisfied that the bankrupt has not committed any of the acts which are a bar to his discharge, the discharge will be granted.

The acts which are a bar to a bankrupt's discharge are set out in section 14, subsection c, as follows:

"The court shall grant the discharge unless satisfied that the bankrupt has (1) committed an offense punishable by imprisonment as provided under this Act; or (2) destroyed, mutilated, falsified, concealed, or failed to keep or preserve books of account or records, from which his financial condition and business transactions might be ascertained, unless the court deems such acts or failure to have been justified under all the circumstances of the case; or (3) obtained money or property on credit, or obtained an extension or renewal of credit, by making or publishing or causing to be made or published in any manner whatsoever, a materially false statement in writing respecting his financial condition; or (4) at any time subsequent to the first day of the twelve months immediately preceding the filing of the petition in bankruptcy, transferred, removed, destroyed, or concealed, or permitted to be removed, destroyed, or concealed, any of his property, with intent to hinder, delay, or defraud his creditors; or (5) has within six years prior to bankruptcy been granted a discharge, or had a composition or an arrangement by way of composition or a wage earner's plan by way of composition confirmed under this Act; or (6) in the course of a proceeding under this Act refused to obey any lawful order of, or to answer any material question approved by, the court; or (7) has failed to explain satisfactorily any losses of assets or deficiency of assets to meet his liabilities: *Provided*, that if, upon the hearing of an objection to a discharge, the objector shall show to the satisfaction of the court that there are reasonable grounds for believing that the bankrupt has committed any of the acts which, under this subdivision c, would prevent his discharge in bankruptcy, then the burden of proving that he has not committed any of such acts shall be upon the bankrupt."

The trustee, a creditor, the United States attorney, or such other attorney as the attorney general may designate, may file objections to and oppose the discharge of a bankrupt. When requested by the court, it is the duty of the United States attorney, located in the judicial district in which the bankruptcy proceeding is pending, to examine into the acts and conduct of the bankrupt. If satisfied that probable grounds exist for the denial of a discharge and that public interest warrants the action, it is his duty to oppose the bankrupt's discharge. Also, if the bankrupt fails to appear at the hearing on his discharge or having appeared refuses to submit himself to examination at the first meeting of creditors or at any subsequent meeting called for his examination, he shall be deemed to have waived his right to a discharge.

In re Lovich et al.
117 F. (2d) 612 (1941)

This was a proceeding in the matter of Bertha Lovich and Bertha Rubin, individually and as copartners trading as the Interstate Drug Company, bankrupts. From an order denying the bankrupts a discharge, bankrupts appealed. Order reversed with directions to grant a discharge.

The bankrupts were two married women who engaged in business as partners under the name of Interstate Drug Co. The business was managed by Boris Lovich, the husband of one partner and brother of the other. In October, 1938, he signed and delivered to a representative of Dun & Bradstreet, Inc., a financial statement of the partnership business. The issuing of such a statement was within the manager's authority, but neither partner ever knew of the statement, nor did the books or records of the partnership contain any mention of it. When the bankrupts came to prepare the "statement of affairs" required to be filed by section 7, sub. a(1), Mrs. Lovich was told by her husband that no financial statement had been issued within the two years immediately preceding the filing of the petition in bankruptcy. She so stated in the statement of affairs to which she made oath on behalf of herself and her partner. This is the false oath relied upon as the ground for refusing the bankrupts their discharge.

Swan, C. J. Concededly Mrs. Lovich swore to a statement that was false; but it is equally undisputed that she believed it to be true. In holding that her good faith was no excuse the District Court adopted the language of the referee's opinion, 34 F. Supp. 85, 86: "If these bankrupts are to be excused from responsibility for the statement that there were no financial statements given, when there were, why we might just as well dispense with the statement of affairs, as an unnecessary and superfluous part of bankruptcy administration; therefore, without imputing any intent to deceive creditors or any fraudulent purpose on their part, I feel obliged to find that this objection is sustained."

This was error. However desirable it may be to assure accuracy in the statement of affairs which the recent amendment requires, the courts may not penalize inaccuracies therein by denial of a discharge unless the statute itself so authorizes. It does not. Not every false oath in relation to a bankruptcy proceeding is made a criminal offense—only those that are "knowingly and fraudulently" given. It must be an intentional untruth with respect to a material matter. Denial of the discharge on the ground of a false oath cannot be supported.

It is necessary, however, to consider whether it may be supported on the second ground of objection alleged by the trustee in bankruptcy. This was based on section 14, sub. c(3) which denies discharge to a bankrupt who has "obtained money or property on credit, or obtained an extension or renewal of credit, by making or publishing or causing to be made or published in any manner whatsoever, a materially false statement in writing respecting his financial condition." The referee dismissed this objection. The District Court, while stating that it could have been sustained, confirmed the referee's order denying the discharge only on the ground of a false oath. We therefore proceed to a discussion of the second ground of objection.

If Boris Lovich were the bankrupt, we should not hesitate to deny him a discharge because of the financial statement. It was relied upon by a creditor, who obtained a copy of it from Dun & Bradstreet, in extending credit. It was proved false in three material respects: the merchandise liabilities were stated as $3,500 when they were in fact $7,658; it was stated there were no loans when in fact the bankrupts owed a loan of $1,000; the net worth was given as $6,700, and the actual net worth as shown by the books was $231. There can be no doubt that the false statements were material and that they were relied on in the granting of credit. The referee excused the bankrupts because of the casual way in which the statement was obtained by Dun & Bradstreet's representative who filled in figures given him by Boris Lovich in conversation and without any reference by the latter to the partnership books. Boris Lovich testified that he regarded all the figures as estimates, as the value of inventory was expressly stated to be. There was, however, nothing in the statement to indicate that the other figures were estimates; they purported to be actual figures. While there are decisions to the effect that a false statement, which can serve as ground for denial of a discharge, must have been knowingly made with intent to deceive, it is also established that a false statement made recklessly without any attempt to ascertain the facts and without any basis for an honest belief in its truth may bar a discharge under section 14, sub. c(3). We believe that the circumstances under which Boris Lovich made the statement would justify the application of this principle, if he were the bankrupt; nevertheless it does not follow as of course that his conduct will bar the discharge of his employers, the bankrupts. As their authorized agent to manage the business, fraud on his part in obtaining credit for them may be imputed to them to affect their rights and obligations with respect to the person defrauded without necessarily affecting their privilege of a discharge under the Bankruptcy Act. Several cases have held that general principles of agency do not apply to require denial of a discharge where the false statement of his agent was not known to the bankrupt, or in any way acquiesced in by him. The denial of a discharge to the present appellants must depend solely on the fact that they entrusted Boris Lovich with general authority to transact their business. No decision has been found which has actually gone to that extreme. In the case of *In re Savarese*, 2 Cir., 209 F. 830, this court was careful to point out that the bankrupt should have known that the agent's statement was false. On principle we think that more should be shown to justify withholding a discharge than that an agent made a fraudulent statement within the scope of a general authority to transact the bankrupt's business. A discharge is a privilege accorded to bankrupts by the statute unless they are chargeable with conduct showing some lack of personal business morality. Laying aside cases of corporate bankrupts, as to which no decision is now required, we believe that when a false statement is made by an agent, some additional facts must exist justifying an inference that the bankrupt knew of the statement and in some way acquiesced in it or failed to investigate its accuracy. No such inference is possible in the case at bar.

QUESTIONS AND PROBLEMS

1. What is the purpose of the Federal Bankruptcy Act?
2. May a solvent person who owes debts file a voluntary petition in bankruptcy and be adjudged a bankrupt?
3. Is insolvency alone sufficient to warrant an involuntary adjudication in bankruptcy?
4. Russell owed Ball $500 which was secured by the pledge of shares of stock valued at $800. While insolvent, Russell paid Ball the $500 in full. Was this a preferential payment and an act of bankruptcy under the provisions of the Bankruptcy Act?
5. In which court would a petition in bankruptcy be filed?
6. The bankruptcy referee appointed the attorney for the bankrupt as trustee of the bankrupt estate. On petition of the creditors should this appointment be set aside?
7. May was adjudged a bankrupt, and in his schedules he listed a debt owing to Briggs which was barred by the statute of limitations. Briggs filed a claim for the amount of the debt. Should the claim be allowed?
8. Is an unliquidated claim provable in bankruptcy?
9. Link borrowed $500 from Hall and as security assigned certain accounts receivable to Hall. At the time of the transaction Hall had no notice or knowledge that Link was insolvent and there was no proof that he was. Link's creditors had knowledge of the assignment. Within four months thereafter Link was adjudged bankrupt. Should the assignment to Hall be set aside as a preferential assignment?
10. Arkin in a written application for a loan failed to list indebtednesses and judgments and stated that he owed no debts. Arkin was adjudged bankrupt. If his creditors oppose his discharge, should his discharge be denied?

CHAPTER XLIII

LABOR RELATIONS

Introduction

In modern society one of the most complex problems encountered in the operation of a business arises in connection with the employment of labor. From an early date the struggle between employer and employee, or as it is known under the common law, the struggle between master and servant has presented a variety of problems. The solution of these problems requires the consideration of many factors, the most important of which are the social, economic, and legal relations of the parties. In some instances it has been necessary to consider religious and racial relations in the solution of labor problems. It is not our purpose to discuss the many factors involved in the solution of modern labor problems; neither shall we attempt a detailed discussion of the legal aspects of such problems; however, we shall discuss some of the fundamental legal principles which have been developed in this field.

According to the laws of England at the time of, and immediately preceding, the colonization of America, we find that a laborer, although nominally a free man, was restricted in most of his activities. His wages and hours of work were fixed, and unless he had a yearly income or was a property owner, he could be forced to work. Instead of having minimum wage laws, the wage laws provided for the establishment of maximum wages. The hours of work for industrial workers were from five in the morning until seven or eight in the evening, and for farm laborers during the harvest season they were from daylight to dark. Only the sons of parents owning land of a value of forty shillings per year could be apprenticed in the more desirable trades. The infliction of criminal punishment for violations of the servants' duties to the master was common. The law was not all on one side. The master owed some duties to the servant. The principal burden of the master was to retain the servant for the year and pay him his wage. At this time society was at the subsistence level and was interested in forcing each member of society to support himself so that he would not become a burden on society.

In the United States, from the time we gained our independence until as late as 1930, the philosophy of individual rights predominated in the field of labor relations. The rights of the employer and employee were defined by their contract which, in theory, was freely negotiated between them. In the early period (1800-1830) the courts held that if two or more laborers combined for the purpose of increasing their wages, they were guilty of the crime of conspiracy. The courts were consistent in that they also held that if two or more employers combined for the purpose of depressing wages, they too were guilty of the crime of conspiracy. By 1850 the courts had abandoned this narrow view. Prior to the depression of 1837 there was some attempt to organize labor associations but the depression crushed this movement. Again in the 1850's, labor associations made some progress but it was not until after the Civil War that they became prominent. The period from the close of the Civil War until about 1880 was marked by labor unrest and violent disturbances. About 1870 the employers began to use the "yellow dog" contract. They required each employee to sign a pledge that he would not join a trade union during the period of his employment. The labor unions ignored the non-union clauses and continued to solicit membership among the employees of firms using the "yellow dog" contract. A trial court issued an injunction enjoining the union and its agents from attempting to induce laborers, who had signed "yellow dog" contracts, from joining the union in violation of their contracts. The case was carried to the United States Supreme Court where the injunction was sustained. This gave the employer a definite advantage over the unions and laborers.

During the first World War a labor truce was declared, but with the close of the war labor troubles broke out anew. In the early years of the twentieth century, several states passed statutes which attempted to outlaw the "yellow dog" contract, but such statutes were of little importance, and in 1915 the United States Supreme Court declared such a statute enacted by a state legislature to be unconstitutional. It was not until the passage of the Norris-LaGuardia Act in 1932 that the "yellow dog" contract was effectively outlawed.

In the final period, from 1932 to date, the right to join a union has been definitely established, the use of the injunction in labor disputes has been curtailed and defined with a greater degree of definiteness, collective bargaining has been introduced, and federal and state commissions and boards have been established to aid in the settlement of labor disputes.

Trade Unions

Trade unions, as a general rule, are organized as unincorporated associations; however, a small number have been incorporated. At common law an unincorporated association was not recognized as having legal capacity. It could not sue or be sued, own property, enter into contracts, nor do any act which required legal capacity. All its activities were carried on in the name of individual members. In the United States in a few early decisions the courts held that a trade union was a partnership but this view was soon abandoned. In England the courts refused to punish the treasurer of a trade union, who had embezzled the funds of the union, on the ground that the union had no legal existence and it could not be a prosecutor.

In 1922, the United States Supreme Court held that an unincorporated union could be sued in its own name and that its funds could be reached by court action. This decision is recognized as established law today; however, the individual members of the union can be held personally liable. A member of an unincorporated association is, in many respects, a principal, and the officers of the association act as his agents.

The union as an unincorporated association may adopt a constitution and rules for the government of the association, and it may set the requirements for membership. The rules adopted must be reasonable and lawful, and the requirements for membership must be such that they do not result in the monopolizing of a trade. Although an unincorporated association may expel members for cause, and as a general rule the courts will not interfere in the internal management of the association, the position of unions in our society is such that the courts do not hesitate to review the expulsion of a member or to consider claimed irregularities in the internal management of the union. In many localities in which closed shop contracts prevail, if a member is expelled from the union, he will be unable to obtain employment at his usual occupation.

Busby et al. v. Electric Utilities Employees Union
147 F. (2d) 865 (1945)

This was an action by Jeff Busby and another (plaintiffs) against Electric Utilities Employees Union, an unincorporated labor union (defendant). Judgment for defendant and plaintiff appealed. Judgment reversed and remanded with directions.

Plaintiffs are attorneys and were employed by defendant to represent it in perfecting its organization and in securing its recognition by the Potomac Electric Power Company, the employer of its members. The defendant refused to pay the plaintiffs' fees and plaintiffs brought suit. The lower court held that the defendant, an unincorporated labor union, was not suable in debt.

Groner, C. J. It is hardly worth while to say that if the question were timed as of a period thirty or forty years ago, the answer would be that under the general rule of the common law a voluntary association, which is neither incorporated nor has otherwise acquired the status of a corporation, or quasi corporation, is not suable in its common name, and this for the reason that it has no legal entity distinguishable from that of its members. In such a case suit might only be brought in the names of all of the individual members. But since the turn of the century the tremendous growth of labor unions, their internal set-up and organization, the extension of their rights and privileges, and the recognition and protection of these in state and federal statutes has resulted in a nearly universal change of viewpoint on the subject of their suability. And this changed viewpoint is by no means confined to courts or legislatures, but is shared, among others, by the leaders of labor.

This change of attitude was anticipated some years earlier by the Supreme Court and the impelling reasons for it are cogently expressed by Chief Justice Taft in the opinion in the Coronado Case, since when the principle has been adopted or followed by statute or court decision, so that today there is substantial agreement that voluntary labor organizations may sue and are suable in their common name and that funds in the common treasury are subject to execution in suits for torts committed and contracts made in the common enterprise. And in the Plasterers' Case, we recognized the drift away from the old rule in saying that because the fictional entity is now recognized by law for the purpose of benefiting and protecting unincorporated associations in both the substantive and adjective senses, as by protection against embezzlement of funds, by giving rights to appeal in statutory arbitrations and before official boards and to represent workers in collective bargaining, so also the fictional entity must in common fairness be recognized for the protection of those dealing with such associations and claiming that in such dealing their legal rights have been violated.

And this right to sue and be sued in the common name, as the Supreme Court said in the Coronado Case, "is after all in essence and principle merely a procedural matter." Substantive rights are unaffected. Members of unions have the same rights and are subject to the same liabilities as before. The entire change relates only to the fact that now they can be sued and can sue by a less cumbersome process. In line with this thought we held in the Plasterers' suit that a judgment obtained in North Carolina against the Plasterers' Union was valid without a state statute authorizing a suit, and that, in thus subjecting the union to suit as an entity, no constitutional right was impaired. Accordingly, we held the North Carolina judgment enforceable in the District of Columbia under the full faith and credit clause of the Constitution. Similarly, we hold that this suit is maintainable in the District of Columbia. And the same right has long been recognized as appropriate in equity through representative suits.

Here, as we have seen, the defendant union, by virtue of Congressional enactment, possesses all the rights and privileges enumerated in the Coronado Case as the reasons for the recognition of the change in the common law rule—the right to maintain strikes and the right of exclusive representation of its members. The embezzlement of union funds has been denounced as a crime since 1910.

Torts and Crimes

A labor union's liability for torts or crimes committed by its members is determined by the application of the law of agency. The union cannot be held liable for the crimes committed by its members. It cannot entertain a criminal intent and, consequently, cannot commit a crime unless criminal intent is not an essential element of the crime.

A labor union is not liable for the torts of its members unless the tort is committed by a member who is representing the union and who commits the tort in the course of and within the scope of his duties to the union. Whether or not the union is liable for the torts of its members is primarily a question of fact. The recent decisions have been uniform in holding that the union may be sued in tort, but the decisions do not clearly define when a member is representing the union nor do the decisions define the course of and the scope of the duties of a union representative.

Contracts

The union and the employer, as a general rule, enter into an agreement which by its terms states the hours, wages, working conditions, seniority rights, and such other matters as are deemed important. The period for which the agreement is to be effective is also stated. In such an agreement the union is acting in behalf of its members. Several important questions in regard to the legal rights and liabilities of the parties affected by such agreements have arisen. If the members of the union refuse to work for the employer under terms of the agreement, what are the liabilities of the union? If the employer refuses to abide by terms of the agreement in his relations with his employees, can the union hold the employer liable for breach of the agreement? Are the individual members of the union bound by the agreement? If so, to what extent are they bound? Can an individual employee hold the employer liable if the employee is discharged in violation of the agreement between the employer and the union or is denied benefits provided for by the terms of such agreement?

The early view of the American courts was that an agreement between a union and an employer had no legal effect. It was no more than a gentleman's agreement and was wholly unenforceable by court action. This view has been abandoned and such agreements are enforced by courts of equity. If the union threatens to abandon the contract and call a strike, the employer will be entitled to an injunction enjoining the strike. Likewise, if an employer, in violation of such an agreement, discharges his union employees and hires in their stead non-union employees, the court will grant the union an injunction enjoining the employer from hiring non-union employees. The decisions are not uniform but the better view is that collective agreements are enforceable by a court of equity. As a general rule, a judgment for damages for breach of such an agreement would not be an adequate remedy; consequently, the cases involving collective contracts have, as a general rule, been equity cases.

The better rule today is that the collective agreement is incorporated into the employment contract of each individual employee, and its provisions are binding on both the employer and the employee. This does not mean that the employee cannot leave the employ of his employer nor that the employer cannot discharge an employee. One of the principal difficulties encountered in working out the relationship of the employer and individual employee is the fact that, as a general rule, the employment is at will. The employee is free to change employers and, as a general rule, the union is not obligated to replace the employee; however, the union takes the view that the employer is not free to discharge the employee at will. The employer may, if he has a valid cause, discharge the employee, but the unions have maintained that the discharge of an employee without cause is grounds for self-help—a strike.

Harper et al. v. Local Union No. 520, International Brotherhood of Electrical Workers et al.
Ct. of Civ. App. Texas, 48 S.W. (2d) 1033 (1932)

This was a suit by Local Union No. 520, International Brotherhood of Electrical Workers and others (plaintiffs) against W. O. Harper and another (defendants). Judgment granting plaintiffs a temporary injunction and defendants appealed. Judgment affirmed.

W. O. Harper and C. C. Linscomb, a copartnership engaged in the business of electrical contractors, entered into an agreement with Local Union No. 520 whereby the partnership agreed to engage only union electricians. The agreement set out in detail the terms on which such union electricians were to be employed. The agreement further provided that it was to be in force for a term of three years. After about one year defendants discharged all their union electricians and employed non-union electricians at lower wages and for longer hours than stipulated in the agreement. The plaintiffs ask for an injunction enjoining the defendants from employing non-union employees.

McClendon, C. J. The general trend of decisions has been to recognize collective bargaining agreements when fairly made and for the lawful purpose of securing employment, shorter working hours, and better working conditions. When so made, such agreements are generally held to be in the public interest, as offering peaceful solutions of labor disputes, and preventing strikes and lockouts, and incidental loss arising from unemployment and violence.

These agreements are now regarded as primarily for the benefit of the members of the union, and under a variety of theories have been held to be enforceable by the members. Some courts have held that the contracts establish usages or customs of trade; a distinction being sometimes drawn between usage and custom. Other courts, holding that the association acts for its members, have applied the general principles of agency. While still others treat the agreement as one made for the benefit of third parties.

Aside from those aspects of the agreement which give rise to legal rights in favor of the individual members of the union as such, who have brought themselves within its purview, the collective agreement is now treated in a number of jurisdictions as a contract also between the organization or group as such and the employer; and, where violated by the former, may be enforced by the latter through appropriate remedy. Instances have arisen where the organization, its officers and members have been enjoined at the instance of employers from calling or inciting a strike, or of engaging in other concerted acts in violation of the collective agreement. Due, no doubt, to the general attitude of aversion on the part of organized labor to interference in labor disputes by court action, resort by labor unions to the courts for redress of grievances has been rare until comparatively recent years; and, as a consequence, there is a paucity of adjudications defining and prescribing the limitations upon the rights of labor unions as parties plaintiff. While the decisions are by no means uniform in many respects upon specific questions that have arisen, generally speaking the courts have sought to apply the recognized principles of contract law to collective bargaining agreements. Differences in decision arise in the main from difference of view in the application to specific situations of generally accepted legal principles.

The right of labor to contract collectively for employment, and for other advantages, such as wage scales, hours of employment, favorable surroundings and working conditions, and the like, is now generally recognized.

In the recent case of *M. & M. Pipe Line Co.* v. *Menke*, 45 S.W. (2d) 344, 345, this court stated a general rule of construction of contracts as follows: "It is a cardinal rule in the construction of contracts that they be given a practical interpretation with a view to effect the intention of the parties as gleaned from the language of the instrument, the subject matter dealt with, the surrounding circumstances, and the objects sought to be accomplished."

When so viewed, we do not believe the agreement is unilateral, in that it imposes no obligation upon the union. While it is true that there is no express agreement on the part of the union to furnish labor at the prices and under the terms and conditions prescribed in the contract, its very purpose and object was to prescribe terms under which the members of the union would work and the contractors would employ. It was therefore, we think, a necessarily implied term of the agreement that the union, its officers and members would collectively abide by the terms of the agreement, and would not collectively or as an organization exercise any right or do any act it or they might otherwise lawfully exercise or do, which was in conflict with any of the terms of the agreement; and that the union would enforce the contract to the extent of its powers over its members under its constitution and by-laws. Clearly, we think, what the contractors were bargaining for and what they obtained under the agreement was freedom from industrial dispute, strike, or collective adverse action on the part of the union, its officers and its members during the term covered by the agreement. As we have already pointed out, this right, if infringed, could be enforced by injunction at the instance of the contractor.

Appellants' second proposition that injunction will not lie at the suit of the union because the contract is one for personal service, which could not be compelled by injunction, and therefore as to that remedy it is lacking in mutuality, is supported by decision in several jurisdictions. We have reached the conclusion, however, that the contract in its collective aspect is not one for personal service. In so far as it may inure to the benefit of the individual members of the union, it does not purport to bind the employers to employ any particular workman, or to continue in the business; nor does it purport to bind any particular workman to work for appellant, or in fact to continue a member of the union, or in the particular line of employment. It does bind the employers, however, to its several terms if they continue in the business; and it becomes a part of the contract of each member of the union on entering the employment of appellant. The right of discharge for any valid reason is not affected by the contract on the one hand; and the right to leave the employment for any valid reason is likewise not affected on the other. The employers and union, its officers and members, are mutually bound by the contract, the former to employ only members of the union in the class of labor specified, pay and observe the stipulated wages and hours of labor, etc.; and the latter to do no act inconsistent with, or obnoxious to, the terms of the contract. They (the union, its officers and members) forego the well-recognized right to strike during the contractual period, to defeat or abridge any stipulation of the collective agreement. As already stated, this implied stipulation of the contract may be enforced by injunction, and we see no valid reason why the same remedy should not be available to the union, if adequate redress may not be otherwise had.

We think it clear that appellees have no adequate remedy at law. As we have seen, there were no specific contracts of employment; and no criterion of practical application for ascertaining the damages that would flow from breach of the collective agreement is suggested. If injunction will not lie, the agreement, in so far as it is to the advantage of appellees, is unenforceable, and might as well be classed as merely a moral obligation or "gentleman's agreement," a view which seems to be upheld by the English courts.

Appellants' third proposition is predicated upon the principle announced in the following quotation from *Polk* v. *Cleveland Ry. Co.*, 20 Ohio App. 317, 151 N.E. 808, 810: "Contracts by which an employer agrees to employ only union labor are contrary to public policy when they take in an entire industry of any considerable proportions in a community so that they operate generally in that community to prevent or seriously deter craftsmen from working at their craft or workmen from obtaining employment under favorable conditions without joining a union."

The general principle announced in this quotation may be conceded; but we do not believe the record brings the case at bar fairly within its purview.

Strikes—Picketing

Until recently both the strike and picketing were held to be illegal. The courts held that although an individual had the right to quit work at will unless he were under contract, an agreement whereby a group of workers were all to quit work at an agreed time was a conspiracy and illegal. Picketing was held to be a tort in that it was an injury to the employer's business. The recent cases have adopted the view that if one person has a legal right to quit his employment at will, he has the right to do the same act in concert with his fellow-workers. The strike is recognized as legal.

Peaceful picketing has been legalized. The courts now hold that under the First Amendment to the Constitution the union and laborers have the right to free speech and that peaceful picketing is a mode of expressing the union's and the laborers' side of the dispute. Legislation which outlaws picketing in all its forms has been held to be unconstitutional. There is no objection to reasonable restrictions pertaining to the number of pickets, or the place, time, or manner of picketing, or other aspects directly related to maintenance of peace and order in the area. The courts have the power to enjoin mass picketing, violence, intimidating conduct, or misrepresentation.

Thornhill v. State of Alabama
310 U.S. 88, 60 S. Ct. 736 (1940)

This was an action by the state of Alabama (plaintiff) against Byron Thornhill (defendant). Defendant was convicted and fined for violating a picketing statute. The conviction was affirmed by the state courts, and defendant appealed to the United States Supreme Court on the ground that the statute under which he was convicted was repugnant to the Constitution of the United States. Conviction reversed.

Thornhill was convicted of the violation of § 3448 of the state code of 1923. This Code section prohibited loitering or picketing. The employees of Brown Wood Preserving Company were out on strike. All but four of the company's employees were members of the local union which was affiliated with the American Federation of Labor. Thornhill was an employee of the company and a member of the union. During the strike the union maintained a picket line twenty-four hours a day. The company had ordered its employees back to work. Thornhill was on picket duty, and when Simpson approached the company's plant to resume work, Thornhill approached Simpson and told him that the employees were out on strike whereupon Simpson went back home. Thornhill did not threaten Simpson nor intimidate him in any manner.

Mr. Justice Murphy delivered the opinion of the Court.

The freedom of speech and of the press, which are secured by the First Amendment against abridgment by the United States, are among the fundamental personal rights and liberties which are secured to all persons by the Fourteenth Amendment against abridgment by a State.

The safeguarding of these rights to the ends that men may speak as they think on matters vital to them and that falsehoods may be exposed through the processes of education and discussion is essential to free government. Those who won our independence had confidence in the power of free and fearless reasoning and communication of ideas to discover and spread political and economic truth. Noxious doctrines in those fields may be refuted and their evil averted by the courageous exercise of the right of free discussion. Abridgment of freedom of speech and of the press, however, impairs those opportunities for public education that are essential to effective exercise of the power of correcting error through the processes of popular government. Mere legislative preference for one rather than another means for combatting substantive evils, therefore, may well prove an inadaquate foundation on which to rest regulations which are aimed at or in their operation diminish the effective exercise of rights so necessary to the maintenance of democratic institutions. It is imperative that, when the effective exercise of these rights is claimed to be abridged, the courts should "weigh the circumstances" and "appraise the substantiality of the reasons advanced" in support of the challenged regulations.

Section 3448 has been applied by the state courts so as to prohibit a single individual from walking slowly and peacefully back and forth on the public sidewalk in front of the premises of an employer, without speaking to anyone, carrying a sign or placard on a staff above his head stating only the fact that the employer did not employ union men affiliated with the American Federation of Labor; the purpose of the described activity was concededly to advise customers and prospective customers of the relationship existing between the employer and its employees and thereby to induce such customers not to patronize the employer. The statute as thus authoritatively construed and applied leaves room for no exceptions based upon either the number of persons engaged in the proscribed activity, the peaceful character of their demeanor, the nature of their dispute with an employer, or the restrained character and the accurateness of the terminology used in notifying the public of the facts of the dispute.

In sum, whatever the means used to publicize the facts of a labor dispute, whether by printed sign, by pamphlet, by word of mouth or otherwise, all such activity without exception is within the inclusive prohibition of the statute so long as it occurs in the vicinity of the scene of the dispute.

We think that § 3448 is invalid on its face. The freedom of speech and of the press guaranteed by the Constitution embraces at the least the liberty to discuss publicly and truthfully all matters of public concern without previous restraint or fear of subsequent punishment. The exigencies of the colonial period and the efforts to secure freedom from oppressive administration developed a broadened conception of these liberties as adequate to supply the public need for information and education with respect to the significant issues of the times.

In the circumstances of our times the dissemination of information concerning the facts of a labor dispute must be regarded as within that area of free discussion that is guaranteed by the Constitution. It is recognized now that satisfactory hours and wages and working conditions in industry and a bargaining position which makes these possible have an importance which is not less than the interests of those in the business or industry directly concerned. The health of the present generation and of those as yet unborn may depend on these matters, and the practices in a single factory may have economic repercussions upon a whole region and affect widespread systems of marketing. The merest glance at state and federal legislation on the subject demonstrates the force of the argument that labor relations are not matters of mere local or private concern. Free discussion concerning the conditions in industry and the causes of labor disputes appears to us indispensable to the effective and intelligent use of the processes of popular government to shape the destiny of modern industrial society. The issues raised by regulations, such as are challenged here, infringing upon the right of employees effectively to inform the public of the facts of a labor dispute are part of this larger problem. We concur in the observation of Mr. Justice Brandeis, speaking for the Court in Senn's case (301 U.S. at 478): "Members of a union might, without special statutory authorization by a State, make known the facts of a labor dispute, for freedom of speech is guaranteed by the Federal Constitution."

It is true that the rights of employers and employees to conduct their economic affairs and to compete with others for a share in the products of industry are subject to modification or qualification in the interests of the society in which they exist. This is but an instance of the power of the State to set the limits of permissible contest open to industrial combatants. It does not follow that the State in dealing with the evils arising from industrial disputes may impair the effective exercise of the right to discuss freely industrial relations which are matters of public concern. A contrary conclusion could be used to support abridgment of freedom of speech and of the press concerning almost every matter of importance to society.

The State urges that the purpose of the challenged statute is the protection of the community from violence and breaches of the peace, which, it asserts, are the concomitants of picketing. The power and the duty of the State to take adequate steps to preserve the peace and to protect the privacy, the lives, and the property of its residents cannot be doubted. But no clear and present danger of destruction of life or property, or invasion of the right of privacy, or breach of the peace can be thought to be inherent in the activities of every person who approaches the premises of an employer and publicizes the facts of a labor dispute involving the latter. We are not now concerned with picketing en masse or otherwise conducted which might occasion such imminent and aggravated danger to these interests as to justify a statute narrowly drawn to cover the precise situation giving rise to the danger.

Legislation

Three federal statutes have been of outstanding importance in determining the rights and liabilities of the parties to labor disputes. In 1890 Congress passed the Sherman Anti-Trust Act which prohibits and makes illegal trusts or conspiracies in restraint of trade. The act does not mention labor unions or combinations of laborers. The courts held that if laborers or labor unions combined with the intent to stop production for the purpose of controlling interstate commerce, the combination was in restraint of trade and illegal. The courts also held that if laborers or unions combined and struck for the purpose of improving wages, hours, working conditions, etc., and that in the course of a strike to obtain such lawful ends, there was an indirect interference with interstate commerce, the acts were not a violation of the act and not illegal under the terms of the act.

In 1914 the Clayton Act was passed by Congress. Several of the provisions of the Clayton Act expressly refer to labor and labor unions. The act expressly states: "That the labor of a human being is not a commodity or article of commerce." It further prohibits the use of restraining orders and injunctions in labor disputes unless necessary to prevent irreparable injury to property or a property right of the party making the application. The act also legalizes the strike and peaceful picketing. The courts have held that the terms of the act were not broad enough to withdraw all combinations of laborers or unions from the prohibitions of the Sherman Anti-Trust Act. Laborers and unions have been held liable under the Sherman Anti-Trust Act if they entered into combinations with the intent to suppress competition in the interstate market so as to monopolize the supply, control its prices, or discriminate between would-be purchasers. In those instances in which unions conspired with employers to obtain control of an interstate market and control the price of the product in that market, the courts have held that the combination was in violation of the Sherman Anti-Trust Act.

After the passage of the Clayton Act, the courts continued to issue injunctions in labor dispute cases. The wording of the provisions of the act in regard to the issuing of restraining orders and injunctions was so broad that it imposed little restriction on the courts, and the injunction was used liberally, especially for the purpose of enjoining picketing. In 1932 the Norris-LaGuardia Act was passed by Congress. The principal purpose of this act was to clarify the powers of the courts to issue injunctions in labor disputes. The act prohibits the use of the injunction as a means of enforcing "yellow dog" contracts. It defines those acts which are permissible in peaceful picketing and prohibits the enjoining of such acts. The act also defines situations in which it prohibits the issuing of an injunction without a public hearing and an opportunity to hear and examine witnesses in open court. Under the provisions of the act a person, accused of violating the terms of the injunction and charged with contempt of court, is entitled to a jury trial before an impartial judge.

The National Labor Relations Act which was passed by Congress in 1935 was "an act to diminish the causes of labor disputes burdening or obstructing interstate and foreign commerce. . . . ." To accomplish this objective, the act gives the employees the right to organize and bargain collectively. It outlaws employer-dominated unions and sets up safeguards which are intended to guarantee to the employees the right to bargain collectively with the employer through representatives of the employees' own choosing. The National Labor Relations Board is established by the act and its functions are set out.

The National Labor Relations Board is charged with the administration of the act and the prevention of unfair labor practices.

The Fair Labor Standards Act of 1938 provides for certain maximum hours and minimum wages in industry. Certain occupations and classes of employees are exempted from the provisions of the act. Executive, administrative, professional and local retailing employees, outside salesmen, employees of retail and service establishments conducting principally an intrastate business are exempt. Also seamen, air transport employees, railroad employees, and agricultural employees are exempt. The minimum wage rate established by the act is: during the first year not less than 25 cents an hour; during the next six years not less than 30 cents an hour; and after the expiration of seven years not less than 40 cents an hour. The act makes provisions for some variations from these rates under stated conditions. The section in regard to maximum hours (Section 7) provides that no employee shall be employed for a workweek of longer than forty-four hours during the first year the act is effective; for a workweek longer than forty-two hours during the second year; and for a workweek of longer than forty hours after the second year "unless the employee receives compensation for his employment in excess of the hours specified at a rate not less than one and one-half times the regular rate at which he is employed." The act provides for a Wage and Hour Division in the Department of Labor whose duty shall be to carry out the provisions of the act.

The several states have passed statutes in the field of labor relations which vary widely in their nature and scope.

QUESTIONS AND PROBLEMS

1. What was the nature of labor legislation in England during the seventeenth century?
2. Could a modern labor union have had a legal existence in the United States prior to 1830?
3. What type of organization has been adopted by the majority of trade unions?
4. Polin, a member of an unincorporated labor union, brought a suit in court in which he charged the officers of the union with having violated the constitution and by-laws of the union and sought redress therefor. Polin was tried by the trial board of the union and was expelled because he brought the court action. There was nothing in the constitution or by-laws of the union which expressly or by implication denied a member the right to bring court action against the officers of the union. Polin brought a suit asking that the union be enjoined from expelling him. Should the injunction be granted?
5. Conn was a member of the Milk Wagon Drivers' Union, an unincorporated labor union. Conn, in violation of a provision of the constitution of the union, solicited the trade of an employer who employed members of the union. After a trial before the trial board of the union, Conn was suspended for ninety days. Without further proceedings before the appeal board of the union, Conn brought suit

for damages against the union and its officers. As a result of the suspension, Conn lost wages for the ninety-day period. Should the court hear and determine Conn's suit?

6. Archer was a member of an unincorporated labor union which was out on a strike. During a dispute with Burch over the merits of the strike, Archer struck and injured Burch. Is the union liable in tort for Archer's act?
7. The Blue Dale Dress Co. entered into an agreement with the Garment Workers Union whereby it agreed not to move its shop or factory from its present location to any place beyond which the public carrier fare would be more than five cents. The Dress Co. had a dispute and thereafter began to move its factory to Philadelphia. The union asked for an injunction enjoining the Dress Co. from moving from the five-cent fare district in New York. Should the injunction be granted?
8. Is a strike legal?
9. In the event of a labor dispute, is it legal to picket the employer?
10. Under the provisions of the Fair Labor Standards Act of 1938, is it permissible for an employee to work a greater number of hours per week than the maximum stated in the Act?

APPENDIX

UNIFORM SALES ACT

PART I

FORMATION OF THE CONTRACT

Section 1. Contracts to Sell and Sales. (1) A contract to sell goods is a contract whereby the seller agrees to transfer the property in goods to the buyer for a consideration called the price.

(2) A sale of goods is an agreement whereby the seller transfers the property in goods to the buyer for a consideration called the price.

(3) A contract to sell or a sale may be absolute or conditional.

(4) There may be a contract to sell or a sale between one part owner and another.

Section 2. Capacities; Liabilities for Necessaries. Capacity to buy and sell is regulated by the general law concerning capacity to contract, and to transfer and acquire property.

Where necessaries are sold and delivered to an infant, or to a person who by reason of mental incapacity or drunkenness is incompetent to contract, he must pay a reasonable price therefor.

Necessaries in this section mean goods suitable to the condition in life of such infant or other person, and to his actual requirements at the time of delivery.

FORMALITIES OF THE CONTRACT

Section 3. Form of Contract or Sale. Subject to the provisions of this act and of any statute in that behalf, a contract to sell or a sale may be made in writing (either with or without seal), or by word of mouth, or partly in writing and partly by word of mouth, or may be inferred from the conduct of the parties.

Section 4. Statute of Frauds. (1) A contract to sell or a sale of any goods or choses in action of the value of $500 or upwards shall not be enforceable by action unless the buyer shall accept part of the goods or choses in action so contracted to be sold or sold, and actually receive the same, or give something in earnest to bind the contract, or in part payment, or unless some note or memorandum in writing of the contract or sale be signed by the party to be charged or his agent in that behalf.

(2) The provisions of this section apply to every such contract or sale, notwithstanding that the goods may be intended to be delivered at some future time or may not at the time of such contract or sale be actually made, procured, or provided, or fit or ready for delivery, or some act may be requisite for the making or completing thereof, or rendering the same fit for delivery; but if the goods are to be manufactured by the seller especially for the buyer and are not suitable for sale to others in the ordinary course of the seller's business, the provisions of this section shall not apply.

(3) There is an acceptance of goods within the meaning of this section when the buyer, either before or after delivery of the goods, expresses by words or conduct his assent to becoming the owner of those specific goods.

SUBJECT MATTER OF CONTRACT

Section 5. Existing and Future Goods. (1) The goods which form the subject of a contract to sell may be either existing goods, owned or possessed by the seller, or goods to be manufactured or acquired by the seller after the making of the contract to sell, in this act called "future goods."

(2) There may be a contract to sell goods, the acquisition of which by the seller depends upon a contingency which may or may not happen.

(3) Where the parties purport to effect a present sale of future goods, the agreement operates as a contract to sell the goods.

Section 6. Undivided Shares. (1) There may be a contract to sell or a sale of an undivided share of goods. If the parties intend to effect a present sale, the buyer, by force of the agreement, becomes an owner in common with the owner or owners of the remaining shares.

(2) In the case of fungible goods, there may be a sale of an undivided share of a specific mass, though the seller purports to sell and the buyer to buy a definite number, weight, or measure of the goods in the mass, and though the number, weight, or measure of the goods in the mass is undetermined. By such a sale the buyer becomes owner in common of such a share of the mass as the number, weight, or measure bought bears to the number, weight, or measure of the mass. If the mass contains less than the number, weight, or measure bought, the buyer becomes the owner of the whole mass and the seller is bound to make good the deficiency from similar goods unless a contrary intent appears.

Section 7. Destruction of Goods Sold. (1) Where the parties purport to sell specific goods, and the goods without the knowledge of the seller have wholly perished at the time when the agreement is made, the agreement is void.

(2) Where the parties purport to sell specific goods, and the goods without the knowledge of the seller have perished in part or have wholly or in a material part so deteriorated in quality as to be substantially changed in character, the buyer may at his option treat the sale:

(*a*) As avoided, or

(*b*) As transferring the property in all of the existing goods or in so much thereof as have not deteriorated, and as binding the buyer to pay the full agreed price if the sale was indivisible, or to pay the agreed price for the goods in which the property passes if the sale was divisible.

Section 8. Destruction of Goods Contracted to Be Sold. (1) Where there is a contract to sell specific goods, and subsequently, but before the risk passes to the buyer, without any fault on the part of the seller or the buyer, the goods wholly perish, the contract is thereby avoided.

(2) Where there is a contract to sell specific goods, and subsequently, but before the risk passes to the buyer, without any fault of the seller or the buyer, part of the goods perish or the whole or a material part of the goods so deteriorate in quality as to be substantially changed in character, the buyer may at his option treat the contract:

(*a*) As avoided, or

(*b*) As binding the seller to transfer the property in all of the existing goods or in so much thereof as have not deteriorated, and as binding the buyer to pay the full agreed price if the contract was indivisible, or to pay the agreed price for so much of the goods as the seller, by the buyer's option, is bound to transfer if the contract was divisible.

THE PRICE

Section 9. Definition and Ascertainment of Price. (1) The price may be fixed by the contract, or may be left to be fixed in such manner as may be agreed, or it may be determined by the course of dealing between the parties.

(2) The price may be made payable in any personal property.

(3) Where transferring or promising to transfer any interest in real estate con-

stitutes the whole or part of the consideration for transferring or for promising to transfer the property in goods, this act shall not apply.

(4) Where the price is not determined in accordance with the foregoing provisions the buyer must pay a reasonable price. What is a reasonable price is a question of fact dependent on the circumstances of each particular case.

Section 10. Sale at a Valuation. (1) Where there is a contract to sell or a sale of goods at a price or on terms to be fixed by a third person, and such third person without fault of the seller or the buyer, can not or does not fix the price or terms, the contract or the sale is thereby avoided; but if the goods or any part thereof have been delivered to and appropriated by the buyer he must pay a reasonable price therefor.

(2) Where such third person is prevented from fixing the price or terms by fault of the seller or the buyer, the party not in fault may have such remedies against the party in fault as are allowed by Parts IV and V of this act.

CONDITIONS AND WARRANTIES

Section 11. Effect of Conditions. (1) Where the obligation of either party to a contract to sell or a sale is subject to any condition which is not performed, such party may refuse to proceed with the contract or sale or he may waive performance of the condition. If the other party has promised that the condition should happen or be performed, such first mentioned party may also treat the non-performance of the condition as a breach of warranty.

(2) Where the property in the goods has not passed, the buyer may treat the fulfilment by the seller of his obligation to furnish goods as described and as warranted expressly or by implication in the contract to sell as a condition of the obligation of the buyer to perform his promise to accept and pay for the goods.

Section 12. Definition of Express Warranty. Any affirmation of fact or any promise by the seller relating to the goods is an express warranty if the natural tendency of such affirmation or promise is to induce the buyer to purchase the goods, and if the buyer purchases the goods relying thereon. No affirmation of the value of the goods, nor any statement purporting to be a statement of the seller's opinion only, shall be construed as a warranty.

Section 13. Implied Warranties of Title. In a contract to sell or a sale, unless a contrary intention appears, there is:

(1) An implied warranty on the part of the seller that in case of a sale he has a right to sell the goods, and that in case of a contract to sell he will have a right to sell the goods at the time when the property is to pass;

(2) An implied warranty that the buyer shall have and enjoy quiet possession of the goods as against any lawful claims existing at the time of the sale;

(3) An implied warranty that the goods shall be free at the time of the sale from any charge or encumbrance in favor of any third person, not declared or known to the buyer before or at the time when the contract or sale is made.

(4) This section shall not, however, be held to render liable a sheriff, auctioneer, mortgagee, or other person professing to sell by virtue of authority in fact or law, goods in which a third person has a legal or equitable interest.

Section 14. Implied Warranty in Sale by Description. Where there is a contract to sell or a sale of goods by description, there is an implied warranty that the goods shall correspond with the description and if the contract or sale be by sample, as well as by description, it is not sufficient that the bulk of the goods corresponds with the sample if the goods do not also correspond with the description.

Section 15. Implied Warranties of Quality. Subject to the provisions of this act and of any statute in that behalf, there is no implied warranty or condition as to the quality or fitness for any particular purpose of goods supplied under a contract to sell or a sale, except as follows:

(1) Where the buyer, expressly or by implication, makes known to the seller

the particular purpose for which the goods are required, and it appears that the buyer relies on the seller's skill or judgment (whether he be the grower or manufacturer or not), there is an implied warranty that the goods shall be reasonably fit for such purpose.

(2) Where the goods are bought by description from a seller who deals in goods of that description (whether he be the grower or manufacturer or not), there is an implied warranty that the goods shall be of merchantable quality.

(3) If the buyer has examined the goods, there is no implied warranty as regards defects which such examination ought to have revealed.

(4) In the case of a contract to sell or a sale of a specified article under its patent or other trade name, there is no implied warranty as to its fitness for any particular purpose.

(5) An implied warranty or condition as to quality or fitness for a particular purpose may be annexed by the usage of trade.

(6) An express warranty or condition does not negative a warranty or condition implied under this act unless inconsistent therewith.

SALE BY SAMPLE

Section 16. Implied Warranties in Sale by Sample. In the case of a contract to sell or a sale by sample:

(*a*) There is an implied warranty that the bulk shall correspond with the sample in quality.

(*b*) There is an implied warranty that the buyer shall have a reasonable opportunity of comparing the bulk with the sample, except so far as otherwise provided in section 47 (3).

(*c*) If the seller is a dealer in goods of that kind, there is an implied warranty that the goods shall be free from any defect rendering them unmerchantable which would not be apparent on reasonable examination of the sample.

PART II

TRANSFER OF PROPERTY AS BETWEEN SELLER AND BUYER

Section 17. No Property Passes Until Goods Are Ascertained. Where there is a contract to sell unascertained goods no property in the goods is transferred to the buyer unless and until the goods are ascertained, but property in an undivided share of ascertained goods may be transferred as provided in section 6.

Section 18. Property in Specific Goods Passes When Parties So Intend. (1) Where there is a contract to sell specific or ascertained goods, the property in them is transferred to the buyer at such time as the parties to the contract intend it to be transferred.

(2) For the purpose of ascertaining the intention of the parties, regard shall be had to the terms of the contract, the conduct of the parties, usages of trade, and the circumstances of the case.

Section 19. Rules for Ascertaining Intention. Unless a different intention appears, the following are rules for ascertaining the intention of the parties as to the time at which the property in the goods is to pass to the buyer.

Rule 1. Where there is an unconditional contract to sell specific goods, in a deliverable state, the property in the goods passes to the buyer when the contract is made and it is immaterial whether the time of payment, or the time of delivery, or both, be postponed.

Rule 2. Where there is a contract to sell specific goods and the seller is bound to do something to the goods, for the purpose of putting them into a deliverable state, the property does not pass until such thing be done.

Rule 3. (1) When goods are delivered to the buyer "on sale or return," or on other terms indicating an intention to make a present sale, but to give the buyer an option to return the goods instead of paying the price, the property passes to the buyer on delivery, but he may revest the property in the seller by returning or tendering the goods within the time fixed in the contract, or, if no time has been fixed, within a reasonable time.

(2) When goods are delivered to the buyer on approval or on trial or on satisfaction, or other similar terms, the property therein passes to the buyer:

(*a*) When he signifies his approval or acceptance to the seller or does any other act adopting the transaction;

(*b*) If he does not signify his approval or acceptance to the seller, but retains the goods without giving notice of rejection, then if a time has been fixed for the return of the goods, on the expiration of such time, and, if no time has been fixed, on the expiration of a reasonable time. What is a reasonable time is a question of fact.

Rule 4. (1) Where there is a contract to sell unascertained or future goods by description, and goods of that description and in a deliverable state are unconditionally appropriated to the contract, either by the seller with the assent of the buyer, or by the buyer with the assent of the seller, the property in the goods thereupon passes to the buyer. Such assent may be expressed or implied, and may be given either before or after the appropriation is made.

(2) Where, in pursuance of a contract to sell, the seller delivers the goods to the buyer, or to a carrier or other bailee (whether named by the buyer or not) for the purpose of transmission to or holding for the buyer, he is presumed to have unconditionally appropriated the goods to the contract, except in the cases provided for in the next rule and in section 20. This presumption is applicable, although by the terms of the contract the buyer is to pay the price before receiving delivery of the goods, and the goods are marked with the words "collect on delivery" or their equivalents.

Rule 5. If the contract to sell requires the seller to deliver the goods to the buyer, or at a particular place, or to pay the freight or cost or transportation to the buyer, or to a particular place, the property does not pass until the goods have been delivered to the buyer or reached the place agreed upon.

Section 20. Reservation of Right of Possession or Property When Goods Are Shipped. (1) Where there is a contract to sell specific goods, or where goods are subsequently appropriated to the contract, the seller may, by the terms of the contract or appropriation, reserve the right of possession or property in the goods until certain conditions have been fulfilled. The right of possession or property may be thus reserved notwithstanding the delivery of the goods to the buyer or to a carrier or other bailee for the purpose of transmission to the buyer.

(2) Where goods are shipped, and by the bill of lading the goods are deliverable to the seller or his agent, or to the order of the seller or of his agent, the seller thereby reserves the property in the goods. But, if except for the form of the bill of lading, the property would have passed to the buyer on shipment of the goods, the seller's property in the goods shall be deemed to be only for the purpose of securing performance by the buyer of his obligations under the contract.

(3) Where goods are shipped, and by the bill of lading the goods are deliverable to the order of the buyer or of his agent, but possession of the bill of lading is retained by the seller or his agent, the seller thereby reserves a right to the possession of the goods as against the buyer.

(4) Where the seller of goods draws on the buyer for the price and transmits the bill of exchange and bill of lading together to the buyer to secure acceptance or payment of the bill of exchange, the buyer is bound to return the bill of lading if he does not honor the bill of exchange, and if he wrongfully retains the bill of lading

he acquires no added right thereby. If, however, the bill of lading provides that the goods are deliverable to the buyer or to the order of the buyer, or is indorsed in blank, or to the buyer by the consignee named therein, one who purchases in good faith, for value, the bill of lading, or goods from the buyer will obtain the property in the goods, although the bill of exchange has not been honored, provided that such purchaser has received delivery of the bill of lading indorsed by the consignee named therein, or of the goods, without notice of the facts, making the transfer wrongful.

Section 21. Sale by Auction. In the case of sale by auction:

(1) Where goods are put up for sale by auction in lots, each lot is the subject of a separate contract of sale.

(2) A sale by auction is complete when the auctioneer announces its completion by the fall of the hammer, or in other customary manner. Until such announcement is made, any bidder may retract his bid; and the auctioneer may withdraw the goods from sale unless the auction has been announced to be without reserve.

(3) A right to bid may be reserved expressly by or on behalf of the seller.

(4) Where notice has not been given that a sale by auction is subject to a right to bid on behalf of the seller, it shall not be lawful for the seller to bid himself or to employ or induce any person to bid at such sale on his behalf, or for the auctioneer to employ or induce any person to bid at such sale on behalf of the seller or knowingly to take any bid from the seller or any person employed by him. Any sale contravening this rule may be treated as fraudulent by the buyer.

Section 22. Risk of Loss. Unless otherwise agreed, the goods remain at the seller's risk until the property therein is transferred to the buyer, but when the property therein is transferred to the buyer the goods are at the buyer's risk whether delivery has been made or not, except that:

(*a*) Where delivery of the goods has been made to the buyer, or to a bailee for the buyer, in pursuance of the contract and the property in the goods has been retained by the seller merely to secure performance by the buyer of his obligations under the contract, the goods are at the buyer's risk from the time of such delivery.

(*b*) Where delivery has been delayed through the fault of either buyer or seller the goods are at the risk of the party in fault as regards any loss which might not have occurred but for such fault.

TRANSFER OF TITLE

Section 23. Sale by a Person Not the Owner. (1) Subject to the provisions of this act, where goods are sold by a person who is not the owner thereof, and who does not sell them under the authority or with the consent of the owner, the buyer acquires no better title to the goods than the seller had, unless the owner of the goods is by his conduct precluded from denying the seller's authority to sell.

(2) Nothing in this act, however, shall affect:

(*a*) The provisions of any factors' acts, recording acts, or any enactment enabling the apparent owner of goods to dispose of them as if he were the true owner thereof.

(*b*) The validity of any contract to sell or sale under any special common law or statutory power of sale or under the order of a court of competent jurisdiction.

Section 24. Sale by One Having a Voidable Title. Where the seller of goods has a voidable title thereto, but his title has not been avoided at the time of the sale, the buyer requires a good title to the goods, provided he buys them in good faith, for value, and without notice of the seller's defect of title.

Section 25. Sale by Seller in Possession of Goods Already Sold. Where a person having sold goods continues in possession of the goods, or of negotiable documents of title to the goods, the delivery or transfer by that person, or by an agent acting for him, of the goods or documents of title under any sale, pledge, or other disposition thereof, to any person receiving and paying value for the same in good faith and without notice of the previous sale, shall have the same effect as if the person making the delivery or transfer were expressly authorized by the owner of the goods to make the same.

Section 26. Creditors' Rights Against Sold Goods in Seller's Possession. Where a person having sold goods continues in possession of the goods, or of negotiable documents of title to the goods and such retention of possession is fraudulent in fact or is deemed fraudulent under any rule of law, a creditor or creditors of the seller may treat the sale as void.

Section 27. Definition of Negotiable Documents of Title. A document of title in which it is stated that the goods referred to therein will be delivered to the bearer, or to the order of any person named in such document is a negotiable document of title.

Section 28. Negotiation of Negotiable Documents by Delivery. A negotiable document of title may be negotiated by delivery:

(*a*) Where by the terms of the document the carrier, warehouseman, or other bailee issuing the same undertakes to deliver the goods to the bearer, or

(*b*) Where by the terms of the document the carrier, warehouseman, or other bailee issuing the same undertakes to deliver the goods to the order of a specified person, and such person or a subsequent indorsee of the document has indorsed it in blank or to bearer.

Where by the terms of a negotiable document of title the goods are deliverable to bearer or where a negotiable document of title has been indorsed in blank or to bearer, any holder may indorse the same to himself or to any other specified person, and in such case the document shall thereafter be negotiated only by the indorsement of such indorsee.

Section 29. Negotiation of Negotiable Documents by Indorsement. A negotiable document of title may be negotiated by the indorsement of the person to whose order the goods are by the terms of the document deliverable. Such indorsement may be in blank, to bearer or to a specified person. If indorsed to a specified person, it may be again negotiated by the indorsement of such person in blank, to bearer or to another specified person. Subsequent negotiation may be made in like manner.

Section 30. Negotiable Documents of Title Marked "Not Negotiable." If a document of title which contains an undertaking by a carrier, warehouseman, or other bailee to deliver the goods to the bearer, to a specified person or order, or to the order of a specified person, or which contains words of like import, has placed upon it the words "not negotiable," "non-negotiable" or the like, such a document may nevertheless be negotiated by the holder and is a negotiable document of title within the meaning of this act. But nothing in this act contained shall be construed as limiting or defining the effect upon the obligations of the carrier, warehouseman, or other bailee issuing a document of title or placing thereon the words "not negotiable," "non-negotiable," or the like.

Section 31. Transfer of Non-negotiable Documents. A document of title which is not in such form that it can be negotiated by delivery may be transferred by the holder by delivery to a purchaser or donee. A non-negotiable document cannot be negotiated and the indorsement of such a document gives the transferee no additional right.

Section 32. Who May Negotiate a Document. A negotiable document of title may be negotiated:

(*a*) By the owner thereof, or

(*b*) By any person to whom the possession or custody of the document has been entrusted by the owner, if, by the terms of the document, the bailee issuing the document undertakes to deliver the goods to the order of the person to whom the possession or custody of the document has been entrusted, or if at the time of such entrusting the document is in such form that it may be negotiated by delivery.

Section 33. Rights of Person to Whom Document Has Been Negotiated. A person to whom a negotiable document of title has been duly negotiated acquires thereby:

(*a*) Such title to the goods as the person negotiating the document to him had or had ability to convey to a purchaser in good faith for value and also such title to the goods as the person to whose order the goods were to be delivered by the terms of the document had or had ability to convey to a purchaser in good faith for value, and

(*b*) The direct obligation of the bailee issuing the document to hold possession of the goods for him according to the terms of the document as fully as if such bailee had contracted directly with him.

Section 34. Rights of Persons to Whom Document Has Been Transferred. A person to whom a document of title has been transferred, but not negotiated, acquires thereby, as against the transferor, the title to the goods, subject to the terms of any agreement with the transferor.

If the document is non-negotiable, such person also acquires the right to notify the bailee who issued the document of the transfer thereof, and thereby to acquire the direct obligation of such bailee to hold possession of the goods for him according to the terms of the document.

Prior to the notification of such bailee by the transferor or transferee of a non-negotiable document of title, the title of the transferee to the goods and the right to acquire the obligation of such bailee may be defeated by the levy of an attachment or execution upon the goods by a creditor of the transferor or by a notification to such bailee by the transferor or a subsequent purchaser from the transferor of a subsequent sale of the goods by the transferor.

Section 35. Transfer of Negotiable Document Without Indorsement. Where a negotiable document of title is transferred for value by delivery, and the indorsement of the transferor is essential for negotiation, the transferee acquires a right against the transferor to compel him to indorse the document unless a contrary intention appears. The negotiation shall take effect as of the time when the indorsement is actually made.

Section 36. Warranties on Sale of Documents. A person who for value negotiates or transfers a document of title by indorsement or delivery, including one who assigns for value a claim secured by a document of title unless a contrary intention appears, warrants:

(*a*) That the document is genuine;

(*b*) That he has a legal right to negotiate or transfer it;

(*c*) That he has knowledge of no fact which would impair the validity or worth of the document, and

(*d*) That he has a right to transfer the title to the goods and that the goods are merchantable or fit for a particular purpose, whenever such warranties would have been implied if the contract of the parties had been to transfer without a document of title the goods represented thereby.

Section 37. Indorser Not a Guarantor. The indorsement of a document of title shall not make the indorser liable for any failure on the part of the bailee who issued the document or previous indorsers thereof to fulfill their respective obligations.

Section 38. When Negotiation Not Impaired by Fraud, Mistake, or Duress. The validity of the negotiation of a negotiable document of title is not impaired by the fact that the negotiation was a breach of duty on the part of the person making the negotiation, or by the fact that the owner of the document was induced by fraud, mistake, or duress to entrust the possession or custody thereof to such person, if the person to whom the document was negotiated or a person to whom the document was subsequently negotiated paid value therefor, without notice of the breach of duty, or fraud, mistake, or duress.

Section 39. Attachment or Levy upon Goods for Which a Negotiable Document Has Been Issued. If goods are delivered to a bailee by the owner or by a person whose act in conveying the title to them to a purchaser in good faith for value would bind the owner and a negotiable document of title is issued for them, they cannot thereafter, while in the possession of such bailee, be attached by garnishment or otherwise or be levied upon under an execution unless the document be first surrendered to the bailee or its negotiation enjoined. The bailee shall in no case be compelled to deliver up the actual possession of the goods until the document is surrendered to him or impounded by the court.

Section 40. Creditors' Remedies to Reach Negotiable Documents. A creditor whose debtor is the owner of a negotiable document of title shall be entitled to such aid from the courts of appropriate jurisdiction by injunction and otherwise in attaching such document or in satisfying the claim by means thereof as is allowed at law or in equity in regard to property which cannot readily be attached or levied upon by ordinary legal process.

PART III

PERFORMANCE OF THE CONTRACT

Section 41. Seller Must Deliver and Buyer Accept Goods. It is the duty of the seller to deliver the goods, and of the buyer to accept and pay for them, in accordance with the terms of the contract to sell or sale.

Section 42. Delivery and Payment Are Concurrent Conditions. Unless otherwise agreed, delivery of the goods and payment of the price are concurrent conditions; that it to say, the seller must be ready and willing to give possession of the goods to the buyer in exchange for the price and the buyer must be ready and willing to pay the price in exchange for possession of the goods.

Section 43. Place, Time, and Manner of Delivery. (1) Whether it is for the buyer to take possession of the goods or for the seller to send them to the buyer is a question depending in each case on the contract, express or implied, between the parties. Apart from any such contract, express or implied, or usage of trade to the contrary, the place of delivery is the seller's place of business if he has one, and if not his residence; but in the case of a contract to sell or a sale of specific goods which to the knowledge of the parties when the contract or the sale was made were in some other place, then that place is the place of delivery.

(2) Where by a contract to sell or a sale the seller is bound to send the goods to the buyer, but no time for sending them is fixed, the seller is bound to send them within a reasonable time.

(3) Where the goods at the time of sale are in the possession of a third person, the seller has not fulfilled his obligation to deliver to the buyer unless and until such third person acknowledges to the buyer that he holds the goods on the buyer's behalf; but as against all others than the seller the buyer shall be regarded as having received delivery from the time when such third person first has notice of the sale. Nothing in this section, however, shall affect the operation of the issue or transfer of any document of title to goods.

(4) Demand or tender of delivery may be treated as ineffectual unless made at a reasonable hour. What is a reasonable hour is a question of fact.

(5) Unless otherwise agreed, the expenses of and incidental to putting the goods into a deliverable state must be borne by the seller.

Section 44. Delivery of Wrong Quantity. (1) Where the seller delivers to the buyer a quantity of goods less than he contracted to sell, the buyer may reject them, but if the buyer accepts or retains the goods so delivered, knowing that the seller is not going to perform the contract in full, he must pay for them at the contract rate. If, however, the buyer has used or disposed of the goods delivered before he knows that the seller is not going to perform his contract in full, the buyer shall not be liable for more than the fair value to him of the goods so received.

(2) Where the seller delivers to the buyer a quantity of goods larger than he contracted to sell, the buyer may accept the goods included in the contract and reject the rest, or he may reject the whole. If the buyer accepts the whole of the goods so delivered he must pay for them at the contract rate.

(3) Where the seller delivers to the buyer the goods he contracted to sell mixed with goods of a different description not included in the contract, the buyer may accept the goods which are in accordance with the contract and reject the rest, or he may reject the whole.

(4) The provisions of this section are subject to any usage of trade, special agreement, or course of dealing between the parties.

Section 45. Delivery in Instalments. (1) Unless otherwise agreed, the buyer of goods is not bound to accept delivery thereof by instalments.

(2) Where there is a contract to sell goods to be delivered by stated instalments, which are to be separately paid for, and the seller makes defective deliveries in respect of one or more instalments, or the buyer neglects or refuses to take delivery of or pay for one or more instalments, it depends in each case on the terms of the contract and the circumstances of the case, whether the breach of contract is so material as to justify the injured party in refusing to proceed further and suing for damages for breach of the entire contract, or whether the breach is severable, giving rise to a claim for compensation, but not to a right to treat the whole contract as broken.

Section 46. Delivery to a Carrier on Behalf of the Buyer. (1) Where, in pursuance of a contract to sell or a sale, the seller is authorized or required to send the goods to the buyer, delivery of the goods to a carrier, whether named by the buyer or not, for the purpose of transmission to the buyer is deemed to be a delivery of the goods to the buyer, except in the cases provided for in section 19, Rule 5, or unless a contrary intent appears.

(2) Unless otherwise authorized by the buyer, the seller must make such contract with the carrier on behalf of the buyer as may be reasonable, having regard to the nature of the goods and the other circumstances of the case. If the seller omits so to do, and the goods are lost or damaged in course of transit, the buyer may decline to treat the delivery to the carrier as a delivery to himself, or may hold the seller responsible in damages.

(3) Unless otherwise agreed, where goods are sent by the seller to the buyer under circumstances in which the seller knows or ought to know that it is usual to insure, the seller must give such notice to the buyer as may enable him to insure them during their transit, and, if the seller fails to do so, the goods shall be deemed to be at his risk during such transit.

Section 47. Right to Examine the Goods. (1) Where goods are delivered to the buyer, which he has not previously examined, he is not deemed to have accepted them unless and until he has had a reasonable opportunity of examining them for the purpose of ascertaining whether they are in conformity with the contract.

(2) Unless otherwise agreed, when the seller tenders delivery of goods to the buyer, he is bound, on request, to afford the buyer a reasonable opportunity of examining the goods for the purpose of ascertaining whether they are in conformity with the contract.

(3) Where the goods are delivered to a carrier by the seller, in accordance with an order from or agreement with the buyer, upon the terms that the goods shall not be delivered by the carrier to the buyer until he has paid the price, whether such terms are indicated by marking the goods with the words "collect on delivery," or otherwise, the buyer is not entitled to examine the goods before payment of the price in the absence of agreement permitting such examination.

Section 48. What Constitutes Acceptance. The buyer is deemed to have accepted the goods when he intimates to the seller that he has accepted them, or when the goods have been delivered to him, and he does any act in relation to them which is inconsistent with the ownership of the seller, or when, after the lapse of a reasonable time, he retains the goods without intimating to the seller that he has rejected them.

Section 49. Acceptance Does Not Bar Action for Damages. In the absence of express or implied agreement of the parties, acceptance of the goods by the buyer shall not discharge the seller from liability in damages or other legal remedy for breach of any promise or warranty in the contract to sell or the sale. But, if, after acceptance of the goods, the buyer fails to give notice to the seller of the breach of any promise or warranty within a reasonable time after the buyer knows, or ought to know of such breach, the seller should not be liable therefor.

Section 50. Buyer Is Not Bound to Return Goods Wrongly Delivered. Unless otherwise agreed, where the goods are delivered to the buyer, and he refuses to accept them, having the right to do so, he is not bound to return them to the seller, but it is sufficient if he notifies the seller that he refused to accept them.

Section 51. Buyer's Liability for Failing to Accept Delivery. When the seller is ready and willing to deliver the goods, and requests the buyer to take delivery, and the buyer does not within a reasonable time after such request take delivery of the goods, he is liable to the seller for any loss occasioned by his neglect or refusal to take delivery, and also for a reasonable charge for the care and custody of the goods. If the neglect or refusal of the buyer to take delivery amounts to a repudiation or breach of the entire contract, the seller shall have the rights against the goods and on the contract hereinafter provided in favor of the seller when the buyer is in default.

PART IV

RIGHTS OF UNPAID SELLER AGAINST THE GOODS

Section 52. Definition of Unpaid Seller. (1) The seller of goods is deemed to be an unpaid seller within the meaning of this act—

(*a*) When the whole of the price has not been paid or tendered.

(*b*) When a bill of exchange or other negotiable instrument has been received as conditional payment, and the condition on which it was received has been broken by reason of the dishonor of the instrument, the insolvency of the buyer, or otherwise.

(2) In this part of this act the term "seller" includes an agent of the seller to whom the bill of lading has been indorsed, or a consignor or agent who has himself paid, or is directly responsible for, the price, or any other person who is in the position of a seller.

Section 53. Remedies of an Unpaid Seller. (1) Subject to the provisions of this act, notwithstanding that the property in the goods may have passed to the buyer, the unpaid seller of goods, as such, has—

(*a*) A lien on the goods or right to retain them for the price while he is in possession of them;

(*b*) In case of the insolvency of the buyer, a right of stopping the goods in transitu after he has parted with the possession of them;

(*c*) A right of resale as limited by this act;

(*d*) A right to rescind the sale as limited by this act.

(2) Where the property in goods has not passed to the buyer, the unpaid seller has, in addition to his other remedies, a right of withholding delivery similar to and coextensive with his rights of lien and stoppage in transitu where the property has passed to the buyer.

UNPAID SELLER'S LIEN

Section 54. When Right of Lien May Be Exercised. (1) Subject to the provisions of this act, the unpaid seller of goods who is in possession of them is entitled to retain possession of them until payment or tender of the price in the following cases, namely:

(*a*) Where the goods have been sold without any stipulation as to credit;

(*b*) Where the goods have been sold on credit, but the term of credit has expired;

(*c*) Where the buyer becomes insolvent.

(2) The seller may exercise his right of lien notwithstanding that he is in possession of the goods as agent or bailee for the buyer.

Section 55. Lien after Part Delivery. Where an unpaid seller has made part delivery of the goods, he may exercise his right of lien on the remainder, unless such part delivery has been made under such circumstances as to show an intent to waive the lien or right of retention.

Section 56. When Lien Is Lost. (1) The unpaid seller of goods loses his lien thereon—

(*a*) When he delivers the goods to a carrier or other bailee for the purpose of transmission to the buyer without reserving the property in goods or the right to the possession thereof;

(*b*) When the buyer or his agent lawfully obtains possession of the goods;

(*c*) By waiver thereof.

(2) The unpaid seller of goods, having a lien thereon, does not lose his lien by reason only that he has obtained judgment or decree for the price of the goods.

STOPPAGE IN TRANSITU

Section 57. Seller May Stop Goods on Buyer's Insolvency. Subject to the provisions of this act, when the buyer of goods is or becomes insolvent, the unpaid seller who has parted with the possession of the goods has the right of stopping them in transitu, that is to say, he may resume possession of the goods at any time while they are in transitu, and he will then become entitled to the same rights in regard to the goods as he would have had if he had never parted with the possession.

Section 58. When Goods Are in Transit. (1) Goods are in transit within the meaning of section 57—

(*a*) From the time when they are delivered to a carrier by land or water, or other bailee for the purpose of transmission to the buyer, until the buyer, or his agent in that behalf, takes delivery of them from such carrier or other bailee;

(*b*) If the goods are rejected by the buyer, and the carrier or other bailee continues in possession of them, even if the seller has refused to receive them back.

(2) Goods are no longer in transit within the meaning of section 57—

(*a*) If the buyer, or his agent in that behalf, obtains delivery of the goods before their arrival at the appointed destination;

(*b*) If, after the arrival of the goods at the appointed destination, the carrier or other bailee acknowledges to the buyer or his agent that he holds the goods on his behalf and continues in possession of them as bailee for the buyer or his agent; and it is immaterial that a further destination for the goods may have been indicated by the buyer;

(*c*) If the carrier or other bailee wrongfully refuses to deliver the goods to the buyer or his agent in that behalf.

(3) If the goods are delivered to a ship chartered by the buyer, it is a question depending on the circumstances of the particular case, whether they are in the possession of the master as a carrier or as agent of the buyer.

(4) If part delivery of the goods has been made to the buyer, or his agent in that behalf, the remainder of the goods may be stopped in transitu, unless such part delivery has been under such circumstances as to show an agreement with the buyer to give up possession of the whole of the goods.

Section 59. Ways of Exercising the Right to Stop. (1) The unpaid seller may exercise his right of stoppage in transitu either by obtaining actual possession of the goods or by giving notice of his claim to the carrier or other bailee in whose possession the goods are. Such notice may be given either to the person in actual possession of the goods or to his principal. In the latter case the notice, to be effectual, must be given at such time and under such circumstances that the principal, by the exercise of reasonable diligence, may prevent a delivery to the buyer.

(2) When notice of stoppage in transitu is given by the seller to the carrier, or other bailee in possession of the goods, he must redeliver the goods to, or according to the directions of, the seller. The expenses of such delivery must be borne by the seller. If, however, a negotiable document of title representing the goods has been issued by the carrier or other bailee, he shall not be obliged to deliver or justified in delivering the goods to the seller unless such document is first surrendered for cancelation.

RESALE BY THE SELLER

Section 60. When and How Resale May Be Made. (1) Where the goods are of a perishable nature, or where the seller expressly reserves the right of resale in case the buyer should make default, or where the buyer has been in default in the payment of the price an unreasonable time, an unpaid seller having a right of lien or having stopped the goods in transitu may resell the goods. He shall not thereafter be liable to the original buyer upon the contract to sell or the sale or for any profit made by such resale, but may recover from the buyer damages for any loss occasioned by the breach of the contract or the sale.

(2) Where a resale is made, as authorized in this section, the buyer acquires a good title as against the original buyer.

(3) It is not essential to the validity of a resale that notice of an intention to resell the goods be given by the seller to the original buyer. But where the right to resell is not based on the perishable nature of the goods or upon an express provision of the contract or the sale, the giving or failure to give such notice shall be relevant in any issue involving the question whether the buyer had been in default an unreasonable time before the resale was made.

(4) It is not essential to the validity of a resale that notice of the time and place of such resale should be given by the seller to the original buyer.

(5) The seller is bound to exercise reasonable care and judgment in making a resale, and subject to this requirement may make a resale either by public or private sale.

RESCISSION BY THE SELLER

Section 61. When and How the Seller May Rescind the Sale. (1) An unpaid seller having a right of lien or having stopped the goods in transitu, may rescind the transfer of title and resume the property in the goods, where he expressly reserved the right to do so in case the buyer should make default, or where the buyer has been in default in the payment of the price an unreasonable time. The seller shall not thereafter be liable to the buyer upon the contract to sell or the sale, but may recover from the buyer damages for any loss occasioned by the breach of the contract or the sale.

(2) The transfer of title shall not be held to have been rescinded by an unpaid seller until he has manifested by notice to the buyer or by some other overt act an intention to rescind. It is not necessary that such overt act should be communicated to the buyer, but the giving or failure to give notice to the buyer of the intention to rescind shall be relevant in any issue involving the question whether the buyer had been in default an unreasonable time before the right of rescission was asserted.

Section 62. Effect of Sale of Goods Subject to Lien or Stoppage in Transitu. Subject to the provisions of this act, the unpaid seller's right of lien or stoppage in transitu is not affected by any sale, or other dispositon of the goods which the buyer may have made, unless the seller has assented thereto.

If, however, a negotiable document of title has been issued for goods, no seller's lien or right or stoppage in transitu shall defeat the right of any purchaser for value in good faith to whom such document has been negotiated, whether such negotiation be prior or subsequent to the notification to the carrier, or other bailee who issued such document, of the seller's claim to a lien or right of stoppage in transitu.

PART V

ACTIONS FOR BREACH OF THE CONTRACT

REMEDIES OF THE SELLER

Section 63. Action for the Price. (1) Where, under a contract to sell or a sale, the property in the goods has passed to the buyer, and the buyer wrongfully neglects or refuses to pay for the goods according to the terms of the contract or the sale, the seller may maintain an action against him for the price of the goods.

(2) Where, under a contract to sell or a sale, the price is payable on a day certain, irrespective of delivery or of transfer of title, and the buyer wrongfully neglects or refuses to pay such price, the seller may maintain an action for the price, although the property in the goods has not passed, and the goods have not been appropriated to the contract. But it shall be a defense to such an action that the seller at any time before the judgment in such action has manifested an inability to perform the contract or the sale on his part or an intention not to perform it.

(3) Although the property in the goods has not passed, if they cannot readily be resold for a reasonable price, and if the provisions of section 64 (4) are not applicable, the seller may offer to deliver the goods to the buyer, and, if the buyer refuses to receive them, may notify the buyer that the goods are thereafter held by the seller as bailee for the buyer. Thereafter the seller may treat the goods as the buyer's and may maintain an action for the price.

Section 64. Action for Damages for Non-acceptance of the Goods. (1) Where the buyer wrongfully neglects or refuses to accept and pay for the goods, the seller may maintain an action against him for damages for non-acceptance.

(2) The measure of damages is the estimated loss directly and naturally resulting, in the ordinary course of events, from the buyer's breach of contract.

(3) Where there is an available market for the goods in question, the measure of damages is, in the absence of special circumstance, showing proximate damage of a greater amount, the difference between the contract price and the market or current price at the time or times when the goods ought to have been accepted, or, if no time was fixed for acceptance, then at the time of the refusal to accept.

(4) If, while labor or expense of material amount are necessary on the part of the seller to enable him to fulfill his obligations under the contract to sell or the sale, the buyer repudiates the contract or the sale, or notifies the seller to proceed no further therewith, the buyer shall be liable to the seller for no greater damages than the seller would have suffered if he did nothing towards carrying out the contract or the sale after receiving notice of the buyer's repudiation or countermand. The profit the seller would have made if the contract or the sale had been fully performed shall be considered in estimating such damages.

Section 65. When Seller May Rescind Contract or Sale. Where the goods have not been delivered to the buyer, and the buyer has repudiated the contract to sell or sale, or has manifested his inability to perform his obligations thereunder, or has committed a material breach thereof, the seller may totally rescind the contract or the sale by giving notice of his election so to do to the buyer.

REMEDIES OF THE BUYER

Section 66. Action for Converting or Detaining Goods. Where the property in the goods has passed to the buyer and the seller wrongfully neglects or refuses to deliver the goods, the buyer may maintain any action allowed by law to the owner of goods of similar kind when wrongfully converted or withheld.

Section 67. Action for Failing to Deliver Goods. (1) Where the property in the goods has not passed to the buyer, and the seller wrongfully neglects or refuses to deliver the goods, the buyer may maintain an action against the seller for damages for non-delivery.

(2) The measure of damages is the loss directly and naturally resulting in the ordinary course of events, from the seller's breach of contract.

(3) Where there is an available market for the goods in question, the measure of damages, in the absence of special circumstances showing proximate damages of a greater amount, is the difference between the contract price and the market or current price of the goods at the time or times when they ought to have been delivered, or, if no time was fixed, then at the time of the refusal to deliver.

Section 68. Specific Performance. Where the seller has broken a contract to deliver specific or ascertained goods, a court having the powers of a court of equity may, if it thinks fit, on the application of the buyer, by its judgment or decree, direct that the contract shall be performed specifically, without giving the seller the option of retaining the goods on payment of damages. The judgment or decree may be unconditional, or upon such terms and conditions as to damages, payment of the price and otherwise, as to the court may seem just.

Section 69. Remedies for Breach of Warranty. (1) Where there is a breach of warranty by the seller, the buyer may, at his election:

(*a*) Accept or keep the goods and set up against the seller, the breach of warranty by way of recoupment in diminution or extinction of the price;

(*b*) Accept or keep the goods and maintain an action against the seller for damages for the breach of warranty;

(*c*) Refuse to accept the goods, if the property therein has not passed, and maintain an action against the seller for damages for the breach of warranty;

(*d*) Rescind the contract to sell or the sale and refuse to receive the goods, or if the goods have already been received, return them or offer to return them to the seller and recover the price or any part thereof which has been paid.

(2) When the buyer has claimed and been granted a remedy in any one of these ways, no other remedy can thereafter be granted.

(3) Where the goods have been delivered to the buyer, he cannot rescind the sale if he knew of the breach of warranty when he accepted the goods, or if he fails to notify the seller within a reasonable time of the election to rescind, or if he fails to return or to offer to return the goods to the seller in substantially as good condition as they were in at the time the property was transferred to the buyer. But if deterioration or injury of the goods is due to the breach of warranty, such deterioration or injury shall not prevent the buyer from returning or offering to return the goods to the seller and rescinding the sale.

(4) Where the buyer is entitled to rescind the sale and elects to do so, the buyer shall cease to be liable for the price upon returning or offering to return the goods. If the price or any part thereof has already been paid, the seller shall be liable to repay so much thereof as has been paid, concurrently with the return of the goods, or immediately after an offer to return the goods in exchange for repayment of the price.

(5) Where the buyer is entitled to rescind the sale and elects to do so, if the seller refuses to accept an offer of the buyer to return the goods, the buyer shall thereafter be deemed to hold the goods as bailee for the seller, but subject to a lien to secure the repayment of any portion of the price which has been paid, and with the remedies for the enforcement of such lien allowed to an unpaid seller by section 53.

(6) The measure of damages for breach of warranty is the loss directly and naturally resulting, in the ordinary course of events, from the breach of warranty.

(7) In the case of breach of warranty of quality, such loss, in the absence of special circumstances showing proximate damage of a greater amount, is the difference between the value of the goods at the time of delivery to the buyer and the value they would have had if they had answered to the warranty.

Section 70. Interest and Special Damages. Nothing in this act shall affect the right of the buyer or the seller to recover interest or special damages in any case where by law interest or special damages may be recoverable, or to recover money paid where the consideration for the payment of it has failed.

PART VI

INTERPRETATION

Section 71. Variation of Implied Obligations. Where any right, duty, or liability would arise under a contract to sell or a sale by implication of law, it may be negatived or varied by express agreement or by the course of dealing between the parties, or by custom, if the custom be such as to bind both parties to the contract or the sale.

Section 72. Rights May Be Enforced by Action. Where any right, duty, or liability is declared by this act, it may, unless otherwise by this act provided, be enforced by action.

Section 73. Rule for Cases Not Provided for by This Act. In any case not provided for in this act, the rules of law and equity, including the law merchant, and in particular the rules relating to the law of principal and agent and to the effect of fraud, misrepresentation, duress or coercion, mistake, bankruptcy, or other invalidating cause, shall continue to apply to contracts to sell and to sales of goods.

Section 74. Interpretation Shall Give Effect to Purpose of Uniformity. This act shall be so interpreted and construed, as to effectuate its general purpose to make uniform the laws of those states which enact it.

Section 75. Provisions Not Applicable to Mortgages. The provisions of this act relating to contracts to sell and to sales do not apply, unless so stated, to any transaction in the form of a contract to sell or a sale which is intended to operate by way of mortgage, pledge, charge, or other security.

Section 76. Definitions. (1) In this act, unless the context or subject matter otherwise requires—

"Action" includes counterclaim, set-off and suit in equity.

"Buyer" means a person who buys or agrees to buy goods or any legal successor in interest of such person.

"Defendant" includes a plaintiff against whom a right of set-off or counterclaim is asserted.

"Delivery" means voluntary transfer of possession from one person to another.

"Divisible contract to sell or sale" means a contract to sell or a sale in which by its terms the price for a portion or portions of the goods less than the whole is fixed or ascertainable by computation.

"Document of title to goods" includes any bill of lading, dock warrant, warehouse receipt, or order for the delivery of goods, or any other document used in the ordinary course of business in the sale or transfer of goods, as proof of the possession or control of the goods, or authorizing or purporting to authorize the possessor of the document to transfer or receive, either by indorsement or by delivery, goods represented by such document.

"Fault" means wrongful act or default.

"Fungible goods" means goods of which any unit is from its nature or by mercantile usage treated as the equivalent of any other unit.

"Future goods" means goods to be manufactured or acquired by the seller after the making of the contract of sale.

"Goods" include all chattels personal other than things in action and money. The term includes emblements, industrial growing crops, and things attached to or forming part of the land which are agreed to be severed before sale or under the contract of sale.

"Order" in sections of this act relating to documents of title means an order by indorsement on the document.

"Person" includes a corporation or partnership or two or more persons having a joint or common interest.

"Plaintiff" includes defendant asserting a right of set-off or counterclaim.

"Property" means the general property in goods, and not merely a special property.

"Purchaser" includes mortgagee and pledgee.

"Purchases" includes taking as a mortgagee or as a pledgee.

"Quality of goods" includes their state or condition.

"Sale" includes a bargain and sale as well as a sale and delivery.

"Seller" means a person who sells or agrees to sell goods, or any legal successor in the interest of such person.

"Specific goods" means goods identified and agreed upon at the time a contract to sell or a sale is made.

"Value" is any consideration sufficient to support a simple contract. An antecedent or pre-existing claim, whether for money or not, constitutes value where goods or documents of title are taken either in satisfaction thereof or as security therefor.

(2) A thing is done "in good faith" within the meaning of this act when it is in fact done honestly, whether it be done negligently or not.

(3) A person is insolvent within the meaning of this act who either has ceased to pay his debts in the ordinary course of business or cannot pay his debts as they become due, whether he has committed an act of bankruptcy or not, and whether he is insolvent within the meaning of the federal bankruptcy law or not.

(4) Goods are in a "deliverable state" within the meaning of this act when they are in such a state that the buyer would, under the contract, be bound to take delivery of them.

Section 76a. Act Does Not Apply to Existing Sales or Contracts to Sell. None of the provisions of this Act shall apply to any sale, or to any contract to sell, made prior to the taking effect of this Act.

Section 76b. No Repeal of Uniform Warehouse Receipt Act or Uniform Bills of Lading Act. Nothing in this Act or in any repealing clause thereof shall be construed to repeal or limit any of the provisions of the Act to Make Uniform the Law of Warehouse Receipts, or of the Act to Make Uniform the Law of Bills of Lading.

Section 77. Inconsistent Legislation Repealed. All acts or parts of acts inconsistent with this act are hereby repealed except as provided in section 76b.

Section 78. Time When the Act Takes Effect. This act shall take effect on the .... day of .... one thousand nine hundred and ....

Section 79. Name of Act. This act may be cited as the Uniform Sales Act.

THE NEGOTIABLE INSTRUMENTS LAW

An Act to Make Uniform the Law of Negotiable Instruments

TITLE I. NEGOTIABLE INSTRUMENTS IN GENERAL

ARTICLE I. FORM AND INTERPRETATION

Section 1. Be it enacted, etc., An instrument to be negotiable must conform to the following requirements:

1. It must be in writing and signed by the maker or drawer;
2. Must contain an unconditional promise or order to pay a sum certain in money;
3. Must be payable on demand, or at a fixed or determinable future time;
4. Must be payable to order or to bearer; and,
5. Where the instrument is addressed to a drawee, he must be named or otherwise indicated therein with reasonable certainty.

Section 2. The sum payable is a sum certain within the meaning of this act, although it is to be paid—

1. With interest; or
2. By stated instalments; or
3. By stated instalments, with a provision that upon default in payment of any instalment or of interest the whole shall become due; or
4. With exchange, whether at a fixed rate or at the current rate; or
5. With costs of collection or an attorney's fee, in case payment shall not be made at maturity.

Section 3. An unqualified order or promise to pay is unconditional within the meaning of this act, though coupled with—

1. An indication of a particular fund out of which reimbursement is to be made, or a particular account to be debited with the amount; or
2. A statement of the transaction which gives rise to the instrument.

But an order or promise to pay out of a particular fund is not unconditional.

Section 4. An instrument is payable at a determinable future time, within the meaning of this act, which is expressed to be payable—

1. At a fixed period after date or sight; or
2. On or before a fixed or determinable future time specified therein; or
3. On or at a fixed period after the occurrence of a special event, which is certain to happen, though the time of happening be uncertain.

An instrument payable upon a contingency is not negotiable, and the happening of the event does not cure the defect.

Section 5. An instrument which contains an order or promise to do any act in addition to the payment of money is not negotiable. But the negotiable character of an instrument otherwise negotiable is not affected by a provision which—

1. Authorizes the sale of collateral securities in case the instrument be not paid at maturity; or
2. Authorizes a confession of judgment if the instrument be not paid at maturity; or
3. Waives the benefit of any law intended for the advantage or protection of the obligor; or
4. Gives the holder an election to require something to be done in lieu of payment of money.

But nothing in this section shall validate any provision or stipulation otherwise illegal.

Section 6. The validity and negotiable character of an instrument are not affected by the fact that—

1. It is not dated; or
2. Does not specify the value given, or that any value has been given therefor; or

3. Does not specify the place where it is drawn or the place where it is payable; or

4. Bears a seal; or

5. Designates a particular kind of current money in which payment is to be made.

But nothing in this section shall alter or repeal any statute requiring in certain cases the nature of the consideration to be stated in the instrument.

Section 7. An instrument is payable on demand:

1. Where it is expressed to be payable on demand, or at sight, or on presentation; or

2. In which no time for payment is expressed.

Where an instrument is issued, accepted, or indorsed when overdue, it is, as regards the person so issuing, accepting, or indorsing it, payable on demand.

Section 8. The instrument is payable to order where it is drawn payable to the order of a specified person or to him or his order. It may be drawn payable to the order of—

1. A payee who is not maker, drawer, or drawee; or
2. The drawer or maker; or
3. The drawee; or
4. Two or more payees jointly; or
5. One or some of several payees; or
6. The holder of an office for the time being.

Where the instrument is payable to order the payee must be named or otherwise indicated therein with reasonable certainty.

Section 9. The instrument is payable to bearer—

1. When it is expressed to be so payable; or

2. When it is payable to a person named therein or bearer; or

3. When it is payable to the order of a fictitious or nonexisting person, and such fact was known to the person making it so payable; or

4. When the name of the payee does not purport to be the name of any person; or

5. When the only or last indorsement is an indorsement in blank.

Section 10. The instrument need not follow the language of this act, but any terms are sufficient which clearly indicate an intention to conform to the requirements hereof.

Section 11. Where the instrument or an acceptance or any indorsement thereon is dated, such date is deemed prima facie to be the true date of the making, drawing, acceptance, or indorsement as the case may be.

Section 12. The instrument is not invalid for the reason only that it is antedated or post-dated, provided this is not done for an illegal or fraudulent purpose. The person to whom an instrument so dated is delivered acquires the title thereto as of the date of delivery.

Section 13. Where an instrument expressed to be payable at a fixed period after date is issued undated, or where the acceptance of an instrument payable at a fixed period after sight is undated, any holder may insert therein the true date of issue or acceptance, and the instrument shall be payable accordingly. The insertion of a wrong date does not avoid the instrument in the hands of a subsequent holder in due course; but as to him, the date so inserted is to be regarded as the true date.

Section 14. Where the instrument is wanting in any material particular, the person in possession thereof has a prima facie authority to complete it by filling up the blanks therein. And a signature on a blank paper delivered by the person making the signature in order that the paper may be converted into a negotiable instrument operates as a prima facie authority to fill it up as such for any amount. In order, however, that any such instrument when completed may be enforced against any person who became a party thereto prior to its completion, it must be filled up strictly in accordance with the authority given and within a reasonable time. But if any such instrument, after completion, is negotiated to a holder in due course, it is valid and effectual for all purposes in his hands, and he may enforce it as if it had been filled up strictly in accordance with the authority given and within a reasonable time.

Section 15. Where an incomplete instrument has not been delivered it will not, if completed and negotiated, without authority, be a valid contract in the hands of any holder, as against any person whose signature was placed thereon before delivery.

Section 16. Every contract on a negotiable instrument is incomplete and revocable until delivery of the instrument for the purpose of giving effect thereto. As between immediate parties, and as regards a remote party other than a holder in due course, the delivery, in order to be effectual, must be made either by or under the authority of the party making, drawing, accepting, or indorsing, as the case may be; and in such case the delivery may be shown to have been conditional, or for a special purpose only, and not for the purpose of transferring the property in the instrument. But where the instrument is in the hands of a holder in due course, a valid delivery thereof by all parties prior to him so as to make them liable to him is conclusively presumed. And where the instrument is no longer in the possession of a party whose signature appears thereon, a valid and intentional delivery by him is presumed until the contrary is proved.

Section 17. Where the language of the instrument is ambiguous or there are omissions therein, the following rules of construction apply:

1. Where the sum payable is expressed in words and also in figures and there is a discrepancy between the two, the sum denoted by the words is the sum payable; but if the words are ambiguous or uncertain, reference may be had to the figures to fix the amount;
2. Where the instrument provides for the payment of interest, without specifying the date from which interest is to run, the interest runs from the date of the instrument, and if the instrument is undated, from the issue thereof;
3. Where the instrument is not dated, it will be considered to be dated as of the time it was issued;
4. Where there is a conflict between the written and printed provisions of the instrument, the written provisions prevail;
5. Where the instrument is so ambiguous that there is doubt whether it is a bill or note, the holder may treat it as either at his election;
6. Where a signature is so placed upon the instrument that it is not clear in what capacity the person making the same intended to sign, he is to be deemed an indorser;
7. Where an instrument containing the words, "I promise to pay," is signed by two or more persons, they are deemed to be jointly and severally liable thereon.

Section 18. No person is liable on the instrument whose signature does not appear thereon, except as herein otherwise expressly provided. But one who signs in a trade or assumed name will be liable to the same extent as if he had signed in his own name.

Section 19. The signature of any party may be made by a duly authorized agent. No particular form of appointment is necessary for this purpose; and the authority of the agent may be established as in other cases of agency.

Section 20. Where the instrument contains or a person adds to his signature words indicating that he signs for or on behalf of a principal, or in a representative capacity, he is not liable on the instrument if he was duly authorized; but the mere addition of words describing him as an agent, or as filling a representative character, without disclosing his principal, does not exempt him from personal liability.

Section 21. A signature by "procuration" operates as notice that the agent has but a limited authority to sign, and the principal is bound only in case the agent in so signing acted within the actual limits of his authority.

Section 22. The indorsement or assignment of the instrument by a corporation or by an infant passes the property therein, notwithstanding that from want of capacity the corporation or infant may incur no liability thereon.

Section 23. When a signature is forged or made without the authority of the person whose signature it purports to be, it is wholly inoperative, and no right to retain the instrument, or to give a discharge therefor, or to enforce payment thereof against any party thereto, can be acquired through or under such signature, unless the party, against whom it is sought to enforce such right, is precluded from setting up the forgery or want of authority.

Article II. Consideration

Section 24. Every negotiable instrument is deemed prima facie to have been issued for a valuable consideration; and every person whose signature appears thereon to have become a party thereto for value.

Section 25. Value is any consideration sufficient to support a simple contract. An antecedent or pre-existing debt constitutes value; and is deemed such whether the instrument is payable on demand or at a future time.

Section 26. Where value has at any time been given for the instrument, the holder is deemed a holder for value in respect to all parties who became such prior to that time.

Section 27. Where the holder has a lien on the instrument, arising either from contract or by implication of law, he is deemed a holder for value to the extent of his lien.

Section 28. Absence or failure of consideration is matter of defense as against any person not a holder in due course; and partial failure of consideration is a defense pro tanto, whether the failure is an ascertained and liquidated amount or otherwise.

Section 29. An accommodation party is one who has signed the instrument as maker, drawer, acceptor, or indorser, without receiving value therefor, and for the purpose of lending his name to some other person. Such a person is liable on the instrument to a holder for value, notwithstanding such holder at the time of taking the instrument knew him to be only an accommodation party.

Article III. Negotiation

Section 30. An instrument is negotiated when it is transferred from one person to another in such manner as to constitute the transferee the holder thereof. If payable to bearer it is negotiated by delivery; if payable to order it is negotiated by the indorsement of the holder completed by delivery.

Section 31. The indorsement must be written on the instrument itself or upon a paper attached thereto. The signature of the indorser, without additional words, is a sufficient indorsement.

Section 32. The indorsement must be an indorsement of the entire instrument. An indorsement, which purports to transfer to the indorsee a part only of the amount payable, or which purports to transfer the instrument to two or more indorsees severally, does not operate as a negotiation of the instrument. But where the instrument has been paid in part, it may be indorsed as to the residue.

Section 33. An indorsement may be either special or in blank; and it may also be either restrictive or qualified, or conditional.

Section 34. A special indorsement specifies the person to whom, or to whose order, the instrument is to be payable; and the indorsement of such indorsee is necessary to the further negotiation of the instrument. An indorsement in blank specifies no indorsee, and an instrument so indorsed is payable to bearer, and may be negotiated by delivery.

Section 35. The holder may convert a blank indorsement into a special indorsement by writing over the signature of the indorser in blank any contract consistent with the character of the indorsement.

Section 36. An indorsement is restrictive, which either—
1. Prohibits the further negotiation of the instrument; or
2. Constitutes the indorsee the agent of the indorser; or
3. Vests the title in the indorsee in trust for or to the use of some other person.
But the mere absence of words implying power to negotiate does not make an indorsement restrictive.

Section 37. A restrictive indorsement confers upon the indorsee the right—
1. To receive payment of the instrument;
2. To bring any action thereon that the indorser could bring;
3. To transfer his rights as such indorsee, where the form of the indorsement authorizes him to do so.
But all subsequent indorsees acquire only the title of the first indorsee under the restrictive indorsement.

Section 38. A qualified indorsement constitutes the indorser a mere assignor of the title to the instrument. It may be made by adding to the indorser's signature the words "without recourse," or any words of similar import. Such an indorsement does not impair the negotiable character of the instrument.

Section 39. Where an indorsement is conditional, a party required to pay the instrument may disregard the condition, and make payment to the indorsee or his transferee, whether the condition has been fulfilled or not. But any person to whom an instrument so indorsed is negotiated, will hold the same, or the proceeds thereof, subject to the rights of the person indorsing conditionally.

Section 40. Where an instrument, payable to bearer, is indorsed specially, it may nevertheless be further negotiated by delivery; but the person indorsing specially is liable as indorser to only such holders as make title through his indorsement.

Section 41. Where an instrument is payable to the order of two or more payees or indorsees who are not partners, all must indorse, unless the one indorsing has authority to indorse for the others.

Section 42. Where an instrument is drawn or indorsed to a person as "Cashier" or other fiscal officer of a bank or corporation, it is deemed prima facie to be payable to the bank or corporation of which he is such officer, and may be negotiated by either the indorsement of the bank or corporation, or the indorsement of the officer.

Section 43. Where the name of a payee or indorsee is wrongly designated or misspelled, he may indorse the instrument as therein described, adding, if he think fit, his proper signature.

Section 44. Where any person is under obligation to indorse in a representative capacity, he may indorse in such terms as to negative personal liability.

Section 45. Except where an indorsement bears date after the maturity of the instrument, every negotiation is deemed prima facie to have been effected before the instrument was overdue.

Section 46. Except where the contrary appears, every indorsement is presumed prima facie to have been made at the place where the instrument is dated.

Section 47. An instrument negotiable in its origin continues to be negotiable until it has been restrictively indorsed or discharged by payment or otherwise.

Section 48. The holder may at any time strike out any indorsement which is not necessary to his title. The indorser whose indorsement is struck out, and all indorsers subsequent to him, are thereby relieved from liability on the instrument.

Section 49. Where the holder of an instrument payable to his order transfers it for value without indorsing it, the transfer vests in the transferee such title as the transferor had therein, and the transferee acquires, in addition, the right to have the indorsement of the transferor. But for the purpose of determining whether the transferee is a holder in due course, the negotiation takes effect as of the time when the indorsement is actually made.

Section 50. Where an instrument is negotiated back to a prior party, such party may, subject to the provisions of this act, reissue and further negotiate the same. But he is not entitled to enforce payment thereof against any intervening party to whom he was personally liable.

Article IV. Rights of the Holder

Section 51. The holder of a negotiable instrument may sue thereon in his own name; and payment to him in due course discharges the instrument.

Section 52. A holder in due course is a holder who has taken the instrument under the following conditions:

1. That it is complete and regular upon its face;
2. That he became the holder of it before it was overdue, and without notice that it had been previously dishonored, if such was the fact;
3. That he took it in good faith and for value;
4. That at the time it was negotiated to him he had no notice of any infirmity in the instrument or defect in the title of the person negotiating it.

Section 53. Where an instrument payable on demand is negotiated an unreasonable length of time after its issue, the holder is not deemed a holder in due course.

Section 54. Where the transferee receives notice of any infirmity in the instrument or defect in the title of the person negotiating the same before he has paid the full amount agreed to be paid therefor, he will be deemed a holder in due course only to the extent of the amount theretofore paid by him.

Section 55. The title of a person who negotiates an instrument is defective within the meaning of this act when he obtained the instrument, or any signature thereto, by fraud, duress, or force and fear, or other unlawful means, or for an illegal consideration, or when he negotiates it in breach of faith, or under such circumstances as amount to a fraud.

Section 56. To constitute notice of an infirmity in the instrument or defect in the title of the person negotiating the same, the person to whom it is negotiated must have had actual knowledge of the infirmity or defect, or knowledge of such facts that his action in taking the instrument amounted to bad faith.

Section 57. A holder in due course holds the instrument free from any defect of title of prior parties, and free from defenses available to prior parties among themselves, and may enforce payment of the instrument for the full amount thereto against all parties liable thereon.

Section 58. In the hands of any holder other than a holder in due course, a negotiable instrument is subject to the same defenses as if it were non-negotiable. But a holder who derives his title through a holder in due course, and who is not himself a party to any fraud or illegality affecting the instrument, has all the rights of such former holder in respect of all parties prior to the latter.

Section 59. Every holder is deemed prima facie to be a holder in due course; but when it is shown that the title of any person who has negotiated the instrument was defective, the burden is on the holder to prove that he or some person under whom he claims acquired the title as holder in due course. But the last-mentioned rule does not apply in favor of a party who became bound on the instrument prior to the acquisition of such defective title.

Article V. Liabilities of Parties

Section 60. The maker of a negotiable instrument by making it engages that he will pay it according to its tenor, and admits the existence of the payee and his then capacity to indorse.

Section 61. The drawer by drawing the instrument admits the existence of the payee and his then capacity to indorse; and engages that on due presentment the instrument will be accepted or paid, or both, according to its tenor, and that if it be dishonored, and the necessary proceedings on dishonor be duly taken, he will pay the amount thereof to the holder, or to any subsequent indorser who may be compelled to pay it. But the drawer may insert in the instrument an express stipulation negativing or limiting his own liability to the holder.

Section 62. The acceptor by accepting the instrument engages that he will pay it according to the tenor of his acceptance; and admits—

1. The existence of the drawer, the genuineness of his signature, and his capacity and authority to draw the instrument; and
2. The existence of the payee and his then capacity to indorse.

Section 63. A person placing his signature upon an instrument otherwise than as maker, drawer or acceptor, is deemed to be an indorser, unless he clearly indicates by appropriate words his intention to be bound in some other capacity.

Section 64. Where a person, not otherwise a party to an instrument, places thereon his signature in blank before delivery, he is liable as indorser, in accordance with the following rules:

1. If the instrument is payable to the order of a third person, he is liable to the payee and to all subsequent parties.
2. If the instrument is payable to the order of the maker or drawer, or is payable to bearer, he is liable to all parties subsequent to the maker or drawer.
3. If he signs for the accommodation of the payee, he is liable to all parties subsequent to the payee.

Section 65. Every person negotiating an instrument by delivery or by a qualified indorsement, warrants—

1. That the instrument is genuine and in all respects what it purports to be;
2. That he has a good title to it;
3. That all prior parties had capacity to contract;
4. That he has no knowledge of any fact which would impair the validity of the instrument or render it valueless.

But when the negotiation is by delivery only, the warranty extends in favor of no holder other than the immediate transferee.

The provisions of subdivision 3 of this section do not apply to persons negotiating public or corporation securities, other than bills and notes.

Section 66. Every indorser who indorses without qualification, warrants to all subsequent holders in due course:

1. The matters and things mentioned in subdivisions 1, 2, and 3 of the next preceding section; and
2. That the instrument is at the time of his indorsement valid and subsisting.

And, in addition, he engages that on due presentment, it shall be accepted or paid, or both, as the case may be, according to its tenor, and that if it be dishonored, and the necessary proceedings on dishonor be duly taken, he will pay the amount thereof to the holder, or to any subsequent indorser who may be compelled to pay it.

Section 67. Where a person places his indorsement on an instrument negotiable by delivery he incurs all the liabilities of an indorser.

Section 68. As respects one another, indorsers are liable prima facie in the order in which they indorse; but evidence is admissible to show that as between or among themselves they have agreed otherwise. Joint payees or joint endorsees who indorse are deemed to indorse jointly and severally.

Section 69. Where a broker or other agent negotiates an instrument without indorsement, he incurs all the liabilities prescribed by section 65 of this act, unless he discloses the name of his principal, and the fact that he is acting only as agent.

Article VI. Presentment for Payment

Section 70. Presentment for payment is not necessary in order to charge the person primarily liable on the instrument; but if the instrument is, by its terms, payable at a special place, and he is able and willing to pay it there at maturity, such ability and willingness are equivalent to a tender of payment upon his part. But except as herein otherwise provided, presentment for payment is necessary in order to charge the drawer and indorsers.

Section 71. Where the instrument is not payable on demand, presentment must be made on the day it falls due. Where it is payable on demand, presentment must be made within a reasonable time after its issue, except that in the case of a bill of exchange, presentment for payment will be sufficient if made within a reasonable time after the last negotiation thereof.

Section 72. Presentment for payment, to be sufficient, must be made—

1. By the holder, or by some person authorized to receive payment on his behalf;
2. At a reasonable hour on a business day;
3. At a proper place as herein defined;
4. To the person primarily liable on the instrument, or if he is absent or inaccessible, to any person found at the place where the presentment is made.

Section 73. Presentment for payment is made at the proper place—

1. Where a place of payment is specified in the instrument and it is there presented;
2. Where no place of payment is specified, but the address of the person to make payment is given in the instrument and it is there presented;
3. Where no place of payment is specified and no address is given and the instrument is presented at the usual place of business or residence of the person to make payment;
4. In any other case if presented to the person to make payment wherever he can be found, or if presented at his last known place of business or residence.

Section 74. The instrument must be exhibited to the person from whom payment is demanded, and when it is paid must be delivered up to the party paying it.

Section 75. Where the instrument is payable at a bank, presentment for payment must be made during banking hours, unless the person to make payment has no funds there to meet it at any time during the day, in which case presentment at any hour before the bank is closed on that day is sufficient.

Section 76. Where the person primarily liable on the instrument is dead, and no place of payment is specified, presentment for payment must be made to his personal representative if such there be, and if, with the exercise of reasonable diligence, he can be found.

Section 77. Where the persons primarily liable on the instrument are liable as partners, and no place of payment is specified, presentment for payment may be made to any one of them, even though there has been a dissolution of the firm.

Section 78. Where there are several persons, not partners, primarily liable on the instrument, and no place of payment is specified, presentment must be made to them all.

Section 79. Presentment for payment is not required in order to charge the drawer where he has no right to expect or require that the drawee or acceptor will pay the instrument.

Section 80. Presentment for payment is not required in order to charge an indorser where the instrument was made or accepted for his accommodation and he has no reason to expect that the instrument will be paid if presented.

Section 81. Delay in making presentment for payment is excused when the delay is caused by circumstances beyond the control of the holder, and not imputable to his default, misconduct, or negligence. When the cause of delay ceases to operate, presentment must be made with reasonable diligence.

Section 82. Presentment for payment is dispensed with:

1. Where after the exercise of reasonable diligence presentment as required by this act cannot be made;
2. Where the drawee is a fictitious person;
3. By waiver of presentment, express or implied.

Section 83. The instrument is dishonored by nonpayment when,—

1. It is duly presented for payment and payment is refused or cannot be obtained; or
2. Presentment is excused and the instrument is overdue and unpaid.

Section 84. Subject to the provisions of this act, when the instrument is dishonored by nonpayment, an immediate right of recourse to all parties secondarily liable thereon accrues to the holder.

Section 85. Every negotiable instrument is payable at the time fixed therein without grace. When the day of maturity falls upon Sunday, or a holiday, the instrument is payable on the next succeeding business day. Instruments falling due on Saturday are to be presented for payment on the next succeeding business day, except that instruments payable on demand may, at the option of the holder, be presented for payment before twelve o'clock noon on Saturday when the entire day is not a holiday.

Section 86. Where the instrument is payable at a fixed period after date, after sight, or after the happening of a specified event, the time of payment is determined by excluding the day from which the time is to begin to run, and by including the date of payment.

Section 87. Where the instrument is made payable at a bank it is equivalent to an order to the bank to pay the same for the account of the principal debtor thereon.

Section 88. Payment is made in due course when it is made at or after the maturity of the instrument to the holder thereof in good faith and without notice that his title is defective.

Article VII. Notice of Dishonor

Section 89. Except as herein otherwise provided, when a negotiable instrument has been dishonored by nonacceptance or nonpayment, notice of dishonor must be given to the drawer and to each indorser, and any drawer or indorser to whom such notice is not given is discharged.

Section 90. The notice may be given by or on behalf of the holder, or by or on behalf of any party to the instrument who might be compelled to pay it to the holder, and who, upon taking it up, would have a right to reimbursement from the party to whom the notice is given.

Section 91. Notice of dishonor may be given by an agent either in his own name or in the name of any party entitled to give notice, whether that party be his principal or not.

Section 92. Where notice is given by or on behalf of the holder, it inures for the benefit of all subsequent holders and all prior parties who have a right of recourse against the party to whom it is given.

Section 93. Where notice is given by or on behalf of a party entitled to give notice, it inures for the benefit of the holder and all parties subsequent to the party to whom notice is given.

Section 94. Where the instrument has been dishonored in the hands of an agent, he may either himself give notice to the parties liable thereon, or he may give notice to his principal. If he gives notice to his principal, he must do so within the same time as if he were the holder, and the principal upon the receipt of such notice has himself the same time for giving notice as if the agent had been an independent holder.

Section 95. A written notice need not be signed, and an insufficient written notice may be supplemented and validated by verbal communication. A misdescription of the instrument does not vitiate the notice unless the party to whom the notice is given is in fact misled thereby.

Section 96. The notice may be in writing or merely oral and may be given in any terms which sufficiently identify the instrument, and indicate that it has been dishonored by nonacceptance or nonpayment. It may in all cases be given by delivering it personally or through the mails.

Section 97. Notice of dishonor may be given either to the party himself or to his agent in that behalf.

Section 98. When any party is dead, and his death is known to the party giving notice, the notice must be given to a personal representative, if there be one, and if with reasonable diligence he can be found. If there be no personal representative, notice may be sent to the last residence or last place of business of the deceased.

Section 99. Where the parties to be notified are partners, notice to any one partner is notice to the firm even though there has been a dissolution.

Section 100. Notice to joint parties who are not partners must be given to each of them, unless one of them has authority to receive such notice for the others.

Section 101. Where a party has been adjudged a bankrupt or an insolvent, or has made an assignment for the benefit of creditors, notice may be given either to the party himself or to his trustee or assignee.

Section 102. Notice may be given as soon as the instrument is dishonored; and unless delay is excused as hereinafter provided, must be given within the times fixed by this act.

Section 103. Where the person giving and the person to receive notice reside in the same place, notice must be given within the following times:

1. If given at the place of business of the person to receive notice, it must be given before the close of business hours on the day following.
2. If given at his residence, it must be given before the usual hours of rest on the day following.
3. If sent by mail, it must be deposited in the post office in time to reach him in usual course on the day following.

Section 104. Where the person giving and the person to receive notice reside in different places, the notice must be given within the following times:

1. If sent by mail, it must be deposited in the post office in time to go by mail the day following the day of dishonor, or if there be no mail at a convenient hour on that day, by the next mail thereafter.
2. If given otherwise than through the post office, then within the time that notice would have been received in due course of mail, if it had been deposited in the post office within the time specified in the last subdivision.

Section 105. Where notice of dishonor is duly addressed and deposited in the post office, the sender is deemed to have given due notice, notwithstanding any miscarriage in the mails.

Section 106. Notice is deemed to have been deposited in the post office when deposited in any branch post office or in any letter box under the control of the post office department.

Section 107. Where a party receives notice of dishonor, he has, after the receipt of such notice, the same time for giving notice to antecedent parties that the holder has after the dishonor.

Section 108. Where a party has added an address to his signature, notice of dishonor must be sent to that address; but if he has not given such address, then the notice must be sent as follows:

1. Either to the post office nearest to his place of residence, or to the post office where he is accustomed to receive his letters; or
2. If he lives in one place, and has his place of business in another, notice may be sent to either place; or
3. If he is sojourning in another place, notice may be sent to the place where he is so sojourning.

But where the notice is actually received by the party within the time specified in this act, it will be sufficient, though not sent in accordance with the requirements of this section.

Section 109. Notice of dishonor may be waived, either before the time of giving notice has arrived, or after the omission to give due notice, and the waiver may be express or implied.

Section 110. Where the waiver is embodied in the instrument itself, it is binding upon all parties; but where it is written above the signature of an indorser, it binds him only.

Section 111. A waiver of protest, whether in the case of a foreign bill of exchange or other negotiable instrument, is deemed to be a waiver not only of a formal protest, but also of presentment and notice of dishonor.

Section 112. Notice of dishonor is dispensed with when, after the exercise of reasonable diligence, it cannot be given to or does not reach the parties sought to be charged.

Section 113. Delay in giving notice of dishonor is excused when the delay is caused by circumstances beyond the control of the holder, and not imputable to his default, misconduct, or negligence. When the cause of delay ceases to operate, notice must be given with reasonable diligence.

Section 114. Notice of dishonor is not required to be given to the drawer in either of the following cases:

1. Where the drawer and drawee are the same person;
2. When the drawee is a fictitious person or a person not having capacity to contract;
3. When the drawer is the person to whom the instrument is presented for payment;
4. Where the drawer has no right to expect or require that the drawee or acceptor will honor the instrument;
5. Where the drawer has countermanded payment.

Section 115. Notice of dishonor is not required to be given to an indorser in either of the following cases:

1. Where the drawee is a fictitious person or a person not having capacity to contract, and the indorser was aware of the fact at the time he indorsed the instrument;
2. Where the indorser is the person to whom the instrument is presented for payment;
3. Where the instrument was made or accepted for his accommodation.

Section 116. Where due notice of dishonor by nonacceptance has been given, notice of a subsequent dishonor by nonpayment is not necessary, unless in the meantime the instrument has been accepted.

Section 117. An omission to give notice of dishonor by nonacceptance does not prejudice the rights of a holder in due course subsequent to the omission.

Section 118. Where any negotiable instrument has been dishonored it may be protested for nonacceptance or nonpayment, as the case may be; but protest is not required except in the case of foreign bills of exchange.

Article VIII. Discharge of Negotiable Instruments

Section 119. A negotiable instrument is discharged:

1. By payment in due course by or on behalf of the principal debtor;
2. By payment in due course by the party accommodated, where the instrument is made or accepted for accommodation;
3. By the intentional cancelation thereof by the holder;
4. By any other act which will discharge a simple contract for the payment of money;
5. When the principal debtor becomes the holder of the instrument at or after maturity in his own right.

Section 120. A person secondarily liable on the instrument is discharged:

1. By any act which discharges the instrument;
2. By the intentional cancelation of his signature by the holder;
3. By the discharge of a prior party;
4. By a valid tender of payment made by a prior party;
5. By a release of the principal debtor, unless the holder's right of recourse against the party secondarily liable is expressly reserved;
6. By any agreement binding upon the holder to extend the time of payment, or to postpone the holder's right to enforce the instrument, unless made with the assent of the party secondarily liable, or unless the right of recourse against such party is expressly reserved.

Section 121. Where the instrument is paid by a party secondarily liable thereon, it is not discharged; but the party so paying it is remitted to his former rights as regards all prior parties, and he may strike out his own and all subsequent indorsements, and again negotiate the instrument, except:

1. Where it is payable to the order of a third person, and has been paid by the drawer; and
2. Where it was made or accepted for accommodation, and has been paid by the party accommodated.

Section 122. The holder may expressly renounce his rights against any party to the instrument, before, at, or after its maturity. An absolute and unconditional renunciation of his rights against the principal debtor made at or after the maturity of the instrument discharges the instrument. But a renunciation does not affect the rights of a holder in due course without notice. A renunciation must be in writing, unless the instrument is delivered up to the person primarily liable thereon.

Section 123. A cancelation made unintentionally, or under a mistake or without the authority of the holder, is inoperative; but where an instrument or any signature thereon appears to have been canceled the burden of proof lies on the party who alleges that the cancelation was made unintentionally, or under a mistake or without authority.

Section 124. Where a negotiable instrument is materially altered without the assent of all parties liable thereon, it is avoided, except as against a party who has himself made, authorized, or assented to the alteration, and subsequent indorsers.

But when an instrument has been materially altered and is in the hands of a holder in due course, not a party to the alteration, he may enforce payment thereof according to its original tenor.

Section 125. Any alteration which changes:
1. The date;
2. The sum payable, either for principal or interest;
3. The time or place of payment;
4. The number or the relations of the parties;
5. The medium or currency in which payment is to be made;

Or which adds a place of payment where no place of payment is specified, or any other change or addition which alters the effect of the instrument in any respect, is a material alteration.

TITLE II. BILLS OF EXCHANGE

Article I. Form and Interpretation

Section 126. A bill of exchange is an unconditional order in writing addressed by one person to another, signed by the person giving it, requiring the person to whom it is addressed to pay on demand or at a fixed or determinable future time a sum certain in money to order or to bearer.

Section 127. A bill of itself does not operate as an assignment of the funds in the hands of the drawee available for the payment thereof, and the drawee is not liable on the bill unless and until he accepts the same.

Section 128. A bill may be addressed to two or more drawees jointly, whether they are partners or not; but not to two or more drawees in the alternative or in succession.

Section 129. An inland bill of exchange is a bill which is, or on its face purports to be, both drawn and payable within this state. Any other bill is a foreign bill. Unless the contrary appears on the face of the bill, the holder may treat it as an inland bill.

Section 130. Where in a bill drawer and drawee are the same person, or where the drawee is a fictitious person, or a person not having capacity to contract, the holder may treat the instrument, at his option, either as a bill of exchange or a promissory note.

Section 131. The drawer of a bill and any indorser may insert thereon the name of a person to whom the holder may resort in case of need, that is to say, in case the bill is dishonored by nonacceptance or nonpayment. Such person is called the referee in case of need. It is in the option of the holder to resort to the referee in case of need or not as he may see fit.

Article II. Acceptance

Section 132. The acceptance of a bill is the signification by the drawee of his assent to the order of the drawer. The acceptance must be in writing and signed by the drawee. It must not express that the drawee will perform his promise by any other means than the payment of money.

Section 133. The holder of a bill presenting the same for acceptance may require that the acceptance be written on the bill, and, if such request is refused, may treat the bill as dishonored.

Section 134. Where an acceptance is written on a paper other than the bill itself, it does not bind the acceptor except in favor of a person to whom it is shown and who, on the faith thereof, receives the bill for value.

Section 135. An unconditional promise in writing to accept a bill before it is drawn is deemed an actual acceptance in favor of every person who, upon the faith thereof, receives the bill for value.

Section 136. The drawee is allowed twenty-four hours after presentment, in which to decide whether or not he will accept the bill; but the acceptance, if given, dates as of the day of presentation.

Section 137. Where a drawee to whom a bill is delivered for acceptance destroys the same, or refuses within twenty-four hours after such delivery, or within such other period as the holder may allow, to return the bill accepted or nonaccepted to the holder, he will be deemed to have accepted the same.

Section 138. A bill may be accepted before it has been signed by the drawer, or while otherwise incomplete, or when it is overdue, or after it has been dishonored by a previous refusal to accept, or by nonpayment. But when a bill payable after sight is dishonored by nonacceptance and the drawee subsequently accepts it, the holder, in the absence of any different agreement is entitled to have the bill accepted as of the date of the first presentment.

Section 139. An acceptance is either general or qualified. A general acceptance assents without qualification to the order of the drawer. A qualified acceptance in express terms varies the effect of the bill as drawn.

Section 140. An acceptance to pay at a particular place is a general acceptance, unless it expressly states that the bill is to be paid there only and not elsewhere.

Section 141. An acceptance is qualified, which is:
1. Conditional, that is to say, which makes payment by the acceptor dependent on the fulfilment of a condition therein stated;
2. Partial, that is to say, an acceptance to pay part only of the amount for which the bill is drawn;
3. Local, that is to say, an acceptance to pay only at a particular place;
4. Qualified as to time;
5. The acceptance of some one or more of the drawees, but not of all.

Section 142. The holder may refuse to take a qualified acceptance, and if he does not obtain an unqualified acceptance, he may treat the bill as dishonored by nonacceptance. Where a qualified acceptance is taken, the drawer and indorsers are discharged from liability on the bill, unless they have expressly or impliedly authorized the holder to take a qualified acceptance, or subsequently assent thereto. When the drawer or an indorser receives notice of a qualified acceptance, he must, within a reasonable time, express his dissent to the holder, or he will be deemed to have assented thereto.

Article III. Presentment for Acceptance

Section 143. Presentment for acceptance must be made:
1. Where the bill is payable after sight, or in any other case, where presentment for acceptance is necessary in order to fix the maturity of the instrument; or
2. Where the bill expressly stipulates that it shall be presented for acceptance; or
3. Where the bill is drawn payable elsewhere than at the residence or place of business of the drawee.

In no other case is presentment for acceptance necessary in order to render any party to the bill liable.

Section 144. Except as herein otherwise provided, the holder of a bill which is required by the next preceding section to be presented for acceptance must either present it for acceptance or negotiate it within a reasonable time. If he fails to do so, the drawer and all indorsers are discharged.

Section 145. Presentment for acceptance must be made by or on behalf of the holder at a reasonable hour, on a business day, and before the bill is overdue, to the drawee or some person authorized to accept or refuse acceptance on his behalf; **and:**

1. Where a bill is addressed to two or more drawees who are not partners, presentment must be made to them all, unless one has authority to accept or refuse acceptance for all, in which case presentment may be made to him only;

2. Where the drawee is dead, presentment may be made to his personal representative;

3. Where the drawee has been adjudged a bankrupt or an insolvent or has made an assignment for the benefit of creditors, presentment may be made to him or to his trustee or assignee.

Section 146. A bill may be presented for acceptance on any day on which negotiable instruments may be presented for payment under the provisions of sections 72 and 85 of this act. When Saturday is not otherwise a holiday, presentment for acceptance may be made before twelve o'clock, noon, on that day.

Section 147. Where the holder of a bill drawn payable elsewhere than at the place of business or the residence of the drawee has not time with the exercise of reasonable diligence to present the bill for acceptance before presenting it for payment on the day that it falls due, the delay caused by presenting the bill for acceptance before presenting it for payment is excused, and does not discharge the drawers and indorsers.

Section 148. Presentment for acceptance is excused, and a bill may be treated as dishonored by nonacceptance, in either of the following cases:

1. Where the drawee is dead, or has absconded, or is a fictitious person or a person not having capacity to contract by bill.

2. Where, after the exercise of reasonable diligence, presentment canot be made.

3. Where, although presentment has been irregular, acceptance has been refused on some other ground.

Section 149. A bill is dishonored by nonacceptance:

1. When it is duly presented for acceptance, and such an acceptance as is prescribed by this act is refused or cannot be obtained; or

2. When presentment for acceptance is excused, and the bill is not accepted.

Section 150. Where a bill is duly presented for acceptance and is not accepted within the prescribed time, the person presenting it must treat the bill as dishonored by nonacceptance or he loses the right of recourse against the drawer and indorsers.

Section 151. When a bill is dishonored by nonacceptance, an immediate right of recourse against the drawers and indorsers accrues to the holder and no presentment for payment is necessary.

Article IV. Protest

Section 152. Where a foreign bill, appearing on its face to be such is dishonored by nonacceptance, it must be duly protested for nonacceptance, and where such a bill which has not previously been dishonored by nonacceptance is dishonored by nonpayment, it must be duly protested for nonpayment. If it is not so protested, the drawer and indorsers are discharged. Where a bill does not appear on its face to be a foreign bill, protest thereof in case of dishonor is unnecessary.

Section 153. The protest must be annexed to the bill, or must contain a copy thereof, and must be under the hand and seal of the notary making it, and must specify:

1. The time and place of presentment;
2. The fact that presentment was made and the manner thereof;
3. The cause or reason for protesting the bill;
4. The demand made and the answer given, if any, or the fact that the drawee or acceptor could not be found.

Section 154. Protest may be made by:

1. A notary public; or
2. By any respectable resident of the place where the bill is dishonored, in the presence of two or more credible witnesses.

Section 155. When a bill is protested, such protest must be made on the day of its dishonor, unless delay is excused as herein provided. When a bill has been duly noted, the protest may be subsequently extended as of the date of the noting.

Section 156. A bill must be protested at the place where it is dishonored, except that when a bill drawn payable at the place of business or residence of some person other than the drawee, has been dishonored by nonacceptance, it must be protested for nonpayment at the place where it is expressed to be payable, and no further presentment for payment to, or demand on, the drawee is necessary.

Section 157. A bill which has been protested for nonacceptance may be subsequently protested for nonpayment.

Section 158. Where the acceptor has been adjudged a bankrupt or an insolvent or has made an assignment for the benefit of creditors, before the bill matures, the holder may cause the bill to be protested for better security against the drawer and indorsers.

Section 159. Protest is dispensed with by any circumstances which would dispense with notice of dishonor. Delay in noting or protesting is excused when delay is caused by circumstances beyond the control of the holder and not imputable to his default, misconduct, or negligence. When the cause of delay ceases to operate, the bill must be noted or protested with reasonable diligence.

Section 160. When a bill is lost or destroyed or is wrongly detained from the person entitled to hold it, protest may be made on a copy or written particulars thereof.

Article V. Acceptance for Honor

Section 161. Where a bill of exchange has been protested for dishonor by nonacceptance or protested for better security and is not overdue, any person not being a party already liable thereon, may, with the consent of the holder, intervene and accept the bill supra protest for the honor of any party liable thereon or for the honor of the person for whose account the bill is drawn. The acceptance for honor may be for part only of the sum for which the bill is drawn; and where there has been an acceptance for honor for one party, there may be a further acceptance by a different person for the honor of another party.

Section 162. An acceptance for honor supra protest must be in writing and indicate that it is an acceptance for honor, and must be signed by the acceptor for honor.

Section 163. Where an acceptance for honor does not expressly state for whose honor it is made, it is deemed to be an acceptance for the honor of the drawer.

Section 164. The acceptor for honor is liable to the holder and to all parties to the bill subsequent to the party for whose honor he has accepted.

Section 165. The acceptor for honor by such acceptance engages that he will on due presentment pay the bill according to the terms of his acceptance, provided it shall not have been paid by the drawee, and provided also, that it shall have been duly presented for payment and protested for nonpayment and notice of dishonor given him.

Section 166. Where a bill payable after sight is accepted for honor, its maturity is calculated from the date of the noting for nonacceptance and not from the date of the acceptance for honor.

Section 167. Where a dishonored bill has been accepted for honor supra protest or contains a reference in case of need, it must be protested for nonpayment before it is presented for payment to the acceptor for honor or referee in case of need.

Section 168. Presentment for payment to the acceptor for honor must be made as follows:

1. If it is to be presented in the place where the protest for nonpayment was made, it must be presented not later than the day following its maturity;

2. If it is to be presented in some other place than the place where it was protested, then it must be forwarded within the time specified in section 104.

Section 169. The provisions of section 81 apply where there is delay in making presentment to the acceptor for honor or referee in case of need.

Section 170. When the bill is dishonored by the acceptor for honor it must be protested for nonpayment by him.

Article VI. Payment for Honor

Section 171. Where a bill has been protested for nonpayment, any person may intervene and pay it supra protest for the honor of any person liable thereon or for the honor of the person for whose account it was drawn.

Section 172. The payment for honor supra protest in order to operate as such and not as a mere voluntary payment must be attested by a notarial act of honor which may be appended to the protest or form an extension to it.

Section 173. The notarial act of honor must be founded on a declaration made by the payer for honor or by his agent in that behalf declaring his intention to pay the bill for honor and for whose honor he pays.

Section 174. Where two or more persons offer to pay a bill for the honor of different parties, the person whose payment will discharge most parties to the bill is to be given the preference.

Section 175. Where a bill has been paid for honor, all parties subsequent to the party for whose honor it is paid are discharged, but the payer for honor is subrogated for, and succeeds to, both the rights and duties of the holder as regards the party for whose honor he pays and all parties liable to the latter.

Section 176. Where the holder of a bill refuses to receive payment supra protest, he loses his right of recourse against any party who would have been discharged by such payment.

Section 177. The payer for honor, on paying to the holder the amount of the bill and the notarial expenses incidental to its dishonor, is entitled to receive both the bill itself and the protest.

Article VII. Bills in a Set

Section 178. Where a bill is drawn in a set, each part of the set being numbered and containing a reference to the other parts, the whole of the parts constitutes one bill.

Section 179. Where two or more parts of a set are negotiated to different holders in due course, the holder whose title first accrues is as between such holders the true owner of the bill. But nothing in this section affects the rights of a person who in due course accepts or pays the part first presented to him.

Section 180. Where the holder of a set indorses two or more parts to different persons he is liable on every such part, and every indorser subsequent to him is liable on the part he has himself indorsed, as if such parts were separate bills.

Section 181. The acceptance may be written on any part and it must be written on one part only. If the drawee accepts more than one part, and such accepted parts are negotiated to different holders in due course, he is liable on every such part as if it were a separate bill.

Section 182. When the acceptor of a bill drawn in a set pays it without requiring the part bearing his acceptance to be delivered up to him, and that part at maturity is outstanding in the hands of a holder in due course, he is liable to the holder thereon.

Section 183. Except as herein otherwise provided where any one part of a bill drawn in a set is discharged by payment or otherwise the whole bill is discharged.

TITLE III. PROMISSORY NOTES AND CHECKS

Article I

Section 184. A negotiable promissory note within the meaning of this act is an unconditional promise in writing made by one person to another signed by the maker engaging to pay on demand, or at a fixed or determinable future time, a sum certain in money to order or to bearer. Where a note is drawn to the maker's own order, it is not complete until indorsed by him.

Section 185. A check is a bill of exchange drawn on a bank payable on demand. Except as herein otherwise provided, the provisions of this act applicable to a bill of exchange payable on demand apply to a check.

Section 186. A check must be presented for payment within a reasonable time after its issue or the drawer will be discharged from liability thereon to the extent of the loss caused by the delay.

Section 187. Where a check is certified by the bank on which it is drawn, the certification is equivalent to an acceptance.

Section 188. Where the holder of a check procures it to be accepted or certified the drawer and all indorsers are discharged from liability thereon.

Section 189. A check of itself does not operate as an assignment of any part of the funds to the credit of the drawer with the bank, and the bank is not liable to the holder, unless and until it accepts or certifies the check.

TITLE IV. GENERAL PROVISIONS

Article I

Section 190. This act may be cited as the Uniform Negotiable Instruments Act.

Section 191. In this act, unless the context otherwise requires—

"Acceptance" means an acceptance completed by delivery or notification.

"Action" includes counterclaim and set-off.

"Bank" includes any person or association of persons carrying on the business of banking, whether incorporated or not.

"Bearer" means the person in possession of a bill or note which is payable to bearer.

"Bill" means bill of exchange, and "note" means negotiable promissory note.

"Delivery" means transfer of possession, actual or constructive, from one person to another.

"Holders" means the payee or indorsee of a bill or note, who is in possession of it, or the bearer thereof.

"Indorsement" means an indorsement completed by delivery.

"Instrument" means negotiable instrument.

"Issue" means the first delivery of the instrument, complete in form, to a person who takes it as a holder.

"Person" includes a body of persons, whether incorporated or not.

"Value" means valuable consideration.

"Written" includes printed, and "writing" includes print.

Section 192. The person "primarily" liable on an instrument is the person who by the terms of the instrument is absolutely required to pay the same. All other parties are "secondarily" liable.

Section 193. In determining what is a "reasonable time" or an "unreasonable time," regard is to be had to the nature of the instrument, the usage of trade or business (if any) with respect to such instruments, and the facts of the particular case.

Section 194. Where the day, or the last day, for doing any act herein required or permitted to be done falls on Sunday or on a holiday, the act may be done on the next succeeding secular or business day.

Section 195. The provisions of this act do not apply to negotiable instruments made and delivered prior to the taking effect hereof.

Section 196. In any case not provided for in this act the rules of the Law Merchant shall govern.

Section 197. Of the laws enumerated in the schedules hereto annexed that portion specified in the last column is repealed.

Section 198. This chapter shall take effect on ....

UNIFORM PARTNERSHIP ACT

PART I

PRELIMINARY PROVISIONS

Section 1. Name of Act. This act may be cited as Uniform Partnership Act.

Section 2. Definition of Terms. In this Act, "Court" includes every court and judge having jurisdiction in the case.

"Business" includes every trade, occupation, or profession.

"Person" includes individuals, partnerships, corporations, and other associations.

"Bankrupt" includes bankrupt under the Federal Bankruptcy Act or insolvent under any state insolvent act.

"Conveyance" includes every assignment, lease, mortgage, or encumbrance.

"Real property" includes land and any interest or estate in land.

Section 3. Interpretation of Knowledge and Notice. (1) A person has "knowl-[illegible]" of a fact within the meaning of this act not only when he has actual knowledge [illegible] but also when he has knowledge of such other facts as in the circumstances sho[illegible]d faith.

(2) A person has "notice" of a fact within the meaning of this act when the person who claims the benefit of the notice

(*a*) States the fact to such person, or

(*b*) Delivers through the mail, or by other means of communication, a written statement of the fact to such person or to a proper person at his place of business or residence.

Section 4. Rules of Construction. (1) The rule that statutes in derogation of the common law are to be strictly construed shall have no application to this act.

(2) The law of estoppel shall apply under this act.

(3) The law of agency shall apply under this act.

(4) This act shall be so interpreted and construed as to effect its general purpose to make uniform the law of those states which enact it.

(5) This act shall not be construed so as to impair the obligations of any contract existing when the act goes into effect, nor to effect any action or proceedings begun or right accrued before this act takes effect.

Section 5. Rules for Cases Not Provided for in This Act. In any case not provided for in this act the rules of law and equity, including the law merchant, shall govern.

PART II

NATURE OF A PARTNERSHIP

Section 6. Partnership Defined. (1) A partnership is an association of two or more persons to carry on as co-owners a business for profit.

(2) But any association formed under any other statute of this state, or any statute adopted by authority, other than the authority of this state, is not a partnership under this act, unless such association would have been a partnership in this

state prior to the adoption of this act; but this act shall apply to limited partnerships except in so far as the statutes relating to such partnerships are inconsistent herewith.

Section 7. Rules for Determining the Existence of a Partnership. In determining whether a partnership exists, these rules shall apply:

(1) Except as provided by section 16, persons who are not partners as to each other are not partners as to third persons.

(2) Joint tenancy, tenancy in common, tenancy by the entireties, joint property, common property, or part ownership does not of itself establish a partnership, whether such co-owners do or do not share any profits made by the use of the property.

(3) The sharing of gross returns does not of itself establish a partnership, whether or not the persons sharing them have a joint or common right or interest in any property from which the returns are derived.

(4) The receipt by a person of a share of the profits of a business is prima facie evidence that he is a partner in the business, but no such inference shall be drawn if such profits were received in payment:

(*a*) As a debt by instalments or otherwise,

(*b*) As wages of an employee or rent to a landlord.

(*c*) As an annuity to a widow or representative of a deceased partner,

(*d*) As interest on a loan, though the amount of payment vary with the profits of the business,

(*e*) As the consideration for the sale of the good-will of a business or other property by instalments or otherwise.

Section 8. Partnership Property. (1) All property originally brought into the partnership stock or subsequently acquired by purchase or otherwise, on ac[illegible] of the partnership is partnership property.

(2) Unless the contrary intention appears, property acquired with pa[illegible] funds is partnership property.

(3) Any estate in real property may be acquired in the partnership name. [illegible]e so acquired can be conveyed only in the partnership name.

(4) A conveyance to a partnership in the partnership name, though without words of inheritance, passes the entire estate of the grantor unless a contrary intent appears.

PART III

RELATIONS OF PARTNERS TO PERSONS DEALING WITH THE PARTNERSHIP

Section 9. Partner Agent of Partnership as to Partnership Business. (1) Every partner is an agent of the partnership for the purpose of its business, and the act of every partner, including the execution in the partnership name of any instrument, for apparently carrying on in the usual way the business of the partnership of which he is a member binds the partnership, unless the partner so acting has in fact no authority to act for the partnership in the particular matter, and the person with whom he is dealing has knowledge of the fact that he has no such authority.

(2) An act of a partner which is not apparently for the carrying on of the business of the partnership in the usual way does not bind the partnership unless authorized by the other partners.

(3) Unless authorized by the other partners or unless they have abandoned the business, one or more but less than all the partners have no authority to:

(*a*) Assign the partnership property in trust for creditors or on the assignee's promise to pay the debts of the partnership.

(*b*) Dispose of the good-will of the business.

(*c*) Do any other act which would make it impossible to carry on the ordinary business of a partnership.

(*d*) Confess a judgment.

(*e*) Submit a partnership claim or liability to arbitration or reference.

(4) No act of a partner in contravention of a restriction on authority shall bind the partnership to persons having knowledge of the restriction.

Section 10. Conveyance of Real Property of the Partnership. (1) Where title to real property is in the partnership name, any partner may convey title to such property by a conveyance executed in the partnership name; but the partnership may recover such property unless the partner's act binds the partnership under the provisions of paragraph (1) of section 9, or unless such property has been conveyed by the grantee or a person claiming through such grantee to a holder for value without knowledge that the partner, in making the conveyance, has exceeded his authority.

(2) Where title to real property is in the name of the partnership, a conveyance executed by a partner, in his own name, passes the equitable interest of the partnership, provided the act is one within the authority of the partner under the provisions of paragraph (1) of section 9.

(3) Where title to real property is in the name of one or more but not all the partners, and the record does not disclose the right of the partnership, the partners in whose name the title stands may convey title to such property, but the partnership may recover such property if the partners' act does not bind the partnership under the provisions of paragraph (1) of section 9, unless the purchaser or his assignee, is a holder for value, without knowledge.

(4) Where the title to real property is in the name of one or more or all the partners, or in a third person in trust for the partnership, a conveyance executed by a partner in the partnership name, or in his own name, passes the equitable interest of the partnership, provided the act is one within the authority of the partner under the provisions of paragraph (1) of section 9.

(5) Where the title to real property is in the names of all the partners a conveyance executed by all the partners passes all their rights in such property.

Section 11. Partnership Bound by Admission of Partner. An admission or representation made by any partner concerning partnership affairs within the scope of his authority as conferred by this act is evidence against the partnership.

Section 12. Partnership Charged with Knowledge of or Notice to Partner. Notice to any partner of any matter relating to partnership affairs, and the knowledge of the partner acting in the particular matter, acquired while a partner or then present to his mind, and the knowledge of any other partner who reasonably could and should have communicated it to the acting partner, operate as notice to or knowledge of the partnership, except in the case of a fraud on the partnership committed by or with the consent of that partner.

Section 13. Partnership Bound by Partner's Wrongful Act. Where, by any wrongful act or omission of any partner acting in the ordinary course of the business of the partnership, or with the authority of his copartners, loss or injury is caused to any person, not being a partner in the partnership, or any penalty is incurred, the partnership is liable therefor to the same extent as the partner so acting or omitting to act.

Section 14. Partnership Bound by Partner's Breach of Trust. The partnership is bound to make good the loss:

(*a*) Where one partner acting within the scope of his apparent authority receives money or property of a third person and misapplies it; and

(*b*) Where the partnership in the course of its business receives money or property of a third person and the money or property so received is misapplied by any partner while it is in the custody of the partnership.

Section 15. Nature of Partner's Liability. All partners are liable.

(*a*) Jointly and severally for everything chargeable to the partnership under sections 13 and 14.

(*b*) Jointly for all other debts and obligations of the partnership; but any partner may enter into a separate obligation to perform a partnership contract.

Section 16. Partner by Estoppel. (1) When a person, by words spoken or written or by conduct, represents himself, or consents to another representing him to any one, as a partner in an existing partnership or with one or more persons not actual partners, he is liable to any such person to whom such representation has been made, who has on the faith of such representation, given credit to the actual or apparent partnership, and if he has made such representation or consented to its being made in a public manner he is liable to such person, whether the representation has or has not been made or communicated to such person so giving credit by or with the knowledge of the apparent partner making the representation or consenting to its being made.

(*a*) When a partnership liability results, he is liable as though he were an actual member of the partnership.

(*b*) When no partnership liability results, he is liable jointly with the other persons, if any, so consenting to the contract or representation as to incur liability, otherwise separately.

(2) When a person has been thus represented to be a partner in an existing partnership, or with one or more persons not actual partners, he is an agent of the persons consenting to such representation to bind them to the same extent and in the same manner as though he were a partner in fact, with respect to persons who rely upon the representation. Where all the members of the existing partnership consent to the representation, a partnership act or obligation results; but in all other cases it is the joint act or obligation of the person acting and the persons consenting to the representation.

Section 17. Liability of Incoming Partner. A person admitted as a partner into an existing partnership is liable for all the obligations of the partnership arising before his admission as though he had been a partner when such obligations were incurred, except that this liability shall be satisfied only out of partnership property.

PART IV

RELATIONS OF PARTNERS TO ONE ANOTHER

Section 18. Rules Determining Rights and Duties of Partners. The rights and duties of the partners in relation to the partnership shall be determined, subject to any agreement between them, by the following rules:

(*a*) Each partner shall be repaid his contributions, whether by way of capital or advances to the partnership property and share equally in the profits and surplus remaining after all liabilities, including those to partners, are satisfied; and must contribute towards the losses, whether of capital or otherwise, sustained by the partnership according to his share in the profits.

(*b*) The partnership must indemnify every partner in respect of payments made and personal liabilities reasonably incurred by him in the ordinary and proper conduct of its business, or for the preservation of its business or property.

(*c*) A partner, who in aid of the partnership makes any payment or advance beyond the amount of capital which he agreed to contribute, shall be paid interest from the date of the payment or advance.

(*d*) A partner shall receive interest on the capital contributed by him only from the date when repayment should be made.

(*e*) All partners have equal rights in the management and conduct of the partnership business.

(*f*) No partner is entitled to remuneration for acting in the partnership business, except that a surviving partner is entitled to reasonable compensation for his services in winding up the partnership affairs.

(*g*) No person can become a member of a partnership without the consent of all the partners.

(*h*) Any difference arising as to ordinary matters connected with the partnership business may be decided by a majority of the partners; but no act in contravention of any agreement between the partners may be done rightfully without the consent of all the partners.

Section 19. Partnership Books. The partnership books shall be kept, subject to any agreement between the partners, at the principal place of business of the partnership, and every partner shall at all times have access to and may inspect and copy any of them.

Section 20. Duty of Partners to Render Information. Partners shall render on demand true and full information of all things affecting the partnership to any partner or the legal representative of any deceased partner or partner under legal disability.

Section 21. Partner Accountable as a Fiduciary. (1) Every partner must account to the partnership for any benefit, and hold as trustee for it any profits derived by him without the consent of the other partners from any transaction connected with the formation, conduct, or liquidation of the partnership or from any use by him of its property.

(2) This section applies also to the representatives of a deceased partner engaged in the liquidation of the affairs of the partnership as the personal representatives of the last surviving partner.

Section 22. Right to an Account. Any partner shall have the right to a formal account as to partnership affairs:

(*a*) If he is wrongfully excluded from the partnership business or possession of its property by his copartners.

(*b*) If the right exists under the terms of any agreement,

(*c*) As provided by section 21,

(*d*) Whenever other circumstances render it just and reasonable.

Section 23. Continuation of Partnership Beyond Fixed Term. (1) When a partnership for a fixed term or particular undertaking is continued after the termination of such term or particular undertaking without any express agreement, the rights and duties of the partners remain the same as they were at such termination, so far as is consistent with a partnership at will.

(2) A continuation of the business by the partners or such of them as habitually acted therein during the term, without any settlement or liquidation of the partnership affairs, is prima facie evidence of a continuation of the partnership.

PART V

PROPERTY RIGHTS OF A PARTNER

Section 24. Extent of Property Rights of a Partner. The property rights of a partner are (1) his rights in specific partnership property, (2) his interest in the partnership, and (3) his right to participate in the management.

Section 25. Nature of a Partner's Right in Specific Partnership Property. (1) A partner is co-owner with his partners of specific partnership property holding as a tenant in partnership.

(2) The incidents of this tenancy are such that:

(*a*) A partner, subject to the provisions of this act and to any agreement between the partners, has an equal right with his partners to possess specific partnership property for partnership purposes; but he has no right to possess such property for any other purpose without the consent of his partners.

(*b*) A partner's right in specific partnership property is not assignable except in connection with the assignment of the rights of all partners in the same property.

(*c*) A partner's right in specific partnership property is not subject to attachment or execution, except on a claim against the partnership. When partnership property is attached for a partnership debt the partners, or any of them, or the representatives of a deceased partner, can not claim any right under the homestead or exemption laws.

(*d*) On the death of a partner his right in specific partnership property vests in the surviving partner or partners, except where the deceased was the last surviving partner, when his right in such property vests in his legal representative. Such surviving partner or partners, or the legal representative of the last surviving partner, has no right to possess the partnership property for any but a partnership purpose.

(*e*) A partner's right in specific partnership property is not subject to dower, courtesy, or allowances to widows, heirs, or next of kin.

Section 26. Nature of Partner's Interest in the Partnership. A partner's interest in the partnership is his share of the profits and surplus, and the same is personal property.

Section 27. Assignment of Partner's Interest. (1) A conveyance by a partner of his interest in the partnership does not of itself dissolve the partnership, nor, as against the other partners in the absence of agreement, entitle the assignee, during the continuance of the partnership, to interfere in the management or administration of the partnership business or affairs, or to require any information or account of partnership transactions, or to inspect the partnership books; but it merely entitles the assignee to receive in accordance with his contract the profits to which the assigning partner would otherwise be entitled.

(2) In case of a dissolution of the partnership, the assignee is entitled to receive his assignor's interest and may require an account from the date only of the last account agreed to by all the partners.

Section 28. Partner's Interest Subject to Charging Order. (1) On due application to a competent court by any judgment creditor of a partner, the court which entered the judgment, order, or decree, or any other court, may charge the interest of the debtor partner with payment of the unsatisfied amount of such judgment debt with interest thereon; and may then or later appoint a receiver of his share of the profits, and of any other money due or to fall due to him in respect of the partnership, and make all other orders, directions, accounts, and inquiries which the debtor partner might have made, or which the circumstances of the case may require.

(2) The interest charged may be redeemed at any time before foreclosure, or in case of a sale being directed by the court may be purchased without thereby causing a dissolution:

(*a*) With separate property, by any one or more of the partners, or

(*b*) With partnership property, by any one or more of the partners with the consent of all the partners whose interests are not so charged or sold.

(3) Nothing in this act shall be held to deprive a partner of his right, if any, under the exemption laws, as regards his interest in the partnership.

PART VI

DISSOLUTION AND WINDING UP

Section 29. Dissolution Defined. The dissolution of a partnership is the change in the relation of the partners caused by any partner ceasing to be associated in the carrying on as distinguished from the winding up of the business.

Section 30. Partnership Not Terminated by Dissolution. On dissolution the partnership is not terminated, but continues until the winding up of partnership affairs is complete.

Section 31. Causes of Dissolution. Dissolution is caused:

(1) Without violation of the agreement between the partners,

(*a*) By the termination of the definite term or particular undertaking specified in the agreement,

(*b*) By the express will of any partner when no definite term or particular undertaking is specified.

(*c*) By the express will of all the partners who have not assigned their interests or suffered them to be charged for their separate debts, either before or after the termination of any specified term or particular undertaking, (*d*) By the expulsion of any partner from the business bona fide in accordance with such a power conferred by the agreement between the partners;

(2) In contravention of the agreement between the partners, where the circumstances do not permit a dissolution under any other provision of this section, by the express will of any partner at any time;

(3) By any event which makes it unlawful for the business of the partnership to be carried on or for the members to carry it on in partnership;

(4) By the death of any partner;

(5) By the bankruptcy of any partner or the partnership;

(6) By decree of court under section 32.

Section 32. Dissolution by Decree of Court. (1) On application by or for a partner the court shall decree a dissolution whenever:

(*a*) A partner has been declared a lunatic in any judicial proceeding or is shown to be of unsound mind,

(*b*) A partner becomes in any other way incapable of performing his part of the partnership contract,

(*c*) A partner has been guilty of such conduct as tends to affect prejudicially the carrying on of the business.

(*d*) A partner wilfully or persistently commits a breach of the partnership agreement, or otherwise so conducts himself in matters relating to the partnership business that it is not reasonably practicable to carry on the business in partnership with him.

(*e*) The business of the partnership can only be carried on at a loss.

(*f*) Other circumstances render a dissolution equitable.

(2) On the application of the purchaser of a partner's interest under sections 27 or 28:

(*a*) After the termination of the specified term or particular undertaking,

(*b*) At any time if the partnership was a partnership at will when the interest was assigned or when the charging order was issued.

Section 33. General Effect of Dissolution on Authority of Partner. Except so far as may be necessary to wind up partnership affairs or to complete transactions begun but not then finished, dissolution terminates all authority of any partner to act for the partnership,

(1) With respect to the partners,

(*a*) When the dissolution is not by the act, bankruptcy or death of a partner; or

(*b*) When the dissolution is by such act, bankruptcy or death of a partner, in cases where section 34 so requires.

(2) With respect to persons not partners, as declared in section 35.

Section 34. Right of Partner to Contribution from Copartners after Dissolution. Where the dissolution is caused by the act, death, or bankruptcy of a partner, each partner is liable to his copartners for his share of any liability created by any partner acting for the partnership as if the partnership had not been dissolved unless

(*a*) The dissolution being by act of any partner, the partner acting for the partnership had knowledge of the dissolution, or

(*b*) The dissolution being by the death or bankruptcy of a partner, the partner acting for the partnership had knowledge or notice of the death or bankruptcy.

Section 35. Power of Partner to Bind Partnership to Third Persons after Dissolution. (1) After dissolution a partner can bind the partnership except as provided in paragraph (3).

(*a*) By any act appropriate for winding up partnership affairs or completing transactions unfinished at dissolution;

(*b*) By any transaction which would bind the partnership if dissolution had not taken place, provided the other party to the transaction

(I) Had extended credit to the partnership prior to dissolution and had no knowledge or notice of the dissolution; or

(II) Though he had not so extended credit, had nevertheless known of the partnership prior to dissolution, and, having no knowledge or notice of dissolution, the fact of dissolution had not been advertised in a newspaper of general circulation in the place (or in each place if more than one) at which the partnership business was regularly carried on, and in the legal periodical, if any, designated by rule of court in such place or places for the publication of legal notices.

(2) The liability of a partner under paragraph (1*b*) shall be satisfied out of partnership assets alone when such partner had been prior to dissolution

(*a*) Unknown as a partner to the person with whom the contract is made; and

(*b*) So far unknown and inactive in partnership affairs that the business reputation of the partnership could not be said to have been in any degree due to his connection with it.

(3) The partnership is in no case bound by any act of a partner after dissolution

(*a*) Where the partnership is dissolved because it is unlawful to carry on the business, unless the act is appropriate for winding up partnership affairs; or

(*b*) Where the partner has become bankrupt; or

(*c*) Where the partner has no authority to wind up partnership affairs; except by a transaction with one who

(I) Had extended credit to the partnership prior to dissolution and had no knowledge or notice of his want of authority; or

(II) Had not extended credit to the partnership prior to dissolution, and, having no knowledge or notice of his want of authority, the fact of his want of authority has not been advertised in the manner provided for advertising the fact of dissolution in paragraph (1*b*II).

(4) Nothing in this section shall affect the liability under section 16 of any person who after dissolution represents himself or consents to another representing him as a partner in a partnership engaged in carrying on business.

Section 36. Effect of Dissolution on Partner's Existing Liability. (1) The dissolution of the partnership does not of itself discharge the existing liability of any partner.

(2) A partner is discharged from any existing liability upon dissolution of the partnership by an agreement to that effect between himself, the partnership creditor and the person or partnership continuing the business; and such agreement may be inferred from the course of dealing between the creditor having knowledge of the dissolution and the person or partnership continuing the business.

(3) Where a person agrees to assume the existing obligations of a dissolved partnership, the partners whose obligations have been assumed shall be discharged from any liability to any creditor of the partnership who, knowing of the agreement, consents to a material alteration in the nature or time of payment of such obligations.

(4) The individual property of a deceased partner shall be liable for all obligations of the partnership incurred while he was a partner but subject to the prior payment of his separate debts.

Section 37. Right to Wind Up. Unless otherwise agreed the partners who have not wrongfully dissolved the partnership or the legal representative of the last surviving partner, not bankrupt, has the right to wind up the partnership affairs; provided, however, that any partner, his legal representative or his assignee, upon cause shown, may obtain winding up by the court.

Section 38. Rights of Partners to Application of Partnership Property. (1) When dissolution is caused in any way, except in contravention of the partnership agreement, each partner, as against his copartners and all persons claiming through them in respect of their interests in the partnership, unless otherwise agreed, may have the partnership property applied to discharge its liabilities, and the surplus applied to pay in cash the net amount owing to the respective partners. But if dissolution is caused by expulsion of a partner, bona fide under the partnership agreement and if the expelled partner is discharged from all partnership liabilities, either by payment or agreement under section 36 (2), he shall receive in cash only the net amount due him from the partnership.

(2) When dissolution is caused in contravention of the partnership agreement the rights of the partners shall be as follows:

(*a*) Each partner who has not caused dissolution wrongfully shall have,

I. All the rights specified in paragraph (1) of this section, and

II. The right, as against each partner who has caused the dissolution wrongfully, to damages for breach of the agreement.

(*b*) The partners who have not caused the dissolution wrongfully, if they all desire to continue the business in the same name, either by themselves or jointly with others, may do so, during the agreed term for the partnership and for that purpose may possess the partnership property, provided they secure the payment by bond approved by the court, or pay to any partner who has caused the dissolution wrongfully, the value of his interest in the partnership at the dissolution, less any damages recoverable under clause (2*a*II) of this section, and in like manner indemnify him against all present or future partnership liabilities.

(*c*) A partner who has caused the dissolution wrongfully shall have:

I. If the business is not continued under the provisions of paragraph (2*b*) all the rights of a partner under paragraph (1), subject to clause (2*a*II), of this section,

II. If the business is continued under paragraph (2*b*) of this section the right as against his copartners and all claiming through them in respect of their interests in the partnership, to have the value of his interest in the partnership, less any damages caused to his copartners by the dissolution, ascertained and paid to him in cash, or the payment secured by bond approved by the court, and to be released from all existing liabilities of the partnership; but in ascertaining the value of the partner's interest the value of the good-will of the business shall not be considered.

Section 39. Rights Where Partnership Is Dissolved for Fraud or Misrepresentation. Where a partnership contract is rescinded on the ground of the fraud or misrepresentation of one of the parties thereto, the party entitled to rescind is, without prejudice to any other right, entitled,

(*a*) To a lien on, or right of retention of, the surplus of the partnership property after satisfying the partnership liabilities to third persons for any sum of money paid by him for the purchase of an interest in the partnership and for any capital or advances contributed by him; and

(*b*) To stand, after all liabilities to third persons have been satisfied, in the place of the creditors of the partnership for any payments made by him in respect of the partnership liabilities; and

(*c*) To be indemnified by the person guilty of the fraud or making the representation against all debts and liabilities of the partnership.

Section 40. Rules for Distribution. In settling accounts between the partners after dissolution, the following rules shall be observed, subject to any agreement to the contrary:

(*a*) The assets of the partnership are:

I. The partnership property,

II. The contributions of the partners necessary for the payment of all the liabilities specified in clause (*b*) of this paragraph.

(*b*) The liabilities of the partnership shall rank in order of payment, as follows:

I. Those owing to creditors other than partners,

II. Those owing to partners other than for capital and profits,

III. Those owing to partners in respect of capital,

IV. Those owing to partners in respect of profits.

(*c*) The assets shall be applied in the order of their declaration in clause (*a*) of this paragraph to the satisfaction of the liabilities.

(*d*) The partners shall contribute, as provided by section 18 (*a*) the amount necessary to satisfy the liabilities; but if any, but not all, of the partners are insolvent, or, not being subject to process, refuse to contribute, the other partners shall contribute their share of the liabilities, and, in the relative proportions in which they share the profits, the additional amount necessary to pay the liabilities.

(*e*) An assignee for the benefit of creditors or any person appointed by the court shall have the right to enforce the contributions specified in clause (*d*) of this paragraph.

(*f*) Any partner or his legal representative shall have the right to enforce the contributions specified in clause (*d*) of this paragraph, to the extent of the amount which he has paid in excess of his share of the liability.

(*g*) The individual property of a deceased partner shall be liable for the contributions specified in clause (*d*) of this paragraph.

(*h*) When partnership property and the individual properties of the partners are in the possession of a court for distribution, partnership creditors shall have priority on partnership property and separate creditors on individual property, saving the rights of lien or secured creditors as heretofore.

(*i*) Where a partner has become bankrupt or his estate is insolvent the claims against his separate property shall rank in the following order:

I. Those owing to separate creditors,

II. Those owing to partnership creditors,

III. Those owing to partners by way of contribution.

Section 41. Liability of Persons Continuing the Business in Certain Cases. (1) When any new partner is admitted into an existing partnership, or when any partner retires and assigns (or the representative of the deceased partner assigns) his rights in partnership property to two or more of the partners, or to one or more of the partners, and one or more third persons, if the business is continued without liquidation of the partnership affairs, creditors of the first or dissolved partnership are also creditors of the partnership so continuing the business.

(2) When all but one partner retire and assign (or the representative of a deceased partner assigns) their rights in partnership property to the remaining partner, who continues the business without liquidation of partnership affairs, either alone or with others, creditors of the dissolved partnership are also creditors of the person or partnership so continuing the business.

(3) When any partner retires or dies and the business of the dissolved partnership is continued as set forth in paragraphs (1) and (2) of this section, with the consent of the retired partners or the representative of the deceased partner, but without any assignment of his right in partnership property, rights of creditors of the dissolved partnership and of the creditors of the person or partnership continuing the business shall be as if such assignment had been made.

(4) When all the partners or their representatives assign their rights in partnership property to one or more third persons who promise to pay the debts and who continue the business of the dissolved partnership, creditors of the dissolved partnership are also creditors of the person or partnership continuing the business.

(5) When any partner wrongfully causes a dissolution and the remaining partners continue the business under the provisions of section 38 (2*b*), either alone or with others, and without liquidation of the partnership affairs, creditors of the dissolved partnership are also creditors of the person or partnership continuing the business.

(6) When a partner is expelled and the remaining partners continue the business either alone or with others, without liquidation of the partnership affairs, creditors of the dissolved partnership are also creditors of the person or partnership continuing the business.

(7) The liability of a third person becoming a partner in the partnership continuing the business, under this section, to the creditors of the dissolved partnership shall be satisfied out of partnership property only.

(8) When the business of a partnership after dissolution is continued under any conditions set forth in this section the creditors of the dissolved partnership, as against the separate creditors of the retiring or deceased partner or the representative of the deceased partner, have a prior right to any claim of the retired partner or the representative of the deceased partner against the person or partnership continuing the business, on account of the retired or deceased partner's interest in the dissolved partnership or on account of any consideration promised for such interest or for his right in partnership property.

(9) Nothing in this section shall be held to modify any right of creditors to set aside any assignment on the ground of fraud.

(10) The use by the person or partnership continuing the business of the partnership name, or the name of a deceased partner as part thereof, shall not of itself make the individual property of the deceased partner liable for any debts contracted by such person or partnership.

Section 42. Rights of Retiring or Estate of Deceased Partner When the Business Is Continued. When any partner retires or dies, and the business is continued under any of the conditions set forth in section 41 (1, 2, 3, 5, 6), or section 38 (2*b*), without any settlement of accounts as between him or his estate and the person or partnership continuing the business, unless otherwise agreed, he or his legal representative as against such persons or partnership may have the value of his interest at the date of dissolution ascertained, and shall receive as an ordinary creditor an amount equal to the value of his interest in the dissolved partnership with interest, or, at his option or at the option of his legal representative, in lieu of interest, the profits attributable to the use of his right in the property of the dissolved partnership; provided that the creditors of the dissolved partnership as against the separate creditors, or the representative of the retired or deceased partner, shall have priority on any claim arising under this section, as provided by section 41 (8) of this act.

Section 43. Accrual of Actions. The right to an account of his interest shall accrue to any partner, or his legal representative, as against the winding up partners or the surviving partners or the person or partnership continung the business, at the date of dissolution in the absence of any agreement to the contrary.

PART VII

MISCELLANEOUS PROVISIONS

Section 44. When Act Takes Effect. This act shall take effect on the........... day of .... one thousand nine hundred and ....

Section 45. Legislation Repealed. All acts or parts of acts inconsistent with this act are hereby repealed.

GLOSSARY OF LEGAL TERMS AND DEFINITIONS

abandoned property (a-ban′doned prop′-er-ti). Property the ownership of which has been relinquished or surrendered by the owner. Such property becomes unowned property.

abatable nuisance (a-ba′ta-bl nu′sans). A nuisance which may be terminated either by the party injured or by suit instituted by him for that purpose.

abet (a-bet′). To abet is to assist. Abetting imparts a positive act in the aid of the commission of an offense.

abeyance (a-ba′ans). The condition of a freehold when there is no person in being in whom it is vested.

ab initio (ab i-nish′i-o). From the beginning. A contract which is void ab initio is void from its inception.

able buyer. A buyer is able who actually has the money to meet the cash payments demanded by the seller.

abridge (a-brij′). To reduce or to cut down a pleading or other writing.

abrogate (ab′ro-gat). To repeal; to make void; to annul.

abscond (ab-skond′). To withdraw clandestinely, to hide, or to conceal one's self, for the purpose of avoiding legal proceedings.

absolute acceptance. The unqualified assent to liability by the drawee on a bill of exchange.

absque injuria (abz′kwe in-ju′ri-a). Without violation of a legal right.

abstract of title. A summary of the conveyances, transfers and other facts relied on as evidence of title, together with all such facts appearing of record which may impair the validity. It should contain a brief but complete history of the title.

abutting owners (a-but′ing o′ners). Those owners whose lands touch the highway or other public places.

acceleration (ak-sel-e-ra′shon). The shortening of the time for the performance of a contract or the payment of a note by the operation of some provision in the contract or note itself.

acceptance (ak-sep′tans). The actual or implied receipt and retention of that which is tendered or offered. The acceptance of an offer is the assent to an offer which is requisite to the formation of a contract. It is either express or evidenced by circumstances from which such assent may be implied.

accession (ak-sesh′on). In its legal meaning it is generally used to signify the acquisition of property by its incorporation or union with other property.

accident (ak′si-dent). An event which takes place without one's foresight or expectation; an event happening by chance; unexpectedly taking place; not in the usual course of things.

accommodation paper. Ordinarily a note or other form of negotiable instrument made for the purpose of enabling the payee to obtain credit, and as such it has no validity until it passes into the hands of a holder for value.

accord (a-kord′). A mutual agreement between debtor and creditor as to the allowance or disallowance of their respective claims and as to the balance struck upon the final adjustment of their accounts and demands on both sides.

accord and satisfaction. The adjustment of a disagreement as to what is due from one person to another, and the payment of the agreed amount.

account (a-kount′). A matter of debt and credit, or demand in the nature of debt and credit, between parties. It implies that one is responsible to another for moneys or other things, either on the score of contract or some fiduciary relation, of a public or private nature, created by law or otherwise.

account stated. An account which has been rendered by one to another and which purports to state the true balance due and which balance is either expressly or impliedly admitted to be due by the debtor.

acknowledge (ak-nol'ej). To own or admit the knowledge of.

acknowledgment (ak-nol'ej-ment). A form for authenticating instruments conveying property or otherwise conferring rights. It is a public declaration by the grantor that the act evidenced by the instrument is his act and deed. Also an admission or confirmation.

acquire (a-kwir'). To make property one's own; to obtain the ownership of or an interest in property.

acquit (a-kwit'). To set free or judicially to discharge from an accusation; to release from a debt, duty, obligation, charge or suspicion of guilt.

act in pais (pah-es'). A judicial or other act performed out of court.

action, common law. The formal demand of one's right from another person or party made and insisted on in a court of justice. At common law certain formal proceedings were followed in bringing suit to enforce such demands. The ordinary common law actions were:

- **covenant** (kuv'e-nant). The remedy which the law assigns for all breaches of a contract under seal.
- **debt** (det). Action which lies for the recovery of a fixed and definite sum of money.
- **ejectment** (e-jekt'ment). Originally ejectment was brought to recover the possession of corporeal hereditaments. By statute in some states it is an action to recover immediate possession of real estate.
- **replevin** (re-plev'in). An action by which an owner recovers the possession of his own goods.
- **trover** (tro'ver). An action for the recovery of damages for the conversion of personal property. In some jurisdictions it includes any action in which the rights of individuals in a personal chattel are determined.

actionable (ak'shon-a-bl). Remedial by an action at law.

action ex contractu (ex kon-trak'tu). An action arising out of the breach of a contract.

action ex delicto (ex de-lik'to). An action arising out of the violation of a duty or obligation created by positive law independent of contract. An action in tort.

adequate remedy at law. A remedy at law which is complete and which is the substantial equivalent of the equitable relief.

adjacent (a-ja'sent). Usually used to designate property which is in the neighborhood of other property but which does not actually touch such other property. Sometimes used to mean "touching" or "contiguous."

adjudge (a-juj'). To give judgment; to decide; to sentence.

adjudicate (ad-ju'di-kat). To adjudge; to settle by judicial decree; to hear or try and determine, as a court.

adjust (a-just'). To settle or to come to a satisfactory agreement so that the parties are in accord in the result. To adjust accounts.

ad libitum (ad lib'i-tum). At pleasure; at will. As in an action where damages are precarious, as in an action for slander the damages are passed ad libitum by the jury.

ad litem (ad li'tem). During the pendency of the action or proceeding.

administrator (ad-min'is-tra-tor). A person appointed by a probate court to settle the estate of a deceased person. His duties are customarily defined by statute. If a woman is appointed she is called the administratrix.

adult (a-dult'). A person who is at least twenty-one years old. One who has reached the age at which he is no longer under the incapacity of infancy.

advisement (ad-viz'ment). When a court takes a case under advisement it delays its decision until it has examined and considered the questions involved.

affidavit (af-i-da'vit). A statement or declaration reduced to writing and sworn or affirmed to before an officer who has authority to administer an oath or affirmation,

affirm (a-ferm'). To confirm a former judgment or order of a court. Also to declare solemnly instead of making a sworn statement.

agent (a'jent). An agent is the substitute or representative of his principal and derives his authority from him.

aggregatio mentium (ag-re-ga'she-o men'she-um). A meeting of the minds. It is a factor essential to the validity of a contract.

aggrieved. One whose legal rights have been invaded by the act of another is said to be aggrieved. Also one whose pecuniary interest is directly affected by a judgment, or whose right of property may be divested thereby, is to be considered a party aggrieved.

aleatory contract (a'le-a-to ri). A contract is aleatory or hazardous when there is a risk on one side or both and when all risks appertaining to the contract and not excepted are assumed by the parties.

alias (a'li-as). Otherwise; also known as; at another time; as formerly.

alibi (al'i-bi). Literally the word means "elsewhere." An alibi as used in the criminal law indicates that the defendant will prove that he did not, and could not have committed the crime because he was not at the scene of the crime at the time of its commission.

alienation (al-yen-a'shon). The voluntary act or acts by which one person transfers his own property to another.

allege (a-lej'). To make a statement of fact; to plead.

allocate (al'o-kat). To allow an appropriate proportion; to apportion; to allot.

allonge (a-lunj'). A paper attached to and made a part of a promissory note, on which paper an endorsement is written.

alongside (a-long'sid). A nautical term meaning that the charterer of a ship is to bring his cargo as near the ship as is practicable.

ambiguity (am-bi-gu'i-ti). Doubtfulness or uncertainty especially in the meaning of language arising from its admitting of more than one meaning.

amend (a-mend'). To improve; to make better by change or modification.

amortize (a-mor'tiz). In modern usage the word means to provide for the payment of a debt by creating a sinking fund or paying in instalments.

ancillary (an'si-la-ri). Auxiliary to. An ancillary receiver is a receiver who has been appointed in aid of, and in subordination to the primary receiver.

anonymous (a-non'i-mous). Without a name.

answer (an'ser). The pleading of a defendant in which he may deny any or all the facts set out in the plaintiff's declaration or complaint.

anticipatory breach (an-tis'i-pa-to-ri). The doctrine of the law of contracts that when the promisor has repudiated the contract before the time of performance has arrived the promisee may sue forthwith.

appeal and error. An appeal brings up questions of fact as well as of law, but upon a writ of error only questions of law apparent on the record can be considered, and there can be no inquiry whether there was error in dealing with questions of fact.

appear (a-per'). To give notice of appearance in an action.

appearance (a-per'ans). The first act of the defendant in court.

appellant (a-pel'ant). A person who files an appeal.

appellate jurisdiction. Jurisdiction to retry and determine an issue which has already been tried in some other tribunal. Also the jurisdiction to review cases as law cases are reviewed at common law.

appellee (ap-e-le'). A party against whom a cause is appealed from a lower court to a higher court. He is called the "respondent" in some jurisdictions.

applicant (ap'li-kant). A petitioner; one who files a petition or application.

appurtenances (a-per'te-nan-ses). An appurtenance is that which belongs to another thing, but which has not belonged to it immemorially; e. g. buildings would be appurtenant to the land.

arbitrate (ar'bi-trat). To submit some disputed matter to selected persons and to accept their decision or award as a substitute for the decision of a judicial tribunal.

argument (ar'gu-ment). The discussion by counsel for the respective parties of their contentions on the law and the facts of the case being tried in order to aid the jury in arriving at a correct and just conclusion.

as per. Commonly used and understood to mean in accordance with, or in accordance with the terms of, or as by the contract authorized. The term is not susceptible of literal translation.

assault (a-salt'). A demonstration of an unlawful intent by one person to inflict immediate injury on the person of another then present.

assignable (a-si'na-bl). Capable of being lawfully assigned or transferred; transferable; negotiable. Also capable of being specified or pointed out as an assignable error.

assignee (as-i-ne'). A person to whom an assignment is made.

assignment (a-sin'ment). A transfer or setting over of property or some right or interest therein, from one person to another. In its ordinary application the word is limited to the transfer of choses in action, e. g. the assignment of a contract.

assignor (as-i-nor′). The maker of an assignment.

assumpsit (a-sump′sit). The form of action brought if one failed to perform a parol agreement either express or implied. The form of action is now brought if one fails to perform any undertaking promissory in its nature.

attachment (a-tach′ment). Taking property into the legal custody of an officer by virtue of the directions contained in a writ of attachment. A seizure under a writ of a debtor's property.

attest (a-test′) To bear witness to; to affirm; to be true or genuine.

attorney-in-fact. A person who is authorized by his principal, either for some particular purpose, or to do a particular act, not of a legal character.

authentication (a-then′ti-ka′shon). Such official attestation of a written instrument as will render it legally admissible in evidence.

authority (a-thor′i-ti). Judicial or legislative precedent; delegated power; warrant.

averment (a-ver′ment). A positive statement of fact made in a pleading.

avoidable (a-voi′da-bl). Capable of being nullified or made void.

bad faith. The term imparts a person's actual intent to mislead or deceive another; an intent to take an unfair and unethical advantage of another.

baggage (bag′aj). Articles of apparel for either use or ornament and such other articles as may be necessary or convenient for the traveler in his journeying.

bail (bal). The release of a person from custody upon the undertaking of two or more persons for him and also upon his own recognizance, that he shall appear to answer the charge against him at the time appointed; the delivery or bailment of a person to his sureties, so that he is placed in their friendly custody instead of remaining in prison.

bailee (ba-lé). The person to whom a bailment is made.

bailment (bal′ment). A delivery of personal property by one person to another in trust for a specific purpose, with a contract, express or implied that the trust shall be faithfully executed and the property returned or duly accounted for when the special purpose is accomplished, or kept until the bailor reclaims it.

bailor (ba′lor). The maker of a bailment; one who delivers personal property to another to be held in bailment.

banc (bangk). A bench; a meeting of all the judges of a court.

banishment (ban′ish-ment). The removal, expulsion or deportation of a person from a country by the political authority thereof on the ground of expediency.

bankable (bang′ka-bl). Capable of being discounted or receivable as cash by a bank.

bank check. An instrument by which a depositor seeks to withdraw funds from a bank.

bankruptcy (bangk′rupt-si). The state of a person who is unable to pay his debts without respect to time; one whose liabilities exceed his assets.

discharge in bankruptcy. An order or decree rendered by a court in bankruptcy proceedings, the effect of which is to satisfy all debts provable against the estate of the bankrupt as of the time when the bankruptcy proceedings were initiated.

bar (bar). As a collective noun it is used to include those persons who are admitted to practice law, members of the bar. The court itself. A plea or peremptory exception of a defendant sufficient to destroy the plaintiff's action.

barratry (bar′a-tri). The habitual stirring up of quarrels and suits; a single act would not constitute the offense.

barter (bar′ter). To exchange one commodity for another; to negotiate for the acquisition of a thing.

bearer (bar′er). The designation of the bearer as the payee of a negotiable instrument signifies that the instrument is payable to the person who seems to be the holder.

bench (bench). A court; the judges of a court; the seat upon which the judges of a court are accustomed to sit while the court is in session.

beneficiaries, third party. A person who is not a party to a contract, agreement or instrument but is, by the terms of the contract, agreement, or written instrument, to receive the promised consideration or some portion of it.

donee beneficiary. A person who is not a party to a contract yet is to receive the consideration promised by way of gift.

creditor beneficiary. A person who is not a party to a contract yet is to receive the consideration contracted for by the promisee in discharge of a debt owed by the promisee to the creditor beneficiary.

benefit of clergy. The exemption of clergymen from trial or punishment for crime excepting before the ecclesiastical court.

bequeath (be-kweth′). Commonly used to denote a testamentary gift of real estate; synonymous to "to devise."

bid (bid). To make an offer at an auction or at a judicial sale. As a noun it means an offer.

bilateral contract (bi-lat′e-ral). A contract in which the promise of one of the parties forms the consideration for the promise of the other; a contract formed by an offer requiring a reciprocal promise.

bill of exchange. An unconditional order in writing by one person to another, signed by the person giving it, requiring the person to whom it is addressed to pay on demand or at a fixed or determinable future time a sum certain in money to order or to bearer.

bill of lading (bil of lad′ing). A written acknowledgment of the receipt of goods to be transported to a designated place and delivered to a named person or to his order.

binder (bin′der). Also called a binding slip,—a brief memorandum or agreement issued by an insurer as a temporary policy for the convenience of all the parties, constituting a present insurance in the amount specified, to continue in force until the execution of a formal policy.

blacklist (blak′list). A document whereby, either voluntarily or in pursuance of a previous arrangement, one person communicates to another or other persons information about a third person which is likely to prevent them from entering into business relations with that third person.

bogus (bo′gus). Spurious, ficticious or sham. A bogus check is a check given by a person upon a bank in which he has no funds.

bona fide (bo′na fi′de). Good faith.

bond (bond). An obligation under seal.

breach of contract. The failure of a party to a contract to comply with the duty he has assumed by the obligation of the contract.

breaking bulk. The division or separation of the contents of a package or container.

brief (bref). A statement of a party's case; usually an abridgment of either the plaintiff's or defendant's case prepared by his attorneys for use of counsel on a trial at law. Also an abridgment of a reported case.

broker (bro′ker). An agent who bargains or carries on negotiations in behalf of his principal as an intermediary between the latter and third persons in transacting business relative to the acquisition of contractual rights, or to the sale or purchase of property the custody of which is not intrusted to him for the purpose of discharging his agency.

brutum fulmen (bru′tum ful′men). Empty or harmless thunder.

buyer's risk. In sales, the risk follows the title and if title to the goods has passed to the buyer the risk of loss or damage to the goods while in transit rests on the buyer.

bylaw (bi′la). A rule or law of a corporation for its government. It includes all self-made regulations of a corporation affecting its business and members which do not operate on third persons, or in any way affect their rights.

call (kal). A notice of a meeting to be held by the stockholders or board of directors of a corporation. Also a demand for payment.

cancellation. The act of crossing out a writing. The operation of destroying a written instrument.

cannon (kan′on). A law; commonly used to indicate a law of the church. Also a church officer who took revenue for conducting service.

capacity (ka-pas′i-ti). A person's ability to understand the nature and effect of the art in which he is engaged and the business which he is transacting.

capias (ka′pi-as). A writ issued for the purpose of securing the person or property of a defendant in a civil action.

caption (kap'shon). A taking; a seizure; the heading or title of a document.

careless (kar'les). Synonymous to the word negligent; lack of care.

carte blanche (kart blonsh). A signed blank instrument intended by the signer to be filled in and used by another person without restriction.

case (kas). A contested question in a court of justice.

case law. The law as laid down in the decisions of the courts. The law extracted from decided cases.

cashier's check. A bill of exchange, drawn by a bank upon itself, and accepted by the act of issuance.

casualty (kaz'u-al-ti). Chance; accident; contingency. A fatal or serious accident.

causa (ka'za). A Roman law term which, in some respects, was analogous to the term "consideration" in our law.

cause of action. A right of action at law arises from the existence of a primary right in the plaintiff, and an invasion of that right by some delict on the part of the defendant, and that the facts which establish the existence of that right and that delict constitute the cause of action.

caveat (ka've-at). A notice filed by an inventor in the United States patent office. A statement of opposition to the probate of a will.

caveat emptor (ka've-at emp'tor). Let the buyer beware. This maxim expresses the general idea that the buyer purchases at his peril, and that there are no warranties, either express or implied, made by the seller.

caveat venditor (ka've-at ven'di-tor). Let the seller beware. It is not accepted as a rule of law in the law of sales.

certainty (ser'tan-ti). Distinctness and accuracy of statement.

certification (ser'ti-fi-ka'shon). The return of a writ; a formal attestation of a matter of fact; the appropriate marking of a certified check.

certified check. A check which has been "accepted" by the drawee bank and has been so marked or certified that it indicates such acceptance.

cestui que trust (ses'twe ke trust). The person for whose benefit property is held in trust by a trustee.

challenge (chal'enj). An objection; an exception; to object; to take exception to.

chancellor (chan'sel-or). A judge of a court of chancery.

chancery (chan'se-ri). In England the high court of chancery is the highest court of judicature in the kingdom next to the parliament.

charge (charj). To charge a jury is to instruct the jury as to the essential law of the case. The first step in the prosecution of a crime is to formally accuse the offender or charge him with the crime.

charter (char'ter). An instrument or authority from the sovereign power bestowing the right or power to do business under the corporate form of organization. Also the organic law of a city or town, and representing a portion of the statute law of the state.

chattel interest. Any interest in land of a less dignity than a freehold estate.

chattel mortgage. An instrument whereby the owner of chattels transfers the title to such property to another as security for the performance of an obligation subject to be defeated on the performance of the obligation.

chattel real. Interests in real estate less than a freehold, such as an estate for years.

chattels (chat'els). Goods both movable and immovable except such as are in the nature of freehold or a part of a freehold.

check (chek). A written order on a bank or banker payable on demand to the person named or his order or bearer and drawn by virtue of credits due the drawer from the bank created by money deposited with the bank.

chose in action (shoz in ak'shon). A personal right not reduced to possession but recoverable by a suit at law.

c. i. f. An abbreviation for cost, freight, and insurance, used in mercantile transactions especially in import transactions.

circuit (ser'kit). A judge's journey in holding court in different places; the district of a judge thus traveling.

citation (si-ta'shon). A writ issued out of a court of competent jurisdiction, commanding the person therein named to appear on a day named to do something therein mentioned.

civil action (siv'il ak'shon). An action brought to enforce a civil right.

claim and delivery. A statutory action which partakes of the common law action of replevin in that its objective is the recovery of specific property when possible.

claimant (kla'mant). One who makes a claim. A voluntary applicant for justice.

clause (klaz). A sentence or paragraph in a written instrument. One of the subdivisions of a written or printed document.

close corporation. A corporation wherein a major part of the persons to whom the corporate powers have been granted have the right to fill vacancies occurring in their ranks.

c. o. d. "Cash on delivery." When goods are delivered to a carrier for a cash on delivery shipment the carrier must not deliver without receiving payment of the amount due.

code (kod). A system of law; a systematic and complete body of law.

codicil (kod'i-sil). Some addition to or qualification of one's last will and testament.

coercion (ko-er'shon). The compulsion actual or presumed by which one is actually or presumably forced to do an act which he would not have done of his own free will and choice.

cognovit (kog-no'vit). To acknowledge an action. A cognovit note is a promissory note which contains an acknowledgment clause.

cohabitation (ko-hab-i-ta'shon). A man and woman openly living together as husband and wife.

collateral attack (ko-lat'e-ral a-tak'). An attempt to impeach a decree, a judgment or other official act in a proceeding which has not been instituted for the express purpose of correcting or annulling or modifying the decree, judgment or official act.

comaker (ko-ma'ker). A person who with another or others signs a negotiable instrument on its face and thereby becomes primarily liable for its payment.

commercial law (ko-mer'shal la). The law which relates to the rights of property and persons engaged in trade or commerce.

commission merchant (ko-mish'on mer'-chant). A person who sells goods in his own name at his own store, and on commission, from sample. Also one who buys and sells goods for a principal in his own name and without disclosing his principal.

common carrier. One who undertakes, for hire or reward, to transport the goods of such of the public as choose to employ him.

compact (kom'pakt). Synonymous to contract.

complaint (kom-plant'). A form of legal process which usually consists of a formal allegation or charge against a party, made or presented to the appropriate court or officer. The technical name of a bill in chancery by which the complainant sets out his cause of action.

composition with creditors. An agreement between creditors and their common debtor and between themselves whereby the creditors agree to accept the sum or security stipulated in full payment of their claims.

conclusive (kon-klo'siv). Decisive, putting an end to debate or question; leading to a conclusion or decision.

concurrent (kon-kur'ent). Running with, simultaneous with. The word is used in different senses. In contracts concurrent conditions are conditions which must be performed simultaneously by the mutual acts required by each of the parties.

condemn (kon-dem'). To appropriate land for public use. To adjudge a person guilty; to pass sentence upon a person convicted of a crime.

condition (kon-dish'on). A provision or clause in a contract which operates to suspend or rescind the principal obligation. A qualification or restriction annexed to a conveyance of lands, whereby it is provided that in the case a particular event does or does not happen, or in case the grantor or grantees do or omit to do a particular act, an estate shall commence, be enlarged or be defeated.

condition precedent. A condition which must happen before either party is bound by the principal obligation of a contract; e. g., one agrees to purchase goods if they are delivered before a stated day. Delivery before the stated day is a condition precedent to one's obligation to purchase.

condition subsequent. A condition which operates to relieve or discharge one from his obligation under a contract.

conditional acceptance. An acceptance of a bill of exchange containing some qualification limiting or altering the acceptor's liability on the bill.

conditional sale (kon-dish'on-al sal). The term is most frequently applied to a sale wherein the seller reserves the title to the goods, though the possession is delivered to the buyer, until the purchase price is paid in full.

confession of judgment. An entry of judgment upon the admission or confession of the debtor without the formality, time or expense involved in an ordinary proceeding.

confusion (kon-fu'zhon). The mingling of goods of different owners into a common mass.

conservator (of an insane person) (kon'-ser-va-tor). A person appointed by a competent court to take care of and oversee the person and estate of an idiot or other incompetent person.

consideration (kon-sid-e-ra'shon). An essential of a valid contract. It consists of either a benefit to the promisor or a detriment to the promisee.

consignee (kon-si-ne). A person to whom goods are consigned, shipped or otherwise transmitted, either for sale or for safe-keeping.

consignment (kon-si'ment). A bailment for sale. The consignee does not undertake the absolute obligation to sell or pay for the goods.

consignor (kon-si'nor). One who sends goods to another on consignment; a shipper or transmitter of goods.

construe (kon'stru). To read a statute or document for the purpose of ascertaining its meaning and effect but in doing so the law must be regarded.

contempt (kon-tempt'). Conduct in the presence of a legislative or judicial body tending to disturb its proceedings, or impair the respect due to its authority or a disobedience to the rules or orders of such a body which interferes with the due administration of law.

contra (kon'tra). Otherwise; disagreeing with; contrary to.

contra bonos moris (kon-tra bo'nos mo'-rez). Contrary to good morals.

contribution (kon-tri-bu'shon). A payment made by each, or by any, of several having a common interest or liability of his share in the loss suffered, or in the money necessarily paid by one of the parties in behalf of the others.

conversion (kon-ver'shon). Any distinct act of dominion wrongfully exerted over another's personal property in denial of or inconsistent with his rights therein. That tort which is committed by a person who deals with chattels not belonging to him in a manner which is inconsistent with the ownership of the lawful owner.

conveyance (kon-va'ans). In its common use it refers to a written instrument transferring the title to land or some interest therein from one person to another. It is sometimes applied to the transfer of the property in personalty.

copartnership (ko-part'ner-ship). A partnership.

corporation (kor-po-ra'shon). An artificial being, invisible, intangible and existing only in contemplation of law. It is exclusively the work of the law, and the best evidence of its existence is the grant of corporate powers by the commonwealth.

corporation de facto (de fak'to). A corporation in fact. An organization which has made a bona fide attempt to organize a corporation under an existing law and which has done business as a corporation but which failed to comply with all the requirements of the law under which it attempted to incorporate.

corporation de jure (de ju're). A corporation which has, in its organization, complied with all the requirements of the law under which it is incorporated and would not be vulnerable to an attack by the state in a quo warranto proceedings.

corporeal (kor-po're-al). Possessing physical substance; tangible; perceptible to the senses.

counterclaim (koun'ter-klam). A claim which, if established, will defeat or in some way qualify a judgment to which the plaintiff is otherwise entitled.

countermand (koun-ter-mand'). To revoke an order previously given.

counter-offer (koun'ter of'er). A cross offer made by the offeree to the offeror.

court of appeals. A court in which appeals from a lower court are heard and disposed of.

court of claims (kort of klams). A Federal tribunal established to hear and investigate claims against the United States. Its opinion is merely advisory.

covenant (kuv'e-nant). The word is used in its popular sense as synonymous to contract. In its specific sense it ordinarily imparts an agreement reduced to writing, and executed by a sealing and delivery.

covenantor (kuv′e-nan-tor). A person who covenants; the maker of a covenant.

coverture (kuv′er-tur). The condition of a married woman.

credible (kred′i-bl). As applied to a witness the word means competent.

crossed checks. A name given to a system recognized as valid in England whereby there is stamped across the check the name of a certain bank through whom it must be presented for payment, and if presented by anyone else it will be dishonored.

Cujus est solum ejus est usque ad coelum et ad inferos (Ku′jus est so′lum, e′jus est us′kwe ad se′lum et ad in′fe-ros). The owner of the soil owns to the heavens and also to the lowest depth.

culpable (kul′pa-bl). Censurable also sometimes used to mean criminal.

cumulative (ku′mu-la-tiv). Adding to or added to something else; by way of increase.

cumulative voting. A method of voting by which an elector entitled to vote for several candidates for the same office may cast more than one vote for the same candidate, distributing among the candidates as he chooses a number of votes equal to the number of candidates to be elected.

curtesy (ker′te-si). Under the early English land law of a man married a woman who had an interest in real estate and issue was born the man was entitled to a life estate in his wife's real estate. This life estate was known as curtesy.

custodia legis (kus-to′di-a le′jis). The custody of the law. When property is lawfully taken, by virtue of legal process, it is in the custody of the law.

custody. The bare control or care of a thing as distinguished from the possession of it.

custom (kus′tum). Something which has by its universality and antiquity acquired the force and effect of law, in a particular place or country, in respect to the subject matter to which it relates; generally practice, judicially noticed without proof.

damages (dam′aj-es). Indemnity to the person who suffers loss or harm from an injury; a sum recoverable as amends for a wrong. An adequate compensation for the loss suffered or the injury sustained.

consequential (kon-se-kwen′shal). Damages which are not produced without the concurrence of some other event attributable to the same origin or cause.

liquidated (lik′wi-da-ted). Damages made certain by the prior agreement of the parties.

nominal. Damages which are recoverable where a legal right is to be vindicated against an invasion which has produced no actual present loss.

date of issue. As the term is applied to notes, bonds, etc., of a series, it usually means the arbitrary date fixed as the beginning of the term for which they run, without reference to the precise time when convenience or the state of the market may permit of their sale or delivery.

deal (del). To engage in mutual intercourse or transactions of any kind.

debenture (de-ben′tur). A written acknowledgment of a debt; specifically an instrument under seal for the repayment of money lent.

debtor (det′or). A person who owes another anything, or who is under obligation, arising from express agreement, implication of law, or from the principles of natural justice, to render and pay a sum of money to another.

deceit (de-set′). A specie of fraud; actual fraud consisting of any false representations or contrivance whereby one person overreaches and misleads another to his hurt.

decide (de-sid). To weigh the reasons for and against and see which preponderates and to be governed by that preponderance.

decision (de-sizh′on). A decision is the judgment of a court, while the opinion represents merely the reasons for that judgment.

declaration (dek-la-ra′shon). The pleadings by which a plaintiff in an action at law sets out his cause of action. An admission or statement subsequently used as evidence in the trial of an action.

declaratory (de-klar′a-to-ri). Explanatory; affirmative; tending to remove doubt.

decree (de-kre′). An order or sentence of a court of equity determining some right or adjudicating some matter affecting the merits of the cause.

deed (ded). A writing, sealed and delivered by the parties; an instrument conveying real property.

de facto (de fak'to). In fact as distinguished from "de jure," by right.

defalcation (de-fal-ka'shon). The word includes both embezzlement and misappropriation and is a broader term than either.

default (de-falt'). Fault; neglect; omission; the failure of a party to an action to appear when properly served with process; the failure to perform a duty or obligation; the failure of a person to pay money when due or when lawfully demanded.

defeasible (of title to property) (de-fe'-zi-bl). Capable of being defeated. A title to property which is open to attack or which may be defeated by the performance of some act.

defend (de-fend'). To oppose a claim or action; to plead in defense of an action; to contest an action suit or proceeding.

defendant (de-fen'dant). A party sued in a personal action.

defendant in error. Any of the parties in whose favor a judgment was rendered which the losing party seeks to have reversed or modified by writ of error and whom he names as adverse parties.

deficiency (de-fish'en-si). That part of a debt which a mortgage was made to secure, not realized by the liquidation of the mortgaged property. Something which is lacking.

defraud (de-frad'). To deprive another of a right by deception or artifice. To cheat; to wrong another by fraud.

dehors (de-horz'). Outside of; disconnected with, unrelated to.

de jure (de ju're). By right; complying with the law in all respects.

del credere agent (del kre'de-re a'jent). An agent who guarantees his principal against the default of those with whom contracts are made.

deliver (de-liv'er). To surrender property to another person.

delusion (de-lu'zhon). A false belief for which there is no reasonable foundation, and which would be incredible, under the given circumstances, to the same person, if of sound mind.

demand (de-mand'). A claim; a legal obligation; a request to perform an alleged obligation; a written statement of a claim.

de minimis non curat lex (de mi'ni-mis non ku'rat lex). The law is not concerned with trifles. The maxim has been applied to exclude the recovery of nominal damages where no unlawful intent or disturbance of a right of possession is shown, and where all possible damage is expressly disproved.

demurrage (de-mer'aj). A compensation for the delay of a vessel beyond the time allowed for loading, unloading or sailing. It is also applied to the compensation for the similar delay of a railroad car.

demurrer (de-mer'er). An objection made by one party to his opponent's pleading, alleging that he ought not to answer it, for some defect in law in the pleading.

de novo, trial (de no'vo). Anew; over again; a second time. A trial de novo is a new trial in which the entire case is retried in all its detail.

dependent covenants. Covenants made by two parties to a deed or agreement which are such that the thing convenated or promised to be done on each part enters into the whole consideration for the covenant or promise on the part of the other, or such covenants as are concurrent, and to be performed at the same time. Neither party to such a covenant can maintain an action against the other without averring and proving performance on his part.

deposition (dep-o-zish'on). An affidavit; an oath; the written testimony of a witness given in the course of a judicial proceeding, either at law or in equity, in response to interrogatories either oral or written, and where an opportunity is given for cross-examition.

depositor (de-poz'i-tor). Any person who shall deposit money or commercial paper in any bank, either on open account subject to check, or to be withdrawn otherwise than by check, whether interest is allowed thereon or not, including holders of demand or time certificates of deposit lawfully issued.

deputy (dep'u-ti). A person subordinate to a public officer whose business and object is to perform the duties of the principal.

descent (de-sent′). Hereditary succession. It is the title whereby a man on the death of his ancestor acquires his estate by right of representation as his heir at law, an heir being one upon whom the law casts the estate immediately at the death of the ancestor, the estate so descending being the inheritance.

descriptio personae (de-skrip′she-o perso′ne). A description of the person, as distinguished from the capacity in which he acts.

detinue (det′i-nu). A common law action, now seldom used which lies where a party claims the specific recovery of goods and chattels unlawfully detained from him.

detriment (det′ri-ment). A detriment is any act or forbearance by a promisee. A loss or harm suffered in person or property.

dictum (dik′tum). The opinion of a judge which does not embody the resolution or determination of the court, and made without argument, or full consideration of the point, and not the professed deliberation of the judge himself.

directed verdict (di-rek′ted ver′dikt). A verdict which the jury returns as directed by the court. The court may thus withdraw the case from the jury whenever there is no competent, relevent and material evidence to support the issue.

discharge (dis-charj′). To unload or deliver a cargo from a vessel. To set a person at liberty who has been in custody. The release or performance of a contract or other obligation.

discount (dis′kount). A loan upon an evidence of debt, where the compensation for the use of the money until the maturity of the debt is deducted from the principal and retained by the lender at the time of making the loan.

dismiss (dis-mis′). To discontinue; to order a cause, motion or prosecution to be discontinued or quashed.

diverse citizenship (di-vers′ sit′i-zn-ship). A term of frequent use in the interpretation of the federal constitutional provision for the jurisdiction of the Federal courts which extends it to controversies between citizens of different states.

divided court (di-vi′ded kort.) A court is so described when there has been a division of opinion between its members on a matter which has been submitted to it for decision.

dividend (div′i-dend). A gain or profit. A fund which a corporation sets apart from its profits to be divided among its members.

document (dok′u-ment). Any matter expressed or described upon any substance by means of letters, figures or marks or by more than one of these means intended to be used, or which may be used, for the purpose of recording that matter.

domain (do-man′). The ownership of land; immediate or absolute ownership. The public lands of a state are frequently termed the public domain.

domicil (dom′i-sil). A place where a person lives or has his home; in a strict legal sense, the place where he has his true, fixed, permanent home and principal establishment, and to which place he has whenever he is absent, the intention of returning.

dominion (property), (do-min′yon). The rights of dominion or property are those rights which a man may acquire in and to such external things as are unconnected with his body.

donee (do-ne′). A person to whom a gift is made.

donor (do′nor). A person who makes a gift.

dower (dou′er). The legal right or interest which his wife acquires by marriage in the real estate of her husband.

draft (draft). A written order drawn upon one person by another, requesting him to pay money to a designated third person. A bill of exchange payable on demand.

drawee (dra-e′). A person upon whom a draft or bill of exchange is drawn by the drawer.

drawer (dra′er). The maker of a draft or bill of exchange.

drummer (drum′er). A person who drums up business; a solicitor of customers or business.

due bill (du bil). An acknowledgment of a debt in writing, not made payable to order.

dummy (dum′i). One posing or represented as acting for himself, but in reality acting for another. A tool or straw man for the real parties in interest.

duress (du-res′). Overpowering of the will of a person by force or fear.

earnest (er'nest). Something given as part of the purchase price to bind the bargain.

easement (ez'ment). A liberty, privilege or advantage in land without profit, existing distinct from the ownership of the soil; the right which one person has to use the land of another for a specific purpose.

edict (e'dikt). A command or prohibition promulgated by a sovereign and having the effect of law.

effects (e-fekts'). As used in wills, the word is held equivalent to personal property. It denotes property in a more extensive sense than goods and includes all kinds of personal property but will be held not to include real property, unless the context discloses an intention on the part of the testator to dispose of his realty by the use of the word.

e. g. An abbreviation for "exempli gratia," meaning for or by the way of example.

ejectment (e-jekt'ment). By statute in some states, it is an action to recover the immediate possession of real property. At common law, it was a purely possessory action, and as modified by statute, though based upon title, it is still essentially a possessory action.

eleemosynary corporation (el-e-mos'i-na-ri kor-po-ra'shon). A corporation created for a charitable purpose or for charitable purposes, such as are constituted for the perpetual distribution of free alms to such purposes as their founders and supporters have directed.

emancipate (e-man'si-pat). To release; to set free. Where a father expressly or impliedly, by his conduct waives his right generally to the services of his minor child, the child is said to be emancipated and he may sue on contracts made by him for his services.

embezzlement (em-bez'l-ment). A statutory offense consisting of the fraudulent conversion of another's personal property by one to whom it has been intrusted, with the intention of depriving the owner thereof, the gist of the offense being usually the violation of relations of fiduciary character.

encumbrance (en-kum'brans). An encumbrance on land is a right in a third person in the land to the diminution of the value of the land, though consistent with the passing of the fee by the deed of conveyance.

enhanced (en-hanst'). Increased. Any increase in value however caused or arising.

entity (en'ti-ti). An existence; a being actual or artificial.

entry (en'tri). Recordation; noting in a record; going upon land; taking actual possession of land. Literally, the act of going into a place after a breach has been effected.

eo nominee (e'o no'mi-ne). By or in that name or designation.

equitable defense (ek'wi-ta-bl de'fens). Any matter which would authorize an application to a court of chancery for relief against a legal liability, but which at law could not be pleaded in bar.

equity (ek'wi-ti). That which in human transactions is founded in natural justice, in honesty and right, and which arises in equity and good conscience; that portion of remedial justice, which is exclusively administered by a court of equity, as counterdistinguished from that portion of remedial justice which is exclusively administered by a court of common law.

error (er'or). A mistake of law or fact; a mistake of the court in the trial of an action.

estate (es-tat'). Technically the word refers only to an interest in land.

estate at will. A lease of lands or tenements to be held at the will of the lessor. Such can be determined by either party.

estate for a term. An estate less than a freehold which is in fact a contract for the possession of land or tenements for some determinate period.

estate for life. An estate created by deed or grant conveying land or tenements to a person to hold for the term of his own life or for the life of any other person or for more lives than one.

estate in fee simple. An absolute inheritance, clear of any conditions, limitations or restrictions to particular heirs. It is the highest estate known to the law and necessarily implies absolute dominion over the land.

estate per autre vie (estate pur o-tr vi). An estate which is to endure for the life of another person than the grantee, or for the lives of more than one, in either of which cases, the grantee is called the tenant for life.

estoppel (es-top'el). That state of affairs which arises when a person executes some deed, or is concerned in or does some act, either of record or in pais, which will preclude him from averring anything to the contrary.

et al. An abbreviation for the Latin "et alius" meaning, and another, also of "et alu" meaning, and others.

et ux. An abbreviation for the Latin "et uxor" meaning, and his wife.

eviction (e-vik'shon). Originally, as applied to tenants, the word meant depriving the tenant of the possession of the demised premises, but technically, it is the disturbance of his possession, depriving him of the enjoyment of the premises demised or any portion thereof by title paramount or by entry and act of the landlord.

evidence (ev'i-dens). That which makes clear or ascertains the truth of the fact or point in issue either on the one side or the other; those rules of law whereby we determine what testimony is to be admitted and what rejected in each case and what is the weight to be given to the testimony admitted.

ex aequo et bono (ex e'quo et bo'no). In equity and good conscience.

exception (ek-sep'shon). An objection; a reservation; a contradiction.

exchange (eks-chanj'). An executed contract which operates by itself as a reciprocal conveyance of the thing given and the thing received in exchange, each of the parties being individually considered in the double light of vendor and vendee. A transfer of money from one person to another at a place more or less distant at an agreed rate of exchange or at the customary rate.

ex debito justitiae (ex de'bi-to jus-ti'-she-e). From a debt of justice; from that which is owing; from one's right; as of right.

ex delicto (ex de-lik'to). From or out of a wrongful act; tortious; tortiously.

executed (ek'se-kut-ed). When applied to written instruments the word is sometimes used as synonymous with the word "signed" and means no more than that but more frequently it imports that everything has been done to complete the transaction; that is that the instrument has been signed, sealed and delivered. An executed contract is one in which the object of the contract is performed.

execution (ek'se-ku'shon). A remedy in the form of a writ or process afforded by law for the enforcement of a judgment. The final consummation of a contract of sale, including only those acts which are necessary to the full completion of an instrument, such as the signature of the seller, the affixing of his seal and its delivery to the buyer.

executor (eg-zek'u-tor). A person who is designated in a will as one who is to administer the estate of the testator.

executory (eg-zek'u-to-ri). Not yet executed; not yet fully performed, completed, fulfilled or carried out; to be performed wholly or in part.

executrix (eg-zek'u-triks). Feminine of executor.

exemption (eg-zemp'shon). A release from some burden, duty or obligation; a grace; a favor; an immunity; taken out from under the general rule, not to be like others who are not exempt.

exhibit (eg-zib'it). A copy of a written instrument on which a pleading is founded, annexed to the pleading and by reference made a part of it. Any paper or thing offered in evidence and marked for identification.

ex industria (ex in-dus'tri-a). On purpose; purposely; intentionally.

exports (eks'portz). Goods exported from the United States to a foreign country.

extension (eks-ten'shon). A lengthening; a continuance; a grant of further time.

ex vi termini (ex vi ter'mi-ni). By the force of the term; by the intrinsic import of the term or expression.

face value (fas' val'u). The nominal or par value of an instrument as expressed on its face; which in the case of a bond is the amount really due including interest.

factor (fak'tor). An agent who not only negotiates a contract of sale or purchase, but is in duty bound to carry it through to performance in behalf of his principal. Hence, he is given either actual or constructive possession of his principal's goods; and it is customary for him to advance money on them. He has implied authority to contract either in his own name without disclosing that of his principal, or in the name of his principal; and a payment to the factor is a complete discharge of his principal's debtor.

fair (far). A large market, open to the public, at which people were encouraged to throng from the surrounding country in large numbers. Fairs were only held at certain seasons and could only be set up by virtue of the king's grant, or by long and immemorial usage and prescription presupposing a grant. Also the word is used to mean justice and equity.

f. a. s. An abbreviation for the expression "free alongside steamer."

fee simple absolute. Same as fee simple. See estates.

felony (fel'on-i). As a general rule all crimes punishable by death or by imprisonment in a state prison are felonies.

feme covert (fem co'vert). A married woman.

feme sole (fem sol). An unmarried woman.

feoffee (fe-fe'). A person to whom a fee is conveyed; a person to whom a feoffment is made.

feoffment (fef'ment). The transfer of a fee, a freehold or a corporeal hereditament by livery of seisin. It operated on the possession, and effected the transmutation thereof.

feoffor (fef-or). A person who conveys a fee; a person who makes a feoffment.

fiction (fik'shon). A false averment on the part of the plaintiff which the defendant is not allowed to traverse, the object being to give the court jurisdiction.

fiduciary (fi-du'shi-a-ri). One who holds goods in trust for another or one who holds a position of trust and confidence.

fieri facias (fi'e-ri fa'she-as). You cause to be made,—an ordinary writ of execution whereby the officer is commanded to levy and sell and to "make" if he can, the amount of the judgment creditors demand.

fiscal (fis'kal). The fiscal affairs of a county are the business transactions of the county, the performance of such duties as the law has defined and placed upon the county board, or such as uniformly pertain to the office of its members.

fixture (fiks'tur). A thing which was originally a personal chattel and which has been actually or constructively affixed to the soil itself or to some structure legally a part of such soil; an article which was once a chattel, but which by being physically annexed or affixed to the realty, has become accessory to it and part and parcel of it.

f. o. b. An abbreviation of "free on board."

forced sale (forst sal). The term generally applies to sales made under the authority of any legal proceedings whether at law or in equity, which seeks to appropriate the property to the payment of debt.

foreman (for'man). The spokesman and presiding member of a jury who is usually elected to that position by the jury itself, but sometimes is appointed by the court.

forfeiture (for'fi-tur). A forfeiture implies a penalty and the word forfeit is often used synonymously with penalty, but in its strict sense a forfeiture implies a divestiture of property without compensation, in consequence of a default or offense.

forwarder (for'war-der). A person who, having no interest in the freight of goods and no ownership or interest in the means of their carriage, undertakes, for hire, to forward them by a safe carrier to their destination.

franchise (fran'chiz). A special privilege conferred by government upon individuals, and which does not belong to the citizens of a country generally, of common right. The word does not mean only the right to be a corporation but it is generic, covering all rights which may be granted by the legislature.

fraud (frad). Conduct which operates prejudicially on the rights of others, and is so intended; deception practiced to induce another to part with property, or surrender some legal right, and which accomplished the end desired.

freehold (fre'hold). Any estate of inheritance or for life in either a corporeal or incorporeal hereditament existing in or arising from real property of free tenure.

fructus industrial (fruk'tus in-dus-tri-a'-lez). Those products of the earth which are annual, and which are raised by yearly planting, and which essentially own their annual existence to the cultivation of man.

fructus naturales (fruk'tus na-tu-ra'lez). Natural fruits—the fruit of trees, perennial bushes and grasses growing from perennial roots.

fungible goods (fun'ji-bl guds). Goods any unit of which is from its nature or by mercantile custom, treated as the equivalent of any other unit.

futures (fu'turs). Contracts for the sale and future delivery of stocks or commodities, wherein either party may waive delivery, and receive or pay, as the case may be, the difference in market price at the time set for delivery.

gamble (gam'bl). To game or play for money.

garnishee (gar-ni-she'). As a noun, the term signifies the person upon whom a garnishment is served, usually a debtor of the defendant in the action. As a verb, the word means to institute garnishment proceedings; to cause a garnishment to be levied on the garnishee.

garnishment (gar'nish-ment). The term denotes a proceeding whereby property, money, or credits of a debtor in possession of another, the garnishee, are applied to the payment of the debts by means of process against the debtor and the garnishee. It is a statutory proceeding based upon contract relations, and can only be resorted to where it is authorized by statute.

general issue (jen'e-ral ish'o). A plea of the defendant amounting to a denial of every material allegation of fact in the plaintiff's complaint or declaration.

gift note (gift not). A donor's promissory note payable to the donee. Such a note is invalid according to the weight of authority.

going business (go'ing biz'ness). An establishment which is still continuing to transact its ordinary business, though it may be insolvent.

good faith (gud fath). An honest intention to abstain from taking an unconscientious advantage of another.

grantee (gran-te'). A person to whom a grant is made.

grantor (gran'tor). A person who makes a grant.

gravamen (gra-va'men). Gist, essence; substance. The grievance complained of; the substantial cause of the action.

guarantor (gar'an-tor). A person who promises to answer for the debt, default or miscarriage of another.

guaranty (gar'an-ti). An undertaking by one person to be answerable for the payment of some debt, or the due performance of some contract or duty by another person, who himself remains liable to pay or perform the same.

guardian (gar'dian). A person (in some rare cases a corporation) to whom the law has intrusted the custody and control of the person, or estate, or both, of an infant, lunatic or incompetent person.

habendum (ha-ben'dum). The second part of a deed or conveyance following that part which names the grantee. It describes the estate conveyed and to what use. It is no longer essential and if included in a modern deed is a mere useless form.

hearing (her'ing). The supporting of one's contentions by argument and if need be by proof. It is an absolute right and if denied to a contestant it would amount to the denial of one of his constitutional rights.

hedging (hej'ing). A market transaction wherein a party buys a certain quantity of a given commodity at the price current on the date of the purchase and sells an equal quantity of the same commodity for future delivery, thereby protecting himself against loss due to fluctuation in the market; for if the price goes down he gains on futures and if the price advances, he loses on futures, but, in either event, he is secure in the profit he has gained on the price of the commodity at the time he purchased it.

heirs (ars). Those persons appointed by law to succeed to the real estate of a decedent, in case of intestacy.

hereditaments (her-e-dit'a-ments). A larger and more comprehensive word than either "land" or "tenements," and meaning anything capable of being inherited, whether it be corporeal, incorporeal, real, personal or mixed.

hinder and delay creditors (hin'der and de-la' kred'i-tors). To impede or retard creditors in their lawful efforts to subject the property of their debtor to the payment of their claims, whether done innocently or with intent to hinder and delay them. A debtor's sale of his property for less than its fair value may be such a hindrance and delay, although innocently made.

holder in due course (hol'der in du kors). A holder who has taken a negotiable instrument under the following conditions:

1. That is complete and regular on its face; 2. That he became the holder of it before it was overdue, and without notice that it had been previously dishonored, if such was the fact; 3. That he took it in good faith and for value; 4. That at the time it was negotiated to him he had no notice of any infirmity in the instrument or defect in the title of the person negotiating it.

holding company (hol'ding kum'pan-i). A corporation the purpose of which is in many instances to circumvent antitrust laws and by which combination among competing corporations is sought to be effected through the absolute transfer of the stocks of the constituent companies to the central "holding" company. This plan is executed by organizing a corporation, often under the laws of a foreign state, to hold the shares of the stock of the constituent companies, their shareholders receiving, upon an agreed basis of value, shares in the holding corporation in exchange therefor.

homestead (hom'sted). In a legal sense the word means the real estate occupied as a home and also the right to have it exempt from levy and forced sale. It is the land, not exceeding the prescribed amount, upon which the dwelling house, or residence, or habitation or abode of the owner thereof and his family reside; and includes the dwelling house as an indispensable part.

illusory (i-lu'so-ri). Deceiving or intending to deceive, as by false appearances; fallaceous. An illusory promise is a promise which appears to be binding but which in fact does not bind the promisor.

immunity (i-mu'ni-ti). A personal favor granted by law, contrary to the general rule.

impanel (im-pan'el). To place the names of the jurors on a panel; to make a list of the names of those persons who have been selected for jury duty; to go through the process of selecting a jury which is to try a cause.

implied (im-plid'). Contained in substance or essence or by fair inference but not actually expressed; deductable by inference or implication.

implied warranty (im-plid wor'an-ti). An implied warranty arises by operation of law and exists without any intention of the seller to create it. It is a conclusion or inference of law, pronounced by the court, on facts admitted or proved before the jury.

import (im-port'). To import goods is to bring them into a country from a foreign country.

inadequacy (in-ad'e-kwa-si). Unequal; insufficient for the purpose to effect the object.

inalienable (in-al'yen-a-bl). Incapable of being aliened, transferred, or conveyed; non-transferable.

in banc (in bangk). With all the judges of the court sitting.

incapacity (in-ka-pas'i-ti). In its legal meaning it applies to one's legal disability, such as infancy, want of authority or other personal incapacity to alter legal relationship.

inception (in-sep'shon). Initial stage. The word does not refer to a state of actual existence, but to a condition of things or circumstances from which the thing may develop; as the beginning of work on a building.

inchoate (in-ko'at). Imperfect; incipient; not completely formed.

incorporeal (in-kor-po're-al). Having no body or substances; intangible; without physical existence.

indebitatus assumpsit (in-de-bi-ta'tus as-sump'sit). Being indebted he undertook. That form of assumpsit which is available for the recovery of any simple common law debt without regard to any express promise to pay the debt. The remedy is also available upon an express contract, when nothing remains to be done but the payment of money. In some states the common-law forms of action are no longer in use.

indemnity (in-dem'ni-ti). An obligation or duty resting on one person to make good any loss or damage another has incurred while acting at his request or for his benefit. By a contract of indemnity one may agree to save another from a legal consequence of the conduct of one of the parties or of some other person.

indenture (in-den'tur). Indentures were deeds which originally were made in two parts formed by cutting or tearing a single sheet across the middle in a jagged or indented line, so that the two parts might be subsequently matched; and they were executed by both grantor and grantee. Later the indenting of the deed was discontinued, yet the term came to be applied to all deeds which were executed by both parties.

independent contractor (in-de-pen′dent kon′trak′tor). One, who, exercising an independent employment, contracts to do a piece of work according to his own methods, and without being subject to the control of his employer except as to the result of his work; one who contracts to perform the work at his own risk and cost, the workmen being his servants, and he being liable for their misconduct.

indictment (in-dit′ment). An accusation founded on legal testimony of a direct and positive character, and the concurring judgment of at least twelve of the grand jurors that upon the evidence presented to them the defendant is guilty.

indorsement (in-dors′ment). Writing on the back of an instrument; the contract whereby the holder of a bill or note transfers to another person his right to such instrument and incurs the liabilities incident to the transfer.

information (in-for-ma′shon). A written accusation of crime preferred by a public prosecuting officer without the intervention of a grand jury.

injunction (in-jungk′shon). A restraining order issued by a court of equity; a prohibitory writ restraining a person from committing or doing an act, other than a criminal act, which appears to be against equity and conscience. There is also the mandatory injunction which commands an act to be done or undone and compels the performance of some affirmative act.

in limine (in lim′i-ne). On the threshold; at the outset.

in personam (in per-so′nam). Against the person.

in re (in re). In the matter; in the transaction.

in rem (in rem). Against a thing and not against a person; concerning the condition or status of a thing.

insolvency (in-sol′ven-si). The word has two distinct meanings. It may be used to denote the insufficiency of the entire property and assets of an individual to pay his debts, which is its general meaning and its meaning as used in the National Bankruptcy Act; but in a more restricted sense, it expresses the inability of a party to pay his debts as they become due in the regular course of his business, and it is so used when traders and merchants are said to be insolvent. This is its meaning as used in the Uniform Sales Act.

in statu quo (in sta′tu kwo). In the situation in which he was.

instrument (in′stru-ment). In its broadest sense, the term includes formal or legal documents in writing, such as contracts, deeds, wills, bonds, leases, and mortgages. In the law of evidence it has still a wider meaning, and includes not merely documents, but witnesses, and things animate and inanimate, which may be presented for inspection.

insurable interest (in-shur′a-bl in-ter′est). Any interest in property the owner of which interest derives a benefit from the existence of the property or would suffer a loss from its destruction. It is not necessary, to constitute an insurable interest that the interest is such that the event insured against would necessarily subject the insured to loss; it is sufficient that it might do so.

inter alia (in-ter a′li-a). Among other things or matters.

interlocutory (in-ter-lok′u-to-ri). In law, that is interlocutory which does not decide the cause, but only settles some intervening matter relating to the cause. The matter thus settled is brought before the court by special motion.

interpleader (in-ter-ple′der). An equitable remedy which lies when two or more persons severally claim the same thing under different titles or in separate interests from another, who, not claiming any title or interest therein himself, and not knowing to which of the claimants he ought in right to render the debt or duty claimed or to deliver the property in his custody, is either molested in an action or actions brought against him, or fears that he may suffer injury from the conflicting claims of the parties.

intervention (in-ter-ven′shon). A proceeding by which one not originally made a party to an action or suit is permitted, on his own application, to appear therein and join one of the original parties in maintaining his cause of action or defense, or to assert some cause of action against some or all of the parties to the proceeding as originally instituted.

intestate (in-tes'tat). A person who has died without leaving a valid will disposing of his property and estate.

in toto (in to'to). In the whole; altogether; wholly.

in transitu (in tran'si-tu). On the journey. Goods are as a rule considered as in transitu while they are in the possession of a carrier, whether by land or water, until they arrive at the ultimate place of their destination and are delivered into the actual possession of the buyer, whether or not the carrier has been named or designated by the buyer.

ipso facto (ip'so fak'to). By the fact itself; by the very fact; by the act itself.

irrelevant (i-rel'e-vant). Not pertinent; not forming or tendering any material issue in the case; redundant.

irreparable injury (i-rep'a-ra-bl in'ju-re). As applied to the law of injunctions, the term means that which cannot be repaired, restored or adequately compensated for in money or where the compensation cannot be safely measured.

irrevocable (i-rev'o-ka-bl). Never to be revoked; never to be abrogated, annulled, or withdrawn. A court will not so interpret the word when such a construction would be unreasonably harsh.

joint (joint). The word joint imparts unity.

joint bank account (joint bangk a-kount'). A bank account of two persons so fixed that they shall be joint owners thereof during their mutual lives, and the survivor shall take the whole on the death of the other.

jointly. Acting together or in concert or co-operating; holding in common or interdependently, not separately. Persons are "jointly bound" in a bond or note when both or all must be sued in one action for its enforcement, not either one at the election of the creditor.

Jointly and Severally. Persons who find themselves "jointly and severally" in a bond or note may all be sued together for its enforcement, or the creditor may select any one or more as the object of his suit.

joint tenancy (joint ten'an-si). An estate held by two or more jointly, with an equal right in all to share in the enjoyments of the land during their lives. Four requisites must exist to constitute a joint tenancy, viz: the tenants must have one and the same interest; the interest must accrue by one and the same conveyance; they must commence at one and the same time; and the property must be held by one and the same undivided possession. If any one of these four elements is lacking, the estate will not be one of joint tenancy. An incident of joint tenancy is the right of survivorship.

judgment (juj'ment). The sentence of the law upon the record; the application of the law to the facts and pleadings. The last word in the judicial controversy; the final consideration and determination of a court of competent jurisdiction upon matters submitted to it in an action or proceeding.

judgment lien (juj'ment le'en). The statutory lien upon the real property of a judgment debtor which is created by the judgment itself. At common law a judgment imposes no lien upon the real property of the judgment debtor and to subject the property of the debtor to the judgment it was necessary to take out an elegit.

judgment n. o. v. (**judgment non obstante veredicto**) (juj'ment non obstan'te vere-dik'to). Judgment notwithstanding the verdict. Under certain circumstances the judge has the power to enter a judgment which is contrary to the verdict of the jury. Such a judgment is a judgment non obstante veredicto.

jurisdiction (ju-ris-dik'shon). The right to adjudicate concerning the subject matter in a given case. The modern tendency is to make the word include not only the power to hear and determine, but also the power to render the particular judgment in the particular case.

jury (ju'ri). A body of laymen, selected by lot, or by some other fair and impartial means, to ascertain, under the guidance of the judge the truth in questions of fact arising either in civil litigation or a criminal process.

justification (jus'ti-fi-ka'shon). A valid defense to an action; a proof made by sureties that they are responsible in the amount of the bond which they have executed.

kite (kit). To secure the temporary use of money by issuing or negotiating worthless papers and then redeeming such paper with the proceeds of similar paper. The word is also used as a noun, meaning the worthless paper thus employed.

laches (lach'ez). The established doctrine of equity that, apart from any question of statutory limitation, its courts will discourage delay and slouth in the enforcement of rights. Equity demands conscience, good faith, and reasonable diligence.

laity (la'i-ti). The laymen or secular persons, as distinguished from the clergy or persons connected with the church.

latent (la'tent). Hidden from view; concealed; not discoverable by ordinary inspection. "The difference between patent and latent is that one is open to observation by ordinary inspection, and the other is not." See Miller v. Moore, 83 Ga. 684.

lawful age (la'ful aj). The age at which one attains majority, that is twenty-one years in England and in most of the United States, and eighteen for girls in some states.

law merchant (la mer'chant). The custom of merchants, or lex mercatorio, which grew out of the necessity and convenience of business, and which, although different from the general rules of the common law, was engrafted into it and became a part of it. It was founded on the custom and usage of merchants and it is today the combined result of reason and experience slowly modified by the necessities and changes in commercial affairs.

leading case (le'ding kas). A case often referred to by the courts and by counsel as having finally settled and determined a point of law.

leading questions (le'ding kwes'chons). Those questions which suggest to the witness the answer desired, those which assume a fact to be proved which is not proved, or which, embodying a material fact, admit of an answer by a simple negative or affirmative.

lease (les). A contract for the possession and profits of land on one side, and a recompense of rent or other income on the other; a conveyance to a person for life, or years, or at will in consideration of a return of rent or other recompense.

legacy (leg'a-si). A bequest; a testamentary gift of personal property. Sometimes incorrectly applied to a testamentary gift of real property.

legal (le'gal). According to the principles of law; according to the method required by statute; by means of judicial proceedings; not equitable.

legitimacy (le-jit'i-ma-si). A person's status embracing his right to inherit from his ancestors, to be inherited from, and to bear the name and enjoy the support of his father.

letter of attorney (let'er of a-ter'ni). A power of attorney; a formal document authorizing some act which shall have a binding effect upon the person who grants the authority. It is usually under seal, and while the want of a seal might not invalidate the instrument as a power of attorney, it is not true that every paper conferring authority upon another is a letter of attorney.

letter of credit (let'er of kred'it). An instrument containing a request (general or special) to pay to the bearer or person named money, or sell him some commodity on credit or give him something of value and look to the drawer of the letter for recompense. It partakes of the nature of a negotiable instrument, but the rules governing bills of exchange and promissory notes are always the same, while letters of credit are to be construed with reference to the particular and often-varying terms in which they may be expressed, the circumstances and intention of the parties to them, and the usage of the particular trade or business contemplated.

levy (lev'i). At common law a levy on goods consisted of an officer's entering the premises where they were and either leaving an assistant in charge of them or removing them after taking an inventory. To-day courts differ as to what is a valid levy, but by the weight of authority there must be an actual or constructive seizure of the goods. In most states, a levy on land must be made by some unequivocal act of the officer indicating his intention of singling out certain real estate for the satisfaction of the debt.

liber (li'ber). A book; a volume; one of the units of a published work; a book in which public records are made.

license (li'sens). A personal privilege to do some act or series of acts upon the land of another, without possessing any estate therein. A permit or authorization to do what, without a license, would be unlawful.

lien (le'en). In its most extensive meaning it is a charge upon property for the payment or discharge of a debt or duty; a qualified right; a proprietary interest, which in a given case, may be exercised over the property of another.

life estate (lif es-tat'). An estate created by deed or grant conveying lands or tenements to a person to hold for the term of his own life, or for the life of any other person, or for more lives than one.

lineal (lin'e-al). In direct line. Lineal heirs are heirs who are related to the deceased in a direct ascending or descending line, as children and grandchildren, parents and grandparents.

lis pendens (lis pen-denz). A pending suit. As applied to the doctrine of lis pendens it is the jurisdiction, power, or control which courts acquire over property involved in a suit, pending the continuance of the action, and until its final judgment therein.

listing contract (lis'ting kon'trakt). A so-called contract whereby an owner of real property employs a broker to procure a purchaser without giving the broker exclusive right to sell. Under such an agreement, it is generally held that the employment may be terminated by the owner at will, and that a sale of the property by the owner terminates the employment.

livery (liv'er-i). Delivery. The act of delivering legal possession of property, as of lands or tenements.

loan (lon). The word imparts a borrowing of money or other personal property by a person who promises to return it.

locus penitentiae (lo'kus pe-ni-ten'she-e). A place of repentance,—the term is applied to the opportunity which a man engaged in the commission of a crime may have to withdraw before its consummation, without incurring its criminality.

magistrate (maj'is-trat). A word commonly applied to the lower judicial officers, such as justices of the peace, police judges, town recorders, and other local judicial functionaries. In a broader sense, a magistrate is a public civil officer invested with some part of the legislative, executive, or judicial power given by the constitution. The President of the United States is the chief magistrate of the nation.

maker (ma'ker). A person who makes or executes an instrument, the signer of an instrument.

mala (ma'la). Bad things; evil things; wicked things.

mala fides (ma'la fi'dez). Bad faith.

malfesance (mal-fe'zans). The doing of an act which a person ought not to do at all. It is to be distinguished from misfeasance, which is the improper doing of an act which a person might lawfully do.

malum in se (ma'lum in se). Evil in and of itself. An offense or act is malum in se which is naturally evil as adjudged by the senses of a civilized community. Acts malum in se are usually criminal acts but not necessarily so.

malum prohibitum (ma'lum pro-hi'bitum). An act which is wrong because it is made so by statute.

mandamus (man-da'mus). We command. It is a command issuing from a competent jurisdiction, in the name of the state or sovereign, directed to some inferior court, officer, corporation, or person, requiring the performance of a particular duty therein specified, which duty results from the official station of the party to whom it is directed, or from operation of law.

manse (mans). A dwelling-house; a habitation; a parsonage.

margin (mar'jin). A deposit by a buyer in stocks with a seller or a stockbroker, as security to cover fluctuations in the market in reference to stocks which the buyer has purchased, but for which he has not paid. Commodities are also traded in on margin.

marshals (mar'shals). Ministerial officers belonging to the executive department of the Federal Government, who with their deputies have the same powers of executing the laws of the United States in each state as the sheriffs and their deputies in such state may have in executing the law of that state.

maxims (mak'sims). Those ancient rules, axioms or postulates of the common law which are general or universal in their application. The authority of these maxims rests entirely upon general reception and usage, and the only method of proving that this or that maxim is a rule of common law, is by showing that it has always been the custom to observe it.

mechanics lien (me-kan'iks le'en). A claim created by law for the purpose of securing a priority of payment of the price or value of work performed and materials furnished in erecting or repairing a building or other structure, and as such it attaches to the land as well as to the buildings erected therein.

merchantable (mer'chan-ta-bl). Of good quality and salable, but not necessarily the best. As applied to articles sold, the word requires that the article shall be such as is usually sold in the market, of medium quality and bringing the average price.

merger (mer'jer). To merge means to sink or disappear in something else; to be swallowed up; to lose identity or individuality.

minor (mi'nor). A person who has not reached the age at which the law recognizes a general contractual capacity, usually twenty-one years.

misdemeanor (mis-de-me'nor). Any crime which is neither punishable by death nor by imprisonment in a state prison.

mistrial (mis-tri'al). "An erroneous trial on account of some defect in the persons trying, as if the jury came from the wrong county; or because there was no issue formed, as if no plea be entered." Wilbridge v. Case 2 Ind. 36, 37.

mitigation of damages (mit-i-ga'shon of dam'aj-es). A term relating only to exemplary damages and their reduction by extenuating circumstances such as provocation or malice. The theory of such mitigation is based on the regard of the law for the frailty of human passions since it looks with some indulgence upon violations of good order which are committed in a moment of irritation and excitement.

moiety (moi'e-ti). One half.

monopoly (mo-nop'o-li). In its broadest meaning, the word signifies the sole power of dealing in an article or doing a specified thing, either generally or in a particular place.

mortgage (mor'gaj). A conveyance of property to secure the performance of some obligation, the conveyance to be void on the due performance thereof.

motive (mo'tiv). The cause or reason that induced a person to commit a crime.

movables (mo'va-bls.) A word derived from the civil law and usually understood to signify the utensils which are to furnish or ornament a house, but it would seem to comprehend personal property generally.

mutuality (mu-tu-al'i-ti). That essential of every contract to make it binding upon both parties at the same time. It is a rule of law that there must be mutuality in a contract; that is, it must be binding upon both parties at the same time, if it is to be deemed valid and enforceable as to either.

necessaries (nes'e-sa-rez). With reference to an infant, the word includes whatever is reasonably necessary for his proper and suitable maintenance, in view of his means and prospects, and the customs of the social circle in which he moves and is likely to move.

negligence (neg'li-jens). The word has been defined as the omission to do something which a reasonable man, guided by those considerations which ordinarily regulate human affairs, would do, or doing something which a prudent and reasonable man would not do.

negotiability (ne-go-shi-a-bil'i-ti). A technical term derived from the usage of merchants and bankers in transferring, primarily, bills of exchange and, afterwards, promissory notes. At common law no contract was assignable, so as to give to an assignee a right to enforce it by suit in his own name. To this rule, bills of exchange and promissory notes, payable to order or bearer, have been admitted exceptions, made such by the adoption of the law merchant.

negotiable instrument (ne-go'shi-a-bl instru-ments). An instrument which may be transferred or negotiated, so that the holder may maintain an action thereon in his own name.

net (net). That which remains after the deduction of all charges and outlays.

no arrival, no sale (no a-ri'val, no sal). A sale of goods "to arrive" or "on arrival," per or ex a certain ship, has been construed to be a sale subject to a double condition precedent, namely, that the ship arrives in port and that when she arrives the goods are on board, and if either of these conditions fails, the contract becomes nugatory.

nominal damages (nom′i-nal dam′aj-es). Damages which are recoverable where a legal right is to be vindicated against an invasion that has produced no actual present loss of any kind, or where there has been a breach of a contract and no actual damages whatever have been or can be shown, or where, under like conditions, there has been a breach of legal duty.

non age (non aj). Under age; under majority; infancy.

non compus mentis (non kom′pos men′-tis). Totally and positively incompetent. The term denotes a person entirely destitute or bereft of his memory or understanding.

nonfeasance (non-fe′zans). In the law of agency, it is the total omission or failure of an agent to enter upon the performance of some distinct duty or undertaking which he has agreed with his principal to do. It is not every omission or failure to perform a duty that will constitute a nonfeasance, but only an omission to perform such distinct duties as he owes to his principal, as distinguished from those which he owes to third persons or to the public in general, as a member of society.

non obstante veredicto (non ob-stan′te ve-re-dik′to). Nothwithstanding the verdict of the jury. See judgment non obstante verdicto.

non-par value stock (non-par val′u stok). Stock of a corporation having no face or par value.

nonsuit (non′sut). A judgment given against the plaintiff when he is unable to prove a case, or when he refuses or neglects to proceed to the trial of the cause after it has been put at issue without determining such issue.

noting protest (not′ing pro′test). The act of making a memorandum on a bill or note at the time of, and embracing the principal facts attending its dishonor. The object is to have a record from which the instrument of protest may be written, so that a notary need not rely on his memory for the fact.

novation (no-va′shon). Under the civil law,—a mode of extinguishing one obligation by another. Under common law, it was at first a transaction whereby a debtor was discharged from his liability to his original creditor by contracting a new obligation in favor of a new creditor by the order of the original creditor. In modern law, it is a mutual agreement, between all parties concerned, for the discharge of a valid existing obligation by the substitution of a new valid obligation on the part of the debtor or another, or a like agreement for the discharge of a debtor to his creditor by the substitution of a new creditor.

nudum pactum (nu′dum pak′tum). A naked promise,—a promise for which there is no consideration.

nuisance (nu′sans). In legal parlance, the word extends to everything that endangers life or health, gives offense to the senses, violates the laws of decency, or obstructs the reasonable and comfortable use of property.

oath (oth). Any form of attestation by which a person signifies that he is bound in conscience to perform an act faithfully and truthfully. It involves the idea of calling on God to witness what is averred as truth, and it is supposed to be accompanied with an invocation of His vengeance, or a renunciation of His favor, in the event of falsehood.

obiter dictum (ob′i-ter dik′tum). That which is said in passing; a rule of law set forth in a court's opinion, but not involved in the case; what is said by the court outside the record or on a point not necessarily involved therein.

objection (ob-jek′shon). In the trial of a case it is the formal remonstrance made by counsel to something which has been said or done, in order to obtain the court's ruling thereon; and when the court has ruled, the alleged error is preserved by the objector's exception to the ruling, which exception is noted in the record.

obligee (ob-li-je′). A person to whom another is bound by a promise or other obligation; a promisee.

obligor (ob′li-gor). A person who is bound by a promise or other obligation; a promisor.

offer (of′er). A proposal by one person to another which is intended of itself to create legal relations on acceptance by the person to whom it is made.

offeree (of′er-e). A person to whom an offer is made.

offeror (of′er-or). A person who makes an offer.

opinion (o-pin′yon). The opinion of the court represents merely the reasons for its judgment, while the decision of the court is the judgment itself.

option (op′shon). A contract whereby the owner of property agrees with another person that he shall have the right to buy the property at a fixed price within a certain time. There are two elements in an option contract: First, the offer to sell, which does not become a contract until accepted; second, the completed contract to leave the offer open for a specified time. These elements are wholly independent and cannot be treated together without great liability to confusion and error. The offer must be considered wholly independent of the contract to leave it open in determining whether or not it has itself ripened into a contract, and the question whether or not there was a valid contract to leave the offer open is wholly immaterial if the offer was in fact accepted before it was withdrawn.

oral (o′ral). By word of mouth; verbal; spoken as opposed to written.

ordinance (or′di-nans). A legislative enactment of a county, or an incorporated city or town.

ostensible authority (os-ten′si-bl a-thor′i-ti). Such authority as a principal, either intentionally or by want of ordinary care, causes or allows a third person to believe the agent to possess. If a principal by his acts had led others to believe that he has conferred authority upon his agent, he cannot be heard to assert, as against third persons who have relied thereon, in good faith, that he did not intend such power.

ostensible partners (os-ten′si-bl part′ners). Members of a partnership whose names are made known and appear to the world as partners, and who in reality are such.

overdraft (o′ver-draft). The withdrawal from a bank by a depositor of money in excess of the amount of money he has on deposit there.

overdraw (o′ver-dra). A depositor overdraws his account at a bank when he obtains on his check or checks from the bank more money than he deposited in the account.

overplus (o′ver-plus). That which remains; a balance left over.

owner's risk (o′ner's risk). A term employed by common carriers in bills of lading and shipping receipts to signify that the carrier does not assume responsiblity for the safety of the goods.

oyer (o′yer). To hear. To demand oyer or to crave oyer was a demand as of right to hear an instrument read. The modern practice is usually to demand the privilege of inspecting the document or to demand a copy of it.

par (par). Par means equal, and par value means a value equal to the face of a bond or a stock certificate. A sale of bonds at par is a sale at the rate of one dollar in money for one dollar in bonds. This is the accepted meaning in the mercantile world.

parol (pa-rol). Oral; verbal; by word of mouth; spoken as opposed to written.

particips criminis (par′ti-seps krim′i-nis). A party to the crime. The term, which, in common acception, means as act that may be visited by an indictment, or other criminal prosecution, but it applies to other transactions contrary to good morals, whether they be immoral per se, or prohibited by statute under penalty, or by a simple prohibition, or as militating against the policy of a statute, or fraud, or other corrupt contract.

parties (par′tez). All persons who are interested in the subject-matter of an action and who have a right to make defense, control the proceedings, examine and cross-examine witnesses, and appeal from the judgment.

partition (par-tish′on). A proceeding the object of which is to enable those who own property as joint tenants or tenants in common, to put an end to the tenancy so as to vest in each a sole estate in specific property or an allotment of the lands and tenements. If a division of the estate is impracticable the estate ought to be sold, and the proceeds divided.

partners (part′ners). Those persons who contribute either property, money or services to carry on a joint business for their common benefit, and who own and share the profits thereof in certain proportions; the members of a partnership.

partnership (part′ner-ship). An association of two or more persons to carry on as co-owners a business for profit.

pass book (pas′ buk). The bank book of a depositor of a bank, in which the cashier or teller, whenever a deposit is made enters the amount and date thereof.

patent (pat′ent). A patent for land is a conveyance of title to government lands by the government; a patent of an invention is the right of monopoly secured by statute to those who invent or discover new and useful devices and processes.

pawn. A pledge; a bailment of personal property as security for some debt or engagement, redeemable on certain terms, and with an implied power of sale on default.

payee (pa-e′). A person to whom a payment is made or is made payable.

pecuniary (pe-ku′ni-a-ri). Financial; pertaining or relating to money; capable of being estimated, computed, or measured by money value.

penal (pe′nal). The words "penal" and "penalty" have many different meanings. Strictly and primarily, they denote punishment, whether corporeal or pecuniary, imposed and enforced by the state for a crime or offense against its laws. But they are also commonly used as including an extraordinary liability to which the law subjects a wrongdoer in favor of the person wronged, not limited to the damages suffered. They are also applied to cases of private contract as when one speaks of the "penal sum" or "penalty" of a bond.

penalty (pen′al-ti). A word which when used in a contract is sometimes construed as meaning liquidated damages, as where the sum named is reasonable, and the actual damages are uncertain in amount and difficult or proof. If, however, it is called a penalty in the contract, it will be held to be a penalty if there is nothing in the nature of the contract to show a contrary intent. An exaction in the nature of a punishment for the nonperformance of an act, or the performance of an unlawful act, and involving the idea of punishment, whether enforced by a civil or criminal action or proceeding.

per curiam (per ku′ri-am). By the court; by the court as a whole.

peremptory challenge (per′emp-to′ri chal′enj). A challenge to a proposed juror which a defendant in a criminal case may make as an absolute right, and which cannot be questioned by either opposing counsel or the court.

performance (per-for′mans). As the word implies, it is such a thorough fulfillment of a duty as puts an end to obligations by leaving nothing to be done. The chief requisite of performance is that it shall be exact.

perjury (per′ju-ri). The willful and corrupt false swearing or affirming, after an oath lawfully administered, in the course of a judical or quasi judical proceeding as to some matter material to the issue or point in question.

per se (per se). The expression means by or through itself; simply, as such; in its own relations.

petition (pe-tish′on). In equity pleading,—a petition is in the nature of a pleading (at least, when filed by a stranger to the suit), and forms a basis for independent action.

pie-powder court (pi′pou-der kort). The court of dusty foot, a court which was held in England by the steward of each fair or market.

plaintiff (plan′tif). A person who brings a suit, action, bill or complaint.

plaintiff in error (plan′tif in er′or). The unsuccessful party to the action who prosecutes a writ of error in a higher court.

plea (ple). A plea is an answer to a declaration or complaint or any material allegation of fact therein which if untrue would defeat the action. In criminal procedure, a plea is the matter which the accused, on his arraignment, alleges in answer to the charge against him.

pledge (plej). A pawn; a bailment of personal property as security for some debt or engagement, redeemable on certain terms, and with an implied power of sale on default.

pledgee (ple-je). A person to whom personal property is pledged by a pledgor.

pledgor (plej′or). A person who makes a pledge of personal property to a pledgee.

possession (pozesh′on). Respecting real property, possession involves exclusive dominion and control such as owners of like property usually exercise over it. The existence of such possession is largely a question of fact dependent on the nature of the property and the surrounding circumstances.

power of attorney (pou′er of a-ter′ni). A written authorization to an agent to perform specified acts in behalf of his principal. The writing by which the

authority is evidenced is termed a letter of attorney, and is dictated by the convenience and certainty of business.

praecipe (pre′si-pe). An order; a command; a writ ordering a person to do some act or to show cause why he should not do it.

precedent (pres′e-dent). A previous decision relied upon as authority. The doctrine of stare decisis, commonly called the doctrine of precedents, has been firmly established in the law. It means that we should adhere to decide cases and settled principles, and not disturb matters which have been established by judicial determination.

preference (pref′er-ens). The act of a debtor in paying or securing one or more of his creditors in a manner more favorable to them than to other creditors or to the exclusion of such other creditors. In the absence of statute, a preference is perfectly good, but to be legal it must be bona fide, and not a mere subterfuge of the debtor to secure a future benefit to himself or to prevent the application of his property to his debts.

prerogative (pre-rog′a-tiv). A sovereign power. Jacob defines it as that power, pre-eminence, or privilege which the king hath or claimeth over and beyond other persons, and above the ordinary course of the common law, in right of his crown.

presumption (pre-zump′shon). A term used to signify that which may be assumed without proof, or taken for granted. It is asserted as a self-evident result of human reason and experience.

prima facie (pri′ma fa′shi-e). At first view or appearance of the business; as a holder of a bill of exchange, indorsed in blank, is prima facie its owner. Prima facie evidence of fact is in law sufficient to establish the fact, unless rebutted.

privies (priv′ez). Persons connected together or having mutual interests in the same action or thing by some relation other than actual contract between them.

privilege (priv′i-lej). A right peculiar to an individual or body.

probate (pro′bat). The word originally meant merely "relating to proof," and later "relating to the proof of wills" but in American law it is now a general name or term used to include all matters of which probate courts have jurisdiction which in many states are the estates of deceased persons and of persons under guardianship.

promise (prom′is). A declaration which gives to the person to whom it is made a right to expect or claim the performance or non-performance of some particular thing.

promisee (prom-i-se′). The person to whom a promise is made.

promisor (prom′i-sor). A person who makes a promise to another; a person who promises.

promoters (pro-mo′terz). The persons who bring about the incorporation and organization of a corporation.

pro rata (pro ra′ta). According to the rate, proportion, or allowance. A creditor of an insolvent estate is to be paid pro rata with creditors of the same class. According to a certain rule or proportion.

prospectus (pro-spek′tus). An introductory proposal for a contract in which the representations may or may not form the basis of the contract actually made; it may contain promises which are to be treated as a sort of floating obligation to take effect when appropriated by persons to whom they are addressed, and amount to a contract when assented to by any person who invests his money on the faith of them.

pro tanto (pro tan′to). For so much; to such an extent.

proximate cause (prok′si-mat kaz). That cause of an injury which, in natural and continuous sequence, unbroken by any efficient intervening cause, produces the injury, and without which the injury would not have occurred.

qualified acceptance (kwol′i-fid ak-sep′-tans). A conditional or modified acceptance. In order to create a contract an acceptance must accept the offer substantially as made; hence a qualified acceptance is no acceptance at all, is treated by the courts as a rejection of the offer made and is in effect an offer by the offeree, which the offeror may, if he chooses, accept and thus create a contract.

quantum meruit (quan-tum me′ru-it). One of the common counts in assumpsit which lies for the value of services rendered.

quasi contract (kwa′si kon′trakt). Sometimes called a contract implied in law, but more properly known as a quasi

contract or constructive contract. It is a contract in the sense that it is remediable by the contractual remedy of assumpsit. The promise is purely fictitious and is implied in order to fit the actual cause of action to the remedy. The liability under it exists from an implication of law that arises from the facts and circumstances independent of agreement or presumed intention.

quasi judicial (kwa′si jo-dish′al). The acts of an officer which are executive or administrative in their character and which call for the exercise of that officer's judgment and discretion are not ministerial acts and his authority to perform such acts is quasi judicial.

qui facit per alium, facit per se (qui fa′sit per a′li-um, fa′sit per se). He who acts by or for himself. The doctrine of the liability of a master for the wrongful acts of his servant rests upon this maxim and the maxim "respondeat superior" and the universal test of the master's liability is whether there was authority express or implied for doing the act.

quitclaim deed (kwit′klam ded). A deed conveying only the right, title and interest of the grantor in the property described, as distinguished from a deed conveying the property itself.

quorum (kwo′rum). That number of persons, shares represented, or officers who may lawfully transact the business of a meeting called for that purpose.

quo warranto (kwo wo-ran′to). By what authority. The name of a writ (and also of the whole pleading) by which the government commences an action to recover an office or franchise from the person or corporation in possession of it.

raising a check (ra′zing a chek). A class of forgery where the signatures on the check are all genuine, but the amount of the check has been increased by the forger's alteration.

ratification (rat′i-fi-ka′shon). The adoption by one in whose name an unauthorized act has been performed by another upon the assumption of authority to act as his agent, even though without any precedent authority whatever, which adoption or ratification relates back, supplies the original authority to do the act, binding the principal so adopting or ratifying to the same extent as if the act had been done in the first instance—by his previous authority. The act of an infant upon reaching his majority affirming a voidable contract made by him during his infancy and giving it the same force and effect as if it had been valid from the beginning.

rebuttal (re-but′al). Testimony addressed to evidence produced by the opposite party; rebutting evidence.

receiver (re-se′ver). An indifferent person between the parties to a cause, appointed by the court to receive and preserve the property or funds in litigation, and receive its rents, issues, and profits, and apply or dispose of them at the direction of the court, when it does not seem reasonable that either party should hold them.

recognizance (re-kog′ni-zans). At common law, an obligation entered into before some court of record or magistrate duly authorized, with a condition to do some particular act, usually to appear and answer to a criminal accusation. Being taken in open court and entered upon the order book, it was valid without the signature or seal of any of the obligors.

recorder (re-kor′der). A public officer of a town or county charged with the duty of keeping the record books required by law to be kept in his office and of receiving and causing to be copied in such books such instruments as by law are entitled to be recorded.

recoupment (re-kop′ment). The doctrine under which in an action for breach of contract, the defendant may show that the plaintiff has not performed the same contract on his part, and may recoup his damages for such breach in the same action, whether liquidated or not.

redemption (re-demp′shon). The buying back of one's property after it has been sold. The right to redeem property sold under an order or decree of court is purely a privilege conferred by, and does not exist independently of, statute.

redress (re-dres′). Remedy; indemnity; reparation.

rejected (re-jek′ted). A claim of a creditor is said to have been rejected when, after having been presented in due form to the proper officer for allowance or approval as a valid claim, it

has been disallowed by that officer in the manner provided at law.

release (re-les'). The giving up or abandoning of a claim or right to a person against whom the claim exists or the right is to be enforced or exercised. It is the discharge of a debt by the act of the party in distinction from an extinguishment which is a discharge by operation of law.

relevancy (rel'e-van-si). The logical relation between proposed evidence and the fact to be established.

remainderman (re-man'der-man). One who is entitled to the remainder of the estate after a particular estate carved out of it has expired.

remedy (rem'e-di). The appropriate legal form of relief by which a remediable right may be enforced.

remit (re-mit'). To pardon; to remand for a new trial or for future proceedings; to transmit. To remit means to send back.

remittitur (re-mit'i-ter). The certificate of reversal issued by an appellate court upon reversing the order or judgment appealed from.

replevin (re-plev'in). A proceeding by which the owner recovers possession of his own goods.

res (rez). The thing; the subject-matter of a suit; the property involved in the litigation; a matter; property; the business; the affair the transaction.

res adjudicata (rez ad-ju-di-ka'ta). A matter which has been adjudicated; that which is definitely settled by a judical decision.

rescind (re-sind'). As the word is applied to contracts, to rescind in some cases means to terminate the contract as to future transactions, while in others it means to annul the contract from the beginning.

residue (rez'i-du). All that portion of the estate of a testator of which no effectual disposition has been made by his will otherwise than in the residuary clause.

respondent (re-spon'dent). The defendant in an action; a party adverse to an appellant in an action which is appealed to a higher court. The person against whom a bill in equity was exhibited.

reversal (re-ver'sal). An annulment or setting aside as the word is used in connection with judgments, its usual meaning contemplates only a reversal by an appellate court; that is, by a court authorized to set aside the judgment.

reversed and remanded (re-verst' and re-mand'ed). Where the judgment of an appellate court concludes with the words, "judgment reversed and cause remanded," unless it is apparent from the opinion of the court that the adjudication was intended to be a final disposition of the cause, the effect of the reversal is only to set aside the judgment of the lower court that a new trial may be had.

reversion (re-ver'shon). The residue of a fee simple remaining in the grantor, to commence in possession after the determination of some particular estate granted out by him. The estate of a landlord during the existence of the outstanding leasehold estate.

reversioner (re-ver'shon-er). A person who is entitled to a reversion.

revocation (rev-o-ka'shon). A withdrawal; a recall; an annulment; a repudiation.

right (rit). When we speak of a person having a right, we must necessarily refer to a civil right as distinguished from the elemental idea of a right absolute. We must have in mind a right given and protected by law, and a person's enjoyment thereof is regulated entirely by the law which creates it.

riparian (ri-pa'ri-an). From the Latin word "riparius" of or belonging to the bank of a river, in turn derived from ripa, a bank, and defined as "pertaining to or situated on the bank of a river;" the word has reference to the bank and not to the bed of the stream.

sanction (sangk'shon). That part of a law which signifies the evil or penalty which will be incurred by the wrongdoer for his breach of it. It is also spoken of as the vindictory part of the law.

satisfaction (sat-is-fak'shon). A performance of the terms of an accord. If such terms require a payment of a sum of money, then "satisfaction" means that such payment has been made.

schedule in bankruptcy (sked'ul in bangk'rup-si). An inventory filed by the bankrupt in bankruptcy proceedings, containing a list of all his property and his credits.

scienter (si-en'ter). In cases of fraud and deceit, the word means knowledge on the part of the person making the representations, at the time when they are made, that they are false. In an action for deceit it is generally held that scienter must be proved.

scintilla of evidence (sin-til'a of ev'i-dens). The least particle of evidence. A slight amount of evidence supporting a material issue.

seal (sel). At common law, a seal is an impression on wax, wafer, or some other tenacious material, but in modern practice the letters "l.s." (locus sigilli) or the word seal enclosed in a scroll, either written or printed, and acknowledged in the body of the instrument to be a seal, are often used as substitutes.

secular (sek'u-lar). Temporal; pertaining to temporal things, things of the world; worldy; opposed to spiritual, holy.

security (se-ku'ri-ti). That which makes the enforcement of a promise more certain than the mere personal obligation of the debtor or promisor, whatever may be his possessions or financial standing. It may be a pledge of property or an additional personal obligation; but it means more than the mere promise of the debtor with property liable to general execution.

seizin (se'zin). In a legal sense, the word means possession of premises with the intention of asserting a claim to a freehold estate therein; it is practically the same thing as ownership; it is a possession of a freehold estate, such as by the common law is created by livery of seizen.

seller's lein (sel'er's le'en. A lien which the vendor of goods has at common law for the whole or the unpaid portion of the purchase price of the goods, where he has parted with title but not with possession. It is in the nature of a pledge raised or created by law upon the happening of the insolvency of the buyer, to secure the unpaid purchase money to the seller.

service (ser'vis). As applied to a process of courts, the word ordinarily implies something in the nature of an act or proceeding adverse to the party served, or of a notice to him.

set-off (set'off). A set-off both at law and in equity, is that right which exists between two parties, each of whom, under an independent contract, owes an ascertained amount to the other, to set off their respective debts by way of mutual deduction, so that, in any action brought for the larger debt, the residue only, after such deduction, shall be recovered.

severable contract (sev'er-a-bl con'trakt). A contract which is not entire or indivisible. If the consideration is single, the contract is entire; but if it is expressly or by necessary implication apportioned, the contract is severable. The question is ordinarily determined by inquiring whether the contract embraces one or more subject-matters, whether the obligation is due at the same time to the same person, and whether the consideration is entire or apportioned.

several (sev'er-al). Separate; distinct, exclusive, individual, appropriated. In this sense it is opposed to common; and it has been held that the word could not be construed as equivalent to respective. More than two but not many.

shareholder (shar'hol'der). See stockholder.

share of stock (shar of stok). The right which its owner has in the management, profits and ultimate assets of the corporation. The tangible property of a corporation and the shares of stock therein are separate and distinct kinds of property and belong to different owners, the first being the property of an artificial person—the corporation —the latter the property of the individual owner.

sheriff (sher'if). The office is a most ancient one, dating back, at least to the time of Alfred, King of England, and the holder thereof has always been the chief executive officer and conservator of the peace in his shire or county.

sight (sit). A term signifiying the date of the acceptance or that of protest for the nonacceptance of a bill of exchange; for example, ten days after sight.

sine qua non (si'ne kwa non). Without which it is not; an indispensable requisite.

situs (si'tus). Location; local position; the place where a person or thing is, is his situs. Intangible property has no actual situs, but it may have a legal situs, and for the purpose of taxation its legal situs is at the place where it

is owned and not at the place where it is owed.

specific performance (spe-sif'ik per-for'-mans). The actual accomplishment of a contract by the party bound to fulfill it; the name of an equitable remedy of very ancient origin the object of which is to secure a decree to compel the defendant specifically to perform his contract, which is nothing more or less than a means of compelling a party to do precisely what he ought to have done without being coerced by a court.

stare decisis (sta're de-si'sis). The doctrine or principle that the decisions of the court should stand as precedents for future guidance.

status quo (sta'tus kwo). The situation in which he was.

stipulation (stip-u-la'shon). An agreement between opposing counsel in a pending action, usually required to be made in open court and entered on the minutes of the court, or else to be in writing and filed in the action, ordinarily entered into for the purpose of avoiding delay, trouble, or expense in the conduct of the action.

stockholder (stok'hol'der). It is generally held that one who hold shares on the books of the corporation is a stockholder and that one who merely holds a stock certificate is not. Stockholders may become such either by original subscription, by direct purchase from the corporation, or by subsequent transfer from the original holder.

stoppage in transitu (stop'aj in tran'zi-tu). A right which the vendor of goods on credit has to recall them, or retake them, on the discovery of the insolvency of the vendee, and it continues so long as the carrier remains in the possession and control of the goods or until there has been an actual or constructive delivery to the vendee, or some third person has acquired a bona fide right in them.

subpoena (sub-(or) su-pe'na). A process the purpose of which is to compel the attendance of a person whom it is desired to use as a witness.

subrogation (sub-ro-ga'shon). The substitution of one person in the place of another with reference to a lawful claim or right frequently referred to as the doctrine of substitution. It is a device adopted or invented by equity to compel the ultimate discharge of a debt or obligation by him who in good conscience ought to pay it. It is the machinery by which the equity of one man is worked out through the legal rights of another.

sui generis (su-i jen'e-ris). Of its own kind; peculiar to itself.

summary proceedings (sum'a-ri pro-sé-dings). Proceedings, usually statutory in the course of which many formalities are dispensed with. But such proceedings are not conducted without proper investigation of the facts, or without notice, or an opportunity to be heard by the person alleged to have committed the act, or whose property is sought to be affected.

summons (sum'onz). A writ or process issued and served upon a defendant in a civil action for the purpose of securing his appearance in the action. In modern practice, the summons serves the same purpose, but it also usually notifies the defendant that if he does not appear within the time specified in the summons, judgment by default will be entered against him.

supra (su'pra). Above; above mentioned; in addition to.

surety (shur'ti). One who by accessory agreement called a contract of suretyship, binds himself with another, called the principal, for the performance of an obligation in respect to which such other person is already bound and primarily liable for such performance.

tacit law (tas'it la). That law which arises out of the silent consent and the custom and usages of the people.

tacking (tak'ing). The adding together of successive periods of adverse possession of persons in privity with each other, in order to constitute one continuous adverse possession for the time required by the statute, to establish title.

tangible (tan'ji-bl). Capable of being possessed or realized; readily apprehensible by the mind; real; substantial; evident.

tariff (tar'if). A schedule or tabulated list of rates.

tenancy (ten'an-si). A tenancy exists when one has let real estate to another to hold of him as landloard. When duly created and the tenant put into possession, he is the owner of an estate for the time being, and has all the usual rights and remedies to defend his possession.

tender (ten′der). An unconditional offer of payment, consisting in the actual production in money or legal tender of a sum not less than the amount due.

tenement (ten′e-ment). A word commonly used in deeds which passes not only lands and other inheritances, but also offices, rents, commons, and profits arising from lands, but usually it is applied exclusively to land, or what is ordinarily denominated real property.

tenor (ten′or). The tenor of an instrument is an exact copy of the instrument. Under the rule that an indictment for forgery must set out in the instrument according to its "tenor," the word imports an exact copy—that the instrument is set forth in the very words and figures.

tenure (ten′ur). In its technical sense, the word means the manner whereby lands or tenements are holden, or the service that the tenant owes his lord. In the latter case there can be no tenure without some service, because the service makes the tenure. The word is also used as signifying the estate in land. The most common tenure by which lands are held in the United States is "fee simple."

testament (tes′ta-ment). Redfield, in his work on Wills defined a last will and testament as the disposition of one's property to take effect after death.

testator (tes-ta′tor). A deceased person who died leaving a will.

testatrix (tes′ta-triks). Feminine of testator.

testimony (tes′ti-mo-ni). In some contexts the word bears the same import as the word "evidence," but in most connections it has a much narrower meaning. Testimony is the words heard from the witnesses in court, and evidence is what the jury considers it worth.

tort (tort). An injury or wrong committed, either with or without force, to the person or property of another. Such injury may arise by nonfeasance, by the malfeasance, or by the misfeasance of the wrongdoer.

tort-feasor (tort′fe′zor). A person who commits a tort; a wrongdoer.

tortious (tor′shus). Partaking of the nature of a tort; wrongful; injurious.

trade fixtures (trad fiks′turs). Articles of personal property which have been annexed to the freehold and which are necessary to the carrying on of a trade.

transcript (tran′skript). A copy of a writing.

transferee (trans-fer-e′). A person to whom a transfer is made.

transferor (trans′fer-or). A person who makes a transfer.

treasure trove (trezh′ur-trov). Any gold or silver in coin, plate or bullion, found concealed in the earth, or in a house or other private place, but not lying on the ground, the owner of the discovered treasure being unknown. Originally, it belonged to the finder, if the owner was not discovered, but afterwards it was adjudged expedient, for purposes of state, and particularly for the coinage, that it should go to the king, whose right thereto depended on the same principles as his right to the goods of an intestate.

trespass (tres′pas). Every unauthorized entry an another's property is a trespass and any person who makes such an entry is a trespasser. In its widest signification, trespass means any violation of law. In its most restricted sense, its signifies an injury intentionally inflicted by force either on the person or property of another.

trial (tri′al). An examination before a competent tribunal, according to the law of the land, of the facts or law put in issue in a cause, for the purpose of determining such issue. When the court hears and determines any issue of fact or law for the purpose of determining the rights of the parties, it may be considered a trial.

trust (trust). A confidence reposed in one person, who is termed trustee, for the benefit of another, who is called the cestui que trust, respecting property, which is held by the trustee for the benefit of the cestui que trust. As the word is used in the law pertaining to unlawful combinations and monopolies, a trust in its original and typical form is a combination formed by an agreement among the stockholders in a number of competing corporations to transfer their shares to an unincorporated board of trustees, and to receive in exchange trust certificates in some agreed proportion to their stockholdings.

trustee (trus-te′). A person in whom property is vested in trust for another.

trustee in bankruptcy (trus-te′ in bangk′-rup-si). The Federal bankruptcy act defines the term as an officer, and he is an officer of the courts in a certain restricted sense, but not in any such sense as a receiver. He takes the legal title to the property of the bankrupt and in respect to suits stands in the same general position as a trustee of an express trust or an executor. His duties are fixed by statute. He is to collect and reduce to money the property of the estate of the bankrupt.

ultra vires act (ul′tra vi′rez akt). An act of a corporation which is beyond the powers conferred upon the corporation.

undertaking (un′der′ta′king). A promise to perform some act; a bond; a recognizance.

unilateral contract (u-ni-lat′e-ral kon′-trakt). A contract formed by an offer or a promise on one side for an act to be done on the other, and a doing of the act by the other by way of acceptance of the offer or promise; that is, a contract wherein the only acceptance of the offer that is necessary is the performance of the act.

usury (u′zhu-ri). The taking more than the law allows upon a loan or for forbearance of a debt. Illegal interest; interest in excess of the rate allowed by law.

utter (ut′er). As applied to counterfeiting, to utter and publish is to declare or assert, directly or indirectly, by words or actions, that the money or note is good. Thus to offer it in payment is an uttering or publishing. To utter and publish a document is to offer directly or indirectly, by words or actions, such document as good and valid. There need be no acceptance by the offeree to constitute an uttering.

valid (val′id). Effective; operative; not void; subsisting; sufficient in law.

vendee (ven-de′). A purchaser of property. The word is more commonly applied to a purchaser of real property, the word "buyer" being more commonly applied to the purchaser of personal property.

vendor (ven′dor). A person who sells property to a vendee. The words "vendor" and "vendee" are more commonly applied to the seller and purchaser of real estate, and the words "seller" and "buyer" are more commonly applied to the seller and purchaser of personal property.

vendue (ven-du′). A sale; a sale at auction.

venire (ve-ni′re). The name of a writ by which a jury is summoned.

venue (ven′u). The word originally was employed to indicate the county from which the jurors were to come who were to try a case, but in modern times it refers to the county in which a case is to be tried.

veracity (ve-ras′i-ti). The words truth, veracity and honesty are almost synonyms each of the other.

verbal (ver′bal). By word of mouth; spoken; oral; parol.

verdict (ver′dikt). The answer of a jury given to the court concerning the matters of fact committed to their trial and examination; it makes no precedent, and settles nothing but the present controversy to which it relates. It is the decision made by the jury and reported to the court, and as such it is an elemental entity which cannot be divided by the judge.

verification (ver′i-fi-ka′shon). The affidavit of a party annexed to his pleadings which states that the pleading is true of his own knowledge except as to matters which are therein stated on his information or belief, and as to those matters, that he believes it to be true. A sworn statement of the truth of the facts stated in the instrument verified.

versus (ver′sus). Against. Vs. and versus have become ingrafted upon the English language; their meaning is as well understood and their use quite as appropriate as the word against could be.

vest (vest). To give an immediate fixed right of present or future enjoyment.

void (void). That which is entirely null. A void act is one which is not binding on either party, and which is not susceptible of ratification.

voidable (voi′da-bl). Capable of being made void; not utterly null, but annullable, and hence that may be either voided or confirmed.

voucher (vou′cher). A written instrument which attests, warrants, maintains and bears witness.

waive (wav). To throw away; to relinquish voluntarily, as a right which one may enforce, if he chooses.

waiver (wa′ver). The intentional relinquishment of a known right. It is a voluntary act, and implies an election by the party to dispense with something of value, or to forego some advantage which he might at his option have demanded and insisted on.

warehouse (war′hous). The word has been defined as a place normally of considerable size, mainly used for the storage of goods in bulk or in large quantities; a place used in connection with a wholesale business for the purpose of storing goods.

warrant (wor′ant). An order authorizing a payment of money by another person to a third person. As a verb, the word means to defend; to guarantee; to enter into an obligation of warranty.

warrant of arrest (wor′ant ov a-rest′). A legal process issued by competent authority, usually directed to regular officers of the law, but occasionally issued to private persons named in it, directing the arrest of a person or persons upon grounds stated therein.

warranty (wor′an-ti). In the sale of a commodity, an undertaking by the seller to answer for the defects therein is construed as a warranty. In a contract of insurance, as a general rule, any statement or description, or any undertaking on the part of the insured on the face of the policy or in another instrument properly incorporated in the policy, which relates to the risk, is a warranty.

wash sales (wosh sals). A stock exchange term designating sales which are merely bets upon the market, in which it is understood between the parties that neither is bound to deliver or accept delivery.

waste (wast). The destruction or material alteration of any part of a tenement by a tenant for life or years, to the injury of the person entitled to the inheritance; an unlawful act or omission of duty on the part of the tenant which results in permanent injury to the inheritance; any spoil or destruction done or permitted with respect to land, houses, gardens, trees, or other corporeal hereditiments, by the tenant thereof, to the prejudice of him in reversion or remainder, or, in other words to the lasting injury of the inheritance.

watered stock (wa′terd stok). Stock issued by a corporation as fully paid up, when in fact it is not fully paid up.

writ (rit). A mandatory precept, issued by the authority and in the name of the sovereigns or the state, for the purpose of compelling the defendant to do something therein mentioned. It is issued by a court or other competent jurisdiction, and is returnable to the same. It is to be under seal and tested by the proper officer, and is directed to the sheriff or other officer lawfully authorized to execute the same.

Year Books (yer buks). The earliest reports of the decisions of the courts of England. The reports are extant in a regular series from the reign of Edward the Second, inclusive. From his time to that of Henry the Eighth the decisions were taken down by the prothonotaries, or chief scribes of the court, at the expense of the crown, and were published annually, and hence they are known as Year Books.

Zone (zon). As a verb, the word is comparatively new and "to zone" means to separate the commercial or industrial districts of a city from the residence district or districts, and to prohibit the establishment of places of business in any designated residence district.

INDEX